FIFTH EDITION

CONTEMPORARY MORAL ISSUES

Wesley Cragg
George R. Gardiner Professor of Business Ethics
York University

Christine M. Koggel
Department of Philosophy
Bryn Mawr College

 **McGraw-Hill
Ryerson**

Toronto Montréal Boston Burr Ridge, IL Dubuque, IA Madison, WI
New York San Francisco St. Louis Bangkok Bogotá Caracas Kuala Lumpur Lisbon
London Madrid Mexico City Milan New Delhi Santiago Seoul Singapore Sydney Taipei

McGraw-Hill Ryerson

CONTEMPORARY MORAL ISSUES
Fifth Edition

ISBN: 0-07-0930104

1 2 3 4 5 6 7 8 9 10 TRI 0 9 8 7 6 5

Printed and bound in Canada.

Vice President, Editorial and Media Technology: Patrick Ferrier
Sponsoring Editor: Leanna MacLean
Developmental Editor: Darren Hick
Marketing Manager: Sharon Loeb
Copy Editor: Jim Zimmerman
Senior Production Coordinator: Jennifer Wilkie
Cover Design: Greg Devitt
Cover Image: Getty Images/Gary S. and Vivian Chapman
Page Layout: JayTee Graphics
Printer: Tri-Graphic Printing

National Library of Canada Cataloguing in Publication

Contemporary moral issues / [edited by] Wesley Cragg, Christine M. Koggel. -- 5th ed.

ISBN 0-07-093010-4

    1. Social ethics. 2. Ethics. I. Cragg, Wesley II. Koggel, Christine M.

HN110.Z9M66 2004   170   C2003-907183-9

Dedication

For Mary and Andy, David, Beth and Paul and George and David

Table of Contents

Chapter 9: Business Ethics 464

Chapter 10: War, Terrorism, and the War against Terrorism 527

Preface to the Fifth Edition

The first edition of *Contemporary Moral Issues* was published in 1983. The anthology is now in its fifth edition, and both the selection of topics and the range of perspectives on the issues have shifted with each new edition. This edition takes up the increasing impact of globalization on Canada and the world. Globalization has opened the doors to increased international trade and economic interdependence, but it has also increased worries over growing disparities in wealth and economic opportunities. Increased immigration and the proliferation of global media networks, e-mail, and the World Wide Web have brought Canadians face to face with moral beliefs and practices very different from those that shaped the judgments of their parents as little as a decade or two ago. Globalization also has opened the doors to new forms of terrorism and international conflict. Renewed examples of genocide, civil war, suicide bombing, global terrorist networks, 9/11, and military responses in the former Yugoslavia, Rwanda, Afghanistan, and Iraq have changed the world in ways that could not have been imagined a decade ago.

These developments are reflected in this edition in a number of ways. Most notably, we have added two chapters, "Business Ethics and Social Responsibility" and "War, Terrorism, and the War against Terrorism," and have updated the chapter on "Poverty."

An explosion of technological developments and vastly improved communications have also reshaped debates on many topics, two of which have been in *Contemporary Moral Issues* since the first edition. The chapter on abortion has been renamed "Abortion and Reproductive Technologies" to reflect important new debates introduced by technological advances such as cloning and stem cell research. These technologies introduce complex moral issues with which Canadians need to grapple as we attempt to formulate policies to regulate their use. The chapter on pornography now includes a discussion of the widespread availability of pornography on the Internet and of its relevance to issues of censorship.

The past two decades have seen an exponential growth in the literature on applied ethics. Many of these recent contributions challenge traditional accounts of morality and have implications for the way in which specific moral issues are discussed. Environmental and business ethicists are challenging traditional views of nature and management. Feminist, race, and disability theorists are exploring the ways in which current structures and beliefs have a detrimental impact on the lives of members of traditionally disadvantaged groups. Significant contributions by these theorists are reflected in the reworked chapter "Equality and Discrimination" that replaces the two chapters on affirmative action and discrimination and have been added to other chapters as well. As an illustration of additions to the fifth edition: Although the law with respect to euthanasia has not changed, discussion of it has, as disability theorists raise questions about the implications of legalizing euthanasia for perceptions of disabled persons. In the case of poverty, recent studies by the economist and philosopher Amartya Sen and by feminist theorists highlight the importance of understanding gender and racial dimensions of poverty both within and across borders, themes that emerge also in the discussion of environmental and business ethics, aboriginal rights, and the war against terrorism.

In some cases, the landscape with respect to specific moral issues has not changed, yet discussion of these issues continues to be important. The chapters on capital punishment and aboriginal rights are examples. Despite the fact that the last execution in Canada took place almost forty years ago, capital punishment is an issue that will not die, in part because questions about the effectiveness of capital punishment as a deterrent, the impact of racism on the imposition of the death penalty, and execution as the just retributive response to murder continue to be hotly debated in the American media with its large Canadian audience. Meanwhile, debates over the extradition of American fugitives from justice, apprehended by Canadian law enforcement officers, and subject to execution by American courts should they be found guilty, have ensured that the moral and constitutional dimensions of capital punishment are not ignored by Canadian courts and the Canadian government.

While there have been significant changes in the legal status of Aboriginal peoples resulting from the Constitution Act of 1982 and subsequent judicial interpretation of its provisions, progress on aboriginal rights seems to be stalled in Canada. The material position of First Nations people has not changed substantially since 1983, and few significant land claim settlements have occurred. As a result, self-government and land rights continue to play a central role in discussions of aboriginal rights.

The fourth edition introduced a new chapter entitled "Tools and Theories." This addition represented a decision to deal more directly with moral theory and its role in the resolution of moral issues. The chapter was designed to provide needed background in understanding those authors included in the anthology who appeal directly to moral theories in developing their positions. It was intended also to provide support for those instructors for whom an introduction to moral theory is a standard feature of their approach to applied ethics. As in the previous edition, the chapter dealing with theory is placed at the end of the book, and this differentiates it from many other moral issues collections. We retain this structure in the fifth edition because we question a number of assumptions about the relation between theory and practice in the analysis of moral problems or issues. Is theory and developing an understanding of its role and importance in addressing practical ethical concerns something that precedes or emerges from ethical deliberation and reflection? Is it really the case that the philosophical examination of practical concerns that have a significant moral dimension typically involves the application of moral theories for the purpose of resolving issues or arriving at sound or morally justifiable conclusions or decisions or actions? This volume does not attempt to address these issues systematically. It is built on an underlying pedagogical principle, namely that students are unlikely to understand the practical relevance of moral theorizing unless they first grapple with moral problems, issues, and concerns, and understand for themselves the need for the tools, skills, and theories that philosophers have constructed in struggling with those same ethical problems, issues, and concerns.

Three features of *Contemporary Moral Issues* have not changed. First, there is the resolve to put the discussion of the issues addressed in a contemporary context. Second, there is the commitment on the part of the editors and publisher to producing a collection that reflects contemporary Canadian perspectives on a wide range of moral issues, perspectives that include contributions not only from the discipline of philosophy, but also from other areas such as law, sociology, history, and politics. A cursory examination of the preceding editions is persuasive evidence of the need, therefore, to update the collection on a regular and systematic basis.

Finally, as with past editions, articles have been selected for one of three reasons: They locate the issue(s) under discussion in an historical or contemporary context and therefore contribute important contextual material. They set out as clearly and sympathetically as possible the kinds of considerations, arguments, and justifications that are having a significant impact on current discussion of the issue(s) in question. Finally, they present an intelligent, relatively accessible philosophical discussion of the issue(s) at hand.

Not all these factors apply to each reading. Hence some of the readings will be seen as inadequate from one or more of a variety of perspectives. The fact that the readings are not all perfect from a philosophical point of view is in our view a virtue and not a defect for the following reasons. Actual debates have flaws. It is important to provide examples of positions that resemble what students will actually encounter as they read newspapers or watch TV or surf the Internet. Students are then challenged to critically evaluate what they are reading, to find the flaws, and to try to fix them or sort through the implications of their analysis for taking a position. Including material drawn from a wide range of sources also ensures that instructors have examples of reasoning and argument viewed as persuasive by participants in ongoing debates that can be subjected to scrutiny and critical examination. Careful use of this opportunity can then be used to demonstrate the value of careful philosophical examination and analysis.

After all is said and done, the purpose of *Contemporary Moral Issues* remains unchanged. Its goal has been to provide a reasonably priced, balanced introduction to the issues that are currently attracting the interest and concern of thoughtful observers of the Canadian scene. We believe that each new edition adds strengths to a longstanding and successful publication. We hope our colleagues and readers will find the results of our work to be useful both as an introduction and as a pedagogical tool.

There are people whose advice, work, and support were invaluable throughout the process of preparing this edition. Our research assistant, Rossella Polera, showed great competence and conscientiousness in finding materials, dealing with permissions, and putting the manuscript together after various revisions. We would also like to thank Sponsoring Editor Leanna MacLean and Developmental Editor Darren Hick, who worked with us from the beginning and attended to the details throughout. Darren's work in soliciting and summarizing reviewer feedback and in consulting with us about them was vital to producing what we believe is an excellent new edition. The reviewer comments themselves were extremely useful during the process of making revisions, selecting new material, creating new chapters, thinking through the structure of each chapter, and putting the book together as a whole. Our thanks go to the very conscientious reviewers, who took the time to make thoughtful and extensive comments. They include: Hilliard Aronovich, University of Ottawa; Jonathan Breslin, McMaster University; Rachel Brown, McGill University; Brian Cupples, University of New Brunswick; Evlyn Fortier, Carleton University; Colin Macleod, University of Victoria; Marilyn Quinn, Niagara College; Peter Trnka, Memorial University; Bob Ware, University of Calgary; Jennifer Welchman, University of Alberta; and Karen Wendling, University of Guelph. Our thanks also go to Kelly Dickson, Margaret Henderson, and Jim Zimmerman, the editors responsible for taking our book through production. Finally, we could not have completed the work without the support of our respective spouses: Mary Cragg, who opened her home to piles of paper and accommodated our sometimes impossible schedules, and Andrew Brook, who was always there to listen and provide valuable insights into the issues and the book as a whole and to whom we dedicate this edition.

Wesley Cragg
Christine M. Koggel

Chapter 1

Euthanasia

Introduction

Rules play a central role in our lives as human beings. They govern much of what we do and how we do it. One reason for the existence of rules is to provide an environment in which individuals can grow and mature without threat to their personal existence. Hence, some of our most important rules are designed to protect the lives of human beings and assure access to needed support and assistance. Rules prohibiting murder are one example. Not surprisingly, rules whose purpose is the protection of human life play a central role in discussions of the morality of euthanasia.

Protection of life, however, is not the only concern at stake. Two others are of particular relevance. First, suffering is a common feature of the human condition and one that human beings almost invariably try to avoid. Many people think that, both collectively and as individuals, we have an obligation to help each other alleviate suffering wherever we can and offer relief if it is available. Second, as moral agents we are assumed capable of thinking through moral problems and deciding how we ought to act. It is sometimes argued that the special significance of being human lies in just this capability. Does it follow that, as autonomous moral agents, we ought to be allowed unlimited freedom to act on our own assessments of what, morally speaking, is required of us in any given situation? The answer here is no. If there were no restrictions on my freedom to act on my own assessment of what is required, the result might well be that your freedom to act as you think right would be seriously reduced or eliminated. This limitation is sometimes expressed by saying that respect for persons as moral agents requires that each person be given as much freedom to act on his or her moral beliefs (or lack of them) as is compatible with others having an equal degree of freedom to do the same.

We now have three principles to consider: the *protection of life principle,* the *avoidance of suffering principle,* and the *moral autonomy principle.* If the first of these principles were the only one that inspired our respect, euthanasia would not generate any moral problems: it would simply be wrong in all cases. If the avoidance of suffering principle were the only one of the three principles worthy of respect, again euthanasia would generate no moral problems. Euthanasia would be morally acceptable if ending someone's life were the only effective way of ending that person's suffering. Finally, if the moral autonomy principle were the only one operative, we might well conclude that it was morally acceptable to respect someone's request to terminate his or her life if we believed that in arriving at this request, he or she was acting as an autonomous moral agent.

In fact, all three principles are widely regarded as worthy of respect. Situations do arise, however, in which it would appear that all three apply but come in conflict. Should that happen, we would be faced with a decision. Which of these principles should have priority? Situations also arise in which a particular principle does not apply to some cases. The moral autonomy principle, for example, cannot help us in those cases in which a person who is suffering does not have or has lost the capacity to decide to end his or her life.

Background Considerations

Societies rooted in the Judeo-Christian tradition have, in the past, thought euthanasia immoral. This attitude reflects the view that human life is sacred and that rules protecting human life should override all other considerations. But should this traditional view continue to command respect? Have medical advances in the twentieth century rendered it obsolete?

The Current Situation

In recent years, the morality of euthanasia has been subjected to increasing scrutiny, largely because of remarkable developments in medical science. Many life-threatening diseases have been conquered, smallpox being but one example. People now are often rescued from serious illness where death would once have been inevitable. Accidents that might once have caused death are no longer fatal. At the same time, our society has made funds available for social and medical services that allow most of us to benefit from these medical advances.

Paradoxically, however, there is another side to this picture. Modern medicine can rescue seriously ill or injured persons from death. But it is not always capable of restoring the capacity to enjoy the life that has been prolonged. Thus, the elderly frequently can be cured of illness, disease, or injury (pneumonia, for example) which in the past might well have resulted in death. But should the cure be effected if the person in question is senile? Children born with serious disabilities that once would have hastened death can be saved using modern medical techniques. But should they be saved if the alternative to death is a life plagued with pain or one affected in detrimental ways by serious mental or physical disabilities?

Four cases in recent years highlight the intensity and significance of the debate these developments have generated. In Montreal, Nancy B., who was paralysed from the neck down by a neurological disease and dependent on a respirator to breath, was allowed by the court to direct that her respirator be unplugged. The courts ruled in her case that to unplug the respirator was not contrary to the criminal code prohibiting anyone from causing or assisting in the death of another person. Rather, it constituted the exercise of the right of any patient to direct her own treatment. The case of Sue Rodriquez, described in the first reading, resulted in a split decision in which the Supreme Court of Canada upheld the law prohibiting assisted suicide. Austin Bastable, who was suffering from advanced multiple sclerosis carried out a public campaign to change the law. In the end, he crossed the border and committed suicide with the help of Dr. Kevorkian, who is a forceful advocate of the legalization of assisted suicide in the United States. Finally, in ending the life of his daughter Tracy, who suffered from cerebral palsy and was a quadriplegic, Robert Latimer was found guilty of second degree murder first by the Saskatchewan courts and then by the Supreme Court of Canada (this case is discussed in the reading by Melanie Rock).

Situations of the kind just described have led people in two directions. Some argue that protection of life is the fundamental and overriding obligation of any society. People who take this view tend to emphasize the dangers of expanding the role of the physician to include decisions to end human life and focus on the importance of palliative care as a morally preferable alternative. Others argue that the traditional view of euthanasia is no longer adequate. In their view, when continued existence has become intolerable through suffering or has lost its meaning because of mental degeneration, disability, or for some other reason, euthanasia is not immoral. Some would go even further. They would argue that members of the medical profession have an obligation to end the lives of those whose suffering has become intolerable or whose capacity to enjoy life has ended.

The view that euthanasia is sometimes justified is frequently defended by appealing to the avoidance of suffering principle. However, the moral autonomy principle has also found a place in current debates. There is a deeply entrenched view in our society that each person should be left free to act on his or her own assessment of what is required in particular situations unless there are strong reasons to the contrary. Applied to the euthanasia debate, this view would seem to imply that both individually and collectively we should respect peoples' decisions to end their lives unless ending their lives will harm others. The moral autonomy principle plays a central role in laws implemented to permit euthanasia in the Netherlands in 2001 and Belgium in 2002.

The Moral Dimension

There are three types of situations in which the problem of euthanasia arises. First, a person may decide that his or her life has become intolerable and request that it be ended as an act of mercy. The request may be direct. Or it may be communicated in a "living will," a document in which people indicate that life should be ended if, for example, they should come to have serious brain damage or serious and irreversible physical disabilities. Euthanasia that is performed in response to such a "direct" request is said to be voluntary.

The problem of euthanasia can also arise in situations in which people are believed to be suffering in an intolerable or pointless way that they would not wish to tolerate but, because of their condition, cannot direct how to be treated. If euthanasia is administered under these conditions, it is nonvoluntary. The assumption is that it is not contrary to the presumed wishes of the person in question. Nevertheless, it is not voluntary because it has not been explicitly requested.

Finally, it is sometimes argued that euthanasia is justified, on occasion, even when the "victim" does not concur, or might not concur, or might reasonably be expected not to concur. We might describe this third possibility as involuntary euthanasia. Infanticide in cases in which a child is seriously disabled (anencephaly, for example) may be an example of involuntary euthanasia, depending on why the action is taken. The Nazi practice of putting mentally defective, ill, old, and other "socially useless" persons to death is another example of involuntary euthanasia. Many fear that legalizing euthanasia may put us on the slippery slope to this sort of devaluation of human life.

Discussions of euthanasia, then, give rise to three questions: Is voluntary euthanasia ever justified? Is nonvoluntary euthanasia ever justified? Is involuntary euthanasia ever justified?

A final distinction should be noted. Some participants in the debate argue that it is important to differentiate between active and passive euthanasia, a distinction that is intended to mark the difference between actively intervening to end a person's life (by administering an injection, for example) and simply not treating a person who has been injured or is ill, knowing that without treatment the person likely will die. Assessing the merits of this distinction is also an essential step in evaluating the morality of euthanasia.

The Readings

The readings begin with the case of Sue Rodriquez, a woman suffering from Lou Gehrig's disease, who petitioned the courts to set aside the criminal law prohibition against euthanasia and assisted suicide. Noting that suicide is not illegal, she argued that in prohibiting assisted suicide, the law discriminated against those like herself who were so physically disabled that they were unable to end their lives without assistance. This case was eventually decided in the Supreme Court of Canada. The Chief Justice at the time, Judge Lamer, argued in a dissenting view that the law was discriminatory and should be stuck down. The effect of his judgment would, among other things, have been to allow Sue Rodriquez the right to an assisted suicide. His judgment sets out the parameters of a euthanasia law that in his view would adequately balance the protection of life and the moral autonomy principles around which so much of the euthanasia debate turns. The majority of the court, however, disagreed with Judge Lamer. In a judgment representing that majority view, Judge Sopinka argues that Criminal Code provisions prohibiting assisted suicide do not constitute unjustifiable discrimination against those unable to end their own lives.

In the second reading, Margaret Somerville argues that we need clarification about the terminology that is used in the euthanasia debate. In particular, she argues that physician-assisted suicide and euthanasia need to be clearly separated from questions about treatment at the end of life. While people ought to be given the right to refuse treatment and to relieve pain, physician-assisted suicide and euthanasia should not be legalized. Somerville answers the question of why there is an interest in legalizing euthanasia now by examining societal and cultural factors such as increased and intense individualism, a death-denying, death-obsessed society, the impact of scientific advances, and a retreat from religious and moral world views to a mechanistic approach to human life. She ends by outlining how the legalization of euthanasia could detrimentally affect the medical profession as well as our views of the meaning of our individual and collective lives.

The third reading by James Rachels can be said to challenge one aspect of Somerville's analysis: the moral significance of the distinction between active and passive euthanasia. If it is acceptable as a way of relieving suffering to let nature take its course when medical intervention could prolong life, then it is equally acceptable, argues Rachels, to intervene to end life when the goal is to ease suffering. Patrick Nowell-Smith, in the fourth reading, also argues in support of the legalization of euthanasia in the case of voluntary euthanasia. His argument emphasizes the avoidance of suffering and the moral autonomy principles.

In the final, difficult but important reading, Melanie Rock examines the concept of suffering and, specifically, the representations of disability as inherently undesirable and persons with disabilities as unhealthy and suffering. These representations, she argues, can be found in the Disability-Adjusted Life Year (DALY), an indicator developed for the World Bank and the World Health Organization to measure human health. Rock uses this complex analysis of discriminatory attitudes about disabled persons to examine the Latimer case, in which questions about what sort of life is worth living were raised in the debate in Canada about whether to charge Robert Latimer with murdering his disabled twelve-year-old daughter Tracy. Rock raises issues important to disability theorists. What effects do policies that allow the termination of lives judged to be of less worth have on those who are currently disabled and on our perception and treatment of them? This question not only is relevant to debates about euthanasia, but also to debates about abortion in which medical technology allows the detection of fetal abnormalities. We also return to issues of disability in Chapter 5 on Equality and Discrimination.

RODRIGUEZ V. BRITISH COLUMBIA (ATTORNEY GENERAL), 1993

Mr. Justice A. Lamer

I. <u>Facts</u>

The facts of this case are straightforward and well known. Sue Rodriguez is a 42-year-old woman living in British Columbia. She is married and the mother of an 8½-year-old son. Ms. Rodriguez suffers from amyotrophic lateral sclerosis (ALS), which is widely known as Lou Gehrig's disease; her life expectancy is between 2 and 14 months but her condition is rapidly deteriorating. Very soon she will lose the ability to swallow, speak, walk and move her body without assistance. Thereafter she will lose the capacity to breathe without a respirator, to eat without a gastrotomy and will eventually become confined to a bed.

Ms. Rodriguez knows of her condition, the trajectory of her illness and the inevitability of how her life will end; her wish is to control the circumstances, timing and manner of her death. She does not wish to die so long as she still has the capacity to enjoy life. However, by the time she no longer is able to enjoy life, she will be physically unable to terminate her life without assistance. Ms. Rodriguez seeks an order which will allow a qualified medical practitioner to set up technological means by which she might, by her own hand, at the time of her choosing, end her life.

Ms. Rodriguez applied to the Supreme Court of British Columbia for an order that s. 241(*b*) of the *Criminal Code*, R.S.C., 1985, c. C-46, be declared invalid, pursuant to s. 24(1) of the *Canadian Charter of Rights and Freedoms*, on the ground that it violates her rights under ss. 7, 12 and 15(1) of the *Charter*, and was therefore, to the extent it prohibits a terminally ill person from committing "physician-assisted" suicide, of no force and effect. . . .

241. Every one who

(*a*) counsels a person to commit suicide, or

(*b*) aids or abets a person to commit suicide,

whether suicide ensues or not, is guilty of an indictable offence and liable to imprisonment for a term not exceeding fourteen years.

The relevant sections of the Charter are as follows:

1. The *Canadian Charter of Rights and Freedoms* guarantees the rights and freedoms set out in it subject only to such reasonable limits prescribed by law as can be demonstrably justified in a free and democratic society.

7. Everyone has the right to life, liberty and security of the person and the right not to be deprived thereof except in accordance with the principles of fundamental justice.

12. Everyone has the right not to be subjected to any cruel and unusual treatment or punishment.

15. (1) Every individual is equal before and under the law and has the right to the equal protection and equal benefit of the law without discrimination and, in particular, without discrimination based on race, national or ethnic origin, colour, religion, sex, age or mental or physical disability. . . .

The principal fear is that the decriminalization of assisted suicide will increase the risk of persons with physical disabilities being manipulated by others. This "slippery slope" argument appeared to be the central justification behind the Law Reform Commission of Canada's recommendation not to repeal this provision. The Commission stated the following in its Working Paper 28, *Euthanasia, Aiding Suicide and Cessation of Treatment* (1892), at p. 46:

> The principal consideration in terms of legislative policy, and the deciding one for the Commission, remains that of possible abuses. There is, first of all, a real danger that the procedure developed to allow the death of those who are a burden to themselves may be gradually diverted from its original purpose and eventually used as well to eliminate those who are a burden to others or to society. There is also the constant danger that the subject's consent to euthanasia may not really be a perfectly free and voluntary act.

While I share a deep concern over the subtle and overt pressures that may be brought to bear on such persons if assisted suicide is decriminalized, even in limited circumstances, I do not think legislation that deprives a disadvantaged group of the right to equality can be justified solely on such speculative grounds, no matter how well intentioned. Similar dangers to the ones outlined above have surrounded the decriminalization of attempted suicide as well. It is impossible to know the degree of pressure or intimidation a physically able person may have been under when deciding to commit suicide. The truth is that we simply do not and cannot know the range of implications that allowing some form of assisted suicide will have for persons with physical disabilities. What we do know and cannot ignore is the anguish of those in the position of Ms. Rodriguez. Respecting the consent of those in her position may necessarily imply running the risk that the consent will have been obtained improperly. The proper role of the legal system in these circumstances is to provide safeguards to ensure that the consent in question is as independent and informed as is reasonably possible.

The fear of a "slippery slope" cannot, in my view, justify the over-inclusive reach of the *Criminal Code* to encompass not only people who may be vulnerable to the pressure of others but also persons with no evidence of vulnerability, and, in the case of the appellant, persons where there is positive evidence of freely determined consent. Sue Rodriguez is and will remain mentally competent. She has testified at trial to the fact that she alone, in consultation with her physicians, wishes to control the decision-making regarding the timing and circumstances of her death. I see no reason to disbelieve her, nor has the Crown suggested that she is being wrongfully influenced by anyone. Ms. Rodriguez has also emphasized that she remains and wishes to remain free *not* to avail herself of the opportunity to end her own life should that be her eventual choice. The issue here is whether Parliament is justified in denying her the ability to make this choice lawfully, as could any physically able person.

While s. 241(*b*) restricts the equality rights of all those people who are physically unable to commit suicide without assistance, the choice for a mentally competent but physically disabled person who additionally suffers from a terminal illness is, I think, different from the choice of an individual whose disability is not life-threatening; in other words, for Ms. Rodriguez, tragically, the choice is not whether to live as she is or to die, but rather when and how to experience a death that is inexorably impending. I do not, however, by observing this distinction, mean to suggest that the terminally ill are immune from vulnerability, or that they are less likely to be influenced by the intervention of others whatever their motives. Indeed, there is substantial evidence that people in this position may be susceptible to certain types of vulnerability that others are not. Further, it should not be assumed that a person with a physical disability who chooses suicide is doing so only as a result of the incapacity. It must be acknowledged that mentally competent people who commit suicide do so for a wide variety of motives, irrespective of their physical condition or life expectancy.

The law, in its present form, takes no account of the particular risks and interests that may be at issue in these differing contexts. The Law Reform Commission used the distinction between these differing contexts to justify its recommendation not to decriminalize assisted suicide in the Working Paper 28, *supra*, at pp. 53-54:

> . . . the prohibition in section 224 is not restricted solely to the case of the terminally ill patient, for whom we can only have sympathy, or solely to his physician or a member of his family who helps him to put an end to his suffering. The section is more general and applies to a variety of situations for which it is much more difficult to feel sympathy. Consider, for example, a recent incident, that of inciting to mass suicide. What of the person who takes advantage of another's depressed state to encourage him to commit suicide, for his own financial benefit? What of the person who, knowing an adolescent's suicidal tendencies, provides him with large enough quantities of drugs to kill him? The "accomplice" in these cases cannot be considered morally blameless. Nor can one conclude that the criminal law should not punish such conduct. To decriminalize *completely* the act of aiding, abetting or counselling suicide would therefore not be a valid legislative policy [Emphasis added.]

I agree with the importance of distinguishing between the situation where a person who is aided in his or her decision to commit suicide and the situation where the decision itself is a product of someone else's influence. However, I fail to see how preventing against abuse in one context must result in denying self-determination in another. I remain unpersuaded by the government's apparent contention that it is not possible to design legislation that is somewhere in between complete decriminalization and absolute prohibition. . . .

To summarize, then, I would make a constitutional exemption available to Ms. Rodriguez, and others, on the following conditions:

(1) the constitutional exemption may only be sought by way of application to a superior court;

(2) the applicant must be certified by a treating physician and independent psychiatrist, in the manner and at the time suggested by McEachern C.J., to be competent to make the decision to end her own life, and the physicians must certify that the applicant's decision has been made freely and voluntarily, and at least one of the physicians must be present with the applicant at the time the applicant commits assisted suicide;

(3) the physicians must also certify:

  (i) that the applicant is or will become physically incapable of committing suicide unassisted, and (ii) that they have informed him or her, and that he or she understands, that he or she has a continuing right to change his or her mind about terminating his or her life;

(4) notice and access must be given to the Regional Coroner at the time and in the manner described by McEachern C.J.;

(5) the applicant must be examined daily by one of the certifying physicians at the time and in the manner outlined by McEachern C.J.;

(6) the constitutional exemption will expire according to the time limits set by McEachern C.J.; and

(7) the act causing the death of the applicant must be that of the applicant him- or herself, and not of anyone else.

I wish to emphasize that these conditions have been tailored to the particular circumstances of Ms. Rodriguez. While they may be used as guidelines for future petitioners in a similar position, each application must be considered in its own context.

VI. Disposition

I would answer the constitutional questions as follows:

1. Does s. 241(b) of the *Criminal Code* of Canada infringe or deny, in whole or in part, the rights and freedoms guaranteed by ss. 7, 12 and 15(1) of the *Canadian Charter of Rights and Freedoms*?

Answer: Yes.

2. If so, is it justified by s. 1 of the *Canadian Charter of Rights and Freedoms* and therefore not inconsistent with the *Constitution Act*, 1982?

Answer: No.

I would therefore allow the appeal, with costs to the appellant against the Attorneys General of British Columbia and Canada, and declare s. 241(*b*) to be of no force or effect, on the condition that the effect of this declaration be suspended for one year from the date of this judgment. During that one-year suspension period, a constitutional exemption from s. 241(*b*) may be granted by superior court on application, on the terms and in accordance with the conditions set out above. In the case of Ms. Rodriguez, in light of the factual record before this Court, it is not necessary for her to make application to a superior court. As long as she satisfies the conditions outlined above, she is granted the constitutional exemption and may proceed as she wishes.

DATED AT OTTAWA this 4th day of August 1993

. . .

SOPINKA J. — I have read the reasons of the Chief Justice and those of McLachlin J. herein. The result of the reasons of my colleagues is that all persons who by reason of disability are unable to commit suicide have a right under the *Canadian Charter of Rights and Freedoms* to be free from government interference in procuring the assistance of others to take their life. They are entitled to a constitutional exemption from the operation of s. 241 of the *Criminal Code*, R.S.C., 1985, c. C-46, which prohibits the giving of assistance to commit suicide (hereinafter referred to as "assisted suicide"). The exemption would apply during the period that this Court's order would be suspended and thereafter Parliament could only replace the legislation subject to this right. I must respectfully disagree with the conclusion reached by my colleagues and with their reasons. In my view, nothing in the *Charter* mandates this result which raises the following serious concerns:

1. It recognizes a constitutional right to legally assisted suicide beyond that of any country in the western world, beyond any serious proposal for reform in the western world and beyond the claim made in this very case. The apparent reason for the expansion beyond the claim in this case is that restriction of the right to the terminally ill could not be justified under s. 15.

2. It fails to provide the safeguards which are required either under the Dutch guidelines or the recent proposals for reform in the states of Washington and California which were defeated by voters in those states principally because comparable and even more stringent safeguards were considered inadequate.

3. The conditions imposed are vague and in some respects unenforceable. While the proposals in California were criticized for failure to specify the type of physician who is authorized to assist and the Dutch guidelines specify the treating physician, the conditions imposed by my colleagues do not require that the person assisting be a physician or impose any restriction in this regard. Since much of the medical profession is opposed to being involved in assisting suicide because it is antithetical to their role as healers of the sick, many doctors will refuse to assist, leaving open the potential for the growth of a macabre specialty in this area reminiscent of Dr. Kevorkian and his suicide machine.

4. To add to the uncertainty of the conditions, they are to serve merely as guidelines, leaving it to individual judges to decide upon application whether to grant or withhold the right to commit suicide. In the case of the appellant, the remedy proposed by the Chief Justice, concurred in by McLachlin J., would not require such an application. She alone is to decide that the conditions or guidelines are complied with. Any judicial review of this decision would only occur if she were to commit suicide and a charge were laid against the person who assisted her. The reasons of McLachlin J. remove any requirement to monitor the choice made by the appellant to commit suicide so that the act might occur after the last expression of the desire to commit suicide is stale-dated.

I have concluded that the conclusion of my colleagues cannot be supported under the provisions of the *Charter*. Reliance was placed on ss. 7, 12 and 15 and I will examine each in turn.

I. Section 7

The most substantial issue in this appeal is whether s. 241(*b*) infringes s. 7 in that it inhibits the appellant in controlling the timing and manner of her death. I conclude that while the section impinges on the security interest of the appellant, any resulting deprivation is not contrary to the principles of fundamental justice. I would come to the same conclusion with respect to any liberty interest which may be involved.

Section 7 of the *Charter* provides as follows:

7. Everyone has the right to life, liberty and security of the person and the right not to be deprived thereof except in accordance with the principles of fundamental justice.

The appellant argues that, by prohibiting anyone from assisting her to end her life when her illness has rendered her incapable of terminating her life without such assistance, by threat of criminal sanction, s. 241(*b*) deprives her of both her liberty and her security of the person. The appellant asserts that her application is based upon (a) the right to live her remaining life with the inherent dignity of a human person, (b) the right to control what happens to her body while she is living, and (c) the right to be free from governmental interference in making fundamental personal decisions concerning the terminal stages of her life. The first two of these asserted rights can be seen to invoke both liberty and security of the person; the latter is more closely associated with only the liberty interest.

(a) *Life, Liberty and Security of the Person*

The appellant seeks a remedy which would assure her some control over the time and manner of her death. While she supports her claim on the ground that her liberty and security of the person interests are engaged, a consideration of these interests cannot be divorced from the sanctity of life, which is one of the three *Charter* values protected by s. 7.

None of these values prevail a priori over the others. All must be taken into account in determining the content of the principles of fundamental justice and there is no basis for imposing a greater burden on the propounder of one value as against that imposed on another. . . .

I find more merit in the argument that security of the person, by its nature, cannot encompass a right to take action that will end one's life as security of the person is intrinsically concerned with the well-being of the living person. This argument focuses on the generally held and deeply rooted belief in our society that human life is sacred or inviolable (which terms I use in the non-religious sense described by Dworkin (*Life's Dominion: An Argument About Abortion, Euthanasia, and Individual Freedom* (1993) to mean that human life is seen to have a deep intrinsic value of its own). As members of a society based upon respect for the intrinsic value of human life and on the inherent dignity of every human being, can we incorporate within the Constitution which embodies our most fundamental values a right to terminate one's own life in any circumstances? This question in turn evokes other queries of fundamental importance such as the degree to which our conception of the sanctity of life includes notions of quality of life as well.

Sanctity of life, as we will see, has been understood historically as excluding freedom of choice in the self-infliction of death and certainly in the involvement of others in carrying out that choice. At the very least, no new consensus has emerged in society opposing the right of the state to regulate the involvement of others in exercising power over individuals ending their lives.

The appellant suggests that for the terminally ill, the choice is one of time and manner of death rather than death itself since the latter is inevitable.

I disagree. Rather it is one of choosing death instead of allowing natural forces to run their course. The time and precise manner of death remain unknown until death actually occurs. There can be no certainty in forecasting the precise circumstances of a death. Death is, for all mortals, inevitable. Even when death appears imminent, seeking to control the manner and timing of one's death constitutes a conscious choice of death over life. It follows that life as a value is engaged even in the case of the terminally ill who seek to choose death over life. . . .

In this case, it is not disputed that in general s. 241(*b*) is valid and desirable legislation which fulfils the government's objectives of preserving life and protecting the vulnerable. The complaint is that the legislation is over-inclusive because it does not exclude from the reach of the prohibition those in the situation of the appellant who are terminally ill, mentally competent, but cannot commit suicide on their own. It is also argued that the extension of the prohibition to the appellant is arbitrary and unfair as suicide itself is not unlawful, and the common law allows a physician to withhold or withdraw life-saving or life-maintaining treatment on the patient's instructions and to administer palliative care which has the effect of hastening death. The issue is whether, given this legal context, the existence of a criminal prohibition on assisting suicide for one in the appellant's situation is contrary to principles of fundamental justice.

Discerning the principles of fundamental justice with which deprivation of life, liberty or security of the person must accord, in order to withstand constitutional scrutiny, is not an easy task. A mere common law rule does not suffice to constitute a principle of fundamental justice, rather, as the term implies, principles upon which there is some consensus that they are vital or fundamental to our societal notion of justice are required. Principles of fundamental justice must not, however, be so broad as to be no more than vague generalizations about what our society considers to be ethical or moral. They must be capable of being identified with some precision and applied to situations in a manner which yields an understandable result. They must also, in my view, be legal principles. The now familiar words of Lamer J. in *Re B.C. Motor Vehicle Act*, [1985] 2 S.C.R. 486, at pp. 512-13, are as follows:

> Consequently, the principles of fundamental justice are to be found in the basic tenets and principles, not only of our judicial process, but also of the other components of our legal system.

> . . . the proper approach to the determination of the principles of fundamental justice is quite simply one in which, as Professor L. Tremblay has written, "future growth will be based on historical roots". . . .

> Whether any given principle may be said to be a principle of fundamental justice within the meaning of s. 7 will rest upon an analysis of the nature, sources, *rationale*

and essential role of that principle within the judicial process and in our legal system, as it evolves.

This Court has often stated that in discerning the principles of fundamental justice governing a particular case, it is helpful to look at the common law and legislative history of the offence in question (*Re B.C. Motor Vehicle Act and Morgentaler, supra*, and *R. v. Swain*, [1991] 1 S.C.R. 933). It is not sufficient, however, merely to conduct a historical review and conclude that because neither Parliament nor the various medical associations had ever expressed a view that assisted suicide should be decriminalized, that to prohibit it could not be said to be contrary to the principles of fundamental justice. Such an approach would be problematic for two reasons. First, a strictly historical analysis will always lead to the conclusion in a case such as this that the deprivation is in accordance with fundamental justice as the legislation will not have kept pace with advances in medical technology. Second, such reasoning is somewhat circular, in that it relies on the continuing existence of the prohibition to find the prohibition to be fundamentally just.

The way to resolve these problems is not to avoid the historical analysis, but to make sure that one is looking not just at the existence of the practice itself (i.e., the continued criminalization of assisted suicide) but at the rationale behind that practice and the principles which underlie it.

The appellant asserts that it is a principle of fundamental justice that the human dignity and autonomy of individuals be respected, and that to subject her to needless suffering in this manner is to rob her of her dignity. The importance of the concept of human dignity in our society was enunciated by Cory J. (dissenting, Lamer C.J. concurring) in *Kindler v. Canada (Minister of Justice)*, [1991] 2 S.C.R. 779, at p. 813. Respect for human dignity underlies many of the rights and freedoms in the *Charter*.

That respect for human dignity is one of the underlying principles upon which our society is based is unquestioned. I have difficulty, however, in characterizing this in itself as a principle of fundamental justice within the meaning of s. 7. While respect for human dignity is the genesis for many principles of fundamental justice, not every law that fails to accord such respect runs afoul of these principles. To state that "respect for human dignity and autonomy" is a principle of fundamental justice, then, is essentially to state that the deprivation of the appellant's security of the person is contrary to principles of fundamental justice because it deprives her of security of the person. This interpretation would equate security of the person with a principle of fundamental justice and render the latter redundant. . . .

The issue here, then, can be characterized as being whether the blanket prohibition on assisted suicide is arbitrary or unfair in that it is unrelated to the state's interest in protecting the vulnerable, and that it lacks a foundation in the legal tradition and societal beliefs which are said to be represented by the prohibition.

Section 241(*b*) has as its purpose the protection of the vulnerable who might be induced in moments of weakness to commit suicide. This purpose is grounded in the state interest in protecting life and reflects the policy of the state that human life should not be depreciated by allowing life to be taken. This policy finds expression not only in the provisions of our *Criminal Code* which prohibit murder and other violent acts against others notwithstanding the consent of the victim, but also in the policy against capital punishment and, until its repeal, attempted suicide. This is not only a policy of the state, however, but is part of our fundamental conception of the sanctity of human life. The Law Reform Commission expressed this philosophy appropriately in its Working Paper 28, *Euthanasia, Aiding Suicide and Cessation of Treatment* (1982), at p. 36:

> Preservation of human life is acknowledged to be a fundamental value of our society. Historically, our criminal law has changed very little on this point. Generally speaking, it sanctions the principle of the sanctity of human life. Over the years, however, law has come to temper the apparent absolutism of the principle, to delineate its intrinsic limitations and to define its true dimensions.

As is noted in the above passage, the principle of sanctity of life is no longer seen to require that all human life be preserved at all costs. Rather, it has come to be understood, at least by some, as encompassing quality of life considerations, and to be subject to certain limitations and qualifications reflective of personal autonomy and dignity. . . .

(iv) <u>Conclusion on Principles of Fundamental Justice</u>

What the preceding review demonstrates is that Canada and other Western democracies recognize and apply the principle of the sanctity of life as a general principle which is subject to limited and narrow exceptions in situations in which notions of personal autonomy and dignity must prevail. However, these same societies continue to draw distinctions between passive and active forms of intervention in the dying process, and with very few exceptions, prohibit assisted suicide in situations akin to that of the appellant. The task then becomes to identify the rationales upon which these distinctions are based and to determine whether they are constitutionally supportable.

The distinction between withdrawing treatment upon a patient's request, such as occurred in the *Nancy B.* case, on the one hand, and assisted suicide on the other has been criticized as resting on a legal fiction — that is, the distinction between active and passive forms of treatment. The criticism is based on the fact that the withdrawal of life supportive measures is done with the knowledge that death will ensue, just as is assisting suicide, and that death does in fact ensue as a result of the action taken. See, for example, the *Harvard Law Review* note "Physician-Assisted Suicide and the Right to Die with Assistance" (1992), 105 *Harv. L. Rev.* 2021, at pp. 2030-31.

Other commentators, however, uphold the distinction on the basis that in the case of withdrawal of treatment, the death is "natural" — the artificial forces of medical technology which have kept the patient alive are removed and nature takes its course. In the case of assisted suicide or euthanasia, however, the course of nature is interrupted, and death results *directly* from the human action taken (E. W. Keyserlingk, *Sanctity of Life or Quality of Life in the Context of Ethics, Medicine and Law* (1979), a study paper for the Law Reform Commission of Canada's Protection of Life Series). The Law Reform Commission calls this distinction "fundamental" (at p. 19 of the Working Paper 28).

Whether or not one agrees that the active vs. passive distinction is maintainable, however, the fact remains that under our common law, the physician has no choice but to accept the patient's instructions to discontinue treatment. To continue to treat the patient when the patient has withdrawn consent to that treatment constitutes battery (*Ciarlariello and Nancy B., supra*). The doctor is therefore not required to make a choice which will result in the patient's death as he would be if he chose to assist a suicide or to perform active euthanasia.

The fact that doctors may deliver palliative care to terminally ill patients without fear of sanction, it is argued, attenuates to an even greater degree any legitimate distinction which can be drawn between assisted suicide and what are currently acceptable forms of medical treatment. The administration of drugs designed for pain control in dosages which the physician knows will hasten death constitutes active contribution to death by any standard. However, the distinction drawn here is one based upon intention — in the case of palliative care the intention is to ease pain, which has the effect of hastening death, while in the case of assisted suicide, the intention is undeniably to cause death. The Law Reform Commission, although it recommended the continued criminal prohibition of both euthanasia and assisted suicide, stated, at p. 70 of the Working Paper, that a doctor should never refuse palliative care to a terminally ill person only because it may hasten death. In my view, distinctions based upon intent are important, and in fact form the basis of our criminal law. While factually the distinction may, at times, be difficult to draw, legally it is clear. The fact that in some cases, the third party will, under the guise of palliative care, commit euthanasia or assist in suicide and go unsanctioned due to the difficulty of proof cannot be said to render the existence of the prohibition fundamentally unjust.

The principles of fundamental justice cannot be created for the occasion to reflect the court's dislike or distaste of a particular statute. While the principles of fundamental justice are concerned with more than process, reference must be made to principles which are "fundamental" in the sense that they would have general acceptance among reasonable people. From the review that I have conducted above, I am unable to discern anything approaching unanimity with respect to the issue before us. Regardless of one's personal views as to whether the distinctions drawn between withdrawal of treatment and palliative care, on the one hand, and assisted suicide on the other are practically compelling, the fact remains that these distinctions are maintained and can be persuasively defended. To the extent that there is a consensus, it is that human life must be respected and we must be careful not to undermine the institutions that protect it.

This consensus finds legal expression in our legal system which prohibits capital punishment. This prohibition is supported, in part, on the basis that allowing the state to kill will cheapen the value of human life and thus the state will serve in a sense as a role model for individuals in society. The prohibition against assisted suicide serves a similar purpose. In upholding the respect for life, it may discourage those who consider that life is unbearable at a particular moment, or who perceive themselves to be a burden upon others, from committing suicide. To permit a physician to lawfully participate in taking life would send a signal that there are circumstances in which the state approves of suicide.

I also place some significance in the fact that the official position of various medical associations is against decriminalizing assisted suicide (Canadian Medical Association, British Medical Association, Council of Ethical and Judicial Affairs of the American Medical Association, World Medical Association and the American Nurses Association). Given the concerns about abuse that have been expressed and the great difficulty in creating appropriate safeguards to prevent these, it can not be said that the blanket prohibition on assisted suicide is arbitrary or unfair, or that it is not reflective of fundamental values at play in our society. I am thus unable to find that any principle of fundamental justice is violated by s. 241(*b*). . . .

LEGALIZING EUTHANASIA: WHY NOW?

Margaret A. Somerville

Until very recently, all countries prohibited euthanasia, although it had been legally tolerated — not legalized, but not prosecuted, provided it complied with various conditions — since the early 1970s in the much studied and cited case of the Netherlands, where it has just been formally legalized.[1] Many countries are now experiencing an unprecedented rise in calls to legalize euthanasia.[2] Some of these demands come from within the profession of medicine.[3] Oregon law[4] now authorizes physicians to prescribe lethal doses of medication for their patients.[5] And the United States Second Circuit Court of Appeals[6] and Ninth Circuit Court of Appeals[7] struck down prohibitions on assisting in suicide[8] as constitutionally invalid, although these decisions were later overturned by the United States Supreme Court. In a then-unique example, the Northern Territory of Australia enacted a bill in 1995 to legalize euthanasia.[9] This legislation was subsequently overruled by the Australian Commonwealth Parliament.

The euthanasia debate is a momentous one. It involves problems that range from the nature and meaning of human life to the most fundamental principles on which societies are based. This debate involves our individual and collective *past* (the ethical, legal, and cultural norms that have been handed down to us as members of families, groups, and societies); the *present* (whether we will change those norms); and the *future* (the impact that any such change would have on those who come after us).

As a result, we must consider the impact of legalizing euthanasia not only at an individual level (which, in the mass media, and therefore in the general public forum, has been the focus of debate) but also at institutional, governmental, and societal levels. And not only in the present but also for the future. We need to consider factual realities, such as the possibilities for abuse that legalizing euthanasia would open up, as well as the effect that doing so would have on the important values and symbols that make up the intangible fabric that constitutes our society and on some of our most important societal institutions.

Definition

Whatever one's personal position on the acceptability of euthanasia, it is essential to know what we mean by that word. I discuss the definition elsewhere in more detail, thus a brief definition will suffice: "Euthanasia is a deliberate act that causes death undertaken by one person with the primary intention of ending the life of another person, in order to relieve that person's suffering."[10] Refusals of treatment — including life-support treatment or artificial hydration and nutrition — and provision of necessary treatment for the relief of pain or other symptoms of serious physical distress are not euthanasia, even if they do shorten life.[11] In the latter case, the primary intention is to respect the right to inviolability — the right not to be touched without consent — or to relieve pain, not to inflict death (as it is in the former case).

The term "physician-assisted suicide" is often used to describe what is really euthanasia. The physician carries out the act that causes death. In physician-assisted suicide, properly so-called, physicians would give patients the means to kill themselves with the intent that patients would so use them. Legally, there is a difference between physician-assisted suicide

From Death Talk: The Case against Ethanasia and Physician-Assisted Suicide, *pp. 101-104, 105-118, 368-371. Reprinted with permission of McGill-Queen's University Press.*

and euthanasia. The latter is homicide, not suicide. It is either murder or manslaughter under the criminal law in the United Kingdom, Australia (except in the Northern Territory before the repeal of its euthanasia law), Canada, and each state of the United States. Criminal liability for physician-assisted suicide would lie in aiding, abetting, or counselling another person to commit suicide. The use of terms such as "physician-assisted suicide" — or even the more ambiguous "physician-assisted death" — to mean euthanasia leads to confusion. But although these interventions are legally distinct crimes (and, some believe, morally distinguishable), at a societal level many of the worries that legalizing them would present would be the same. From this perspective, they can be discussed together.[12] Unless some distinction must be made, therefore, in this chapter I use the word *euthanasia* to include physician-assisted suicide.

It is necessary, and only honest, to state at the outset where one stands. I am against legalization. I cannot argue against euthanasia from an empirical base, however. Carrying out euthanasia constitutes a very serious criminal offence in the vast majority of jurisdictions; consequently, research may not be undertaken to produce "hard" evidence of the impact that legalizing it would have. Opponents of legalization are therefore open to the criticism and challenge that their arguments are purely speculative and lacking in scientific rigour. This difficulty has become manifest in another way. The burden of proof has somehow shifted from those who promote legalization to those who oppose it — a lamentable situation. How ironic that the norm that we must not kill must now be defended more vigorously than its opposite.

The problem of producing evidence is not as severe for those who are pro-euthanasia because they base their case on respect for individual autonomy, the failure of palliative care to relieve all suffering, and the allegation, often, that physicians are secretly practising euthanasia anyway. They can use polls and surveys — which have the appearance, at least, of producing "hard" data — to show that many people believe they should have a right of access to euthanasia, that the suffering of some terminally ill patients cannot be relieved, and that some physicians admit to carrying out euthanasia. The fact that it is easier to establish the case for legalization than against it, moreover, could distort the process of making a decision about legalizing euthanasia and, consequently, the ultimate decision. Other factors could have the same effect. It would be an interesting research project to compare the number of pro- and of anti-euthanasia articles in leading medical journals and to examine the reasons for any discrepancies found between these numbers. I predict that a substantial majority would be pro-euthanasia. If so, we would need to take care that the popularity of that position does not unjustifiably influence the decision.

A Necessary Question: Why Now?

Why are we considering legalizing euthanasia now, after our society has prohibited it for almost two milennia?[13] It is true that the population is aging; modern medicine has extended our life span, with the result that it is more likely now than in the past that we will die of chronic degenerative diseases, not acute ones. It is also true that many countries lack adequate palliative care, and some physicians are ignorant about treatments for the relief of pain and suffering, while others either fail or refuse to provide them. Medical practice, too, has also changed. A lifetime relationship with "the family doctor" is largely a relic of the past, and the feeling of isolation that people can experience in seeking help from health-care professionals is probably a reflection of the wider isolation that individuals and families experience. But the capacity to relieve pain and suffering has improved remarkably. Not one of the bottom-line conditions usually seen as linked with the call for euthanasia — that terminally ill people want to die and that we can kill them — is new. These factors have been part of the human condition for as long as humans have existed. Why, then, are we considering such a radically different response to this situation?

Societal and Cultural Causes

I suggest that the principal cause is not a change in the situation of individuals who seek euthanasia; rather, it is profound changes in our postmodern, secular, Western, democratic societies. Some of these changes involve trends that have been emerging since the eighteenth century, but only recently have they all co-existed and each has overwhelmingly dominated its opposite, or countervailing, trend. The factors I single out here do not constitute a comprehensive list. They are not all of the same nature, so they are not all treated in the same way or depth. Indeed, I mention some very briefly. In any case, each requires a much more thorough examination. And my conclusions about their strength, causal link to euthanasia, or impact are clearly open to challenge. My aim is to provide a rough map — a somewhat impressionistic overview — of the societal and cultural factors giving rise to and influencing the movement to legalize euthanasia. There are, moreover, still strong forces that resist the legalization of euthanasia, most notably the Catholic Church, evangelical Christian churches, Orthodox Judaism, and Islam.

Individualism

Our society is based on "intense individualism," even in connection with death and bereavement — possibly, individualism to the exclusion of any real sense of community. If this highly individualistic approach is applied to euthanasia, especially in a society that gives pre-eminence to personal autonomy and self-determination, it is likely to result in the belief that euthanasia is acceptable.[14] There seems to be either a total lack of consciousness or a denial that this kind of individualism can undermine the intangible infrastructure on which society rests, the communal and cultural fabric. Individualism untempered by concern and recognition of a duty to protect and promote community will inevitably result in destruction of the community. Thus, although legalizing euthanasia is a result of unbridled individualism, the former would also promote the latter, at least in terms of tipping the balance between the individual and the community further towards the individual.

Almost all the justifications for legalizing euthanasia focus primarily on the dying person who wants it. Indeed, it is usually considered unacceptable to promote the case for euthanasia by arguing that it would benefit others or society, except possibly as a secondary gain. Here are two examples of such a secondary gain. People would be relieved of the burden of caring for terminally ill people. And countries with publicly funded health-care systems (such as those in the United Kingdom, Canada, and Australia), and Medicare and Medicaid in the United States — all countries in which the legalization of euthanasia has recently been a focus of controversy — would save limited health-care resources for allegedly more beneficial uses. This reticence to mention benefits to others or society might be changing, however. In the American case of *Lee v. Oregon*,[15] the trial court noted that the defendant's argument in support of the constitutional validity of the Oregon Death with Dignity Act[16] allowing physician-assisted suicide would reduce the financial burdens caused by terminal illness.

There is yet another sense in which intense individualism might give rise to calls for euthanasia. In postmodern Western societies, death is largely a medical event that takes place in a hospital or other institution and is perceived as occurring in great isolation — patients are alone, separated from those they love and the surroundings with which they are familiar. Death has been institutionalized, depersonalized, and dehumanized. Intense individualism and seeking to take control, especially through euthanasia, are predictable and even reasonable responses to the circumstances. To avoid legalizing euthanasia, therefore, we must give death a more human scale and face.[17]

Mass Media

At first, we created our collective story in each other's physical presence. Later on, we had books and print media, which meant we could do so at a physical distance from each other. Now, for the first time, we can do so through film or television and, consequently, at a physical distance from — but still in sight of — each other no matter where we live on the planet. We do not know how this shift will affect the stories we tell each other to create our shared story, our societal and cultural paradigm — the store of values, attitudes, beliefs, commitments, and myths — that informs our collective life and, through that, our individual lives, and helps to give them meaning. Creating a shared story through the mass media could alter the balance between the various components that make it up. In particular, we might engage in too much "death talk" and too little "life talk." We can be most attracted to that we most fear, and the mass media provide an almost infinite number of opportunities to indulge our fear of, and attraction to, death.

Failure to take into account societal- and cultural-level issues related to euthanasia is connected with "mediatization" of our societal dialogues in general and the one about euthanasia in particular. We see the stories that make up these dialogues only as they are presented by the mass media, an avenue that introduces additional ethical issues — those of "media ethics." It makes dramatic and emotionally gripping television to feature an articulate, courageous, forty-two-year-old divorced woman who is dying of amyotrophic lateral sclerosis, begging to have euthanasia made available and threatening to commit suicide while she is still able — thus leaving her eight-year-old son even sooner — if she is refused access. This scenario describes Sue Rodriguez, who became a national figure in taking her case for euthanasia to the Supreme Court of Canada. In 1993 the court denied her that right by a majority of five to four, with a plurality of dissenting judgments.[18]

The arguments against euthanasia, based on the harm it would do to society in both the present and the future, are much more difficult to present in the mass media than arguments for euthanasia. Anti-euthanasia arguments do not make dramatic and compelling television. Visual images are difficult to find. Viewers do not personally identify with these arguments, which come across as abstractions or ideas, in the same way they do with those of dying people who seek euthanasia. Society cannot be interviewed on television and become a familiar, empathy-evoking figure to the viewing public. Only if euthanasia were legalized and there were obvious abuses — such as proposals to use it on those who want to continue living — could we create comparably riveting and gripping images to communicate the case against euthanasia. Consider *The Children of Men* by P.D. James, set in the year 2025.[19] The novel's first chapter features a scene in which many elderly people die through mass euthanasia. That description evokes a powerful anti-euthanasia response in readers.

The vast exposure to death we are subjected to in both current affairs and entertainment programs might have overwhelmed our sensitivity to the awesomeness of death and, likewise, of inflicting it. Gwynne Dyer has described research showing that human beings have an innate resistance to killing each other, and that this resistance is operative even among soldiers in battle — unless they have been desensitized in order to overcome it. Frighteningly, children are subjected to the techniques developed to achieve this desensitization through their exposure to violence in the mass media.[20] Reports from the 1990s on violent crime in major American cities have shown a drop in the crime rate. But "youth crimes — particularly violent crimes by the young [the super-predators] — are increasing and will continue to increase."[21]

Ironically, the most powerful way in which the case against euthanasia has been presented on television is probably through Dr Jack Kevorkian's efforts to promote euthanasia and the revulsion they evoked in many viewers, including those who support euthanasia. A documentary film about a Dutch physician providing euthanasia to a terminally ill patient who requested it has a similar impact.[22] The film, telecast on prime-time television in Canada and the United States, elicited a chill in many viewers,[23] and condemnation for exploiting both the patient and euthanasia itself.[24] If capital punishment were televised, viewers might be horrified enough to demand its abolition. But the opposite could also occur. People might be as fascinated as they once were by public executions. This personal closeness to, or distance from, the infliction of death is an important difference between euthanasia and physician-assisted suicide. Everyone, including the physician, is more distant from the infliction of death in the latter case than in the former. In the Northern Territory of Australia, where euthanasia was legalized briefly,[25] a computer-activated "suicide machine" that could be triggered by the terminally ill person was developed and used for carrying out the first death.[26] We distance ourselves from inflicting death even when doing so is legal.

When it comes to euthanasia, it could be argued, people react one way in theory and another in practice. It is much easier to approve of euthanasia in theory than in practice, which probably reflects moral anxiety about euthanasia and an ethical intuition as to its dangers. That reaction should send a deep warning, which should be heeded. The difference might also partly explain why polls on euthanasia show that, even when over 75 per cent of those polled say that they approve of it, under 50 per cent of those same people actually vote for it[27] — except in the case of the Oregon Death with Dignity Act of 1994. Maybe these people like "death talk"[28] more than "death practice." It is also possible that the survey instruments used in these polls are not well designed and, therefore, give rise to confused or ambiguous results.[29]

Denial and Control of Death and Death Talk

As I say several times in this book, ours is a death-denying, death-obsessed society.[30] Those who no longer adhere to the practice of institutionalized religion, at any rate, have lost their main forum for engaging in death talk. As humans, we need to engage in it if we are to accommodate the inevitable reality of death into the living of our lives. And we must do that if we are to live fully and well. Arguably, our extensive discussion of euthanasia in the mass media is an example of contemporary death talk. Instead of being confined to an identifiable location and an hour a week, it has spilled out into our lives in general. This exposure makes it more difficult to maintain the denial of death, because it makes the fear of death more present and "real." One way to deal with this fear is to believe that we have death under control. The availability of euthanasia could support that belief. Euthanasia moves us from chance to choice concerning death. (The same movement can also be seen at the beginning of human life, when it results from the use of new reproductive and genetic technologies at conception or shortly thereafter.[31]) Although we cannot make death optional, we can create an illusion that it is by making its timing, and the conditions and ways in which it occurs, a matter of choice.[32]

Fear

We are frightened not only as individuals, however, but also as a society. Collectively, we express the fear of crime in our streets. But that fear, though factually based, might also be a manifestation of a powerful and free-floating fear of death in general. Calling for the legalization of euthanasia could be a way of symbolically taming and civilizing death — reducing our fear of its random infliction through crime. If euthanasia were experienced as a way of converting death by chance to death by choice, it would offer a feeling of increased control over death and, therefore, decreased fear. We tend to use law as a response to fear, often in the misguided belief that the law will increase our control over the things that frighten us and so augment our safety.

Legalism

It is not surprising that we have, to varying degrees, become a legalistic society. The reasons are complex and include the use of law as a means of ordering and governing a society of strangers, as compared with one of intimates.[33] Matters such as euthanasia, which would once have been the topic of moral or religious discourse, are now explored in courts and legislatures, especially through concepts of individual human rights, civil rights, and constitutional rights. Man-made law (legal positivism), as compared with divinely ordained law or natural law, has a very dominant role in establishing the values and symbols of a secular society. In the euthanasia debate, it does so through the judgments and legislation that result from the "death talk" that takes place in "secular cathedrals" — courts and legislatures. It is to be expected that those trying to change society's values and symbols would see this debate as an opportunity to further their aims and, consequently, seek the legalization of euthanasia.

Materialism and Consumerism

Another factor, which I can mention only in passing, is that our society is highly materialistic and consumeristic. It has lost any sense of the sacred, even of the "secular sacred"[34] (although some scholars in the field of religious studies, such as Paul Nathanson, put forward an interesting case for the vitality of "secular religion"[35]). The result favours a pro-euthanasia position, because a loss of the sacred fosters the idea that wornout people may be equated with wornout products; both can then be seen primarily as "disposal" problems.

Mystery

Our society is intolerant of mystery. We convert mysteries into problems. If we convert the mystery of death into the problem of death, euthanasia (or, even more basically, a lethal injection) can be seen as a solution. As can be seen in descriptions of death by euthanasia — for instance, that of a young man dying of AIDS[36] — euthanasia can function as a substitute for the loss of death rituals, which we have abandoned at least partly to avoid any sense of mystery. A sense of mystery might be required also to "preserve . . . room for hope."[37] And euthanasia could be a response "based on a loss of faith in what life may still have in store for us. Perhaps, what is needed . . . is a different kind of faith in life and in the community of caregivers."[38] This need is especially acute in situations of serious illness. If the interactions I have just outlined are occurring, I postulate a complex relation between some degree of comfort with a sense of mystery and being able to elicit in others and experience ourselves hope and trust. This leads to a question: Could the loss of mystery — and of hope, faith, and trust — be generating nihilism in both individuals and society? And could calls for the legalization of euthanasia be one expression of it?

The loss of mystery has been accompanied by a loss of wonder and awe, both of which we need in some form as humans. Also lost is the sense that we, as humans, are sacred in any meaning of this word (that we are, at least, "secular sacred").[39] These losses are connected in both their nature and their causes, but they might not be inseparable. We might be able to retain some of these senses (for instance, a sense of the sacred) and not others (a sense of awe, at least in the form of traditional taboos used to elicit awe).

Impact of Scientific Advances

Among the most important causes of our loss of the sacred is extraordinary scientific progress, especially because science and religion are viewed as antithetical.[40] New genetic discoveries and new reproductive technologies have given us a sense that we understand the origin and nature of human life and that therefore we may manipulate — or even "create" — life. Transferring these sentiments to the other end of life would support the view that euthanasia is acceptable. Euthanasia would be seen as a correlative and consistent development with the new genetics; its acceptance would be expected. According to this view, as I have noted elsewhere, it is no accident that we are currently concerned with both eugenics (good genetics — good at birth) and euthanasia (good death — good at death, of no trouble to anyone else). Yet another connection between genetics and euthanasia could arise from a new sense of our ability to ensure genetic immortality — seeing ourselves as an immortal gene — and, as a result, some reduction of anxiety about the annihilation presented by death.

The paradigms used to structure knowledge in general have been influenced by genetic theory. These paradigms have already been the bases for new schools of thought in areas well beyond genetics. They can challenge traditional concepts of what it means to be human and what is required to respect human life. For instance, evolutionary psychology, a subcategory of sociobiology, sees the characteristics usually identified as unique markers of being human — our most intimate, humane, altruistic, and moral impulses — as the product of our genes and their evolution.[41] At a macrogenetic level, deep concern about overpopulation (as compared with earlier fears of extinction due to underpopulation) might, likewise, have diminished a sense of sacredness in relation to human life.

But countervailing trends, such as the environmental protection movement, are beginning to emerge. A powerful recognition of innate dependence on the ecological health of our planet has resurrected a sense of the "secular sacred" by reidentifying the absolute necessity of respectful human-Earth relations.[42] Moreover, science can be linked with the sacred; it just depends on how we view it. Rather than assuming that the new genetics is a totally comprehensive explanation of life, for example, we can experience it as a way of deepening our sense of awe and wonder at what we now know — but even more powerfully at what, as a result of this new knowledge, we now know we do *not* know.[43] We can, in other words, see the new genetics and other sciences as only some of the lenses through which we are able to search for "the truth."

Competing World Views

Though immensely important in itself, the debate over euthanasia might be a surrogate for yet another, even deeper, one. Which of two irreconcilable world views will form the basis of our societal and cultural paradigm? As discussed in a previous chapter, there is also a third world view — the "pure mystery" view. It rejects euthanasia on the ground that it is prohibited by religious commandment. Important as such commandments are to their adherents, in secular societies they cannot be used directly as the basis for public policy on euthanasia. Consequently, this view is not discussed further here.

According to one of the other two world views, we are highly complex, biological machines whose most valuable features are our rational, logical, cognitive functions. This world view is in itself a mechanistic approach to human life. Its proponents support euthanasia as being, in appropriate circumstances, a logical and rational response to problems at the end of life. (Being anti-euthanasia can, of course, be just as logical and rational a response.[44])

I hesitate to refer to Nazi atrocities because they can readily be distinguished from situations in which the use of euthanasia is currently being proposed. It is easy to argue that those horrific abuses were different in kind from any that would occur if euthanasia were to be legalized in our society. But consider the question about the Nazi doctors that George Annas and Michael Grodin describe as "among the most profound questions in medical ethics": "How could physician healers turn into murderers?"[45] David Thomasma, citing the work of Robert Proctor,[46] states that the primary answer is that "society, itself, was primed to develop a *biological basis for its political platforms*."[47] I propose that current efforts to legalize euthanasia might reflect a connection of these same two factors, but in the reverse order. Those who are pro-euthanasia are, at one level, seeking a political platform for a solely or predominantly biological view of human life — especially in terms of having it form an important element in any new societal paradigm. As I have noted elsewhere, this view can be called the "gene machine" or "pure science" position.[48] Its far-reaching impact and consequences should, at the least, cause us to think carefully before taking any steps to legalize euthanasia.

The other world view (which for some people is expressed through religion, but can be, and possibly is for most people, held independently of religion, at least in a traditional or institutional sense) is that human life consists of more than its biological component, wondrous as that is. It involves a mystery — at least the "mystery of the unknown" — of which we have a sense through intuitions, especially moral ones. Again, as I have already proposed, this world view includes a sense of a "space for (human) spirit" and the "secular sacred." It sees death as part of the mystery of life, which means that, to respect life, we must respect death. Although we might be under no obligation to prolong the lives of dying people, we do have an obligation not to shorten their lives deliberately. There are some fine, but immensely important, distinctions to be made when it comes to grey areas of decision-making at the end of life. Giving pain-relief treatment that is necessary to relieve pain, but that could or would shorten life, would be morally, ethically, and legally different from giving a lethal injection to end life deliberately. This view may be called the "science-spirit" position.[49]

Impact on Medicine

We need to consider how the legalization of euthanasia could affect the profession of medicine and its practitioners. Euthanasia takes both beyond their fundamental roles of caring, healing, and curing whenever possible. It involves them, no matter how compassionate their motives, in the infliction of death on those for whom they provide care and treatment. It can be described as "a merciful act of clinical care"[50] and, therefore, it can seem appropriate for physicians to administer. But the same act is accurately described as "killing," too. This means that euthanasia places "the very soul of medicine on trial."[51] We need to be concerned about the impact that legalization would have on the institution of medicine — not only in the interests of protecting it for its own sake but also because of the harm to society that damage to the profession would cause.

With the decline of organized religion in many postmodern, secular, pluralistic societies, it is difficult to find consensus on the fundamental values that create society and establish its ethical and legal "tone" — those that provide the "existential glue" that holds society together. Many people do not personally identify with the majority of societal institutions. There are very few institutions, if any, with which everyone identifies except for those — such as medicine — that make up the health-care system. These, therefore, are important when it comes to carrying values, creating them, and forming consensus around them. We must take great care not to harm their capacities in these regards and, consequently, must ask whether legalizing euthanasia would run a high risk of causing this type of harm.

Can we imagine teaching medical students how to administer euthanasia — how to kill their patients? A fundamental value and attitude that we reinforce in medical students, interns, and residents is an absolute repugnance to killing patients.[52] If physicians were authorized to administer euthanasia it would no longer be possible to teach that repugnance. Maintaining this repugnance and, arguably, the intuitive recognition of a need for it, are demonstrated in the outraged reactions against physicians carrying out capital punishment when laws provide for them to do so.[53] We do not consider their involvement acceptable — not even for those physicians who personally are in favour of capital punishment. We, as a society, need to say powerfully, consistently, and unambiguously that killing each other is wrong. Physicians are very important carriers of this message, partly because they have opportunities (not open to members of society in general) to kill people.

It is sometimes pointed out that many societies justify one form of killing by physicians: abortion. This procedure was justified, traditionally, on the grounds that it was necessary to save the life of the mother. We now have liberalized abortion laws, which reflect a justification that hinges on the belief that the fetus is not yet a person in a moral or legal sense. In justifying abortion, attention is focused on the woman's right to control her body; access to abortion is considered necessary to respect this right. Besides, it is argued, abortion is aimed primarily not at destroying the fetus but at respecting women's reproductive autonomy. Indeed, when destroying the fetus is the primary aim — as it is in sex selection — even those who agree with abortion on demand often regard it as morally unacceptable. And the rarity of third-trimester abortions in most countries shows that, once we view the fetus as a "person," we do not find killing it acceptable.[54] Consequently, legalized euthanasia would be unique in that the killing involved could not be justified on the grounds either that it is necessary to protect the life of another (which, as well as being the justification for some abortions, is also that for the other examples of legally sanctioned killing — self-defence, "just" war, and, in theory and in part, capital punishment) or that it does not involve taking the life of a person (the justification used for some abortions). Euthanasia would seem likely to affect physicians' attitudes and values, therefore, in ways that, arguably, abortion does not.

We need to consider whether patients' and society's trust in their treating physicians and the profession of medicine depends in large part on this absolute rejection by physicians of intentionally inflicting death. Moreover, we cannot afford to underestimate the desensitization and brutalization that carrying out euthanasia would have on physicians. Keep in mind that the same might be true of abortion. We should remain open-minded about this possibility — even if we believe women should have a right of access to safe, legal abortion. Sometimes, dealing with new ethical issues can cause us to review ones we believe have already been settled ethically. It could be that rightful concerns about the impact on physicians of their being involved in euthanasia would cause us to reconsider the effect of abortion on physicians involved in it. In short, one problem with the position of those who promote abortion on demand is that it threatens to continue undermining the link between medicine and respect for life. Some will argue in response that abortion is "different." But that is another debate, which I will not explore here.

It is sometimes remarked that physicians have difficulty in accepting death, especially the deaths of their patients. This attitude raises the question of whether, in inculcating a total repugnance to *killing*, we have evoked a repugnance to *death* as well. In short, there might be confusion between inflicting death and death itself. We know that failure to accept death, when allowing death to occur would be appropriate, can lead to overzealous and harmful measures to sustain life. We are most likely to elicit a repugnance to killing while fostering an acceptance of death — and we are most likely to avoid confusion between a repugnance to killing and a failure to accept death — if we speak of and seek to convey a repugnance to *killing*, when that is the appropriate word (although it is an emotionally powerful one), instead of death. Achieving these aims would be very difficult in the context of legalized euthanasia.

The Art of Medicine

Finally, I propose that it is a very important part of the art of medicine to sense and respect the mystery of life and death, to hold this mystery in trust, and to hand it on to future generations — especially future generations of physicians. We need to consider deeply whether legalizing euthanasia would threaten this art, this trust, and this legacy.

Conclusion

Every country will need to decide whether to legalize euthanasia. Making this choice will be, and will require, a complex process. It is crucial that all of us in each of our roles — whether as concerned citizens, professional organizations, or policy-makers — engage in the euthanasia debate.

This debate will involve many questions about euthanasia at both the individual and societal levels, but three of the most important are the following. First, would legalization be most likely to help us in our search for meaning in our individual and collective lives? Second, how do we want our grandchildren and great-grandchilden to die? And third, in relation to human death, what memes (fundamental units of cultural information that are inherited by being passed from generation to generation) do we want to pass on?

NOTES

1. M.A. Somerville, "Song of Death: The Lyrics of Euthanasia," *Journal of Contemporary Health Law and Policy* 9 (1993): 1–76. See chapter 3 above.
2. New York State Task Force on Life and Law, *When Death Is Sought: Assisted Suicide and Euthanasia in the Medical Context* (Albany: New York State Task Force on Life and the Law, 1994); G.J. Annas, "Death by Prescription: The Oregon Initiative," *New England Journal of Medicine* 331 (1994): 1240–3; House of Lords, *Report of the Select Committee on Medical Ethics* (London: HMSO, 1994); Report of the Special Senate Committee on Euthanasia and Assisted Suicide, *Of Life and Death* (Ottawa: Supply and Services Canada, 1995).
3. Editorial, "The Final Autonomy," *Lancet* 346 (1995): 259.
4. The Oregon Death with Dignity Act 1994 (Ballot Measure 16).
5. *Lee v. State of Oregon* 891 F. Supp. 1429 (D. Or. 1995).
6. *T. Quill and others v. Vacco* 80 F. Supp. 3rd. 716 (1996) (US Court of Appeals Second Circuit).

7. *Compassion in Dying v. State of Washington* 79 F. Supp. 790 (1996) (U.S. Court of Appeals, Ninth Circuit). The United States Supreme Court later overturned this decision. See chapter 7 below.

8. Somerville, "The Song of Death."

9. Rights of the Terminally Ill Act 1995, Legislative Assembly of the Northern Territory of Australia.

10. See references cited in note 2, Somerville, "The Song of Death," and M.A., Somerville, "Euthanasia," correspondence, *Lancet* 345 (1995): 1240–1.

11. See Somerville, "Euthanasia," and "The Song of Death"; House of Lords, *Report*; Special Senate Committee, *Of Life and Death.*

12. J.J. Fins and M.D. Bacchetta, "Framing the Physician-Assisted Suicide and Voluntary Active Euthanasia Debate: The Role of Deontology, Consequentalism, and Clinical Pragmatism," *Journal of the American Geriatric Society* 43 (1995): 563–8.

13. Katherine K. Young, "A Cross-Cultural Historical Case against Planned Self-Willed Death and Assisted Suicide," *McGill Law Journal* 39 (1994): 657–707.

14. Somerville, "The Song of Death."

15. *Lee v. State of Oregon.*

16. The Oregon Death with Dignity Act, 1994.

17. M.A. Somerville, "Unpacking the Concept of Human Dignity in Human(e) Death: Comments on 'Human Dignity and Disease, Disability, and Suffering,' by Sylvia D. Stolberg," *Human Medicine* 11 (1995): 148–51. See chapter 16(b) below.

18. *Rodriguez v. Canada (A.G.),* [1993] 3 SCR 519 (sub nom. *Rodriguez v. British Columbia*) (*A.G.*) 107 DLR (4th) 342.

19. P.D. James, *The Children of Men* (New York: Knopf, 1993).

20. Gwynne Dyer, "Learning to Kill," Montreal *Gazette*, 15 December 1995, B3.

21. R. Rodriguez, "The Coming Mayhem," Los Angeles *Times*, 21 January 1996, M1.

22. "Death on Request," Ikon Television Network, 1994.

23. "Death on Request" (excerpts), *Prime Time Live*, 8 December 1994.

24. H. Hendin, "Selling Death and Dignity," *Hastings Center Report* 25, 3 (1995): 19–23.

25. Somerville, "Song of Death."

26. P. Parrs, "Suicide Program Makes Me Uneasy," Montreal *Gazette*, 25 May 1996, E21.

27. Somerville, "Song of Death."

28. M.A. Somerville, "'Death Talk' in Canada: The Rodriguez Case," *McGill Law Journal* 39 (1994): 602–17 (see chapter 4); Somerville, "Song of Death."

29. G. Kolata, "Nurses Reported Hastening Patients' Deaths," Montreal *Gazette*, 23 May 1996, A1, A2 (reprinted from the *New York Times*).

30. E. Becker, *The Denial of Death* (New York: Free Press, 1973); D. Callahan, *The Troubled Dream of Life: Living with Mortality* (New York: Simon & Schuster, 1993).

31. M.A. Somerville, "Just 'Gene Machines' or Also 'Secular Sacred': From New Science to a New Societal Paradigm," *Policy Options* 17, 2 (1996): 3–6. See chapter 1 above, "Euthanasia, Genetics, Reproductive Technologies, and the Search for a New Societal Paradigm."

32. Somerville, "Song of Death."

33. Carol Gilligan, *In a Different Voice: Psychological Theory and Women's Development* (Cambridge, Mass.: Harvard University Press, 1982).

34. Somerville, "Just 'Gene Machines.'"

35. Some scholars in the field of religious studies point out that "religion" is alive and well even in societies that purport either to be secular or to "separate church and state." Paul Nathanson, for example, has done a great deal of research on what he calls "secular religion" (primarily in his book *Over the Rainbow: The Wizard of Oz as a Secular Myth of America* [Albany: State University of New York Press, 1989] and in his article "I Feel, Therefore I Am: The Princess of Passion and the Implicit Religion of Our Time," *Implicit Religions* 2, 2 [1999]: 59–87). By "secular religion," he refers to massively popular world views that are secular in a technical sense (because they do not mediate the sacred, which is the defining feature of religion), but religious in a functional sense. Secular religions function on both the individual level and the collective (but not necessarily official) level. They can take either explicit forms (such as the movements based on political ideologies and the public ceremonies of state-sponsored "civil religions") or

implicit ones (such as the neo-Romanticism that finds expression in phenomena as different as television talk shows and public response to the death of Princess Diana). Directly or indirectly, secular religions explain universal features of the human condition (such as death, sacrifice, love, or home). Directly or indirectly, intentionally or unintentionally, movies and even television shows are often either "secular myths" or "secular parables" (about the way things are now, the way things once were in some primaeval golden age, and the way things will be again for those who "see the light"). Secular religions satisfy the universal need for rituals to mark the great events of life (such as birth, death, and coming of age for individuals, and independence or historic catastrophes for communities). They confer identity, meaning, and purpose (as in the personal quest for self-realization or the struggle for a common cause such as environmentalism). They provide exemplary heroes (such as movie stars and rock singers or political activists and martyrs). The only religious function they do not have is mediating the sacred (which, being *sui generis*, is not a synonym for morality, justice, compassion, truth, or anything else that can be "understood" in either emotional or cognitive terms).

36. M. Seguin, *A Gentle Death* (Toronto: Key Porter, 1994).
37. C.S. Lewis, *A Grief Observed* (London: Faber & Faber, 1961), 27–8.
38. H.R. Moody, *Ethics in an Aging Society* (Baltimore: Johns Hopkins University Press, 1992), 86; cited in D.C. Thomasma, "The Ethics of Physician-Assisted Suicide," in J.M. Humber et al., eds., *Physician-Assisted Death* (Totowa, NJ: Humana Press, 1994), 105.
39. Somerville, "Just 'Gene machines.'"
40. D.C. Dennett, "Darwin's Dangerous Idea," *The Sciences* 35 (1995): 34–40.
41. R. Wright, *The Moral Animal: Evolutionary Psychology and Everyday Life* (New York: Pantheon Books, 1994); M. Ruse, "The Significance of Evolution," in P. Singer, ed., *A Companion to Ethics* (Cambridge, Mass.: Blackwell, 1991), 500–10.
42. Brian Swimme and T. Berry, *The Universe Story: From the Primordial Flaring Forth to the Econozoic Era* (San Francisco: Harper, 1992).
43. Somerville, "Just 'Gene machines.'"
44. I am indebted to Paul Nathanson for this insight (personal communication, June 2000).
45. G.J. Annas and M.A. Grodin, eds., *The Nazi Doctors and the Nuremberg Code: Human Rights in Human Experimentation* (New York: Oxford University Press, 1992), 3.
46. R.N. Proctor, "Nazi Doctors, Racial Medicine, and Human Experimentation," in G.J. Annas and M.A. Grodin, eds., *The Nazi Doctors and the Nuremberg Code* (New York: Oxford University Press, 1992), 18–19.
47. Thomasma, "The Ethics of Physician-Assisted Suicide," 118 (emphasis added).
48. Somerville, "Just 'Gene machines.'"
49. Ibid.
50. Institute of Medical Ethics Working Party on the Ethics of Prolonging Life and Assisting Death, "Assisted Death," *Lancet* 336 (1990): 610–13.
51. W. Gaylin et al., "Doctors Must Not Kill," referred to, without citation, in D.W. Brock, "Voluntary Active Euthanasia," *Hastings Center Report*, 22, 2 (1992): 16 and note 14.
52. N. Lickiss, untitled piece, in S. Chapman and S. Leeder, eds., *The Last Right? Australians Take Sides on the Right to Die* (Sydney: Mandarin, 1995), 92–8.
53. Editorial, "Doctors and Death Row," *Lancet* 341 (1993): 209–10; R.D. Truog and T.A. Brennan, "Participation of Physicians in Capital Punishment," *New England Journal of Medicine* 329 (1993): 1346–50; H. Wolinsky, "U.S. Physicians Debate Capital Punishment," *Lancet* 346 (1995): 43.
54. *Roe v. Wade* 410 U.S. 113 (1973 USSC).

QUESTIONS

1. Margaret Somerville argues that being clear about how key concepts such as "euthanasia" and "physician-assisted suicide" are defined is important. How does she define each of these terms? Why is this important to Somerville's argument?

2. Somerville provides several reasons for the current interest in legalizing euthanasia. Which reasons, if any, do you find convincing and why? Do you think that providing reasons for the current interest in legalizing euthanasia helps us to understand the issues and resolve the debate on euthanasia? Why or why not?

3. Somerville argues that we need to consider the facts with respect to the implications of legalizing euthanasia, both on the medical profession and on societal values and structures. What does Somerville take these implications to be? Do you find them convincing? Why or why not?

4. In Somerville's view, how would the legalization of euthanasia affect the medical profession?

ACTIVE AND PASSIVE EUTHANASIA

James Rachels

The distinction between active and passive euthanasia is thought to be crucial for medical ethics. The idea is that it is permissible, at least in some cases, to withhold treatment and allow a patient to die, but it is never permissible to take any direct action designed to kill the patient. This doctrine seems to be accepted by most doctors, and it is endorsed in a statement adopted by the House of Delegates of the American Medical Association on 4 December 1973:

> The intentional termination of the life of one human being by another — mercy killing — is contrary to that for which the medical profession stands and is contrary to the policy of the American Medical Association.
>
> The cessation of the employment of extraordinary means to prolong the life of the body when there is irrefutable evidence that biological death is imminent is the decision of the patient and/or his immediate family. The advice and judgement of the physician should be freely available to the patient and/or his immediate family.

However, a strong case can be made against this doctrine. In what follows I will set out some of the relevant arguments, and urge doctors to reconsider their views on this matter.

To begin with a familiar type of situation, a patient who is dying of incurable cancer of the throat is in terrible pain, which can no longer be satisfactorily alleviated. He is certain to die within a few days, even if present treatment is continued, but he does not want to go on living for those days since the pain is unbearable. So he asks the doctor for an end to it, and his family joins in the request.

Suppose the doctor agrees to withhold treatment, as the conventional doctrine says he may. The justification for his doing so is that the patient is in terrible agony, and since he is going to die anyway, it would be wrong to prolong his suffering needlessly. But now notice this. If one simply withholds treatment, it may take the patient longer to die, and so he may suffer more than he would if more direct action were taken and a lethal injection given. This fact provides strong reason for thinking that, once the initial decision not to prolong his agony has been made, active euthanasia is actually preferable to passive euthanasia, rather than the reverse. To say otherwise is to endorse the option that leads to more suffering rather

From The New England Journal of Medicine, *vol. 292, no. 2 (9 January 1975), pp. 78–80. Copyright 1975 Massachusetts Medical Society. Reprinted by permission of* The New England Journal of Medicine.

than less, and is contrary to the humanitarian impulse that prompts the decision not to prolong his life in the first place.

Part of my point is that the process of being 'allowed to die' can be relatively slow and painful, whereas being given a lethal injection is relatively quick and painless. Let me give a different sort of example. In the United States about one in 600 babies is born with Down's syndrome. Most of these babies are otherwise healthy — that is, with only the usual pediatric care, they will proceed to an otherwise normal infancy. Some, however, are born with congenital defects such as intestinal obstructions that require operations if they are to live. Sometimes, the parents and the doctor will decide not to operate, and let the infant die. Anthony Shaw describes what happens then:

> When surgery is denied [the doctor] must try to keep the infant from suffering while natural forces sap the baby's life away. As a surgeon whose natural inclination is to use the scalpel to fight off death, standing by and watching a salvageable baby die is the most emotionally exhausting experience I know. It is easy at a conference, in a theoretical discussion to decide that such infants should be allowed to die. It is altogether different to stand by in the nursery and watch as dehydration and infection wither a tiny being over hours and days. This is a terrible ordeal for me and the hospital staff — much more so than for the parents who never set foot in the nursery.[1]

I can understand why some people are opposed to all euthanasia, and insist that such infants must be allowed to live. I think I can also understand why other people favour destroying these babies quickly and painlessly. But why should anyone favour letting 'dehydration and infection wither a tiny being over hours and days'? The doctrine that says a baby may be allowed to dehydrate and wither, but may not be given an injection that would end its life without suffering, seems so patently cruel as to require no further refutation. The strong language is not intended to offend, but only to put the point in the clearest possible way.

My second argument is that the conventional doctrine leads to decisions concerning life and death made on irrelevant grounds.

Consider again the case of the infants with Down's syndrome who need operations for congenital defects unrelated to the syndrome to live. Sometimes, there is no operation, and the baby dies, but when there is no such defect, the baby lives on. Now, an operation such as that to remove an intestinal obstruction is not prohibitively difficult. The reason why such operations are not performed in these cases is, clearly, that the child has Down's syndrome and the parents and the doctor judge that because of that fact it is better for the child to die.

But notice that this situation is absurd, no matter what view one takes of the lives and potentials of such babies. If the life of such an infant is worth preserving what does it matter if it needs a simple operation? Or, if one thinks it better that such a baby should not live on, what difference does it make that it happens to have an unobstructed intestinal tract? In either case, the matter of life and death is being decided on irrelevant grounds. It is the Down's syndrome, and not the intestines, that is the issue. The matter should be decided, if at all, on that basis, and not be allowed to depend on the essentially irrelevant question of whether the intestinal tract is blocked.

What makes this situation possible, of course, is the idea that when there is an intestinal blockage, one can 'let the baby die', but when there is no such defect there is nothing that can be done, for one must not 'kill' it. The fact that this idea leads to such results as deciding life or death on irrelevant grounds is another good reason why the doctrine would be rejected.

One reason why so many people think that there is an important moral difference between active and passive euthanasia is that they think killing someone is morally worse than letting someone die. But is it? Is killing, in itself, worse than letting die? To investigate this issue, two cases may be considered that are exactly alike except that one involves killing whereas the other involves letting someone die. Then, it can be asked whether this difference makes any difference to the moral assessments. It is important that the cases be exactly alike, except for this one difference, since otherwise one cannot be confident that it is this difference and not some other that accounts for any variation in the assessments of the two cases. So, let us consider this pair of cases:

In the first, Smith stands to gain a large inheritance if anything should happen to his six-year-old cousin. One evening while the child is taking his bath, Smith sneaks into the bathroom and drowns the child, and then arranges things so that it will look like an accident.

In the second, Jones also stands to gain if anything should happen to his six-year-old cousin. Like Smith, Jones sneaks in planning to drown the child in his bath. However, just as he enters the bathroom Jones sees the child slip and hit his head, and fall face down in the water. Jones is delighted; he stands by, ready to push the child's head back under if it is necessary, but it is not necessary. With only a little thrashing about, the child drowns all by himself, 'accidentally', as Jones watches and does nothing.

Now Smith killed the child, whereas Jones 'merely' let the child die. That is the only difference between them. Did either man behave better, from a moral point of view? If the difference between killing and letting die were in itself a morally important matter, one should say that Jones's behaviour was less reprehensible than Smith's. But does one really want to say that? I think not. In the first place, both men acted from the same motive, personal gain, and both had exactly the same end in view when they acted. It may be inferred from Smith's conduct that he is a bad man, although that judgement may be withdrawn or modified if certain further facts are learned about him — for example, that he is mentally deranged. But would not the very same thing be inferred about Jones from his conduct? And would not the same further considerations also be relevant to any modification of this judgement? Moreover, suppose Jones pleaded, in his own defence, 'After all, I didn't do anything except just stand there and watch the child drown. I didn't kill him; I only let him die.' Again, if letting die were in itself less bad than killing, this defence should have at least some weight. But it does not. Such a 'defence' can only be regarded as a grotesque perversion of moral reasoning. Morally speaking, it is no defence at all.

Now, it may be pointed out, quite properly, that the cases of euthanasia with which doctors are concerned are not like this at all. They do not involve personal gain or the destruction of normal healthy children. Doctors are concerned only with cases in which the patient's life is of no further use to him, or in which the patient's life has become or will soon become a terrible burden. However, the point is the same in these cases: the bare difference between killing and letting die does not, in itself, make a moral difference. If a doctor lets a patient die, for humane reasons, he is in the same moral position as if he had given the patient a lethal injection for humane reasons. If his decision was wrong — if, for example, the patient's illness was in fact curable — the decision would be equally regrettable no matter which method was used to carry it out. And if the doctor's decision was the right one, the method used is not in itself important.

The AMA policy statement isolates the crucial issue very well; the crucial issue is 'the intentional termination of the life of one human being by another'. But after identifying this issue, and forbidding 'mercy killing', the statement goes on to deny that the cessation of treatment is the intentional termination of a life. This is where the mistake comes in, for what is the cessation of treatment, in these circumstances, if it is not 'the intentional termination of the life of one human being by another'? Of course it is exactly that, and if it were not, there would be no point to it.

Many people will find this judgement hard to accept. One reason, I think, is that it is very easy to conflate the question of whether killing is, in itself, worse than letting die, with the very different question of whether most actual cases of killing are more reprehensible than most actual cases of letting die. Most actual cases of killing are clearly terrible (think, for example, of all the murders reported in the newspapers), and one hears of such cases every day. On the other hand, one hardly ever hears of a case of letting die, except for the actions of doctors who are motivated by humanitarian reasons. So one learns to think of killing in a much worse light than of letting die. But this does not mean that there is something about killing that makes it in itself worse than letting die, for it is not the bare difference between killing and letting die that makes the difference in these cases. Rather, the other factors — the murderer's motive of personal gain, for example, contrasted with the doctor's humanitarian motivation — account for different reactions to the different cases.

I have argued that killing is not in itself any worse than letting die; if my contention is right, it follows that active euthanasia is not any worse than passive euthanasia. What arguments can be given on the other side? The most common, I believe, is the following:

> The important difference between active and passive euthanasia is that, in passive euthanasia, the doctor does not do anything to bring about the patient's death. The doctor does nothing, and the patient dies of whatever ills already afflict him. In active euthanasia, however, the doctor does something to bring about the patient's death: he kills him. The doctor who gives the patient with cancer a lethal injection has himself caused his patient's death; whereas if he merely ceases treatment, the cancer is the cause of the death.

A number of points need to be made here. The first is that it is not exactly correct to say that in passive euthanasia the doctor does nothing, for he does do one thing that is very important: he lets the patient die. 'Letting someone die' is certainly different, in some respects, from other types of action — mainly in that it is a kind of action that one may perform by way of not performing certain other actions. For example, one may let a patient die by way of not giving medication, just as one may insult someone by way of not shaking his hand. But for any purpose of moral assessment, it is a type of action none the less. The decision to let a patient die is subject to moral appraisal in the same way that a decision to kill him would be subject to moral appraisal: it may be assessed as wise or unwise, compassionate or sadistic, right or wrong. If a doctor deliberately let a patient die who was suffering from a routinely curable illness, the doctor would certainly be to blame for what he had done, just as he would be to blame if he had needlessly killed the patient. Charges against him would then be appropriate. If so, it would be no defence at all for him to insist that he didn't 'do anything'. He would have done something very serious indeed, for he let his patient die.

Fixing the cause of death may be very important from a legal point of view, for it may determine whether criminal charges are brought against the doctor. But I do not think that this notion can be used to show a moral difference between active and passive euthanasia. The reason why it is considered bad to be the cause of someone's death is that death is regarded as a great evil — and so it is. However, if it has been decided that euthanasia —

even passive euthanasia — is desirable in a given case, it has also been decided that in this instance death is no greater an evil than the patient's continued existence. And if this is true, the usual reason for not wanting to be the cause of someone's death simply does not apply.

Finally, doctors may think that all of this is only of academic interest — the sort of thing that philosophers may worry about but that has no practical bearing on their own work. After all, doctors must be concerned about the legal consequences of what they do, and active euthanasia is clearly forbidden by the law. But even so, doctors should also be concerned with the fact that the law is forcing upon them a moral doctrine that may be indefensible, and has a considerable effect on their practices. Of course, most doctors are not now in the position of being coerced in this matter, for they do not regard themselves as merely going along with what the law requires. Rather, in statements such as the AMA policy statement that I have quoted, they are endorsing this doctrine as a central point of medical ethics. In that statement, active euthanasia is condemned not merely as illegal but as 'contrary to that for which the medical profession stands', whereas passive euthanasia is approved. However, the preceding considerations suggest that there is really no moral difference between the two, considered in themselves (there may be important moral differences in some cases in their *consequences*, but, as I pointed out, these differences may make active euthanasia, and not passive euthanasia, the morally preferable option). So, whereas doctors may have to discriminate between active and passive euthanasia to satisfy the law, they should not do any more than that. In particular, they should not give the distinction any added authority and weight by writing it into official statements of medical ethics.

NOTES

1. Shaw, Anthony, "Doctor, Do We Have a Choice?" *The New York Times Magazine*, 30 January 1972, p. 54.

QUESTIONS

1. James Rachels argues that in some cases, to simply withhold treatment rather than provide a lethal injection is to "endorse the option that leads to more suffering rather than less and is contrary to the humanitarian impulse that prompts the decision not to prolong life in the first place." How would Sopinka or Somerville respond to Rachels' claim in light of the arguments they offer to support their view that euthanasia should not be legalized?

2. Rachels suggests that if it is morally acceptable not to operate on a Down's syndrome baby thus ensuring that it will die of dehydration and starvation, it must also be morally acceptable to give such a baby a lethal injection. Is he right about this? Is it morally acceptable to treat Down's syndrome children in this way? Is this an example of the slippery slope that concerns those opposed to euthanasia such as Sopinka, Somerville, and Rock?

3. Does Rachels' comparison of the man who drowns a child and a man who allows a child to drown without intervening to save its life show that where euthanasia is concerned there is no morally relevant difference between active and passive euthanasia?

4. Rachels offers the following argument: most people would agree that a doctor who lets a patient die if it is within his or her power to provide a medical remedy is just as

culpable, morally speaking, as a doctor who actively intervenes to kill a patient. On pain of inconsistency, these same people should therefore accept that "letting die" has the same moral quality for a doctor as killing. Is this a sound argument? How would you propose to assess its validity?

THE RIGHT TO DIE

Patrick Nowell-Smith

Do we have a right to die at a time and in a manner of our own choice? That this question is being more and more urgently asked is due to two changes, one technological and one social, that have occurred in our lifetime. Modern medical technology has virtually eliminated the main killer diseases of the past; in particular the introduction of antibiotics has made possible the prevention and cure of pneumonia, a disease that used to be called "the dying man's friend." Human beings can be kept biologically alive, though unconscious, almost indefinitely.

As for the social change, before the First World War there could hardly have been an adult who had never watched over a parent, baby, child, neighbour, or friend and seen him die. In short, death was familiar. And *accepted*. Sad, to be sure; often very sad indeed. But it was nonetheless accepted as part of the natural order of things, talked about openly, and frequently dealt with in literature. All that has changed. Apart from those professionally concerned, few of us have ever seen a corpse unless it was laid out for viewing. Most of us will die in an institution. Death has replaced sex as the unmentionable topic.

Euthanasia is commonly divided into "active" (killing) and "passive" (letting die), a distinction that will be challenged later. It is also divided into "voluntary" (at the request or with the consent of the person) and "involuntary" (without such consent). The legal position in the United Kingdom is simple. Before 1961 suicide had always been a common law crime, and aiding suicide was therefore automatically a crime as well. But when, in 1961, the crime of suicide was abolished, a new statutory offence of *aiding* suicide was introduced, except in Scotland. Active euthanasia was always treated as murder, and still is. So much for the law on paper, which is pretty much the same in all common law jurisdictions.

However, this severity toward mercy killing and aiding suicide is in practice greatly mitigated by the wide powers of sentencing which our legal system accords to judges, especially when the issue is one of passive rather than active euthanasia. If a doctor allows a grossly deformed baby to die, he will be discharged if he can show that his decision not to treat the baby was standard medical practice; and there are many cases which are not even prosecuted. In cases of active euthanasia judges almost always impose a very light sentence or no sentence at all, when the motive was clearly compassion.

Since the methods most of us would choose to commit suicide require the illegal co-operation of others, it is clear that we have at best a very restricted *legal* right to die at a time and in a manner of our own choice. Whether or not we have a *moral* right which ought to be reflected in the law depends on the type of moral theory we take as a starting-point. On a theory which starts from the concept of individual rights, we have a right to do anything we like provided there are no good reasons for prohibiting what we want to do — for example that

Published by permission of the author. Copyright jointly held by ICUS and Paragon House Publishers.

it infringes on the equal right of another. The countervailing reasons can be divided into the religious, the moral, and the practical.

Of the religious reasons little need be said. It is argued that we are not the absolute owners of our own lives, but hold them in trust from a God who gave them to us, so that the times of our dying should be chosen, not by us, but by God. But whatever the theoretical merits of this argument, it would be wrong to base any prohibition solely on the grounds that others have a religious objection to what someone proposes to do.

The main categories of moral theories are the *right-based* and the *utilitarian*. For a rights theorist, the right to life, the right not to be killed, is the most fundamental of all rights. When rights are listed, it always comes first, for the very good reason that to deprive someone of life is to deprive him at one blow of all his rights, of all possibility of earthly enjoyment. But if we grant, as no doubt we all do, that everyone has a right to life, it follows at once that we have a right to choose to die. For it is a feature of all rights that they can be invoked or not *at the option of the right-holder*. If you owe me ten dollars, I have a right to demand and get ten dollars from you. But I have no *duty* to demand repayment; I may, if I choose, waive my right — in this example forgive the debt. Similarly, the correlative of my right to life is your duty not to kill me; but I can release you from this duty by requesting you to kill me or giving my consent. To deny this is to confuse the right to life with the duty, if there is one, to go on living.

In special circumstances there may be such a duty. For example, if a person is the only breadwinner of a family and has no life insurance, it may well be his duty to struggle on against his desire to die. For some few of us, perhaps, some larger loyalty, even the national interest, might require us to forego our right to die. But such considerations are rare and not likely to figure in the type of case that leads people to advocate a more liberal law on euthanasia. Their concern is for people who, either from incurable disease or from extreme old age, are unlikely to be able to contribute substantially to the good of others.

A large majority of the people who join voluntary euthanasia societies are people in their sixties and seventies who are still enjoying life but do not like what they see in front of them in a society in which more than three-quarters of us will die in institutions. They ask for the various guides to self-deliverance issued by some of these societies not because they want to use the information now, but because they want the security of knowing that, in the words of John Donne, the keys of their prison house are in their own hands. The following letter sent to the Canadian society Dying with Dignity is typical.

> I am seventy-nine years of age, in relatively vigorous health and constantly amused with life while it lasts. But I saw my mother and my father, years apart, in the same chronic care hospital suffering helplessly for months when they might have been quietly released; and this makes me dread a similar fate unless the law is changed so that one can choose, if still able, to slip away in dignity from the inhumane methods many hospitals employ today to keep one from dying a natural death.

Inevitably some people will be sad when a person dies; but that sadness will come to them anyway, and it should be lessened rather than increased by the thought that the person they loved died as he wished to die.

But what if no one is willing to kill me or to help me die? What then becomes of my right to choose death? This objection can be met by pointing out that the right to life and its corollary, the right to die, are only *negative* rights. My right to life imposes on you a duty not to kill me without my consent, but it imposes on you no duty to keep me alive (though, for other reasons, you may have such a duty). The same is true of the right to die. Supporters of voluntary euthanasia are not asking for "death on demand." They are not asking that anyone be saddled with a duty to kill a person who asks for death. They assert only that neither a person who asks for help in dying nor a person who gives that help is committing a moral wrong, and they claim that this moral position should be reflected in our criminal law.

If we look at the question from the point of view of utilitarianism, we get the same result. The utilitarian judges the morality of an action by assessing the good and the evil consequences, for the agent and all others concerned, of either doing something or not doing it. Obviously such calculations are not easy; but they are not always impossible. *Ex hypothesi*, a person who asks for death has come to the conclusion that, for him, dying is better than staying alive. He may be mistaken; but often this is very unlikely, and in any case he is the best judge of his own interests. As for the interests of others, his choice of death will be morally right so long as the benefit for them of his remaining alive is less than the burden on them and on him.

Let us now turn to the practical arguments, according to which, even if the moral admissibility of voluntary euthanasia were conceded, proposals to change the law would run into insuperable difficulties. First, it is argued that no proposal to change the law has any chance of success unless it has the support of the medical profession, which, it is said, it will never have. "Doctors vary in their approach to passive euthanasia but the profession condemns legalised active voluntary euthanasia."[1] Nevertheless, there are some British physicians who practise active voluntary euthanasia, but it is difficult to find out just how many there are. Since such an admission would, under present British law, be a confession of murder, it is understandable that they do not openly admit it.

On the other hand, voluntary active euthanasia is now practised openly in Holland, where there are between 5000 and 6000 cases a year.[2] The procedure starts with an application by the patient. A team is then formed consisting of a doctor and a nurse, a pastor if the patient asks for one, and others as appropriate.[3] The team discusses the application with the patient, and then either grants or refuses it. Some years ago, Dr. Pieter Admiraal, a leading proponent of the practice, was convicted of aiding suicide, but was discharged on the grounds that his actions had been medically necessary. "What made Dr. Admiraal's actions acceptable were (1) the patient's voluntary and spontaneous requests, (2) the rational and 'durable' nature of the requests, (3) the presence of unacceptable and 'endless' suffering, and (4) Dr. Admiraal's consultation with his colleagues."[4] If the consensus of medical opinion could change in the course of a few years in Holland, it could change in other countries too.

The second type of practical objection comes from lawyers, who, like doctors, are on the whole opposed to active euthanasia and the assistance of suicide. In 1984 the Law Reform Commission of Canada's report *Euthanasia, Suicide, and Cessation of Treatment* recommended that the law on active euthanasia and aiding suicide should not be changed. One of its arguments for this conservative stance was that the law in action is much less severe than the law on paper:

> Our legal system has internal mechanisms which offset the apparent harshness of the law. It is possible that in *some* circumstances the accused would be allowed to plead guilty to a lesser charge. . . . Finally in *truly exceptional circumstances*, the authorities already have it within their discretion to decide not to prosecute.[5]

But this is cold comfort indeed, since the circumstances in which people wish to die are, even now, not "truly exceptional"; and as the population ages and the power of medical technology increases such circumstances are likely to become even more common.

Many doctors and paramedics would like to put an end to suffering they know to be hopeless; but they are law-abiding people, and they have a special need to be careful of their reputations. That they are less inclined than they used to be to follow their humane inclinations is due to fear of possible prosecution and of malpractice suits if they do not pull out all the stops to keep a patient alive. It is not fair to say to them, as the Commission in effect does, "What you are doing is against the law, but we *may* turn a blind eye."

The Commission's second argument was that any relaxation of the law could lead to mistakes and to serious abuses. This is a weighty argument, and it will be considered later; but it is surprising that the Commission did not consider the possibility of building safeguards against abuse into a more liberal law. Perhaps the reason for this omission was that it relied most heavily on its third argument: that relaxation of the law would be "morally unacceptable to the majority of the Canadian people."[6] This, however, is not a moral question, but a question of empirical fact, and the Commission should surely have produced some evidence to support its view. But not only did it cite no evidence; it ignored such evidence as there was. In 1968, the Canadian Institute for Public Opinion (the Gallup Poll) had asked the following narrowly worded question:

> When a person has an incurable disease that causes great suffering, do you or do you not think that competent doctors should be allowed by law to end the patient's life through mercy-killing, if the patient has made a formal request in writing?

Forty-five percent of the firm answers were yes, 43 no. In 1974 the proportion was 55 to 35 percent. By 1978 the favourable replies outnumbered the unfavourable by more than two to one, and this result was repeated in 1984. In Britain a similar 1969 survey showed 51 percent in favour of active voluntary euthanasia. By 1976 the fraction had increased to 69 percent; in 1985 it was 72 percent. In the United States, though the proportion of favourable replies was lower, the trend was similar. In 1973 the Harris Poll showed only 37 percent in favour; by 1985 the figure had reached 61 percent.[7]

This disparity between legal and popular thinking is also shown by the many cases in which even newspapers of a generally conservative complexion have criticized a court decision. One example must suffice. In December 1984 an 84-year-old lady who had many reasons for ending her life tried to commit suicide by taking a lethal drug. She had a legal right to do so; but, fearful that the attempt might not succeed, she asked a friend, Mrs. Charlotte Hough, to sit with her and to place a plastic bag over her head after she had lost consciousness. Mrs. Hough did so and reported her action to the police. Initially she was charged with murder, but because of the uncertainty as to whether the death was due to the drug or to the plastic bag, the charge was reduced to attempted murder. She pleaded guilty, and was sentenced to nine months' imprisonment, a sentence upheld on appeal.[8] The judge said that although he had the greatest sympathy for Mrs. Hough, a prison sentence was necessary to uphold the law. On this *The Sunday Times* commented:

> What is often morally right in this sensitive area remains legally incorrect because, as a nation, we tend to sweep discussion of death under the carpet. In 1976 Baroness Wootton introduced a bill into the House of Lords which would have brought a modicum of good

sense and regulation to the subject of euthanasia. But it was not supported. As a result, uncounted numbers of people kept alive by medical science, often die without dignity. . . . Mrs. Hough's crime was compassion and it served to underline once more the need for better legislation governing voluntary euthanasia and the dangers of being without it. People should be allowed to die on their own terms and, as Barbara Wootton once wrote, "not those of nature's cruelty or doctors' ingenuity."[9]

The third type of objection arises from the possibility that mistakes will be made and abuses will occur. It would be a pity, it is said, if someone were to choose death when a cure for his condition was just around the corner. As it stands, this objection is based on a misunderstanding of the nature of biomedical research. The time that elapses between someone's thinking of a new drug or a new application of a known drug and its actual availability is to be measured, not in weeks or months, but in years. So, if there is really a new treatment likely to be available soon, that fact will be known. The patient should be told what the treatment can do for him now or in the near future and left to choose whether or not to hang on and hope for the best. New cures apart, it is true that people whose case seemed hopeless have recovered to lead meaningful lives; so it may well be true that some of those who chose to die would also have recovered. But, from the nature of the case, we can never know whether a person who chooses to die would have recovered, and since cases of unexpected recovery are rare, it must be presumed that in most cases they would not.

The possibility that a more liberal law might be abused is a much more serious objection. How can we be sure that when a patient chooses death the choice is *fully voluntary*? Obviously this opens one of the most notorious cans of worms in the history of philosophy. Aristotle defined a voluntary action as one not taken under compulsion or due to ignorance,[10] and no one has been able to improve significantly on that definition. But this raises the problem of what counts as compulsion. Subtle pressures which would not amount to coercion in law might be put on old people to sign their own death warrants, for example, by greedy heirs who want to inherit sooner rather than later; and even if there is little to inherit, family members might want to get the old person off their backs. Senility, even without the aid of high technology, can last quite a time and people who need constant care can be a great nuisance. It is also tempting for family members to insinuate that the old person really has a duty to get out of the way.

A more liberal law to mitigate the uncertainties and inhumanity of our current laws is urgently needed; but the problem of devising adequate safeguards is one, not for philosophers, but for lawyers. For the law has great experience of dealing with problems of coercion and constraint in other areas. The validity of a contract may depend on whether the parties freely consented to its terms; and in many crimes the guilt of the accused depends on whether or not he intended of his own free will to commit the crime. So we might insist that possible sources of coercion be fully investigated, that the would-be suicide has been fully informed of the options, and that his will has been expressed several times over a stipulated period. Under the Dutch system the most serious abuses — coercion and fraud — are all but eliminated since active voluntary euthanasia is practised openly, only in hospitals, and after consultations so wide that there can be no reasonable doubt that the patient's request is uncoerced, considered, and durable.

Passive euthanasia (letting die), whether voluntary or not, is now generally accepted except by the more fervent right-to-life groups. But, while most religious leaders, doctors, and lawyers consider it morally acceptable, they still regard active euthanasia as morally wrong. Their morality can be summed up in Clough's often-quoted words, "Thou shalt not kill, but needst not strive/Officiously to keep alive." But what, if any, is the difference?

There is certainly a conceptual difference between killing and letting die. A lifeguard who holds a child's head under water till he drowns certainly kills the child; a lifeguard who sits on the bank watching the child drown as certainly does not. He lets the child die. But is there any *morally relevant* difference between these two cases? Is not the lifeguard in the second case just as culpable, just as responsible for the death of the child as the lifeguard in the first? The law has long accepted the principle that acts of omission can be just as criminal as acts of commission, and popular morality accepts that they can be just as reprehensible.

If a baby is born with Tay-Sachs disease or anencephalic, it is routine practice to prescribe "nursing care only" and when the baby dies this is thought of as a merciful dispensation of Providence. But in this sort of case the physician intentionally causes death, for all that he causes it, not by action but by refraining from taking action. So there is no moral superiority of passive over active euthanasia here, and if the former is allowed to be morally permissible (as it generally is), the latter is also permissible. In fact, if there is any moral superiority here at all, it lies with active euthanasia, since, assuming the baby to be conscious, its suffering will be shorter. On this point the conventional moral position seems to be simply confused.

The fundamental principle of medical ethics has always been that a physician should act in the best interest of his patient, and this principle has been reaffirmed by two eminent bodies, the World Medical Assembly[11] and the United States President's Commission for the Study of Ethical Problems in Medicine and Biomedical and Behavioral Research.[12] Both of these bodies advocate passive euthanasia as often preferable to the use of "extraordinary" measures to keep a person alive. What neither of them asks, however, is whether letting someone die, even with the best possible care while dying, is really better for that person than giving him a quicker release.

The question of what is in a person's best interests is not an easy one to answer and the World Medical Assembly did not try to answer it. But the President's Commission did.

> In its report *Deciding to Forego Life-sustaining Treatment* the Commission says that all patients have an interest in well-being and that, in addition to this, normal adult or competent patients also have an interest in self-determination. . . . In other words, seriously disabled infants should, according to the Commission, not have their lives sustained if their lives are likely to contain more suffering and frustrated desires than happiness and satisfactions.[13]

In line with the Commission's thinking, the United States Surgeon General recommended that an infant who cannot be nourished orally "should not be put on hyperalimentation for a year and a half . . . but should be provided with a bed and food by mouth knowing that it was not going to be nutritious" and thus allowed to die.[14] But once it has been decided that it is better for the baby to die than to be kept alive by extraordinary means, would it not be in his best interests to die quickly rather than slowly and perhaps painfully?

> In one recently publicized case, an 85-year-old patient starved himself to death over a 47-day period. But who would seriously want to suggest that it is in the patient's best interests to be dehydrated and starved to death? It appears that the World Medical Assembly and the American President's Commission would.[15]

If there is no moral difference between passive and active euthanasia, it is illogical to accept the former and reject the latter; and if there is a moral difference *in favour of* active euthanasia, current medical practice is immoral as well.

In the case, not of an infant, but of a competent patient who, in addition to an interest in general well-being, has an interest in self-determination, the inconsistency of the Commission's position is even more glaring, since it says that a competent person's interest in and right to self-determination is paramount.

> Competent patients should be allowed to die when, from their point of view, life in a distressing or seriously debilitating condition is no longer worthwhile. Different patients will decide differently under similar circumstances. These goals and values ought to be respected. Hence, the Commission says, "no uniform, objective determination can be adequate — whether defined by society or by health care professionals."
>
> No objective determination can be adequate, the Commission states, because normal adult persons have an overriding interest in self-determination, that is, in the exercise of their "capacity to form, revise, and pursue his or her own plans for life." It is self-determination, the Commission suggests, which gives persons an element of worth and dignity.[16]

But if the right to self-determination really has the paramount status which the Commission accords to it, it must surely extend to include a right to die at a time and in a manner of one's own choice.

Postscript

I have argued that changes in the law of common law jurisdictions are urgent, that such changes will not occur without the support of the medical profession, and that, to judge from the polls, public opinion is more liberal on these issues. But opinion polls are notoriously unreliable, because the respondents are often unaware of the complexities of the issues underlying the questions put. Other evidence suggests that the public is, on the whole, indifferent. For example, though it is growing fast, the total membership of the 27 right-to-die societies that exist in 17 countries remains very small.

What we need to bring about is a change in our whole society's attitude toward death and dying. Instead of sweeping it under the carpet, we must learn again to accept it as our forefathers did, as not only the inevitable, but the natural end to earthly life. My own ideal death is that of Socrates, who took poison and died discussing the immortality of the soul with his friends. To be sure, his reason for choosing to die was that he had been condemned to death by the law of his country, which he felt bound to obey. But change that story a little: Socrates is growing old; he can no longer handle his stonemason's tools with his old skill, and worst of all, he can no longer match his friends in philosophic discussion. Life has no more that he values to offer him. So he accepts death, not knowing what is to come, having enjoyed life to the end.

NOTES

1. *Handbook of Medical Ethics* (British Medical Association, 1980), p. 31.
2. John Dawson, "An open and gentle death," *News Review* (British Medical Association), Vol. 12, No. 1 (January 1986), p. 22.

3. Pieter V. Admiraal, "Active voluntary euthanasia," *Newsletter* (Voluntary Euthanasia Society, London), No. 24 (May 1985).
4. Dawson, *op. cit.*, p. 23.
5. Law Reform Commission of Canada, *Euthanasia, Suicide, and Cessation of Treatment* (Ottawa, 1984). Emphasis added.
6. *Ibid*.
7. *Newsletter* (Voluntary Euthanasia Society, London), No. 24 (May 1985), p. 5.
8. *Ibid.*, No. 23, pp. 1–2.
9. *The Sunday Times* (London), December 16, 1984.
10. Aristotle, *Nicomachean Ethics*, III, 1110a.
11. "Statement on terminal illness and boxing, October 1983," *Medical Journal of Australia*, Vol. 141 (1984), p. 549. I am indebted for this and the following references to Dr. Helga Kuhse of the Centre for Human Bioethics, Monash University, Australia.
12. *Deciding to Forego Life-sustaining Treatment* (Washington: U.S. Government Printing Office, 1983).
13. Helga Kuhse, "Euthanasia — again," *Medical Journal of Australia*, Vol. 142 (1985), p. 612.
14. Quoted by Peter Singer and Helga Kuhse, "The future of Baby Doe," *New York Review of Books*, No. 31 (1984), pp. 17–22.
15. Kuhse, *op. cit.*, p. 611.
16. *Ibid.*, p. 612.

QUESTIONS

1. Contrary to Somerville's account, Patrick Nowell-Smith argues that the commitment of our society to religious freedom implies that religious objections to euthanasia should not be allowed to influence the debate on the legalization of euthanasia. Whose account do you find more convincing and why?

2. Let us grant that all human beings have a right to life. Does it follow, as Nowell-Smith suggests, that everyone has a right to waive his or her right to go on living and ask that his or her life be ended?

3. A recurring theme in the discussion of euthanasia is the problem of preventing the abuse of legislation that allows euthanasia under specified conditions. Are the concerns of Somerville in this regard adequately dealt with by Nowell-Smith?

DISCOUNTED LIVES? WEIGHING DISABILITY WHEN MEASURING HEALTH AND RULING ON 'COMPASSIONATE' MURDER

Melanie Rock

Introduction

The study of suffering has become an important vein of research in medical anthropology (*Desjarlais*; *Green* and *Kleinman*). The research usually situates suffering in poor countries often ruled by very oppressive governments. Consequently, many of these studies imply that suffering is incompatible with liberal governance.

Reprinted from Social Science and Medicine, *Vol. 51, Rock, "Discounted Lives? Weighing Disability when Measuring Health and Ruling on 'Compassionate' Murder," pp, 407–417, Copyright 2000, with permission from Elsevier. Online 3 May, 2000. Department of Social Studies of Medicine, McIntyre Medical Sciences Building, 3655 Drummond Street, McGill University, Montreal, Quebec, Canada H3G 1Y6.*

By analysing representations of disability that prevail in the international public health field and in a liberal democracy such as Canada, I hope to extend this research agenda on suffering. These representations mostly equate disability with pathology, so disability appears inherently undesirable. It follows that most people with disabilities would surely choose "normal" bodies if only they could, and that a body with disabilities is a body in the throes of suffering. In fact, social policy experts, medical personnel and anthropologists alike often conflate disability with disease, illness and sickness. The theoretical foundations in contemporary medical anthropology even appear to preclude the possibility of experiencing "health" alongside disability, or other "socially devalued states" subject to medical treatment (*Young*, 1992). Perhaps this equation of disability with disease, illness and sickness explains why few anthropologists have considered disability per se, although this situation has begun to change (*Ingstad & Reynolds Whyte*, 1995).

Specifically, this paper aims to elaborate on the politics of suffering by considering the Disability-Adjusted Life Year (DALY) alongside a controversial murder case. The DALY was developed for the World Bank and the World Health Organisation under the leadership of Christopher Murray of the Harvard School of Public Health. It has quickly gained prominence as a health indicator. In measuring health, the DALY regards disability as pathology — as disease in need of elimination. The DALY does not, therefore, measure social, economic or individual resources that may affect the impact of bodily circumstances. It deems time lived with a disability as having less worth than time spent in "perfect health."

Meanwhile, the Latimer case has sparked heated debate in Canada about when a life with disabilities is worth living, whether such a life has the same worth as a life "free" from disability, and who should make these judgements. The case concerns a father killing his daughter with disabilities. The case has already reached the Supreme Court of Canada once and will likely return. [Decided Jan. 18, 2001.]

The DALY and the Latimer case can be juxtaposed to unearth a common thread: the claim that life lived with disabilities has less value than life lived without disabilities, based on evidence of "suffering" derived from biomedical expertise. That is, the DALY and the Latimer affair can be considered in parallel, rather than directly compared, to show how ascriptions of "suffering" buttress judgements about quality of life. In the process, prevalent ideas about "normal" bodies come to the fore.

This paper will argue that efforts to evaluate the relative "health" of various "types" of bodies signal efforts to evaluate the worth of certain people: assessments of the "health" of particular "types" of bodies cannot escape assessments of the quality of the lives lived in such bodies. Some people are "discounted"[1] whenever human lives are deemed "not worth living," or simply worth less than others.

The Latimer Affair

The Latimer case provides an entry point for considering how cultural conventions about suffering interlace with Western expert knowledge about disability.

On 24 October, 1993, Tracy Latimer died while her mother and siblings attended church near the family farm. She was 12 years old. Within 2 weeks, Robert Latimer, her father, admitted to killing her. After two trials, the legal status of the case remains unresolved. In the first trial, though charged with first degree murder, Robert Latimer was found guilty of second degree murder (*R. v. Latimer*, 1994). His conviction and sentence — life in prison without parole for 10 years, the minimum for this offence — struck many commentators as unduly harsh. The Supreme Court of Canada eventually heard the case, and ordered a new trial because of a "flagrant abuse of process and interference with the administration of justice" (*R. v. Latimer*, 1997, p. 6). Indeed, counsel for the Crown and a police officer had prepared a questionnaire, which subsequently guided unrecorded interviews with some potential jurors. The instrument included questions on issues such as religion, abortion and mercy killing (*Mitchell*, 1995). Five of those interviewed served on the jury that convicted the accused (*R. v. Latimer*, 1997, pp. 6, 3–4).

The decision from the new trial came down in November 1997: Robert Latimer was again found guilty of second degree murder. This time, the judge exempted him from the minimum penalty for this crime. Instead, his sentence numbered 2 years less a day, and he was to serve half of that time on probation. Robert Latimer, the judge decreed, had suffered enough already (*Globe & Mail*, 1997). Both sides appealed this ruling.

In November 1998, the Saskatchewan Court of Appeal announced its ruling (*Roberts*, 1998). Robert Latimer was once again found guilty of second degree murder, but this time he was given the minimum sentence for this crime. That is, the Court of Appeal overturned the constitutional exemption to reduce his sentence to less than two years, granted in the November 1997 trial. Robert Latimer appealed again, and the Supreme Court granted his appeal. The Supreme Court will likely hear this case again in 2000. Meanwhile, Robert Latimer is out on bail. [Decision: Conviction/and sentence of life in prison with a mandatory minimum of 10 years' imprisonment for second-degree murder should be upheld.]

Robert Latimer's defence revolves around the claim that he acted out of compassion, out of love. This claim requires evidence that can stand up in a court of law. The bald "facts" about Tracy Latimer's life, and that of her family's, read as follows in the Supreme Court decision:

> Tracy suffered from extreme cerebral palsy and was quadriplegic. As a result of her physical condition, she was largely immobile and bedridden, and was physically unable to take care of herself. Her family provided her with constant care. Eating was a difficult task, and Tracy had to be spoon-fed. Unfortunately, even with this assistance, she could not consume a sufficient amount of nutrients, and as a result experienced weight loss. It is undisputed that Tracy was in constant pain. As well, despite the administration of medication, Tracy experienced five to six seizures every day (*R. v. Latimer*, 1997, p. 9).

Note how heavily the "facts of the case" in this "neutral" document rely on biomedicine for evidence of suffering. The prosecution and defence also invoke biomedicine, and as will be shown below, so do disability-rights activists who contend that her father committed cold-blooded murder.

These activists claim that the legal process and especially public debate has put Tracy Latimer's "quality of life" rather than her father's actions on trial. A coalition of six disability-rights groups participated in the latest appeal. This coalition also intervened when the Supreme Court of Canada heard the case in 1997. (The Canadian justice system permits select groups to outline their position in cases heard by provincial appeal courts and the Supreme Court of Canada.) A few excerpts from *Latimer Watch*, a bulletin for activists to share information and views connected to the Latimer affair, illustrate how disability rights activists regard this case and surrounding debates.

In an opinion piece first published in a city daily, a father writes:

I believe an even more serious conviction was in order. Think about it: He picked his defenceless daughter up, carried her into his truck, put a tube in the window, started the engine, stood back — and watched her die. He then carried her dead body back to her crib and called emergency crews to say his daughter had died in her sleep. He put his daughter down, it's as simple as that. She was not a farm animal (*Braid*, 1997).

The writer's son has disabilities similar to Tracy Latimer's. Given his personal experience, he reports that most people expect him to defend Robert Latimer.

Jim Derksen, a prominent disability activist, had scathing remarks about an interview with Robert Latimer and his wife, which was broadcast on a television news program:

I would like to know why the [Canadian Broadcast Corporation's] *National Magazine* allowed the murderer to represent the best interest of his victim. Where were the voices of persons who have benefited from the hip joint and feeding-tube surgeries Tracy's murderer denied her based on his own prejudice against such treatments? Those of us with gastrotomies so that we can eat through feeding tubes, with skeletons surgically altered so that we can live in health without pain, say to Robert Latimer that we are not mutilated, not tormented, not terrorized. We have been helped; Tracy Latimer has been murdered (*Derksen*, 1997a).

Derksen refuses to accept that having disabilities makes life unbearable, in part by portraying biomedicine's technical capacities in a positive light. Thus, he disputes the inevitability of her discomfort.

Derksen also critiques legislation proposed by a Canadian law professor (*Sneiderman*, 1997). This statute would reduce charges for killings motivated by "compassion." The courts would decide whether the accused had killed to end the suffering of the victim, and if the "ordinary person" would feel sympathy for the person killed. Yet, he writes, "It is the defining experience of most people I know who live with visible disabilities, that 'ordinary persons' will tell us they would rather be dead than be disabled as we are" (*Derksen*, 1997b).

As shown here, disability activists register profound offence at the conflation of disability with pathology, and suffering more generally. Gregor Wolbring, who advocates for disability rights in Canada and internationally, says bluntly, "Having a disability does not equal suffering" (*Wolbring*, 1997). Equality for people with disabilities arguably demands recognition of their differences — not charity, cures or sympathy (*Rioux*, 1994). Unlike formal equality theory, which implies determining the extent to which a given disability departs from "normality," this rival approach contends that achieving equality will mean accommodating divergence from the "norm": otherwise, designations such as "poor quality of life" may legitimate an unequal social status for people with disabilities (*Bach*, 1994).

Canada has achieved an international reputation for approaching disability as a human rights issue (*Rioux & Richler*, 1995), not least because its constitution outlaws discrimination based on mental or physical disability (*Canadian Charter of Rights and Freedoms*, *1982*, s. 15). Nevertheless, the Latimer affair suggests that most Canadians view disability as indicative of suffering, especially but not exclusively when physical pain seems involved. Thus, when someone kills a person with "poor quality of life," many Canadians believe that the penalties for ending the life of an "ordinary person" should not apply. Moreover, many

Canadians contend that Robert Latimer acted morally when he ended his daughter's life because he ended her "suffering."

Unpacking the Disability-Adjusted Life Year (DALY)

The Latimer case may seem to be of parochial relevance. However, representations of disability and suffering in the Latimer affair mirror those invoked internationally when measuring health and allocating resources. The DALY embodies such representations. The DALY equates death with the absence of functioning; perfect health means full functioning; and health is reduced by anomalous limitations on what a body can do (*Murray* and *Murray*). This formulation, firmly rooted in the modern West, deploys utilitarian terms to codify a universal human body.

Some medical anthropologists acknowledge that the DALY embodies culturally based assumptions, but they still regard it as an innovative way of measuring suffering that can usefully inform health policy around the world (*Desjarlais et al.*, 1995). Policy makers indeed face choices about whether to emphasise the prevention of disabilities or to invest more heavily in measures that enhance the lives of people with disabilities. Resources appear finite, and so rational heads must presumably prevail. The DALY can ostensibly muster political will and direct it toward improving health through a proper balance between efforts to prevent and treat pathologies (*Murray*, 1996, p. 67). This measure was first used in 1993 (*World Bank*, 1993). Since then, it has gained favour with many researchers (*Bowie et al.*, 1997, for example), and notoriety among others (*Anand & Hanson*, 1997, for example).

A Brief History of Quantification in Public Health

The DALY's emergence and rapid adoption cannot be understood without reference to the history of quantification in public health. Although general indicators of non-fatal health outcomes first became a significant issue in the 1960s (*Murray*, 1994), arguments to consider "quality of life" date back at least 150 years. John Stuart Mill claimed, "It is better to be a human being dissatisfied than a pig satisfied; better to be Socrates dissatisfied than a fool satisfied" (*Mill*, 1861 in; *Olsen*, 1997, p. 626). Since eradicating diseases remains a prominent goal in international public health, statistics on death, which deal with such things as infant mortality and mean life expectancy, predominate in this field.

Since the 1918 influenza epidemic, webs — not chains — of causation seem to account best for mortality rates (*Kunitz* and *Mendelsohn*). The "web of causation" approach regards disease and disease agents as necessary but insufficient causes of death. It directly implicates individual actions and socio-economic conditions. For example, this approach would imply explaining why certain people die or suffer injuries in traffic accidents, whether because of poor road conditions or drunk driving. Therefore, models specifying webs of causation reflect deeply rooted assumptions about society, free will, and the requirements of justice (*Kunitz*, 1987, p. 402).

Researchers, policy makers and the public in many countries perceive objectivity as a key requirement of justice. In public health research and related policy, "objectivity" seems to mean impersonality (*Porter*, 1992). This approach to objectivity leads to decisions ostensibly based purely on principles, since impersonalising judgement aims to remove partisanship from policy decisions affecting health. In this light, it is not surprising to learn that the political dimensions of health indicators have received little attention (*Murray* and *Olsen*).

Impersonalising judgement implies putting trust in numbers instead of officials, but trust in numbers requires trust in the experts who compile and analyse the figures. Achieving the carapace of impersonality often implies quantifying the value of human lives (*Porter*, 1992). By equating specified cases analogically according to select criteria, and then aggregating them, quantification "makes up" classes of people (*Hacking*, 1986). Resource allocation in health care illustrates the enormous power of quantification: "impersonal" calculations may determine to whom health care resources flow (*Porter*, 1992). Increasingly, by suggesting ways of allocating health care resources, "prescriptions" based on quantitative analysis can counter clinical priorities and limit physicians' professional power (*Osborne* and *Rose*).

The DALY: Rationale, Uses and Components

The DALY extends the concern with morbidity, which has a strong presence in epidemiological studies of "developed" countries, to "developing" ones. Simultaneously, it preserves the concern with "premature" death that characterises the epidemiology of "developing" countries, with its focus on eradicating infectious disease. A measure combining mortality and morbidity information was first attempted over 30 years ago, but soon became mired in controversy (*Murray*, 1994, p. 429). Combined measures, and the DALY in particular, purport to enable just resource allocation by enhancing dialogue on the major health challenges facing humanity (*Murray*, 1994, p. 429; *Murray*, 1996, p. 67).

The DALY was developed for three main reasons. First, its creators wanted to facilitate inclusion of nonfatal health outcomes in debates on international health policy (*Murray*, 1996, p. 1). That is, they wanted to highlight suffering, including mental distress, not captured by mortality measures. Second, the DALY's creators aimed to uncouple population health assessment from advocacy, with the goal of enhancing objectivity (*Murray*, 1996, pp. 1–2). It seems decision makers often receive studies produced by advocates of particular policy options, when they actually require non-partisan figures. Third, the DALY was designed for use in cost-effectiveness analysis, necessary for making "fair" resource allocation decisions (*Murray*, 1996, p. 2). This third aim helps explain why the World Bank, in collaboration with the World Health Organisation, sponsored the development of this measure.

In fact, the measure first appeared in a World Bank report (World Bank, 1993). The latest *Global Burden of Disease* study, released in 1997, also deploys this measure. It found that the substantial impact of neuropsychiatric conditions receives insufficient recognition. It also found that developed regions account for precisely 11.6% of the world-wide burden from all causes of death and disability, yet consume 90.2% of health expenditures world-wide (*Murray & Lopez*, 1997). As suggested by these figures, while designed mostly with "developing" countries in mind, researchers are beginning to use the DALY to evaluate relative health and resource allocation patterns in "developed" countries. A recent study, for example, analyses data for an English region with a view to tailoring resource allocation to fit epidemiological patterns (*Bowie et al.*, 1997).

Consistent with a concern for universal justice, the DALY purports to measure health in the same ways around the world. The emphasis on collective priorities sets the DALY apart from quality-of-life indicators derived from surveying individuals about their willingness to live with various health conditions (*Murray*, 1996, pp. 23–24). Measuring functional limitations, rather than individuals' stated personal preferences and reported health status, ostensibly enhances objectivity (*Murray*, 1994). However, this approach has met with criticism: individual and socio-economic resources arguably mediate "burdens" imposed by disability, and people with disabilities do not necessarily bear all or even most of these "burdens" (*Anand & Hanson*, 1997). But the DALY emphasises pathology lodged in individual bodies, presumed amenable to elimination through concerted human effort. The degree of pathology estimates the "burden" on diagnosed individuals, families, and society.

In seeking to "measure health by the degree of deprivation experienced by a person in being able to use one's own body" (*Murray & Archarya*, 1997, p. 724), the DALY clearly treats disability as pathology, and pathology as suffering. To ensure "objectivity," the DALY follows the definition of disability in the *International Classification of Impairments, Disabilities and Handicaps* or ICIDH (*World Health Organisation*, 1980). This schema proposes that diseases lead to pathologies, which become manifest in impairments, disabilities and handicaps. Impairment refers to the impact at the level of the organ system; disability refers to the impact on individual functioning; and handicap refers to the consequences, which depend on the social and physical environment. This classification scheme assigns the Parsonian sick role to people with disabilities, suggesting that people with disabilities cannot participate in society nor can they sustain "customary" relationships with others (*Pfeiffer*, 1998).

While the DALY measures individual functioning, and therefore disability, it does try to account for the impact, on average, of various conditions. Thus, it arguably measures the "average level of handicap" (*Murray*, 1996, p. 34). Murray rejects measuring handicap per se rather than disability because he contends that efforts to minimise "handicaps" would most benefit people who already enjoy personal, social and economic advantages. For example, he claims that a focus on the reduction of handicaps could lead to preventing intellectual disabilities among the rich and well-educated but not among poor people (*Murray*, 1996, p. 33). He appears to suggest that reducing handicaps experienced by people who are better off than the average in every way except in biological terms, would be easiest and most efficient. Moreover, efforts to minimise the impact of a disabling condition on affected individuals may reinforce inequalities because these efforts would be most likely to succeed among privileged people. Thus, Murray implies that improving the average level of individual functioning promotes global equality. That is why the DALY seeks to measure bodily functioning, not the degree of disadvantage experienced due to limitations on bodily functioning.

In explaining the DALY's emphasis on functional limitations, Murray acknowledges that stated preferences depend largely on the social context. This variation, he explains, may obstruct objectivity and social justice. He invokes the "happy slave" conundrum identified by de Toqueville, wherein a slave claims to be content but only because this individual has been conditioned to expect very little (*de Toqueville*, 1839 in; *Murray*, 1996, p. 31). That some slaves may have been happy, says Murray, does not make slavery acceptable. "By analogy, the adaptive powers of man [sic] should not make the prevention or rehabilitation of those with a nonfatal health outcome less valuable" (*Murray*, 1996, p. 31). In the next breath, he claims that only perversion would suggest that deafness not be prevented just because people who are deaf have adapted to their situation. Many deaf people, by contrast, see themselves as members of an oppressed culture, not as afflicted individuals (*Crouch*, 1997). If people with disabilities report health and happiness, Murray suggests, it is because they suffer from false consciousness.

Comparing disability and slavery implies that people with disabilities are unfairly trapped in their "diseased" bodies. Accordingly, measuring "handicap" would arguably do a disservice to people with disabilities by, in effect, measuring "adaptation." Furthermore, it implies that people with disabilities form a class of people who, like slaves, cannot provide valid information about how they experience the world. To represent the "disability experience," as discussed below, the DALY relies upon professional opinion when determining the "cost" or "loss" of a disability.

The qualifications necessary to judge the quality of life experienced by people with disabilities is a crucial issue in designing and using health status measures. In concluding a review article about these measures, Nord observes that

> Health state valuation studies are generally based on proxies. That is, subjects are asked to consider states that they have not experienced themselves. Applying the results of any of these studies in decision-making clearly presupposes that judgements by proxies correctly reflect the relative disutility of different states of illness or disability as perceived by patients in those states. In general, far too little is known about this issue (*Nord*, 1992, p. 567).

As Murray acknowledges (*Murray*, 1996, pp. 29–30) and as witnessed in the Latimer case, many activists contend that people with disabilities can best judge their circumstances. Disability activists also emphasise that the environment largely determines how much their disabilities "burden" them, their families and society more generally. Certain scholars share this view, arguing that disability is not necessarily a burden and that time spent with a disability is not time lost (*Chamie* and *Pfeiffer*). Proponents of the DALY seemingly dismiss these considerations. Instead, they emphasise "objective" biomedical expertise, encompassing variation in individuals' ability to cope with adversity (*Murray & Archarya*, 1997, pp. 710–711). The impact of socio-economic resources does not enter into the equation.

According to DALY's champions, accounting for variation in individual and social resources would violate the principle of treating likes alike (*Murray & Archarya*, 1997). This principle is based on formal equality theory, which demands homogeneous treatment of people with "similar" conditions (*Rioux*, 1994). As for the DALY, formal equality means scaling people according to their degree of disability. Through this scaling process and the logic of cost-effectiveness, it implies that fewer resources should flow to people with disabilities than people without disabilities.

It is important to note that cost-utility or cost-effectiveness studies[2] need not imply that fewer resources flow to people with disabilities than to people without disabilities. When the DALY formula is used, money spent on rehabilitation seems like money well-spent. But spending money on "perfectly healthy" people may seem even more advisable.

> For example, a treatment which enables a person in a wheelchair to live another year (without altering the person's existing disability) prevents fewer DALYs than the same treatment given to a perfectly healthy person. This is because, given his existing disability (weighted, say, at a value of 1/2), he is permanently suffering half a DALY per year.
>
> Extending his life by a year thus only averts half a DALY (assuming an age weight of unity and no discounting), whereas extending the life of a perfectly able-bodied person averts a whole DALY (*Anand & Hanson*, 1997, p. 700).

Therefore, *Anand and Hanson* (1997, p. 702) argue that resource allocation decisions based on the DALY arguably stand to entrench disadvantage among people with disabilities. It also bears noting that the only form of investment in people with disabilities that seems warranted by the DALY formula is "rehabilitation." Even then, it might seem preferable to divert money that could be spent on rehabilitation to interventions that promise greater "health" among the already "healthy." In sum, a cost-effectiveness or cost-utility analysis can endorse resource allocations in favour of people with disabilities, depending upon the criteria used to evaluate "health" and "health" benefits.

The DALY equates "effectiveness" with "health" and it equates "health" with the absence of disabilities. As a result, it favours rehabilitation (compared with modifying the physical or social environment) and investment in people without disabilities (or with "minor" disabilities). If the DALY quantified "adaptation," on the other hand, extending the lives of people with disabilities would seem more cost-effective than preventing disability in the first place (*Murray* 1996, p. 30). That is, measuring the degree of impact that a disability has would encourage investments that would minimise any negative consequences experienced as a result of having a disability.

> Consider the hypothetical individual who suffers a spinal court transection at age 25. Immediately after the injury the individual might assign a very low preference weight for his health state. With time the individual will adapt to his paraplegia, and serial assessments of his preference weight might steadily rise. Which preference should be used for burden of disease or cost-effectiveness analyses: the adapted or the pre-adapted weight? The coping/adaptation phenomenon has profound resource implications: using pre-adapted weights will make prevention and rehabilitation look more cost-effective, but life extension for those with paraplegia will appear less cost-effective. Using the adapted weights will make prevention and rehabilitation much less attractive in cost-effectiveness terms, but it will make life extension more cost-effective (*Murray & Archarya*, 1997), p. 713.

Measuring "adaptation" could also render attractive a range of interventions that could augment social inclusion and "quality of life" — but that do not "rehabilitate" or extend life — for people with disabilities, such as personal assistance with work-related activities. But to reiterate, the DALY does not consider what might cause more people with disabilities to report better "health," except for interventions that would improve "functioning."

As noted above, the DALY formula implies that disabilities can make life unworthy of living. The DALY ranks the most "severe" class of disabilities as only slightly less burdensome than "premature" death. Furthermore, multiple disabilities may yield a score worse than death (*Murray*, 1996, pp. 41–42). According to the DALY formula, Tracy Latimer was in fact living a fate worse than death. Her combined disability score would exceed at least 1.2, where one equals "premature" death and zero equals "perfect health."

"Perfect health" implies an absence of pathology, but also minimises conditions associated with the onset of disease. Since the mid-nineteenth century, pathology contrasts with normality (*Canguilhem*, 1989 [1943, 1966]). This contrast expresses a shift in emphasis toward defining "normal people," and away from the Enlightenment preoccupation with human nature. Concern with specifying normality produced an "avalanche of numbers," needed to draw "normal" curves; normality serves simultaneously as an abstract average and a goal (*Hacking*, 1990). Therefore, governing bodies can always undertake measures aimed at improvement. Typically, improvement implies eliminating, preventing or lessening pathology in hopes of ever more normal people, in terms of both bodily qualities and sheer numbers. Biomedicine bears the indelible imprint of this mandate. Epidemiology, which provides biomedicine with a bird's eye view of the distribution of disease, can pinpoint injustices by showing that social and economic conditions produce suffering — glossed as pathology — at diverging rates in different locales.

Originally, the DALY divided "burden" into six categories on a scale between perfect health and death. Limited ability to perform at least one recreational, educational, reproductive or occupational activity meant a person fit the "least disabled" category, the "most disabled" category included people requiring assistance with activities of daily living, such as eating, personal hygiene or toilet use. A group of "independent experts" ranked the relative "burden" associated with each of the six categories (*Murray*, 1994, p. 439).

Four criticisms of this approach were considered when, in 1995, the measure underwent revision. These criticisms were: the categories did not apply well to children; the lack of a formalised protocol made it difficult to reproduce the process for scaling various disabilities in terms of their social undesirability; the weight assigned to the first category on the scale overstated the degree of "burden" imposed by "mild" conditions; and finally, the panel of experts charged with assigning the disability weights did not have to consider the policy implications of their decisions (*Murray*, 1996, p. 34). This last criticism seems somewhat ironic, given the goal of "impersonal" decision-making that informed the DALY's development.

Instead of estimating the magnitude of disability, as in the original version, the revised disability scale stems from the "person trade-off" method (*Nord* and *Nord*).[3] The DALY team designed a protocol using this method with health care providers in mind, "so that less time needs to be invested to describe each of these conditions," and not because these professionals necessarily have "better" judgement (*Murray*, 1996, pp. 26–37).[4] Over two days at the World Health Organisation's headquarters, an international panel assigned a numerical value to "the average individual with the condition described taking into account the average social response or milieu" (*Murray*, 1996, p. 38). Expertise as a health care professional apparently provides the knowledge necessary to accomplish this task, even if the terms seem vague. Yet Murray interprets the "high degree of consensus" that developed, despite "diverse cultural backgrounds," as evidence for the measure's validity. He also finds comfort in the close match of the reference group's ranking with eight other groups of professionals that have followed the protocol (*Murray*, 1996, p. 39).

The first phase of the protocol includes a series of questions about extending life to people with and without disabilities. For example, participants decided whether they would rather purchase one year of life for a thousand "perfectly healthy" individuals, or for two thousand "blind individuals." In the second phase, participants chose between rehabilitating people with disabilities and extending life for "perfectly healthy" individuals.[5] After eliminating differences in the rankings established by each participant during the two phases, discussion aimed at consensus among the participants (*Murray*, 1996, pp. 35–36).

The participants repeated this process for twenty-two conditions, giving each condition a score between perfect health and death. These conditions, grouped into seven categories, serve as indicators for ranking disabilities not specifically considered by the panel (*Murray*, 1996, pp. 39–40). Among the indicator conditions in the current version of the DALY, dementia ranks below Down syndrome; deafness is about on par with a below-the-knee amputation; and it is better to have a major unipolar depression than severe migraines.

Let us now revisit the "happy slave" conundrum. The abolition of slavery in the West marks a modern concern with not treating people as property (*Strathern*, 1996). The condemnation of slavery may distract us from recognising that commodification of people occurs in virtually all societies, although it takes diverse forms. Think of wage labour and bridewealth, for example. Recognising that exchange and value-setting are commodification's signature (*Appadurai*, 1986), we may gain new insights into the DALY. It invokes the possibility of exchanging people with disabilities for people without disabilities, and exchanging longer "normal" lives for "rehabilitated" bodies. That these exchanges do not take effect when calculating the DALY should not prevent us from commodification processes inherent to its formula and its use in guiding resource allocation. While the DALY proposes hypothetical exchanges, it is a practical tool. It values human life with various bodily conditions to enable policy decisions.

Concluding Remarks

Calls to complement "thin" columns of numbers with qualitative research have become common in medical anthropology (*Kleinman*, 1995, pp. 68–92; *Trostle & Sommerfeld*, 1996, for example). Such arguments recognise that ethnography — encompassing narratives and historical research — can provide a welcome antidote to quantitative research about the body, thereby enhancing understanding. Evoking "the context," however, is never straightforward. Considering the DALY alongside Robert Latimer's position provides a very different perspective from that of disability rights activists. This paper suggests that we need a "thick" account of "thin" measures of suffering, such as the DALY. We need to account for why the DALY and other health measures have a particular form.

The DALY reflects a desire to measure health and death correctly so as to allocate resources fairly, and eventually, achieve better living conditions among the world's people. The Latimer case, endowed with embodied experience and visceral reactions, seems cut from an altogether different cloth than public health issues. It focuses on the health and death of one individual. Public debate surrounding this legal case has often turned on whether or not Tracy Latimer had a conscious existence beyond physical pain. Relatedly, many Canadians believe that her parents bore the brunt of the pain involved, through empathy and through limits placed on their own lives by raising this daughter. If Tracy Latimer could experience physical pain but not happiness, and if relieving her physical pain would mean an even more anomalous body, then "normality" would appear to have limits. By contrast, the DALY imagines "normality" as limitless in human populations, and indeed universal but for injustice. The DALY thus portrays "premature" death and observable pathologies as preventable, and even "unnatural."

The DALY implies a belief that Robert Latimer's defence explicitly invokes: bodily anomalies always indicate pain, be it emotional or physical or a combination of the two. Emotional pain presumes consciousness of a particular sort — that of "ordinary" people who would prefer a "normal" life. The DALY suggests that preventing or treating anomalies in the future will result in less suffering, on average. Insofar as individuals' anomalous bodies affect others (kin, "society"), deviations from the "normal" body serve as proxy markers for the sum total of "suffering" involved. The DALY does not encompass the possibility of perpetuating pronounced deviations from the "normal" body through biomedical interventions, even as these interventions aim to extend or ameliorate life. This possibility rears its head in the Latimer affair.

While the Latimer affair and the DALY display some crucial differences as regards pain and normality, both involve converting people into cases. Generally, converting people into cases implies that people are fungible, that lives are interchangeable. The Latimer affair is a legal case, while the DALY converts people into statistical cases. The DALY formula's treatment of disability derives from deliberation about hypothetical cases generated to fix the exchange value of various bodies. The DALY suggests that life without disabilities replace life with disabilities in the future. Meanwhile, confessed killers like Robert Latimer must usually "pay" for their crimes in Euro-America, but how? If not by "giving" their own lives, then through some other form of suffering, typically incarceration. Precisely because two lives are never completely alike, those who analyse cases must grapple with difference. The Latimer affair and the DALY both involve the assertion that some lives have more worth because they involve less "suffering." Once closely examined, therefore, the DALY exhibits some ideas about suffering that resound in the Latimer affair.

Although the goal of a "normal" body infuses biomedicine, some bodies are more "normal" than others. By extension, some populations are more "normal" than others. Disability activists and allied scholars claim that the DALY and the Latimer case presumptuously exclude disability from "normality." They argue that disability is not coterminous with pain — whether physical or emotional — nor with illness, sickness or disease. By invoking human rights, they counter the suggestion that unusual bodies are necessarily pathological bodies in need of "compassion." Crucially, those who claim that people with disabilities may enjoy life do not always oppose biomedical treatment. But when proposing resource allocations, they do not always privilege biomedical interventions. Furthermore, they maintain that disability is "normally" found in all human populations, not least in societies committed to social equality. As Pfeiffer puts it,

> Disability is a natural part of life. Everyone will be disabled. Perhaps a person will be disabled for only moments before death from a massive heart attack or in an automobile accident; but most people will spend a significant amount of time in their life as a person with a disability. It cannot be avoided. Therefore, it is important to say that people with disabilities have a right to be different and a right to be treated equally with people without disabilities (*Pfeiffer*, 1998, p. 519).

In the discourse of disability activists and allied scholars, the population rather than the individual body serves as the base unit, such that people with disabilities rightfully form a geographically dispersed population nested within other populations (such as nations).

Any reduction in Robert Latimer's punishment because he killed out of "compassion," disability activists maintain, discounts the lives of citizens with disabilities. Recall that Robert Latimer was originally charged with first degree murder, that sentencing him for the minimum penalty for second degree murder produced public outcry, and that he has appealed even that sentence. The DALY, meanwhile, explicitly rates life lived with a disability as less desirable than life lived without a disability. Considering the DALY and the Latimer affair together reveals a shared logic, even the rudiments of a common metric, for conceptualising what it is to suffer. As the Latimer affair makes especially clear, however, "suffering" is contested terrain.

The prosecution, the defence, pundits and activists in the Latimer affair invoke biomedical expertise, so crucial for compelling claims about bodily conditions. The attribution of "suffering" in the DALY also relies on biomedical expertise. That is, the mantle of biomedical authority seems to inform the positions advanced by all the players considered here. Clearly, biomedicine does not have a single perspective on disability. It follows that no single "biomedical model" of disability exists. Biomedicine does take the desirability of a "normal" body as its starting point, yet "perfectly normal" bodies seem in short supply.

Some medical anthropologists, sensitive to power relations, have pointed out that appropriations of suffering depend on depicting actual people (*Das* and *Kleinman*), however abstractly formulas or court cases represent individual circumstances. This paper has elaborated on this moral concern about representations by highlighting how expertise construes suffering as a "really real" phenomenon in the first place, sometimes through commodifying processes.

Doing so has exposed a paradox. Anthropologists, economists and other social scientists often remain committed to normalising the body — in its individual and collective dimensions — even when critiquing biomedicine. Therefore, social scientists' critiques of biomedicine often implicitly depend upon the idea that "normal" and "pathological" states exist, and that "pathology" should be avoided. Notably, a "social model" of disability (as opposed to a "biomedical model") and characterisations of "social suffering" (as opposed to disease) both depend heavily on biomedicine's tenets, for both rely upon a distinction between what is "normal" and what is "pathological," a distinction which is crucial to biomedicine. In particular, a "social model" of disability and "social suffering" invoke pathology. Instead of locating pathology *in* the body, however, the literature on "social suffering" and that premised upon a "social model" of disability locate pathology in relationships *between* bodies. They sometimes portray the "social" relationships constitutive of biomedicine and governments as being capable of generating pathology, in the form of inequality for example. By implication, social scientists cannot take their understandings of "normalcy," "pathology," or "suffering" for granted.

Acknowledgements

Alberto Cambrosio, Margaret Lock, Janalyn Prest, George Weisz, and Allan Young provided vital counsel as I prepared this paper. Dominique Béhague also provided valuable insights about the DALY and international public health. Carl Elliot asked a question that pushed my thinking on commodification when I presented an earlier version of this paper at the Canadian Bioethics Society meetings in October 1998. Bill Harvey, Tod Chambers, Jane Chambers-Evans, Kathryn Morgan, and Gregor Wolbring provided much-appreciated encouragement on that occasion. In addition, I am indebted to Ernie Lightman for much of my appreciation of the uses and abuses of cost-benefit, cost-effectiveness, and cost-utility analyses. As a result of working as a researcher at the Roeher Institute from 1994 to 1997, I gained a heightened awareness of issues affecting people with disabilities. I wish to acknowledge funding for my doctoral studies from the Social Science and Humanities Research Council of Canada. I also benefit from membership in a research team studying "Body, Memory and Identity," funded by the Quebec government's Fonds pour la Formation de Chercheurs et l'Aide à la Recherche.

REFERENCES

Anand, S. and Hanson, K., 1997. Disability-adjusted life years: a critical review. *Journal of Health Economics* 16, pp. 685–702. *Abstract / PDF (913 K)*

Appadurai, A., 1986. Introduction: commodities and the politics of value. In: Appadurai, A., Editor, 1986. *The social life of things: Commodities in cultural perspective*, Cambridge University Press, Cambridge.

Bach, M., 1994. Quality of life: Questioning the vantage points for research. In: Rioux, M.H. and Bach, M., Editors, 1994. *Disability is not measles: New research paradigms in disability*, The Roeher Institute, North York, ON.

Bowie, C., Beck, S., Bevan, G., Raftery, J., Silverton, F. and Stevens, A., 1997. Estimating the burden of disease in an English region. *Journal of Public Health Medicine* 19 1, pp. 87–92. *Abstract-MEDLINE | Abstract-EMBASE*

Braid, T. (1997). The misery Latimer ended was his own (originally published in the *Edmonton Sun*). *Latimer Watch*, 25 November, http://www.pcs.mb.ca/~ccd/lwintro.html.

Canadian Charter of Rights and Freedoms. (1982), Ottawa, ON.

Canguilhem, G. (1989). [1943, 1966]. *The Normal and the Pathological*. Zone Books, New York.

Chamie, M., 1995. What does morbidity have to do with disability? *Disability and Rehabilitation* 17, pp. 323–337. *Abstract-PsycINFO | Abstract-MEDLINE | Abstract-EMBASE*

Crouch, R.A., 1997,. Letting the deaf be deaf: reconsidering the use of cochlear implants in prelingually deaf children. *Hastings Centre Report* 27 4, pp. 14–21. *Abstract-MEDLINE*

Das, V., 1977. Sufferings, theodicies, disciplinary practices, appropriations. *International Social Science Journal* 49 4, pp. 563–572.

Derksen, J. (1997a). Consumers monitor CBC: Jim Derksen critiques The National's interview with Robert Latimer. *Latimer Watch*, 28 November, http://www.pcs.mb.ca/~ccd/lwintro.html.

Derksen, J. (1997b). Jim Derksen speaks out: Murder is never compassionate. *Latimer Watch*, 27 December, http://www.pcs.mb.ca/~ccd/lwintro.html.

Desjarlais, R., Eisenberg, L., Good, B. and Kleinman, A., 1995. *World mental health: Problems and priorities in low-income countries*, Oxford University Press, New York.

Globe and Mail, 1997. Latimer released on bail: Farmer to appeal conviction, sentence, for killing disabled daughter. *Globe and Mail* 20 December, p. A14.

Green, L., 1998. Lived lives and social suffering: problems and concerns in medical anthropology (Introduction to special issue: The embodiment of violence). *Medical Anthropological Quarterly* 12 1, pp. 3–7.

Hacking, I., 1986. Making up people. In: Heller, H.C., Sosna, M. and Wellbery, D.E., Editors, 1986, *Reconstructing individualism: Autonomy, individuality and the self in western thought*, Stanford University Press, Stanford.

Hacking, I., 1990. *The taming of chance*, Cambridge University Press, Cambridge.

Hammit, J.K., 1993. Discounting health increments (Editorial). *Journal of Health Economics* 12, pp. 117–120.

Ingstad, B. and Reynolds Whyte, S., 1995. *Disability and Culture*, University of California Press, Berkeley, Los Angeles.

Kleinman, A., 1995. *Writing at the margin: Discourse between anthropology and medicine*, University of California Press, Berkeley.

Kleinman, A., Das, V. and Lock, M., Editors, 1997. *Social suffering*, University of California Press, Berkeley.

Kleinman, A. and Kleinman, J., 1997. The appeal of experience; the dismay of images: Cultural appropriations of suffering in our times. In: Kleinman, A., Das, V. and Lock, M., Editors, 1997. *Social suffering*, University of California Press, Berkeley.

Kunitz, S., 1987. Explanations and ideologies of mortality patterns. *Population and Development Review* 13 3, pp. 379–408. *Abstract-GEOBASE | Abstract-EconLit.*

Mendelsohn, J.A., 1998. From eradication to equilibrium: how epidemics became complex after World War I. In: Lawrence, C. and Weisz, G., Editors, 1998. *Greater than the whole: Holism in western biomedicine 1920–1950*, Oxford University Press, Oxford.

Mill, J.S., 1861. *Utilitarianism*, Bobbs-Merril, Indianapolis.

Mitchell, A., 1995. Latimer entitled to new trial: gossip revealed that RCMP questioned potential jurors about ethical beliefs on mercy killing. *Globe and Mail* 26 October, p. A2.

Murray, C.J., 1994. Quantifying the burden of disease: the technical basis for disability-adjusted life years. *Bulletin of the World Health Organisation* 72 3, pp. 429–445. *Abstract-MEDLINE*

Murray, C.J. and Lopez, A.D., 1994. Quantifying disability: data, methods and results. *Bulletin of the World Health Organisation* 72 3, pp. 481–494. *Abstract-EMBASE* | *Abstract-MEDLINE*

Murray, C.J. and Lopez, A.D., 1997. Global mortality, disability, and the contribution of risk factors: Global Burden of Disease Study. *Lancet* 349 9063, pp. 1436–1442. *SummaryPlus* | ***Full Text + Links*** | *PDF (79K)*

Murray, C.J.L., 1996. Rethinking DALYs. In: Murray, C.J.L. and Lopez, A.D., Editors, 1996. *The global burden of disease: A comprehensive assessment of mortality and disability from diseases, injuries, and risk factors in 1990 and projected to 2020.* Harvard University Press, Cambridge, MA.

Murray, C.J.L. and Archarya, A.K., 1997. Understanding DALYs. *Journal of Health Economics* 16, pp. 703–730. *Abstract* | *PDF (1401 K)*

Nord, E., 1992. Methods for quality adjustment of life years. *Social Science and Medicine* 34, pp. 556–569. *Abstract*

Nord, E., 1995. The person trade-off approach to valuing health care programs. *Medical Decision Making* 15, pp. 201–208. *Abstract-EMBASE* | *Abstract-MEDLINE*

Olsen, J.A., 1993. On what basis should health be discounted? *Journal of Health Economics* 12, pp. 39–53. *Abstract*

Olsen, J.A., 1997. Theories of justice and their implications for priority setting in health care. *Journal of Health Economics* 16, pp. 625–639. *Abstract* | *PDF (649 K)*

Osborne, T., 1993. On liberalism, neo-liberalism and the "liberal profession" of medicine. *Economy and Society* 22 3, pp. 345–356.

Pfeiffer, D., 1998. The ICIDH and the need for its revision. *Disability and Society* 13 4, pp. 503–523. *Abstract-PsycINFO* | ***Full Text*** via CrossRef

Porter, T., 1992. Objectivity as standardization: the rhetoric of impersonality in measurement, statistics and cost-benefit analysis. *Annals of Scholarship* 9, pp. 19–59.

R. v. Latimer. (1994). 124 Saskatchewan R. 180 (Q.B.).

R. v. Latimer. (1997). Robert W. Latimer v. Her Majesty the Queen. Supreme Court of Canada on appeal from the Court of Appeal for Saskatchewan, 6 February.

Rioux, M., 1994. Towards a concept of equality of well-being: overcoming the social and legal construction of inequality. *Canadian Journal of Law and Jurisprudence* 7 1, pp. 127–147.

Rioux, M. and Richler, D., 1995. Count us in: lessons from Canada on strategies for social change. In: Philpot, T. and Ward, L., Editors, 1995. *Values and visions: Changing ideas in services for people with learning difficulties*, Butterworth-Heinman, Oxford.

Roberts, D. (1998). Latimer gets life, vows to appeal. *Globe and Mail* 24 November, A1, A10.

Rose, N. and Miller, P., 1992. Political power beyond the state: problematics of government. *British Journal of Sociology* 43 2, pp. 173–205.

Sneiderman, B., 1997. The Latimer [*R. v. Latimer* [1995] 8 W.W.R. 609] mercy-killing case: a rumination on crime and punishment. *Health Law Journal* 5, pp. 1–26. *Abstract-MEDLINE*

Strathern, M., 1996. Cutting the network. *Journal of the Royal Anthropological Institute* 2 n.s., pp. 517–535.

de Toqueville, A., 1839. *Democracy in America*.

Trostle, J.A. and Sommerfeld, J., 1996. Medical anthropology and epidemiology. *Annual Review of Anthropology* 25, pp. 253–274. ***Full Text*** via CrossRef

Wolbring, G. (1997). Gregor Wolbring responds to Marilynne Seguin of Death with Dignity and reveals their ableist bias. *Latimer Watch*, 28 November, http://www.pcs.mb.ca/~ccd/lwintro.html.

World Bank, 1993. *World Development Report 1993: Investing in health*, Oxford University Press, New York.

World Health Organisation, 1980. *International classification of impairments, disabilities and handicaps*, World Health Organisation, Geneva.

Young, A., 1982. The anthropologies of illness and sickness. *Annual Review of Anthropology* 11, pp. 257–285. *Abstract-GEOBASE | Abstract-PsycINFO*

NOTES

1. In this regard, "discounting" refers to the common practice of reducing the value assigned to a good or service so that it corresponds more precisely with the true worth of that good or service. As I will demonstrate below, this practice also applies at times to people. Notably, when the "good" in question is "health," the valuation process encompasses human bodies and the people inhabiting such bodies. The bodies in question may exist in an imagined future, as when economists seek to assess the "health benefit" that would accrue to a particular population as a result of interventions such as improved sanitation or better clinical treatment methods (*Hammit* and *Olsen*). Indeed, economists typically use the term "discounting" when evaluating future benefits. When the benefit in question is human "health," these efforts implicitly assign a value to human lives, to people. In fact, they seek to quantify the social values associated with different "health states." In operationalising social values, they express — and contribute to the codification of — conceptions of "suffering."

2. Cost-utility health analysis involves expressing the benefit of an intervention in terms of the number of quality-adjusted life years gained as a result of the intervention. The DALY is an example of a cost-utility measure. Cost-effectiveness analysis involves expressing the impact of an intervention as a ratio between the benefit of that intervention and the costs incurred to produce that benefit. The benefits may be measured in a variety of ways, including by using a cost-utility measure such as the DALY. Costs are measured monetarily, and may include the monetisation of "in-kind" inputs such as unpaid labour.

3. *Nord* (1992) illustrates the differences between magnitude estimation, standard gamble, time trade-off and person trade-off as follows, where A is equivalent to a life year weight of 0.4 and B is equivalent to a life year weight of 0.8: **Magnitude estimation** — I think state A is half as good as state B; **Standard gamble**: I think it is just as good to gamble with the chance of 0.4 of getting well immediately and a chance of 0.6 of dying immediately as to live with certainty in state A; **Time trade-off**: I think that it is just as good to live 0.4 of a year as healthy as living 1 year in state A; **person trade-off**: I think that is just as good to cure 1 person in state A as curing three people in state B.

4. In a recent scathing critique of the WHO's International Classification of Impairments, Disabilities and Handicaps (ICIDH), which undergirds the DALY and many other health-related quality of life measures, Pfeiffer (1992, p. 51) asserts that "if, in the judgement of experts, a person does not presently have a sufficiently high qualify of life due to 'impairments, functional states, perceptions and social opportunities' which are the outcome of 'disease, injury, treatment or policy,' then that person will not, ought not to receive "the benefits of health expenditures. A clear statement of the ideal of Eugenics."

5. The person trade-off method is admittedly "quite demanding" to apply in making resource-allocation decisions: the results obtained can depend heavily on the clarity of the decision context

presented to the participants, on how the arguments are presented and on the choice of start points in numerically ranking the options (*Nord*, 1995, p. 201). By way of comparison with the DALY, the scenarios recently deployed "in various small-scale studies conducted in Norway" did not ask participants to choose between whether to extend life to people with and without disabilities, nor were participants asked to indicate a preference for rehabilitating people with disabilities or extending life for "perfectly healthy" individuals. Instead, through a series of questions framing the scenario, they were asked to indicate preferences for helping two groups of people with disabilities, where one group is "worse off" (in terms of physical functioning) than the other (see *Nord*, 1995 for details). The differences between the scenarios described by Nord and those used in assigning weights to different bodily states in the DALY could have considerable implications in determining the flow of resources. But both involve modelling how best to distribute various degrees of "health" among types of people, whose merit is defined in relation to their bodily capacities.

QUESTIONS

1. What is the Disability-Adjusted Life Year (DALY)? How is this measure relevant to the debate on euthanasia?
2. What does Melanie Rock mean by the phrase "the politics of suffering"? How, if at all, does this relate to Somerville's argument that it is important to separate questions about treatment at the end of life from ending life itself?
3. How does Rock use the DALY to shed light on the Latimer case? Do you find her argument convincing? Why or why not?
4. How would Rock respond to Rachels' example of the child with Down's syndrome?
5. Rock states that "any reduction in Robert Latimer's punishment because he killed out of 'compassion,' disability activists maintain, discounts the lives of citizens with disabilities." What is the argument for this claim? Do you find this sort of argument against euthanasia convincing? Why or why not?

SUGGESTIONS FOR FURTHER READING

Court Decisions

- *R. v. Latimer*. Supreme Court of Canada. June 14, 2001 [2001] 1 S.C.R. The Supreme Court reviewed the decision of the Court of Appeal for Saskatchewan and determined that the mandatory minimum sentence for second degree murder in the case of Robert Latimer ending the life of his disabled daughter does not constitute cruel and unusual punishment.

Reports and Web sites

- *Of Life and Death: Final Report*. Parliament of Canada. Report of the Special Committee on Euthanasia and Assisted Suicide. 1995. URL: *http://www.parl.gc.ca/english/senate/com-e/euth-e/rep-e/lad-tc-e.htm*
- *Quality End-of-Life Care: The Right of Every Canadian*. Subcommittee to update "Of Life and Death" of the Standing Senate Committee on Social Affairs, Science and Technology. Final Report, Chaired by Sharon Carstairs. 2000.

- *Consensus Guidelines on Analgesia and Sedation in Dying Intensive Care Unit Patients*. University of Toronto Joint Centre for Bioethics. Laura Hawryluck et al. August 2002. As the title suggests, this report provides guidelines for the treatment of dying patients.
- Not Dead Yet. URL:
  http://www.notdeadyet.org/
  An organization representing the interests of disabled persons opposing euthanasia and assisted suicide. The Web site includes links to court cases and other Web sites on the issue of euthanasia.

Books

- E. W. Keyserlingk, *Sanctity of Life or Quality of Life in the Context of Ethics, Medicine and Law* (Minister of Supply and Services, 1979). This is a report prepared as a background study for the Law Reform Commission of Canada. The report studies the concepts of "sanctity of life" and "quality of life" in depth and goes on to make a series of proposals. Although the focus of the Commission work is law reform, this report is primarily ethical in nature.
- Ronald Dworkin, *Life's Dominion: An Argument About Abortion, Euthanasia and Individual Freedom* (New York: Knopf, 1993). In this book, Dworkin describes the recent history of the abortion and euthanasia controversies in the United States and elsewhere. He argues that in the end, respect for human dignity requires respect for human freedom and freedom of choice both with regard to abortion and euthanasia.
- Ruth Enns, *A Voice Unheard: The Latimer Case and People with Disabilities* (Halifax: Fernwood, 1999). In this book, Enns examines the Latimer case, arguing that people with disabilities have perspectives that challenge mainstream interpretations of "mercy" killing, including the actions of Robert Latimer in the case of his disabled daughter.
- Margaret Battin, Rosamond Rhodes, and Anita Silvers, eds. *Physician Assisted Suicide: Expanding the Debate* (New York: Routledge, 1998). An important collection of articles covering various aspects of the debate from conceptual to medical to legal to religious issues. The book includes "The Philosophers' Brief," a brief formulated by six prominent moral philosophers, Ronald Dworkin, Thomas Nagel, Robert Nozick, John Rawls, Thomas Scanlon, and Judith Jarvis Thomson, supporting the right to physician-assisted suicide.
- Marvin Kohl, ed. *Beneficent Euthanasia* (Buffalo: Prometheus Books, 1975) and *Infanticide and the Value of Life* (Buffalo: Prometheus Books, 1978). These books are excellent collections of articles on the subjects of euthanasia and infanticide, viewed from many perspectives, religious and secular, pro and con.
- John Ladd, ed. *Ethical Issues Relating to Life and Death* (Oxford: Oxford University Press, 1979). This volume includes articles by a number of notable authors and takes up many of the issues touched on in the first two chapters of this book.

Articles

- Douglas Walton, "Splitting the Difference: Killing and Letting Die," *Dialogue*, vol. 20, no. 1, 1981. In this article, Walton explores the distinction between killing and letting die. In particular, he examines the position of James Rachels (in this volume), who has written extensively in defence of euthanasia and who concludes that there is no morally relevant distinction to be made between active and passive euthanasia.

- Margaret Battin, "Euthanasia: The Way We Do It, the Way They Do It?" *Journal of Pain and Symptom Management*, vol. 6, no. 5, 1991. Battin examines the history of and rationale for current euthanasia practices in the Netherlands, Germany, and the United States to argue that the United States can and should support physician-assisted suicide.
- Daniel Callahan, "When Self-Determination Runs Amok," *Hastings Center Report*, March-April 1992. In this article, Callahan presents several arguments from the perspectives of patients, doctors, and society as a whole against allowing voluntary euthanasia.
- Daniel Callahan, "Killing and Allowing to Die," in *Medical Ethics: Basic Ethics in Action* edited by M. Boylan (New Jersey: Prentice-Hall, 2000). In this article, Callahan distinguishes between killing another person and allowing a person to die from an incurable disease. He argues that allowing someone to die without using heroic means to prolong life is justified.
- Leon Kass, "Why Doctors Must Not Kill," *Commonwealth* 118 (August 9, 1991). In this article, Kass outlines reasons why doctors dedicated to healing the sick should not kill patients, even terminally ill ones. He argues that "the physician-euthanizer is a deadly self-contradiction."

Chapter 2

Abortion and Reproductive Technologies

Introduction

Abortion is a complex moral issue involving important questions about procreative choice, status of the unborn, welfare of children, responsibilities of fathers, involvement of the medical profession, and interests of the state. All of these dimensions bring into sharp relief each of the principles of protection of life, avoidance of suffering, and moral autonomy introduced in the previous chapter. This chapter begins with an examination of these principles in the case of abortion and then turns to some of the issues introduced by reproductive technologies. It will become clear that these principles take on new meaning in the contemporary context of technologies that promise increased choice about when and how to reproduce and that raise questions about who is affected by these choices and when human life itself begins.

Having children has become widely viewed as a matter of choice and not a matter of necessity or obligation. Many people now believe that if having children is really a matter of choice, the terminating of a pregnancy by abortion should, like the use of birth control, be a matter of choice.

Why might a woman choose to have an abortion? Sometimes the procedure is therapeutic. For example, the pregnancy might have become a threat to the life or health of the mother; it might be the result of rape or incest; or the mother may fear that she will be unable to cope with a child for psychological or financial reasons. Sometimes the reason may centre on the child. It may simply be unwanted by the mother, or the parents and doctors may have concluded that there is a substantial risk the child will be born with severe mental or physical disabilities. Finally, abortion may be requested for what might be called reasons of convenience. Either the pregnancy or parenthood may conflict with the lifestyle of one or the other parent. Or amniocentesis may indicate that the child that has been conceived is not of the desired sex. While not exhaustive, this list and grouping of reasons provides a starting point for assessing the relevance of the principles of protection of life, moral autonomy, and avoidance of suffering to the issue of abortion.

The life and welfare of a woman seeking to terminate an unwanted pregnancy are clearly central to a discussion of the morality of abortion. But there is a second life involved. It is a long-held view in our society that protecting human life is a central, morally obligatory task. We do not, as a rule, leave those whose lives are in danger to fend for themselves. Moreover, as will be shown in Chapter 5 on Equality and Discrimination, it is also true that extending such protection to *all* human beings, regardless of factors such as race, sex, religion, or disability has been a difficult and frequently unsuccessful struggle. The abortion debate, because of the problem of determining the point in human development at which someone acquires the status of an equal member of the community with the rights and protections that confers, evokes echoes of the age-old struggle for human rights. One reason that has been given for opposing abortion is that the welfare of many "marginal" (disabled, sick, or rejected) individuals might well be jeopardized by widespread access to and use of abortion procedures. As discussed in the previous chapter, the need to consider the rights of persons with disabilities is also a factor in debates about euthanasia.

So far, our discussion highlights what many see as the central aspect of the abortion debate: the conflict between a woman's right to choose and the right to life of the fetus. If the interests of a mother are in conflict with those of the child she is carrying, whose interest should prevail? As is reflected in some of the readings, many take the task of explicating and settling whose rights are primary and in what contexts are central to resolving the abortion debate. But there are also reasons for understanding abortion not simply as a matter of individual rights, but as a social issue that raises questions about societal responsibilities for the welfare of others.

All societies are inevitably involved in the creation of rules concerning procreation, child nurture, and child-rearing. In our society this concern takes the form of providing medical and other facilities for the care of women who are pregnant. Further, we have laws that govern the treatment of both mother and child before and after birth. Caring for children may not be the sole prerogative of the biological parents, but the law presumes this to be their responsibility unless they demonstrate otherwise. However, barring further technological developments, only women can bear children. Moreover, in our society, women continue to be responsible for most of the childrearing activities. As will be shown in the readings, some take these factors about women's roles to be relevant to a discussion of abortion. More recent concerns raised by reproductive technologies in the areas of surrogate motherhood, in vitro fertilization, frozen embryos, and so on provide additional reasons for taking questions about what constitutes a family, women's roles, and inequalities in access and financial resources to be relevant to issues of human reproduction more generally. Modern technological advances that assist reproduction provide good examples of how the current discussion of abortion has been broadened to include issues other than those of the status of the fetus and the woman's right to choose.

Background Considerations

To a considerable degree, abortion as we usually encounter it today is a phenomenon made possible by advances in modern medicine. There are, of course, records of abortions and attempted abortions going back to the beginning of recorded time. However, it is only in this century that medical science has developed to the point where an abortion, properly performed in the first twelve weeks of pregnancy, poses little risk to the life or health of the person seeking the abortion.

There is another side to the story, however. The knowledge that allows for relatively safe abortions has also provided the basis for remarkable developments in the field of fetal medicine. Sophisticated techniques exist for diagnosing genetic and other disorders; blood transfusions are possible; and fetal surgery both inside and outside the womb is now a reality.

Thus modern medicine has become a means for enhancing the quality of life of a child by intervening to correct problems prior to birth. But it has also become both a means for providing information that may well lead to a request for abortion and a means for procuring that abortion with a minimum of risk.

Current Situation

It is worth reminding ourselves that the legal status of abortion in Canada has changed quite dramatically over a few years. Since those changes stem directly from social, political, and moral debate, knowledge of them is essential to a balanced understanding of the issue.

Prior to 1969, abortion was prohibited by the Canadian Criminal Code. In 1969, the Code was amended to allow for therapeutic abortions approved by a hospital committee comprising three doctors. Hospitals were permitted but not required to perform approved abortions.

It is generally agreed that the drafters of the 1969 law were seeking a middle ground between those who were of the view that continuing a pregnancy was a private matter to be resolved by women faced with unwanted pregnancies in accordance with values of their own choosing and those who believed that abortion was a form of murder. Perhaps not surprisingly, therefore, the law was from its inception the subject of controversy. Some thought it too restrictive and unfair in its application. Others thought it too lenient because it seemed to allow abortion on demand, at least in large urban settings.

Shortly after the new law came into effect, Dr. Henry Morgentaler challenged its moral and legal validity by setting up a private abortion clinic in Montreal and performing abortions in apparent contravention of the new law. He was subsequently charged with performing an illegal abortion and found not guilty by a jury. The verdict was subsequently overturned on appeal, and a verdict of guilty put in its place. That verdict was appealed to the Supreme Court of Canada, which in 1973 confirmed it and the 1969 law.

In 1982, Canada found itself with a new constitution, an important part of which was the Charter of Rights. This was a significant new development and in the view of the law's opponents justified a new legal challenge. That challenge was once again mounted by Dr. Morgentaler who opened a private abortion clinic in Toronto and performed abortions in apparent defiance of the Criminal Code. Dr. Morgentaler was once again charged under the Criminal Code. Once again, a jury returned a verdict of not guilty. Both the trial and the verdict were very controversial for a variety of reasons. On appeal, the Ontario Supreme Court concluded that the 1969 law was consistent with the new Charter of Rights and ordered a new trial. A majority of the Supreme Court of Canada disagreed. Some of the reasons are set out in the readings that follow. The resulting judgment, represented by Supreme Court Justice Bertha Wilson in the first reading, ruled that the 1969 law was contrary to the Charter and therefore unconstitutional.

Faced with this decision, the government of Canada undertook to draft a new law. When the law was presented to Parliament, however, it failed to gain the necessary majority. Hence, for the moment at least, the criminal law is no longer an obstacle in the path of women seeking an abortion. However, the procedure remains controversial. Various public opinion polls have suggested that a majority of Canadians do not regard abortion as a purely private matter and believe that it should be controlled in some fashion by legislation. Furthermore, right to life groups have continued to lobby for laws that would protect human life from conception onward.

In practice, abortion is not uniformly available throughout the country. Some hospitals refuse to permit the procedure. Others are reluctant to give it a high priority in light of other demands on their facilities. Some provinces, Quebec for example, have facilitated access to abortion by recognizing and encouraging the creation of abortion clinics. Other provinces have been more reluctant to take this step and have resisted the creation of clinics for this purpose. All of these factors indicate that the topic continues to be actively debated in our society.

In terms of the law, our society is now faced with three options. The first is to leave things as they now are. A second option is to attempt to define in law the reasons for which abortion should be allowed, prohibiting it in all other cases. For example, Parliament might seek to prohibit abortion except in carefully defined extenuating circumstances. A third option is to determine a point in gestation after which abortion should be prohibited.

Interest in formulating law with respect to abortion, however, can be said to have been superseded by an interest in formulating law to regulate the use of new reproductive technologies. Many countries have responded to the proliferation of medical technology to assist reproduction by proposing legislation (the final reading, Bill C-13, is Canada's attempt to formulate legislation).

The Moral Dimension

The abortion issue, like a number of the issues to be examined in later chapters, raises two closely related but distinct groups of questions. First, what is the morality of abortion? Is abortion ever morally justified? If so, under what conditions? The second set of issues is concerned with whether access to abortion should be regulated by law. Should we prohibit by law abortions that the community believes are not morally justified? Much of our law reflects our moral values. Yet not everything we judge to be immoral is unlawful. For example, most of us would probably agree that, as a rule, promises should not be broken. Yet the law enforces only some promises and not others. Reasons for enforcing by law some moral values and not others will be explored in later chapters.

For the discussion of abortion, as well as for the discussion of a number of other issues raised in later chapters, it is important that these questions be distinguished. We prize our right to form our own moral assessments and to act on those assessments. Laws created to control human behaviour circumscribe individual liberty. Thus, limiting the freedom of individuals by creating laws is a moral issue in itself. Paradoxically, failing to limit freedom of choice can also limit the freedom of individuals. This is one of the reasons the creation of laws restricting individual liberty is sometimes a moral imperative. This paradox can be illustrated by the problem of abortion. The freedom to choose for oneself to have an abortion is a very significant one to many people. But the freedom accorded to adults in this area has a direct impact on the freedom of the child, as yet unborn, to grow and mature as he or she will if the pregnancy is not terminated.

An unavoidable problem in the discussion of human development concerns the point at which we become members of the human community, with all the protection its system of rules is designed to ensure. Is an unborn child a person? The question might, at first glance, seem a simple one. Unfortunately, in this case, first glances are deceptive. Human development from conception to birth is gradual; there are no sudden qualitative changes clearly signalling that the unborn child is now a member of the human community. Indeed, even birth, though traumatic, generates no significant, sharp, qualitative changes in a child. And so we are left with a clear dilemma. Do the moral and legal rules generated by the human community to offer a social environment in which human development can continue through childhood to adulthood extend to those who are not yet born? Can they be extended to those entities created in a lab for purposes of in vitro fertilization, stem cell research, or cloning? And, perhaps more importantly, should those rules be so extended?

There are other dimensions to be considered as well. As we have seen, an abortion may be requested because the parents of the unborn child have discovered that their child, if born, will be disabled in some way, and have concluded that, from the child's own point of view, it is better that it should not be born. Approaching abortion from this point of view creates serious moral tensions, similar in many respects to those raised by involuntary euthanasia. Those concerned with the morality of abortion are faced with the challenge of resolving those tensions.

The involvement of the medical profession is unavoidable and this dimension raises another set of questions. Do doctors have moral obligations to unborn children similar in nature to their obligations to other patients? If undertaking an abortion in the later stages of pregnancy, does the doctor have a moral obligation to use techniques most likely to result in a live birth? Or does the mother have a moral right to decide, when a live birth is possible, that it will or will not occur? Whose decisions about the life of the fetus should prevail in those cases in which modern technology allows doctors to use clinically "dead" mothers as incubators for fetuses that are not yet viable or in which it allows researchers to create human life in laboratories? Does medical technology in the areas of in vitro fertilization, surrogacy, and cloning affect debates on abortion? This last question emphasizes the importance of being clear and up to date about what technology allows, a point that is illustrated in the definitions provided in the last reading's excerpt of Bill C-13.

Lastly, there is a dimension that explores the idea that social and political factors are relevant to an examination of the morality of abortion. Although women's roles are changing in our society, they continue to have primary responsibility for the caring and rearing of children. Does this factor provide an additional argument for respecting women's deliberations and decisions regarding abortion? Is there a sense in which engagement in childrearing activities gives women a different or privileged way of reasoning through moral dilemmas such as abortion? If so, how does this thinking about abortion differ from questions about the status of the fetus that have framed the traditional debate on abortion? Does a consideration of social and political factors help us understand fathers' responsibilities for childcare? Is an examination of social and political factors relevant to current debates about stem cell research, cloning, surrogacy, and in vitro fertilization? This last set of questions introduces some of the issues relevant to the later chapters on discrimination and poverty.

The Readings

The first set of readings set out the legal background to current discussions of abortion in Canada: extracts from Madam Justice Bertha Wilson's judgment in the Morgentaler case supporting the majority view that the 1969 Criminal Code provisions were in conflict with sections of the Canadian Charter of Rights and Freedoms; and, extracts from Justice McIntyre's dissenting judgment arguing that the abortion law was a legitimate use of legislative power and not in conflict with the Charter.

The Supreme Court judgment written by Madam Justice Wilson rests in large measure on a distinction between private and public morality. That distinction was first made by John Stuart Mill, an eighteenth-century philosopher whose ideas have influenced modern thinking in a number of significant ways (his seminal ideas on Utilitarianism are included in the Tools and Theories chapter). It is important because it provides a criterion for determining those areas of social life with which the law has a legitimate concern and those areas that are properly regarded as private and beyond the law's reach. The idea that morality can be divided into a public and a private sphere is one of the central themes in several chapters and is subjected to critical analysis by a number of contributors to this book. It is particularly important in discussions of pornography and the issues it raises.

In the second reading, Jane English examines the issue of the status of the fetus by finding a middle position between extreme conservative and liberal views. While she rejects the view that a fetus is a person from the moment of conception, she also takes issue with the liberal view that abortion is a purely private matter regardless of the development of a fetus. By using criteria that point to psychological and social features of personhood, English argues that early in pregnancy a human fetus is not sufficiently well developed to be properly described as a person. Hence, early abortions are not morally objectionable. In the later stages of pregnancy, however, a human fetus is a person and abortion does generate legitimate moral worries.

The third reading by Jason T. Eberl provides an account of personhood different from the one provided by English, one that Eberl argues can also settle some of the issues with respect to new reproductive technologies. Eberl uses a Thomistic framework to argue that personhood begins when ensoulment begins: at the moment when implantation of the zygote in the uterus occurs. He then argues that this conception of when personhood begins has moral implications not only for abortion but also for medical procedures such as stem cell research, in vitro fertilization, and abortifacient contraceptives.

The fourth reading "Abortion Through a Feminist Ethics Lens" provides a feminist perspective on the issue of abortion, one that also has implications for debates about new reproductive technologies. Susan Sherwin distinguishes between feminist and non-feminist approaches and argues that questions about the status of the fetus cannot be settled in abstraction from women's lives. The issue of abortion cannot be properly understood unless it is placed in the context of the lives of women and the kinds of inequalities they continue to experience. In that context, she argues, the value of a human fetus can be properly determined and the justifiability of abortion defended.

In the fifth reading, Laura Shanner and Jeffrey Nisker also broaden the analysis from questions about the status of the fetus to the broader social and political issues introduced by technologies that are thought to enhance women's choices with respect to reproduction. They raise concerns about family relationships, informed choice, gender inequality, and the commercialization of reproduction. They then use this analysis as a way to guide legal and policy issues with respect to assisted reproductive technologies. The final reading, Bill C-13, is Canada's most recent attempt at legislation that delineates restrictions on the use of technologies to assist human reproduction.

DR. HENRY MORGENTALER V. HER MAJESTY THE QUEEN, 1988

[The 1988 judgement of the Supreme Court of Canada]

Madam Justice Bertha Wilson

The Right to Liberty

. . .

The *Charter* is predicated on a particular conception of the place of the individual in society. An individual is not a totally independent entity disconnected from the society in which he or she lives. Neither, however, is the individual a mere cog in an impersonal machine in which his or her values, goals and aspirations are subordinated to those of the collectivity. The individual is a bit of both. The *Charter* reflects this reality by leaving a wide range of activities and decisions open to legitimate government control while at the same time placing limits on the proper scope of that control. Thus, the rights guaranteed in the *Charter* erect around each individual, metaphorically speaking, an invisible fence over which the state will not be allowed to trespass. The role of the courts is to map out, piece by piece, the parameters of the fence.

The *Charter* and the right to individual liberty guaranteed under it are inextricably tied to the concept of human dignity. Professor Neil MacCormick,* *Legal Right and Social Democracy: Essays in Legal and Political Philosophy*, speaks of liberty as "a condition of human self-respect and of that contentment which resides in the ability to pursue one's own conception of a full and rewarding life" (p. 39). He says at p. 41:

> To be able to decide what to do and how to do it, to carry out one's own decisions and accept their consequences, seems to me essential to one's self-respect as a human being, and essential to the possibility of that contentment. Such self-respect and contentment are in my judgment fundamental goods for human beings, the worth of life itself being on condition of having or striving for them. If a person were deliberately denied the opportunity of self-respect and that contentment, he would suffer deprivation of his essential humanity.

Dickson C.J. in *R. v. Big M Drug Mart Ltd.* makes the same point at p. 346:

> It should also be noted, however, that an emphasis on individual conscience and individual judgment also lies at the heart of our democratic political tradition. The ability of each citizen to make free and informed decisions is the absolute prerequisite for the legitimacy, acceptability, and efficacy of our system of self-government. It is because of the centrality of the rights associated with freedom of individual conscience both to basic beliefs about human worth and dignity and to a free and democratic political system that American jurisprudence has emphasized the primary or "firstness" of the First Amendment. It is this same centrality that in my view underlies their designation in the *Canadian Charter of Rights and Freedoms* as "fundamental." They are the *sine qua non* of the political tradition underlying the *Charter*.

Excerpts from the 1988 judgement of the Supreme Court of Canada. Reproduced by permission of Supply and Services Canada, 1996.

* *Regius Professor of Public Law and the Law of Nature and Nations, University of Edinburgh.*

It was further amplified in Dickson C.J.'s discussion of *Charter* interpretation in *R. v. Oakes*, [1986] 1 S.C.R. 103, at p. 136:

> A second contextual element of interpretation of s. 1 is provided by the words "free and democratic society." Inclusion of these words as the final standard of justification for limits on rights and freedoms refers the Court to the very purpose for which the *Charter* was originally entrenched in the Constitution: Canadian society is to be free and democratic. The Court must be guided by the values and principles essential to a free and democratic society which I believe embody, to name but a few, respect for the inherent dignity of the human person, commitment to social justice and equality, accommodation of a wide variety of beliefs, respect for cultural and group identity, and faith in social and political institutions which enhance the participation of individuals and groups in society. The underlying values and principles of a free and democratic society are the genesis of the rights and freedoms guaranteed by the *Charter* and the ultimate standard against which a limit on a right or freedom must be shown, despite its effect, to be reasonable and demonstrably justified.

The idea of human dignity finds expression in almost every right and freedom guaranteed in the *Charter*. Individuals are afforded the right to choose their own religion and their own philosophy of life, the right to choose with whom they will associate and how they will express themselves, the right to choose where they will live and what occupation they will pursue. These are all examples of the basic theory underlying the *Charter*, namely that the state will respect choices made by individuals and, to the greatest extent possible, will avoid subordinating these choices to any one conception of the good life.

Thus, an aspect of the respect for human dignity on which the *Charter* is founded is the right to make fundamental personal decisions without interference from the state. This right is a critical component of the right to liberty. Liberty, as was noted in *Singh*, is a phrase capable of a broad range of meaning. In my view, this right, properly construed, grants the individual a degree of autonomy in making decisions of fundamental personal importance. . . .

The question then becomes whether the decision of a woman to terminate her pregnancy falls within this class of protected decisions. I have no doubt that it does. This decision is one that will have profound psychological, economic and social consequences for the pregnant woman. The circumstances giving rise to it can be complex and varied and there may be, and usually are, powerful considerations militating in opposite directions. It is a decision that deeply reflects the way the woman thinks about herself and her relationship to others and to society at large. It is not just a medical decision; it is a profound social and ethical one, as well. Her response to it will be the response of the whole person.

It is probably impossible for a man to respond, even imaginatively, to such a dilemma not just because it is outside the realm of his personal experience (although this is, of course, the case) but because he can relate to it only by objectifying it, thereby eliminating the subjective elements of the female psyche which are at the heart of the dilemma. As Noreen Burrows* has pointed out in her essay on "International Law and Human Rights: the Case of Women's Rights," in *Human Rights: From Rhetoric to Reality*, the history of the struggle for human rights from the eighteenth century on has been the history of men struggling to assert their dignity and common humanity against an overbearing state apparatus. The more recent struggle for women's rights has been a struggle to eliminate discrimination, to achieve

---

* *Lecturer in European Law, University of Glasgow.*

a place for women in a man's world, to develop a set of legislative reforms in order to place women in the same position as men (pp. 81–82). It has not been a struggle to define the rights of women in relation to their special place in the societal structure and in relation to the biological distinction between the two sexes. Thus, women's needs and aspirations are only now being translated into protected rights. The right to reproduce or not to reproduce, which is an issue in this case, is one such right and is properly perceived as an integral part of modern woman's struggle to assert *her* dignity and worth as a human being.

Given then that the right to liberty guaranteed by s. 7 of the *Charter* gives a woman the right to decide for herself whether or not to terminate her pregnancy, does s. 251 of the *Criminal Code* violate this right? Clearly it does. The purpose of the section is to take the decision away from the woman and give it to a committee. Furthermore, as the Chief Justice correctly points out, the committee bases its decision on "criteria entirely unrelated to [the pregnant woman's] priorities and aspirations." The fact that the decision whether a woman will be allowed to terminate her pregnancy is in the hands of a committee is just as great a violation of the woman's right to personal autonomy in decisions of an intimate and private nature as it would be if a committee were established to decide whether a woman should be allowed to continue her pregnancy. Both these arrangements violate the woman's right to liberty by deciding for her something that she has the right to decide for herself. . . .

Re: Section 2(a)

In my view, the deprivation of the s. 7 right with which we are concerned in this case offends s. 2(a) of the *Charter*. I say this because I believe that the decision whether or not to terminate a pregnancy is essentially a moral decision, a matter of conscience. I do not think there is or can be any dispute about that. The question is: Whose conscience? Is the conscience of the woman to be paramount or the conscience of the state? I believe, for the reasons I gave in discussing the right to liberty, that in a free and democratic society it must be the conscience of the individual. Indeed, s. 2(a) makes it clear that this freedom belongs to "everyone," *i.e.*, to each of us individually. . . .

In *R. v. Big M Drug Mart Ltd., supra*, Dickson C.J. made some very insightful comments about the nature of the right enshrined in s. 2(a) of the *Charter* at pp. 345–47:

> Beginning, however, with the Independent faction within the Parliamentary party during the Commonwealth or Interregnum, many, even among those who shared the basic beliefs of the ascendant religion, came to voice opposition to the use of the State's coercive power to secure obedience to religious precepts and to extirpate nonconforming beliefs. The basis of this opposition was no longer simply a conviction that the State was enforcing the wrong set of beliefs and practices but rather the perception that belief itself was not amenable to compulsion. Attempts to compel belief or practice denied the reality of individual conscience and dishonoured the God that had planted it in His creatures. It is from these antecedents that the concepts of freedom of religion and freedom of conscience became associated, to form, as they do in s. 2(a) of our *Charter*, the single integrated concept of "freedom of conscience and religion."
>
> What unites enunciated freedoms in the American First Amendment, in s. 2(a) of the *Charter* and in the provisions of other human rights documents in which they are associated, *is the notion of the centrality of individual conscience and the inappropriateness of governmental intervention to compel or to constrain its manifestation.* [my emphasis] In *Hunter v. Southam Inc., supra*, the purpose of the *Charter* was identified,

at p. 155, as "the unremitting protection of individual rights and liberties." It is easy to see the relationship between respect for individual conscience and the valuation of human dignity that motivates such unremitting protection.

It should also be noted, however, that an emphasis on individual conscience and individual judgment also lies at the heart of our democratic political tradition. The ability of each citizen to make free and informed decisions is the absolute prerequisite for the legitimacy, acceptability, and efficacy of our system of self-government. [my emphasis] It is because of the centrality of the rights associated with freedom of individual conscience both to basic beliefs about human worth and dignity and to a free and democratic political system that American jurisprudence has emphasized the primacy or "firstness" of the First Amendment. It is this same centrality that in my view underlies their designation in the Canadian Charter of Rights and Freedoms as "fundamental." They are the sine qua non of the political tradition underlying the Charter.

Viewed in this context, the purpose of freedom of conscience and religion becomes clear. *The values that underlie our political and philosophic traditions demand that every individual be free to hold and to manifest whatever beliefs and opinions his or her conscience dictates, provided inter alia only that such manifestations do not injure his or her neighbours or their parallel rights to hold and manifest beliefs and opinions of their own.* [my emphasis] Religious belief and practice are historically prototypical and, in many ways, paradigmatic of conscientiously held beliefs and manifestations and are therefore protected by the *Charter*. Equally protected, and for the same reasons, are expressions and manifestations of religious non-belief and refusals to participate in religious practice. It may perhaps be that freedom of conscience and religion extends beyond these principles to prohibit other sorts of governmental involvement in matters having to do with religion. For the present case it is sufficient in my opinion to say that whatever else freedom of conscience and religion may mean, it must at the very least mean this: government may not coerce individuals to affirm a specific religious belief or to manifest a specific religious practice for a sectarian purpose. I leave to another case the degree, if any, to which the government may, to achieve a vital interest or objective, engage in coercive action which s. 2(*a*) might otherwise prohibit.

The Chief Justice sees religious belief and practice as the paradigmatic example of conscientiously held beliefs and manifestations and as such protected by the *Charter*. But I do not think he is saying that a personal morality which is not founded in religion is outside the protection of s. 2(*a*). Certainly, it would be my view that conscientious beliefs which are not religiously motivated are equally protected by freedom of conscience in s. 2(*a*). In so saying I am not unmindful of the fact that the *Charter* opens with an affirmation that "Canada is founded upon principles that recognize the supremacy of God. . . ." But I am also mindful that the values entrenched in the *Charter* are those which characterize a free and democratic society.

As is pointed out by Professor C.E.M. Joad*: *Guide to the Philosophy of Morals and Politics*, the role of the state in a democracy is to establish the background conditions under which individual citizens may pursue the ethical values which in their view underlie the good life. He states at p. 801:

For the welfare of the state is nothing apart from the good of the citizens who compose it. It is no doubt true that a State whose citizens are compelled to go right is more

---

* *Then Head of Department of Philosophy and Psychology, Birkbeck College, University of London.*

efficient than one whose citizens are free to go wrong. But what then? To sacrifice free-dom in the interests of efficiency is to sacrifice what confers upon human beings their humanity. It is no doubt easy to govern a flock of sheep; but there is no credit in the governing, and, if the sheep were born as men, no virtue in the sheep.

Professor Joad further emphasizes at p. 803 that individuals in a democratic society can never be treated "merely as means to ends beyond themselves" because:

> To the right of the individual to be treated as an end, which entails his right to the full development and expression of his personality, all other rights and claims must, the democrat holds, be subordinated. I do not know how this principle is to be defended any more than I can frame a defence for the principles of democracy and liberty.

Professor Joad stresses that the essence of a democracy is its recognition of the fact that the state is made for man and not man for the state (p. 805). He firmly rejects the notion that science provides a basis for subordinating the individual to the state. He says at pp. 805–6:

> Human beings, it is said, are important only in so far as they fit into a biological scheme or assist in the furtherance of the evolutionary process. Thus each generation of women must accept as its sole function the production of children who will consti-tute the next generation who, in their turn, will devote their lives and sacrifice their inclinations to the task of producing a further generation, and so on ad infinitum. This is the doctrine of eternal sacrifice — "jam yesterday, jam tomorrow, but never jam today." For, it may be asked, to what end should generations be produced, unless the individuals who compose them are valued in and for themselves, are, in fact, ends in themselves? There is no escape from the doctrine of the perpetual recurrence of gen-erations who have value only in so far as they produce more generations, the perpetu-al subordination of citizens who have value only in so far as they promote the interests of the State to which they are subordinated, except in the individualist doctrine, which is also the Christian doctrine, that the individual is an end in himself.

It seems to me, therefore, that in a free and democratic society "freedom of conscience and religion" should be broadly construed to extend to conscientiously held beliefs, whether grounded in religion or in a secular morality. Indeed, as a matter of statutory interpretation, "conscience" and "religion" should not be treated as tautologous if capable of independent, although related, meaning. Accordingly, for the state to take sides on the issue of abortion, as it does in the impugned legislation by making it a criminal offence for the pregnant woman to exercise one of her options, is not only to endorse but also to enforce, on pain of a further loss of liberty through actual imprisonment, one conscientiously held view at the expense of another. It is to deny freedom of conscience to some, to treat them as means to an end, to deprive them, as Professor MacCormick puts it, of their "essential humanity." Can this comport with fundamental justice? Was Blackmun J. not correct when he said in *Thornburgh, supra*, at p. 2185:

> A woman's right to make that choice freely is fundamental. Any other result . . . would protect inadequately a central part of the sphere of liberty that our law guarantees equally to all.

Legislation which violates freedom of conscience in this manner cannot, in my view, be in accordance with the principles of fundamental justice within the meaning of s. 7. . . .

Re: Section 1

In my view, the primary objective of the impugned legislation must be seen as the protection of the foetus. It undoubtedly has other ancillary objectives, such as the protection of the life and health of pregnant women, but I believe that the main objective advanced to justify a restriction on the pregnant woman's s. 7 right is the protection of the foetus. I think this is a perfectly valid legislative objective.

Miss Wein submitted on behalf of the Crown that the Court of Appeal was correct in concluding that "the situation respecting a woman's right to control her own person becomes more complex when she becomes pregnant, and that some statutory control may be appropriate." I agree. I think s. 1 of the *Charter* authorizes reasonable limits to be put upon the woman's right having regard to the fact of the developing foetus within her body. The question is: At what point in the pregnancy does the protection of the foetus become such a pressing and substantial concern as to outweigh the fundamental right of the woman to decide whether or not to carry the foetus to term? At what point does the state's interest in the protection of the foetus become "compelling" and justify state intervention in what is otherwise a matter of purely personal and private concern?

In *Roe v. Wade, supra,* the United States Supreme Court held that the state's interest became compelling when the foetus became viable, *i.e.,* when it could exist outside the body of the mother. As Miss Wein pointed out, no particular justification was advanced by the Court for this selection of viability as the relevant criterion. The Court expressly avoided the question as to when human life begins. Blackmun J. stated at p. 159:

> We need not resolve the difficult question of when life begins. When those in the respective disciplines of medicine, philosophy, and theology are unable to arrive at any consensus, the judiciary, at this point in the development of man's knowledge, is not in a position to speculate as to the answer.

He referred, therefore, to the developing foetus as "potential life" and to the state's interest as "the protection of potential life."

Miss Wein submitted that it was likewise not necessary for the Court in this case to decide when human life begins although she acknowledged that the value to be placed on "potential life" was significant in assessing the importance of the legislative objective sought to be achieved by s. 251. It would be my view, and I think it is consistent with the position taken by the United States Supreme Court in *Roe v. Wade*, that the value to be placed on the foetus as potential life is directly related to the stage of its development during gestation. The undeveloped foetus starts out as a newly fertilized ovum; the fully developed foetus emerges ultimately as an infant. A developmental progression takes place in between these two extremes and, in my opinion, this progression has a direct bearing on the value of the foetus as potential life. It is a fact of human experience that a miscarriage or spontaneous abortion of the foetus at six months is attended by far greater sorrow and sense of loss than a miscarriage or spontaneous abortion at six days or even six weeks. This is not, of course, to deny that the foetus is potential life from the moment of conception. Indeed, I agree with the observation of O'Connor J. dissenting in *City of Akron v. Akron Center for Reproductive*

Health, Inc., supra, at p. 461 (referred to by my colleague Beetz J. in his reasons) that the foetus is potential life from the moment of conception. It is simply to say that in balancing the state's interest in the protection of the foetus as potential life under s. 1 of the *Charter* against the right of the pregnant woman under s. 7 greater weight should be given to the state's interest in the later stages of pregnancy than in the earlier. The foetus should accordingly, for purposes of s. 1, be viewed in differential and developmental terms: see Sumner*: *Abortion and Moral Theory*, pp. 125–28.

As Professor Sumner points out, both traditional approaches to abortion, the so-called "liberal" and "conservative" approaches, fail to take account of the essentially developmental nature of the gestation process. A developmental view of the foetus, on the other hand, supports a permissive approach to abortion in the early stages of pregnancy and a restrictive approach in the later stages. In the early stages the woman's autonomy would be absolute; her decision, reached in consultation with her physician, not to carry the foetus to term would be conclusive. The state would have no business inquiring into her reasons. Her reasons for having an abortion would, however, be the proper subject of inquiry at the later stages of her pregnancy when the state's compelling interest in the protection of the foetus would justify it in prescribing conditions. The precise point in the development of the foetus at which the state's interest in its protection becomes "compelling" I leave to the informed judgment of the legislature, which is in a position to receive guidance on the subject from all the relevant disciplines. It seems to me, however, that it might fall somewhere in the second trimester. Indeed, according to Professor Sumner (p. 159), a differential abortion policy with a time limit in the second trimester is already in operation in the United States, Great Britain, France, Italy, Sweden, the Soviet Union, China, India, Japan and most of the countries of Eastern Europe although the time limits vary in these countries from the beginning to the end of the second trimester (*cf.* Isaacs, Stephen L., "Reproductive Rights 1983: An International Survey" [1982–83], 14 *Columbia Human Rights Law Review* 311, with respect to France and Italy).

Section 251 of the *Criminal Code* takes the decision away from the woman at *all* stages of her pregnancy. It is a complete denial of the woman's constitutionally protected right under s. 7, not merely a limitation on it. . . . It cannot be saved under section 1 (of the *Charter*).

Mr. Justice Wm. R. McIntyre

The Right to Abortion and s. 7 of the Charter

The judgment of my colleague, Wilson J., is based upon the proposition that a pregnant woman has a right, under s. 7 of the *Charter*, to have an abortion. The same concept underlies the judgment of the Chief Justice. He reached the conclusion that a law which forces a woman to carry a foetus to term, unless certain criteria are met which are unrelated to her own priorities and aspirations, impairs the security of her person. That, in his view, is the effect of s. 251 of the *Criminal Code*. He has not said in specific terms that the pregnant woman has the right to an abortion, whether therapeutic or otherwise. In my view, however, his whole position depends for its validity upon that proposition, and that interference with the right constitutes an infringement of her right to security of the person. It is said that a law which forces a woman to carry a foetus to term unless she meets certain criteria unrelated to her own priorities and aspirations interferes with security of her person. If compelling a

---

* *Professor of Philosophy, University of Toronto.*

woman to complete her pregnancy interferes with security of her person, it can only be because the concept of security of her person includes a right not to be compelled to carry the child to completion of her pregnancy. This, then, is simply to say that she has a right to have an abortion. It follows, then, that if no such right can be shown, it cannot be said that security of her person has been infringed by state action or otherwise. . . .

It cannot be said that the history, traditions and underlying philosophies of our society would support the proposition that a right to abortion could be implied in the *Charter*. The history of the legal approach to this question, reflective of public policy, was conveniently canvassed in the Ontario Court of Appeal in this case in these terms, at pp. 364–66:

> *History of the Law of Abortion*
> The history of the law of abortion is of some importance. At common law procuring an abortion before quickening was not a criminal offence. Quickening occurred when the pregnant woman could feel the foetus move in her womb. It was a misdemeanour to procure an abortion after quickening: *Blackstone's Commentaries on the Laws of England*, Book 1, pp. 129–30. The law of criminal abortion was first codified in England in *Lord Ellenborough's Act* 1803 (U.K.), c. 58. That Act made procuring an abortion of a quick foetus a capital offence and provided lesser penalties for abortion before quickening. After the *Offences Against the Person Act*, 1861 (U.K.), c. 100, s. 58, no differentiation in penalty was made in England on the basis of the stage of foetal development. The offence was a felony and the maximum penalty life imprisonment. The *Infant Life (Preservation) Act*, 1929 (U.K.), c. 34, gave greater protection to a viable foetus by creating the offence of child destruction where a child capable of being born alive was caused to die except in good faith to preserve the life of the mother. In *R. v. Bourne*, [1939] 1 K.B. 687, the prohibition against abortion both at common law and by statute was held to be subject to the common law defence based upon the necessity of saving the mother's life.
>
> The earliest statutory prohibition in Canada against attempting to procure an abortion is to be found in "An Act respecting Offences against the Person," 1869 (Can.), c. 20, ss. 59 and 60. The Act was based on *Lord Ellenborough's Act* and the *Offences Against the Person Act*, 1861. The provisions relating to abortion were included in the Canadian *Criminal Code* in 1892 (1892 [Can.], c. 29, ss. 272 to 274), and with slight changes were included in the Codes of 1906 (R.S.C. 1906, c. 146, ss. 303 to 306); 1927 (R.S.C. 1927, c. 36, ss. 303 to 306) and 1954 (1953–54 (Can.), c. 51, ss. 237 and 238).
>
> Section 251(1) made it clear that Parliament regarded procuring an abortion as a very serious crime for which there was a maximum sentence of imprisonment for life.
>
> In 1969, Parliament alleviated the situation by the addition to s. 251 of ss. (4), (5), (6) and (7) as exculpatory provisions by 1968–69, c. 38, s. 18. These subsections provided that it was not a criminal act to procure an abortion where the continuation of the pregnancy would or would be likely to endanger the life or health of a female person.
>
> . . . By defining criminal conduct more narrowly, these amendments reflected the contemporary view that abortion is not always socially undesirable behaviour.

As the Court of Appeal said, the amendments to the *Criminal Code* which imported s. 251 are indicative of a changing view on this question, but it is not possible to erect upon the words of s. 251 a constitutional right to abortion.

. . . I would conclude that, save for the provisions of the *Criminal Code*, which permit abortion where the life or health of the woman is at risk, no right of abortion can be found in Canadian law, custom or tradition, and that the *Charter*, including s. 7, creates no further right. Accordingly, it is my view that s. 251 of the *Code* does not in its terms violate s. 7 of the *Charter*.

ABORTION AND THE CONCEPT OF A PERSON*

Jane English

Introduction

The abortion debate rages on. Yet the two most popular positions seem to be clearly mistaken. Conservatives maintain that a human life begins at conception and that therefore abortion must be wrong because it is murder. But not all killings of humans are murders. Most notably, self defense may justify even the killing of an innocent person.

Liberals, on the other hand, are just as mistaken in their argument that since a fetus does not become a person until birth, a woman may do whatever she pleases in and to her own body. First, you cannot do as you please with your own body if it affects other people adversely.[1] Second, if a fetus is not a person, that does not imply that you can do to it anything you wish. Animals, for example, are not persons, yet to kill or torture them for no reason at all is wrong.

At the center of the storm has been the issue of just when it is between ovulation and adulthood that a person appears on the scene. Conservatives draw the line at conception, liberals at birth. In this paper I first examine our concept of a person and conclude that no single criterion can capture the concept of a person and no sharp line can be drawn. Next I argue that if a fetus is a person, abortion is still justifiable in many cases; and if a fetus is not a person, killing it is still wrong in many cases. To a large extent, these two solutions are in agreement. I conclude that our concept of a person cannot and need not bear the weight that the abortion controversy has thrust upon it.

I

The several factions in the abortion argument have drawn battle lines around various proposed criteria for determining what is and what is not a person. For example, Mary Anne Warren[2] lists five features (capacities for reasoning, self-awareness, complex communication, etc.) as her criteria for personhood and argues for the permissibility of abortion because a fetus falls outside this concept. Baruch Brody[3] uses brain waves. Michael Tooley[4] picks having-a-concept-of-self as his criterion and concludes that infanticide and abortion are justifiable, while the killing of adult animals is not. On the other side, Paul Ramsey[5] claims a certain gene structure is the defining characteristic. John Noonan[6] prefers conceived-of-humans and presents counterexamples to various other candidate criteria. For instance, he argues against viability

From Canadian Journal of Philosophy, vol. 5, no. 2 (October 1975), pp. 233–43. Reprinted by permission of the Canadian Journal of Philosophy, the Jane English Memorial Trust Fund and the University of Calgary Press.

* I am deeply indebted to Larry Crocker and Arthur Kuflik for their constructive comments.

as the criterion because the newborn and infirm would then be non-persons, since they cannot live without the aid of others. He rejects any criterion that calls upon the sorts of sentiments a being can evoke in adults on the grounds that this would allow us to exclude other races as non-persons if we could just view them sufficiently unsentimentally.

These approaches are typical: foes of abortion propose sufficient conditions for personhood which fetuses satisfy, while friends of abortion counter with necessary conditions for personhood which fetuses lack. But these both presuppose that the concept of a person can be captured in a strait jacket of necessary and/or sufficient conditions.[7] Rather, "person" is a cluster of features, of which rationality, having a self-concept and being conceived of humans are only part.

What is typical of persons? Within our concept of a person we include, first, certain biological factors: descended from humans, having a certain genetic make-up, having a head, hands, arms, eyes, capable of locomotion, breathing, eating, sleeping. There are psychological factors: sentience, perception, having a concept of self and of one's own interests and desires, the ability to use tools, the ability to use language or symbol systems, the ability to joke, to be angry, to doubt. There are rationality factors: the ability to reason and draw conclusions, the ability to generalize and to learn from past experience, the ability to sacrifice present interests for greater gains in the future. There are social factors: the ability to work in groups and respond to peer pressures, the ability to recognize and consider as valuable the interests of others, seeing oneself as one among "other minds," the ability to sympathize, encourage, love, the ability to evoke from others the responses of sympathy, encouragement, love, the ability to work with others for mutual advantage. Then there are legal factors: being subject to the law and protected by it, having the ability to sue and enter contracts, being counted in the census, having a name and citizenship, the ability to own property, inherit, and so forth.

Now the point is not that this list is incomplete, or that you can find counterinstances to each of its points. People typically exhibit rationality, for instance, but someone who was irrational would not thereby fail to qualify as a person. On the other hand, something could exhibit the majority of these features and still fail to be a person, as an advanced robot might. There is no single core of necessary and sufficient features which we can draw upon with the assurance that they constitute what really makes a person; there are only features that are more or less typical.

This is not to say that no necessary or sufficient conditions can be given. Being alive is a necessary condition for being a person, and being a U.S. Senator is sufficient. But rather than falling inside a sufficient condition or outside a necessary one, a fetus lies in the penumbra region where our concept of a person is not so simple. For this reason I think a conclusive answer to the question whether a fetus is a person is unattainable.

Here we might note a family of simple fallacies that proceed by stating a necessary condition of personhood and showing that a fetus has that characteristic. This is a form of the fallacy of affirming the consequent. For example, some have mistakenly reasoned from the premise that a fetus is human (after all, it is a human fetus rather than, say, a canine fetus), to the conclusion that it is a human. Adding an equivocation on "being," we get the fallacious argument that since a fetus is something both living and human, it is a human being.

Nonetheless, it does seem clear that a fetus has very few of the above family of characteristics, whereas a newborn baby exhibits a much larger proportion of them — and a two-year-old has even more. Note that one traditional anti-abortion argument has centered on pointing out the many ways in which a fetus resembles a baby. They emphasize its development ("It already has ten fingers . . .") without mentioning its dissimilarities to adults (it still has gills and a tail). They also try to evoke the sort of sympathy on our part that we only feel toward other persons ("Never to laugh . . . or feel the sunshine?"). This all seems to be a relevant way to argue, since its purpose is to persuade us that a fetus satisfies so many of the important features on the list that it ought to be treated as a person. Also note that a fetus near the time of birth satisfies many more of these factors than a fetus in the early months of development. This could provide reason for making distinctions among the different stages of pregnancy, as the U.S. Supreme Court has done.[8]

Historically, the time at which a person has been said to come into existence has varied widely. Muslims date personhood from fourteen days after conception. Some medievals followed Aristotle in placing ensoulment at forty days after conception for a male fetus and eighty days for a female fetus.[9] In European common law since the seventeenth century, abortion was considered the killing of a person only after quickening, the time when a pregnant woman first feels the fetus move on its own. Nor is this variety of opinions surprising. Biologically, a human being develops gradually. We shouldn't expect there to be any specific time or sharp dividing point when a person appears on the scene.

For these reasons I believe our concept of a person is not sharp or decisive enough to bear the weight of a solution to the abortion controversy. To use it to solve the problem is to clarify *obscurum per obscurius*.

II

Next let us consider what follows if a fetus is a person after all. Judith Jarvis Thomson's landmark article, "A Defense of Abortion,"[10] correctly points out that some additional argumentation is needed at this point in the conservative argument to bridge the gap between the premise that a fetus is an innocent person and the conclusion that killing it is always wrong. To arrive at this conclusion, we would need the additional premise that killing an innocent person is always wrong. But killing an innocent person is sometimes permissible, most notably in self defense. Some examples may help draw out our intuitions or ordinary judgments about self defense.

Suppose a mad scientist, for instance, hypnotized innocent people to jump out of the bushes and attack innocent passers-by with knives. If you are so attacked, we agree you have a right to kill the attacker in self defense, if killing him is the only way to protect your life or to save yourself from serious injury. It does not seem to matter here that the attacker is not malicious but himself an innocent pawn, for your killing of him is not done in a spirit of retribution but only in self defense.

How severe an injury may you inflict in self defense? In part this depends upon the severity of the injury to be avoided: you may not shoot someone merely to avoid having your clothes torn. This might lead one to the mistaken conclusion that the defense may only equal the threatened injury in severity; that to avoid death you may kill, but to avoid a black eye you may only inflict a black eye or the equivalent. Rather, our laws and customs seem to say that you may create an injury somewhat, but not enormously, greater than the injury to be avoided. To fend off an attack whose outcome would be as serious as rape, a severe beating or the loss of a finger, you may shoot; to avoid having your clothes torn, you may blacken an eye.

Aside from this, the injury you may inflict should only be the minimum necessary to deter or incapacitate the attacker. Even if you know he intends to kill you, you are not justified in shooting him if you could equally well save yourself by the simple expedient of running away. Self defense is for the purpose of avoiding harms rather than equalizing harms.

Some cases of pregnancy present a parallel situation. Though the fetus is itself innocent, it may pose a threat to the pregnant woman's well-being, life prospects or health, mental or physical. If the pregnancy presents a slight threat to her interests, it seems self defense cannot justify abortion. But if the threat is on a par with a serious beating or the loss of a finger, she may kill the fetus that poses such a threat, even if it is an innocent person. If a lesser harm to the fetus could have the same defensive effect, killing it would not be justified. It is unfortunate that the only way to free the woman from the pregnancy entails the death of the fetus (except in very late stages of pregnancy). Thus a self defense model supports Thomson's point that the woman has a right only to be freed from the fetus, not a right to demand its death.[11]

The self defense model is most helpful when we take the pregnant women's point of view. In the pre-Thomson literature, abortion is often framed as a question for a third party: do you, a doctor, have a right to choose between the life of the woman and that of the fetus? Some have claimed that if you were a passer-by who witnessed a struggle between the innocent hypnotized attacker and his equally innocent victim, you would have no reason to kill either in defense of the other. They have concluded that the self defense model implies that a woman may attempt to abort herself, but that a doctor should not assist her. I think the position of the third party is somewhat more complex. We do feel some inclination to intervene on behalf of the victim rather than the attacker, other things equal. But if both parties are innocent, other factors come into consideration. You would rush to the aid of your husband whether he was attacker or attackee. If a hypnotized famous violinist were attacking a skid row bum, we would try to save the individual who is of more value to society. These considerations would tend to support abortion in some cases.

But suppose you are a frail senior citizen who wishes to avoid being knifed by one of these innocent hypnotics, so you have hired a bodyguard to accompany you. If you are attacked, it is clear we believe that the bodyguard, acting as your agent, has a right to kill the attacker to save you from a serious beating. Your rights of self defense are transferred to your agent. I suggest that we should similarly view the doctor as the pregnant woman's agent in carrying out a defense she is physically incapable of accomplishing herself.

Thanks to modern technology, the cases are rare in which a pregnancy poses as clear a threat to a woman's bodily health as an attacker brandishing a switchblade. How does self defense fare when more subtle, complex and long-range harms are involved?

To consider a somewhat fanciful example, suppose you are a highly trained surgeon when you are kidnapped by the hypnotic attacker. He says he does not intend to harm you but to take you back to the mad scientist who, it turns out, plans to hypnotize you to have a permanent mental block against all your knowledge of medicine. This would automatically destroy your career which would in turn have a serious adverse impact on your family, your personal relationships and your happiness. It seems to me that if the only way you can avoid this outcome is to shoot the innocent attacker, you are justified in so doing. You are defending yourself from a drastic injury to your life prospects. I think it is no exaggeration to claim that unwanted pregnancies (most obviously among teenagers) often have such adverse lifelong consequences as the surgeon's loss of livelihood.

Several parallels arise between various views on abortion and the self defense model. Let's suppose further that these hypnotized attackers only operate at night, so that it is well known that they can be avoided completely by the considerable inconvenience of never leaving your house after dark. One view is that since you could stay home at night, therefore if you go out and are selected by one of these hypnotized people, you have no right to defend yourself. This parallels the view that abstinence is the only acceptable way to avoid pregnancy. Others might hold that you ought to take along some defense such as Mace which will deter the hypnotized person without killing him, but that if this defense fails, you are obliged to submit to the resulting injury, no matter how severe it is. This parallels the view that contraception is all right but abortion is always wrong, even in cases of contraceptive failure.

A third view is that you may kill the hypnotized person only if he will actually kill you, but not if he will only injure you. This is like the position that abortion is permissible only if it is required to save a woman's life. Finally we have the view that it is all right to kill the attacker, even if only to avoid a very slight inconvenience to yourself and even if you knowingly walked down the very street where all these incidents have been taking place without taking along any Mace or protective escort. If we assume that a fetus is a person, this is the analogue of the view that abortion is always justifiable, "on demand."

The self defense model allows us to see an important difference that exists between abortion and infanticide, even if a fetus is a person from conception. Many have argued that the only way to justify abortion without justifying infanticide would be to find some characteristic of personhood that is acquired at birth. Michael Tooley, for one, claims infanticide is justifiable because the really significant characteristics of person are acquired some time after birth. But all such approaches look to characteristics of the developing human and ignore the relation between the fetus and the woman. What if, after birth, the presence of an infant or the need to support it posed a grave threat to the woman's sanity or life prospects? She could escape this threat by the simple expedient of running away. So a solution that does not entail the death of the infant is available. Before birth, such solutions are not available because of the biological dependence of the fetus on the woman. Birth is the crucial point not because of any characteristics the fetus gains, but because after birth the woman can defend herself by a means less drastic than killing the infant. Hence self defense can be used to justify abortion without necessarily thereby justifying infanticide.

III

On the other hand, supposing a fetus is not after all a person, would abortion always be morally permissible? Some opponents of abortion seem worried that if a fetus is not a full-fledged person, then we are justified in treating it in any way at all. However, this does not follow. Non-persons do get some consideration in our moral code, though of course they do not have the same rights as persons have (and in general they do not have moral responsibilities), and though their interests may be overridden by the interests of persons. Still, we cannot just treat them in any way at all.

Treatment of animals is a case in point. It is wrong to torture dogs for fun or to kill wild birds for no reason at all. It is wrong Period, even though dogs and birds do not have the same rights persons do. However, few people think it is wrong to use dogs as experimental animals, causing them considerable suffering in some cases, provided that the resulting research will probably bring discoveries of great benefit to people. And most of us think it all right to kill birds for food or to protect our crops. People's rights are different from the consideration we give to animals, then, for it is wrong to experiment on people, even if others might later benefit a great deal as a result of their suffering. You might volunteer to be a subject, but this would be supererogatory; you certainly have a right to refuse to be a medical guinea pig.

But how do we decide what you may or may not do to non-persons? This is a difficult problem, one for which I believe no adequate account exists. You do not want to say, for instance, that torturing dogs is all right whenever the sum of its effects on people is good —

when it doesn't warp the sensibilities of the torturer so much that he mistreats people. If that were the case, it would be all right to torture dogs if you did it in private, or if the torturer lived on a desert island or died soon afterward, so that his actions had no effect on people. This is an inadequate account, because whatever moral consideration animals get, it has to be indefeasible, too. It will have to be a general proscription of certain actions, not merely a weighing of the impact on people on a case-by-case basis.

Rather, we need to distinguish two levels on which consequences of actions can be taken into account in moral reasoning. The traditional objections to Utilitarianism focus on the fact that it operates solely on the first level, taking all the consequences into account in particular cases only. Thus Utilitarianism is open to "desert island" and "lifeboat" counterexamples because these cases are rigged to make the consequences of actions severely limited.

Rawls' theory could be described as a teleological sort of theory, but with teleology operating on a higher level.[12] In choosing the principles to regulate society from the original position, his hypothetical choosers make their decision on the basis of the total consequences of various systems. Furthermore, they are constrained to choose a general set of rules which people can readily learn and apply. An ethical theory must operate by generating a set of sympathies and attitudes toward others which reinforces the functioning of that set of moral principles. Our prohibition against killing people operates by means of certain moral sentiments including sympathy, compassion and guilt. But if these attitudes are to form a coherent set, they carry us further: we tend to perform supererogatory actions, and we tend to feel similar compassion toward person-like non-persons.

It is crucial that psychological facts play a role here. Our psychological constitution makes it the case that for our ethical theory to work, it must prohibit certain treatment of non-persons which are significantly person-like. If our moral rules allowed people to treat some person-like non-persons in ways we do not want people to be treated, this would undermine the system of sympathies and attitudes that makes the ethical system work. For this reason, we would choose in the original position to make mistreatment of some sorts of animals wrong in general (not just wrong in the cases with public impact), even though animals are not themselves parties in the original position. Thus it makes sense that it is those animals whose appearance and behavior are most like those of people that get the most consideration in our moral scheme.

It is because of "coherence of attitudes," I think, that the similarity of a fetus to a baby is very significant. A fetus one week before birth is so much like a newborn baby in our psychological space that we cannot allow any cavalier treatment of the former while expecting full sympathy and nurturative support for the latter. Thus, I think that anti-abortion forces are indeed giving their strongest arguments when they point to the similarities between a fetus and a baby, and when they try to evoke our emotional attachment to and sympathy for the fetus. An early horror story from New York about nurses who were expected to alternate between caring for six-week premature infants and disposing of viable 24-week aborted fetuses is just that — a horror story. These beings are so much alike that no one can be asked to draw a distinction and treat them so very differently.

Remember, however, that in the early weeks after conception, a fetus is very much unlike a person. It is hard to develop these feelings for a set of genes which doesn't yet have a head, hands, beating heart, response to touch or the ability to move by itself. Thus it seems to me that the alleged "slippery slope" between conception and birth is not so very slippery. In the early stages of pregnancy, abortion can hardly be compared to murder for psychological reasons, but in the latest stages it is psychologically akin to murder.

Another source of similarity is the bodily continuity between fetus and adult. Bodies play a surprisingly central role in our attitudes toward persons. One has only to think of the philosophical literature on how far physical identity suffices for personal identity or Wittgenstein's remark that the best picture of the human soul is the human body. Even after death, when all agree the body is no longer a person, we still observe elaborate customs of respect for the human body; like people who torture dogs, necrophiliacs are not to be trusted with people.[13] So it is appropriate that we show respect to a fetus as the body continuous with the body of a person. This is a degree of resemblance to persons that animals cannot rival.

Michael Tooley also utilizes a parallel with animals. He claims that it is always permissible to drown newborn kittens and draws conclusions about infanticide.[14] But it is only permissible to drown kittens when their survival would cause some hardship. Perhaps it would be a burden to feed and house six more cats or to find other homes for them. The alternative of letting them starve produces even more suffering than the drowning. Since the kittens get their rights second hand, so to speak, *via* the need for coherence in our attitudes, their interests are often overridden by the interests of full-fledged persons. But if their survival would be no inconvenience to people at all, then it is wrong to drown them, *contra* Tooley.

Tooley's conclusions about abortion are wrong for the same reason. Even if a fetus is not a person, abortion is not always permissible, because of the resemblance of a fetus to a person. I agree with Thomson that it would be wrong for a woman who is seven months pregnant to have an abortion just to avoid having to postpone a trip to Europe. In the early months of pregnancy when the fetus hardly resembles a baby at all, then, abortion is permissible whenever it is in the interests of the pregnant woman or her family. The reasons would only need to outweigh the pain and inconvenience of the abortion itself. In the middle months, when the fetus comes to resemble a person, abortion would be justifiable only when the continuation of the pregnancy or the birth of the child would cause harms — physical, psychological, economic or social — to the woman. In the late months of pregnancy, even on our current assumption that a fetus is not a person, abortion seems to be wrong except to save a woman from significant injury or death.

The Supreme Court has recognized similar gradations in the alleged slippery slope stretching between conception and birth. To this point, the present paper has been a discussion of the moral status of abortion only, not its legal status. In view of the great physical, financial and sometimes psychological costs of abortion, perhaps the legal arrangement most compatible with the proposed moral solution would be the absence of restrictions, that is, so-called abortion "on demand."

So I conclude, first, that application of our concept of a person will not suffice to settle the abortion issue. After all, the biological development of a human being is gradual. Second, whether a fetus is a person or not, abortion is justifiable early in pregnancy to avoid modest harms and seldom justifiable late in pregnancy except to avoid significant injury or death.

NOTES

1. We also have paternalistic laws which keep us from harming our own bodies even when no one else is affected. Ironically, anti-abortion laws were originally designed to protect pregnant women from a dangerous but tempting procedure.
2. Mary Anne Warren, "On the Moral and Legal Status of Abortion," *Monist* 57 (1973), p. 55.
3. Baruch Brody, "Fetal Humanity and the Theory of Essentialism," in Robert Baker and Frederick Elliston (eds.), *Philosophy and Sex* (Buffalo, N.Y., 1975).

4. Michael Tooley, "Abortion and Infanticide," *Philosophy and Public Affairs* 2 (1971).
5. Paul Ramsey, "The Morality of Abortion," in James Rachels, ed., *Moral Problems* (New York, 1971).
6. John Noonan, "Abortion and the Catholic Church: a Summary History," *Natural Law Forum* 12 (1967), pp. 125–131.
7. Wittgenstein has argued against the possibility of so capturing the concept of a game. *Philosophical Investigations* (New York, 1958), pp. 66–71.
8. Not because the fetus is partly a person and so has some of the rights of persons, but rather because of the rights of person-like non-persons. This I discuss in part III below.
9. Aristotle himself was concerned, however, with the different question of when the soul takes form. For historical data, see Jimmye Kimmey, "How the Abortion Laws Happened," Ms. 1 (April, 1973), pp. 48ff and John Noonan, *loc. cit.*
10. J.J. Thomson, "A Defense of Abortion," *Philosophy and Public Affairs* 1 (1971).
11. *Ibid.*, p. 52.
12. John Rawls, *A Theory of Justice* (Cambridge, Mass., 1971), pp. 3–4.
13. On the other hand, if they can be trusted with people, then our moral customs are mistaken. It all depends on the facts of psychology.
14. *Op. cit.*, pp. 40, 60–61.

QUESTIONS

1. Why does Jane English think that the question "Is a fetus a person"? cannot be given an unambiguous answer? What reasons does she give for thinking that answering the question is not essential to determining the morality of abortion?
2. Can you extract from English's account her view of what it is to be a person? In your view, would having a clear and unambiguous answer to this question make a difference in determining the morality of abortion?
3. Are English's reasons for viewing abortion in the earlier stages of gestation as morally unproblematic sound? What reasons does she have for her view that abortion in the later stages of gestation is morally objectionable?
4. Is English correct in concluding from her own arguments that the law should not seek to prohibit abortion at any point in the gestational cycle?

THE BEGINNING OF PERSONHOOD: A THOMISTIC BIOLOGICAL ANALYSIS

Jason T. Eberl

Introduction

In the arena of bioethical enquiry, one of the newest and most controversial subjects is embryonic stem cell (ES cell) research. This research involves the harvesting of stem cells from human embryos. Stem cells are 'the primordial, largely undifferentiated cells of an organism. "Totipotent" stem cells are capable of forming all cells of the body. In an early human embryo, each such cell theoretically has the potential to become a human being.'[1] The potential medical advances that such research provides would be of enormous benefit. The use of harvested ES cells to grow new bodily tissues and organs for those who suffer from

From *Bioethics*, Vol. 14, No. 2, 2000, pp. 134–157. Reprinted by permission of Blackwell Publishers Ltd.

diseases requiring organ transplant could virtually eliminate the need for human organ donation. Moral concerns about ES cell research arise from the manner in which the embryos,
from which the ES cells are harvested, are produced. For pro-life institutions and organizations, such as the Roman Catholic Church, the use of aborted human fetuses as sources of
harvested ES cells is a clear moral wrong. However, there is ambiguity concerning the
morality of artificially producing human zygotes[2] which are never destined to be implanted
into a uterus, being created for the sole purpose of harvesting their ES cells.

In order to respond to such ambiguity, as well as that surrounding the moral permissibility
of other biomedical procedures, I wish to enquire into the beginnings of human personhood.
This enquiry is different from the question 'When does a human life begin?' As far as human
'life' *per se*, it is, for the most part, uncontroversial among the scientific and philosophical community that life begins at the moment when the genetic information contained in the sperm and
ovum combine to form a *genetically unique cell*. However, what is controversial is whether this
genetically unique cell should be considered a human *person*. In what follows, I will examine
both philosophical and scientific endeavors to provide an answer to the question, 'When did *I*,
a human person, begin?' The answer to this question will serve as a basic premise for arguing
whether the artificial production of embryos for the sole purpose of harvesting their ES cells,
as well as certain other biomedical procedures,[3] are morally permissible.

Thomas Aquinas provides a plausible foundation for building a theory of human personhood
and its origin due to his persistent focus on the human person as essentially a being composed
of the integrated components of intellective soul and material body. Aquinas, unlike many others of his time,[4] argued that one must consider both the body and the soul of a human being,
understanding their interaction, in order to have a complete theory of human *personhood*.

Thus, my approach to the question of human personhood within a Thomistic framework
will consider both biological and metaphysical aspects of human persons. As Philip Smith
states, 'The fact that Aquinas' metaphysics is grounded in the order that reason discovers in
nature rather than imposes upon it, not only allows, but demands that the scientific information
on fetal development be incorporated into the discussion on the beginnings of personhood.'[5]

To answer the biological aspect of the question of when human personhood begins, I will
refer to the arguments presented by Eric Olson in his book, *The Human Animal*[6] and Norman
Ford in his book, *When Did I Begin?*[7] I utilize these two thinkers because they, as I, approach
biological data on the beginnings of human life with an eye to the issue of when personhood
begins. I will relate the considered arguments and positions to Aquinas' account of body and
soul.

Thomistic Metaphysics

A necessary preamble to this discussion is to present and explain the key relevant concepts
in Aquinas' metaphysics. The first section concerns Aquinas' understanding of the relationship between *form* (soul) and *matter* (body). This section will include Aquinas' contention
that a material human body and the soul (form) which defines it are inseparably linked. The
second section will consider Aquinas' metaphysics of *ensoulment*, i.e., the instantiation of a
human soul in a human biological organism. In the third section, I will give Aquinas' definition of 'person' and briefly compare it with two other conceptions of 'person' from Peter
Singer and Michael Tooley. This metaphysical groundwork will define the necessary conditions to validly assert, from a Thomistic perspective, whether or not there is a human soul,
and thus a human person, present at the earliest stages of biological life.

Form and Matter

Thomas Aquinas held an Aristotelian view with respect to the nature of human persons. The primary characteristic of this view is that a human person is essentially a composite unified being. This means that the *essence* of human personhood is an integration of both of its required components: *form* and *matter*. Form is understood in Aristotelianism to be the defining principle by which matter takes on a certain *individuated nature*. Form is basically that by which an instance of matter possesses certain defining qualities (e.g., having a particular shape, size, color, texture, smell, ability to reproduce, ability to sense, ability to form abstract concepts, etc.) in an integrated unity. For Aquinas and Aristotle, matter cannot exist without form, and form does not exist apart from matter.[8] With respect to living beings, there are three types of form and they are all referred to by both Aristotle[9] and Aquinas[10] by the term 'soul' (*psyche* and *anima*, respectively). Soul is best characterized as the dynamic unifying principle of a living being's activities and end (*telos*).[11] There are three different types of soul: *vegetative*, *sensitive*, and *intellective*. Each of these types is defined by its respective set of powers. All three types function as the organizing principle of matter.

The vegetative soul is found in plants and all higher biological organisms.[12] It endows them with the powers of life, nutrition, and growth. The sensitive soul is found in animals and human beings. It endows them with the powers of sensation, imagination, and awareness of particular objects. The intellective soul is found only in human beings and is the principle of endowment of the powers of rational thought, as well as the human biological powers proper to the functioning of the intellective soul.

The soul is the form of the body for living beings. It is the organizing principle of all physical aspects of living beings. All types of form are essentially integrated with the matter they inform. They cannot exist separate from matter. Thus, the essence of human personhood requires both the form and the matter together; i.e., the presence of a human person requires that there be matter (a body) organized as an individual *human* body by an intellective soul (the appropriate form of a human person).

Another aspect of the Thomistic/Aristotelian relationship of form and matter is that form *individuates* matter. Without form, there is no distinction between one instance of matter and another. In fact, Aquinas contends that such 'prime matter' (i.e., matter without form) does not exist. All instances of matter are informed and each is thus a separate individual from other instances of informed matter. Therefore, to say that there is an instance of informed matter is to say that there is *an individual substance*. The body of a plant, informed by a vegetative soul, is distinct from the body of another plant that is informed by a numerically different vegetative soul. With respect to humans, a human body which is informed by an intellective soul is distinct from another human body which is informed by a numerically distinct intellective soul.

Metaphysics of Ensoulment[13]

Each of the three type of soul consists of a unique set of powers and these powers correspond to certain biological capacities and functions. I assert that the relation of psychological instantiation (ensoulment) to biological instantiation is accomplished by matching the powers of the soul with the corresponding biological capacities which the soul informs. Aquinas argues for this position that the powers of the soul and biological capacities correspond to each other in the *Summa Theologiae* Ia., Q. 90, A. 4, ad. 1: 'as the soul is naturally the form of the body, it was necessarily created, not separately, but in the body'.[14]

I do not intend by this to say that the biological capacities precede the powers of the soul. In fact, Aquinas and Aristotle explicitly argue the reverse. I merely contend that if certain powers of the soul are actualized, then the corresponding biological capacities will be actualized. By *modus tollens*, if the biological capacities are not actualized, then the corresponding powers of the soul are not actualized.

When is the human soul instantiated in the matter of the biological organism? In the Thomistic/Aristotelian framework, form (soul) must metaphysically, but not temporally, precede matter (biological organism), because it is the form that defines the nature of the matter. Thus, the soul informs the nature of the biological organism not before, nor after, but *at the same moment* as the biological organism is instantiated. As Philip Smith points out,

> Since [the soul] is the organizing principle of a living organism, the substantial form is the source of a being's internal unity and the root of its specific activity and growth. Thus, while we cannot directly experience this form, we can infer its reality by observing a being's activity. ... By examining a thing's operations, we can learn something about the source of its operations or its substantial form.[15]

To understand what kind of form (soul) informs the matter of a particular organism, we must observe the activities of that organism. The presence of activities proper to a particular type of soul allows the inference of the presence of that type of soul.

For example, if an organism is observed to have the capacity to respirate, reproduce, take in nutrition, etc., it can be concluded that it is informed by a vegetative soul. If an organism is observed to not only be alive, but also has the capacity for sensory awareness of its environment and has the proper sensory organs, then one can conclude that it is informed by a sensitive soul. Finally, if an organism is observed to be alive, capable of sensation, and has, or is developing, the organs necessary for intellectual thought, then that organism can be said to be informed by an intellective soul—the one type of soul that, for Aquinas, defines a person.

Definition of Personhood

Aquinas adopts the definition of 'person' that Boethius' offers in his treatise *Contra Eutychen et Nestorium* III. The best English translation of the technical definition is 'individual substance of a rational nature'.[16] The two key relevant terms are 'individual' and 'rational.' I interpret Aquinas as intending, by the use of these two terms, that a person must consist of *one, ongoing ontology* and a *soul* which endows it with the power of *rationality*, i.e., intellect. Hence, for Aquinas, a person is an *individual, continuous biological organism informed by an intellective soul*.

Included in this definition of 'person' is the contention that the mere presence of the intellective soul is sufficient for personhood. The actualization of all of the soul's essential *powers* of personhood is not necessary. That is, the informed biological organism need not be *actually* capable of rational thought for it to be considered a person. Aquinas, in this respect, differs from Peter Singer, who contends that personhood is not acquired until the biological organism *actualizes* the essential powers of personhood, *viz.*, rational thought, autonomous choice, self-consciousness, etc. For Aquinas, the endowment of the essential powers of personhood is sufficient for actual personhood.

Aquinas' conception of the necessary conditions for personhood seems to be in agreement with Michael Tooley's understanding of personhood. On p. 146 of his book *Abortion and Infanticide*,[17] Tooley summarizes his position concerning the necessary and sufficient conditions for personhood. Of the four essential qualities of personhood that Tooley identifies (having a non-momentary interest, rationality, being an agent, and self-consciousness), not one of them is considered by him to be a necessary condition for personhood; though, he holds that having a non-momentary interest and being an agent may each, in themselves, be a sufficient condition for personhood. It seems as if Tooley and Aquinas are in agreement that the essential qualities, or powers, of personhood need not be actualized for a person to be present. Tooley and Aquinas also seem to be in agreement when Tooley asserts at least one necessary condition for personhood: 'a continuing mental substance'.[18] Although Aquinas does not hold the human intellective soul (considered by itself) to be a 'substance,' in the technical Aristotelian understanding of that term, he does contend that psychological (mental) continuity is necessary for personhood in the sense that there must be the continuous presence of an human intellective soul.

With this Thomistic metaphysical framework in mind, I will now present the arguments of Olson and Ford as to when the biological requirements of ensoulment are met. The basic requirement is an ongoing, ontologically unique, biological organism which, in its activities, exemplifies the powers of the intellective soul.

Olson and the Biological Approach

Olson holds that the continuous existence of a human biological organism is necessary and sufficient for personhood. In a Thomistic framework, however, I contend that the continuous existence of a human biological organism is necessary, but not sufficient, for personhood. As already described above, for Aquinas, the instantiation of an intellective soul informing the biological organism is also necessary for personhood. However, while I disagree with Olson on this point, his arguments for the beginning of the continuous existence of a human biological organism are salient, because the continuous existence of such is a necessary component of human personhood for Aquinas.

Olson argues that the beginning of a human person as an individual living continuous[19] biological organism is

> When the cells that develop into the fetus (as opposed to the placenta) become specialized and begin to grow and function in a coordinated manner. They develop bilateral symmetry around the 'primitive streak', the ancestor of the spinal cord. At this point, twinning is no longer possible: cutting away half the cells would not result in two smaller living embryos, but would simply cause death. ... Only at this point do we have a multicellular organism and not merely a mass of living cells stuck together.[20]

The key to Olson's argument for the beginning of a human person not occurring before this point in fetal development is the *totipotency* of the mass of cells that make up the blastocyst before it becomes implanted in the uterine wall. 'Totipotency' means that, prior to implantation, each cell or group of cells has the power to separate from the rest of the zygote, divide by cellular mitosis, and develop into a multicellular organism. It is a due to this totipotency of pre-implantation cells that identical twins, triplets, etc. are able to occur. One or more cells break away from the cluster, divide (mitosis), and develop into a second (or third, fourth, etc.) organism. Since each cell or group of cells is its own unique individual biological entity and has the capacity to separate and develop into a distinct multicellular biological organism, it cannot be said that there is already an individual human organism at this point. In potentiality, there are, practically speaking, one or a few individual human organisms present.[21]

One could respond to this conclusion by asserting that there is one individual human organism in potentiality, if the case were that twinning did not occur. I argue that this response fails because, before the point at which twinning becomes impossible, there is both the potential for a single organism and for multiple organisms to develop. Neither potential is any *more potential*, or closer to being actual, than the other is. In other words, any zygote has the potential to twin, prior to implantation. One may argue that one of the potentialities would have an advantage over the other if there were some type of genetic encoding for twinning that determines whether or not it will occur. However, at the present time of scientific discovery, it is not known whether such is the case or not.

Ford and the Biological Approach

Olson builds his case upon the work done by Norman Ford in his book, *When did I begin?* I will give a brief outline of Ford's arguments against the human individual beginning prior to implantation and the formation of the 'primitive streak'.[22] Then, I will relate Ford's (and Olson's) conclusion to Aquinas' metaphysical account of ensoulment.

Ford begins with the argument in favor of the human individual beginning at the moment of fertilization.[23] The basic case being made is that there is strong biological evidence that an *ontologically* and *genetically* unique individual human organism begins a career of biological development at the moment of fertilization.[24] Ford counters that, at the moment of fertilization, there is only a genetically distinct biological entity, not an ongoing ontologically distinct entity:

> Biologists speak about one's genetic or biological identity or genome being established at fertilization. This is unique for each individual. Except in the case of identical twins, no two persons have the same genetic constitution or genotype. … [But] the genetic code in the zygote does not suffice to constitute or define a human individual in an ontological sense. Identical twins have the same genetic code but they are distinct ontological individuals.[25]

The first cell, which results after fertilization is complete, has a unique genetic identity and a unique ontological identity *as a biological cell*. However, it does not have a unique ontological identity *as a human being*. This is due to there existing, after the first mitotic event, two cells, which have the same *genetic* identity, but are *ontologically* distinct. The same follows for every event of cellular mitosis until the point is reached when mitosis can no longer occur which results in ontologically distinct beings, i.e., identical twinning is no longer possible.

One could counter that twinning does not lead to the conclusion that there is not an ontologically unique individual to begin with, if it were the case that the second (twin) ontological individual grows out of the material of the first without the first losing its ontological status. I contend, however, that this does not seem to be a likely case since there is no way to differentiate the two different ontologies. Cells remain undetermined for quite some time as to where they will go and what role they will play in the developing organism. The same indeterminism can come into play in some cases of twinning in which the two organisms share cell clusters for a great deal of the developmental process.[26] To which organism each set of cells will ultimately go is largely undetermined. Therefore, there is both a sharing of ontology and a lack of completely individuated ontology in each organism.[27]

There is another important implication of the indeterminacy factor for the cells of the zygote. A great number of the zygote's cells, when they become differentiated from other cells, are utilized to form extraembryonic material (trophoblast).[28] These cells do not contribute to the 'embryo proper'. Only the cells in the ICM (Inner Cell Mass) are differentiated from those that form the trophoblast to form the embryo itself. Furthermore, there is no strict determiner for which cells will form the trophoblast and which will form the ICM. Ford points out that it is just a matter of which cells are spatially located in relation to other cells and the outer membrane (zona pellucida) that places different cells into one of the two sets.

The stage at which this differentiation has occurred is called the *morula* stage. Ford argues that, as I indicated above,

> at the morula stage, it is extremely difficult to establish the presence of the sort of unity that would be required for the cluster of cells to be an actual ontological individual. There does not appear to be any strict commitment or rigid predetermination in cells from the earliest cleavages to become the inner cells. ... The relatively independent behaviour of the individual cells, together with the indeterminate and uncommitted nature of their developmental potential within the cluster of cells as a whole, seems to be incompatible with the individuation of the morula itself as a distinct ontological individual.[29]

In a separate article, Ford contends that 'it is only at the primitive streak stage that specific cells are destined to form the entire embryo and fetus. This means that the cells within the zona pellucida are not yet sufficiently activated to form one integrated living body.'[30] Based on experiments conducted that resulted in *chimeric* sheep (i.e., a sheep formed out of 'the cells of genetically dissimilar embryos'), Ford concludes 'that purposeful development [from a zygote to an embryo] occurs *between* cells rather than *within* a multicellular individual'.[31]

However, the question now arises that once the cells have differentiated at the end of the morula stage into the trophoblast and ICM, could it be said that the ICM constitutes an ongoing ontologically unique individual? Ford states that there is still indeterminate differentiation that occurs as the zygote implants itself in the uterine wall.[32] Some of the cells of the ICM, formed before implantation, will not, in the end, form part of the embryo proper, but will form extraembryonic material.[33] Thus, it still cannot be said that there is a unique individual entity until all the cells that will contribute to the formation of the embryo proper are determined to that end and no other. Prior to strict cell determination, there is more than one entity present in the zygote, embryo proper and extraembryonic material, and they can not be completely differentiated from each other.

Another way of approaching this issue is to argue that the entire 'new biological entity'[34] is the human organism. Couldn't it be said that the embryo proper, placenta, umbilical cord, and any other extraembryonic biological material together constitute one unique human organism? If this is the case, then the human organism, at the moment of birth, removes a significant portion of itself (the embryo proper) from the placenta, and, after a time, completely sheds the placenta and umbilical cord which are no longer necessary.[35]

Ford, however, rejects this possible scenario because he sees no reason for considering the placenta as part of the embryo proper that is discarded after birth. He cites two supporting reasons: 1. When a baby is stillborn, we do not mourn for the placenta and bury it along with the rest of the baby; 2. In some non-human mammals, a placenta will form even in cases where no embryo is present. Thus, the placenta is best considered as a separate biological entity from the embryo proper. It is the embryo proper alone that will continue to develop into an infant and adult human being.

Now, I will present Ford's argument for when the human person does begin[36] and will follow with a Thomistic account, compatible with Ford, of the event of ensoulment.[37] According to current biological data, fourteen to nineteen days after fertilization, the new biological entity has completed the implantation process in the uterine wall. By this point, all cells are determined as to whether they will form part of the embryo proper or extraembryonic material. The key event that occurs next is the formation of the primitive streak and the beginning of the functioning fetal heart. This indicates the presence of a new unique self-sustaining human individual that will grow and develop into an infant and adult human being which are numerically identical to it. Furthermore, twinning is no longer possible after the formation of the primitive streak. The last possible occurrence of twinning is if two primitive streaks are formed.

Ford sums up his positions and refers to *ensoulment* for the first time:

> The appearance of the primitive streak is an important landmark, indicating the position of the embryo proper with the main features of the new individual's body plan. *This appears to be the stage of development when the cells of the epiblast first become organized through this primitive streak into one whole multicellular individual living human being, possessing for the first time a body axis and bilateral symmetry. Its developing cells are now integrated and subordinated to form a single heterogeneous organic body that endures with its own ontological as well as biological identity through all its subsequent stages of growth and development. A new human individual begins once the matter of the epiblastic cells become one living body, informed or actuated by a human form, life-principle or soul that arises through the creative power of God. The appearance of one primitive streak signals that only one embryo proper and human individual has been formed and begun to exist. Prior to this stage it would be pointless to speak about the presence of a true human being in an ontological sense. A human individual could scarcely exist before a definitive human body is formed. As mentioned earlier, the formation of an ontological individual with a truly human nature and rational ensoulment must coincide.*[38]

While Ford's insistence on a 'definitive human body' here may seem arbitrary, I hold that it is precisely what is required in a Thomistic framework. For Aquinas, in order to say that there is a human person, there must, at minimum, be an intellective soul informing a human body. The minimum requirements of a 'definitive human body' are what are at issue in Ford's discussion and this article. The answer is that a definitive human body exists when there is biological material present that will, in the absence of interruption in the natural course, develop into an adult human biological organism and *nothing else*. As Ford argues, before the formation of the primitive streak, there is biological material that will naturally form things other than an adult human biological organism, e.g., extraembryonic material or a possible second adult human biological organism.

The presence of such material that does not belong to the embryo proper may *prima facie* not seem like a threat to the metaphysical argument that there is a 'definitive' embryonic human body present amidst the extra material. One may argue that the inability to differentiate which cells of the zygote will constitute extraembryonic material and which will constitute the embryo proper is merely an epistemological problem and has no bearing on the metaphysical reality that there is a definitive human body present within the cell cluster. I disagree with such an argument, because the epistemological problem of differentiating which cells will constitute which entity (embryo proper, twin embryo, or extraembryonic material) is due to the lack of a metaphysical determining factor for cell differentiation. *Contra* what my interlocutor may argue, there is no metaphysical fact-of-the-matter concerning which cells constitute the embryo proper which is merely not known, or knowable, by current scientific understanding. The only metaphysical fact-of-the-matter concerning the differentiation of pre-implantation cells is that they are *not* differentiated in any way. It is merely due to chance occurrence that some cells, rather than others, will end up in the proper position to be cells of the embryo proper.[39] There is no hidden metaphysical mechanism of cell determination present in the zygote.

Accepting Ford's and Olson's accounts of when occurs the instantiation of a unique individual human biological organism which will maintain biological continuity across its development into an infant and adult, my final concern is to relate this biological answer to a psychological answer to the question of when personhood begins. I have argued above that, for a Thomist, a complete account of personhood must include both the biological and psychological factors that constitute a human person. The soul is the set of endowments and powers that actualize the biological and psychological activities that constitute the human body and intellect.

Thomistic Answer to When Ensoulment Occurs

According to Ford and Olson, the human soul is instantiated at the end of implantation when the primitive streak begins to form. It is only at this point that the activities proper to the human intellective soul are observed.[40] However, it is not necessary to say that *all* of the soul's powers must be actualized at that moment. The actualization of the soul's different powers occurs as the corresponding biological capacities develop. Another reason that it is not until the point of implantation that there can be said to be instantiation of the intellective soul is due to the requirement that there be *individuated* matter present. Prior to implantation, the cluster of cells does not form a unique individual entity. Rather, they are a collection of several individual entities. Because of the remaining possibility of twinning, there cannot be said to be one individual instance of matter, i.e., one body. There are possibly two or more bodies present. Therefore, it cannot be said that there is one intellective soul informing the matter of the zygote. Once implantation occurs, twinning is no longer possible, and cell differentiation between the embryo proper and extraembryonic material is complete, the instance of matter that is the embryo proper can be said to be an *individual* instance of matter, informed by *one* form, *viz.*, the intellective soul.

At the formation of the primitive streak, there is a living biological organism, capable of nutrition and growth,[41] developing the earliest biological tools necessary for sensation, imagination, and rational thought (being that all of these powers are tied to the brain and spinal cord that develop from the primitive streak). Therefore, at this point, the powers proper to the vegetative type of soul are actualized (life, nutrition, growth) and the powers proper to the sensitive type of soul are informing the biological organism to develop the tools necessary to actualize the powers of sensation and imagination. Also, the powers proper to the intellective type of soul are informing the same development in order to actualize the power of rational thought.[42] The specific powers of sensation and intellection are not themselves actualized until the required organs begin to function. However, the soul itself is active by informing the body to develop the required organs. Therefore, I conclude that the human person is instantiated as an individual complete biological organism with the powers of life, sensation, and rational thought (i.e., a being with both a body and a human intellective soul) at the moment the primitive streak begins to form, division of the organism (i.e., twinning) is no longer possible, and cells which form the embryo proper are determined to that end and no other.

I wish to note here, as Smith does on p. 206 of this article that the point of implantation is merely used as the reference point for when the primitive streak begins to form and twinning is no longer possible. There is no apparent causal influence of the event of uterine implantation over the possibility of twinning. Twinning is the key to determining an embryo's being an individual substance informed by an intellective soul. Therefore, if it were discovered that twinning was still possible after implantation, say up until the second trimester; then, my argument would be that there is no intellective soul, or human person, present until the second trimester. Such a contention would present a problem of reconciling the lack of an intellective soul with the formation of the primitive streak, which would still occur at implantation and is an activity proper, I have argued above, to the intellective soul. However, the fact-of-the-matter is that twinning is not possible after implantation and this corresponds to the formation of the primitive streak. That these two key events coincide is supporting evidence that both events are due to the fact that it is at this point that the intellective soul is instantiated in the embryonic matter.

The Nature of the Zygote

One matter I must now address concerns the nature of the zygote. Before there exists the developing individual biological organism, there exists, in its place, a cluster of cells, dividing and differentiating among themselves, which contain *human* DNA. Based on the evidence and arguments presented above, I contend that this cell cluster can best be understood as human biological *material*, but not a unified living human organism. There is no soul informing this cluster of cells that constitute the zygote. It is merely biological material that contains human DNA. One reason I make this contention is that each cell of the cluster does not exist as a *self-sustaining* biological organism. Although each cell operates independently of the other cells in the cluster (and has the capacity to be separated from the other cells, divide, and form a new cell cluster), it is not a *viable* biological organism operating under its own internal life-principle (vegetative soul). If that were the case, then the cell would be able to take in nourishment and sustain its own existence as single-celled amoebae have the capacity to do. However, this is not the case. Removed from the special environment provided by the different components of the female reproductive system, these cells would not be capable of sustaining their own existence and would quickly die.[43]

In adopting this stance toward the nature of the zygote, I am departing from strict Thomistic embryology. However, this departure is necessary and justified because Aquinas did not have the benefit of the embryological data available today. Aquinas[44] contends that there is a vegetative soul informing the zygote from the moment of conception. However, this vegetative soul is not numerically identical to the set of vegetative powers of the intellective soul; i.e., Aquinas contends that there is no intellective soul present at this point. Aquinas holds that this vegetative soul is later annihilated and replaced by a sensitive soul which includes both vegetative and sensitive powers. This soul is later annihilated and replaced by the intellective soul that includes vegetative, sensitive and intellective powers. As one can see, I could maintain allegiance to Aquinas' view and still hold the thesis that the zygote does not contain an intellective soul. However, holding that there is a vegetative soul informing the zygote implies that it is a *unified* living organism. This is inconsistent with the arguments of Ford and Olson, which have led to the conclusion that there is not a unified organism extant before implantation. Therefore, having adopted Ford and Olson's position, I must depart from Aquinas on this issue.

Two Types of Potentiality

At this point, I must pause to introduce a technical distinction in Thomistic metaphysics: the distinction between a *passive potentiality* and an *active potentiality*. This is best illustrated by example. Every time a heterosexual couple engage in genital sexual intercourse without the interference of any natural or artificial contraceptives, each ejaculated sperm has the potential to fertilize an ovum, if present, and cause a new biological entity to begin to form. This is an example of a *passive potentiality*, and the entity that can be figuratively said to exist in this fashion is far removed from the actualized biological organism that possesses an intellective soul and is on the developmental path toward full actualization of the essential powers of human personhood.

Here is another illustrative example. If I am sitting at home watching TV, I have the potential to get up and walk to the store. But, if I am already walking down the street in the direction of the store with the intention to complete my journey to the store, that is a different type of potentiality (one much closer to actualization). This latter type of potentiality is an *active potentiality*, as opposed to a *passive potentiality*.

The term 'passive' is used because the actualization of the relevant capacities requires an extra component (what Tooley terms a 'positive causal factor')[45] to act upon the subject so that the subject may actualize its relevant capacities. In the case of the sperm, its potential for actualizing a new human person depends upon the presence of an ovum to act upon it with its set of chromosomes. In the case of my walking to the store, while I am sitting in my chair, an extra component, *viz.*, a decision to get up and go to the store, is required for me to actually get up and go to the store. However, if I am already walking to the store, then this decision is already present. Only an additional component, e.g., my deciding not to finish walking to the store or some barricade blocking me from getting to the store (what Tooley terms a 'negative causal factor'),[46] can prevent my potential for completing my journey to the store from being actualized.

With these distinctions in mind, I assert that a sperm or ovum that exists independently of the other only has a *passive potentiality* for human personhood. I further contend that a fertilized zygote also has only a *passive potentiality* for human personhood, which implies that it is not yet an actual person. Why? Because, in addition to unique genetic identity (which the zygote does possess), ongoing ontological identity is required (which the zygote does not possess since it is capable of twinning into two or more distinct ontologies); and the latter is only achieved by the addition of another positive causal factor, *viz.*, the intellective soul.[47]

Therefore, until the moment when twinning is no longer possible, there is no actual human person present, because there is no basis for contending that there is a human soul informing the matter of the zygote. Nevertheless, it seems counter-intuitive to assert that both a sperm cell and a fertilized zygote share the same type of potentiality. One tends to think that there is an important difference between the two types of biological material, even though they both require the addition of a key positive causal factor to become a unified human biological organism.

Tooley offers a solution to this dilemma by recognizing that there is a *range* of passive potentiality. Two things may both have only a passive potentiality to be something else, but one of the two may be *closer* to actualizing that potentiality than the other. How? One may have a need of fewer positive causal factors to fulfill its potentiality. In this case, the sperm first requires union with an ovum, and then instantiation of an intellective soul, to fulfill its potentiality for human personhood. The fertilized zygote has already achieved union with an ovum; it requires only the instantiation of the intellective soul to fulfill its potentiality. Thus, it could be contended, in agreement with the general intuition, that the fertilized zygote is, to a large degree, closer to being an actual human person than the sperm cell is. In fact, one could say that, since the zygote has the requisite DNA programming, it has an active potentiality *for further biological development* toward becoming the individual human biological organism that is informed by the intellective soul. However, it would still have only a passive potentiality for *human personhood* — since it requires the additional positive causal factor, *viz.*, the intellective soul.

Ethical Implications

I will now proceed to address the ethical implications that follow from the conception of a zygote as having merely a passive potentiality for personhood. I wish to first note that, while the zygote is not a human *person*, it is still *human* in the sense that it contains a complete set of human DNA. Thus, as stated above, it could be said that the zygote, while having only a passive potentiality for personhood, has an active potentiality for biological development toward becoming a human biological organism, which is informed by an intellective soul. Due to this active potentiality for human biological development, I contend that the zygote should not be treated frivolously.[48] Nothing should interfere with the natural process of cell mitosis and differentiation unless it has a commensurate value. Defining what outcomes would be of commensurate value is a separate and daunting task. I follow with a couple examples of morally contentious acts, which may have a commensurate value to that of the zygote.

ES Cell Research

Richard Doerflinger, the associate director of the pro-life activities office of the National Conference of Catholic Bishops (NCCB), has suggested that 'supposing that the laboratory-produced stem-cell clusters are not true human embryos but only resemble them ... the research could go forward'.[49] Doerflinger and the NCCB may contend that the human zygotes produced *in vitro* for the purpose of ES cell harvesting are indeed truly human by re-asserting the Roman Catholic Church's claim that inviolable human life begins at the completion of the process of conception. My argument, however, is that even if such laboratory-produced zygotes do contain human DNA in the cells that constitute the cluster, that is not sufficient for claiming that there is either an actual human person present, or a potential human person present – 'potential' in the sense of an active potentiality. Such laboratory-produced ES cell clusters would resemble a human person only in terms of being potential persons in the sense of a passive potentiality.

In Vitro Fertilization

Allowing a woman to conceive and bear children of her own and her partner's genetic make-up is a good thing. However, the process of *in vitro* fertilization and implantation of zygotes into the uterus, by which a woman who would otherwise be unable to conceive children of her own can do so, has the consequence of allowing the destruction of a small number of fertilized zygotes.[50] But, if the above thesis is true, then there has been no loss of human persons. What was destroyed in this process was human biological material that was not informed by an intellective soul. Such zygotes have none of the endowments associated with the intellective soul, even in active potentiality. At most, they are potentially (in the sense of passive potentiality) the recipients of an intellective soul – nothing more.

Furthermore, we can take into account the scientific evidence that a number of naturally fertilized zygotes do not implant in the uterus following conception. The result is a natural (spontaneous) abortion. Since this is the case, it seems odd to believe that God (or whatever agent is responsible for creation) would permit the needless death of so many persons. It seems more reasonable to conceive of them as naturally rejected biological material — not persons.

Procured Abortion and Abortifacient Contraceptives

With respect to the abortion issue, my thesis is not practically applicable since procured abortions cannot occur until after the mother is aware that she is pregnant. Usually, implantation and the instantiation of an intellective soul have occurred by that point. However, my thesis could be used to argue in favor of the use of certain artificial contraceptives that are morally rejected otherwise. Some people accept the moral permissibility of using artificial contraceptives such as condoms or spermicidal jelly, but object to the use of an IUD or the 'morning-after' pill, because they function as abortifacients, i.e., they cause spontaneous abortions.[51] According to my thesis, for such people, artificial contraceptives which function as abortifacients would be morally permissible, if the contraceptives are utilized to achieve an end of commensurate value; for the spontaneous abortion occurs before the implantation process begins.

An example of a case in which there may be justifiable use of such contraceptives involves a schizophrenic woman who is on medication (e.g., haldol) which would likely lead to severe limb malformation of the fetus if she should become pregnant. In this case, it seems better that she not become pregnant. Therefore, the use of abortifacient contraceptives (which have a higher success rate of preventing pregnancy than other contraceptives, such as condoms) may be justified considering that preventing the birth of a severely physically deformed child is commensurate with the loss of a zygote which has only a passive potentiality for becoming a human person.

Conclusion

As is apparent, this combination of scientific discovery and philosophical reflection does not provide a definitive answer to the issue of the beginning of human personhood and the moral implications thereof. However, a plausible and coherent Thomistic conception of human personhood and its origins sheds light upon the critical subject of morally evaluating certain relevant actions under a natural law, deontological, or utilitarian ethical system.[52]

NOTES

1. Russell Shaw 'Moral Concerns Persist on Stem-cell Research' *Our Sunday Visitor* 87/40 (1999), p. 3.
2. Such zygotes are 'human' in that they contain human DNA. I am differentiating the terms 'embryo' and 'zygote' in the sense that 'embryo' refers to the developing human organism present

after the blastocyst (cell cluster) has implanted in the uterine wall and begun to develop primitive tissues and organs. 'Zygote' refers to the pre-implantation biological material which consists of a cluster of cells from the moment of fertilization until the completion of the implantation process, at which time the embryo becomes distinct from the placenta and other extraembryonic material. Thus, whenever I utilize the term 'zygote', the adjective 'pre-implantation' is understood.

3. Some of the other issues I will address in this paper include *in vitro* fertilization, procured abortion, and the use of artificial contraceptives which function as abortifacients, i.e., cause the spontaneous abortion of a fertilized zygote to occur within the uterus.

4. E.g., the Manicheeans, who actually pre-date Aquinas by several centuries but still had influence in the 13th century, held that only the spirit (i.e., soul) defined what a human person is, that the physical body was a hindrance to that spirit, and that a person should make every attempt to remove themselves from their corporeal prison. They even went so far as to argue against procreation, claiming that it was a great evil to take part in trapping another spirit into a body.

5. Philip Smith 'The Beginning of Personhood: A Thomistic Perspective' *Laval Theologique et Philosophique* 39/2 (1983), pp. 197–8. Cf. Thomas Aquinas *Commentary on Nicomachean Ethics* Vol. 1: Bk. I, Lect. 1, C. I. Litzinger, trans. (Chicago: Henry Regnery Co., 1964), p. 6.

6. Eric Olson *The Human Animal: Personal Identity Without Psychology* (New York: Oxford University Press, 1997).

7. Norman Ford *When Did I Begin?* (New York: Cambridge University Press, 1988).

8. An illustrative example utilized by Aristotle in his *De Anima* is that of a seal imprinted on wax. The seal *informs* the wax to take on a definite shape and texture that allows an observer to recognize the seal in the wax. The seal does not exist separate from the wax (one cannot physically abstract the seal from the wax), nor can the wax exist without having the shape and texture of the seal, or some other shape and texture.

9. Cf. Aristotle *De Anima*.

10. Cf. Thomas Aquinas *Summa Theologiae* Ia., Treatise on Man.

11. I am grateful to Fr. John Kavanaugh, S.J. for suggesting this characterization of 'soul'. Understanding the soul in this way allows for it to be considered either as a *substance*, in the Aristotelian sense, or as merely a collection of attributes. For more on this debate concerning the nature of the soul in Aristotle, cf. Herbert Granger *Aristotle's Idea of the Soul*, Philosophical Studies Ser. 48 (Netherlands: Kluwer, 1996).

12. I believe that if Aquinas and Aristotle had access to today's biological knowledge, they would be inclined to include bacteria, amoebae, and the like in their set of living organisms with a vegetative soul.

13. 'Ensoulment' refers to the moment that the human soul informs the matter of the human body.

14. Thomas Aquinas *Summa Theologiae* Vol. 1, Fathers of the English Dominican Province, trans. (New York: Benziger, 1948), p. 461.

15. Smith, pp. 203-4. The term 'substantial form' is a technical term used by Aquinas which I have not utilized in this article. Simply understood, the substantial form of a thing 'x' which is of kind 'F', as opposed to what can be called an *accidental* form of 'x', is that which is the organizing principle of 'x' such that 'x' is 'F'. Without the substantial form that informs the matter of 'x', 'x' would not be 'F'. For an example of this, substitute, 'x' with 'Socrates' and 'F' with 'human.' For the purposes of this article, one can equate a human person's substantial form with what I have termed the 'human soul' or 'intellective soul'.

16. Cf. Thomas Aquinas, *Summa Theologiae* Ia., Q. 29, A. 1. Boethius' original Latin is '*naturae rationabilis individua substantia*'.

17. Michael Tooley *Abortion and Infanticide* (Oxford: Clarendon Press, 1983).

18. Tooley, p. 146.

19. Olson is primarily concerned with the question of one's continuous personal identity. I agree that such continuity is a key factor in the matter of defining personhood. However, having already established that the basic Thomistic requirement of personhood is a suitable biological organism informed by an intellective soul, the additional requirement of continuity is not specifically addressed in this article. Keep in mind, however, that Olson's arguments for the biological beginning of human personhood presupposes the requirement of continuity. Thus, I presuppose it as a basic requirement as well.

20. Olson, p. 91.

21. Theoretically, there are an infinite number of potential individual organisms; if each cell separated, began to develop, and then split apart again before implantation, and so on *ad infinitum*. This is biologically impossible, though.

22. The 'primitive streak' is a group of cells that divide the developing organism symmetrically. The primitive streak will eventually develop into the brain and spinal cord.

23. 'Fertilization' occurs when the 23 chromosomes from the sperm cell unite with the 23 chromosomes from the ovum.

24. Referring to a 'moment of fertilization' is somewhat inaccurate, since the joining of sperm and ovum is a process. However, one can refer to a 'moment' when the two sets of 23 chromosomes cease to exist as two distinct sets and become one set of 46 chromosomes. This, too, may be a process of fusion; in which case, the 'moment' would be best considered as the completion of the process.

25. Ford 1988, p. 117.

26. In the case of 'joined twins' (a.k.a., Siamese twins), the two organisms continue to share cell clusters (now in the form of organs and tissue at the end of the gestational period). In these cases, we say that there are two distinct ontologies, but it is still difficult to differentiate where one ends and the other begins due to the overlap in shared organs such as a heart or liver. However, this difficulty in differentiation does not entail it is not possible at all to demarcate two distinct bodies. One could contend that differentiation of the two bodies could be made due to distinctions in the control of organ functions by the two individual brain systems.

27. Cf. Ford 1988, pp. 133–5.

28. Cf. Ford 1988, p. 124.

29. Ford 1988. pp. 148–9

30. Norman Ford 'Fetus' *Encyclopedia of Applied Ethics* Vol. 2, Ruth Chadwick, ed. (San Diego: Academic Press, 1998), p. 291.

31. Ford 1998, p. 292.

32. Cf. Ford 1988, p. 161.

33. Fr. Kavanaugh pointed out to me that we could perhaps say the same thing with respect to fingernails or hair. Does the fact that these parts of our body are eventually discarded upset the developed organism's biological unity? If not, as would seem to be the case, then this argument cannot be used against the ICM being a biological unity. I respond, however, that the two cases are not analogous. Fingernails and hair are, at one time, part of the developed organism's body, and then at some later time are discarded and no longer part of the body. The undifferentiated cells of the ICM, however, because they are undifferentiated, can never be said to be part of the embryo proper.

34. This refers to all biological components that have formed since fertilization. It includes both the embryo proper and all extraembryonic material.

35. This scenario, with reference to the placenta and umbilical cord being shed from the organism after a certain amount of time, concerns what would happen naturally if there were no medical intervention in the birth and development process (i.e., the umbilical cord is not artificially severed, thereby dividing the embryo proper and the placenta before a natural process would have done so).

36. Ford's account is the same as Olson's.

37. Cf. Ford 1988, ch. 6.

38. Ford 1988, pp. 171–2; italics original.

39. As was reported above, Ford's biological data indicates that spatial location plays a role in ultimately determining which cells form what entities. However, there is no metaphysical determining factor that dictates the proper spatial location of each cell. As cells move around in the blastocyst formation, nothing but random chance places them in whatever spatial location at which they end up.

40. The following paragraph highlights what these observed activities are.

41. Before implantation and the presence of a unified human biological organism, there is human biological material that contains human DNA, but is not informed by an intellective soul.

42. By distinguishing the different types of soul, I am not asserting that there are three souls present. I am merely marking out, as Aristotle and Aquinas do, the different sets of powers proper to the different types of soul. It should be understood, however, that there is *one* human soul that consists of all these sets of powers.

43. This is the same case as that which concerns the cells present in a human hair follicle. If the follicle is removed from the body, the cells will continue to live for a short period of time, but quickly perish because they are no longer sustained by the vegetative powers of the human soul.
44. Cf. Thomas Aquinas *Summa Theologiae* Ia., Q. 118, A. 2, ad. 2.
45. Cf. Tooley, pp. 166–8; n. 47 below.
46. Cf. Tooley, pp. 166–8; n. 47 below.
47. This contention that the zygote has only a passive potentiality for personhood is in agreement with Tooley's conception of 'passive potentiality' presented on pp. 166–8 of *Abortion and Infanticide*. Tooley states that an object 'x' has only a passive potentiality for acquiring a property (in this case, personhood) if other things could act upon it in such a way as to bring about the acquisition of the property. Tooley implies in this statement that 'x' does not contain within itself all of the *positive causal factors* (i.e., factors which are necessary for 'x' to do something, *viz.*, acquire the property of personhood). My Thomistic account agrees with this notion in that I hold that the human intellective soul must act on 'x' (i.e., the zygote) by informing it with the essential powers of personhood as active potentialities, which will be actualized as the developmental process continues, guided by the soul. Without the intellective soul, the zygote does not have all of the positive causal factors required for it to acquire personhood. In fact, it is lacking the *key* positive casual factor — the intellective soul.
48. Ford makes a note of this way of considering the zygote as bestowing upon it more moral weight than the sperm or unfertilized ovum: 'Others believe respect should be shown to a nonpersonal early embryo [zygote] which, on account of its genetically human life and genome, has the inherent developmental potential to become a human individual and person, thanks to the support of the mother's favorable uterine environment. It is claimed that this intrinsic potency and proximity to becoming an actual human individual and person suffice to establish a duty of moral respect. This claim is greater when it is coupled with a belief in the sanctity of the formative process established by God' (Ford 1998, pp. 292–3).
49. Shaw, p. 3.
50. In the *in vitro* procedure, a small number of fertilized zygotes (usually between 3 and 5) are injected into the woman's uterus. With luck, one may implant itself in the uterine wall and begin to develop into a human organism. The other, unimplanted, zygotes are naturally ejected from the woman's body during her period — spontaneous abortion. Those who have a strong pro-life ethic (e.g., the Roman Catholic Church) argue against the moral permissibility of *in vitro* fertilization for this reason, among others.
51. The Roman Catholic Church univocally rejects the use of any type of artificial contraceptive, irrespective of whether or not it functions as an abortifacient. Thus, my contention in this section is not addressed to the Church.
52. I cite these specific ethical systems because they are widely held by contemporary philosophers and the thesis of this article has moral implications for evaluating relevant actions within all three systems. I am grateful to Fr. John Kavanaugh, Dr. Janet Smith, Miguel Endara, and referees of this journal for comments on earlier drafts; as well as to participants at the 1999 Eastern Regional Meeting of the Society of Christian Philosophers who offered helpful comments.

QUESTIONS

1. Why does Jason Eberl think it is important to distinguish the question "when does a human life begin?" from the question "when does personhood begin"? What is his account of personhood and how does it differ from English's account?
2. What does Eberl mean when he says that his account of personhood considers both biological and metaphysical aspects of human persons? What are the aspects of each?
3. How does Eberl use the distinction between passive and active potentiality to determine the status of the sperm, the ovum, the fertilized zygote, and the human person? Do the sperm and ovum have the same passive potentiality in his account?

4. What does Eberl's account of personhood imply for the issues of procured abortion and abortifacient contraceptives? What does his account of personhood imply for stem cell research and *in vitro* fertilization?
5. Can Eberl's analysis be used to formulate policy with respect to these issues?

ABORTION THROUGH A FEMINIST ETHICS LENS

Susan Sherwin

Although abortion has long been an important issue in bioethics, the distinctive analysis of feminist ethics is generally overlooked in the discussion. Authors and readers commonly presume a familiarity with the feminist position and equate it with other liberal defenses of women's right to choose abortion; but feminist ethics yields a different analysis of the moral questions surrounding abortion from that usually offered by liberal abortion arguments.[1] Although feminists agree with some of the conclusions of nonfeminist arguments on abortion, they often disagree with the way the issues are formulated and with the reasoning that is offered in the mainstream literature.

Feminist reasoning in support of women's right to choose abortion is significantly different from the reasoning used by nonfeminist supporters of similar positions. For instance, most feminist accounts evaluate abortion policy within a broader framework, according to its place among the social institutions that support the subordination of women. In contrast, most nonfeminist discussions of abortion consider the moral or legal permissibility of abortion in isolation; they ignore (and thereby obscure) relevant connections with other social practices, including the ongoing power struggle within sexist societies over the control of women and their reproduction. Feminist arguments take into account the actual concerns that particular women attend to in their decision-making on abortion, such as the nature of a woman's feelings about her fetus, her relationships with her partner, other children she may have, and her various obligations to herself and others. In contrast, most nonfeminist discussions evaluate abortion decisions in their most abstract form (for example, questioning what sort of being a fetus is); from this perspective, specific questions of context are deemed irrelevant. In addition, nonfeminist arguments in support of choice about abortion are generally grounded in masculinist conceptions of freedom (such as privacy, individual choice, and individuals' property rights with respect to their own bodies), which do not meet the needs, interests, and intuitions of many of the women concerned.

Feminists also differ from nonfeminists in their conception of what is morally at issue with abortion. Nonfeminists focus exclusively on the morality and legality of performing abortions, whereas feminists insist that other issues, including the accessibility and delivery of abortion services, must also be addressed. Disputes about abortion arise even at the stage of defining the issue and setting the moral parameters for discussion. Although many nonfeminist bioethicists agree with feminists about which abortion policies should be supported, they tend to accept the proposals of the antifeminists as to what is morally at issue in developing that policy.

Thus although feminists welcome the support of nonfeminists in pursuing policies that grant women control over abortion decisions, they generally envision policies for this purpose that are very different from those considered by their nonfeminist sympathizers. Feminist ethicists promote a model for addressing the provision of abortion services different from the one conceived in traditional bioethical arguments. For example, Kathleen McDonnell urges feminists to develop an explicitly "'feminist morality' of abortion. . . . At its root it would be characterized by the deep appreciations of the complexities of life, the refusal to polarize and adopt simplistic formulas" (McDonnell 1984, 52). Here I propose one conception of the shape such an analysis should take.

Women and Abortion

The most obvious difference between feminist and nonfeminist approaches to abortion lies in the relative attention each gives in its analysis to the interests and experiences of women. Feminist analysis regards the effects of unwanted pregnancies on the lives of women individually and collectively as the central element in the moral examination of abortion; it is considered self-evident that the pregnant woman is the subject of principal concern in abortion decisions. In many nonfeminist accounts, however, not only is the pregnant woman not perceived as central, she is often rendered virtually invisible. Nonfeminist theorists, whether they support or oppose women's right to choose abortion, generally focus almost all their attention on the moral status of the fetus.[2]

In pursuing a distinctively feminist ethics, it is appropriate to begin with a look at the role of abortion in women's lives. The need for abortion can be very intense; no matter how appalling and dangerous the conditions, women from widely diverse cultures and historical periods have pursued abortions. No one denies that if abortion is not made legal, safe, and accessible in our society, women will seek out illegal and life-threatening abortions to terminate pregnancies they cannot accept. Antiabortion activists seem willing to accept this cost, although liberals definitely are not; feminists, who explicitly value women, judge the inevitable loss of women's lives that results from restrictive abortion policies to be a matter of fundamental concern.

Antiabortion campaigners imagine that women often make frivolous and irresponsible decisions about abortion, but feminists recognize that women have abortions for a wide variety of compelling reasons. Some women, for instance, find themselves seriously ill and incapacitated throughout pregnancy; they cannot continue in their jobs and may face insurmountable difficulties in fulfilling their responsibilities at home. Many employers and schools will not tolerate pregnancy in their employees or students, and not every woman is able to put her job, career, or studies on hold. Women of limited means may be unable to take adequate care of children they have already borne, and they may know that another mouth to feed will reduce their ability to provide for their existing children. Women who suffer from chronic disease, who believe themselves too young or too old to have children, or who are unable to maintain lasting relationships may recognize that they will not be able to care properly for a child when they face the decision. Some who are homeless, addicted to drugs, or diagnosed as carrying the AIDS virus may be unwilling to allow a child to enter the world with the handicaps that would result from the mother's condition. If the fetus is a result of rape or incest, then the psychological pain of carrying it may be unbearable, and the woman may recognize that her attitude to the child after birth will be tinged with bitterness. Some women learn that the fetuses that they carry have serious chromosomal anomalies and consider it best to prevent them from being born with a condition that is bound to cause them to suffer. Others, knowing the fathers to be brutal and violent, may be unwilling to subject a child to the beatings or incestuous attacks they anticipate; some may have no other realistic way to remove the child (or themselves) from the relationship.[3]

Finally, a woman may simply believe that bearing a child is incompatible with her life plans at the time. Continuing a pregnancy may have devastating repercussions throughout a woman's life. If the woman is young, then a pregnancy will likely reduce her chances of pursuing an education and hence limit her career and life opportunities: "The earlier a woman has a baby, it seems, the more likely she is to drop out of school; the less education she gets, the more likely she is to remain poorly paid, peripheral to the labor market, or unemployed, and the more children she will have" (Petchesky 1985, 150). In many circumstances, having a child will exacerbate the social and economic forces already stacked against a woman by virtue of her sex (and her race, class, age, sexual orientation, disabilities, and so forth). Access to abortion is necessary for many women if they are to escape the oppressive conditions of poverty.[4]

Whatever the specific reasons are for abortion, most feminists believe that the women concerned are in the best position to judge whether abortion is the appropriate response to a pregnancy. Because usually only the woman choosing abortion is properly situated to weigh all the relevant factors, most feminists resist attempts to offer general, abstract rules for determining when abortion is morally justified.[5] Women's personal deliberations about abortion involve contextually defined considerations that reflect their commitments to the needs and interests of everyone concerned, including themselves, the fetuses they carry, other members of their household, and so forth. Because no single formula is available for balancing these complex factors through all possible cases, it is vital that feminists insist on protecting each woman's right to come to her own conclusions and resist the attempts of other philosophers and moralists to set the agenda for these considerations. Feminists stress that women must be acknowledged as full moral agents, responsible for making moral decisions about their own pregnancies. Women may sometimes make mistakes in their moral judgments, but no one else can be assumed to have the authority to evaluate and overrule their judgments.[6]

Even without patriarchy, bearing a child would be a very important event in a woman's life, because it involves significant physical, emotional, social, and (usually) economic changes for her. The ability to exert control over the incidence, timing, and frequency of childbearing is often tied to a woman's ability to control most other things she values. Because we live in a patriarchal society, it is especially important to ensure that women have the authority to control their own reproduction.[7] Despite the diversity of opinion found among feminists on most other matters, most feminists agree that women must gain full control over their own reproductive lives if they are to free themselves from male dominance.[8]

Moreover, women's freedom to choose abortion is linked to their ability to control their own sexuality. Women's subordinate status often prevents them from refusing men sexual access to their bodies. If women cannot end the unwanted pregnancies that result from male sexual dominance, then their sexual vulnerability to particular men may increase, because caring for an(other) infant involves greater financial needs and reduced economic opportunities for women.[9] As a result, pregnancy often forces women to become dependent on particular men. Because a woman's dependence on a man is assumed to entail her continued sexual loyalty to him, restriction of abortion serves to commit women to remaining sexually accessible to particular men and thus helps to perpetuate the cycle of oppression.

In contrast to most nonfeminist accounts, feminist analyses of abortion direct attention to how women get pregnant. Those who reject abortion seem to believe that women can avoid unwanted pregnancies "simply" by avoiding sexual intercourse. These views show little appreciation for the power of sexual politics in a culture that oppresses women. Existing patterns of sexual dominance mean that women often have little control over their sexual lives. They may be subject to rape by their husbands, boyfriends, colleagues, employers, customers, fathers, brothers, uncles, and dates, as well as by strangers. Often the sexual coercion is not even recognized as such by the participants but is the price of continued "good will" — popularity, economic survival, peace, or simple acceptance. Many women have found themselves in circumstances where they do not feel free to refuse a man's demands for intercourse, either because he is holding a gun to her head or because he threatens to be emotionally hurt if she refuses (or both). Women are socialized to be compliant and accommodating, sensitive to the feelings of others, and frightened of physical power; men are socialized to take advantage of every opportunity to engage in sexual intercourse and to use sex to express dominance and power. Under such circumstances, it is difficult to argue that women could simply "choose" to avoid heterosexual activity if they wish to avoid pregnancy. Catharine MacKinnon neatly sums it up: "The logic by which women are supposed to consent to sex [is]: preclude the alternatives, then call the remaining option 'her choice'" (MacKinnon 1989, 192).

Furthermore, women cannot rely on birth control to avoid pregnancy. No form of contraception that is fully safe and reliable is available, other than sterilization; because women may wish only to avoid pregnancy temporarily, not permanently, sterilization is not always an acceptable choice. The pill and the IUD are the most effective contraceptive means offered, but both involve significant health hazards to women and are quite dangerous for some.[10] No woman should spend the thirty to forty years of her reproductive life on either form of birth control. Further, both have been associated with subsequent problems of involuntary infertility, so they are far from optimal for women who seek to control the timing of their pregnancies.

The safest form of birth control involves the use of barrier methods (condoms or diaphragms) in combination with spermicidal foams or jelly. But these methods also pose difficulties for women. They are sometimes socially awkward to use. Young women are discouraged from preparing for sexual activity that might never happen and are offered instead romantic models of spontaneous passion; few films or novels interrupt scenes of seduction for a partner to fetch contraceptives. Many women find their male partners unwilling to use barrier methods of contraception, and they often find themselves in no position to insist. Further, cost is a limiting factor for many women. Condoms and spermicides are expensive and are not covered under most health care plans.[11] Only one contraceptive option offers women safe and fully effective birth control: barrier methods with the backup option of abortion.[12]

From a feminist perspective, the central moral feature of pregnancy is that it takes place in women's bodies and has profound effects on women's lives. Gender-neutral accounts of pregnancy are not available; pregnancy is explicitly a condition associated with the female body.[13] Because only women experience a need for abortion, policies about abortion affect women uniquely. Therefore, it is important to consider how proposed policies on abortion fit into general patterns of oppression for women. Unlike nonfeminist accounts, feminist ethics demands that the effects of abortion policies on the oppression of women be of principal consideration in our ethical evaluations.

The Fetus

In contrast to feminist ethics, most nonfeminist analysts believe that the moral acceptability of abortion turns entirely on the question of the moral status of the fetus. Even those who support women's right to choose abortion tend to accept the premise of the antiabortion proponents that abortion can be tolerated only if we can first prove that the fetus lacks full personhood.[14] Opponents of abortion demand that we define the status of the fetus either as a being that is valued in the same way as other humans and hence is entitled not to be killed or as a being that lacks in all value. Rather than challenging the logic of this formulation, many defenders of abortion have concentrated on showing that the fetus is indeed without significant value (Tooley 1972, Warren 1973); others, such as L. W. Sumner (1981), offer a more subtle account that reflects the gradual development of fetuses and distinguishes between early fetal stages, where the relevant criterion for personhood is absent, and later stages, where it is present. Thus the debate often rages between abortion opponents, who describe the fetus as an "innocent," vulnerable, morally important, separate being whose life is threatened and who must be protected at all costs, and abortion supporters, who try to establish that fetuses are deficient in some critical respect and hence are outside the scope of the moral community. In both cases, however, the nature of the fetus as an independent being is said to determine the moral status of abortion.

The woman on whom the fetus depends for survival is considered as secondary (if she is considered at all) in these debates. The actual experiences and responsibilities of real women are not perceived as morally relevant to the debate, unless these women too, can be proved innocent by establishing that their pregnancies are a result of rape or incest.[15] In some contexts, women's role in gestation is literally reduced to that of "fetal containers"; the individual women disappear or are perceived simply as mechanical life-support systems.[16]

The current rhetoric against abortion stresses that the genetic makeup of the fetus is determined at conception and the genetic code is incontestably human. Lest there be any doubt about the humanity of the fetus, we are assailed with photographs of fetuses at various stages of development that demonstrate the early appearance of recognizably human characteristics, such as eyes, fingers, and toes. Modern ultrasound technology is used to obtain "baby's first picture" and stimulate bonding between pregnant women and their fetuses (Petchesky 1987). That the fetus in its early stages is microscopic, virtually indistinguishable to the untrained eye from fetuses of other species, and lacking in the capacities that make human life meaningful and valuable is not deemed relevant by the self-appointed defenders of the fetus. The antiabortion campaign is directed at evoking sympathetic attitudes toward a tiny, helpless being whose life is threatened by its own mother; the fetus is characterized as a being entangled in an adversarial relationship with the (presumably irresponsible) woman who carries it (Overall 1987). People are encouraged to identify with the "unborn child," not with the woman whose life is also at issue.

In the nonfeminist literature, both defenders and opponents of women's right to choose abortion agree that the difference between a late-term fetus and a newborn infant is "merely geographical" and cannot be considered morally significant. Daniel Callahan (1986), for instance, maintains a pro-choice stand but professes increasing uneasiness about this position in light of new medical and scientific developments that increase our knowledge of embryology and hasten the date of potential viability for fetuses; he insists that defenders of women's right to choose must come to terms with the question of the fetus and the effects of science on the fetus's prospects apart from the woman who carries it. Arguments that focus on the similarities between infants and fetuses, however, generally fail to acknowledge that a fetus inhabits a woman's body and is wholly dependent on her unique contribution to its maintenance, whereas a newborn is physically independent, although still in need of a lot of care.[17] One can only view the distinction between being in or out of a woman's womb as morally irrelevant if one discounts the perspective of the pregnant woman; feminists seem to be alone in recognizing the woman's perspective as morally important to the distinction.[18]

In antiabortion arguments, fetuses are identified as individuals; in our culture, which views the (abstract) individual as sacred, fetuses qua individuals are to be honored and preserved. Extraordinary claims are made to establish the individuality and moral agency of fetuses. At the same time, the women who carry these fetal individuals are viewed as passive hosts whose only significant role is to refrain from aborting or harming their fetuses. Because it is widely believed that a woman does not actually have to do anything to protect the life of her fetus, pregnancy is often considered (abstractly) to be a tolerable burden to protect the life of an individual so like us.[19]

Medicine has played its part in supporting these attitudes. Fetal medicine is a rapidly expanding specialty, and it is commonplace in professional medical journals to find references to pregnant women as "the maternal environment." Fetal surgeons now have at their disposal a repertoire of sophisticated technology that can save the lives of dangerously ill fetuses; in light of the excitement of such heroic successes, it is perhaps understandable that women have disappeared from their view. These specialists see the fetuses as their patients, not the women who nurture the fetuses. As the "active" agents in saving fetal lives (unlike the pregnant women, whose role is seen as purely passive), doctors perceive themselves as developing independent relationships with the fetuses they treat. Barbara Katz Rothman observes: "The medical model of pregnancy, as an essentially parasitic and vaguely pathological relationship, encourages the physician to view the fetus and mother as two separate patients, and to see pregnancy as inherently a conflict of interests between the two" (Rothman 1986, 25).

Perhaps even more distressing than the tendency to ignore the woman's agency altogether and view her as a passive participant in the medically controlled events of pregnancy and childbirth is the growing practice of viewing women as genuine threats to the well-being of the fetus. Increasingly, women are described as irresponsible or hostile toward their fetuses, and the relationship between them is characterized as adversarial. Concern for the well-being of the fetus is taken as license for doctors to intervene to ensure that women comply with medical "advice." Courts are called upon to enforce the doctors' orders when moral pressure alone proves inadequate, and women are being coerced into undergoing unwanted cesarean deliveries and technologically monitored hospital births (Annas 1982; Rodgers 1989; Nelson and Milliken 1990). Some states have begun to imprison women for endangering their fetuses through drug abuse and other socially unacceptable behaviors (Annas 1986). Mary Anne Warren reports that a bill was recently introduced in an Australian state that makes women liable to criminal prosecution "if they are found to have smoked during pregnancy, eaten unhealthful foods, or taken any other action which can be shown to have adversely affected the development of the fetus" (Warren 1989, 60).

In other words, some physicians have joined antiabortion campaigners in fostering a cultural acceptance of the view that fetuses are distinct individuals who are physically, ontologically, and socially separate from the women whose bodies they inhabit and that they have their own distinct interests. In this picture, pregnant women are either ignored altogether or are viewed as deficient in some crucial respect, and hence they can be subject to coercion for the sake of their fetuses. In the former case, the interests of the women concerned are assumed to be identical with those of the fetus; in the latter, the women's interests are irrelevant, because they are perceived as immoral, unimportant, or unnatural. Focus on the fetus as an independent entity has led to presumptions that deny pregnant women their roles as active, independent, moral agents with a primary interest in what becomes of the fetuses they carry. The moral question of the fetus's status is quickly translated into a license to interfere with women's reproductive freedom.

A Feminist View of the Fetus

Because the public debate has been set up as a competition between the rights of women and those of fetuses, feminists have often felt pushed to reject claims of fetal value, in order to protect women's needs. As Kathryn Addelson (1987) has argued, however, viewing abortion in this way "rips it out of the context of women's lives." Other accounts of fetal value are more plausible and less oppressive to women.

On a feminist account fetal development is examined in the context in which it occurs, within women's bodies, rather than in the isolation of imagined abstraction. Fetuses develop in specific pregnancies that occur in the lives of particular women. They are not individuals housed in generic female wombs or full persons at risk only because they are small and subject to the whims of women. Their very existence is relationally defined, reflecting their development within particular women's bodies; that relationship gives those women reason to be concerned about them. Many feminists argue against a perspective that regards the fetus as an independent being and suggest that a more accurate and valuable understanding of pregnancy would involve regarding the pregnant woman "as a biological and social unit" (Rothman 1986, 25).

On this view, fetuses are morally significant, but their status is relational rather than absolute. Unlike other human beings, fetuses do not have any independent existence; their existence is uniquely tied to the support of a specific other. Most nonfeminist accounts have ignored the relational dimension of fetal development and have presumed that the moral status of fetuses could be resolved solely in terms of abstract, metaphysical criteria of personhood as applied to the fetus alone (Tooley 1972; Warren 1973). Throughout much of the nonfeminist literature, commentators argue that some set of properties (such as genetic heritage, moral agency, self-consciousness, language use, or self-determination) will entitle all who possess it to be granted the moral status of persons. They seek some feature by which we can neatly divide the world into moral persons (who are to be valued and protected) and others (who are not entitled to the same group privileges).

This vision, however, misinterprets what is involved in personhood and what is especially valued about persons. Personhood is a social category, not an isolated state. Persons are members of a community, and they should be valued in their concrete, discrete, and different states as specific individuals, not merely as conceptually undifferentiated entities. To be a morally significant category, personhood must involve personality as well as biological integrity.[20] It is not sufficient to consider persons simply as Kantian atoms of rationality, because persons are embodied, conscious beings with particular social histories. Annette Baier has developed a concept of persons as "second persons," which helps explain the sort of social dimension that seems fundamental to any moral notion of personhood:

A person, perhaps, is best seen as one who was long enough dependent upon other persons to acquire the essential arts of personhood. Persons essentially are *second* persons, who grow up with other persons. . . . The fact that a person has a life *history*, and that a people collectively have a history depends upon the humbler fact that each person has a childhood in which a cultural heritage is transmitted, ready for adolescent rejection and adult discriminating selection and contribution. Persons come after and before other persons (Baier 1985: 84–5).

Persons, in other words, are members of a social community that shapes and values them, and personhood is a relational concept that must be defined in terms of interactions and relationships with others.[21]

Because humans are fundamentally relational beings, it is important to remember that fetuses are characteristically limited in the "relationships" in which they can "participate"; within those relationships, they can make only the most restricted "contributions."[22] After birth human beings are capable of a much wider range of roles in relationships with a broad variety of partners; that very diversity of possibility and experience leads us to focus on the abstraction of the individual as a constant through all these different relationships. Until birth, however, no such variety is possible, so the fetus must be understood as part of a complex entity that includes the woman who currently sustains the fetus and who will, most likely, be principally responsible for it for many years to come.

A fetus is a unique sort of human entity, then, for it cannot form relationships freely with others, and others cannot readily form relationships with it. A fetus has a primary and particularly intimate sort of "relationship" with the woman in whose womb it develops; connections with any other persons are necessarily indirect and must be mediated through the pregnant woman. The relationship that exists between a woman and her fetus is clearly asymmetrical, because she is the only party to it who is capable of even considering whether the interaction should continue; further, the fetus is wholly dependent on the woman who sustains it, whereas she is quite capable of surviving without it.

Most feminist views of what is valuable about persons reflect the social nature of individual existence. No human, especially no fetus, can exist apart from relationships; efforts to speak of the fetus itself, as if it were not inseparable from the woman in whom it develops, are distorting and dishonest. Fetuses have a unique physical status — within and dependent on particular women. That gives them also a unique social status. However much some might prefer it to be otherwise, no one other than the pregnant woman in question can do anything to support or harm a fetus without doing something to the woman who nurtures it. Because of this inexorable biological reality, the responsibility and privilege of determining a fetus's specific social status and value must rest with the woman carrying it.

Many pregnancies occur to women who place a very high value on the lives of the particular fetuses they carry and choose to see their pregnancies through to term, despite the possible risks and costs involved; it would be wrong of anyone to force such a woman to terminate her pregnancy. Other women, or some of these same women at other times, value other things more highly (for example, their freedom, their health, or previous responsibilities that conflict with those generated by the pregnancies), and so they choose not to continue their pregnancies. The value that women ascribe to individual fetuses varies dramatically from case to case and may well change over the course of any particular pregnancy. The fact that fetal lives can neither be sustained nor destroyed without affecting the women who support them implies that whatever value others may attach to fetuses generally or to specific fetuses individually should not be allowed to outweigh the ranking that is assigned to them by the pregnant women themselves.

No absolute value attaches to fetuses apart from their relational status, which is determined in the context of their particular development. This is not the same, however, as saying that they have no value at all or that they have merely instrumental value, as some liberals suggest. The value that women place on their own fetuses is the sort of value that attaches to an emerging human relationship.

Nevertheless, fetuses are not persons, because they have not developed sufficiently in their capacity for social relationships to be persons in any morally significant sense (that is, they are not yet second persons). In this way they differ from newborns, who immediately begin to develop into persons by virtue of their place as subjects in human relationships; newborns are capable of some forms of communication and response. The moral status of fetuses is determined by the nature of their primary relationship and the value that is created there. Therefore, feminist accounts of abortion emphasize the importance of protecting women's rights to continue or to terminate pregnancies as each sees fit.

The Politics of Abortion

Feminist accounts explore the connections between particular social policies and the general patterns of power relationships in our society. With respect to abortion in this framework, Mary Daly observes that "one hundred percent of the bishops who oppose the repeal of antiabortion laws are men and one hundred percent of the people who have abortions are women. . . . To be comprehended accurately, they [arguments against abortion] must be seen within the context of sexually hierarchical society" (Daly 1973, 106).

Antiabortion activists appeal to arguments about the unconditional value of life. When we examine their rhetoric more closely, however, we find other ways of interpreting their agenda. In addition to their campaign to criminalize abortion, most abortion opponents condemn all forms of sexual relations outside of heterosexual marriage, and they tend to support patriarchal patterns of dominance within such marriages. Many are distressed that liberal abortion policies support permissive sexuality by allowing women to "get away with" sex outside of marriage. They perceive that ready access to abortion supports women's independence from men.[23]

Although nonfeminist participants in the abortion debates often discount the significance of its broader political dimensions, both feminists and antifeminists consider them crucial. The intensity of the antiabortion movement correlates closely with the increasing strength of feminism in achieving greater equality for women. The original American campaign against abortion can be traced to the middle of the nineteenth century, that is, to the time of the first significant feminist movement in the United States (Luker 1984). Today abortion is widely perceived as supportive of increased freedom and power for women. The campaign against abortion intensified in the 1970s, which was a period of renewed interest in feminism. As Rosalind Petchesky observes, the campaign rested on some powerful symbols: "To feminists and antifeminists alike, it came to represent the image of the 'emancipated woman' in her contemporary identity, focused on her education and work more than on marriage or childbearing; sexually active outside marriage and outside the disciplinary boundaries of the parental family; independently supporting herself and her children; and consciously espousing feminist ideas" (Petchesky 1984, 241). Clearly, much more than the lives of fetuses is at stake in the power struggle over abortion.

When we place abortion in the larger political context, we see that most of the groups active in the struggle to prohibit abortion also support other conservative measures to maintain the forms of dominance that characterize patriarchy (and often class and racial oppression as well). The movement against abortion is led by the Catholic church and other conservative religious institutions, which explicitly endorse not only fetal rights but also male dominance in the home and the church. Most opponents of abortion also oppose virtually all forms of birth control and all forms of sexuality other than monogamous, reproductive sex; usually, they also resist having women assume positions of authority in the dominant public institutions (Luker 1984). Typically, antiabortion activists support conservative economic measures that protect the interests of the privileged classes of society and ignore the needs of the oppressed and disadvantaged (Petchesky 1985). Although they stress their commitment to preserving life, many systematically work to dismantle key social programs that provide life necessities to the underclass. Moreover, some current campaigns against abortion retain elements of the racism that dominated the North American abortion literature in the early years of the twentieth century, wherein abortion was opposed on the grounds that it amounted to racial suicide on the part of whites.[24]

In the eyes of its principal opponents, then, abortion is not an isolated practice; their opposition to abortion is central to a set of social values that runs counter to feminism's objectives. Hence antiabortion activists generally do not offer alternatives to abortion that support feminist interests in overturning the patterns of oppression that confront women. Most deny that there are any legitimate grounds for abortion, short of the need to save a woman's life — and some are not even persuaded by this criterion (Nicholson 1977). They believe that any pregnancy can and should be endured. If the mother is unable or unwilling to care for the child after birth, then they assume that adoption can be easily arranged.

It is doubtful, however, that adoptions are possible for every child whose mother cannot care for it. The world abounds with homeless orphans; even in the industrialized West, where there is a waiting list for adoption of healthy (white) babies, suitable homes cannot always be found for troubled adolescents, inner-city, AIDS babies, or many of the multiply handicapped children whose parents may have tried to care for them but whose marriages broke under the strain.

Furthermore, even if an infant were born healthy and could be readily adopted, we must recognize that surrendering one's child for adoption is an extremely difficult act for most women. The bond that commonly forms between women and their fetuses over the full term of pregnancy is intimate and often intense; many women find that it is not easily broken after birth. Psychologically, for many women adoption is a far more difficult response to unwanted pregnancies than abortion. Therefore, it is misleading to describe pregnancy as merely a nine-month commitment; for most women, seeing a pregnancy through to term involves a lifetime of responsibility and involvement with the resulting child and, in the overwhelming majority of cases, disproportionate burden on the woman through the child-rearing years. An ethics that cares about women would recognize that abortion is often the only acceptable recourse for them.

Expanding the Agenda

The injunction of feminist ethics to consider abortion in the context of other issues of power and oppression means that we need to look beyond the standard questions of its moral and legal acceptability. This implies, for instance, that we need to explore the moral imperatives of ensuring that abortion services are actually available to all women who seek them. Although medically approved abortions are technically recognized as legal (at least for the moment) in both Canada and the United States, many women who need abortions cannot obtain them; accessibility is still associated with wealth and privilege in many regions.[25] In Canada vast geographical areas offer no abortion services at all, so unless the women of those regions can afford to travel to urban clinics, they have no meaningful right to abortion. In the United States, where there is no universal health insurance, federal legislation (under the Hyde amendment) explicitly denies the use of public money for abortions. Full ethical discussion of abortion reveals the necessity of removing the economic, age, and racial barriers that currently restrict access to medically acceptable abortion services.[26]

The moral issues extend yet further. Feminism demands respect for women's choices; even if the legal and financial barriers could be surpassed, this condition may remain unmet. The focus of many political campaigns for abortion rights has been to make abortion a matter of medical, not personal, choice, suggesting that doctors (but not necessarily women) can be trusted to choose responsibly. Feminists must insist on respect for women's moral agency. Therefore feminism requires that abortion services be provided in an atmosphere that is supportive of the choices that women make. This could be achieved by offering abortions in centers that deal with all matters of reproductive health in an open, patient-centered manner, where respectful counseling on all aspects of reproductive health is available.[27]

Furthermore, the moral issues surrounding abortion include questions of how women are treated when they seek abortions. All too frequently hospital-based abortions are provided by practitioners who are uneasy about their role and treat the women involved with hostility and resentment.[28] Health care workers involved in providing abortions must recognize that abortion is a legitimate option that should be carried out with respect and concern for the physical, psychological, and emotional well-being of the patient. In addition, we need to turn our moral attention to the effects of antiabortion protests on women. Increasingly, many antiabortion activists have personalized their attacks and focused their energies on harassing the women who enter and leave abortion clinics, thereby requiring them to pass a gauntlet of hostile protesters to obtain abortions. Such arrangements are not conducive to positive health care, so these protests, too, must be subject to moral criticism within the ethics of health care.

Feminist ethics promotes the value of reproductive freedom, which is defined as the condition under which women are able to make truly voluntary choices about their reproductive lives. Women must have control over their reproduction if patriarchal dominance over women is to be brought to an end. In addition to reliable and caring abortion services, then, women also need access to safe and effective birth control, which would provide them with other means of avoiding pregnancy.[29]

Moreover, we must raise questions about the politics of sexual domination in this context. Many men support women's right to abortion because they perceive that if women believe that they can engage in intercourse without having to accept an unwanted pregnancy, they will become more sexually available. Some of the women who oppose abortion resist it for this very reason; they do not want to support a practice that increases women's sexual vulnerability. Feminists need to develop an analysis of reproductive freedom that includes sexual freedom as it is defined by women, not men. Such an analysis would, for example, include women's right to refuse sex. Because this right can only be assured if women have power equal to men's and are not subject to domination because of their sex, women's freedom from oppression is itself an element of reproductive freedom.

Finally, it is important to stress that feminist accounts do not deny that fetuses have value. They ask that fetuses be recognized as existing within women's pregnancies and not as separate, isolated entities. Feminists positively value fetuses that are wanted by the women who carry them; they vigorously oppose practices that force women to have abortions they do not want. No women should be subjected to coerced abortion or sterilization. Women must be assured of adequate financial and support services for the care of their children, so that they are not forced to abort fetuses that they would otherwise choose to carry. Further, voluntarily pregnant women should have access to suitable pre- and postnatal care and nutrition, lest wanted fetuses be unnecessarily harmed or lost.

Feminists perceive that far more could be done to protect and care for fetuses if the state directed its resources toward supporting women who choose to continue their pregnancies, rather than draining those resources to police the women who try to terminate undesired pregnancies. Unlike their conservative counterparts, feminists recognize that caring for the women who maintain the lives of fetuses is not only a more legitimate policy than is regulating them but also probably more effective at ensuring the health and well-being of more fetuses and, ultimately, of more infants.

In sum, then, feminist ethics demands that moral discussions of abortion reflect a broader agenda than is usually found in the arguments put forth by bioethicists. Only by reflecting on the meaning of ethical pronouncements on actual women's lives and the connections that exist between judgments on abortion and the conditions of domination and subordination can we come to an adequate understanding of the moral status of abortion in a particular society.

NOTES

1. Much of the philosophic literature on abortion characterizes the possible moral positions on the issue as falling within three slots along a continuum: conservative (no abortions are morally acceptable, except, perhaps, when the woman's life is at stake), moderate (abortions are permissible under certain circumstances), or liberal (abortion should be available "on demand"). See, e.g., Wertheimer (1971) or Sumner (1981).
2. Technically, the term "fetus" does not cover the entire period of development. Medical practitioners prefer to distinguish between differing stages of development with such terms as "conceptus," "embryo" (and, recently, "pre-embryo"), and "fetus." Because these distinctions are not relevant to the discussion here, I follow the course common to discussions in bioethics and feminism and use the term "fetus" to cover the entire period of development from conception to the end of pregnancy through either birth or abortion.
3. Bearing a child can keep a woman within a man's sphere of influence against her will. The Canadian news media were dominated in the summer of 1989 by the story of Chantel Daigle, a Quebec woman who faced injunctions granted to her former boyfriend by two lower courts against her choice of abortion before she was finally given permission for abortion by the Supreme Court of Canada. Daigle's explanation to the media of her determination to abort stressed her recognition that if she was forced to bear this child, she would never be free from the violent father's involvement in her life.
4. Feminists believe that it is wrong of society to make childbearing a significant cause of poverty in women, but the reality of our social and economic structures in North America is that it does. In addition to their campaigns for greater reproductive freedom for women, feminists also struggle to ensure that women receive greater support in child-rearing; in efforts to provide financial stability and support services to those who provide care for children, feminists would welcome the support of those in the antiabortion movement who sincerely want to reduce the numbers of abortions.
5. Among the exceptions here, see Overall (1987), who seems willing to specify some conditions under which abortion is immoral (78–79).
6. Critics continue to base the debate on the possibility that women might make frivolous abortion decisions; hence they want feminists to agree to setting boundaries on acceptable grounds for choosing abortion. Feminists, however, should resist this injunction. There is no practical way of

drawing a line fairly in the abstract; cases that may appear "frivolous" at a distance often turn out to be substantive when the details are revealed. There is no evidence to suggest that women actually make the sorts of choices worried critics hypothesize about: for example, the decision of a woman eight-months pregnant to abort because she wants to take a trip or gets in "a tiff" with her partner. These sorts of fantasies, on which demands to distinguish between legitimate and illegitimate personal reasons for choosing abortion rest, reflect an offensive conception of women as irresponsible. They ought not to be perpetuated. Women seeking moral guidance in their own deliberations about choosing abortion do not find such hypothetical discussions of much use.

7. In her monumental historical analysis of the early roots of Western patriarchy, Lerner (1986) determined that patriarchy began in the period from 3100 to 600 B.C., when men appropriated women's sexual and reproductive capacity; the earliest states entrenched patriarchy by institutionalizing the sexual and procreative subordination of women to men.

8. Some women claim to be feminist yet oppose abortion; some even claim to offer a feminist argument against abortion (see Callahan 1987). For reasons that I develop in this chapter, I do not believe a thorough feminist analysis can sustain a restrictive abortion policy, although I do acknowledge that feminists need to be wary of some of the arguments proposed in support of liberal policies on abortion.

9. The state could do a lot to ameliorate this condition. If it provided women with adequate financial support, removed the inequities in the labor market, and provided affordable and reliable child care, pregnancy need not so often lead to a woman's dependence on a particular man. That it does not do so is evidence of the state's complicity in maintaining women's subordinate position with respect to men.

10. The IUD has proven so hazardous and prone to lawsuits, it has been largely removed from the market in the United States (Pappert 1986). It is also disappearing from other Western countries but is still being purchased by population-control agencies for use in the developing world (LaCheen 1986).

11. For a more detailed discussion of the limitations of current contraceptive options, see Colodny (1989); for the problems of cost, see esp. 34–35.

12. See Petchesky (1985), esp. chap. 5, where she documents the risks and discomforts associated with pill use and IUDs and the increasing rate at which women are choosing the option of diaphragm or condom, with the option of early, legal abortions as backup.

13. Eisenstein (1988) has developed an interesting account of sexual politics, which identifies the pregnant body as the central element in the cultural subordination of women. She argues that pregnancy (either actual or potential) is considered the defining characteristic of all women, and because it is not experienced by men, it is classified as deviance and considered grounds for different treatment.

14. Thomson (1971) is a notable exception to this trend.

15. Because she was obviously involved in sexual activity, it is often concluded that the noncoerced woman is not innocent but guilty. As such, she is judged far less worthy than the innocent being she carries within her. Some who oppose abortion believe that an unwanted pregnancy is a suitable punishment for "irresponsible" sex.

16. This seems reminiscent of Aristotle's view of women as flowerpots where men implant the seed with all the important genetic information and the movement necessary for development and the woman's job is that of passive gestation, like the flowerpot. See Whitbeck (1973) and Lange (1983).

17. Some are so preoccupied with the problem of fetuses being "stuck" in women's bodies that they seek to avoid this geographical complication altogether, completely severing the ties between woman and fetus. For example, Bernard Nathanson, an antiabortion activist with the zeal of a new convert, eagerly anticipates the prospect of artificial wombs as alternative means for preserving the lives of fetuses and "dismisses the traditional reverence for birth as mere 'mythology' and the act of birth itself as an 'insignificant event'" (cited in McDonnell 1984, 113).

18. Cf. Warren (1989) and Tooley (1972).

19. The definition of pregnancy as a purely passive activity reaches its ghoulish conclusion in the increasing acceptability of sustaining brain-dead women on life-support systems to continue their functions as incubators until the fetus can be safely delivered. For a discussion of this trend, see Murphy (1989).

20. This apt phrasing is taken from Petchesky (1985), 342.
21. E.g., Held (1987b) argues that personhood is a social status, created by the work of mothering persons.
22. Fetuses are almost wholly individuated by the women who bear them. The fetal "contributions" to the relationship are defined by the projections and interpretations of the pregnant woman in the latter stages of pregnancy, if she chooses to perceive fetal movements in purposeful ways (e.g., "it likes classical music, spicy food, exercise").
23. See Luker (1984), esp. chaps. 6 and 7, and Petchesky (1985), esp. chaps. 7 and 8, for documentation of these associations in the U.S. antiabortion movement and Collins (1985), esp. chap. 4, and McLaren and McLaren (1986) for evidence of similar trends in the Canadian struggle.
24. See McLaren and McLaren (1986) and Petchesky (1985).
25. When abortion was illegal, many women nonetheless managed to obtain abortions, but only the relatively privileged women with money were able to arrange safe, hygienic abortions; poor women were often constrained to rely on dangerous, unacceptable services. In the United States court rulings have ensured that rich and middle-class women have, for the moment, relatively easy access to well-run clinics and hospitals, but because public hospitals are mostly unwilling to offer abortion services and federal law prohibits the use of Medicaid funding for abortion, many poor women still find legal, safe abortions out of reach (Petchesky 1985). In Canada, too, abortion services are most readily available to middle-class, urban, mature women. This suggests that financial circumstances may be a more significant factor in determining women's access to abortion than abortion's legal status.
26. Some feminists suggest we seek recognition of the legitimacy of nonmedical abortion services. This would reduce costs and increase access dramatically, with no apparent increase in risk as long as services were provided by trained, responsible practitioners who were concerned with the well-being of their clients. It would also allow the possibility of increasing women's control over abortion. See, e.g., McDonnell (1984).
27. For a useful model of such a center, see Van Wagner and Lee (1989).
28. A poignant collection of some women's unfortunate experiences with hospital abortions is offered in *Telling Our Secrets*, produced by CARAL (1990).
29. Therefore, the Soviet model, in which abortions have been relatively accessible, is also unacceptable, because there the unavailability of birth control forces women to rely on multiple abortions to control their fertility.

QUESTIONS

1. Susan Sherwin distinguishes between feminist and non-feminist approaches to abortion. Based on her way of making the distinction, would you classify the approaches to abortion of English and Eberl as feminist or non-feminist? Why?
2. What is it to be a 'second person'? Is this a helpful idea for understanding the morality of abortion?
3. Compare Sherwin's account of personhood with Eberl's account, and in particular, with his account of the different role that the sperm and ovum have in determining the status of the zygote.
4. Sherwin argues that women facing an unwanted pregnancy should be free to make their decision to have an abortion in light of their own values. What are the key steps in her reasoning that lead her to that conclusion?
5. Does Sherwin offer convincing reasons for thinking that the development of fetal medicine should not play a decisive role in determining the rights of the unborn? Compare her views on this issue with those of Eberl.
6. Do you agree that, if the abortion debate is broadened in the way Sherwin suggests in her closing paragraph, the case for limiting access to abortion is seriously undermined? In your view, should the debate be broadened in this way?

7. In what ways can Sherwin's feminist approach shed light on the moral dilemmas presented by new reproductive technologies?

BIOETHICS FOR CLINICIANS: ASSISTED REPRODUCTIVE TECHNOLOGIES

Laura Shanner and Jeffrey Nisker

The waiting room walls display Picasso's *Maternité* and photo collages of babies born in this busy fertility clinic. Rachel sits alone, glad that Ray could not leave work today. Both in their late 20s, they assumed it would be easy to have a baby when they felt ready. After several months of trying, Rachel has just had another period. She feels depressed, discouraged and guilty that she is unable to become pregnant. She feels like a failure. She appreciates the many choices open to her but still feels that she really has only one: to have a child or be somehow "incomplete." She and Ray are increasingly irritable when together, so they withdraw into themselves. Their sexual relationship grows more formulaic each month. They are embarrassed when family, friends and coworkers ask "when?" or "why is it taking so long?" Rachel no longer sees her friends just as friends, but as mothers or almost-mothers; she increasingly declines social invitations to avoid child-centred conversation. She is beginning to panic that she will never get pregnant. After seeing a television documentary on infertility and reproductive technologies, Rachel asked her family physician to refer her here, to an infertility specialist.

What are assisted reproductive technologies?

The first assisted reproductive technology (ART) was noncoital insemination, which may be intrauterine or intravaginal, using sperm either from a donor or from the woman's partner. Sperm has been almost exclusively from anonymous donors, as opposed to sperm from known donors, since 1970.

Hormonal ovarian stimulation can be used to treat anovulation or may increase the likelihood of conception in idiopathic infertility by increasing the number of mature oocytes. Ovarian stimulation may also accompany intrauterine insemination.

With in vitro fertilization (IVF), multiple ova are matured through hormonal stimulation and retrieved by transvaginal ultrasound-guided needle aspiration. Fertilization occurs in the laboratory either by adding sperm to the culture medium or by injecting a single sperm into the ovum (intracytoplasmic sperm injection).[1] Resulting embryos may be transferred to the woman's uterus or cryopreserved for future use. In rare cases preimplantation genetic diagnosis may be used for specific genetic disorders.[2] Embryos may be transferred to the woman who produced the ovum (standard IVF), to another infertile woman (embryo donation) or to a woman who is contracted to carry the pregnancy for someone else (a "surrogate" mother). Embryos may also be donated for research.

Future reproductive possibilities include the creation of offspring genetically identical to an existing or deceased person (reproductive cloning), and the development of fetuses in mechanical wombs (ectogenesis).

From "Bioethics for clinicians: 26. Assisted reproductive technologies," *Reprinted from Canadian Medical Association Journal, 164 (11). May 29, 2001, pages 1589–1594 by permission of the publisher, © 2001 Canadian Medical Association.*

Why are assisted reproductive technologies important?

ARTs can be very helpful for certain patients. However, ethical concerns have been raised both about the inherent nature of certain techniques and the specific contexts in which many techniques are used.[3] ARTs are unique among medical procedures because they aim specifically to create new individuals and family relationships. The ethics of ARTs must be understood within this social context, which is often characterized by tension among competing interests.

Ethics

Family relationships

Although most infertility treatments are sought by a woman and man in a close relationship, as many as 5 adults may play parenting roles in ARTs: the genetic mother and father (ovum and sperm providers), the gestational mother and the intended social parents. Each party has his or her own interests and vulnerabilities. Any offspring who result are the most vulnerable of all, since they could not consent to the arrangements that will profoundly shape their developing identities. The interests of potential offspring must therefore always be central to reproductive choices.

IVF allows a woman to gestate a fetus genetically unrelated to her, either as the recipient of an ovum or embryo donation or as a contracted surrogate mother. Both genetic and gestational mothers are biological mothers, but neither is consistently identified as the legal mother.[4,5] A recent US case involving all 5 possible reproductive collaborators left the resulting child without any legal parent until she was 3 years old.[6] Other family variations — such as women who bear their own genetic grandchildren, postmenopausal pregnancies and reproduction by members of same-sex couples — challenge social, legal and historical norms. These new possibilities often leave family members without social or legal support.

Donor anonymity protects the privacy of donors and recipients, but it undermines the interests of offspring regarding their genetic medical history and ancestral heritage. We should consider carefully the role of secrecy in close family relationships and guard against the temptation to cut moral corners to ensure a supply of donors. Child-centred reproduction favours openness of donor records, but families often struggle with whether, when and how to share donor information with the offspring.

Preimplantation genetic diagnosis allows parents to diagnose conditions before pregnancy has been initiated, thus avoiding situations in which mid-trimester pregnancy termination might be sought.[2] Despite consensus that genetic diagnosis should focus on severe diseases rather than traits such as sex or appearance,[7] the definitions of "disease" remain unclear. Another question is whether the advantages of avoiding abortion warrant the extension of IVF with preimplantation genetic diagnosis to fertile couples.

Informed choice

Informed consent[8] requires full disclosure and fair representation of all potential medical, social and emotional outcomes and risks. Unfortunately, we often lack sufficient information to provide the full disclosure needed for truly informed choice.[9] Supportive counselling can assist patients to make these profoundly meaningful life choices[10,11,12] and to prepare realistically for suboptimal outcomes such as medical complications, multiple births, pregnancy loss and having no pregnancy at all.

Many clinicians try to create an optimistic atmosphere through the choice of the program name, the decorative use of baby pictures and the wording of their informational materials. Although these positive images may support patients through a trying procedure, they may also become manipulative. An emphasis on success rates masks failure rates; both sides of this truth are essential to the patient's decision to proceed. News media may also skew perceptions of new treatments with references to "miracle babies" and medical breakthroughs while downplaying associated risks and uncertainties.

Research

Research on the efficacy, long-term safety and psychosocial implications of most ARTs remains incomplete, but recent studies are beginning to address these concerns. Although many of the techniques questioned by the Royal Commission on New Reproductive Technologies[7] have since been proven effective,[13,14] new techniques are rapidly introduced into clinical use without patients (and many clinicians) appreciating that they are still experimental. Explicit clarification must be made among procedures that are experimental, innovative, common but not yet validated, and truly validated, with special attention to possible risks. Key factors that motivate research — including desires to overcome infertility, to be helpful, to achieve professional advancement and to acquire financial gain — have resulted in rapid technical advancements that outpace social and ethical reflection.

Research on embryos must be understood as a women's health matter, since embryos cannot be acquired without first retrieving ova from women. When ova or embryos are sought for use in research, the fundamental ethical consideration must therefore be the well-being of the donor.[15] The research question must be compelling and scientifically important, not merely a matter of interest. Clinicians must avoid potential conflicts of interest between the patient's or donor's best medical care and the interests of research or financial gain.[16,17] The demand for ova and embryos for research is expected to increase as a result of recent advances in stem cell research for possible tissue transplantation.[18,19,20]

Fertility protection has received very little research funding to date. Medical research, education and practice should emphasize the protection and restoration of reproductive health, where possible, above methods that merely circumvent infertility.[7]

Gender issues

The desire to have a child is significantly influenced by societal assumptions about women's mothering role and, to a lesser extent, about men's virility as a mark of masculinity.[10,11] Gender issues are thus central to the ethics of assisted reproduction. Until recent generations, women were denied most education and employment opportunities, thus leaving very few opportunities for financial and social success outside of motherhood. This "pronatalist" social imperative for women to have children dates to ancient times and retains its power despite critical scrutiny in 20th century feminism.[3,4,21,22] Indeed, ARTs have made it harder for some women to end their pursuit of maternity.[10,23] The social imperative to reproduce may have important implications for informed consent.

For many infertile people, reproductive expectations prompt devastating feelings of inadequacy and abnormality.[10,11,12] These perceptions are often gender-specific ("pregnancy makes a woman complete" or "real men get women pregnant"), but they may also be expressed as general perceptions of failure. Some aspects of treatment may also cause gender-specific distress: many men feel humiliated at producing a sperm sample through masturbation,[12] and some women feel that repeated internal exams are similar to sexual violence.[10]

Embryo status

The ethical and legal status of human embryos has long been a core ethical concern in ARTs.[24] The range of legal definitions include embryos as persons, embryos as property or objects, and embryos as a unique category.[5] The Supreme Court of Canada has consistently held that fetuses are "unique" but not persons under the law, and it would likely treat embryos similarly. Health Canada's working group on embryo research also adopted the third option, identifying human embryos as having special status as a human entity but less than children or adults, and it recommended that embryos not be created specifically for research purposes.[15] Religious views must be considered both in policy contexts and in helping specific patients select their most appropriate treatment options. All major religions attach special meaning to embryos, although significant disagreement exists about the details of embryo status. The Vatican considers embryos to be persons from conception and rejects IVF because it separates sex and reproduction.[25] Conservative and Orthodox Judaism both attach greater but varying significance to embryos after the 40th day of conception, while both the Sunni and Shia branches of Islam believe that ensoulment (the condition for being a person) occurs around the fourth month of gestation.[26] Protestant Christian views vary widely, considering personhood to arise anywhere from conception to birth.

Access

The distress caused by infertility clearly deserves a helpful and sympathetic response. The difficulty lies in ensuring access to medically necessary and appropriate treatment while avoiding inappropriate overuse at both micro (individual patient) and macro (health policy) levels. Restriction on public funding for ARTs promotes suboptimal treatment for less wealthy women,[27] and free enterprise often promotes the use of incompletely tested technology. Providing the safest and best available treatment for a patient's needs is essential to ethical health care service.

At a macro level, accountability and justice in the distribution of resources[28] create new tensions and frustrations in a publicly funded health care system. Decisions regarding whether to cover specific health care interventions must be justified by continual evidence-based assessment of the intervention's safety and effectiveness, the full costs of the intervention to the health care system (e.g., total costs per successful outcome and the costs of complications)[29,30] and the availability and comparative results of other options. Values-based assessments include balancing competing health care priorities and the right of fair access to the best available interventions across all types of health care needs. The social effects of increased usage, such as reinforcement of pronatalist attitudes in the case of assisted reproduction, must also be considered. Canada has one of the few remaining publicly funded health care systems that does not cover IVF. One author of this paper is committed to full IVF funding for all patients, whereas the other struggles to reconcile fair access to treatment with competing policy considerations.

Social factors have also been used as criteria for access to ARTs. Concern for the well-being of future children stemming from clear evidence (e.g., a prospective parent's history of violence or substance abuse) must be distinguished from social biases that might be unfounded (e.g., same-sex couples or single parents). The community's interest to avoid supporting more children on welfare must be balanced against interests in parenting regardless of socioeconomic status. Pregnancy in women of advanced age challenges stereotypes of "normal" motherhood and raises the concern that the parents' good health and life expectancies may end before the child reaches maturity.

Commercializing Reproduction

Markets in human gametes, embryos and pregnancy raise widespread ethical alarm.[31] Despite chronic and life-threatening shortages of blood and transplant organs, the sale of these tissues is widely rejected and is in most instances illegal.[5] Normally, the only appropriate payment for tissue donations is reimbursement for direct expenses such as travel. It is unclear why reproductive tissues are treated differently.

Women who provide reproductive tissues or services tend to be from lower socioeconomic groups, whereas recipients tend to be more socially and economically advantaged. Reducing treatment costs by "sharing" ova or embryos[32] is a form of sale: the donor's treatment is paid for by the recipient in exchange for acquisition of gametes or embryos. "Sharing" programs may also undermine informed consent, as the strong desire to have children (and thus to attempt IVF) may overshadow the implications of donation for both the donor and recipient.

Gamete providers who are influenced by financial or other considerations rather than informed commitment to donor parenting may later regret the possible creation of unknown offspring. Such regrets may be especially severe if the donor later experiences infertility or, in sharing programs, a failure of IVF to result in the birth of a child.

Law

Although most Western countries have adopted legislation to govern ARTs, Canada to date largely has not. The handling of sperm is regulated under the Food and Drug Act of 1996, the Excise Tax Act (for imported sperm) and the Family Acts of Quebec, Newfoundland and the Yukon Territory.[5] The Supreme Court of Canada ruled in *ter Neuzen* v. *Korn*[33] that no implied warranty exists for sperm quality under the British Columbia Sale of Goods Act. The Human Tissue Gift Act in several provinces would seem to extend to sold or donated reproductive tissues, but it has not been enforced in fertility centres.[5] Quebec is the only province to regulate ovum donation, stipulating the gestational mother as the legal mother of the offspring.[34]

Restricted access to ARTs may raise Charter challenges regarding a right to reproduce.[5,35,36] Ontario is the only province to fund IVF treatments, but only in cases of bilateral blockage of the fallopian tubes in accordance with recommendations of the Royal Commission on New Reproductive Technologies.[7] The provinces do cover several other forms of assisted reproduction and fertility restoration, such as intrauterine insemination, non-IVF ovarian stimulation and surgical repair of varicoceles or fallopian tubes. In 1999 a Nova Scotia couple argued that infertility is a disability under section 15 of the Charter, making it discriminatory to exclude intracytoplasmic sperm injection from medicare coverage.[37] The discrimination question remains unsettled, as the trial court noted that other infertility treatments are available to infertile people. Both trial and appellate courts, however, affirmed the provincial right to limit medicare coverage of specific procedures on the grounds of expense, effectiveness and medical necessity. The plaintiffs have appealed to the Supreme Court of Canada.

Policy

Government

The Royal Commission on New Reproductive Technologies (1989–1993) issued 293 recommendations and emphasized a need for an ongoing, federal-level regulatory body.[7] Necessary legislation has been stalled since then by multiple cabinet shuffles and 3 federal elections. In July 1995, then-Minister of Health Diane Marleau asked for a voluntary moratorium on specific ART practices including transgenic research, ectogenesis, cloning, the creation of embryos specifically for research and commercialization of human reproductive tissues. In 1996, federal Bill C-47 would have created criminal penalties for the practices listed in the moratorium, but the bill expired without a vote before a federal election. An Advisory Committee on Reproductive and Genetic Technologies was also established in 1996 to advise the minister in drafting new legislation, and several additional working groups have advised Health Canada on topics such as embryo research[15] and genetic testing. In April 2000, Minister of Health Allan Rock announced that comprehensive legislation to regulate ARTs would be introduced that year, but once again it was stalled by an autumn election. In April 2001, he announced that it would be introduced in May to the House of Commons Standing Committee on Health.

Professional Associations

The Canadian Fertility and Andrology Society (CFAS) and the Society of Obstetricians and Gynaecologists of Canada (SOGC) developed guidelines for practitioners of assisted reproduction in 1990[38] and 1998.[39] In conjunction with the Canadian Council on Health Services Accreditation, the CFAS and the SOGC are also developing accreditation guidelines for ART laboratories. The Canadian Medical Association, the CFAS and the SOGC were concerned with the criminalization of procedures as outlined in Bill C-47 and continue to discuss their recommendations for regulation with the federal government.

Empirical Studies

Canada has no registry for the comprehensive collection of data on IVF outcomes according to diagnosis and age. The United Kingdom's Human Fertilisation and Embryo Authority (HFEA) 1999 annual report[40] listed the following live birth rates across 24 889 IVF cycles initiated during 1997/98: 14.9% among women with tubal disease, 16.3% among women with endometriosis and 17.2% among couples with unexplained infertility. The live birth rate for 9295 cycles of intracytoplasmic sperm injection was 20.7%. The University of Ottawa infertility program's statistics for 422 IVF cycles initiated in 1999 reported a live birth rate per initiated cycle of 29.0% among women under 35 years of age, 18.4% among women aged 35–37, 9.2% among those aged 38–40 and 0% among women over 40 years of age.[41]

Because multiple births increase the risk of perinatal death, low birth weight and neonatal complications, the physician has an obligation to minimize these risks.[30,42,43] Ovulation induction with menotropins, especially if IVF is not used, greatly increases the risk of multiple pregnancy. Patients must be monitored carefully to ensure that multiple pregnancy does not occur; ovulation-inducing drugs, therefore, should not be prescribed by clinicians without sufficient training in their use.[43] The 1999 HFEA report indicated that 47% of babies born from IVF come from multiple pregnancy, a statistic largely unchanged from 1994.[40] To reduce multiple pregnancy, it has been strongly recommended that no more than 3 embryos be returned to the uterus at one time; no more than 2 would, except in unusual circumstances, be best for younger women with ovaries that respond well to menotropins.[44]

Ovarian hyperstimulation syndrome may pose serious and even life-threatening complications for women undergoing ovarian stimulation.[45,46] Lacking conclusive evidence, an increased risk of ovarian cancer has been reported[47] and more recently disputed.[48] Small risks of punctured bladder, damaged blood vessels and pelvic inflammatory disease accompany ovum retrieval.

No increase in observable major abnormalities has been identified in children conceived in vitro, but certain genetic causes of infertility may be passed to offspring conceived by means of intracytoplasmic sperm injection.[49]

How Should I Approach Assisted Reproductive Technologies in Practice?

Infertility and ARTs pose challenges not just for fertility specialists, but also for general practitioners, gynecologists and others providing care for people with fertility concerns.

Women initiate most fertility inquiries, both because they see their physicians more frequently and because social norms assign them greater reproductive responsibility. Their male partners should never be ignored, however, either medically or emotionally.

As in all areas of medicine, invasive or potentially dangerous treatments must be reserved until options with less risk have been exhausted. Contributors to infertility, including alcohol, medications, diet, stress, occupational exposures and other lifestyle factors should be addressed in both partners. Education about reproductive and sexual physiology may increase the chances of conception for some patients. Underlying health problems that contribute to infertility should be investigated and treated appropriately.

For most patients, waiting a year or longer before initiating treatment is appropriate, but advanced age and specific indicators of infertility may suggest accelerated investigation and treatment. Most patients will need reassurance and attention to general health promotion in the interim.

To ensure truly informed consent, all fertility centres should present easily understood tables of live birth rates across all initiated cycles (not merely those that proceeded to ovum retrieval or embryo transfer)[7] specified by cause of infertility and age. Maternal and perinatal complications should be included. Primary care physicians and specialists alike must assist patients to acquire and appreciate these data.

Supportive counselling must be readily available from primary care physicians[12] as well as from professionals with expertise in the psychosocial dynamics of family, marriage and infertility. Both partners should be encouraged to address personal concerns (e.g., self-esteem), external pressures from family or others, gender expectations, religious or ethnic beliefs, and options such as adoption or not having children. It is especially important for patients to prepare for potential negative outcomes such as medical side effects, miscarriage, perinatal complications, multiple births, social and legal complications involving reproductive collaborators, or the failure of treatments to produce the healthy child they desire to raise. Sadly, ARTs more often than not fail to result in a live birth.

Referring physicians must ensure detailed, ongoing communication with the specialists and remain important allies as the patients decide whether to attempt, continue or discontinue ARTs. Although negative outcomes are understandably devastating, even the birth of a child may not fully relieve the distress of being unable to reproduce "normally," and continuing support may be needed for the family.[50]

The Case

Rachel's case illustrates both the psychosocial pain of the imperative to reproduce and the influence of media, family and even the clinic's decor on the patient's thinking. Ray's distress is of note and should not be ignored. Physicians play important roles in supporting those who wish to become parents and in educating patients about impediments to fertilization and ways to promote conception. Both Rachel and Ray should be examined thoroughly to rule out known causes of infertility and to address any underlying health concerns or lifestyle choices that inhibit fertility. Whether or not a specific cause of infertility is found, the couple should be encouraged to promote general good health and to enjoy their sexual relationship. However, treatment should not be denied on the grounds that the cause of the infertility is unknown. Supportive counselling should be offered to assist Rachel and Ray to cope with their current stresses and maintain a positive self-image, whatever their decision about pursuing treatment. If a referral to a specialist is made, assistance should be given to help them reach truly informed and voluntary choices about how to proceed and to prepare for the stresses and possible outcomes of ART protocols.

NOTES

1. Martin RH, Nisker JA, Daya S, Miron P, Parish B. Intracytoplasmic sperm injection. Policy statement: ethical issues in assisted reproduction. *J Soc Obstet Gynaecol Can* 1999;21(4):369-75.
2. Nisker JA, Gore-Langton RE. Pre-implantation genetic diagnosis: a model of progress and concern. *J Soc Obstet Gynaecol Can* 1995;17(3):247-62.
3. Purdy LM. Assisted reproduction. In: Kuhse H, Singer P, editors. *A companion to bioethics*. Oxford (UK): Blackwell; 1998. p. 163-72.
4. Rothman BK. *Recreating motherhood*. New York: WW Norton; 1989.
5. Mykitiuk R, Wallrap A. Regulating reproductive technologies in Canada. In: Downie JG, Caulfield TA, editors. *Canadian health law and policy*. Markham (ON): Butterworth; 1999. p. 303-52.
6. *Marr. of Buzzanca* [1998]. 3/10/98 CA 4/3 G022147.
7. Royal Commission on New Reproductive Technologies. *Proceed with care: final report*. Ottawa: The Commission; 1993.
8. Etchells E, Sharpe G, Walsh P, Williams JR, Singer PA. Bioethics for clinicians: 1. Consent. *CMAJ* 1996;155(2):177-80. Available: www.cma.ca/cmaj/vol-155/0177.htm
9. Shanner L. Informed consent and inadequate medical information [letter]. *Lancet* 1995;346:251.
10. Zolbrod A. *Men, women and infertility: intervention and treatment strategies*. New York: Lexington Books; 1993.
11. Leiblum SR, editor. *Infertility: psychological issues and counseling strategies*. New York: John Wiley & Sons; 1997.
12. Michaels E. FPs can play important role in treatment of infertile patients, counsellors say. *CMAJ* 1996;154(10):1559-61. Available: www.cma.ca/cmaj/vol-154/1559.htm
13. Alsalili M, Yuzpe A, Tummon I, Parker J, Martin J, Daniel S, et al. Cumulative pregnancy rates and pregnancy outcome after in-vitro fertilization: > 5000 cycles at one centre. *Hum Reprod* 1995;10(2):470-4.
14. Pinheiro RC, Lambert J, Bernard F, Mauffette F, Miron P. Effectiveness of in vitro fertilization with intracytoplasmic sperm injection for severe male infertility. *CMAJ* 1999;161(11):1397-401. Available: www.cma.ca/cmaj/vol-161/issue-11/1397.htm

15. Discussion Group on Embryo Research. *Research on human embryos in Canada: final report.* Ottawa: Health Policy Division, Health Canada; 1995.

16. Weijer C, Dickens B, Meslin EM. Bioethics for clinicians: 10. Research ethics. *CMAJ* 1997;156(8):1153-7. Available: www.cma.ca/cmaj/vol-156/issue-8/1153.htm

17. Lemmens T, Singer PA. Bioethics for clinicians: 17. Conflict of interest in research, education and patient care. *CMAJ* 1998;159(8):960-5. Available: www.cma.ca/cmaj/vol-159/issue-8/0960.htm

18. Shanner L. *Embryonic stem cell research: Canadian policy and ethical considerations.* Ottawa: Health Canada; 2001.

19. National Bioethics Advisory Commission. *Ethical issues in human stem cell research.* Vol 1. Rockville (MD): The Commission; 1999.

20. Canadian Institutes of Health Research. *Human stem cell research: opportunities for health and ethical perspectives. A discussion paper.* Ottawa: The Institute; 2001. Available: www.cihr.ca/news/forums/stem_cell/issues_e.shtml (accessed 2001 Apr 24).

21. Sherwin S. *No longer patient: feminist ethics and health care.* Philadelphia: Temple University; 1992.

22. Purdy LM. *Reproducing persons: issues in feminist bioethics.* Ithaca (NY): Cornell University; 1996.

23. Kozolanka K. Giving up: the choice that isn't. In: Klein RE, editor. *Infertility: women speak out about their experiences of reproductive medicine.* London: Pandora; 1989. p. 121-30.

24. Steinbock B. *Life before birth: the moral and legal status of embryos and fetuses.* New York: Oxford University Press; 1992.

25. Congregation for the Doctrine of the Faith. *Instruction on respect for human life in its origin and on the dignity of procreation.* Vatican City; 1987.

26. National Bioethics Advisory Commission. Summary of presentations on religious perspectives relating to research involving human stem cells, May 7, 1999 [Appendix E]. In: *Ethical issues in human stem cell research.* Vol 1. Rockville (MD): The Commission; 1999.

27. Nisker JA. Rachel's ladders or how societal situation determines reproductive therapy. *Hum Reprod* 1996;11(6):1162-7.

28. McKneally MF, Dickens BM, Meslin EM, Singer PA. Bioethics for clinicians: 13. Resource allocation. *CMAJ* 1997;157(2):163-7. Available: www.cma.ca/cmaj/vol-157/issue-2/0163.htm

29. Neumann PJ, Gharib SD, Weinstein MC. The cost of a successful delivery with in vitro fertilization. *N Engl J Med* 1994;331(4):239-43.

30. Callahan TL, Hall JE, Ettner SL, Christiansen CL, Greene MF, Crowlet WF. The economic impact of multiple-gestation pregnancies and the contribution of assisted-reproduction techniques to their incidence. *N Engl J Med* 1994;331(4): 244-9.

31. Cohen CB. Selling bits and pieces of humans to make babies: *The gift of the Magi* revisited. *J Med Philos* 1999;24(3):288-306.

32. Nisker JA. In quest of the perfect analogy for using in vitro patients as oocyte donors. *Womens Health Issues* 1997;7(4):241-7.

33. *ter Neuzen* v. *Korn* [1995] 3 SCR 674.

34. *Civil Code of Quebec* (CCQ). art. 53 [ad. 1991, c.64].

35. Shanner L. The right to procreate: when rights claims have gone wrong. *McGill Law Journal* 1995;40(4):823-7.

36. Ontario Law Reform Commission. *The prohibition of artificial contraception technologies: Is there a right to procreate? Report on human artificial reproduction and related matters.* Toronto: Ministry of the Attorney General; 1985.

37. *Cameron* v. *Nova Scotia (Attorney General)* [1999]. NSJ. No. 33, DRS 99-01803, SH No. 137396.

38. Reid RL. *Ethical considerations of the new technologies: a report of the combined ethics committee of the Canadian Fertility and Andrology Society and the Society of Obstetricians and Gynaecologists of Canada.* Toronto: Ribosome; 1990.

39. Martin RH, Nisker JA. Ethical issues in assisted reproduction. *J Soc Obstet Gynaecol Can* 1998;20(13):1235-41.

40. Human Fertilisation and Embryology Authority. *Annual reports.* London (UK): The Authority.

41. Assisted reproductive technology pregnancy success rates, 1999. Ottawa: Fertility Centre,

University of Ottawa; 1999. Available: www.conceive.org/success.htm#ART (accessed 2001 Apr 24).

42. Barrett J, Bocking A. Management of twin pregnancies [two parts]. *J Soc Obstet Gynaecol Can* 2000;22:519-29, 607-10.

43. Klotzko AJ. Medical miracle or medical mischief? The saga of the McCaughey septuplets. *Hastings Cent Rep* 1998;28(3):5-8.

44. Templeton A, Morris JK. Reducing the risk of multiple births by transfer of two embryos after in vitro fertilization. *N Engl J Med* 1998;339(9):573-7.

45. Abramov Y, Elchalal U, Schenker JG. Severe OHSS: an "epidemic" of severe OHSS. A price we have to pay? *Hum Reprod* 1999;14(9):2181-3.

46. World Health Organization. *Summary report: consultation on the place of in vitro fertilization in infertility care*. Copenhagen: WHO; 1990 June 18-22.

47. *Long-term effects on women from assisted conception*. Canberra: National Health and Medical Research Council, Commonwealth of Australia; 1995.

48. Venn A, Watson L, Bruinsma F, Giles G, Healy D. Risk of cancer after use of fertility drugs with in-vitro fertilisation. *Lancet* 1999;354:1586-90.

49. Page DC, Silber S, Brown LG. Men with infertility caused by AZFc deletion can produce sons by intracytoplasmic sperm injection, but are likely to transmit the deletion and infertility. *Hum Reprod* 1999;14(7):1722-6.

50. Harper P, Aitken J, editors. *A child is not the cure for infertility: National Workshop on Infertility, report of proceedings*; Sept 1981. Melbourne (Australia): Institute of Family Studies, Citizen's Welfare Service of Victoria; 1982.

QUESTIONS

1. Laura Shanner and Jeffrey Nisker argue that the ethics of assisted reproductive technologies must be understood within a social context in which they create new individuals and family relationships and have implications for them. How does this argument differ from Eberl's evaluation of the moral implications of assisted reproductive procedures such as in vitro fertilization?

2. What implications for family relationships are highlighted by Shanner and Nisker? Which implications do you take to be positive? Which negative? How might these implications inform policies with respect to specific assisted reproductive technologies?

3. What do Shanner and Nisker mean when they suggest that the desire to have a child is significantly influenced by assumptions about gender roles? What does this account suggest about gender roles? What does it suggest about policies with respect to assisted reproductive technologies?

4. Are issues of financial and social access to assisted reproductive technologies relevant to questions of policy? Why or why not?

5. How has the Shanner and Nisker analysis of assisted reproductive technologies influenced your thinking about the case of the infertile Rachel that opens this reading?

HOUSE OF COMMONS OF CANADA BILL C-13: AN ACT RESPECTING ASSISTED HUMAN REPRODUCTION

Her Majesty, by and with the advice and consent of the Senate and House of Commons of Canada, enacts as follows:

SHORT TITLE

1. This Act may be cited as the *Assisted Human Reproduction Act*.

PRINCIPLES

2. The Parliament of Canada recognizes and declares that

(*a*) the benefits of assisted human reproductive technologies and related research for individuals and for society in general can be most effectively secured by taking appropriate measures for the protection and promotion of human health, safety, dignity and rights in the use of these technologies and in related research;

(*b*) the health and well-being of children born through the application of these technologies must be given priority in all decisions respecting their use;

(*c*) while all persons are affected by these technologies, women more than men are directly and significantly affected by their application;

(*d*) the principle of free and informed consent must be promoted and applied as a fundamental condition of the use of human reproductive technologies;

(*e*) trade in the reproductive capacities of women and men and the exploitation of children, women and men for commercial ends raise health and ethical concerns that justify their prohibition; and

(*f*) human individuality and diversity, and the integrity of the human genome, must be preserved and protected.

INTERPRETATION AND APPLICATION

3. The following definitions apply in this Act.

"Agency" means the Assisted Human Reproduction Agency of Canada established by subsection 21(1).

"assisted reproduction procedure" means any controlled activity referred to in section 10 that is performed for the purpose of creating a human being.

"chimera" means

(*a*) an embryo into which a cell of any non-human life form has been introduced; or

(*b*) an embryo that consists of cells of more than one embryo, foetus or human being.

"consent" means fully informed and freely given consent that is given in accordance with the applicable law governing consent.

"controlled activity" means an activity that may not be undertaken except in accordance with sections 10 to 12.

"donor" means

(*a*) in relation to human reproductive material, the individual from whose body it was obtained, whether for consideration or not; and

(*b*) in relation to an *in vitro* embryo, a donor as defined in the regulations.

"embryo" means a human organism during the first 56 days of its development following fertilization or creation, excluding any time during which its development has been suspended, and includes any cell derived from such an organism that is used for the purpose of creating a human being.

"foetus" means a human organism during the period of its development beginning on the fifty-seventh day following fertilization or creation, excluding any time during which its development has been suspended, and ending at birth.

"gene" includes a nucleotide sequence, and an artificially created gene or nucleotide sequence.

"genome" means the totality of the deoxyribonucleic acid sequence of a particular cell.

"health reporting information" means information provided under this Act respecting

(*a*) the identity, personal characteristics, genetic information and medical history of donors of human reproductive material and *in vitro* embryos, persons who have undergone assisted reproduction procedures and persons who were conceived by means of those procedures; and

(*b*) the custody of donated human reproductive materials and *in vitro* embryos and the uses that are made of them.

"human clone" means an embryo that, as a result of the manipulation of human reproductive material or an *in vitro* embryo, contains the same nuclear deoxyribonucleic acid sequence as is found in the cell of a living or deceased human being, foetus or other embryo.

"human reproductive material" means a sperm, ovum or other human cell or a human gene, and includes a part of any of them.

"hybrid" means

(*a*) a human ovum that has been fertilized by a sperm of a non-human life form;

(*b*) an ovum of a non-human life form that has been fertilized by a human sperm;

(*c*) a human ovum into which the nucleus of a cell of a non-human life form has been introduced;

(*d*) an ovum of a non-human life form into which the nucleus of a human cell has been introduced; or

(*e*) a human ovum or an ovum of a non-human life form that otherwise contains haploid sets of chromosomes from both a human being and a non-human life form.

"*in vitro* embryo" means an embryo that exists outside the body of a human being.

"licence" means a licence issued in respect of a controlled activity or premises under section 40.

"Minister" means the Minister of Health.

"ovum" means a human ovum, whether mature or not.

"sperm" means a human sperm, whether mature or not.

"surrogate mother" means a female person who carries an embryo or foetus derived from the genes of a donor or donors with the intention of surrendering the child at birth to a donor or another person.

4.   This Act is binding on Her Majesty in right of Canada or a province.

PROHIBITED ACTIVITIES
5. (1) No person shall knowingly

(*a*) create a human clone, or transplant a human clone into a human being;

(*b*) create an *in vitro* embryo for any purpose other than creating a human being or improving or providing instruction in assisted reproduction procedures;

(*c*) for the purpose of creating a human being, create an embryo from a cell or part of a cell taken from an embryo or foetus or transplant an embryo so created into a human being;

(*d*) maintain an embryo outside the body of a woman after the fourteenth day of its development following fertilization or creation, excluding any time during which its development has been suspended;

(*e*) for the purpose of creating a human being, perform any procedure or provide, prescribe or administer any thing that would ensure or increase the probability that an embryo will be of a particular sex, or that would identify the sex of an *in vitro* embryo, except to prevent, diagnose or treat a sex-linked disorder or disease;

(*f*) alter the genome of a cell of a human being or *in vitro* embryo such that the alteration is capable of being transmitted to descendants;

(*g*) transplant a sperm, ovum, embryo or foetus of a non-human life form into a human being;

(*h*) for the purpose of creating a human being, make use of any human reproductive material or an *in vitro* embryo that is or was transplanted into a non-human life form;

(*i*) create a chimera, or transplant a chimera into either a human being or a non-human life form; or

(*j*) create a hybrid for the purpose of reproduction, or transplant a hybrid into either a human being or a non-human life form.

(2) No person shall offer to do, or advertise the doing of, anything prohibited by this section.

(3) No person shall pay or offer to pay consideration to any person for doing anything prohibited by this section.

6. (1) No person shall pay consideration to a female person to become a surrogate mother, offer to pay such consideration or advertise that it will be paid.

(2) No person shall accept consideration for arranging for the services of a surrogate mother, offer to make such an arrangement for consideration or advertise the arranging of such services.

(3) No person shall pay consideration to another person to arrange for the services of a surrogate mother, offer to pay such consideration or advertise the payment of it.

(4) No person shall counsel or induce a female person to become a surrogate mother, or perform any medical procedure to assist a female person to become a surrogate mother, knowing or having reason to believe that the female person is under 18 years of age.

7. (1) No person shall purchase, offer to purchase or advertise for the purchase of sperm or ova from a donor or a person acting on behalf of a donor.

(2) No person shall

(*a*) purchase, offer to purchase or advertise for the purchase of an *in vitro* embryo; or

(*b*) sell, offer for sale or advertise for sale an *in vitro* embryo.

(3) No person shall purchase, offer to purchase or advertise for the purchase of a human cell or gene from a donor or a person acting on behalf of a donor, with the intention of using the gene or cell to create a human being or of making it available for that purpose.

(4) In this section, "purchase" or "sell" includes to acquire or dispose of in exchange for property or services.

8. (1) No person shall make use of human reproductive material for the purpose of creating an embryo unless the donor of the material has given written consent, in accordance with the regulations, to its use for that purpose.

(2) No person shall remove human reproductive material from a donor's body after the donor's death for the purpose of creating an embryo unless the donor of the material has given written consent, in accordance with the regulations, to its removal for that purpose.

(3) No person shall make use of an *in vitro* embryo for any purpose unless the donor has given written consent, in accordance with the regulations, to its use for that purpose.

9. No person shall obtain any sperm or ovum from a donor under 18 years of age, or use any sperm or ovum so obtained, except for the purpose of preserving the sperm or ovum or for the purpose of creating a human being that the person reasonably believes will be raised by the donor.

CONTROLLED ACTIVITIES

10. (1) No person shall, except in accordance with the regulations and a licence, alter, manipulate or treat any human reproductive material for the purpose of creating an embryo.

(2) No person shall, except in accordance with the regulations and a licence, alter, manipulate, treat or make any use of an *in vitro* embryo.

(3) No person shall, except in accordance with the regulations and a licence, obtain, store, transfer, destroy, import or export

   (*a*) a sperm or ovum, or any part of one, for the purpose of creating an embryo; or

   (*b*) an *in vitro* embryo, for any purpose.

11. (1) No person shall, except in accordance with the regulations and a licence, combine any part or any proportion of the human genome specified in the regulations with any part of the genome of a species specified in the regulations.

(2) The following definitions apply in this section.

"human genome" means the totality of the deoxyribonucleic acid sequence of the human species.

"species" means any taxonomic classification of non-human life.

12. (1) No person shall, except in accordance with the regulations and a licence,

   (*a*) reimburse a donor for an expenditure incurred in the course of donating sperm or an ovum;

   (*b*) reimburse any person for an expenditure incurred in the maintenance or transport of an *in vitro* embryo; or (*c*) reimburse a surrogate mother for an expenditure incurred by her in relation to her surrogacy.

(2) No person shall reimburse an expenditure referred to in subsection (1) unless a receipt is provided to that person for the expenditure.

13. No person who is licensed to undertake a controlled activity shall undertake it in any premises except in accordance with a licence permitting the use of the premises for that controlled activity.

SUGGESTIONS FOR FURTHER READING

Supreme Court Decision

* *Chantal Daigle v. Jean-Guy Tremblay*. Supreme Court of Canada [1989] 2 S.C.R. This judgment resulted from a request made by Jean-Guy Tremblay for an injunction by the Court to prevent Chantal Daigle, with whom he had conceived a child, from having an abortion. The injunction was granted by a Quebec Court and confirmed by the Quebec Court of Appeal. The Supreme Court unanimously overruled the decision taken by the lower courts.

Reports and Web Sites

* Canada. Royal Commission on New Reproductive Technologies. *Proceed with Care: Final Report of the Royal Commission on New Reproductive Technologies* (Ottawa: Supply and Services Canada, 1993). In addition to the final two-volume report, this Royal Commission chaired by Patricia Baird produced fifteen volumes of Research Studies and separately authored reports and bibliographies. One of these reports, volume 1 of the Research Studies called *New Reproductive Technologies: Ethical Aspects*, was designed to set the ethical framework for examining the issues.
* Laura Shanner, *Embryonic Stem Cell Research: Canadian Policy and Ethical Considerations*. A Report for Health Canada, Policy Division. March 31, 2001. This article provides a detailed description of stem cell research and a framework for considering the ethical issues.
* Health Canada. Legal Services. *Guide to the Proposals for Legislation Governing Assisted Human Reproduction*. April 2001.
* United States Conference of Catholic Bishops. Department of Pro-Life Activities. URL: http://www.usccb.org/prolife/index.htm
  This Web site provides information about the Catholic Church's position on various issues such as abortion, contraception, partial birth abortion, fetal research, *in vitro* fertilization, stem cell research, and cloning as well as euthanasia and assisted suicide.
* Religious Coalition for Reproductive Choice. URL: http://www.rcrc.org/
  The Religious Coalition for Reproductive Choice states that its goal is to "work to ensure reproductive choice through the moral power of religious communities. The Coalition seeks to give clear voice to the reproductive issues of people of color, those living in poverty, and other underserved populations. Comprised of national Christian, Jewish and

other religious organizations, the Religious Coalition provides opportunities for religious people to examine and articulate their own pro-choice positions."

Books

- L.W. Sumner, *Abortion and Moral Theory* (Princeton, N.J.: Princeton University Press, 1981). This book, referred to by Justice Wilson in the *Morgentaler* decision, defends a view similar to that of Jane English. Sumner argues for a developmental view of the point at which a human fetus becomes a human being with a right to life.
- Maureen Muldoon (ed.). *The Abortion Debate in the United States and Canada: A Source Book* (New York: Garland, 1991). This book is a compendium of sources of material relevant to the abortion debate. Its chapter headings are: "Demographics, Sociological Research, and Opinions"; "Philosophical Perspectives on Abortion"; "The Positions of Religious Denominations"; "The Advocates and Advocate Groups"; and "Law and Politics." This last chapter identifies the significant court decisions and legislative initiatives over the past two decades in both the United States and Canada.
- Christine Overall, *Ethics and Human Reproduction: A Feminist Analysis* (Boston: Unwin Hyman, 1987). In this book, the author reviews the development of new reproductive technologies and their implications for women. The purpose of the book is to explore the value context appropriate for the decisions and policy development that the new reproductive technologies are making unavoidable.
- Christine Overall (ed.), *The Future of Human Reproduction* (Toronto: Women's Press, 1989). This anthology gathers together a number of important essays by feminist scholars on the topic of human reproduction.
- Ian Gentles (ed.), *A Time to Choose Life: Women, Abortion and Human Rights* (Toronto: Stoddart, 1990). This book is a collection of articles that reflect on the implications for the development of social policy in Canada of the Supreme Court judgment striking down the abortion law. The various authors argue that in spite of the Supreme Court judgment and perhaps even because of it, Canadians should be concerned with the protection of prenatal human life.
- Susan Wolf (ed.), *Feminism & Bioethics: Beyond Reproduction* (New York: Oxford University Press, 1996). This book is a collection of articles by prominent feminist bioethicists on topics ranging from abortion to assisted reproduction to euthanasia to health care more generally.

Articles

- Judith Jarvis Thomson, "A Defense of Abortion," *Philosophy & Public Affairs*, vol. 1, no. 1 (Fall 1971). A classic article on abortion in which Thomson grants, for the sake of argument, that the fetus is a person from conception onwards, but then argues that it does not follow from this that abortion is morally wrong. By imagining cases analogous to that of the mother and fetus in which the two principles of protection of life and moral autonomy come into conflict, Thomson appeals to the reader's sense that terminating a life may not always be morally wrong. In many cases, she argues, the mother's right to decide what happens in and to her body overrides the right to life of the fetus.
- Edward W. Keyserlingk, "The Unborn Child's Right to Prenatal Care," *Health Law in Canada*, Fall, 1982. This article points to the apparent inconsistency of legal systems that allow abortion without legal impediment while extending the protection of the law to unborn children in other respects.

- John T. Noonan Jr., "An Almost Absolute Value in Human History," in *The Morality of Abortion: Legal and Historical Perspectives* (Cambridge, Mass.: Harvard University Press, 1970). The book in which this article appears is a widely quoted study of the history of abortion and its legal treatment. The book contains a number of other articles by prominent commentators and is one of the early collections of philosophical essays to address what has become a topic of wide philosophical debate.
- Donald B. Marquis, "Why Abortion is Immoral," *Journal of Philosophy*, v. 86 (1989). By examining the deficiencies in the arguments concerning the status of the fetus on both sides of the debate, Marquis argues that "abortion is, except possibly in rare cases, seriously immoral, that it is in the same moral category as killing an innocent human being."
- Michael Tooley, "In Defense of Abortion and Infanticide," *Philosophy & Public Affairs*, v. 2, no. 2 (Fall 1972). Tooley argues that neither abortion nor infanticide are matters of moral concern because neither fetuses nor very young infants have the right to life.
- Mary Ann Warren, "On the Moral and Legal Status of Abortion," *The Monist*, v. 57, no. 1 (January 1973). In this article, Warren provides criteria that define personhood and then argues that a fetus does not fall within the parameters of what constitutes a "person."
- Celia Wolf-Devine, "Abortion and the 'Feminine Voice,'" *Public Affairs Quarterly*, vol. 3, no. 3 (July 1989). Celia Wolf-Devine summarizes arguments presented by those feminists who defend the idea that women have a distinctive "feminine voice" that reasons about moral problems in terms of our interconnectedness with others and our responsibilities to care for others. Wolf-Devine then locates a tension in a feminist defence of abortion that appears to support individual choice at the same time as it emphasizes our responsibilities to care for others.
- Ronald Dworkin, "Playing God: Genes, Clones, and Luck," in the 6th edition of *Morality and Moral Controversies* edited by John Arthur (New Jersey: Prentice-Hall, 2002). In this article, Dworkin lays out the arguments for and against the use of genetic engineering.
- Bonnie Steinbock, "Surrogate Motherhood as Prenatal Adoption," in the 6th edition of *Morality and Moral Controversies* edited by John Arthur (New Jersey: Prentice-Hall, 2002). In this article, Steinbock addresses arguments for the use of surrogate arrangements and moral objections to the practice of surrogacy.

Chapter 3

Capital Punishment

Introduction

Our discussion of abortion and euthanasia directed our attention to three principles: the *protection-of-life principle*, the *avoidance-of-suffering principle*, and the *moral-autonomy* principle. However, as we reflected on why these issues are important, some fundamental characteristics of human existence have begun to emerge. First, human beings need the cooperation of others in meeting even their most basic needs. When that cooperation is not forthcoming, survival is not a possibility. Secondly, each of us is remarkably vulnerable to violence: We are easily hurt or killed. And our capacity to protect ourselves against unprovoked attack without the help of others is quite limited. In view of these facts, securing the conditions under which people can see to their needs and pursue their various goals and objectives free from unprovoked attack is essential both for individuals and for the communities in which they live.

How is this accomplished? One way is to win agreement on basic principles whose purposes are to protect human life and to create social conditions that will permit and encourage cooperation. We have already identified three such principles. It would not be difficult to add to the list. For example, values such as honesty, fairness, generosity, loyalty, and courtesy also play important roles in creating conditions under which people can live together in harmony, satisfy their basic needs, and accomplish their various goals.

Another way of accomplishing this task is to create a legal system. It is for this reason that many of the most important issues that arise in modern societies have both a legal and a moral dimension.

The need to have people respect basic moral and legal rules and values is the source of a fundamental moral question: What actions are individuals and groups justified in taking to protect themselves from those who refuse to respect what are widely accepted as fundamental rules or values governing social interaction? For example, what are people entitled to do when they encounter others who are prepared to abuse, coerce, or even kill in the pursuit of their objectives?

These questions can arise in three different contexts: First, what actions are individuals justified in taking in the name of self-defence or in the defence of others? Second, what actions are communities justified in taking to ensure that the law is respected? Finally, what actions are groups, communities, or nations justified in taking in the name of self-defence?

These are thematic questions that are addressed in different ways in several chapters in the book. The third question, for example, is central to the discussion of the use of military force and the justification of war which we examine in Chapter Ten. The purpose of this chapter is to explore the second of these questions. Specifically, is it morally acceptable, using powers accorded to the state, to impose capital punishment on those who fail to respect what many regard as the most fundamental rule of a society, the prohibition of murder?

Capital punishment, like the topics of euthanasia and abortion, raises profound questions about the values that ought to govern the lives of human beings living in complex social environments. Like the topics of euthanasia and abortion, it also brings into sharp relief each of the principles introduced in the first two chapters: protection of life, avoidance of suffering, and moral autonomy. What sets this topic apart, however, is the apparently paradoxical role these principles play in justifications of capital punishment. Capital punishment involves a deliberate act on the part of the state to end a human life. And while in many jurisdictions executions are increasingly designed to ensure that persons being executed do not die in a deliberately painful way, the threat of execution would not be described as the most severe form of punishment that can be inflicted for breaking the law and therefore would not be regarded by some as the most effective deterrent available to the state in the enforcement of law unless it imposed significant suffering on those condemned to death. In short, the purpose of capital punishment is to protect life by taking life and to avoid suffering by imposing suffering. These characteristics make capital punishment a compelling moral issue.

Background Considerations

Capital punishment is thought of today as a punishment inflicted on persons who have been found guilty of murder. But the idea that capital punishment should be reserved only for murderers has gained wide acceptance only in this century. At one time in English history, for example, the penalty of death could be imposed for the theft of anything worth more than 12 pence. Blackstone, an influential eighteenth-century commentator on the law, discovered 166 crimes punishable by death in English law. By 1810, there were 300 offences, including forgery, for which the death penalty could be imposed in England.

The view that capital punishment should be reserved for murder is the product of more than one hundred years of law reform, the result of which has been increasing moderation in the use of capital punishment in many countries in the Western world.

Execution by hanging for murder has been a feature of Canadian law throughout our history. Until the 1950s murder was rather broadly defined as the unlawful killing of a human being by someone who intended to bring about the victim's death or who intended to inflict bodily harm on the victim, and where the harm inflicted resulted in the victim's death. For such a crime the mandatory sentence was death by hanging. A judge had no discretion in the matter and only the Governor General, acting on the advice of the Canadian government, could intervene to prevent the execution from taking place. Such interventions were relatively rare.

Toward the end of the 1950s support for moderation in the use of capital punishment began to grow. It resulted first in a decision that no one under the age of 18 was to be executed. A second step was taken in 1960: the law was altered to differentiate between murder and capital murder. Capital murder, for which capital punishment was the mandatory sentence, comprised those murders which were planned and deliberate. The change was not intended to be a step in the direction of the abolition of capital punishment. Nevertheless, from 1957 to 1963, the Conservative government commuted 80 percent of all death sentences. And from 1963 to 1967, the Liberal government commuted one hundred percent of all death sentences. Thus, by 1967 abolition of capital punishment had in fact come about, though in law capital punishment continued to exist.

By 1967, substantial pressure for the formal abolition of capital punishment was being felt by the government. The result was a bill restricting capital murder to situations in which the victim was a police officer or a prison guard. All other acts of murder were to result in a sentence of life imprisonment. The bill was to remain in force for an experimental period of five years. After a stormy debate, the bill was adopted in a vote in which members were free of party discipline and could vote according to what they believed to be right. In 1973, the same bill was renewed for a further five-year period by a vote of 119 in favour, 106 opposed. At the same time, public-opinion polls suggested that a majority of Canadians wished to return to a wider definition of capital murder.

Between 1967 and 1977 all death sentences were commuted to life imprisonment by the Governor General on the advice of the government.

The final step toward the abolition of capital punishment was taken in 1978 when capital punishment was eliminated. Murder is now classified as first-degree murder or second-degree murder. If a murder is planned or deliberate, carried out for pay, or committed in the course of an actual or attempted hijacking of an aircraft, kidnapping, sexual assault with or without a weapon, or aggravated sexual assault, or if the victim is a police officer or prison employee or the murderer has been convicted of murder before, it is first-degree murder. Most other acts of murder are second-degree. Both are punishable by a mandatory sentence of life imprisonment. However, persons convicted of first-degree murder must serve a minimum sentence of 25 years before they are eligible for parole. A conviction for second-degree murder now results in a minimum of ten years in jail before becoming eligible for parole.

The Current Situation

As just noted, capital punishment was abolished in Canada in 1978. However, debate about its merits as a response to crimes involving murder did not come to an end at that time. Right through the 1980s, opinion polls indicated that a substantial majority of Canadians wanted capital punishment reintroduced at least for some crimes. Not surprisingly, throughout that period, there were continuous efforts to put the issue back on the national political agenda.

In 1987, capital punishment was back on the parliamentary agenda. A motion to reinstate capital punishment was introduced. A contentious national debate followed. Public opinion polls once again suggested that a majority of Canadians supported reinstatement. However, when the vote, in which members of Parliament were free to follow their conscience, was taken on the floor of the House of Commons, the motion was defeated by a vote of 148 to 127. This did not stop the debate which then continued through the 1990s. From time to time, individual members of Parliament and both the Alliance and the Conservative political parties have called for further parliamentary debate. A referendum on the issue has also been proposed. However, the issue has not returned for resolution by vote to the parliamentary agenda. There is an interesting footnote, however, to the story of the abolition of capital punishment in Canada. Although it was abolished for civilian crimes in 1978, it remained a punishment for offences under the military provisions long after it was abolished for offences under the Criminal Code. In 1998, this anomaly was resolved when capital punishment was quietly abolished for military offences through provisions in an omnibus "housekeeping" bill.

The issue of capital punishment has also been vigorously debated in other countries. In England, capital punishment was abolished for civilian offences in 1965 by a free vote in the House of Commons. As in Canada, opinion polls at the time of abolition indicated that as much as 79% of the British people were opposed to abolition. In 1969, abolition was reaffirmed by vote in the House of Commons, a situation that has continued to the present.

The current situation in the United States is quite different. There, criminal law falls within the jurisdiction of state legislatures. As a result, the situation varies from state to state. In 1972, the Supreme Court of the United States prohibited executions because of serious concerns about the fairness in the application of capital punishment laws. Many states then revised their laws and in 1976, the US Supreme Court cleared the way for the resumption of executions. Today, in addition to the federal government, 38 states have statutes allowing for and in some cases requiring capital punishment. As of the year 2000, a total of 3,593 inmates were on death row, 85 of whom were actually executed. Although lethal injection is now the most common method of execution, lethal gas, hanging, electrocution, and firing squads continue to be used.

According to Amnesty International, 84 nations still have capital punishment. They report that at least 3,048 people were executed worldwide in 2001. Of these executions, at least 2,468 were carried out in China.

The Moral Dimension

Any form of punishment inflicts suffering on the offender being punished. For that reason, punishment needs to be justified. The death penalty is a particularly severe form of punishment because it inflicts suffering on an offender by taking his life. How then can a society that claims to be committed to the view that human life is sacred tolerate capital punishment?

Those who endorse the death penalty tend to justify their position by appealing to one of two views. The first view is that, because the protection of human life is a fundamental obligation which the community has toward its members, it must do everything it legitimately can to deter those who might otherwise commit murder. Capital punishment is the most effective deterrent available and so is justified. In short, capital punishment is a means of securing respect for the principle that both individually and collectively we have an obligation to preserve and respect human life.

Evaluating the merits of the view that capital punishment is justified as a deterrent requires that we address two questions: First, does the threat of capital punishment deter people from committing murder? Some have argued that it does not. They point to a host of studies undertaken in several countries over the past several decades which have failed to provide any evidence for the view that capital punishment is a deterrent to murder. Others have argued that the studies which have been done are inconclusive; further, the suggestion that capital punishment is not a deterrent conflicts with practical experience and common sense. Assessing the merits of these conflicting points of view is a theme which runs through several of the readings.

There is a second question to be considered. Let us assume for the moment that the death penalty is a deterrent. Does it follow that capital punishment is justified? Many people are prepared to accept that it does. But for others, harming some individuals as a way of securing benefits for others is not acceptable, particularly when taking human life is involved.

Let us turn now to a second view, namely, that justice requires that those who break the law should be punished. According to this view justice requires that offenders receive the punishment they deserve for the crime which they have committed. That is, the punishment should fit the crime. The punishment which those who commit murder deserve, that is the punishment which fits the crime of murder, is death.

Assessing the merits of this view requires, once again, that we address two questions: First, does justice require that those who break the law be punished? A complex variety of arguments have been advanced by those who reject a "just deserts" view of punishment. Some have suggested that those who commit serious crimes such as murder are not autonomous moral agents responsible for their actions; rather they are mentally ill; or they are victims of their upbringing or their environment. The findings of the social sciences are frequently cited in support of these arguments. Others argue that we are never justified in imposing suffering in the form of punishment unless we can establish that punishment will serve to reform or rehabilitate the offender, or that it will result in benefits to the community. Obviously, reform or rehabilitation of the offender is not the point of capital punishment. And empirical research has failed to establish that capital punishment reduces the volume of crime in general or murder in particular. Hence, they conclude that capital punishment is immoral.

Those who advocate capital punishment on the grounds that execution is the fitting punishment for those who commit murder must address a second question. Let us assume that justice requires that those who break the law be punished. Does it follow that execution is a just punishment for those who commit murder? This question requires serious consideration. Murder is frequently committed in a moment of uncontrollable anger or while the offender is heavily intoxicated. Frequently the victim is closely related to the murderer, a husband or wife, a parent, or a son or daughter. Of course, not all cases of murder fall into this category. But here, too, there are objections. For example, courts have been known to make mistakes. Innocent people have been found guilty in the past. This has led some to argue that the death penalty is simply too final a punishment to be inflicted by fallible human institutions. Those who commit very serious crimes such as murder should be given very long prison sentences, to leave open the possibility for errors to be corrected.

The Readings

Because capital punishment is no longer practised in Canada, our courts have not had to examine it directly from a legal and constitutional perspective. In this respect, Canadian jurisprudence is quite different from that of the United States where the constitutionality of capital punishment has been extensively tested in the courts and has been the subject of important American Supreme Court judgements. However, the Canadian Supreme Court has not escaped debating this issue entirely.

First in 1991 and again in 2001, the Supreme Court of Canada was asked to determine the constitutionality of decisions on the part of the Canadian government to extradite back to the United States people wanted for murder in that country. In both cases, the accused argued against extradition on the grounds that if extradited, they faced the death penalty if found guilty.

In the first of these two cases,[1] the majority ruled that given the history of the sanction in Canada, the lack of consensus in Parliament on those occasions when the issue was addressed and voted on, and the continuing public debate about its reinstatement, capital punishment was not seen by Canadians as morally abhorrent or absolutely unacceptable. Extraditing an accused to the United States where he might face execution therefore was not unconstitutional. A minority of the court argued in contrast that capital punishment was regarded with abhorrence by Canadians and was a cruel and unusual punishment of the sort

---

[1] *This case is indexed in the legal literature as "Kindler v. Canada" (Minister of Justice, 1991). It is not included among the readings in this chapter.*

prohibited by the Charter of Rights and Freedoms. Extradition of an accused to a jurisdiction in which he might be executed therefore was judged to be unconstitutional.

In 2001, a similar case was referred to the Supreme Court for decision. In this case, the Court reversed its decision and concluded that the extradition of persons who faced the death penalty if found guilty was contrary to core Canadian values. In coming to its judgement, the Court reviewed carefully the wide-ranging debate in Canada, the United States, the United Kingdom, and elsewhere both for and against capital punishment. Their judgement, the *United States vs. Burns*, is set out in the first reading.

The Supreme Court judgement is followed by a speech in defence of capital punishment by John Stuart Mill made in the British Parliament in 1868. Many of Mill's points are still being argued today. For example, Mill emphasizes the role of executions in deterring violent crime.

One of the significant aspects of discussions and debates designed to resolve moral issues is the way in which people in search of the truth can vary in their interpretation of empirical data or what we might describe as matters of fact. An example is disagreements about whether capital punishment deters homicide. This is an important, though complex and difficult issue. It is addressed in our third reading by Rosalind Simson who uses the debate about whether capital punishment deters homicide as a case study. Her investigation requires that she set out and evaluate the deterrence argument for capital punishment. She then asks whether the fact that people disagree on what looks like a matter of fact proves that the traditional ideal of objectivity in the pursuit of knowledge is mistaken. Her conclusion, namely that people's circumstances and moral values do quite legitimately colour their pursuit of the truth, is one that needs careful consideration. It is a theme that is addressed, though less explicitly, in a number of places in this anthology. Examples include Brian Slattery's discussion of Native land rights in Chapter Six and Conrad Brunk's discussion of Professionalism and Responsibility in the Technological Society in Chapter Nine.

Alan Brudner's article then shifts the focus of discussion. Justifying punishment by reference to its consequences, he argues, is a mistake. Retributivism with its emphasis on just deserts offers a more convincing alternative. But does it follow that capital punishment is therefore justified? Brudner offers a cautious no to this question.

THE UNITED STATES VS. BURNS

2001 SCC 7 - Supreme Court of Canada

1   THE COURT — Legal systems have to live with the possibility of error. The unique feature of capital punishment is that it puts beyond recall the possibility of correction. In recent years, aided by the advances in the forensic sciences, including DNA testing, the courts and governments in this country and elsewhere have come to acknowledge a number of instances of wrongful convictions for murder despite all of the careful safeguards put in place for the protection of the innocent. The instances in Canada are few, but if capital punishment had been carried out, the result could have been the killing by the government of innocent individuals. The names of Marshall, Milgaard, Morin, Sophonow and Parsons signal prudence and caution in a murder case. Other countries have also experienced revelations of wrongful convictions, including states of the United States where the death penalty is still imposed and carried into execution.

2   The possibility of a miscarriage of justice is but one of many factors in the balancing process which governs the decision by the Minister of Justice to extradite two Canadian citizens, Glen Sebastian Burns and Atif Ahmad Rafay, to the United States. A competing principle of fundamental justice is that Canadians who are accused of crimes in the United States can ordinarily expect to be dealt with under the law which the citizens of that jurisdiction have collectively determined to apply to offences committed within their territory, including the set punishment.

3   Awareness of the potential for miscarriages of justice, together with broader public concerns about the taking of life by the state, as well as doubts about the effectiveness of the death penalty as a deterrent to murder in comparison with life in prison without parole for 25 years, led Canada to abolish the death penalty for all but a handful of military offences in 1976, and subsequently to abolish the death penalty for all offences in 1998.

4   The abolitionist view is shared by some, but not a majority, of the United States. Michigan, Rhode Island and Wisconsin in fact abolished the death penalty for murder in the 1840s and 1850s, years before the first European state, Portugal, did so, and over a century before Canada did. At present, 12 states are abolitionist while 38 states retain the death penalty. The State of Washington, in which the respondents are wanted for trial on charges of aggravated first degree murder, is a retentionist state.

5   The extradition of the respondents is sought pursuant to the *Extradition Treaty between Canada and the United States of America*, Can. T.S. 1976 No. 3 (the "treaty" or the "extradition treaty") which permits the requested state (in this case Canada) to refuse extradition of fugitives unless provided with assurances that if extradited and convicted they will not suffer the death penalty. The Minister declined to seek such assurances because of his policy that assurances should only be sought in exceptional circumstances, which he decided did not exist in this case.

6   The respondents contend that Canada's principled abolition of the death penalty at home, and its spirited advocacy of abolition internationally, confirm Canadian acceptance of abolition as a fundamental principle of our criminal justice system. This principle, they say, combined with the respondents' Canadian citizenship and the fact that they were 18 years old at the time of the alleged offences, constitutionally prohibits the Minister from extraditing them to a foreign jurisdiction without assurances that they will not face a penalty which Canada, as a society, does not permit within its own borders.

7   The Minister contends, on the other hand, that persons who are found to commit crimes in foreign countries forfeit the benefit of Canada's abolitionist policy. The Constitution does not require Canada, on this view, to project its internal values onto the world stage, and to insist as a condition of extradition that a requesting state view capital punishment in the same light as our domestic legal system does.

8   We agree that the *Canadian Charter of Rights and Freedoms* does not lay down a constitutional prohibition in all cases against extradition unless assurances are given that the death penalty will not be imposed. The Minister is required (as he did here) to balance on a case-by-case basis those factors that favour extradition with assurances against competing factors that favour

extradition without assurances. We hold, however, for the reasons which follow, that such assurances are constitutionally required in all but exceptional cases. We further hold that this case does not present the exceptional circumstances that must be shown before the Minister could constitutionally extradite without assurances. By insisting on assurances, Canada would not be acting in disregard of international extradition obligations undertaken by the Canadian government, but rather exercising a treaty right explicitly agreed to by the United States. We thus agree with the result, though not the reasons, reached by a majority of the judges of the British Columbia Court of Appeal in this case. The Minister's appeal must therefore be dismissed.

I. <u>Facts</u>

9 The crimes alleged against the respondents were, as the Minister contends, "brutal and shocking cold blooded murder[s]." The father, mother and sister of the respondent Rafay were found bludgeoned to death in their home in Bellevue, Washington, in July 1994. Both Burns and Rafay, who had been friends at high school in British Columbia, admit that they were at the Rafay home on the night of the murders. They claim to have gone out on the evening of July 12, 1994 and when they returned, they say, they found the bodies of the three murdered Rafay family members. The house, they say, appeared to have been burgled.

10 However, if the confessions allegedly made by the respondents to undercover RCMP officers are to be believed, the three members of the Rafay family were bludgeoned to death by the respondent Burns while the respondent Rafay watched. Burns allegedly told an undercover RCMP officer that he had killed the three victims with a baseball bat while wearing only underwear so as not to get blood on his clothes. Rafay's father, Tariq Rafay, and mother, Sultana Rafay, were beaten to death in their bedroom. The force used was so violent that blood was spattered on all four walls and the ceiling of the room. The respondent Rafay's sister, Basma Rafay, was beaten about the head and left for dead in the lower level of the house. She later died in hospital. Burns allegedly explained that following the attacks, he had a shower at the Rafay home to clean off the victims' blood. The discovery of hairs with Caucasian characteristics in the shower near the master bedroom, where the two parents were killed, supports this story. There is also evidence of dilute blood covering large sections of the shower stall. The respondents allegedly told the police that they drove around the municipality disposing of various items used in the killings as well as some of the parents' electronic devices, apparently to feign a burglary. The respondent Rafay is also alleged to have told the officer the killings were "a necessary sacrifice in order that he could get what he wanted in life." With the death of all other members of his family, Rafay stood to inherit his parents' assets and the proceeds of their life insurance. Burns, it is alleged, participated in exchange for a share in the proceeds under an agreement with Rafay. He was, the prosecution alleges, a contract killer.

11 The Bellevue police suspected both of the respondents but did not have enough evidence to charge them. When the respondents returned to Canada, the Bellevue police sought the cooperation of the RCMP in their investigation of the murders. The RCMP initiated an elaborate and in the end, they say, productive undercover operation. An RCMP officer posed as a crime boss and subsequently testified that, after gaining the confidence of the respondents, he repeatedly challenged them to put to rest his professed scepticism about their stomach for serious violence. The respondents are alleged to have tried to reassure him by bragging about their respective roles in the Bellevue murders.

12   The respondents assert their innocence. They claim that in making their alleged confessions to the police they were play-acting as much as the undercover policeman to whom they confessed. At this stage of the criminal process in Washington, they are entitled to the presumption of innocence. What to make of it all will be up to a jury in the State of Washington.

13   The respondents were arrested in British Columbia and a committal order was issued for their extradition pending the decision of the Minister of Justice on surrender. The then Minister, Allan Rock, signed an unconditional Order for Surrender to have both of the respondents extradited to the State of Washington to stand trial without assurances in respect of the death penalty. If found guilty, the respondents will face either life in prison without the possibility of parole or the death penalty. Washington State provides for execution by lethal injection unless the condemned individual elects execution by hanging (Revised Code of Washington §10.95.180(1)).

II. The Minister's Decision

. . . the Minister proceeded on the assumption that the death penalty would be sought by the prosecutors in the State of Washington. . . .

IV. Relevant Constitutional and Statutory Provisions

Canadian Charter of Rights and Freedoms

1.   The *Canadian Charter of Rights and Freedoms* guarantees the rights and freedoms set out in it subject only to such reasonable limits prescribed by law as can be demonstrably justified in a free and democratic society.

6.   (1) Every citizen of Canada has the right to enter, remain in and leave Canada.

. . .

7.   Everyone has the right to life, liberty and security of the person and the right not to be deprived thereof except in accordance with the principles of fundamental justice.

12. Everyone has the right not to be subjected to any cruel and unusual treatment or punishment.

32. (1) This Charter applies

(*a*) to the Parliament and government of Canada in respect of all matters within the authority of Parliament including all matters relating to the Yukon Territory and Northwest Territories; and

(*b*) to the legislature and government of each province in respect of all matters within the authority of the legislature of each province.

Constitution Act, 1982

52. (1) The Constitution of Canada is the supreme law of Canada, and any law that is inconsistent with the provisions of the Constitution is, to the extent of the inconsistency, of no force or effect.

Extradition Act, R.S.C. 1985, c. E-23 (as am. by S.C. 1992, c. 13)

25. (1) Subject to this Part, the Minister of Justice, on the requisition of a foreign state, may, within a period of ninety days after the date of a fugitive's committal for surrender, under the hand and seal of the Minister, order the fugitive to be surrendered to the person or persons who are, in the Minister's opinion, duly authorized to receive the fugitive in the name and on behalf of the foreign state, and the fugitive shall be so surrendered accordingly.

. . .

VI. <u>Revised Code of Washington</u>

10.95.030. Sentences for aggravated first degree murder

(1) Except as provided in subsection (2) of this section, any person convicted of the crime of aggravated first degree murder shall be sentenced to life imprisonment without possibility of release or parole. A person sentenced to life imprisonment under this section shall not have that sentence suspended, deferred, or commuted by any judicial officer and the indeterminate sentence review board or its successor may not parole such prisoner nor reduce the period of confinement in any manner whatsoever including but not limited to any sort of good-time calculation. The department of social and health services or its successor or any executive official may not permit such prisoner to participate in any sort of release or furlough program.

(2) If, pursuant to a special sentencing proceeding held under RCW 10.95.050, the trier of fact finds that there are not sufficient mitigating circumstances to merit leniency, the sentence shall be death. . . .

. . .

VII. <u>Analysis</u>

The evidence amply justifies the extradition of the respondents to Washington State to stand trial on charges of aggravated first degree murder. Under the law of that state, a conviction would carry a minimum sentence of imprisonment for life without the possibility of release or parole. If the prosecutors were to seek the death penalty, they would have the burden of persuading the jury that "there are not sufficient mitigating circumstances" in favour of the respondents. If the jury is so satisfied, the death penalty would be administered by lethal injection or (at the option of the convicted individual), by hanging. If the jury is not so satisfied, the convicted murderer is locked up for life without any possibility of release or parole. An individual convicted of aggravated first degree murder in Washington State thus will either die in prison by execution or will die in prison eventually by other causes. Those are the possibilities. Apart from executive clemency, the State of Washington does not hold out the possibility (or even the "faint hope") of eventual freedom.

The respondents' position is that the death penalty is so horrific, the chances of error are so high, the death row phenomenon is so repugnant, and the impossibility of correction is so draconian, that it is simply unacceptable that Canada should participate, however indirectly, in its imposition. While the government of Canada would not itself administer the lethal injection or erect the gallows, no executions can or will occur without the act of extradition by the Canadian government. The Minister's decision is a prior and essential step in a process that may lead to death by execution.

. . .

We affirm that it is generally for the Minister, not the Court, to assess the weight of competing considerations in extradition policy, but the availability of the death penalty, like death itself, opens up a different dimension. The difficulties and occasional miscarriages of the criminal law are located in an area of human experience that falls squarely within "the inherent domain of the judiciary as guardian of the justice system": *Re B.C. Motor Vehicle Act*, *supra*, at p. 503. It is from this perspective, recognizing the unique finality and irreversibility of the death penalty, that the constitutionality of the Minister's decision falls to be decided.

. . .

8. *Factors that Arguably Favour Extradition Without Assurances*

. . .

A state seeking Canadian cooperation today may be asked to yield up a fugitive tomorrow. The extradition treaty is part of an international network of mutual assistance that enables states to deal both with crimes in their own jurisdiction and transnational crimes with elements that occur in more than one jurisdiction. Given the ease of movement of people and things from state to state, Canada needs the help of the international community to fight serious crime within our own borders. Some of the states from whom we seek cooperation may not share our constitutional values. Their cooperation is nevertheless important. The Minister points out that Canada satisfies itself that certain minimum standards of criminal justice exist in the foreign state before it makes an extradition treaty in the first place.

. . .

9. *Countervailing Factors that Arguably Favour Extradition Only with Assurances*

We now turn to the factors that appear to weigh against extradition without assurances that the death penalty will not be imposed.

(a) Principles of Criminal Justice as Applied in Canada

The death penalty has been rejected as an acceptable element of criminal justice by the Canadian people, speaking through their elected federal representatives, after years of protracted debate. Canada has not executed anyone since 1962. Parliament abolished the last legal vestiges of the death penalty in 1998 (*An Act to amend the National Defence Act and to make consequential amendments to other Acts*, S.C. 1998, c. 35) some seven years after the decisions of this Court in *Kindler* and *Ng*. In his letter to the respondents, the Minister of Justice emphasized that "in Canada, Parliament has decided that capital punishment is not an appropriate penalty for crimes committed here, and I am firmly committed to that position."

. . .

It is incontestable that capital punishment, whether or not it violates s.12 of the *Charter*, and whether or not it could be upheld under s.1, engages the underlying values of the prohibition against cruel and unusual punishment. It is final. It is irreversible. Its imposition has been described as arbitrary. Its deterrent value has been doubted. Its implementation necessarily causes psychological and physical suffering. It has been rejected by the Canadian Parliament for offences committed within Canada. Its potential imposition in this case is thus a factor that weighs against extradition without assurances.

(b) <u>The Abolition of the Death Penalty Has Emerged as a Major Canadian Initiative at the International Level, and Reflects a Concern Increasingly Shared by Most of the World's Democracies</u>

. . .

Amnesty International reports that in 1948, the year in which the Universal Declaration of Human Rights was adopted, only eight countries were abolitionist. In January 1998, the Secretary-General of the United Nations, in a report submitted to the Commission on Human Rights (U.N. Doc. E/CN.4/1998/82), noted that 90 countries retained the death penalty, while 61 were totally abolitionist, 14 (including Canada at the time) were classified as abolitionist for ordinary crimes and 27 were considered to be abolitionist *de facto* (no executions for the past 10 years) for a total of 102 abolitionist countries. At the present time, it appears that the death penalty is now abolished (apart from exceptional offences such as treason) in 108 countries. These general statistics mask the important point that abolitionist states include all of the major democracies except some of the United States, India and Japan ("Dead Man Walking Out", *The Economist*, June 10-16, 2000, at p. 21). According to statistics filed by Amnesty International on this appeal, 85 percent of the world's executions in 1999 were accounted for by only five countries: the United States, China, the Congo, Saudi Arabia and Iran.

. . .

10. *An Accelerating Concern About Potential Wrongful Convictions Is a Factor of Increased Weight Since Kindler and Ng Were Decided*

The avoidance of conviction and punishment of the innocent has long been in the forefront of "the basic tenets of our legal system". It is reflected in the presumption of innocence under s. 11(*d*) of the *Charter* and in the elaborate rules governing the collection and presentation of evidence, fair trial procedures, and the availability of appeals. The possibility of miscarriages of justice in murder cases has long been recognized as a legitimate objection to the death penalty, but our state of knowledge of the scope of this potential problem has grown to unanticipated and unprecedented proportions in the years since *Kindler* and *Ng* were decided. This expanding awareness compels increased recognition of the fact that the extradition decision of a Canadian Minister could pave the way, however unintentionally, to sending an innocent individual to his or her death in a foreign jurisdiction.

(a) The Canadian Experience

Our concern begins at home. There have been well-publicized recent instances of miscarriages of justice in murder cases in Canada. Fortunately, because of the abolition of the death penalty, meaningful remedies for wrongful conviction are still possible in this country.

The first of a disturbing Canadian series of wrongful murder convictions, whose ramifications were still being worked out when *Kindler* and *Ng* were decided, involved Donald Marshall, Jr. He was convicted in 1971 of murder by a Nova Scotia jury. He served 11 years of his sentence. He was eventually acquitted by the courts on the basis of new evidence. In 1989 he was exonerated by a Royal Commission which stated that:

> The criminal justice system failed Donald Marshall, Jr. at virtually every turn from his arrest and wrongful conviction for murder in 1971 up to, and even beyond, his acquittal by the Court of Appeal in 1983. The tragedy of the failure is compounded by evidence that this miscarriage of justice could — and should — have been prevented, or at least corrected quickly, if those involved in the system had carried out their duties in a professional and/or competent manner. That they did not is due, in part at least, to the fact that Donald Marshall, Jr. is a Native.

(Royal Commission on the Donald Marshall, Jr., Prosecution, *Digest of Findings and Recommendations* (1989), at p. 1)

In June 1990, a further commission of inquiry recommended that Marshall receive a compensation package consisting, among other things, of a payment for pain and suffering and monthly annuity payments guaranteed over a minimum period of 30 years, at the end of which he will have received in excess of $1 million. The miscarriage of justice in his case was known at the time *Kindler* and *Ng* were decided. What was not known was the number of other instances of miscarriages of justice in murder cases that would surface in subsequent years in both Canada and the United States.

In 1970, David Milgaard was convicted of murder by a Saskatchewan jury and sentenced to life imprisonment. He served almost 23 years in jail. On two occasions separated by almost 22 years, it was held by Canadian courts that Milgaard was given the benefit of a fair trial, initially by the Saskatchewan Court of Appeal in January 1971 in *R. v. Milgaard* (1971), 2 C.C.C. (2d) 206, leave to appeal refused (1971), 4 C.C.C. (2d) 566n, and subsequently by this Court in Reference re Milgaard (Can.), [1992] 1 S.C.R. 866. There was no probative evidence that the police had acted improperly in the investigation or in their interviews with any of the witnesses, and no evidence that there had been inadequate disclosure in accordance with the practice prevailing at the time. Milgaard was represented by able and experienced counsel. No serious error in law or procedure occurred at the trial. Notwithstanding the fact that the conviction for murder followed a fair trial, new evidence surfaced years later. This Court, on a special reference, considered that "[t]he continued conviction of Milgaard would amount to a miscarriage of justice if an opportunity was not provided for a jury to consider the fresh evidence" (p. 873). In 1994, Milgaard commenced proceedings against the Government of Saskatchewan for wrongful conviction and in 1995 he sued the provincial Attorney General personally after the latter had told the media he believed Milgaard was guilty of the murder. DNA testing in 1997 ultimately satisfied the Saskatchewan government that Milgaard had been wrongfully convicted. In May 2000 another individual was prosecuted and convicted for the same murder. His appeal is pending before the Saskatchewan Court of Appeal. Compensation in the sum of $10 million was paid to Milgaard. The history of the wrongful conviction of David Milgaard shows that in Canada, as in the United States, a fair trial does not always guarantee a safe verdict.

Of equal concern is the wrongful conviction for murder of Guy Paul Morin who was only 25 years old when he was arrested on April 22, 1985, and charged with the first degree murder of a child named Christine Jessop who was his next door neighbour. While initially acquitted by an Ontario jury, he was found guilty at a second jury trial in 1992. DNA testing carried out while the second appeal was pending before the Ontario Court of Appeal, more than 10 years after his initial arrest, exonerated him. His appeal was then uncontested, and he received an apology from the Attorney General of Ontario, compensation of $1.25 million, and the establishment of a commission (the Kaufman Inquiry) to look into the causes of the wrongful conviction. In his 1998 Report, the Commissioner, a former judge of the Quebec Court of Appeal, concluded:

> The case of Guy Paul Morin is not an aberration. By that, I do not mean that I can quantify the number of similar cases in Ontario or elsewhere, or that I can pass upon the frequency with which innocent persons are convicted in this province. We do not know. What I mean is that the causes of Mr. Morin's conviction are rooted in systemic problems, as well as the failings of individuals. It is no coincidence that the same systemic problems are those identified in wrongful convictions in other jurisdictions worldwide.

(Commission on Proceedings Involving Guy Paul Morin, *Report* (1998), vol. 2, at p. 1243)

Thomas Sophonow was tried three times for the murder of Barbara Stoppel. He served 45 months in jail before his conviction was overturned in 1985 by the Manitoba Court of Appeal. It was not until June 2000 that the Winnipeg police exonerated Sophonow of the killing, almost 20 years after his original conviction. The Attorney General of Manitoba recently issued an apology to Mr. Sophonow and mandated the Honourable Peter Cory, recently retired from this Court, to head a commission of inquiry which is currently looking into the conduct of the investigation and the circumstances surrounding the criminal proceedings, both to understand the past and to prevent future miscarriages of justice. The commission will also examine the issue of compensation.

In 1994, Gregory Parsons was convicted by a Newfoundland jury for the murder of his mother. He was sentenced to life imprisonment with no eligibility for parole for 15 years. Subsequently, the Newfoundland Court of Appeal overturned his conviction and ordered a new trial. Before that trial could be held, Parsons was cleared by DNA testing. The provincial Minister of Justice apologized to Parsons and his family and asked Nathaniel Noel, a retired judge, to conduct a review of the investigation and prosecution of the case and to make recommendations concerning the payment of compensation.

These miscarriages of justice of course represent a tiny and wholly exceptional fraction of the workload of Canadian courts in murder cases. Still, where capital punishment is sought, the state's execution of even one innocent person is one too many.

In all of these cases, had capital punishment been imposed, there would have been no one to whom an apology and compensation <u>could</u> be paid in respect of the miscarriage of justice (apart, possibly, from surviving family members), and no way in which Canadian society with the benefit of hindsight could have justified to itself the deprivation of human life in violation of the principles of fundamental justice.

Accordingly, when Canada looks south to the present controversies in the United States associated with the investigation, defence, conviction, appeal and punishment in murder cases, it is with a sense of appreciation that many of the underlying criminal justice problems are similar. The difference is that imposition of the death penalty in the retentionist states inevitably deprives the legal system of the possibility of redress to wrongfully convicted individuals.

(b) The U.S. Experience

Concerns in the United States have been raised by such authoritative bodies as the American Bar Association which in 1997 recommended a moratorium on the death penalty throughout the United States because, as stated in an ABA press release in October 2000:

> The adequacy of legal representation of those charged with capital crimes is a major concern. Many death penalty states have no working public defender systems, and many simply assign lawyers at random from a general list. The defendant's life ends up entrusted to an often underqualified and overburdened lawyer who may have no experience with criminal law at all, let alone with death penalty cases.

> The U.S. Supreme Court and the Congress have dramatically restricted the ability of our federal courts to review petitions of inmates who claim their state death sentences were imposed in violation of the Constitution or federal law.

> Studies show racial bias and poverty continue to play too great a role in determining who is sentenced to death.

The ABA takes no position on the death penalty as such (except to oppose it in the case of juveniles and the mentally retarded). Its call for a moratorium has been echoed by local or state bars in California, Connecticut, Ohio, Virginia, Illinois, Louisiana, Massachusetts, New Jersey and Pennsylvania. The ABA reports that state or local bars in Florida, Kentucky, Missouri, New Mexico, North Carolina and Tennessee are also examining aspects of the death penalty controversy.

On August 4, 2000, the Board of Governors of the Washington State Bar Association, being the state seeking the extradition of the respondents, unanimously adopted a resolution to review the death penalty process. The Governor was urged to obtain a comprehensive report addressing the concerns of the American Bar Association as they apply to the imposition of the death penalty in the State of Washington. In particular, the Governor was asked to determine "[w]hether the reversal rate of capital cases from our state by the federal courts indicates any systemic problems regarding how the death penalty is being implemented in Washington State."

Other retentionist jurisdictions in the United States have also expressed recent disquiet about the conduct of capital cases, and the imposition and the carrying out of the death penalty. These include:

(i) Early last year Governor George Ryan of Illinois, a known retentionist, declared a moratorium on executions in that state. The Governor noted that more than half the people sentenced to die there in the last 23 years were eventually exonerated of murder. Specifically, Illinois exonerated 13 death row inmates since 1977, one more than it actually executed. Governor Ryan said ". . . I have grave concerns about our state's shameful record of convicting innocent people and putting them on death row." He remarked that he could not support a system that has come "so close to the ultimate nightmare, the state's taking of innocent life" (Governor Ryan Press Release, January 31, 2000).

(ii) The Illinois moratorium followed closely in the wake of a major study on wrongful convictions in death penalty cases by the *Chicago Tribune* newspaper, and a conference held at Northwestern University School of Law: see L. B. Bienen, "The Quality of Justice in Capital Cases: Illinois as a Case Study" (1998), 61 *Law & Contemp. Probs*. 193, at p. 213, fn. 103. The study examined the 285 death penalty cases that had occurred in Illinois since capital punishment was restored there. "The findings reveal a system so plagued by unprofessionalism, imprecision and bias that they have rendered the state's ultimate form of punishment its least credible" (*Chicago Tribune*, November 14, 1999).

(iii) One of the more significant exonerations in Illinois was the case of Anthony Porter who came within 48 hours of being executed for a crime he did not commit (*Chicago Tribune*, December 29, 2000, at p. N22).

(iv) Both the New Hampshire House of Representatives and Senate voted to abolish the death penalty last year, although the measure was vetoed by the Governor. It is noteworthy that New Hampshire has not executed anyone since 1939 (*New York Times*, May 19, 2000, at p. 16, and May 20, 2000, at p. 16).

(v) In May 1999, the Nebraska legislature approved a bill that imposed a two-year moratorium on executions in that state and appropriated funds for a study of the issue. That initiative was vetoed by the Governor. However, the legislature unanimously overrode part of the veto so that the study could proceed.

(vi) Senator Russ Feingold of Wisconsin introduced a bill in Congress in April 2000 calling on the federal government and all states that impose the death penalty to suspend executions while a national commission reviews the administration of the death penalty.

(vii) On September 12, 2000, the United States Justice Department released a study of the death penalty under federal law. It was the first comprehensive review of the federal death penalty since it was reinstated in 1988. The data shows that federal prosecutors were almost twice as likely to recommend the death penalty for black defendants when the victim was non-black than when he or she was black. Moreover, a white defendant was almost twice as likely to be given a plea agreement whereby the prosecution agreed not to seek the death penalty. The study also revealed that 43 percent of the 183 cases in which the death penalty was sought came from 9 of the 94 federal judicial districts. This has led to concerns about racial and geographical disparity. The then Attorney General Janet Reno said that she was "sorely troubled" by the data and requested further studies (*New York Times*, September 12, 2000, at p. 17).

Foremost among the concerns of the American Bar Association, the Washington State Bar Association and other bodies who possess "hands-on" knowledge of the criminal justice system, is the possibility of wrongful convictions and the potential state killing of the innocent. It has been reported that 43 wrongfully convicted people have been freed in the United States as a result of work undertaken by The Innocence Project, a clinical law program started in 1992 at the Cardozo School of Law in New York. See, generally, B. Scheck, P. Neufeld, and J. Dwyer, *Actual Innocence: Five Days to Execution and Other Dispatches from the Wrongly Convicted* (2000). One of the authors, Peter Neufeld testified on June 20, 2000 to the House of Representatives' Committee on the Judiciary that "DNA testing only helps correct conviction of the innocent in a narrow class of cases; most homicides do not involve biological evidence that can be determinative of guilt or innocence."

Finally, we should note the recent Columbia University study by Professor James Liebman and others which concludes that 2 out of 3 death penalty sentences in the United States were reversed on appeal: *A Broken System: Error Rates in Capital Cases, 1973-1995* (June 12, 2000). The authors gathered and analyzed all of the available cases from the period of 1973 to 1995, the former being the year that states began to enact new death penalty statutes following the United States Supreme Court's decision in *Furman*, *supra*, invalidating the existing regimes. Collection of the data for the study began in 1991, the year *Kindler* and *Ng* were decided. In their executive summary, the authors report that "the overall rate of prejudicial error in the American capital punishment system was 68%." These errors were detected at one of three stages of appeal in the American legal system. The authors say that with "so many mistakes that it takes three judicial inspections to catch them" there must be "grave doubt about whether we *do* catch them all" (emphasis in original). The authors point out in footnote 81 that "[b]etween 1972 and the beginning of 1998, 68 people were released from death row on the grounds that their convictions were faulty, and there was too little evidence to retry the prisoner" and as of May 2000 "the number of inmates released from death row as factually or legally innocent apparently has risen to 87, including nine released in 1999 alone." For an abridged version of the Liebman study, see "Capital Attrition: Error Rates in Capital Cases, 1973-1995" (2000), 78 *Tex. L. Rev.* 1839.

It will of course be for the United States to sort out the present controversy surrounding death penalty cases in that country. We have referred to some of the reports and some of the data, but there is much more that has been said on all sides of the issue. Much of the evidence of wrongful convictions relates to individuals who were saved prior to execution, and can thus be presented as evidence of the system's capacity to correct errors. The widespread expressions of concern suggest there are significant problems, but they also demonstrate a determination to address the problems that do exist. Our purpose is not to draw conclusions on the merits of the various criticisms, but simply to note the scale and recent escalation of the controversy, particularly in some of the retentionist states, including the State of Washington.

(c) The Experience in the United Kingdom

Countries other than Canada and the United States have also experienced their share of disclosure of wrongful convictions in recent years. In the United Kingdom, in 1991, the then

Home Secretary announced the establishment of a Royal Commission on Criminal Justice (the Runciman Commission) to examine the effectiveness of the criminal justice system in securing the conviction of the guilty and the acquittal of the innocent. In making the announcement, the Home Secretary referred to such cases as the "Birmingham Six" which had seriously undermined public confidence in the administration of criminal justice. The report of the Commission, pointing to potential sources of miscarriage of justice, was presented to the British Parliament in 1993. The new *Criminal Appeal Act*, adopted in 1995, created the Criminal Cases Review Commission, an independent body responsible for investigating suspected miscarriages of criminal justice in England, Wales and Northern Ireland and referring appropriate cases to the Court of Appeal.

The Criminal Cases Review Commission started its casework in April 1997. As of November 30, 2000, it had referred 106 cases to the Court of Appeal. Of these, 51 had been heard, 39 convictions quashed, 11 upheld and one remained under reserve. The convictions overturned by the court as unsafe included 10 convictions for murder. In two of the overturned murder convictions, the prisoners had long since been hanged.

In *R. v. Bentley (Deceased)*, [1998] E.W.J. No. 1165 (QL) (C.A.), the court posthumously quashed the murder conviction of Derek Bentley who was executed on January 28, 1953. The Crown had alleged that Bentley and an accomplice had embarked upon "a warehouse-breaking expedition" during which a police officer was killed. It was argued that the trial judge had erred in summing up to the jury. It was also argued that fresh evidence made the conviction unsafe. The Lord Chief Justice, Lord Bingham, said about the summing up in this case (at para. 78):

> It is with genuine diffidence that the members of this court direct criticism towards a trial judge widely recognised as one of the outstanding criminal judges of this century [Lord Goddard C.J.]. But we cannot escape the duty of decision. In our judgment the summing up in this case was such as to deny the appellant that fair trial which is the birthright of every British citizen.

After quashing the conviction on this basis, Lord Bingham C.J. said (at para. 95):

> It must be a matter of profound and continuing regret that this mistrial occurred and that the defects we have found were not recognised at the time.

It does not appear that the Court of Appeal gave much weight to the fresh evidence, though one component of this evidence (dealing with the taking of the appellant's statement) was said to provide "additional support" (para. 130) for the conclusion that the conviction was unsafe.

Another recent case is *R. v. Mattan*, [1998] E.W.J. No. 4668 (QL) (C.A.). Mahmoud Hussein Mattan was convicted of murdering a Cardiff shopkeeper in 1952. The shopkeeper's throat had been cut. On August 19, 1952, the Court of Criminal Appeal refused his application for leave to appeal. He was hanged in Cardiff Prison on September 8, 1952. Fresh evidence came to light in 1969 but the Home Secretary declined in February 1970 to have the case reopened. The Commission, however, referred the matter to the Court of Appeal, which found that Crown had failed to disclose highly relevant evidence to the defence. In the result, the conviction was quashed. Near the end of its judgement, the Court of Appeal stated that "[i]t is, of course, a matter for very profound regret that in 1952 Mahmoud Mattan was convicted and hanged and it has taken 46 years for that conviction to be unsafe." It also observed that the case demonstrates that "capital punishment was not perhaps a prudent culmination for a criminal justice system which is human and therefore fallible" (para. 39).

The U.K. experience is relevant for the obvious reason that these men might be free today if the state had not taken their lives. But there is more. These convictions were quashed not on the basis of sophisticated DNA evidence but on the basis of frailties that perhaps may never be eliminated from our system of criminal justice. It is true, as the English Court of Appeal noted in *Mattan*, that the present rules require far more disclosure on the part of the Crown. And it is true that there was some blood on the shoes of Mattan that could now be shown by DNA testing not to have belonged to the victim. But there is always the potential that eyewitnesses will get it wrong, either innocently or, as it appears in the case of *Mattan*, purposefully in order to shift the blame onto another. And there is always a chance that the judicial system will fail an accused, as it apparently did in *Bentley*. These cases demonstrate that the concern about wrongful convictions is unlikely to be resolved by advances in the forensic sciences, welcome as those advances are from the perspective of protecting the innocent and punishing the guilty.

(d) Conclusion

The recent and continuing disclosures of wrongful convictions for murder in Canada, the United States and the United Kingdom provide tragic testimony to the fallibility of the legal system, despite its elaborate safeguards for the protection of the innocent. When fugitives are sought to be tried for murder by a retentionist state, however similar in other respects to our own legal system, this history weighs powerfully in the balance against extradition without assurances.

11. *The "Death Row Phenomenon" Is of Increasing Concern Even to Retentionists*

The evidence filed on this appeal includes a report by Chief Justice Richard P. Guy, Chief Justice of the State of Washington, dated March 2000 entitled "Status Report on the Death Penalty in Washington State." In the report the Chief Justice notes the following statistics relevant to the present discussion:

— Since 1981, 25 men have been convicted and sentenced to death. Four have had their judgments reversed by the federal courts, 2 have had their sentences reversed by the Washington State Supreme Court, and 3 have been executed.
— The case of one defendant who was sentenced to be executed 18 years ago is still pending.
— Two of the three executed defendants chose not to pursue appeals to the federal courts.
— For cases completed in the federal courts, state and federal review has taken an average of 11.2 years.
— State review after conviction has averaged 5.5 years.

In his introduction to the Status Report, the Chief Justice made the following observations (at p. 2):

Because a death sentence is irreversible, opportunities for proving innocence in addition to those furnished in other felony cases are offered to the defendant in order to avoid erroneous executions. The importance of the review system is illustrated by the current situation in Illinois, a state in which 12 men have been executed since the 1980s but another 13 men sentenced to death have been exonerated. Appellate review of their cases resulted in reversal of their judgments after they were able to prove their innocence through the use of newly discovered DNA techniques or for other reasons.

These statistics are comparable to the degree of delay on "death row" that concerned the European Court of Human Rights in *Soering, supra*. The evidence was that if Soering were to be sentenced to death under Virginia law he would face an average of six to eight years on death row. The European Court commented on the serious human rights consequences of holding a convict under the threat of death for a prolonged length of time at para. 106:

> However well-intentioned and even potentially beneficial is the provision of the complex of post-sentence procedures in Virginia, the consequence is that the condemned prisoner has to endure for many years the conditions on death row and the anguish and mounting tension of living in the ever-present shadow of death.

In *Pratt v. Attorney General for Jamaica, supra*, at p. 783, the Judicial Committee of the Privy Council ruled against the decision of the Jamaican government which sought to carry out death sentences against two appellants who had been on death row for over 14 years. Lord Griffiths for the Committee stated at p. 786:

> In their Lordships' view a state that wishes to retain capital punishment must accept the responsibility of ensuring that execution follows as swiftly as practicable after sentence, allowing a reasonable time for appeal and consideration of reprieve. It is part of the human condition that a condemned man will take every opportunity to save his life through use of the appellate procedure. If the appellate procedure enables the prisoner to prolong the appellate hearings over a period of years, the fault is to be attributed to the appellate system that permits such delay and not to the prisoner who takes advantage of it. Appellate procedures that echo down the years are not compatible with capital punishment. The death row phenomenon must not become established as a part of our jurisprudence. [Emphasis added.]

The role of the death row phenomenon in extradition proceedings was not conclusively determined by this Court in *Kindler*. Cory J., with whom Lamer C.J. concurred, was of the view that it would be wrong to extradite someone who would face the death row phenomenon: see pp. 822-24. Sopinka J. did not deal with the question while McLachlin J. (at p. 856) alluded to "the complexity of the issue." La Forest J. was critical of the concept. He said (at p. 838):

> While the psychological stress inherent in the death row phenomenon cannot be dismissed lightly, it ultimately pales in comparison to the death penalty. Besides, the fact remains that a defendant is never forced to undergo the full appeal procedure, but the vast majority choose to do so. It would be ironic if delay caused by the appellant's taking advantage of the full and generous avenue of the appeals available to him should be viewed as a violation of fundamental justice; . . .

There is now, however, as is shown in the report of Chief Justice Guy of Washington State, *supra*, a widening acceptance amongst those closely associated with the administration of justice in retentionist states that the finality of the death penalty, combined with the determination of the criminal justice system to satisfy itself fully that the conviction is not wrongful, seems inevitably to provide lengthy delays, and the associated psychological trauma. It is apposite to recall in this connection the observation of Frankfurter J. of the United States Supreme Court, dissenting, in *Solesbee v. Balkcom*, 339 U.S. 9 (1950), at p. 14, that the "onset of insanity while awaiting execution of a death sentence is not a rare phenomenon." Related concerns have been expressed by Breyer J., dissenting from decisions not to issue writs of *certiorari* in *Elledge v. Florida*, 119 S. Ct. 366 (1998), and *Knight v. Florida*, 120 S. Ct. 459 (1999). In the latter case, Breyer J. cited a Florida study of inmates which showed that 35 percent of those committed to death row attempted suicide.

The death row phenomenon is not a controlling factor in the s. 7 balance, but even many of those who regard its horrors as self-inflicted concede that it is a relevant consideration. To that extent, it is a factor that weighs in the balance against extradition without assurances.

12. *The Balance of Factors in This Case Renders Extradition of the Respondents Without Assurances a Prima facie Infringement of their Section 7 Rights*

Reviewing the factors for and against unconditional extradition, we conclude that to order extradition of the respondents without obtaining assurances that the death penalty will not be imposed would violate the principles of fundamental justice.

The Minister has not pointed to any public purpose that would be served by extradition <u>without</u> assurances that is not substantially served by extradition <u>with</u> assurances, carrying as it does in this case the prospect on conviction of life imprisonment without release or parole. With assurances, the respondents will be extradited and be made answerable to the legal system where the murders took place. The evidence shows that on previous occasions when assurances have been requested of foreign states they have been forthcoming without exception. (See, for example, Ministerial Decision in the Matter of the Extradition of Lee Robert O'Bomsawin, December 9, 1991; Ministerial Decision in the Matter of the Extradition of Rodolfo Pacificador, October 19, 1996.) There is no basis in the record to support the hypothesis, and counsel for the Minister did not advance it, that the United States would prefer no extradition at all to extradition with assurances. Under Washington State law it by no means follows that the prosecutor will seek the death penalty if the respondents are extradited to face charges of aggravated first degree murder.

It is true that if assurances are requested, the respondents will not face the same punishment regime that is generally applicable to crimes committed in Washington State, but the reality is that Washington requires the assistance of Canada to bring the respondents to justice. Assurances are not sought out of regard for the respondents, but out of regard for the principles that have historically guided this country's criminal justice system and are presently reflected in its international stance on capital punishment.

International experience, particularly in the past decade, has shown the death penalty to raise many complex problems of both a philosophic and pragmatic nature. While there remains the fundamental issue of whether the state can ever be justified in taking the life of a human being within its power, the present debate goes beyond arguments over the effectiveness of deterrence and the appropriateness of vengeance and retribution. It strikes at the very ability of the criminal justice system to obtain a uniformly correct result even where death hangs in the balance.

International experience thus confirms the validity of concerns expressed in the Canadian Parliament about capital punishment. It also shows that a rule requiring that assurances be obtained prior to extradition in death penalty cases not only accords with Canada's principled advocacy on the international level, but is also consistent with the practice of other countries with whom Canada generally invites comparison, apart from the retentionist jurisdictions in the United States.

The "balancing process" mandated by *Kindler* and *Ng* remains a flexible instrument. The difficulty in this case is that the Minister proposes to send the respondents without assurances into the death penalty controversy at a time when the legal system of the requesting country is under such sustained and authoritative <u>internal</u> attack. Although rumblings of this controversy in Canada, the United States and the United Kingdom pre-dated *Kindler* and *Ng*, the concern has grown greatly in depth and detailed proof in the intervening years. The imposition of a moratorium (*de facto* or otherwise) in some of the retentionist states of the United States attests to this concern, but a moratorium itself is not conclusive, any more than the lifting of a moratorium would be. What is important is the recognition that despite the best efforts of all concerned, the judicial system is and will remain fallible and reversible whereas the death penalty will forever remain final and irreversible.

The arguments in favour of extradition without assurances would be as well served by extradition with assurances. There was no convincing argument that exposure of the respondents to death in prison by execution advances Canada's public interest in a way that the alternative, eventual death in prison by natural causes, would not. This is perhaps corroborated by the fact that other abolitionist countries do not, in general, extradite without assurances.

The arguments against extradition without assurances have grown stronger since this Court decided *Kindler* and *Ng* in 1991. Canada is now abolitionist for all crimes, even those in the military field. The international trend against the death penalty has become clearer. The death penalty controversies in the requesting State — the United States — are based on pragmatic, hard-headed concerns about wrongful convictions. None of these factors is conclusive, but taken together they tilt the s.7 balance against extradition without assurances.

Accordingly, we find that the Minister's decision to decline to request the assurances of the State of Washington that the death penalty will not be imposed on the respondents as a condition of their extradition, violates their rights under s.7 of the *Charter*.

13. *Extradition of the Respondents Without Assurances Cannot Be Justified Under Section 1 of the Charter*

The final issue is whether the Minister has shown that the violation of the respondents' s.7 rights that would occur if they were extradited to face the death penalty can be upheld under s.1 of the *Charter* as reasonable and demonstrably justifiable in a free and democratic society. The Court has previously noted that it would be rare for a violation of the fundamental principles of justice to be justifiable under s.1: *Re B.C. Motor Vehicle Act*, *supra*, at p. 518. Nevertheless, we do not foreclose the possibility that there may be situations where the Minister's objectives are so pressing, and where there is no other way to achieve those objectives other than through extradition without assurances, that a violation might be justified. In this case, we find no such justification.

The Minister must show that the refusal to ask for assurances serves a pressing and substantial purpose; that the refusal is likely to achieve that purpose and does not go further than necessary; and that the effect of unconditional extradition does not outweigh the importance of the objective: *R. v. Oakes*, [1986] 1 S.C.R. 103. In our opinion, while the government objective of advancing mutual assistance in the fight against crime is entirely legitimate, the Minister has not shown that extraditing the respondents to face the death penalty without assurances is necessary to achieve that objective.

The Minister cites two important policies that are integral to Canada's mutual assistance objectives, namely, (1) maintenance of comity with cooperating states; and (2) avoiding an influx to Canada of persons charged with murder in retentionist states for the purpose of avoiding the death penalty.

With respect to the argument on comity, there is no doubt that it is important for Canada to maintain good relations with other states. However, the Minister has not shown that the means chosen to further that objective in this case — the refusal to ask for assurances that the death penalty will not be exacted — is necessary to further that objective. There is no suggestion in the evidence that asking for assurances would undermine Canada's international obligations or good relations with neighbouring states. The extradition treaty between Canada and the United States explicitly provides for a request for assurances and Canada would be in full compliance with its international obligations by making it. More and more states are becoming abolitionist and reserving to themselves the right to refuse to extradite unconditionally, as already mentioned.

In *Soering*, *supra*, the European Court of Human Rights held that, in the circumstances of that case, extradition of a West German national from the United Kingdom to face possible execution in the United States would violate the European Convention on Human Rights. West Germany was willing to try Soering in Germany on the basis of his nationality. The European Court ruled that the option of a trial of Soering in West Germany was a "circumstance of relevance for the overall assessment under Article 3 in that it goes to the search for the requisite fair balance of interests and to the proportionality of the contested extradition decision in the particular case" (para. 110) and that "[a] further consideration of relevance is that in the particular instance the legitimate purpose of extradition could be achieved by another means which would not involve suffering of such exceptional intensity or duration" (para. 111). By "another means", the court had in mind the trial of Soering in West Germany. In the present appeal as well, "the legitimate purpose of extradition could be achieved by another means", namely extradition with assurances, in perfect conformity with Canada's commitment to international comity.

We have already addressed the speculative argument that an American government might prefer to let accused persons go without trial by refusing to give assurances. As European states now routinely request assurances that the death penalty will not be imposed on an extradited person, there is little indication that U.S. governments would ever refuse such guarantees. A state seeking to prosecute a serious crime is unlikely to decide that if it cannot impose the ultimate sanction — the death penalty — it will not prosecute at all. Seeking assurances that the death penalty will not be imposed does not amount to asking for lawlessness.

An issue could also arise where a treaty did not contain an assurance clause equivalent to Article 6 of the Canada-U.S. treaty. The argument would then be raised that the Canadian government violated the s. 7 rights of fugitives by failing to insist on such a provision. That issue is not raised by the facts of this case and we leave consideration of the point to an appeal where it is fully argued.

As noted, the Minister's second argument is that it is necessary to refuse to ask for assurances in order to prevent an influx to Canada of persons who commit crimes sanctioned by the death penalty in other states. This in turn would make Canada an attractive haven for persons committing murders in retentionist states. The "safe haven" argument might qualify as a pressing and substantial objective. Indeed, it was accepted as such in *Kindler*, *supra*, by both La Forest J. (at p. 836) and McLachlin J. (at p. 853).

International criminal law enforcement including the need to ensure that Canada does not become a "safe haven" for dangerous fugitives is a very legitimate objective, but there is no evidence whatsoever that extradition to face life in prison without release or parole provides a lesser deterrent to those seeking a "safe haven" than the death penalty, or even that fugitives approach their choice of refuge with such an informed appreciation of tactics. If Canada suffers the prospect of being a haven from time to time for fugitives from the United States, it likely has more to do with geographic proximity than the Minister's policy on treaty assurances. The evidence as stated is that Ministers of Justice have on at least two occasions (since *Kindler* and *Ng*) refused to extradite without assurances, and no adverse consequences to Canada from those decisions were brought to our attention. The respondents pointed out that "[s]ince the execution by the United States of two Mexican nationals in 1997, Mexican authorities have consistently refused to extradite anyone, nationals or non-nationals, in capital cases without first seeking assurances" (respondents' factum, at para. 63).

The fact is, however, that whether fugitives are returned to a foreign country to face the death penalty or to face eventual death in prison from natural causes, they are equally prevented from using Canada as a safe haven. Elimination of a "safe haven" depends on vigorous law enforcement rather than on infliction of the death penalty once the fugitive has been removed from the country.

We conclude that the infringement of the respondents' rights under s. 7 of the *Charter* cannot be justified under s. 1 in this case. The Minister is constitutionally bound to ask for and obtain an assurance that the death penalty will not be imposed as a condition of extradition.

VIII. Conclusion

The outcome of this appeal turns on an appreciation of the principles of fundamental justice, which in turn are derived from the basic tenets of our legal system. These basic tenets have not changed since 1991 when *Kindler* and *Ng* were decided, but their application in particular cases (the "balancing process") must take note of factual developments in Canada and in relevant foreign jurisdictions. When principles of fundamental justice as established and understood in Canada are applied to these factual developments, many of which are of far-reaching importance in death penalty cases, a balance which tilted in favour of extradition without assurances in *Kindler* and *Ng* now tilts against the constitutionality of such an outcome. For these reasons, the appeal is dismissed.

SPEECH IN FAVOUR OF CAPITAL PUNISHMENT (1868)

John Stuart Mill

. . . It would be a great satisfaction to me if I were able to support this Motion. It is always a matter of regret to me to find myself, on a public question, opposed to those who are called

Reprinted from Hansard's Parliamentary Debates, *3rd Series, 21 April 1868 (London, 1868).*

— sometimes in the way of honour, and sometimes in what is intended for ridicule — the philanthropists. Of all persons who take part in public affairs, they are those for whom, on the whole, I feel the greatest amount of respect; for their characteristic is, that they devote their time, their labour, and much of their money to objects purely public, with a less admixture of either personal or class selfishness, than any other class of politicians whatever. On almost all the great questions, scarcely any politicians are so steadily and almost uniformly to be found on the side of right; and they seldom err, but by an exaggerated application of some just and highly important principle. On the very subject that is now occupying us we all know what signal service they have rendered. It is through their efforts that our criminal laws — which within my memory hanged people for stealing in a dwelling house to the value of 40s. — laws by virtue of which rows of human beings might be seen suspended in front of Newgate by those who ascended or descended Ludgate Hill — have so greatly relaxed their most revolting and most impolitic ferocity, that aggravated murder is now practically the only crime which is punished with death by any of our lawful tribunals; and we are even now deliberating whether the extreme penalty should be retained in that solitary case. This vast gain, not only to humanity, but to the ends of penal justice, we owe to the philanthropists; and if they are mistaken, as I cannot but think they are, in the present instance, it is only in not perceiving the right time and place for stopping in a career hitherto so eminently beneficial. Sir, there is a point at which, I conceive, that career ought to stop. When there has been brought home to any one, by conclusive evidence, the greatest crime known to the law; and when the attendant circumstances suggest no palliation of the guilt, no hope that the culprit may even yet not be unworthy to live among mankind, nothing to make it probable that the crime was an exception to his general character rather than a consequence of it, then I confess it appears to me that to deprive the criminal of the life of which he has proved himself to be unworthy — solemnly to blot him out from the fellowship of mankind and from the catalogue of the living — is the most appropriate, as it is certainly the most impressive, mode in which society can attach to so great a crime the penal consequences which for the security of life it is indispensable to annex to it. I defend this penalty, when confined to atrocious cases, on the very ground on which it is commonly attacked — on that of humanity to the criminal; as beyond comparison the least cruel mode in which it is possible adequately to deter from the crime. If, in our horror of inflicting death, we endeavour to devise some punishment for the living criminal which shall act on the human mind with a deterrent force at all comparable to that of death, we are driven to inflections less severe indeed in appearance, and therefore less efficacious, but far more cruel in reality. Few, I think, would venture to propose, as a punishment for aggravated murder, less than imprisonment with hard labour for life; that is the fate to which a murderer would be consigned by the mercy which shrinks from putting him to death. But has it been sufficiently considered what sort of a mercy this is, and what kind of life it leaves to him? If, indeed, the punishment is not really inflicted — if it becomes the sham which a few years ago such punishments were rapidly becoming — then, indeed, its adoption would be almost tantamount to giving up the attempt to repress murder altogether. But if it really is what it professes to be, and if it is realized in all its rigour by the popular imagination, as it very probably would not be, but as it must be if it is to be efficacious, it will be so shocking that when the memory of the crime is no longer fresh, there will be almost insuperable difficulty in executing it. What comparison can there really be, in point of severity, between consigning a man to the short pang of a rapid death, and immuring him in a living tomb, there to linger out what may be a long life in the hardest and most monotonous toil, without any of its alleviations or rewards

— debarred from all pleasant sights and sounds, and cut off from all earthly hope, except a slight mitigation of bodily restraint, or a small improvement of diet? Yet even such a lot as this, because there is no one moment at which the suffering is of terrifying intensity, and, above all, because it does not contain the element, so imposing to the imagination, of the unknown, is universally reputed a milder punishment than death — stands in all codes as a mitigation of the capital penalty, and is thankfully accepted as such. For it is characteristic of all punishments which depend on duration for their efficacy — all, therefore, which are not corporal or pecuniary — that they are more rigorous than they seem; while it is, on the contrary, one of the strongest recommendations a punishment can have, that it should seem more rigorous than it is; for its practical power depends far less on what it is than on what it seems. There is not, I should think, any human infliction which makes an impression on the imagination so entirely out of proportion to its real severity as the punishment of death. The punishment must be mild indeed which does not add more to the sum of human misery than is necessarily or directly added by the execution of a criminal. As my hon. Friend the Member for Northampton (Mr Gilpin) has himself remarked, the most that human laws can do to anyone in the matter of death is to hasten it; the man would have died at any rate; not so very much later, and on the average, I fear, with a considerably greater amount of bodily suffering. Society is asked, then, to denude itself of an instrument of punishment which, in the grave cases to which alone it is suitable, effects its purposes at a less cost of human suffering than any other; which, while it inspires more terror, is less cruel in actual fact than any punishment that we should think of substituting for it. My hon. Friend says that it does not inspire terror, and that experience proves it to be a failure. But the influence of a punishment is not to be estimated by its effect on hardened criminals. Those whose habitual way of life keeps them, so to speak, at all times within sight of the gallows, do grow to care less about it; as, to compare good things with bad, an old soldier is not much affected by the chance of dying in battle. I can afford to admit all that is often said about the indifference of professional criminals to the gallows. Though of that indifference one-third is probably bravado and another third confidence that they shall have the luck to escape, it is quite probable that the remaining third is real. But the efficacy of a punishment which acts principally through the imagination, is chiefly to be measured by the impression it makes on those who are still innocent; by the horror with which it surrounds the first promptings of guilt; the restraining influence it exercises over the beginning of the thought which, if indulged, would become a temptation; the check which it exerts over the graded declension towards the state — never suddenly attained — in which crime no longer revolts, and punishment no longer terrifies. As for what is called the failure of death punishment, who is able to judge of that? We partly know who those are whom it has not deterred; but who is there who knows whom it has deterred, or how many human beings it has saved who would have lived to be murderers if that awful association had not been thrown round the idea of murder from their earliest infancy? Let us not forget that the most imposing fact loses its power over the imagination if it is made too cheap. When a punishment fit only for the most atrocious crimes is lavished on small offences until human feeling recoils from it, then, indeed, it ceases to intimidate, because it ceases to be believed in. The failure of capital punishment in cases of theft is easily accounted for; the thief did not believe that it would be inflicted. He had learnt by experience that jurors would perjure themselves rather than find him guilty; that Judges would seize any excuse for not sentencing him to death, or for recommending him to mercy; and that if neither jurors nor Judges were merciful, there were still hopes from an authority above both. When things had come to this pass it was high time to give up the vain attempt. When it is impossible to inflict a punishment, or when its infliction becomes a public scandal, the idle threat cannot too soon disappear from the statute book. And in the case of the host of offences which were formerly capital, I heartily rejoice that it did become impracticable to execute the law. If the same state of public feeling comes to exist in the case of murder; if the time comes when jurors refuse to find a murderer guilty; when Judges will not sentence him to death, or will recommend him to mercy; or when, if juries and Judges do not flinch from their duty, Home Secretaries, under pressure of deputations and memorials, shrink from theirs, and the threat becomes, as it became in the other cases, a mere *brutum fulmen*; then, indeed, it may become necessary to do in this case what has been done in those — to abrogate the penalty. That time may come — my hon. Friend thinks that it has nearly come. I hardly know whether he lamented it or boasted of it; but he and his Friends are entitled to the boast; for if it comes it will be their doing, and they will have gained what I cannot but call a fatal victory, for they will have achieved it by bringing about, if they will forgive me for saying so, an enervation, an effeminancy, in the general mind of the country. For what else than effeminancy is it to be so much more shocked by taking a man's life than by depriving him of all that makes life desirable or valuable? Is death, then, the greatest of all earthly ills? *Usque adeone mori miserum est?* Is it, indeed, so dreadful a thing to die? Has it not been from of old one chief part of a manly education to make us despise death — teaching us to account it, if an evil at all, by no means high in the list of evils; at all events, as an inevitable one, and to hold, as it were, our lives in our hands, ready to be given or risked at any moment, for a sufficiently worthy object? I am sure that my hon. Friends know all this as well, and have as much of all these feelings as any of the rest of us; possibly more. But I cannot think that this is likely to be the effect of their teaching on the general mind. I cannot think that the cultivating of a peculiar sensitiveness of conscience on this one point, over and above what results from the general cultivation of the moral sentiments, is permanently consistent with assigning in our own minds to the fact of death no more than the degree of relative importance which belongs to it among the other incidents of our humanity. The men of old cared too little about death, and gave their own lives or took those of others with equal recklessness. Our danger is of the opposite kind, lest we should be so much shocked by death, in general and in the abstract, as to care too much about it in individual cases, both those of other people and our own, which call for its being risked. And I am not putting things at the worst, for it is proved by the experience of other countries that horror of the executioner by no means necessarily implies horror of the assassin. The stronghold, as we all know, of hired assassination in the 18th century was Italy; yet it is said that in some of the Italian populations the infliction of death by sentence of law was in the highest degree offensive and revolting to popular feeling. Much has been said of the sanctity of human life, and the absurdity of supposing that we can teach respect for life by ourselves destroying it. But I am surprised at the employment of this argument, for it is one which might be brought against any punishment whatever. It is not human life only, not human life as such, that ought to be sacred to us, but human feelings. The human capacity of suffering is what we should cause to be respected, not the mere capacity of existing. And we may imagine somebody asking how we can teach people not to inflict suffering by ourselves inflicting it? But to this I should answer — all of us would answer — that to deter by suffering from inflicting suffering is not only possible, but the very purpose of penal justice. Does fining a criminal show want of respect for property, or imprisoning him, for personal freedom? Just as unreasonable is it to think that to take the life of a man who has taken that of another is to show want of regard for human life. We show, on the contrary, most emphatically our regard for it, by the adoption of a rule that he who violates that right in another forfeits it for himself, and that while no other crime that he can commit deprives him of his right to live, this shall. There is one argument against capital punishment, even in extreme cases, which I cannot deny to have weight — on which my hon. Friend justly laid great stress, and which never can be entirely got rid of. It is this — that if by an error of justice an innocent person is put to death, the mistake can never be corrected; all compensation, all reparation for the wrong is impossible. This would be indeed a serious objection if these miserable mistakes — among the most tragical occurrences in the whole round of human affairs — could not be made extremely rare. The argument is invincible where the mode of criminal procedure is dangerous to the innocent, or where the Courts of Justice are not trusted. And this probably is the reason why the objection to an irreparable punishment began (as I believe it did) earlier, and is more intense and more widely diffused, in some parts of the Continent of Europe than it is here. There are on the Continent great and enlightened countries, in which the criminal procedure is not so favourable to innocence, does not afford the same security against erroneous conviction, as it does among us; countries where the Courts of Justice seem to think they fail in their duty unless they find somebody guilty; and in their really laudable desire to hunt guilt from its hiding places, expose themselves to a serious danger of condemning the innocent. If our own procedure and Courts of Justice afforded ground for similar apprehension, I should be the first to join in withdrawing the power of inflicting irreparable punishment from such tribunals. But we all know that the defects of our procedure are the very opposite. Our rules of evidence are even too favourable to the prisoner; and juries and Judges carry out the maxim, 'It is better that ten guilty should escape than that one innocent person should suffer', not only to the letter, but beyond the letter. Judges are most anxious to point out, and juries to allow for, the barest possibility of the prisoner's innocence. No human judgement is infallible; such sad cases as my hon. Friend cited will sometimes occur; but in so grave a case as that of murder, the accused, in our system, has always the benefit of the merest shadow of a doubt. And this suggests another consideration very germane to the question. The very fact that death punishment is more shocking than any other to the imagination, necessarily renders the Courts of Justice more scrupulous in requiring the fullest evidence of guilt. Even that which is the greatest objection to capital punishment, the impossibility of correcting an error once committed, must make, and does make, juries and Judges more careful in forming their opinion, and more jealous in their scrutiny of the evidence. If the substitution of penal servitude for death in cases of murder should cause any declaration in this conscientious scrupulosity, there would be a great evil to set against the real, but I hope rare, advantage of being able to make reparation to a condemned person who was afterwards discovered to be innocent. In order that the possibility of correction may be kept open wherever the chance of this sad contingency is more than infinitesimal, it is quite right that the Judge should recommend to the Crown a commutation of the sentence, not solely when the proof of guilt is open to the smallest suspicion, but whenever there remains anything unexplained and mysterious in the case, raising a desire for more light, or making it likely that further information may at some future time be obtained. I would also suggest that whenever the sentence is commuted the grounds of the commutation should, in some authentic form, be made known to the public. Thus much I willingly concede to my hon. Friend; but on the question of total abolition I am inclined to hope that the feeling of the country is not with him, and that the limitation of death punishment to the cases referred to in the Bill of last year will be generally considered sufficient. The mania which existed a short time ago for paring down all our punishments seems to have reached its limits, and not before it was time.

We were in danger of being left without any effectual punishment, except for small offences. What was formerly our chief secondary punishment — transportation — before it was abolished, had become almost a reward. Penal servitude, the substitute for it, was becoming, to the classes who were principally subject to it, almost nominal, so comfortable did we make our prisons, and so easy had it become to get quickly out of them. Flogging — a most objectionable punishment in ordinary cases, but a particularly appropriate one for crimes of brutality, especially crimes against women — we would not hear of, except, to be sure, in the case of garrotters, for whose peculiar benefit we re-established it in a hurry, immediately after a Member of Parliament had been garrotted. With this exception, offences, even of an atrocious kind, against the person, as my hon. and learned Friend the Member for Oxford (Mr Neate) well remarked, not only were, but still are, visited with penalties so ludicrously inadequate, as to be almost an encouragement to the crime. I think, Sir, that in the case of most offences, except those against property, there is more need of strengthening our punishments than of weakening them; and that severer sentences, with an apportionment of them to the different kinds of offences which shall approve itself better than at present to the moral sentiments of the community, are the kind of reform of which our penal system now stands in need. I shall therefore vote against the Amendment.

QUESTIONS

1. Mill argues that capital punishment is "the least cruel mode in which it is possible adequately to deter from the crime" of murder. What support does he offer for this view? How would he respond to the concern evinced by the Supreme Court of Canada (*The United States vs. Burns*) for the history of wrongful convictions in Canada, the United States, and elsewhere? What would Mill say in response to the Supreme Court of Canada discussion of "The Death Row Phenomenon"?
2. Is Mill's view that capital punishment is an effective deterrent subject to empirical confirmation? Review your answer in light of Rosalind Simson's discussion of the deterrent effect of capital punishment in the next reading.
3. Mill voices a view that is also heard frequently today, namely that penalties in place for dealing with crime, particularly violent crime, are too lenient. Do you think the Supreme Court judgement (*The United States vs. Burns*) deals adequately with this concern in the case of Burns and Raffy, who were accused of the "cold blooded" murder of the father, mother, and sister of Raffy, one of the persons accused of the crime?

DOES CAPITAL PUNISHMENT DETER HOMICIDE?: A CASE STUDY OF EPISTEMOLOGICAL OBJECTIVITY

Rosalind S. Simson

Philosophers, natural and social scientists, and scholars in general traditionally believed that anyone seeking knowledge of the world should be "objective." This meant that people should gather and assess evidence with a detachment and disinterest achieved by setting aside any influences exerted by either their individual and societal circumstances or their

From Metaphilosophy, *Vol. 32, No. 3 April 2001. Reprinted with permission from Blackwell Publishers Ltd.*

moral values.[1] Objectivity of this sort was thought to be both a goal to strive for and a goal that really good knowledge seekers actually achieve.

In recent years, feminists and others engaged in what Evelyn Fox Keller calls "science studies"[2] have argued that scientists and other knowledge seekers historically have been far less successful in achieving detached, disinterested perspectives than they typically believed. Knowledge seekers have always been influenced by their particular situations and moral values. These have affected the problems scholars have chosen to study, the funding they have received, the types of evidence they have sought out, noticed, and acknowledged, the methodologies they have used, and the types of hypotheses they have formulated and deemed acceptable. Much recent feminist writing has been devoted to arguing that scientific and other accounts that traditionally were thought to be objective are, in fact, informed by male-oriented perspectives and values.[3]

The type of critique of the traditional view of knowledge seeking that I have just described has yielded many important insights. By itself, though, it does not challenge the traditional ideal of objectivity. It simply shows that much of what historically passed for objective really was not objective in the traditional sense. Indeed, even if it were established that knowledge seekers have *never* succeeded in achieving totally detached, disinterested perspectives, this by itself would not undermine the traditional ideal of objectivity. Unattainable goals are not necessarily bad goals. For example, being considerate of all others is a worthy ideal, regardless of whether anyone has ever totally succeeded in this quest.

My project in this paper is to examine the more radical claim made by many feminists and others engaged in "science studies" that the traditional ideal of objectivity is misguided.[4] This claim implies that people who sincerely want to know about the world are altogether epistemically justified in allowing their individual and societal situations and moral values to influence their inquiries. On the one hand, I am sympathetic to this radical idea, and my first goal in this paper is to support the view that the traditional ideal of objectivity is wrongheaded and should be replaced. On the other hand, however, I believe that the traditional ideal of objectivity is based on some core precepts that one should be careful not to abandon. Therefore my second goal is to outline a possible alternative ideal for knowledge seeking that sees a central role for situational and value influences, but nevertheless retains the core precepts of the traditional ideal.

I propose to undertake this project as a case study, because I believe that these issues can be dissected more clearly through a concrete example than in the abstract. The question I want to analyze is this: Is capital punishment more effective than protracted prison terms in deterring people, other than the sentenced person, from committing murder? I believe that this example is extremely well-suited to my purposes for several reasons. First, it is a clearly factual question worthy of considerable attention because of its prominent role in the current debate about the death penalty. Second, social scientists have researched this question extensively but have failed to reach a consensus on the proper conclusions to be drawn from their data. And third, people who study the research typically have difficulty detaching themselves from both their values concerning the morality of executing persons convicted of murder and from features of their own personal situations that make the death penalty an important concern for them.

I

Let me begin by briefly summarizing the main points of controversy about whether capital punishment deters homicide better than long-term imprisonment. The modern research began with a series of studies on capital punishment and deterrence conducted in the 1950s and 1960s by Thorsten Sellin. These studies made two sorts of comparisons of homicide rates: (1) they compared these rates in geographically contiguous states, some of which had capital punishment and some of which did not, and (2) they compared these rates over time in single states that had authorized capital punishment during some time periods but not others. The goal was to determine whether the homicide rate has been lower when capital punishment has been in effect than when it has not. Sellin concluded from these studies that capital punishment "has no discernible effect as a deterrent to murder."[5]

In the mid 1970s Isaac Ehrlich challenged Sellin, charging that his studies had too many uncontrolled variables. Ehrlich argued that Sellin failed to take account of some possibly relevant differences between the contiguous states that he compared and some potentially important changes in social conditions that might have occurred over time in the single states that he studied. In addition, Ehrlich argued that instead of only considering whether a state did or did not have a death penalty statute, Sellin should have focused on the important variable of how likely it was that an offender in a state that authorized the death penalty would actually be convicted and executed. Ehrlich used regression analysis — a methodology often employed in the social sciences — to analyze states' execution and homicide data for 1933–67, taking into account such variables as unemployment rates, per capita incomes, the youthfulness of the populations, arrest rates in murder cases, and conviction rates of murder suspects. He concluded that "on the average the tradeoff between the execution of an offender and the lives of potential victims it might have saved was of the order of magnitude of one for eight for the period 1933–67 in the United States" — in other words, that each execution during that period deterred eight murders.[6]

Ehrlich's studies have been widely attacked by social scientists who have agreed with both his criticisms of Sellin and his basic methodology, but whose own studies using this methodology found no evidence that capital punishment deters homicide better than long-term imprisonment. Scholars have made a host of objections to Ehrlich, but I will mention only a few. One is technical, concerning the types of equations he used to analyze data. Another is that the homicide rate data available to Ehrlich failed to make an important distinction between murders for which death is and is not the maximum penalty. A last objection is that Ehrlich did not succeed in his attempt to identify all the relevant variables. For example, he took into account neither changes in the availability of guns during the time period he studied nor a shortening of prison sentences that in some jurisdictions occurred contemporaneously with the abolition of capital punishment.[7] Some social scientists who have conducted studies using Ehrlich's methodology have even concluded that capital punishment has been associated with higher, not lower, homicide rates.[8]

The repudiation of Ehrlich, however, has not been unanimous. Most notably, in the mid-1980s Stephen Layson, a student of Ehrlich's, conducted studies that used Ehrlich's methodology but also accounted for additional variables, incorporated updated data, and measured homicide rates somewhat more reliably. His conclusion, still being roundly attacked on the grounds that his improvements were inadequate to resolve Ehrlich's difficulties, was that every execution deters as many as eighteen homicides.[9]

Lastly, one other noteworthy type of study that has been conducted periodically over the past forty or so years has examined homicide rates shortly preceding and following highly publicized executions. The operating principle here is that a reliable assessment of the deterrent power of capital punishment depends on controlling the variable of whether would-be killers in particular jurisdictions *believe* that punishment by death is a serious possibility there. A few of these studies observed declines in homicide rates during the two weeks following well-publicized executions but rebound effects afterward. Most other studies found no declines whatsoever, and a small number found increases.[10]

II

People who have surveyed the research on the deterrent effects of capital punishment on homicide differ in their conclusions. Very few see in the studies strong evidence of a causal connection between capital punishment and lower homicide rates. Ehrlich and Layson hold distinctly minority viewpoints, and even those sympathetic to their work typically agree that the studies raise a host of questions.

The main issue of disagreement is whether the studies are inconclusive or instead provide compelling evidence that capital punishment is no more effective than long-term imprisonment in deterring homicide. People who hold the latter view typically point out that the vast majority of studies find no correlation between the presence of capital punishment and lower homicide rates. Of course, evidence of such a correlation may emerge in the future. The position of those persuaded that capital punishment does not deter homicide, however, is summarized by this statement by Sellin: "It is impossible to prove that there are no unicorns. All that we can prove is that we've found none so far. If the end result of a long argument . . . is nothing more than a statement that a particular theory can't be disproved, you are probably safe in putting it in the same class as unicorns."[11]

People who consider the research findings to be inconclusive, on the other hand, typically point to Ehrlich and Layson's studies and to some of the research on highly publicized executions to argue that the deterrence hypothesis has not been effectively refuted. In their view, the most significant lesson to be learned from the research is how difficult it is to identify all the applicable variables and to get accurate, relevant, statistics on the homicide rate. Moreover, some commentators suggest that even if the overall homicide rate is unaffected by capital punishment, substantial further research is needed to determine whether this might be the result of countervailing forces. Perhaps some types of homicides are deterred by the threat of death, whereas others are encouraged by it. For example, racial and ethnic minorities who are disproportionately represented on death row may be deterred by the threat of capital punishment. By contrast, whites — particularly those from higher social classes — may assume from execution patterns that society condones killing by "good" people when they are confident of having a just cause.[12]

III

People's views on whether capital punishment deters homicide better than long-term imprisonment typically appear to be generated by the sort of detached, disinterested knowledge seeking envisioned by proponents of the traditional ideal of objectivity. Research on attitudes toward the death penalty has yielded some interesting findings. Although supporters and opponents of capital punishment often cite their beliefs about its deterrent effectiveness as one reason for their positions on the death penalty, studies indicate that these beliefs play only a small role in determining their positions. When asked if they would oppose the death

penalty if it could be proven that it is not a superior deterrent, most capital punishment supporters said they would still favor it based on their moral belief that killing murderers is
necessary for justice. By the same token, when asked if they would favor the death penalty
if it could be proven that it is a superior deterrent, most capital punishment opponents said
that they would still oppose it based on their moral belief that killing for the purpose of retribution is wrong. Moral beliefs about retributivism, therefore, appear to be key to people's
positions on capital punishment.[13]

Since positions on the death penalty generally are not rooted in beliefs about its deterrent
effect, it is striking to see the disparity in belief between opponents and proponents of the
death penalty on the question of deterrence. Whereas approximately 60 percent of the overall population believes that capital punishment is a superior deterrent to homicide,[14] this
belief is held by a much higher percentage of death penalty proponents and a very much
lower percentage of death penalty critics. One study found that 93 percent of supporters
agreed that "the death penalty is a more effective deterrent than life imprisonment," while 92
percent of opponents disagreed.[15] This disparity only makes sense if one assumes that people's ideas about the morality of retributivism influence their views regarding the factual
question of how well capital punishment deters homicide.[16]

The influence of moral values that I have just described seems to extend not only to the
population in general, but also to those who have closely studied the empirical data on capital punishment and deterrence. Scholars who argue that the death penalty is inhumane or
uncivilized tend to be persuaded that it does not deter homicide, whereas those who argue on
retributivist grounds that it is necessary for justice tend to consider the deterrence issue unsettled.[17] A striking example of the association I am suggesting here can be found in the U.S.
Supreme Court's opinions in *Gregg v. Georgia*, a 1976 case that upheld the constitutionality
of capital punishment as long as judges and juries are given standards to use in deciding when
to impose death sentences. In a plurality opinion joined by Justices Powell and Stevens,
Justice Stewart expresses support for retributivist arguments and then asserts the following
about the research on capital punishment's effectiveness as a deterrent to homicide: "The
results simply have been inconclusive. . . . [T]here is no convincing empirical evidence either
supporting or refuting this view."[18] By contrast, Justice Marshall, in a dissenting opinion,
rejects both the retributivist arguments of the plurality opinion and Justice Stewart's assessment of the evidence on the effectiveness of capital punishment as a deterrent. He cites
approvingly a report by a United Nations Committee: ". . . [T]he data which now exist show
no correlation between the existence of capital punishment and lower rates of capital crime."[19]

People's interpretations of the research on capital punishment as a deterrent often appear
to be influenced by not only moral views regarding retributivism but also by personal and
societal situations. For example, most police officers and other government officials charged
with crime control consider the studies inconclusive. Indeed, they generally believe affirma-
tively that capital punishment does deter homicide.[20] On the other hand, a great number of
African Americans, whose representation on death row is disproportionately high, appear to
view the studies as settling the case against deterrence.[21]

IV

The case that I have just examined poses a challenge to the traditional ideal of objectivity.
According to this ideal, the influences of values and situations on knowledge seeking
described in Section III are illegitimate. More precisely, those wanting to know the effec-

tiveness of capital punishment as a deterrent to homicide are not epistemically justified in allowing their analyses of the research to be swayed by their moral beliefs or situationally based concerns; they ought to struggle to resist such influences. I believe that this traditional view is untenable. Although, as I discuss in Section V, I think that values and situations can sometimes influence knowledge seeking in improper ways, I am convinced that some such influences are quite appropriate and should be taken into account. To support this claim, this section offers examples of two types of influence I consider appropriate. I suggest that people in varying situations and with different moral values may reasonably approach the studies on deterrence with different expectations about the amount of evidence needed for the studies to be persuasive. Thus, someone who believes that killing is always immoral, except in cases of self-defense, may be epistemically justified in demanding less evidence than many others do before believing that capital punishment is not a superior deterrent to homicide. Similarly, a law enforcement official immersed in the business of crime control may be epistemically justified in demanding more evidence than many others do before accepting that capital punishment fails to deter homicide more effectively than long-term imprisonment.

Consider, for example, Oliver Officer, a hypothetical chief of police for a major city and Betty Barrister, a partner in a small law firm who frequently takes on appeals from prisoners on death row. Both would like to see more conclusive studies of the effects of capital punishment on the homicide rate. In view of the large number of variables to be controlled and the enormous amount of data to be collected, however, it is unlikely that significantly less controversial research will be produced any time soon. As conscientious knowledge seekers interested in this issue, should Officer and Barrister decide, based on the current research, that capital punishment is not a superior deterrent to homicide or instead suspend belief pending further research?

The risk in believing now, based on the existing evidence, that capital punishment deters homicide no better than long-term imprisonment is that one may be mistaken. Future studies may produce evidence that the death penalty has a superior deterrent effect on at least particular kinds of homicides. Officer may be very worried about making such a mistake because he has taken on the enormous responsibility of trying to control crime and safeguard a city. The claim that capital punishment has no particular effectiveness as a deterrent is often used to bolster arguments for abolishing capital punishment. It may be an important consideration for those undecided about the morality of retributivism. Officer will naturally be wary of abolitionist arguments as long as there is any uncertainty about the death penalty's deterrent effects. His cautiousness, furthermore, may be enhanced by the realization that his beliefs on the deterrent effectiveness of capital punishment may shape social policy. Lawmakers voting on capital punishment often take to heart the opinions of people in positions like his.

Barrister, by contrast, may have a very different set of concerns. Because she is not personally responsible for controlling crime, she may be less worried than Officer about mistakenly believing that capital punishment is no better a deterrent than long-term imprisonment. She may be more worried than Officer, however, about the risks inherent in suspending belief on this matter pending further investigation. Suppose that Barrister's work with death row inmates has led her to staunchly oppose capital punishment, because it has made her keenly aware of the extent to which one's ability to secure top quality counsel and pay for expert witnesses affects one's chances of being sentenced to death. Suppose, furthermore, that Barrister realizes that failing to take a position on the death penalty's ineffectiveness as a deterrent means giving up an important argument against capital punishment. In light of the increasing number of states enacting death penalty statutes and carrying out executions, Barrister may be especially wary of waiting for more evidence before believing that capital punishment has no particular effectiveness as a deterrent to homicide.

Officer and Barrister are both looking at the same evidence in a sincere and conscientious attempt to learn whether capital punishment is a superior deterrent to homicide. They hold the evidence to different standards, thus reaching different conclusions, because one is more concerned about the risk of holding a mistaken belief about the death penalty's effectiveness as a deterrent, whereas the other is more concerned about the risk of having no belief on this matter at all. Avoiding error and believing what is true are both important, though often incompatible, epistemic goals.[22] The traditional ideal of objectivity does not recognize the existence of these different, and often competing, goals. Certainly, it offers no "objective" way of determining in any particular instance either how much weight one should give to each goal or which goal should take precedence.

I am not arguing that Officer and Barrister would necessarily make the same choices between epistemic goals with regard to other beliefs. Consider, for instance, the proposition that there is not extremely strong evidence to support the conclusion that capital punishment fails to be a superior deterrent. If, as in the previous example, Officer were primarily concerned with avoiding error, he would suspend belief in this claim. I suggest, however, that Officer may believe this proposition, because the different stakes in this case may cause him to give greater priority to the goal of holding true belief. Unlike the previous example, this belief in no way poses a threat to Officer's ability to safeguard the city.

My point is simply that when considering any *particular* candidate for belief, it is both appropriate and sensible for conscientious knowledge seekers (like Officer and Barrister) to allow factors specific to their own situations to guide their choices of epistemic goals. They should not struggle to resist these influences. As a result, a law enforcement official like Officer and a lawyer like Barrister may be equally epistemically justified in their different views on the deterrent effectiveness of capital punishment.

I would offer a similar analysis of the legitimacy of allowing one's moral beliefs about killing and retribution to influence one's interpretation of the data concerning capital punishment's effectiveness in deterring homicide. Suppose that Linda Letlive believes that killing, except in cases of self-defense, is always immoral, whereas Peter Payback maintains that killing those convicted of murder is required for justice. The belief that capital punishment fails to deter homicide better than long-term imprisonment fits neatly into Letlive's system of beliefs. Although there is no inconsistency in Payback's believing both that capital punishment is required for justice *and* that it is not a superior deterrent, the latter belief no doubt creates some conflict for him. Like Officer in the previous example, Payback may fear that without the argument that capital punishment has a superior deterrent effect, it may be more difficult to persuade voters and legislators to support death penalty statutes. He may, therefore, be more wary than Letlive of mistakenly believing, based on the available data, that capital punishment is not a better deterrent to homicide than long-term imprisonment. In this case, Payback may be more concerned than Letlive with the epistemic goal of avoiding error.

By the same token, Letlive may be more concerned than Payback about the prospect of suspending belief pending further investigation. Suppose that she is both distressed about the homicide rate and persuaded that the death penalty is immoral, and so is eager for society to put resources into finding other strategies for reducing the murder rate. As a result of these concerns, Letlive may hold the belief that capital punishment is not a superior deterrent to a lower standard of proof than does Payback. Unlike Payback, in other words, her major epistemic goal in assessing the deterrent effect of capital punishment is not avoiding error, but rather achieving true belief.

Again, the traditional ideal of objectivity does not distinguish between these different epistemic ends. Nor does it explain how people in a particular context can make a principled choice between them in a detached, disinterested, "objective" way. I maintain that it is perfectly appropriate and reasonable for people to consult their moral values for guidance in making a choice of epistemic goals. For this reason, I suggest that both Letlive and Payback are epistemically justified in their different views of how well capital punishment deters homicide.

I am not saying that all cases are entirely like the one that I have just described. People who differ in their situations and moral values often are not epistemically justified in holding different beliefs concerning particular factual matters. For example, there are many cases in which the evidence for a particular claim is so strong that people who differ in their epistemic goals nevertheless are epistemically justified in believing the claim. The analysis in this section, however, is still applicable to these instances. Even when the evidence for a claim is very strong, it typically remains possible that, for some individual in unusual circumstances, the consequences of making an error would be so devastating that he or she would be epistemically justified in suspending belief. Thus, I suggest that assessments of factual claims always require people, consciously or unconsciously, to make choices about epistemic goals and, as I have argued, these choices cannot be made in a context-free, value-neutral way.

V

Although I have argued that the traditional ideal of objectivity is untenable, I believe that this ideal is based on two crucial precepts that a viable conception of knowledge seeking must be careful not to abandon. The first is that knowledge seekers are not entitled to whatever beliefs suit their own particular, and possibly idiosyncratic, situations and moral values. The other is that knowledge is not determined by people in positions of power or by those whose moral values are widely shared. It is worth noting that most scholars engaged in "science studies" agree on this. Certainly, most feminists do. Typically, feminists have been critical of accounts and theories in the various disciplines that are informed by the situations and moral values of the dominant male perspective. Moreover, the point of these feminist critiques often is not simply that one can see matters differently; it is that these accounts and theories are androcentrically biased and should be replaced by something better.

What is needed, then, is an ideal for seeking knowledge that would replace the traditional ideal of objectivity but nevertheless would incorporate the two precepts just discussed.[23] This substitute ideal would sanction some but not all kinds of influences of values and situations on epistemically justified belief. Moreover, it would offer guidance to conscientious knowledge seekers wishing to proceed in epistemically principled ways that would not require them to struggle to dissociate themselves from the influences of their circumstances and moral values. I do not claim to be able to offer a full-fledged account of such an ideal, but I can offer some suggestions about its components.

First, before adopting a position on a particular matter, knowledge seekers should attempt to ascertain the often partisan views of individuals from a broad range of situations and with a wide spectrum of moral values. For example, those studying the data on how well capital punishment deters homicide ideally would ask, "What do philosophers, psychologists, social scientists, community leaders from a variety of sectors of society, law enforcement officials, convicted murderers, and so forth make of the studies that have been done? Moreover, what conclusions are drawn by those who believe that it is always immoral to kill except in self-defense, those who believe that killing people convicted of murder is necessary for justice, and those who are undecided about their moral views on these issues?"

One reason for seeking out a diversity of interested viewpoints is to solicit ideas for further studies that might be conducted. For example, police officers might have ideas about specific circumstances worth studying in which the death penalty might be a particularly effective deterrent — e.g., cases in which prisoners serving life sentences attempt to escape by killing the police officers charged with transporting them. African American community leaders might have suggestions about how to interview convicted African American murderers to try to ascertain what motivated their actions. A frequent complaint made by feminists is that mainstream investigations often "conceal data" by failing to ask various pertinent questions.[24] Soliciting a variety of viewpoints should make it less likely that this will occur.

Soliciting input from many interested parties may also expand the range of possible interpretations of data that are considered. For example, those trying to understand the existing data on deterrence might consult both psychologists and convicted murderers for ideas about whether the threat of execution would be likely to deter or encourage various categories of potential killers. Moreover, people on all sides of the moral debate can benefit from becoming aware of the ways in which those with differing moral views tend to interpret the data.

Lastly, people with different situations and moral values may perceive rather different reasons for considering either error avoidance or truth seeking to be more compelling epistemic ends when deciding which interpretations are supported by the data. It is quite common for people not even to notice that they are making choices between epistemic ends. Contemplating a variety of viewpoints will help them to become aware of these choices and to think carefully about the basis for them.

A second proposed goal for those seeking knowledge is to be open-minded in considering the spectrum of views generated by people with varying situations and moral values. This is a different kind of open-mindedness from the one prescribed by the traditional ideal of objectivity. The latter encourages people to strive for disinterestedness by trying to eliminate the influences of their situations and moral values. The ideal I propose asks people to embrace these influences by making judgments only after they have examined their own as well as others' interested perspectives.

To be open-minded in the way I am suggesting, people must be aware of their own situations and values and the influence these have on their own inquiries. One of the most harmful consequences of the traditional ideal of objectivity is that its insistence that detached, disinterested perspectives are desirable and attainable encourages blindness to the role played by one's own values and circumstances. Such encouragement, coupled with people's typically strong sensitivity to the influence of others' values and situations, tends to bias people in favor of their own views or those of others with values and backgrounds similar to their own.

Open-mindedness of the sort that I am advocating may occasionally require a person to be somewhat deferential to perspectives he or she is ill-equipped to evaluate. As advocates of so-called "standpoint epistemology" have argued, not all viewpoints are equally conducive to insightful perception.[25] In some respects this is widely acknowledged. For example, someone unschooled in social science methodology obviously cannot expect to evaluate the mathematics of an attempt to use regression analysis to assess the deterrent effects of capital punishment. More controversially, but I think equally validly, a white, middle class person with a supportive family may be unable to fathom the psychological perspective of a poor, African American teenager from a fractured family who contemplates murder. The views of convicted murderers from similar backgrounds might be particularly instructive in this regard. I certainly am not suggesting that people avoid scrutinizing viewpoints they have difficulty understanding, but I am proposing that they treat such viewpoints, especially when they come from marginalized members of society, with an extra measure of respect.

While good knowledge seekers should strive for open-mindedness, I propose, thirdly, that they should be suspicious and even intolerant of some types of situational and value influences. This follows from the claim that not all perceptual vantage points are equal. I cannot offer criteria for identifying illegitimate situational and value influences, but I can offer some extreme examples to explain what I have in mind. Suppose that someone's thinking about the deterrent value of capital punishment is influenced by the belief that it is not a severe moral problem if a state sometimes executes people it knows are innocent because it believes those executions will deter potential murderers. Similarly, suppose that a person's beliefs about capital punishment and deterrence are influenced by the very recent murder of her only child, or that a police officer's thinking is driven by an acute fear of personal attack. Holding patently immoral values or being in highly emotionally charged situations may not pose significant obstacles to finding innovative data sources or formulating hypotheses worthy of consideration. I suggest, however, that evaluations of data influenced by such values or situations are insufficiently principled to be deserving of the respect for which I argued in Section IV.

Fourth, and lastly, seekers of knowledge must always have as their goal the discovery and interpretation of evidence. This is a requirement for what has sometimes been called "epistemic responsibility."[26] As I have argued, people's circumstances and moral values can guide them in such matters as designing empirical studies, finding and identifying data, generating hypotheses, and setting standards for how much evidence is needed to substantiate these hypotheses. People are not epistemically justified, however, in holding beliefs that are aligned with their moral values or personal situations but clearly incompatible with any reasonable interpretations of the evidence. For example, people who believe that killing murders is morally required for justice would not be epistemically justified in concluding from the existing studies that capital punishment *does* deter homicide. The data are simply too controversial to support this conclusion. One can reach this conclusion only by ignoring the evidence and believing what one's circumstances or values lead one to want to believe.[27]

VI

As I have indicated, I do not see my proposals as a fully developed account of an ideal for knowledge seeking that can replace the traditional ideal. One point that deserves more attention is the issue of how to identify illegitimate influences of circumstances and moral values. Another is the question of how to decide when to defer to perspectives that one is poorly equipped to evaluate. I hope, however, that the account I have offered here is at least a beginning. It provides a basic framework for evaluating the efforts of those who consciously acknowledge the situations and moral values that compose their epistemic standpoints. Moreover, it offers some guidelines that knowledge seekers can look to in attempting to proceed in conscientious, epistemically principled ways.[28]

NOTES

1. Advocates of the traditional view of objectivity generally do not exclude the influence of epistemic values — e.g., that comprehensive explanations are better than ad hoc explanations.
2. Evelyn Fox Keller, "Science and its Critics," *Academe*, Sept.–Oct. 1995, p. 10.
3. The feminist literature abounds with examples. See, for instance, Ruth Hubbard, "Have Only Men Evolved?" in *Discovering Reality: Feminist Perspectives on Epistemology, Metaphysics, Methodology, and Philosophy of Science*, ed. Sandra Harding and Merrill Hintikka (Dordrecht, Holland: D. Reidel, 1983), pp. 45–69; Naomi Scheman, "Individualism and the Objects of Psychology," also in *Discovering Reality*, pp. 225–44; and Anne Fausto-Sterling, "Hormones and Aggression: An Explanation of Power?" in *Myths of Gender: Biological Theories About Women and Men*, 2nd ed. (New York: Basic Books, 1992), pp. 123–55.
4. This radical position has its roots in Thomas Kuhn's *The Structure of Scientific Revolutions* (Chicago: Univ. of Chicago Press, 1962). More recent proponents include, for example, Barry Barnes and David Bloor, "Relativism, Rationalism, and the Sociology of Knowledge," in *Rationality and Relativism*, ed. Martin Hollis and Steven Lukes (Cambridge, Mass.: MIT Press, 1982), pp. 21–47; Donna Haraway, *Primate Visions: Gender, Race and Nature in the World of Modern Science* (New York: Routledge, 1989); and Nancy Fraser and Linda J. Nicholson, "Social Criticism Without Philosophy: An Encounter Between Feminism and Postmodernism," in *Feminism/Postmodernism*, ed. Linda J. Nicholson (New York: Routledge, 1990), pp. 19–38.
5. Thorsten Sellin, *Capital Punishment* (New York: Harper & Row, 1967), p. 138. A recent study by the *New York Times* conducted along lines similar to Sellin's reached the same conclusion for the years 1978–98 as Sellin reached for the period he studied. See Raymond Bonner and Ford Fessenden, "States With No Death Penalty Share Lower Homicide Rates," *New York Times*, Late Ed., 22 Sept. 2000, Sec. 1, p. 1, col. 1.
6. Isaac Ehrlich, "The Deterrent Effect of Capital Punishment: A Question of Life and Death," *American Economic Review*, 65 (1975), p. 398.
7. For discussions of the objections to Ehrlich, see Franklin E. Zimring and Gordon Hawkins, *Capital Punishment and the American Agenda* (Cambridge: Cambridge Univ. Press, 1986) pp. 175–81; Hans Zeisel, "The Deterrent Effect of the Death Penalty: Facts v. Faith," in *The Death Penalty in America*, 2nd ed. (New York: Oxford Univ. Press, 1982), pp. 129–32; and Samuel Cameron, "A Review of the Econometric Evidence on the Effects of Capital Punishment," *The Journal of Socio-Economics*, 23, No. 1–2 (1994), pp. 202–206.
8. See William J. Bowers and Glenn L. Pierce, "The Illusion of Deterrence in Isaac Ehrlich's Research on Capital Punishment," *Yale Law Journal*, 85 (Dec. 1975), pp. 187–208; and William J. Bowers and Glenn L. Pierce, "Deterrence or Brutalization: What is the Effect of Executions?" *Crime and Delinquency*, 26 (1980), pp. 453–84.
9. Stephen Layson, "Homicide and Deterrence: A Reexamination of the United States Time-Series Evidence," *Southern Economic Journal*, 52 (1985), pp. 68–89. For criticism of Layson, see James Alan Fox and Michael L. Radelet, "Persistent Flaws in Econometric Studies of the Deterrent Effect of the Death Penalty," *Loyola of L.A. Law Review*, 23, No. 1 (November 1989), pp. 29–44.
10. For a summary of these studies, see William C. Bailey and Ruth D. Peterson, "Murder, Capital Punishment, and Deterrence: A Review of the Evidence and an Examination of Police Killings," *Journal of Social Issues*, 50, No. 2 (1994), pp. 56–58.
11. Thorsten Sellin, *The Penalty of Death* (London: Sage, 1980), p. 144. Examples of other scholars who agree with Sellin are Zeisel, pp. 132–33; Craig Haney and Deana Dorman Logan, "Broken Promise: The Supreme Court's Response to Social Science Research on Capital Punishment," *Journal of Social Issues*, 50, No. 2 (1994), p. 88; and Zimring and Hawkins. Zimring and Hawkins remark, "[t]he death penalty is about as relevant to controlling violent crimes as rain-dancing is to controlling the weather." (p. 14).
12. For the view that the studies are inconclusive see Ernest Van Den Haag, "Why Capital Punishment?" *Albany Law Review*, 54, No. 3/4 (1990), p. 509; and Walter Berns, *For Capital Punishment: Crime and the Morality of the Death Penalty* (New York: Basic, 1979), pp. 87–127.
13. See Phoebe C. Ellsworth and Samuel R. Gross, "Hardening of the Attitudes: Americans' Views on the Death Penalty," *Journal of Social Issues*, 50, No. 2 (1994), pp. 26–33.

14. Ellsworth and Gross, p. 27.

15. Ellsworth and Gross, p. 27. Although this study was conducted in 1974, a time when a higher percentage of people than today cited their belief that the death penalty is a deterrent to crime as the basis for their endorsement of capital punishment, the statistics nevertheless dramatically illustrate the point in the text. Even in 1974, the percentage of people who based their support for capital punishment on a belief in its value as a deterrent to crime was far lower than could possibly account for the disparity in opinion about whether capital punishment does in fact act as such a deterrent.

16. Another example of moral values influencing factual beliefs in the capital punishment area concerns value influences on jurors' factual beliefs about the guilt or innocence of defendants in capital cases. Social scientists have conducted numerous studies of both actual jurors in real cases and of people serving as jurors in video-taped simulated cases. These studies have consistently found that people who oppose the death penalty are more likely than those who support it to conclude, based on the evidence presented at trial, that defendants in capital cases are innocent of the charges against them. See Claudia L. Cowan, William C. Thompson, and Phoebe C. Ellsworth, "The Effects of Death Qualification on Jurors' Predisposition to Convict and on the Quality of Deliberation," *Law and Human Behavior*, 8 (1984) pp. 53–79.

17. Compare, for example, the arguments on retribution and deterrence offered by death penalty opponents Anthony G. Amsterdam, "Capital Punishment," *The Stanford Magazine*, Fall/Winter 1977, and Zimring and Hawkins with those offered by death penalty proponents Van Den Haag, 1990, and Berns. Berns charges that the reason a majority of scholars conclude from the research that capital punishment is not a superior deterrent to homicide is "that most studies of deterrence were undertaken by criminologists who were inveterate opponents of capital punishment, and their opposition . . . may have influenced their work" (Berns, p. 92). Of course, there are exceptions to the association I am suggesting here. See, for example, Igor Primoratz, *Justifying Legal Punishment* (London: Humanities, 1989), pp. 155–69, who offers a retributivist defense of capital punishment while rejecting the claim that the death penalty is a superior deterrent to homicide.

18. *Gregg v. Georgia*, 428 U.S. 153, 185 (1976) (plurality opinion of Stewart, J.). The opinion then goes on to state that, regardless of the empirical evidence, for some would-be murderers — e.g., those who contemplate murder for hire — "the death penalty undoubtedly is a significant deterrent." (pp. 185–86). Haney and Logan point out (pp. 87–90) that Justice Stewart's position in *Gregg* on the effectiveness of capital punishment as a deterrent has served as precedent in various subsequent court opinions concerning the constitutionality of specific aspects of capital punishment.

19. *Gregg v. Georgia*, 428 U.S. 153, 233 (1976) (Marshall, J., dissenting).

20. See "Establishing Constitutional Procedures for the Imposition of Capital Punishment," Report of the Senate Judiciary Committee, *Congressional Record*, 17 January 1980, pp. 7–14.

21. Existing studies of attitudes toward the death penalty do not expressly address the question of how members of different racial groups view the issue of whether capital punishment is a superior deterrent to homicide. I base the claim I make in the text on two considerations: 1) statistics show that African Americans oppose capital punishment in far greater number than whites do (see Ellsworth and Gross, p. 22); and 2) people who oppose capital punishment generally are persuaded that the evidence clearly establishes that the death penalty deters homicide no better than long-term imprisonment.

22. The existence of these competing epistemic goals was first noted by William James, "The Will to Believe," *New World*, June 1896; rpt. in his *Essays in Pragmatism*, ed. Alburey Castell (New York: Hafner, 1948), pp. 99–100. Others have refined the idea. For example, Alvin Goldman distinguishes between the "reliability" and the "power" of a process, method, or a system. Reliability "consists in a tendency to produce a high truth ratio of beliefs." "A reliable process, method, or procedure is an antidote to error." Power, by contrast, "is the capacity . . . to produce a large number of true beliefs." Power is "the antidote to ignorance." "A method or system can be very reliable without being very powerful; and a method or system can be pretty powerful but not terribly reliable." Alvin I. Goldman, *Epistemology and Cognition* (Cambridge, Mass.: Harvard Univ. Press, 1986), pp. 26–27.

23. For examples of authors who have taken this general approach, see Sandra Harding, "Rethinking Standpoint Epistemology: What is 'Strong Objectivity'?" in *Feminist Epistemologies*, ed. Linda

Alcoff and Elizabeth Potter (New York: Routledge, 1993), pp. 49–82; Donna Haraway, "Situated Knowledges: The Science Question in Feminism and the Privilege of Partial Perspective," *Feminist Studies*, 14, No. 3 (1988), pp. 575–99; and Helen E. Longino, *Science as Social Knowledge* (Princeton Univ. Press, 1990), Chapter 4.

24. See, for example, Nancy Hartsock, "The Feminist Standpoint: Developing the Ground for a Specifically Feminist Historical Materialism," in Harding and Hintikka, pp. 283–310; and Kathryn Pyne Addelson, "Moral Revolution," in *Women and Values: Readings in Recent Feminist Philosophy*, ed. Marilyn Pearsall, 3rd ed. (Belmont, Calif.: Wadsworth, 1999), pp. 328–43.

25. See, for example, Hartsock, "The Feminist Standpoint," and Dorothy Smith, *The Conceptual Practices of Power: A Feminist Sociology of Knowledge* (Boston: Northeastern Univ. Press, 1990).

26. For discussions of the notion of "epistemic responsibility," see, for example, Lorraine Code, *Epistemic Responsibility* (Hanover, N.H.: Univ. Press of New England, 1987) and Rosalind Simson, "Values, Circumstances, and Epistemic Justification," *The Southern Journal of Philosophy*, XXXI, No. 3 (1993).

27. Ellsworth and Gross cite an interesting experiment that was conducted on two groups of people — one group that initially believed that capital punishment does deter homicide and the other that initially believed that it does not. Both were given a pair of fictitious studies, one that supplied data strongly supporting the deterrence hypothesis and the other that supplied data strongly refuting it. In each case the subjects accepted the evidence that favored the position they originally held and simply rejected the contrary evidence. Clearly, this is an example of improper knowledge seeking, regardless of the people's reasons for initially believing as they did.

28. I would like to thank Eugen Baer, Richard Bensel, Scott Brophy, Ben Daise, Patricia Kerr, Steven Lee, Risa Lieberwitz, Richard W. Miller, Neelam Sethi, Henry Shue, and especially Gary Simson for their helpful comments on earlier drafts of this paper.

QUESTIONS

1. People disagree quite sharply about whether capital punishment actual deters murder. Are these disagreements empirically resolvable? Does it matter whether they are resolvable?

2. Why does the debate about the deterrence value of capital punishment raise questions, in Rosalind Simson's view, about the objectivity of knowledge?

3. Simson concludes that when coming to conclusions about empirical questions, people are justified in allowing "factors specific to their own situation" as well as their moral beliefs to influence their interpretation of empirical issues. How does she defend this view?

4. Simson argues that the traditional view of the objectivity of knowledge is based on two precepts that are sound and should not be abandoned. What are those precepts, why are they important, and why in her view should they not be abandoned?

RETRIBUTIVISM AND THE DEATH PENALTY

Alan Brudner

A reasoned approach to the death penalty presupposes a comprehensive theory of punishment. A comprehensive theory of punishment is an account of punishment which distinguishes it from arbitrary and unjust violence and which, in doing so, provides a criterion for the legitimate deprivation of rights. Whether or not the death penalty is just, whether it should or should not be retained or restored can be decided only with reference to the criterion of justice generated by a true account of punishment.

Since Beccaria, the argument for the abolition of the death penalty has customarily been advanced from within the framework of a utilitarian theory of punishment. According to this theory, punishment is an expression of the impulse for self-defence moralized by the feeling of sympathy.[1] Whereas the former is rooted in the self-regarding desire for pleasure and aversion to pain, the latter allows us to transcend the narrow bounds of self and identify our own with collective pleasures and pains. Thus punishment is collective self-defence. Since the aim of collective defence is what constitutes punishment as a moral phenomenon in contradistinction to private revenge, it alone can provide grounds for the legitimate pursuit of the aim. For punishment is an evil that can be justified only as a means of avoiding greater evil; that is, only if its social benefits exceed its social costs.[2] That punishment is an evil follows from the hedonistic psychology and ethics of utilitarian thought. For Bentham the good at which all human beings aim is happiness, understood as the excess of pleasure over pain. Therefore the good at which all just policy must aim is the maximization of pleasure in the social aggregate. Now punishment inflicts suffering and so belongs in the debit column of the social utility ledger. It is acceptable, therefore, only if it yields a return of pleasure greater than its cost in pain. The benefits to be derived from punishment are: deterrence of potential offenders, the protection of society against actual offenders, and the rehabilitation of the criminal. Accordingly, the decision as to whether a particular instance of punishment is moral or immoral is basically an accounting decision. If the punishment works more harm than good, or if the same benefits can be obtained at less cost in suffering, then the punishment is unjust in the only sense intelligible to a utilitarian. It is especially the latter criterion that has provided the major focus for policy research on the death penalty and that has structured whatever rational debate one can find on the subject. Once the utilitarian premises are granted, it remains to determine by means of empirical studies whether, as compared with long-term imprisonment, the death penalty is either a uniquely effective deterrent to murder or a uniquely effective protection against those convicted of murder. Of its rehabilitative effects nothing need be said.

From a utilitarian standpoint the death penalty is difficult to justify. The statistical evidence fails to confirm (though neither does it decisively refute) the common intuition that capital punishment deters potential murderers and protects society from actual ones more effectively than incarceration for life.[3] It is true that no study of the deterrent effect of capital punishment can be conclusive, since it is impossible to compare the effects of retention and abolition within the same jurisdiction over the same time period. But since the burden of justification rests with those who would take a life, inconclusive data ought properly to weigh in favor of abolition. Ernest van den Haag has, to be sure, formulated a retentionist

From the University of Toronto Law Journal, *Vol. XXX, No. 4, 1980. Reprinted by permission of University of Toronto Press Incorporated.*

case that takes into account the lack of firm proof for the marginal deterrent value of the death penalty.[4] He argues that, given our uncertainty about deterrence, capital punishment should be retained in order to minimize the costs of our being wrong. The risk of causing unnecessary suffering to the criminal is preferable to that of exposing innocent people to murderers who might have been deterred. Though ingenious, this argument can, I think, be countered on utilitarian grounds. One could point out that, in retaining capital punishment, we choose the alternative that carries a risk of injustice over the one which carries none. For if we abolish the death penalty and people murder who would have been deterred, we have committed no injustice because we could not have known they would be deterred. But if we retain it and execute someone in vain, then we have done wrong in killing someone without sufficient reason. A more plausible justification of capital punishment from a utilitarian perspective is that of John Stuart Mill, who simply challenged the commonplace assumption that life imprisonment inflicts less suffering on the criminal than death.[5] Yet even this point argues less in favor of capital punishment than for granting the convict the right to choose, and so merely shifts the moral dilemma from capital punishment to suicide or euthanasia.

Were the utilitarian account of punishment the true one, therefore, we should have no doubt but that the movement toward abolition in the western world is securely grounded in reason, and that opposition to this movement, however broadly based, can be justly disregarded. However, a number of legal philosophers have insistently called attention to shocking inadequacies in the theory, and the result of their efforts is that the classic or pure utilitarian position outlined above now stands discredited even among philosophers whom one could still class as utilitarians.[6] As yet little has been done to assess the implications of this development for the moral status of the death penalty.[7] Such an assessment is, however, an urgent necessity, because the downfall of utilitarianism directs our attention once again to retributivism, a theory of punishment that has traditionally furnished arguments in favor of the death penalty.[8] Accordingly, the next section of this paper recapitulates the main objections to the utilitarian position and argues that recent efforts to rescue it by retreating to a qualified utilitarianism are in vain. The succeeding sections attempt both to vindicate retributivism as the only morally defensible account of punishment and to explore its implications for the death penalty. I intend to show that, far from specifically enjoining capital punishment for first-degree murder, retributivism provides grounds for favouring abolition as an ideal, though also for opposing it in circumstances which make the realization of the ideal imprudent.

The test of an adequate theory of punishment is whether it can save, provide an explicit ground for, and so confirm the prephilosophic distinction between punishment and arbitrary violence. Sense-perception alone cannot distinguish between murder and judicial killing, or between abduction and judicial detention. Our common-sense conviction that a difference nonetheless exists must therefore remain a prejudice vulnerable to skeptical questioning unless a philosophy of punishment can disclose the real basis of the distinction and so confirm it to rational insight. Now there are two levels at which thought can seek to clarify punishment. At one level it attempts merely to analyse the concept of punishment, to isolate the various elements implicit in its definition that distinguish it from wrongful injury. Although this approach yields important results, it can never produce a "justification" of punishment, for it deals only with a conventional object, with what we mean by punishment, without ever showing that what we mean has a foundation in reality. Thus analysis merely describes — it cannot confirm — the content of moral opinion.

The second level is that of theory. Here thought aims at a scientific account of the phenomenon of punishment. Rather than analysing an abstract concept, it seeks to disclose the real nature of the thing. The effect of such a theory may well be to debunk the common opinion regarding the essential distinction between judicial and criminal force, or it may be to confirm that opinion — that is, to provide a justification of punishment. But although only theory can justify punishment, the analytic approach is a necessary preliminary, because it alone can provide standards for the verification of theory. By specifying the conceptual elements of the distinction between punishment and violence, analysis furnishes the criteria by which we can assess the validity of justificatory theories of punishment.

There are at least three factors which distinguish punishment from violence for common sense. One of these is purpose. Punishment differs from unjust violence in that it is directed towards a good that is genuinely common — that is, common both to those who punish and to him that is punished — while unjust violence aims at some particular or exclusive interest. It is this factor of aim that distinguishes punishment not only from criminal aggression but also from that form of violence with which it is in all other essential respects identical, namely, revenge. Second, punishment differs from unjust violence in that it is intrinsically related to desert. Punishment, we may say, is the deserved infringement of a right. That it is connected with desert further implies that punishment can only be (a) a reaction to wrongdoing, and (b) a measured reaction — measured, that is, to the gravity of the wrong. The question as to the meaning and criterion of an appropriate measure is of course the crucial one in a discussion of the death penalty, and I shall return to it presently. For now let us simply say that implicit in the notion of punishment (as connected with desert) is a relation of fitness between punishment and crime. This means that penalties must be measured not only to the seriousness of the objective but also to the degree of subjective responsibility, since it is responsibility alone that constitutes wrongdoing. Thus civilized criminal codes recognize various degrees of culpable homicide ranging from manslaughter to first-degree murder, the degrees of guilt or desert corresponding to degrees of intent (or what is called *mens rea*), and they prescribe penalties which vary in severity according to the degree of intent. The converse of this principle of proportionality is that of strict liability, according to which the intention of the individual is irrelevant to the determination either of guilt or of the appropriate statutory penalty. Accordingly, a morally sound theory of punishment must (a) justify punishment with reference to a good that is genuinely universal, (b) save the connection between punishment and wrongdoing, and (c) save the rule of proportionality as between punishment and crime.

As has been frequently argued, the utilitarian theory fails on all three counts. In the first place, it views punishment as an evil inflicted on one individual for the benefit of others. The criminal is sacrificed, or used as a means, to the welfare of the majority, so that punishment becomes indistinguishable from the criminal use of force. Secondly, the utilitarian theory can countenance "punishment" of the innocent. This is because it defines just punishment in terms of aims that are only contingently related to desert. If punishment is justified by its deterrent effect, then in circumstances which made the risks of disclosure worth bearing, the state could legitimately fabricate evidence against an innocent man in order to make an example of him. Moreover, collective or vicarious punishment could, in extreme cases, also be socially expedient, and where expedient, just. And if punishment is justified by the protection it affords society, then justified in certain cases are preventive detention and the indeterminate sentence — that is, punishment related not to actual wrongdoing but to expected wrongdoing. From the standpoint of self defence, waiting for a known psychopath to strike is absurd.

What of the requirement that punishment be proportioned to the offence? At first sight the utilitarian theory seems to preserve this relation, at least with respect to the nature of the objective act. Deterrence requires that the punishment be severe enough to make the crime a bad risk to the potential offender; utilitarian justice demands that it be no more severe than what is needed to deter the crime, and no more socially injurious than the crime unpunished. Furthermore, penalties must be so graded that anyone embarking on a criminal course will be encouraged to commit the less rather than the most harmful offence. However, we must recall that deterrence is only one of three aims contemplated by utilitarian punishment, and that of these three only deterrence looks to the crime. The goals of self-protection and reform have regard not to the offence but to the offender. They consider the criminal in terms of psychological rather than legal categories: not as the responsible author of a particular offence but as a dangerous or deviant personality, the subject of unique characterological attributes and propensities of which the crime is but a particular manifestation. Accordingly, since a penal practice which aimed exclusively at minimum deterrence would accomplish these other goals only accidentally, utilitarianism must fix penalties which leave sufficient room for judicial discretion in imposing individualized sentences. In doing so, however, it defines the moral degree of punishment by reference to something other than the offence, hence in a way that subverts the rule of natural justice requiring that punishments be proportioned to crimes. On utilitarian principles the pathological petty offender may warrant more severe punishment than the "normal" armed robber.

It is questionable, moreover, whether utilitarianism preserves the rule of proportionality respecting punishment and responsibility. Bentham, to be sure, claimed that it did. He argued that the circumstances recognized in the common law as excusing or extenuating wrongdoing — namely, accident, insanity, coercion, and provocation — are all confirmed by utilitarian theory as factors which render punishment "inefficacious."[9] Punishment of the insane, for example, would serve no useful deterrent purpose; and punishing a provoked crime with the same severity as a premeditated one would mean paying more than is necessary for the deterrence purchased, since a man provoked is not the rational maximizer of utilities envisaged by Benthamite psychology. Bentham, however, was wrong on two counts. He was wrong, first of all, in supposing that because the threat of punishment in cases where intent is absent is useless for deterrence, it is also useless for other utilitarian goals. From the standpoint of self-protection, for example, doing away with excusing conditions might conceivably be socially beneficial, for it would eliminate the opportunities that criminals now have for deceiving juries. He was wrong, secondly, in supposing that because the threat of punishment in such cases is useless for particular deterrence, it is also useless for general deterrence. As H.L.A. Hart has pointed out, punishing the insane will not deter them from striking again, but it may effectively deter others, especially if they know that a defence of insanity will do them no good.[10] From the standpoint of deterrence, in other words, excusing conditions are just so many loopholes in the law which the unscrupulous may be encouraged to exploit. Furthermore, persons engaged in an activity governed by a statute of strict liability are likely to exercise added caution, knowing that a plea of accident or of reasonable mistake will not excuse them; indeed they may be discouraged from undertaking the activity altogether. For all these reasons it can be said that any conduct which society wants to prevent is more effectively prevented by a statute of strict liability than by one which recognizes excusing or extenuating conditions. Hence the requirement of natural justice that responsibility be a condition of criminal liability finds in utilitarianism only contingent support. No doubt the question of responsibility would still be relevant for a utilitarian at the sentencing stage, where it would serve to indicate the kind of reformative or protective measures that need to be taken.[11] But adapting measures of social hygiene to the mental condition of the offender is a far different thing from proportioning punishments to legal responsibility. And it would be a sheer accident if their results were congruent. A crime of passion deserves less punishment than a calculated one; but the offender may require a more prolonged period of "treatment."

There have been several recent attempts to rescue the utilitarian position from the moral anomalies to which it leads. The weakest consist in definitionally limiting punishment to mean infliction of pain on the deserving, as if by calling "punishment" of the innocent by some other name utilitarians could stop worrying about sanctioning it.[12] Others have held that punishing innocents is condemned by a utilitarianism rightly interpreted, one that judges the morality of acts by their utility not in isolated circumstances but when generalized as a rule.[13] If sacrificing innocent persons for the sake of deterrence were standard policy, it is argued, the costs in terms of public anxiety would far outweigh the benefits of a reduced crime rate. Yet surely it is quite consistent with "rule-utilitarianism" for governments to empower themselves to use all expedient means (including collective punishment) for coping with emergencies, provided that the type of emergency is specified in law and is sufficiently grave to warrant such extraordinary powers. Because, in other words, it is possible to formulate rules not only for the general case but also for exceptional circumstances of a given type, rule-utilitarianism cannot, any more than act-utilitarianism, absolutely exclude punishing innocents under the colour of right. A third defence is in the nature of a strategic retreat. Professor Hart has acknowledged the pitfalls of a thoroughly consistent utilitarianism yet sees no need to discard it once it is suitably qualified. Deterrence and self-protection continue to justify punishment in general but cannot alone guide us in determining whom and how much to punish. For these questions principles (e.g., that punishment be only for an offence) must be applied that limit the extent to which the individual can be sacrificed for social ends — principles that guarantee a calculable world in which choices have a bearing on one's fate.[14] This solution is similar to that of John Rawls, in that it consists in splitting up the phenomenon of punishment into the general institution and the particular applications and in applying different moral criteria to each — a salutary eclecticism.[15] Whereas social utility justifies the former, principles associated with (but, according to Hart, not exclusive to) retributive punishment must guide us in the latter.

A number of rejoinders can be made to this argument. First, the splitting up of punishment in this way denies the organic link between the universal and its particularization. Just as a law is properly a law only if it is regularly enforced, so a set of penalties affixed to rules is a system of punishment only insofar as the penalties are imposed for violations of the rules. Conversely, a specific imposition of a sanction is an instance of punishment only insofar as it is carried out under the system of rules and procedures defining the legal use of force. While distinct, therefore, the institution of punishment and its particular applications are united in essence; neither is apart from the other. Consequently, one cannot coherently adopt one set of principles to govern the institution of punishment and another set to govern its concrete applications. Taking a utilitarian position on the universal commits one to taking it on the particular as well, because the latter is the realization of the former. Of course one may wish to limit the application of deterrence and security considerations by other values, but either these values are likewise grounded in social utility or they are not. If they are not, then we must abandon utilitarianism as a general justifying theory. If they are, then they lie at the mercy of the utilitarian calculus and so cannot serve as an unconditional stop to the encroachments of society. Secondly, the mixed theory of punishment is designed to extricate utilitarianism only from the charge that it justifies punishment of the innocent. It is no answer to the objection that utilitarianism fails to provide a morally acceptable justification for punishing the guilty. On the mixed theory, law-breakers are still harmed to satisfy the particular interests of others. Finally, the solution of Hart and Rawls involves a refusal to submit to rigorous standards of theoretical adequacy. The test of a theory of a natural phenomenon is the empirical one of whether it is confirmed by the observed facts. The test of a theory of a moral phenomenon is the dialectical one employed by Socrates. If an account of the phenomenon (e.g., courage, justice, punishment) logically entails, or is consistent with, consequences that involve the collapsing of the phenomenon into its opposite (e.g., punishment into arbitrary violence), then the account must be abandoned as a resting point, because it has failed to grasp the thing's specific essence. Certainly one cannot think to have rescued it by holding it aloof from its contradictions. Had Cephalus replied to Socrates in *Republic I*, "While I grant that in certain circumstances paying one's debts may work injustice, and that in those cases difference principles would have to guide us, nevertheless I maintain that justice in general is paying one's debts," he would have responded in the manner of Hart and Rawls. It might be objected, however, that the utilitarian theory of punishment offers not an account of punishment in this explanatory sense but only as a set of justifying conditions, and so is not rigorously committed to all its logical implications. But this is not the case. The utilitarian position is ultimately an answer to the question, What is punishment? It offers criteria and conditions for distinguishing authentic punishment from arbitrary violence. Explanation and justification are thus inextricably meshed: what justifies punishment is also what constitutes its essence and vice-versa. The utilitarian position is thus a full-fledged "account" of punishment, which, to be tenable, must offer non-collapsible criteria for distinguishing it from criminal force.

Given the very serious deficiencies of the utilitarian account of punishment, the impressive array of statistics adduced to question the superior deterrent force of the death penalty suddenly becomes irrelevant. Whether or not capital punishment is a uniquely effective deterrent to murder or the only sure-fire means of self protection is beside the point if these criteria are not the ones we should be using to determine the justice of capital punishment. But not only are these questions theoretically irrelevant. Inasmuch as they orient research that determines our policy, they implicate us in immorality, because they suppose the criteria of an immoral view of punishment.

Let us then consider the chief rival to the utilitarian account of punishment and inquire as to the implications it bears for the death penalty. I refer to the retributivist account, the classic formulations of which are by Immanuel Kant and G.W.F. Hegel.[16] In contrast to utilitarianism, the retributive theory views punishment as a moral good rather than as an evil requiring justification in terms of extrinsic advantages. Whether or not punishment yields these advantages is irrelevant to its justification, because the principal end of punishment is neither to deter, nor to protect, nor to reform, but to annul wrong and thereby vindicate right. This is not to say that the retributivist is indifferent to these other goals or regards them as improper objects of policy. The criteria of reform, deterrence, and protection do have their place, but it is a very subordinate one. Specifically, they are relevant only to the secondary question of how we shall punish and not to the primary question of whether we have the right to punish. Furthermore, even within the limits of the secondary question (with which we are here concerned) they have relevance only *after* the moral issue has been settled and what remains is merely the choice, judicial or administrative, between various morally acceptable types and measures of punishment. For the retributivist the sole criterion of just punishment as well as of a just measure of punishment is whether it annuls the wrong.

But precisely how, we may ask, does punishment annul wrong? "Can the shrieks of a wretch recall from time, which never reverses its course, deeds already accomplished?" thundered Beccaria. Obviously punishment cannot undo the deed, for the past is irrevocable. And yet by "annulment" of the wrong retributivists must mean something more than mere restitution, for restitution is not punishment. According to Hegel, punishment annuls wrong by demonstrating the non-being of the criminal principle, which might otherwise have seemed to possess validity.[17] The principle of crime is the claim to a right of the arbitrary and unrestrained freedom of the will. Seen in this way, crime is more than, as Plato thought, a sickness in the individual soul; it is a challenge to the natural moral order underpinning civilized society. This is because it denies the validity of natural law and gives this denial itself a show of validity. Punishment, then, is the denial of the denial and so the vindication or reaffirmation of natural law. It is, in other words, the objective demonstration that the criminal claim is without natural support or sanction, without reality.

Because it looks backward to a crime over and done with rather than forward to its social effects, retributive punishment has always seemed to utilitarians a relic of more barbarous times, a mere rationalization of the lust for revenge. In part this judgment reflects the utilitarian's rationalist suspicion of popular sentiment, in which he is wont to see only vulgar prejudice and blind emotionalism. Beccaria saw in the penal law of his time only "the accumulated errors of centuries," and this attitude finds its modern counterpart in the demand to keep separate the questions, Why do men punish? and What justifies punishment?[18] On the other hand, because of his commitment to natural law, the retributivist is more inclined to see in public opinion a dim perception of moral truth. And he is thus also inclined to see his task as one of providing a rational account of action already in itself moral rather than one of excogitating a criterion of morality to which society may be indifferent. To his utilitarian critic, therefore, the retributivists would reply that his punishment is not a form of revenge, but that revenge and punishment are both forms of natural retribution, punishment being alone the adequate form because emancipated from subjective interest. He would, moreover, counter with the charge that whereas utilitarianism plays havoc with our common-sense notions of penal justice, retributivism confirms them.

First of all, retributivism justifies punishment by reference to a good that is genuinely common. Punishment vindicates human rights. It thus affirms and makes objective the real rights of the criminal himself, who, in asserting a right to unlimited freedom, had undermined right as such, his own no less than others'. In receiving punishment, therefore, the criminal is subjected not to someone else's good, but to his own true good, hence to his own rational will. His autonomy and dignity are thus respected.

Secondly, retributivism accounts for the connection between punishment and desert. If punishment is the vindication of right against wrong or the denial of a denial, then it logically presupposes wrongdoing. Thus retributivism condemns punishment of the innocent. Furthermore, if what requires annulment is not the criminal deed itself but rather its claim to validity, then clearly intent or *mens rea* is saved as a determinant of wrongdoing and hence of criminal desert. Retributivism thus condemns strict liability.

Thirdly, retributivism saves the rule of proportionality respecting the relation between punishment and crime. The punishment must annul the wrong. This it does by demonstrating the self-contradictoriness — that is, the inherent nullity — of the criminal act. If I steal, I deny the existence of property even for me. My act recoils upon itself and so destroys itself.

Now punishment simply brings home this contradiction, or is this contradiction objectively manifest? I assert a right to unbridled freedom; I thereby deny the existence of right, which denial punishment brings home to me by depriving me of mine. I am the author of my punishment, inasmuch as the latter is simply the inner consequence of my deed. "The Eumenides sleep," says Hegel, "but crime awakens them, and hence it is the very act of crime itself which vindicates itself."[19] Now this account of punishment explains the demand that the punishment fit the crime. Punishment must be related to the gravity of the wrong because it must signify nothing but the recoiling of the criminal's own act against itself. Only as such is punishment natural retribution and not another act of violence. It is in this sense that Hegel speaks of the criminal's "right" to punishment — that is, to be subjected only to the consequences immanent in his act and never to the alien exigencies of society.[20] To punish the offender in accordance with the principle laid down by his deeds is to honour his human subjectivity, his essential self-determination, while to fix penalties according to the requirements of deterrence or correction is to degrade him to an object and a tool. Moreover, only if the measure of punishment is derived from the deed itself does the punishment logically annul the wrong. Were a fine the penalty for murder, we would feel that murder had not been sufficiently repaid, hence not decisively invalidated. The Biblical *lex talionis* as well as the common opinion that the criminal incurs a debt that can be discharged only by suffering the appropriate punishment are prephilosophic apprehensions of punishment as nemesis.

Before considering the implications of retributivism for the death penalty, I should briefly mention a third view of punishment often linked with retributivism but in reality quite distinct from it. Variously referred to as the denunciatory, the reprobative, or the expressive view of punishment, this theory holds that punishment is the emphatic denunciation of crime by society, an authoritative expression of disapproval that both vents popular indignation towards the criminal and reaffirms the positive morality of a people. The most frequently quoted exponent of this view is Sir James Fitzjames Stephen, a Victorian judge and the author of *Liberty, Equality, Fraternity*, a contemporary attack on Mill's *On Liberty*. "It is highly desirable," wrote Stephen in 1883, "that criminals should be hated, that punishments inflicted upon them should be so contrived as to give expression to that hatred, and to justify it so far as the public provision of means for expressing and gratifying a healthy natural sentiment can justify and encourage it."[21] A somewhat more temperate version of this position was expressed by Lord Justice Denning in hearings before the Royal Commission on Capital Punishment. "The punishment inflicted for grave crimes," said Denning, "should adequately reflect the revulsion felt by the great majority of citizens for them. It is a mistake to consider the objects of punishment as being deterrent or reformative or preventive and nothing else. . . . The ultimate justification of any punishment is not that it is a deterrent, but that it is the emphatic denunciation by the community of a crime."[22] Denning thus opposed the denunciatory view of punishment to the deterrence school and saw it as implying a retentionist position on the death penalty. The vilest of crimes demanded the most emphatic of all denunciations. Nevertheless, the two positions are not as incompatible as they may seem, nor does the denunciatory theory necessarily entail retention of capital punishment. If the public condemnation of crime is held to be desirable as a salutary outlet for moral indignation and as a vindication of social norms, then the denunciatory theory is a species of utilitarianism, and the rivalry between it and the deterrence school is a rivalry between siblings. It has thus been quite a simple matter in practice for utilitarian policy-makers to assimilate the criterion of reprobative power to their own theoretical framework and to formulate alternatives to the death penalty which take into account this desideratum.

On the other hand, if the apparent opposition between the denunciatory and the deterrence schools conceals a fundamental agreement, the affinity between the former and the retributivists masks a real opposition. There is, to be sure, an element of denunciation in retributive punishment, but the author of this condemnation is nature rather than society. Punishment expresses the objective nemesis of crime, not the revulsion of men. Of course feelings of revenge, revulsion, and moral indignation enter into punishment, but they have nothing to do with its essence or justification. In retributive punishment, furthermore, denunciation is linked to a principle of fitness in the light of which one can distinguish between natural retribution and human violence. By itself the denunciatory theory contains no such principle; it sets a minimum limit to punishment but not a maximum. In short, the question as to whether a particular punishment is sufficient to denounce a crime is indeed relevant to the issue of a just measure, but it has to be developed out of a morally acceptable theory of punishment in general. The denunciatory theory is not such a one. Either it justifies punishment by reference to the social benefits of denouncing crime, in which case it is a disguised utilitarianism; or it justifies punishment as an expression, good in itself, of moral indignation, without bothering to explain why this feeling should lend moral weight to violence. We do not allow anger as an excuse, let alone a moral justification, for assault or homicide; why then should we admit it just because it is also self-righteous?

What guidance does the classic retributivist theory offer in the matter of capital punishment? It is usually assumed that retributivism logically entails retention of the death penalty for first-degree murder because of its apparent confirmation of the *lex talionis*. Certainly this connection was maintained by Kant, for whom fitness meant, quite simply, equality. The murderer must die, insists Kant, because "there is no sameness of kind between death and remaining alive even under the most miserable conditions, and consequently there is also no equality between the crime and the retribution unless the criminal is judicially condemned and put to death."[23] Theorists of punishment have had little difficulty in demolishing this conception of justice, thinking in having done so to have dealt a death-blow to retributivism. If by equality is meant equality in kind, then we must repay theft with theft, adultery with adultery, forgery with forgery, and so on. If equal value is meant, then we must punish mass murderers on a scale repugnant to our moral sense. Moreover, even if it were possible to compare qualitatively different injuries in terms of their painfulness according to an average preference scale, the commensurability of crimes and punishment would be destroyed as soon as we added considerations of *mens rea* to the balance. For although suffering can be compared with suffering, how can suffering be compared with wickedness?[24] All these and other arguments are useful and valid against the *lex talionis*, but against retributivism itself they are quite harmless. For the demand that, as the criminal has done, so shall it be done to him is merely a sensuous representation or image of the inner identity of crime and its nemesis. The conceptual likeness is represented by the popular imagination as a qualitative (or quantitative) one, and, as in the allegory of the cave, the representation is taken for the thing represented. That retributive justice has nothing to do with crude conceptions of equality was emphasized by Hegel. While agreeing that equivalence is the criterion of justice in the distribution of punishment, he pointed out that "in crime, as that which is characterized at bottom by the infinite aspect of the deed, the purely external, specific character vanishes."[25] In other words, the injury to be annulled by punishment is not the determinate injury done to the victim but the noumenal injury done to the moral order. Hence the measure of punishment is properly derived not from the qualitative or quantitative aspects of the crime (as in revenge) but from its moral significance. The seriousness of the criminal's infringement of Right must be matched by an infringement of his right of "equal" weight. Since, however, the first of these variables eludes measurement in quantitative terms, "equal weight" cannot mean more than "proportionate severity." That is to say, the principle of equivalence properly understood translates into the rather vague demand for a graded proportionality, whereby more serious crimes are punished with severer penalties. Thus retributivism does not specifically enjoin the death penalty for first-degree murder, but neither of course does it absolutely condemn it. This result is not as unenlightening as it may seem, for that capital punishment is neither a moral imperative nor a moral wrong is no trivial conclusion.

Can we, however, go further? Can retributivism offer any guide as to how to go about matching punishments to crimes? Let us immediately grant the argument that, given the impossibility of assigning values to degrees of "seriousness" or "wickedness," we cannot fit penalties to offences according to the principle of proportionality literally construed. We may regard murder as a more serious crime than robbery, but as we have no way of assigning a numerical ratio to this comparison, we cannot achieve proportional equality between the relative severity of punishments and the relative seriousness of crimes. But although there is no principle of fitness by which we could establish natural correspondences between specific penalties and specific crimes, we can at least seek considerations relevant to determining the overall severity of the punishment scale taken by itself. And I want now to suggest that such considerations may be supplied by the retributivist understanding of mercy.

The charge is often heard that retributivism leaves no room for mercy, that it establishes not only the right to punish but also the positive duty to do so, so that any waiving of the right appears, on this theory, to be itself an injustice.[26] I shall argue, however, that it is not retributivism as such which leads to this conclusion so much as Kant's metaphysical assumptions, and that Hegel offers a metaphysical context for retributivism significantly different from Kant's, one that saves mercy. Furthermore, the difference between the two accounts of mercy will suggest a criterion for determining whether and for what crimes death is an appropriate punishment.

Let us first notice what Kant says about the right to pardon. In *The Metaphysical Elements of Justice* he writes:

> The right to pardon a criminal . . . is certainly the most slippery of all the rights of the sovereign. By exercising it he can demonstrate the splendor of his majesty and yet thereby wreak injustice to a high degree. With respect to crime of one subject against another, he absolutely cannot exercise this right, for in such cases exemption from punishment constitutes the greatest injustice toward his subjects. Consequently he can make use of this right to pardon only in connection with an injury committed against himself.[27]

Kant is clearly uneasy about the right to pardon; indeed, he is totally at a loss to account for it and would restrict its application to the crime of treason. This is precisely what one would expect from a philosopher who regards punishment as a categorical imperative, an unconditional duty to be performed for its own sake and irrespective of its consequences. Kant would have the whole human race perish rather than exempt a criminal from punishment, for "if legal justice perishes, then it is no longer worthwhile for men to remain alive on this earth."[28]

Now consider what Hegel says about the right to pardon.

> The right to pardon criminals arises from the sovereignty of the monarch since it is this alone which is empowered to actualize Spirit's power of making undone what has been done and wiping out a crime by forgiving and forgetting it.

Pardon is the remission of punishment, but it does not annul the law. On the contrary, the law stands and the pardoned man remains a criminal as before. This annulment of punishment may take place through religion, since something done may by Spirit be made undone in Spirit. But the power to accomplish this on earth resides in the king's majesty alone and must belong solely to his self-determined decision.[29]

Here there is no uneasiness. The right of pardon exhibits the majesty, the supreme self-confidence of Spirit in its cosmic authority, and Hegel places no limitations on its exercise. How can we account for this difference within retributivism between the Kantian and Hegelian attitudes towards mercy?

The answer lies, I believe, in their different understandings of the basis of human dignity. For Kant, the individual's dignity, and thus his title to rights, rests on his sharing the common personality of the human species. This common personality — Kant's pure ego — is a human essence abstracted from the empirical personality, which is ruled by self-love and which remains as a fixed reality opposed to the rational self. Now the fixed reality or naturalness of the self-seeking person poses an ever-present challenge to the objective reality of human dignity. For Kant this dignity is inherently insecure, because it is nothing more than a subjective claim asserted over against a hostile nature, a claim that must therefore be continually vindicated through the external conquest of its antithesis. From this perspective, therefore, to grant mercy to a criminal would be to leave standing the claim of selfishness to validity and thus to leave justice unsatisfied.

For Hegel, by contrast, the basis of human dignity is not solely a human essence of personality. It is a transcendent or divine Personality of which human selfhood is a subordinate though essential element. And this divine Person is no mere abstraction which leaves evil as a fixed reality outside it. Rather it is a Spirit which itself submits to negation by evil in order that, by the annulment of evil's claim to positive reality, its sovereignty might be objectively manifest. Stated otherwise, the natural (self-centred) will is for Hegel not primary and absolute, but is rather posited within the divine ground as an appearance of something independent, in order that, by the demonstration of its independence as appearance, the divine ground of being might be vindicated as such.[30] This means that the naturalness of egoism is inherently a show, a passing phase in the self-reintegration of Spirit. Punishment is just the practical demonstration that the right of egoism is a mere show, and this constitutes its justification. But now mercy is a more perfect demonstration of this truth. For Kant, mercy was opposed to justice because it meant leaving unrefuted the claim of egoism to reality. For Hegel, mercy is a form of justice because it is itself the refutation of that claim. The passage quoted above suggests a distinction as well as a relation between divine and human forgiveness. Divine forgiveness flows from the divine nature as that which incorporates as a constituent element of itself the individual's alienation from, and return to, the divine ground. From the divine standpoint, therefore, mercy is reconciled with justice because, far from leaving the natural will in its otherness, it is the very process of positing and conquering it. Human forgiveness flows from the recognition that divine mercy robs evil of its power of being and so establishes man's dignity beyond threat of subversion.[31] Thus, not even from the human standpoint is mercy opposed to justice, for it too attests to the nullity of evil. Like punishment, mercy presupposes wrongdoing; but it affirms that the wrong is insignificant, that its claim to validity is a mock claim, that it is powerless to prevail against right. This, then, is how mercy can have a place within a retributive theory of punishment. Mercy, no less than punishment, "wipes out" the wrong, not by repaying it but by forgetting it.

Now the relevance of all this to the death penalty is simply this. If the purpose of punishment is to vindicate human rights against the pretended validity of the criminal act, it seems consequent to suppose that the severity of punishment in any epoch will depend on the perceived magnitude of the threat that crime poses to the reality of human dignity. A claim of human worth resting on the supposed sovereignty of individual personhood finds its sole objective confirmation in outward possessions. It will therefore see in any offence against property an infinite challenge to itself and punish it accordingly. Since, moreover, the absolutization of the isolated person brings the state of nature into political society, the penal system will take upon itself the enforcement of the law of private revenge, centralizing without reconstituting it. Retribution will thus take the form of the qualitative and quantitative redress of personal injury, and torture, the giving back of pain for pain, will be the paradigmatic form of punishment.[32] On the other hand, a claim of dignity resting, like Kant's, on the assumed sovereignty of a common humanity (and hence of law) will view this dignity as established independently of external things, though still challenged by a natural will now regarded as evil. Since the state of nature is here abrogated as a normative principle, the law of retaliation will be reinterpreted as the impersonal vengeance of the general will, and minutely differentiated corporal punishments will give way to the uniform abstraction of imprisonment, corresponding to the abstraction of crime as an offence against right in general. Moreover, since it is now the principle of the criminal will and not the criminal act itself that challenges the objective reality of human worth, punishments will be adjusted more subtly to the evil quality of the will, and, in particular, the death penalty will be reserved for the only crime which, by destroying the body, also destroys the person. Finally, a people confident that human dignity is no mere subjective claim pitted against an indifferent nature but an objective fact rooted in a divinely governed cosmos; a people confident, in short, that the human personality cannot be destroyed will be inclined to temper punishment with mercy. We may imagine, therefore, that there exists an ideal penal code corresponding to the highest strength of the human spirit and in which the death penalty perhaps plays no part. But like representative government, this simply best penal code is not suited to all peoples at all stages of their moral development. At any stage, the strength of the basis of self-definition will determine the scale of punishments needed to preserve and reinforce the positive morality (understood as a particular perception of natural morality) on which the social order is founded. And any attempt to impose a higher, less severe code on a people unprepared for it risks undermining the belief in a natural moral order on which depends the conviction of personal worth as well as the habit of self-restraint.

Somewhat surprisingly, therefore, retributivism issues in a counsel of pragmatism with respect to the use of the death penalty. It leads to the Montesquieuian conclusion that that penal code is best which suits the "spirit" of a people, by which is here understood the system of life-organizing beliefs regarding the foundation of human value. Not to be confused with this result is the conclusion of Beccaria, who thought that the scale of punishments ought to be relative to the level of civility of a people, the more savage requiring stronger deterrents. The question legislators must ask is not how much punishment is needed to deter potential criminals in the present state of society, but how much is needed to reassure decent men in the present state of their self-knowledge. Obviously these questions lead to different oracles. The first directs us to data on differential crime rates, the second to public opinion.

NOTES

1. Mill, "Utilitarianism," in Lerner (ed.), *Essential Works of John Stuart Mill* (1961), 236.
2. Bentham, *The Principles of Morals and Legislation* (Darien, Hafner 1970), 170.
3. Sellin, "Death and Imprisonment as Deterrents to Murder," in Bedau (ed.), *The Death Penalty in America* (1964) 274-284; Sellin, "Does the Death Penalty Protect Municipal Police?" in Bedau, 284-301; Sellin, "Effect of Repeal and Reintroduction of the Death Penalty on Homicide Rates," in Bedau, 339-343. Stronger, though still not conclusive, evidence for the uniquely effective deterrent force of the death penalty is offered by Ehrlich, "The Deterrent Effect of Capital Punishment," 65 *American Economic Review* (1975), 397-417.
4. Van Den Haag, "On Deterrence and the Death Penalty," 78 *Ethics* (1968), 280-287. See also Goldberg, "On Capital Punishment," 85 *Ethics* (1974) 67-74.
5. Mill, "Speech in Favor of Capital Punishment," 1868 in Ezorsky (ed.), *Philosophical Perspectives on Punishment* (1972), 271-278.
6. See, e.g., Mabbott, "Punishment," 48 Mind (1939); McCloskey, "A Non-utilitarian Approach to Punishment," 8 *Inquiry* (1965); Armstrong, "The Retributivist Hits Back," 70 *Mind* (1961).
7. See, however, Hart, "Murder and the Principles of Punishment," in Hart, *Punishment and Responsibility* (1968), 54-89. My disagreements with Hart will be spelled out below.
8. For a recent retributivist argument in favor of retention see Berns, *For Capital Punishment* (1979).
9. Bentham, supra note 2, 172-175.
10. Hart, *Punishment and Responsibility*, supra note 7, 77 and passim.
11. See Wootton, *Social Science and Social Pathology* (1959), ch. 8, and Crime and the Criminal Law (1963) 47-57.
12. Quinton, "On Punishment," in Acton (ed.), *The Philosophy of Punishment* (1969), 55-64.
13. Rawls, "Two Concepts of Rules," in Acton, supra note 12, 105-114.
14. Hart, *Punishment and Responsibility*, supra note 2, 22-24, 44-49, 80-81, 181-183.
15. Rawls, supra note 13.
16. Kant, *The Metaphysical Elements of Justice* (trans. Ladd, 1965), 99-108; Hegel, *Hegel's Philosophy of Right* (trans. Knox, 1952), paras. 90-103.
17. *Philosophy of Right*, supra note 16, paras. 97, 99.
18. Beccaria, *On Crimes and Punishments* (trans. Paolucci, 1963), 9; Hart, *Punishment and Responsibility*, supra note 2, 74.
19. *Philosophy of Right*, supra note 16, addition to para. 101.
20. Ibid. para. 100.
21. Stephen, *A History of the Criminal Law of England* (1883), Volume 2, 81.
22. Quoted in Ezorsky, supra note 5, 250.
23. Kant, supra note 16, 102.
24. The problems in matching punishments to crimes are discussed in two recent articles. See Wertheimer, "Should the Punishment Fit the Crime?" 3 *Social Theory and Practice* (1975), 403-423; Goldman, "The Paradox of Punishment," 9 *Philosophy and Public Affairs* (1979), 42-58.
25. Hegel, supra note 16, para. 101.
26. This accusation has been repeated by Honderich, *Punishment: The Supposed Justifications* (1969), 12-13. Here we may note that it is really utilitarianism that abolishes mercy. The latter presupposes the right to punish; it is a forgoing of the right. Now if the circumstances of utility give us the right to punish, then we must do so, since to forgo the right is to satisfy the criminal's interest at the expense of the general welfare, which is to commit an injustice. On the other hand, if considerations of utility lead us to forgo punishment, this is not to show mercy, for we had no right to punish.
27. Kant, supra note 16, 107-108.
28. Ibid., 100.
29. Hegel, supra note 16, para. 282 and addition.
30. Hegel, *The Phenomenology of Mind* (trans. Baillie, 1931), 93-94, 96-99, 789-790, 806-807.
31. Hegel, *Early Theological Writings* (trans. Knox, 1971), 224-244; *Phenomenology of Mind*, supra note 30, 6680-679.
32. See Foucault, *Discipline and Punish* (trans. Sheridan, 1977), 32-69.

QUESTIONS

1. Based on the materials in this chapter, can you construct a utilitarian or what is sometimes called a forward-looking justification of punishment? What are the central strengths and weaknesses to this approach?
2. What are Alan Brudner's objections to utilitarian justifications of punishment?
3. Brudner argues that retributivism offers the only morally defensible account of punishment. Why? Do you find his arguments persuasive?
4. What is Brudner's view of capital punishment? Is it persuasive?

SUGGESTIONS FOR FURTHER READING

Books

- Hugo Adam Bedau, *Matters of Life and Death*, ed. Tom Regan (New York: Random House, 1980). In the fifth chapter, "Capital Punishment," Bedau explores the various justifications for capital punishment. (Regan's book is a useful resource for exploring the issues of abortion and euthanasia as well as capital punishment.)
- Walter Berns, *For Capital Punishment* (New York: Basic Books Inc., 1979). The various arguments against capital punishment are set out and systematically examined and rejected. The author then constructs a defence of capital punishment.
- David Chandler, *Capital Punishment in Canada* (Toronto: McClelland and Stewart, 1976). The author describes his book as a study in the sociology of law. It provides a background study of the history of capital punishment in Canada. Key debates in Parliament are set out; the positions of political parties and individuals are described and analyzed and conclusions with respect to the capital punishment debate are suggested.
- *Crime and Delinquency* is a journal published by the American National Council on Crime and Delinquency. Their October 1980 issue is devoted to the topic of capital punishment. The other articles in this volume are, for the most part, opposed to the use of capital punishment. The emphasis is on research designed to establish the effect of capital punishment on the occurrence of murder. One particularly interesting article argues that there is no evidence that capital punishment deters people from committing murder; and that there is empirical evidence suggesting that capital punishment has a brutalizing effect — that is to say, that capital punishment is actually a stimulant to murder.

Government Reports

These reports should be available in the public-documents section of your university library.

- *Capital Punishment: New Material 1965-1972*. This was prepared for the Solicitor-General of Canada in 1972 as a resource document for the public and for Parliament in the 1972 abolition debate. It is an update of a similar study done in 1965. The report, though somewhat out of date, provides an interesting summation of the arguments for and against capital punishment.

- *A Study of the Deterrent Effect of Capital Punishment with Special Reference to the Canadian Situation*. This research report was prepared by E.A. Fattah for the department of the Solicitor-General as a resource document to be used in the debate of 1972. The report is a somewhat dated but highly regarded study. Much of the information it contains is still of value.

Articles

- Anthony G. Amsterdam, "Race and the Death Penalty," *Criminal Justice Ethics*, Vol. 7, No. 2 (Summer/Fall 1988). This article, which was included in the 4th edition of *Contemporary Moral Issues*, examines the practice of capital punishment in the United States. The author argues that American courts have not found a way to apply capital punishment in a way that does not discriminate against people of colour and that it should therefore be abolished.
- M. Costanzo, "Just revenge: Costs and consequences of the death penalty," in S. Satris (Ed) *Taking sides: Clashing views on controversial moral issues* (7th edition) (Guilford, Conn: McGraw-Hill/Dushkin), 2002. The author argues against the death penalty calling it "costly, arbitrary, discriminatory, prone to error, and without deterrent value."
- Richard C. Dieter, "The Death Penalty in Black and White: Who Lives, Who Dies, Who Decides," Death Penalty Information Center, Washington, D.C., June 1998. The author is the Executive Director of the Death Penalty Information Center. The article provides the results of two studies that the author describes as underscoring "the continuing injustice of racism in the application of the death penalty."
- E.A. Fattah, "Is Capital Punishment a Unique Deterrent?," *Canadian Journal of Criminology*, Vol. 23, No. 3 (July 1981). This article, which is found in all previous editions of *Contemporary Moral Issues*, looks at two questions. Does capital punishment deter murder? Secondly, does capital punishment deter murder more effectively than other less morally objectionable alternatives such as life imprisonment. The author concludes that the empirical evidence does not support the view that capital punishment is a more effective deterrent than other onerous sentences such as life imprisonment.
- E.A. Fattah, "Perceptions of Violence, Concern about Crime, Fear of Victimization and Attitudes to the Death Penalty," *Canadian Journal of Criminology*, Vol. 21, No. 1 (January 1979). This is an empirical survey of available information and studies of attitudes in Canada and the United States with a view to discovering relationships among the factors indicated. The findings suggest that the attitude toward the death penalty is stable, resistant to change, and not "greatly influenced by the level of general concern about crime, or by the degree of personal fear of victimization."
- J. Feinberg, "The Expressive Function of Punishment," *The Monist*. La Salle, Illinois, Vol. 49 (1965), No. 3. Over the past two or three decades there has developed in legal and government circles the view that denunciation of crime is a central purpose of punishment. Among punishments, capital punishment is the strongest tool of denunciation available; therefore, capital punishment is appropriate where the most emphatic form of denunciation is required — namely, murder. This view is set out and defended by Feinberg in this article, which is reprinted in *Punishment*, referred to below. For a critical assessment of Feinberg's argument see "Crime, Punishment and Emphatic Denunciation," my article printed in the special issue, Vol. 11, No. 1 (November 1981), of *The Laurentian University Review* devoted to the topic "Law and Justice." It is argued

here that the justification of punishment as denunciation is at root simply a variation on the deterrence justification. For such a view to support the use of capital punishment it would have to be shown that capital punishment is a unique deterrent. Adopting a view similar to that developed by Fattah in this chapter, the argument is that it is not. The article is available from me on request.

- James M. Galliher and John F. Galliher, "A 'commonsense' theory of deterrence and the 'ideology' of science: the New York state death penalty debate," *Journal of Criminal Law and Criminology*, Fall 2001. This is an analysis of the nature of the arguments used in public debates in New York State and Kansas to justify capital punishment. The authors propose that there are three central arguments that are not easily tested that taken together form what the authors describe as a commonsense theory of punishment. This "commonsense theory" which, they argue, is impervious to empirical evidence showing that the death provides the public justification for death penalty legislation.

- Daniel McDermott, "A Retributivist Argument against Capital Punishment," *Journal of Social Philosophy*, Vol. 32, No. 3, Fall 2001. Retributivism provides a common platform for the justification of capital punishment. Examples of arguments of this kind can be found in the "Books" reading list above. This article challenges the view that just retribution provides an adequate basis for defending capital punishment.

- Thomas Gabor, Kwing Hung, Stephen Mihorean, and Catherine St-Onge, "Canadian homicide rates: a comparison of two data sources," *Canadian Journal of Criminology*, Vol. 44, No. 3, July 2002. This article is an empirical examination of the reliability of Canadian homicide statistics.

On Punishment in General

Discussion of the merits of capital punishment inevitably leads to discussions on the justification of punishment. A good deal of worthwhile material is available on this issue. For example, the Law Reform Commission of Canada has prepared a number of reports and commissioned a number of studies. Of these the following are certainly of interest:

- *The Meaning of Guilt* (Working Paper 2). In this paper the Commission argues that punishment is justified in the name of fairness to those who obey the law and in the name of self-defence.

- *Imprisonment and Release* (Working Paper 11). As the title suggests, this study examines the justification of punishment and what that justification implies for sentencing and imprisonment.

- *Studies on Sentencing* (Working Paper 3). This paper includes two studies of interest. The first, by John Hogarth (then chairman of the B.C. Police Commission), examines alternatives to our adversarial system of justice with their implications for the imposition of punishment. The second (by Paul Weiler, professor of law at Osgoode Law School), "The Reform of Punishment," examines a variety of theories of punishment. A deterrence justification is rejected and a retribution model advanced.

- *Fear of Punishment*. This study was published in 1976. It contains two essays. The first, by E.A. Fattah, is "Deterrence: A Review of the Literature." The second, "Deterrent Effects of Punishment for Breaking and Entering and Theft," is an empirical analysis.

- Robert L. Misner, "A strategy for mercy," William and Mary Law Review, April 2000. One of the tensions that theories of punishment frequently addresses is the tension between justice and mercy. Both are regarded widely as virtues. Yet most approaches to criminal punishment appear to leave little room for the exercise of mercy. This article explores that tension.

- Finally, a good source of articles written from a philosophical perspective on the subject of punishment is *Punishment,* edited by Gertrude Ezorsky and published by the State University of New York Press (1972).

Audiovisual Resources

- As is the case for the topics of abortion and euthanasia, the Ontario Education Authority has produced two half-hour videotapes on capital punishment. The first tape is called "The Last Hangings in Canada." It is built around an account of the last days of the last two people to be executed in Canada and includes discussions with a number of academics, American prison personnel who supervised executions, and a number of men on death row in American prisons at the time of filming. The second, "Capital Punishment," is a round-table discussion. Participants include Hugo Bedau and Walter Berns, both of whose work is included in this chapter.
- Finally, a 1996 American film called *Dead Man Walking* explores a relationship between a man on death row in the United States and a Roman Catholic nun. The story takes the viewer through a series of appeals, through the final hours of the prisoner's life, and into the death chamber, where the prisoner is executed by lethal injection.

Chapter 4

Pornography

Introduction

The concept of moral autonomy explored in the first two chapters on euthanasia and abortion also plays a central role in discussions of the morality of censorship, particularly the censorship of pornographic materials. How do we assess the limits beyond which the exercise of freedom on the part of some becomes an unacceptable threat to the freedom or well-being of others? How do we assess freedom and well-being in the context of the vast proliferation and availability of pornography on the Internet? Can limitations to freedom and harms to well-being be conceived as affecting group members as well as individuals? These questions provide a focus for the discussions of this chapter.

Background Considerations

The Criminal Code of Canada from its earliest formulations has contained provisions restricting the circulation of obscene material. The 1892 Code prohibited the sale or display of anything that tended to "corrupt public morals" or was "disgusting" or "immoral." It also banned the use of postal services for the transmission of anything that was "immoral," "obscene," or "indecent." The law did provide, however, that serving the public good was an adequate defence to an obscenity charge.

The Code was expanded in 1927 to include the sale, public display, circulation, distribution, and possession of "obscene" materials or "materials tending to corrupt public morals." No further major change was made until shortly after the Second World War, when the Code was expanded once more to include crime comics — material that through the use of pictures depicted the commission of real or fictitious crimes. The Code was also revised to remove any reference to "the tendency to corrupt public morals."

The 1950s were a period of social change. Increasing wealth and sophisticated printing and distribution techniques led to dramatic increases in the circulation of pornographic materials. Concern with this trend resulted in the creation of a Senate Committee on Salacious and Indecent Literature. The committee hearings provided a public forum for debate, and individuals and groups used the occasion to set out their views. Those who advocated stricter control argued that the Criminal Code should be strengthened. There was clear concern about the involvement of children.

Those who opposed further regulation did so on two grounds. Some argued that current provisions provided adequate control. Others argued that any control limited freedom of speech, interfered with the right of adults to read what they wished, and was objectionable except where needed to protect people from direct harm.

In 1958, a series of changes was proposed to Parliament by the Minister of Justice, Davie Fulton, who presented his amendments with two objectives in mind. To begin with, there was no statutory definition of obscenity. Prior to 1958, material was judged obscene by the courts if it had a "tendency to deprave and corrupt those whose minds were open to such immoral influences and into whose hands a publication of the sort in question might fall." This test, laid down by a British judge, Chief Justice Cockburn, in the case of *R. v. Hicklin* in 1868, was known as the Hicklin test. However, this test had come under severe criticism as being subjective and open to uneven application. Davie Fulton proposed in his amendments to supplement this test with a more objective standard. The courts were to regard as obscene "any publication a dominant characteristic of which was the undue exploitation of sex or of sex and crime, horror, cruelty, and violence." Fulton was also concerned to stem the circulation of what he described in the House of Commons as "the kind of muck on the newsstands against which our main efforts in this definition are directed." The aim, therefore, was to strengthen control of pornographic materials.

The proposed amendments were adopted in 1959 under s. 159 of the Criminal Code (now s. 163 and included in the first reading). This legislation regarding obscenity remains to this day.

It is perhaps ironic that legislation designed to reduce the amount of objectionable material in circulation had the opposite effect. The key to this development was the case of *Queen v. Brodie,* which was finally decided in the Supreme Court and in which the Court was asked to determine whether the unexpurgated text of *Lady Chatterley's Lover* was an obscene publication under the 1959 provisions of the Criminal Code. The Court decided, five votes to four, that it was not. Although the Supreme Court was divided on a number of issues, its decision had a decisive impact on Canadian law and its treatment of obscene materials. To begin with, the Hicklin test ceased to be used. This in itself had a liberalizing impact. Second, a book could be judged obscene only if undue exploitation of sex was a dominant theme of the whole publication. Judgment could no longer be based on passages taken out of context. Further, artistic merit could now be considered, with the result that today it is unlikely that works of serious literary merit could be judged obscene under the Code no matter how explicit their treatment of subjects defined by the law as obscene. Finally, the notion of "community standards" was introduced. A publication could be judged obscene only if it exceeded community standards of tolerance.

The 1970s saw a strong renewal of public concern with pornography in response to a flood of increasingly explicit, widely circulated, pornographic publications. Relaxation of legal controls was widely criticized. By 1977 a number of private-members' bills dealing with pornography had been proposed. The government of the day felt itself under increasing pressure to tighten legislative controls. The result was a decision to examine all the proposed amendments to the Criminal Code through public hearings to be conducted by the Justice and Legal Affairs Committee of the House of Commons.

The pattern followed in the hearings was similar, in many respects, to that of the Senate inquiry that had taken place two decades previously. Those who advocated stricter controls called for an objective test of obscenity. There was a sharply focused desire to eliminate child pornography. And the theme of violence played a significant role in the discussions. Those opposed to increased control argued that current provisions were adequate if properly applied and pointed to the undesirable aspects of censorship in any form.

The committee reported in 1978 and indicated that it was concerned with the depiction and advocacy "in clear and explicit terms" of such activities as "sodomy, cunnilingus, fellatio, incest, masturbation, bestiality, necrophilia, sadism, and masochism." It argued that "the effect of this type of material is to reinforce male-female stereotypes to the detriment of both sexes," and went on to say that "such literature attempts to make degradation, humiliation, victimization and violence in human relationships appear normal and acceptable." The committee concluded that Canadians were justified in controlling the circulation of this kind of material and proposed a series of amendments. However, the report was not acted upon.

Another government report, *Pornography and Prostitution in Canada: Report of the Special Committee on Pornography and Prostitution*, chaired by Paul Fraser and written in 1985, concluded that "with respect to pornography, its availability and its control, it is overwhelmingly apparent that the current legal proscriptions are unsatisfactory to everyone." Once again, changes were proposed in 1987 in response to that report and growing public concern. However, as in the past, the proposed amendments generated serious controversy, and the proposed legislation died on the order paper.

A landmark Supreme Court decision in 1992 determined the issue of censorship with respect to pornography. In *R. v. Butler*, a unanimous 9-0 decision by the Justices held that pornography depicting child sex and violent, degrading, or dehumanizing sex is illegal in Canada. The first set of readings in this chapter are excerpts from that case.

Concern with pornography has not been an exclusively Canadian phenomenon. Over the past two decades, studies have been commissioned in both the United States and Great Britain. The resulting reports (mentioned in the Suggested Readings at the end of the chapter) have concluded that, in spite of obvious public concern, research has not established conclusively that exposure to pornography stimulates an increase in sexual crimes such as rape or indecent exposure. On the basis of these findings, these committees have recommended that, because controls limit freedom of choice and expression, and because no direct harm in the form of criminal activity can be proven to result from exposure to such materials, legislative control of pornographic material should be reduced or eliminated. A different approach to dealing with pornography and its effects has been explored in the United States by feminists Catharine MacKinnon and Andrea Dworkin, whose attempt to have legislation implemented failed when challenged by the courts as unconstitutional. They argued that because of what pornographers and the pornography industry do to women, restrictions are needed to promote women's equality.

The Current Situation

Pornography today is big business. Moreover, if the report of the Justice and Legal Affairs Committee is to be believed, a substantial portion of the business is controlled by organized crime in the United States. Of course, not all pornography is illegal, as a visit to the magazine shelf of the corner store would quickly reveal. Of the ten best-selling magazines in the U.S. today, six are explicitly sexual in content. Three examples are *Hustler*, *Playboy*, and *Penthouse*.

The public attitude toward pornography is not easy to gauge. Over the past ten years the courts have accepted a wider range of materials as not exceeding community standards of tolerance. At the same time, Parliament has been under constant political pressure since the mid-1970s to strengthen the law. Some of this pressure has come from feminists who argue that because pornography depicts women in ways that communicate messages about their unequal and subordinate status, restricting its circulation is one strategy for achieving the goal of equality. Discussions of as well as challenges to this feminist analysis of pornography are evident in the reasoning of the Supreme Court Justices in the *Butler* case and in the readings by Lorenne Clark and Wendy McElroy.

Recently, concerns about child pornography have been raised by the courts. In one case a father was questioned for having pictures of his child in the bathtub developed at a local drug store. In 2001, the Supreme Court examined the issue of the possession of child pornography in its decision, *R. v. Sharpe*. It ruled that restrictions to freedom of speech are justifiable to prevent harm to children that results from the production and collection of child pornography. Two exceptions were outlined: "(1) any written material or visual representation created by the accused alone, and held by the accused alone, exclusively for his or her own personal use; and (2) any visual recording, created by or depicting the accused, provided it does not depict unlawful sexual activity and is held by the accused exclusively for private use."

Pornography continues to be controversial, as rapid technological developments have made it possible for people to freely access information on the Internet. Pornography is now readily available in virtually every home by computer. As outlined in the final reading by Susan Dwyer, these developments raise new and difficult problems with respect to how we think about pornography and its effects. In summary, the nature and availability of pornography continue to pose vexing questions for Canadians both as individuals and as a community.

The Moral Dimension

Some people believe that pornography is beneficial, in part because it provides an outlet for sexual fantasies that might otherwise find expression in violent or coercive behaviour. None of the readings in this chapter adopts this stance, though some of the readings examine it. Others have argued that pornography is a form of sexual expression that is simply a matter of personal preference, and, as such, neutral with respect to public morality if participation is voluntary and those participating are adults capable of deciding their own lifestyle. This view, too, is examined in the readings. Much more common is the view that pornography is objectionable either because of the way it depicts human sexuality and because of the sexual morality it appears to advocate, or because of specific and common ingredients such as violence or the way it represents women or children.

However, the debate does not end here, for two reasons. First, those who feel quite strongly that pornography is seriously objectionable face further questions: Should pornography be censored in general or only in certain cases? If in certain cases, how do we define pornography so as to target only that material which is objectionable? For those who do not feel strongly on the subject, a slightly different question is raised: When is a majority entitled to override the moral autonomy of individuals and impose, by law, a standard of conduct?

We have already examined possible answers to this last question. In the first three chapters, we have seen it argued that communities are justified in creating legal constraints on individual autonomy in order to protect human life or to prevent harm. People should be allowed to pursue their own lifestyle and determine their own behaviour up to the point at which the behaviour begins to harm themselves or others. A dominant question around which the pornography debate often revolves is whether the voluntary use of pornography by some is harmful to non-users, members of particular groups, or the community at large.

The suggestion that the basic issue in assessing the justifiability of censorship is its harmfulness for non-users carries with it a deceptive air of simplicity and masks several difficulties with respect to determining the harm of pornography. In its most basic form, harm is associated with direct physical harm resulting in death or injury. But there are more complex dimensions to the concept. We can cause *psychological* harm through insults or misrepresentations or discriminatory behaviour. Furthermore, at a social level each of us is dependent on others in a wide variety of ways. That dependence results in cooperation. But cooperation is possible only if there are shared rules and patterns of behaviour. If confidence in those rules and patterns of behaviour is undermined, the consequences can be damaging. For example, yelling "Fire!" in a crowded theatre may well cause panic. Panic is a state of mind in which confidence in normal rules or patterns of behaviour has collapsed. The results of these psychological and social aspects are invariably harmful, but their effects can be described as indirect.

Even if we could reach agreement about the kinds of harm relevant to an assessment of pornography, there is an additional difficulty in determining the level of harm. Are all types of harm to be given equal weight? Or do some kinds of harm have a higher priority than others? If so, how are the priorities to be determined? That is, by reference to what system of values are decisions to be made?

A third type of difficulty complicates the debate about the harm of pornography. Even if we agree on what we are looking for, how do we trace in a definitive way the impact of pornography on its users and on the community generally? The answer might be thought to be relatively straightforward: We can set up research studies designed to provide us with the facts. The simplicity of the suggestion hides the complexity of the situation. The tools available to social scientists in analyzing and explaining human conduct are not precision instruments. In addition, there are serious moral limitations on the kinds of studies that are allowed.

The task of measuring harm for purposes of restricting pornography is complicated in a fourth way. Where does the onus of proof lie? Should we take the view that obscenity legislation is justified only if substantial harm can be demonstrated to flow from free and uncontrolled circulation of pornography? Or should we take the view that until pornography is shown to be harmless, legislative control is justified? Furthermore, should we resolve this issue in the case of pornography differently than we would in the case of pollution or safety standards? The question is important, at least in part because available research about the effect of pornography on users and on the community is inconclusive.

Thus far, we have four difficulties that lie in the way of ready agreement on the consequences of exposure to pornography. Yet another difficulty arises when we consider the possibility that the relevant harm of pornography is not only harm to individuals, but harm to members of particular groups. It may be that the most important characteristic of pornography is its impact on how people think about others and the world in which they live. Some people are opposed to anti-Semitic literature not because research shows it leads directly to harm to Jews. In fact, it is unlikely that any direct cause/effect relationship could be demonstrated. Rather, the concern is with the way in which such literature affects how its users and members of society generally think about or see themselves and others. The harmful impact of pornography may as a consequence be at the level of ideas or concepts or attitudes. Some argue that pornography perpetuates beliefs about the inferiority of women, beliefs that result in discrimination and unequal treatment. The idea that groups can be harmed in ways that justify restrictions to individual freedom is central to the discussion of discrimination in the next chapter and will be a recurring theme in many of the remaining chapters.

The Readings

In the previous section we identified several types of difficulty that lie in the way of agreement on the nature and impact of pornography. Each is encountered in the readings that follow.

The first reading is drawn from the 1992 Supreme Court decision in *Butler*. Speaking for the majority, Justice Sopinka ruled that the standard of "undue exploitation" as defined in s. 163 of the Criminal Code is appropriate. Because it can be reasonably concluded that pornography causes harm both directly and indirectly, the restriction on freedom of expression is justified.

A second group of readings by Leo Groarke and Lorenne Clark defend censorship, but each presents a different analysis of the kind of harm that justifies restricting pornography. The reading by Groarke makes use of the traditional liberal distinction articulated by John Stuart Mill between private and public morality. The distinction justifies state interference with individual freedom only when failure to intervene will result in direct harm to others. Using this standard, Groarke targets violent pornography and argues that placing limits on its production and circulation is in keeping with traditional liberal justifications for restricting individual freedom.

Lorenne Clark agrees with the conclusion reached by Groarke regarding censorship. However, she rejects the liberal distinction between private and public morality. She argues that the kind of liberty this distinction has traditionally supported has resulted in inequalities for women in both the public and private spheres. Because pornography endorses messages about women's inferior status, it causes harm to women as a group. Censorship of pornography can then be justified as one of a number of strategies for promoting women's equality.

In the fourth reading, Wendy McElroy rejects the analyses presented thus far regarding the harms of pornography and the justifications for censorship. She presents a series of challenges to the kind of radical feminist analysis provided by Lorenne Clark. She defends a libertarian approach, which she refers to as "individualist feminism," in which she views pornography as serving the important function of enhancing human sexual diversity and women's right to choose, "regardless of the content of their choices."

The final reading by Susan Dwyer examines the debate on pornography in the contemporary context of the widespread availability of pornography on the Internet. Dwyer accepts the importance of the right to freedom of speech. She argues that the issue of pornography should be moved from the public and legal realm of questions about censorship to the moral realm of questions about character development. Dwyer asks us to consider the effects of pornography on the formation of moral character. She argues that the way pornography is consumed on-line facilitates character corruption and makes it the kind of behaviour that is risky with respect to moral development.

DONALD VICTOR BUTLER V. HER MAJESTY THE QUEEN, 1992

[Supreme Court of Canada, 1992]

Mr. Justice J. Sopinka

1. Facts and Proceedings

In August 1987, the appellant, Donald Victor Butler, opened the Avenue Video Boutique located in Winnipeg, Manitoba. The shop sells and rents "hard core" videotapes and magazines as well as sexual paraphernalia. Outside the store is a sign which reads:

> Avenue Video Boutique; a private members only adult video/visual club. Notice: if sex oriented material offends you, please do not enter. No admittance to persons under 18 years.

On August 21, 1987, the City of Winnipeg Police entered the appellant's store with a search warrant and seized all the inventory. The appellant was charged with 173 counts in the first indictment: three counts of selling obscene material contrary to s. 159(2)(*a*) of the *Criminal Code*, R.S.C. 1970, c. C-34 (now 163(2)(*a*)), 41 counts of possessing obscene material for the purpose of distribution contrary to s. 159(1)(*a*) (now 163(1)(*a*)) of the *Criminal Code*, 128 counts of possessing obscene material for the purpose of sale contrary to s. 159(2)(*a*) of the *Criminal Code* and one count of exposing obscene material to public view contrary to s. 159(2)(*a*) of the *Criminal Code*. . . .

2. Relevant Legislation

Criminal Code, R.S.C., 1985, c. C-46.

163. (1) Everyone commits an offence who,

(*a*) makes, prints, publishes, distributes, circulates, or has in his possession for the purpose of publication, distribution or circulation any obscene written matter, picture, model, phonograph record or other thing whatever; or

(*b*) makes, prints, publishes, distributes, sells or has in his possession for the purpose of publication, distribution or circulation a crime comic.

(2) Every one commits an offence who knowingly, without lawful justification or excuse,

(*a*) sells, exposes to public view or has in his possession for such a purpose any obscene written matter, picture, model, phonograph record or other thing whatever;

(*b*) publicly exhibits a disgusting object or an indecent show;

(*c*) offers to sell, advertises or publishes an advertisement of, or has for sale or disposal, any means, instructions, medicine, drug or article intended or represented as a method of causing abortion or miscarriage; or (*d*) advertises or publishes an advertisement of any means, instructions, medicine, drug or article intended or represented as a method for restoring sexual virility or curing venereal diseases or diseases of the generative organs.

(3) No person shall be convicted of an offence under this section if he establishes that the public good was served by the acts that are alleged to constitute the offence and that the acts alleged did not extend beyond what served the public good.

(4) For the purposes of this section, it is a question of law whether an act served the public good and whether there is evidence that the act alleged went beyond what served the public good, but it is a question of fact whether the acts did or did not extend beyond what served the public good.

(5) For the purposes of this section, the motives of an accused are irrelevant.

(6) Where an accused is charged with an offence under subsection (1), the fact that the accused was ignorant of the nature or presence of the matter, picture, model, phonograph record, crime comic or other thing by means of or in relation to which the offence was committed is not a defence to the charge.

(7) In this section, "crime comic" means a magazine, periodical or book that exclusively or substantially comprises matter depicting pictorially

(*a*) the commission of crimes, real or fictitious; or

(*b*) events connected with the commission of crimes, real or fictitious, whether occurring before or after the commission of the crime.

(8) For the purposes of this Act, any publication a dominant characteristic of which is the undue exploitation of sex, or of sex and any one or more of the following subjects, namely, crime, horror, cruelty and violence, shall be deemed to be obscene.

3. Issues

The following constitutional questions are raised by this appeal:

1. Does s. 163 of the *Criminal Code* of Canada, R.S.C, 1985, c. C-46, violate s. 2(*b*) of the *Canadian Charter of Rights and Freedoms*?

2. If s. 163 of the *Criminal Code* of Canada, R.S.C., 1985, c. C-46, violates s. 2(b) of the *Canadian Charter of Rights and Freedoms*, can s. 163 of the *Criminal Code* of Canada be demonstrably justified under s. 1 of the *Canadian Charter of Rights and Freedoms* as a reasonable limit prescribed by law?

4. <u>Analysis</u>

The constitutional questions, as stated, bring under scrutiny the entirety of s. 163. However, both lower courts as well as the parties have focused almost exclusively on the definition of obscenity found in s. 163(8). Other portions of the impugned provision, such as the reverse onus provision envisaged in s. 163(3) as well as the absolute liability offence created by s. 163(6), raise substantial *Charter* issues which should be left to be dealt with in proceedings specifically directed to these issues. In my view, in the circumstances, this appeal should be confined to the examination of the constitutional validity of s. 163(8) only. . . .

Pornography can be usefully divided into three categories: (1) explicit sex with violence, (2) explicit sex without violence but which subjects people to treatment that is degrading or dehumanizing, and (3) explicit sex without violence that is neither degrading nor dehumanizing. Violence in this context includes both actual physical violence and threats of physical violence. Relating these three categories to the terms of s. 163(8) of the *Code*, the first, explicit sex coupled with violence, is expressly mentioned. Sex coupled with crime, horror or cruelty will sometimes involve violence. Cruelty, for instance, will usually do so. But, even in the absence of violence, sex coupled with crime, horror or cruelty may fall within the second category. As for category (3), subject to the exception referred to below, it is not covered.

Some segments of society would consider that all three categories of pornography cause harm to society because they tend to undermine its moral fibre. Others would contend that none of the categories cause harm. Furthermore there is a range of opinion as to what is degrading or dehumanizing. See *Pornography and Prostitution in Canada: Report of the Special Committee on Pornography and Prostitution* (1985) (the Fraser Report), Vol. 1, at p. 51. Because this is not a matter that is susceptible of proof in the traditional way and because we do not wish to leave it to the individual tastes of judges, we must have a norm that will serve as an arbiter in determining what amounts to an undue exploitation of sex. That arbiter is the community as a whole.

The courts must determine as best they can what the community would tolerate others being exposed to on the basis of the degree of harm that may flow from such exposure. Harm in this context means that it predisposes persons to act in an anti-social manner as, for example, the physical or mental mistreatment of women by men, or, what is perhaps debatable, the reverse. Anti-social conduct for this purpose is conduct which society formally recognizes as incompatible with its proper functioning. The stronger the inference of a risk of harm the lesser the likelihood of tolerance. The inference may be drawn from the material itself or from the material and other evidence. Similarly evidence as to the community standards is desirable but not essential.

In making this determination with respect to the three categories of pornography referred to above, the portrayal of sex coupled with violence will almost always constitute the undue exploitation of sex. Explicit sex which is degrading or dehumanizing may be undue if the risk of harm is substantial. Finally, explicit sex that is not violent and neither degrading nor dehumanizing is generally tolerated in our society and will not qualify as the undue exploitation of sex unless it employs children in its production.

If material is not obscene under this framework, it does not become so by reason of the person to whom it is or may be shown or exposed nor by reason of the place or manner in which it is shown. The availability of sexually explicit materials in theatres and other public places is subject to regulation by competent provincial legislation. Typically such legislation imposes restrictions on the material available to children. See *Nova Scotia Board of Censors v. McNeil*, [1978] 2 S.C.R. 662. . . .

Does the prevention of the harm associated with the dissemination of certain obscene materials constitute a sufficiently pressing and substantial concern to warrant a restriction on the freedom of expression? In this regard, it should be recalled that in *Keegstra, supra*, this Court unanimously accepted that the prevention of the influence of hate propaganda on society at large was a legitimate objective. Dickson C.J. wrote with respect to the changes in attitudes which exposure to hate propaganda can bring about:

> . . . the alteration of views held by the recipients of hate propaganda may occur subtly, and is not always attendant upon conscious acceptance of the communicated ideas. Even if the message of hate propaganda is outwardly rejected, there is evidence that its premise of racial or religious inferiority may persist in a recipient's mind as an idea that holds some truth, an incipient effect not to be entirely discounted. . . .
>
> The threat to the self-dignity of target group members is thus matched by the possibility that prejudiced messages will gain some credence, with the attendant result of discrimination, and perhaps even violence, against minority groups in Canadian society. [At pp. 747-48.]

This Court has thus recognized that the harm caused by the proliferation of materials which seriously offend the values fundamental to our society is a substantial concern which justifies restricting the otherwise full exercise of the freedom of expression. In my view, the harm sought to be avoided in the case of the dissemination of obscene materials is similar. In the words of Nemetz C.J.B.C. in *R. v. Red Hot Video Ltd.* (1985), 45 C.R. (3d) 36 (B.C.C.A.), there is a growing concern that the exploitation of women and children, depicted in publications and films can, in certain circumstances, lead to "abject and servile victimization" (at pp. 43-44). As Anderson J.A. also noted in that same case, if true equality between male and female persons is to be achieved, we cannot ignore the threat to equality resulting from exposure to audiences of certain types of violent and degrading material. Materials portraying women as a class as objects for sexual exploitation and abuse have a negative impact on "the individual's sense of self-worth and acceptance".

In reaching the conclusion that legislation proscribing obscenity is a valid objective which justifies some encroachment of the right to freedom of expression, I am persuaded in part that such legislation may be found in most free and democratic societies. As Nemetz C.J.B.C. aptly pointed out in *R v. Red Hot Video, supra*, for centuries democratic societies have set certain limits to freedom of expression. He cited (at p. 40) the following passage of Dickson J.A. (as he then was) in *R. v. Great West News Ltd.*, [1970] 4 C.C.C. 307 (Man. C.A.):

> . . . all organized societies have sought in one manner or another to suppress obscenity. The right of the state to legislate to protect its moral fibre and well-being has long been recognized, with roots deep in history. It is within this frame that the Courts and Judges must work. [At p. 309.]

The advent of the *Charter* did not have the effect of dramatically depriving Parliament of a power which it has historically enjoyed. It is also noteworthy that the criminalization of obscenity was considered to be compatible with the *Canadian Bill of Rights*. As Dickson J.A. stated in *R. v. Prairie Schooner News Ltd.* (1970), 1 C.C.C. (2d) 251:

> Freedom of speech is not unfettered either in law or civil law. The *Canadian Bill of Rights* was intended to protect, and does protect, basic freedoms of vital importance to all Canadians. It does not serve as a shield behind which obscene matter may be disseminated without concern for criminal consequences. The interdiction of the publications which are the subject of the present charges in no way trenches upon the freedom of expression which the *Canadian Bill of Rights* assures. [At p. 271.]

The enactment of the impugned provision is also consistent with Canada's international obligations. (*Agreement for the Suppression of the Circulation of Obscene Publications* and the *Convention for the Suppression of the Circulation of and Traffic in Obscene Publications*).

Finally, it should be noted that the burgeoning pornography industry renders the concern even more pressing and substantial than when the impugned provisions were first enacted. I would therefore conclude that the objective of avoiding the harm associated with the dissemination of pornography in this case is sufficiently pressing and substantial to warrant some restriction on full exercise of the right to freedom of expression. The analysis of whether the measure is proportional to the objective must, in my view, be undertaken in light of the conclusion that the objective of the impugned section is valid only insofar as it relates to the harm to society associated with obscene materials. Indeed, the section as interpreted in previous decisions and in these reasons is fully consistent with that objective. The objective of maintaining conventional standards of propriety, independently of any harm to society, is no longer justified in light of the values of individual liberty which underlie the Charter. . . .

Finally, I wish to address the arguments of the interveners, Canadian Civil liberties Association and Manitoba Association for Rights and Liberties, that the objectives of this kind of legislation may be met by alternative, less intrusive measures. First, it is submitted that reasonable time, manner and place restrictions would be preferable to outright prohibition. I am of the view that this argument should be rejected. Once it has been established that the objective is the avoidance of harm caused by the degradation which many women feel as "victims" of the message of obscenity, and of the negative impact exposure to such material has on perceptions and attitudes towards women, it is untenable to argue that these harms could be avoided by placing restrictions on access to such material. Making the materials more difficult to obtain by increasing their cost and reducing their availability does not achieve the same objective. Once Parliament has reasonably concluded that certain acts are harmful to certain groups in society and to society in general, it would be inconsistent, if not hypocritical, to argue that such acts could be committed in more restrictive conditions. The harm sought to be avoided would remain the same in either case.

It is also submitted that there are more effective techniques to promote the objectives of Parliament. For example, if pornography is seen as encouraging violence against women, there are certain activities which discourage it — counselling rape victims to charge their assailants, provision of shelter and assistance for battered women, campaigns for laws against discrimination on the grounds of sex, education to increase the sensitivity of law enforcement agencies and other governmental authorities. In addition, it is submitted that education is an under-used response.

It is noteworthy that many of the above suggested alternatives are in the form of *responses* to the harm engendered by negative attitudes against women. The role of the impugned provision is to control the dissemination of the very images that contribute to such attitudes. Moreover, it is true that there are additional measures which could alleviate the problem of violence against women. However, given the gravity of the harm, and the threat to the values at stake, I do not believe that the measure chosen by Parliament is equalled by the alternatives which have been suggested. Education, too, may offer a means of combating negative attitudes to women, just as it is currently used as a means of addressing other problems dealt with in the *Code*. However, there is no reason to rely on education alone. It should be emphasized that this is in no way intended to deny the value of other educational and counselling measures to deal with the roots and effects of negative attitudes. Rather, it is only to stress the arbitrariness and unacceptability of the claim that such measures represent the sole legitimate means of addressing the phenomenon. Serious social problems such as violence against women require multi-pronged approaches by government. Education and legislation are not alternatives but complements in addressing such problems. There is nothing in the *Charter* which requires Parliament to choose between such complementary measures.

Balance Between Effects of Limiting Measures and Legislative Objective

The final question to be answered in the proportionality test is whether the effects of the law so severely trench on a protected right that the legislative objective is outweighed by the infringement. The infringement on freedom of expression is confined to a measure designed to prohibit the distribution of sexually explicit materials accompanied by violence, and those without violence that are degrading or dehumanizing. As I have already concluded, this kind of expression lies far from the core of the guarantee of freedom of expression. It appeals only to the most base aspect of individual fulfilment, and it is primarily economically motivated.

The objective of the legislation, on the other hand, is of fundamental importance in a free and democratic society. It is aimed at avoiding harm, which Parliament has reasonably concluded will be caused directly or indirectly, to individuals, groups such as women and children, and consequently to society as a whole, by the distribution of these materials. It thus seeks to enhance respect for all members of society, and non-violence and equality in their relations with each other.

I therefore conclude that the restriction on freedom of expression does outweigh the importance of the legislative objective.

PORNOGRAPHY, CENSORSHIP, AND OBSCENITY LAW IN CANADA[1]

Leo Groarke

Recent discussions of pornography and censorship focus on the question whether violence in pornography legitimates new restrictions on freedom of expression. In 1987, the Canadian government proposed new laws that would prohibit such material.[2] Though I take issue with some aspects of their proposals, I defend restrictions on violent pornography, arguing that it is a mistake to think they violate traditional limits on freedom of expression. I conclude that the censorship of pornography can be made compatible with free speech, and that commentators who have defended and attacked censorship — among them, Feinberg, Cohen, Clark, Lederer,[3] and North American civil libertarians — have mistakenly assumed that this is not the case.

Examples of the images and themes that have fuelled debates about pornography and censorship are enumerated by Laura Lederer in her introduction to the anthology *Take Back the Night: Women on Pornography*. She describes the investigations undertaken by the California group Women Against Violence in Pornography and the Media. In one three-month period, they viewed twenty-six pornographic films to gain some understanding of their content. Twenty-one of the films featured rape, sixteen celebrated bondage and torture, two were films of child molestation, and two condoned the killing of women for sexual satisfaction. In their investigation of pornographic magazines, members of the group found stories, articles, and photographs that glorified pain, violence against women, kidnapping, and assault and torture for sexual stimulation. As Thelma McCormack remarks in her discussion of similar material,

> A new hard-edged sado-masochistic pornography has appeared in which women are mutilated and abused with chains, whips and fists. The women in this pornography are presented as seeking and enjoying their own punishment, while violence heightens the erotic excitement of both partners.[4]

Many commentators respond to such trends by calling for censorship, but McCormack and others still reject it. The basis of their views is an appeal to freedom of expression and it is in this sense the heart of the debate on censorship.

The classic defence of freedom of expression is John Stuart Mill's *On Liberty*. It is difficult to exaggerate its influence, and it is enough for us to note that its account of freedom of expression has become a rarely questioned part of liberal theory that is routinely invoked by contemporary theorists, both in discussions of pornography and in the more general accounts of justice proposed by influential thinkers like John Rawls, Jan Narveson,[5] and Michael Walzer.

The crux of Mill's account is his claim that freedom is a general good that must be maximized, and his consequent conclusion that "the only purpose for which power can be rightfully exercised over any member of a civilized community, against his will, is to prevent harm to others."[6] Given this principle, freedom of expression is a fundamental right, for the expression of thoughts and opinions does not itself harm others. The freedom this implies must, says Mill, include the freedom to live as one chooses, so long as one does not transgress the rights of others. As Mill himself puts it:[7]

From Windsor Review of Legal and Social Issues, *vol. 2 (May 1990). Reprinted by permission of Leo Groarke.*

This, then, is the appropriate region of human liberty. It comprises, first, the inward domain of consciousness, demanding liberty of thought and feeling, absolute freedom of opinion and sentiment on all subjects. . . . The liberty of expressing and publishing opinions . . . [is] almost of as much importance as the liberty of thought itself and resting in great part on the same reasons, is practically inseparable from it. Secondly, the . . . liberty of tastes and pursuits, of framing the plan of our life to suit our own character, of doing as we like, subject to such consequences as may follow, without impediment from our fellow creatures, so long as what we do does not harm them, even though they should think our conduct foolish, perverse, or wrong.

Elsewhere, Mill contends that we must not infringe on freedom of expression even when it becomes "intemperate" and is "pushed to an extreme."[8] It is natural to conclude that he would oppose the censorship of pornography, for viewing it does not itself cause harm to others. *On Liberty* does allow the prohibition of public actions that "are a violation of good manners,"[9] and this may justify a ban on the public display of pornographic matter, but has no implications for its use in private.[10]

In response to this interpretation of Mill, Kathleen Okruhlik has argued that Mill would accept the censorship of pornography, for current psychological research links the viewing of pornography to subsequent harm and violence against women. This is, she concludes, a case where the state can legitimately prohibit a particular action (the publication of pornography) because it causes harm to others. The research she cites[11] is important, and we shall see that her conclusion contains an important element of truth, but it is based on an account of harm that is broader than the one that Mill allows. At most, the publication and viewing of pornography harms others indirectly — in the sense that they may lead to other acts (rape, assault, for instance), which cause actual harm. Mill does not, however, allow the state to interfere with acts that are only indirectly harmful. On the contrary, he explicitly declares that we must permit all acts that do not harm others "directly and in the first instance."[12] According to his account, all such acts are "self-regarding" and should not be prohibited.

Mill's unwillingness to allow the state to interfere with indirectly harmful acts is clear when he discusses drunkenness and other "extravagances" that may lead to other acts that are directly harmful. Rather than argue for a ban on such activities, he holds that individuals have the responsibility to ensure that their extravagances do not lead to harmful acts and that society may intervene only when they abrogate this responsibility.

I fully admit that the mischief which a person does to himself may seriously affect, both through their sympathies and their interests, those nearly connected with him and, in a major degree, society at large. When [and only when], by conduct of this sort, a person is led to violate a distinct and assignable obligation to any other person or persons, the case is taken out of the self-regarding class. . . . If a man, through intemperance or extravagance becomes unable to pay his debts, or having undertaken the moral responsibility of a family, becomes from the same cause incapable of supporting or educating them, he is deservedly reprobated and might be justly punished; but it is for the breach of duty to his family or creditor, not for the extravagance. . . .

. . . [T]he merely contingent . . . injury which a person causes society by conduct which neither violates any specific duty to the public, nor occasions perceptible hurt to any assignable individual except himself . . . is one which society can afford to bear, for the sake of the greater good of human freedom.[13]

It is, on this account, the harmful effects that may be produced by one's self regarding habits, not the habits and attitudes themselves that must be the focus of reproach and legal sanction. If the habitual viewing of violent pornography leads someone to commit a rape, for example, it would seem to follow that they can be justly punished, but it is for the rape rather than the habits that precipitated it.

In answer to such considerations, it might be said that the distinction between directly and indirectly harmful acts may sometimes be ignored. When someone yells "Fire!" in a crowded theatre, the effects are so immediate and so obvious that we might, for example, count this as an attempt at direct harm. Such cases have little consequence for the questions we are discussing here, however, for such a situation is not analogous to the viewing of pornography, which is not so obvious and immediate an attempt to provoke harm. Rather, the viewing of pornography can better be compared to the situation Mill discusses when he argues that "an opinion that corn dealers are starvers of the poor, or that private property is robbery, ought to be unmolested when . . . circulated through the press."[14] Such claims obviously promote a view of corn dealers and the owners of private property that might inflame someone who reads them, thus precipitating violence. Mill is not, however, willing to suppress such remarks on this account though he does claim that context can make them unacceptable — as when they are yelled to an angry mob gathered outside the residence of a corn dealer.[15] In the latter, *but not the former*, case the difference between directly and indirectly harmful acts is, on Mill's account, insignificant. Yet it is the former case that is analogous to the publication of pornography, and it seems to follow that the link between it and harm is not direct enough to provide sufficient grounds for censorship.

One might still defend the censorship of pornography by arguing that we should extend Mill's ban on harmful acts so that it applies to indirectly harmful acts, but such a move is difficult to justify. It must be granted that some indirectly harmful acts lead to actual harm, but this is the price of liberty and the prohibition of such acts is compatible with the most extreme paternalism. Gambling in the stock market, consuming alcohol, betting on horse races, watching crime on television, frequenting pool halls, and attending soccer games and rock and roll concerts may lead to harmful acts, but it is difficult to justify the suggestion that we should ban them on these grounds. Analogous restrictions on freedom of expression are still more difficult to justify, for the publication of anything that fuels emotions — stories that offend religious convictions (e.g., Salman Rushdie's *The Satanic Verses*), government exposés, and harsh criticisms of any individual or groups — may be indirectly harmful, for they may lead, in one way or another, to anger and ultimately violence. The censorship of material that may be indirectly harmful, therefore, implies an enormous infringement on the freedom of expression, which is difficult to make compatible with free political discussion.

It may seem to follow that Mill's defence of freedom of expression is incompatible with the censorship of pornography, but it would be a mistake to draw this conclusion. For although Mill does not accept the prohibition of all indirectly harmful acts, he does allow the state to interfere in specific cases, and a careful look at *On Liberty* shows that he would hold that the state can justifiably suppress freedom of expression in cases where individuals promote harm to others. This is not a principle he explicitly propounds, but it can be deduced from his discussion of the promotion of self-regarding acts of which society disapproves. There is, he says in this regard, "considerable force" in the arguments for interfering with anyone who "makes it his occupation, for subsistence of pecuniary gain, to promote" self-regarding acts that "society and the State consider to be an evil."[16] Taking fornication and gambling as examples, he claims that they must be accepted, but that the question whether one should be allowed to be a pimp or the keeper of a gambling house "is one of those which lie on the exact boundary line . . ." between what is and what is not acceptable.[17] This is enough to show that Mill would not tolerate the attempt to benefit by promoting directly harmful acts, for they are more objectionable than the self-regarding acts in question, and the attempt to promote them must, therefore, cross the boundary line between what should and should not be tolerated. Mill himself does not discuss such cases, but this is not because he thinks they are acceptable, but because he cannot envision such a possibility.

At first glance, it may seem that this account of Mill implies a new restriction on freedom of expression, but the principle that individuals may not promote harm to others is not a radically new suggestion. On the contrary, it is the implicit basis of laws against inciting an offence, aiding and abetting, conspiracy, intimidation, threatening, and counselling an offence. In all these cases, actions are prohibited because they promote harm to others, even though they themselves are only indirectly harmful and lead at most to other acts that are the immediate cause of harm. The extent to which the promotion of harm to others is rejected in standard legal principles is seen in the law of torts, which defines "defamation" as any visible or audible matter or act that tends "to diminish the esteem, respect, goodwill or confidence in which the plaintiff is held, or to excite adverse, derogatory or unpleasant feelings against him."[18] Defamation is not, it should be emphasized, confined to communication that actually harms another's reputation, but applies to any communication that has *a general tendency* to this effect.

Given limits on freedom of expression that rule out the promotion of harm to others, the censorship of a great deal of contemporary pornography can be justified, for it suggests that kidnapping, rape, assault, and torture are a legitimate means of achieving sexual satisfaction. It is the explicit promotion of harm that this implies that distinguishes it from other indirectly harmful acts (e.g., drinking and gambling) that cannot be legitimately prohibited. Within the arena of free speech, publications that may indirectly lead to harm by stirring up emotions are, in contrast, permissible as long as they do not suggest that violence and the infringement of other people's rights are appropriate. Much violent pornography does not literally state that rape, assault, torture, etc., is acceptable, but this is still its obvious message, as is clear from its heroes (men and sometimes women who perpetrate assault, torture, and violence), its lack of compassion for their victims, and its complete disregard and insensitivity to the unacceptability of the acts that it depicts. To imagine something similar in a more explicitly political realm, we would have to imagine political pamphlets that glorified or made light of the vivid torture of political opponents. In both cases, the promotion of violence that this implies is a clear case where freedom of expression is used to condone the harm to others that Mill and traditional legal sanctions both reject.

Though she does not discuss the links between her views and traditional accounts of freedom of expression, Rosemarie Tong[19] recognizes this aspect of contemporary pornography in an analysis she has proposed. Arguing that violent pornography defames women as a class, she proposes "group libel" as a means of preventing the dissemination of "degrading thanatica" (from the Greek thanatos for "death"). Appropriate plaintiffs and damages can, she suggests, be determined by standard libel law principles, while injunctions against the future publication of similar materials may be adopted as a remedy.[20]

Such moves are in keeping with a rejection of the promotion of harm to others, but there are many practical problems with such a strategy. Thus the courts have not been receptive to the notion of group libel on the grounds that it is difficult to define defamed groups,[21] injunctions are possible only in very restricted circumstances,[22] and the cost of civil actions would impede them. As Tong herself suggests, group libel is an "undeveloped" legal concept. Changes to obscenity law therefore seem a better answer to contemporary pornography, although they could have an effect similar to the one that she defends.

We can better understand the proposed defense of the censorship of violent pornography if we compare it to censorship as it presently operates in North America. Originally, both Canadian and United States courts employed the common law test of obscenity — the "Hicklin test" enunciated by Lord Cockburn, chief justice of the Court of Queen's Bench in 1868. It asks ". . . whether the tendency of the matter charged as obscenity is to deprave and corrupt those whose minds are open to such immoral influences, and into whose hands a publication of this sort may fall."[23]

In American courts, the Hicklin test was first rejected when Judge Augustus Hand ruled that James Joyce's *Ulysses* was not obscene.[24] In lieu of Hicklin, he proposed a new standard that emphasized the dominant theme of a work as viewed by the average reader. In 1957, the United States Supreme Court confirmed this rejection of Hicklin in *Roth v. U.S.* Roth further held that obscenity was "utterly without redeeming social importance" and not protected by the First Amendment. In 1973, in *Miller v. California*, the Supreme Court established as the present test of obscenity the questions:

(a) whether the "average person, applying contemporary community standards" would find that the work, taken as a whole appeals to the prurient interest . . .
(b) whether the work depicts or describes, in a patently offensive way, sexual conduct specifically defined by the applicable state law, and
(c) whether the work, taken as a whole, lacks serious literary, artistic, political, or scientific value.

According to Miller, local communities must be appealed to in determining standards of tolerance, though it is unclear whether these communities are states or smaller units.

In Canada, the Hicklin test was modified by the introduction of the Criminal Code[25] definition of obscenity in 1959. Subsection 159 (8) of the code states that

any publication a dominant characteristic of which is the undue exploitation of sex, or of sex and any one or more of the following subjects, namely crime, horror, and violence, shall be deemed to be obscene.[26]

Originally intended as a mechanism that would support the Hicklin test, case law soon adopted the Criminal Code definition as an exhaustive test. Initially introduced as a remedy to the "vague subjective" common law criteria,[27] it soon proved to be inadequate, and case law turned to "the community standards test,"[28] employing community standards to establish what constitutes the "undue exploitation" central to the statutory definition of obscenity.

In 1985, the Supreme Court of Canada made possible a broader understanding of obscenity, suggesting that community standards were merely one of a number of ways to measure undue exploitation. Any legal definition of undueness must, it declared, also encompass publications that might pass the community standards test but are harmful to members of society and, therefore, society as a whole.[29] In *R v. Wagner*, the Alberta Court of Appeal subsequently concluded that video tapes could be judged obscene if they could result in probable harm to the public.[30] Sociological studies, research, and experiments of the kind we have already noted were accepted as evidence that could establish the probability of such harm.

Unlike courts in the United States, Canadian courts interpret their appeal to community standards as an appeal on a national rather than a local level.[31] Despite this difference, obscenity law has, for the most part, been applied similarly in both jurisdictions.[32] For our purposes, the important point is that obscenity law is founded, in both cases, on an appeal to community attitudes and opinions. The legal constitutionality of such appeals under the Canadian Charter of Rights and Freedoms[33] has yet to be decided by the Supreme Court,[34] but there is, from a moral point of view, no way to escape the conclusion that present day obscenity law represents an arbitrary infringement on freedom of expression. Indeed, it would be difficult to find a clearer example of the "tyranny of the majority," which prompted Mill's defence of freedom of expression. As he says repeatedly, the imposition of the majority's view on other individuals is the most serious threat to liberty in a democratic state, and freedom of expression must protect us from such interference. Instead, obscenity law as it is now exercised has the opposite effect, enforcing the majority's view of what is unacceptable and obscene.

I have already argued that there are instances where the censorship of pornography can be justified, but this censorship should not be confused with censorship as it now operates in North America. In the cases in question, pornography is unacceptable because it promotes harm to others and *not* because the views expressed contravene the views of the community. The conflict between the rationale behind present-day obscenity law and censorship, which is compatible with traditional accounts of freedom of expression, is very clearly seen in the decision, by the British Columbia Court of Appeal, that sexually explicit material can be deemed to be obscene even when no violence is involved and women are not subjugated to degrading and dehumanizing roles.[35] Though I know of no such case, it is also easy to imagine how the standard appeal to community standards of tolerance might be used to justify restrictions that allow society to act against material it finds politically offensive — e.g., the defence of gay and lesbian rights. Any such action is, however, an arbitrary infringement on freedom of expression, which endorses the principle that society can interfere with individual expression it finds disagreeable even if it has no clear connection to direct harm to others.

American and Canadian appeals to obscenity law are, it should be noted, also problematic from a practical point of view, for they are vague and indeterminate. "The determination of 'community standards' by the experts appearing in obscenity trials is . . . left largely to their hunches, impressions and subjective judgments."[36] The uncertain and inconsistent standard this implies makes it difficult to apply obscenity law and asks defendants to abide by standards that are not clearly demarcated in the first place. Within such a context, those involved in obscenity trials have good reason to criticize the unavailability of advance notice that specific materials are obscene. It is in view of the vague, subjective, and indeterminate nature of Canadian obscenity law that it has been called "the most muddled law in Canada." In a 1948 decision in the United States, Judge Struble of Ohio captured the frustration that surrounds obscenity law in both the United States and Canada when he remarked that "'obscenity' is not a legal term. It cannot be defined so that it will mean the same thing to all people, all the time, everywhere. Obscenity is very much a figment of the imagination." This may overstate the case, but it is hard to deny that the vagueness and inconsistency of present-day standards of obscenity supports Lawrence Tribe's suggestion that "the American Supreme Court's bare majority in 1973 for yet another definition of the obscene and yet another set of rationales for its suppression has produced a formula as likely to be as unstable as it is unintelligible."

Instead of resolving these practical problems, many of those who have attacked pornography have proposed analyses that are likely to exacerbate them. Helen Longino has, for example, argued that the degradation of women and their portrayal "as mere sexual objects to be exploited and manipulated" is what is unacceptable in present-day pornography.[37] The Canadian Parliament's Standing Committee on Justice and Legal Affairs endorsed a similar account of obscenity in 1978, suggesting that we define it in terms of degradation and humiliation. In *R v. Towne Cinema Theatres Ltd.*[38] Madam Justice Wilson concurred with the majority decision, but further defined the undue exploitation of sex prohibited by the present law to include degrading and dehumanizing treatments of sex. What is exploitative, degrading, and dehumanizing is very much a matter of individual taste, however, and changes to obscenity law along these lines would allow for arbitrary infringements on freedom of expression rather than a clear account of what should and should not be censored. It is a similar lack of clear criteria that created the present appeal to community standards in the first place, and it is likely that courts would be forced to use some such standards in interpreting such notions. The end result is likely to be yet another version of the practical problems that presently exist.

One finds a more promising attempt to deal with the problems with present-day obscenity law in the changes to the Canadian Criminal Code proposed in 1987 — changes that are founded on detailed definitions of "pornography" and "erotica."[39] Pornography is defined to include written and visual matter that shows (or incites, promotes, encourages, or advocates) "a person causing, attempting to cause or appearing to cause, in a sexual context, permanent or extended impairment of the body or bodily functions of that person or any other person," or "sexually violent conduct, including sexual assault and any conduct in which physical pain is inflicted or apparently inflicted on a person by that person or any other person in a sexual context."[40] A person is guilty of "dealing in pornography" if he or she "imports, makes, prints, publishes, distributes," and so forth, pornography as it is defined.

Such legislation is in keeping with the account of the limits of freedom of expression I have defended, but goes too far when it prohibits material that depicts consenting sexual acts that do not involve harm to others, e.g., consenting intercourse or masturbation.[41] The proposed prohibitions on the public display of erotica are especially heavy-handed, prohibiting erotica that may be in keeping with public taste and the rejection of the promotion of harm that I have already elaborated.[42] As many commentators have pointed out, there seems no way to justify such infringements on freedom of expression. Judging by the account I have proposed, the emphasis on sex, which continues to be the cornerstone of obscenity law, is very much misguided, for it is the promotion of harm that can justifiably be prohibited and it follows that objectionable material may contain no sex at all.

A further problem with the proposed changes to Canadian law is their failure to make clear enough the distinction between material that depicts and promotes harm to others. It must in this regard be emphasized that some specific film, book, video, sign, etc., must be judged by considering its attitude to the content it includes. A film that contains a rape scene is not ipso facto unacceptable, and the crucial factor is whether it condones the rape. A magazine, like *Brutal Trio*, which glorifies rape as a means of sexual stimulation should be prohibited, while an anti-rape film like *Scream From Silence* (which graphically portrays a rape) cannot legitimately be censored. Rather, its attempt to dispel myths that make rape acceptable is a laudable attempt to reinforce the principle that harm to others is unacceptable — the very principle attacked by objectionable pornography. It is in view of this principle that unacceptable pornography should be defined as material that *incites, advocates, promotes or, encourages* (and not merely as material that "depicts") harm to others. The context in which a particular publication is presented may, therefore, be important to a determination of its status as pornography. The publication of Marquis de Sade's *One Hundred and Twenty Days of Sodom* may, for example, be permissible as a basis for the study of history or sexual deviance though it should be published in a way that reflects the attitude this implies. It is one thing to make it available for serious study, it is another to publish and promote it as illustrated popular bedtime reading. Dworkin and MacKinnon have suggested one way to allow such contexts in their proposal to amend the Minneapolis Code of Ordinance on Civil Rights in a way that would ban "trafficking in pornography," for their amendment would exempt public libraries from this ban.

Accepting the limit on censorship implied by a consideration of the attitude that is displayed by pornographic material, it should by now be clear that the censorship of violent pornography proposed by the Canadian government can be made compatible with liberal notions of freedom of expression. The key to such censorship is the principle that the promotion of harm to others should not be tolerated, a principle that can be used to justify the changes to obscenity law that prohibit such material, though not the changes that allow a broader censorship.

In closing, it should perhaps be noted one should not expect the proposed censorship to eliminate every problematic case, even though it will eradicate much of the vagueness inherent in the present appeal to community standards. A definition of obscenity that focuses on the promotion of harm will substantially clarify obscenity law, but questions of intent and meaning are inherently difficult and complex. Indeed, the problems they produce are not unique to censorship and inevitably permeate any legal system. It is impossible to anticipate every possible problem here, and it must instead be said that such censorship must be refined by a discussion of a multitude of examples, and that this is best accomplished by case law and the evolution this implies. Granting the need for such discussion, the fundamental principle behind the account of obscenity I have proposed is (unlike the principles behind present-day obscenity law) relatively straightforward and easily applied.[43] More importantly perhaps, it provides a basis for obscenity that is very much in keeping with traditional accounts of freedom of expression.

NOTES

1. For detailed references, see the version of the present paper published in the *Windsor Review of Legal and Social Issues*, Vol. II, May 1990.
2. The legislation died on the order paper when Parliament was dissolved for the federal election in 1988.
3. Laura Lederer, ed., *Take Back the Night: Women on Pornography* (New York: William Morrow & Company, 1980); ". . . the liberal approach . . . presents pornography as just one more aspect of our ever expanding sexuality" (19).
4. Thelma McCormack, "Passionate Protests: Feminists and Censorship," *Canadian Forum* (March, 1980).
5. Jan Narveson, *The Libertarian Idea* (Philadelphia: Temple University Press, 1988). Narveson discusses the issues raised in the present paper on pp. 284-95, but his account is inconclusive and does not address the distinctions I make here.
6. John Stuart Mill, *On Liberty* (Markham: Penguin Books, 1974), 68.
7. Ibid., 71.
8. Ibid., 116-17, 81.
9. Ibid., 148.

10. In very extreme cases where the making of ("snuff") pornography depends on actual rape and murder, the state must intervene, but this leaves the bulk of pornography untouched.

11. For relevant material, see supra, note 1.

12. Supra, note 6 at 71. It is important to separate: (1) the distinction between directly and indirectly harmful acts, and (2) the distinction between acts which are always or only sometimes directly harmful. Mill allows society to take action against the latter when he suggests that acts may be forbidden if they promote "a definite risk of damage" or "probability of damage," ibid., pp. 149 and 163, though he fails to give a precise account of how much risk warrants prohibition. The important point is that the acts that might thus be prohibited (drunken driving, for example) cause direct harm when they cause harm, and that this aspect of Mill's discussion is not, therefore, applicable to the viewing of pornography, which is at most indirectly harmful.

13. Ibid., 148-49.

14. Ibid., 119.

15. Ibid., 119.

16. Ibid., 168-69.

17. Ibid., 170.

18. *Black's Law Dictionary*, 5th ed. (St. Paul: West Publishing Co., 1983), 217. See also P. Lewis, ed., *Gatley on Libel and Slander*, 8th ed. (London: Sweet and Maxwell, 1981).

19. Rosemarie Tong, "Feminism, Pornography and Censorship," *Social Theory and Practice* 8 (1982).

20. Ibid., 12. A similar approach is discussed in Susan G. Cole, *Pornography and the Sex Crisis* (Toronto: Amanita Enterprises, 1989), 95-106. For a detailed discussion of group libel, see David Reisman, "Democracy and Defamation: Control of Group Libel," *Columbia Law Review* (1942) 42:727.

21. Especially as different individuals (including different individuals from the groups that have allegedly been defamed) disagree over the question whether pornography is objectionable.

22. *Natural Resources Ltd. v. Saturday Night Ltd.* (1910), 2 O.W.N. 9. See *Robinson v. Adams* (1924), 56 O.L.R. 217 (C.A.) for the principles outlining the limited cases where an injunction should be granted.

23. *R v. Hicklin* (1868), 3 L.R.Q.B. 360.

24. *United States v. One Book Called "Ulysses"*: 5 F. Supp. 182 (S.D.N.Y., 1983) affirmed 72 F. 2d 705 (2d Cir. 1934). See L. Tribe, *American Constitutional Law* (Mineola: The Foundation Press Inc. 1978), 659.

25. *Canadian Criminal Code*, S.C. 1953-54 c. 51.

26. Ibid., a. 159(8), as am. S.C. 1959, c. 41, s. 11.

27. Canada, House of Commons Debates 1959, Vol. V, p. 5517, Standing Committee on Justice and Legal Affairs, "Report on Pornography" by the Hon. E. Davie Fulton in *House of Commons Journal*, Vol. 123, No. 86, 1978.

28. *R v. Brodie; R v. Times Square Cinemas Ltd.* (1971), 3 O.R. 688, 4 C.C.C. (2d) 229 (C.A.).

29. *R v. Towne Cinema Theatres Ltd.* [1985] 1 S.C.R. 494, 18 D.L.R. (4th) 1.

30. *R v. Wagner* (1986), 26 C.C.C. (3d) 242, 43 Alta. L.R. (2d).

31. *R v. Times Square Cinemas Ltd.*, supra; *R v. Adriadne Dev. Ltd.* (1974), 19 C.C.C. (2d) 49, 8 N.S.R. (2dd) 560.

32. "The definitions of obscenity in these two countries, although developing from different sources, have been interpreted and applied similarly." R.E. Dean, *Obscenity Standards in Canada and the United States: A Comparative Study in Constitutional Law* (Ph.D. Dissertation, University of Tennessee, 1974), 11.

33. *Canadian Charter of Rights and Freedoms*, 1 of the *Constitution Act*, 1982, being Schedule B of the *Canada Act* 1982 (U.K.) 1982, c. 11.

34. Lower court rulings on the issue are found in the decisions of the British Columbia Court of Appeal in *R v. Red Hot Video* (1985), 15 C.R.R. 206, 18 C.C.C. (3d) 1, and the Ontario Court of Appeal in *Re Ontario Film and Video Appreciation Society and the Ontario Board of Censors* (1984), 7 C.R.R. 129, 5 D.L.R. (4th) 766. In *R v. Butler* (1989), 50 C.C.C. (3d) 97, 60 M.R. (2d) 82, the Manitoba Court of Queen's Bench ruled in favour of prohibitions on obscene material if their purpose is to protect people from, among other things, material that effectively reduces the human, equality, or other Charter rights of individuals (but not if their purpose is to control the morals of society).

35. *R v. Pereira-Vasquez* (1988),43 C.C.C. (3d) 82, 26 B.C.L.R. (2d) 273.
36. Supra, note 49, 532.
37. Supra, note 7.
38. *R v. Towne Cinema Theatres Ltd.,* [1985] 1 S.C.R. (S.C.C.), 494.
39. Bill C-54, *An Act to Amend the Criminal Code and other Acts in Consequence Thereof,* 2d Sess., 33d Parl., 1986-87, s. 1.
40. Ibid. at 1 a(ii) & 1 a(iii).
41. Ibid. at 1 a(vi).
42. Though "erotica" is defined very broadly to include almost any vaguely sexual representation, section 159.7 would make it an offence to publicly display it.
43. It should be emphasized that such censorship implies a very specific restriction on freedom of expression and cannot be rejected on the grounds that other kinds of censorship have often been abused (Leach and other critics of censorship seem oblivious to the differences that distinguish different kinds of censorship).

QUESTIONS

1. Is John Stuart Mill right in thinking that freedom is a general good that must be maximized? Why or why not?
2. Is Mill's view that "the only purpose for which power can be rightfully exercised over any member of a civilized community against his will is to prevent harm to others" sound? How would you test its validity?
3. Leo Groarke argues that censoring some kinds of pornography is compatible with Mill's principle. What reasons does he give for this view? Are they convincing? Why or why not?
4. The fact that censoring some kinds of pornography is compatible with Mill's principle does not show that violent pornography should be censored. Does Groarke provide convincing arguments to show that the kind of pornography that he thinks should be censored is sufficiently harmful to warrant this kind of legal intervention?

SEXUAL EQUALITY AND THE PROBLEM OF AN ADEQUATE MORAL THEORY: THE POVERTY OF LIBERALISM

Lorenne Clark

One of the fundamental principles endorsed by a liberal ethic is that there must be some areas of one's life in which one has the freedom to do what one wants, free from interference by others. It has been argued that there simply are some areas of life which are none of the law's business. For those familiar with the Wolfenden Report on Homosexuality in England, and the subsequent debate that this started both within and outside academic circles, this phrase, "none of the law's business," will have an all too familiar ring. Philosophically, this is reflected in debates about which areas of one's life should be essentially characterized by negative freedom, the ability to act free of restraints and scrutiny of others. Legally, it is reflected in debates about privacy, about the areas of one's life into which others should be

This is a shortened version of a paper originally published in In Search of the Feminist Perspective: The Changing Potency of Women, *Mary Kathryn Shirley and Rachel Emma Vigier, eds. Toronto: Resources for Feminist Research, Special Publication no. 5 (Spring 1979). Reprinted by permission of Lorenne Clark.*

legally prohibited from interfering.[1] There is virtually no one who would want to say that we should have no negative liberty or no privacy, but the debate still rages as to which areas of one's life should be guaranteed as areas of negative liberty through the creation of a legal right to privacy.

The difficulty is that no one has found a satisfactory method of drawing the boundaries between the private and other areas of life. In the past, the boundary was thought to be a *natural* one, based on the traditional distinction between the public and the private. The private just *was* "the private," and, as such should be guaranteed as an area of negative liberty and fully protected by means of a legally enforceable right to privacy. This was the basis of the argument in the Wolfenden Report. Here it was alleged that sexual relations between consenting adults simply are none of the law's business and the underlying rationale was that such behaviour should justifiably be left to the absolute discretion of individuals because it has effects on no one other than the participants. This was the rationale provided by John Stuart Mill in "On Liberty," and which was reiterated and defended by Herbert Hart in *Law, Liberty, and Morality*.[2] The best defence of this liberal tenet is the view developed by Mill that the law is justified in prohibiting actions if and only if doing them results in the inability of others to exercise rights of a similar kind. The underlying view is that rights should be distributed equally, which entails that no one can have rights the exercise of which would prevent others from exercising similar rights. The difficulty with the position is that it is virtually impossible to say with certainty of any action or pattern of behaviour that it has in principle no potential effects on others, either in terms of causing harm, or in terms of limiting the effective exercise of rights. Thus it is impossible *in principle* to draw a defensible boundary between the public and the private.

And certainly it has been indefensible to draw the legal boundary on the basis of the historical division between public and private. As is now abundantly clear, privacy functioned historically to protect those who were privileged to begin with. Privacy was a consequence of the ownership of private property, and, hence, was a commodity purchased with property. It has been a privilege accorded those of wealth and high social status. But more importantly from a feminist perspective, it protected not only the dominant class in the Marxist sense, but the dominant sex-class as well. The traditionally "private" was the sphere of the personal, home and hearth. And that area was the area within which women and children were forms of private property under the exclusive ownership and control of males. As the person in whom the absolute personality of the family rested, male heads of households had virtually absolute rights over their wives and children. The family, clearly, was not and is not a partnership of equals. There is no mutuality in the marital relations and the rights and duties are decidedly one-sided.

Of course it is not the concept of privacy which is responsible for this state of affairs. But in drawing a boundary between the historically private and public, for the purpose of entrenching a legal right to privacy in the area of the traditionally private, it certainly functioned to condone and encourage the abusive and unjustified practices which were possible within this unequal relation. As is now clear, the family has been characterized by a great deal of physical violence. The legitimate basis of authority in the family is physical coercion, and it is and has been regularly relied on to secure to the male head of the house the attitudes and behaviours he wants. Women, much less children, had no right to protest such behaviour but were expected to suffer it, willingly, or otherwise. Thus, the last place feminists want to see a right to privacy is in the family. What possible sense can be made of the notion of being a consenting adult when one is in a relation in which one has no right to say no? Clearly, if we want privacy at all, where we do not want it is in the home.

The area of life most in need of regulation and control in the interest of creating more liberty and equality for women is the area of the traditionally private and personal. But greater liberty and equality for women can be purchased only at the cost of less liberty, and loss of status, for men. To the extent that women are given more rights within marriage, men are less able to do as they please; what was before permissible would now be either mandatory, as, for example, in making it a duty for men to share the housework and childcare, or prohibited, as for example in allowing a charge of rape between spouses. Within terms of the basic principle, such changes are justified. The past operation of the law has permitted many forms of behaviour which in fact caused physical and other direct and tangible harms to others, and which certainly prevented the effective exercise of like rights on the part of others. On the principle of like liberties for all, marriage must be turned into a relation of mutuality, and the relationships within it must be subject to regulation and control.

Why, then, has the demand for privacy centred so exclusively on preserving the traditional domain of male privilege? And why do the staunchest defenders of that view fail to see that in invoking these principles within a domain characterized by fundamental sexual inequality they are in fact both reinforcing that inequality and sanctioning its worst abuses? Thus, at the very least, adherents of the liberal ethic must acknowledge that there is no *natural* basis for deciding on what is private and what is public for the purpose of entrenching a legal right to privacy, and that the traditional area of the private is the area most in need of loss of privacy, in the name of promoting greater positive liberty and greater equality. How this fares on a purely utilitarian principle is of course problematic, for since men and women each make up roughly half the population, we cannot be sure that the benefits to women will in fact outweigh the losses to men.

In my view, the whole debate about privacy has been totally miscast because it has relied on the historical division between public and private. Thus, its liberal adherents continue to stress the need for privacy in just the areas where it is least defensible. Where we need the most protection, the legally enforceable right to prevent others from gaining access to information about us, and from disseminating that information to others without either our knowledge or our consent, is in the public world, the world of computers and charge-cards, credit ratings, and security forces. But this will mean much more regulation and control of the people and institutions which determine the structure and organization of the economic and social order. It will mean confronting the dominant class and the dominant sex in the public as well as the private sphere, and we should hardly be surprised to find that we are forced to part company with radical adherents of the liberal ethic. Equality cannot flourish without limiting the privileges some already have in both the private and the public spheres because the inequalities of the present system were a product of the unequal attribution of rights in the first instance; thus greater equality and liberty for those least advantaged under the present system necessitates placing restrictions on the privileged rights of those who are presently most advantaged. And since this must be done by creating obligations either to do or to forbear actions previously permitted, it can be accomplished only at the expense of negative liberty.

While the principles of the liberal ethic itself do not require the historical division between public and private, it has certainly been presupposed in liberal thinking about these issues. Recognition of the extent to which this has played a role must lead to a reappraisal of what it is that people should be at liberty to do, and it must find a basis for this which does not rest on traditional views of the different spheres of life, and the different roles of the sexes.

What is needed, at base, is a reappraisal of what is *harmful*. That, too, has historically been defined in terms of what the dominant sex and the dominant economic class find "harmful." An analysis of rape law demonstrates that point as well as anything could. Physically coerced sexual intercourse has been regarded as constituting a redressable harm if and only if the female victim was a dependent female living under either parental or matrimonial control, and in possession of those qualities which made her desirable as a piece of sexual and reproductive property available for the exclusive use of a present or future husband.[3] I dare say that when we start pressing for legal reform which will prohibit sexual harassment on the job we will find few adherents of liberalism rallying to our cause. It remains to be seen whether or not liberalism can survive and transcend the limitations of its own historical perspective, but in so far as it must renounce much of its accepted thinking about what sorts of actions individuals ought to be free to do, and must recognize that negative liberty must at least temporarily take a back seat to the promotion of equality, I cannot say I am hopeful about the outcome. But the ethics of liberalism will not do as the moral framework for the achievement of sexual equality unless it can meet this challenge.

But it is clear from a consideration of the issue of pornography that so far at least the ethics of liberalism has been unable to rethink its concept of harm in a way which is consistent with sexual equality. Feminists and civil libertarians are now at complete loggerheads over the issue. The trend among feminists is clear. More and more of them are coming to see that pornography is a species of hate literature.[4] To achieve its impact, it relies on depicting women in humiliating, degrading, and violently abusive situations. To make matters worse, it frequently depicts them willingly, even avidly, suffering and inviting such treatment. As is obvious to even the naivest of eyes, such recreations of heterosexual behaviour and relationships feed traditional male fantasies about both themselves and women.

Pornography is a method of socialization; it is the tangible, palpable embodiment of the imposition of the dominant sexual system which is a part of the dominant sex-class system. It is a vivid depiction of how to deploy male sexuality in just the way that will achieve maximum effect in maintaining the *status quo*. Pornography would be neither desired nor tolerated within any system other than one which sprang from the differential attribution of rights of ownership in which women and children are forms of sexual property, and in which they must either like it or quite literally lump it. It is the obverse of a morality which stresses female passivity and submissiveness, and it encourages the actualization of such states through active aggression and violence. Pornography has very little to do with sex, certainly with any conception of egalitarian sexual relations between the sexes, but it has everything to do with showing how to use sexuality as an instrument of active oppression, and that is why it is wrong. Some allege that it also feeds female fantasies about themselves and men, but that is certainly being questioned, at least in so far as it can be said that there is any hard empirical data to support it.[5]

That there should be no laws prohibiting the manufacture, sale, and distribution of pornography has traditionally and increasingly been defended as a freedom of speech, and freedom of press, issue. It is alleged that the reading or viewing of such material does not cause harm, or that if it does, it is harm only to those who willingly consent to it. The premise that it doesn't cause harm is defended by arguing that it relates only to the fantasy level and does not translate itself into interpersonal behaviour. And it goes further than this to argue that, indeed, it provides a healthy outlet, a cathartic effect, for those who might otherwise be tempted to act out their fantasies. Those who oppose pornography, particularly those who advocate its prohibition, are treated as Victorian prudes with sexual hang-ups. Women who object to it are seen as uptight, unliberated, and just not "with it" sexually speaking.

The general principle underlying the liberal view is of course that expressed by Mill in "On Liberty," who argued against any form of censorship on the ground that it was only through the free flow of information that the true and false could be separated. Prohibitions against the dissemination of any form of information functions to preserve the *status quo* and to prevent the development of a critically reflective morality which is itself necessary to pave the way for needed social change. The principle has much to be said for it. But that cannot change the fact that when it is uncritically made to apply within a domain characterized by inequality and by frankly abusive behaviour, a domain which is fundamentally shaped by a framework of social relations and institutions which makes all sexual relationships between men and women fundamentally coercive in nature,[6] it is bound to produce results which will be unacceptable because harmful to those who are in the pre-existing inferior position and who stand to be most affected by the attitudes and beliefs, as well as the practices, of those who use it.

The liberal argument has been that such material isn't harmful at all, and certainly cannot be seen as harmful to anyone other than the user, if harmful even to him. It isn't harmful because it functions merely to inflame male sexual desire. What is the harm if all it does is give a guy a bit of a rush? And it is right here that we must begin our critique. Surely we must acknowledge at least two things. First, it is not "normal" to get one's rushes from just anything. Secondly, if one gets desirable reactions from things which create a clear and substantial risk to others, then one can justifiably be prohibited from getting them that way. Persons who get their sexual stimulation from watching the atrocities perpetrated against the Jews during the Holocaust are not regarded as "normal," and rightly so. Furthermore, we do not feel that we are infringing any legitimate rights of others in preventing them access to material designed to provide sexual stimulation by this means. And the reasons for that are at least two-fold. First, as history has made all too clear, actions of this particular species do not remain at the level of mere fantasy. They have been acted out on the grand scale, so grand as to make any rational and reflective person aware that the possibility of a correlation between thought and action is at least strong enough to justify the imposition of prohibitions against material of this sort. Second, it stems from recognizing that even if the actual actions themselves are not acted out, the attitudes and beliefs of the persons enjoying them reflect attitudes toward the objects of the actions which are in themselves intrinsically bad and which are bound to produce practical effects in real life, if only to be expressed in bigoted and racist attitudes. All of the same arguments apply to material which depicts black people in degrading, humiliating, and abusive circumstances. Such material is, in itself, an affront to the dignity of the objects depicted, not least because they *are* being depicted purely as objects, dehumanized and depersonalized instruments for the satisfaction of someone else's perverted tastes.

The same case can be made with respect to heterosexual pornography.[7] As Camille Le Grand puts it, "pornography teaches society to view women as less than human. It is this view which keeps women as victims."[8] The typical way in which women are depicted in pornography certainly reflects a view of them as inferior to men, as inherently masochistic, and as primarily of value as instrument for the satisfaction of male lust. That is, in itself, intrinsically offensive to women, and is a straightforward objective affront to their dignity as equal persons. So on that ground alone, pornography ought to be prohibited just as we prohibit material depicting other social groups in such a fashion.

Of course, we could hardly argue within the parameters of our present culture that it is abnormal for males to react as they do to pornography. It is, unfortunately, all too normal, at least where we have any notion of statistical normality in mind. But neither is it unusual for rape victims to feel shamed, humiliated, and degraded by being raped; this is "normal" in the culture, but from any more rational perspective, it certainly is not "normal" in any normative sense. Much of recent efforts around the issue of rape have been designed specifically to change the perspective which rape victims have on that experience. Rape victims can come to see the assaultive behaviour perpetrated against them as legitimizing the anger which is appropriate to the nature of the attack. In short, it is possible both to identify the specific effects of socialization within a male supremacist and sexually coercive society, and to off-set those effects with appropriate reconceptualization of the event. Women can come to identify the masochism and victimization into which they have been socialized, and can then act both to counteract it, and to be sublimely angry at a culture which socialized them into that mode. So, too, it should be possible for men to identify the sadism and attitudes of sexual aggressivity into which they are socialized and so act both to counteract them, and to be angry at a social system that produced that response. In short, *it is not a mark of personal depravity or immorality to be aroused by such material*. Given the cultural pattern of which it is a manifestation that is not at all surprising. Indeed, it is just what we would expect. But what must be recognized is that it is a socialized response, and that it is a response about which men should be both concerned and angry. And certainly, once its cultural roots are exposed, it is a response which should not be seen as needing or justifying the sale and distribution of the material which elicited it. Women must object to pornography because it both reflects and reinforces the patterns of socialization appropriate to a system based on the unequal status of the sexes, in which women are consistently regarded and treated as the inferiors, and the sexual property, of men. The socialization it brings about is *in itself* a limitation of the autonomy of women. Men ought to object to it for the same reason, and they ought to recognize that the socialization it brings about in terms of their self-images and internalized standards of conduct is also intrinsically undesirable given any commitment to the notion of sexual equality. To the extent that men are able to internalize the conviction that women and men are equal persons, they must recognize that the pleasurable responses they get from pornography are inappropriate to that conviction and are destructive to their ability to form self-images consistent with it. But that does not entail that they are in any sense to blame for those responses: they had as little choice about that as they did about their names. But we have, then, given strong arguments in support of the view that the eliciting of a pleasurable response is not in itself any reason to condone the sale and distribution of pornography, and that a proper understanding of the nature and causes of that response gives men as well as women solid grounds for objecting to the material which occasioned it. I believe that many more men would be able to understand and accept the feminist perspective on pornography if they could come to realize that they are not responsible for their sexual responses to it given the patterns of socialization which exist to mould us all into a set of social relations which institutionalizes male aggression and female passivity.

Thus, pornography is intrinsically harmful, both to women and to men. However, that does not end the argument with defenders of liberalism because their argument then moves on to the assertion that the harm to women is not direct enough to justify the legal prohibition of pornography. Frankly, I think that the argument that pornography is intrinsically offensive to the dignity of women ought to carry the day, but in the interests of completeness I want to go on to consider the other arguments that are brought to pornography's defence. Apart from this notion of an intrinsic harm and infringement of the rights of women, it will be argued that even if pornography is harmful to the user, it does not lead to direct harm to women, because the fantasies it supports remain fantasies, and it in fact prevents direct harm to women through its cathartic effect. I may say at the outset that I'm not at all impressed with either of these arguments. So far as the first is concerned, there is plenty of hard evidence available which supports the contention that modeling has a powerful effect on human behaviour. Studies of wife and child abuse consistently attest to the fact that there is a strong correlation between those who are abusers and those who come from family situations which were themselves abusive. The battered child becomes the battering parent; the son who witnessed his father battering his mother, and who was himself battered, becomes a battering husband.[9] Also, the evidence about the effect of violence depicted on television on the behaviour of children also points strongly in this direction.[10] People tend to act out and operationalize the behaviour that they see typically acted out around them. And surely that is hardly surprising. It is what has kept civilization going. If we weren't able to perpetuate the patterns of behaviour developed through cultural organization we wouldn't have come very far. So far as I know, however, there is no hard data to support the catharsis theory. It is a theory espoused by those who are looking for a rationale, though doubtless it has its roots in their awareness that they read pornography but don't rape and brutalize women. But raping and brutalizing women isn't the only harm that can be perpetrated against women. But so far there is little empirical support offered for the view that pornography feeds only the fantasy. Most psychiatric literature dealing with the "perversions" asserts that some people remain content with the fantasy while others do not.[11] But no one knows what differentiates the one who does actualize it from the one who doesn't. If this argument is going to be effective, it must be empirically demonstrated that this is so, and surely we cannot predict until the data are in that those who don't so outnumber those who do that we should, in the interests of an open society, tolerate the risk that some will. And since we are all imprisoned by the cultural stereotypes and the patterns of socialization appropriate to a society based on sexual coercion, how can those who do read it assert with certainty that they do not cause harm to women? They are hardly the best judges! As rape makes clear again, there is nowhere greater difference in perception than there is in the confusion surrounding rape and seduction. The men believe they are merely seducing, but the women perceive it as rape! And who is to judge? Certainly it is intrinsically unfair to permit only those who are the perpetrators of such behaviour to have a say in its interpretation.

While the liberal principle behind opposition to censorship is based on a recognition that desirable social change requires public access to information which challenges the beliefs and practices of the *status quo*, what it does not acknowledge is that information which supports the *status quo* through providing role models which advocate the use or threat of coercion as a technique of social control directed at a clearly identifiable group depicted as inferior, subordinate, and subhuman works against the interest both of desirable social change and of the members of the subgroup so identified. This has been clearly acknowledged in the case of violently anti-Semitic and other forms of racist literature. The same principles apply with respect to violently anti-female literature, and the same conclusion should follow. But this cannot come about until it is recognized and acknowledged that the dissemination of such material is itself a harm to the members of the group involved. It remains to be seen whether liberalism can accomplish this, but until it does, we cannot hope for its support on this issue.

In refusing to count as "harms" actions and practices which serve the interest of the dominant sex by reinforcing the patterns and effects of modes of socialization which support the sexist system, it renders itself incapable of changing that system and of promoting greater equality and positive liberty for women. Liberalism serves the interest of the dominant sex and the dominant class, though it contains within itself the potential for promoting greater equality and greater positive liberty for all. It can realize this potential, however, only by reconceptualizing harm in a way consistent with sex and class equality, and by recognizing that negative liberty must take second place to the promotion of equality at least until we have achieved a framework of enforceable rules which guarantees equality within both the public and the private spheres. When no one is allowed to do what is harmful to others, and/or what prevents them from effectively exercising liberty rights to autonomy and equality consistent with the equal attribution and effective exercise of like rights on the part of others, then we will have achieved a state in which liberty is concrete, and not a chimera which upholds the liberty of some at the expense of inequality to the rest. As women we are members of the disadvantaged sex. We are thus acting contrary to the interests of our sex in accepting any position which does not place the achievement of legally enforceable sexual equality at the forefront of its program.

That entails that we have to challenge traditional concepts of harm, and of liberty as the absence of restraint. We have been successful in removing most of the legal restraints which made both equality and liberty impossible, and that was the stage at which the ethics of liberalism served our purpose. But it has now outlived its usefulness to us. The achievement of *real*, rather than merely *possible*, equality and liberty now depends on placing effective, enforceable restraints on others; we can expect little support from liberalism as we move into this stage of our liberation.

NOTES

1. A more detailed account of the relationship between the philosophical and legal debates, as well as a discussion of the complexity of the legal issue of privacy itself, is found in Clark, Lorenne M.G., "Privacy, Property, Freedom, and the Family," *Philosophical Law*, (Ed.) R. Bronaugh, Greenwood Press, Conn., 1978.
2. Hart, H.L.A., *Law, Liberty, and Morality*, O.U.P. London, 1963. This was Hart's answer to the objections raised by Lord Devlin to the recommendations and theory expressed in the Wolfenden Report. Devlin's position on this and other related matters is found in Devlin, Lord Patrick, *The Enforcement of Morals*, O.U.P., London, 1965.
3. For a discussion of the way in which the historical evolution and conception of rape law functioned to maintain the sexual *status quo*, and indeed continues to produce just the results we should expect to find with respect to the treatment and handling of rape cases within the criminal justice system, see Clark, Lorenne M.G., and Lewis, Debra J., *Rape: The Price of Coercive Sexuality*, The Women's Press, Toronto, 1977.
4. Among the articles that spring readily to mind are Morgan, Robin, "Theory and Practice: Pornography and Rape," *Going Too Far*, Random House, N.Y., 1977, Ch. IV, pp. 163-169; Russell, Diana, "Pornography: A Feminist Perspective," unpublished paper; Brownmiller, Susan, *Against Our Will*, Simon & Schuster, N.Y., 1975, pp. 394-396; and Shear, Marie, "Free Meat Talks Back," *J. of Communication*, Vol. 26, No. 1, Winter, 1976, pp. 38-39.
5. For an excellent discussion of the way in which the empirical research that has been done on obscenity reflects a decidedly male bias, see McCormack, Thelma, "Machismo in Media Research: A Critical Review of Research on Violence and Pornography," *Social Problems*, Vol. 25, No. 5, 1978, pp. 544-555.
6. Clark and Lewis, *Rape: The Price of Coercive Sexuality*, Chs. 7 and 8 in particular.
7. Indeed, it is true of male homosexual pornography as well. But in the interest of not legislating in the interest of others, I am not advocating that we should prohibit this species of pornography. If men object to it, as in my view they should, whether homo- or heterosexual, it is up to them to express their opposition. Certainly I do not wish to infringe the rights homosexuals have to look at what they like, even though I cannot say with certainty that I am not adversely affected by it.
8. Quoted in Russell, Diana, "Pornography: A Feminist Perspective," op. cit., p. 7, no reference given.

9. See, for example, Martin, Del, *Battered Wives*, Glide Publications, San Francisco, 1976, pp. 22-23; Pizzey, Erin, *Scream Quietly or the Neighbours Will Hear*, Penguin Books, England, 1974, Ch. 4; Van Stolk, Mary, *The Battered Child in Canada*, McClelland & Stewart, Toronto, 1972, pp. 23-27.
10. Bandura, A., Ross, D., and Ross, S.A., "Transmission of Aggression through Imitation of Aggressive Models," *J. Abnormal and Social Psychology*, 63, No. 3, 575-582.
11. Kraft-Ebbing, Richard von, *Psychopathia Sexualis*, 11th ed. rev. and enlarged, Stuttgart, 1901, pp. 94-95; Freud, S., *Introductory Lectures on Psycho-Analysis*, Standard Edition, 16:306.

QUESTIONS

1. Is Lorenne Clark right in thinking that the separation of law and morality as it relates to human sexuality and reproduction is not sound?
2. In what respects does Clark's critique of the public-private distinction differ from the account provided by Groarke?
3. Is the idea of harm used by those opposing the censorship of pornography adequate? Or is it in need of revision as Clark suggests?
4. To what extent does the idea of harm suggested by Clark differ from that suggested by the authors of the other selections?
5. Is pornography a species of hate literature?
6. Does pornography reinforce a sexist view of women? If so, does this fact provide adequate grounds for censorship?

LIBERAL FEMINISM: THE GLIMMER OF HOPE

Wendy McElroy

In the maelstrom of anti-pornography hysteria, liberal feminism often provides the few voices of sanity heard above the storm. Liberal organizations like Feminists for Free Expression (FFE) have consistently and courageously stood up against measures like the Victims of Pornography Compensation Act, and for sexual expression. Some liberal feminists like Nadine Strossen have been staunch and tireless in their defense of freedom of speech. It is difficult to imagine better companions in the fight for sexual choice.

Other liberals seem to have forgotten their roots and are now willing to sacrifice free speech for the greater good of protecting women from pornography.

There is a growing schism within liberal feminism, which threatens to disrupt such key liberal organizations as the National Organization for Women (NOW) and the American Civil Liberties Union (ACLU).

What are the arguments that are causing such turmoil in liberal ranks?

Liberal Feminist Arguments Against Censorship

In general, liberal feminists offer three types of arguments against censoring pornography: Freedom of speech is a necessary condition for human freedom; the suppression of pornography will hurt women (in the several ways presented below); and, pornography offers certain benefits to women.

Let us examine the first two arguments. The third will be discussed in the following chapter.

Freedom of speech is a necessary condition for human freedom.

This argument says little about women's relationship to pornography, except in the most general sense. Even feminists who believe porn degrades and humiliates women sometimes argue against censorship as the greater threat. These are the feminists who say: As a woman I am appalled by *Playboy* . . . but as a writer I understand the need for free speech.

Such feminists are not pro-pornography. They are anti-censorship. They argue on several grounds: Great works of art and literature would be banned; the First Amendment would be breached; political expression would be suppressed; and a creative culture requires freedom of speech.

The suppression of pornography will hurt women.

This argument specifically addresses the relationship of women to pornography. But, again, it is not so much a defense of pornography as it is an attack on censorship. Liberal feminists point to the real problems involved in implementing the anti-pornography program. Among the insightful questions they ask are:

Who Will Act as Censor?

Whoever acts as censor will wield tremendous power, because words such as *degrading* are so subjective they will be interpreted to mean whatever the censor wants them to. In the August 1993 *Virginia Law Review*, Nadine Strossen worries that the anti-pornography definitions are so vague that they could be used against homosexual and lesbian material:

"It is not clear whether Andrea Dworkin or Catharine MacKinnon would classify homoerotic photographs or films as 'pornography.' Although their model law defines 'pornography' as the 'sexually explicit subordination of *women* through pictures, and/or words,' it expressly stipulates that even images of men could be interpreted as portraying the subordination of women."[1]

The state that banned Margaret Sanger because she used the words *syphilis* and *gonorrhea* is no different, in principle, than the one that interprets obscenity today.

There will be nothing — not even the paper shield of the First Amendment — to stand between the state and feminist literature. There will be no protection even for the feminist classics such as *Our Bodies, Ourselves*, which provided a generation of women with an explicit glimpse of their own sexuality.

Inevitably, censorship will be used against the least popular views, against the weakest members of society — including feminists and lesbians. When the Canadian Supreme Court decided (1992) to protect women by restricting the importation of pornography, one of the first targets was a lesbian/gay bookstore named Glad Day Bookstore, which had been on a police "hit list." Canadian officials also targeted University and radical bookstores. Among the books seized by Canadian customs were two books by Andrea Dworkin: *Pornography: Men Possessing Women* and *Women Hating*.

Even narrowing the definition of pornography to include only the depiction of explicit violence would not protect feminist works. It would not, for example, protect Susan Brownmiller's pivotal *Against Our Will*, which offers a "history" of rape, complete with graphic detail. Nor would it exempt Kate Millett's *The Basement*, a novel-chronicle of sexual torture.

Doesn't the Anti-Pornography Crusade Perpetuate the Myth of Women as Victims?

Refusing to acknowledge the contracts of women in pornography places them in the same legal category as children or mental incompetents. In Indianapolis, the anti-pornography ordinance argued that women, like children, needed special protection under the law:

"Children are incapable of consenting to engage in pornographic conduct. . . . By the same token, the physical and psychological well-being of women ought to be afforded comparable protection, for the coercive environment . . . vitiates any notion that they consent or 'choose' to perform in pornography."[2]

This attitude of "I'm a helpless victim" could easily backfire on women who may be required to prove they are able to manage their own finances, or to handle custody of their own children. Moreover, the idea of men "emotionally or verbally coercing" women reenforces the concept of men as intellectually and psychologically stronger than women. It is the old "Man of Steel/Woman of Kleenex" myth.

Who Will Protect Women from the Anti-Feminist Conservatives, with Whom Radical Feminists Are Aligning?

By joining hands with conservatives, anti-pornography feminists have strengthened the political power of the Religious Right, who attack abortion and other fundamental rights of women. Radical feminists are being used. For example, in 1992, the promotional material of the conservative National Coalition Against Pornography featured quotes from Andrea Dworkin; in other contexts, these same people crucify her as a lesbian.

This alliance may be a tragic mistake for women's rights. With tragic results. Feminists are lending credibility and power to organizations which will turn on a dime against them.

Aren't Radical Feminists Diverting Attention from the Real Issues That Confront Women?

Feminists used to address the complex network of cultural, political, and biological factors that contributed to the real issues confronting women. Now the beginning and ending of all discussion seems to be the specter of patriarchy — of white male culture in league with capitalism. Pornography is merely one aspect of this single-minded assault. Radical feminist analysis is imposed on all forms of women's sexuality, including childbirth.

Consider the furor that is brewing around the New Reproductive Technologies (NRTs), which have been called "the pornography of pregnancy." These technologies — which include *in vitro* fertilization, surrogate motherhood, and embryo transfer — are behind the recent news stories announcing that sixty-year-old women are giving birth. Men have always been able to become parents at sixty; that door has just opened for women.

The NRTs raise many questions of medical and genetic ethics, including: how to redefine the family, what of population control; and what of world hunger. For radical feminists, however, there is but one issue. Medical science and technology are the products of white male culture, which oppresses women; therefore, the NRTs are medicalized terror conducted against women.

(Interestingly enough, the women who clamor for such medical procedures are dismissed in the same manner as women in pornography: namely, they are said to be brainwashed and no longer capable of true consent.)

Patriarchy seems to be blamed for everything from sexual harassment to stretch marks. It is a common saying: When all you have is a hammer, everything looks like a nail. When your ideology sounds only one note, all songs are in the same key.

Increasingly, violence against women seems to be linked — almost attributed — to one source: pornography. This is not an opening up of feminist theory and consciousness; it is a closing down.

Doesn't Blaming Pornography Exonerate Rapists?

To blame words or images for the actions of people is simplistic. It retards any real examination into what motivates violent crimes, such as rape. Radical feminists are handing a "pornography made me do it" excuse to rapists. Nothing should be allowed to mitigate the personal responsibility of every man who physically abuses a woman.

Radical feminists are allowing men to introduce "extenuating circumstances" into their defense. For example, in appealing *Schiro v. Clark*,[3] the defendant — a rapist — argued that in sentencing, the judge had failed to take into account his consumption of "rape" pornography. Fortunately, his argument fell deservedly flat.

How Can Women Chronicle Their Oppression if They Do Not Have Access to Its History?

Censorship removes the evidence of women's oppression and limits their ability to learn from it. For example, if it had been up to Comstock and his nineteenth-century censorship drive, no evidence of the fledgling birth control movement would have survived. The record of this struggle survives only because individuals preserved periodicals and pamphlets, which were archived decades later by universities and historical societies.

How much lesbian history will be available if censorship prevails?

The Flaw in Liberal Feminist Arguments

Those liberals who defend pornography do not generally address the ideological underpinnings of the onslaught against it. They continue to view anti-porn feminists as fellow travelers, instead of seeing them as dangerous companions.

One reason for this is that liberal feminists share many of the ideological assumptions underlying the radical feminist attack. For example, both liberal and radical feminists condemn the free market for making a profit by using women as "body parts." Both believe that the commercialization of sex demeans women. In an essay meant to defend the rights of pornographers, Lisa Steel comments: "Sexist representation of women . . . is all part of the same system that, in the service of profits, reduces society to 'consumer groups.' And marketing is every bit as conservative as the military . . . we pay dearly for the 'rights' of a few to make profits from the rest of us."[4]

Is this a defense or an attack?

Liberal feminists also tend to use the radical feminist definition of pornography — a definition tremendously slanted in favor of censorship. Once women accept the anti-pornography definition, it is difficult to arrive at any position other than censorship. The Canadian sociologist Jill Ridington argues for free speech. Nevertheless, she defines pornography as: ". . . a presentation . . . of sexual behavior in which one or more participants are coerced, overtly or *implicitly*, into participation; or are injured or abused physically or *psychological-*

ly; or in which an *imbalance of power* is obvious, or *implied* . . . and in which such behavior can be taken to be advocated or endorsed." (Emphasis added.)[5]

By this definition, what isn't pornography? What can't be interpreted as an imbalance of power? Since almost every sexual presentation is capable of causing psychological harm to someone, almost every presentation can be considered pornographic.

Pornography needs stauncher advocates.

Fortunately, it has them. . . .

NOTES

1. *Virginia Law Review,* August 1993, p. 1118.
2. Indianapolis-Mercer Country; Indiana, General Ordinances Nos. 24 and 25 (1984), amendments to code of Indianapolis and Marion Country.
3. *Schiro v. Clark,* 63 F.2d. 962, 972 (7th Cir. 1992).
4. Lisa Steel, "A Capital Idea," *Women Against Censorship,* ed. Varda Burstyn (Vancouver, Can.: Douglas & McIntyre, 1985), p. 63.
5. Jill Ridington, as quoted in *Women Against Censorship,* p. 34.

INDIVIDUALIST FEMINISM: A TRUE DEFENSE OF PORNOGRAPHY

Wendy McElroy

Individualist feminism provides the best defense of pornography because its ideology is the mirror image of radical feminism, from which the most effective attack on porn is coming. Individual feminism insists on the principle of self-ownership: a woman's body, a woman's right. It insists that women be free to choose, regardless of the content of their choices.

The key concept here is *choice*, which is present whenever a woman acts without physical coercion. Certainly, it is present whenever the woman herself says the actions are voluntary, because she is the only person truly capable of judging that claim. The peaceful choices of every woman must be respected; the voice of every woman should be heard.

This is a profoundly individualistic approach, which leaves little room for class analysis as presented by anti-porn feminists. Such feminists view individual rights and personal preferences as irritating bumps on the road to the greater good of class interest. To them, "the personal is political."

To individualist feminists, the personal is personal. There is a political door that closes to separate and protect individuals from society. People call this protection by different names: the Bill of Rights, self-ownership, individual rights, or natural law. In the shadow of this protection, individual women make decisions about matters that concern them and them alone. For example, they decide about sex.

This is not to say that one woman's sexual choices cannot have implications for another woman, or an impact upon her. Every action you take and every word you utter can impact upon another human being. Exhaling can have an impact, especially if you have a cold or some other contagious disease. The question is: At what point does another woman have a right to restrict your actions on the grounds of self-protection?

Individualist feminism answers: When, and only when, those actions involve physical force, threat of force, or fraud. In the absence of force, women should be free to make any and every sexual choice they wish.

I may not personally approve of their choices. I may find their choices distasteful. Nevertheless, every choice a woman makes enriches me, because it expands my range of alternatives — even if it is an alternative I can't imagine ever pursuing myself.

The nineteenth-century individualist feminist Lillian Harman made a similar point:

> I consider uniformity in mode of sexual relations as undesirable and impractical as enforced uniformity in anything else. For myself, I want to profit by my mistakes . . . and why should I be unwilling for others to enjoy the same liberty? If I should be able to bring the entire world to live exactly as I live at present, what would that avail me in ten years, when as I hope, I shall have a broader knowledge of life, and my life therefore probably changed.[1]

To repeat: the key is choice. With regard to pornography, this means: Let individual women decide for themselves. Let them weigh the evidence and come to their own conclusions.

But what of the women who are upset by the mere fact that pornography exists? Aren't they "forced" to live in a pornographic world? In a word, yes. Women who like pornography force others to live in a pornographic world in the same manner that women who lack taste in clothes force others to live with their fashion sense. *Every* peaceful act can affect someone else. Again, the question is: Do the effects deny to anyone what they have the right to demand?

The answer is no. My decision to consume pornography in no way infringes on another woman's ability to walk right past it. She can express her disapproval — through speaking out, picketing, and boycott. What she must not do is introduce the force of law.

The mere fact that some women are upset by the presence of pornography tells us very little. It tells us nothing about whether porn is right or wrong, valuable or useless. After all, feminism distresses a great many people. Yet feminists would argue that the movement should not only be tolerated, it should be nurtured. They consider women's rights to have a positive, rather than a negative effect on society — even if it causes distress. Perhaps the same is true of the graphic depiction of sex.

This is the position I maintain. I argue that the benefits pornography provides to women far outweigh any of its disadvantages. But, at its root, the argument for pornography is not utilitarian.

Pornography should be defended out of respect for women's choices and for human sexual diversity.

NOTES

1. Lillian Harman as quoted in Hal D. Sears, *The Sex Radicals,* p. 258.

QUESTIONS

1. In your view, does Wendy McElroy provide a fair assessment of the kind of feminist analysis offered by Lorenne Clark?
2. McElroy is critical of both radical and liberal feminist analyses of pornography. What sorts of objections does she raise against liberal feminism's defence of pornography?
3. McElroy claims that in practice censorship laws have tended to target material such as homosexual pornography and even radical feminist pro-censorship literature. Do you think this sort of evidence of what happens in practice should influence policies regarding censorship?
4. What is individualist feminism? Why does McElroy say that it is the best defence of pornography? Do you agree with McElroy that "women should be free to make any and every sexual choice they want"?

CAUGHT IN THE WEB: SEXUAL FANTASIZING, CHARACTER, AND CYBERPORNOGRAPHY

Susan Dwyer

In a culture committed to individual liberty and value pluralism, any critique of sexually explicit material runs the risk of being misunderstood. Criticisms of pornography are apt to be thought of as symptomatic of sexual prudishness or as recommendations for censorship. Now, while some critiques of pornography have been just that, most are far more complicated. For example, different feminist theorists have claimed both that being "for" pornography and being "against" pornography are inconsistent with feminist goals.[1] And a good number of pornography's defenders are not defenders of pornography *per se*, but of more noble or abstract things, like the right to free speech or the "right to moral independence."[2]

Interesting and important as they are, the quite sophisticated moral, political, and legal debates about pornography of the past three decades have tended to obscure our intuitive — some would say, naive — reactions to pornography. To say these reactions are naive, however, is not to denigrate them. I believe they are manifestations of deep, though tacit, moral judgments. I also believe that we will have more success talking to one another about pornography itself as well as about what we should or should not do about it, if we pay attention to these intuitive reactions. For they are resilient, and we will be left unsatisfied by the best of arguments, if those arguments fail either to respect or explain away these judgments.

In this paper, I present a moral critique of pornography that attempts to accommodate some intuitive moral judgments about certain kinds of sexual fantasizing. The central idea is that some pornography is morally problematic because it provides the raw material for and helps to nurture a class of morally bad actions; namely, sexual fantasizing about a variety of harms to oneself and/or to others. Sexual fantasizing is something we deliberately and consciously *do*. We construct fantasies that please us and return to them over the course of our lives. Indeed, empirical evidence suggests that sexual fantasies are among the most enduring elements of our respective psychologies. But, some kinds of sexual fantasizing are morally risky. A person runs a serious risk of compromising her character if she persistently and deliberately engages in an activity that yokes sexual pleasure and satisfaction to conscious thoughts of degradation, humiliation, and violence. And, as I shall explain below, there is reason to believe that this risk is significantly increased when pornography is consumed on-line.

Put so bluntly, my critique is ripe for both types of misinterpretation I mentioned at the outset. No matter how they are gussied up, one might say, claims about the character-corrupting potential of pornography are nothing more than thinly veiled expressions of nose-wrinkling disgust at what turns other people on sexually. Alternatively, an objector might conclude from the mention of pornography's *harms* that the critique is simply a long-winded call for the legal prohibition of pornography. But both of these *are* misinterpretations. Explaining why my critique is not merely sexual prudery masquerading as moral argument will take some time, and a good deal of this paper is devoted to that task. Dispensing with the second misinterpretation is (moderately) easier.

Precisely because the harm of some pornography is what it is — the facilitation of character-corruption — the state can neither be an effective nor an appropriate agent in addressing that harm. The criminal law is an effective restraint on many (though perhaps not enough) people who would harm others. And various paternalistic laws — for example, regarding the use of motorcycle helmets and seat belts — protect our physical selves. But the state and the law are ill-equipped to deal with our characters.[3] The state cannot enact successful coercive policies to make us better people, in the very personal and intimate sense of having better characters. Our characters are our own business, where this does not mean that they are immune from evaluation (far from it). Rather, our characters are essentially *our* projects. The impetus for both the development and reform of character must come from within. Of course, other people can be helpful or instrumental in modifying our characters. But those others need to be intimate particulars; people who know us, not the faceless, bureaucratic state. Requests or recommendations for change must be motivated by love and respect, and not backed up by police powers. Hence, the very nature of the critique I offer makes censorship irrelevant.[4]

To reiterate: the proposition I wish to defend is that some pornography is morally problematic insofar as it plays a role (perhaps a pivotal one) in morally dangerous sexual fantasizing. It will be helpful to begin with an example.

Morally Problematic Sexual Fantasizing: An Example

Dennis fantasizes about the following: he moves to a foreign city where he takes up residence in an abandoned building. He meets a young man in a club and brings him back to his place. For a sum of money, the young man agrees to allow Dennis to perform a sex act on him. After a while, Dennis kills him. This is the first of several killings, some of which Dennis participates in with two other men. The killings all occur in a sexual context; Dennis and his collaborators either have sex with their victims or masturbate while one or the other of them beat or torture their victim.[5] Dennis becomes aroused when he engages in this fantasy and he deliberately calls it to mind when he masturbates. Sometimes he focuses on it when he has sex with a partner.

Now imagine two worlds, World A and World B, in all respects like the actual world, except that in World A, many people sexually fantasize about the sorts of things Dennis does, and in World B no one does. Take it as given that the Dennis's of World A never act out what they fantasize about. Which is the morally preferable world?

Many people would *like* to be able to say "Neither." Given the option of living in World A or World B, many would *like* to be able to say that it would not matter. But, I believe, some honest reflection will reveal that we are not indifferent to the fact that people around us engage in such fantasizing. Now, arguably, World A is closer to the actual world, and so we do not have the option of living apart from such fantasizers. If the fantasies and their authors bother us, then the best we can do is not think about them.[6]

The previous thought experiment does not establish very much. However, it helps brings to awareness an intuitive unease many people feel about certain types of fantasizing. Is such intuitive unease sufficient to support the judgment that sexual fantasizing like Dennis's is morally problematic? Not at all. Our intuitions here are only prima facie evidence of some deeper judgments. Digging down to those judgments will require dispensing with the widely held view that a moral critique of sexual fantasizing is simply a non-starter.

Two main assumptions underlie this view. First, there is the thought that fantasizing is essentially "inner." We fantasize in the privacy of our own minds; as long as our fantasizing does not "spill over" into overt behavior, then it cannot be criticized; and if fantasizing does so "spill over," then it is our behavior (and not our fantasizing) that is the proper target of evaluation. Second, it might be thought that there is something about *sexual* fantasizing in particular that renders it off limits to moral criticism. Sexual fantasizing is one way in which we attempt to satisfy our sexual desires. Many of these desires are opaque to us — we do not understand them, and since we seem simply to find ourselves with them, we cannot be held responsible for having them.

Let us now critically examine these assumptions.

Fantasizing as Inner

A common view is that fantasizing is essentially "inner." Killing a rival is morally wrong; merely fantasizing about killing her is not. And, in the vast majority of cases, there is little reason to think that fantasizing about X-ing makes actual X-ing more likely.

Fantasizing *is* inner, in some sense of that term that also describes thinking in general. It is one among many ways in which we exercise our imaginations. However, fantasizing is not something that merely *happens* to us. It may be distinguished from having fleeting thoughts, or being subject to unbidden or intrusive images. Rather, fantasizing is typically something we deliberately and consciously *do*. Since this claim is central to my overall argument it is worth pausing to consider the distinction between *actions* and *happenings* more closely.

My shrugging to indicate that I do not know the answer to your question is an *action*, whereas the very same movement, say, my shoulders going up and down when I hiccup, is a *happening*. Or, consider a comedian's hilarious prat falls. His intentional and deliberate behavior is quite different from that of the person who is tripped up on the street or who falls over during an epileptic fit. A comedian's falling is funny precisely because he *means* to fall. In general, we can say a person's *actions* are explained in terms of his beliefs, desires, and intentions, whereas *happenings* — for example, his mere bodily motions — are fully explicable in terms of physiological goings-on.[7]

Undoubtedly, there are cases of compulsive fantasizing, just are there cases of compulsive hand-washing. However, in the usual case, a person fantasizes for a reason: in order to distract, please, or motivate herself. So, despite its "location" inside our heads, fantasizing is properly described as a type of *action*.

As I noted above, it might be conceded that some fantasizing can be morally criticized, but only if that fantasizing leads to harmful overt behavior. About a man with sadistic sexual fantasies we might say "They're all in his head. He is not hurting anyone. And maybe his fantasizing in this way is what keeps him from actually doing such things." But this is just beside the point, once we recognize that fantasizing is a type of action. For the purpose of moral evaluation, it does not matter whether a particular instance of fantasizing is associated with *another* action. My stabbing you is morally wrong irrespective of whether, having enjoyed it so much, I go on to stab someone else, or whether, filled with a new sense of your own mortality, you go on to be a great philanthropist. Similarly, we can make sense of the idea that you act wrongly when you break your promise to take me to a baseball game, even though our not going makes it possible for me to do more work on my book. Hence, an instance of fantasizing need not lead to some other bad action in order to be morally bad itself.

The moral status of an action is not determined exclusively and exhaustively by its actual consequences. Some actions, like those described above, may be judged on the basis of their intrinsic features alone. The consequences of our actions are not morally irrelevant. However they are not *all* that is morally relevant. If we focus exclusively upon the consequences of our actions, we ignore a large part of what comprises our moral lives. We respond not only to the results of one another's overt behavior but also to one another's beliefs, desires, intentions, and characters; in short, to each other's moral *agency*. If this is right, then it is at least arguable that a person's fantasizing can be morally bad whether or not he acts out his fantasy.

So far, I have argued that fantasizing is an action, and hence that it is morally evaluable. Moreover, an action can be morally bad irrespective of its actual consequences. This much might be granted, but in order to make my case, I must also address the concern that specifically *sexual* fantasizing may not be morally evaluated.

Sexual Fantasizing is Different

Many people balk at the idea of morally judging sexual fantasizing. But their reasons for doing so are various and often not very articulate. I think we can identify three quite different concerns. I shall discuss each in turn.

In the first place, there is a familiar practical objection. To engage in the moral evaluation of sexual fantasizing puts us at the beginning of an unpleasant slippery slope. When it comes to making judgments about people's sexual lives, the track record is not good. For example, the erroneous judgment that homosexual sexual desire is morally perverse continues to play a significant role in the unjust treatment of homosexuals. The worry here is not that sexually fantasizing is constitutionally immune from evaluation or that it is always morally neutral or morally good. Rather, the concern is that it would be better if we did not engage in the evaluation of sexual fantasies or desires at all.

I take this concern seriously.[8] However, it bears emphasizing that moral evaluation does not by itself warrant any particular state action. If we assume otherwise, if we forswear the moral evaluation of some human practices simply because we worry about what use might be made of those evaluations, then we effectively hold ourselves hostage to the irrationality and ill will of others. More importantly, as I will try to make clearer below, when an agent engages in moral evaluation and moral judgment, he need not limit himself to evaluation of and judgment about the actions of *others*. Being a moral agent essentially involves turning those critical faculties on *oneself*, at least every now and then.

In the second place, skepticism about the moral evaluation of sexual fantasizing might be based on an influential idea that the content of an episode of sexual fantasizing — that is, what the sexual fantasy is about — is indeterminate. No one, not even the person fantasizing can be sure that rape fantasies, say, are *really* about rape.

This line of reasoning, which has been a favorite of defenders of pornography, has a distinguished lineage. In his paper, "A Child is Being Beaten," Freud notes that the fantast herself can and does assume different roles in her fantasy. In the case he discusses, sometimes she is a third party spectator of a beating, sometimes she is the child, and sometimes she is doing the beating.[9] From Freud we also inherit the idea that our dreams are saturated with symbolism. If this claim is true, then our dreams cannot be read literally and are always open to interpretation. Many people are inclined to believe that our sexual fantasies are like dreams in this respect.

It is telling, I think, that the (alleged) indeterminancy of fantasies is invariably invoked when the fantasies in question concern events which are, in some quite straightforward way, problematic. When someone fantasizes about puppies and fresh apple pie, or about living a successful and happy life, the urge to interpret diminishes to zero. This indicates that our first instinct is to read fantasies literally. It is only when we do not like what we see that we welcome and come to find plausible our therapist's complicated story about "narcissistic wounds" and the like.[10] When the content of our fantasizing disturbs us, it is natural to seek reassurances that neutralize the elements of those fantasies we do not like. However, there is little evidence to suggest that a cigar is not just a cigar most of the time.

The third concern about the moral evaluation of sexual fantasizing begins in the recognition that sexual fantasizing is one way in which persons satisfy their desires. Then it is argued that there is a world of difference between our sexual desires and our non-sexual desires. In particular, it might be said that we have less control over the former than we have over the latter: we just seem to find ourselves with certain sexual desires.

All this may be true. But it is insufficient to establish that sexual fantasizing cannot be morally evaluated. For even if we are not responsible for our sexual desires, which I doubt,[11] fantasizing is not unavoidable. As I have already stressed, fantasizing is a deliberate and intentional action. And for this reason it is an optional response to desire.

This is borne out by the empirical evidence. Sexual fantasizing appears to be almost universal across the species. And psychologists suggest it is the most common sort of fantasizing in which humans engage. Sexual fantasies are a type of a "repeating" fantasy, meaning that individuals return to the same sexual fantasies over and over again. While there is considerable variation between people's sexual fantasies, all appear to be highly scripted and durable. Ethel Person likens a decision to fantasize to a decision to take down a favorite book from an inner and familiar library, and writes,

> Once a fantasy is invoked, the fantasizer savors, lingers on, or revises the most exciting, pleasing, or soothing part of his or her mental creation, whirling it around in the mind until arriving at the 'version' that is most gratifying, often slowing the fantasy down at the most stimulating point, and speeding it up at moments that have begun to seem boring, improving on the dialogue, adding new touches to glamorize the setting.[12]

And Harold Leitenberg and Kris Henning write,

> In general . . . most sexual fantasies appear to be *deliberate* patterns of thought designed to stimulate or enhance pleasurable sexual feelings regardless of whether the fantasies involve reminiscing about past sexual experiences, imagining anticipated future activity, engaging in wishful thinking, or having daydreams that are exciting to imagine without any desire to put them into practice [emphasis added].[13]

We cannot, therefore, assume that sexual fantasizing is inexorably driven by desires. We choose to fantasize: fantasizing is action. And where our fantasizing is in the service of desire-satisfaction, we can be held responsible for it whether or not we are responsible for the relevant desires. It is crucial not to mistake the apparent helplessness of arousal and orgasm that accompanies sexual fantasizing for a lack of control over the fantasizing itself.

Whatever else it may be, fantasizing cannot be said to be off limits to moral evaluation just by dint of its being inner, private, or about sex. Neither is it the case that the moral status of fantasizing (sexual or non-sexual) depends upon the probability of its issuing in overt behavior. Still, to argue that sexual fantasizing is morally evaluable is not yet to give an account of what makes sexual fantasizing morally bad when it is. It is to that issue that I now turn.

We are unquestionably the authors of our sexual fantasies: we consciously choose the scenario we imagine, we embellish it, edit it, and so on. It would be seriously disingenuous of a person to say that she had *no* control over the elements of her fantasies, or that when she conjures up a particular scene, its "real" meaning is utterly opaque to her. After all, fantasizing, and sexual fantasizing in particular, is essentially self-gratificatory. We fantasize about the things that please us.

Recall Dennis. He fantasizes about what pleases him. He consciously and deliberately conjures up his favorite scenario of sexual debasement and torture, and he concentrates on it to have an orgasm. To say that the content of a fantasy pleases the fantast is to say that he takes a pro-attitude toward that content. Sexual arousal on the basis of fantasizing would hardly be possible if we did not adopt such an attitude, if only for as long as we are fantasizing. The particular pro-attitude a person takes to the content of his sexual fantasies is usefully described by the term *eroticization*, where, as John Corvino suggests, to eroticize an activity is to "actively regard [. . .] the activity with sexual desire."[14] Hence, whether or not the fantast delights in his fantasizing (as the sexual sadist does) or is horrified by it (as we might imagine some pedophiles are), by eroticizing what he does, the fantast adopts a pro-attitude towards the activity he fantasizes about.

It is easy to be repelled by the content of Dennis's fantasy. But that repulsion by itself is not sufficient to warrant moral judgments about Dennis's fantasizing. So what does make some sexual fantasizing morally problematic?

Actions and Character

As I mentioned earlier, at least on reflection, few of us believe that consequences are *all* that matter morally. We judge lying and the breaking of promises morally wrong, whether or not those actions have bad consequences. But an appeal to the violation of moral principles or duties of the sort that underpin our judgments about lying and promise-breaking will not help here. For it is not really plausible to say that I transgress a specific moral principle or that I violate a particular duty when I engage in certain kinds of fantasizing. But more to the point, it is hard to see how one could specify the relevant principles or obligations in a non-question-begging way. We cannot explain the moral badness of certain sorts of fantasizing by saying that those activities violate the principle, "It is morally wrong to fantasize about harming others." For the truth of such a principle is precisely what is in question.

A more promising approach emerges if we think about the relations between action, character, and moral agency. Moral agency refers to set of abilities or capacities: the ability to deliberate between options for action, taking into account not only one's own well-being, but the well-being of others; the capacity to recognize when a situation demands a moral response of some kind, for example, rendering assistance to strangers or not serving prime rib at a dinner for vegetarian friends; a sensitivity to the moods, emotions, and commitments of others; the ability to persevere when the going gets tough and to resist distractions to important projects; and the disposition to seek coherence among one's commitments, expectations, and efforts (integrity).

Moral beings possess these abilities in varying degrees, and while some seem naturally well-endowed, others must labor to acquire and develop them. Variability also exists in the ways in which the capacities and abilities that constitute moral agency are exercised: there are moral virtuosi and moral amateurs. Talk of a person's character is usefully construed as shorthand for whatever grounds and enables these practical competencies, where we can think of these grounds as the maxims — the regulative ideals — to which she holds herself and to which she believes she ought to hold herself. It is crucial to recognize that a person's character is not simply a laundry list of beliefs. First, because it is not only the *content* of a person's moral beliefs that matter but also her *attitudes* toward those beliefs. Central to the notion of character is the idea that a person endorses — at the very least, accepts — certain principles of right action. Second, in order to ground moral competencies across a life, the regulative ideals to which a person is committed (that is, which she endorses) must be ordered in some way; they might, for example, be hierarchically ordered from most general to most specific, or lexically ordered according to some other principle. A mere concatenation of practical principles will not deliver the kind of stability over time that is a hallmark of character. Moreover, where there is no ordering of practical principles, inconsistencies are more likely; the kind of stability required for the exercise of moral agency is absent.

But this does not mean that character is static. Indeed, precisely the opposite is true. While the experience of living a life as a reflective rational being will have the effect of reinforcing some elements of our characters, each of us is always a work in progress. New challenges can reveal aspects of our character of which we had been unaware; we might embrace these elements, or, finding them to be inconsistent with other more familiar and more important elements, we might seek to eliminate them. Despite the fact that human beings (as rational beings) are self-reflective, we are not utterly transparent to ourselves. In part, then, having a character involves the ongoing activity of self-scrutiny, self-discovery, and self-adjustment.

The dynamic nature of character indicates three ways in which actions and character are related. First and most obviously, a person's overt actions are evidence of the nature of his character. It is through observing the actions a person typically performs that we attribute to him a certain type of character. Less obviously, perhaps, a person's non-overt actions are evidence at least for *him* about the direction his character is taking. Second, some actions — actions for which the agent has a settled disposition, actions he reliably performs — are not merely evidence of his character; they express, in the sense of being constitutive elements of, that character. Finally, a person can attempt to perform a certain type of action because he wants eventually to acquire a settled disposition to perform that action. He wants, that is, for the maxim or practical principle determining that type of action to be an element of his character. We cannot construct a character out of nothing, and we are committed to some practical principles simply in virtue of being the kinds of creatures we are.[15] But beyond the basics, we have considerable latitude in fine-tuning our characters, making certain traits part of who we are.

An example will help tie these claims about moral agency, character, and action together. Imagine that George, a man who has never paid much attention to the ways in which gender makes a difference in the world, develops a friendship with a feminist theorist whom he respects. She talks to him about the many subtle ways in which gender structures the social world, often to the advantage of men and the disadvantage of women. George believes that men and women are equal and that if women are badly treated just on account of being women, this is a very bad thing. George worries that he has been oblivious to the effects of gender hierarchy; he does not want to be a person who discriminates unfairly, offends, and so on. So George decides that he needs to pay more attention to gender, and as a practical exercise to keep gender before his consciousness, he decides always to use the feminine pronoun in his writing, except for instances where to do so would be a blatant absurdity — for example, he cannot refer to his brother as "she." Over time, the action of using the feminine pronoun makes George more sensitive to gender. He notices things he had not noticed before, and he formulates practical principles that constrain the way he acts in situations where gender is relevant. Through habitually acting in a certain way, he improves his moral agency. He is now more sensitive to morally significant facts around him.[16]

George's story is, we might say, a success story. But the interplay between action, character, and moral agency that allows for human flourishing also allows for corruption. Habitually performing bad actions or actions which desensitize one to morally salient facts can seriously hinder the project of character development. Endorsing the wrong kinds of practical principles is corrosive of character. Consider again our sexual fantast Dennis. Here is a man who appears to endorse actions that might seriously undermine his character and thus his moral agency. He takes deep pleasure in fantasizing about harming others and he does so habitually. One ought not be the sort of person who takes sexual pleasure in the debasement of others. And one ought not act in ways that constitute being that sort of person.[17]

This completes my argument for the claim that certain types of sexual fantasizing are morally risky on account of the ways in which they undermine moral agency and corrode character. With this in hand, we can now turn to a consideration of pornography.

Pornography and Sexual Fantasizing

As enjoyable as sexual excitement is, pornography's popularity would be surprising if all it did was provide the color and sound for our inner black and white, silent movies. Undoubtedly, pornography supplies its consumers with novel elements for their sexual fantasies as well as new ideas for their flesh-and-blood sexual encounters. More significantly, pornography concretizes existing sexual fantasies, providing enduring and substantive representations of what might otherwise exist "just" in people's heads.

The implications of the publication and distribution of representations of sexual fantasies must not be underestimated. Like many other cultural discourses, pornography provides us with language and concepts, a framework within which to ground and organize our sexual experience. In this way, pornography and sexual fantasizing are mutually legitimating. The very existence of an industry devoted to producing sexual arousal — despite the fact that some people persist in thinking that pornography is marginal — tells us that it is okay to derive sexual pleasure from fantasizing in certain ways. Moreover, when a person sees the major elements of their favorite sexual fantasy acted out with real people he can rest assured that he is not deviant; he can infer that others are turned on in similar ways. (Hence the widely used therapeutic strategy of normalization, which involves dealing with a client's distress about her sexual desires and fantasies by suggesting that she is not alone in having them.)

Ethel Person sums up the relation between pornography and sexual fantasizing in the following way:

> . . . works like the *Story of O* and the writings of the Marquis de Sade have become part of a cultural debate on the prevalence, meaning, and legitimacy of sadomasochistic fantasies and practices. But these works could never have achieved their popularity if they did not speak to deep-seated fantasies shared by large numbers of people. Probably their popularity helped legitimize such fantasies, which in turn helped to make them even more available to consciousness and therefore more widespread.[18]

By supplying us with a constant supply of new and old sexual ideas, pornography permits and encourages us to engage in unbounded sexual fantasizing. This is precisely why some theorists defend pornography, seeing it as a tool of liberation. No doubt some pornography can be liberating, it can be, but pornography like Dennis Cooper's story (described above) facilitates and helps to legitimize sexual fantasizing that is morally risky.

Before I move to discuss cyberpornography, I want to deal with an objection which I am sure has already occurred to the reader. It will be said that a good deal of bondage and discipline and sadomasochistic pornography is produced by and for members of the BDSM community — adults who consensually engage in various kinds of sexual torture. Visit a typical BDSM Web site and one will usually find — along with pictures of "masters" and "slaves" — some statement about "play" etiquette; that is, a list of do's and don't's for sexual scenes, which emphasizes the importance of mutual consent. Members of the BDSM community are quick to condemn those who seek sexual satisfaction from the actual debasement and abuse of others. They and others might claim that pornography that is about *pretend* or *simulated* degradation, humiliation, and abuse is not vulnerable to the present critique. For the fantasies that this material stimulates and reinforces are not fantasies about doing real harm to anyone.

All this might be so, but it is beside the point. No one can say with certainty that *all* members of the BDSM community are "only playing." And even if they are, there is still room for concern. For what is it to be sexually aroused by fantasies of simulated degradation, or, by extension, by the "actual simulation" of sexual torture? In a response to Patrick Hopkins's defense of sadomasochism, Corvino insightfully undermines any confidence we might have had that sadomasochists are turned on only by the simulation of certain practices. He questions the psychological possibility of eroticizing a "simulation qua simulation." Corvino writes,

> True, SM participants frequently attend to the pleasure of their partners, and to that extent, they are mindful of features that distinguish their activities from actual violence. But they are also mindful of features that occur in the 'real' case: the spanking, the quickened heartbeat, the gasps and groans. When they eroticize these features, SM participants . . . seem to be eroticizing not simulations qua simulations, but domination and its manifestations. The simulation is not the object of arousal; rather, it is the vehicle for the object of arousal.[19]

If Corvino is right, then, to some extent, even participants in consensual BDSM practices take pro-attitudes toward such things as sexual torture, bondage, submission, and domination. Adopting such attitudes, and more to the point, actively encouraging them in oneself is not obviously consistent with the maintenance of a sound character.

Cyberpornography

Cyberpornography may be more effective in facilitating and legitimizing sexual fantasizing than traditional forms of print and video pornography. This is not just because cyberporn is more accessible than other forms of pornography, though that is a factor. Rather the very form of cyberporn determines a unique experience of consumption. Accessing and enjoying cyberporn implicates the consumer's agency in interesting ways.

Cyberporn *is* far more accessible than other types of pornography in at least two senses. First, it is easier to get at the material; opening Netscape Navigator takes less time than driving to the local video store or sex shop. Second, cyberporn can be delivered directly and privately to one's home. Hence, one traditional barrier to getting hold of pornography — embarrassment — is removed. But while these facts might prompt more people to try pornography and prompt others to try more pornography, they do not yet suggest that cyberporn is morally more risky than print and video pornography.

Some critics have argued otherwise, claiming that the ready availability of porn online gives rise to addiction. The research and literature on Internet addiction — of a sexual and non-sexual kind — is highly controversial.[20] But in any case, it is beside the point for the argument under consideration here. If cyberporn is addictive, that would be unfortunate; but only in the sense that *any* addiction is a bad thing. Addiction compromises a person's agency, and distracts or prevents him from engaging in a full range of valuable life projects. The present thesis is narrower, having to do with morally risky sexual fantasizing.

It is trivial to note that the Internet has changed and continues to alter the ways in which many people obtain information and communicate with one another. However, what has gone relatively unexplored are the ways in which individual use of the technology changes the *user*.[21] It is, therefore, worth thinking about the phenomenology of computer-mediated communications and other human-Internet interactions. In what remains, I will offer some speculative remarks about two features of consuming cyberporn which, I believe, serve to buttress the claim that cyberporn is more morally dangerous than traditional print and video pornography.

First, consider the experience of browsing the World Wide Web. The ease of browsing (for *anything*) online, the speed at which vast quantities of information can be procured might lead us to think that the Web is the ultimate desire-satisfaction machine. Want something? Open your favorite search engine or database, and what you desire is only a click or two away. This is certainly true when the desire in question is quite specific, for example, when I want to know the business hours of my local IKEA store or the directions to a restaurant. Such a desire is easily satisfied and, once it is, I have little motivation to continue browsing.

However, typically, we browse the Web precisely because we do not quite know what we want. Either we have no specific question for which we seek an answer, or we do not know what is "out there" about a particular topic. Consider finding out about alternative treatments for some recently diagnosed medical condition. The experience of this type of browsing is quite different from the experience of browsing in order to answer a precise query. When I do not have a particular question in mind, I have to work harder to get useful information. And in some cases, what counts as useful information is constructed as I browse, somewhat after the fashion of the game Twenty Questions. When I browse, I am continually offered new links to different sites. My desire, inchoate to begin with, is tweaked, refined, heightened; each link promises that the next site will be what I am looking for. In this way, my motivation for staying on-line is continuously energized.

The genius of Web browsing is that it feeds off desires, many of which the activity of browsing itself helps to create and to amplify, and some of which, by design, will never be satisfied. Purveyors of cyberporn exploit this aspect of the technology quite effectively. Go to the Web with a general curiosity about sexually explicit material (search engine keyword: "XXX") or with a specific sexual interest (search engine keyword: "BBW" or "BCT")[22] and you will be provided with more sites than you know what to do with. More importantly, cyberpornographers have deliberately built their sites in ways that make it very difficult for a consumer to leave them. Open a pornography site and try to close the browser window. The chances are that you will be bumped to another (pornography) site. Soon you will have dozens of browser windows open on your desktop. And the escalation of unsatiated desire continues.[23]

Browsing cyberporn is rarely just like browsing racks of print pornography or watching a lot of videos. To be sure, it has two similar effects; namely, it provides content for many new and different fantasies and, by its very existence, serves to legitimize the fantasies of its consumers. However, cyberporn also has the effect of keeping consumers engaged in the business of sexual fantasizing longer. First, the ways in which cyberporn is delivered to consumers helps to construct desires which are in turn prevented from being satisfied; one is always encouraged to go to another and then another site. Such "movement" is relatively effortless, and the chain of new sites to which consumers are bumped is often characterized by increasingly "extreme" content. (The term *extreme* is the industry's own.) Furthermore, this rapid delivery of images keeps alive fantasies that the consumer might otherwise have ceased having for want of imagination or because they strike him as "too bizarre." Because of the unique nature of consuming pornography on-line, consumers' sexual fantasizing is facilitated in previously unimaginable ways.

A potential objection at this point helps to highlight a second relevant aspect of the experience of consuming cyberporn. In light of the above, someone might say that consumers of cyberporn can hardly be held responsible for the sexual fantasizing in which they engage while on-line or as a result of viewing cyberporn. For have I not just suggested that the medium itself compromises agency? Cyberporn consumers are deliberately manipulated. As a result of being "trapped" or "caught" in Web sites, certain fantasies are forced on them.

It must be conceded that users of technology are changed in more or less significant ways by that experience. But even cyborgs — those who see their machines as literal sexual prostheses — do not for that reason cease to be responsible agents. Nonetheless, I think that the cyberporn consumer's *sense* of his own agency is compromised. The genuine and deliberate activities of opening the first site, consciously following links, downloading images, and repeating the exercise can feel quite passive. The material is delivered to one's desk top. Most of the time, one does not have to do anything (except stay on-line) to find out about new sites. And opening a site requires just a click of the mouse. Moreover, the intense privacy of consuming porn on-line can make it seem as if one is not actively engaged in any way. Rather the illusion is created that one's fantasizing and on-line pornography have serendipitously converged. In this way, the consumer is positively discouraged by the medium itself from keeping his own agency and responsibility for fantasizing in focus.

To summarize these speculations: consuming cyberporn, by its very nature, facilitates sexual fantasizing — often, of a morally problematic sort (when consumers are bumped to more extreme sites), and simultaneously masks from the consumer his own agency in the act of consumption. The consumer's character is thus doubly threatened: morally risky sexually fantasizing is facilitated in quite aggressive ways, and the fantast's agency, his own complicity in such actions, is rendered obscure.

Conclusion

The moral critique of pornography I have offered here must be distinguished from more familiar arguments that cite pornography's (allegedly) harmful effects. No part of it depends on dubious claims about pornography's causal effects on overt behavior. My concern is with the character-corroding effects of sexual fantasizing that is made possible and nurtured by certain types of sexually explicit material. In contrast to so-called harm-based objections to pornography, on my account, the agency — and thus the personal responsibility — of pornography's consumers is never in doubt. Throughout, I have taken our intuitive reactions seriously, and I have attempted to "unpack" those intuitions in an effort to show that they are often reflective of deeper, difficult to articulate moral judgments. Finally, it bears emphasizing yet again that this line of argument does not by itself imply restrictive public policies concerning pornography either on- or off-line. If anything, this particular moral critique of pornography would seem to make the prospects of state intervention quite poor. For we are and should be skeptical of *state*-imposed limitations on our freedom directed at the goal of making us better moral agents. That said, the present discussion is not without practical relevance. Each of us has a responsibility to make judgments about *our own* actions and attitudes. This is the sense in which morality is as much self-regarding as it is other-regarding. For the moral status of any social activity, like the consumption of pornography, may be analyzed in terms of its effects on its practitioners as well as on others.[24]

NOTES

1. For the idea that being "for" pornography is consistent with feminist goals, see Wendy McElroy, *XXX: A Woman's Right to Pornography* (New York: St. Martin's Press, 1995), and Alison Assiter and Avedon Carol, eds., *Bad Girls and Naughty Pictures* (London: Pluto Press, 1993). For the idea that being "for" pornography is inconsistent with feminist goals, see Laura Lederer, ed., *Take Back the Night: Women on Pornography*, (New York: William Morrow & Co., 1980), and Catharine A. MacKinnon, *Only Words* (Cambridge, MA: Harvard University Press, 1993). The debate between feminists has sometimes been rancorous; see Dorchen Leidholdt and Janice Raymond, eds., *The Sexual Liberals and the Attack on Feminism* (New York: Pergamon Press, 1990).

2. See Nadine Strossen, *Defending Pornography: Free Speech, Sex, and the Fight For Women's Rights* (New York: Scribner, 1995) and Ronald Dworkin, "Do We Have a Right to Pornography?" *Oxford Journal of Legal Studies* 1 (1981), pp. 177-212; reprinted in his *A Matter of Principle* (Cambridge, MA: Harvard University Press, 1985), pp. 335-372.

3. Some evidence of this is revealed in the now well-known Canadian Supreme Court decision, *R. v. Butler* [1992] 1 S.C.R. 452. At issue in this case was whether section 163 (8) of the Criminal Code, which outlaws obscenity, constitutes an unjustified infringement of free speech as guaranteed by Section 2 (b) of the Canadian Charter of Rights and Freedoms. The Court ruled that it did not. Because some of the language in the majority opinion referred to the potential threat of certain types of pornography to women's equality, many scholars hailed the *Butler* decision as a victory in the battle for women's equality. But a closer reading of the opinion reveals the Court was actually engaged in legal moralism — that is, in an attempt to legislate a particular *moral* view about certain kinds of sexual behavior (and representations of such behavior) that some people might judge to be degrading. Since the received view (in Canada and the United States) is that courts have no business legislating morality, in *Butler* the Court was forced to disguise its problematic action in the rhetoric of threats to women's equality, when its actual intention was to prohibit the publication and consumption of sexual images the justices and future judges would deem degrading. A full defense of this charge would require a separate paper. Two points must suffice for present purposes. Firstly, the majority opinion in *Butler* is at least quite ambivalent

about whether the moral attitudes of citizens are something the law may and can control. In several places, Justice Sopinka explicitly declares the Court's opposition to legal moralism. Yet, on account of the fact that the available empirical evidence does not establish a causal connection between obscene pornography and actual sexual violence, the Court retreats to defending the prohibition of obscenity in terms of the presumption "that exposure to images bears a causal relationship to changes in attitudes and beliefs (p. 503)." Secondly, in allowing individual judges' opinions to substitute for the actual judgments of Canadians regarding whether some depicted sexual activity is degrading or dehumanizing, the *Butler* ruling effectively opened the door for the unilateral judicial imposition of a particular moral point of view. It is not merely coincidental that the seizure of gay and lesbian pornography was among the immediate effects of the *Butler* decision. Gay and lesbian pornography is hardly problematic *just* on account of it representing same-sex sex. But some judges clearly think it is. In any case, it should be clear that preventing access to genuinely problematic pornography is neither necessary nor sufficient for preventing character-corruption.

4. For the record, I am somewhat of a free speech absolutist. See my "Free Speech," *Sats: The Nordic Journal of Philosophy* 2 (2001), pp. 80-97.
5. The content of this fantasy is drawn from an excerpt of Dennis Cooper's story "Numb", originally published in his *Frisk* (New York: Grove/Atlantic, 1991) and reprinted in *Forbidden Passages: Writings Banned in Canada*, introductions by Pat Califia and Janine Fuller (Pittsburgh: Cleis Press, 1995), pp. 151-160. I do not know whether this story describes the content of a sexual fantasy Mr. Cooper himself has. However, the story is intended as a piece of gay erotica, and it might be someone's fantasy.
6. Indeed, I suspect that people's reluctance to judge sexual fantasizing — either their own or others' — is better explained by the wish to avoid paying close attention to the content of sexual fantasies than by a deep moral commitment regarding psychological freedom or some such thing.
7. To complicate matters, we might also want to specify a middling range of movements which are neither quite actions nor merely happenings; for example, unthinkingly drumming one's fingers during a tedious meeting or bobbing one's foot while listening to music. Typically, we do not *decide* to move our bodies in these ways, but once we become aware that we are doing so, we can stop.
8. Consider the case of 22 year-old Ohio resident Brian Dalton. Having served a few months for a child pornography conviction in 1998, Dalton was on parole in July 2001, when his parole officer discovered Dalton's journal during a routine search. The journal contained descriptions of Dalton's violent sexual fantasies involving fictional children said to be ten or eleven years of age. A grand jury indicted Dalton of two felony counts under an Ohio law that prohibits the creation of obscene material involving minors. He was sentenced to seven years in prison. See Bob Herbert, "The Thought Police," *The New York Times*, Thursday, July 19, 2001.
9. Sigmund Freud, "A Child is Being Beaten," in *Selected Writings*, vol. 10 (Harmondsworth: Penguin, 1979). See also the discussion in Jean Grimshaw, "Ethics, Fantasy, and the Self-Transformation," in *Ethics* (Royal Institute of Philosophy Supplement, 35) edited by A. Phillips Griffiths (Cambridge: Cambridge University Press, 1993), pp. 145-158.
10. For a summary of what she aptly describes as the "chaos of theories" each purporting to explain women's masochistic sexual fantasies, see Sandra Bartky, *Femininity and Domination: Studies in the Phenomenology of Oppression* (New York: Routledge, 1990), pp. 52-54.
11. There is little reason to think that our sexual desires are any "purer" than our non-sexual desires, in the sense that our sexual desires are wholly biologically determined. Our sexuality, like other aspects of our being, is mediated by both biological and cultural factors. See, for example, Martha C. Nussbaum, "Constructing Love, Desire, and Care," in *Sex, Preference, and the Family*, edited by David M. Estlund and Martha C. Nussbaum (New York: Oxford University Press, 1997), pp. 17-43.
12. Ethel Person, *By Force of Fantasy: How We Make Our Lives* (New York: Basic Books, 1995), p. 35.
13. Harold Leitenberg and Kris Henning, "Sexual Fantasy," *Psychological Bulletin* 117 (1995), pp. 469-496, 470.
14. John Corvino, "Naughty Fantasies," *Southwest Philosophy Review* 18 (2002), pp. 213-220, 214.
15. The idea that human persons have some native moral endowment is an ancient though controversial one. For a defense see my "Moral Competence," in *Philosophy and Linguistics*, edited by

Kumiko Murasugi and Robert Stainton (Boulder, CO: Westview Press, 1999), pp. 169-190. See Sissela Bok, "What Basis for Morality? A Minimalist Approach," *The Monist* 76 (1993), pp. 348-359 for a non-nativist account of a universal morality.

16. For a more detailed account of what we can imagine to be George's developmental trajectory and of the relation between character and practical rationality see Martha C. Nussbaum, "The Discernment of Perception: An Aristotelian Conception of Private and Public Rationality," in her *Love's Knowledge: Essays on Philosophy and Literature* (New York and Oxford: Oxford University Press, 1990), pp. 54-105.

17. These remarks hold outside the domain of sexual fantasizing. Consider other kinds of inner goings-on, like emotions. Being overjoyed at and privately gloating about another's misfortune, irrespective of whether one actually laughs in the face of the other, are evil states of mind. Voluntary gloating is morally bad action. One ought not be the kind of person who performs such actions. See, for example, A.C. Ewing, "The Justification of Emotions," *Proceedings of the Aristotelian Society*, supp. Vol. 31 (1957), pp. 59-74; S.I. Benn, "Wickedness," *Ethics* 96 (1985), pp. 795-810; and Robert Merihew Adams, "Involuntary Sins," *The Philosophical Review* 94 (1985), pp. 3-31.

18. Ethel Person, *By Force of Fantasy*, p. 94.

19. Corvino, "Naughty Fantasies," p. 214.

20. See Alvin Cooper, Coralie R. Scherer, Sylvain C. Boies, and Bary L. Gordon, "Sexuality on the Internet: From Sexual Exploration to Pathological Expression," *Professional Psychology: Research and Practice* 30 (1999), pp. 154-156; Stephen F. Davis, Brandy G. Smith, Karen Rodrigue, and Kim Pulvers, "An examination of Internet usage on two college campuses," *College Student Journal* 33 (1999), pp. 257-261; and Jennifer P. Schneider, "Effects of cybersex addiction on the family: Results of a survey," *Sexual Addiction and Compulsivity* 7 (2000), pp. 31-58.

21. Some preliminary research indicates that we are likely to say things on-line that we would never dare say in face-to-face situations. For example, conversations in company chat rooms, where users are anonymous, have come close to being libelous. See Reed Abelson, "By the Water Cooler in Cyberspace, the Talk Turns Ugly," *The New York Times*, Sunday, April 29, 2001. See also Sherry Turkle, *Life on the Screen: Identity in the age of the Internet* (New York: Simon and Schuster, 1995).

22. For cyberporn neophytes, these are the standard acronyms for Big Beautiful Women and Ball and Cock Torture.

23. "Porn sites now, some 30% of which are estimated to be content-free are little more than ads for other sites, electronically 'booby-trapped' with blind links and pop-up consoles and windows designed to gain hits and to send the surfer to other sites. This practice, known as 'click-through farming,' marks a relatively new development in advertising strategy, supplanting the old banner system, where one 'click-through,' that is, the act of mouse-clicking on an ad banner, might pay as much as 15 cents for sending a potential customer to a specific site. Now, if you hit a so-called free site, full page ads that look like tables of contents pop up, or new browser windows open spontaneously in dizzying layers, sending you to several other sites. . . . Attempts to close the windows only generates more of them, including JavaScript-launched 'consoles' that linger long after the original site has been left. The race to close windows faster than they pop-up is on. Clicking on thumbnail images or buttons on a slick console page that might offer 'amateur orgy' or 'naughty schoolgirl' images, instead of linking you to any images, will send you to another site, whose URL, normally appearing in the browser's status bar, has been obscured by a JavaScript program. And should you decide that you have had enough, and exit the original page, an exit console will pop up which usually points surfers back to the first site. Trapped in a loop, surfers return to the original site again and again without realizing it." (Michael Uebel, "Toward a Symptomatology of Cyberporn," *Theory and Event* 3 (2000) at http://muse.jhu.edu/journals/theory_and_event/v003/3.4uebel.html, para.55).

24. Many thanks to the following people for useful discussion and provocative questions: Robert Cavalier, Felmon Davis, Christine Koggel and her students at Bryn Mawr College, Alex London, Patrick McCroskery, Eduardo Mendieta, Paul Pietroski, Jennifer Saul, Mandy Simons, Sarah Stroud, and Carol Voeller.

QUESTIONS

1. Susan Dwyer claims that her examination of pornography makes the issue of censorship irrelevant. What is her argument for this claim? According to Dwyer, where should the attention be placed and why?
2. Dwyer provides an example of sexual fantasizing that she takes to be morally problematic. Is it problematic in your view? Is all sexual fantasizing morally problematic?
3. How does Dwyer address the objection that making judgments about morally problematic sexual fantasizing puts us on the slippery slope to making discriminatory judgments about people's sexual lives and practices?
4. In what ways does Dwyer's account of the harms of pornography differ from those presented by Groarke, Clark, and McElroy?
5. In Dwyer's view, what is it about cyberpornography that makes it particularly worrisome with respect to issues of character development and agency? Has Dwyer's analysis changed your thinking with respect to either engaging in sexual fantasizing or surfing the Internet?

SUGGESTIONS FOR FURTHER READING

Court Cases

- *R. v. Sharpe*. Supreme Court of Canada. 2001 SCC 2. File No.: 27376. A ruling in which the Supreme Court determined that restrictions to freedom of speech are justifiable to prevent harm to children that results from the production and collection of child pornography. It then delineated exceptions in the form of diaries, drawings, and videos for private use.

Canadian Government Reports

- *Limits of Criminal Law - Obscenity: A Test Case* (Working Paper 10) prepared by the Law Reform Commission of Canada and published in 1975. This report sets the discussion within the context of an analysis of the function of the criminal law with respect to censoring pornographic materials.
- *Pornography and Prostitution in Canada* is the report of a committee commissioned by the Canadian government and chaired by Paul Fraser. It submitted its findings in 1985.
- Industry Canada (1997). "The Cyberspace is not a No Law Land." URL: http://strategis.ic.gc.ca/epic/internet/insmt-gst.nsf/vwGeneratedInterE/sf08058e.html
  This report by Industry Canada provides an analysis of how Canadian law applies to content-related Internet liability in the areas of copyright and trademarks, privacy and defamation, obscenity, child pornography, and hate literature.

Other Government Reports

- *The Report on the Commission on Obscenity and Pornography* (New York: Bantam Books, 1970). One of the first government reports commissioned by the U.S. government to study the effects of pornography on users.

- *Report of the Attorney General's Commission on Pornography* (Washington, D.C.: United States Government Printing Office, 1986). This report, prepared by the Meese Commission, suggests that, contrary to the findings of the 1970 U.S. commission, exposure to some types of pornography has harmful consequences.
- *Obscenity and Film Censorship*, the report of a committee commissioned by the British government and chaired by Bernard Williams, a prominent British philosopher. The report was published under the same title by Cambridge University Press in 1979.

Books

- Alison Assiter, *Pornography, Feminism and the Individual* (London: Pluto Press, 1989). The author takes issue with radical feminists who seek the total elimination of pornography as well as with liberals who see censorship as an unjustified violation of individual liberty. The book argues that "the consumption of pornography is an individualist pursuit that violates the autonomy of those who model for pornographic films and magazines but that it is a symptom rather than a cause of the power relations that exist within our society."
- F.M. Christensen, *Pornography: The Other Side* (New York: Praeger, 1990). This book explores the "other side" of the censorship debate, arguing that anti-pornography campaigns are themselves morally evil and rest on irrational attitudes toward human sexuality.
- David Copp and Susan Wendell (eds.), *Pornography and Censorship: Scientific, Philosophical and Legal Studies* (Buffalo: Prometheus Books, 1983). This anthology reviews a wide range of arguments both for and against the censorship of pornography. It includes an extensive evaluation of the results of research into the harmfulness of pornography. It also includes the Williams report referred to above.
- Laura Lederer (ed.), *Take Back the Night: Women on Pornography* (New York: Morrow, 1980). This collection is representative of the early feminist analysis of pornography. It includes essays that are critical of studies used in the Copp collection, referred to above, as evidence that pornography does not have harmful social consequences.
- *Pornography and Sexual Violence: Evidence of the Links* (London: Everywoman, 1988). This is the published transcript of the 1983 hearings in Minneapolis, Minnesota, of the MacKinnon/Dworkin Ordinance referred to in some of the readings. The book includes the text of the ordinance as well as the testimony of women who came before the hearings to give personal accounts of how they had been harmed by pornography.
- Catharine MacKinnon, *Only Words* (Cambridge, MA: Harvard University Press, 1993). In this book as well as in chapters of *Feminism Unmodified: Discourses in Life and Law* (Harvard University Press, 1987), MacKinnon sets out her analysis of the harms of pornography, both to individual women and to women as a group. She calls for restrictions along the lines sketched in the Minneapolis civil rights ordinance.
- Susan Dwyer (ed.), *The Problem of Pornography* (Belmont: Wadsworth, 1995). A collection of papers covering various topics in the pornography debate, including definitions, pornography and equality, pornography and sexuality, and pornography and speech acts. The collection includes an interesting philosophical exchange between Ronald Dworkin and Rae Langton about the tension between liberty and the principle of equality as it relates to the issue of pornography.
- Carole S. Vance (ed.), *Pleasure and Danger: Exploring Female Sexuality* (Boston: Routledge, 1984). A collection of papers originating at a conference held at Barnard

College in New York in 1982 called, "Towards a Politics of Sexuality." Many of the papers challenge a feminist analysis that emphasizes the dangers of pornography at the expense of making it difficult for women to explore sexuality and express desire.

Films

- *Not a Love Story* and *Give Me Your Soul*. Films about pornography produced by the Canadian National Film Board in 1981 and 2000 respectively.
- *Killing Us Softly* is the first of two films, the second of which is *Still Killing Us Softly*, put out by the Media Education Foundation. These films examine the role of the advertising industry in perpetuating myths and stereotypes about women and sexuality.

Chapter 5

Equality and Discrimination

Introduction

In the introduction to the discussion of euthanasia, three principles that have a central role in the discussion of contemporary moral issues — the protection-of-life principle, the avoidance-of-suffering principle, and the moral-autonomy principle — were introduced. There is a fourth principle, what we shall call the *principle of equal worth*, that has an equally important role to play in discussions of contemporary moral issues. The principle of equal worth is implicit in the previous chapter's exploration of the notion of group harm; that is, the idea that pornography harms women as a group. One of the central tasks of this chapter is to bring the significance of the principle of equal worth into focus. We will then appreciate that this principle plays a role in virtually all of the remaining chapters.

In modern democratic societies of the sort in which we live we often forget that discrimination on grounds of race, sex, ethnic origin, disability, and so on has a long and deeply entrenched history. That history reveals that some people have been explicitly judged as having inferior worth and deserving of unequal treatment. It is easy to forget that slavery was an institution in our society until less than two centuries ago, that visible minorities often have difficulty finding jobs and adequate housing because of skin colour, and that women have been and, in the view of many, still are actively discouraged from following career paths open to men because of their sex.

These examples of discrimination bring into sharp relief an idea discussed in the chapters on euthanasia and abortion with respect to issues of disability and in the pornography chapter with respect to women's inequality. It is not only individuals who can be harmed by the actions and attitudes of others, but groups as well. Discriminatory actions, of the kind illustrated above, result from judgments that certain individuals are inferior merely because they are members of particular groups. Discrimination is widely thought to be morally unacceptable because it prevents people who are discriminated against from participating fully in the life of their society for irrelevant or immoral reasons.

Indeed, the elimination of discrimination is thought to be so central to creating a just society that the principle of equal worth is found in all modern charters, bills, and declarations of human rights. The United Nations' Universal Declaration of Human Rights adopted in 1948 is a good example. It proclaims that "all human beings are born free and equal in dignity and rights" and that "everyone is entitled to all the rights and freedoms set forth in this Declaration, without distinction of any kind, such as race, colour, sex, language, religion, political or other opinion, national or social origin, property, birth or other status."

The UN declaration is one example of numerous articulations of our current commitment to equality. However, propounding a commitment to the principle of equal worth is but one step on the road to actually achieving equality. Our emergence from a long history in which discrimination against members of particular groups was overt and explicitly defended in legislation and theory continues to make the topic of discrimination current and important for several reasons. Identifying at least two of these now will serve to highlight the complexity of issues of discrimination.

First, different groups experience discrimination in diverse ways and at multiple levels, and this creates different sorts of inequalities and disadvantages for particular groups. This complexity with respect to kinds of inequality and discrimination provides a second reason for identifying discrimination as an important topic of investigation. Even though we have reached agreement that the principle of equal worth ought to be foundational to a just society, this does not yet tell us what is needed to satisfy the principle in particular social contexts and specific cases. In fact, it will become clear that even within liberal societies there is a great deal of disagreement about what counts as a justifiable application of the principle of equal worth. This chapter will introduce some of the main concepts and begin the exploration of issues central to a discussion of discrimination. These issues will then be examined in more detail in many of the remaining chapters.

Background Considerations

Canada is a signatory country to the Universal Declaration of Human Rights and many other international human rights agreements. In Canada, enshrining human rights into law is a fairly recent phenomenon. One of the first pieces of antidiscrimination legislation, "An Act to prevent the Further Introduction of Slaves and to limit the term of Enforced Servitude within this Province," was passed in the province of Upper Canada in 1793. One of its objectives was to free the children of slaves once they reached the age of twenty-five. It remained in force until 1833 when Britain abolished slavery throughout the British Empire. However, up until 1944 the message given in court decisions dealing with cases of racial discrimination was that discrimination was not illegal. In 1940, the Supreme Court ruled in *Christie v. York Corporation* that no wrong was done to Christie, a black man who was refused entry to a tavern in the Montreal Forum. Christie's claim for damages sought for humiliation was dismissed because, in the words of Justice Rinfret: "The general principle of the law of Quebec is that of complete freedom of commerce. Any merchant is free to deal as he may choose with an individual member of the public." In 1944, Ontario passed the *Ontario Racial Discrimination Act*, which was to change this view that human rights were subordinate to the rights of property and commerce. The Act prohibited public endorsements of discrimination on the basis of "race or creed" and specifically targeted the public display of "whites only" signs. This act allowed the Ontario High Court in 1945 to prevent the prohibition of the sale of land to Jews.

Paralleling the advances made against discrimination on the basis of "race or creed" was the fight for women's rights. In 1916, women were granted voting rights for the first time in Manitoba, Saskatchewan, and Alberta. They won the vote federally in 1918. In 1916, Emily Murphy became one of the first woman magistrates in the British Empire. Soon after, her judgments were challenged, based on the argument that she did not qualify as a person under the *British North America Act*. In 1927, Murphy and four other women from Alberta requested a constitutional interpretation to determine the eligibility of women for appointment to the

Senate. In what has become known as "the Persons Case," the Supreme Court ruled that only men were eligible under the "qualified persons" provision in Section 24 of the *BNA Act*. Murphy appealed to the British Privy Council, the final interpreter of the *BNA Act* at that time, and won the case in 1929, when it ruled that the word persons "*may* include members of both sexes." The following year, Cairine Wilson became the first woman senator.

Women's participation in politics and the labour force was practically negligible in the decades that followed. During the Second World War, an exemption was made when women were recruited into jobs left vacant by men who had joined the armed forces. However, when the war was over, women were laid off and their jobs made available to returning armed forces personnel. Policies providing incentives to stay home and raise children were also instituted. In 1967, Florence Bird was the first woman to head a royal commission, the Royal Commission on the Status of Women. In many of the first attempts to enact human rights into provincial codes, sex was absent from the lists that enumerated the grounds for discrimination.

The first Bill of Rights in Canada was enacted by the province of Saskatchewan in 1947. It prohibited discrimination on the basis of race, creed, religion, colour, ethnic or national origin. In 1951, Ontario enacted the first *Fair Employment Practices Act*. This legislation was important because it expanded procedures for investigating complaints, launching inquiries, and seeking redress, and made noncompliance with the Act an offense. After the Canadian Bill of Rights was enacted in 1960, various individual provinces introduced human rights codes. Notable among these was the 1962 Ontario consolidation of various antidiscrimination provisions into a comprehensive human rights code and the *Canadian Human Rights Act*, first passed in 1977, excerpts of which lead the readings in this chapter.

The Current Situation

In 1982, the Canadian Charter of Rights and Freedoms was enacted. Section 15, the equality rights section of the Charter, came into force three years later on April 17, 1985. Section 15 of the Charter states:

> 15. (1) Every individual is equal before and under the law and has the right to the equal protection and equal benefit of the law without discrimination and, in particular, without discrimination based on race, national or ethnic origin, colour, religion, sex, age or mental or physical disability.
>
> 15. (2) Subsection (1) does not preclude any law, program or activity that has as its object the amelioration of conditions of disadvantaged individuals or groups including those that are disadvantaged because of race, national or ethnic origin, colour, religion, sex, age or mental or physical disability.

The delay in implementation of Section 15 was intended to allow time for federal and provincial governments to amend any legislation that did not conform to the section. If anything, this was an acknowledgment of the possibly far-reaching effects of the equality provisions, Subsection (2) of which permits affirmative action measures designed to alleviate inequalities. The Charter has been viewed as a powerful tool for righting the imbalance of decades of discrimination and unequal access.

The government and various concerned groups responded to the equality rights provisions in Section 15 by providing an abundance of research into its potential effects. An example was the Royal Commission on Equality in Employment headed by Judge Rosalie Abella. Its report, *Equality in Employment*, provides factual information on four groups about whom the government was particularly concerned, namely, women, the disabled, native people, and visible minorities. The Commission also made recommendations for alleviating the discrimination and disadvantages suffered by these groups. A more recent report, *Embracing Change in the Federal Public Service: Task Force on the Participation of Visible Minorities in the Federal Public Service* was published in 1999 with updates issued in 2002.

Cases invoking Section 15 of the Charter are only now finding their way into the courts. Some take the 1989 Supreme Court decision in *Andrews v. Law Society of B.C.* to be an important contribution to the project of articulating Canada's own vision of what constitutes equality. The 1999 Supreme Court decision *Law v. Canada (Minister of Employment and Immigration)* is another important case that interprets the equality provisions in the Charter on the issue of discrimination on the basis of age.

In recent years, eight same-sex couples challenged the law that requires that marriage be between "one man and one woman" as offending their right to equality as guaranteed by Section 15(1) of the Canadian Charter. In the June 2003 decision *Halpern v. Canada (Attorney General)*, the Ontario Court of Appeal agreed and ruled that the "dignity of persons is violated by the exclusion of same-sex couples from the institution of marriage." Shortly after, the federal government announced that it would not challenge the ruling, but instead introduce legislation allowing same-sex marriage. If successful, this would make Canada only the third country after the Netherlands and Belgium to legalize same-sex marriage. Some take these developments to be a charting of new and exciting territory, one that departs from the direction taken by our neighbours to the south. Others view the interpretations of equality and the new legislation as either unnecessary or unjustifiable applications of the principle of equal worth.

The Moral Dimension

Making wise choices requires the capacity to discriminate between and among things and people in ways designed to help us accomplish our objectives. We applaud the ability to distinguish things that are well made from things that are not. And normally, it is a compliment to describe someone as a person of discriminating taste. Viewed from this perspective, discrimination is an unavoidable feature of human life. Discrimination is normally considered to be unjustified, however, when it interferes arbitrarily with the application of the moral autonomy principle by unfairly limiting the capacity of some individuals to participate fully in the life of their community, or enjoy the rights, privileges, and benefits to which, morally speaking, they are entitled.

The principle of equal worth is an important one for several reasons. Articulating some of them here will give us an idea of the various complex dimensions of discrimination. First, our emergence from a long history in which discrimination against certain groups was defended and entrenched in laws and behaviour should undermine confidence that we have succeeded in eliminating discrimination and achieving equality. While legal barriers that once prohibited some people from participating as full members of a community have been removed, informal barriers in the form of discriminatory beliefs, judgments, and actions continue to have an impact on the freedom and opportunities of individuals who are members of traditionally disadvantaged groups.

Second, an examination of the nature of discrimination and of its various manifestations raises issues concerning the connections and conflicts between the principle of equal worth and the principle of moral autonomy. What sort of barriers to the full exercise of autonomy stand in the way of those who are disadvantaged because their membership in a group continues to determine in advance their life prospects and goals? Does an emphasis on individual freedom in abstraction from social and political contexts of discrimination prevent us from understanding certain limitations of freedom and autonomy experienced by those who are members of traditionally disadvantaged groups? Are group inequalities exacerbated in a society that prizes an individual's freedom from the interference of law and policy? Can policies that attempt to alleviate discrimination against groups be justified when they infringe on the freedom of other individuals?

This set of questions about individual freedom and group inequality raises another set of questions that suggest a third important dimension in a discussion of the principle of equal worth. Does discrimination have an impact on how individuals who are members of disadvantaged groups see themselves and the world? If there are differences in perspectives on societies and social relations, does it follow that only those individuals who are members of a particular group can understand or interpret the experiences of that group? Is what members of disadvantaged groups say about their experiences important to understanding discrimination for the purpose of eliminating conditions of inequality?

Taken together, all of the questions posed thus far demonstrate the complexity of the moral issues surrounding discrimination. The questions also point to a fourth and final reason for acknowledging the importance of the principle of equal worth, one that is introduced in this chapter and developed more fully in the chapters that follow. The principle of equal worth is grounded on the assumption that all people are equal. But how do we apply this principle when we are confronted with particular cases of inequality? In the tradition of Western political thought, theorists have developed two different approaches to applying the principle of equal worth.

On the one side are those theorists who believe that equality is achieved when legal barriers to obtaining certain goods are removed: each person is then taken to have the same opportunity as anyone else to participate in society and acquire his or her share of social, educational, and economic goods. This approach to satisfying the principle of equal worth has been referred to as "formal equality," an approach that advocates that everyone be treated the same or equally no matter what their differences. Under formal equality, the emphasis is on individual and negative freedom, the freedom from artificial barriers and state interference in the lives of citizens.

Other theorists have pointed out that removing legal barriers and providing equal treatment have not resulted in vast improvements to the condition or prospects of disadvantaged groups. These theorists conclude that the damage and injustice that have been inflicted on groups that have suffered from discrimination can only be overcome if they are given special, favourable consideration whose purpose is to bring the members of those groups to a position where they are treated equally as a matter of course. This second approach to the principle of equal worth is generally referred to as "substantive equality." The suggestion is that achieving meaningful or substantive equality sometimes requires respecting difference and providing special treatment. Special educational opportunities, job training, affirmative action programs, as well as rights to welfare are examples of positive measures endorsed by substantive equality theorists. While these measures limit the freedom of some individuals, they have the effect of increasing the freedom of members of traditionally disadvantaged groups by broadening their range of opportunities and improving their life prospects. We will note that moral justifications for special treatment or positive measures are central to the discussions in the remaining chapters on poverty and the right to welfare, aboriginal rights, and environmental ethics.

The Readings

The first group of readings set out the legal background to current discussions of discrimination in Canada. The first includes excerpts from the most recent version of the *Canadian Human Rights Act* and the second is a report mandated by the government to review the purpose and the grounds of the *Act* to ensure that it reflects contemporary equality principles. This 2000 report entitled *Promoting Equality: A New Vision* outlines concepts central to equality analysis, such as systemic discrimination, equal opportunity, and accommodation. It also provides recommendations for revisions to the *Act*.

The readings in the second group discuss the moral dimensions of various manifestations of discrimination: whether and what sorts of restrictions to individual freedom are experienced by members of different disadvantaged groups; whether differences do exist and can form the basis for justifying different or unequal treatment; and whether and what sorts of positive measures designed to address inequalities by providing special treatment can be morally justified.

The first reading in this group introduces us to issues of race. The report from *The Toronto Star* is one of a multipart series on racial profiling in Toronto's police force. It provides data that show that blacks in Toronto are much more likely to be stopped, questioned, searched, and charged by police. This aspect of racial discrimination in the justice system connects with information learned in the chapter on capital punishment. The reading by Peggy McIntosh that follows continues the examination of race by exploring the concept of white privilege. McIntosh provides an extensive list of conditions that attach to being white, a way of being that is assumed to be normal and neutral. These conditions point to the kinds of advantages and privileges that are invisible and taken for granted. McIntosh ends by examining some of the ways in which being male and heterosexual also provide a set of privileges.

In the third reading in this group, Marilyn Frye examines the concept of sexism. She provides numerous descriptions and examples that would appear to support the idea that there are relevant differences between the sexes that justify assigning different roles to women. Frye argues, however, that these differences are constructed in and through social practices and political contexts that have assumed women's inferiority and unequal status. The results are manifested in the various aspects of sexism that, Frye argues, need our moral attention.

The fourth reading by Alex Wellington focuses on discrimination on the basis of sexual orientation. Wellington questions the idea that sexual orientation is a difference that justifies unequal treatment. She argues that a purely formal equality approach can form the moral justification for same sex-marriage. By rejecting the accounts of harm that some argue would result from state-sanctioned same-sex marriage, Wellington concludes that formal equality demands that same-sex couples be treated in the same way and be given the same benefits as heterosexual couples.

In the final reading, J.E. Bickenbach carefully outlines the complexities involved in describing and understanding disability to argue that the inequalities associated with disabilities result from public perceptions and beliefs about the capacities of people with disabilities. Bickenbach evaluates a "civil rights" approach to disability, one that dominates the treatment of discrimination and focuses on addressing discriminatory actions. He argues that while this approach has resulted in changes to both the physical environment to accommodate people with disabilities and to attitudes and stereotypes about disability, it has not succeeded in broadening the range of choices available to people with disabilities. A better approach, he argues, is one that views disability as a condition each of us does or will experience in a lifetime. Issues of disability can then be seen as issues of the fair distribution of social goods, including positive liberty.

CANADIAN HUMAN RIGHTS ACT

R.S., 1985, c. H-6 May 2000

CHAPTER H-6

An Act to extend the laws in Canada that proscribe discrimination

SHORT TITLE

Short title **1.** This Act may be cited as the *Canadian Human Rights Act.*
1976-77, c. 33, s. 1.

PURPOSE OF ACT

Purpose **2.** The purpose of this Act is to extend the laws in Canada to give effect, within the purview of matters coming within the legislative authority of Parliament, to the principle that all individuals should have an opportunity equal with other individuals to make for themselves the lives that they are able and wish to have and to have their needs accommodated, consistent with their duties and obligations as members of society, without being hindered in or prevented from doing so by discriminatory practices based on race, national or ethnic origin, colour, religion, age, sex, sexual orientation, marital status, family status, disability or conviction for an offence for which a pardon has been granted.
R.S., 1985, c. H-6, s. 2; 1996, c. 14, s. 1; 1998, c. 9, s. 9.

PART I
PROSCRIBED DISCRIMINATION

General

Prohibited grounds of discrimination **3.** (1) For all purposes of this Act, the prohibited grounds of discrimination are race, national or ethnic origin, colour, religion, age, sex, sexual orientation, marital status, family status, disability and conviction for which a pardon has been granted.

Idem

(2) Where the ground of discrimination is pregnancy or child-birth, the discrimination shall be deemed to be on the ground of sex.

R.S., 1985, c. H-6, s. 3; 1996, c. 14, s. 2.

Multiple grounds of discrimination

3.1 For greater certainty, a discriminatory practice includes a practice based on one or more prohibited grounds of discrimination or on the effect of a combination of prohibited grounds.

1998, c. 9, s. 11.

Orders regarding discriminatory practices

4. A discriminatory practice, as described in sections 5 to 14.1, may be the subject of a complaint under Part III and anyone found to be engaging or to have engaged in a discriminatory practice may be made subject to an order as provided in sections 53 and 54.

R.S., 1985, c. H-6, s. 4; 1998, c. 9, s. 11.

Discriminatory Practices

Denial of good, service, facility or accommodation

5. It is a discriminatory practice in the provision of goods, services, facilities or accommodation customarily available to the general public

(*a*) to deny, or to deny access to, any such good, service, facility or accommodation to any individual, or

(*b*) to differentiate adversely in relation to any individual,

on a prohibited ground of discrimination.

1976-77, c. 33, s. 5.

Denial of commercial premises or residential accommodation

6. It is a discriminatory practice in the provision of commercial premises or residential accommodation

(*a*) to deny occupancy of such premises or accommodation to any individual, or

(*b*) to differentiate adversely in relation to any individual,

on a prohibited ground of discrimination.

1976-77, c. 33, s. 6.

Employment

7. It is a discriminatory practice, directly or indirectly,

(*a*) to refuse to employ or continue to employ any individual, or

(*b*) in the course of employment, to differentiate adversely in relation to an employee,

on a prohibited ground of discrimination.

1976-77, c. 33, s. 7.

Employment applications, advertisements

8. It is a discriminatory practice

(*a*) to use or circulate any form of application for employment, or

(*b*) in connection with employment or prospective employment, to publish any advertisement or to make any written or oral inquiry

that expresses or implies any limitation, specification or preference based on a prohibited ground of discrimination.

1976-77, c. 33, s. 8.

Employee organizations

9. (1) It is a discriminatory practice for an employee organization on a prohibited ground of discrimination

(*a*) to exclude an individual from full membership in the organization;

(*b*) to expel or suspend a member of the organization; or

(*c*) to limit, segregate, classify or otherwise act in relation to an individual in a way that would deprive the individual of employment opportunities, or limit employment opportunities or otherwise adversely affect the status of the individual, where the individual is a member of the organization or where any of the obligations of the organization pursuant to a collective agreement relate to the individual.

Exception

(2) Notwithstanding subsection (1), it is not a discriminatory practice for an employee organization to exclude, expel or suspend an individual from membership in the organization because that individual has reached the normal age of retirement for individuals working in positions similar to the position of that individual.

(3) [Repealed, 1998, c. 9, s. 12]

R.S., 1985, c. H-6, s. 9; 1998, c. 9, s. 12.

Discriminatory policy or practice

10. It is a discriminatory practice for an employer, employee organization or employer organization

(*a*) to establish or pursue a policy or practice, or

(*b*) to enter into an agreement affecting recruitment, referral, hiring, promotion, training, apprenticeship, transfer or any other matter relating to employment or prospective employment,

that deprives or tends to deprive an individual or class of individuals of any employment opportunities on a prohibited ground of discrimination.

R.S., 1985, c. H-6, s. 10; 1998, c. 9, s. 13(E).

Equal wages

11. (1) It is a discriminatory practice for an employer to establish or maintain differences in wages between male and female employees employed in the same establishment who are performing work of equal value.

Assessment of value of work

(2) In assessing the value of work performed by employees employed in the same establishment, the criterion to be applied is the composite of the skill, effort and responsibility required in the performance of the work and the conditions under which the work is performed.

Separate establishments

(3) Separate establishments established or maintained by an employer solely or principally for the purpose of establishing or maintaining differences in wages between male and female employees shall be deemed for the purposes of this section to be the same establishment.

Different wages based on prescribed reasonable factors

(4) Notwithstanding subsection (1), it is not a discriminatory practice to pay to male and female employees different wages if the difference is based on a factor prescribed by guidelines, issued by the Canadian Human Rights Commission pursuant to subsection 27(2), to be a reasonable factor that justifies the difference.

Idem

(5) For greater certainty, sex does not constitute a reasonable factor justifying a difference in wages.

No reduction of wages

(6) An employer shall not reduce wages in order to eliminate a discriminatory practice described in this section.

Definition of "wages"

(7) For the purposes of this section, "wages" means any form of remuneration payable for work performed by an individual and includes

(*a*) salaries, commissions, vacation pay, dismissal wages and bonuses;

(*b*) reasonable value for board, rent, housing and lodging;

(*c*) payments in kind;

(*d*) employer contributions to pension funds or plans, long-term disability plans and all forms of health insurance plans; and

(*e*) any other advantage received directly or indirectly from the individual's employer.

1976-77, c. 33, s. 11.

Publication of discriminatory notices, etc.

12. It is a discriminatory practice to publish or display before the public or to cause to be published or displayed before the public any notice, sign, symbol, emblem or other representation that

(*a*) expresses or implies discrimination or an intention to discriminate, or

(*b*) incites or is calculated to incite others to discriminate

if the discrimination expressed or implied, intended to be expressed or implied or incited or calculated to be incited would otherwise, if engaged in, be a discriminatory practice described in any of sections 5 to 11 or in section 14.

1976-77, c. 33, s. 12; 1980-81-82-83, c. 143, s. 6.

Hate messages

13. (1) It is a discriminatory practice for a person or a group of persons acting in concert to communicate telephonically or to cause to be so communicated, repeatedly, in whole or in part by means of the facilities of a telecommunication undertaking within the legislative authority of Parliament, any matter that is likely to expose a person or persons to hatred or contempt by reason of the fact that that person or those persons are identifiable on the basis of a prohibited ground of discrimination.

Exception

(2) Subsection (1) does not apply in respect of any matter that is communicated in whole or in part by means of the facilities of a broadcasting undertaking.

Interpretation

(3) For the purposes of this section, no owner or operator of a telecommunication undertaking communicates or causes to be communicated any matter described in subsection (1) by reason only that the facilities of a telecommunication undertaking owned or operated by that person are used by other persons for the transmission of that matter.

1976-77, c. 33, s. 13.

Harassment

14. (1) It is a discriminatory practice,

(*a*) in the provision of goods, services, facilities or accommodation customarily available to the general public,

(*b*) in the provision of commercial premises or residential accommodation, or

(*c*) in matters related to employment,

to harass an individual on a prohibited ground of discrimination.

Sexual harass-
ment

(2) Without limiting the generality of subsection (1), sexual harassment shall, for the purposes of that subsection, be deemed to be harassment on a prohibited ground of discrimination.
1980-81-82-83, c. 143, s. 7.

Retaliation

14.1 It is a discriminatory practice for a person against whom a complaint has been filed under Part III, or any person acting on their behalf, to retaliate or threaten retaliation against the individual who filed the complaint or the alleged victim.
1998, c. 9, s. 14.

Exceptions

15. (1) It is not a discriminatory practice if
(*a*) any refusal, exclusion, expulsion, suspension, limitation, specification or preference in relation to any employment is established by an employer to be based on a *bona fide* occupational requirement;
(*b*) employment of an individual is refused or terminated because that individual has not reached the minimum age, or has reached the maximum age, that applies to that employment by law or under regulations, which may be made by the Governor in Council for the purposes of this paragraph;
(*c*) an individual's employment is terminated because that individual has reached the normal age of retirement for employees working in positions similar to the position of that individual;
(*d*) the terms and conditions of any pension fund or plan established by an employer, employee organization or employer organization provide for the compulsory vesting or locking-in of pension contributions at a fixed or determinable age in accordance with sections 17 and 18 of the *Pension Benefits Standards Act, 1985*;
(*e*) an individual is discriminated against on a prohibited ground of discrimination in a manner that is prescribed by guidelines, issued by the Canadian Human Rights Commission pursuant to subsection 27(2), to be reasonable;
(*f*) an employer, employee organization or employer organization grants a female employee special leave or benefits in connection with pregnancy or child-birth or grants employees special leave or benefits to assist them in the care of their children; or
(*g*) in the circumstances described in section 5 or 6, an individual is denied any goods, services, facilities or accommodation or access thereto or occupancy of any commercial premises or residential accommodation or is a victim of any adverse differentiation and there is *bona fide* justification for that denial or differentiation.

Accommodation
of needs

(2) For any practice mentioned in paragraph (1)(*a*) to be considered to be based on a *bona fide* occupational requirement and for any practice mentioned in paragraph (1)(*g*) to be considered to have a *bona fide* justification, it must be established that accommodation of the needs of an individual or a

class of individuals affected would impose undue hardship on the person who would have to accommodate those needs, considering health, safety and cost.

PROMOTING EQUALITY: A NEW VISION 2000

PART ONE: INTRODUCTION

CHAPTER 1
Summary of the Mandate, Consultation and Research Process

On April 8, 1999, the Honourable Anne McLellan, Minister of Justice, announced the establishment of an independent Panel to conduct a review of the *Canadian Human Rights Act*. The Act had not been comprehensively reviewed since it was passed in 1977.

Our mandate was to examine the purpose of the Act and the grounds listed in it, to ensure that the Act kept current with human rights and equality principles. We were also asked to review the scope and jurisdiction of the Act, including the exceptions contained in it. Our mandate also included a review of the current complaints-based model and to make recommendations for enhancing or changing the model to improve protection from discrimination, while ensuring that the process was efficient and effective. We were also asked to consider the powers (including the audit powers under the *Employment Equity Act*) and procedures of the Canadian Human Rights Commission and the Human Rights Tribunal. Notably, the equal pay provisions were not part of our mandate.

. . .

CHAPTER 2
The Context of the Canadian Human Rights Act

The *Canadian Human Rights Act* works with other laws to protect human rights. The Act applies to federal private businesses as well as the federal government and the governments of the Northwest Territories and Nunavut. In contrast, the *Canadian Charter of Rights and Freedoms*, which also prohibits discrimination, only applies to governments.

Each province and territory also has a human rights act that covers businesses and organizations within their jurisdictions. For example, discrimination in housing and other types of accommodation would be brought to a provincial or territorial human rights commission.

The Act applies to all employers and providers of goods, services, facilities and accommodation within the legislative power of the federal Parliament. In addition, it deals with hate messages where a person acts individually or together with a group of persons to create hate messages about a person or persons protected by the grounds in the Act, whether those messages are communicated by telephone or by any other means of telecommunication within the ability of Parliament to regulate.

Specifically, the Act applies to the federal government, including the Canadian Forces and the Royal Canadian Mounted Police, and governmental agencies. It applies to approximately

The Report of the Canadian Human Rights Act Review Panel Promoting Equality: A New Vision, 2000, *Justice Canada. Reproduced with the permission of the Minister of Public Works and Government Services, 2003, and Courtesy of the Department of Justice Canada.*

48 Crown Corporations such as the Canadian Broadcasting Corporation and the Canadian Film Development Corporation. It also applies to individuals and corporations carrying on the business of inter-provincial and international transportation by road, rail, air, ferry, pipeline and shipping and navigation. Further, it applies to those in the telecommunications business, including broadcasting, and to the postal service. It covers the chartered banks. It also applies to a special group of businesses which Parliament has declared to be for the general advantage of Canada, such as feed mills, grain elevators and some mining operations. It applies to the nuclear energy business, including uranium mining and processing . . . .

CHAPTER 3
The Purpose and Language of the Canadian Human Rights Act

Issue. We examined whether the purpose provision in the Act should be amended to recognize developments in the concept of discrimination since 1977 and whether its language should be updated to reflect any change in the purpose of the Act.

The Importance of a Purpose Clause. The purpose of the CHRA is set out in section 2 as follows:

> PURPOSE OF ACT
> The purpose of this Act is to extend the laws in Canada to give effect, within the purview of matters coming within the legislative authority of Parliament, to the principle that all individuals should have an opportunity equal with other individuals to make for themselves the lives that they are able and wish to have and to have their needs accommodated, consistent with their duties and obligations as members of society, without being hindered in or prevented from doing so by discriminatory practices based on race, national or ethnic origin, colour, religion, age, sex, sexual orientation, marital status, family status, disability or conviction of or an offence for which a pardon has been granted.

This statement of the purpose has been very important in the interpretation of the protection provided by the Act, its remedial focus and the concept of discrimination itself. Looking at the history of the interpretation of the purpose clause in the Act is instructive in providing an insight into the development of the concept of discrimination over the past two decades.

In the early 1980s, the courts were of the view that human rights legislation was meant to deal only with intentional (or direct) discrimination. This was consistent with the idea that equality meant that everyone should be treated in the same way. As long as an employer did not intend to deny employment because of religion or race, then there was a sufficient amount of equality. This has become known as a formalistic kind of equality. It meant that as long as employees could comply with rules made with the majority in mind, then there was no harm to be alleviated by human rights law.

Adverse Effect Discrimination. In *Bhinder v. Canadian National Railway* (1985), the Supreme Court of Canada decided that the broad aim and purpose of the Act covered adverse effect discrimination. The Court held that an employment rule that required all employees to wear hard-hats for safety reasons discriminated against Sikh employees whose religious principles forbade any head-covering but a turban.

This decision meant that the Act prohibited not just acts of direct discrimination where individuals were expressly excluded from employment or services because of personal characteristics connected with the listed grounds of discrimination, but also that the Act prohibited conditions of employment and accessibility to services which did not expressly single out a group of employees but had a negative effect on them because of their personal characteristics. The Court felt that the purpose of the Act to eliminate and remedy discrimination required the recognition of the fact that a discriminatory act was harmful whether intended or not.

The concept of adverse effect discrimination was an important step towards a more comprehensive understanding of discrimination. It meant that employers and service providers could not ignore the effect of their policies on employees and customers based on the prohibited grounds.

This development initiated a legal recognition of the fact that each person is different and has different needs and capacities. The Supreme Court of Canada held in the companion case to *Bhinder, O'Mally v. Simpson-Sears* (1985), that where a company policy adversely affected an employee because of her religion (Mrs. O'Malley could not work on Saturday because she was a Seventh Day Adventist), the employer had to show that it tried to accommodate her religious needs to the point that it caused undue hardship to the business. In *Alberta Human Rights Commission v. Central Alberta Dairy Pool* (1990), the Court decided the duty to accommodate was triggered whenever an employment rule had an adverse discriminatory effect on an employee.

Systemic Discrimination. Though adverse effect was a powerful device for analyzing whether a policy had a discriminatory effect on individuals contrary to the purpose of the Act, it was not a comprehensive concept of discrimination. This came with the idea of systemic discrimination adopted by the Supreme Court of Canada in another case under the Act.

In *Action Travail des Femmes v. Canadian National Railway* (1987), the Court decided that a purposive approach to interpreting the Act required the recognition of another form of discrimination with potentially greater consequences in terms of the number of people affected. This was called systemic discrimination.

The Court stated that ". . . systemic discrimination in an employment context is discrimination that results from the simple operation of established procedures of recruitment, hiring, and promotion, none of which is necessarily designed to promote discrimination . . . ." It called for systemic remedies, such as the employment equity order made by the Tribunal in that case. The Court wrote that "to combat systemic discrimination, it is essential to create a climate in which both negative practices and negative attitudes can be challenged and discouraged."

Looking at discrimination in this way recognizes that human activities, such as employment and the provision of services, proceed on the basis of assumptions and value judgments about the capacities and needs of individuals. These assumptions often reflect ideas about the place in society of certain individuals because of their personal characteristics. This in turn may be reflected in the way the workplace is ordered, in the terms and conditions of employment, and in decisions about who should be hired and promoted. While some of these assumptions may be accurate, others are harmful, in that they create barriers to the full participation of individuals in the workplace or in access to services.

The idea of systemic discrimination exposed the underlying causes of much discrimination in the workplace. These causes related to the way employers and service providers treated differences between individuals. Differences in the needs and capacities of employees based on their disabilities, their family responsibilities or religions were assumed to be of insufficient importance to be accommodated in the system or were simply overlooked. For example, a workplace designed with the assumption that all employees are able-bodied will create barriers for others. These barriers exist and prevent some people from participating, whether or not the assumption is conscious or whether the effects are intended.

In fact, the idea of systemic discrimination allowed for the next extension of the concept of discrimination which was to question why employment and service systems were based on the assumption that there was such a thing as a "normal" employee or customer. The underlying assumption was that anyone who was not a "normal" employee or consumer was a "special interest" whose needs had to be accommodated based on this normal standard subject to a cost limit. Categorizing an interest as "special" suggests that society has a choice about whether to recognize it or not.

We think the language in the Act should be changed to reflect the fact that, at least as far as the Act extends, there should be no such choice and that these are not "special" interests. It should reflect the idea that everyone should have the same right to participate in the matters covered by the Act. This involves adopting the notion of "substantive equality" which requires an acceptance of the fact that everyone is different and that positive measures may be needed to ensure that some individuals may participate as fully as others. These equalization measures should not be looked on as "special" measures, but rather as simply what it takes to recognize the right of everyone to participate as fully as they can in work and services. The Act should refer to the goal of full participation. The concept of "substantive equality" needs to be actualized in order to permit full participation.

The Remedial Purpose of the Act. The Supreme Court of Canada considered the purpose provision of the Act in *Robichaud v. Canada* (1987). The question at issue was whether the government was responsible for sexual harassment of one of its employees by one of its managers. The Court considered the purpose provision of the Act and the proposition that human rights legislation must be interpreted to give effect to its purposes. That meant that "...the Act (s. 2) seeks "to give effect" to the principle of equal opportunity for individuals by eradicating invidious discrimination" and not by punishing discriminators. The main concern of the Act was removing discrimination and redressing socially undesirable conditions, so motive or intent was not important.

In this case, the Court rejected theories of criminal and fault-based liability. It expanded the liability of employers for actions of employees based on the idea that only employers had the power to change the workplace, rather than on the idea that employers should be responsible only for the actions they authorized employees to do, which would exclude liability for sexual harassment not authorized by employers. This was a new type of statutory liability tailored to the purposes of the Act and made liable the person who could take remedial action to remove undesirable conditions.

The Court also was of the view that the educational function of the Act could also suffer if the employer were not liable for acts of employees.

The *Robichaud* case provides a working basis for some changes to the Act. The employer or service provider has control over the workplace or the way in which services are provided. This forms a secure policy basis for a positive duty to eliminate discrimination in areas within its control. The *Robichaud* case also exemplifies the Court's view that the prime purpose of human rights legislation is remedial. It is also meant to prevent discrimination and to provide education about discrimination.

The *Robichaud* and the *Action Travail des Femmes* cases suggest that our recommendations should, whenever possible, reflect an approach that will remedy systemic discrimination and attach liability to those who can take action to ensure that the principle of equality is advanced in the future.

The Perspective of the Act. The Court considered the purpose clause of the Act to justify the intrusion that section 13 (which makes repeated telecommunicated hate messages a discriminatory practice) made on freedom of expression in *Canadian Human Rights Commission v. Taylor* (1990). In that case, Taylor was found liable for hate messages contrary to section 13 of the Act. Taking into account the purpose provision of the Act, the majority of the Court was of the view that "...messages of hate propaganda undermine the dignity and self-worth of target group members and, more generally, contribute to disharmonious relations among various racial, cultural and religious groups, as a result eroding the tolerance and open-mindedness that must flourish in a multi-cultural society which is committed to the idea of equality."

The majority of the Court thus looked at the prohibition of hate messages from the point of view of those affected. This is an important orientation. This is found now in the current view of the Court about the perspective from which the equality guarantee in the Charter should be viewed. That is, the alleged discriminatory law should be looked at from the point of view of the reasonable person in circumstances similar to that of the claimant, taking into account the relevant contextual factors.

The Need for a Purpose Clause. We are of the view that a purpose provision in the Act is necessary.

The current provision has been sufficient to permit some of the major revolutions in our understanding of discrimination, the basis of liability and the perspective for viewing discrimination. We considered whether the present purpose clause should be changed to reflect developments in the concept of discrimination since 1977. In our view, the purpose provision should set the tone for the Act's approach to ensuring equality without discrimination. At the same time it should not freeze the development of the concepts of equality or discrimination.

The general purpose of the Act must be to ensure the achievement of equality in the way the concept has come to be understood in the evolutionary process described above.

Equal Opportunity. The current purpose provision states that the Act is meant to assist individuals who are able to make "for themselves" the lives they wish and "are able" to have, consistent with their obligations to society. The Act then aims at ensuring equal opportunity without the hindrance or prevention by discrimination based on listed grounds. The concept of having one's needs accommodated as part of the aspirations of individuals was added to section 2 in June 1998 to reflect the addition of a new provision expressly adding the duty to accommodate in section 15 of the Act, rather than as a major shift in the protections of the Act.

The purpose provision serves a strong symbolic function. The term "equal opportunity" may be somewhat outmoded now. However, the concept is still full of promise based on the idea that all individuals have unique abilities and aspirations. The concept has also shown itself capable of supporting an evolving concept of discrimination, from direct to adverse effect/accommodation to systemic discrimination. However, it may not fully express the idea that attainment of equality may require more than simply equal competition for jobs and services in the marketplace. It does not fully encompass the idea that some individuals may need some positive action to ensure that they are equal in participation in employment and services.

Recent Developments in the Concepts of Discrimination and Accommodation. Through amendments to the Act in June of 1998, an employer or employee association wishing to establish that a job requirement came from within the *bona fide* occupational requirement (BFOR) exception of the Act, now has to show that they have attempted to accommodate the individual or class of individuals to the point of undue hardship taking into consideration health, safety and cost. If a BFOR can be established, the Act provides that the requirement is not discriminatory. In other words, as worded now, the BFOR is part of the definition of what constitutes a prohibited discriminatory practice.

We heard at our consultations and read in the submissions that we received from employers they were unhappy with the June, 1998 amendment to the Act that added the duty to accommodate to the point of undue hardship. They were mainly concerned that the amendment limited the factors that can be taken into account in assessing undue hardship to health, safety and cost. They were concerned that such matters as the effect of accommodations on matters covered by a collective agreement, such as seniority or shift preferences, could not be considered in this assessment. They felt they had received guidance from the Tribunal and arbitrators on what the duty to accommodate meant, and that the amendment would require them to re-litigate many issues they felt were resolved.

After the Act was amended to make this change, the approach established by the amendments was also established by the Supreme Court of Canada as the standard *bona fide* occupational requirement analysis in the case of *British Columbia v. British Columbia Government and Service Employees' Union* released in September, 1999. In that case, the question was whether certain physical fitness requirements for the job of forest firefighter were justified as *bona fide* occupational requirements. The Court held that its earlier approach that discrimination had to be categorized either as direct discrimination (where the defence was the *bona fide* occupational requirement) or as adverse effect discrimination (for which the defence was accommodation to the point of undue hardship) was too complex, unrealistic and artificial. Instead, all discrimination in employment must be justified by a *bona fide* occupational requirement that takes into account the duty to accommodate to the point of undue hardship.

One of the reasons for the Court's change of view was its concern that only the adverse effect analysis required a consideration of accommodation. Further, it did not require an examination of the question of whether the employment rule was based on a discriminatory standard, for example, one that was based on a male-only concept of who should normally be doing the job. This allowed systemic discrimination in the workplace to continue insofar as it maintained an employment structure based on under-inclusive ideas about who should be doing the work.

The Court said that the new *bona fide* occupational requirement standard required employers to accommodate as much as reasonably possible the characteristics of individual employees when setting the workplace standard. This would suggest an amendment that would place a positive duty on employers and service providers to eliminate discrimination in the workplace and in the way in which services are provided. The Supreme Court of Canada said: "They must build conceptions of equality into workplace standards." This is also consistent with the duty imposed on employers covered by the *Employment Equity Act* to identify and plan to eliminate barriers to employment for the groups targeted by that Act.

In light of this, we do not wish to re-open the discussion surrounding the June, 1998 amendments to the Act and turn back the clock on the protection provided by these new provisions.

Further, we think the proposed amendment should make clear that this positive duty includes an affirmative duty for employers and service providers to accommodate to the point of undue hardship. This would be consistent with the idea that accommodation of differences is not a defensive, and therefore unusual matter, but is part of the recognition that everyone is different and should be able to participate to their potential. This is also a lesson that we can take from the Supreme Court's recent decision.

Should the Act Protect Only Disadvantaged Groups? The Act now prohibits discrimination on the eleven groups listed in section 3. It does not provide a definition of discrimination, other than to describe discriminatory practices, usually in terms of an adverse differentiation or denial on a prohibited ground. It does not focus its protection only on individuals who have suffered disadvantage based on personal characteristics that have traditionally been connected with disadvantageous treatment resulting in persistent patterns of discrimination.

The Supreme Court of Canada has focused the protection of anti-discrimination provisions in the Charter and human rights legislation on individuals who suffer disadvantage connected to identifiable personal characteristics. Though the Court has not said that only members of disadvantaged groups can make use of the Charter equality protections, it has stated that that the social reality is such that they will be less likely than members of advantaged groups to have difficulty in demonstrating discrimination (*Nancy Law v. Canada* [1999]). Though we did hear submissions that it be made clear that the Act was meant to help only disadvantaged groups, this might fall short of the Court's view that there may be cases where others could make a discrimination claim.

Thus, the Act could focus on ensuring equality for all rather than restricting the protection of the Act to disadvantaged groups. However, we are of the view, in accord with the current state of the law in Canada, that the idea of equality in the Act encompasses positive measures to remedy inequality and the need to take account of disadvantage.

A Definition of Discrimination? The Act now prohibits certain defined discriminatory practices. A typical example is section 7, which prohibits refusals to employ or to continue to employ, or adverse differentiation in the course of employment based on the listed grounds.

Other human rights Acts define discrimination. For example, Manitoba defines it to mean differential treatment on the basis of being an actual or presumed member of a group defined by a listed personal characteristic rather than personal merit, or being associated with such a person, or differential treatment simply on the basis of a listed personal characteristic or the refusal of reasonable accommodation based on a listed characteristic.

In essence, the Supreme Court of Canada has generally interpreted the human rights Acts as having the same purposes and prohibitions despite variations in wording and has, in fact, said that discrimination has the same meaning as under the Charter. This has not resulted in a conservative interpretation of the Acts. Rather, all the human rights Acts and the Charter share the broad, liberal interpretation the courts have provided. We can perhaps conclude that little turns on the definition of discrimination in the Act. Our main concern must be to not restrict its future development.

Though a definition of discrimination serves an educational function, a more elaborate definition might cause as much confusion as it avoided. Further, a definition could freeze the concept so that it would not develop in the future.

Create a Duty to Ensure Equality Without Discrimination. While it may not be a good idea to define discrimination, it is time to cast the language of the Act in a more positive way, to create a duty on the part of employers and service providers to promote equality and eliminate discrimination in much the same way that the *Canada Labour Code* creates a general duty for employers to ensure the protection of the safety and health of its employees at work (s. 124).

The Act could provide for a similar duty for employers and service providers under the Act to ensure equality without discrimination for their employees and consumers, and recognize that accommodation is needed to ensure that all may participate. Such an approach would be much more consistent with the broad purposes of the Act than simple prohibitions of discrimination. It would also be consistent with an approach that is much more proactive in eliminating systemic discrimination, one that would provide detail for the employer and service provider's duty through statutory requirements and guidelines and best practices codes.

This change in the language of the Act should not change the meaning of discrimination. Rather, it should signal a change in the approach to attain the purpose of the Act.

Referring to Canada's International Equality Obligations in a Premable. The current Act grew out of the concerns of the international community since the Second World War about the elimination of discrimination. It does not expressly state the connection between the Act and Canada's international obligations.

Canada has bound itself to a considerable number of international equality obligations. Some provincial and territorial human rights legislation refer in their preambles to the *Universal Declaration of Human Rights* and some generally to other international obligations.

We think it would be appropriate to make this connection in a preamble to the Act. The preamble of human rights legislation has been used to determine the purpose of such legislation. For example, in *O'Malley v. Simpsons-Sears* (1985), the Supreme Court of Canada described the fundamental nature of human rights legislation. The Court used the preamble to the Alberta human rights legislation for the same purpose in *Vriend v. Alberta* (1998), when it ordered that Alberta human rights legislation must be treated as though it prohibited discrimination on the ground of sexual orientation, because failing this, the law was in breach of the Charter. It is important that this general link be made with the international tradition from which our domestic human rights is developed.

We think that both a preamble and a purpose clause are useful. The preamble could identify the broad aims of the Act, including the relevance of Canada's commitment to achieve equality. The purpose section could identify more precisely the principles underlying the Act.

Recommendations:

1. We recommend that the Act have a preamble referring to the various international agreements that Canada has entered into that refer to equality and discrimination.
2. We recommend that the Act contain a purpose clause in conformity with the principle of the advancement of equality of all in Canada and the elimination of all forms of dis-

crimination, including systemic discrimination, taking into account patterns of disadvantage in our society.

3. We recommend that the language of the Act be premised on a duty of employers and service providers to ensure equality without discrimination in the workplace and in the provision of services. We recommend that the duty to ensure equality include a duty to provide accommodation to the point of undue hardship.

RACE AND CRIME

Toronto Star, October 20, 2002

Black drivers confronted by the flashing lights of a police cruiser often worry if they're being pulled over for the colour of their skin.

Officers deny that happens. Now, for the first time, empirical evidence suggests police have indeed been targeting black drivers in Toronto.

Police traffic offence data, obtained and analyzed by The Star, shows a disproportionate number of blacks ticketed for violations that routinely surface only after a stop has been made.

These "out-of-sight" traffic offences include failing to update a driver's licence with a change of address, driving without a licence, driving without insurance, or driving while under suspension. Police usually discover such violations only after a motorist has been pulled over. And, in the absence of any other charge, it isn't clear why drivers involved in these offences were stopped in the first place.

It's assumed random checks would generate a pattern of charges that mimics the racial distribution of drivers in society as a whole. So the rate at which minority drivers are charged is often used, in the U.S., as a bellwether for racial profiling.

Canadian authorities refrain from studying the issue. Toronto's police services board has ordered its officers not to analyze raw race-based crime data, arguing racists might use the resulting statistics to stigmatize ethnic communities.

Police follow that rule, and don't record race statistics for the purpose of ethnic analysis. They do, however, list skin colour in most arrest reports when describing a person charged. It's routine in arrests for major crimes, while a record of skin colour occurs less often for simple traffic offences.

The Star, through a freedom of information request, obtained a police database listing all Toronto arrests and charges dating back to 1996. An analysis of more than 7,500 out-of-sight violations found that skin colour was listed in about two-thirds of cases where drivers were ticketed with only this type of offence. And black drivers were carrying a heavy load of charges.

Almost 34 per cent of all drivers charged with out-of-sight violations were black, in the group where race was listed. Yet, according to the latest census figures, Toronto's black community represents just 8.1 per cent of the city's population. By contrast, 62.7 per cent of Toronto's population is white, but whites account for 52.1 per cent of motorists charged with out-of-sight traffic offences.

From "Police target black drivers; Star analysis of traffic data suggests racial profiling," *Toronto Star, October 20, 2002. Reprinted with permission.*

Black men, between 25 and 34 years of age, seem to warrant special attention. They were issued 39.3 per cent of tickets for out-of-sight violations in that age group. Yet, they represented 7.9 per cent of Toronto's population in that age category.

Chief Julian Fantino disputed The Star's findings in an interview Friday. He questioned that his officers record racial data when charging drivers with traffic violations. And he vehemently opposed any suggestion officers use racial profiling in deciding whom they'll pull over.

"We do not do racial profiling. We do not deal with people on the basis of their ethnicity, their race, or any other factor. We deal with people in situations for what it is that we're mandated to do. We're not perfect people but you're barking up the wrong tree," Fantino said.

Susan Eng, a Toronto lawyer and former head of the Toronto Police Services Board, opposes keeping race-based arrest statistics. But she supports tracking the skin colour of everyone subjected to a traffic stop by police.

"Remember, the person being measured (wouldn't be) the person of colour, but the person dealing with the person of colour," said Eng, a past director of Urban Alliance on Race Relations. "We're measuring discrimination and racism. We're not dealing with behaviour by certain racial groups."

North York's race relations committee recently recommended police do exactly what Eng suggests — document race, age, and other personal details about everyone pulled over, along with justification for the stop.

That request, made to Fantino and the police services board, has so far gone unheeded. Racial profiling — targeting specific groups — is a common practice and has been devastating to the black community, says Margaret Parsons, executive director of the African Canadian Legal Clinic. Young blacks, especially, feel stigmatized and are left with a deep-rooted fear and mistrust of police.

"I don't think if you ask any African Canadian or African American ... they won't have a story," Parsons said. "It's humiliating, and it's frightening, to have a police car come up in the middle of the night with lights blazing."

Grace-Edward Galabuzi said he had been pulled over by police several times in his youth, for no evident reason, and questioned for up to 30 minutes.

"It's sadly inevitable for young black men," lamented the 40-year-old community activist and researcher at the Centre for Social Justice. One stop was particularly ironic. He was pulled over driving from Pearson International Airport, in an upscale Audi 4000, having just flown home from an Ottawa conference on police harassment. The officer refused to give Galabuzi a reason for the stop, arguing that "security reasons" prevented him from explaining his actions. Galabuzi, then 29, complained to the officer about this "humiliating" scrutiny but was warned not to cause trouble. Heeding that caution, he stopped protesting and was allowed to go on his way.

Undue attention from police underlines the black community's own perceptions of racism, said Scot Wortley, professor of criminology at the University of Toronto.

"The community does experience this as racist. The community does experience this as intrusive. It does experience it as evidence that Canadian society is not fair."

Wortley's 1997 study, called "The Usual Suspects: Race, Police Stops and Perceptions of Criminal Justice," is among the most detailed work on racial profiling done in Canada. Almost 1,300 people in Toronto — randomly selected whites, blacks, and Chinese — were asked about their contacts with police. About 28 per cent of blacks reported being stopped at least once in a two-year period, compared to 14.6 per cent of whites, and 18.2 per cent of Chinese contacted for the study.

In other research, Wortley and U of T colleague Julian Tanner asked more than 3,000 Toronto high school students about their experiences with police.

More than half of the 474 black students participating in the study reported being stopped by police two or more times over a two-year period. Almost 1,300 white students were interviewed, but only 22.7 per cent said they were stopped by police over the same time.

Tanner and Wortley concluded "racial profiling directly contributes to the over-representation of black people in the criminal justice system."

To illustrate, Wortley suggests picturing two groups, one black and one white, of equal size — perhaps 1,000 people. Then consider that in each of those groups the rate of drug dealing is precisely the same: 1 in 10 people deal crack, a total of 100 in each group.

If authorities were policing these groups identically, with race playing absolutely no role, the number of dealers arrested from each group should always be the same.

When races are profiled, however, police assume blacks are more likely to be dealing drugs, and stop more black people. Because of the extra attention, police would naturally find more black law-breakers. If the ratio of stops was 5:1, black to white, the police would charge 50 black dealers for every 10 white dealers.

"What the statistics don't show is that 90 per cent of the white drug dealers got away," said Wortley, "and that half the black dealers got away." Still, at the end of the year, police statistics would "prove" drug-dealing is centred in the black community. Which, of course, would justify continued profiling. "It can be a self-fulfilling prophecy," he said. Seek, and you shall find.

The higher proportion of blacks charged also affects attitudes, Wortley said. Black men who have experienced profiling, perceived or real, are less inclined to be polite. Faced with that attitude, an officer would be more inclined to lay a charge, he said. "Although you'll always get the police saying, 'this is not true,' the pieces of the puzzle, in all the data, point in one direction ... racism in the justice system." Toronto police deny using racial profiling but many blacks are convinced of it.

More than a dozen young black Torontonians shared their experiences with Star reporters. All but a few asked that their names not be published, for fear of reprisal.

"When I'm driving with my brother, and he sees a cop in the rearview mirror, he's shook," said one 17-year-old. "But when I'm with a white friend, and he sees a cop in the rearview mirror, he's still chillin'."

"I've had so many experiences with police," said a 25-year-old professional, "that I just immediately become aware when they're around and make sure I'm driving carefully and going the limit."

An 18-year-old student said he wasn't intimidated by police. "When I see a cop I keep walking, but if I see him coming at me I just stand right in his way. I'm not trying to be an activist, but I know I don't have a criminal record, so if they're staring at me, I'm staring at them.

"What do I have that they want? I didn't do the streets no harm. I didn't cause them no trouble. So what did I do? I try not to let them make me scared."

Police should record racial information about the people they stop and search, says Osgoode Hall law professor David Tanovich.

"Frankly, I wish they did keep the statistics — to confirm who is stopped so we can see, and actually have evidence, of whether there are disproportionate stops."

Marie Chen, a lawyer with the African Canadian Legal Clinic, said racial profiling is particularly insidious in Canada because, unlike in the United States, authorities here refuse to acknowledge it. "Police will deny that they have a policy of profiling," said Chen. "But when you talk to police officers, they'll tell you they know it's happening."

There is little recourse for victims of profiling, Chen said. Ontario's Progressive Conservative government shut down the independent Public Complaints Commission in 1997, forcing people alleging misconduct by officers to file grievances directly with police.

"The complaints system is toothless," Chen said.

Despite its flaws, using the complaints system is still better than trying to take on police in a confrontational way, warns Bromley Armstrong, a Jamaican-born Canadian who has served on numerous race committees over the past five decades. "They say the older you get, the wiser you get. My philosophy is that if you are doing nothing wrong, then you don't have to get into a shouting match with police," said Armstrong.

When young blacks argue with police, after being stopped, it usually ends badly for them, with charges laid and legal bills to face, he said. But if enough black people file complaints about racial profiling, senior police commanders may get the message and finally do something about it, Armstrong said.

WHITE PRIVILEGE AND MALE PRIVILEGE: A PERSONAL ACCOUNT OF COMING TO SEE CORRESPONDENCES THROUGH WORK IN WOMEN'S STUDIES

Peggy McIntosh

Through work to bring materials and perspectives from Women's Studies into the rest of the curriculum, I have often noticed men's unwillingness to grant that they are over-privileged in the curriculum, even though they may grant that women are disadvantaged. Denials which amount to taboos surround the subject of advantages which men gain from women's disadvantages. These denials protect male privilege from being fully recognized, acknowledged, lessened, or ended.

Thinking through unacknowledged male privilege as a phenomenon with a life of its own, I realized that since hierarchies in our society are interlocking, there was most likely a phenomenon of white privilege which was similarly denied and protected, but alive and real in its effects. As a white person, I realized I had been taught about racism as something which puts others at a disadvantage, but had been taught not to see one of its corollary aspects, white privilege, which puts me at an advantage.

I think whites are carefully taught not to recognize white privilege, as males are taught not to recognize male privilege. So I have begun in an untutored way to ask what it is like to have white privilege. This paper is a partial record of my personal observations, and not a scholarly analysis. It is based on my daily experiences within my particular circumstances.

I have come to see white privilege as an invisible package of unearned assets which I can count on cashing in each day, but about which I was "meant" to remain oblivious. White privilege is like an invisible weightless knapsack of special provisions, assurances, tools, maps, guides, codebooks, passports, visas, clothes, compass, emergency gear, and blank checks.

Since I have had trouble facing white privilege, and describing its results in my life, I saw parallels here with men's reluctance to acknowledge male privilege. Only rarely will a man go beyond acknowledging that women are disadvantaged to acknowledging that men have unearned advantage, or that unearned privilege has not been good for men's development as human beings, or for society's development, or that privilege systems might ever be challenged and *changed*.

I will review here several types or layers of denial which I see at work protecting, and preventing awareness about, entrenched male privilege. Then I will draw parallels, from my own experience, with the denials which veil the facts of white privilege. Finally, I will list 46 ordinary and daily ways in which I experience having white privilege, within my life situation and its particular social and political frameworks.

Writing this paper has been difficult, despite warm receptions for the talks on which it is based.[1] For describing white privilege makes one newly accountable. As we in Women's Studies work reveal male privilege and ask men to give up some of their power, so one who writes about having white privilege must ask, "Having described it, what will I do to lessen or end it?"

The denial of men's overprivileged state takes many forms in discussions of curriculum change work. Some claim that men must be central in the curriculum becauses they have done most of what is important or distinctive in life or in civilization. Some recognize sexism in the curriculum but deny that it makes male students seem unduly important in life. Others agree certain *individual* thinkers are blindly male-oriented but deny that there is any systemic tendency in disciplinary frameworks or epistemology to over-empower men as a group. Those men who do grant that male privilege takes institutionalized and embedded forms are still likely to deny that male hegemony has opened doors for them personally. Virtually all men deny that male overreward alone can explain men's centrality in all the inner sanctums of our most powerful institutions. Moreover, those few who will acknowledge that male privilege systems have over-empowered them usually end up doubting that we could dismantle these privilege systems. They may say they will work to improve women's status, in the society or in the university, but they can't or won't support the idea of lessening men's. In curricular terms, this is the point at which they say that they regret they cannot use any of the interesting new scholarship on women because the syllabus is full. When the talk turns to giving men less cultural room, even the most thoughtful and fair-minded of the men I know well tend to reflect, or fall back on, conservative assumptions about the inevitability of present gender relations and distributions of power, calling on precedent or sociobiology and psychobiology to demonstrate that male domination is natural and follows inevitably from evolutionary pressures. Others resort to arguments from "experience" or religion or social responsibility or wishing and dreaming.

After I realized, through faculty development work in Women's Studies, the extent to which men work from a base of unacknowledged privilege, I understood that much of their oppressiveness was unconscious. Then I remembered the frequent charges from women of color that white women whom they encounter are oppressive. I began to understand why we are justly seen as oppressive, even when we don't see ourselves that way. At the very least, obliviousness of one's privileged state can make a person or group irritating to be with. I began to count the ways in which I enjoy unearned skin privilege and have been conditioned into oblivion about its existence, unable to see that it put me "ahead" in any way, or put my people ahead, overrewarding us and yet also paradoxically damaging us, or that it could or should be changed.

My schooling gave me no training in seeing myself as an oppressor, as an unfairly advantaged person, or as a participant in a damaged culture. I was taught to see myself as an individual whose moral state depended on her individual moral will. At school, we were not taught about slavery in any depth; we were not taught to see slaveholders as damaged people. Slaves were seen as the only group at risk of being dehumanized. My schooling followed the pattern which Elizabeth Minnich has pointed out: whites are taught to think of their lives as morally neutral, normative, and average, and also ideal, so that when we work to benefit others, this is seen as work that will allow "them" to be more like "us." I think many of us know how obnoxious this is attitude can be in men.

After frustration with men who would not recognize male privilege, I decided to try to work on myself at least by identifying some of the daily effects of white privilege in my life. It is crude work, at this stage, but I will give here a list of special circumstances and conditions I experience which I did not earn but which I have been made to feel are mine by birth, by citizenship, and by virtue of being a conscientious law-abiding "normal" person of goodwill. I have chosen those conditions which I think in my case *attach somewhat more to skin-color privilege* than to class, religion, ethnic status, or geographic location, though of course all these other factors are intricately intertwined. As far as I can see, my Afro-American co-workers, friends, and acquaintances with whom I come into daily or frequent contact in this particular time, place, and line of work cannot count on most of these conditions.

1. I can if I wish arrange to be in the company of people of my race most of the time.
2. I can avoid spending time with people whom I was trained to mistrust and who have learned to mistrust my kind or me.
3. If I should need to move, I can be pretty sure of renting or purchasing housing in an area which I can afford and in which I would want to live.
4. I can be pretty sure that my neighbors in such a location will be neutral or pleasant to me.
5. I can go shopping alone most of the time, pretty well assured that I will not be followed or harassed.
6. I can turn on the television or open to the front page of the paper and see people of my race widely represented.
7. When I am told about our national heritage or about "civilization," I am shown that people of my color made it what it is.
8. I can be sure that my children will be given curricular materials that testify to the existence of their race.
9. If I want to, I can be pretty sure of finding a publisher for this piece on white privilege.
10. I can be pretty sure of having my voice heard in a group in which I am the only member of my race.
11. I can be casual about whether or not to listen to another woman's voice in a group in which she is the only member of her race.
12. I can go into a music shop and count on finding the music of my race represented, into a supermarket and find the staple foods which fit with my cultural traditions, into a hairdresser's shop and find someone who can cut my hair.
13. Whether I use checks, credit cards, or cash, I can count on my skin color not to work against the appearance of financial reliability.
14. I can arrange to protect my children most of the time from people who might not like them.

15. I do not have to educate my children to be aware of systemic racism for their own daily physical protection.

16. I can be pretty sure that my children's teachers and employers will tolerate them if they fit school and workplace norms; my chief worries about them do not concern others' attitudes toward their race.

17. I can talk with my mouth full and not have people put this down to my color.

18. I can swear, or dress in second hand clothes, or not answer letters, without having people attribute these choices to the bad morals, the poverty, or the illiteracy of my race.

19. I can speak in public to a powerful male group without putting my race on trial.

20. I can do well in a challenging situation without being called a credit to my race.

21. I am never asked to speak for all the people of my racial group.

22. I can remain oblivious of the language and customs of persons of color who constitute the world's majority without feeling in my culture any penalty for such oblivion.

23. I can criticize our government and talk about how much I fear its policies and behavior without being seen as a cultural outsider.

24. I can be pretty sure that if I ask to talk to "the person in charge," I will be facing a person of my race.

25. If a traffic cop pulls me over or if the IRS audits my tax return, I can be sure I haven't been singled out because of my race.

26. I can easily buy posters, post-cards, picture books, greeting cards, dolls, toys, and children's magazines featuring people of my race.

27. I can go home from most meetings of organizations I belong to feeling somewhat tied in, rather than isolated, out-of-place, outnumbered, unheard, held at a distance, or feared.

28. I can be pretty sure that an argument with a colleague of another race is more likely to jeopardize her chances for advancement than to jeopardize mine.

29. I can be pretty sure that if I argue for the promotion of a person of another race, or a program centering on race, this is not likely to cost me heavily within my present setting, even if my colleagues disagree with me.

30. If I declare there is a racial issue at hand, or there isn't a racial issue at hand, my race will lend me more credibility for either position than a person of color will have.

31. I can choose to ignore developments in minority writing and minority activist programs, or disparage them, or learn from them, but in any case, I can find ways to be more or less protected from negative consequences of any of these choices.

32. My culture gives me little fear about ignoring the perspectives and powers of people of other races.

33. I am not made acutely aware that my shape, bearing, or body odor will be taken as a reflection on my race.

34. I can worry about racism without being seen as self-interested or self-seeking.

35. I can take a job with an affirmative action employer without having my co-workers on the job suspect that I got it because of my race.

36. If my day, week, or year is going badly, I need not ask of each negative episode or situation whether it has racial overtones.

37. I can be pretty sure of finding people who would be willing to talk with me and advise me about my next steps, professionally.

38. I can think over many options, social, political, imaginative, or professional, without asking whether a person of my race would be accepted or allowed to do what I want to do.

39. I can be late to a meeting without having the lateness reflect on my race.
40. I can choose public accommodation without fearing that people of my race cannot get in or will be mistreated in the places I have chosen.
41. I can be sure that if I need legal or medical help, my race will not work against me.
42. I can arrange my activities so that I will never have to experience feelings of rejection owing to my race.
43. If I have low credibility as a leader, I can be sure that my race is not the problem.
44. I can easily find academic courses and institutions which give attention only to people of my race.
45. I can expect figurative language and imagery in all of the arts to testify to experiences of my race.
46. I can choose blemish cover or bandages in "flesh" color and have them more or less match my skin.

I repeatedly forgot each of the realizations on this list until I wrote it down. For me, white privilege has turned out to be an elusive and fugitive subject. The pressure to avoid it is great, for in facing it I must give up the myth of meritocracy. If these things are true, this is not such a free country; one's life is not what one makes it; many doors open for certain people through no virtues of their own. These perceptions mean also that my moral condition is not what I had been led to believe. The appearance of being a good citizen rather than a troublemaker comes in large part from having all sorts of doors open automatically because of my color.

A further paralysis of nerve comes from literary silence protecting privilege. My clearest memories of finding such analysis are in Lillian Smith's unparalleled *Killers of the Dream* and Margaret Andersen's review of Karen and Mamie Fields' *Lemon Swamp*. Smith, for example, wrote about walking toward black children on the street and knowing they would step into the gutter; Andersen contrasted the pleasure which she, as a white child, took on summer driving trips to the south with Karen Fields' memories of driving in a closed car stocked with all necessities lest, in stopping, her black family should suffer "insult, or worse." Adrienne Rich also recognizes and writes about daily experiences of privilege, but in my observation, white women's writing in this area is far more often on systemic racism than on our daily lives as light-skinned women.[2]

In unpacking this invisible knapsack of white privilege, I have listed conditions of daily experience which I once took for granted, as neutral, normal, and universally available to everybody, just as I once thought of a male-focused curriculum as the neutral or accurate account which can speak for all. Nor did I think of any of these perquisites as bad for the holder. I now think that we need a more finely differentiated taxonomy of privilege, for some of these varieties are only what one would want for everyone in a just society, and others give license to be ignorant, oblivious, arrogant, and destructive. Before proposing some more finely tuned categorization, I will make some observations about the general effects of these conditions on my life and expectations.

In this potpourri of examples, some privileges make me feel at home in the world. Others allow me to escape penalties or dangers which others suffer. Through some, I escape fear, anxiety, or a sense of not being welcome or not being real. Some keep me from having to hide, to be in disguise, to feel sick or crazy, to negotiate each transaction from the position of being an outsider or, within my group, a person who is suspected of having too close links with a dominant culture. Most keep me from having to be angry.

I see a pattern running through the matrix of white privilege, a pattern of assumptions which were passed on to me as a white person. There was one main piece of cultural turf; it was my own turf, and I was among those who could control the turf. I could measure up to the cultural standards and take advantage of the many options I saw around me to make what the culture would call a success of my life. *My skin color was an asset for any move I was educated to want to make.* I could think of myself as "belonging" in major ways, and of making social systems work for me. I could freely disparage, fear, neglect, or be oblivious to anything outside of the dominant cultural forms. Being of the main culture, I could also criticize it fairly freely. My life was reflected back to me frequently enough so that I felt, with regard to my race, if not to my sex, like one of the real people.

Whether through the curriculum or in the newspaper, the television, the economic system, or the general look of people in the streets, we received daily signals and indications that my people counted, and that others *either didn't exist or must be trying, not very successfully, to be like people of my race.* We were given cultural permission not to hear voices of people of other races, or a tepid cultural tolerance for hearing or acting on such voices. I was also raised not to suffer seriously from anything which darker-skinned people might say about my group, "protected," though perhaps I should more accurately say *prohibited,* through the habits of my economic class and social group, from living in racially mixed groups or being reflective about interactions between people of differing races.

In proportion as my racial group was being made confident, comfortable, and oblivious, other groups were likely being made unconfident, uncomfortable, and alienated. Whiteness protected me from many kinds of hostility, distress, and violence, which I was being subtly trained to visit in turn upon people of color.

For this reason, the word "privilege" now seems to me misleading. Its connotations are too positive to fit the conditions and behaviors which "privilege systems" produce. We usually think of privilege as being a favored state, whether earned, or conferred by birth or luck. School graduates are reminded they are privileged and urged to use their (enviable) assets well. The word "privilege" carries the connotation of being something everyone must want. Yet some of the conditions I have described here work to systemically overempower certain groups. Such privilege simply *confers dominance,* gives permission to control, because of one's race or sex. The kind of privilege which gives license to some people to be, at best, thoughtless and, at worst, murderous should not continue to be referred to as a desirable attribute. Such "privilege" may be widely desired without being in any way beneficial to the whole society.

Moreover, though "privilege" may confer power, it does not confer moral strength. Those who do not depend on conferred dominance have traits and qualities that may never develop in those who do. Just as Women's Studies courses indicate that women survive their political circumstances to lead lives which hold the human race together, so "under-privileged" people of color who are the world's majority have survived their oppression and lived survivors' lives from which the white global minority can and must learn. In some groups, those dominated have actually become strong through *not* having all of these unearned advantages, and this gives them a great deal to teach the others. Members of so-called privileged groups can seem foolish, ridiculous, infantile or dangerous by contrast.

I want, then, to distinguish between earned strength and unearned power conferred systemically. Power from unearned privilege can look like strength when it is in fact permission to escape or to dominate. But not all of the privileges on my list are inevitably damaging. Some, like the expectation that neighbors will be decent to you, or that your race will not count against you in court, should be the norm in a just society and should be considered as the entitlement of everyone. Others, like the privilege not to listen to less powerful people, distort the humanity of the holders as well as the ignored groups. Still others, like finding one's staple foods everywhere, may be a function of being a member of a numerical majority in the population. Others have to do with not having to labor under pervasive negative stereotyping and mythology.

We might at least start by distinguishing between positive advantages which we can work to spread, to the point where they are not advantages at all but simply part of the normal civic and social fabric, and negative types of advantage which unless rejected will always reinforce our present hierarchies. For example, the positive "privilege" of belonging, the feeling that one belongs within the human circle, as Native Americans say, fosters development and should not be seen as privilege for a few. It is, let us say, an entitlement which none of us should have to earn; ideally it is an *unearned entitlement*. At present, since only a few have it, it is an *unearned advantage* for them. The negative "privilege" which gave me cultural permission not to take darker-skinned Others seriously can be seen as arbitrarily conferred dominance and should not be desirable for anyone. This paper results from a process of coming to see that some of the power which I originally saw as attendant on being a human being in the U.S. consisted in *unearned advantage* and *confirmed dominance,* as well as other kinds of special circumstance not universally taken for granted.

In writing this paper I have also realized that white identity and status (as well as class identity and status) give me considerable power to choose whether to broach this subject and its trouble. I can pretty well decide whether to disappear and avoid and not listen and escape the dislike I may engender in other people through this essay, or interrupt, take over, dominate, preach, direct, criticize, or control to some extent what goes on in reaction to it. Being white, I am given considerable power to escape many kinds of danger or penalty as well as to choose which risks I want to take.

There is an analogy here, once again, with Women's Studies. Our male colleagues do not have a great deal to lose in supporting Women's Studies, but they do not have a great deal to lose if they oppose it either. They simply have the power to decide whether to commit themselves to more equitable distributions of power. They will probably feel few penalties whatever choice they make; they do not seem, in any obvious short-term sense, the ones at risk, though they and we are all at risk because of the behaviors which have been rewarded in them.

Through Women's Studies work I have met very few men who are truly distressed about systemic, unearned male advantage and conferred dominance. And so one question for me and others like me is whether we will be like them, or whether we will get truly distressed, even outraged, about unearned race advantage and conferred dominance and if so, what we will do to lessen them. In any case, we need to do more work in identifying how they actually affect our daily lives. We need more down-to-earth writing by people about these taboo subjects. We need more understanding of the ways in which white "privilege" damages white people, for these are not the same ways in which it damages the victimized. Skewed white psyches are an inseparable part of the picture, though I do not want to confuse the kinds of damage done to the holders of special assets and to those who suffer the deficits. Many, perhaps most, of our white students in the U.S. think that racism doesn't affect them because they are not people of color; they do not see "whiteness" as a racial identity. Many men likewise think that Women's Studies does not bear on their own existences because they are not female; they do not see themselves as having gendered identities. Insisting on the universal *effects* of "privilege" systems, then, becomes one of our chief tasks, and being more explicit about the *particular* effects in particular contexts is another. Men need to join us in this work.

In addition, since race and sex are not the only advantaging systems at work, we need to similarly examine the daily experience of having age advantage, or ethnic advantage, or physical ability, or advantage related to nationality, religion, or sexual orientation. Prof. Marnie Evans suggested to me that in many ways the list I made also applies directly to heterosexual privilege. This is a still more taboo subject than race privilege: the daily ways in which heterosexual privilege makes married persons comfortable or powerful, providing supports, assets, approvals, and rewards to those who live or expect to live in heterosexual pairs. Unpacking that content is still more difficult, owing to the deeper imbeddedness of heterosexual advantage and dominance, and stricter taboos surrounding these.

But to start such an analysis I would put this observation from my own experience: The fact that I live under the same roof with a man triggers all kinds of societal assumptions about my worth, politics, life, and values, and triggers a host of unearned advantages and powers. After recasting many elements from the original list I would add further observations like these:

1. My children do not have to answer questions about why I live with my partner (my husband).
2. I have no difficulty finding neighborhoods where people approve of our household.
3. My children are given texts and classes which implicitly support our kind of family unit, and do not turn them against my choice of domestic partnership.
4. I can travel alone or with my husband without expecting embarrassment or hostility in those who deal with us.
5. Most people I meet will see my marital arrangements as an asset to my life or as a favorable comment on my likability, my competence, or my mental health.
6. I can talk about the social events of a weekend without fearing most listeners' reactions.
7. I will feel welcomed and "normal" in the usual walks of public life, institutional and social.
8. In many contexts, I am seen as "all right" in daily work on women because I do not live chiefly with women.

Difficulties and dangers surrounding the task of finding parallels are many. Since racism, sexism, and heterosexism are not the same, the advantaging associated with them should not be seen as the same. In addition, it is hard to disentangle aspects of unearned advantage which rest more on social class, economic class, race, religion, region, sex, and ethnic identity than on other factors. Still, all of the oppressions are interlocking, as the Combahee River Collective statement of 1977 continues to remind us eloquently.[3]

One factor seems clear about all of the interlocking oppressions. They take both active forms which we can see and embedded forms which as a member of the dominant group one is taught not to see. In my class and place, I did not see myself as racist because I was taught to recognize racism only in individual acts of meanness by members of my group, never in invisible systems conferring unsought racial dominance on my group from birth. Likewise, we are taught to think that sexism or heterosexism is carried on only through individual acts of discrimination, meanness, or cruelty toward women, gays, and lesbians, rather than in invisible systems conferring unsought dominance on certain groups. Disapproving of the systems won't be enough to change them. I was taught to think that racism could end if white individuals changed their attitudes; many men think sexism can be ended by individual changes in daily behavior toward women. But a man's sex provides advantage for him whether or not he approves of the way in which dominance has been conferred on his group. A "white" skin in the United States opens many doors for whites whether or not we approve of the way dominance has been conferred on us. Individual acts can palliate, but cannot end, these problems. To redesign social systems we need first to acknowledge their colossal unseen dimensions. The silences and denials surrounding privilege are the key political tool here. They keep the thinking about equality or equity incomplete, protecting unearned advantage and conferred dominance by making these taboo subjects. Most talk by whites about equal opportunity seems to me now to be about equal opportunity to try to get into a position of dominance while denying that *systems* of dominance exist.

It seems to me that obliviousness about white advantage, like obliviousness about male advantage, is kept strongly inculturated in the United States so as to maintain the myth of meritocracy, the myth that democratic choice is equally available to all. Keeping most people unaware that freedom of confident action is there for just a small number of people props up those in power, and serves to keep power in the hands of the same groups that have most of it already. Though systemic change takes many decades, there are pressing questions for me and I imagine for some others like me if we raise our daily consciousness on the perquisites of being lightskinned. What will we do with such knowledge? As we know from watching men, it is an open question whether we will choose to use unearned advantage to weaken hidden systems of advantage, and whether we will use any of our arbitrarily-awarded power to try to reconstruct power systems on a broader base.

I have appreciated commentary on this paper from the Working Papers Committee of the Wellesley College Center for Research on Women, from members of the Dodge seminar, and from many individuals, including Margaret Andersen, Sorel Berman, Joanne Braxton, Johnnella Butler, Sandra Dickerson, Marnie Evans, Beverly Guy-Sheftall, Sandra Harding, Eleanor Hinton Hoytt, Pauline Houston, Paul Lauter, Joyce Miller, Mary Norris, Gloria Oden, Beverly Smith, and John Walter.

NOTES

1. This paper was presented at the Virginia Women's Studies Association conference in Richmond in April, 1986, and the American Educational Research Association conference in Boston in October, 1986, and discussed with two groups of participants in the Dodge seminars for Secondary School Teachers in New York and Boston in the spring of 1987.
2. Andersen, Margaret, "Race and the Social Science Curriculum: A Teaching and Learning Discussion." *Radical Teacher,* November, 1984, pp. 17-20. Smith, Lillian, *Killers of the Dream,* New York, 1949.
3. "A Black Feminist Statement," The Combahee River Collective, pp. 13–22 in Hull, Scott, Smith, eds., *All the Women Are White, All the Blacks Are Men, But Some of Us Are Brave: Black Women's Studies.* The Feminist Press, 1982.

QUESTIONS

1. Peggy McIntosh provides a list of circumstances and conditions of being white, ones which she takes to be so merely by "virtue of being a conscientious law-abiding 'normal' person of good will." What does she mean by this? What is the purpose of the list?
2. Select four items from the list and ask yourself if these reflect your own experiences or ones you take to be the experiences of white people. Can this exercise inform one about the nature of racism? In what ways is this exercise useful for explaining the phenomenon of racial profiling as described in the previous reading from *The Toronto Star*?
3. In what ways might McIntosh's delineation of white privilege challenge an account of formal equality as an individual's freedom to pursue life goals and projects without interference from the state?
4. Do you think that McIntosh's account of white privilege has implications for policies with respect to racism?
5. McIntosh draws parallels between white, male, and heterosexual privilege. What are some of the similarities? What are some of the differences?

SEXISM

Marilyn Frye

The first philosophical project I undertook as a feminist was that of trying to say carefully and persuasively what sexism is, and what it is for someone, some institution or some act to be sexist. This project was pressed on me with considerable urgency because, like most women coming to a feminist perception of themselves and the world, I was seeing sexism everywhere and trying to make it perceptible to others. I would point out, complain and criticize, but most frequently my friends and colleagues would not see that what I declared to be sexist was sexist, or at all objectionable.

As the critic and as the initiator of the topic, I was the one on whom the burden of proof fell — it was I who had to explain and convince. Teaching philosophy had already taught me that people cannot be persuaded of things they are not ready to be persuaded of; there are certain complexes of will and prior experience which will inevitably block persuasion, no matter the merits of the case presented. I knew that even if I could explain fully and clearly what I was saying when I called something sexist, I would not necessarily be able to convince various others of the correctness of this claim. But what troubled me enormously was that I could not explain it in any way which satisfied me. It is this sort of moral and intellectual frustration which, in my case at least, always generates philosophy.

The following was the product of my first attempt to state clearly and explicitly what sexism is:

> The term 'sexist' in its core and perhaps most fundamental meaning is a term which characterizes anything whatever which creates, constitutes, promotes or exploits any irrelevant or impertinent marking of the distinction between the sexes.[1]

When I composed this statement, I was thinking of the myriads of instances in which persons of the two sexes are treated differently, or behave differently, but where nothing in the real differences between females and males justifies or explains the difference of treatment or behavior. I was thinking, for instance, of the tracking of boys into Shop and girls into Home Ec, where one can see nothing about boys or girls considered in themselves which seems to connect essentially with the distinction between wrenches and eggbeaters. I was thinking also of sex discrimination in employment — cases where someone otherwise apparently qualified for a job is not hired because she is a woman. But when I tried to put this definition of 'sexist' to use, it did not stand the test.

Consider this case: If a company is hiring a supervisor who will supervise a group of male workers who have always worked for male supervisors, it can scarcely be denied that the sex of a candidate for the job is relevant to the candidate's prospects of moving smoothly and successfully into an effective working relationship with the supervisees (though the point is usually exaggerated by those looking for excuses not to hire women). Relevance is an intrasystematic thing. The patterns of behavior, attitude and custom within which a process goes on determine what is relevant to what in matters of describing, predicting or evaluating. In the case at hand, the workers' attitudes and the surrounding customs of the culture make a difference to how they interact with their supervisor and, in particular, *make* the sex of the supervisor a relevant factor in predicting how things will work out. So then, if the company hires a man, in preference to a more experienced and knowledgeable woman, can we explain our objection to the decision by saying it involved distinguishing on the basis of sex when sex is irrelevant to the ability to do the job? No: sex is relevant here.

So, what did I mean to say about 'sexist'? I was thinking that in a case of a candidate for a supervisory job, the reproductive capacity of the candidate has nothing to do with that person's knowing what needs to be done and being able to give properly timed, clear and correct directions. What I was picturing was a situation purified of all sexist perception and reaction. But, of course. *If* the whole context were not sexist, sex would not be an issue in such a job situation; indeed, it might go entirely unnoticed. It is precisely the fact that the sex of the candidate is relevant that is the salient symptom of the sexism of the situation.

I had failed, in that first essay, fully to grasp or understand that the locus of sexism is primarily in the system or framework, not in the particular act. It is not accurate to say that what is going on in cases of sexism is that distinctions are made on the basis of sex when sex is irrelevant; what is wrong in cases of sexism is, in the first place, that sex *is* relevant; and then that the making of distinctions on the basis of sex reinforces the patterns which make it relevant.

In sexist cultural/economic systems, sex is always relevant. To understand what sexism is, then, we have to step back and take a larger view.

Sex-identification intrudes into every moment of our lives and discourse, no matter what the supposedly primary focus or topic of the moment is. Elaborate, systematic, ubiquitous and redundant marking of a distinction between two sexes of humans and most animals is customary and obligatory. One *never* can ignore it.

Examples of sex-marking behavior patterns abound. A couple enters a restaurant; the headwaiter or hostess addresses the man and does not address the woman. The physician addresses the man by surname and honorific (Mr. Baxter, Rev. Jones) and addresses the woman by given name (Nancy, Gloria). You congratulate your friend — a hug, a slap on the back, shaking hands, kissing; one of the things which determines which of these you do is your friend's sex. In everything one does one has two complete repertoires of behavior, one for interactions with women and one for interactions with men. Greeting, storytelling, order-giving and order-receiving, negotiating, gesturing deference or dominance, encouraging, challenging, asking for information: one does all of these things differently depending upon whether the relevant others are male or female.

That this is so has been confirmed in sociological and socio-linguistic research,[2] but it is just as easily confirmed in one's own experience. To discover the differences in how you greet a woman and how you greet a man, for instance, just observe yourself, paying attention to the following sorts of things: frequency and duration of eye contact, frequency and type of touch, tone and pitch of voice, physical distance maintained between bodies, how and whether you smile, use of slang or swear words, whether your body dips into a shadow curtsy or bow. That I have two repertoires for handling introductions to people was vividly confirmed for me when a student introduced me to his friend, Pat, and I really could not tell what sex Pat was. For a moment I was stopped cold, completely incapable of action. I felt myself helplessly caught between two paths — the one I would take if Pat were female and the one I would take if Pat were male. Of course the paralysis does not last. One is rescued by one's ingenuity and good will; one can invent a way to behave as one says "How do you do?" to a human being. But the habitual ways are not for humans: they are one way for women and another for men.

Interlaced through all our behavior is our speaking — our linguistic behavior. Third person singular pronouns mark the sex of their referents. The same is true for a huge range of the nouns we use to refer to people ('guy', 'boy', 'lady', 'salesman', etc., and all the terms which covertly indicate the sex of the referent, like 'pilot', 'nurse', etc.), and the majority of given proper names ('Bob', 'Gwen', etc.).* In speaking, one constantly marks the sexes of those one speaks about.

The frequency with which our behavior marks the sexes of those we interact with cannot be exaggerated. The phenomenon is absolutely pervasive and deeply entrenched in all the patterns of behavior which are habitual, customary, acceptable, tolerable and intelligible. One can invent ways of behaving in one situation or another which are not sex-marking, which do not vary with the sexes of the persons involved, but if one were to succeed in removing sex-marking from one's behavior altogether, one's behavior would be so odd as to precipitate immediate crises of intelligibility and strenuous moral, religious or aesthetic objections from others. Everything one did would seem strange. And this is a matter of no small moment. We are a gregarious species. Our lives depend on our abilities to interact with others in relations of work, of exchange and of sympathy. What one cannot do without seeming excessively odd or unintelligible, one cannot do without severe disturbance to patterns of interaction upon which one's life depends. Sex-marking behavior is not optional; it is as obligatory as it is pervasive.

Closely connected with habitual and obligatory sex-marking is a constant and urgent need to know or be able to guess the sex of every single person with whom one has the slightest

---

* Languages differ in their degree of "gender-loading" and there is evidence that these differences correlate with differences in the ages at which children "attain gender identity." In "Native Language and Cognitive Structures — A Cross-cultural Inquiry," Alexander Z. Guiora and Arthur Herold detail this evidence. They characterize English as having "minimal" gender-loading, Hebrew as having "maximum gender-loading" and Finnish as having "zero." If English, whose gender-marking seems so very prevalent to me, is an example of "minimal gender-loading," it seems safe to assume that gender-marking in human languages is indeed a significant factor in human experience generally. (The Guiora and Herold article may be requested from Dr. Guiora at Box No. 011, University Hospital, The University of Michigan, Ann Arbor, Michigan 48109). I am indebted to Barbara Abbott for bringing this article to my attention.

or most remote contact or interaction. If we are going to mark people's sexes in every situation, then we have to know their sexes. I needed to know whether "Pat" was endowed with a clitoris or a penis prior to making the first step in getting acquainted. If I am writing a book review, the use of personal pronouns to refer to the author creates the need to know whether that person's reproductive cells are the sort which produce ova or the sort which produce sperm. I cannot ask the time of day without first knowing or presuming I know my informant's potential role in reproduction. We are socially and communicatively helpless if we do not know the sex of everybody we have anything to do with, and for members of such a species as ours, such helplessness can be life-threatening. Our habitual behavior patterns make knowledge of each person's sex both pervasively pertinent and of the *first* importance. Furthermore, the importance and urgency of having such knowledge is intensified by another sort of factor which I think most people rarely notice because they *do* usually know the sexes of others.

In a culture in which one is deemed sinful, sick or disgusting (at least) if one is not heterosexual, it is very important to keep track of one's sexual feelings and the sexes of those who inspire them. If one is permitted sexual expression or gratification, or even mere feeling, with persons of one sex but not of the other, one has to know what sex each person is before one can allow one's heart to beat or one's blood to flow in erotic enjoyment of that person. Much of our ordinary and apparently nonsexual interaction and communication involves elements of sexual or erotic message, and these are *rigidly* regulated by sex taboos, including the taboo on homosexuality. The adjustment or maladjustment of these messages to the sex of the person in question can have wonderful or disastrous consequences. The thought that one might misapprehend the sex of another conjures nothing less than the holy dread of unwitting violation of powerful taboo. Thus all the tension connected with sexual taboo and repression intensifies the urgency of being acceptable and intelligible, and our need to know everyone's sex carries much of the weight of an acute and emotionally fraught survival need.

The pressure on each of us to guess or determine the sex of everybody else both generates and is exhibited in a great pressure on each of us to *inform* everybody all the time of our sex. For, if you strip humans of most of their cultural trappings, it is not always that easy to tell without close inspection which are female, which are male. The tangible and visible physical differences between the sexes are not particularly sharp or numerous. Individual variation along the physical dimensions we think of as associated with maleness and femaleness are great, and the differences between the sexes could easily be obscured by bodily decoration, hair removal and the like. One of the shocks, when one does mistake someone's sex, is the discovery of how easily one can be misled. We could not ensure that we could identify people by their sex virtually any time and anywhere under any conditions if they did not announce themselves, did not *tell* us in one way or another.

We do not, in fact, announce our sexes "in one way or another." We announce them in a thousand ways. We deck ourselves from head to toe with garments and decorations which serve like badges and buttons to announce our sexes. For every type of occasion there are distinct clothes, gear and accessories, hairdos, cosmetics and scents, labeled as "ladies'" or "men's" and labeling us as females or males, and most of the time most of us choose, use, wear or bear the paraphernalia associated with our sex. It goes below the skin as well. There are different styles of gait, gesture, posture, speech, humor, taste and even of perception, interest and attention that we learn as we grow up to be women or to be men and that label and announce us as women or as men. It begins early in life: even infants in arms are color coded.

That we wear and bear signs of our sexes, and that this is compulsory, is made clearest in the relatively rare cases when we do not do so, or not enough. Responses ranging from critical to indignant to hostile meet mothers whose small children are not immediately sex-identifiable, and hippies used to be accosted on the streets (by otherwise reserved and polite people) with criticisms and accusations when their clothing and style gave off mixed and contradictory sex-announcements. Anyone in any kind of job placement service and any Success Manual will tell you that you cannot expect to get or keep a job if your clothing or personal style is ambiguous in its announcement of your sex. You don't go to a job interview wearing the other sex's shoes and socks.

The buzz on this last example indicates another source of pressure to inform each other of our sexes, namely, once again, the requirement that one be and appear heterosexual. Queerly enough, one appears heterosexual by informing people of one's sex *very* emphatically and *very* unambiguously, and one does this by heaping into one's behavior and upon one's body ever more and more conclusive sex-indicators. For homosexuals and lesbians who wish to pass as heterosexual, it is these indicators that provide most of the camouflage; for those who wish to avoid being presumed heterosexual, the trick is to deliberately cultivate ambiguous sex-indicators in clothes, behavior and style. In a culture in which homosexuality and lesbianism are violently and almost universally forbidden, and heterosexuality is announced by announcing one's sex, it always behooves one to announce one's sex.

The information as to what sex one is is always wanted, and supplying it is always appropriate to one's own and others' most constant and pervasive interests — interests in being and remaining viable in the available human community.

The intense demand for marking and for asserting what sex each person is adds up to a strenuous requirement that there *be* two distinct and sharply dimorphic sexes. But, in reality, there are not. There are people who fit on a biological spectrum between two not-so-sharply defined poles. In about 5 percent of live births, possibly more, the babies are in some degree and way not perfect exemplars of male and female. There are individuals with chromosome patterns other than XX or XY and individuals whose external genitalia at birth exhibit some degree of ambiguity. There are people who are chromosomally "normal" who are at the far ends of the normal spectra of secondary sex characteristics — height, musculature, hairiness, body density, distribution of fat, breast size, etc. — whose overall appearance fits the norm of people whose chromosomal sex is the opposite of theirs.[3]

These variations not withstanding, persons (mainly men, of course) with the power to do so actually *construct* a world in which men are men and women are women and there is nothing in between and nothing ambiguous; they do it by chemically and/or surgically altering people whose bodies are indeterminate or ambiguous with respect to sex. Newborns with "imperfectly formed" genitals are immediately "corrected" by chemical or surgical means, children and adolescents are given hormone "therapies" if their bodies seem not to be developing according to what physicians and others declare to be the norm for what has been declared to be that individual's sex. Persons with authority recommend and supply cosmetics and cosmetic regimens, diets, exercises and all manner of clothing to revise or disguise the too-hairy lip, the too-large breast, the too-slender shoulders, the too-large feet, the too-great or too-slight stature. Individuals whose bodies do not fit the picture of exactly two sharply dimorphic sexes are often enough quite willing to be altered or veiled for the obvious reason that the world punishes them severely for their failure to be the "facts" which would verify the doctrine of two sexes. The demand that the world be a world in which there are exactly two sexes is inexorable, and we are all compelled to answer to it emphatically, unconditionally, repetitiously and unambiguously.

Even being physically "normal" for one's assigned sex is not enough. One must *be* female or male, actively. Again, the costumes and performances. Pressed to acting feminine or masculine, one colludes (co-lude: play along) with the doctors and counselors in the creation of a world in which the apparent dimorphism of the sexes is so extreme that one can only think there is a great gulf between female and male, that the two are, essentially and fundamentally and naturally, utterly different. One helps to create a world in which it seems to us that we *could* never mistake a woman for a man or a man for a woman. We never need worry.

Along with all the making, marking and announcing of sex-distinction goes a strong and visceral feeling or attitude to the effect that sex-distinction is the most important thing in the world: that it would be the end of the world if it were not maintained, clear and sharp and rigid; that a sex-dualism which is rooted in the nature of the beast is absolutely crucial and fundamental to all aspects of human life, human society and human economy. Where feminism is perceived as a project of blurring this distinction, antifeminist rhetoric is vivid with the dread that the world will end if the feminists have their way.[4] Some feminists' insistence that the feminist goal is not a "unisex" society is defensive in a way that suggests they too believe that culture or civilization would not survive blurring the distinction. I think that one of the sources of the prevalence and profundity of this conviction and dread is our immersion in the very behavior patterns I have been discussing.

It is a general and obvious principle of information theory that when it is very, very important that certain information be conveyed, the suitable strategy is redundancy. If a message *must* get through, one sends it repeatedly and by as many means or media as one has at one's command. On the other end, as a receiver of information, if one receives the same information over and over, conveyed by every medium one knows, another message comes through as well, and implicitly: the message that this information is very, very important. The enormous frequency with which information about people's sexes is conveyed conveys implicitly the message that this topic is enormously important. I suspect that this is the single topic on which we most frequently receive information from others throughout our entire lives. If I am right, it would go part way to explaining why we end up with an almost irresistible impression, unarticulated, that the matter of people's sexes is the most important and most fundamental topic in the world.

We exchange sex-identification information, along with the implicit message that it is very important, in a variety of circumstances in which there really is no concrete or experientially obvious point in having the information. There are reasons, as this discussion has shown, why you should want to know whether the person filling your water glass or your tooth is male or female and why that person wants to know what you are, but those reasons are woven invisibly into the fabric of social structure and they do not have to do with the bare mechanics of things being filled. Furthermore, the same culture which drives us to this constant information exchange also simultaneously enforces a strong blanket rule requiring that the simplest and most nearly definitive physical manifestations of sex difference be hidden from view in all but the most private and intimate circumstances. The double message of sex-distinction and its pre-eminent importance is conveyed, in fact, in part *by* devices which systematically and deliberately cover up and hide from view the few physical things which do (to a fair extent) distinguish two sexes of humans. The messages are overwhelmingly dissociated from the concrete facts they supposedly pertain to, and from matrices of concrete and sensible reasons and consequences.

Small children's minds must be hopelessly boggled by all this. We know our own sexes, and learn to think it a matter of first importance that one is a girl or a boy so early that we do not remember not knowing — long before physical differences in our young bodies could make more than the most trivial practical differences. A friend of mine whose appearance and style have a little bit about them that is gender-ambiguous walked past a mother and child, and heard the child ask the mother, "Is she a man or a woman?" The struggle to divine some connection between social behavior and physical sex, and the high priority of it all, seem painfully obvious here.

If one is made to feel that a thing is of prime importance, but common sensory experience does not connect it with things of obvious concrete and practical importance, then there is mystery, and with that a strong tendency to the construction of mystical or metaphysical conceptions of its importance. If it is important, but not of mundane importance, it must be of transcendent importance. All the more so if it is *very* important.*

This matter of our sexes must be very profound indeed if it must, on pain of shame and ostracism, be covered up and must, on pain of shame and ostracism, be boldly advertised by every means and medium one can devise.

There is one more point about redundancy that is worth making here. If there is one thing more effective in making one believe a thing than receiving the message repetitively, it is rehearsing it repetitively. Advertisers, preachers, teachers, all of us in the brainwashing professions, make use of this apparently physical fact of human psychology routinely. The redundancy of sex-marking and sex-announcing serves not only to make the topic seem transcendently important, but to make the sex-duality it advertises seem transcendently and unquestionably *true*.

It is quite a spectacle, really, once one sees it, these humans so devoted to dressing up and acting out and "fixing" one another so everyone lives up to and lives out the theory that there are two sharply distinct sexes and never the twain shall overlap or be confused or conflated; these hominids constantly and with remarkable lack of embarrassment marking a distinction between two sexes as though their lives depended on it. It is wonderful that homosexuals and lesbians are mocked and judged for "playing butch-femme roles" and for dressing in "butch-femme drag," for nobody goes about in full public view as thoroughly decked out in butch and femme drag as respectable heterosexuals when they are dressed up to go out in the evening, or to go to church, or to go to the office. Heterosexual critics of queers' "role-playing" ought to look at themselves in the mirror on their way out for a night on the town to see who's in drag. The answer is, everybody is. Perhaps the main difference between heterosexuals and queers is that when queers go forth in drag, they know they are engaged in theater — they are playing and they know they are playing. Heterosexuals usually are taking it all perfectly seriously, thinking they are in the real world, thinking they *are* the real world.

---

* For some readers it will be useful to note a connection here with H.P. Grice's doctrine of conversational implicatures. There is a conversational "rule" to the effect that a speaker should "be relevant." As audiences we assume information given us is relevant, and if we cannot see its relevance we generally assume the relevance is to something hidden or that we are somehow missing something others see; or we invent a relevance by reconstruing the information as about something other than it initially appeared to be about. (Grice, "Logic and Conversation," *The Logic of Grammar*, edited by Donald Davidson and Gilbert Harman (Dickenson Publishing Company, Inc., Encino, California and Belmont, California [1975], pp. 64–75).

Of course, in a way, they are the real world. All this bizarre behavior has a function in the construction of the real world.

Sex-marking and sex-announcing are equally compulsory for males and females; but that is as far as equality goes in this matter. The meaning and import of this behavior is profoundly different for women and for men.

Imagine. . .

A colony of humans established a civilization hundreds of years ago on a distant planet. It has evolved, as civilizations will. Its language is a descendant of English.

The language has personal pronouns marking the child/adult distinction, and its adult personal pronouns mark the distinction between straight and curly pubic hair. At puberty each person assumes distinguishing clothing styles and manners so others can tell what type she or he is without the closer scrutiny which would generally be considered indecent. People with straight pubic hair adopt a style which is modest and self-effacing and clothes which are fragile and confining; people with curly pubic hair adopt a style which is expensive and prepossessing and clothes which are sturdy and comfortable. People whose pubic hair is neither clearly straight nor clearly curly alter their hair chemically in order to be clearly one or the other. Since those with curly pubic hair have higher status and economic advantages, those with ambiguous pubic hair are told to make it straight, for life will be easier for a low-status person whose category might be doubted than for a high-status person whose category might be doubted.

It is taboo to eat or drink in the same room with any person of the same pubic hair type as oneself. Compulsory heterogourmandism, it is called by social critics, though most people think it is just natural human desire to eat with one's pubic-hair opposite. A logical consequence of this habit, or taboo, is the limitation to dining only singly or in pairs — a taboo against banquetism, or, as the slang expression goes, against the group gulp.

Whatever features an individual male person has which tend to his social and economic disadvantage (his age, race, class, height, etc.), one feature which never tends to his disadvantage in the society at large is his maleness. The case for females is the mirror image of this. Whatever features an individual female person has which tend to her social and economic advantage (her age, race, etc.), one feature which always tends to her disadvantage is her femaleness. Therefore, when a male's sex-category is the thing about him that gets first and most repeated notice, the thing about him that is being framed and emphasized and given primacy is a feature which in general is an asset to him. When a female's sex-category is the thing about her that gets first and most repeated notice, the thing about her that is being framed and emphasized and given primacy is a feature which in general is a liability to her. Manifestations of this divergence in the meaning and consequences of sex-announcement can be very concrete.

Walking down the street in the evening in a town or city exposes one to some risk of assault. For males the risk is less; for females the risk is greater. If one announces oneself male, one is presumed by potential assailants to be more rather than less likely to defend oneself or be able to evade the assault and, if the male-announcement is strong and unambiguous, to be a noncandidate for sexual assault. If one announces oneself female, one is presumed by potential assailants to be less rather than more likely to defend oneself or to evade the assault and, if the female-announcement is strong and unambiguous, to be a prime candidate for sexual assault. Both the man and the woman "announce" their sex through style of gait, clothing, hair style, etc., but they are not equally or identically affected by announcing their sex. The male's announcement tends toward his protection or safety, and the female's announcement tends toward her victimization. It could not be more immediate or concrete; the meaning of the sex-identification could not be more different.

The sex-marking behavioral repertoires are such that in the behavior of almost all people of both sexes addressing or responding to males (especially within their own culture/race) generally is done in a manner which suggests basic respect, while addressing or responding to females is done in a manner that suggests the females' inferiority (condescending tones, presumptions of ignorance, overfamiliarity, sexual aggression, etc.). So, when one approaches an ordinary well-socialized person in such cultures, if one is male, one's own behavioral announcement of maleness tends to evoke supportive and beneficial response and if one is female, one's own behavioral announcement of femaleness tends to evoke degrading and detrimental response.

The details of the sex-announcing behaviors also contribute to the reduction of women and the elevation of men. The case is most obvious in the matter of clothing. As feminists have been saying for two hundred years or so, ladies' clothing is generally restrictive, binding, burdening and frail; it threatens to fall apart and/or to uncover something that is supposed to be covered if you bend, reach, kick, punch or run. It typically does not protect effectively against hazards in the environment, nor permit the wearer to protect herself against the hazards of the human environment. Men's clothing is generally the opposite of all this — sturdy, suitably protective, permitting movement and locomotion. The details of feminine manners and postures also serve to bind and restrict. To be feminine is to take up little space, to defer to others, to be silent or affirming of others, etc. It is not necessary here to survey all this, for it has been done many times and in illuminating detail in feminist writings. My point here is that though both men and women must behave in sex-announcing ways, the behavior which announces femaleness is in itself both physically and socially binding and limiting as the behavior which announces maleness is not.

The sex-correlated variations in our behavior tend systematically to the benefit of males and the detriment of females. The male, announcing his sex in sex-identifying behavior and dress, is both announcing and acting on his membership in a dominant caste — dominant within his subculture and to a fair extent across subcultures as well. The female, announcing her sex, is both announcing and acting on her membership in the subordinated caste. She is obliged to inform others constantly and in every sort of situation that she is to be treated as inferior, without authority, assaultable. She cannot move or speak within the usual cultural norms without engaging in self-deprecation. The male cannot move or speak without engaging in self-aggrandizement. Constant sex-identification both defines and maintains the caste boundary without which there could not be a dominance-subordination structure.

The forces which make us mark and announce sexes are among the forces which constitute the oppression of women, and they are central and essential to the maintenance of that system.

Oppression is a system of interrelated barriers and forces which reduce, immobilize and mold people who belong to a certain group, and effect their subordination to another group (individually to individuals of the other group, and as a group, to that group). Such a system could not exist were not the groups, the categories of persons, well defined. Logically, it presupposes that there are two distinct categories. Practically, they must be not only distinct but relatively easily identifiable; the barriers and forces could not be suitably located and applied if there were often much doubt as to which individuals were to be contained and reduced, which were to dominate.[5]

It is extremely costly to subordinate a large group of people simply by applications of material force, as is indicated by the costs of maximum security prisons and of military suppression of nationalist movements. For subordination to be permanent and cost effective, it is necessary to create conditions such that the subordinated group acquiesces to some extent in the subordination. Probably one of the most efficient ways to secure acquiescence is to convince the people that their subordination is inevitable. The mechanisms by which the subordinate and dominant categories are defined can contribute greatly to popular belief in the inevitability of the dominance/subordination structure.

For efficient subordination, what's wanted is that the structure not appear to be a cultural artifact kept in place by human decision or custom, but that it appear *natural* — that it appear to be a quite direct consequence of facts about the beast which are beyond the scope of human manipulation or revision. It must seem natural that individuals of the one category are dominated by individuals of the other and that as groups, the one dominates the other.[6] To make this seem natural, it will help if it seems to all concerned that members of the two groups are *very* different from each other, and this appearance is enhanced if it can be made to appear that within each group, the members are very like one another. In other words, the appearance of the naturalness of the dominance of men and the subordination of women is supported by anything which supports the appearance that men are very like other men and very unlike women, and that women are very like other women and very unlike men. All behavior which encourages the appearance that humans are biologically sharply sex-dimorphic encourages the acquiescence of women (and, to the extent it needs encouragement, of men) in women's subordination.

That we are trained to behave so differently as women and as men, and to behave so differently toward women and toward men, itself contributes mightily to the appearance of extreme natural dimorphism, but also, the *ways* we act as women and as men, and the *ways* we act toward women and toward men, mold our bodies and our minds to the shapes of subordination and dominance. We do become what we practice being.

Throughout this essay I have seemed to beg the question at hand. Should I not be trying to prove that there are few and insignificant differences between females and males, if that is what I believe, rather than assuming it? What I have been doing is offering observations which suggest that if one thinks there are biologically deep differences between women and men which cause and justify divisions of labor and responsibility such as we see in the modern patriarchal family and male-dominated workplace, one may *not* have arrived at this belief because of direct experience of unmolested physical evidence, but because our customs serve to construct that appearance; and I suggest that these customs are artifacts of culture which exist to support a morally and scientifically insupportable system of dominance and subordination.[7]

But also, in the end, I do not want to claim simply that there are not socially significant biologically grounded differences between human females and males. Things are much more complex than that.

Enculturation and socialization are, I think, misunderstood if one pictures them as processes which apply layers of cultural gloss over a biological substratum. It is with that picture in mind that one asks whether this or that aspect of behavior is due to "nature" or "nurture." One means, does it emanate from the biological substratum or does it come from some layer of the shellac? A variant on this wrong picture is the picture according to which enculturation or socialization is something mental or psychological, as opposed to something physical or biological. Then one can think of attitudes and habits of perception, for instance, as "learned" versus "biologically determined." And again, one can ask such things as whether men's aggressiveness is learned or biologically determined, and if the former is asserted, one can think in terms of changing them while if the latter is asserted, one must give up all thought of reform.

My observations and experience suggest another way of looking at this. I see enormous social pressure on us all to act feminine or act masculine (and not both), so I am inclined to think that if we were to break the habits of culture which generate that pressure, people would not act particularly masculine or feminine. The fact that there are such penalties threatened for deviations from these patterns strongly suggests that the patterns would not be there but for the threats. This leads, I think, to a skeptical conclusion: we do not know whether human behavior patterns would be dimorphic along lines of chromosomal sex if we were not threatened and bullied; nor do we know, if we assume that they would be dimorphous, *what* they would be, that is, *what* constellations of traits and tendencies would fall out along that genetic line. And these questions are odd anyway, for there is no question of humans growing up *without* culture, so we don't know what other cultural variables we might imagine to be at work in a culture in which the familiar training to masculinity and femininity were not going on.

On the other hand, as one goes about in the world, and in particular as one tries out strategies meant to alter the behaviors which constitute and support male dominance, one often has extremely convincing experiences of the *inflexibility* of people in this respect, of a resistance to change which seems to run much, much deeper than willingness or willfulness in the face of arguments and evidence. As feminist activists, many of us have felt this most particularly in the case of men, and it has sometimes seemed that the relative flexibility and adaptability of women and the relative rigidity of men are so widespread within each group respectively, and so often and convincingly encountered, that they must be biologically given. And one watches men and women on the streets, and their bodies seem so different — one hardly can avoid thinking there are vast and profound differences between women and men without giving up the hard won confidence in one's powers of perception.

The first remedy here is to lift one's eyes from a single culture, class and race. If the bodies of Asian women set them apart so sharply from Asian men, see how different they are also from Black women; if white men all look alike and very different from white women, it helps to note that Black men don't look so like white men.

The second remedy is to think about the subjective experience we have of our *habits*. If one habitually twists a lock of one's hair whenever one is reading and has tried to break this habit, one knows how "bodily" it is; but that does not convince one it is genetically determined. People who drive to work every day often take the same route every day, and if they mean to take another route one day in order to do an errand on the way, they may find themselves at work, conveyed along the habitual route, without having revised the decision to do the errand. The habit of taking that course is mapped into one's body; it is not a matter of a decision — a mental event — that is repeated each day upon a daily re-judgment of the reasonableness of the course. It is also not genetic. We are animals. Learning is physical, bodily. There is not a separate, nonmaterial "control room" where socialization, enculturation and habit formation take place and where, since it is nonmaterial, change is independent of bodies and easier than in bodies.

Socialization molds our bodies; enculturation forms our skeletons, our musculature, our central nervous systems. By the time we are gendered adults, masculinity and femininity *are* "biological." They are structural and material features of how our bodies are. My experience suggests that they are changeable just as one would expect bodies to be — slowly, through constant practice and deliberate regimens designed to remap and rebuild nerve and tissue. This is how many of us *have* changed when we chose to change from "women" as culturally defined to "women" as we define ourselves. Both the sources of the changes and the resistances to them are bodily — are among the possibilities of our animal natures, whatever those may be.

But now "biological" does not mean "genetically determined" or "inevitable." It just means "of the animal."

It is no accident that feminism has often focused on our bodies. Rape, battering, reproductive self-determination, health, nutrition, self-defense, athletics, financial independence (control of the means of feeding and sheltering ourselves). And it is no accident that with varying degrees of conscious intention, feminists have tried to create separate spaces where women could exist somewhat sheltered from the prevailing winds of patriarchal culture and try to stand up straight for once. One needs space to *practice* an erect posture; one cannot just will it to happen. To retrain one's body one needs physical freedom from what are, in the last analysis, physical forces misshaping it to the contours of the subordinate.

The cultural and economic structures which create and enforce elaborate and rigid patterns of sex-marking and sex-announcing behavior, that is, create gender as we know it, mold us as dominators and subordinates (I do not say "mold our minds" or "mold our personalities"). They construct two classes of animals, the masculine and the feminine, where another constellation of forces might have constructed three or five categories, and not necessarily hierarchically related. Or such a spectrum of sorts that we would not experience them as "sorts" at all.

The term 'sexist' characterizes cultural and economic structures which create and enforce the elaborate and rigid patterns of sex-marking and sex-announcing which divide the species, along lines of sex, into dominators and subordinates. Individual acts and practices are sexist which reinforce and support those structures, either as culture or as shapes taken on by the enculturated animals. Resistance to sexism is that which undermines those structures by social and political action and by projects of reconstruction and revision of ourselves.

NOTES

1. "Male Chauvinism — A Conceptual Analysis," *Philosophy and Sex*, edited by Robert Baker and Frederick Elliston (Prometheus Books, Buffalo, New York, 1975), p. 66. The inadequacies of such an account of sexism are reflected in the inadequacies of a standard legal interpretation of

what sex discrimination is as it is analyzed by Catharine A. MacKinnon in *Sexual Harassment of Working Women* (Yale University Press, New Haven and London, 1979), cf. Chapters 5 and 6. See also my review of this book, "Courting Gender Justice," *New Women's Times Feminist Review*, No. 17, September-October 1981, pp. 10–11.

2. See, for example, such works as *Body Politics: Power, Sex and Nonverbal Communication*, by Nancy Henley (Prentice-Hall, Englewood Cliffs, New Jersey, 1977); *Language and Sex: Difference and Dominance*, edited by Barrie Thorne and Nancy Henley (Newbury House Publishers, Rowley, Massachusetts, 1975); and *Gender and Nonverbal Behavior*, edited by Clara Mayo and Nancy M. Henley (Springer-Verlag, New York, 1981).

3. I rely here on lectures by Eileen Van Tassell in which she interpreted the generally available data on sex-characteristics, sex-differences and sex-similarities. One can refer, in particular, to *Man and Woman, Boy and Girl*, by John Money and Anke A. Ehrhardt (The Johns Hopkins University Press, 1972) and *Intersexuality*, edited by Claus Overzier (Academic Press, New York and London, 1963). See also, for instance: "Development of Sexual Characteristics," by A.D. Jost in *Science Journal*, Volume 6, No. 6 (especially the chart on page 71) which indicates the variety of "sex characteristics" which occurs in normal females and males; and "Growth and Endocrinology of the Adolescent," by J. M. Tanner in *Endocrine and Genetic Diseases of Childhood*, edited by L. Gardner (Saunders, Philadelphia & London, 1969), which tries to give clinical standards for evaluating the hormonal status of adolescent youth, and in which the author characterizes individuals which are well within the normal curve for males as "feminized males," thus, by implication, as "abnormal" males; and similarly, *mutatis mutandis*, for females.

4. See, for example, *Sexual Suicide*, by George F. Gilder (Quadrangle, New York, 1979). For an eloquent example of the Victorian version of this anxiety and the world view which underlies it, see "The Emancipation of Women," by Frederic Harrison in *Fortnightly Review*, CCXCVII, October 1, 1891, as quoted in a talk given by Sandra Siegel at the Berkshire Conference on Women's History, April 1981, entitled "Historiography, 'Decadence,' and the Legend of 'Separate Spheres' in Late Victorian England," which connects Victorian conceptions of civilization and the separateness and differentness of women and men.

5. See "Oppression," in this collection.

6. See "Feminist Leaders Can't Walk On Water," by Lorraine Masterson, *Quest: A Feminist Quarterly* (Volume II, Number 4, Spring, 1976), especially pp. 35–36 where the author refers to Paulo Freire's *Pedagogy of the Oppressed* and speaks to the special case of women's belief that our subordination is inevitable because rooted in biology.

7. Cf., the early and powerful article by Naomi Weisstein, "Psychology Constructs the Female," in *Woman in Sexist Society: Studies in Power and Powerlessness*, edited by Vivian Gornick and Barbara K. Moran (Basic Books, Inc., New York, 1971). Weisstein documents clearly that neither laypersons nor psychologists are the least bit dependable as observers of sex-correlated traits of people, and that theories of sex-difference based on "clinical experience" and based on primate studies are scientifically worthless.

QUESTIONS

1. Why does Marilyn Frye revise her initial definition of sexism as that which promotes or exploits any irrelevant distinction between the sexes?

2. According to Frye, why do we need to examine the system or framework and not the particular discriminatory act in order to explore the moral dimensions of sexism?

3. Frye provides examples of the marking of the distinction between the sexes. Do you think these examples succeed in revealing aspects of the immorality of sexism?

4. What does Frye mean when she says that "whatever features an individual male person has which tend to his social and economic disadvantage (his age, race, class, height, etc.), one feature which never tends to his disadvantage in the society at large is his maleness"? Evaluate this claim in light of McIntosh's analysis of privilege.

5. Frye suggests that her analysis of sexism can also be applied to an analysis of discrimination on the basis of sexual orientation. How would this analysis differ from McIntosh's? How would it differ from the analysis that follows in the reading by Alex Wellington?

WHY LIBERALS SHOULD SUPPORT SAME SEX MARRIAGE

Adrian Alex Wellington

This paper is about the state sponsorship of same sex unions, or about "family values, queer-style," as one commentator has put it.[1] The simple claim of this paper is that gays, lesbians, and bisexuals should have the right to legally marry if they so choose.[2] This simple claim can be characterized as a claim about formal equality — the same sex marriage bar is a denial of the formal equality rights of lesbians, gays,[3] and bisexuals. However, the simple claim does not adequately capture the complexity of the issue, either for those who argue against same sex marriage or for those who argue for it.

In this paper I will present a more complex version of the above argument in the context of contemporary secular liberalism. The argument can be broken down into the following components:

1. In a liberal society, sexual relations between consenting adults is beyond the purview of the state — "the state has no business in the bedrooms of the nation."[4]
2. It is not possible to justify anything other than a functional account of marriage in contemporary secular liberal society.
3. If some relationships — namely opposite sex ones — are to be given state sponsorship, there must be rational reasons consistent with liberal principles to deny that sponsorship to analogous relationships.
4. On a functional account of marriage same sex relationships are analogous to opposite sex relationships.
5. As a matter of formal equality, same sex unions should be entitled to state sponsorship.
6. Any other arguments against the provision of state sponsorship to same sex unions could only make claim to liberal principles by reference to some formulation of the harm principle.
7. There is no valid argument against same sex marriage based on the grounds of harm consistent with the harm principle.

All of these claims taken together provide a compound argument for the claim that gays, lesbians, and bisexuals should have the right to participate in state sponsored same sex unions if they so choose. The policy claim that corresponds to my argument is that legislative reform would be required in order to ensure the provision of that right.

The main claim of this paper is that as a matter of social justice liberalism requires the provision of the opportunity for state sponsorship and state recognition of same sex couples.

From the Journal of Social Philosophy, *v. 26, no. 3 (Winter 1995), pp. 5–32. Reprinted by permission of the* Journal of Social Philosophy.

The paper is concerned with an issue of political philosophy — whether a commitment to liberalism entails a commitment to support the rights of lesbians, gays, and bisexuals to marry persons of the same sex, should they so desire. Whether gays, lesbians, and bisexuals should choose to exercise the option, if available, of marrying persons of the same sex is a separate issue. The position that liberalism must, as a matter of political philosophy, recognize the validity of same sex marriage as an option for gays, lesbians, and bisexuals as well as for heterosexuals (should any heterosexuals choose to marry persons of the same sex) is distinct from the position that state sponsorship of same sex marriages should be pursued as a strategy for achieving gay rights or gay liberation. One can acknowledge that liberalism entails the commitment to support state sponsorship of same sex marriage without insisting that lesbians, gays, and bisexuals should participate in, or even advocate the provision of the opportunity to participate in same sex marriages.

I

This paper begins with certain crucial assumptions about the basic claims of liberalism and the fluidity of human sexuality and emotional attachment. The first basic claim of liberalism as a broadly defined concept is the claim that each person in a liberal society should be able to determine for her/himself just what constitutes the "good life." Corollary to that claim is another basic claim that the state should be neutral between conceptions of the "good life." The third basic claim is that liberal society not only need not, but actually should not, be based on any specific picture of "human nature." A liberal society is one in which there are many diverse conceptions of "human nature," as with conceptions of the "good life," and that none should be accorded primacy or specific state endorsement. The fourth basic claim is that legal intervention in the lives of the members of a liberal society should be constrained as far as possible by the notion of liberty contained in the formulation of the harm principle.[5]

The claims concerning human sexuality and emotional attachment are simpler, but probably no less contentious. These claims are that human beings as a species have a remarkably diverse range of potential sexual practices and emotional affiliations. Even given tremendous levels of socialization aimed at producing compulsory heterosexuality, many people resist this socialization and choose to reject, partly or completely, heterosexuality. One can assume that many more people would adopt homosexuality or bisexuality in practice or identify with either by inclination if those socialization pressures were ameliorated. The picture of a traditional marriage is that of heterosexual adults taking on a pair bonding union sanctioned by religion and/or the state involving fidelity and reproduction. Yet, many, many people who enter into the state of marriage, who partake of the status of the social practice of marriage, actually do not adhere to that traditional picture. Many marriages do not rest upon fidelity, and many marriages do not result in procreation. Further, many marriages are between parties, or involve parties, who do not primarily perceive themselves as heterosexual.

It seems clear that a liberal conception of sexuality must be one that recognizes the contingency of heterosexuality. There may be many subcultures or segments of a liberal society — religious fundamentalists, certain kinds of anti-homosexual moralists — which do not accept the assertion of heterosexuality as contingent. These groups may wish to entrench heterosexuality socially, morally, and legally, yet the very fact that they seek to entrench it and to force compliance with the norm of heterosexuality itself attests to the very contingency of the norm. It is because some people are unwilling to live in compliance with the norm, and are able to resist the supposed necessity of the norm, that these groups wish to adopt harsh measures of policing and enforcement of the norm. These groups who categorically oppose the assertion of contingent heterosexuality, nevertheless, are only part of liberal society. Liberal society also includes those who wish to partake in homosexual or bisexual pair bonding unions as well as those who wish to, or at least are willing to, tolerate such unions.

A liberal society is one that rests upon the provision of choice for individuals to determine what sorts of people they want to be, as well as what sorts of lives they want to lead. Part of the choices that one undertakes during the process of self construction and life construction is whether, and to what extent, to participate in pair bonding unions. In a society which is premised upon the separation of religion and democratic governance, indicated by the institution of civil marriage, these unions must be interpreted in the context of liberal and not religious norms. Despite the holdover of religious notions in the wording of the marriage ceremony itself, it is clear that people can engage in the practice of marriage without any specific commitment to religious conceptions of marriage. Marriage thus becomes a state sanctioned pair bonding union, an affirmation of state endorsement of the pair bonding itself. There is no requirement that one engage in heterosexual practices with one's marriage partner, and no requirement that one attempt to produce children. The only conditions one need meet in order to undertake civil marriage are that the partners are of opposite sex, of sufficient age, legally sane, and not too closely related (consanguinity conditions).[6] Of course, the partners must also be able to pay the required fee for the ceremony.

It is interesting to note that once the religious basis for marriage is removed or at least elided that there is no longer any rational reason — rational in the sense of related to the purpose of the practice — to insist that parties to a civil marriage be of the opposite sex. A civil marriage is a self-defining ceremony, intended to accord a certain social status. The state cannot require that marriage partners endorse and live up to the ideal of fidelity, or endorse and live by the norm of heterosexuality, or endorse and live in accordance with the intention to reproduce. The marriage union in a secular liberal society is one that is interpreted by the parties in the context of the purported absence of teleological conceptions of human nature and of state sanctioned conceptions of the good life. The parties themselves determine what marriage means to them, and shape the practice to their needs and wants. How then can the state insist upon the condition that parties must be of opposite sexes in order to participate in that kind of practice?

Marriages are intended to be unions, unions which apparently automatically create "couples" and then "families." There are of course couples outside of marriage and marriage partners who do not perceive themselves to be couples. There are of course families outside of marriage and marriages which do not actually function like families. The point is that civil marriages produce a certain kind of coupling — state sanctioned coupling. Other than the requirement that the parties be adults and be of opposite sex, the civil marriage ceremony can be tailored by the parties to incorporate their values and beliefs and preferences. The parties can undertake civil marriage in order to attain the social status of marriage but intend to be "unfaithful" to one another sexually with persons of the opposite or same sex. The parties can intend to be celibate, to avoid procreation or to engage in procreation, to have sex only with each other, or to never have sex with each other. In other words, marriage does not depend upon any particular set of sexual or emotional practices. Why then does it depend upon an arbitrary condition of membership in the opposite sex to one's intended partner?

If a homosexual person can marry another homosexual person of the opposite sex or a heterosexual person of the opposite sex, or a bisexual person marry a homosexual or heterosexual person of the opposite sex, why should lesbians, gays, and bisexuals be excluded from marrying a homosexual or bisexual or heterosexual person of the same sex? Heterosexuals are also prevented from marrying a heterosexual or homosexual person of the same sex as well. If one looks at marriage in the context of a liberal conception of the practice, divorced from the religious interpretation of the practice and the historical background of the practice, these restrictions make no sense. Apart from social prejudice and discrimination, there is no reason to insist that individuals of the same sex cannot form couples in the same way that parties to marriage form couples. Civil marriage is a self-defining, self-obligating union. The parties will determine what the union provides for them, and what need they have for the state sanction — from expression of commitment to tax breaks. Same sex couples are no less capable of determining this than opposite sex couples.

One does not have to able to recognize the capacity in oneself to respond sexually to persons of either sex or of the same sex in order to recognize that the capacity exists in many others. One does not have to be able to recognize the capacity in oneself to form emotional affiliations with persons of either sex or of the same sex in order to recognize that the capacity exists in many others. There is no biological, or psychological reason that human beings must have sex or emotional affiliations only with persons of the opposite sex. There are only political or social reasons that motivate people to insist that heterosexuality is natural, or normal. Liberals are predisposed to resist arguments of the form that it is only "natural" or "normal" for humans to be X or to do Y. On my reading of liberalism the central driving force behind the adoption of liberal political philosophy and policy historically was to counteract precisely those kind of arguments in favor of the divine right of monarchs or in favor of religious morality. Divorce is one of the clearest examples of the movement towards a secularization of social practices that were initially the exclusive preserve of religion.

It seems clear that secular liberal societies can no longer rely upon outdated and archaic religious notions about the purposes of coupling and specifically of marriage. The attempts of courts to deal with common law opposite sex coupling point to several interesting things about contemporary civil marriage. The courts in some cases have attempted to develop functional characterizations of "spouses" and thus functional definitions of "couples."[7] These definitions include factors like the following: Did the parties share a bank account? Did the parties own property in common? Did the parties visit each other's relatives? Did the parties purchase shared items? Did the parties entertain guests together? Did the parties divide up household chores between them? Did the parties share meals? Did the parties provide nurturance and caring for each other when ill?

It is obvious that all these factors apply equally to same sex couples as to opposite sex couples. Same sex couples share bank accounts, own property in common, visit each other's relatives, purchase shared items, entertain guests together, divide up household chores, share meals, and provide nurturance and care for each other when ill. And of course, same sex couples, like opposite sex couples, have sex with each other. Any functional characterization of a couple — which I would argue is the only kind that could be endorsed by a full-fledged liberalism — is going to apply equally to same sex couples as to opposite sex couples.

If functional definitions are appropriate to determine whether unmarried couples were or are effectively married, and thus fall under "common law" marriage provisions of family law, then would functional definitions not be appropriate to determine whether same sex couples are suitable candidates for characterizations of "spouses" and thus suitable candidates to be deemed effectively married as well? Same sex couples look indistinguishable from opposite couples on the basis of functional definitions — that is, the differences among particular opposite and same sex couples would be as great as differences between opposite and same sex couples. The only reason that same sex couples do not fall under "common law" marriage provisions of family law is that same sex couples cannot marry, and thus they cannot be "effectively married." I should point out that "common law" marriage designation has to do with both the division of property and family assets, and the custody of, and access to, children. Both of these factors can be relevant to same sex couples who may own property together, have been in a relationship of economic dependence and support, and have children together (not the children of both of them together, but the children of each of them who they parent together or the children they have adopted together or singly previously).

None of the criteria in a functional definition of "spouse" — a person with whom one may share a bank account, own property, visit relatives, purchase shared items, entertain guests, divide up household chores, share meals, and have sex, and for whom one may provide nurturance and care — are gender specific. All are functional and relational. The significant issue in the determination of "spouse" is whether the two people relate to each other, and think of each other, in the manner of a "couple." What is a couple then, on this account, is a provisional definition that is something along the lines of a "voluntary relation premised on intimacy and connection." This phrase is my choice of wording; similar ideas based on functional definitions are suggested by the wording found in domestic partnership provisions and in certain court decisions.[8] My functional definition of marriage explicitly excludes the requirement of procreation, or even intended procreation. It is inconsistent, I argue, with a liberal account of marriage to include such a requirement. Thus, there is no basis to the attempt to privilege procreative or potentially procreative heterosexual marriage to encourage reproduction. Such an attempt could not be justified on my account.

Of course, the phrase "voluntary relation premised on intimacy and connection" could apply to affairs, and special friendships, so what needs to be added is the clause intended to produce the union of coupling. Thus, it is self-defining. What is distinctive about "couples" is that two people self-identify as a couple, and then other people identify those two people as a couple. There is no reason, once the notion of "couple" is characterized as functional and self-defining, to restrict the notion to opposite sex couples. And then if marriage is simply the legitimation by state sanction of self-defined, functional couples, there is no reason to restrict civil marriage to opposite sex couples.

The argument might be made that a significant feature of marriage is that the status of marriage represents a certain expression of social approval for the union. Thus, the state provides for couples to marry to express social approval for opposite sex coupling. It is of course arguments like this that make advocates of gay rights argue that gays, lesbians, and bisexuals need to have the opportunity to marry in order to be accorded the expression of social approval for their unions. The idea is that marriage is a legitimating social practice — that the status of marriage legitimates the coupling. Therefore, some lesbians, gays, and bisexuals wish to have their same sex coupling legitimated. The counter argument then is that "society," whatever that is, does not wish to bestow social approval on same sex coupling. Therefore, same sex couples should not be provided with the option of legitimating state sanctioned marriage.

This counter argument does not work, for several reasons. One reason is that people who marry engage in myriad forms of coupling which are not socially approved by large segments of the population — for example, childless marriages (by choice), open marriages, adulterous marriages, opportunistic marriages or marriages of convenience (for immigration purposes, for example), tabloid marriages ("grandmother- or grandfather-aged person marries teen" type of thing). It simply is not the case that whatever unions result from opposite sex marriages would be subject to social approval. It is not simply by virtue of the fact that parties are of opposite sexes that civil marriage expresses social approval. Another reason is that many, many people do support the idea of state sanctioned social approval for same sex unions. Obviously, most if not all gays, lesbians, and bisexuals support the idea of state sanctioned social approval for same sex unions.[9] Whether or not all gays, lesbians, and bisexuals would actually want to participate in the practice of same sex marriages, they would nevertheless not want to endorse a continuation of a source of discrimination against gays, lesbians, and bisexuals. There may be some homosexuals who object to the campaign for gay marriage, but the basis of their denial of support may be something other than a wish to see discrimination against gays, lesbians, and bisexuals continued.

It is also the case that some heterosexuals who would not wish to have the option to undertake same sex marriages for themselves would still support the provision of state sanctioned same sex marriages to those who do want them. Liberals are notorious for arguing for the rights of people to do things that liberals themselves may not want to do, and that other people (non liberals) do not support for anyone. Why should same sex marriage be any different? A liberal society is one in which the fullest possible range of options for human flourishing is to be encouraged, consistent with the need for respect of the civil rights and liberties of individuals. One important civil liberty is the freedom to engage in a state sanctioned union. The only possible reason that a liberal could have for rejecting same sex marriage is that the practice would in some way violate the harm principle.

It is important to clarify why the harm principle is even relevant in this context. The harm principle purports to stipulate the conditions under which the state could legitimately interfere with the liberty of its citizens; it sets out the bounds of individual liberty which must be respected by liberal government. The harm principle is clearly germane to the issue of whether (homosexual) sodomy should be subject to criminal prohibition.[10] It makes sense therefore to apply the harm principle to that issue, but it is less clear why the harm principle should be applied to the issue of same sex marriage. There are several reasons why the application may be problematic.

Criminal prohibitions against sexual activity between consenting adults obviously violate the liberty of those subject to them. Thus, these prohibitions could only be justified if there was sufficient reason to do so, reasons which satisfy the requirements of the harm principle. If it could be shown that some harm — harm of the sort envisaged by Mill — results from the activity, then the prohibition could be justified. It cannot be shown that any harm of the sort envisaged by Mill results from the activity, and thus the criminal prohibition of homosexual activity cannot be justified. Any justifications of such criminal prohibitions could only be based on illiberal principles and prejudices.

The question of permitting homosexual marriage does not involve any clear violation of liberty. It could be argued that marriage law is an instance of power-conferring and entitlement-allocating legislation. Marriage law determines which couples are entitled to state sanction for their unions, and which couples are not. Marriage constitutes "an affirmation by the state, a larger-than-life acknowledgment of one's relationship, a seal of approval."[11] The question of whether the state can legitimately deny same sex couples the right to marry seems thus to be a question of equality. Are same sex couples equal to opposite sex couples, such that they should be entitled to the same state sponsorship of their unions? I argue that on a functional account of marriage formal equality would dictate that same sex couples are entitled to the same state sponsorship as opposite sex couples. I also argue that a functional account of marriage is the only type of account consistent with contemporary secular liberal society.

It should be sufficient, then, to say that the same sex marriage bar violates the formal equality of gays, lesbians, and bisexuals. Yet, it is not sufficient because the literature addressing the issue of same sex marriage does not facilitate a straightforward treatment in terms of formal equality. To respond to the objections that have been raised by critics of homosexual marriage, it is necessary to depart from a neat and simple analysis of equality.

The critics of homosexual marriage (both straight and gay) are not satisfied with the characterization of the issue as one of formal equality. Those critics who object to homosexual marriage because they object to homosexuality will not accept the claim of equality between same sex couples and opposite sex couples. That claim is contentious for them, and their response to that claim is typically to point out some kind of harm that is imputed to homosexual marriage. Those critics who object to homosexual marriage, or at least raise concerns about the pursuit of state sponsorship, but who do not object to homosexuality *per se* are concerned with issues of substantive equality. To address same sex marriage in the context of substantive equality is to talk about benefit and disbenefit, it is to talk about harm to interests.

Some readers might wonder whether the kind of harm that is being discussed in this section of the paper is really the kind of harm that Mill would have had in mind when he proposed the Harm Principle. I have two responses to that potential interjection. Firstly, what Mill would have had in mind is not determinative of the articulation of harm to be covered by the Principle for contemporary society. The debates over hate literature, pornography, and the limits of free speech are not really foreshadowed in Mill's formulation, yet these issues have become an integral part of how the Harm Principle is understood in contemporary liberal society. Secondly, the kinds of harms that are covered by the term stigmatization include the loss of jobs, physical assaults ("gay bashing"), and other violations of the civil rights of gays, lesbians, and bisexuals. These are certainly the kinds of things Mill's own formulation would have been intended to cover.

On the usual reading of Mill's harm principle, preventing harm to others is the only justified rationale for state interference with the liberty of individuals.[12] I propose to apply a variant of the harm principle which can accommodate the concerns about putative harm raised by both sets of critics of same sex marriage, but still does justice to liberal principles. That variant is the following: the only justification for the denial by the state of a benefit required by formal equality is that the provision of that benefit would harm others in the society. Thus, as a matter of public policy, the state must sponsor power-conferring or entitlement-allocating legislation required by formal equality unless it can be shown that significant harm (of the kind covered by the harm principle) would result from that sponsorship. It could be argued that my formulation has departed so far from Mill's principle that it could not be included under the same label. Nevertheless, I think that the term harm is irreplaceable in this context — since it is harm that justifies the denial of state benefits. My version could be called the State Benefits Version of the Harm Principle.

The objections to same sex marriage which need to be countered involve conceptions of harm. I contend that in order to make sense of the objections, and in order to make a valid case for state sponsorship, it is necessary to respond to the assertions about putative harm. I have found that the most efficacious way to do so is to examine the application of my proposed formulation of the harm principle in the context of the legitimation of homosexual marriage.

II

There are effectively two distinct sets of criticisms of same sex marriage on the grounds of imputed harm resulting from state sanction. One set of criticisms includes several variations on the idea that allowing same sex marriages will bring about a threat to the nuclear family, marriage in general, or even to society. This set of criticisms is based on a claim that I will call the Harm to Heterosexuality claim. The other set of criticisms includes several variations on the idea that advocating and pursuing state sponsorship of same sex marriage will bring about a threat to the goals and objectives of gay liberation. This set of criticisms is based on a claim that I will call the Harm to Homosexuality claim. The objection to same sex marriage can make use of conceptions of harm that are either symbolic or empirical, or both. In other words, the kind of harm that is imputed can be harm that can be determined and measured empirically or it can be symbolic harm that is simply perceived.

The Harm to Heterosexuality is supposed to consist in the threat that same sex marriages pose to opposite sex marriages, harm in the form of decline in the sanctity of the institution of marriage, inconsistency with traditional definitions of family, or even in the most extreme articulations of the position, harm in the form of a contribution to an overall breakdown in social order. People who make these kinds of criticisms are motivated by the rejection of gay rights and liberation, and often even a "fear and loathing" of homosexuality.

Many versions of the Harm to Heterosexuality position are premised upon religious conceptions of sex, family, and society. As such, the harm that is claimed tends to be more symbolic than empirical. Insofar as the Harm to Heterosexuality position is based upon religious conceptions of sex, family, and society, it is easily dispensed with in the context of a discussion of liberalism. Given that liberalism requires the separation of church and state, it cannot be argued that the state should outlaw same sex marriages because such marriages are inconsistent with religious morality. Insofar as the Harm to Heterosexuality position is based upon some empirical sounding claim about actual harm to the institutions of marriage and family, or to "society" itself, it is obvious that this would have to be based on some kind of evidence. What kind of evidence could one possibly produce to argue that same sex marriages would erode the institutions of marriage and family?

Someone who wants to claim that same sex marriages will produce some kind of distinct social harm has to be able to show what harm is caused by the state sponsorship of marriage that is distinct from the harm that is imputed to same sex relationships themselves. Same sex coupling will continue with or without state sponsorship, and even with or without criminalization of some of the acts that are targeted as part of an attempt to outlaw homosexuality. People who object to same sex marriage may also object to homosexuality, but the point is that to make any kind of a case for why a liberal society should not provide legal sanction for relationships that are already occurring, an argument specifically against state sponsorship of marriage is needed. If liberalism is based, as I want to argue, on the notions of privacy, autonomy, and individual liberty, no argument against homosexuality based on mere moral or social disapproval is acceptable. There has to be evidence of actual harm that will be experienced by members of the society that amounts to more than mere offense at the actions or choices of others. Therefore, the critics of same sex marriage cannot argue that they object to state sponsorship because they object to homosexuality and state sponsorship legitimates homosexuality.

What quickly becomes clear once one looks at the various articulations of the Harm to Heterosexuality position is that it is difficult to separate the objection to same sex marriage from the objection to homosexuality. It is of course important to be able to separate these objections, because the only basis a liberal could accept for outlawing, or denying legitimacy to, same sex relationships, is that those relationships will actually cause harm to others. If we recognize that the harm that can be considered is not harm that consists of mere offense, then the symbolic element of the objection is disallowed. That leaves the empirical element of the objection.

One candidate for the requisite kind of harm that is proposed is the potential for gay marriage to undermine the legitimacy of straight marriage. This claim can be understood in two ways: one in which the delegitimation consists of symbolic harm to the institution and the other in which the delegitimation consists of actual harm to the institution in the form of decreased participation. The notion of symbolic harm to the sanctity of heterosexual marriage rests upon illiberal commitments and concerns, and thus does not raise issues germane to the consideration of what liberals should support.

The notion of the latter form of harm, one of decreased participation, underlies the claim that the opportunity for gay marriage will weaken the institution of heterosexual marriage. Yet, as others have pointed out, this argument rests upon (at least one) fallacy. As one commentator puts it, "[g]ay marriage could only delegitimize straight marriage if it were a real alternative to it."[13] That is, it could only delegitimize it if those who would otherwise participate in straight marriage chose to participate instead in gay marriage. Obviously, heterosexuals will continue to marry other heterosexuals. The people who will no longer participate in straight marriages if offered the opportunity to participate in gay marriages will be gays, lesbians, and bisexuals. Assuming that some gays who marry straights do so in order to be married and to have families, and not simply to avoid social stigma, then they would continue to do so. Those gays who marry straights in order to stay closeted and to avoid social stigma would continue to do so as long as the social stigmatization continues. Of course, the legalization of gay marriage would contribute to the erosion of the social stigma surrounding homosexuality, which would in turn encourage lesbians, gays, and bisexuals to participate in gay marriage. None of this suggests that there would be any real threat of significantly decreased participation in heterosexual marriage.

It thus seems as if the objection to same sex marriage characterized in terms of harm rests solely upon the objection to homosexuality itself. There is no argument against marriage of same sex persons that is not an argument against homosexuality. I want to assert that there is no valid empirical evidence that same sex relationships, in and of themselves, cause actual harm to any other persons. The claim that these relationships are harmful to the participants — even assuming there could be shown to be a factual basis to this dubious supposition — is of course an irrelevant claim, given liberalism's *prima facie* commitment to non-paternalism. It is particularly illegitimate when the paternalism is based on contentious moral, religious, or social conceptions of the "good" of the intended beneficiaries of the paternalism.[14]

The Harm to Homosexuality is supposed to consist in the threat that state sponsorship poses to the achievement of gay liberation and to the project of reconceiving heterosexuality, homosexuality, and relations between the sexes. People who make these kinds of claims are motivated by a commitment to gay liberation, and to some articulations of gay rights — ones that do not amount to presumption of the notion of "sameness" between gays and straights but rather assume the notion of "difference" between gays and straights. The position of those in gay, lesbian, and bisexual communities[15] who reject the pursuit of state sponsorship for same sex relationships, is not of course that there is anything wrong with same sex relationships. Their position is that there is something wrong with state sponsorship, and something wrong with marriage.

It should be pointed out that those in lesbian, gay, and bisexual communities who raise objections to the prospect of gay marriage do so largely on grounds of strategy and tactics. The debate over gay marriage within gay, lesbian, and bisexual communities is mainly a debate over the priority of different venues or policies for the allocation of resources and the expenditure of efforts. The discussion in much of the literature thus addresses the advisability of pursuing gay marriage as a strategy for gay activists, and raises concerns about the diversion of efforts and resources from other significant issues. These debates — whether putting too much effort into this one option will divert efforts from other options that may be more central to sexual liberation, whether the pursuit of domestic partnership legislation should take priority over removal of the same sex marriage bar,[16] whether the potential backlash from the pursuit of this particular option will have repercussions, or whether the gay, lesbian, and bisexual community is too divided over the option to make it a priority — could all be seen to involve questions about goals and strategies for queer activism.[17] For instance, some "regard domestic partnership agreement registration as a distraction from the need to gain full rights to marry with full access to benefits and protections," while others perceive that registration is better because it "recognizes alternative family structures."[18] These questions about which is the better target begin with the assumption that gays, lesbians, and bisexuals are entitled to equality and then move to the attempt to articulate and clarify the appropriate way to characterize and pursue that equality.

The point is that gays, lesbians, and bisexuals who call into question the desirability of gay marriage generally do not dispute the position that the opposite sex requirement of marriage laws is "socially discriminatory and offensive to the basic liberal principles that underlie human rights legislation."[19] Even those who raise objections to same sex marriage do not deny that the same sex marriage bar is illiberal. Yet, it is still possible to construct an objection to state sponsorship to same sex marriage that imputes some type of potential harm that would result from the policy. This objection could take several different forms:

1. one based on an objection to perceived conformity to "straight standards;[20]
2. one based on an objection to the oppressive patriarchal nature of the institution of marriage; and
3. one based on an objection to the involvement of the state in the regulation of lesbian, gay, and bisexual intimate relationships. These objections tend to overlap and are difficult to disentangle.

The first form of the objection, based on rejection of the perceived conformity to "straight standards" inherent in same sex marriage, implies that the pursuit of conformity on the part of some gays, lesbians, and bisexuals — namely those who would want to get married — could indirectly harm the interests of those who would not want to get married, and thus who do not conform. The harm would consist of the further stigmatization of those lesbians, gays, and bisexuals who choose not to get married once the option becomes available.[21]

It is possible to construct the imputed argument along the following lines. Homosexual sex is stigmatized and a cause for oppression of gays, lesbians, and bisexuals. If homosexuals could marry, those who would already tend to benefit from certain social privileges (class, race, ethnicity, and so forth) will likely be the ones to exercise the option. Those homosexuals who do not marry will be further stigmatized and oppressed, relative to the otherwise more privileged homosexuals who will marry.[22]

It is difficult to determine in what sense there would be more stigmatization or oppression of the lesbians, gays, and bisexuals who choose not to marry — absolutely or in terms of perception of relative privilege. It is at least partly an empirical question. What is relevant to the issue in question is whether the provision of state sponsorship for same sex marriage would result in more harm overall, harm of the sort that is germane to liberalism.

The significant issue for the question of whether liberalism should support same sex marriage is whether the resulting "extra" stigmatization would result from the provision of same sex marriage itself, or would be an unintended byproduct of pre-existing homophobia.[23] It is unclear whether the stigmatization of non-married or single gays, lesbians, and bisexuals would be more after the option of state sponsored same sex marriage is available or whether it would be the same amount of stigmatization, but would seem more in relation to the other married gays, lesbians, and bisexuals. That is, it is unclear whether it would be extra stigmatization or simply continuing stigmatization. Either way, the "extra" stigmatization should be the focus of additional efforts to reduce and eventually overcome homophobic societal attitudes. Unless one could show that denying same sex couples the right to marry would, in and of itself, decrease the stigmatization, it is necessary to address the resulting harm by other measures than continuing the same sex marriage bar.

The first objection to same sex marriage can be presented still more abstractly, in terms of the "politics of validating difference,"[24] and a general critique of "rights discourse" and "rights claims." The presumption is that there is something one could identify as lesbian and gay identity and culture that resists assimilation. There is no denial, however, that some gays and lesbians as individuals do not resist, and even welcome, assimilation. The concern is that whenever society extends rights to some previously disenfranchised group of persons — in this case the lesbians, gays, and bisexuals who do want to get married — then other members of the group who "forswear or forego such rights risk being even more marginalized than before."[25] The objection seems to highlight the tension between individual rights which would be asserted by the group of same sex couples who want to marry, and collective interests which would be represented by the interests of the remainder of the group, the non-marrying gays and lesbians.[26]

The second form of the Harm to Homosexuality objection is the claim that marriage is an oppressive institution which lesbians and gay men should condemn, rather than lobby to join.[27] There are two different aspects of characterizing the harm of marriage in this objection. One aspect concerns the patriarchal nature of marriage as a social institution.[28] The other aspect emphasizes the balance of benefits and burdens that marriage may provide for particular same sex couples. The latter aspect is related to the former in that the reason some couples would not realize the potential benefits of marriage would have to do with the underlying oppressive features, and structural constraints of society. What Nitya Duclos calls the "hierarchy of privilege" ensures that some couples — whether opposite sex or same sex couples — will benefit more from the bundle of benefits that constitute marriage.[29] The provision of state-sponsored marriage for same sex couples will also have effects on cohabiting same sex couples that may or may not be welcomed by those cohabiting couples.

Both aspects of the second objection — the particular and the general — have in common the focus on marriage. It is marriage as a social institution that is an oppressive patriarchal institution. It is marriage as a particular legislative scheme that has better or worse effects for particular couples. The important point for the purposes of this paper is that the putative harm does not result from the provision of same sex marriage, but rather from marriage itself. For the liberal, the question is whether it is justifiable for the state to continue to deny to same sex couples the option that is available to opposite sex couples — to participate in the potentially undesirable, arguably harmful institution of marriage. The liberal rejection of paternalism entails that individuals should be allowed to choose for themselves whether or not to participate in activities that may be harmful to themselves. The issue is not the desirability of marriage, but the desirability of the right.[30]

Several feminists have argued for the position that while marriage may be oppressive in its present form, it need not always be that way. Marriage, the argument goes, is a creature of law dependent upon the power of the state; as such, it is an historically and culturally contingent institution.[31] The further claim is made that same sex marriage could have the potential to "disrupt both the gendered definition of marriage and the assumption the marriage is a form of socially, if not legally, prescribed hierarchy".[32] At the very least, same sex marriages would require the rethinking of the content of the marriage vows and the exercise of linguistic creativity to replace the "husband" and "wife" terminology. These improvements would have symbolic value, and would contribute to the larger project of reforming marriage as a social institution. Same sex marriage, then, would produce no distinctive harm and might even ameliorate the current harm produced by marriage.

What makes the issue complicated is that it is possible to characterize the benefits that would accrue to lesbians, gays, and bisexuals upon provision of the right to state sponsorship of same sex marriage in two ways. One way is to emphasize the benefits that would be realized by individual members of same sex couples who could participate in marriage. The other way is to emphasize the benefits that would be realized by all queers consisting of increased tolerance of homosexuality and increased legitimacy for same sex unions. Some advocates of state sponsorship of same sex marriage argue that it is actually the "issue most likely to lead ultimately to a world free of discrimination against lesbians and gay men."[33] The characterization of benefits — the determination of which benefits will result and who specifically will benefit — is addressed in the literature in the context of the identification of attendant harms — the determination of which harms will result and who specifically will be harmed.

It is important to distinguish between the claim that same sex couples should be entitled to equal treatment with opposite sex couples — whether through domestic partnership arrangements or civil marriage — and the claim that these legal measures should be the focus of advocacy and struggle for gay rights. It is also important to distinguish between the claim that the right to choose X — for example, the right to choose to marry — will benefit those for whom X is a likely option and the claim that the right to choose X is a benefit to only those who do choose X. There is a difference between the concern that gay activists should not direct their energies to the pursuit of marriage and domestic partnership arrangements because only some gays and lesbians would want to participate in these institutions and the claim that only those who (will) participate in those institutions will be benefited by the existence of the choice.

The objection to same sex marriage based on the rejection of conformity should properly locate the harm in homophobia. The objection to same sex marriage based on the suspicion of marriage should properly locate the harm in marriage itself. The objection to same sex marriage based on the perniciousness of state regulation of sexuality should properly locate the harm in the combination of homophobia and marriage itself. It is obvious why queers would be suspicious of any manifestation of state regulation of sexuality.[34] The question, however, is whether gays, lesbians, and bisexuals would be worse off with the provision of state sponsorship for same sex coupling. It is hard to see how they would be. The problem rests with state initiatives that amount to the entrenchment of intolerance of homosexuality.

According to the third form of the Harm to Homosexuality objection, marriage simply presents yet another vehicle of state regulation of sexuality. Marriage, however, does present some potential for protection from state regulation and other benefits. Nitya Duclos lists four objectives of the advocates of gay and lesbian marriage:

1. "to revolutionize marriage and force society to rethink its collective views of sex and sexuality;"
2. to provide validation and legitimation of same sex relationships;
3. to enable lesbian and gay families to partake in the range of socioeconomic benefits of marriage;
4. to legitimate gay and lesbian relationships in the eyes of courts to help lesbians and gays keep their children.[35]

It is clear that merely removing the obstacles to same sex marriage is not going to be sufficient for the realization of these objectives.

State sponsorship of same sex coupling will entail toleration of homosexuality, but it alone will not provide for respect and full equality without other social, political, legal, and economic changes.[36] For example, changes in judicial attitudes and child custody legislation will be necessary for the achievement of the fourth objective.[37] The effect of marriage breakdown will cause same sex couples to come under the purview of courts under divorce legislation. Same sex couples who separate and divorce will be subject to provisions concerning division of property, support, and custody of children. For some people, that will be a benefit and for others that will be a burden. The point is that it is not same sex marriage that increases the points of contact but the legislative regime governing marriage and divorce. The fear of state regulation should not amount to a fear of same sex marriage, but rather a fear of homophobia and a fear of the potential effects of the legislative regime governing marriage and divorce. Thus, harm would result from homophobia and the effects of marriage and divorce, but not from same sex marriage itself.

The consideration of the Harm to Homosexuality objections points to the need to distinguish between formal and substantive equality. The conceptions of harm contained in the various forms of the objection indicate concerns of substantive equality. The question of whether same sex couples should be denied the state sponsorship available to opposite sex couples is really a question of formal equality. The position of this paper is that the same sex marriage bar is a clear denial of formal equality for gay, lesbians and bisexuals. It is important to make clear, then, the relation between formal equality and substantive equality on this issue, if there is any relation.

The opponents to same sex marriage who are motivated by some version of the Harm to Homosexuality objection could be making one of three different claims about the effects of same sex marriage on substantive equality. These three claims are:

1. same sex marriage would increase substantive equality;
2. same sex marriage would decrease substantive equality; or
3. same sex marriage would neither decrease nor increase substantive equality.

On the basis of the above discussion it seems that the three forms of the Harm to Homosexuality objection — the rejection of conformity, the suspicion of marriage, and the fear of state regulation — all attempt to implicate same sex marriage in the charge of jeopardizing substantive equality.

I have tried to argue, however, that what actually jeopardizes substantive equality is not the possibility of same sex marriage, in and of itself, but the effects of pre-existing inequalities resulting from homophobia, the legal regime governing marriage and divorce, and other social inequalities. I would contend then, that same sex marriage at the least could be said to neither decrease nor increase substantive equality. It may even increase substantive equality if the claims concerning the potential liberatory effects of same sex marriage upon the institution of marriage are viable. The provision of state sponsored same sex marriage would certainly further the pursuit of formal equality for homosexuals, and for that reason it is incumbent upon liberals to support it.

NOTES

1. Chris Bull, "Till Death Do Us Part", *The Advocate*, Issue 643, November 30, 1993, 40 at 41. As Bull and others point out gays and lesbians are "openly marrying, raising children, and demanding official recognition of their partners as spouses." Bull says that same sex marriage is the "new hot issue in the nation's [the U.S.] gay and lesbian community." See Michelangelo Signorile's article "Bridal Wave" for an account of how the issue is developing in Hawaii, which may end up being the first U.S. state to legally recognize homosexual marriages.
2. Gays and lesbians have been participating in commitment ceremonies (also called bonding or union ceremonies) for some time, but these, of course, do not have the "stamp of approval" nor the legal consequences of state-sponsored marriage. In Canada, several challenges to the exclusion of same sex couples from legal provisions concerning "spouses" are working their way through the courts. These challenges are typically based on equality claims involving section 15 of the Canadian Charter of Rights and Freedoms. See Bruce Ryder's "Equality Rights and Sexual Orientation: Confronting Heterosexual Family Privilege", *Canadian Journal of Family Law*, Volume 9, 1990, 39 for more on the specifics of the Canadian context.
3. As per common usage, I will assume that gay refers to gay men and lesbian refers to gay women. Some people take the term "queer" to refer to gay men, lesbian women, bisexual women, bisexual men, transsexuals, and transvestites collectively.
4. This is the gist of what then Prime Minister Pierre Elliot Trudeau said when recommending the decriminalization of any sexual activity between consenting adults in private. This claim is a prior assumption to my version of a functional definition of marriage.
5. Clearly, I am developing my formulation of liberalism and its basic assumptions and commitments in reliance upon certain exponents of the liberal tradition — namely John Stuart Mill in *On Liberty*, Ronald Dworkin in "Liberalism," from Hampshire, ed., *Public and Private Morality*, and Joel Feinberg in *Harmless Wrongdoing*. There is a vast literature on liberalism, but interestingly very little of that literature that I am aware of actually addresses the question of a liberal position on the state sponsorship of same sex marriages.
6. These are the usual conditions for marriage – there will likely be some variation among jurisdictions. Nitya Duclos, in "Some Complicating Thoughts on Same Sex Marriage," says the common bars to marriage include: "minimum age limits, insanity, absence of consent (mistake, duress, and fraud), prohibited degrees of affinity and consanguinity, and a prior existing marriage." Nitya Duclos, "Some Complicating Thoughts on Same Sex marriage", *Law and Sexuality: A Review of Lesbian and Gay Legal Issues*, Volume 1, Summer 1991, 31 at 44, fn. 48.

7. Nan Hunter, in "Marriage, Law and Gender: A Feminist Inquiry", points out that the functionalist approach — which posits the identification of objective criteria to determine which relationships are the functional equivalents to marriage — underlay the recognition of common law marriage. See Nan Hunter, "Marriage, Law and Gender", *Law and Sexuality: A Review of Lesbian and Gay Issues*, Volume 1, Summer 1991, 9 at 21 ff.

8. The San Francisco Domestic Partnership law states "[d]omestic partners are two adults who have chosen to share one another's lives in an intimate and committed relationship of mutual caring, who live together, and who have agreed to be jointly responsible for basic living expenses incurred during the Domestic Partnership". See Appendix A: San Francisco Domestic Partnership Ordinance (1990) in David Chambers's article "Tales of Two Cities: AIDS and the Legal Recognition of Domestic Partnerships in San Francisco and New York", *Law and Sexuality: A Review of Lesbian and Gay Legal Issues*, Volume 2, Summer 1992, 181 at 204. The New York Court of Appeals found in *Braschi v. Stahl Associates* that a gay couple must be treated as a family in relation to New York's rent control law. The Court found that the couple satisfied the following criteria: "the exclusivity and longevity of the relationship, the level of emotional and financial commitment, the manner in which the parties have conducted their everyday lives and held themselves out to society, and the reliance placed upon one another for daily family services". Chambers provides an extended discussion of that case from p. 192 ff. See Hunter, supra, p. 23.

9. I should point out that the support is often a qualified support, for a series of complicated reasons. I will touch briefly on some of those reasons in the section concerning the Harm to Homosexuality objection to same sex marriages below, but it will not be possible for me to do justice in this paper to the fascinating complexity of the debates over same sex marriage in the lesbian, gay and bisexual community. For some sense of what the issues are see the papers by Nitya Duclos, Mary Dunlap and Nan Hunter in the Symposium on Lesbian and Gay Marriage in *Law and Sexuality: A Review of Lesbian and Gay Legal Issues*, Volume 1, Summer 1991 and see the papers by Thomas Stoddard and Paula Ettelbrick in *Lesbian and Gay Marriage*, edited by Suzanne Sherman. See also Chris Bull, "Till Death Do Us Part", supra, and Michelangelo Signorile, "Bridal Wave", *Out*, December/January 1994, 69.

10. Laws in several states in the United States which criminalize sodomy do not distinguish between heterosexual and homosexual sodomy. Yet, in *Bowers vs. Hardwick* the Georgia law was challenged by a homosexual man and the court dealt with the issue as if the law were intended to outlaw homosexual sodomy. In Canada, the federal criminal code was amended in May 1969 to remove the criminalization of any sexual acts between consenting adults.

11. Harlon Dalton, "Reflections on the Lesbian and Gay Marriage Debate", *Law and Sexuality: A Review of Lesbian and Gay Legal Issues*, Volume 1, Summer 1991, 1 at 7.

12. This general conception covers both narrower and broader conceptions of the Harm Principle. See Lyons, "Liberty and Harm to Others", for a discussion of the debate over how narrowly or broadly Mill's principle — which he calls the Principle of Liberty — should be construed. Brown argues that the principle should cover only harm producing conduct and Lyons argues that it should be expanded to include harm preventing conduct, which may not itself be harm producing — for example, good samaritan behaviour and joint cooperation behaviour. My conception differs from that of both of these versions in that I focus on the justification of the denial of state benefits rather than the justification of the interference with liberty.

13. Andrew Sullivan, in "Here Comes the Groom: A (Conservative) Case for Gay Marriage", *The New Republic*, August 28, 1989, 20. Catherine MacKinnon points out that "persons secure in their heterosexuality would not be threatened by the availability of this option", ie. gay marriage. MacKinnon, *Feminism Unmodified: Discourses on Life and Law*, Harvard University Press, 1987, at 27.

14. Michael Levin, in "Why Homosexuality is Abnormal," for example, attempts to provide a teleological account of the harm that homosexuality presents. If his argument were persuasive, then paternalism would seem to follow. Michael Ruse's discussion of the claim that homosexuality is unnatural in "Is Homosexuality Bad Sexuality?" tends to undercut Levin's claims. Both papers can be found in *Moral Controversies: Race, Class, and Gender in Applied Ethics*, edited by Steven Jay Gold, Wadsworth, 1993.

15. It would be inaccurate and inappropriate to speak of "the" gay, lesbian, and bisexual community; but it would be equally inaccurate and inappropriate to speak of "the" gay, "the" lesbian, or "the" bisexual community. There are communities, and communities within communities. It might be possible to speak of a community of communities, but even that might be misleading. One can get a sense of the remarkable range of conceptions of equality for gays, lesbians and bisexuals and of the range of recommended strategies from reading Paul Berman's essay "Democracy and Homosexuality", in *The New Republic,* and from the following books (two of which Berman reviews): Bruce Bawer, *A Place at the Table: The Gay Individual in American Society*; Mark Blasuis, *A Politics of Sexuality: The Emergence of a Lesbian and Gay Ethos*; Diana Fuss, *Essentially Speaking: Feminism, Nature and Difference*; Marshall Kirk and Hunter Madsen, *After the Ball: How America Will Conquer Its Fear and Hatred of Gays in the 1990s*; Shane Phelan, *Identity Politics: Lesbian Feminism and the Limits of Community*; Michelangelo Signorile's *Queer in America: Sex, the Media and the Closets of Power*. There are many more references that could be given, but this list is sufficient to cover the range from separatist liberation perspectives to conservative assimilationist perspectives. Chris Bull's article in the *Advocate*, "Till Death Do Us Part" and Michelangelo Signorile's article in *Out*, "Bridal Wave" gave some indication of the range of positions on same sex marriage among gays and lesbians.

16. See David Chambers, "Tales of Two Cities: AIDS and the Legal Recognition of Domestic Partnerships in San Francisco and New York". Domestic Partnership ordinances have been enacted by municipalities in various U.S. cities. The domestic partnership arrangements usually contain a requirement that same sex couples register as partners — "two people who have chosen to share one another's lives in an intimate and committed relationship of mutual caring". Chambers, *supra*, at 185. The other feature of the arrangements is the provision by public and private employers that those couples who have registered will be entitled to the benefits provided to "spouses". Domestic Partnership regimes in the U.S. have usually been open to both homosexual and heterosexual unmarried couples. See Dunlap, at 94 and Posner, at 313–314 on the arrangements in Denmark and Sweden. Richard Posner's discussion is part of a larger work, *Sex and Reason*, Harvard University Press, 1992.

17. Many of the discussions of the issue by gay and lesbian activists focus on this aspect. For example, Michael Lowenthal in "Wedding Bells and Whistles" says that "[w]inning domestic-partnership privileges won't lead to acceptance for all lesbians and gay men, only for those in domestic partnerships". He then goes on to say: "[r]ather than lobbying for policies that will benefit only those who choose to register domestic partnerships, we should be fighting for the fundamental civil rights that will guarantee equal treatment for us all". See Lowenthal, *The Advocate*, December 4, 1993, 5.

18. Suzanne Sherman points to the divided opinion on the topic among the interviewees for her book, *Lesbian and Gay Marriage: Private Commitments, Public Ceremonies*, Temple University Press, 1992. See p. 8.

19. Nitya Duclos, "Some Complicating Thoughts on Same Sex Marriage", *supra* at 31. Paula Ettelbrick, one of those most strongly opposed to same sex marriages admits that: "[w]hen analyzed from a standpoint of civil rights, certainly lesbians and gay men should have a right to marry". Ettelbrick, "Since When Is Marriage a Path to Liberation?", in Sherman, ed., *Lesbian and Gay Marriage*, at 21.

20. Michael Lowenthal says in "Wedding Bells and Whistles" that he was part of efforts to obtain legal recognition of domestic partnerships but came to realize that the administration of the college where he worked "would accept us only to the degree that we conformed to straight standards". Lowenthal, p. 5.

21. The objection is framed this way by Mary Dunlap in "The Lesbian and Gay Marriage Debate: A Microcosm of Our Hopes and Troubles in the Nineties", *Law and Sexuality: A Review of Lesbian and Gay Legal Issues*, Volume 1, Summer 1991, 63 at 78 and Nan Hunter in "Marriage, Law and Gender . . .", *supra*, at 12. Dunlap asks "If Outlaws Can Have In-Laws Then Won't Those Without In-Laws Become Outer Outlaws?" Nitya Duclos discusses the issue several times in "Some Complicating Thoughts on Same Sex Marriage". Paula Ettelbrick says, "gay marriage, instead of liberating gay sex and sexuality, would further outlaw all gay and lesbian sex that is not performed in a marital context". See Ettelbrick, "Since When Is Marriage a Path to Liberation?", *supra*, at 23.

22. This is a reconstruction of the various positions presented in the papers by Hunter, Duclos, and Ettelbrick.

23. Homophobia has become a common term for the unjust denial of civil rights to homosexuals, as well as to the irrational fear and hatred of homosexuals and homosexuality. The term was initially used in psychiatric literature to refer to the 'phobia' that one might be a homosexual oneself. The term has taken on a broader meaning, one which functions in many respects analogously to sexism, racism, ableism, and classism. The term heterosexism is often used in the same contexts as homophobia.

24. Nan Hunter, supra, at 11.

25. Harlon Dalton, "Reflections on the Lesbian and Gay Marriage Debate", supra, at 5. As Dalton points out, "legal rights would never be extended if the bare fact that a subset of the class might thereby be disadvantaged were deemed to constitute a sufficient ground for inaction". He goes on to say that it is still problematic to pursue policies which will have the unintended effects of favouring some class members over others.

26. While this conflict is most readily treated as a conflict between individual and collective interests, it can also be conceived as a conflict between different collective interests and thus competing versions of collective rights – the interests of assimilationists and the interests of anti-assimilationists respectively. C.f. Leslie Green, "Two Views of Collective Rights". *Canadian Journal of Law and Jurisprudence*, Volume 4(2), 1991, 315 at 325.

27. Hunter, supra, at 11. Hunter identifies two arguments that opponents to same sex marriage within lesbian, gay, and bisexual communities have relied on: the one about assimilation and stigmatization and the other one about the oppressiveness of marriage. Duclos and Dunlap also provide extensive discussion of the claim concerning marriage.

28. See Duclos, Dunlap, and Hunter for extensive discussions of marriage as a patriarchal institution. Duclos points out that the provision of same sex marriage may serve to legitimate marriage, which would have bad consequences for heterosexually identified women. It is of course the legitimation of marriage that would have the bad consequences.

29. Dunlap, supra at 86 reproduces the following list of rights enjoyed by persons who marry: the right to obtain health insurance, bereavement leave, and make decisions when the partner is incapacitated; the right to visit the partner in hospitals, jails, mental institutions and other places restricted to family members; the right to claim dependency deductions and statuses; the right to claim estate and gift tax benefits; the right to file joint tax returns; the right of inheritance (particularly in case of intestacy); the right to sue for infliction of emotional distress by injury to the partner, for loss of consortium, wrongful death and other personal injuries; the right to claim marital communication privilege; the right to live in housing for married persons; and more. See Duclos, pp. 52–53 for a more extensive list. Duclos also sets out a list of burdens the marriage brings, which includes the following: "spouse in the house" rules for state welfare assistance; "spouse's" credit history taken into account in credit rating; disentitlement from government student loans on the basis of "spouse's" income; anti-nepotism rules in employment, and more. See Duclos, supra, at 53–54 for the complete list.

30. Thomas Stoddard makes this point in "Why Gay People Should Seek the Right to Marry", in Sherman, ed., *Lesbian and Gay Marriage*, at 18.

31. Nan Hunter, supra, at 13. See also Dunlap and Duclos for similar arguments.

32. Hunter, supra, at 16. As Catherine MacKinnon puts it in "Not By Law Alone" from *Feminism Unmodified: Discourses on Life and Law*: "I do think it might do something amazing to the entire institution of marriage to recognize the unity of "two" persons between whom no superiority or inferiority could be presumed on the basis of gender". MacKinnon, supra, at 27.

33. Thomas Stoddard, "Why Gay People Should Seek the Right to Marry", supra at 17.

34. See Dunlap for an extensive discussion of the harmful effects of the *Bowers v. Hardwick* decision and other homophobic state measures.

35. Duclos, supra, at 42.

36. Nan Hunter suggests that more encompassing changes be based on "gender dissent", which she says does not connote identity based on sexual orientation but rather conveys an active intent to disconnect power from gender and conveys an adversary relationship to dominance. Hunter, supra, at 29–30. She argues that the pursuit of domestic partnership laws should complement the pursuit of legalizing lesbian and gay marriage, and that "neither strategy is complete without the

other". Hunter, supra, at 26. For more, on domestic partnership agreements, see David Chambers, "Tales of Two Cities . . .", supra.

37. It is interesting, and disconcerting, to note that the Danish government which provided the right to marry for same sex couples by an act of Parliament still restricted the right of lesbian and gay couples to adopt children. There would be no rationale for the continuing restriction on a liberal treatment of the issue such as I have been developing. See Dunlap, supra, at 94.

QUESTIONS

1. According to Alex Wellington, what are the basic tenets of liberalism?
2. What aspects of the functional definition of heterosexual couples does Wellington see as analogous to the case for same-sex couples?
3. Why is the harm principle relevant to an analysis of the issue of same-sex marriage? Wellington identifies two distinct sets of criticisms of same-sex marriage that have relied on an account of harm. What are they? What reasons does Wellington give for rejecting these accounts of harm?
4. Does Wellington provide a convincing case for seeing same-sex couples as the same as heterosexual couples and, thus, deserving of equal treatment under the law?

DISABILITY AND EQUALITY

Jerome E. Bickenbach

When census-takers first tried to count the number of their citizens with mental or physical disabilities it proved to be surprisingly difficult. They found that two people with precisely the same medical condition — a visual impairment, spinal injury, cerebral palsy, neurosis or depression — often experience the condition in very different ways. Some will be limited in what they can do, others will not. They also discovered something sociologists had known for years: disability is not merely a medical condition, it is a negative social status that people may, justifiably, be reluctant to apply to themselves. Disability, it turns out, is a complex notion, both logically and sociologically. But a careful analysis of it has shed light on the wider issue of human diversity and the political ideal of equality.

Although philosophers have only very recently thought much about disability, it has been scrutinized by other disciplines for decades. The profession of physical therapy, for example, broke away from medicine in part because of the practical need to distinguish the medical domain of pathologies and impairments — which affect cells, tissues, organs and other parts of people — from the disfunctionings and inabilities that limit the range of activities people perform in the world as they find it. Social psychologists have emphasized the role of stereotyping and stigmatization in the construction of the public perception of disability. Economists, for their part, have analyzed disability as a limitation on the repertoire of functional capacities of people. And political theorists have identified disability as an administrative category used to set people apart for special treatment, sometimes to their advantage, but usually not.

In 1980, the World Health Organization published a remarkable document that brought together many of these isolated strains of thought about disability. It was called the

Reprinted by permission of Jerome E. Bickenbach.

International Classification of Impairments, Disabilities, and Handicaps (or ICIDH), and, though designed primarily as a classification tool, it embodied a sophisticated three-part analysis of disability in terms of Impairments, Disabilities* and Handicaps:

An Impairment is any loss or abnormality of physiological, psychological or anatomical structure or function, described and explained by biomedical scientists. Sometimes, an Impairment forms the physical basis of a Disability, defined as a restriction or lack of an ability to perform an activity in the manner or range considered normal. This transition is not inevitable, not only because some Impairments are so trivial they normally would not limit significant abilities (for example, being born with a thumb that is a millimetre shorter than normal), but also because people with a potentially disabling Impairment are not disabled because, for them in their circumstances, lacking that ability has no affect on their lives (for example, being unable to tolerate very hot weather if one lives out one's life in the arctic). Having a Disability, in short, is in part a function of the physical and social circumstances in which one lives.

Lastly, the complex phenomenon of disability includes the aspect of Handicap, defined as those disadvantages that are created by the social reception of perceived Impairments or Disabilities. If I am ridiculed for my limp, or prohibited from being a school teacher because of my blindness, or denied a place in the movie theatre because I am in a wheelchair, then I am disadvantaged (I am denied benefits and opportunities available to others) because of the reception of my perceived Impairment or Disability. Handicaps, in a word, are denials of equality based on perceived Disability or Impairment.

But why 'perceived' Disability or Impairment? Because, interestingly, since Handicaps are the products of stigma, stereotype, ill-will, pity, misperception, ignorance, or benign neglect, it is the perception, not the reality, that is important. Suppose I am denied an apartment because the landlord thinks that I have AIDS (when in fact I do not). Were I HIV serio-positive I would have an Impairment, and would eventually have a collection of Disabilities as well; and if I were denied the apartment for these reasons, then I would have a Handicap. But if I am falsely believed to have AIDS, and denied an apartment on that ground, I still have a Handicap, since I am still disadvantaged because of someone's perception of my physical state.

The WHO model helpfully explains why the purely medical understanding of disability is incomplete. There is no direct, causal link between Impairments, Disabilities and Handicaps: each aspect of disability interacts with the background social and physical context in which the person lives, and it is the interaction, not just the physical or mental condition, that yields Disabilities and Handicaps. This model of disability is sometimes called the ecological model because of the essential role played by environment factors (social, attitudinal, physical) in the creation of the various dimensions of disability.

Understanding disability ecologically, or interactively, helps also to clarify basic confusions about what it means to have a disability. First of all, many Disabilities involve chronic Impairments that do not get better. So, if one is blind, or an amputee, or post-polio, the 'problems' one faces are not really medical, but rehabilitative: getting around, finding employment, acquiring and using prosthetic devices. To insist that Disability is a medical problem, moreover, can be stigmatizing. People with medical problems we believe have a responsibility to see a physician, follow her advice, and get better. But if Disability is medicalized, people with Disabilities will be viewed either as irresponsible, or as medical 'failures'.

---

* *From now on, to avoid confusion, the specially defined WHO motion will be capitalized (Disability) while the ordinary, inclusive and ambiguous notion will be left in lower case.*

Secondly, Disabilities often, and Handicaps always, are created by social circumstances wholly separate from the Impairment a person may have, and this has obvious, and profound, social and political consequences. Suppose I am in a wheelchair and I wheel up to the front door of a building that has no ramp. I might describe my situation by saying, either that I am unable to enter the building, because of my Impairment, or else that I am unable to enter because of the absence of a ramp. The word 'able' and its cognants (including 'ability') are ambiguous in this respect. But notice that in the first case the problem is functional, while in the second, it is architectural. In the first case, if medicine and rehabilitative therapy can do nothing, then I cannot enter the building because of my inability; but in the second case, I cannot enter the building because it is inaccessible.

How does our interactive notion of Disability help us here? It does by insuring that we describe the situation accurately: my Disability (being unable to get into the building) is the result of what happens when my Impairment interacts with a particular architectural environment. This means that my Disability can be 'fixed' by altering the environment: first of all, and for many purposes, by giving me a wheelchair; but, secondly, as in this instance, by providing a ramp or elevator.

The ecological model, in another words, makes it clear that there are two distinct social responses to Impairments and Disabilities: On the one hand, we can direct social and individual resources to try to *correct* the Impairment or Disability. In the standard case, this would mean either looking for a medical therapy or cure, where possible and appropriate, or else a rehabilitative response. Performing surgery to alter the configuration of muscles in my legs, or training me to walk by means of exercises and physical therapy are thus modes of correction.

But on the other hand, we can direct social and individual resources to altering the physical or social environment in order to *accommodate* a person's functional limitations. Wheelchairs and ramps are accommodations; so too are alterations in job descriptions that make it possible for me to work on one floor rather than having to go up and down stairs, or changes in employers' attitudes to hiring people in wheelchairs, or passing legislation that requires governments to put ramps in public buildings and to share the cost of doing so in private employment sites, and on and on. An accommodation alters that part of the social and physical environment that Disables people who have Impairments.

Significantly, though, the line between correction and accommodation is drawn politically, not medically. Take the case of finding employment for people with disabilities. As a society we are faced with a choice: should we correct the person by providing her or him with new or augmented skills in order to overcome the physical obstacles in the workplace; or should we make the workplace accessible to the person with a Disability by means of accommodations. (For years physiotherapists trained people in wheelchairs to 'jump' curbs so that they could get around; now we put in curb cuts.) Although medical and other expertise is obviously relevant to our decision, ultimately our choice is grounded in our political and moral understanding of what society owes to people with disabilities. We need to ask ourselves, what does equality demand?

Hence the third philosophically important consequence of the ecological model is that it identifies the social-political dimension of disability. In nearly every nation, some provision is made for people with disabilities; in the wealthier, Western countries social policy for and on behalf of people with disabilities constitutes a substantial portion of what is usually called the 'welfare state': disability pensions, worker's compensation, medical insurance, drug and assistive device programmes, mental health care, vocational rehabilitation, and so on.

Increasingly too, anti-discrimination laws have extended protection to those who are Handicapped by discrimination on the basis of disability. The three-part WHO model makes it clear that this complex social policy addresses different aspects of disability: Impairment issues (medical care, medications, chronic care); Disability issues (rehabilitation, assistive devices, architectural and other accommodations); and Handicap Issues (anti-discrimination protections; accommodation requirements; access to services).

In recent years, with the ecological approach to disability in hand, advocates for people with disabilities have made the link, both as a matter of political theory and practice, between the nature of Disability and Handicap and the political ideal and promise of equality. These efforts have been primarily in the political arena, where, for example in the United States, we have witnessed an increased politicalization of people with disabilities which has resulted in legislation such as the *Americans with Disabilities Act*. At the theoretical level, though, there remains much turmoil, and considerable need for philosophical investigation that goes to the very heart of the theory of political and social equality.

It is clear that whatever our social policy arrangements happen to be, wherever we choose to draw the line between correction and accommodation, and whether we have legal protections against discrimination or not, at bottom the politics of disability rests on the political value of equality. Bluntly put, the issue comes to this: What does a social and political commitment to equality require in the case of people with disabilities?

So far — but the day is still young in theorizing about disability — two major strategies have been tried to answer this question. One approach, and to date by far the most popular, is to characterize all forms and manifestations of Handicaps as discriminatory denials of equality of opportunity. Treatment is discriminatory, on this account, if it is either insulting, demeaning, trivializing or marginalizing, or else if it indirectly disadvantages people with disabilities by failing to provide them with the resources required to meet the needs created by their Impairments and Disabilities. This means that people with disabilities constitute a kind of minority group who have historically faced systemic discrimination. The solution is political action to ensure protection against discrimination, through explicit anti-discrimination legislation and system-wide changes to remedy the marginalized status of people with disabilities, as a group.

As a political strategy, the civil rights approach (as this first strategy may be called) is a proven success. Born out of the consumer and civil rights movements of the 1960s, the disability rights movement can be credited with nearly every change in attitude and treatment of people with disabilities in the last two decades — from curb cuts and accessible bathrooms, to programs to integrate developmentally disabled children into the public schools to protections of the rights of people in mental institutions. As it has matured, the civil rights approach has adopted some of the theoretical developments introduced by feminists and black theorists, notably identity politics and separatist cultures (as evidenced by the Deaf Culture).

Another strategy, still in its infancy, might be called the universalistic, or distributive justice, approach. It is founded on the principle that disability is not the characteristic of some discrete and insular minority of people, it is rather a human phenomenon experienced by everyone, to one degree or another, and at one time or another. On this account, a failure to make public transportation accessible, or to integrate people with different cognitive abilities into schools, are not acts of discrimination but rather instances of distributive injustice. By catering to people whose range of abilities falls within an artificially narrow range we call 'normal', our society and its economic institutions, public and private, are unfairly and irrationally privileging one group of people over another. Equality is best served by distributive justice, and justice requires that the range of variation in human abilities and capabilities should not be artificially narrowed to advantage some at the expense of others.

The universalistic approach has the advantage of providing a theoretical answer to why disability is an issue of political equality. Since Disabilities and Handicaps are limitations on an individual positive liberty — the freedom to do or become what a person chooses — to the extent that these limitations are socially-constructed, they are instances of unjust distribution of positive liberty across members of society. People who are currently not disabled (the disability rights community jokingly calls these people TABs — the 'temporarily able bodied') enjoy a disproportionate share of the benefits from social arrangements because the existing social environment has been arbitrarily designed to cater to their range of abilities. Moreover, they enjoy these benefits, not because they deserve them, but simply because of good luck: in the 'natural lottery' they happened to be born without potentially Disabling conditions, or they happen not to have Disabling accidents. On the other hand, people who came out differently in the natural lottery and as a result cannot perform within the socially-constructed and artificially narrow range of abilities enjoy fewer social benefits, and must confront more socially-created burdens that limit their positive freedom.

From the point of view of distributive justice, the appropriate response to this situation is to remove the unfairness by redistributing positive liberty more equitably across the population. That may be accomplished either by correcting, or by accommodating or both. Those who are reaping the unearned benefits of the natural lottery (the TABs) can in fairness be required to return this unearned benefit (or, alternatively, to take on their fair share of social burdens) through the standard social redistributive mechanisms of taxation and regulation. This is not a matter, it should be noted, of punishing the TABs for their discriminatory behaviour; it is rather a matter of securing a more equitable distribution of the positive liberty that it is society's obligation to secure for all its citizens.

The universalistic approach, in other words, focuses our social energies on the task of finding the right balance of correction and accommodation that can secure full equality of social participation for everyone, regardless of their functional capacities. The civil rights approach, by contrast, is diverted from this important, and extremely difficult task, by two preliminary tasks: first, that of determining whether a particular person with a Disability has been disadvantaged because of an act of discrimination; and secondly, assigning responsibility for the discrimination in order to determine who must repair the damage caused by it. The first task determines the eligibility of the complainant, the second, the identity of the culprit. In practice, both of these tasks require an adjudicator (such as a judge or tribunal) and, in fairness, the opportunity for the putative culprit to defend herself. All of these take up time, and social resources, both of which could be more fruitfully expended on the task of securing equality through redistribution.

Another contrast between the two strategies is illuminating. To employ the notion of discrimination in order to remedy a Handicap the person with the disability can not themselves have contributed to the creation of the Handicap, since it would be unfair to hold one person responsible for a disadvantage that the victim has helped to create. That means that it matters how the Impairment or Disability came about, and in particular, it matters whether the person with the disability is in part, or entirely, to blame for it (by leading a risky or unhealthy life, for example). So, on the civil rights approach, if someone is denied employment because they are in a wheelchair, it will make a difference to the social response to the discrimination whether the individual acquired the Disability innocently or brought it on themselves through careless living.

The universalistic approach does not see it this way. Here we do not care how the Disability was acquired, or who was to blame for it, but merely whether the individual has access to a fair share of positive liberty, in order to participate equally in all areas of social life. Knowing about a person's risky or careless life habits is important, for these habits are themselves Disabilities that may need to be corrected or accommodated. But, on the universalistic approach, being denied employment because you are in a wheelchair is unjust, irrespective on why you are in the wheelchair or whose fault it is that you are.

Now, although historically the civil rights approach has proven its usefulness, the universalistic or distributive justice approach may in the long run prove to have a stronger theoretical foundation. In part this is because many of the basic assumptions of the civil rights approach are dubious. For example, it is doubtful whether people with disabilities constitute a distinct minority group, or that all of the systemic Handicaps that they face are the product of discrimination (unless that term is given an uncomfortably wide, and loose, characterization). Intuitively, it makes more sense to say that, unlike race, ethnicity, gender, and religion, disability is a universal feature of the human condition, shared by all to one degree or another. Indeed, the ultimate Handicap may just be that of assuming that disability is confined to one group of people.

To prove its theoretical superiority, however, the universalistic approach to disability must secure the link between disability, understood on the ecological model, and the political and moral value of equality. That in turn requires what so far has not been successfully achieved, namely, a theory of distributive justice that takes disability seriously. So far, most theories of distributive justice treat disability as a 'special case' that can be added on to a theory of justice designed primarily for 'normal people'. Increasingly, political and moral philosophers are turning to the ecological understanding of disability as a cure for their unaccommodating accounts of equality and justice.

FURTHER READING

Amundson, Ron "Disability, Handicap, and the Environment" (1992) 9 *Journal of Social Philosophy*

Bickenbach, Jerome *Physical Disability and Social Policy* (Toronto, University of Toronto Press, 1993)

Goffman, Erving *Stigma: Notes on the Maintenance of Spoiled Identity* (Englewood Cliffs, NJ, Prentice Hall, 1963)

Hahn, Harlan "The Politics of Physical Differences: Disability and Discrimination" (1988) 44 *Journal of Social Issues* 39

McCluskey, Martha "Rethinking Equality and Difference: Disability Discrimination in Public Transportation" (1988) 97 *Yale Law Journal* 863

Minow, Martha *Making All the Difference: Inclusion, Exclusion, and American Law* (Ithaca, NY, Cornell University Press, 1990)

Oliver, Michael *Understanding Disability: From Theory to Practice* (London, MacMillan, 1996)

Zola, Irving K. "Toward the Necessary Universalizing of a Disability Policy" (1989) 67 *The Milbank Quarterly* 401

QUESTIONS

1. What are the definitions of "Impairment," "Disabilities," and "Handicaps" offered by the World Health Organization?
2. What does Jerome Bickenbach mean by an ecological model? Do you think this idea helps us to understand the nature of disability?
3. What are the differences between a civil rights approach and a distributive justice approach to issues of disability? What reasons does Bickenbach give for saying that the civil rights approach has limitations?
4. Bickenbach claims that "it makes more sense to say that, unlike race, ethnicity, gender, and religion, disability is a universal feature of the human condition, shared by all to one degree or another." How does Bickenbach use this claim to defend a distributive justice approach? Do you think this claim has implications for other issues of discrimination examined in this chapter?

SUGGESTIONS FOR FURTHER READING

Court Cases

- Supreme Court of Canada. *Action Travail des Femmes v. Canadian National Railway Co. et al. Dominion Law Reports* 40 D.L.R. (4th), 1987. A case that ruled it was within the jurisdiction of the Canadian Human Rights Tribunal to order CN to instate quotas for the hiring of women.
- Supreme Court of Canada. *Law Society of British Columbia et al. v. Andrews et al.* 1989. The Court examined the question of whether the citizenship requirement for entry into the legal profession contravened Section 15 of the Charter. This examination resulted in the first attempt by the Supreme Court to interpret the equality provisions in Section 15 of the Charter.
- Court of Appeal for Ontario. *Halpern v. Canada (Attorney General)* June 10, 2003. DOCKET: C39172 and C39174. A case that ruled that the violation of eight couples' equality rights under s. 15(1) of the *Charter* was not justified under s. 1 of the *Charter* and that the Attorney General of Canada failed to show that the objectives of excluding same-sex couples from marriage are pressing and substantial.

Canadian Government Reports

- Canada. Royal Commission on Equality in Employment. *Report of the Commission on Equality in Employment.* (Ottawa: Supply and Services Canada, 1984). This final report of a commission chaired by Judge Rosalie S. Abella as well as the background papers, *Research Studies of the Commission on Equality in Employment*, provides an introduction to equality theory in the context of an examination of the disadvantages and inequalities experienced in Canada by visible minorities, people with disabilities, women, and Native people.
- Canada. Parliament. House of Commons. Standing Committee on Justice and Legal Affairs. Sub-Committee on Equality Rights. *Equality For All: Report of the Parliamentary Committee on Equality Rights.* Ottawa: Supply and Services, 1985.

- Canadian Advisory Council on the Status of Women. *Canadian Charter Equality Rights for Women: One Step Forward or Two Steps Back?* Ottawa: Canadian Advisory Council on the Status of Women, 1989.
- Canada. House of Commons Standing Committee on Human Rights and the Status of Disabled Persons. *A Consensus for Action: The Economic Integration of Disabled Persons.* Ottawa: Supply and Services, 1990.
- Canada. Task Force on the Participation of Visible Minorities in the Federal Public Service. *Embracing Change in the Federal Public Service.* 1999.

Books and Web Sites

- *Race, Gender, and Affirmative Action: Resource Page for Teaching.* URL: http://www-personal.umich.edu/%7Eeandersn/biblio.htm
  This Web site provides an extensive annotated bibliography of resources on race, gender, and affirmative action. It includes court cases related to U.S. court cases including the landmark University of Michigan affirmative action case as well as links to and citations of a number of other resources.
- Anne Bayefsky and Mary Eberts, eds., *Equality Rights and the Canadian Charter of Rights and Freedoms* (Toronto: Carswell, 1985). This collection of essays explores the ways in which interpretations of the Charter may affect various disadvantaged groups. It includes chapters that discuss aspects of discrimination on the grounds of ethnicity, religion, sex, age, mental and physical disability, marital status, and sexual orientation.
- Carl E. James, ed., *Perspectives on Racism and the Human Services Sector: A Case for Change* (Toronto: University of Toronto Press, 1996). A collection of essays by Canadian academics, lawyers, public servants, and policy workers that "examines race and racism in Canada from historical and contemporary perspectives and explores the extent to which these factors operate within social services systems related to immigration, settlement, the justice system, health, and education."
- Will Kymlicka, ed., *The Rights of Minority Cultures* (Oxford: Oxford University Press, 1995). A collection of essays on the rights of minority cultures by prominent political theorists such as Joseph Raz, Jeremy Waldron, Michael Walzer, Iris Marion Young, and Allen Buchanan.
- D. Kelly Weisberg, ed., *Feminist Legal Theory: Foundations* (Philadelphia: Temple University Press, 1993). This book is a comprehensive collection of essays that examine the treatment of difference in law and social policy. While the focus is on issues of gender, the book contains a broader and more general discussion of discrimination and equality theory.
- Evelyn Kallen, *Ethnicity and Human Rights in Canada.* 2nd ed. (Toronto: Oxford University Press, 1995). This book examines key issues central to the concerns of Canada's three major ethnic constituencies: aboriginal peoples, racial and ethnic immigrant groups, and Franco-Québécois.

Articles

The sources cited in the bibliographies by the individual authors in this chapter will be helpful for identifying material on different issues of discrimination. This list supplements those sources and provides perspectives on the issues different from those in the chapter.

- J.R. Lucas, "Because You are a Woman," *Philosophy* 48 (1973) 161-171. Lucas argues that sex is a relevant difference that justifies different treatment.
- Laurence Thomas, "Sexism and Racism: Some Conceptual Differences," *Ethics* v. 90, January 1980. Thomas compares the issues of racism and sexism and argues that, unlike racism, sexism is tied to the positive self-concept of men in a way that racism is not tied to the positive self-concept of whites. This difference, he argues, suggests that sexism is more difficult to erase than racism.
- Kwame Anthony Appiah, "Racisms" in *Anatomy of Racism* edited by David Theo Goldberg. University of Minnesota Press, 1990. Appiah distinguishes aspects of racism. Appiah argues that racialism, the view that people divide up into distinct races and possess traits and tendencies that are not shared with member of other races, is false. He then examines the theoretical and moral difficulties of two other theories of race that he refers to as intrinsic and extrinsic racism.
- Cornel West, "The New Cultural Politics of Difference," *October*, vol. 53 (Summer 1990). West argues that because the history and experiences of African Americans have been suppressed or ignored, it is morally incumbent on societies to give such groups a forum for representing and expressing those experiences and challenging existing stereotypes. Art is one such forum that serves this purpose.
- James O. Young, "Should White Men Play the Blues?" *Journal of Value Inquiry*, vol. 28 (1984). Young uses the context of art to argue against programs and policies, for example, that base decisions about allocating funds or restricting public displays of works by particular artists on considerations of cultural or group representation. White men, Young argues, can and should play the blues.
- David Theo Goldberg, "Racist Exclusions," *Philosophical Forum* 26 (1) Fall 1994. Goldberg argues that the standard view of racism as an "irrational prejudice predicated upon the arbitrary and so morally irrelevant category of 'race'" fails to capture critical features of racism and what is wrong with it.
- Jeffrey Jordon, "Is it Wrong to Discriminate on the Basis of Homosexuality?" *Journal of Social Philosophy*, v. 26, no. 1 (Spring 1995). This article discusses the issue of same-sex marriages and argues that it is morally permissible to discriminate against homosexuals because public sentiments favour the "neutral" approach of not giving public recognition to same-sex marriages.
- Christine Overall, "Heterosexuality and Feminist Theory," *Canadian Journal of Philosophy*, v. 20, no. 1 (March 1990), 1-17. Overall argues that because our institutions enforce heterosexuality in a myriad of ways, it is problematic to view homosexuality as "abnormal." As an institution, heterosexuality contributes to women's unequal status in relationships and reduces their choices for sexual expression.

Chapter 6

Aboriginal Rights

Introduction

Moral issues often focus on individuals. Euthanasia, abortion, and capital punishment are examples of issues of this kind. Is it morally acceptable for members of the medical profession to assist those who want to die to do so? Is abortion a matter appropriately left to a woman and her doctor? Is a society morally justified in executing individuals who commit murder?

Moral issues can also be generated by the interaction of individuals who are members of particular groups with other individuals or groups. This adds a degree of complexity as we have seen in our discussion of pornography, discrimination, and equality. Pornography is of moral concern because of the possible implications of its use by some for individual non-users and for women as a group. Discussions of equality and discrimination take as their focus individuals identified by group membership: race, creed, sex, and so on.

A third focus for moral issues is the relationship of groups to other groups. Each of us is affected in significant ways by our membership in groups. In many ways, our identity as individuals is shaped by the families and communities in which we are raised and live. It is also shaped by the way in which the groups, communities, society, and culture we are or are seen to be a part of are regarded by other groups, communities, or cultures. Working out appropriate relationships between and among groups is therefore extremely important. It is also extremely complex. The relationship between Canadians generally and the aboriginal peoples who occupied that part of North America now known as Canada well before the arrival of European settlers is a case in point.

Background Considerations

The relationship of the Native people with the dominant Canadian majority has been an uneasy one virtually from the point of first contact. Substantially different views of the land are one reason for this. From the time Europeans first discovered North America they regarded the land as unoccupied. They had no qualms about using it for their own purposes, settling on it, and claiming it for the countries from which they had come.

However, this view had an odd quality to it. For the land *was* occupied by people with well-developed and effective though largely informal political and legal systems. Land and "ownership" played a part in their social system, but a part quite different from that assigned to it by the Europeans who landed on their shores. In their view, land was not something which could be owned by individuals or by groups as European law defined ownership. It could only be used and shared. And so it was shared with the first settlers and later through the medium of treaties with the governments they brought with them or formed after their arrival.

One result of these differing attitudes was that the treaties signed by Native peoples and their representatives with British and Canadian governments were interpreted in different and often incompatible ways by those involved. The European view was that the treaties involved agreements to surrender ownership of the land in return for reservations on which the Native people involved could live together with whatever other considerations were included in the treaties. Yet how could the Native people surrender land that in their view they did not own? The result has been conflicting views of what the signatories to the various treaties were in fact agreeing to. And where no treaties were signed, serious conflicts have developed about the status of the original inhabitants who continue to occupy the land.

Because they are a relatively insignificant percentage of the Canadian population, the Native people have been largely unsuccessful in obtaining political solutions to the disputes that have arisen with the dominant culture. As a result, until recently they have had to rely on the courts to resolve outstanding disagreements. This has been particularly true of land claims that have arisen in areas of the country where treaties have never been signed. Consequently, serious disputes generally have been resolved in the context of legal principles that are essentially foreign to the Native outlook.

The Current Situation

The status of Canada's Native peoples is today very much in flux. That there have been significant and permanent changes in their legal status is hard to deny. The Constitution Act of 1982 which recognized and affirmed the existing aboriginal and treaty rights of Canada's aboriginal people (Section 35) has been decisive in this regard. Significant special collective aboriginal rights are now enshrined in Canadian law. As Brian Slattery points out in his contribution to this chapter, these constitutional provisions mark a basic shift in the legal status of Canada's first inhabitants.

This shift is reflected in the report of The Royal Commission on Aboriginal Peoples that argued that one of the special collective rights protected by the 1982 Constitution is the right to self-government. Section 35 of the 1982 Constitution has also altered how the courts and the federal and provincial governments have approached land claim issues in recent years. (See the discussion of the case of Sparrow, a Supreme Court judgment, in Brian Slattery's contribution in the readings that follow.) Finally, the Canadian government has acknowledged, apologized, and begun to provide compensation for the harm caused by the assimilation policies that led to the placement of Aboriginal children in residential schools distant from their homes and isolated from their language and culture.

In spite of these developments, Aboriginal/government relations have continued to be marked by conflict, hostility, and controversy. The Oka (Quebec) confrontation in the summer of 1990 is an example. So to are the armed confrontations that followed in Ontario (Camp Ipperwash) and British Columbia. Most recently, Canada has seen serious conflict and confrontation over Native fisheries in both New Brunswick and British Columbia.

Conflict and controversy over the political status of Canada's Native people as well as their role in federal and provincial constitutional and political discussions and negotiations have also impacted Canadian political life. Anger over the failure of political leaders to include Aboriginal concerns in the Meech Lake constitutional negotiations played a decisive role in the defeat of that accord when Elijah Harper, a Native member of the Manitoba legislature, refused to give his agreement to the ratification process which required unanimous consent in the Manitoba legislature and the unanimous agreement of all ten provinces. In contrast, the Charlottetown agreement did acknowledge self-government demands on the part of prominent Native leaders, though this was not enough to win its acceptance in a referendum that followed its negotiation.

In the absence of the constitutional backing of the Charlottetown Accord, governments have turned to local, regional, and provincial negotiations. These initiatives have not been without results. In Manitoba, for example, significant steps have been taken toward self-government. A ground-breaking agreement has been reached by the federal and provincial governments with the Nisga'a people of northern British Columbia. And finally, the Department of Native Affairs in Ottawa, long a symbol of entrenched colonial and paternalistic attitudes, is being phased out.

It remains the case, however, that Canadians are a long way from consensus on how to resolve long-standing problems and disagreements with the Aboriginal peoples. Changes in the political climate through the 1990s have resulted in provincial governments committed to reduce both expenditures and the size and role of government. Statements by some influential political leaders suggest that the position articulated by Pierre Elliott Trudeau on behalf of the federal government in 1969 (see the readings that follow) continues to have considerable appeal for large segments of the Canadian population and some of their political leaders. At the same time, statistics show that on virtually every available measure of social welfare, income, employment, housing, infant mortality, longevity, health, and so on, people of Native descent are much the least favoured of Canadians economically and socially.

For all these reasons, the issues raised in the chapter are significant ones that continue to attract attention and debate.

The Moral Dimension

Because the moral issues surrounding the treatment and status of Canada's Aboriginal people arise from and are articulated from within diverse cultures and histories, they are particularly difficult to set out in an uncontroversial way. Are historical grievances resolvable? How are land claims to be settled when the land from which Native people have been excluded has been taken up, settled, and developed by non-Native people for whom those lands provide homes, jobs, and for many an essential part of their way of life? Do Canadians living today have an obligation to compensate Native people for assimilation policies imposed by Canadian governments now long since out of office that have left deep scars still being felt today and likely to be felt in the future by Natives and Native communities affected by those policies? How are resources that Natives have relied on historically to support their communities and their way of life to be shared with non-Natives who are also dependent on access to those resources for jobs and incomes?

These issues and many others arising from the historical encounter of Native and non-Native peoples in Canada are the focus of the readings that follow.

The Readings

We begin with Section 35 of the Constitution Act of 1982. This is followed by two contrasting views of how to approach the righting of past wrongs suffered by Canada's Aboriginal peoples. Pierre Elliott Trudeau, speaking from the perspective of government policy in the 1960s, argues that the most effective way to confront the "Native issue" is to move from special status toward full integration into the political and legal life of the country. A reading by George Erasmus and Joe Sanders, two distinguished Native spokespeople, challenges Trudeau's reading of Canadian history and the values that should shape the resolution of Native grievances arising from that history. They point to occupation of what we know of today as Canada by First Nations, fully sovereign and self-governing. They speak of broken agreements and promises, distorted accounts of the history of encounters between First Nation inhabitants and European settlers, the injustices of the Indian Act, and the battle to have their rights recognized that the Canada's Native people continue to wage to this day.

In our fourth reading, Brian Slattery takes up the discussion of the "correct" interpretation of Canadian history viewed through the prism of constitutional evolution. He points to two dominant visions or models of Canadian constitutional history. One model, the Imperial Model, sees the Constitution as an outgrowth of European legal traditions. This model leaves very little room for Native views of Canadian history set out by Aboriginal leaders such as George Erasmus. The other model, the Organic Model, roots the Constitution in Canadian history and traditions. This second model acknowledges the distinctive contributions of Aboriginal peoples and their long-standing relations with the Crown.

Michael McDonald then examines, from a philosophical perspective, a range of arguments that have been used in public debate to try to determine the nature and extent of Native rights. He concludes that aboriginal rights are grounded on land rights which in turn derive from the fact that Native peoples are the original inhabitants of what is now known as Canada. His conclusions in this regard are then critically examined by David Gauthier who defends a contrasting position.

Finally, Jack Stevenson asks whether there is a moral principle that has broad cultural acceptance and acceptability by reference to which the issues in question can be evaluated and resolved. He argues that there is such a principle; he calls it "the personal security principle."[1] Applying this principle specifically to the issue of land ownership leads him to conclude that the basic claims of Canada's Native peoples are well-founded. Further, a just resolution of those claims will require that the demand for self-government be recognized.

NOTES

1. One theme that those reading Stevenson's article might like to pursue is the similarity between the notion of personal security that he develops and the more recent concept of human security that has in recent years become an organizing concept for the development and pursuit of Canadian foreign policy.

RIGHTS OF THE ABORIGINAL PEOPLES OF CANADA

The Constitution Act of 1982: Section 35

> **35.** (1) The existing aboriginal and treaty rights of the aboriginal peoples of Canada are hereby recognized and affirmed.
>
> (2) In this Act, "aboriginal peoples of Canada" includes the Indian, Inuit and Métis peoples of Canada.

REMARKS ON INDIAN ABORIGINAL AND TREATY RIGHTS

[Part of a speech given August 8, 1969, in Vancouver, British Columbia]

Prime Minister P.E. Trudeau

I think Canadians are not too proud about their past in the way in which they treated the Indian population of Canada and I don't think we have very great cause to be proud.

We have set the Indians apart as a race. We've set them apart in our laws. We've set them apart in the ways the governments will deal with them. They're not citizens of the province as the rest of us are. They are wards of the federal government. They get their services from the federal government rather than from the provincial or municipal governments. They have been set apart in law. They have been set apart in the relations with government and they've been set apart socially too.

So this year we came up with a proposal. It's a policy paper on the Indian problem. It proposes a set of solutions. It doesn't impose them on anybody. It proposes them — not only to the Indians but to all Canadians — not only to their federal representatives but to the provincial representatives too and it says we're at the crossroads. We can go on treating the Indians as having a special status. We can go on adding bricks of discrimination around the ghetto in which they live and at the same time perhaps helping them preserve certain cultural traits and certain ancestral rights. Or we can say you're at a crossroads — the time is now to decide whether the Indians will be a race apart in Canada or whether it will be Canadians of full status. And this is a difficult choice. It must be a very agonizing choice to the Indian peoples themselves because, on the other hand, they realize that if they come into the society as total citizens they will be equal under the law but they risk losing certain of their traditions, certain aspects of a culture and perhaps even certain of their basic rights and this is a very difficult choice for them to make and I don't think we want to try and force the pace on them any more than we can force it on the rest of Canadians but here again is a choice which is in our minds whether Canadians as a whole want to continue treating the Indian populations as something outside, a group of Canadians with which we have treaties, a group of Canadians who have as the Indians, many of them claim, aboriginal rights, or whether we will say well forget the past and begin today and this is a tremendously difficult choice because, if — well, one of the things the Indian bands often refer to are their aboriginal rights and in our policy, the way we propose it, we say we won't recognize aboriginal rights. We will recognize treaty rights. We will recognize forms of contract which have been made with the Indian people by the Crown and we will try to bring justice in the area and this will mean that perhaps the treaties shouldn't go on forever. It's inconceivable, I think, that in a given society one section of the society have a treaty with the other section of the society. We must be all equal under the laws and we must not sign treaties amongst ourselves and many of these treaties, indeed, would have less and less significance in the future anyhow but things that in the past were covered by the treaties like things like so much twine or so much gun powder and which haven't been paid, this must be paid. But I don't think that we should encourage the Indians to feel that their treaties should last forever within Canada so that they be able to receive their twine or their gun powder. They should become Canadians as all other Canadians and if they are prosperous and wealthy they will be treated like the prosperous and wealthy and they will be paying taxes for the other Canadians who are not so prosperous and not so wealthy whether they be Indians or English Canadians or French or Maritimers and this is the only basis on which I see our society can develop as equals. But aboriginal rights, this really means saying, "We were here before you. You came and you took the land from us and perhaps you cheated us by giving us some worthless things in return for vast expanses of land and we want to re-open this question. We want you to preserve our aboriginal rights and to restore them to us." And our answer — it may not be the right one and may not be one which is accepted but it will be up to all of our people to make your minds up and to choose for or against it and to discuss with the Indians — our answer is "no."

If we think of restoring aboriginal rights to the Indians, well, what about the French who were defeated at the Plains of Abraham? Shouldn't we restore rights to them? And what about the Acadians who were deported — shouldn't we compensate for this? And what about the other Canadians, the immigrants? What about the Japanese Canadians who were so badly treated at the end of or during the last war? What can we do to redeem the past? I can only say as President Kennedy said when he was asked about what he would do to compensate for the injustices that the Negroes had received in American society. We will be just in our time. This is all we can do. We must be just today.

QUESTIONS

1. Does it matter that the Native peoples were the first people in Canada?
2. If we restore rights to the Native peoples, must we then restore rights to other groups in Canada who feel a grievance? Are the Native peoples a special case?

CANADIAN HISTORY: AN ABORIGINAL PERSPECTIVE?

George Erasmus and Joe Sanders

Aboriginal Sovereignty

When non-native people first came to this continent some five hundred years ago, indigenous peoples lived all across the Americas. It is a matter of historical record that before the arrival of Europeans, these First Nations possessed and exercised absolute sovereignty over

From Nation to Nation Aboriginal Sovereignty and the Future of Canada, *edited by Diane Engels and John Bird. Reprinted by permission of Stoddart Publishing Co. Ltd., Don Mills, Ont.*

what is now called the North American continent. Hundreds of tribal communities, made up of a variety of nations and representing at least ten linguistic groups, lived in what is now known as Canada, from Newfoundland to Vancouver Island.

It was not possible to find "empty" land in the Americas. All the land was being used by the First Nations. Our people decided their own citizenship. They had a wide variety and diversity of governmental systems, almost all of them regulating their activities and the relations among their members with a degree of formality. The way they dealt with the Europeans is ample proof of their capacity to enter into relations with foreign powers: they made a number of treaties with the French and British Crowns, and many of the colonies survived because of the assistance First Nations gave to the European settlers.

Our people knew how to survive in this part of the world. They knew all of their valleys and mountains and rivers. They had names in their own languages for all of these places. They believed that all things had their place, from even the smallest insect and the smallest leaf. And they were taught to respect life and all living things. Our people were living lives that must have been of a much higher quality than people now live in Canada.

It was unfortunate that early Christian leaders believed that our people did not understand why human beings were here on earth. Our people did not think there were gods in every leaf. But they did think that everything around was given by the Creator. They believed that there was one supreme being, that there was purpose in all of this, and that the purpose did not end when we died.

Our people were not a war-like people, but they did defend their interests. Our territorial boundaries were clearly defined. Although First Nations had many disputes with neighbours in their history, they eventually arrived at peaceful arrangements with one another.

Our people understood what the non-native people were after when they came amongst our people and wanted to treaty with them, because they had done that many times amongst themselves. They recognized that a nation-to-nation agreement, defining the specific terms of peaceful coexistence, was being arranged.

Broken Agreements

When our people treated with another nation, each nation's interests, its pride, and its word were at stake. The word of the agreement, the treaty, was given in a very sacred way. And it was not very easily broken.

So it was quite amazing to our people — and it took them a long, long time to realize — that they could sit with other people whose religious leaders were present, and who would be virtually lying to our people as they were executing the treaty. Even before the document reached London or Paris or Ottawa, they were already forgetting the solemn promises they had made. That never happened on the side of the indigenous people.

It didn't help that the European interpretation of a treaty, often differing radically from the First Nation's interpretation or understanding, significantly altered the intent of the original agreement. For example, ownership of land in the Anglo-Canadian "fee simple" sense of title was foreign to the thinking and systems of First Nations. Land was revered as a mother from which life came, and was to be preserved for future generations as it had been from time immemorial. Land was used for common benefit, with no individual having a right to any more of it than another. A nation's traditional hunting grounds were recognized by its neighbours as "belonging" to that nation, but this was different from the idea of private ownership. For the most part, the boundaries were not delineated, although some nations in British Columbia had systems of identifying their boundaries and passing on custodial responsibilities. First Nations peoples, then and now, believe that they live *with* the land, not simply on it.

As our people understood it, they had agreed to allow peaceful settlement by non-native people in large parts of their valleys and mountains and on rivers, but at the same time native people would retain large tracts of land on which they would govern themselves; on which our institutions would continue to survive; where we would nurture our children; where our languages and our culture would flourish; where we could continue our lives; where we could hunt if we wished, plant crops if we wished, fish if we wished. And where, if we wanted to, we could also be educated in a formal way to become doctors, lawyers or whatever we wished.

The history of the settlement of Canada shows that non-native people, represented by federal, provincial and local governments, have continued to break the original agreements. Hunting, fishing, trapping and gathering sections of treaties that were to protect the aboriginal way of life have continued to be changed by Canadian government policies, regulations and legislation. The original land base agreed to at treaty time has continued to be expropriated for bridges, municipal expansion, military exercises and railway and highway right-of-ways, generally without compensation. In many cases, First Nations are still waiting to have the land entitlement of one-hundred-year-old treaties fulfilled.

Rewriting History

Non-native people have even distorted history. It is very difficult to find a history textbook in any province of this country that accurately tells the story of how our two peoples came together. Instead, there are books in which we are still being called pagans and savages, without an accurate reflection of the solemn agreements that were made and which indicate that indigenous people were to continue to govern themselves.

Native people have the enormous job of tapping people on the shoulder and saying, "This is not the way it's supposed to be. This is not the way we are supposed to be coexisting. We aren't supposed to be the poorest of the poor in our land." Our people have an understanding of the early agreements that the school books usually ignore.

In 1763, three years after the French and British resolved their differences in Canada and recognized Britain as the European power here, the Crown of Great Britain laid down a process in the Royal Proclamation that set forth the Crown's policy on land negotiations. That policy has never been revoked. In the Royal Proclamation, the Crown recognized that any lands possessed by First Nations in what was then British North America, would be reserved for them, unless, or until, they ceded that land to the Crown.

The Proclamation could be regarded as the first major legal link between First Nations and the British Crown. And by virtue of that Proclamation, it can be said that First Nations became protected states of the British, while being recognized as sovereign nations competent to maintain the relations of peace and war and capable of governing themselves under that protection. Under international law, a weaker power does not surrender its right to self-government merely by associating with a stronger power and taking its protection.

Between 1781 and Canadian Confederation in 1867, some First Nations signed treaties with the Crown under which they ceded rights and privileges to certain lands. In return, they were to obtain certain treaty rights. These treaties represented further legal links between those nations and the Crown. But again, there is no evidence that sovereignty was surrendered.

Canadian courts, since the latter part of the nineteenth century, have relegated the First Nations' treaties with the Crown almost to the level of private law contracts, thereby denying their status as treaties in the sense of international law. Yet the Supreme Court of Canada repeated in the *R. v. Simon* case that First Nations' treaties are unique and share some of the features of international treaties. If the agreements were "treaties among sovereign nations" in the eighteenth and nineteenth centuries, how could their status be changed without the consent of First Nations?

In 1867, the British North America Act (later renamed the Constitution Act 1867) provided for internal self-government in Canada by European settlers. First Nations were not a party to the Confederation that was established, nor to the drafting of the British North America Act. Nevertheless, subsection 91(24) provided that the federal Parliament would have the authority to legislate for "Indians and lands reserved for the Indians" to the exclusion of the provincial legislatures. By virtue of that subsection, the First Nations were placed under the legislative power of the federal government as agent of the Crown, but not under its territorial jurisdiction.

Certain other treaties were executed between some of the First Nations and the Crown after Confederation. In many cases it is evident that treaties were imposed upon First Nations and that their leaders had little choice but to consent. The treaties were written in English and the Crown's negotiators often misrepresented the contents.

Today it may be argued that many of those treaties are "unequal" or "unconscionable" or "unfair" in both substance and procedure. Even so, First Nations did not perceive the treaties as being a surrender of sovereignty.

The Indian Act

In 1876, the federal government passed its first Indian Act, "the first consolidation of the laws pertaining to Indians." The Indian Act was passed by the federal government because it had exclusive legislative responsibility for Indians and lands reserved for Indians, but First Nations themselves had no input into it. Neither did First Nations' citizens have any part in electing the politicians who legislated the Indian Acts, since native people were not allowed to vote federally until 1960.

In the early days of European settlement, it is likely that native self-government continued for some time because First Nations had the numbers and the strength at that time to warrant recognition. But as time went on, that changed. During the first sixty years of this century, our people were in the most despicable, colonizing, racist situation imaginable. Under the control of Indian agents, they could not leave their reserves without passes. They were not legally in charge of a single thing that happened on their land.

The same Department of Indian Affairs that controlled our lives through Indian agents until only recently still exists today. It has 4000 civil servants, and its primary function is to maintain control over native people.

The Indian Act still controls every facet of our lives. It allows a certain amount of local self-government, but there is not a single thing on which we can make a law that does not have to go to a department official. That official is usually a bureaucrat whose face we've never seen and who has never seen the community. And yet he has total power to determine whether he is going to pass a dog law, a local development law, a garbage law or any law requiring departmental approval. He doesn't have to give a reason; he can just deny it. No other municipal government in this country is up against that kind of control. Surely it only exists in parts of the world where an occupying army wants to ensure that the population is completely submissive.

Today, every time we see a movement beginning among indigenous people somewhere in this country, the Department of Indian Affairs finds some way to divide those people — discredit their organization, discredit their leadership, create an opposition group, fund an opposition group.

Some day the Department of Indian Affairs should vanish off the face of the earth. There must be a time when the kind of colonial, dictatorial control that is ruining our lives comes to an end. We must have freedom at some point.

Retaining Our Rights: The Ongoing Saga

Despite all of this, the Royal Proclamation of 1763 is still alive and well. That means that where there are no treaties the land belongs to the First Nations, and no Canadian government — whether provincial or federal — should be developing our resources and extracting royalties and taxes from them. There should be indigenous governments and institutions for aboriginal people.

In some cases in this country, we have treaties over a hundred years old by which, very clearly, original land was to have been set aside for native people. After a hundred years and more, the land still hasn't been put aside. Meanwhile, governments have repeatedly invited people from all over the world to come cut down our trees and get a square mile . . . two square miles . . . ten square miles of land. Although everyone agrees that our people have lived here for thousands of years, because the federal government has not recognized First Nations' title, there is not a square centimetre that is recognized as indigenous territory.

First Nations regularly confront governments with their claims to entitlement, and the governments can't deny the validity of such claims. But instead of recognizing land as indigenous territory, they seek to "settle" claims by exchanging historic rights for "fee simple" ownership, so the land can be treated like every other piece of private property in Canada.

Take, for example, the territory we call Denendeh, otherwise known as the western Northwest Territories. The Dene know they have always owned this land, but the federal government refuses to acknowledge our indigenous title. Recently the smallest group of Dene, the Gwitch'in, negotiated an agreement with the federal government to get property title to a portion of the land in exchange for extinguishing historic claims. Outside of this one agreement, no Dene land has ever been surrendered. Yet there is not even a small piece of the vast remaining territory that a Dene can use to build a home. Instead, our people must use a foreign system of government to obtain a building permit.

At the same time, it is clear that the Canadian public has always been on the side of some kind of just, equitable recognition and implementation of both aboriginal rights and treaty rights.

Despite the irony of this state of affairs, First Nations were not even party to the drafting of the renewed Constitution of 1982. The governments did agree, however, that First Nations leaders should be invited to participate in subsequent constitutional conferences to identify and define their rights for inclusion in the Canadian Constitution.

That was the first time in their relationship with the Crown that First Nations were consulted about the Constitution, albeit only to a very limited degree. They were, in effect, merely invited to establish and defend their rights. If First Nations had not participated, it is conceivable that non-native governments would have unilaterally identified and defined those rights.

Finding a Genuine Solution

What is it that our people are after? Simply this: We want to sit down across the table from the leaders of this country and come up with a genuine solution that will be acceptable both to indigenous nations and to the people who have come here from elsewhere.

We think there are sufficient land and resources in this country to allow First Nations to retain enough of their original territory where their own institutions can be sovereign.

We don't want to scare Canadians with our terminology. No one is scared in this country by the fact that Ontario or Manitoba can make laws in education and not a single power in the world can do anything about it. They are sovereign in their area of jurisdiction. We, likewise, want to have clear powers over our territories.

Canada is already set up for it, because we have a confederation that lends itself very easily to what our people are asking for. We have the federal government, we have federal powers. We have provinces, we have provincial powers. We have some areas where the two overlap. We could easily have a third list of First Nation powers.

We are prepared to negotiate. But we definitely need enough control over our lives that we can grow, we can flourish, we can prosper. Our people no longer want to be in a situation where you can have a mine right outside your door but the resources from that mine go to somebody else, the employers come from somewhere else, the employees come from somewhere else, the caterers come from somewhere else, and the decision as to *when* that mine is going to be developed is made somewhere else. This kind of development leads to social disruption. The mobile out-of-town workforce, continuing high unemployment, racism, pollution and the disturbance of hunting, fishing and trapping grounds all take their toll when we don't have the power to make decisions affecting our people.

There has to be a peaceful way to share. And if we can't do it in Canada, with the few people we have here, how will any other parts of the world ever be able to settle their situations?

But native people are losing their patience. It's very clear that our people are not going to sit back and take the treatment we have had to take in the past. That much is guaranteed.

The Canadian people must continue to push their governments to sit down with First Nations and negotiate a just and acceptable solution, to reflect what the Canadian polls say Canadian people want. Native people by themselves, it is obvious, are not going to get the Canadian government to take that step.

QUESTIONS

1. Compare and contrast the vision of Canada set out in this reading with that implied by Trudeau's 1969 policy statement.
2. In light of this reading of Canadian history, are Natives who become frustrated with the slow pace of discussions on resolving long-standing grievances justified in resorting to violence to accomplish the goal of self-government, as some have in recent years? If not, at what point would violence become justifiable? Is there a morally sound answer to this question?

THE ORGANIC CONSTITUTION: ABORIGINAL PEOPLES AND THE EVOLUTION OF CANADA

Brian Slattery

I. Introduction

> What we don't like about the Government is their saying this: "We will give you this much land." How can they give it when it is our own? We cannot understand it. They have never bought it from us or our forefathers. They have never fought and conquered our people and taken the land in that way, and yet they say now that they will give us so much land—our own land. ... [O]ur forefathers for generations and generations past had their land here all around us; chiefs have had their own hunting grounds, their salmon streams, and places where they got their berries; it has always been so.[1]

This statement could have been made yesterday, or a decade ago, or a century ago. In fact, it was made in 1888, by David Mackay of the Nishga Nation of British Columbia, while addressing a Royal Commission visiting the Nishga Territory.

In the same year that Mackay met the Royal Commission, the Judicial Committee of the Imperial Privy Council in London was considering arguments on the nature of indigenous land rights in Canada. At that time, the Privy Council was the final court of appeal for Canada, as well as for other British colonies. The case, *St. Catherine's Milling & Lumber Co. v. R.*,[2] did not directly involve native peoples. It was a dispute between Canada and Ontario over which government reaped the benefits of an Indian treaty ceding lands to the Crown. Lord Watson delivered the Privy Council's decision. He referred to the provisions of *The Royal Proclamation, 1763*,[3] an imperial instrument protecting Indian lands, and went on to say:

> The territory in dispute has been in Indian occupation from the date of the proclamation until 1873 [when it was ceded by the native inhabitants to the Crown]. ... Their possession, such as it was, can only be ascribed to the general provisions made by the royal proclamation in favour of all Indian tribes then living under the sovereignty and protection of the British Crown. It was suggested in the course of the argument for the Dominion, that inasmuch as the proclamation recites that the territories thereby reserved for Indians had never "been ceded to or purchased by" the Crown, the entire property of the land remained with them. That inference is, however, at variance with the terms of the instrument, which shew that the tenure of the Indians was a personal and usufructuary right, dependent upon the good will of the Sovereign.[4]

Lord Watson seemed to think that whatever land rights the Aboriginal people possessed were ascribable to the bounty of the Crown, as manifested in the *Royal Proclamation, 1763*. Even then, these rights were held at the "good will of the Sovereign." The contrast with Mackay's outlook is striking.

In recent years, the Privy Council's views on aboriginal land rights have fallen into partial disrepute, due to an important series of Supreme Court decisions.[5] Nevertheless, some of the basic assumptions that underlie Lord Watson's remarks are still surprisingly influential.

The Canadian legal system has been slow to come to terms with the perspective implicit in David Mackay's speech: "We, the First Peoples of Canada, are autonomous peoples, with our own laws and lands, our own systems of government and justice. We are the original custodians of this land that we now share with you. You are the newcomers. We are not beholden to you for our basic rights and status."

One reason why the courts have had difficulty in accommodating this viewpoint is their attachment to a conception of the Constitution deeply rooted in Canada's colonial past—what may be called the Imperial Model of the Constitution. In its classic form, the Imperial Model involves a number of basic tenets, which interconnect and reinforce one another. As we will see, these tenets have never won complete acceptance in the courts and in recent times have fallen increasingly under a cloud. Nevertheless, in one form or another, the Imperial Model has had a remarkable influence on the thinking of lawyers and judges over the past century and a half. And, in the absence of anything better to replace it, it continues to provide the tacit matrix for much legal thinking about the Constitution. In this paper, I will examine the basic precepts of the Imperial Model and then propose an alternative to it, following some guideposts laid down in the recent jurisprudence of the Supreme Court.

II. The Imperial Model

There are six basic canons that together make up the Imperial Model. The first holds that when Europeans began settling in North America in the sixteenth and seventeenth centuries, the native inhabitants of the continent had no legal status or rights under the international law of the times. On this view, Aboriginal nations did not qualify as international entities because of such factors as their modest size, mobile lifestyle, diffuse political structures, and religious beliefs. Moreover, these groups did not have any international rights to the territories they occupied, which as a matter of law were vacant and open to appropriation by others.[6]

On this view, then, the incoming French and British were able to gain sovereignty over large expanses of North America simply by "discovering" and exploring them, performing symbolic acts of appropriation, or founding small settlements along the sea coasts and riverbanks. In this relatively effortless fashion, France is thought to have gained an enormous American empire which, as depicted in standard historical atlases, stretched from the Gulf of the St. Lawrence River through the Great Lakes as far west as the Prairies and as far south as the mouth of the Mississippi River. For its part, Great Britain obtained original title to extensive regions along the Atlantic coast and around Hudson Bay and later augmented its American empire by conquest and cession from France in 1713 and 1763.[7] So, according to this approach, Canada's international title to its current territories is grounded in British title, which in turn partly derives from that of France. In no case does Canada's title stem from the original title held by indigenous peoples, for they had no international legal rights to their territories in the first place.

So, according to the Imperial Model, the *factual* process by which Aboriginal peoples joined the Canadian federation does not affect the *legal* account of how Canada came to be. Whether that process was coercive or consensual, whether it proceeded unilaterally or by agreement, whether it occurred in the seventeenth century or only in the twentieth century, the genesis of Canada remains the same in the eyes of the law. The only recognized actors in the drama are European states and their colonial progeny, and so the plot centres on their comings and goings. When Aboriginal peoples appear on the stage, they are mere bitplayers and stand-ins.

This account of our legal evolution is rounded out by a complementary understanding of the Canadian Constitution. According to the second tenet of the Imperial Model, our basic constitutional framework finds its roots in British law. The Constitution consists primarily of statutes passed by the Imperial Parliament, as supplemented by unwritten principles of British constitutional law. These statutes include the *Constitution Act, 1867* [8] and its successors, which established the basic federal structure of Canada, and, more recently, the *Constitution Act, 1982* [9] and the *Canadian Charter of Rights and Freedoms*, [10] which, although drafted in Canada, were enacted by the British Parliament at Canada's request. Since 1982, Canada has been able to amend its Constitution without having to resort to Westminster. However, according to the Imperial Model, our newfound capacity to pass amendments locally does not alter the fact that the Canadian Constitution is rooted historically in British law and still largely embodied in statutes enacted by the British Parliament.

The third tenet of the Imperial Model extends this point one stage further. It holds that all governmental authority in Canada emanates notionally from the Canadian Crown, which acts as the successor of the British Imperial Crown. This authority is exercised in the Crown's name by the federal and provincial governments and by subordinate bodies holding delegated powers. Taken together, these bodies completely exhaust the field of governmental power in Canada. So, Aboriginal peoples do not have any inherent jurisdiction over their lands or peoples. Whatever governmental authority they possess stems from the Crown by way of delegation. According to the Imperial Model, in pre-European times indigenous peoples had little that could be described as true "jurisdiction." However, even supposing that they originally held such jurisdiction, this ended when the Crown gained sovereignty over them.

Under the fourth tenet of the Imperial Model, the main body of our ordinary law also traces its origins to European sources. In Quebec, private matters are regulated by the *Code civil*, [11] which, as originally enacted in 1866, codified the laws of Lower Canada (based on the *Coutume de Paris*) on the pattern of the Napoleonic *Code civil*. [12] In the other provinces and territories, the private law is based on English common law, as imported by settlers or adopted by statute. The laws of indigenous Canadian peoples have no recognized status in Canada. Any native custom that existed in pre-contact days was too uncertain and flexible to merit the name "law." [13] In any event, it was automatically superseded when French and English laws were introduced. As a result, aboriginal custom cannot be applied by our courts except where adopted by statute.

We now come to the fifth tenet of the Imperial Model, which deals with the question of land rights. It holds that Aboriginal peoples do not have any legal rights to their traditional lands, except where these rights have been recognized by a Crown act. [14] All land rights in Canada are deemed to stem from the Crown, either directly or indirectly. There is no such thing as "aboriginal title" in Canadian law, in the sense of land rights that spring from long-time use and occupation under customary law. If any such rights had existed prior to European contact, they came to an end when the French and British Crowns gained sovereignty and imposed their own land systems. Whatever land rights indigenous peoples possess in modern times are necessarily based on Crown acts or statutory provisions.

The sixth and final tenet of the Imperial Model holds that the historical agreements concluded by Aboriginal peoples with the French and British Crowns cannot be characterized as international treaties because, as already seen, Aboriginal peoples were never recognized as sovereign entities in international law. [15] Moreover, these agreements are not recognized in domestic Canadian law, whether as constitutional instruments or simple contracts. Whatever legal force they have stems from statutory provisions, such as section 88 of the *Indian Act*. [16]

Considered globally, the Imperial Model has three main characteristics. First, it takes an unreservedly Eurocentric view of our laws and institutions, tracing them to sources in Great Britain or France. Second, it portrays governmental authority as stemming ultimately from a single source, the Crown. Third, it subscribes to the positivist creed that law and governmental institutions are the product of legislation, grounded ultimately in the sovereign's power to command obedience. In short, the Imperial Model portrays the Constitution as (1) *alien* in origin; (2) *monistic* in structure; and (3) *positive* in nature.

Two basic premises underlie and inform the Imperial Model. The first holds that the indigenous peoples of Canada originally lacked any international status, territorial title, jurisdiction, laws, or land rights. We may call this *the doctrine of a legal vacuum*, because it supposes that North America was juridically "empty" when Europeans arrived. The second principle maintains that, even if Aboriginal nations had originally possessed certain laws and rights prior to contact, they automatically lost them when European powers gained control, in the absence of explicit recognition or confirmation. This may be described as *the doctrine of radical discontinuity*, because it posits a complete legal rupture between the periods before and after the Crown's arrival.[17]

When reduced to its basic elements, the Imperial Model is clearly wrong in principle and profoundly out of harmony with our history and traditions. Canada is not, after all, the poor, hobbled creature of eighteenth and nineteenth century British expansionist designs, as the Imperial Model seems to assume. To the contrary, Canada is an independent, multinational federation, with an autonomous Constitution rooted in several centuries of shared and divergent national experiences. The task before us is to reform our basic understanding of the Constitution so as to allow these rich bodies of experience to be tapped. We have to move from a framework grounded in imperial history to a framework more open to local history, tradition, and perspectives.

In reality, this process has been underway for more than two decades. The turning point was the split decision of the Supreme Court of Canada in the *Calder* case,[18] decided in 1973. While the judges disagreed on the result, a clear majority recognized the existence of aboriginal land rights as a matter of Canadian common law. However, the strongest impetus for change came only in 1982, when Canada formally patriated its Constitution. The new constitutional package contained several provisions dealing specifically with the rights of Aboriginal peoples. The most important of these provisions is section 35(1), which states:

> The existing aboriginal and treaty rights of the aboriginal peoples of Canada are hereby recognized and affirmed.[19]

The section goes on to explain that the Aboriginal peoples of Canada include the Indian, Inuit, and Métis peoples, and that the rights in question are guaranteed equally to men and women. Section 35 represents a basic shift in our understanding of the constitutional foundations of Canada. As the Supreme Court held in the leading case of *Sparrow*, decided in 1990:

> [T]he context of 1982 is surely enough to tell us that this is not just a codification of the case law on aboriginal rights that had accumulated by 1982. Section 35 calls for a just settlement for aboriginal peoples. It renounces the old rules of the game under which the Crown established courts of law and denied those courts the authority to question sovereign claims made by the Crown.[20]

This decision opens the window, then, to a new conception of the Constitution, one that places less emphasis on imperial claims and pronouncements. This new approach may be called the Organic Model, because it emphasizes that the Constitution is the product of slow and continuing growth, as molded in part by local Canadian influences and traditions.[21]

III. The Organic Model

This new Model takes issue with the six basic canons of the Imperial Model. First and most fundamentally, the Organic Model maintains that the French and British Crowns did not acquire title to North America by virtue of "discovery" and "occupation," as though the continent were a desert island. North America was not legally vacant at the time Europeans arrived. It was the domain of a large variety of independent nations and peoples, which were the custodians of the territories they controlled. In most cases, Aboriginal nations were never conquered militarily. In the early years, they frequently entered into alliances and trading partnerships with incoming European states. As Aboriginal-European contacts became more extensive and important, and as the balance of power gradually tilted to the European side, there was a slow process of accommodation whereby Aboriginal peoples were constrained to accept piecemeal the suzerainty of the Crown in return for its protection. In some instances, this arrangement was the fruit of understandings reached in treaty sessions; in others, it was the result of informal processes whereby the Crown's suzerainty was gradually extended and acquiesced in; more rarely, it was the product of war or overt coercion. The important point is that Aboriginal nations were active *participants* in the lengthy processes that eventually gave rise to the federation of Canada.

So, Canada's modern links with its territories are in part the fruit of historical relationships with Aboriginal peoples, who were the original stewards of the land, and whose long-standing presence here dwarfs the relatively brief span of European settlement. In other words, Canada's international title is grounded to some extent in the ancient occupation of indigenous nations. Canada represents, at some level, a *merging* of the sovereignties of its various component nations, with Aboriginal peoples retaining a measure of their original autonomy.

Second, under the Organic Model, our basic constitutional law is not limited to such enactments as the *Constitution Acts* of 1867 and 1982. These enactments depend for their legitimacy on a more fundamental body of law, which may be called the common law of the Constitution. This law has undergone a long period of gestation and has drawn nourishment from a variety of sources, including local practices and traditions. Among other things, the common law of the Constitution provides the framework linking Aboriginal peoples with the governmental institutions recognized in the statutory portions of the Constitution.

More specifically, the constitutional law relating to Aboriginal peoples is grounded in ancient practices generated by interaction between Aboriginal nations and British and French officials in eastern North America during the seventeenth and eighteenth centuries. By the close of the Seven Years' War, when France withdrew in favour of Great Britain, these practices had crystallized into a distinctive body of "common" or unwritten law. This body of law was neither European nor Aboriginal in origin or substance, but drew elements from both sides to produce a unique set of intersocietal rules, known in modern times as *the doctrine of aboriginal rights*. This common law was partially manifested in such instruments as the *Royal Proclamation, 1763*,[22] which reassured Aboriginal peoples of their land rights. But the *Proclamation* was not the source of the law in question; it only reflected and gave voice to a much larger body of intersocietal custom.

The common law doctrine of aboriginal rights has many facets, which the courts are still in the process of articulating. However, its main effect, I suggest, is to recognize the internal autonomy, customary laws, and land rights of Aboriginal peoples, within a federal super-structure linking them with the broader Canadian community.

The Organic Model supports a third premise. Generally speaking, Aboriginal peoples emerged from their dealings with the Crown as partially autonomous entities living under the Crown's protection, with the right to govern their internal affairs. Over the years, this common law status was whittled away by statute, and was often ignored by governmental officials and forgotten by the general public. However, it remains the essential historical background against which the modern position of Aboriginal peoples must be understood. Under the Organic Model, it is also a central element in the panoply of aboriginal rights recognized in section 35 of the *Constitution Act, 1982*.

According to this view, the aboriginal right of self-government does not flow from the Crown and does not depend on governmental grant or recognition. It is an inherent right. However, the right of self-government is not unlimited in scope and it does not support a claim to independence. It operates under the aegis of the Canadian Constitution, and confers powers consistent with the needs and circumstances of Aboriginal peoples and their historical links with the larger community.

According to a fourth premise, our laws in private matters are not restricted to those emanating from England and France; they include aboriginal laws, as applied within native communities. These laws are not static, forever preserved in their original state like flies in amber; they are living things, which evolve over time and adapt to new needs and circumstances.

Fifth, under Canadian common law, Indian, Inuit, and Métis peoples hold aboriginal rights to their traditional lands, except where these rights have been lawfully qualified by statute or agreement. These land rights are not based on Crown grant or statutory recognition; they arise from long-standing occupation under customary law. Aboriginal title confers communal rights of use and possession and constitutes a form of collective title, which cannot be alienated by private sale but may only be surrendered or shared by way of agreement with the Crown. Aboriginal title is not confined to so-called "traditional" uses, practised at the time of European contact. It allows indigenous peoples to adapt their lands to whatever purposes serve their current needs, and permits a broad range of modern uses, including agriculture, forestry, mining, and tourism.

Finally, the Organic Model holds that early treaties concluded between Aboriginal nations and European powers were often international in nature, in the sense that they were concluded between independent, self-governing political entities, each with their own territories. However, as the balance of power gradually shifted, treaties increasingly reflected the predominance of the European partner and embodied the latter's claims of suzerainty. These later treaties operated increasingly at the domestic level, contributing to the formation of the Canadian Constitution and the common law doctrine of aboriginal rights. However, it would be wrong to think that the international and domestic spheres can be neatly severed. Under the Organic Model, an historic international treaty between Aboriginal and European entities might today carry certain domestic effects, and a domestic treaty might have modern international consequences. What is clear, for our purposes, is that aboriginal treaties not only contributed in a general way to the evolution of the Constitution, but also supplied part of its federal structure. This situation, sometimes described as "treaty federalism," has now been formally recognized and consolidated in section 35 of the *Constitution Act, 1982*.

The Organic Model, then, has three main features, which contrast with those of the Imperial Model. First, the Organic Model holds that the Constitution is rooted ultimately in Canadian soil rather than in Europe, while acknowledging the important influences of Great Britain and France. Second, the Model subscribes to a pluralist conception of the sources of law and authority, viewing the Crown as the constitutional trustee of coordinate spheres of jurisdiction rather than their exclusive source. Third, the Model rejects the positivist view that our most fundamental laws are embodied in legislation and are grounded ultimately on the sovereign's power to command obedience; rather, it portrays the law as immanent in our collective practices and traditions, which, in turn, reflect more basic values and principles. In summary, the Organic Model views the Constitution as (1) *indigenous* to Canada, rather than an alien import; (2) *complex* in structure, rather than monistic; and (3) fundamentally *customary* in nature, rather than composed simply of positive law.

Two basic principles lie at the foundations of the Organic Model. The first rejects the view that North America was a legal vacuum at the time of European contact. It holds that America was the domain of a variety of aboriginal polities, possessing international status, territorial title, jurisdiction, laws, and land rights, with the capacity to enter into international treaties and other relations. This view forms the core of what we have called *the doctrine of aboriginal rights*. The second principle denies that aboriginal laws, jurisdiction, and land rights were automatically terminated when European powers gained sovereignty. It maintains that these rights presumptively remained in force under the new regime, as necessarily modified by the advent of the Crown. We may call this the *doctrine of continuity*.[23]

Thus, the Organic Model encourages us to broaden our conception of the sources of Canadian law and to recognize the diverse roles that Indian, Inuit, and Métis peoples have played in the formation of this country and its Constitution. It suggests that Aboriginal peoples should be viewed as active participants in generating the basic norms that govern us—not as people on the fringes, helpless victims, or recipients of constitutional handouts from the government or the courts, but as contributors to the evolution of our Constitution and most fundamental laws. In short, aboriginal conceptions of law and rights really count—not as curiosities of another time and place or as the denizens of exotic legal pigeonholes, but as a fundamental part of our living legal traditions.

More generally, the Organic Model opens up the Constitution to a variety of perspectives that have long been excluded or assigned to the periphery of our collective life. The Model represents a further stage in the long process of decolonization that Canada has undergone since 1867. If we have been slow to free ourselves from the trammels of imperial rule, preferring to accomplish by gradual processes of evolution what others have effected abruptly by force of arms, we have been even slower to embark on the task of internal decolonization. It is only a Canadian, perhaps, who would prefer the silent shifting of constitutional paradigms in the night to the tumultuous drama of a Boston Tea Party or a Bastille. Nevertheless, as an astute observer of the Commonwealth once said: "There is much to be said for stealth and subtlety as methods of revolution, if revolution there must be."[24]

NOTES

1. Quoted in *Calder* v. *British Columbia (A.G.)*, [1973] S.C.R. 313 at 319 [hereinafter *Calder*].
2. (1888), 14 A.C. 46 (P.C.) [hereinafter *St. Catherine's Milling*].
3. (U.K.), reprinted in R.S.C. 1985, App. II, No. 1 [hereinafter *Royal Proclamation, 1763*]. An accurate copy of the original printed text is found in C.S. Brigham, ed., *British Royal*

Proclamations Relating to America (Worcester, Mass.: American Antiquarian Society, 1911) at 212-18.

4. *St. Catherine's Milling, supra* note 2 at 54.

5. See especially *Calder, supra* note 1; *Guerin* v. *Canada*, [1984] 2 S.C.R. 335 [hereinafter *Guerin*]; *R.* v. *Sioui*, [1990] 1 S.C.R. 1025; and *R.* v. *Sparrow*, [1990] 1 S.C.R. 1075 [hereinafter *Sparrow*]; *R.* v. *Van der Peet*, [1996] 2 S.C.R. 507; *Delgamuukw v. British Columbia*, [1997] 3 S.C.R. 1010; *R.* v. *Marshall*, [1999] 3 S.C.R. 456; *R.* v. *Powley*, 2003 SCC 43 (not yet reported).

6. For a striking expression of this viewpoint, see *R.* v. *Syliboy*, [1929] 1 D.L.R. 307 at 313 (N.S. Co. Ct.) [hereinafter *Syliboy*]. The Supreme Court of Canada expressed its disapproval of this passage in *Simon v. R.*, [1985] 2 S.C.R. 387 at 399.

7. See, for example, the maps in D.G.G. Kerr, *Historical Atlas of Canada*, 3d rev. ed. (Don Mills, Ont.: Nelson & Sons, 1975) at 22-23 and 30-31; and H.C. Darby & H. Fullard, eds., *The New Cambridge Modern History* vol, XIV, *Atlas*, (Cambridge: Cambridge University Press, 1970) at 196-98.

8. (U.K.), 30 & 31 Vict., c. 3 (formerly *British North America Act, 1867*), reprinted in R.S.C. 1985, App. II, No. 5 [hereinafter *Constitution Act, 1867*].

9. Schedule B of the *Canada Act 1982* (U.K.), 1982, c. 11 [hereinafter *Constitution Act, 1982*].

10. Part I of the *Constitution Act, 1982, ibid.* [hereinafter *Charter*].

11. *Code civil du Québec*, L.Q. 1991, c. 64.

12. See the historical account in J.E.C. Brierley & R.A. Macdonald, eds., *Quebec Civil Law: An Introduction to Quebec Private Law* (Toronto: Emond Montgomery, 1993) at 5-32.

13. See, for example, the remarks of McEachern C.J. in *Delgamuukw v. British Columbia* (1991), 79 D.L.R. (4th) 185 at 447 (B.C.S.C.).

14. This was the holding of the British Columbia Court of Appeal in *Calder v. British Columbia (A.G.)* (1970), 13 D.L.R. (3d) 64. The correctness of this holding was thrown in doubt by the Supreme Court of Canada on further appeal, *supra* note 1, and was finally laid to rest by the Supreme Court in *Guerin, supra* note 5.

15. See, for example, *Syliboy, supra* note 6.

16. R.S.C. 1985, c. I-5.

17. For more detailed discussion of these doctrines, see B. Slattery, *Ancestral Lands, Alien Laws: Judicial Perspectives on Aboriginal Title* (Saskatoon: University of Saskatchewan Native Law Centre, 1983).

18. *Supra* note 1.

19. *Constitution Act, 1982, supra* note 9.

20. *Supra* note 5 at 1105-06, quoting N. Lyon, "An Essay on Constitutional Interpretation" (1988) 26 Osgoode Hall L.J. 95 at 100.

21. For fuller treatment of various aspects of the Organic Model, see my papers: "The Independence of Canada" (1983) 5 Sup. Ct. L. Rev. 369; "Understanding Aboriginal Rights" (1987) 66 Can. Bar Rev. 727; "Aboriginal Sovereignty and Imperial Claims" (1991) 29 Osgoode Hall L.J. 681; and "First Nations and the Constitution: A Question of Trust" (1992) 71 Can. Bar Rev. 261.

22. *Supra* note 3.

23. See Slattery, *supra* note 17.

24. R.T.E. Latham, *The Law and the Commonwealth* (London: Oxford University Press, 1949) at 534.

QUESTIONS

1. Why does Brian Slattery refer to his model of the Constitution as the "Organic Model"?
2. How does he justify his view that the Organic Model is the appropriate model for interpreting the evolution of the Canadian Constitution?
3. Does Slattery provide a good basis for rejecting the position taken by P.E. Trudeau?

4. Does the Organic Model, as Brian Slattery describes it, capture and give adequate constitutional expression to the Aboriginal view of Canadian history as set out by George Erasmus and Joe Sanders?

ABORIGINAL RIGHTS

Michael McDonald

How would you respond to the question "What sorts of treatment do the native peoples of Canada deserve?"

Since native peoples are amongst the most underprivileged Canadians, you might respond on the basis of your attitude to the poor. Thus, if you believe that Canadians should have welfare rights, then you would claim that Indians like other Canadians should not be allowed to fall below some national standard of minimum welfare. You may believe that this is best done through providing a guaranteed annual income or through the provision of various goods (such as food and housing) and various services (such as medical care and job training). You would then find yourself in agreement with Prime Minister Trudeau who in 1969 said that native people

> . . . should become Canadians as all other Canadians and if they are prosperous and wealthy they will be treated like the prosperous and wealthy and they will be paying taxes for the other Canadians who are not so prosperous and not so wealthy whether they be Indians of English Canadians or French or Maritimers and this is the only basis on which I see our society can develop as equals.

On the other hand, another person might make a libertarian response and deny that anyone has a right to welfare. He might argue that no one deserves "free passage" — that everyone should work his own way. The debate would then be joined over a whole set of familiar issues. What are the relative merits of free enterprise and planned economies? What does "equal opportunity" involve? How much may the government interfere in citizens' lives? And so the argument will wend its way over time-worn paths until one or both of you get tired and change the subject.

A very effective way of changing the subject is changing it so that you both wind up on opposite sides of the original question with you arguing against any special treatment for "the poor Indians" and your libertarian opponent demanding that they receive significant advantages from white society. I think this reversal is likely to happen if you shift the topic from welfare rights to aboriginal rights. Topic shifts of this sort, those which get the attacker and defender of a particular *status quo* to change places, very often provide interesting material for the political philosopher. Such is the case with aboriginal rights.

Reprinted from Contemporary Issues in Political Philosophy, *ed. William Shea and John King-Farlow, Academic Publications Inc., New York.*

I. Entitlement Theory

What is the reason for this reversal in position?

I would suggest that there is something different about the ways in which we ground welfare and aboriginal rights. That is, when we argue for someone's having a welfare right we usually base our arguments on quite different sorts of premises than when we argue for aboriginal rights. The initial problem is then to characterize these sorts of differences.

Fortunately, this task has been made easier by the recent publication of *Anarchy, State, and Utopia* (New York, 1974) by Robert Nozick, who defends Locke's libertarian political philosophy. He argues that neither more nor less than the minimum or night watchman state of *laissez-faire* economics can be justified. In the course of this argument, he has to explain how people may legitimately have the exclusive use of various things, i.e., how they may come to own things. It is this discussion of "justice in holdings" that sheds light on the salient differences between welfare and aboriginal rights.

According to Nozick there are two primary ways in which I can have a just holding. If the object is unowned, I may under certain conditions come to own it; this is called "justice in the original acquisition of holdings." If the object is owned, then its owner may under certain conditions transfer it to me; this is called "justice in the transfer of holdings." Thus, for example, if you want to find out if the Atlantic salmon in my freezer is mine, you would want to know how I came to have the fish in my freezer: if I caught it, stole it, bought it, received it as a gift, etc. In short, you would ask for a history of ownership. The fish is mine if its original acquisition was just, and all subsequent transfers, if any, are also just. Insofar as you can trace this history, you can determine if I have *clear* title. To the extent that you cannot trace this history, it is not clearly mine, e.g., if all you know is that a friend gave it to me but you have no way of knowing how he got it, you can't say for certain that it really is mine.

If you get a clear history and then find that the original acquisition or one of the subsequent transfers was unjust, then you or someone else has the problem of deciding how to rectify this injustice in holdings. The rectification of injustice in holdings is the third part of Nozick's theory of just ownership. Thus, if you find out that my generous friend stole the salmon from a seafood store, you'll have to decide whether or not you should tell me to return it.

Now let us imagine that you decide to settle the question of my ownership of the salmon by using welfare principles solely. Let us assume that whatever welfare criterion you intend to use will only apply to the two of us in this case. First, you appeal to "need." You say that you are hungry and desperately short of protein, while I am not; since needs should be satisfied, you should have the fish. Say that I ignore that plea, so you try a hedonic appeal: you claim that you will enjoy eating the salmon much more than I will; hence, by the greatest happiness principle, you should have the salmon. It is not difficult in either appeal to imagine how I would have to respond to prove that I have a better title to the fish according to the criterion used. I would argue that I am needier than you or that I would really enjoy it more than you. Further it is not difficult to imagine the two criteria coming into conflict: you need the protein, but I would enjoy the dinner more. Then we would have to sort out which criterion takes precedence, e.g., that needs take precedence over wants. It is also not difficult to foresee some of the problems we might have in applying these considerations: how can I compare my need or enjoyment with yours, how can we properly take into account the effects of giving the fish to you or to me on each of our future needs or enjoyments, how do we know what counts as a "need" as opposed to what counts as a "want"? These are all problems which make up the bulk of philosophical debate about utilitarianism.

In our argument about who has the better welfare claim to the fish we proceed in a quite different way than we did earlier in trying to decide if the fish was a just holding of mine. Then we asked if the salmon had been justly acquired by me or justly transferred to me; in short, we looked backwards in time to see how the fish came into my possession. In the second case, we applied welfare criteria by looking to our present and future conditions to decide the issue according to our relative positions on the scale of need or enjoyment. Two major differences in the determination of ownership stand out in these cases: these are different attitudes to (a) the past and the future, and (b) the characteristics of the affected parties. Both (a) and (b) require some further explanation.

Regarding (a), we have seen that what mattered in determining justice in holdings were the acquisitions and transfers of the object; that is to say, the principle for the determination of ownership was *historical*. In the use of welfare criteria, we looked only at present and future considerations, viz. the relative degrees to which my or your having the fish would meet present and future needs or yield present and future enjoyment. Here we decided who owned the salmon on the basis of *end-results*. Our approach in the second case was *a*historical.

Regarding (b), you will recall that in the application of the welfare criteria we were concerned with the degree to which each of us had or lacked certain characteristics: if you were needier or would enjoy it more, then the fish should be yours. We were concerned in this case with the resulting *patterns* of the alternative distributions. In the first case, however, we proceeded without reference to patterns. There were no characteristics (such as need) which I might or might not have that would be determinative of the question of my ownership. It mattered not why I caught the fish (e.g., that I was trying to satisfy my hunger or pass the time of day) or even what I would do with it (e.g., eat it, throw it back in the stream, or use it for fertilizer). Nor did it matter why someone transferred it to me (e.g., because I paid for it, because I am his son, or because he simply felt like it). In fact it doesn't even matter if I have a freezer full of Atlantic salmon and you have none or even no food at all. Justice in holdings is *unpatterned* in that there is no natural dimension (what I call a "characteristic") or set of dimensions according to which the distribution of goods should take place.

II. Aboriginal Rights

We can now see how Nozick's approach to justice in holdings, which he calls "entitlement theory," ties in with the topic of aboriginal rights. Aboriginal rights are none other than original acquisition rights which haven't been transferred to anyone else. To defend the aboriginal rights of Canada's native peoples necessarily involves us in presenting a theory of original acquisition. Moreover, we must be willing to defend our theory of original acquisition against not only rival theories of original acquisition, but also against non-entitlement theories of ownership.

At the beginning of this paper, the argument about providing help to native people was carried on between a person who held a non-entitlement theory of the distribution of goods and one who held an entitlement theory. As you recall, one argued that native people should be helped on the basis of need. This, we have just seen, is an argument based on end-results and patterns. The other disputant argued that native people were not entitled to help. This argument is essentially historical and unpatterned.

Introducing aboriginal rights into the argument forced a change in the disputants' positions because it introduced a historical and unpatterned basis for the native people's entitlement. Now it was possible for the libertarian defender of property rights to argue that the natives had been dealt a historic injustice which stands in need of rectification. The defender of welfare rights must reject this approach, not because native people shouldn't receive significant benefits, but because in his view the only true basis for the reception of benefits is need. That is, he was arguing that benefits should be distributed in a patterned way with a view to the end-results achievable.

Now it is important to realize that we cannot simply let the disputants "agree to disagree." In practical terms, we are talking about claims to at least half of Canada. According to Peter Cumming and Neil Mickenberg in the second edition of *Native Rights in Canada* (Toronto, 1972), aboriginal claims have been superseded by treaties for less than one half of Canada. This would leave standing aboriginal claims to British Columbia, Quebec, the Maritimes, the Yukon, and parts of the Northwest Territories. Think of what this means to established settlements and to plans for Northern development. Remember, too, that "the natives are restless": they have been pressing their claims in the courts (in 1973 the Supreme Court of Canada split four to three against admitting an aboriginal claim), over the bargaining table (in Quebec native people have received a large cash and land settlement for allowing the James Bay Project to proceed in a scaled down form), at the barricades (in British Columbia), and before a royal commission (Mr. Justice Berger is carrying out an investigation of the effect of the proposed Mackenzie Valley Pipeline on native peoples). The questions of aboriginal rights is a real, not an ivory-tower, question.

In my examination of this question, I do not intend to say much more about non-entitlement theories except by way of contrast to entitlement theories. I shall instead focus on various problems that I see in the application of Nozickian and Lockean entitlement theories to the question of aboriginal rights in Canada. I will argue that some of the problems anticipated in such an application of entitlement theory can be adequately handled, but that other problems — particularly those at the core — are much more difficult and may well be insurmountable.

I shall proceed by presenting a number of objections to an entitlement defence of aboriginal rights. I shall first state the objection in the broad and general way it occurs in non-philosophical discussion. Here I have tried to draw upon statements made by politicians, lawyers, and native people, as well as from discussions I've had with students and colleagues. This response will consist, first, in sorting out various objections that have been confused and run together in the non-philosophical context. After that, I shall see what kind of reply can be made within an entitlement theory. I have tried to give each objection a name which suggests the sort of objection made and renders the arguments easier to remember. This mnemonic aid is important because the arguments are often interrelated and used together for or against aboriginal rights.

A. The Vandals Argument

This is the kind of argument that Trudeau has used:

> If we think of restoring aboriginal rights to the Indians, well, what about the French who were defeated at the Plains of Abraham? Shouldn't we restore rights to them? What about the Acadians who were deported — shouldn't we compensate for this? And what about the other Canadians, the immigrants? What about the Japanese Canadians who were so badly treated at the end [of] or during the last war?

A similar position was taken by many Americans in response to James Forman's demand that American churches and synagogues pay $500 million as reparations for years of slavery. In his book, *The Case for Black Reparations* (New York, 1973), Yale law professor Boris Bittker cites the *New York Times* response to Forman: "There is neither wealth nor wisdom enough in the world to compensate for all the wrongs in history."

An objector might ask if the descendants of the Roman victims of the Vandals' sack of Rome in 453 A.D. should be able to sue the Vandals' descendants? Here, however, we see the need to distinguish two separate objections. The first is what I shall call "Historical Disentanglement," and the second "Arbitrariness."

A.1. Historical Disentanglement. The first objection rests on practical difficulties in sorting out historical issues. The problem is to find out who is a descendant of the victims of an injustice and who is a descendant of the perpetrators of that injustice. In the Vandals' case the problems seem well-nigh insuperable. Even if some sorting out is possible, there will probably be enough intermarriage to confuse most cases thoroughly. Intermarriage has been alleged a serious barrier to reparations to blacks in the United States.

In the case we are considering, however — that of native Canadians — we can get some powerful assistance from the facts. A quarter of a million Indians are registered under the Indian Act of 1951 as members of recognized bands. While we may have problems with the fairness of some of the provisions of that Act (e.g., Indian women who marry non-Indian males are deregistered and non-Indian females who marry Indian males are automatically registered), the fact remains that we have an accurate, though somewhat incomplete, record of many descendants of the purported victims of injustice. The cases of the unregistered Indians and of the Metis are more difficult, but we have two important facts which will help disentangle matters. First, these people have regarded themselves as native people. And secondly, they have been regarded by white Canadians as natives insofar as they have been objects of the same informal extra-legal distinctions (including racial prejudices) as those under the Indian Act. It should not prove to be too difficult to arrive at a consensus on who is or is not a native person amongst the Metis and other unregistered claimants of this status.

This, of course, leaves the question of tracing the descendants of those purported to have violated aboriginal title. Here again the facts help us — in this case it is the legal fact that only the Crown could seize land. In the case of New France, we can regard the Crown as the inheritor of whatever title France had to aboriginal lands.

It is also possible that we might in hard cases make use of a test Nozick suggests for determining the descendants of victims and perpetrators on the grounds that *persistent* inequalities are most likely a result of historical injustice. (While Nozick does not suggest "persistency" as a criterion here, I think it might make his suggestion more plausible.)

A.2. Arbitrariness. The second distinct element in the Vandals Argument is that suggestion that the defender of aboriginal rights wants to make an arbitrary and invidious distinction between rectifying the injustices done to aboriginal peoples and the injustices done to non-aboriginal Canadians. This is, I think, what Trudeau was asking, namely, how could we defend rectifying the injustices done to the Indians and ignore the injustices done by our nation to the French, the Acadians, and Japanese?

Trudeau goes on to say that we cannot "redeem the past"; we can only be "just in our time." This seems to let us argue that if we can't wholly rectify all the injustices we have ever done, then we needn't rectify any. The most favourable interpretation that I can put on

Trudeau's conclusion is that we may have to face a multiplicity of competing claims of all sorts including a number of competing claims for the rectification of past injustices. We may then not be able to do everything that we ought ideally to do; in an imperfect world we may have to pay our most morally pressing debts in full and make only token payments on the remainder. There need be no arbitrariness in the recognition of aboriginal rights, for we can still recognise other past and present injustices. We may not be able to fully satisfy all the claims for rectification, but that isn't arbitrary either — there is no obligation to do more than one can.

B. The Forefathers Argument

There is another way of taking Trudeau's conclusion that we cannot redeem the past, and that is to say that we are only responsible for our sins and not for the sins of our fathers. How can I be blamed for what my French-Canadian ancestors did to the Indians of New French? How can anyone do more than be just in his own time?

Let's sort out this argument.

B.1 Backwards Causation. The first thing to clarify is whether saying that I ought to rectify injustice X involves saying that I am one of X's causes. If my children ruin my neighbor's prize roses, may I not have an obligation to make reparations? If I do, it needn't be the case that in so doing I am admitting that it was I who tramped through the roses. I may not even have to admit that it was somehow my fault that my children were in the garden. I may have told my children to stay out of the garden. Moreover, I may have done the best I can to instill in them a sense of respect for others' property. Then there is nothing more I should have done. (After all, there are outward bounds like child abuse for determining how far a parent can go in instructing his children.) Indeed my children may not have acted deliberately, purposely, or even intentionally; it was an accident pure and simple, for which even they are not to blame. But there it is: the roses are ruined, and I am the one who should set it right.

The point is that "responsibility" can be used in a variety of ways. Sometimes it is used to indicate causality, in which case contemporaneousness or precedence in time is essential. But in the rose garden case, it was used to indicate who was *liable* for damages. The concept of liability is most highly developed within the law, but we do use it outside the law in our ordinary attributions or moral responsibility. The question then is whether anyone today has liability for the past violations (if any) of aboriginal rights.

There is a further confusion in this argument. This is to claim that backwards causation must be involved because I can only have obligations of my own making. Thus, I could have an obligation to contemporary native peoples respecting aboriginal rights only if I had undertaken to respect these rights, i.e., if I made a promise to or contract with their ancestors. It will take only a moment's reflection, however, to see that many obligations we have are not entered into voluntarily (or involuntarily either), e.g., not to kill, to express gratitude for favours received, to be kind, and to be honest.

B.2. Benefits Received. In (B.1) I didn't really so much respond to the Forefathers Argument as clear the way for a response to it. That liability-responsibility is different from causal-responsibility is important; nevertheless, it does not tell us if Canadians today have liability-responsibility for violations of aboriginal title. Neither does knowing that all obligations are not of our own making tell us if the rectification of this putative injustice is our responsibility.

A much more telling response is an analogy with the receipt of stolen goods. If person *A* steals person *B*'s watch and then makes a present of it to *C*, do we think that *C* has an obligation to return it to *B* even though he had no idea that he was in receipt of stolen goods when he accepted the watch? Surely, the answer is "Yes!" We might go on to say that *A* owes *C* something (an apology at minimum) for inconveniencing and embarrassing him. We would, I think, give the same answer even if the thief *A* can't recompense *C* (say that *A* is now dead). It is worth noting here that no one is blaming *C* for *A*'s stealing *B*'s watch or even for unwittingly accepting stolen property. *C* needn't feel any guilt about either of these matters. He should, however, feel guilt if he doesn't return the watch to *B*. I see no reason to change our views about returning the watch if instead of talking about *B* and *C* we talk about their heirs. I would not extend this to *A*'s heirs, however, who presumably have not benefitted either from *A*'s theft, itself, or the gift of the watch to *C*.

The parallels with the case of aboriginal rights should be fairly obvious. Non-Indians have in Canada benefitted (albeit in very unequal degrees) from the noncompensated supersession of aboriginal title. This is not to say that non-Indians *today* refused to compensate native people for the loss of aboriginal rights *during* the last and preceding centuries. These non-Indians certainly can't be held responsible for being born into this society or for immigrating to it. In this respect, breast-beating over what has been done to the "poor native" is neither due nor appropriate. Guilt is appropriate only if nothing is done to remedy injustices in the treatment of native people including, in particular, the rectification of past injustices.

Of course, the case for reparations becomes more difficult if we change the analogy somewhat. For example, what, if anything, does *C* owe *B* if after *C* receives the watch he loses it? It would be different if *C* were keeping *B*'s watch in trust for *B*, for then he could well be responsible for not losing it. This problem posed by lost or ruined articles seems quite likely to occur with the passage of significant periods of time. If we are talking about *C*'s and *B*'s great-grandchildren, the odds are that by this time the watch has been lost or no longer works.

That is, I think, the kind of thing that Bittker has in mind when he says that there would be no case for reparations to blacks if in the period since the Civil War there had been an unbroken ascent up to a present state of genuine equality. That is, the argument here is that reparations are not due if the relative advantage seized by the act of injustice gets lost or equalized in the course of history, so that it no longer makes any difference. It is *not* crucial to this argument that *both* the benefits accruing to the oppressors and their heirs and the evils suffered by the victims and their heirs no longer remain. It is enough to have the first without the second.

B.3. Inheritance. There is a way of taking the Forefathers Argument that avoids the reply just advanced (B.2.). There I argued that if you can inherit benefits, you can inherit burdens chargeable against those benefits. This is like having to pay estate taxes and creditors before receiving an inheritance. As we have just seen, if you inherit nothing, you do not have any obligation (save, perhaps, "a debt of honour") to pay any debts chargeable against the estate. This suggests that there would be no aboriginal rights if there were no rights to make bequests; that is, aboriginal rights disappear if no one may rightfully inherit anything.

Native people could use this as an effective *ad hominem* argument in pressing their case. They could say to the rich and powerful in our society that Indians and Inuit will give up their claims to aboriginal rights if the rich and powerful will surrender all the property that they have inherited. This would not mean the end of private property but only the aspect of it — which I call "bequeathability." Other aspects of private property would remain (viz. rights of alienability, exclusive use, security, management, income, and so forth) but these "standard incidents" of property would be limited to the life of the holder. (To make this suggestion effective, we would have to set a limit to the life of corporations, for under our laws these "artificial persons" can be immortal.)

C. The Double Wrong Argument

The objection here is that to rectify one injustice another will have to be done, so that in rectifying the injustice done to the native people an injustice will have to be done to non-native Canadians by taking away from them land or the profit therefrom which they have in good faith purchased and improved. Moreover, the settlement of aboriginal claims will impose an enormous burden on those who in some cases are already disadvantaged.

The main response to this has already been made in the Forefathers Argument (B.2.). No one has a right to receive and retain what is not another's to give. "Good faith" here excuses one from complicity in the original theft: one is not to blame for the theft, so one needn't feel guilty about it. It does not excuse one from returning the stolen goods or the equivalent. Remember that we are working within the context of entitlement theory; justice in holding demands, justice in acquisition, and transfers. To give weight to the claims of those who have unjust holdings is just the sort of thing end-result theorists would do.

Nevertheless, the entitlement theorist can reduce the practical force of this objection by pointing out that third party beneficiaries (here, non-Indian and non-Inuit property owners) must return what remains of that which was wrongfully transferred to them. Given the ravages of time, one may not have to surrender any of one's own goods in making this reparation because nothing of value remains. I say "may not" because among the benefits received from the stolen property is that there is less drain on one's own resources. Thus, in the watch analogy, C or his heirs may benefit from not having to purchase watches of their own because they have the use of the watch stolen from B. So if the watch breaks after a few years while in C's possession, B might ask for rent for the use of his watch over the years before it broke. If C is now bankrupt, there may be little B can get (unless it is the case that entitlement theory would demand that C work the rent off). If it is the case that in addition to bankruptcy C also dies, then B cannot demand that C's would-be heirs pay for it out of their own justly acquired resources (including working the debt off). Death without the transmission of a benefice would seem on the entitlement theory to end the case for repayment simply because the unjust holding no longer exists. Presumably, in this wealthy nation, most of the benefit has been transmitted to us.

A final remark on the plight of the small property holder. According to the principles of rectification of injustice in holdings, it surely must be the case that those who have benefitted most from unjust holdings owe more than those who have benefitted least. Keeping in mind the complications about inheritance discussed earlier, it should be the case that in a society like ours, in which most wealth — especially capital — remains concentrated in a few families, the wealthiest would have the most to lose by the recognition of aboriginal rights. Here I would think especially of those who have benefitted most from the exploitation of natural resources (like gas, oil, and minerals) in the areas in question, particularly Alberta, the North, and B.C. Of course, it has already been argued (B.3.) that these same people have the most to lose by denying aboriginal claims for they would thereby undermine their own claims to inherited wealth.

D. The Sovereignty Argument

In an article in *The Globe and Mail* (21 February 1973), Cumming has suggested that one possible reason for the Government's reluctance to recognise aboriginal rights is the fear that in so doing there would be a recognition of aboriginal sovereignty over the lands in question, to wit, Trudeau's reference to the Plains of Abraham. This is evident, too, in the same speech when Trudeau says, "It's inconceivable, I think, that in a given society one section of society have a treaty with another section of society." Trudeau is not the only politician in Canada's history to express concern about holding the country together; this is a country which has been plagued by threats of separatism — from Quebec, the West, and the Maritimes.

If it is the case that the recognition of aboriginal rights would necessarily involve a recognition of a separate aboriginal nation or nations then it is not clear what an entitlement theorist like Nozick would say. Nozick's invisible hand explanation of the emergence of a dominant protection agency as the (minimal) state never comes to grips with the fact that there is more than one nation in this complicated world. The fact of nationalism should also have some effect on Nozick's proposal for utopia — allowing diverse experiments in types of communities *within* a single nation. Are nationalists entirely wrong when they think that they must have control over the state and not just over the community? Another interesting way of putting this question is to ask what sorts of self-determination (determination particularly of a group's identity) are not possible in a libertarian society. Leaving aside these complex and difficult questions, it is possible to argue that if sovereignty is an issue here, then surely we must talk about more than justice in holdings.

The simplest way of dealing with this objection is to deny, as Cumming does, that sovereignty and property rights are connected except in an indirect way. In ordinary disputes over land ownership, neither claimant is trying to set up an independent nation. The adjudication usually follows the laws of the nation in which the property is situated. Although in a few difficult cases there can be arguments about which of two nation's laws are applicable, the dispute is primarily about ownership and only secondarily about sovereignty. It should be pointed out that no less an entitlement theorist like Locke claimed that rights to property are quite independent of rights to rule, for he maintained that property rights should survive changes in government including violent changes brought about by war.

E. The Litigation Argument

The general argument here is that claims to aboriginal title are unlike ordinary property claims. They are not amenable to the usual sorts of tests used by the courts to decide property rights. In particular many aboriginal claims are such as to deny courts the use of a most effective procedure for deciding between rival claims in cases where due to the passage of time both records are missing and memories are uncertain, namely, "prescription" which is "the operation of time as a vestitive fact." If this is correct, then how can anyone maintain that aboriginal claims can be settled in the same way as ordinary disputes about ownership? Indeed, how can anyone maintain that they are property rights at all?

This argument can be taken in part as a necessary corrective to the oversimplified reply that I just advanced against the Sovereignty Argument. There I argued that sovereignty and property were different kinds of rights. This may have left the impression that all property rights are alike and that aboriginal rights are like other property-rights. Neither of these contentions is true.

I agree with A.M. Honore that "property" is probably best thought of in terms of a list of "the standard incidents of ownership." This would be a list of the rights which a property owner has in the standard, full-blown case. It would include rights of physical possession, use, derivation of profit and capital, security, management, and so forth. One would probably also have to say something about the duties of ownership as well, in particular the prohibition of harmful use. If some of these incidents are missing in a particular case, we could still talk about "property-rights." In fact all the Indian treaties deny Indians the liberty of converting their reserves into capital, i.e., they may not alienate their lands, only the Crown may. In this sense, reserves could be seen as belonging to a particular people in perpetuity, not just to its present-day occupants; thus, future generations would have patrimonial rights. Aboriginal land claims involve the same kind of arrangement. (I should add here that if a whole people, conceived as a group extending across time into the future, can have property rights, then such right might well play havoc with many of the positions that Nozick defends on the basis of actions in a free market).

So part of my reply to this argument is that while aboriginal titles may lack some of the standard incidents of property it may well be possible to still think of them as property rights. To properly establish this reply would require a great deal more space than I presently have. I think more needs to be said, however, about this argument along somewhat different lines.

First, there is the issue of "prescription." In the law it is the case that the passage of time can extinguish or establish ownership. This is determined by time limits established by custom or statute. For example, in some jurisdictions if you have made use of part of someone else's land as a right-of-way for twenty years, then the courts will uphold your right to continue to do so and thus bar the landowner from preventing your passage. Thus time has given you a right you formerly did not have and extinguished a property-right that the landowner had. The point of prescription is quite straightforward: the passage of time is used as a conclusive evidence because it simplifies the work of the courts in determining ownership. Thus, the jurist Savigny said, "All property is founded in adverse possession ripened by prescription."

The problem for aboriginal claims is that in many cases the land claimed is not now and has not been occupied by the claimants at all or on an exclusive basis for many years more than the limits set by law for the extinguishment of title. Yet it seems unfair therefore to deny title even though it is fair to do so in ordinary cases. In ordinary cases the law protects the property-owner's exercise of his property-rights before the period of prescription has elapsed. That is, if he wants to prevent his title from lapsing, he need only take action. Thus, in the right-of-way case, the property-owner can put up a "no trespassing" sign before the twenty years are out; this completely extinguishes your claim to a legally guaranteed right-of-way. If it is illegal to post the sign, then using the passage of time to effect a transfer of title would be unfair. The parallel here is that native peoples have not been given an opportunity to present their aboriginal claims, either through the courts or directly to government.

Secondly, the Litigation Argument does raise important doubts about the appropriate *forum* for the determination of the value and extent of various aboriginal claims. Cumming says that "the court is by far the least appropriate forum for dealing with aboriginal rights" because "litigation is expensive, time-consuming, and abounds with technical difficulties." He proposes instead that there be direct negotiations between the government and native people. Thus, this is essentially a practical, not an in-principle concern.

Thirdly, the Litigation Argument hints at a problem which will concern us in the next and final section. The problem, as seen from the perspective of this Argument, concerns the relationship between particular property-rights and the existing legal system. One way of finding the general area of difficulty is to ask if there can be property without laws. If there cannot be property without laws (as has been argued by generations of contractarians, Kant among them), then is property merely a creature of law? If property-rights can only be created and destroyed by law, what must be said about the entitlement theorists' claim that we have a natural right to "estate" in addition to "life and liberty"? In the next section I will consider some of these questions.

F. The Acquisition Arguments

Thus far, in all the objections and replies, I have tried to apply entitlement theory to the question of aboriginal rights. If I am right, then a number of interesting and plausible objections to entitlement theory and its application can be answered. In neither the objections nor the replies have I asked if native people actually have a claim to these lands on the basis of just original acquisition; for the sake of argument I have assumed that they do, and then gone to ask whether such claims should be recognised. Obviously, if native people in general or in particular did *not* make a just original acquisition of the land, the whole case for aboriginal rights fails. This would now show that all the native people's claims to land ownership are null and void, but it would remove the most important and the largest claims.

There is more than this practical issue at stake here. The whole entitlement theory rests on original acquisition. If the justice of an original acquisition is called into question then so also, Nozick says, are all subsequent transfers. If *all* original acquisitions can be called into question, then, perhaps, all claims to property rights are challengeable. One way of calling all aboriginal acquisitions into question is to deny that sense can be made of the concept of "original acquisition." Another way would be to deny that original acquisition as imagined by entitlement theorists can be a basis for rightful ownership.

So now I will turn to the "keystone" issue. I should say that some of the sharpest criticisms of the original acquisition doctrine come from Nozick himself. He writes in an almost ironic, or shall I say, "contrapuntal" way that involves the reader and enlivens debate. I will present four objections and responses. The responses, I should indicate, are partial and do not, I think, save entitlement theory (though, curiously enough, they save aboriginal rights).

F.1. The Jus Tertii Argument. One way of challenging aboriginal rights *within* the framework of entitlement theory is to deny that the Indians and Inuit had made original and just acquisition. This could be denied on the grounds that Indians and Inuit weren't the first human beings in Canada and that Indians and Inuit acquired the northern half of this continent by force. In any event, given the lack of records of property acquisition, it could be claimed that no one can know for certain if the native people's ancestors acquired the lands justly as either first possessors or as a result of just transfer. This would at the very least make aboriginal claims suspect.

The argument presented here rests on a claim like the following: if Bill's acquisition of Blackacres from Alice is unjust, then Chuck's acquisition of the land from Bill need not follow the rules of just transfer in order to get as good, or better, title than Bill has to Blackacres. The underlying contention is that if title is, so to speak, "spoiled" at any point the property is simply up for grabs. Here I am assuming that the just owner Alice is not laying claim to Blackacres and that Chuck is in no way acting on behalf of Alice. The question is not, then, one of Chuck's rectifying an injustice done to Alice by Bill. The objection rests on the contention that given Alice's not laying or transferring her claim to another, Bill's act of injustice returns Blackacres to an ownerless situation from which Chuck may claim it.

Before questioning this contention, I would note that even accepting this reasoning there still is a difference between showing that Bill's title is spoiled and raising a suspicion that it may not be clear. In some cases, it simply is impossible for a possessor to prove that he has clear title; however, this does not mean that others can prove that he does not. Surely the burden of proof rests on those who charge wrongful possession.

Now as to the argument itself, it is worth noting that the practice under common law is not to establish ownership *absolutely* but *only relatively*, i.e., to decide who has a *better* right to possess. It would, I believe, be the case that a court would hold that Bill has a better title to Blackacres than Chuck and Alice has a better title to Blackacres than Bill. Regardless of the court's decision, it is certainly more convenient for a court to decide matters in this relative way (adjudicating only between the rival claims presented to it) rather than trying to do this once and for all (which would involve ruling on every conceivable claim). In this case, the court would settle the dispute between Bill and Chuck leaving it to others such as Alice to bring suit separately.

Which approach should an entitlement theorist adopt — that unjust acquisition or transfer returns the object to an ownerless condition or that it simply "weakens" the possessor's title? I wonder if in answering this question we will have to fall back on utilitarian considerations, e.g., about which procedure would be the most orderly and least disruptive for a given society. I am not sure how this question would be decided on purely entitlement grounds. That is, I don't know what *natural* rights to the ownership of Blackacres are held by Bill as opposed to Chuck. I would suspect that this cannot be determined without a *policy* decision about the rules governing property. Entitlement theory does not say which is the appropriate way of deciding ownership in this case. If this is right then it indicates an important gap in entitlement theory, for it means that the theory of justice in holdings has to be patched up by resorting to utilitarianism.

Apropos the question of aboriginal rights, it would seem that if we proceed on the basis of who has better title rather than on the basis of who has absolute title, then native people's claims would seem to be stronger than those of successive possessors.

F.2 The Spoilage Argument. In *The Second Treatise of Government*, Locke presents an objection to his view of justice in original acquisition:

> That if gathering the Acorns, or other Fruits of the Earth, & c. makes a right to them, then any one may *ingross* as much as he will.

Locke says that this is not so; one may take "as much as one can make use of to any advantage of life before it spoils . . . Whatever is beyond this, is more than his share and belongs to others." Locke grounds this limitation of original acquisition on God's will: "Nothing was made by God for Man to spoil or destroy." Yet it is clear that God's will is not capricious, for as Locke says earlier:

> God, who hath given the World to Men in common, hath also given them reason to make use of it to the best advantage of Life and convenience.

Men then have a right to self-preservation which entitles them to take the means thereto, viz. by acquiring the necessaries of life. Self-preservation grounds appropriation and sets limits to it.

Now it could be argued that the spoilage provision sets the limits too widely in that it allows me to refuse to share my bounty with my starving neighbours so long as I can use that bounty for "the best advantage of [my] Life and convenience." Matters are weighted heavily in favour of the propertied and against those without property. But let us for the sake of argument accept spoilage as an outward limit of just original acquisition. We can then ask whether native peoples violated the spoilage principle in acquiring these lands. If they did and if the Europeans who came here could make use of the wasted portions, then aboriginal claims may be defensible on the grounds of wastage.

If this question is answerable, it would have to be on the basis of historical evidence; however, it is fair for the philosopher to ask about the determination of the criteria for wastage and spoilage: by what marks do we identify something as waste? Here it is tempting to ask if the thing in question is used for anyone's benefit. But will any minute amount of incremental benefit suffice to justify ownership or must there be some standard margin of benefit for this use to count here for title? Must there also be standards of efficient use? Would there be a combined standard, e.g., "Makes the best use of X for the greatest benefit"? Any benefit or efficiency standard would seem to be hopelessly utilitarian and redistributivist. On the other hand, having no standards at all would effectively deny a right of self-preservation to those without property and the correlative duty to share for the propertied.

If we try to fix on some mid-point (i.e., having a spoilage provision which is compatible with entitlement theory), then the question is how to justify our selection of standards on an entitlement basis. This is a particularly troublesome question in the case of aboriginal rights. In many cases an advanced agricultural and industrialised economy came into contact with a hunting, fishing, and gathering economy. The patterns of resource use were bound to be different. What would appear as under-utilisation in one economy might appear as over-utilisation in the other. Clearly Canada's native peoples made ingenious use of the often harsh environment, but their uses could not support the numbers of people that present-day uses can. (In this paper I am being deliberately silent about how much longer we can continue our use-patterns.) However, if we move in the direction of giving title to the Europeans rather than the native peoples, then we would have to surrender our ownership claims to any society which could support more people here more efficiently. This seems quite obviously in direct opposition to the whole thrust of an *entitlement* theory: if I am entitled to something, if it's *mine*, then I should within the limit of non-harmfulness be able to use it as efficiently or as inefficiently as I wish for whosoever's advantage I choose. This would accord with Nozick's slogan: "From each as they choose, to each as they are chosen."

Tentatively, then, if we are willing to deny the right of self-preservation and more especially the correlative duty of sharing when necessary to provide it, then we can still hold the entitlement theory and so avoid the conceptual difficulties posed by the spoilage principle.

F.3. The "Proviso" Argument. Spoilage is not the only limit Locke sets to original acquisition; he also suggests what Nozick calls "the Lockean Proviso," namely that there be "enough and as good left in common for others." This Nozick says, "is meant to ensure that the position of others is not worsened." Thus, we can imagine a parallel argument to the Spoilage Argument being advanced against aboriginal rights on the grounds that aboriginal possession violated the enough-and-as-good proviso.

Factually, this is going to be a tricky argument to work out for not only must it be shown that the native people did not leave enough and as good to the immigrants, but also that the immigrants have taken just enough to rectify this violation of the proviso. This will be very hard to prove, given the relative wealth of natives and immigrants. At present, indeed, native people could justifiably argue that the immigrants haven't left enough and as good to them.

Here, as in the Spoilage Argument, there are serious conceptual problems in determining the appropriate criteria. Nozick advances two interpretations of the Proviso:

> Someone may be made worse off by another's appropriation in two ways: first by losing the opportunity to improve his situation by a particular appropriation or any one, and second, by no longer being able to use freely (without appropriation) what he previously could.

Nozick accepts the second or "weaker requirement" and not the first or "the stringent requirement." The difference between the two seems to be between characterizing the proviso as applying to appropriation (ownership) or to use. But then it must be remembered that earlier Nozick says that the central core of the notion of a property right in X is "the right to determine what shall be done with X." If I have a right to use X, then would I not have a property right in X?

Be that as it may, Nozick argues that those who are unable to appropriate (because everything is now owned) are likely to be compensated for this restriction on their liberty by having their prospects increased by a system which allows (virtually unlimited) private acquisition. Nozick says the free market will make up for their loss of acquisition and/or use rights. The point is to compensate these people enough for not being able to appropriate or use what they could have had they been born earlier. Nozick suggests that the level of compensation can be determined by getting "an estimate of the general economic importance of appropriation."

But this, I suggest, won't do for several reasons. First, if this isn't forcing on someone a kind of compensation that he doesn't want, then in the case of those who really want to make acquisitions the state will have to take something away from various property-owners. Secondly, as my colleague Jan Narveson has argued, the level of compensation will probably have to be set high enough to amount to a tidy guaranteed annual income. Thirdly, it isn't clear how much compensation is to be given to any particular propertyless person. Does he get as much as he would have been likely to get if he were in the position of the last person who acquired property or as much as if he were the first person to acquire property? In either case, the primary basis for distribution (his acquisitiveness) seems suspiciously patterned. Fourth, if the benefits of a free market economy really do provide enough compensation, then why does it seem so unlikely that anyone who has more than a little property, e.g., E.P. Taylor, would want to change places with one of these people who can't acquire any property because everything is owned?

All of which suggests that on a *pure* entitlement theory — one which is based on historical entitlement — there would be no room for the Proviso. On a pure entitlement theory if you are born after all the accessible and useful unowned objects have been taken up by your predecessors, you are simply out of luck. The denial of the Proviso would also seem to be in agreement with Nozick's criticisms of Rawls' contention that a system of natural liberties allows distribution on morally arbitrary grounds — that the distribution of natural talents is not on the basis of desert leads Rawls to design the social system to compensate for this "arbitrariness" by favouring (other things being equal) the least talented in the distribution of goods. Nozick criticises this is a "manna-from-heaven" model that totally ignores who has made these goods, i.e., Rawls ignores the crucial fact of historical entitlement. Similarly, the Proviso seems to ignore the crucial fact of appropriation.

Finally, as in the Spoilage Argument, we can ask what it is to leave "enough and as good"? If the standard is *usability*, then do we adopt the native peoples' idea of what is usable or the non-native immigrants? If we defend the latter, then in effect we are denying native peoples their ways of life. According to the Proviso, this would seem to demand that we compensate the native peoples for that loss. Yet is that something for which adequate compensation is possible other than allowing them to maintain their standards of use and so their way of life? Would not "the base line for comparison" be very high indeed then?

F.4. The Invalid Acquisition Arguments. In both the Spoilage and Proviso Arguments, aboriginal title was challenged on the grounds that Indians and Inuit had acquired too much, i.e., more than they were entitled to acquire. It is possible to raise a different objection by claiming that they failed to acquire anything or scarcely anything at all. The heart of this contention is that native peoples did not perform the appropriate acquisitive acts. We get a variety of objections of this kind based on different views of what is an appropriate act of acquisition, that is depending on what sorts of human actions bring things out of a state of ownerlessness into a state of property. Before trying to get this argument off the ground, it is worth noting that both Nozick and Locke start with the assumption that before individual acquisition things are in an ownerless condition (the *res nullis* doctrine); there is another school of thought that assumes that before private acquisition takes place, things are held in common by all men (the *res communae* doctrine).

The major problem in raising this objection is fixing on some kind(s) of action that can be plausibly regarded as acts of original acquisition, i.e., upon the *rites* that generate property *rights*. Nozick raises very serious problems about Locke's criterion for ownership, namely that one owns that with which one has mixed one's labour. He asks about the boundaries of such an acquisition:

> If a private astronaut clears a place on Mars, has he mixed his labour with (so that he comes to own) the whole planet, the whole uninhabited universe, or just a particular plot?

Nozick also asks why mixing one's labour with something isn't simply throwing one's labour away, and if it isn't, then why should one have title to more than the value (if any) added by one's labour? If "mixing labour" is the acquisitive act, then surely these and related questions must be convincingly answered if entitlement theory is to proceed.

We have already seen that if usage is made the standard there are serious problems in determining whose standard of use should prevail. In fact, it would seem that an entitlement theorist should shy away from recognising usage as the acquisitive action, for anyone could take your title to X away from you by finding a better use of X (if you are already using it) or putting it to use for the first time (if you haven't used it yet). I would think that an entitlement theorist should say that it is solely up to X's owner whether and to what use X shall be put. Yet it is Locke who denies that the Indians of America have any ownership rights beyond what they use for food and clothing; English settlers have rights to the land itself because they till it. In short, Locke denies aboriginal rights because the Indians don't use the land in the same way as the English immigrants.

Perhaps, then, it will be suggested that acquisitive actions are *conventional* — literally consisting in the conventions (customs or laws) of a particular people. Thus in one society you own only what you actually have in hand or on your person at the moment, while in another you own whatever bears your mark, and in still another society you own only those things entered in the central ownership registry. Of course, there will be problems when societies with different ownership conventions each want to make exclusive use of the same objects. Each society (assuming no overlap in conventions) can say that the other society's people haven't really acquired the goods in question because of a failure to follow the appropriate conventions. I do not see how an entitlement theorist can say which set of conventions (in part, presumably, adopted for non-arbitrary reasons having to do with different patterns of usage) should prevail on the basis of entitlement theory; it seems to me that he must resort to patterned and, in the end, possibly redistributivist considerations. I think it is on the basis of these considerations that our society will have to deal with the contention (if it can be proven) that the Indian treaties are invalid because the whites and the Indians had totally different conceptions of ownership.

Conclusions

First, I hope to have shown in my consideration of entitlement theory that a number of plausible objections to it (A) through (E), can be answered. These are essentially peripheral objections. Once we get to the core of the theory, however, serious and, I would maintain, insurmountable problems arise. The entitlement theory of original acquisition cannot be maintained without resort to non-entitlement considerations — patterns, end-results, and pure conventions. To cleanse entitlement theory of these additions will make it so unattractive that it cannot be accepted as a theory of justice in holdings.

Secondly, and somewhat surprisingly, I think that I have made out the case for aboriginal rights. I claim that this country ought to recognise aboriginal rights *on the basis of original acquisition*. Of course, this conclusion depends on the validity of my claim that the only rationale that is advanced and is plausible for the present system of holdings in Canada is entitlement theory. I contend that it is on the basis of entitlement theory alone, that we could ever hope to justify the way in which most holdings are distributed in Canada. Just because entitlement theory won't work does not mean that our society won't proceed as if it does. The argument for aboriginal rights is provisional. But it ought to obtain until we are willing to redistribute holdings in this country on a truly just basis.

QUESTIONS

1. If we grant Canada's original peoples aboriginal rights, does it follow from Michael McDonald's argument that we cease to have any obligations to provide welfare?
2. McDonald's arguments about property rights are based on a concept of property derived from Western European thought. Yet the Native peoples reject the idea (so important to our way of thinking) that land can be owned or acquired as property. Does this affect McDonald's argument?

3. If entitlement theory won't work, should our society proceed as though it were a valid theory? Do we need to create a new theory?

ABORIGINAL RIGHTS AND THE PROBLEMS OF OWNERSHIP

David Gauthier

McDonald begins with the question, "What sorts of treatment do the native peoples of Canada deserve?" He mentions two very different answers: (i) "Canadians should have welfare rights . . . [so] Indians . . . should not be allowed to fall below some national standard of minimum welfare"; (ii) "no one deserves 'free passage' . . . everyone should work his own way" (p. 27). McDonald then proposes to "shift the topic from welfare rights to aboriginal rights" (ibid.), suggesting that those who defend special welfare rights for Indians (because of their endemic poverty) will reject special aboriginal rights, whereas those who reject special welfare rights (because they reject all such rights) will find that they must defend aboriginal rights.

It is the second part of this reversal which primarily concerns McDonald. Those who reject welfare rights usually defend rights of appropriation. Everyone has a right to what he justly appropriates or justly acquires by transfer, and since this effectively exhausts rights to things, there can be no further welfare rights. But the native peoples were the original appropriators of Canada. Therefore. . . .

McDonald then considers a number of objections to this entitlement theory, which derives from the work of Nozick. His conclusion is that "The entitlement theory of original acquisition cannot be maintained without resort to non-entitlement considerations . . . [However] it is on basis [sic] of entitlement theory alone, that we could ever hope to justify the way in which most holdings are distributed in Canada. Just because entitlement theory won't work does not mean that our society won't proceed as if it does" (pp. 47–48). And so proceeding, "this country ought to recognise aboriginal rights *on the basis of original acquisition*" (p. 47).

My concern with this ingenious argument will be restricted here to McDonald's discussion of objections to the supposition that native peoples did indeed acquire Canada. In particular, referring to the Lockean basis of Nozick's theory, he discusses the *spoilage argument* and the *"proviso" argument*.

Rightful acquisition is limited by spoilage; one may not waste what one acquires. Did the natives, then, waste North America? Were Europeans entitled to appropriate the wasted portions, so that aboriginal rights were not violated by such appropriation?

McDonald argues that it is unclear how the condition of spoilage is to be specified. ". . . by what marks do we identify something as waste? Here it is tempting to ask if the thing in question is used for anyone's benefit. But will any minute amount of incremental benefit suffice to justify ownership or must there be some standard margin of benefit for this use to count here for title? Must there also be standards of efficient use? . . . Any benefit or efficiency standard would seem to be hopelessly utilitarian and redistributivist. On the other hand, having no standards at all would effectively deny a right of self-preservation to those without property and the correlative duty to share for the propertied."

From a review in Dialogue *of Michael McDonald's "Aboriginal Rights."*

This issue is particularly vexed in the sphere of aboriginal rights, where the native pattern of use differs significantly from the newcomers' pattern. "Clearly Canada's native peoples made ingenious use of the often harsh environment, but their uses could not support the numbers of people that present-day use can . . . However, if we move in the direction of giving title to the Europeans rather than the native peoples, then we would have to surrender our ownership claims to any society which could support more people here more efficiently. This seems quite obviously in direct opposition to the whole thrust of an *entitlement* theory . . ."(pp. 43–44). Hence — despite the harsh consequence of rejecting a right of self-preservation — the native claim to aboriginal acquisition can, McDonald holds, be defended against the spoilage objection.

Against McDonald, I should urge the following form of the spoilage objection. Let us grant that, in the state of nature, a group of persons, A, is entitled to appropriate as much land as its members are able to use in any way at all. However, should another group, B, of would-be appropriators appear on the scene, and should this group possess a superior technology to A, then B would be entitled to appropriate, from A, as much as would leave A with land sufficient, using B's superior technology, to maintain at least as many persons as before, with at least as rich an assortment of material goods, and at least as wide a range of opportunities (though perhaps a different range), *provided B* makes its technology effectively available to A.

The rationale for my version of the spoilage objection brings us to the "proviso" argument. Rightful appropriation is limited by leaving, in Locke's word, "enough and as good for others"; this Nozick entitles the Lockean proviso. McDonald supposes the objector to argue that Indian appropriation violates this proviso, in not leaving enough land and as good for the Europeans. I do not think that this can be made to work (nor does McDonald). However, I do hold that the Europeans can justify their appropriation of much of North America by an appeal to the proviso. For in a state of nature, one is entitled to appropriate as much as does not worsen the situation of others, even if one takes from others what they previously, and legitimately, appropriated. In a state of nature, one's title is good *only* against actions which would worsen one's situation. Only under the conventional agreement which constitutes society can there be a stronger title.

The spoilage argument may be understood as a form of the "proviso" argument. To waste what one appropriates is to leave others worse off than if what one wasted had been left free for others to appropriate. The original inhabitants of North America did not appropriate wastefully, given their technology, and so the Europeans could take most of North America from its original inhabitants without violating the Lockean proviso.

Summarily, then, my account is this. The Indians and Eskimo appropriated North America, and their appropriation did not in itself worsen the situation of anyone else. Hence it was legitimate. However, it was not indefeasible, for it could be overridden, in the state of nature, by any group which could leave the original inhabitants better off then they were under their initial appropriation. The Europeans, who were in a state of nature with respect to the Indians and Eskimo, by making available their superior technology, were in a position to make such an overriding appropriation, not of all of North America, but of so much as to leave the original inhabitants with a combination of land and technology superior to their initial combination.

This will put aboriginal rights into a manageable framework. It will not extinguish them, but will severely limit them. McDonald's position would require us to recognize aboriginal rights to all of Canada, with the exception (probably empty) of those rights which have been legitimately exchanged in an agreement not based on force or fraud. My account will instead require us to recognize only such rights as will leave the original inhabitants better off than prior to our coming. Since, of course, we did not provide the Indians and Eskimo with effective access to our technology, and since we did not ensure that they were left sufficient land so that they would be as well off as before our coming, we shall not find the recognition of aboriginal rights costless. But the cost is one that we may realistically consider ourselves able and willing to pay, and one that can be defended by a non-arbitrary application of the Lockean proviso to questions of appropriation in a state of nature.

QUESTIONS

1. David Gauthier concludes that Locke's approach to property rights is sound and can be applied to problems of aboriginal rights. How does Gauthier reach this conclusion?
2. Has Gauthier found a sound set of reasons for the view that we can treat the Native peoples justly without taking the radical step urged by Michael McDonald?

ABORIGINAL LAND RIGHTS IN NORTHERN CANADA

J.T. Stevenson

Introduction

I believe that the usual approach to aboriginal land claims in Canada is profoundly misguided. We have imposed our political and legal system on the native peoples and have forced them to argue for their rights in terms of our current culture. In so doing, we have ignored their point of view and not addressed some fundamental issues.

Canada's Constitution Act 1982, fortunately, requires (Part IV, S. 37[2]) a constitutional conference, which is to discuss "the identification and definition of the rights" of aboriginal peoples. We thus have the opportunity, indeed the duty, to look at the whole question of land claims philosophically, in a manner broader and deeper than usual.

A Standard Approach

According to the political/legal system that developed in the course of the industrial revolution, land is treated as property, as something that can be owned, as something alien to us but over which we have dominion. In this liberal tradition, the owner of a property has, on the face of it, the sole and despotic right to do whatsoever he wills with it. Land is also treated as a commodity, as something that can be bought and sold and that has value determined by its market price. There is an elaborate legal system for determining who owns what, for settling disputes, and for regulating the use of property. The state may, exercising its ultimate power of sovereignty, expropriate land and give as compensation other commodities (money, goods, services) equal to the market value of the land.

Within this framework, we argue whether or not native peoples really own the land where they reside. Some say they do because of the right of first possession. They thus confer on

J.T. Stevenson, 1993. Reprinted with permission of J.T. Stevenson.

the native peoples despotic powers over the land that the native peoples never exercised, never even conceived themselves as possessing, and do not (if they can keep their own ways) want. Others say that they do not own it because, as the judicial Committee of the British Privy Council put it in the eighteenth century, the inhabitants were "so low on the scale of social organization that their usages and conceptions are not to be reconciled with the institutions and legal ideas of a civilized society." In similar fashion, some have recently argued that the natives may "own" the land but that we can simply take it from them because they have a technologically inferior culture — provided we offer them, whether they want it or not, our superior culture. A third position, sometimes taken by our courts, is that the natives have a limited ownership in the form of usufruct rights. This means, roughly, that ultimate ownership resides with the Crown but, because of traditional usage and customs, the natives have the right, say, to hunt and fish on certain lands. Much debate has revolved around the issue of compensation for land claims, which presupposes that the aboriginal peoples have some sort of legal entitlement to their lands but that the Crown in right of Canada, being sovereign, can expropriate land and determine an adequate form of compensation.

Why Wrong

All this, I say, is misguided. It proceeds on the assumptions of a particular culture and its political/economic legal regime, when the issue is cross-cultural and concerns the adequacy of that regime. What rarely gets a serious hearing is the native point of view.[1] The native peoples did not traditionally regard their land as something over which they had sovereign dominion, as something they owned and could do with as they pleased. The land and its other inhabitants were regarded, according to their laws, as something essential to their well-being, as something to be used with respect, care, and moderation, as something to be shared and preserved for future generations of all living things. In our terms, we might say that they regarded themselves, in a fashion, as stewards of the land with not only rights but obligations respecting it. They believed they had a very special relation with the land, which we may call religious, spiritual, or philosophical, but which, in any case, was expressed by them in myth, legend, symbol, and ceremony. Their land was not a property and commodity. It may be particularly hard for us to understand how and why the native peoples feel that their individual, personal identity is intimately connected to their relation to the land. Yet, to treat them fairly, it is vital that we make an effort to do so.

Purpose and Plan of Discussion

Because we tend to dismiss their view as primitive, mytho-poetical, or mystical rather than civilized, scientific, and rational, I shall try to explain or translate it into rational and scientific terms, the terms of philosophy, anthropology, and psychology. Some things, especially the experiential dimension, get lost in this translation, but, one hopes, the translation will provide a small bridge of understanding and sympathy.

Thus I shall present an argument designed not only to support certain conclusions, but to serve as a thread tying together a set of considerations usually overlooked in discussing aboriginal land claims. It will tie individual identity and a personal security right, on the one hand, to group rights to culture and land, on the other.

I make three background assumptions: (1) that natural justice requires that we first listen to the voices of the claimants, the native peoples, in their own terms rather than assume that we know best what is good for them; (2) that we should appeal to moral principles that are cross-cultural and find as much other common ground as possible; (3) that in tracing the consequences of our actions we should appeal to the most realistic and well-evidenced scientific theories available.

My discussion focusses on land claims in the Yukon and Northwest Territories because of the special opportunities and dangers faced by people there: on the one hand, they have not yet suffered as much disruption as native peoples in the South; on the other hand, they face severe threats because of the rush to exploit the nonrenewable resources of the northern frontier and have made specific claims on us. While the experiences of the southern aboriginals will be used as evidence in the empirical steps in the argument, a solution to the problems of southern Amerindians and Metis will be particularly difficult and I say nothing directly on the question. I hope, however, that the discussion will indirectly illuminate some aspects of their problems and those of other cultural minorities.

The discussion proceeds as follows. In the second section the problem is presented as it is understood and expressed by native peoples themselves. The claims are then interpreted and summarized in terms that may be more familiar to us so that we can have a common understanding of the problem. In the third section I set out and interpret a widely accepted, cross-cultural moral principle, so that discussion can proceed on a common normative basis. The fourth section outlines a difficult empirical step in the argument: it attempts to express, in terms of theories from anthropology and psychology, the central native view that their individual identity and hence personal security is tied up with their relation to their land. It turns out, I believe, that once again we can find common ground. In the fifth section the argument is restated briefly and certain conclusions, both positive and negative, are drawn. Note that much of the basic evidence has had to be relegated to footnotes.

Native Voices

Let us listen attentively to a carefully chosen but representative selection of native voices in the North that present the problems as *they* see them.

A. To the Indian people our land really is our life. Without our land we cannot — we could no longer exist as people. [Note: "as people" not "as a people."] If our land is destroyed, we too are destroyed. If you people ever take our land you will be taking our life. (Richard Nerysoo)

Every time the white people come to the North or come to our land and start tearing up the land, I feel as if they are cutting up our own flesh because that is the way we feel about our land. It is our flesh. (Georgina Tobac)

B. Ever since they came in I couldn't make a living out of the country. This is my trouble now. There is all kinds of money made around me with the oil, and they don't give me anything. They don't think that I am a person living there. (Johnny Klondike)

C. [They suggest] that we give up our land and resources to the richest nation [the U.S.A. which wanted a pipeline built] in the world; not the poorest. We are threatened with genocide only so the rich and powerful can become more rich and more powerful.

I suggest, in any man's view, that is immoral. If our Indian nation is being destroyed so that poor people of our world might get a chance to share this world's riches, then as Indian people, I am sure we would seriously consider giving up our resources. But do you really expect us to give up our life and our lands so that those few people who are the richest and most powerful in the world today can maintain and defend their own immoral position of privilege?

That is not our way. (Phillip Blake)

D. For myself, I find it very hard to identify with anybody because I have nobody to turn to. My people don't accept me any more because I got an education, and the white people won't accept me because I am not the right colour. So like, a lot of people keep saying, "O.K., we've got to educate these young native people, so that they can become something." But what good is it if a person has no identity? I can't really identify with anybody and I'm lost. I'm just sort of a person hanging in the middle of two cultures and doesn't know which way to go. (Roy Fabian)

E. The Dene have the right to recognition, self-determination, and on-going growth and development as a People and a Nation.

The Dene, as aboriginal people, have a special status under the Constitution of Canada.

The Dene, as aboriginal people, have the right to retain so much of their traditional lands, and under such terms, as to ensure their independence and self-reliance, traditionally, economically and socially.

There will, therefore, be within Confederation, a Dene Government with jurisdiction over a geographical area and over subject matters now within the jurisdiction of either the Government of Canada or the Government of the Northwest Territories. (Proposed by the Dene as an "Agreement in Principle between the Dene Nation and Her Majesty the Queen in Right of Canada.")[2]

Interpretation

Taking into account the cultural context, we can translate these statements into our terms as follows. A: The people believe that they live in a complex, symbiotic relation with the land and its ecosystems; that is, their environment, culture, and personal identity are closely interwoven in a balanced system. B: They believe they are being economically marginalized and treated as non-persons. C: They believe that they are being treated unjustly, that their vital interests are being sacrificed for the less important or trivial interests of those already well-off. D: They believe the form of the enculturation process into white society that is imposed on them prevents or destroys a healthy personality integration. E: They believe they need and have the right to some forms of political and social self-determination. This, in summary but I believe fair fashion, is the native position. My argument will try to elucidate, in particular, A and D.

Let us try to find common ground, both morally and intellectually.

The Personal-Security Principle

One cross-cultural and widely accepted normative principle that is relevant is stated in the UN Charter of Human Rights (1948) — often called "the conscience of mankind" — to which Canada is a subscriber. It says (Article 3): "Everyone has the right to life, liberty and the security of person." Of course, like other abstract legal and moral principles, it must be interpreted to be applied; and its application clarifies and enriches its meaning. I shall focus on the personal-security aspect of this right — Everyone has the right to personal security — and I shall spell out what this means.[3]

Content of Right

We would agree that arbitrary, capricious killing, such as indulged in by Idi Amin in Uganda, would violate this right; as similarly would the more systematic holocaust of the Nazi regime in Germany. Hacking off a person's limbs or reducing him to slavery while keeping him alive would also be clearly prohibited. Of course the right is defeasible. That is to say, it can be overridden: we can kill in self-defence; the criminal can lose his liberty; the surgeon who mutilates a cancer patient to save his life does not violate the patient's security right. So some thought is required in applying the principle.

Such thought, I believe, will lead us to recognize that the right to the security of our person extends beyond life and limb to matters affecting basic personality structure. Many modern states, alas, practise forms of torture that leave a person alive and unmutilated but nevertheless personally destroyed. A person may, for instance, be subjected to sensory deprivation, electro-shock, and hallucinogenic drugs. As a result, he may be prey to chronic anxiety, feelings of guilt and worthlessness, and alternating passivity and rage; he may be unable to function economically and socially; he may suffer from anomie — a state in which normative standards of conduct and belief are weak or lacking, a state that is characterized by disorientation, anxiety, and isolation; he may lack purpose or meaning in his life and be unable to persevere in projects and establish normal social relations; he may lapse into alcoholism and chronic delinquency; he may be so overwhelmed by anxiety and depression that he commits suicide. In short, he may be turned into a human derelict.

Such can be the effects of torture. But, as we shall see, similar effects can be produced unintentionally by other methods and can be observed on reserves and in urban centres throughout Canada. I suggest that the personal security right protects us not only against physical death, mutilation and enslavement, but against such psychic destruction and mutilation.

Qualifications

To avoid controversy as much as possible, let us put a construction on the personal-security right. (1) The right obliges us to acts of omission rather than commission. We may not have to help or enhance a person's security, but we are required to refrain from positive acts that harm personal security. (2) These harms must be serious and substantial. In the myriad of social interactions we engage in, we daily harm other people, intentionally or otherwise: we inflict, for instance, little blows on their pride and self-esteem. But here we speak only of those major blows or the death of a thousand cuts, which strike at the core of personality, which sap our capacity to cope, which in a strong sense destroy and mutilate us. (3) The forbidden harms to be culpable or blameworthy must be foreseeable and avoidable. When we act, we sometimes "know not what we do" or "can't help what we do." We act in ignorance or unintentionally or we produce effects by accident or we couldn't have done otherwise. We speak here, however, only of what a reasonable person in the light of currently available knowledge would expect as the probable consequences of his actions where there is a genuine choice available. Of course, people who are educated or in responsible positions with special access to information and with powers to act will be less able than others to plead ignorance or unavoidability. (4) Since personal security is so important, the onus of proof should be on the agent, but the burden of proof is on me to assure that I am not violating the personal security of those affected by my act. To reverse the onus would mean that the patient or potential victim would have to calculate the consequences of other people's actions and prevent or avoid consequences which would harm his, the victim's, personal security. Second, instead of setting as the level of proof required — what might be reasonable given the importance of the matter — that I refrain from acting unless it is beyond a reasonable doubt that I am harming no one's personal security, let us be conservative and impose a weaker test. I should not act unless the balance of probabilities indicates that I will not be harming someone's personal security. (5) There will be, for psychic personal security as for physical security, defeasibility conditions that prevent absurd applications of the right. Thus, for example, if I am a paedophile whose personality is integrated around my desire to sexually molest children, you do not violate my personal security right if you prevent me from acting on this desire and thereby drastically upset my personality. The personal security rights of children in those circumstances override those of paedophiles.

The problem now is to indicate how, in certain circumstances, it is possible to violate psychic personal security by disrupting a person's relationship to his environment and way of life.

The Evidence of Science

Political and ethical arguments in philosophy usually rely, in part, on views about human nature and society. Often they are theories from the seventeenth and eighteenth centuries; for instance, the psychology of Thomas Hobbes or the anthropology of Jean-Jacques Rousseau. I have thought it wiser to appeal to the much better evidence theories of the twentieth century. And from the plethora of available opinion I have made choices that I cannot here defend in the space available. I can only invite the reader to do what the writer has done: immerse himself in the literature, examine the evidence and try to make a judicious choice; one that avoids as much as possible ideological prejudices.

Systems Analysis

We have become accustomed to the idea of applying systems analysis to our environment, to regarding it as an ecosystem: a set of elements (land, air, water, plants, and animals) connected by a complex web of interdependencies and feedback loops which maintain the system in a delicate balance. For example, a lake, with its water quality, plants, fish, and aquatic animals, may form such a system. The system may absorb some shocks and regain its balance: the lake may, after over-fishing, regenerate the fish stock. But sometimes a shock will be catastrophic: the flow of nutrients into the lake may so increase (more sewage, detergents, and so on) that an algae bloom occurs, oxygen is depleted, the fish die, and we have a eutrophied lake with different forms of life in it. It is not always easy to tell which shocks will be catastrophic. For example, the human body can recover from massive bleeding and many broken bones (as in a car accident) but completely succumb to the administration of enough white powder to cover a pinhead (say the powder is strychnine). If we want to act on a system without destroying it, we need to understand its critical elements and relations, how it will respond to changed conditions and how it may adapt.

It is important to note at this point that the native belief that the natural world forms a complex, interdependent system of which the native peoples are an integral part should not be dismissed as mere primitive or magical thought. It is a view they forged in the struggle for existence and it is based on thousands of years of experience and empirical observation. Although not expressed in our theoretical terms and differing in many details, the general approach is consistent with our most advanced biological science. In their own way, the native peoples got there first.

I suggest that this common ground of a systems mode of thought can be extended from biology to our understanding of society, culture, and the development of personal identity. Two main points will be made. First, a physical and biological environment, a culture and social system in which people earn a living, and the way in which human beings grow and are nurtured into mature personalities in that culture — all three — should be regarded as one system. Second, the personal security of native peoples has been attacked by European settlers at two critical points — in their livelihood from the land and in the nurturance of their children. Let us see how.

Anthropology

The culture of a human society is an integrated pattern of behaviour that includes thought, speech, action, and artifacts, and depends on our capacity for learning and transmitting knowledge to succeeding generations. According to anthropologist Marvin Harris, we may distinguish those broad elements of culture that interact in important ways.[4]

Harris distinguishes an infrastructure, which consists of modes of production and reproduction. The mode of production, Harris says, is "The technology and practices employed for expanding or limiting basic subsistence production, especially the production of food and other forms of energy, given the restrictions and opportunities provided by a specific technology interacting with a specific habitat." The mode of reproduction is "The technology and the practices employed for expanding, limiting and maintaining population size." Harris notes a structure of a domestic and political economy: "the organization of reproduction, production, exchange, and consumption within and between bands, villages, chiefdoms, states, and empires." He also defines a superstructure: "the conscious and unconscious cognitive goals, categories, rules, plans, values, philosophies and beliefs" that are expressed in behaviour generally and often particularly in rituals, religion, art, music, dance, games, literature, and so on.

These interacting elements form a cultural system that can be stable or unstable, concordant or discordant, that can grow or decline, live or die. Some shocks to the system will be easily absorbed; others will produce dramatic changes and be catastrophic.

Harris has advanced a fruitful approach to anthropology, which he calls the "research program of cultural materialism." It says, very roughly: look first to infrastructural elements when attempting to explain the riddles of culture. A disruption in the infrastructure of a culture, for example, a major change in the way land is used, can have dramatic impacts on its other elements, such as its belief and value system and the way it nurtures its offspring into persons. I believe Harris has demonstrated in certain cases the fruitfulness of this approach. I have in mind, for instance, his elegant, plausible, and powerful analysis of the sacred cow taboo in India, which explains a wide range of facts (such as different sex ratios amongst adult cattle in different regions of India) but which other theories leave inexplicable and puzzling.

I am relying on his approach in stressing the importance of land use to the question of a personal-security right. A sudden and drastic disruption of the relation between a people and its environment can reverberate, through elements of its culture, to the very foundations of human personality. But to see how this can be so, we need to add a theory from psychology to the one from anthropology, in order to connect culture and personality development. My views on this are drawn largely from the work of Erik Erikson, Jean Piaget, and Bruno Bettelheim.[5] Each general point made will be followed by an illustration.

Psychology

Persons, in an important sense, are made not born.[6] We know that without some decent system of training and nurturing — the systems can vary within certain broad limits — biological human beings will not develop the cognitive, emotional, and social capacities for personhood at all or will have severe personality disorders. Our practices may be unconscious (based on habit and tradition) but even apparently trivial details can have deep effects on personality structure. A proper understanding of the phenomena requires an integrated approach to personality development.

> We are speaking of three processes, the somatic process, the ego process, and the societal process. In the history of science these three processes have belonged to three different scientific disciplines — biology, psychology, and the social sciences — each of which studied what it could isolate, count, and dissect: single organisms, individual minds, and social aggregates. . . . Unfortunately this knowledge is tied to the conditions under which it was secured: the organism undergoing dissection or examination; the mind surrendered to experiment or interrogation; social aggregates spread out on statistical tables. In all of these cases, then, a scientific discipline prejudiced the matter under observation by actively dissolving its total living situation in order to be able to make an isolated section of it amenable to a set of instruments or concepts.[7]

We now know more and can do better. We know something about how culture — the mode of reproduction, the domestic economy, and elements of the superstructure such as myths and legends — plays an important role in the development of personality. Thus anthropology is linked to psychology. We can also recognize the existence of normal pathways of development and critical stages in those paths such that an event which would be relatively harmless at most stages may have profound consequences at a critical stage. We also know something of the importance of systemic consistency and appropriateness: two methods of child-rearing, each separately successful, may, when combined, produce a severely conflicted personality; a method that produces a personality successful in one culture may not be appropriate for producing the type of personality required for success in another culture. Finally, let us note that the destruction or mutilation of personality can occur after childhood. Indeed, Erikson's work on the so-called identity-crisis of early adulthood was triggered by clinical observations of young men suffering from war-induced psychoneuroses and led to his investigations of the developmental stages and crises of the whole human life cycle.

So, in the clinical investigation of individual pathology we need to take into account differences rooted in biology (genetics), critical stages and events in personality development, and the social-cultural-historical setting in which they take place.

Let us now return to the native question. First, contrary to common European belief — which vacillated between regarding Indians as noble, untutored children of nature and regarding them as depraved, untutored savages — native peoples have elaborate child-rearing systems that have produced integrated personalities well-adapted to their culture.

Up to recent decades child training has been an anthropological no man's land. Even anthropologists living for years among aboriginal tribes failed to see that these tribes trained their children in some systematic way. Rather, the experts tacitly assumed with the general public that savages had no child training at all and that primitives grew up "like little animals" — an idea which in the overtrained members of our culture arouses either angry contempt or romantic elation.

The discovery of primitive child-training systems makes it clear that primitive societies are neither infantile stages of mankind nor arrested deviations from the proud progressive norms which we represent: they are a complete form of mature human living, often of a homogeneity and simple integrity which we at times might well envy.[8]

Application

Let me illustrate now the foregoing general discussion. Erikson was asked to investigate the causes of widespread behavioural and personality disorders amongst Dakota Indian children in U.S. government schools.[9] He found that in the first years of their lives they were brought up in a way which, through traditional techniques of child transport, breastfeeding, weaning, and so on, was well suited to produce personalities adapted to a culture based on the buffalo hunt. Then the children were thrust into schools well suited to produce, as personalities, the factory workers needed in an industrial society. The Indian children were deeply conflicted cognitively (e.g., in their structuring of space and time) and emotionally. Moreover, neither form of training was suited to the actual economic basis of their society. The reserves on which they were confined would support neither a hunting culture nor an industrial one. The inconsistency and inappropriateness of their upbringing left them with identity confusions, expressed in their feelings and behaviour. (Recall the statement of Roy Fabian.) Their prospects were poverty and the cycle of the welfare syndrome. The trouble started when their cultural infrastructure was destroyed — the buffalo wiped out and their lands seized — and was compounded by the efforts made to enculturate the children into white society.

Similar stories can be told about Indian bands across Canada. It was once thought that a solution could be found in residential schools, where native children would be separated from the influence of their families and thoroughly indoctrinated in the fundamentals of white society. Little was understood about the importance of critical stages of development and the effects of experiences in infancy; little regard was given to the milieu to which the children would return. The result was a catastrophe for several generations of aboriginal peoples.

If you want a recipe for the destruction of personality, one such would be this: destroy the material basis of a culture; force the people into an environment which provides little means for economic activity; foster the culture of poverty and dependency by means of minimal handouts; make ignorant and racist attacks on the structure and superstructure of what remains of the culture; as the adults disintegrate from these shocks, experiment blindly with their children.

I have sketched an integrated theory from anthropology and psychology which enables us to trace and understand some of the effects of our actions. Is it consistent with the native view of the matter? I believe so. When a native women says that interfering with her land is "cutting up our own flesh," this should not be dismissed as the far-fetched, special pleading of an ignorant primitive. She may well be expressing, metaphorically, what we may express using scientific jargon. And the grounds of the belief may not be altogether different from ours: she may be expressing the native belief in the complex dependencies of the individual/social/environmental system, as well as the results of her own observations of shocks to that system.

In any case the facts must be explained. There is massive evidence of widespread personal pathology amongst Southern Canadian aboriginal peoples.[10] It can be seen with the naked eye on reserves and in urban ghettos; it is described in personal accounts by those affected; it shows up in the statistics on poverty, anomie, school failures, alcoholism, family break-down, crime, and suicide. How are these changes in individual human lives to be explained?

Many Euro-Canadians and other whites give a racist explanation: somehow the aborigi-nals are genetically inferior, lacking in intelligence and adaptability. (Winnipeg magistrate Isaac Rice: "There is something in their blood. I don't know what it is but an Indian and alco-hol just don't mix . . . I have never come across a married Indian couple.")[11] The facts do not bear them out.

Even those racists who offer the evidence of IQ testing to support (however inadequate-ly) their claims that blacks are genetically inferior have been unable to make similar claims about the aboriginal population. And it is the case that, historically, the Amerindian and Inuit peoples have shown a high degree of adaptability and cultural variation.[12]

The plain fact is that the aboriginal peoples of the Americas have been subjected to a long series of massive assaults equivalent to genocide. Sometimes it has been the genocide (in the strict sense) of politicians, generals, and settlers who conducted campaigns — still going on in the jungles of the Amazon — of slaughter and germ warfare.[13] Sometimes it has been the unexpected effect of well-intentioned efforts by politicians, economists, missionaries, and educators.

We need to be warned particularly against the latter: the politicians who, to preserve tra-ditional life-styles, have deported Indians to reservations which cannot support that life-style or any other decent one; the economists who, under the aegis of the crude doctrines of their dismal science, turn all rights into commodities to be bought and sold at market evaluation and try to force natives into marginal positions in the wage economy; the Christians who, not understanding their meaning and spiritual significance, ban the Potlatch, the Sun-dance, the White Dog Feast as superstitious and barbarous, and replace them with a ceremony in which the body and blood of a man/god is consumed; the teachers who, to civilize and educate, transport little children hundreds of miles from their families and communities and whip them for speaking their native tongues; the philosophers who, in their ignorance, settle Indian land claims by means of *a priori* quibbles amongst themselves. As for you and me, have we ever thought to help the native peoples by offering them as a compensation for their lands the blessings of our philosophy, religion, political theory, economics, technology, and education? And to what effect?

Conclusions

Argument Summarized

So far I have argued (a) that the widely recognized personal-security right protects us against psychic destruction and mutilation; (b) that there are well attested scientific theories in anthropology and psychology that can explain how the disruption of a culture's infrastruc-ture (particularly land use) and other key sectors can produce personal pathology; (c) that there is abundant evidence that such pathology is widespread amongst Southern native peo-ples who have been subjected to massive cultural assaults; and (d) that racist and genetic explanations of the facts are implausible. It follows, then, that the personal security rights of Southern native peoples have probably been violated by the political, economic and other cultural arrangements — particularly those affecting their relation to the land — that we have forced upon them. This conclusion is in general agreement with what the native peoples themselves claim. Because of ignorance, our past wrongs may not be culpable; but, since we should now know better, future ones of the same sort would be.

First Conclusion

We can draw, then, a negative conclusion concerning aboriginal land rights in Northern Canada: namely, we must not impose a settlement that would violate the personal security rights of the peoples of those territories. This rules out certain types of proposals. For example, it rules out the radical proposals of the Liberals' 1969 White Paper, "Statement of the Government of Canada on Indian Policy."[14]

The 1969 White Paper, in the name of enlightened liberalism and perhaps in fear of Québécois separatism, proposed to abolish all forms of special status for aboriginal peoples and to force a quick-march enculturalization into industrial civilization. Those who couldn't adapt would be left to the tender mercies of provincial welfare legislation. Although the White Paper, as such, was shelved after a storm of protest, the underlying ideology and attitudes are still very much alive. They must be resisted and the implications for federalism accepted.

To be fair to the native people, we will have to give up some of our passion for symmetry and homogenization in political arrangements: a province is a province and all must be treated the same; all must have the same legal and social system; every Canadian must have exactly the same rights and must be able to move anywhere in the country without changing status. In a confederation allowing for various forms and degrees of special status for ethnic groups — whether aboriginals, Québécois or Newfoundlanders — it may seem that we are giving group rights priority over individual rights. But we are not really faced with a choice between individualism and collectivism. For as I tried to show in the case of the native peoples — a primary right to personal security can require, for its implementation, the recognition of certain group rights to land and culture. To violate the latter is, in certain circumstances, to violate the former.

Second Conclusion

Does this negative conclusion imply a *status quo* policy that would freeze development and prohibit change? Would it imply that Northern aboriginals be hived off in wilderness ghettos (reminiscent of the Bantustans of South Africa) and left to fend for themselves? No. The implication is only a modest conservatism which rules out certain kinds of forced change, change of the sort imposed on natives in the past.

Northern natives have already made changes from their traditional ways. They made a swift and successful adaptation from a nomadic/hunting/gathering culture to a nomadic/hunting/trading one, two or three hundred years ago. They desire further change now.

The nature and pacing of cultural change, however, must not be too drastic and swift for successful adaptation. Basic economic change should centrally and positively involve native skills and knowledge — as did the swift adaptation to the fur-trade economy — rather than something like the social and economic marginalization of natives in the later agricultural and industrial changes in the South. The changes should allow for the forms of personal and group autonomy required for successful adaptation and the development of healthy personalities.

These principles of successful change suggest a positive conclusion. The form of land settlement demanded by native peoples in the North is reasonable and consistent with their personal security rights. They want some form of self-determination within Confederation, perhaps through the creation of two new provinces, Denedeh and Nunavut, with their own special rules for land ownership and use. They want a mixed economy based principally on renewable resources which they can manage, with controlled and limited exploitation of non-renewable resources. They want control over education and other cultural institutions so that these can be made amenable to their changing needs and traditions.

In short, they believe that without balanced, carefully timed changes — changes over which they have a large measure of control — in the infrastructure, structure, and superstructure of their culture, they will be destroyed, not only as a people, but as people, not only as a group but as individuals. And, as I have tried to show, they are probably right.

NOTES

1. I am particularly indebted to E. Newbery and J. Dumont of the Native Studies Department of Laurentian University for providing me with reading materials used in their course, "North American Native People: Tradition and Culture." These were most useful in gaining some insight into the native perspective. A standard ethnographic work is Diamond Jenness, *The Indians of Canada*, 4th ed., Ottawa: National Museum of Canada, 1958. See also Dennis and Barbara Tedlock, *Teachings from the American Earth: Indian Religion and Philosophy*, New York: Liveright, 1975. A classic account of shamanism on the world scale is Mircea Eliade, *Shamanism: Archaic Techniques of Ecstasy*, Princeton: Princeton University Press, 1964. For a more personal attempt to understand the phenomena, see James Dumont, "Journey to Day-light Land — Through Ojibway Eyes," *Laurentian Review*, Vol. VIII, No. 2, 1976.

2. The quotation from Phillip Blake and the Dene Proposed Agreement are taken from *Dene Nation: The Colony Within*, ed. by Mel Watkins, Toronto: University of Toronto Press, 1977. The other native voices are from Mr. Justice Thomas R. Berger, *Northern Frontier, Northern Homeland: the Report of the Mackenzie Valley Pipeline Inquiry*. Vol. 1, Ottawa: Ministry of Supply and Services Canada, 1977. The latter in particular is highly recommended for its comprehensiveness, insight, and compassion.

3. For a massive compendium of international work on human rights since World War II, see Louis B. Sohn and Thomas Buergenthal, *International Protection of Human Rights*, Indianapolis: The Bobbs-Merril Co. Inc., 1973. For accounts of torture in the modern world, see the bulletins of Amnesty International. For a set of case studies and an insightful theoretical account of forms of psychological torture, see Robert Jay Lifton, *Thought Reform and the Psychology of Totalism: A Study of "Brainwashing" in China*, New York: W.W. Norton and Company, 1969.

4. For an argumentative survey of anthropological theories, see Marvin Harris, *The Rise of Anthropological Theory: A History of Theories of Culture*, New York: Harper & Row, 1968. For a popular, accessible survey of anthropology, see Peter Farb, *Humankind*, Boston: Houghton Mifflin Co., 1978. The position in the text is drawn from Harris's *Cultural Materialism: the Struggle for a Science of Culture*, New York: Random House, 1979. For a study of the sacred cow taboo and other case studies, see the latter and the more popular works, *Cows, Pigs, Wars and Witches: The Riddles of Culture*, New York: Vintage Books, 1978 and *Cannibals and Kings: The Origins of Cultures*, New York: Vintage Books, 1978. Harris's position bears some marked similarities with and departures from orthodox Marxist accounts of culture and social change. The present writer, while relying heavily on Harris, (a) finds important technical difficulties with the epistemology of his emic/etic distinction and (b) deplores the absence of a sophisticated psychological theory — whence the emphasis on (a) the significance of "native voices" and (b) developmental psychology in my account.

5. See Erik Erikson's seminal work, drawing upon but extending in important ways the Freudian revolution in psychology, *Childhood and Society*, 2nd ed., New York: W.W. Norton and Company, Inc., 1963, especially Part Two: "Childhood in Two American Indian Tribes." See also: *Insight and Responsibility*, New York: W.W. Norton and Company, Inc., 1964 and *Identity: Youth and Crisis*, New York: W.W. Norton and Company, Inc., 1968. An accessible survey of Piaget's theory can be found in *Piaget's Theory of Intellectual Development* by Herbet Ginsburg and Sylvia Opper, Englewood Cliffs: Prentice-Hall Inc., 1969. Some insights into the importance of myths and legends in child-nurturing among Amerindians were drawn from Hyemeyohsts Storm, *Seven Arrows*, New York: Harper & Row, 1972 and backed up by the child psychiatrist Bruno Bettelheim's *The Uses of Enchantment: The Meaning and Importance of Fairy Tales*, New York: Vintage Books, 1977. See also his *Love Is Not Enough*, New York: Avon Books, 1971 and *The Informed Heart*, New York: Avon Books, 1971.

6. I do not attempt to unravel here the complex relations amongst personhood, personal identity, and personality. But, as noted, I am drawing on the work of psychologists in personality theory. I am also assuming that certain human beings who have not developed into "full persons" — or who have declined from that state and become human derelicts — still have rights.

7. *Childhood and Society*, p. 36.

8. *Ibid.*, p. 111.

9. *Ibid.*, Part Two.

10. For a brutally frank, first-hand account of conditions on some Indian reserves, see Heather Robertson, *Reservations Are for Indians*, Toronto: James Lewis & Samuel, 1970. For statistics and an indication of the relation between personal pathology (in the form of alcoholism) and crime see Douglas A. Schmeiser et al., *The Native Offender and the Law*, prepared for the Law Reform Commission of Canada, 1974. See also the Hawthorn Committee Report, *A Survey of the Contemporary Indians of Canada*, 1967. It would be grossly unfair to those whom I have described as "human derelicts" produced by culture shock to leave the impression that they are without hope. The "powerful, baffling, cunning" disease of alcoholism, the chief form of personal pathology amongst native peoples, can be successfully fought through the cross-cultural program of Alcoholics Anonymous. A multi-faceted approach is required, but key elements seem to be a rediscovery of cultural roots and a form of spiritual growth. For theoretical perspectives, see Herbert Fingarette, *The Self in Transformation*, New York: Harper & Row, 1965 and Erik Erikson's *Young Man Luther, New York: W.W. Norton & Co., Inc., 1962,* and *Gandhi's Truth*, New York: W.W. Norton & Co., Inc., 1969. For relevant personal perspectives, see Lame Deer/Richard Endoes, *Lame Deer: Seeker of Visions*, New York: Simon & Schuster, 1972, and Maria Campbell, *Halfbreed*, Toronto: McClelland and Stewart-Bantam Ltd., 1979. The creativity that can flourish amidst personal and cultural chaos is illustrated in the life of Norval Morrisseau: see his *Legends of My People: The Great Ojibway* (illustrated and told by Morrisseau, ed. by Selwyn Dewdney), Toronto: McGraw-Hill Ryerson Ltd., 1965, and Lister Sinclair and Jack Pollock, *The Art of Norval Morrisseau*, Toronto: Methuen, 1979.

11. The remarks of Magistrate Rice are quoted in James Burke, *Paper Tomahawks: From Red Tape to Red Power*, Winnipeg: Queenston House Publishing Inc., 1976.

12. For an account of Amerindian adaptability and cultural evolution see Peter Farb, *Man's Rise to Civilization, as Shown by the Indians of North America from Primeval Times to the Coming of the Industrial State*, New York: Avon Books, 1971. An antidote to Hollywood glamorization of European settlements is the revisionist history, *Bury My Heart at Wounded Knee: An Indian History of the American West*, by Dee Brown, New York: Bantam Books, 1972.

13. Perhaps the first commission of deliberate germ warfare was by the British general Lord Jeffrey Amherst in 1763 when he had smallpox-infested blankets and handkerchiefs distributed to his Indian enemies. (See Farb, p. 298).

14. For an Indian reaction to the 1969 White Paper, see Harold Cardinal, *The Unjust Society*, Edmonton: M.G. Hurtig Ltd., 1969.

QUESTIONS

1. Is there a right to personal security? Is it a universal right? How would you relate the personal-security principle to the protection-of-life or the avoidance-of-suffering principles that were introduced in earlier chapters?
2. Do J.T. Stevenson's arguments apply only to those Native groups who have not signed treaties?
3. Do you think Stevenson has provided convincing reasons for rejecting the position outlined by Trudeau?
4. Does respect for the personal-security principle imply acceptance of some form of self-government on the part of Canada's Native peoples?

SUGGESTIONS FOR FURTHER READING

- Because the matter of land claims has, throughout our history, been treated as a legal matter, much of the background discussion of the issues involved has been developed by our courts. In turn, commentary by legal scholars attempting to interpret and evaluate legal decisions has influenced social and political debate in significant ways. For that reason, the bibliography that follows has three sections. The first lists a number of cases that have had an important impact on the way in which our ideas about the moral foundation of land and self-government claims has been articulated. In this section, D.L.R. refers to the *Dominion Law Reports*. S.C.C. refers to a series of reports that set out the findings of the Supreme Court of Canada. Both series can be found in law libraries and often in other libraries as well; both D.L.R. and S.C.C. references are provided in each case. The second group identifies legal commentaries that provide insight into the legal and social dimensions of the issues involved, as well as the writing of philosophers on the subject.

Important Cases

- *Calder v. Attorney-General of British Columbia* (1973), 34 D.L.R. (3D) 145 (S.C.C.) This case dealt with a land claim by the Nishga people in northern British Columbia. The decision proved to be significant in its acceptance of aboriginal land rights even though the Court split evenly on the question. The Nishga people did have a legitimate claim to the land for which they were seeking title.
- *Delgamuukw v. The Queen* (1991), 79 D.L.R. (4th) 185 (B.C.S.C.) This judgment reflects a traditional form of reasoning with regard to Native land claims that has its roots in Privy Council judgments of the last century.
- *Guerin v. The Queen* (1984), 13 D.L.R. (4th) 321 (S.C.C.) The Court decided that the government had a trustlike responsibility to use its powers respecting Native lands in a manner that reflected Native interests and concerns.
- *Simon v. The Queen* (1984), 13 D.L.R. (4th) 390 (S.C.C.) This case had to do with a treaty signed with Aboriginal peoples in the 1750s. The Court ruled that the treaty was still valid and blocked the application of provincial game laws in the area concerned.
- *R. v. Sioui* (1990), 70 D.L.R. (4th) 427 (S.C.C.) In this case, the Court was asked to consider whether Huron customary law continued to have authority given a treaty signed with

incoming British forces in the eighteenth century. The Court upheld the treaty, said its provisions were still valid, and gave Huron customary law precedence over provincial law in the matter at issue.

- *R. v. Sparrow* (1990), 70 D.L.R. (4th) 385 (S.C.C.) This case provided the Supreme Court with its first opportunity to interpret Section 35 of the Constitution Act of 1982, which recognizes existing aboriginal and treaty rights. The Court held that this section guarantees protection to any aboriginal or treaty right that had not been completely extinguished prior to 1982 even if the exercise of the right had been narrowly constrained. What this meant was that the Court could then review the way in which exercise of the right had been regulated and decide whether the restrictions were justifiable.

Books and Articles

- Michael Asch, *Home and Native Land: Aboriginal Rights and the Canadian Constitution* (Toronto: Methuen, 1984). Writing from an anthropological point of view, this writer explores the idea of Aboriginal self-government and argues for its acceptability.
- Leroy Little Bear, Menno Bolt, and J. Anthony Log, eds., *Pathways to Self-Determination: Canadian Indians and the Canadian State* (Toronto: University of Toronto Press, 1985). This is an anthology with Native and non-Native contributors on the topic of self-determination and self-government.
- Menno Bolt and J. Anthony Long, eds., *The Quest for Justice: Aboriginal People and Aboriginal Rights* (Toronto: University of Toronto Press, 1985). This book is an anthology that takes up a variety of issues arising from the idea of aboriginal rights.
- Hugh Brody, *Maps and Dreams: Indians and the British Columbia Frontier* (Toronto: Penguin, 1983). The chapters in this book alternate between accounts of personal experiences with Natives and their culture and thematic discussions of the issues raised by those experiences.
- Diane Engelstad and John Bird, eds., *Nation to Nation: Aboriginal Sovereignty and the Future of Canada* (Concord, Ontario: Anansi Press, 1992). This is a book which attempts to tell the story of Aboriginal/Canadian relations down through the years from the perspective of both Aboriginal and non-Aboriginal authors. It has three parts. In the first, authors describe the pursuit of sovereignty to the 1990s. Part II describes how Aboriginal people have been working out their visions of sovereignty and self-determination within the realities of their own communities. Part III looks at the non-Native support for aboriginal rights.
- Kent McNeil, *Common Law Aboriginal Title* (Oxford: Clarendon Press, 1989). The author's purpose in this book is to argue that aboriginal land title can be grounded in English common law.
- Dennis McPherson and Doug Rabb, *Indian from the Inside* (Lakehead, Ontario: Lakehead University, 1991). This book, which is available from Lakehead University, was prepared by Doug Rabb, a philosopher teaching at that university, and Dennis McPherson, a Native social worker and graduate of Lakehead University, for use in a philosophy course entitled "Native Canadian World Views." It attempts to construct an understanding of Native thinking on a wide range of issues.
- J.R. Miller, *Skyscrapers Hide the Heavens: A History of Indian-White Relations in Canada* (Toronto: University of Toronto Press, 1989). The title of this book explains its content.

- Anastasia M. Shkilnky, *A Poison Stronger Than Love: The Destruction of an Ojibwa Community* (New Haven: Yale University Press, 1985). The author describes the effect on an Ojibwa community of a move from traditional lands to a new reserve. The move was necessitated by mercury pollution in the rivers on which the community depended.
- Brian Slattery, "Aboriginal Sovereignty and Imperial Claims: Reconstructing North American History," *Osgoode Hall Law Journal*, vol. 29, no. 4 (1991). In this paper, the author examines and rejects the thesis central to the approach of European law that Aboriginal America was vacant territory when first discovered by Europeans. He then attempts to identify basic principles of justice that could provide the reference points for fair settlement of aboriginal land and sovereignty claims.
- — "The Hidden Constitution: Aboriginal Rights in Canada," *American Journal of Comparative Law*, vol. 32 (1984): 361. Most analyses of Native rights start from assumptions central to European political and legal traditions. Brian Slattery argues in this paper that an adequate view of aboriginal rights in Canada cannot be grounded on those assumptions alone. In this paper, he examines the history of diplomatic relations between the imperial powers who, for a wide variety of reasons, found it necessary to negotiate with the Native people to secure their imperial objectives and constructs from his study a view of aboriginal rights based on the character of the diplomatic relations that resulted.
- "Symposium on Aboriginal Land Rights," *Australian Journal of Philosophy,* vol. 68, no. 3 (September 1990). This issue of the journal carries two articles, "Land Rights and Aboriginal Sovereignty" and "Land, Well-Being and Compensation," that explore the issue of aboriginal rights from an Australian perspective. These articles have the virtue of examining the range of issues faced by Canadians as they have arisen in the Australian context and provide a good basis for comparing the development of land claims and self-government questions in the two countries.
- Mary Ellen Turpel, "Aboriginal Peoples and the Canadian Charter: Interpretive Monopolies, Cultural Differences," *Canadian Human Rights Yearbook*, vol. 6 (1989–90): 3. The theme of this book is that because of significant cultural differences, Canadian courts should take into consideration the Native point of view in interpreting the Constitution and its bearing on aboriginal rights.

Chapter 7

Poverty

Introduction

Poverty has features distinct from the issues examined thus far. To begin with, unlike abortion, euthanasia, capital punishment, or censorship, poverty is not the obvious or intended consequence of individual or government decision making. Poverty is clearly not a problem that can be solved by individuals acting alone. It is not even clear that it is a problem that can be solved by national governments, since poverty is not just a local but also a global phenomenon. Poverty is also in many respects a hidden or disguised problem. There seem to be three reasons for this: First, none of us can be certain we will not face the reality of a painful death. No one with an extended network of family or friends can be sure that people close to them will not be touched directly or indirectly by an unwanted pregnancy. But many of us seem to believe that whatever else life might have in store for us, poverty, at least, is something we can guard carefully against. At least one reason for this belief is central to liberal theory itself: the formal equality principle, as outlined in the Equality and Discrimination chapter, holds that each person has the freedom to compete for and obtain economic and social goods if not interfered with by others or by the state.

This last observation points to a second factor that plays a role, sometimes hidden, sometimes explicit, when the topic is under discussion. A conception that takes individuals to be free when not interfered with by others or by the state leads to the belief that those who are poor are responsible for their condition. For many who are not poor, being poor is considered a morally blameworthy condition, one that can be avoided by planning and hard work. As a consequence, poverty often carries with it a kind of social stigma. People who find themselves gripped by poverty are frequently ashamed of their condition and often stigmatized by others because they do not have material goods considered important to leading a good or comfortable life.

A third factor that makes poverty a hidden or disguised problem differentiates poverty from issues central to the chapter on equality and discrimination. While members of most traditionally disadvantaged groups identify and can be identified on the basis of features such as skin colour, disability, or gender, those living in poverty do not identify and are not identifiable in the same way. Although many countries define poverty by level of income and identify those who are poor on this basis, how poverty is defined, who counts as poor, and what it means to live in poverty remain controversial, particularly at the level of government policy.

Though distinctive in many respects, poverty does intersect with each of the principles that have guided our introductory discussions throughout this book. Poverty is life-threatening. The mortality rates of children born into poverty are much higher than is the case generally where poverty is not a factor. Those who are poor are much less able to ward off life-threatening illness or to recover from serious and even not-so-serious accidents than those with a reasonable income. Hence, it is difficult to avoid the conclusion that if we have an obligation to protect life and prevent harm, then we have an obligation to respond to the causes and incidences of poverty.

Suffering and poor quality of life are also frequent companions because of poor health care, inadequate shelter, limited educational opportunities, and so on. If there is a general obligation to attempt to alleviate suffering, then surely there is an obligation to seek to alleviate suffering brought on by poverty. The same would appear to apply to the moral autonomy principle. If being poor determines what one can eat and wear, where one can live, and what educational and job opportunities are available, then poverty clearly impedes the ability of those afflicted by it to direct their own lives in accordance with values of their own choosing.

Finally, it is widely thought that poverty is a condition that both invites and attracts discrimination. Poverty seems to hit the members of traditionally disadvantaged groups examined in the previous two chapters more than others: people of colour, women, disabled persons, and Aboriginals. If this claim is true, then the equal-worth principle also has applicability to this issue.

The difficulty, however, is to work out what application the principles have in this case and what they generate by way of rights and obligations. For reasons already set out, this task is not an easy one.

Background Considerations

As individuals, all of us at some points in our lives depend on others for our survival and well-being. Throughout human history, human beings have felt an obligation to respond to those who do not have or cannot obtain the basic goods needed to survive and flourish. They have done so in a variety of ways. Many societies have assigned the responsibility to lend a helping hand to families. Some societies have understood responses to poverty to be a religious obligation often associated with tithing, the giving of alms, or charitable donations. Indeed, European societies throughout their history have relied heavily on religious and charitable institutions in dealing with the poor. This pattern continues to be an influential one in our society today as evidenced by soup kitchens, food banks, clothing drives, and a plethora of charitable organizations that are supported by donations from private citizens.

In the last century, dealing with poverty came to be seen as a government responsibility. In Canada, the impetus for this development can be traced to the Great Depression of the 1930s. Faced with social devastation resulting from the collapse of the economy, populist political movements took shape with a view to persuading the country that the pursuit of social justice should be accepted as a government responsibility. Rooted most firmly on the Prairies in the first instance, these movements led to the creation of a new party, the CCF (the Co-operative Commonwealth Federation), which won office in Saskatchewan in 1944. The result was, among other things, the first provincial public health insurance program, which then served as the model for the national public heath insurance program, which today provides a standard of medical services to all Canadians regardless of ability to pay. This development was accompanied by federal and provincial legislation creating a comprehensive social welfare safety net whose goal has been, among other things, to alleviate the effects of poverty in its various forms.

Although currently the focus of increasing debate and controversy, the social safety net put in place in the 1950s and '60s constituted this country's principal response to the problem of poverty. For example, poverty for senior citizens was reduced when old age pensions were introduced during this time (though changing government policy is reducing this trend). Publicly funded social welfare, though varying in form from country to country, is today the basic response to poverty in Western industrialized societies.

At the international level, the picture is a good deal less clear. A fundamental form of response in First World countries to poverty in Third World countries is donations on the part of individuals to international aid and famine relief agencies such as the Red Cross, Save the Children, and so on. Western governments have also created publicly funded agencies such as the Canadian International Development Agency (CIDA), much of whose work has been designed to reduce poverty by fostering conditions of economic development. Finally, international organizations such as the United Nations have attempted to focus world attention on poverty and to stimulate and coordinate efforts to alleviate it.

The Current Situation

For the past several years, Canada has ranked high, and for several years first, in the United Nations' *Human Development Report* as the best place in the world to live as measured by reference to health, education, and income. Despite this ranking, however, there are great disparities in the distribution of income in this country. If we accept Statistics Canada low-income cut-offs as the definition of poverty, then in 1994, over 16 percent of Canadians were living below the poverty line. Again in 1994, using Statistics Canada low-income cut-offs, people living in poverty included 57 percent of single-parent mothers under the age 65 with children under the age of 18, 89 percent of single mothers under the age of 25, and 1.3 million, or 19.1 percent of Canadian children. In the same year, a total of 226,000 families and 367,000 unattached people had incomes that amounted to less than half of what the National Council of Welfare describes as the poverty line. A 2002 report produced by the Canadian Centre for Policy Alternatives, excerpts of which are included in the readings, analyzes data from Statistics Canada dating back to 1970 to show that the gap between the rich and the poor is increasing. It reports that "the wealthiest 50% of family units controlled an almost unbelievable 94.4% of the wealth, leaving only 5.6% for the bottom 50%."

Nor is poverty particularly easy to escape in Canada. Many of those who are employed have part-time jobs that pay the minimum wage and have no benefits. Many of those living below what the National Welfare Council has defined as the poverty line are what have come to be called the "working poor." Equally important, with cutbacks in government spending and private sector downsizing, people who once thought they had secure, well-paying jobs are now finding themselves unemployed with very uncertain job prospects.

All of this is being accompanied today by an ideological shift that has resulted in austerity budgets and significant reductions in social welfare programs, unemployment insurance, and other social safety net provisions.

Poverty is clearly a matter of concern for Canadians. However, it is a problem of much greater proportions internationally. According to the 1999 United Nations *Human Development Report*, the income of the poorest 20 percent of the world's population has been declining steadily over the past 15 years. Their share of the world's income is now only 1.4 percent, while the richest 20 percent of the world's population now receives 85 percent of the world's income. Disparities between rich and poor are enormous. As an illustration, the combined assets of the world's top three billionaires are more than the combined annual GNP of all least-developed countries. Set out in human terms, what these disparities in income signal is a world in which great wealth coexists with great poverty.

The Moral Dimension

The fact of poverty raises two questions viewed from a moral perspective: Do individuals who are relatively well-off have an individual or a collective moral obligation to seek to alleviate poverty? If the answer to this question is yes, then what is the nature of those responsibilities? Posed this way, these questions appear simple. Yet they hide a complex range of moral perplexities. As individuals and as a society, if we decide that pornography is immoral and should not be allowed, we can refuse to consume it and we can support government measures designed to render it illegal. The same could be said of the other issues addressed elsewhere in this book. Responding to the phenomenon of poverty is another matter.

It is true that individuals can choose to share their wealth with the poor. Indeed many do just this. However, charity raises moral quandaries. It can be demeaning, however well-intentioned. It can create dependence as well as the illusion that problems are being solved when in fact they are not. Further, taken by itself, it is unlikely that the problem of poverty in today's world can be effectively addressed by private generosity, however important such gestures might be as acts of social solidarity.

Government intervention is an obvious alternative response to poverty. Whatever else may be said for or against it, legislative responses can be effective. The introduction of policies such as public medical insurance and government-financed old age pensions, for example, clearly has had and continues to have a positive impact on the lives of many Canadians. At the same time, however, legislatively imposed transfers of wealth from one group to another inevitably raise issues of justice, efficiency, and effectiveness. Opposition to these policies is evident in government policies in Canada and the United States that have cut social welfare programs or implemented strict controls on who qualifies for this aid. As we found out in the chapter on equality and discrimination, there is disagreement among liberal theorists about whether positive measures such as affirmative action or welfare policies are justifiable infringements on individual freedom.

The problems are even more acute at the international level, where legislative tools are mostly non-existent. Here the favoured tool is international aid. At this level, the pursuit of social justice and charity seem once more to converge with implications and consequences that are notoriously difficult to predict and assess. Additional complications arise when aid or actions by rich countries, banks, and multinational corporations is contingent on poor countries adopting policies that may very well affect the well-being of its own citizens in detrimental ways. We will examine some of these issues in this chapter and in the chapters on business ethics and terrorism and war that follow.

Even assuming the existence of policy instruments adequate to the task, we are faced with determining how much is enough. When it comes to alleviating poverty, how far do the obligations of individuals and states extend?

None of these questions is easily addressed. All of them are touched on in one form or another in the readings that follow.

The Readings

We begin with selected articles from the *International Covenant on Economic, Social and Cultural Rights*. The Covenant is significant because it specifies what its signatories thereby agree are universal rights and the obligations of governments that follow from their recognition. The second reading is an extract from the United Nations' millennium report *We The Peoples: The Role of the United Nations in the 21st Century*. The report articulates eight millennium goals, the first of which is to adopt the target of halving the proportion of people living in extreme poverty by 2015. The reading points to both the progress that has been made globally in this century and the problems that still remain with respect to eradicating extreme poverty and hunger.

The third reading discusses poverty in Canada. In this report by the Canadian Centre for Policy Alternatives, Steve Kerstetter provides data indicating that the gap between the rich and the poor is growing and that this inequality in wealth perpetuates inequalities in opportunity and status that need to be addressed at the national level. This report provides the background for the argument made by Bruce Porter in the fourth reading. Porter uses the twentieth anniversary of the Canadian Charter of Rights and Freedoms as the occasion for arguing that poverty and homelessness in Canada call for reading into the Charter the social and economic rights recognized in international documents such as the *International Covenant on Economic, Social and Cultural Rights*. The fifth reading, an excerpt from the December 2002 Supreme Court Decision in *Gosselin v. Quebec*, can be said to be a rejection of Porter's call for this interpretation of the Charter. In it, the Supreme Court ruled that Louise Gosselin, who had her monthly assistance reduced from $434 to $170 by Quebec's Social Assistance Law, did not have a positive right to welfare.

In the sixth reading, Christine Koggel examines the standard definitions of poverty. The absolute definition, used in many government reports in the U.S. and Canada, measures poverty by setting an income level below which individuals are no longer able to satisfy basic needs of food, shelter, clothing, and health. The relative definition, used by international bodies such as the United Nations Population Fund and the United Nations Children's and Education Fund, takes poverty to be a relative state describing people whose incomes *and* lifestyles lag far behind the average in the society in which they live. Koggel argues that the relative definition more adequately captures the moral wrongs of poverty than does the absolute definition with its focus on the basic income needed to satisfy essential needs. She builds on the relative definition by using insights from relational theory to argue that the perspectives of those whose lives are lived in poverty are important for understanding poverty and for designing policies to alleviate it both nationally and globally.

The final reading is by Amartya Sen, a Nobel Prize winner in economics well known for his work on famine and for the influence his work has had on the United Nations' *Human Development Reports*. In this reading, Sen discusses property rights in the context of famines and hunger. He then evaluates and supports the thesis that human beings have a right not to be hungry.

INTERNATIONAL COVENANT ON ECONOMIC, SOCIAL AND CULTURAL RIGHTS

United Nations

PREAMBLE

The States Parties to this Convention,

Considering that, in accordance with the principles proclaimed in the Charter of the United Nations, recognition of the inherent dignity and of the equal and inalienable rights of all members of the human family is the foundation of freedom, justice and peace in the world,

Recognizing that these rights derive from the inherent dignity of the human person,

Recognizing that, in accordance with the Universal Declaration of Human Rights, the ideal of free human beings enjoying freedom from fear and want can only be achieved if conditions are created whereby everyone may enjoy his economic, social and cultural rights, as well as his civil and political rights,

Considering the obligation of States under the Charter of the United Nations to promote universal respect for, and observance of, human rights and freedoms,

Realizing that the individual, having duties to other individuals and to the community to which he belongs, is under a responsibility to strive for the promotion and observance of the rights recognized in the present Covenant,

Agree upon the following articles:

PART I

Article 1

1. All peoples have the right of self-determination. By virtue of that right they freely determine their political status and freely pursue their economic, social and cultural development.

2. All peoples may, for their own ends, freely dispose of their natural wealth and resources without prejudice to any obligations arising out of international economic cooperation, based upon the principle of mutual benefit, and international law. In no case may a people be deprived of its own means of subsistence.

PART II

Article 2

1. Each State Party to the present Covenant undertakes to take steps, individually and through international assistance and co-operation, especially economic and technical, to the

maximum of its available resources, with a view to achieving progressively the full realization of the rights recognized in the present Covenant by all appropriate means, including particularly the adoption of legislative measures.

2. The States Parties to the present Covenant undertake to guarantee that the rights enunciated in the present Covenant will be exercised without discrimination of any kind as to race, colour, sex, language, religion, political or other opinion, national or social origin, property, birth or other status.

Article 3

The States Parties to the present Covenant undertake to ensure the equal right of men and women to the enjoyment of all economic, social and cultural rights set forth in the present Covenant.

Article 4

The States Parties to the present Covenant recognize that, in the enjoyment of those rights provided by the State in conformity with the present Covenant, the State may subject such rights only to such limitations as are determined by law only in so far as this may be compatible with the nature of these rights and solely for the purpose of promoting the general welfare in a democratic society.

Part III

Article 6

1. The States Parties to the present Covenant recognize the right to work, which includes the right of everyone to the opportunity to gain his living by work which he freely chooses or accepts, and will take appropriate steps to safeguard this right.

2. The steps to be taken by a State Party to the present Covenant to achieve the full realization of this right shall include technical and vocational guidance and training programmes, policies and techniques to achieve steady economic, social and cultural development and full and productive employment under conditions safeguarding fundamental political and economic freedoms to the individual.

Article 7

The States Parties to the present Covenant recognize the right of everyone to the enjoyment of just and favourable conditions of work which ensure, in particular:

(a) Remuneration which provides all workers, as a minimum, with:

(i) Fair wages and equal remuneration for work of equal value without distinction of any kind, in particular women being guaranteed conditions of work not inferior to those enjoyed by men, with equal pay for equal work;

> *(ii)* A decent living for themselves and their families in accordance with the provisions of the present Covenant;

(b) Safe and healthy working conditions;

(c) Equal opportunity for everyone to be promoted in his employment to an appropriate higher level, subject to no considerations other than those of seniority and competence;

(d) Rest, leisure and reasonable limitation of working hours and periodic holidays with pay, as well as remuneration for public holidays.

Article 9

The States Parties to the present Covenant recognize the right of everyone to social security, including social insurance.

Article 11

1. The States Parties to the present Covenant recognize the right of everyone to an adequate standard of living for himself and his family, including adequate food, clothing and housing, and to the continuous improvement of living conditions. The States Parties will take appropriate steps to ensure the realization of this right, recognizing to this effect the essential importance of international co-operation based on free consent.

2. The States Parties to the present Covenant, recognizing the fundamental right of everyone to be free from hunger, shall take, individually and through international cooperation, the measures, including specific programmes, which are needed:

(a) To improve methods of production, conservation and distribution of food by making full use of technical and scientific knowledge, by disseminating knowledge of the principles of nutrition and by developing or reforming agrarian systems in such a way as to achieve the most efficient development and utilization of natural resources;

(b) Taking into account the problems of both food-importing and food-exporting countries, to ensure an equitable distribution of world food supplies in relation to need.

Article 12

1. The States Parties to the present Covenant recognize the right of everyone to the enjoyment of the highest attainable standard of physical and mental health.

Article 13

1. The States Parties to the present Covenant recognize the right of everyone to education. They agree that education shall be directed to the full development of the human personality and the sense of its dignity, and shall strengthen the respect for human rights and fundamental freedoms. They further agree that education shall enable all persons to participate effectively in a free society, promote understanding, tolerance and friendship among all nations and all racial, ethnic or religious groups, and further the activities of the United Nations for the maintenance of peace.

FREEDOM FROM WANT

Kofi A. Annan, Secretary-General, United Nations

In the past half-century the world has made unprecedented economic gains. Countries that a mere generation ago were struggling with under-development are now vibrant centres of global economic activity and domestic well-being. In just two decades, 15 countries, whose combined populations exceed 1.6 billion, have halved the proportion of their citizens living in extreme poverty. Asia has made an astounding recovery from the financial crisis of 1997-1998, demonstrating the staying power of its economies—though Asia's poor have not yet regained lost ground.

Chief among the human development success stories since the 1960s are the increase in life expectancy in developing countries, from 46 to 64 years; the halving of infant mortality rates; an increase of more than 80 per cent in the proportion of children enrolled in primary school; and the doubling of access to safe drinking water and basic sanitation.

While more of us enjoy better standards of living than ever before, many others remain desperately poor. Nearly half the world's population still has to make do on less than $2 per day. Approximately 1.2 billion people —500 million in South Asia and 300 million in Africa— struggle on less than $1. People living in Africa south of the Sahara are almost as poor today as they were 20 years ago. With that kind of deprivation comes pain, powerlessness, despair and lack of fundamental freedom—all of which, in turn, perpetuate poverty. Of a total world labour force of some 3 billion, 140 million workers are out of work altogether, and a quarter to a third are underemployed.

The persistence of income inequality over the past decade is also troubling. Globally, the 1 billion people living in developed countries earn 60 per cent of the world's income, while the 3.5 billion people in low-income countries earn less than 20 per cent. Many countries have experienced growing internal inequality, including some of those in transition from communism. In the developing world, income gaps are most pronounced in Latin America, followed closely by sub-Saharan Africa.

Extreme poverty is an affront to our common humanity. It also makes many other problems worse. For example, poor countries—especially those with significant inequality between ethnic and religious communities—are far more likely to be embroiled in conflicts

Excerpted from We the Peoples: The Role of the United Nations in the 21st Century, *Kofi A. Annan, Secretary-General United Nations. Reprinted by permission.*

than rich ones. Most of these conflicts are internal, but they almost invariably create problems for neighbours or generate a need for humanitarian assistance.

Moreover, poor countries often lack the capacity and resources to implement environmentally sound policies. This undermines the sustainability of their people's meagre existence, and compounds the effects of their poverty.

Unless we redouble and concert our efforts, poverty and inequality may get worse still. World population recently reached 6 billion. It took only 12 years to add the last billion, the shortest such span in history. By 2025, we can expect a further 2 billion— almost all in developing countries, and most of them in the poorest. We must act now.

I call on the international community at the highest level—the Heads of State and Government convened at the Millennium Summit—to adopt the target of halving the proportion of people living in extreme poverty, and so lifting more than 1 billion people out of it, by 2015. I further urge that no effort be spared to reach this target by that date in every region, and in every country.

History will judge political leaders in the developing countries by what they did to eradicate the extreme poverty of their people—by whether they enabled their people to board the train of a transforming global economy, and made sure that everyone had at least standing room, if not a comfortable seat. By the same token, history will judge the rest of us by what we did to help the world's poor board that train in good order.

There is a growing consensus on what must be done for us to reach this paramount goal— and it can be reached. I wish to highlight a number of specific areas for particular attention by the Summit.

Achieving Sustained Growth

Our only hope of significantly reducing poverty is to achieve sustained and broad-based income growth. South Asia, and even more so sub-Saharan Africa, will have to make significant gains.

The latest poverty figures illustrate the challenge. They show a decrease in the overall number of people living on $1 a day. A closer look reveals that this is due almost entirely to progress in East Asia, notably China, where poverty reduction is closely associated with strong rates of growth. Indeed, recent studies show an almost perfect correlation between growth and poverty reduction in poor countries—a 1 per cent increase in GDP brings a corresponding increase in the incomes of the poorest 20 per cent of the population. Only in the societies with the greatest inequalities does growth fail to benefit the poor.

So what are some of the critical ingredients of success?

Expanding access to the opportunities of globalization is one. Those countries that have achieved higher growth are those that have successfully integrated into the global economy and attracted foreign investment. Over the past 25 years, Asia has grown at an annual rate of 7 per cent and Latin America at 5 per cent. The countries that have been largely left out of globalization have fared the worst. That includes substantial parts of sub-Saharan Africa.

Some people fear that globalization makes inequality worse. The relationship between the two is complex. With the exception of the economies in transition, recent increases in income gaps are largely the result of technological changes that favour higher skilled workers over less skilled ones. As the economic benefits of education and skills increase, so does income inequality between the people who have them and those who do not. This is true both within and among countries. Globalization may exacerbate these differences, but it does not cause them. Increased global competition may also restrain income gains in relatively higher wage countries, though to date this effect has been felt mainly in the industrialized countries.

Another major source of income inequality within countries is gender discrimination in wages, property rights and access to education. Here globalization, on the whole, may be having some positive effects.

In the developing countries, the labour force engaged in global production typically includes a large proportion of women—whether in textiles, electronics, data processing or chip manufacturing. In many cases, these women work in conditions and for wages that are appalling, and which we must strive to improve. But the fact of their employment also has important benefits.

These new employment opportunities enable women to expand the range of critical choices open to them. They can delay marriage, for example, as a result of which fertility rates often decline. They and their children often gain access to more and better nutrition, health care and education. As the survival rates of their children increase, fertility rates will decline further. The increase in female employment and earnings may also lead to changes in the perceived "social value" of a female child, which means that parents and society at large may become more willing to give girls greater access to education, health care and nutrition.

It is now widely accepted that economic success depends in considerable measure on the quality of governance a country enjoys. Good governance comprises the rule of law, effective state institutions, transparency and accountability in the management of public affairs, respect for human rights, and the participation of all citizens in the decisions that affect their lives. While there may be debates about the most appropriate forms they should take, there can be no disputing the importance of these principles.

A fair and transparent public expenditure and taxation system is another key ingredient. Revenues must be used wisely to help the poor, and to make sound investments in physical and social infrastructure for all. Excessive regulation, by contrast, impedes economic performance and slows growth.

Certain practices clearly do not constitute good governance by any definition. If a succession of military dictators in a resource-rich country in a poor part of the world siphon off as much as $27 billion of the public's money, economic performance and the poor are likely to suffer. Those responsible for such abuses, and the international banks that eagerly transfer their funds to safe havens, must be held accountable.

Other forms of institutionalized corruption are far less extreme but may, nevertheless, seriously distort economic incentives, limit economic growth and result in low levels of support for the poor.

Nothing is more inimical to pro-growth, anti-poverty objectives than armed conflict. It must pain us all beyond description to see a war between two of Africa's poorest countries drag on into yet a third year, having already taken an estimated 55,000 lives, and with 8 million people in one of the countries threatened by famine. Internal conflicts in other parts of Africa have lasted even longer, and have destroyed the lives and livelihoods of many more millions of Africans.

Sustained and broad-based growth also requires investments in health and education, as well as other social policies. The United Nations conferences in the 1990s spelled these out in considerable detail; I shall recommend both a health and an education initiative.

Better-educated and healthier people are empowered to make better choices and lead fuller lives, which also makes them more productive and their economies more competitive. Similarly, all the evidence indicates that extending equal opportunities to women and girls has multiplier effects for entire families and even communities. As a supplement to universal social programmes, school lunches and other targeted initiatives for the poor have an economic as well as a social purpose.

Finally, appropriate levels and types of support from the global community—public and private—are needed for development targets to be reached. I shall address this dimension of the challenge separately.

In short, experience confirms some fundamental truths: growth is a necessary, though not sufficient, condition for reducing poverty and income inequality. The surest route to growth is through successfully engaging in the global economy. But that must be combined with effective social policies: advances in education for all, health for all and gender equality. Success rests on a strong foundation in governance. And it requires external support.

RAGS AND RICHES: WEALTH INEQUALITY IN CANADA

Steven Kerstetter

Rags and Riches: Wealth inequality in Canada analyzes data from Statistics Canada's Survey of Financial Security and previous surveys by the federal agency dating back to 1970. The focus of the surveys was accumulated wealth or net worth rather than current income. Wealth was defined as all personal assets minus all personal debts. This study includes regional data never before published that were commissioned and paid for by the Canadian Centre for Policy Alternatives—BC Office. This research was made possible through an inequality endowment fund provided by the Government of British Columbia.

Key Findings

Canadians may view their country as a land of opportunity, but it also a land of deep and abiding inequality in the distribution of personal wealth.

- The wealthiest 10 percent of family units held 53 percent of the wealth in 1999. The wealthiest 50 percent of family units controlled an almost unbelievable 94.4 percent of the wealth, leaving only 5.6 percent for the bottom 50 percent.
- The poorest 10 percent of family units have *negative* average wealth or more debts than assets. Average wealth adjusted for inflation for the poorest 10 percent actually declined by 28 percent from -$8,031 in 1970 to -$10,656 in 1999.
- Average wealth adjusted for inflation for the richest 10 percent of family units increased from $442,468 in 1970 to $980,903 in 1999—an increase of 122 percent.

Gaps between rich and poor are evident in the statistics for each of Canada's regions. There are also large differences in wealth across the regions themselves.

From "Rags and Riches: Wealth Inequality in Canada," *Canadian Centre for Policy Alternatives, December 2002, pp. 4-5. Reprinted by permission. Please also refer to CCPA's Web site: www.policyalternatives.ca.*

- Average wealth overall tends to increase from east to west. Average wealth in the Atlantic region was $122,798 in 1999, and the average for Quebec was $155,198. Both those figures were well below the averages of $221,110 for Ontario, $213,114 for the three Prairie provinces and $251,253 for BC.
- Most of the differences in average regional wealth are the result of differences in wealth among the richest family units in each region. Differences in average wealth for the poorest and middle family units are smaller.

Financial security is an elusive goal for many Canadians. Financial *insecurity* may actually be the norm these days and financial security the exception to the rule.

- Poor people are least able to withstand any kind of financial crisis because they have so few assets and often have outstanding debts. People in the middle may be squeezed because so much of their wealth is tied up in housing. Only people with above-average wealth enjoy true financial security because they have sizable financial assets in addition to housing and other non-financial assets.
- The poorest 20 percent of family units had financial assets of only $1,974 on average in 1999, and their average income in 1998 (the last full year before the latest Statistics Canada survey) was only $18,698. If their current income suddenly disappeared, their financial assets alone would be enough to keep the family going for barely five weeks.
- The richest 20 percent of family units had average financial assets of $262,186 in 1999 and average income of $62,518 in 1998. The financial assets were enough to replace normal income for more than four years.

Housing is the single largest asset of Canadians and also their single largest debt. However, financial assets play a more significant role in explaining the skewed distribution of wealth in Canada.

- The estimated value of all principal residences in 1999 was $1.1 trillion, or 38 percent of all total personal assets. Mortgages on principal residences totaled $304 billion, or 66 percent of total personal debt.
- About 60 percent of family units were homeowners, and the other 40 percent were renters. The median wealth of homeowners with mortgages was $111,807 in 1999, and the median wealth of homeowners without mortgages was $259,200. The median wealth of renters was only $8,000.
- Housing has a surprisingly small impact on the overall skewed distribution of wealth. The richest 20 percent of family units had 70.4 percent of all personal wealth in 1999. After subtracting housing assets and mortgage debt, the richest group has 76.2 percent of the wealth.

Wealth in Canada varies by family type, age, housing status, education and current income. But there are rich and poor in every category.

- Families tend to be much better off than people living alone, because many families have two incomes rather than one. Older people tend to be better off than younger people because they have had more time to accumulate assets and pay off their debts.

- Despite the general link between age and wealth, it would be wrong to conclude that all older people are well-to-do. Even in the older age groups starting at age 45, roughly one in five family units had total wealth of no more than $30,000 in 1999.
- The family units most likely to be wealthy are those with high current incomes. Families with incomes of $75,000 or more in 1998 after federal and provincial income taxes had average wealth of $583,517 in 1999.
- Differences in educational attainment have less bearing on wealth than might be expected. However, this may be the legacy of an era where education was less important as a determinant of income.

The assets, debts and wealth of all Canadians combined rose substantially over the years, but not everyone wound up better off. Poor family units—notably lone-parent families and young people—gained little or even lost ground.

- Family units headed by persons under age 25 saw their median wealth fall from $1,474 in 1970 to a mere $150 in 1999 after adjustments for inflation.
- Lone-parent families headed by either women or men saw their median wealth go from $1,870 in 1984 to $3,656 in 1999 after adjustments for inflation.

The tax policies of the federal government and some provincial governments in recent years have conferred huge benefits on Canada's wealthiest people, the one group capable of fending for themselves. Meanwhile, Canada's social safety nets and programs of special importance to the poor have been weakened by cuts in government support.

- In 1999, 72 percent of the $420 billion in RRSPs and other registered savings plans was held by the richest 20 percent of family units. The richest 20 percent also owned 94 percent of the $92 billion in stocks outside RRSPs, and 81 percent of the $80 billion in mutual and investment funds outside RRSPs. RRSPs and other registered plans, capital gains, and stock dividends all get preferred income tax treatment.
- Canada is one of the few developed countries in the world that has no inheritance taxes, estate taxes or wealth transfer taxes. Such taxes ensure some measure of equality of opportunity, and promote democratic values by placing limits on inherited wealth.
- The percentage of unemployed workers receiving unemployment insurance benefits from Ottawa was cut in half during the 1990s. Provincial governments have kept welfare incomes far below the poverty line in all parts of the country in recent years.

The findings of this study have significant implications for public policy in Canada. Governments would do well to rethink their policies of recent times, and move Canada back on the path towards a "just society."

REWRITING THE CHARTER AT 20

Bruce Porter

If the Canadian Charter of Rights and Freedoms[1] were scheduled for a twenty-year overhaul and update, I think many would agree that we would want to try to correct its failure to address in any meaningful way the growing social and economic inequalities in Canadian society and the widespread poverty and homelessness in the midst of unprecedented affluence. The proliferation of hunger and homelessness in Canada belies the Charter's promise of a more egalitarian and just society and has left many of the most disadvantaged in Canada on the outside of our so-called "rights revolution."

Last year, when the Canadian Human Rights Review Panel, chaired by former Justice La Forest, traveled across the country to hear from human rights and equality seeking groups about what they would look for in a revised Canadian Human Rights Act (CHRA),[2] it was virtually unanimous among equality seeking constituencies that increasingly widespread and severe poverty and homelessness among the most vulnerable and disadvantaged groups in Canada must be recognized as a national human rights crisis. These issues, everyone seemed to agree, go to the very core of equality, security, and dignity that are at the heart of Canadians' conceptions of human rights and must be addressed not only as issues of social policy but also as human rights violations subject to legal remedy.[3]

A similar consensus has emerged at the international level among United Nations human rights treaty monitoring bodies reviewing Canada's compliance with our international human rights obligations. These bodies have expressed alarm and shock at the growing crisis of poverty and homelessness in Canada and at the fact that Canadian courts and governments appear unwilling to recognize the effects of unprecedented cuts to social programs and resulting hunger and homelessness as violations of rights under the Charter and human rights legislation.[4]

Our governments have tried to dismiss the growing concerns among U.N. bodies by pointing to the fact that Canada has perched proudly atop the United Nations Development Program Human Development Index for the last six years. What they fail to appreciate is that from the perspective of international law and those who monitor its compliance, a high average standard of living and increased economic prosperity for the majority does not make the destitution of some members of our society more tolerable. Rather, poverty and homelessness in Canada is more abhorrent because it is completely unnecessary and almost invariably a matter of legislative or administrative choice. Our governments have chosen to ignore the interests of the most marginalized and disadvantaged groups and governed primarily for what J.K. Galbraith calls the "Contented Electoral Majority."[5]

Some would say, of course, that these legislative and administrative choices are somehow exempt from judicial review under the Charter and that these are issues beyond the competence and legitimate role of the courts. Yet as Justice Wilson noted in *Andrews*, relying on the words of John Hart Ely: "The whole point of the approach is to identify those groups in society to whose needs and wishes elected officials have no apparent interest in attending. If the approach makes sense, it would not make sense to assign its enforcement to anyone but the courts."[6] When governments cater exclusively to majority interests at the expense of the fundamental human rights of those at the margins, surely the promise of the Charter is that

From Rewriting the Charter at 20 or Reading it Right: The Challenge of Poverty and Homelessness in Canada: The Canadian Charter of Rights and Freedoms: Twenty Years Later, *Bruce Porter, 2002. Reprinted by permission.*

the courts will step in to protect and safeguard their rights. That promise has not been fulfilled for those living in poverty in Canada.

One of the reasons for this is that when poor people claim their rights under the Charter to equality or security of the person, they may appear to courts to be seeking remedies to a category of rights which is not explicitly included in the Charter. Poor people experience discrimination by governments primarily in relation to refusals to address economic deprivation. The type of government action or inaction that denies poor people equality or security of the person is usually linked with a failure to provide for economic need or a denial of basic social or economic rights such as housing. Thus, when the most disadvantaged in Canadian society advance claims to dignity, equality, and security, they are at the same time advancing claims to rights which, under international law, are categorized as "social and economic rights."

Central to the Universal Declaration of Human Rights,[7] and to most subsequent human rights treaties ratified by Canada is the right to an adequate standard of living, including the right to adequate food and the right to adequate housing.[8] We do not find those rights, or other social and economic rights, explicitly enumerated in the Charter. Does that mean that the Charter has to be re-written to include social and economic rights if those living in poverty are to be included in its guarantees of dignity, equality, and security? That is the question I want to briefly explore.

The lack of explicit recognition of social and economic rights in Canadian law has been a matter of growing concern at the U.N. Committee on Economic, Social and Cultural Rights, which monitors Canada's compliance with the International Covenant on Economic, Social and Cultural Rights (ICESCR).[9] With respect to human rights legislation in Canada, the Committee has recommended the explicit inclusion of economic, social, and cultural rights.[10] This has also been the solution advocated by many within Canada. As Canada's Chief Commissioner of Human Rights has observed:

> [It] is difficult to argue that poverty is not a human rights issue, given the devastating impact it has on people's lives ... The international community has recognized for some time that human rights are indivisible, and that economic and social rights cannot be separated from political, legal or equality rights. It is now time to recognize poverty as a human rights issue here at home as well.[11]

Most equality seeking and human rights groups appearing before Justice La Forest's Task Force last year also called for the inclusion of social and economic rights in the CHRA, including the right to an adequate standard of living and the right to adequate housing as basic rights which could be claimed and adjudicated before a tribunal.[12]

If a twenty year "tune up" were on the agenda for the Charter, I am sure the U.N. Committee on Economic, Social and Cultural Rights as well as most equality seeking groups in Canada would express similar support for the inclusion of social and economic rights there. Adding to the Charter explicit reference to social and economic rights such as the right to adequate food, clothing and housing, social security, work freely chosen, healthcare and education would serve to update the Charter in light of recent developments in international human rights and help to overcome what seems to be a strong judicial resistance, at least at lower courts, to address the pressing human rights issues in Canada that are of growing concern both internationally and domestically.

International human rights law has seen significant advances in the area of social and economic rights since the Charter was first drafted. At that time, the International Covenant on Economic, Social and Cultural Rights had only recently come into force. Though declared by the United Nations to be indivisible and interdependent with civil and political rights, social and economic rights were still, in 1981, in the institutional backwaters of the U.N. in comparison to civil and political rights. Civil and political rights were monitored and adjudicated by a specially constituted treaty monitoring body under the International Covenant on Civil and Political Rights (ICCPR)[13] — the U.N. Human Rights Committee — which reviewed governments' five year periodic reports under that Covenant and also received and adjudicated individual complaints of violations.[14] Social and economic rights, on the other hand, had no official treaty monitoring body. They were reviewed by various ineffective working groups within the Economic and Social Council, were subject to no complaints procedure, and had virtually no jurisprudence. Because they require resources and are subject to "progressive realization" over time, social and economic rights such as the right to adequate food, clothing and housing, were considered more as policy commitments than as enforceable human rights.[15]

A lot has changed in the last twenty years. The ICESCR was given its own Committee in 1986 which has developed more rigorous state party review and developed General Comments on various rights and obligations under the Covenant, including the right to adequate housing[16] and the right to food;[17] the obligations with respect to particular groups such as persons with disabilities[18] and older persons;[19] and on the general nature of state party obligations, particularly with respect to the provision of legal remedies.[20] Experts have convened from around the world, first in Limburg and more recently in Maastricht to develop guidelines on violations of economic, social, and cultural rights.[21] At the urging of the World Conference on Human Rights in Vienna, the U.N. Committee on Economic, Social and Cultural Rights has prepared a Draft Optional Protocol which would establish a complaints and adjudication procedure similar to that which exists under the ICCPR.[22]

With the expansion of the human rights treaty monitoring system at the United Nations in the 1980s and the adoption of treaties dealing with the rights of groups such as women and children, the indivisibility of social and economic rights and civil and political rights has become an institutional reality. The Convention on the Rights of the Child[23] adopted in 1989, recognizes a broad range of economic and social rights of children and now enjoys almost universal ratification.[24]

Virtually all regional treaty bodies now have incorporated review and adjudication of social and economic rights. The forty member Council of Europe, for example, has adopted an updated and revised European Social Charter which includes rights such as the right to decent housing and the right to "protection against poverty and social exclusion" and provides for a complaints procedure.[25] Most other regional human rights systems now provide in some manner for the adjudication of social and economic rights.

The United Nations and regional human rights bodies are struggling to respond, although arguably too slowly, to an urgent need for internationally enforceable social and economic rights in the new global economy. When the primary market in which corporations competed was circumscribed by national borders and protectionist trade barriers, governments were relatively free to set the rules of the competition. They could establish minimum wages, health and safety protections, labour standards, and social programs and set appropriate taxation rates through which to pay for them. In the new international economy, however, governments are too often governed by the market they regulate: by their credit ratings, their ability to compete for investment, their need to sell their products in the global market, and by the decisions of trade panels about the legality of domestic regulatory measures. Without a new emphasis on social and economic rights that can be applied both internationally and domestically as universal norms, social policy can easily be held hostage to global competition.

These developments have brought new domestic challenges to social and economic rights in all countries. Certainly the challenges facing Canadian society have altered dramatically since parliamentarians debated and framed the provisions of a new Charter of Rights back in 1980-81. If our parliamentarians at that time had gone to the Parliamentary Library to look into the problem of "homelessness" in Canada they would have found only a couple of reports dealing with transient men in larger cities living in inadequate rooming houses or "flop houses".[26] They would not have imagined that after twenty years of unprecedented economic prosperity, there would be thousands in Canada who sleep on the streets or in grossly inadequate shelters for the homeless. Most parliamentarians would have had no idea what a "food bank" was. The first food bank only opened in Edmonton in 1981. It would have been unimaginable to them that twenty years later three quarters of a million people, including over 300,000 children, would rely every month on emergency assistance from a national network of over 615 food banks and over 2,000 agencies providing limited emergency food.[27]

These developments, occurring to various degrees in all countries, raise new challenges to domestic constitutional regimes. Many of the world's newer constitutional democracies have responded by providing, at least in some form, for the adjudication of social and economic rights, either through the direct application of international human rights law in domestic courts or through the inclusion of specified social and economic rights in national constitutions.

An example with which many in the Canadian Bar Association (CBA) will be familiar is South Africa, where the CBA has forged important research and support networks for advocates working under the new Constitution. South Africa's final Constitution includes a broad range of social and economic rights that are fully justiciable, including the right "to have access to" "adequate housing", "health care services, including reproductive health care", "sufficient food and water" and "social security, including, if they are unable to support themselves and their dependents, appropriate social assistance."[28] Their Constitutional Court recently released its first ruling which applied the right to have access to adequate housing. The Court found that various levels of government failed to fulfill their constitutional responsibilities when 390 adults and 510 children were living on a sports field without tents or facilities after having been forced to vacate a squatter settlement.[29] Surely if a government facing a horrific AIDS crisis and with considerably fewer resources than Canada is prepared to be held constitutionally accountable to these fundamental norms of international human rights law, we in Canada should be.

It is interesting to note that as early as 1990, when Canada was experiencing a serious housing crisis and after the International Year of Shelter for the Homeless in 1987 had brought new attention to the right to housing in international law, a Liberal Housing Task Force co-chaired by Paul Martin recommended that the Charter be amended to include the right to adequate housing and other social and economic rights.[30] Mr. Martin argued at that time that while many of the rights in the Charter tend to be seen as "negative" rights, it is increasingly important to recognize the positive obligations of governments:

... [S]ince the middle of the Great Depression and particularly from the end of World War II, we have moved into an era where government decides not only that certain rights are available but also undertakes an obligation to provide the means whereby the rights may be enjoyed. In Canada, the most obvious example of those types of rights and corresponding obligations can be seen with respect to minority language rights, health care and education.

The Task Force believes that it is a healthy sign in a democracy for new rights to be created. It is therefore not unusual at this time in our history to have positive rights creating a State or government obligation. The question then becomes how best can a right to housing, or even to shelter, be expressed.

.... In order to find a definition and legal description of housing rights, it is instructive to look at specific international covenants to which Canada is a signatory. These covenants are also significant in that they highlight the fact that Canada, as a member of the international community, has recognized the universal need for a rights declaration dealing with adequate housing.

... though Canada is a signatory to these international covenants, some of the matters contained in them, such as housing, tend still to be looked upon only as worthy goals of social and economic policy rather than legally enforceable rights.

... The Task Force believes that those searching for adequate, affordable housing may be better served by giving them some form of constitutionally guaranteed right to shelter.[31]

The 1990 Task Force concluded by recommending that the constitutional recognition of the right to housing should be placed on the agenda of the next First Ministers' Meeting.

Today, of course, telling homeless people that they need to wait for the Charter to be re-written by the First Ministers to protect their right to housing is to condemn them to a lengthy, if not eternal, exile from Canada's constitutional democracy. Before we propose to re-write the Charter to include social and economic rights like the right to housing, we should make sure we are reading the one we've got right, and that poor peoples' claims to dignity and security could not receive an appropriate hearing and response in the context of the present Charter. For while the Charter may seem old to some, it is relatively new for poor people. The first Charter challenge to poverty and homelessness to reach the Supreme Court of Canada will be heard in the autumn.[32] It is a bit early in their rights claiming history to be telling poor people that they need to re-write the Charter if they want to have their claims to dignity, equality, and security heard.

While we do not have in the Charter an enumeration of particular social and economic rights, we still have two all-important, open-ended provisions which were the result of hard fought battles back in 1980–81. First, there is the broad guarantee of the right to "life, liberty and security of the person" in section 7, duplicating the wording of the broad, overarching guarantee in article two of the Universal Declaration, and situated within a Constitution which uniquely excludes the right to property in order to ensure that regulatory measures important to the community at large and to the personal security of individuals are not subject to challenge by more advantaged corporate interests. And second, there is a substantive guarantee of the equal benefit of the law in section 15. Neither of these rights conforms to the "negative rights" paradigm described by Paul Martin. Both have been recognized by the Supreme Court as being "hybrid" rights, made up of positive and negative components.[33]

Open ended, substantive rights such as these are particularly well equipped for providing remedies to more specific substantive rights enumerated and codified in international human rights law. The Supreme Court has embraced the well established principle of international law that domestic law should be interpreted in a manner that conforms to international legal obligations and it has done so specifically in relation to social and economic rights. It was in the context of invoking the right to work under the ICESCR that the majority of the Supreme Court embraced Chief Justice Dickson's important precept that "the Charter should generally be presumed to provide protection at least as great as that afforded by similar provisions in international human rights documents which Canada ratified."[34] The Supreme Court has recognized that while corporate property rights were deliberately excluded from the Charter and cannot be read back into it through section 7, this is not true of social and economic rights which might be claimed by those living in poverty. It has recognized that section 7 may be interpreted to include rights in the ICESCR such as "rights to social security, equal pay for equal work, adequate food, clothing and shelter."[35] It has found that section 7 obliges governments to provide legal aid or counsel for poor people in custody cases where there is an issue of security of the person at stake.[36]

Considering the status of the Convention on the Rights of the Child as an interpretive framework for administrative discretion, Justice L'Heureux-Dubé asserted for the majority of the Court in *Baker* that international law is "a critical influence on the interpretation of the scope of the rights included in the Charter."[37] She further elaborated on that principle in *Ewanchuk*, noting that "our Charter is the primary vehicle through which international human rights achieve a domestic effect"[38] and that the equality guarantee, along with the guarantee of security of the person, will be particularly important vehicles for incorporating international human rights norms, as these two rights "embody the notion of respect of human dignity and integrity."[39]

Canada's unique approach to equality should thus act as an appropriate vehicle for providing domestic legal effect to many of the substantive obligations toward disadvantaged groups contained in the ICESR and the Convention on the Rights of the Child, The Convention on the Elimination of All Forms of Discrimination Against Women and other human rights treaties. As the U.N. Committee on Economic, Social and Cultural Rights put it in the Committee's General Comment on the Domestic Application of the Covenant:

> ... when a domestic decision maker is faced with a choice between an interpretation of domestic law that would place the state in breach of the Covenant and one that would enable the State to comply with the Covenant, international law requires the choice of the latter. Guarantees of equality and non-discrimination should be interpreted, to the greatest extent possible, in ways which facilitate the full protection of economic, social and cultural rights.[40]

In its first decisions under section 15 in *Andrews* and *Turpin* in 1989, the Supreme Court affirmed that the equality guarantee is the broadest of all guarantees, underpinning all other rights, that it has a strong remedial component, and that its purposes are "in remedying or preventing discrimination against groups suffering social, political and legal disadvantage in our society."[41] In the *Eldridge*[42] case, deaf patients in British Columbia challenged the fact that there was no sign language interpretation provided when it was necessary to adequate healthcare. When the B.C. government had declined to fund a non-profit provider of these services they argued that their right to the equal benefit of the healthcare system had been infringed. Government lawyers argued that the right to equality ought only to protect against inequalities created by government action, not to authorize courts to require governments to allocate resources to particular issues of disadvantage that were not directly caused by government action. Justice La Forest, on behalf of a unanimous Supreme Court of Canada, forcefully rejected that argument, stating that:

> To argue that governments should be entitled to provide benefits to the general population without ensuring that disadvantaged members of society have the resources to take full advantage of those benefits bespeaks a thin and impoverished vision of s. 15(1).[43]

It is difficult to see how government action or inaction depriving single mothers and their children, people with disabilities, youth, others enumerated, or analogous groups of adequate food, clothing, and housing would fall outside of this broad guarantee of substantive equality.

While the Supreme Court's evolving approach to equality and security of the person is properly informed by modern developments in international human rights law, it is also a retrieval of the original promise of the Charter, and its broad affirmation of social justice as a fundamental foundation of our constitutional democracy. Chief Justice Dickson wrote in *Oakes* in 1986 of the values and principles essential to a free and democratic society which must guide Charter interpretation, including "respect for the inherent dignity of the human person, commitment to social justice and equality, accommodation of a wide variety of beliefs, respect for cultural and group identity, and faith in social and political institutions which enhance the participation of individuals and groups in society."[44]

As Justice Cory noted in *Vriend*, the guarantee of substantive equality at the core of the Charter evokes the promise of a "just society" in which all individuals live in dignity — arduous and difficult as it may be to attain, but well worth the effort.[45] We were certainly reminded in September 2000, watching historical clips of Pierre Elliott Trudeau, of how inseparable were our expectations of the Charter twenty years ago from the ideal of a just and inclusive society based on universal dignity and social justice. As the young Trudeau wrote in 1961 in an article on "Economic Rights" for the *McGill Law Journal*, unless society evolves "an entirely new set of values" and produces the services that private enterprise is failing to produce "any claim by lawyers that they have done their bit by upholding civil liberties will be dismissed as a hollow mockery."[46]

Without being naively nostalgic, I think it is true to say that in 1981, governments' commitments and ability to, in the words of section 36 of the Constitution, "promote the well-being of Canadians and to provide essential public services of reasonable quality to all Canadians" was an assumed commitment and obligation behind the rights entrenched in the Charter. Rights and obligations were two sides of the same coin. Canadians had lived under the guarantee of the Canada Assistance Plan Act for 15 years, in which the entitlement to an adequate level of financial assistance for anyone in need, regardless of the cause of need, was a core social right, and one which was subject to judicial review and remedy.[47] These social rights and constitutional commitments were inextricably interwoven with the Charter's guarantees of individual rights.[48] They were part of the Charter's promise, and we should not have to re-write the Charter to demand that its promise be realized.

In the twelve years since the Supreme Court issued its first decisions under section 15, affirming the primacy of the guarantee of equality and the over-riding purpose of alleviating social and historical disadvantage, almost half a million more households have fallen into poverty. The number of single mothers living in poverty has increased by more than 50 percent to over 300,000, and their poverty has in many cases deepened to the point of extreme destitution.[49] The number of homeless women and children living in shelters in Toronto has increased by 130 percent.[50] Surely this is not the version of substantive equality for which the Ad Hoc Committee of Women fought so hard back in 1981.

Rosemary Billings, in her Introduction to *The Taking of Twenty-Eight*,[51] quotes Linda Ryan-Nye as saying, after the lobbying for women's rights in the Charter over 20 years ago, that although constitutional equality was "a helluva lot to lose it was not a helluva lot to gain." Rights still have to be claimed after the writing is over. Twenty years after the Charter, most of the work remains to be done, at least in terms of realizing the Charter's promise for those living in poverty, most of whom are women. Our Charter, informed by its history and nurtured with new developments in international human rights, is a solid foundation on which social and economic rights can be claimed by the most disadvantaged in society. But we need to make place for people living in poverty in our rights revolution.

People living in poverty bringing forward claims under sections 7 and 15 of the Charter, the primary vehicles for giving domestic effect to international human rights obligations, have been told, essentially, that their issues of equality and security are not included under the Charter. Rather than attracting additional judicial attention and concern because their claims intersect with internationally recognized social and economic rights, their claims have been rejected for this reason. Let me give three examples which have been particularly disturbing to the U.N. Committee on Economic, Social and Cultural Rights.

Eric Fernandes, a person with a severe degenerative muscular disease, argued that his rights to equality and security ought to include special assistance for attendant care necessary for him to live in dignity in his home rather than be confined for the rest of his life to a hospital room. Under international law this would be a straightforward claim to adequate housing and medical care and under the Charter, it would seem to be a straightforward claim to substantive equality. The Manitoba Court of Appeal, however, rejected this claim precisely because it could be construed as a claim to a right to adequate housing. The Court stated that "the desire to live in a particular setting does not constitute a right protected under s.7 of the Charter." As for the rights of persons with disabilities to positive action by government, the Court found that this right does not extend to situations where the disadvantage of disability is exacerbated by poverty:

> Fernandes is not being disadvantaged because of any personal characteristic or because of his disability. He is unable to remain community-based because he has no caregiver, because he must rely on public assistance and because the facilities available to meet his needs are limited.[52]

Another case which provoked some astonishment at the United Nations was that of *Masse v. Ontario (Ministry of Community and Social Services)*,[53] in which twelve Ontario social assistance recipients, including seven sole support mothers, asked the Ontario Court (General Division) to reverse a twenty-two percent cut in provincial social assistance rates on the basis that it would deprive them of basic necessities and force many into homelessness. Some of the uncontroverted evidence in the case showed that the cuts would lead to significant increases in homelessness and would dislocate approximately 120,000 families, including 67,000 single mothers from their homes.[54] The court described the effects of the cuts in the following terms:

The daily strain of surviving and caring for children on low and inadequate income is unrelenting and debilitating. All recipients of social assistance and their dependants will suffer in some way from the reduction in assistance. Many will be forced to find other accommodation or make other living arrangements. If cheaper accommodation is not available, as may well be the case, particularly in Metropolitan Toronto, many may become homeless.[55]

The court nevertheless accepted the pleadings of the Attorney General of Ontario "that the plight of welfare recipients, although urgent and serious, relates to their inability to provide for themselves." O'Brien J. found that "S. 7 does not provide the applicants with any legal rights to minimal social assistance. The legislature could repeal the social assistance statutes". [56] Both of these cases were denied leave to the Supreme Court of Canada. Ironically, it is Canada's first Charter challenge to poverty and homelessness, launched in 1989, which will be the first to be heard by the Supreme Court.[57]

Louise Gosselin was subject to a regulation in Quebec's Social Assistance Law which reduced the assistance for those who were employable and under thirty and not engaged in workfare or training programs, from $434 a month to $170 a month. It was largely undisputed that no one can find adequate food, clothing, and housing in Montreal for this amount. Ms. Gosselin was periodically homeless and slept in shelters. When she rented a room in a boarding house she had no money left for food. A man from whom she was receiving food attempted to rape her. She lived for a winter in an apartment without heat. She resorted at times to prostitution and to making herself sexually available to a man for whom she had no affection in exchange for shelter and food.[58]

The trial judge rejected Ms. Gosselin's claim largely on the basis that economic or social rights such as the right to an adequate standard of living, protected under international human rights law, are not enforceable rights under the Charter. Poverty, the judge found, is frequently the result of "internal" causes. Poor people, he noted, smoke at twice the average rate of Canadians, are under-educated, psychologically vulnerable, and have a weak work ethic.[59] The Quebec Court of Appeal upheld the decision, but the dissenting judgment of Robert, J., drew extensively on the fundamental importance of social and economic rights in international law as an interpretive framework for human rights legislation and the Canadian Charter.[60]

The lower court decisions in all of these cases show a common theme: that the substantive approach to equality or security of the person affirmed by the Supreme Court in other contexts, ought not to be applied to address poverty and homelessness. To do so, the courts seem to believe, would be to read into the Charter social and economic rights. While it defies common sense to suggest that the deprivation of adequate food, clothing, and housing in these cases did not engage directly the equality and security interests protected by the Charter, the lower courts rejected these claims essentially because the claimants' disadvantage was, in part, linked to their poverty, and to remedy poverty or homelessness is to grant a remedy for a violation of an "economic" right.

Courts in these and other cases in which poor peoples' Charter claims have been dismissed have also made reference to concerns about the unique competence of legislatures to determine matters of social and economic policy. It is noteworthy, however, that in none of the cases was the challenged decision a legislated one. Most of the decisions engaging poor peoples' equality and security, in fact, are regulatory changes and administrative decisions, made behind closed doors, with no hearings, no consultation, and no debate.

This is not to say that courts ought not to avoid unnecessary tampering with legislative decision-making. Finding the line and developing the criteria for making these distinctions is an ongoing project. The distinction between social, economic, and cultural rights on the one hand, and civil and political rights on the other, however, seems to be of no value in distinguishing between occasions when courts ought to intervene and those when they ought to defer to parliament. At worst, such a distinction encourages courts to abandon those who need their protection the most. As Justice McLachlin (as she then was) put it:

> Parliament has its role: to choose the appropriate response to social problems within the limiting framework of the constitution. But the courts also have a role to determine, objectively and impartially, whether Parliament's choice falls within the limiting framework of the constitution. The courts are no more permitted to abdicate their responsibility than is Parliament. To carry judicial deference to the point of accepting Parliament's view simply on the basis that the problem is serious and the solution difficult, would be to diminish the role of the courts in the constitutional process and to weaken the structure of rights upon which our constitution and our nation is founded.[61]

The Supreme Court, it seems, has begun to chart a different course than that followed by the lower courts in poverty related cases. Rather than declaring certain categories of rights claims to be non-justiciable because they engage with social and economic rights, the Court has found it preferable to exercise appropriate deference in the context of particular cases, and at various stages of the Charter analysis. In the *Eldridge* case, for example, the Court left it up to the government to choose from the "myriad options available to the government that may rectify the unconstitutionality of the current system."[62] The South African Constitutional Court followed the same approach in its recent decision with respect to the right to housing, mandating the South African Human Rights Committee to work with the various levels of government in fashioning an appropriate remedy. In this way, courts and legislators may fashion new relationships to meet the new challenges of poverty and homelessness.

Perhaps, if my optimism about the Supreme Court proves ill-founded, I will be arguing, a year from now that we must re-write the Charter to protect the fundamental rights of those in Canada whose equality and security is assaulted daily by the ordeal and indignities of poverty.[63] I hope, instead, to be applauding the Supreme Court's decision to allow Ms. Gosselin's appeal and that all of us will be explaining to Jeffrey Simpson that the Court did not re-write the Charter or read new rights into it, so as to give judges more power to make social policy. Rather, we will explain, the Court read the Charter right and decided to include poor people in our constitutional democracy, which may not, after all, prove so old at twenty.[64]

NOTES

1. Part I of the Constitution Act, 1982, being Schedule B to the Canada Act 1982 (U.K.), 1982, c. 11 [hereinafter Charter or Canadian Charter].
2. R.S.C. 1985, c. H-6.
3. See Summaries of Non-Governmental Organizations Roundtable Consultations, Halifax, Nova Scotia, September 28th and 29th 1999; Montréal, September 30/October 1, 1999; Ottawa: October 18th and 19th, 1999; Toronto: October 20th and 21st, 1999; Vancouver: October 25th and 26th, 1999; Edmonton, Alberta: October 27th and 28th, 1999, online at <www.chrareview.org>.

4. For descriptions of the emerging consensus with U.N. treaty monitoring bodies about poverty and homelessness in Canada, see B. Porter, "Judging Poverty: Using International Human Rights Law to Refine the Scope of Charter Rights," 15 *JLSP* 2000 and Craig Scott, "Canada's International Human Rights Obligations and Disadvantaged Members of Society: Finally into the Spotlight?" (1999) 10:4 *Constitutional Forum* 97.

5. J. K. Galbraith, *The Culture of Contentment* (Boston: Houghton Mifflin, 1992) at p. 15

6. J.H. Ely, *Democracy and Distrust* (Cambridge: Harvard University Press, 1980) at 151, cited in Andrews supra note 49 at 152.

7. Universal Declaration of Human Rights, GA Res. 217(III) UN GAOR, 3d Sess., Supp. No. 13, UN Doc. A/810 (1948) 71.

8. Article 25(1) of the Universal Declaration provides that: "Everyone has the right to a standard of living adequate for the health and well-being of himself and of his family, including food, clothing, housing and medical care and necessary social services, and the right to security in the event of unemployment, sickness, disability, widowhood, old age or other lack of livelihood in circumstances beyond his control." Other social and economic rights recognized under the Universal Declaration include the right to "social security" and to the realization of social and economic rights "indispensable for [a person's] dignity and the free development of his [or her] personality" under Article 22; the right to work, to free choice of employment, to protection against unemployment, and to remuneration ensuring "an existence worthy of human dignity, and supplemented, if necessary, by other means of social protection" under Article 23; and the right to education under Article 26.

9. Article 6 of the ICESCR guarantees "the right to work, which includes the right of everyone to the opportunity to gain his living by work which he freely chooses or accepts..." Article 9 recognizes "the right of everyone to social security, including social insurance." Article 10 declares that "The widest possible protection and assistance should be accorded to the family ... particularly ... while it is responsible for the care and education of dependent children." Article 11(2), in terms similar to the Universal Declaration, guarantees: "the right of everyone to an adequate standard of living for himself and his family, including adequate food, clothing and housing, and to the continuous improvement of living conditions." M. Craven, *The International Covenant on Economic, Social and Cultural Rights* (Oxford: Clarendon Press, 1995).

10. United Nations Economic and Social Council, Committee on Economic, Social and Cultural Rights, Official Records, 1994, Supplement No.3 *Consideration of Reports Submitted by States Parties Under Articles 16 and 17 of the Covenant: Concluding Observations of the Committee on Economic, Social and Cultural Rights (Canada)*, Geneva, 10 June 1993, E/C 12/1993/19 [hereinafter *Concluding Observations, CESCR, 1993*] at paragraph 9; United Nations Economic and Social Council, Committee on Economic, Social and Cultural Rights, *Consideration of Reports Submitted by States Parties Under Articles 16 and 17 of the Covenant: Concluding Observations of the Committee on Economic, Social and Cultural Rights (Canada)*, 10 December 1998, E/C.12/1/Add.31 [hereinafter *Concluding Observations, CESCR, 1998*] at paragraph 51.

11. Canadian Human Rights Commission, *Annual Report* 1997 (Ottawa: Canadian Human Rights Commission, 1998) 2.

12. Among the organizations supporting the inclusion of social and economic rights are the Charter Committee on Poverty Issues (CCPI), the National Anti-Poverty Organization (NAPO), Equality for Gays and Lesbians Everywhere (EGALE), The African Canadian Legal Clinic, Action travail des femmes, La table féministe de concertation provinciale de L'Ontario, National Association of Women and the Law (NAWL), the Council of Canadians with Disabilities (CCD), Coalition of Persons with Disabilities (Newfoundland and Labrador) and Independent Living Resource Centre (St. John's, Newfoundland), Metro Toronto Chinese & Southeast Asian Legal Clinic, Affiliation of Multicultural Societies & Service Agencies of B.C. (AMSSA) and the Canadian Council for Refugees (CCR). See Summaries of Non-Governmental Organizations Roundtable Consultations, Halifax, Nova Scotia, September 28th and 29th, 1999; Montréal, September 30/October 1, 1999; Ottawa: October 18th and 19th, 1999; Toronto: October 20th and 21st, 1999; Vancouver: October 25th and 26th, 1999; Edmonton, Alberta: October 27th and 28th, 1999, online at <www.chrareview.org>.

13. International Covenant on Civil and Political Rights, 19 December 1966, 999 U.N.T.S. 171, Can. T.S. 1976 No. 47 (entered into force 23 March 1976, accession by Canada 19 May 1976).

14. International Covenant on Civil and Political Rights, (First) Optional Protocol, Adopted Dec. 19, 1966 999 U.N.T.S. 302 (entered into force Mar. 23, 1976).

15. For a description of changes since the early1980s see B. Porter, "Socio-economic Rights Advocacy - Using International Law: Notes from Canada" (July 1999) 2:1 *Economic & Social Rights Review* 1.

16. See United Nations Economic and Social Council, Committee on Economic, Social and Cultural Rights, Sixth Sess., General Comment No. 4 The Right to Adequate Housing (Article 11(1) of the Covenant), Geneva, 13 December 1991, E/1992/23; United Nations Economic and Social Council, Committee on Economic, Social and Cultural Rights, Sixteenth Sess., 28 April - 16 May 1997, General Comment No. 7 The Right to Adequate Housing (article 11.1 of the Covenant): Forced Evictions, Geneva, 20 May 1997, E/C.12/1997/4.

17. United Nations Economic and Social Council, Committee on Economic, Social and Cultural Rights, Twentieth Sess., 26 April - 14 May 1999, General Comment No. 12 The Right to Adequate Food (article 11.1), Geneva, 12 May 1999, E/C.12/1999/5.

18. United Nations Economic and Social Council, Committee on Economic, Social and Cultural Rights, Eleventh Sess., 38th Mtg., 25 November 1994, General Comment No. 5 Persons with Disabilities, Geneva 25 November 1994, E/C.12/1994/13.

19. United Nations Economic and Social Council, Committee on Economic, Social and Cultural Rights, Thirteenth Sess., 39th Mtg., 20 November - 8 December 1995, General Comment No. 6 The Economic, Social and Cultural Rights of Older Persons, Geneva, 24 November 1995, E/1996/22 as reported in (1996) 3:2 I.H.R.R. at 253.

20. United Nations Committee on Economic, Social and Cultural Rights, Nineteenth Session General Comment No. 9: The Domestic Application of the Covenant, Committee on Economic, Social and Cultural Rights, Geneva, 16 November - 4 December 1998, E/C.12/1998/24 [hereinafter General Comment No. 9].

21. Limburg Principles on the Implementation of the International Covenant on Economic, Social and Cultural Rights, UN doc. E/CN.4/1987/17; reproduced in *Human Rights Quarterly*, Vol. 9 (1987), pp. 122-135; Maastricht Guidelines on Violations of Economic, Social and Cultural Rights in *Human Rights Quarterly*, Vol. 20 (1998).

22. Draft Optional Protocol to the International Covenant on Economic, Social and Cultural Rights, UN doc. E/CN.4/1997/105.

23. Convention on the Rights of the Child, 20 November 1989, Can T.S. 1992 No. 3; UN Doc. A/RES/44/25 (entered into force 2 September 1990 and in force for Canada 28 May 1990) [hereinafter CRC].

24. The CRC recognizes, *inter alia*, the right of the child to "the enjoyment of the highest attainable standard of health and to facilities for the treatment of illness and rehabilitation of health" (Article 24); "the right to benefit from social security, including social insurance" (Article 26); and "the right of every child to a standard of living adequate for the child's physical, mental, spiritual, moral and social development" (Under Article 27(1)). Article 27(3) states that: "States Parties, in accordance with national conditions and within their means, shall take appropriate measures to assist parents and others responsible for the child to implement this right and shall in case of need provide material assistance and support programmes, particularly with regard to nutrition, clothing and housing." The United States has refused to ratify the ICESCR and is one of only two countries to refuse to ratify the CRC, the other being Rwanda.

25. European Social Charter (Revised), 3 May 1996, E.T.S. No. 163 (entered into force 1 July 1999) in B.H. Wester ed., *International Law and World Order: Basic Documents* (May 1997) at Vol. 3, Doc III.3.16d. especially Part II. at Part IV, Article C in reference to the Additional Protocol to the European Social Charter Providing for a System of Collective Complaints, 9 November 1995, E.T.S. No. 158 (entered into force 1 July 1998).

26. See, for example, Toronto Social Planning Council, *Report on Homelessness* (City of Toronto, 1976).

27. Canadian Association of Food Banks, *Hunger Count2000: A Surplus of Hunger*, Prepared by Beth Wilson and Carly Steinman (Toronto, October, 2000). The first food bank in Canada opened later in 1981 in Edmonton.

28. Constitution of the Republic of South Africa 1996, Act 108 of 1996 at sections 26(1) and 27(1). For a full discussion of the standard of judicial review of social and economic rights under South

Africa's Constitution, see Sandra Liebenberg, "Socio-Economic Rights," in M. Chaskalson et al eds., *Constitutional Law of South Africa*, 3rd Revision Service (Johannesburg: Juta & Co. Ltd, 1996).

29. *The Government of South Africa v. Grootboom*, Case CCT 11/00, 4 October 2000.

30. Paul Martin and Joe Fontana, *Report of the National Liberal Caucus Task Force on Housing* (National Liberal Caucus, Parliament of Canada, 1990).

31. *Report of the Liberal Housing Task Force*, (Ottawa, Parliament of Canada, 1990).

32. *Louise Gosselin v. Quebec (Attorney General)* (S.C.C. File No. 27418). The case referred to here was subsequently heard by the Supreme Court of Canada on October 29, 2001 and the decision was released December 19, 2002. See *Gosselin v. Quebec (Attorney General)* 2002 SCC 84, and footnote 63 below.

33. On sections 7 and 15 as "hybrid" rights incorporating positive and negative components, see *Schachter v. Canada*, [1992] 2 S.C.R. 679 at 702, 721. For the Supreme Court's subsequent consideration of positive obligations under section 15, see B. Porter, "Beyond *Andrews*: Substantive Equality and Positive Obligations After *Eldridge* and *Vriend*" (1998) 9 *Constitutional Forum* 71.

34. *Slaight Communications v. Davidson* [1989] 1 S.C.R. 1038 at 1056.

35. *Irwin Toy v. Attorney General of Quebec* [1989] 1 S.C.R. 927 at 1003-04.

36. *New Brunswick (Minister of Health and Community Services v. G. (J.)* [1999] S.C.J. No. 47.

37. *Baker v. Canada (Minister of Citizenship and Immigration)*, [1999] S.C.J. No. 39 at paragraph 70.

38. Ibid. at 365.

39. *R. v. Ewanchuk*, [1999] 1 S.C.R. 330 at paragraph 73.

40. United Nations Committee on Economic, Social and Cultural Rights, Nineteenth Session General Comment No. 9: The Domestic Application of the Covenant, Committee on Economic, Social and Cultural Rights, Geneva, 16 November - 4 December 1998, E/C.12/1998/24 at paragraphs 14, 15.

41. *R. v. Turpin*, [1989] 1 S.C.R. 1296 at 1332.

42. *R. v. Eldridge* [1997] 3 S.C.R. 624 [hereinafter Eldridge].

43. Ibid. at 677-78.

44. *R. v. Oakes*, [1986] 1 S.C.R. 103 at 136.

45. *Vriend v. Alberta*, [1998] 1 S.C.R. 493 (per Cory, J.) at paragraph 68.

46. Pierre Trudeau, "Economic Rights" *McGill Law Journal*, 1961.

47. In the same year that the Charter came into effect, Jim Finlay, a social assistance recipient in Manitoba, sought standing to challenge provincial non-compliance with the adequacy requirements of CAP. In *Finlay v. Canada (Minister of Finance)*, [1986] S.C.R. 607, it was subsequently determined that an affected individual had public interest standing to challenge provincial non-compliance with the adequacy requirements of CAP. Subsequently, in a 5-4 judgment, the Court found in *Finlay v. Canada (Minister of Finance)* [1993] 1 S.C.R. 1080 that Manitoba had not violated the adequacy requirements by imposing a 15 percent deduction for recovery of overpayments. Sopinka, J., writing for the majority, found that CAP "requires assistance to be provided in an amount that is compatible, or consistent, with an individual's basic requirements" but provides for some flexibility and for the recovery of overpayments.

48. Martha Jackman, "The Protection of Welfare Rights Under The Charter", 20 *Ottawa L. Rev.* 257 at 259-283.

49. National Council on Welfare *Poverty Profile*: 1998, Vol. 113 (Autumn, 2000).

50. City of Toronto *Homelessness Report* 2001.

51. Penney Kome, *The Taking of Twenty-Eight: Women Challenge the Constitution* (Toronto: The Women's Press, 1983).

52. *Fernandes v. Manitoba (Director of Social Services (Winnipeg Central))* 93 D.L.R. (4th) 402 at pp, 414-415. This decision was denied leave by the Supreme Court of Canada.

53. *Masse v. Ontario Ministry of Community and Social Services* (1996), 134 D.L.R. (4th) 20, leave to appeal to Ontario Court of Appeal denied (1996), 40 *Admin. L.R.* 87N, leave to appeal to the Supreme Court of Canada denied (1996), 39 C.R.C. (2d) 375 [hereinafter *Masse*].

54. Affidavit of Michael Ornstein, Application Record, Volume II, Tab 15; Affidavit of Gerard Kennedy, Application Record, Volume II, Tab 14 in *Masse v. Ontario*, Ont. Ct. (Gen. Div.) Court File No. 590/95.

55. Ibid at 69 (per Corbett J.).

56. Ibid at 42-43.

57. *Gosselin v. Quebec (Attorney General)* 2002 SCC 84, supra f.n. 31.

58. Testimony of L. Gosselin, Record Vol. 1, pp. 106-127. *Gosselin v. Québec (Procureur Général)* [1992] R.J.Q. 1647 at pp. 1676–77.

59. *Gosselin v. Québec (Procureur Général)* [1992] R.J.Q. 1647 at pp. 1676-77.

60. *Louise Gosselin c. Procureur général du Québec* (6 April 1999) Montreal 500-09-001092-923 (C.A.).

61. *RJR-MacDonald Inc. v Canada (A.G.)*, [1995] 3 S.C.R. 199 at paragraph 136.

62. *Eldridge*, supra, at 631-32.

63. As it turns out, the Supreme Court of Canada's decision in *Gosselin*, released on December 19, 2002, was neither the inclusive reading of the Charter I had hoped for nor the rejection of social and economic rights I had feared. The decision to dismiss the appeal, supported by a slim majority of five to four, showed a disturbing lack of empathy or understanding of the indignity of poverty and homelessness among some of the justices. On the other hand, Justice Arbour, supported by Justice L'Heureux Dubé, wrote a strong dissent in support of including in the scope of "security of the person" the right to adequate food, clothing, housing and other necessities, and placing positive obligations on governments to provide adequate financial assistance to those in need. Significantly, six of the seven remaining justices, though not agreeing that the right to security of the person had been breached in this case, refused to rule out the possibility that in a future case such a "novel" interpretation of security of the person might be adopted. The justices were sharply divided on their assessment of the evidence in this case and the interpretive issues raised in my presentation remain undecided.

   We did not meet with Jeffrey Simpson about the decision. Predictably, he wrote in his column the day after the decision of his alarm at this "very near thing", and at the fact that the majority of the Court had signaled that in a future case, the Court may be prepared to find that the right to security of the person "empowers courts to instruct the government to do certain things to underpin economic and social rights." See Jeffery Simpson, "Talk About a Very Near Thing," *The Globe and Mail*, (December 20, 2002).

64. Jeffrey Simpson, a columnist in the *Globe and Mail* newspaper, is well known for his relentless tirades against what he sees as increasing judicial intrusions on parliament's domain under the Canadian Charter of Rights and Freedoms.

QUESTIONS

1. According to Bruce Porter, does the Charter need to be rewritten to address issues of poverty and homelessness in Canada?

2. Porter claims that Canada fares badly at the international level when it comes to judgments about its treatment of poverty and homelessness. What is Porter's argument for this claim?

3. Porter argues that "poor people experience discrimination by governments primarily in relation to refusals to address economic deprivation." Do you think that discrimination on the basis of wealth is a form of discrimination similar to or different from the kinds of discrimination discussed in Chapter 5? Provide reasons for your answer.

4. Porter's hope that the December 2002 Supreme Court decision in *Gosselin v. Quebec* would interpret Section 7 of the Charter as supporting economic rights to social welfare did not come to pass. The reading that follows provides excerpts from the Supreme Court decision. What are the reasons provided by the majority justices for rejecting this interpretation of the Charter? In your view, does Porter have reason to be optimistic that the door was left open for interpreting the Charter in this way in the future?

GOSSELIN V. QUEBEC (ATTORNEY GENERAL)

2002 SCC 84. File No.: 27418 2001: October 29; 2002: December 19

Madam Justice C.J. McLachlin (and Gonthier, Iacobucci, Major, and Binnie J.J.)

B. Does the Social Assistance Scheme Violate Section 7 of the Canadian Charter?

75   Section 7 states that "[e]veryone has the right to life, liberty and security of the person" and "the right not to be deprived" of these "except in accordance with the principles of fundamental justice". The appellant argues that the s. 7 right to security of the person includes the right to receive a particular level of social assistance from the state adequate to meet basic needs. She argues that the state deprived her of this right by providing inadequate welfare benefits, in a way that violated the principles of fundamental justice. There are three elements to this claim: (1) that the legislation affects an interest protected by the right to life, liberty and security of the person within the meaning of s. 7; (2) that providing inadequate benefits constitutes a "deprivation" by the state; and (3) that, if deprivation of a right protected by s. 7 is established, this was not in accordance with the principles of fundamental justice. The factual record is insufficient to support this claim. Nevertheless, I will examine these three elements.

76   The first inquiry is whether the right here contended for — the right to a level of social assistance sufficient to meet basic needs — falls within s. 7. This requires us to consider the content of the right to life, liberty and security of person, and the nature of the interests protected by s. 7.

77   As emphasized by my colleague Bastarache J., the dominant strand of jurisprudence on s. 7 sees its purpose as guarding against certain kinds of deprivation of life, liberty and security of the person, namely, those "that occur as a result of an individual's interaction with the justice system and its administration": *New Brunswick (Minister of Health and Community Services) v. G. (J.)*., [1999] 3 S.C.R. 46, at para. 65. "[T]he justice system and its administration" refers to "the state's conduct in the course of enforcing and securing compliance with the law", (*G. (J.)*, at para. 65). This view limits the potential scope of "life, liberty and security of person" by asking whom or what s. 7 protects against. Under this narrow interpretation, s. 7 does not protect against all measures that might in some way impinge on life, liberty or security, but only against those that can be attributed to state action implicating the administration of justice: see *Reference re ss. 193 and 195.1(1)(c) of the Criminal Code* (Man.), [1990] 1 S.C.R. 1123 (the "*Prostitution Reference*"), at pp. 1173-74, *per* Lamer J. (as he then was), writing for himself; *B. (R.) v. Children's Aid Society of Metropolitan Toronto*, [1995] 1 S.C.R. 315, at paras. 21-23, *per* Lamer C.J., again writing for himself alone; and *G. (J.)*, *supra*, for the majority. This approach was affirmed in *Blencoe v. British Columbia (Human Rights Commission)*, [2000] 2 S.C.R. 307, 2000 SCC 44, *per* Bastarache J. for the majority.

From Gosselin v. Quebec (Attorney General), *2002 SCC 84. File No. 27418; 2002: October 29; 2002: December 19; paras. 75 to 84.*

78   This Court has indicated in its s. 7 decisions that the administration of justice does not refer exclusively to processes operating in the criminal law, as Lamer C.J. observed in *G. (J.)*, *supra*. Rather, our decisions recognize that the administration of justice can be implicated in a variety of circumstances: see *Blencoe*, *supra* (human rights process); *B. (R.)*, *supra*, (parental rights in relation to state-imposed medical treatment); *G. (J.)*, *supra*, (parental rights in the custody process); *Winnipeg Child and Family Services v. K.L.W.*, *[2000] 2/519*, 2000 SCC 48 S.C.R. (liberty to refuse state-imposed addiction treatment). Bastarache J. argues that s. 7 applies only in an adjudicative context. With respect, I believe that this conclusion may be premature. An adjudicative context might be sufficient, but we have not yet determined that one is *necessary* in order for s. 7 to be implicated.

79   In my view, it is both unnecessary and undesirable to attempt to state an exhaustive definition of the administration of justice at this stage, delimiting all circumstances in which the administration of justice might conceivably be implicated. The meaning of the administration of justice, and more broadly the meaning of s. 7, should be allowed to develop incrementally, as heretofore unforeseen issues arise for consideration. The issue here is not whether the administration of justice is implicated — plainly it is not — but whether the Court ought to apply s. 7 despite this fact.

80   Can s. 7 apply to protect rights or interests wholly unconnected to the administration of justice? The question remains unanswered. In *R. v. Morgentaler*, [1988] 1 S.C.R. 30, at p. 56, Dickson C.J., for himself and Lamer J. entertained (without deciding on) the possibility that the right to security of the person extends "to protect either interests central to personal autonomy, such as a right to privacy". Similarly, in *Irwin Toy Ltd. v. Quebec (Attorney General)*, [1989] 1 S.C.R. 927, at p. 1003, Dickson C.J., for the majority, left open the question of whether s. 7 could operate to protect "economic rights fundamental to human ... survival". Some cases, while on their facts involving the administration of justice, have described the rights protected by s. 7 without explicitly linking them to the administration of justice: *B.(R.)*, *supra*; *Winnipeg Child and Family Services v. K.L.W.*, *supra*.

81   Even if s. 7 could be read to encompass economic rights, a further hurdle emerges. Section 7 speaks of the right *not to be deprived* of life, liberty and security of the person, except in accordance with the principles of fundamental justice. Nothing in the jurisprudence thus far suggests that s. 7 places a positive obligation on the state to ensure that each person enjoys life, liberty or security of the person. Rather, s. 7 has been interpreted as restricting the state's ability to *deprive* people of these. Such a deprivation does not exist in the case at bar.

82   One day s. 7 may be interpreted to include positive obligations. To evoke Lord Sankey's celebrated phrase in *Edwards v. Attorney-General for Canada*, [1930] AC 124, the *Canadian Charter* must be viewed as "living tree capable of growth and expansion within its natural limits": see *Reference Re Provincial Electoral Boundaries (Sask.)*, [1991] 2 S.C.R. 158, at p. 180, *per* McLachlin J. It would be a mistake to regard s. 7 as frozen, or its content as having been exhaustively defined in previous cases. In this connection, LeBel J.'s words in *Blencoe*, *supra*, at para. 188 are apposite:

> We must remember though that s. 7 expresses some of the basic values of the Charter. It is certainly true that we must avoid collapsing the contents of the Charter and perhaps of Canadian law into a flexible and complex provision like s. 7. But its importance is such

for the definition of substantive and procedural guarantees in Canadian law that it would be dangerous to freeze the development of this part of the law. The full impact of s. 7 will remain difficult to foresee and assess for a long while yet. Our Court should be alive to the need to safeguard a degree of flexibility in the interpretation and evolution of s. 7 of the Charter.

The question therefore is not whether s. 7 has ever been — or will ever be — recognized as creating positive rights. Rather, the question is whether the present circumstances warrant a novel application of s. 7 as the basis for a positive state obligation to guarantee adequate living standards.

83   I conclude that they do not. With due respect for the views of my colleague Arbour J., I do not believe that there is sufficient evidence in this case to support the proposed interpretation of s. 7. I leave open the possibility that a positive obligation to sustain life, liberty, or security of person may be made out in special circumstances. However, this is not such a case. The impugned program contained compensatory "workfare" provisions and the evidence of actual hardship is wanting. The frail platform provided by the facts of this case cannot support the weight of a positive state obligation of citizen support.

84   In view of my conclusions under s. 15(1) and s. 7 of the *Canadian Charter*, the issue of justification under s. 1 does not arise. Nor does the issue of *Canadian Charter* remedies arise.

POVERTY AND GLOBAL JUSTICE

Christine M. Koggel

Human rights, development, nationhood, the environment, labor, culture, population growth, education, health care, and poverty are just some of the issues being reshaped by the phenomenon of globalization. In general terms, globalization represents increased flows of technology, trade, information, markets, capital, and people themselves. An overarching feature of globalization is that we live in a context of *economic* globalization, one in which the dominance of markets, multinational corporations, and world trade organizations shape the issues and circumscribe its effects on people. These features of economic globalization reflect the dominance of liberal theory and policies on the world stage. While the hope was and continues to be that economic globalization in the form of market structures and liberal trade policies can create opportunities, ease suffering, and reduce poverty, statistics show that there are persistently high levels of poverty and ever-growing gaps between the rich and the poor both within and across borders.

The United Nations Development Program's (UNDP) 1999 *Human Development Report* discloses that "people living in the highest-income countries had 86% of world GDP — the bottom fifth just 1%. ... The world's 200 richest people more than doubled their net worth in

This paper was first presented to the Greater Philadelphia Philosophy Consortium Symposium, "Human Needs and Global Justice", in January 2003. I would like to thank the organizers, participants, and members of the audience and, in particular Audrey Brokes, David Crocker, Ashok Gangadean, Bob Dostal, and Hugh Lacey. I would also like to thank Sally Scholz, Gerry Cohen, and Andrew Brook for their contributions to the revision process. Reprinted by permission.

the four years to 1998, to more than $1 trillion. The assets of the top three billionaires are more than the combined GNP of all least developed countries and their 600 million people" (UNDP, 1999, 3). In its annual report two years later, the UNDP declares that "despite a reduction in the relative differences between many countries, absolute gaps in per capita income have increased" (UNDP, 2001, 16).

Inequalities are not limited to huge gaps in wealth between rich and poor countries. An ever-growing gap between the rich and the poor, increased levels of poverty, and high incidences of child poverty characterize some of the richest countries in the world. After detailing these facts for the situation in Canada, the Canadian Centre for Policy Alternatives in its report *Rags and Riches* (excerpts of which are in the third reading of this chapter), goes on to say: "[i]t is no consolation to Canadians, but wealth in the United States is even more concentrated than it is in Canada. Between 1983 and 1998, the share of wealth held by the richest 20 percent of family units rose from 81.3 percent to 83.4 percent at the expense of all the other groups. ... The largest gains took place within the richest one percent of family units, from 33.8 percent of all the personal wealth in 1983 to 38.1 percent of all the wealth in 1998" (Kerstetter 2002, 14). In its 2000 report, *A League Table of Child Poverty in Rich Nations*, UNICEF ranks the United States 22 out of 23 industrialized countries for having the highest percentage of children living in poverty: 22.4 percent of its children live in poverty (United Nations Children's Fund 2000).

It seems uncontroversial to state that living in poverty with its day to day struggles to satisfy basic needs such as food and shelter results in unequal life prospects on a variety of fronts: premature mortality, persistent health problems, reduced opportunities for education and employment, low levels of self-respect, and little power to suggest policy or implement change. Moreover, data links the likelihood of being poor with membership in groups already disadvantaged by factors such as race, ethnicity, gender, and disability, factors that in turn perpetuate a cycle of poverty by solidifying stereotypes about what it means to be poor both within and across the borders of rich and poor nations. The idea that poverty is a moral and social wrong that ought to be eliminated may have intuitive appeal, yet as John Jones points out in a survey of philosophical work on poverty, "[a]part from some normative inquiry concerning poverty (which generally focuses on the problem of distributive justice and not on poverty per se), one finds virtually no conceptual analysis, philosophical interpretation or phenomenological description of poverty. It is not clear to me why this is so. It may be that philosophers conceive poverty to be an unproblematic idea, essentially economic in character" (Jones 1986–87, 557).

This paper has four main purposes. I begin by raising objections to the idea that poverty is merely economic in character by providing a critical analysis of the two definitions of poverty used in international and national measures. Contrasting the absolute and relative definitions of poverty will reveal that poverty is about more than the income one has. As captured in relative definitions, interpersonal comparisons point to the relevance of *gaps* between the rich and poor and this matters to an assessment of poverty and its effects on people. These insights are then used to question some of the assumptions about the justice and/or necessity of inequalities in wealth in ordinary discourse and in philosophical accounts. I then turn to accounts of distributive justice and in particular liberal justifications for inequalities in wealth. Here I outline briefly G. A. Cohen's persuasive critique of the incentive argument in Rawls's theory of justice. I use this discussion to introduce the role and importance of perspectives for a proper understanding of poverty and to argue that we need to take them into account in formulating policies sensitive to the particularities of cases and locations. By revealing the relevance of the perspectives of those whose lives are lived in poverty, I detail an account of the inequalities and injustices of poverty that tend to go unnoticed in standard definitions, philosophical accounts, and economic measures of poverty. I conclude by applying insights from the conceptual analysis of poverty, the critical evaluation of liberal theory, and the role of perspectives to issues of poverty in the global context.

1. Poverty: Absolute or Relative?

If the injustice of poverty has intuitive appeal, why has data about ever increasing gaps between the rich and the poor both within and across borders not translated into massive citizen protest and the political will to redistribute the vast wealth concentrated in the hands of an increasingly small percentage of people? There are many reasons, but I want to examine just two: 1) how poverty is defined reveals deep-rooted assumptions about what it is like to live in poverty, who is responsible for it, and what needs to be done to alleviate it; and 2) liberal justifications for inequalities in wealth reflect entrenched beliefs about the necessity and/or justice of an unequal distribution of wealth that in turn support prevailing beliefs about poverty and acceptable levels of it. First the analysis of how poverty is defined.

The United States ranks 22 out of 23 for child poverty under the relative definition of poverty that is used and defended by UNICEF, but 11 out of 23 under the absolute definition, a measure favored by the U.S. for defining poverty. The absolute definition measures the level of poverty independently of cultural or social circumstances by determining the precise level of income, below which a person cannot afford the basic necessities of life. Under this definition, poverty is a term reserved for those who are unable to purchase a fixed minimum package of goods and services needed for basic survival. With this measure, the U.S. poverty line is then converted into the respective currencies of the other industrialized countries to provide the U.S. ranking of 11 on a global scale. While 11 out of 23 is still a shameful showing for the richest country in the world, the U.S. poverty line shows that Americans have quite a high income in comparison to the vast majority of people in other countries. It is then all too easy to believe that if people in other countries can survive on much less by way of income, then surely Americans can. But there is more going on with respect to beliefs about poverty in the mind set of those living in what is taken to be the land of opportunity.

Liberal theorists have always been prepared to justify the necessity and/or justice of inequalities in wealth. These justifications emerge from the role that negative rights to non-interference have played in liberal theory: citizens should have the freedom to live their lives as they see fit and the state should not interfere by instituting measures that redistribute the wealth that individuals acquire by their own means and through free exchange with others. The central importance of liberty is evident in Nozickean desert or entitlement based arguments for inequalities in wealth. People are either entitled to or deserve their wealth when they produce it themselves or have it transferred to them voluntarily. On this account, the absence of formal barriers as specified in constitutional rights to political and civil liberties is both necessary and sufficient for ensuring that each person has the freedom to live life as they choose and the opportunity to use their talents and abilities to acquire the material and social goods they need and want. This kind of liberal theorist has resisted declaring positive or economic rights to food, shelter, or work as rights that ought to be guaranteed to each and every citizen.

When equality of opportunity is understood as satisfied when there are no formal barriers that prevent people from competing for and obtaining jobs and goods, those living in poverty tend to be viewed as responsible for their condition because they have the same opportunity as anyone else to change their circumstances if they so desire. The result is that many believe that welfare policies need to be restricted or eliminated because those on welfare are perceived as willfully unemployed, stuck in a rut of dependency, lacking initiative, utterly failing to contribute to society, or buying luxury items they neither need nor deserve. They could try harder to get a job, they could get a better job through education and training opportunities, and they could be more frugal in spending the money they have or get through welfare. These underlying beliefs were evident in Ontario a few years ago when the then provincial finance minister responded to protests about his government's cuts to welfare by producing a grocery list of items that people on welfare could buy to live on the reduced income he had put in place. He outlined ways in which to save money by, for example, buying damaged tins of food or cheap brands. The list was as offensive in its implication that the poor just need to learn how to shop and save as it was in the media response to it, which was to all too readily accept that the poor take easy handouts and do not even spend that money wisely.

This example from real life politics shows that measuring poverty in absolute terms makes it possible for politicians to address poverty by merely calibrating the level of income that defines poverty and thereby minimizing the reality of it. This strategy was evident in remarks by the head of the U.S. Census Bureau, who in lowering the poverty line in 1999 for a four person family living in the U.S. from $16,780 to $14,945 was quoted as saying that Americans are now "winning the war on poverty" and "millions of people ... are living better lives." The insensitivity and wrong headedness of this strategy of redefining poverty by lowering the poverty line was captured by a Missouri motel housekeeper who in having her *same* level of income now defined as above the poverty line was reported in email lists as having said: "I never dreamed I'd ever become middle-class. America truly is the land of opportunity."

The housekeeper's comment is more perspicuous than one might at first think. UNICEF argues that the United States in its reliance on an absolute measure of poverty breaks faith with its professed ideals of freedom and equality of opportunity. Not only is there no sense in which children, for example, can be said to be responsible for the conditions of poverty into which they are born, but the simple fact is that "the children of the poor simply do not have the same opportunities as the children of the non-poor. Whether measured by physical and mental development, health and survival rates, educational achievement or job prospects, income or life expectancies, those who spend their childhood in poverty of income and expectation are at a marked and measurable disadvantage" (UNICEF 2000, 1). In other words, they neither have the same freedom or opportunity as those who are not poor.

Thus far, I have suggested that we need to know what the lives of people with low incomes are actually like as a way to raise problems with defining poverty in terms of income levels alone. Michael Katz argues that merely concentrating on income levels make "[p]oor people seem cardboard cutouts, figures in single dimensions, members of inferior categories, rarely complex, multifaceted, even contradictory in the manner of other persons. Their poverty therefore results from some attribute, a defect in personality, behaviour, or human capital" (Katz 1989, 236). This insight about the importance of knowing about people and their circumstances will turn out to be central to my analysis of what is missing in both absolute and relative definitions of poverty. But first I need to discuss the relative definition of poverty because features of it will introduce the importance of interpersonal comparisons for assessing inequalities in wealth and its effects on people.

As described by UNICEF, the relative measure defines poverty as "the falling behind, by more than a certain degree, from the average income and life-style enjoyed by the rest of the society in which one lives" (UNICEF 2000, 4). The general idea behind the relative definition is that poverty needs to be conceived as a *relative* state describing people whose incomes and lifestyles lag far behind the average in the society *in which they live*. An approach to poverty that uses a relative definition reveals inequalities that go beyond that which is evident in lives lived at or below some fixed level of income needed to survive. Under the relative definition, one could have the basic necessities and yet be living in poverty because one does not have access to many of the material and social goods that the majority enjoy. UNICEF argues that the relative measure "most accurately reflects the equality of opportunity that has long been the boast and battle-cry of industrialized nations" (UNICEF 2000, 5). What this means is that if my level of income dictates that I cannot send my child to the schools with greater resources that rich children go to, my child cannot be said to have an equal opportunity. Or if my level of income dictates that my child cannot get the same level of health care as those with more money, then this can affect my child's capacity to prevent illness and disease from affecting her opportunities to learn and develop, to hold a job, to have children, and to care and be cared for. While levels of income obviously matter, the relative definition pays attention to what those levels of income mean in terms of my life prospects and opportunities as compared to fellow citizens.

Being able to compare my situation with those who are better off draws attention to restrictions on freedoms and opportunities, restrictions that not only determine what I am able to compete for and obtain but how I perceive myself, my society, and my role in it. As I will go on to argue, these are features of a relational account more generally that are accentuated when we take perspectives into account. For now, it is important to note that relative measures allow interpersonal comparisons that more easily have us pay attention to the effects of inequalities in wealth than do absolute measures that fix attention on income alone. For those defending relative measures, the size of the gaps in wealth and the number of people who fall on one or the other side of the gap matter in judgments about how individuals fare relative to others in their society.

Perhaps better than any other theorist, Amartya Sen captures why interpersonal comparisons permitted by relative measures matter to an assessment of poverty. Sen argues that income alone will not provide sufficient information about poverty and that relative measures, including those that compare the lives and life prospects of people across borders, are relevant to an understanding of poverty. In *Development as Freedom*, Sen cites data that show that "even though the per capita income of African Americans in the United States is considerably lower than that of the white population, African Americans are very many times richer in income terms than the people of China or Kerala (even after correcting for cost-of-living differences)" (Sen 1999, 21). And yet "African Americans have an *absolutely* lower chance of reaching mature ages than do people of many third-world societies, such as China, or Sri Lanka, or parts of India (with different arrangements of health care, education, and community relations)" (Sen 1999, 6). Measured by income alone, African Americans would seem to be doing well in comparison to people in most parts of the world. Sen argues that we need to expand the information base to take into account deprivations and various unfreedoms that go beyond one's capacity to buy basic goods needed for survival.

As is well-known, Sen defends a capabilities approach, one that focuses on freedoms to avoid premature mortality, undernourishment, and ill health and to pursue goals and objectives that one has reason to value. Sen uses data on cross cultural differences to argue that we need to pay attention to what people are able to be and to do and not on their incomes alone. He thinks income matters, but argues that poverty is best understood as the deprivation of capabilities. On Sen's account, the absolute measure may tell us that income levels for virtually all Americans are higher than those for people in many parts of the world. But it does not tell us about deprivations and inequalities suffered by some Americans that turn out to be worse than those suffered by people in parts of the world that are taken to be much poorer in terms of levels of income alone.

We can develop this analysis further in ways that Sen does not. An account that uses a relative measure can show why it is worse to live with less in a society where others are much better off than it is to be at a lower standard of living in a society where the wealth is more equally distributed. The injustices are even more apparent in societies where massive amounts of wealth are concentrated in the hands of a few people who seem to be lucky rather than deserving; lucky to be born with talents, for example, that a particular society happens to value and reward. It can then be said that even if the worse off in Florida are better off than the worse off in Cuba in absolute terms of levels of income, there are still good reasons for saying that the worse off in Cuba are better off for not suffering in an inegalitarian society.[1] Larry Temkin argues that the more apparent the inequalities in wealth are to those who are worse off, the more legitimate are their complaints and the stronger the justification for removing the inequalities in wealth or reducing the number of people who have a lot less. But he does not tell us why exactly except to say that this judgment fits with egalitarian intuitions.[2] Sen points out that being unable to avoid premature mortality, to remain healthy, to get an education, and to find work are deprivations that can be as apparent for people in rich countries as they are for people in poor countries. I want to argue that to suffer these deprivations in rich countries where some or many around you do not is also to suffer from low self-respect, a sense of powerlessness, and a lack of solidarity and community with fellow members. These are inequalities that can be revealed through the interpersonal comparisons allowed by relative measures, but they tend to be missed. My key argument is that noticing them requires that we be aware of the perspectives from which the interpersonal comparisons are made.

That we miss these aspects of the effects of inequalities in wealth, become complacent about doing anything about them, or rationalize them points to beliefs central to liberal theory and held by those who are advantaged. I have already discussed libertarian desert and entitlement type arguments that justify inequalities in wealth. I want to turn to a brief discussion of Rawls's version of egalitarianism. It is liberal theory's strongest case for paying attention to and reducing inequalities in wealth because Rawls's theory concentrates on improving the situation of the least well-off. By using Cohen's critique of Rawls as a starting point, I begin to outline how perspectives can reveal what is missing in both the absolute and relative definitions of poverty.

2. Justifications for Inequalities in Wealth

Rawls rejects desert, entitlement, and utilitarian justifications for inequalities in wealth. The difference principle, the second of two principles of justice emerging from the original position, justifies inequalities in wealth but only if they are to the benefit of the least well-off. The gist of Rawls's argument is that inequalities in wealth serve as an incentive for the talented in a society to work harder and produce more than they would if everyone had the same amount of material goods. Moreover, because the rich and talented are motivated to work harder when they have more material goods, they generate the kind of wealth and opportunities that allow everyone to benefit, particularly the least well-off.

UNICEF identifies the incentive argument as at work in American complacency about high levels of poverty: "the supposedly high level of child poverty in the United States might be said to reveal nothing more than the higher degree of income inequality which is what provides the incentives to make the United States what it is — the richest country on earth" (UNICEF 2000, 5). But increasing overall wealth is not how Rawls defends the incentive argument. Even the least generous interpretations of the difference principle show Rawls would certainly not support the inequalities in wealth present in the U.S. or Canada, for example. Rawls uses the position of the least well-off and a preparedness to improve conditions for those in this position as the only justification for inequalities in wealth. Yet, it is far from clear that the incentive argument justifying inequalities in wealth would be supported if the position of the least well-off was indeed represented in the original position. Cohen develops this line of argument in ways that prove useful for presenting my case for the importance of perspectives to an analysis of inequalities in wealth and an adequate understanding of poverty.

Cohen mounts a case against the inequalities in wealth justified by the difference principle on the grounds that it violates a condition of community. To be part of a community, citizens need to be able to provide what Cohen refers to as "comprehensive justifications" (Cohen 1995, 347), justifications that can pass what he calls "the interpersonal test" and stand as justified when uttered by any member of society to any other member. Cohen argues that the incentive argument seems reasonable when it is uttered in statements that take the following third-person form: "because the talented rich will not work as hard if they do not have incentives such as greater wealth, everyone will be made worse off ". However, the incentive argument cannot serve as a comprehensive justification for inequality when it is uttered by the talented rich in first-person interpersonal statements that take the following form: "because I, a talented rich person, will not work as hard unless I have incentives such as greater wealth, you, the poor, will be worse off ". On the lips of the talented rich and presented to the poor, the incentive argument fails to explain why the talented rich will not work as hard and thereby worsen the condition of the less well-off unless there are inequalities in wealth. In Cohen's words, the incentive "argument is generally presented in thoroughly third-personal terms and, relatedly, as though no question arises about the attitudes and choices of the rich people it mentions. When, by contrast, we imagine a talented rich person himself affirming the argument, the background issues of equality and obligation come clearly into view, and, if I am right, the rich are revealed to be out of community with the poor in respect of the economic dimension of their lives" (Cohen 1995, 354).

It seems clear to the rich and talented that inequalities in wealth are necessary because from their point of view they act as incentives. It is less clear, however, that the least well-off perceive things in the same way. Cohen hints at this objection when he tries out the following justificatory move by a rich person to a poor person: "'if you were in our shoes you would feel the same way'" (Cohen 1995, 369). The reply he imagines a poor person could give hints at the significance of perspectives: "'[n]either of us really knows how I would behave. Not all rich people market maximize as a matter of course, and I hope that, if I were rich, I would not belong to the vast majority that do, *especially if I retained a lively sense of what it is like to be in the condition I am now actually in*'" (Cohen 1995, 370, my emphasis). Having a lively sense of what it is like to be poor provides a perspective on incentives that may differ from that held by those who are rich and talented. From the perspective of the poor, that the rich and talented need or want greater wealth indicates that they are more likely to be motivated by self-interest, greed, or market maximization than by a sense of justice or fellow feeling for community members. These motivations are evident in our own context where an ethos of market maximization has many rich people experience tax measures that redistribute wealth as coercive rather than just and fair.

In *Perspectives on Equality*, I argue that the perspectives of members of various disadvantaged groups can provide valuable insights into kinds of inequality and the structures that perpetuate them (Koggel 1998). Being poor is likely to give one a different perspective on a structure that assumes inequalities in wealth are necessary or just. Living in a society in which these assumptions are made and inequalities in wealth are not only taken to be inevitable but just makes it prudent for those who are poor to accept the way things are. But this acceptance comes with costs that are more readily recognized by those who live in poverty. Cohen argues that the poor are out of community with respect to the economic dimension of their lives. I would argue that they are out of community in a broader sense than with respect to inequalities in material goods alone. In our society, there are no means such as Cohen's interpersonal test for those who are poor to voice their objections, demand justifications, or even to be heard. Furthermore, prevalent beliefs that being poor or living on welfare means one is "lazy," "taking handouts," "unwilling to work," "mismanaging someone else's hard earned money" or "free loading" result in the kind of powerlessness that makes what people say about their conditions or about the structures that perpetuate them appear to be irrelevant or even wrongheaded. Moreover, when stereotypes are internalized in ways that destroy self-respect, they can create the kind of self-doubt that silences those living in poverty altogether. As Jean Harvey points out, "the individual is wrongly convinced that, being unemployed and desperately poor, he is socially 'unimportant' and has no right to address 'important' people — like famous politicians discussing welfare cuts — and 'take up their valuable time' by trying to give accurate information on what inescapable poverty involves" (Harvey 1999, 112–113).

Earlier, I argued that relative measures that make use of interpersonal comparisons are important. We can now understand why it is important to reveal who does the judging about the inequalities and who has the power to set policies for addressing them. This aspect of what it means to make comparisons is obvious, but easily missed. Comparisons always take for granted a particular perspective from which judgments of inequality are made. When the perspectives assumed and reflected in norms, standards, and practices are those of the advantaged, various inequalities suffered by those who are poor and disadvantaged are made invisible or ignored. On my account, the perspectives of the disadvantaged are valuable vantage points for revealing these inequalities. Moreover, on my account, perspectives put a face on poverty. They reveal who is poor, who is likely to be poor, what poverty does to people, and why generalized policies that treat all poor people as the same will not work.

Let us now return to the stereotypes discussed earlier to highlight the positive role that perspectives can play in an understanding of poverty and how to address it. Those living in poverty or on welfare are perceived as "taking easy handouts," "lazy," or "in a rut of dependency." They are not perceived as full members of the community who have managed to make it on their own by using their talents, working hard, managing their finances well, and contributing to the wealth of the country. In fact, they are vulnerable to judgments about being responsible for their state of affairs. This is not to say that these descriptions do not fit some people who are poor. However, an account that takes perspectives seriously holds that we cannot make general statements about responsibility, laziness, or even lack of contribution to a society until we know a lot more about the particularities of people's lives from their perspectives. Nor are we justified in implementing welfare policies without this knowledge about the people involved and the details of their lives. For example, it is relevant to an analysis of justice to learn that statistics show a strong correlation between those who are living in poverty and those who are members of particular groups: women, disabled people, and people of color. It is difficult to explain or justify their greater representation in the ranks of the poor based on beliefs that all members of traditionally disadvantaged groups deserve less by way of material and social goods or just do not have capabilities that allow them to compete for or obtain material and social goods.

Learning about these inequalities based on factors such as gender, race, class, and disability undermines the legitimacy of current and fashionable policies of cuts to welfare or of forcing people to pass stringent tests in order to have their basic needs met. Three examples will help to elucidate these points about the importance of perspectives for revealing and challenging norms, beliefs, and policies. To qualify for welfare, the single mother who needs to prove that she cannot "work," when she considers child rearing to be valuable work, is forced to accept these norms about the meaning of work and to reject her own priorities and values regarding children. If the income she gets through welfare cannot cover the cost of childcare or job training, she often becomes trapped in a cycle of poverty: unable to get a job because she cannot afford childcare or without access to job training and thus dependent on the (often restricted) income from the state. People with disabilities can more easily "prove" that they cannot "work," but getting a fixed income determined as sufficient for meeting the basic needs of an able bodied person will not address the specific needs of being unable to use public transportation or get into workplaces or pay for expensive medical devices and treatment above what an income for basic goods can provide. Lastly, the combination of low minimum wages and high costs of living make it virtually impossible for the working poor to pay for food and shelter even when they do double shifts of day and night work. These facts about the lives of the working poor and from the perspectives of those living them is made vivid in *Nickel and Dimed*, where reporter Barbara Ehrenreich lived the life of the working poor and in the process discovered the hardships and uncovered the myths (Ehrenreich 2001). The result in all three cases of knowing the details of actual lives and of kinds of people who are poor undermines stereotypes of the poor as lazy, taking easy handouts, or unknowledgeable about spending money. It also challenges the current trend of cutting or reducing welfare.

In all these examples, listening to and learning from people most directly affected by low income or welfare policies can teach politicians and ordinary citizens that certain policies have detrimental effects not only on income, opportunities, well-being, or life-prospects, but also on levels of self respect and power for individuals, for members of disadvantaged groups, and for whole communities. Self-respect is undermined when members of a community have their freedom to satisfy basic human needs and pursue what they value restricted on a number of fronts and in a variety of ways. Self-respect is also undermined when members of a community do not have conditions that support and respect their attempts to be considered and to contribute to and participate in the very social and political institutions that shape the kinds of lives they can lead. Finally, and most importantly, perceptions and self-perceptions of diminished self-respect reduce and often eliminate the power that the poor have to suggest policies or implement change.

Responsible learning of perspectives is needed for understanding inequalities of various kinds and for devising policies for eliminating them. Making perspectives relevant underscores the importance of accountability to oneself, to others, and to the community as a whole for an adequate account of poverty and for shaping policies to address it. While relative measures have the important feature of allowing interpersonal comparisons, comparisons and judgments need to be free of contaminating biases and stereotypes that reflect and entrench beliefs about poverty and what is justified or acceptable by way of inequalities in wealth. Poverty is not only about living at or below the level of subsistence. It is also about how people are treated and how they regard themselves. It is about issues of powerlessness, loss of dignity and respect, and exclusion from one's community and meaningful participation in it. Perspectives provide concrete details about the kind of lives that are invisible in definitions of poverty and in the numbers that these definitions produce. In fact, reliance on absolute measures that define and identify who is poor can work to reinforce both the stereotypes of people who are poor and the moral judgments that are attached to these stereotypes.

Taking perspectives seriously allows us to confront stereotypes and to learn how particular structures restrict one's capacity to meet basic needs and to make choices that improve life prospects for oneself and future generations. This approach that defends the role of perspectives to an understanding of poverty is all the more important in a world that reflects the rise of multinational corporations, international financial institutions, and world trade organizations and the power they have to shape relationships of inequality and powerlessness in various locations. Responsible learning of poverty and its effects on people situated in contexts very different from our own will be difficult. At this juncture in world history, the work of development ethicists and postcolonial feminists who explore issues of if, when, and how it is appropriate for rich Western nations and individuals in them to make judgments about the policies and practices in Third World countries becomes increasingly important.

3. Globalization and Inequalities in Wealth

Features of economic globalization have magnified relationships of power between countries that are rich and poor in ways that perpetuate inequalities in wealth and shape its effects on people. Economic globalization has meant that capital and corporations can move easily across borders in ways that allow multinational corporations to utilize labor markets in particular ways in specific Third World countries to maximize profits. Economic globalization makes it possible for commodities consumed by people in rich countries to be manufactured by forced child labor or for starvation wages in poor countries where there are no worker rights of health and safety protection and where union organizing is actively discouraged. Moreover, Third World countries that have little or no environmental protection legislation can have their resources degraded and depleted by those same corporations that accumulate vast amounts of wealth. If citizens of a country protest, multinational corporations can easily move to more politically stable investment zones, thereby putting pressure on governments of poor countries to squelch the citizen protest within their own borders.

There is no question that multinational corporations have had a positive effect on individual lives and communities as a whole. They have provided job opportunities, increased household income and national wealth, and decreased unemployment rates. An approach that takes perspectives seriously warns that measuring increases in income levels or providing generalized interpersonal comparisons do not give us the full picture of the inequalities that remain or are created by the changed conditions. We need to be aware of the ways in which opportunities can be enhanced in some domains, such as providing jobs where none existed before, at the same time as opportunities in other domains, such as having a say about work and living conditions or being able to care for children, can be reduced. Moreover, there are many factors, both local and global, that are relevant to inequalities, some that may be alle-

viated in particular locations or in specific areas of a person's life and others that are created or exacerbated in particular locations and domains. As examples, global corporate
employers often utilize specific sectors and features of labor markets in Third World countries to the detriment of groups already disadvantaged. Changing local factors can generate
further disadvantage when, for example, government policies are dictated by trade agreements, or a falling currency, or unemployment rates, or the exit of global corporations into
more profitable locations. Other local factors such as discrimination of ethnic minorities or
of members of particular groups can also determine who gets to work, what kind of work
they get to do, and whether they can be active participants in their communities. Providing
details of places, practices, policies, and people is central to a full understanding of inequalities in wealth and power that are created and perpetuated in the global context.

Feminist postcolonial theory is useful for telling us why an account of poverty needs to
uncover the ways in which power at the global level of multinational corporations and financial institutions intersects with and utilizes power at the local level of beliefs, practices, and
traditions.[3] In the process of providing this context specific and detailed analysis, we uncover the ways in which local understandings of gender, race, caste, and disability, for example,
are often employed by global corporations in ways that perpetuate inequalities in some
domains or create new ones in specific locations. This kind of analysis reveals the ways in
which forces of power at the global level sometimes intersect with, sometimes utilize, sometimes destabilize, and sometimes intensify relations of power at the local level and always in
diverse and complicated ways. We need this information for devising effective policies for
addressing power imbalances created by ever growing gaps in wealth within and between
rich and poor countries.

Chandra Mohanty's work exemplifies this strategy of emphasizing the importance of the
overarching factor of economic globalization *and* paying attention to its specific manifestation at local levels where members of disadvantaged groups are affected in varied ways and
both positively and negatively. Mohanty argues that we need to know about the ways in
which factors of race, class, and ethnicity intersect with and also reflect, shape, and sustain
relations of power in specific contexts. Mohanty uses examples of women's work to highlight the importance of providing detailed descriptions of the concrete realities of the lives
of working women in specific social contexts (Mohanty 1997). This sort of account takes
women's experiences as told in narratives and manifested in grassroots activities and sites of
resistance to be central to shaping policy. A contextual and perspectival approach broadens
the information base for evaluating poverty by highlighting how global forces of power
shape features of poverty differently for different people and in different places. Perhaps
more importantly, the enriched understanding of poverty gained from taking perspectives
seriously is vital for conceiving people as agents who in forming coalitions at local and global levels can devise effective policies for alleviating the specific effects of poverty in their
own locations.

In this paper I have defended the importance of the interpersonal comparisons endorsed
by relative measures because they expand an understanding of poverty as being about more
than having a low income. I have argued for expanding the analysis of poverty yet further by
acknowledging the relevance of perspectives for capturing what generalized interpersonal
comparisons can and often exclude. An approach that makes perspectives central to the
analysis tells us that generalizations captured by data, whether of income levels or deprivations in health, education, and opportunities do not reveal the whole story of poverty as experienced by people in rich countries or in contexts of varied beliefs, practices, customs, and

colonial histories and traditions. It also does not tell us how overarching features of economic globalization impact on and affect the lives of specific people in diverse ways in different places. To devise policies for addressing poverty in our context of economic globalization, we need this detail of context, lives, and experiences that a perspectival approach can provide. Ignoring the relevance of perspectives in information gathering risks the further entrenchment of assumptions, biases, and stereotypes that reflect the norms and practices of the dominant and powerful. In a global context of increasing gaps between the rich and the poor both within and across borders, ignoring perspectives also risks the further entrenchment of relationships of power that silence and exclude those who are poor from full membership in their own communities and from meaningful participation in global discourse and protest about the course of economic globalization.

The kinds of inequalities that put the poor out of community with the rich are not limited to the economic inequalities on which liberal theory has tended to focus or even on a set of capability deprivations that the poor suffer in relation to the rich. In a global context of entrenched expectations that inequalities in wealth are necessary and assumptions that they are just, other inequalities such as diminished self-respect and dignity and lack of power to affect change are difficult to perceive let alone address. Katz writes: "Even in the language of social science, as well as in ordinary conversation and political rhetoric, poor people usually remain outsiders, strangers to be pitied or despised, helped or punished, ignored or studied, but rarely full citizens, members of a larger community on the same terms as the rest of us" (Katz 1989, 167). I have argued that taking perspectives seriously brings people and the details of their lives into sharp focus. I have also argued that this strategy that works to uncover dominant norms and upset relations of power is increasingly important in our context of economic globalization.

NOTES

1. I am grateful to Samantha Brennan for providing this example of how relative measures matter. Contrary to Rawls's assumption that it is not rational for those who are less well off to envy those who are better off, this account suggests that one is and indeed should be "downcast by the knowledge or perception that others have a larger index of primary social goods" (Rawls, 1971, 143).
2. Temkin defends an individualist (Temkin 1993, 281) and comparative (Temkin 1993, 33) account of egalitarianism that allows judgments about better and worse inequalities to emerge from comparing the situations of individuals with respect to other individuals. Temkin argues that his account does not provide a precise or complete set of judgments, yet there are some general judgments about inequalities that emerge from intuitions that he takes to be fairly universal and firm: the more apparent the inequalities in wealth and the greater the number of those who are worse off in comparison to those who are well off, the worse the inequality.
3. Some examples of this work are contained in Alexander, M. Jaqui and Mohanty, Chandra, eds., *Feminist Genealogies, Colonial Legacies, Democratic Futures* (New York: Routledge, 1997); and Narayan, Uma and Sandra Harding, eds., *Decentering the Center: Philosophy for a Multicultural, Postcolonial, and Feminist World* (Bloomington: Indiana University Press, 2000).

BIBLIOGRAPHY

Alexander, M. Jaqui and Mohanty, Chandra, eds. 1997. *Feminist Genealogies, Colonial Legacies, Democratic Futures*. New York: Routledge.

Cohen, G. A. 2000. *If You're an Egalitarian, How Come You're So Rich?* Cambridge, MA: Harvard University Press.

——. 1995. "Incentives, Inequality, and Community." In *Equal Freedom: Selected Tanner Lectures on Human Values*, ed. Stephen Darwall, pp. 331-397. Ann Arbor: University of Michigan Press.

Ehrenreich, Barbara. 2001. *Nickel and Dimed: On (Not) Getting By in America*. New York: Henry Holt.

Harvey, Jean. 1999. *Civilized Oppression*. Lanham, MD: Rowman & Littlefield.

Jones, John D. 1986-87. "Poverty as a Living Death: Toward a Phenomenology of Skid Row". *Philosophy Research Archives*, v. XII.

Katz, Michael B. 1989. *The Undeserving Poor: From the War on Poverty to the War on Welfare*. New York: Pantheon.

Kerstetter, Steve. 2002. *Rags and Riches: Wealth Inequality in Canada*. Vancouver: Canadian Centre for Policy Alternatives.

Koggel, Christine M. 2003. "Globalization and Women's Paid Work: Expanding Freedom?" *Feminist Economics, Special Issue on the Ideas and Work of Amartya Sen*. Volume 9, no. 2.

—— . 2003. "Equality Analysis in a Global Context: A Relational Approach." *Feminist Moral Philosophy*, edited by Samantha Brennan. *Canadian Journal of Philosophy*. Supplementary Volume, no. 28.

—— . 1998. *Perspectives on Equality: Constructing a Relational Theory*. Lanham. MD: Rowman & Littlefield.

Mohanty, Chandra. 1988. "Under Western Eyes: Feminist Scholarship and Colonial Discourses." *Feminist Review* 30: 61-88.

—— . 1997. "Women Workers and Capitalist Scripts: Ideologies of Domination, Common Interests, and the Politics of Solidarity." In *Feminist Genealogies, Colonial Legacies, Democratic Futures*, ed. M. J. Alexander and C. Mohanty, pp. 3-29. New York: Routledge.

Narayan, Uma and Sandra Harding, eds. 2000. *Decentering the Center: Philosophy for a Multicultural, Postcolonial, and Feminist World*. Bloomington: Indiana University Press.

Rawls, John. 1971. *A Theory of Justice*. Cambridge, MA: Harvard University Press.

Sen, Amartya. 1999. *Development as Freedom*. New York: Anchor Books.

—— . 1992. *Inequality Reexamined*. Cambridge, MA: Harvard University Press.

Temkin, Larry S. 1993. *Inequality*. New York: Oxford University Press.

United Nations. 2000. *We the Peoples: The Role of the United Nations in the 21st Century*. New York: Department of Public Information.

United Nations Children's Fund. 1999. *Child Poverty Across Industrialized Nations*. Florence: UNICEF.

—— . 2000. *A League Table of Child Poverty in Rich Nations*. Florence: UNICEF.

United Nations Development Program. 2001. *Human Development Report 2001*. New York: Oxford University Press.

——-——. 1999. *Human Development Report 1999*. New York: Oxford University Press.

United Nations Population Fund. 2000. *The State of World Population 2000*. UNPF.

QUESTIONS

1. What is the absolute definition of poverty? What is the relative definition? According to Christine Koggel, why do definitions matter to an understanding of poverty?

2. What are some of the traditional liberal arguments against social welfare policies surveyed by Koggel? Do you find them convincing? Why or why not?

3. John Rawls argues that inequalities in wealth are justified only if they are to the benefit of the least well-off. What is his argument for this account of what justice demands? Would his account of what justice demands radically change the distribution of wealth in our society?

4. What is G.A. Cohen's critique of Rawls's justification for inequalities in wealth? Do you find it convincing?

5. Koggel argues that Cohen's critique of Rawls can be further expanded to highlight the role of perspectives in an account of inequalities in wealth. What can perspectives reveal with respect to understanding poverty and devising policies for eliminating it?

6. Koggel suggests that perspectives can play a role in an account of poverty in our global context of the power of multinational corporations and their increasing presence in developing countries. Do you agree? How does this differ from Bruce Porter's analysis in the previous reading and Amartya Sen's in the reading that follows?

PROPERTY AND HUNGER

Amartya Sen

In an interesting letter to Anna George, the daughter of Henry George, Bernard Shaw wrote: "Your father found me a literary dilettante and militant rationalist in religion, and a barren rascal at that. By turning my mind to economics he made a man of me." I am not able to determine what making a man of Bernard Shaw would exactly consist of, but it is clear that the kind of moral and social problems with which Shaw was deeply concerned could not be sensibly pursued without examining their economic aspects. For example, the claims of property rights, which some would defend and some (including Shaw) would dispute, are not just matters of basic moral belief that could not possibly be influenced one way or the other by any empirical arguments. They call for sensitive moral analysis responsive to empirical realities, including economic ones.

Moral claims based on intrinsically valuable rights are often used in political and social arguments. Rights related to ownership have been invoked for ages. But there are also other types of rights which have been seen as "inherent and inalienable," and the American Declaration of Independence refers to "certain unalienable rights," among which are "life, liberty and the pursuit of happiness." The Indian constitution talks even of "the right to an adequate means of livelihood." The "right not to be hungry" has often been invoked in recent discussions on the obligation to help the famished.

Rights: Instruments, Constraints, or Goals?

Rights can be taken to be morally important in three different ways. First, they can be considered to be valuable *instruments* to achieve other goals. This is the "instrumental view," and is well illustrated by the utilitarian approach to rights. Rights are, in that view, of no intrinsic importance. Violation of rights is not in itself a bad thing, nor fulfillment intrinsically good. But the acceptance of rights promotes, in this view, things that are ultimately important, to wit, utility. Jeremy Bentham rejected "natural rights" as "simple nonsense," and "natural and imprescriptible rights" as "rhetorical nonsense, nonsense upon stilts." But he attached great importance to rights as instruments valuable to the promotion of a good society, and devoted much energy to the attempt to reform appropriately the actual system of rights.

The second view may be called the "constraint view," and it takes the form of seeing rights as *constraints* on what others can or cannot do. In this view rights are intrinsically

From Economics and Philosophy, *v. 4 (1998), pp. 57–68. Reprinted by permission of Amartya Sen and Cambridge University Press.*

important. However, they don't figure in moral accounting as goals to be generally promoted, but only as constraints that others must obey. As Robert Nozick has put it in a powerful exposition of this "constraint view": "Individuals have rights, and there are things no person or group may do to them (without violating their rights)." Rights "set the constraints within which a social choice is made, by excluding certain alternatives, fixing others, and so on."

The third approach is to see fulfillments of rights as goals to be pursued. This "goal view" differs from the instrumental view in regarding rights to be intrinsically important, and it differs from the constraint view in seeing the fulfillment of rights as goals to be generally promoted, rather than taking them as demanding only (and exactly) that we refrain from violating the rights of others. In the "constraint view" there is no duty to help anyone with his or her rights (merely not to hinder), and also in the "instrumental view" there is no duty, in fact, to help unless the right fulfillment will also promote some other goal such as utility. The "goal view" integrates the valuation of rights — their fulfillment and violation — in overall moral accounting and yields a wider sphere of influence of rights in morality.

I have argued elsewhere that the goal view has advantages that the other two approaches do not share, in particular, the ability to accommodate integrated moral accounting including inter alia the intrinsic importance of a class of fundamental rights. I shall not repeat that argument here. But there is an interesting question, of dual roles of rights in the sense that some rights may be *both* intrinsically important and instrumentally valuable. For example, the right to be free from hunger could — not implausibly — be regarded as being valuable in itself as well as serving as a good instrument to promote other goals such as security, longevity or utility. If so, both the goal view and the instrumental view would have to be simultaneously deployed to get a comprehensive assessment of such a right. This problem of comprehensiveness is a particularly important issue in the context of Henry George's discussion of rights, since he gave many rights significant dual roles.

The instrumental aspect is an inescapable feature of every right, since irrespective of whether a certain right is intrinsically valuable or not, its acceptance will certainly have other consequences as well, and these, too, have to be assessed along with the intrinsic value of rights (if any). A right that is regarded as quite valuable in itself may nevertheless be judged to be morally rejectable if it leads to disastrous consequences. This is a case of the rights playing a *negative* instrumental role. It is, of course, also possible that the instrumental argument will *bolster* the intrinsic claims of a right to be taken seriously. I shall presently argue that such is the case in George's analysis with the right of labor to its produce.

There are two general conclusions to draw, at this stage, from this very preliminary discussion. First, we must distinguish between (1) the intrinsic value of a right, and (2) the overall value of a right taking note inter alia of its intrinsic importance (if any). The acceptance of the intrinsic importance of any right is no guarantee that its overall moral valuation must be favorable. Second, no moral assessment of a right can be independent of its likely consequences. The need for empirical assessment of the effects of accepting any right cannot be escaped. Empirical arguments are quite central to moral philosophy.

Property and Deprivation

The right to hold, use and bequeath property that one has legitimately acquired is often taken to be inherently valuable. In fact, however, many of its defenses seem to be actually of the instrumental type, e.g., arguing that property rights make people more free to choose one kind of a life rather than another. Even the traditional attempt at founding "natural property rights" on the principles of "natural liberty" (with or without John Locke's proviso) has some instrumental features. But even if we do accept that property rights may have some intrinsic value, this does not in any way amount to an overall justification of property rights, since property rights may have consequences which themselves will require assessment. Indeed, the causation of hunger as well as its prevention may materially depend on how property rights are structured. If a set of property rights leads, say, to starvation, as it well might, then the moral approval of these rights would certainly be compromised severely. In general, the need for consequential analysis of property rights is inescapable whether or not such rights are seen as having any intrinsic value.

Consider Henry George's formula of giving "the product to the producer." This is, of course, an ambiguous rule, since the division of the credits for production to different causal influences (e.g., according to "marginal productivities" in neoclassical theory, or according to human efforts in classical labor theory) is inevitably somewhat arbitrary, and full of problems involving internal tensions. But no matter how the ambiguities are resolved, it is clear that this rule would give no part of the socially produced output to one who is unemployed since he or she is producing nothing. Also, a person whose productive contribution happens to be tiny, according to *whichever* procedure of such accounting we use, can expect to get very little based on this so-called "natural law." Thus, hunger and starvation are compatible with this system of rights. George thought that this would not occur, since the economic reforms he proposed (including the abolition of land rights) would eliminate unemployment, and provision for the disabled would be made through the sympathetic support of others. These are empirical matters. If these empirical generalizations do not hold, then the outlined system of rights would yield a serious conflict. The property rights to one's product (however defined) might be of some intrinsic moral importance, but we clearly must also take note of the moral disvalue of human misery (such as suffering due to hunger and nutrition-related diseases). The latter could very plausibly be seen as having more moral force than the former. A positive intrinsic value of the right to one's product can go with an overall negative value, taking everything into account.

I have tried to argue elsewhere — not in the context of disputing these moral theories but in trying to understand the causation of famines in the modern world — that famines are, in fact, best explained in terms of failures of entitlement systems. The entitlements here refer, of course, to legal rights and to practical possibilities, rather than to moral status, but the laws and actual operation of private ownership economies have many features in common with the moral system of entitlements analyzed by Nozick and others.

The entitlement approach to famines need not, of course, be confined to private ownership economies, and entitlement failures of other systems can also be fruitfully studied to examine famines and hunger. In the specific context of private ownership economies, the entitlements are substantially analyzable in terms, respectively, of what may be called "endowments" and "exchange entitlements." A person's endowment refers to what he or she initially owns (including the person's own labor power), and the exchange entitlement mapping tells us what the person can obtain through exchanging what he or she owns, either by production (exchange with nature), or by trade (exchange with others), or a mixture of the two. A person has to starve if neither the endowments, nor what can be obtained through exchange, yields an adequate amount of food.

If starvation and hunger are seen in terms of failures of entitlements, then it becomes immediately clear that the total availability of food in a country is only one of several variables that are relevant. Many famines occur without any decline in the availability of food.

For example, in the Great Bengal famine of 1943, the total food availability in Bengal was not particularly bad (considerably higher than two years earlier when there was no famine), and yet three million people died, in a famine mainly affecting the rural areas, through rather violent shifts in the relative purchasing powers of different groups, hitting the rural laborers the hardest. The Ethiopian famine of 1973 took place in a year of average per capita food availability, but the cultivators and other occupation groups in the province of Wollo had lost their means of subsistence (through loss of crops and a decline of economic activity, related to a local drought) and had no means of commanding food from elsewhere in the country. Indeed, some food moved *out* of Wollo to more prosperous people in other parts of Ethiopia, repeating a pattern of contrary movement of food that was widely observed during the Irish famines of the 1840s (with food moving out of famine-stricken Ireland to prosperous England which had greater power in the battle for entitlements). The Bangladesh famine of 1974 took place in a year of *peak* food availability, but several occupation groups had lost their entitlement to food through loss of employment and other economic changes (including inflationary pressures causing prices to outrun wages). Other examples of famines without significant (or any) decline in food availability can be found, and there is nothing particularly surprising about this fact once it is recognized that the availability of food is only one influence among many on the entitlement of each occupation group. Even when a famine *is* associated with a decline of food availability, the entitlement changes have to be studied to understand the particular nature of the famine, e.g., why one occupation group is hit but not another. The causation of starvation can be sensibly sought in failures of entitlements of the respective groups.

The causal analysis of famines in terms of entitlements also points to possible public policies of prevention. The main economic strategy would have to take the form of increasing the entitlements of the deprived groups, and in general, of guaranteeing minimum entitlements for everyone, paying particular attention to the vulnerable groups. This can, in the long run, be done in many different ways, involving both economic growth (including growth of food output) and distributional adjustments. Some of these policies may, however, require that the property rights and the corresponding entitlements of the more prosperous groups be violated. The problem, in fact, is particularly acute in the short run, since it may not be possible to engineer rapid economic growth instantly. Then the burden of raising entitlements of the groups in distress would largely have to fall on reducing the entitlements of others more favorably placed. Transfers of income or commodities through various public policies may well be effective in quashing a famine (as the experience of famine relief in different countries has shown), but it may require substantial government intervention in the entitlements of the more prosperous groups.

There is, however, no great moral dilemma in this if property rights are treated as purely *instrumental*. If the goals of relief of hunger and poverty are sufficiently powerful, then it would be just right to violate whatever property rights come in the way, since — in this view — property rights have no intrinsic status. On the other hand, if property rights are taken to be morally inviolable irrespective of their consequences, then it will follow that these policies cannot be morally acceptable even though they might save thousands, or even millions, from dying. The inflexible moral "constraint" of respecting people's legitimately acquired entitlements would rule out such policies.

In fact this type of problem presents a reductio ad absurdum of the moral validity of constraint-based entitlement systems. However, while the conclusions to be derived from that approach might well be "absurd," the situation postulated is not an imaginary one at all. It is based on studies of actual famines and the role of entitlement failures in the causation of mass starvation. If there is an embarrassment here, it belongs solidly to the consequence-independent way of seeing rights.

I should add that this dilemma does not arise from regarding property rights to be of intrinsic value, which can be criticized on other grounds, but not this one. Even if property rights *are* of intrinsic value, their violation may be justified on grounds of the favorable consequences of that violation. A right, as was mentioned earlier, may be intrinsically valuable and still be justly violated taking everything into account. The "absurdum" does not belong to attaching intrinsic value to property rights, but to regarding these rights as simply acceptable, regardless of their consequences. A moral system that values both property rights and other goals — such as avoiding famines and starvation, or fulfilling people's right not to be hungry — can, on the one hand, give property rights intrinsic importance, and on the other, recommend the violation of property rights when that leads to better overall consequences (*including* the disvalue of rights violation).

The issue here is not the valuing of property rights, but their alleged inviolability. There is no dilemma here either for the purely instrumental view of property rights or for treating the fulfillment of property rights as one goal among many, but specifically for consequence-independent assertions of property rights and for the corresponding constraint-based approaches to moral entitlement of ownership.

That property and hunger are closely related cannot possibly come as a great surprise. Hunger is primarily associated with not owning enough food and thus property rights over food are immediately and directly involved. Fights over that property right can be a major part of the reality of a poor country, and any system of moral assessment has to take note of that phenomenon. The tendency to see hunger in purely technocratic terms of food output and availability may help to hide the crucial role of entitlements in the genesis of hunger, but a fuller economic analysis cannot overlook that crucial role. Since property rights over food are derived from property rights over other goods and resources (through production and trade), the entire system of rights of acquisition and transfer is implicated in the emergence and survival of hunger and starvation.

The Right Not to Be Hungry

Property rights have been championed for a long time. In contrast, the assertion of "the right not to be hungry" is a comparatively recent phenomenon. While this right is much invoked in political debates, there is a good deal of skepticism about treating this as truly a right in any substantial way. It is often asserted that this concept of "right not to be hungry" stands essentially for nothing at all ("simple nonsense," as Bentham called "natural rights" in general). That piece of sophisticated cynicism reveals not so much a penetrating insight into the practical affairs of the world, but a refusal to investigate what people mean when they assert the existence of rights that, for the bulk of humanity, are not in fact guaranteed by the existing institutional arrangements.

The right not to be hungry is not asserted as a recognition of an institutional right that already exists, as the right to property typically is. The assertion is primarily a moral claim as to what should be valued, and what institutional structure we should aim for, and try to guarantee if feasible. It can also be seen in terms of Ronald Dworkin's category of "background rights" — rights that provide a justification for political decisions by society in abstract. This interpretation serves as the basis for a reason to change the existing institutional structure and state policy.

It is broadly in this form that the right to "an adequate means of livelihood" is referred to in the Constitution of India: "The state shall, in particular, direct its policy towards securing . . . that the citizens, men and women equally, have the right to an adequate means of livelihood." This does not, of course, offer to each citizen a guaranteed right to an adequate livelihood, but the state is asked to take steps such that this right could become realizable for all.

In fact, this right has often been invoked in political debates in India. The electoral politics of India does indeed give particular scope for such use of what are seen as background rights. It is, of course, not altogether clear whether the reference to this right in the Indian constitution has in fact materially influenced the political debates. The constitutional statement is often cited, but very likely this issue would have figured in any case in these debates, given the nature of the moral and political concern. But whatever the constitutional contribution, it is interesting to ask whether the implicit acceptance of the value of the right to freedom from hunger makes any difference to actual policy.

It can be argued that the general acceptance of the right of freedom from acute hunger as a major goal has played quite a substantial role in preventing famines in India. The last real famine in India was in 1943, and while food availability per head in India has risen only rather slowly (even now the food availability per head is no higher than in many sub-Saharan countries stricken by recurrent famines), the country has not experienced any famine since independence in 1947. The main cause of that success is a policy of public intervention. Whenever a famine has threatened (e.g., in Bihar in 1967–68, in Maharashtra in 1971–73, in West Bengal in 1978–79), a public policy of intervention and relief has offered minimum entitlements to the potential famine victims, and thus have the threatening famines been averted. It can be argued that the quickness of the response of the respective governments (both state and central) reflects a political necessity, given the Indian electoral system and the importance attached by the public to the prevention of starvation. Political pressures from opposition groups and the news media have kept the respective governments on their toes, and the right to be free from acute hunger and starvation has been achieved largely because it has been seen as a valuable right. Thus the recognition of the intrinsic moral importance of this right, which has been widely invoked in public discussions, has served as a powerful political instrument as well.

On the other hand, this process has been far from effective in tackling pervasive and persistent undernourishment in India. There has been no famine in post-independence India, but perhaps a third of India's rural population is perennially undernourished. So long as hunger remains non-acute and starvation deaths are avoided (even though morbidity and mortality rates are enhanced by undernourishment), the need for a policy response is neither much discussed by the news media, nor forcefully demanded even by opposition parties. The elimination of famines coexists with the survival of widespread "regular hunger." The right to "adequate means" of *nourishment* does not at all seem to arouse political concern in a way that the right to "adequate means" to *avoid starvation* does.

The contrast can be due to one of several different reasons. It could, of course, simply be that the ability to avoid undernourishment is not socially accepted as very important. This could be so, though what is socially accepted and what is not is also partly a matter of how clearly the questions are posed. It is, in fact, quite possible that the freedom in question would be regarded as a morally important right if the question were posed in a transparent way, but this does not happen because of the nature of Indian electoral politics and that of news coverage. The issue is certainly not "dramatic" in the way in which starvation deaths and threatening famines are. Continued low-key misery may be too familiar a phenomenon to make it worthwhile for political leaders to get some mileage out of it in practical politics. The news media may also find little profit in emphasizing a non-spectacular phenomenon — the quiet survival of disciplined, non-acute hunger.

If this is indeed the case, then the implications for action of the goal of eliminating hunger, or guaranteeing to all the means for achieving this, may be quite complex. The political case for making the quiet hunger less quiet and more troublesome for governments in power is certainly relevant. Aggressive political journalism might prove to have an instrumental moral value if it were able to go beyond reporting the horrors of visible starvation and to portray the pervasive, non-acute hunger in a more dramatic and telling way. This is obviously not the place to discuss the instrumentalities of practical politics, but the endorsement of the moral right to be free from hunger — both acute and non-acute — would in fact raise pointed questions about the means which might be used to pursue such a goal.

Moral Assessment and Social Relations

. . . If there is one thing that emerges sharply from the discussion I have tried to present in this paper, it is the importance of factual analysis for moral assessment, including moral scrutiny of the acceptability and pursuit of specific rights. This is so even when the right in question is acknowledged to have intrinsic moral value, since valuing a right is not the same thing as accepting it. To affirm acceptability independently of consequences can be peculiarly untenable, as was discussed in analyzing entitlements and hunger. In assessing the claims of property rights, of the right not to be hungry, the examination cannot be confined to issues of basic valuation only, and much of the challenge of assessment lies in the empirical analysis of causes and effects. In the world in which we live — full of hunger as well as wealth — these empirical investigations can be both complex and quite extraordinarily important. The big moral questions are frequently also deeply economic, social, or political.

QUESTIONS

1. What is the difference between rights seen as instruments, rights seen as constraints, and rights seen as goals? Which of these three accounts of the nature of rights does Amartya Sen advocate?
2. Sen argues that hunger is typically the result of an inadequate distribution of entitlements rather than an inadequate supply of food. Explain his views in this regard.
3. What is a property right? What bearing do property rights have on the problem of hunger?
4. In Sen's view, which should take priority, property rights or what he describes as the moral disvalue of human misery?
5. Sen concludes that "if there is one thing that emerges sharply from the discussion I have tried to present in this paper, it is the importance of factual analysis for moral assessment." What leads him to this conclusion? Do you agree?

SUGGESTIONS FOR FURTHER READING

As Amartya Sen points out in his contribution to this chapter, facts are of crucial importance in building a critical understanding of an issue such as poverty. The facts about poverty, however, are constantly being updated. What is needed to keep abreast of current information is not specific publications but rather reliable sources of information. There are many such sources. What follows are just a few that are readily accessible.

- The Canadian Council on Social Development publishes a fact book, *Canadian Fact Book on Poverty*, which includes information about the changing face of poverty, comparisons with poverty in other countries, and poverty data for the provinces and large cities. These reports as well as other statistical data are available from CCSD, 441 MacLaren St., 4th floor, Ottawa ON K2P 2H3, tel:613-236-8977/fax:236-2750. URL: http://www.ccsd.ca/facts.html
- Citizens for Public Justice is a non-partisan national Christian organization of citizens which promotes justice in Canadian public affairs. It has a strong research wing that studies and reports from an ethical perspective on public issues including the issue of poverty. It is located in Toronto at #311, 229 College St. (M5T 1RA) tel: 416-979-2443. e-mail: cjp@web.apc.org.
- The National Council of Welfare, referred to in the introduction to this chapter, publishes annual *Poverty Profiles*, the latest of which reports on 1994. These reports are available from the Council (2nd floor, 1010 Somerset St. West, Ottawa ON K1A 0J9, tel: 613-957-2961). URL: http://www.ncwcnbes.net/
- The National Anti-Poverty Organization has a wealth of material on the subject of poverty. They can be reached at: 316-256 King Edward Ave., Ottawa ON K1N 7M1, tel: 613-789-0242. e-mail: NAPO@web.apc.org. URL: http://www.napo-onap.ca/
- *Human Development Reports* are published for the United Nations Development Program (UNDP). The United Nations began preparing these reports in 1990. They are published annually and can be found in the public documents sections of libraries, in United Nations bookstores in a number of cities across the country, or at the United Nations itself. They provide a wealth of information about human development in all parts of the world.
- *Country Reports on Health, Nutrition, Population, and Poverty*. These are World Bank country reports that provide statistics on intra-country data between rich and poor countries with respect to health, nutrition, population, and poverty. URL: http://www.worldbank.org/poverty/health/data/index.htm
- *Child Poverty Across Industrialized Nations* and *A League Table of Child Poverty in Rich Nations* by the United Nations Children's Fund and *The State of World Population* by the United Nations Population Fund are other UN publications providing data about specific aspects of poverty in the global context.

Books

- *Policy Options* is a periodical which is published ten times a year by the Institute for Research on Public Policy. Its July-August issue is devoted to a discussion by several contributors from several points of view of welfare and unemployment in Canada.
- Christopher Sarlo, *Poverty in Canada* (2nd ed.) (Vancouver: The Fraser Institute, 1996). This is an updated version of the same book which was published in 1994. It challenges the definition of poverty widely used by organizations such as those referred to above and

then undertakes a detailed analysis of the extent of poverty in light of its own definition. The author argues that poverty is considerably less prevalent in Canada than is widely reported as being the case by the media.

- Christopher Sarlo, *Popular Myths about Poverty*. (Vancouver, The Fraser Institute, 2001). URL: http://www.oldfraser.lexi.net/publications/forum/2001/07/section_14.html
- Robin Broad, (ed.) *Global Backlash: Citizen Initiatives for a Just World Economy*. (Lanham, MD: Rowman & Littlefield, 2002). A collection of articles by various international organizations and scholars on the topics of globalization, poverty, and human rights.

Articles

- Nigel Dower, "World Poverty" in *A Companion to Ethics* edited by Peter Singer (Oxford: Blackwell, 1991). This article argues that there is an obligation to relieve world poverty "though not a relentless, overburdening one."
- Garrett Hardin, "Carrying Capacity as an Ethical Concept" is found in many moral issues texts including *Applied Ethics: A Multicultural Approach*, 3rd edition edited by Larry May et al. (New Jersey: Prentice-Hall, 2002). In this well-known article, Harding argues against the view that the wealthy nations of the world have an obligation to help nations that are poor.
- Andrew Belsey, "World Poverty, Justice and Equality," in *International Justice and the Third World: Studies in the Philosophy of Development* edited by Robin Attfield and Barry Wilkins (London: Routledge, 1992). Belsey argues that poverty in the global context is best examined as a characteristic of the economic and political inequalities that exist between Third World countries of the South and capitalist First World countries of the North.
- Trudy Govier, "The Right to Eat and the Duty to Work," *Philosophy of Human Sciences*, vol. 5 (1975). Govier examines three different views of the responsibilities of a modern state confronted with the issue of poverty. She ties the discussion of welfare to basic moral principles and rights such as the right to life and argues that supportive welfare systems are justified as preconditions for the exercise of important human rights.
- Susan James, "The Duty to Relieve Suffering," *Ethics* 93, October 1982. The author argues that our duty to prevent harm is greater than people usually are prepared to admit. The way to persuade people of this fact is to take existing beliefs seriously and to help people to understand their implications for responding to suffering. Appealing to moral theory is not likely to achieve the same results.
- Peter Marin, "Helping and Hating the Homeless" in *Harpers Magazine*, January 1987. This is an insightful exploration of the nature of poverty and the people in its grip. The author describes who the poor are and where they come from, their reasons and motives for living in poverty, and the paradoxes and challenges they pose for modern America.
- Kai Nielsen, "Arguing for Equality," in *Philosophic Exchange* 1986 published by the Center for Philosophic Exchange, State University of New York. In this paper, Kai Nielsen defends the thesis that for there to be a free society there must be an extensive equality of living conditions across that society. Contrary to the widely held opposing view, he argues that large disparities in wealth and income are not compatible with freedom.

- Alistair Macleod, "Economic Inequality: Justice and Incentives," In *Economic Rights: Private Rights and Public Interests* edited by K. Kipnis and D. Meyers. (New Jersey: Rowman and Allanheld, 1985). Macleod examines one of the most common arguments for inequality in the distribution of resources: the need for incentives. He argues that standard justifications of incentives leading to inequality in the distribution of resources are not persuasive.
- Peter Singer, "Rich and Poor" from *Practical Ethics* edited by the same author (Cambridge: Cambridge University Press, 1979). This is another widely read article in which Peter Singer argues for the very strong view that those who are well-off have an obligation to share their wealth with the poor to the point where to do so would make them less well-off than those they are helping.

Chapter 8

Environmental Ethics

Introduction

In this chapter, we turn to a topic that is in a number of respects unique among the topics considered to this point. To begin with, the topics we have taken up in previous chapters have been the subject of discussion for centuries, and in some cases for much of human history. In contrast, environmental issues have emerged as the focus of sustained public ethical discussion and debate only recently. One of the challenges of this chapter is understanding why this is so. Second, the focus of discussion in previous chapters has been on articulating the values and principles that should guide human interaction.

Environmental concerns connect the values and principles that guide or ought to guide human interaction. Poverty, discrimination, equality, and environmental degradation are all closely related. Environmental protection has become a key issue in business ethics. And the environment is an inevitable casualty in war. However, the topic of environmental ethics takes us beyond concerns simply about the values and principles that should guide human interaction. With this chapter we also look to see whether the principles that have emerged from our discussion of these other topics apply or ought to apply to our interaction with other sentient creatures, and with the environment generally.

Background Considerations

Until relatively recently, environmental issues have not been the subject of sustained or widespread ethical scrutiny. Why this is so is itself a matter of considerable controversy and debate, some of which is referred to directly or alluded to in the readings which follow. Two factors, however, seem uncontroversially relevant: First, until this century, human population has expanded, if at all, only quite slowly. There are no doubt many complex reasons for this. But certainly, exposure to disease and limitations on the capacity to produce and distribute food were important factors. In the twentieth century, however, these limiting conditions were radically altered. The explosion in medical knowledge resulted in the eradication of communicable diseases such as smallpox, dramatic improvements in public health standards, the capacity to control infections through the use of antibiotics, and so on. The result has been declining rates of infant mortality and significantly increased lifespan for much of the world's population.

A second factor, related to the first, has been the explosion of knowledge in science and technology. Human beings can now quite literally move mountains, change the direction of the flow of water across continents, produce energy cheaply in response to exponentially increasing demand, and create new technologies, new products, new chemicals, and now, new life forms of a sort and at a speed that is unique in human history.

The result of this is a rapidly increasing human population and an increasingly more powerful capacity on the part of that population to change the natural world in environmentally significant ways.

The Current Situation

Today we find ourselves faced with a situation unique in human history. Our numbers are growing rapidly. The green revolution made possible by scientific advances in the field of agriculture has to date allowed the increased agricultural production needed to feed a rapidly expanding human population. However, the changes that made this possible have not been without significant environmental impact. One of the most important concerns is soil depletion resulting from agriculture based on new technologies. A second is the impact of chemicals on human and other life forms. The history of DDT is a good illustration of this phenomenon. It is relevant in this regard that, despite remarkable advances in agriculture and the ability to distribute food from one part of the world to another, starvation is common, and many people today do not have enough to eat, as our discussion of poverty illustrates.

Equally important is the fact that advances in scientific technology have opened the door to industrial activity the byproducts of which have caused far-reaching and very damaging environmental impacts. In some respects, the most dramatic evidence of this is global warming. The suggestion that modern industrial activity has the capacity to alter climates globally illustrates the magnitude of changes that have brought to environmental issues an urgent ethical dimension.

Global warming, however, is just one of the many significant environmental issues we face today. Others include the pollution of land and water; deforestation; soil depletion; the extinction of species; the impact of new farming technologies on the welfare of animals; the disposal of waste in all its forms, including radioactive wastes resulting from the production of nuclear energy; and energy consumption (Canadians consume more energy per person than the people of almost any other country in the world).

One of the concepts that has emerged from the discussion of these issues is that of sustainable development. Popularized by the Brundtland Commission, this notion is now central to environmental debates. In the words of the Commission itself, development is sustainable if it "meets the needs of the present without compromising the ability of future generations to meet their own needs." Despite its broad appeal, however, the notion of sustainable development has been vigorously challenged by many environmentalists who have concluded that the capacity of the earth to absorb further development has now been exhausted. Environmental protection or conservation, they argue, requires nothing less than a dramatic change in the way particularly those in the advanced industrial countries live, as well as the way we human beings understand our place in nature.

A final important component of this picture is the role of government in responding to what many see as a developing environmental crisis. This is essentially a public policy issue having to do with environmental regulation. Throughout much of the second half of the last century, there was increasing momentum at least in the industrialized world toward increasingly strict environmental regulation. The result is that it is not uncommon to have environmental assessments precede the launch of large industrial projects. Recent changes in the political coloration of provincial and federal governments in Canada, however, are now leading to a reassessment of this trend. Hence, the role of governments in addressing environmental concerns has itself become a matter of ethical analysis and debate.

The Moral Dimension

What then are the moral dimensions of these wide-ranging environmental concerns? As it turns out, this is not an easy question to answer for reasons that often characterize moral deliberation but are particularly acute when environmental issues are under discussion. First is the challenge of simply getting the facts straight. This may not seem a particularly challenging problem. After all, getting one's facts straight is an important first step in resolving any moral issue. Environmental issues are a particular challenge, however. This is typically because the factual components of environmental issues can be very complex and are often contested. This is why the resolution of disputes is so often handed over to experts. This in turn means that the relevant facts are often assembled by scientists and communicated in technical language that non-scientists typically have a good deal of trouble understanding. As a consequence, public discussions of the ethical dimension of environmental issues are frequently shunted aside.

This in turn leads to a second important consideration. To this point in the book, our focus has been more or less exclusively on the obligations we have as human beings to other human beings individually or collectively. Environmental ethics challenges that focus. In particular it requires that we think carefully about whether our obligations as human beings extend only to other human beings. Or do the kinds of principles we have been articulating — the protection-of-life principle, the avoidance-of-suffering principle, the moral-autonomy principle, and the equal-worth principle — apply also to other sentient creatures and perhaps also to the natural environment itself? For example, ensuring the preservation of wild fur-bearing animals is of obvious importance for anyone whose life depends on trapping. But if it could be established that the well-being of human beings would not be affected by the disappearance of fur-bearing animals, would protecting them or ensuring their survival have any moral significance? Answering this kind of question is central to the emerging field of environmental ethics.

Finally, we need to be aware of a third important dimension of environmental ethics, namely the notion of sustainable development. Sustainable development or what is sometimes referred to as sustainability picks up all the themes canvassed to this point in the discussion but asks in addition: Do we also have obligations to the future or more specifically to future generations? If so, are these obligations similar to those we have to the present? Finally, how are our obligations to the future, assuming we have such obligations, to be balanced against those we have to the present?

These questions are not of purely academic interest. The answers we give to them could have significant implications for the way in which those currently alive eat, work, and play.

The Readings

In the discussions that follow, environmental issues are explored from a variety of perspectives. Northrop Frye sets out some of the historical and intellectual dimensions of traditional Canadian attitudes to the environment. In our second reading, Mary Midgley in "Duties Concerning Islands" criticizes theories that ignore the social and cultural dimensions of morality and treat individuals as though they were "social atoms" whose moral obligations extend only to other human beings who are in a position to hinder or help them as they pursue their individual interests. Rather, she argues, human beings have a much wider range of obligations or duties of care and responsibility to a wide range of people and things who are not in a position to help or harm them in any way. This includes the duty not to gratuitously destroy things even if doing so cannot be shown to have harmful implications for other human beings.

The focus then shifts to an evaluation of deep ecology, an environmental philosophy that has attempted to set out, in a systematic and holistic way, a comprehensive understanding of our relation and responsibility as human beings to the environment. It is a view that implies that the protection-of-life, avoidance-of-suffering, moral-autonomy, and equal-worth principles do have moral force in describing our obligations to the environment. Tom Regan explores the claims of the deep ecology philosophy sympathetically but ultimately rejects them. He argues, nevertheless, that animals, being sentient, do have rights that human beings ought to respect. Jan Narveson then questions Regan's position, arguing against Regan and Midgley for a view of morality which roots moral obligations in contractual relations between and among existing human beings.

In the last article in the chapter, Andrew Brook examines the ethics of waste disposal, using nuclear waste as a test case. He points out that the waste produced as a result of uranium mining and the use of nuclear fuels is highly toxic and will be for thousands of years. Furthermore, no permanent solution has been found to its long-term safe disposal. Central to his discussion is the idea of sustainable development, that is to say, our obligations to future generations and "creatures, ecosystems, and the biosphere as a whole."

CANADA: NEW WORLD WITHOUT REVOLUTION

Northrop Frye

Canada, with four million square miles and only four centuries of documented history, has naturally been a country more preoccupied with space than with time, with environment rather than tradition. The older generation, to which I have finally become assigned, was brought up to think of Canada as a land of unlimited natural resources, an unloving but rich earth-mother bulging with endless supplies of nickel and asbestos, or, in her softer parts, with the kind of soil that would allow of huge grain and lumber surpluses. The result of such assumptions is that many of our major social problems are those of ecology, the extinction of animal species, the plundering of forests and mines, the pollution of water, as the hundreds of millions of years that nature took to build up our supplies of coal and oil are cancelled out in a generation or two. The archaeologists who explore royal tombs in Egypt and Mesopotamia find they are almost always anticipated by grave robbers, people who got there first because they had better reasons for doing so than the acquisition of knowledge. We are the grave robbers of our own resources, and posterity will not be grateful to us. There is, however, a growing understanding that our situation is not simply one of people against planes, or whatever the current issue may be, but of soil and trees and water against concrete and tarmac.

Excerpt from "Canada: New World Without Revolution," in Divisions on a Ground: Essays on Canadian Culture *copyright © 1982 by Northrop Frye. Reprinted with the permission of House of Anansi Press.*

These spatial and environmental problems have a temporal dimension as well. Our history began in the seventeenth century, the age of Baroque expansion in Europe, where the countries advancing most rapidly into the future were those on the Atlantic seaboard. Rapid advance is usually followed either by rapid decline or by a rapid change in some other direction: even by then Spain and Portugal had passed their meridian of growth, and France soon turned back to its European preoccupations. If the French had held Canada they might well have sold it, as they did Louisiana. What is important is not nationality but cultural assumptions. The Baroque age was an age of intense belief in the supremacy of human consciousness over nature. It had discovered something of the technological potential of mathematics, once mathematics had become attached to a powerful social organization. It was not an age of individualism, as is often said, but an age of relatively enlightened despotism, and in some ways very like the dawn of civilization in the Near East, when the pyramids of Egypt and the ziggurats of Babylon emerged as dramatic witness to what men could do when united under a sufficiently strong social will. Both then and in the Baroque period, mathematics, and the appearance of geometrical patterns in the human environment, was a symbol of aggressiveness, of imperialistic domination. We can see the results all over our country, in the grid patterns of our cities, the concession lines that divide up the farmland into squares, the railways and highways that emphasize direction through landscape rather than accommodation to it. Improvement in such communications always means a wider and straighter path through nature, and a corresponding decline of interest in it. With the coming of the aeroplane, even the sense of passing through a natural environment disappears. Our attitude to nature is reflected in our social environment, the kind we build ourselves. Washington was a city designed for automobiles rather than pedestrians long before there were any automobiles: Los Angeles, a city never designed at all, seems to have broken through the control even of the automobile. It was, after all, named after angels, who traditionally do not travel through space but simply manifest themselves elsewhere.

The religion that the British and French brought to the New World was not a natural monotheism, like the Algonquin worship of a Great Spirit, nor an imperial monotheism like that of the Stoics, but a revolutionary monotheism, with a God who took an active and partisan role in history; and like all revolutionary movements, including Marxism in our time, it equipped itself with a canon of sacred books and a dialectical habit of mind, a mental attitude in which the neighboring heresy is much more bitterly hated than the total rejection of the faith. The dialectical habit of mind produced the conception of the false god, a conception hardly intelligible to an educated pagan. All false gods, in the Christian view, were idols, and all idolatry came ultimately from the belief that there was something numinous in nature. The Christian teaching was that there were no gods in nature; that nature was a fellow-creature of man, and that all the gods that had been discovered in it were devils. We have derived many benefits from this attitude, but it had a more sinister side: it tended to assume that nature, not being inhabited or protected by gods or potentially dangerous spirits, was simply something available for human exploitation. Everywhere we look today, we see the conquest of nature by an intelligence that does not love it, that feels no part of it, that splits its own consciousness off from it and looks at it as an object. The sense of the absolute and unquestionable rightness of man's conquest over nature extended to other cultures regarded as being in a "state of nature." The primary principle of white settlement in this country, in practice if not always in theory, was that the indigenous cultures should be destroyed, not preserved or continued or even set apart.

The spokesman for the Baroque phase of this attitude is Descartes, whose fundamental axiom, "I think, therefore I am," rested on a desire to derive human existence from human consciousness, and to see that consciousness as being in a different world from the nature which for Descartes was pure extension in space. This attitude, in itself a logical development from the traditional Christian view of nature, got so far away from idolatry that it became a kind of idolatry in reverse, the idol this time being human consciousness itself, separated from nature. We live today in a social environment which is a triumph of Cartesian consciousness; an abstract and autonomous world of interlocking co-ordinates, in which most of our imagination is focussed not on nature but on the geometrical shapes that we have imposed on nature. My own few childhood memories of big cities are full of a kind of genial clutter: crowds of people on streets, shops with their doors open, theatres with glittering lights; and certainly the exhilaration of this had much to do with the attractiveness of cities for those in smaller centres a generation or two ago. Much of it of course remains, but it is becoming clearer that each advance of technology is accompanied by an advance in introversion, and less sense of public use. Many of the streets now in these same cities, with their deserted sidewalks and cars whizzing up and down the road past scowling fortress-like buildings, show us the kind of anti-community symbolized for me by University Avenue in Toronto and by the areas in Los Angeles where pedestrians are regarded as vagrants. The amount of mental distress caused by living in an environment which expresses indifference or contempt for the perspectives of the human body is very little studied: one might call it proportion pollution.

My own university is in the middle of a big industrial city: this means great masses of box-lunch students, who commute in and out from distant suburbs and take their courses with little experience of a real university community, of the kind that Cardinal Newman regarded as the "idea" of the university. The surrounding streets keep steadily turning into anonymous masses of buildings that look eyeless in spite of being practically all windows. Many of them seem to have had no architect, but appear to have sprung out of their excavations like vast toadstools. City planners speak of the law of conserving the plan, meaning that Bloor Street in Toronto or Sherbrooke Street in Montreal are still where those streets originally were even though there has been a total metamorphosis of the buildings on them. But even this law, which seems at first sight like a concession to a sense of tradition, is really a means of confining change to the inorganic. And as we shuttle from a pigeon-hole in a high-rise apartment to another pigeon-hole in an office, a sense of futility and humiliation takes possession of us that we can now perhaps see in its historical dimension.

As civilization has "progressed" from ax to bulldozer, the growing withdrawal from nature paralyzes something natural in ourselves. A friend of my wife's, an interior decorator, remarked that she had a group of neurotic clients whom it seemed impossible either to please or to get rid of, and she suddenly realized that they had something in common: they all lived in high-rise apartments at a level above the trees. A withdrawal from nature extends into a growing withdrawal from human society itself. I mentioned the increasing introversion that technology brings with it: the aeroplane is more introverted than the train; the super-highway, where there is a danger of falling asleep, more introverted than the most unfrequented country road. The international airport, completely insulated even from the country it is in, is perhaps the most eloquent symbol of this, and is parodied in Stanley Kubrick's movie *2001*, where the hero lands on the moon, dependent on human processing even for the air he breathes, and finds nothing to do there except to phone his wife back on earth, who is out.

A revolutionary habit of mind, being founded on the sense of a crucial break in time at some point, the Exodus from Egypt, the Incarnation of Christ, the flight of Mohammed, the October Revolution in Russia, has a hostility to continuous tradition built into it. In Moslem countries everything that happened before Mohammed's time is part of the age of ignorance. Guides in developing countries, especially Marxist ones, want to show tourists the achievements of their own regime, and often get angry or contemptuous when the tourists want to see the cultural products of the old exploiting days. Similarly with our own culture. The Puritans in Massachusetts were in communion with the Puritans in Norwich who petitioned the Cromwellian government to pull down a useless and cumbersome cathedral which was a mere relic of superstition. Even the Jesuit missionaries, for all their zeal and devotion, still assumed that the Indians, so long as they were heathen, were a part of subconscious nature, and that only Christianity could incorporate them into a fully human society. A cultural sense thus got started which was still operative until quite recently. My late friend Charles Currelly, the founder of the Archaeological Museum in Toronto, was horrified by the indifference with which the authorities of his day regarded the British Columbia totem poles, and by the eagerness with which they were ready to sell them off to anyone whom they thought would be fool enough to want them. What we are now beginning to see is that an original belief in the rightness of destroying or ignoring a so-called "savage" culture develops toward a contempt for our own. In Margaret Atwood's very ironic novel *Surfacing*, the heroine, trying to get back to an original identity represented by the Quebec forests, finds that she has to destroy everything cultural that she possesses, or, as she says: "everything from history must be eliminated."

The revolutionary aspect of white settlement extended from religion into economics, as entrepreneur capitalism developed. Every technological change brought with it a large-scale shift in population centres. The skyline of Toronto sixty years ago was dominated by the spires of the great churches: now the churches are points of depression within the skyline. My moral is not the shift of interest from spiritual to financial administration: my moral is rather that the churches themselves are now largely without parishes, the population, at least the church-going part of it, having moved elsewhere. Similarly Canada is a land of ruins to an extent that the less spacious countries of Europe would not dare to be: ghost towns at exhausted mines or the divisional points of old railways remind us how quickly our economy can scrap not merely a building but an entire city. As Earle Birney remarks, the country is haunted by its lack of ghosts, for a ghost town has no ghosts: it is only one of the rubbish heaps that spring up in an economy of waste. We may remember Sam Slick on the beauties of Niagara Falls:

> "It would be a grand speck to get up a jint stock company for factory purposes, for such another place for mills ain't to be found atween the poles. Oh dear!" said I, "only think of the cardin' mills, fullin' mills, cotton mills, grain mills, saw mills, plaster mills, and gracious knows what sort o' mills might be put up there . . . and yet them goneys the British let all run away to waste."

For Sam Slick the ideal thriving mill town of this sort was Lowell in Massachusetts, where my father started in business, and it was a sad day for both of us when I took him there as an old man, after all the mills had been moved to the south, and he saw only the empty shell of the town he once knew. One question that such events raise is obviously: what can or should be preserved of what is no longer functional, and has little interest in itself apart from being a part of our past?

Whatever the answer, our social environment is a revolutionary one in which the main forces are indiscriminately destructive. This has to some extent always been true. Once there was a great city called Nineveh, so great that, according to the Book of Jonah, it took three days to journey across it. Then, quite suddenly, Nineveh disappeared under the sand, where it remained for nearly three thousand years. This kind of destruction from enemy action without is a greater danger now, as hydrogen bombs would leave nothing for the sand to preserve; but along with it is the even more insidious sense of destruction from within, destruction that proceeds from the very nature of technology itself, not impossibly inspired by some death wish in ourselves. The only possible economic alternative to capitalism, we feel, is socialism, but if capitalism is a destroyer, socialism is even more of one, because more committed to technology. In ancient Egypt one of the first things a new Pharaoh often did was to deface his predecessor's monuments: this is still our rhythm of life, but it is largely an unconscious one, except when rationalized as progress.

The violence of our almost unmanageable cities is bringing about another great population shift, as people move out of them and back to smaller centres. We are beginning to see a very large cycle of history turning here, and with this is slowly growing another social vision. Ecology, the sense of the need for conserving natural resources, is not a matter of letting the environment go back to the wilderness, but of finding some kind of working balance between man and nature founded on a respect for nature and its inner economies. As part of natural ecology, we are also developing some sense of the need for a kind of human ecology, of conserving not only our natural but our cultural and imaginative resources. Again, this is not simply a matter of leaving alone everything that is old: it is a way of life that grows out of a sense of balance between our present and our past. In relation to the natural environment, there are two kinds of people: those who think that nature is simply there to be used by man, and those who realize that man is himself a part of nature and will destroy himself if he destroys it. In relation to time and human history, there are also two kinds of people: those who think that the past is dead, and those who realize that the past is still alive in us. A dead past left to bury its dead ends in a dead present, a society of sleepwalkers, and a society without a memory is as senile as an individual in the same plight.

QUESTIONS

1. Northrop Frye suggests that "our attitude toward nature is reflected in our social environment." What evidence does he provide in support of this view? Is it convincing? Can you find evidence in your social environment that would support this claim?
2. Frye sees a relationship between natural ecology (conserving natural resources) and "human ecology" (conserving cultural and imaginative resources). Do you think that a good case can be made for the existence of such a relationship?

DUTIES CONCERNING ISLANDS

Mary Midgley

Had Robinson Crusoe any duties?

When I was a philosophy student, this used to be a familiar conundrum, which was supposed to pose a very simple question; namely, can you have duties to yourself? Mill, they correctly told us, said no. "The term duty to oneself, when it means anything more than prudence, means self-respect or self-development, and for none of these is anyone accountable to his fellow-creatures."[1] Kant, on the other hand, said yes. "Duties to ourselves are of primary importance and should have pride of place . . . nothing can be expected of a man who dishonours his own person."[2] There is a serious disagreement here, not to be sneezed away just by saying, "It depends on what you mean by duty." Much bigger issues are involved — quite how big has, I think, not yet been fully realized. To grasp this, I suggest that we rewrite a part of Crusoe's story, in order to bring in sight a different range of concerns.

> 19 Sept. 1685. This day I set aside to devastate my island. My pinnance being now ready on the shore, and all things prepared for my departure, Friday's people also expecting me, and the wind blowing fresh away from my little harbour, I had a mind to see how all would burn. So then, setting sparks and powder craftily among certain dry spinneys which I had chosen, I soon had it ablaze, nor was there left, by the next down, any green stick among the ruins. . . .

Now, work on the style how you will, you cannot make that into a convincing paragraph. Crusoe was not the most scrupulous of men, but he would have felt an invincible objection to this senseless destruction. So would the rest of us. Yet the language of our moral tradition has tended strongly, ever since the Enlightenment, to make that objection unstateable. All the terms which express that an obligation is serious or binding — duty, right, law, morality, obligation, justice — have been deliberately narrowed in their use so as to apply only in the framework of contract, to describe only relations holding between free and rational agents. Since it has been decided *a priori* that rationality admits of no degrees and that cetaceans are not rational, it follows that, unless you take either religion or science fiction seriously, we can only have duties to humans, and sane, adult, responsible humans at that. Now the morality we live by certainly does not accept this restriction. In common life we recognize many other duties as serious and binding, though of course not necessarily overriding. If philosophers want to call these something else instead of duties, they must justify their move.

We have here one of those clashes between the language of common morality (which is of course always to some extent confused and inarticulate) and an intellectual scheme which arose in the first place from a part of that morality, but has now taken off on its own claims of authority to correct other parts of its source. There are always real difficulties here. As ordinary citizens, we have to guard against dismissing such intellectual schemes too casually; we have to do justice to the point of them. But, as philosophers, we have to resist the opposite temptation of taking the intellectual scheme as decisive, just because it is elegant and satisfying, or because the moral insight which is its starting point is specially familiar to us. Today, this intellectualist bias is often expressed by calling the insights of common

From Environmental Philosophy, *eds. Robert Elliot and Aaron Gare, published by University of Queensland Press, 1983. Reprinted by permission of University of Queensland Press.*

morality mere "intuitions." This is quite misleading, since it gives the impression that they have been reached without thought, and that there is, by contrast, a scientific solution somewhere else to which they ought to bow — as there might be if we were contrasting common sense "intuitions" about the physical world with physics or astronomy. Even without that word, philosophers often manage to give the impression that whenever our moral views clash with any simple, convenient scheme, it is our *duty* to abandon them. Thus, Grice states:

> It is an inescapable consequence of the thesis presented in these pages that certain classes cannot have natural rights: animals, the human embryo, future generations, lunatics and children under the age of, say, ten. In the case of young children at least, my experience is that this consequence is found hard to accept. But it is a consequence of the theory; it is, I believe, true; and I think we should be willing to accept it. At first sight it seems a harsh conclusion, but it is not nearly so harsh as it appears.[3]

But it is in fact extremely harsh, since what he is saying is that the treatment of children ought not to be determined by their interests but by the interests of the surrounding adults capable of contract, which, of course, can easily conflict with them. In our society, he explains, this does not actually make much difference, because parents here are so benevolent that they positively want to benefit their children, and accordingly here "the interests of children are reflected in the interests of their parents." But this, he adds, is just a contingent fact about us. "It is easy to imagine a society where this is not so," where, that is, parents are entirely exploitative. "In this circumstance, the morally correct treatment of children would no doubt be harsher than it is in our society. But the conclusion has to be accepted." Grice demands that we withdraw our objections to harshness, in deference to theoretical consistency. But "harsh" here does not mean just "brisk and bracing," like cold baths and a plain diet. (There might well be more of those where parents do feel bound to consider their children's interests.) It means "unjust." Our objection to unbridled parental selfishness is not a mere matter of tone or taste; it is a moral one. It therefore requires a moral answer, an explanation of the contrary *value* which the contrary theory expresses. Grice, and those who argue like him, take the ascetic, disapproving tone of those who have already displayed such a value, and who are met by a slovenly reluctance to rise to it. But they have not displayed that value. The ascetic tone cannot be justified merely by an appeal to consistency. An ethical theory, which, when consistently followed through, has iniquitous consequences, is a bad theory and must be changed. Certainly we can ask whether these consequences really are iniquitous, but this question must be handled seriously. We cannot directly conclude that the consequences cease to stink the moment they are seen to follow from our theory.

The theoretical model which has spread blight in this area is, of course, that of social contract, and, to suit it, that whole cluster of essential moral terms — right, duty, justice and the rest — has been progressively narrowed. This model shows human society as a spread of standard social atoms, originally distinct and independent, each of which combines with others only at its own choice and in its own private interest. This model is drawn from physics, and from seventeenth-century physics, at that, where the ultimate particles of matter were conceived as hard, impenetrable, homogeneous little billiard balls, with no hooks or internal structure. To see how such atoms could combine at all was very hard. Physics, accordingly, moved on from this notion to one which treats atoms and other particles as complex items, describable mainly in terms of forces, and those are the same kind of forces which operate outside them. It has abandoned the notion of ultimate, solitary, independent individuals. Social-contract theory, however, retains it.

On this physical — or archaeo-physical — model, all significant moral relations between individuals are the symmetrical ones expressed by contract. If, on the other hand, we use a biological or "organic" model, we can talk also of a variety of asymmetrical relations found within a whole. Leaves relate not only to other leaves, but to fruit, twigs, branches and the whole tree. People appear not only as individuals, but as members of their groups, families, tribes, species, ecosystems and biosphere, and have moral relations as part to these wholes. The choice between these two ways of thinking is not, of course, a simple once-and-for-all affair. Different models are useful for different purposes. We can, however, reasonably point out, firstly, that the old physical pattern does make all attempts to explain combination extremely difficult; and, secondly, that since human beings actually are living creatures, not crystals or galaxies, it is reasonable to expect that biological ways of thinking will be useful in understanding them.

In its own sphere, the social contract model has of course been of enormous value. Where we deal with clashes of interest between free and rational agents already in existence, and particularly where we want to disentangle some of them from some larger group that really does not suit them, it is indispensable. And for certain political purposes during the last three centuries these clashes have been vitally important. An obsession with contractual thinking, and a conviction that it is a cure-all, are therefore understandable. But the trouble with such obsessions is that they distort the whole shape of thought and language in a way which makes them self-perpetuating, and constantly extends their empire. Terms come to be defined in a way which leaves only certain moral views expressible. This can happen without any clear intention on the part of those propagating them, and even contrary to their occasional declarations, simply from mental inertia. Thus, John Rawls, having devoted most of his long book to his very subtle and exhaustive contractual view of justice, remarks without any special emphasis near the end that "we should recall here the limits of a theory of justice. Not only are many aspects of morality left aside, but no account can be given of right conduct in regard to animals and the rest of nature."[4] He concedes that these are serious matters. "Certainly it is wrong to be cruel to animals and the destruction of a whole species can be a great evil. The capacity for feelings of pleasure and pain and for the forms of life of which animals are capable clearly impose duties of compassion and humanity in their case." All this is important, he says, and it calls for a wider metaphysical enquiry, but it is not his subject. Earlier in the same passage he touches on the question of permanently irrational human beings, and remarks that it "may present a difficulty. I cannot examine this problem here, but I assume that the account of equality would not be materially affected."[5] Won't it though? It is a strange project to examine a single virtue — justice — without at least sketching in one's view of the vast background of general morality which determines its shape and meaning, including, of course, such awkward and noncontractual virtues as "compassion and humanity." It isolates the duties which people owe each other *merely as thinkers* from those deeper and more general ones which they owe each other as beings who feel. It cannot, therefore, fail both to split a man's nature and to isolate him from the rest of the creation to which he belongs.

Such an account may not be *Hamlet* without the prince, but it is *Hamlet* with half the cast missing, and without the state of Denmark. More exactly, it is like a history of Poland which regards Russia, Germany, Europe and the Roman Church as not part of its subject. I am not attacking Rawls' account on its own ground. I am simply pointing out what the history of ethics shows all too clearly — how much our thinking is shaped by what our sages *omit* to mention. The Greek philosophers never really raised the problem of slavery till towards the end of their speech, and then few of them did so with conviction. This happened even though it lay right in the path of their enquiries into political justice and the value of the individual soul. Christianity did raise that problem, because its class background was different and because the world in the Christian era was already in turmoil, so that men were not presented with the narcotic of a happy stability. But Christianity itself did not, until quite recently, raise the problem of the morality of punishment, and particularly of eternal punishment. This failure to raise central questions was not, in either case, complete. One can find very intelligent and penetrating criticisms of slavery occurring from time to time in Greek writings — even in Aristotle's defence of that institution.[6] But they are mostly like Rawls' remark here. They conclude that "this should be investigated some day." The same thing happens with Christian writings concerning punishment, except that the consideration, "this is a great mystery," acts as an even more powerful paralytic to thought. Not much more powerful, however. Natural inertia, when it coincides with vested interest or the illusion of vested interest, is as strong as gravitation.

It is important that Rawls does not, like Grice, demand that we toe the line which would make certain important moral views impossible. Like Hume, who similarly excluded animals from justice, he simply leaves them out of his discussion. This move ought in principle to be harmless. But when it is combined with an intense concentration of discussion on contractual justice, and a corresponding neglect of compassion and humanity, it inevitably suggests that the excluded problems are relatively unimportant. This suggestion is still more strongly conveyed by rulings which exclude the nonhuman world from rights, duties and morality. Words like "rights" and "duties" are awkward because they do indeed have narrow senses approximating to the legal, but they also have much wider ones in which they cover the whole moral sphere. To say "they do not have rights," or "you do not have duties to them" conveys to any ordinary hearer a very simple message; namely, "they do not matter." This is an absolution, a removal of blame for ill treatment of "them," whoever they may be.

To see how strong this informal, moral usage of "rights" is, we need only look at the history of that powerful notion, the "rights of man." These rights were not supposed to be ones conferred by law, since the whole point of appealing to them was to change laws so as to embody them. They were vague, but vast. They did not arise, as rights are often said do, only within a community, since they were taken to apply in principle everywhere. The immense, and on the whole coherent, use which has been made of this idea by reform movements shows plainly that the tension between the formal and the informal idea of "right" is part of the word's meaning, a fruitful connection of thought, not just a mistake. It is therefore hard to adopt effectively the compromise which some philosophers now favour, of saying that it is indeed wrong to treat animals in certain ways, but that we have no duties to them or that they have no rights.[7] "Animal rights" may be hard to formulate, as indeed are the rights of humans. But "no rights" will not do. The word may need to be dropped entirely. The compromise is still harder with the word "duty," which is rather more informal, and is more closely wedded to a private rather than political use.

Where the realm of right and duty stops, there, to ordinary thinking, begins the realm of the optional. What is not a duty may be a matter of taste, style or feeling, of aesthetic sensibility, of habit and nostalgia, of etiquette and local custom, but it cannot be something which demands our attention whether we like it or not. When claims get into this area, they can scarcely be taken seriously. This becomes clear when Kant tries to straddle the border. He says that we have no direct duties to animals, because they are not rational, but that we should treat them properly all the same because of "indirect" duties which are really duties to our own humanity.[8] This means that ill-treating them (a) might lead us to ill-treat humans, and (b) is a sign of a bad or inhumane disposition. The whole issue thus becomes a contingent one of spiritual style or training, like contemplative exercises, intellectual practice or, indeed, refined manners.[9] Some might need practice of this kind to make them kind to people, others might not, and, indeed, might get on better without it. (Working off one's ill-temper on animals might make one treat people *better*.) But the question of cruelty to animals cannot be like this, because it is of the essence to such training exercises that they are internal. Anything that affects some other being is not just practice, it is real action. Anyone who refrained from cruelty *merely* from a wish not to sully his own character, without any direct consideration for the possible victims, would be frivolous and narcissistic.

A similar trivialization follows where theorists admit duties of compassion and humanity to noncontractors, but deny duties of justice. Hume and Rawls, in making this move, do not explicitly subordinate these other duties, or say that they are less binding. But because they make the contract element so central to morality, this effect appears to follow. The priority of justice is expressed in such everyday proverbs as "be just before you're generous." We are therefore rather easily persuaded to think that compassion, humanity and so forth are perhaps emotional luxuries, to be indulged only after all debts are paid. A moment's thought will show that this is wrong. Someone who receives simultaneously a request to pay a debt and another to comfort somebody bereaved or on their death bed is not as a matter of course under obligation to treat the debt as the more urgent. He has to look at circumstances on both sides, but in general we should probably expect the other duties to have priority. This is still more true if, on his way to pay the debt, he encounters a stranger in real straits, drowning or lying on the road. To give the debt priority, we probably need to think of his creditor as also being in serious trouble — which brings compassion and humanity in on both sides of the case.

What makes it so hard to give justice a different clientele from the other virtues, as Hume and Rawls do, is simply the fact that justice is such a pervading virtue. In general, all serious cases of cruelty, meanness, inhumanity and the like are also cases of injustice. If we are told that a certain set of these cases does not involve injustice, our natural thought is that these cases must be *trivial*. Officially, Hume's and Rawls' restriction is not supposed to mean this. What, however, is it supposed to mean? It is forty years since I first read Hume's text, and I find his thought as obscure now as I did then. I well remember double-taking then, going back over the paragraph for a point which, I took it, I must have missed. Can anyone see it?

> Were there a species of creatures intermingled with men, which, though rational, were possessed of such inferior strength, both of body and mind, that they were incapable of all resistance, and could never, upon the highest provocation, make us feel the effects of their resentment; the necessary consequence, I think, is that we should be bound by the laws of humanity to give gentle usage to these creatures, but should not, properly speaking, lie under any restraint of justice with regard to them, nor could they possess any right or property, exclusive of such arbitrary lords. Our intercourse with them could not be called society, which supposes a degree of equality, but absolute command on one side and servile obedience on the other. . . . This is plainly the situation of men with regard to animals.[10]

I still think that the word "justice," so defined, has lost its normal meaning. In ordinary life we think that duties of justice become *more* pressing, not less so, when we are dealing with the weak and inarticulate, who cannot argue back. It is the boundaries of prudence which depend on power, not those of justice. Historically, Hume's position becomes more understandable when one sees its place in the development of social-contract thinking. The doubtful credit for confining justice to the human species seems to belong to Grotius, who finally managed to ditch the Roman notion of *jus naturale*, natural right or law, common to all species. I cannot here discuss his remarkably unimpressive arguments for this.[11] The point I want to make here is simply in reference to the effect of these restrictive definitions of terms like "justice" on people's view of the sheer size of the problems raised by what falls outside them.

Writers who treat morality as primarily contractual tend to discuss noncontractual cases briefly, casually and parenthetically, as though they were rather rare. Rawls' comments on the problem of mental defectives are entirely typical here. We have succeeded, they say, in laying most of the carpet; why are you making this fuss about those little wrinkles behind the sofa? This treatment confirms a view, already suggested by certain aspects of current politics in the United States, that those who fail to clock in as normal rational agents and make their contracts are just occasional exceptions, constituting one more "minority" group — worrying, no doubt, to the scrupulous, but not a central concern of any society. Let us, then, glance briefly at their scope, by roughly listing some cases which seem to involve us in noncontractual duties. (The order is purely provisional and the numbers are added just for convenience.)

Human Sector	1.	The dead
	2.	Posterity
	3.	Children
	4.	The senile
	5.	The temporarily insane
	6.	The permanently insane
	7.	Defectives, ranging down to "human vegetables"
	8.	Embryos, human and otherwise
Animal Sector	9.	Sentient animals
	10.	Nonsentient animals
Inanimate Sector	11.	Plants of all kinds
	12.	Artefacts, including works of art
	13.	Inanimate but structured objects — crystals, rivers, rocks, etc.
Comprehensive	14.	Unchosen groups of all kinds, including families and species
	15.	Ecosystems, landscapes, villages, warrens, cities, etc.
	16.	Countries
	17.	The Biosphere
Miscellaneous	18.	Oneself
	19.	God

No doubt I have missed a few, but that will do to go on with. The point is this: if we look only at a few of these groupings, and without giving them full attention, it is easy to think that we can include one or two as honorary contracting members by a slight stretch of our conceptual scheme, and find arguments for excluding the others from serious concern entirely.

But if we keep our eye on the size of the range, this stops being plausible. As far as sheer numbers go, this is no minority of the beings with whom we have to deal. We are a small minority of them. As far as importance goes, it is certainly possible to argue that some of these sorts of beings should concern us more and others less: we need a priority system. But, to build it, *moral* arguments are required. The various kinds of claims have to be understood and compared, not written off in advance. We cannot rule that those who, in our own and other cultures, suppose that there is a direct objection to injuring or destroying some of them, are always just confused, and mean only, in fact, that this item will be needed for rational human consumption.[12]

The blank antithesis which Kant made between rational persons (having value) and mere things (having none) will not serve us to map out this vast continuum. And the idea that, starting at some given point on this list, we have a general licence for destruction, is itself a moral view which would have to be justified. Western culture differs from most others in the breadth of destructive licence which it allows itself, and, since the seventeenth century, that licence has been greatly extended. Scruples about rapine have been continually dismissed as irrational, but it is not always clear with what rational principles they are supposed to conflict. Western destructiveness has not in fact developed in response to a new set of disinterested intellectual principles demonstrating the need for more people and less redwoods, but mainly as a by-product of greed and increasing commercial confidence. Humanistic hostility to superstition has played some part in the process, because respect for the nonhuman items on our list is often taken to be religious. It does not have to be. Many scientists who are card-carrying atheists can still see the point of preserving the biosphere. So can the rest of us, religious or otherwise. It is the whole of which we are parts, and its other parts concern us for that reason.

But the language of rights is rather ill-suited to expressing this, because it has been developed mainly for the protection of people who, though perhaps oppressed, are in principle articulate. This makes it quite reasonable for theorists to say that rights belong only to those who understand them and can claim them. When confronted with the "human sector" of our list, these theorists can either dig themselves in, like Grice, and exclude the lot, or stretch the scheme, like Rawls, by including the hypothetical rational choices which these honorary members *would* make if they were not unfortunately prevented. Since many of these people seem less rational than many animals, zoophiles have, then, a good case for calling this second device arbitrary or specious, and extending rights to the border of sentience. Here, however, the meaning of the term "rights" does become thin, and when we reach the inanimate area, usage will scarcely cover it. (It is worth noticing that long before this, when dealing merely with the "rights of man," the term often seems obscure, because to list and specify these rights is so much harder than to shout for them. The word is probably of more use as a slogan, indicating a general direction, than as a detailed conceptual tool.) There may be a point in campaigning to extend usage. But to me it seems wiser on the whole not to waste energy on this verbal point, but instead to insist on the immense variety of kinds of beings with which we have to deal. Once we grasp this, we ought not to be surprised that we are involved in many different kinds of claim or duty. The dictum that "rights and duties are correlative" is misleading, because the two words keep rather different company, and one may be narrowed without affecting the other.

What, then, about duties? I believe that this term can properly be used over the whole range. We have quite simply got many kinds of duties to animals,[13] to plants and to the biosphere. But to speak in this way we must free the term once and for all from its restrictive contractual use, or irrelevant doubts will still haunt us. If we cannot do this, we shall have to exclude the word "duty," along with "rights" from all detailed discussion, using wider words like "wrong," "right" and "ought" instead. This gymnastic would be possible but inconvenient. The issue about duty becomes clear as soon as we look at the controversy from which I started, between Kant's and Mill's views on duties to oneself. What do we think about this? Are there duties of integrity, autonomy, self-knowledge, self-respect? It seems that there are. Mill is right, of course, to point out that they are not duties to someone in the ordinary sense. The divided self is a metaphor. It is as natural and necessary a metaphor here as it is over, say, self-deception or self-control, but it certainly is not literal truth. The form of the requirement is different. Rights, for instance, certainly do not seem to come in here as they often would with duties to other persons; we would scarcely say, "I have a right to my own respect." And the *kind* of things which we can owe ourselves are distinctive. It is not just chance who they are owed to. You cannot owe it to somebody else, as you can to yourself, to force him to act freely or with integrity. He owes that to himself, the rest of us can only remove outside difficulties. As Kant justly said, our business is to promote our own perfection and the happiness of others; the perfection of others is an aim which belongs to them.[14] Respect, indeed, we owe both to ourselves and to others, but Kant may well be right to say that self-respect is really a different and deeper requirement, something without which all outward duties would become meaningless. (This may explain the paralyzing effect of depression.)

Duties to oneself, in fact, are duties with a different *form*. They are far less close than outward duties to the literal model of debt, especially monetary debt. Money is a thing which can be owed in principle to anybody, it is the same whoever you owe it to, and if by chance you come to owe it to yourself, the debt vanishes. Not many of our duties are really of this impersonal kind; the attempt to commute other sorts of duties into money is a notorious form of evasion. Utilitarianism however wants to make all duties as homogeneous as possible. And that is the point of Mill's position. He views all our self-concerning motives as parts of the desire for happiness. Therefore he places all duty, indeed all morality, on the outside world, as socially required restrictions of that desire — an expression, that is, of other people's desire for happiness.

> We do not call anything wrong, unless we mean that a person ought to be punished in some way or another for doing it; if not by law, by the opinion of his fellow-creatures; if not by opinion, by the reproaches of his own conscience. This seems the real turning point of the distinction between morality and simple expedience. It is a part of the notion of Duty in every one of its forms, that a person may rightly be compelled to fulfil it. Duty is a thing which may be *exacted* from a person, as one exacts a debt.[15]

To make the notion of wrongness depend on punishment and public opinion in this way instead of the other way round is a bold step. Mill did not mind falling flat on his face from time to time in trying out a new notion for the public good. He did it for us, and we should, I think, take proper advantage of his generosity, and accept the impossibility which he demonstrates. The concepts cannot be connected this way round. Unless you think of certain acts as wrong, it makes no sense to talk of punishment. "Punishing" alcoholics with aversion therapy or experimental rats with electric shocks is not really punishing at all; it is just deterrence. This "punishment" will not make their previous actions wrong, nor has it anything to do with morality. The real point of morality returns to Mill's scheme in the Trojan horse of "reproaches of his own conscience." Why do *they* matter? Unless the conscience is talking sense — that is, on Utilitarian principles, unless it is delivering the judgment of society — it should surely be silenced. Mill, himself a man of enormous integrity, deeply concerned about autonomy, would never have agreed to silence it. But, unless we do so, we shall have to complicate his scheme. It may well be true that, in the last resort and at the deepest level, conscience and the desire for happiness converge. But in ordinary life and at the everyday level they can diverge amazingly. We do want to be honest but we do not want to be put out. What we know we ought to do is often most unwelcome to us, which is why we call it duty. And whole sections of that duty do not concern other people directly at all. A good example is the situation in Huxley's *Brave New World*, where a few dissident citizens have grasped the possibility of a fuller and freer life. Nobody else wants this. Happiness is already assured. The primary duty of change here seems to be that of each to himself. True, they may feel bound also to help others to change, but hardly in a way which those others would *exact*. In fact, we may do better here by dropping the awkward second party altogether and saying that they have a duty *of* living differently — one which will affect both themselves and others, but which does not require, as a debt does, a named person or people *to* whom it must be paid. Wider models like "the whole duty of man" may be more relevant.

This one example from my list will, I hope, be enough to explain the point. I cannot go through all of them, nor ought it to be necessary. Duties need *not* be quasi-contractual relations between symmetrical pairs of rational human agents. There are all kinds of other obligations holding between asymmetrical pairs, or involving, as in this case, no outside beings at all. To speak of duties to things in the inanimate and comprehensive sectors of my list is not necessarily to personify them superstitiously, or to indulge in chatter about the "secret life of plants."[16] It expresses merely that there are suitable and unsuitable ways of behaving in given situations. People have duties *as* farmers, parents, consumers, forest dwellers, colonists, species members, shipwrecked mariners, tourists, potential ancestors and actual descendants, etc. As such, it is the business of each not to forget his transitory and dependent position, the rich gifts which he has received, and the tiny part he plays in a vast, irreplaceable and fragile whole.

It is remarkable that we now have to state this obvious truth as if it were new, and invent the word "ecological" to describe a whole vast class of duties. Most peoples are used to the idea. In stating it, and getting back into the centre of our moral stage, we meet various difficulties, of which the most insidious is possibly the temptation to feed this issue as fuel to long-standing controversies about religion. Is concern for the nonhuman aspects of our biosphere necessarily superstitious and therefore to be resisted tooth and nail? I have pointed out that it need not be religious. Certified rejectors of all known religions can share it. No doubt, however, there is a wider sense in which any deep and impersonal concern can be called religious — one in which Marxism is a religion. No doubt, too, all such deep concerns have their dangers, but certainly the complete absence of them has worse dangers. Moreover, anyone wishing above all to avoid the religious dimension should consider that the intense individualism which has focused our attention exclusively on the social contract model is itself thoroughly mystical. It has glorified the individual human soul as an object having infinite and transcendent value; has hailed it as the only real creator; and bestowed on it much of the panoply of God. Nietzsche, who was responsible for much of this new theology,[17] took over from the old theology (which he plundered extensively) the assumption that all the rest of creation mattered only as a frame for humankind. This is not an impression which any disinterested observer would get from looking around at it, nor do we need it in order to take our destiny sufficiently seriously.

Crusoe then, I conclude, did have duties concerning this island, and with the caution just given we can reasonably call them duties *to* it. They were not very exacting, and were mostly negative. They differed, of course, from those which a long standing inhabitant of a country has. Here the language of *fatherland* and *motherland*, which is so widely employed, indicates rightly a duty of care and responsibility which can go very deep, and which long-settled people commonly feel strongly. To insist that it is really only a duty to the exploiting human beings is not consistent with the emphasis often given to reverence for the actual trees, mountains, lakes, rivers and the like which are found there. A decision to inhibit all this rich area of human love is a special manoeuvre for which reasons would need to be given, not a dispassionate analysis of existing duties and feelings. What happens, however, when you are shipwrecked on an entirely strange island? As the history of colonization shows, there is a tendency for people so placed to drop any reverence and become more exploitative. But it is not irresistible. Raiders who settle down can quite soon begin to feel at home, as the Vikings did in East Anglia, and can, after a while, become as possessive, proud and protective towards their new land as the old inhabitants. Crusoe himself does, from time to time, show this pride rather touchingly, and it would, I think, certainly have inhibited any moderate temptation, such as that which I mentioned, to have a good bonfire. What keeps him sane through his stay is in fact his duty to God. If that had been absent, I should rather suppose that sanity would depend on a stronger and more positive attachment to the island itself and its creatures. It is interesting, however, that Crusoe's story played its part in developing that same icy individualism which has gone so far towards making both sorts of attachment seem corrupt or impossible. Rousseau delighted in *Robinson Crusoe*, and praised it as the only book fit to be given to a child, *not* because it showed a man in his true relation to animal and vegetable life, but because it was the bible of individualism. "The surest way to raise him [the child] above prejudice and to base his judgments on the true relations of things, is to put him in the place of a solitary man, and to judge all things as they would be judged by such a man in relation to their own utility. . . . So long as only bodily needs are recognized, man is self-sufficing . . . the child knows no other happiness but food and freedom."[18] That false atomic notion of human psychology — a prejudice above which nobody ever raised Rousseau — is the flaw in all social-contract thinking. If he were right, every member of the human race would need a separate island—and what, then, would our ecological problems be? Perhaps, after all, we had better count our blessings.

NOTES

1. John Stuart Mill, *Essay on Liberty* (London: Dent, Everyman's Library, 1910), chap. 4, p. 135.
2. Immanuel Kant, *"Duties to Oneself,"* in *Lectures on Ethics*, trans. Louis Infield (London: Methuen, 1930), p. 118.
3. G.R. Grice, *Grounds for Moral Sentiments* (Cambridge: Cambridge University Press, 1967), pp. 147–149.
4. John Rawls, *A Theory of Justice* (Oxford: Oxford University Press, 1972), p. 512.
5. Ibid., p. 510.
6. Aristotle, Politics 1. 3–8; cf., idem, *Nicomachean* Ethics 7, 2.
7. For example, John Passmore, *Man's Responsibility for Nature* (London: Duckworth, 1974), pp. 116–117, H.J. McCloskey, "Rights," *Philosophical Quarterly* 15 (1965).
8. Nor will it help for philosophers to say "it is not the case that they have rights." Such pompous locutions have either no meaning at all, or the obvious one.
9. Immanual Kant, "Duties towards Animals and Spirits," in *Lectures on Ethics*, p. 240.
10. David Hume, "An Enquiry concerning the Principles of Morals," in *Hume's Moral and Political Philosophy*, ed. H.E. Aiben (New York: Hafner, 1949), app. 3, pp. 190–191.

11. A point well discussed by Stephen R.L. Clark, *The Moral Status of Animals* (Oxford: Clarendon Press, 1977), pp. 12–13.
12. For details, see John Rodman, "Animal Justice: The Counter-Revolution in Natural Right and Law," *Inquiry* 22, nos. 1–2 (Summer 1979).
13. A case first made by Jeremy Bentham, *An Introduction of the Principles of Moral and Legislation*, chap. 17, and well worked out by Peter Singer, *Animal Liberation* (New York: Avon, 1975), Chaps. 1, 5 and 6.
14. Immanuel Kant, *Preface to the Metaphysical Elements of Ethics*, section "Introduction to Ethics," 4 and 5.
15. John Stuart Mill, *Utilitarianism* (London: Dent, Everyman's Library, 1910), chap. 5, p. 45.
16. P. Thompkins and C. Bird, *The Secret Life of Plants* (New York: Harper and Row, 1973), claimed to show, by various experiments involving electrical apparatus, that plants can feel. Attempts to duplicate their experiments have, however, totally failed to produce any similar results. (See A.W. Galston and C.L. Slayman, "The Secret Life of Plants," *American Scientist* 67 [1973]: 337.) It seems possible that the original results were due to a fault in the electrical apparatus. The attempt shows, I think, one of the confusions which continually arise from insisting that all duties must be of the same form. We do not need to prove that plants are animals in order to have reason to spare them. The point is well discussed by Marian Dawkins in her book *Animal Suffering* (London: Chapman and Hall, 1981), pp. 117–119.
17. See particularly, Friedrich Nietzsche, *Thus Spake Zarathustra* 3, section "Of Old and New Tables"; and *The Joyful Wisdom* (otherwise called *The Gay Science*), p. 125 (the Madman's Speech). I have discussed this rather mysterious appointment of man to succeed God in a paper called "Creation and Originality," *Heart & Mind: The Varieties of Moral Experience* (Brighton: The Harvester Press, 1981).
18. Barbara Foxley, trans., *Emile* (London: Dent, Everyman's Library, 1966), pp. 147–148.

QUESTIONS

1. What is it about social contract theory that leads Midgley to say that it is excessively individualistic in orientation? Is she right to suggest that one indication social contract theory is not sound is that it is based on a physical rather than a biological model of the ways in which individuals relate?
2. If my friend has no right to ask me for help, does it follow that I have no duty or obligation to offer it?
3. Did Crusoe have a duty not to destroy his island once it was of no further use to him? Would the situation change if it could be shown to be of no further use to anyone?

HONEY DRIBBLES DOWN YOUR FUR

Tom Regan

> *For Dogen, the others who are "none other than myself" include mountains, rivers, and the great earth. When one thinks like a mountain, one thinks also like the black bear and this is a step . . . to deep ecology which requires openness to the black bear, becoming truly intimate with the black bear, so that honey dribbles down your fur as you catch the bus to work.*

From Environmental Ethics: Philosophical and Policy Perspectives, *edited by Philip P. Hanson. Burnaby: Institute for the Humanities/SFU Publications, 1986, pp. 99–113. Reprinted by permission of the Institute for the Humanities.*

Robert Aitken, Roshi "Gandhi, Dogen and Deep Ecology" quoted by John Seed, "Anthropocentrism Questioned," *Ecophilosophy V,* George Sessions and Bill Devall, eds., p. 14.

I imagine there would be more on my mind than the honey dribbling down my fur if I were to become truly intimate with the black bear as I caught the bus to work. I imagine I would be terrified by the sights and sounds of urban life. And the smells. There would be nothing inviting about the interior of the bus — or its dreaded occupants — unless the bear with whom I was truly intimate was a cute fellow, near domestication from human contact. But then my sympathetic participation in his form of life, however episodic, would be less of a step to deep ecology. A more or less tame bear is more or less the shadow of a bear.

Perhaps, though, I am to think like a bear, not in my urban environment, but in his wild one. The honey dribbling down my fur is the remains of a recent adventure. With him I remember the dense fragrance of wildflowers, sweet to the nose; somewhere, nearby, the source, hidden from the careless eye. But it was found, and, amid the buzzing protestations of the bees, we had drunk the heavy liquid, chewed the catacombed interior, and now, with honey dribbling down my fur, I am setting out in search of new satisfaction — a fish from the nearby stream, a drink from the spring.

Though not easy, this imaginary participation in a bear's life is intelligible. Because we share a common fund of experience with the black bear, we can project ourselves into his life, at least to a limited, perhaps evanescent, extent, whether we imagine ourselves as a bear in his, or in our, environment. If we have the time and inclination, we can — or so I believe — feel his pain, grow thirsty and hungry with him, take pleasure in the presence of companions, taste the honey. Our sympathetic participation in his life will — or can — make us more sensitive to his needs, less willing to unthinkingly frighten him or destroy the wilderness that is his home. Thinking like a bear, in a word, can raise our ursine consciousness. To drink honey like a bear is a step to becoming less self-centered, indeed, less species-centered, in our thinking. And it is in this respect that it is a step to deep ecology.

"Deep ecology" is the name now commonly given to a constellation of views about our proper relationship to the natural order. First introduced by the Norwegian philosopher Arne Naess[1], the name marks the distinction between

1) views that assess the morality of our interactions with nature and its inhabitants exclusively in terms of human interests (what here will be called "anthropocentric environmental ethics" or "anthropocentrism"); and

2) views that assess the morality of our interactions in ways that are not wholly anthropocentric ("nonanthropocentric environmental ethics" or "nonanthropocentrism"). Views of the former type are more or less 'shallow'; those of the latter type, more or less 'deep.'

The "more-or-less" of this contrast in many ways is as important as the basic contrast itself. In the shallow camp, for example, we find those who think that our obligations, as they involve the nonhuman world, are to be fixed exclusively in terms of the interests of the present generation of human beings; but we also find those who would include the interests of generations not yet born.[2] And among a view of either sort there are those who compute human interests exclusively in terms of economic criteria (for example, the criterion of willingness-to-pay), while others deny that our aesthetic and political values, for example, are reducible to units in, or are adequately reflected by, even the most refined economic theory.[3] The class of anthropocentric environmental ethics, in short, is anything but a theoretical monolith. It is home to great diversity.

The same is true of the 'deep' side of the distinction. There are some who allow the relevance of the interests of individual human beings in determining the ethics of our dealings with nature; others are openly hostile to what humans want or prefer, stridently misanthropic.[4] Some think that species *as such* have value, while others (often called "holists") think right and wrong are to be fixed by weighing the effects of what we do for *ecosystems*, possibly even the whole biosphere.[5]

We do not as yet have a full typology of the two major classes of environmental ethics — anthropocentric and nonanthropocentric. Already we know enough, however, to understand why the differences between theories belonging to the same class are no less important than their similarities. We also know why thinking like a bear is, or at least can be, a step to deep ecology. To the extent that our imagining-our-way-into-the-bear's-skin raises our ursine consciousness, makes us less species-centered in thinking about how we should act when it comes to our sometimes fatal interactions with the natural order, to that extent we are moved away from an exclusively anthropocentric environmental ethic. Not just human interests, but also the interests of the black bear must somehow find a place in our moral deliberation and judgement. And not only the interests of the black bear. Our imaginative penetration of the bear's way of life will not have taught us much if the lives of other, relevantly similar animals, whether domestic or wild, are ignored. If we can feel the honey dribbling down our fur, we can also taste the salt with the cow at the lick, smell the blood of the wounded caribou with the wolf, and, with the dog, hear the familiar tread of the master on the stairs.

I think any ethical theory laying claim to our rational assent must be at least this deep — must, that is, recognize the independent moral status, the direct moral relevance, of animals such as these. It is not clear how, or whether, one can 'prove' that this is so; it is not clear how, or whether, one can 'prove' any moral belief of this sort.[6] What one can do is consider the assumptions and implications of anthropocentrism and ask how rationally and morally satisfactory they are. For example, if a given theory considers *human* pain and suffering morally relevant but denies the moral relevance of the pain and suffering of the black bear, then it seems to be rationally defective. For pain is pain, and pain is in itself undesirable, to whomsoever it may occur, whether beast or human.[7] Or if a theory assumes that moral principles are the rules self-interested agents agree to have imposed on everyone's behavior, and claims that one has duties directly *only* to those individuals who are capable of entering into such agreements (or *contracts*), then one wants to protest, I think, that the theory's implications are morally skewed.[8] A young child, for example, lacks the abilities necessary for contracting; the theory implies, therefore, that we can do no wrong directly to the child, that we have no direct duties in this case, and so *do no wrong to the child* if, for example, we spend an evening's amusement torturing her. But if, as I assume, thoughtful people will agree that we *owe it to the child* not to torture her, despite her inability to contract, then it cannot be rational to deny that we owe it to a dog not to torture him, because *he* lacks the abilities required to contract. For these reasons, then, though not only for these, I do not myself believe that any version of anthropocentrism is rationally or morally satisfactory.

These sketchy objections to anthropocentric environmental ethics must face serious problems of their own. One does not offer a sound objection to a moral theory unless the objection is *of a kind* that is both relevant and fair. How moral theories *are* to be fairly and relevantly assessed, however, is a highly divisive issue, one that cannot be even *superficially* examined on this occasion.[9] As is always true in philosophy, questions outnumber answers. If those of us involved in this conference are to make any progress in our attempt to answer some of our questions about environmental ethics, we must assume that we can agree on how we should answer others. So let us assume, for the sake of argument — and this is a large assumption, certainly — that I am right: No version of anthropocentrism is adequate. Some form of nonanthropocentric environmental ethic, some specimen of a (more or less) deep ecology, must be where the truth lies. Our question then becomes, Which one? Or, alternatively, How deep?

One answer is: Deeper than you've gone so far. And one way to suggest the depth others would have us plumb is to recall the passage quoted at the outset. For Dogen, it will be recalled, not only became "truly intimate" with the black bear; he also "thought as a mountain." So, to understand our moral place in nature's scheme of things, the passage suggests, we must not only enter imaginatively into the lives of nonhuman animals; we must also enter imaginatively into the mute majesty of mountains — and, by implication, of oceans, stars, rocks, forests, or, in a word, *all* that dwell therein. To think like a black bear, on this view, is a step to deep ecology, but it is only a step, failing by itself to complete the journey of a thousand miles to the true environmental ethic.

What shall we make of the injunction to think like a mountain? Peter Singer gives part of the correct answer, I think, when he states that "such imagining yields a perfect blank."[10] Unlike the case of the black bear, with whom we share a real, even if comparatively small, family of experiences, a mountain is not a conscious individual and so has no experiences in common with us. This is why, were I to attempt to imagine being a mountain, the result would be "a perfect blank" — that is, no awareness. Thus, if, in order to demonstrate the need for an environmental ethic that is deeper than one that requires consideration of what benefits and harms nonhuman animals, we must first think the thoughts of a mountain, and given, as seems obvious, that the attempt to do this yields *no thoughts at all*, then the need for a deeper environmental ethic has not been demonstrated.

Singer and many others believe the lesson to be learned from this exercise is simple: the boundary of morality is sentience, where by "sentience" is meant the capacity to experience pleasure and pain. When that capacity is present, then there is something to take into account, something of direct moral importance; when it is absent, then there is nothing of direct moral relevance to consider. Black bears are in; Black Mountain is out. Let us call this view *sentientism*. Is this as far, as deep, as we can or should go in our search for a nonanthropocentric environmental ethic?

If the only theory of value that required our serious consideration was one that reduces value to certain mental states or feelings, or, more particularly, if the only view of this sort worthy of our assent was hedonism (pleasant mental states have positive, painful mental states have negative, value), then we wouldn't have a serious choice. Sentientism would win hands down. But philosophical plots are never this simple. There are important theories of value that differ from, and are inconsistent with, any unqualified version of a mental state theory, including hedonism. Of particular relevance in the present context is a view of the sort we find in Kant, where it is individuals, not their mental states, that are said to have a distinctive kind of value, what we'll call *inherent value*. Kant, it is true, offers his vision of inherent value in the course of developing a very famous anthropocentric theory,[11] so the relevance of his ideas to nonanthropocentric environmental ethical theories needs to be approached indirectly. But let us set out some of the important features of the idea of inherent value as this applies to individual human beings, as, on Kant's view, it does; then we will be able to understand what it would mean to apply this idea to those who are not human.[12]

A large part of the characterization of inherent value, or what Kant refers to as "end in itself", is negative. Among the defining characteristics are the following:

1. The inherent value of an individual human being is not reducible to, and is incommensurate with, the value of that individual's mental states. A normally happy person, for example, is not of greater inherent value than someone who is chronically depressed. Our inherent value does not wax or wane with changes in the hedonic tone of our lives.

2. The inherent value of an individual human being is not reducible to, nor does it vary with, the individual's usefulness relative to the interests of others. A surgeon, for example, has no greater inherent value, even assuming her greater utility, than a dishwasher.

3. The inherent value of an individual human being is not reducible to, nor does it vary according to the possession of, the individual's skills or other virtues, including moral virtues. Wayne Gretzky is neither more nor less inherently valuable than the substitute right wing on the company hockey team, and Sister Theresa has no greater inherent value than a woman doing time for child abuse.

4. An individual human being's inherent value is not dependent on, and is not reducible to, the attitudes and beliefs others have toward, or about, him. Those who are loved and idolized are no more valuable, inherently, than those who are hated and despised, and persons who belong to 'lower' classes are not less inherently valuable than those who belong to 'higher' classes (e.g., Untouchables and Brahmins in India).

Though not complete, the foregoing remarks about inherent value at least should suggest how the idea offers something on which to pin our (presumed) egalitarian hopes. If, as the idea allows, all who have inherent value have it equally, then the noble vision of the equality among 'all men' may have found a home in theory. For differ though we do in many ways — in terms of our skills, for example, or our moral character and usefulness to others — we are all the same, all equal, when it comes to possessing this fundamental value, inherent value. Each of us is, in Kant's terminology, an end in himself or herself, and no one of us who is, is so to a lesser or greater degree than anyone else. Moreover, if this much is true, then we can glimpse both the spirit and the letter of Kant's proscription against treating one another "as means merely." This I do, for example, whenever I treat you as if your value as an individual is reducible to your usefulness to me or, less self-centeredly, to some group, even the public at large. To treat you thus is to treat you as if you were a thing, a tool, a mere resource, whose purpose for being is to advance the interests of others.

Now, types of value, like entities generally, ought not to be multiplied beyond necessity. Why, then, introduce a second, quite different, kind of value (inherent value) if one kind of value (the value of mental states, such as pleasure) is enough? The short answer some philosophers give is that value of this latter kind just isn't enough. Unless our individual, equal inherent value is postulated, these thinkers believe — (and Kant is one member of this group, I believe) — the moral theory we will be left holding will be unequal to the task of providing a fully adequate account of moral right and wrong. In particular, such a theory will allow, possibly encourage, us to treat the individual *merely as a means* to some supposedly desirable end (for example, the general welfare). To the extent that such treatment of the individual is wrong, and assuming that any and all theories that fail to recognize our equal inherent value imply that it is not, to that extent we have good reason to deny their validity as theories and postulate our equal inherent value.

That this value is postulated in our case is not unimportant. Kant, for example, makes it abundantly clear that our value as ends-in-ourselves is not observed by the senses, nor 'intuited' by the intellect in its *a priori* exercise. The status of inherent value in our moral theorizing, he implies, is analogous to the status of electrons in our theorizing in physics. In the latter case, we postulate that there are electrons in order both to unify and explain what we know, or what we think we know, about the physical order; analogously, then, we postulate inherent value in order to unify and explain what we know, or think we know, about the moral order. We know — or at least many of us think we know — that it is wrong to treat any human person merely as a means, regardless of race, sex, age, intellect, virtue, economic standing, etc.; and it is only by postulating our equal inherent value, or so some moral philosophers believe, that we are able to explain why this is wrong and bring unity to other, related beliefs about the wrongful treatment of the individual (for example, that it is wrong to execute a native youth known to be innocent of a crime in order to avert a race riot in the community).

The concept of inherent value, then, has important uses in anthropocentric ethical views. But it also holds promise for views that are nonanthropocentric. It has been argued, for example — and convincingly, to my mind[13] — that possession of inherent value rationally cannot be limited only to human persons but instead must be attributed to nonhuman animals like the black bear — to animals, that is, who, like human persons, are the experiencing subjects of a life that matters to them as individuals, independently of their usefulness to others. Indeed, the grounds for postulating inherent value in the case of these animals are the same as those we have for doing so in the case of human persons — namely, in order to unify and explain what we know, or think we know, at least on reflection, about the moral ties that bind us to these animals. Thus, though the notion of inherent value or its equivalent (e.g., Kant's concept of "end in itself") historically has been a major theme of anthropocentrism in ethics, there is no reason why it cannot play a leading role in nonanthropocentric theories.

Like sentientism, theories that are built on the notion of inherent value ("inheritism," if this verbal barbarism will be forgiven me) can move us in the direction of a deep ecology. How deep? Here we encounter an enormously important difference between the two kinds of theory. *By definition* sentientism limits those individuals of direct moral concern to those who have *mental states*, to those who are conscious. Everything else, whether individual, group, or system, fails to possess what is of direct moral significance, so that nonsentient nature in general is consigned, in John Rodman's graphic phrase, to "to the realm of thinghood."[14] Mountains, rivers, deserts, prairies, wetlands — all wilderness, wherever it may be, lacks what it takes to be of direct moral relevance. So long as we do not embrace panpsychism, everything lacking consciousness remains beyond the moral pale.

Inheritism, by contrast, is theoretically open-minded at this point. Notwithstanding the fact that theories of both human and animal rights deploy this notion, and despite the fact that both the humans and animals in question are conscious, it remains true that *there is nothing in the notion of inherent value itself that necessarily limits its possession to what is capable of having mental states, to what is conscious. Anything* that has a value that is not reducible to its utility for others, or to how others feel about it, or to its virtues, or to how happy or miserable it is, to that extent *can* have inherent value. Whether a strong case can be made for believing that it *actually* has such value will depend on our showing more than that these negative tests are passed, but there is nothing in the nature of these tests themselves that entails that something lacking consciousness cannot possess value of this kind.

Once this much is seen, we should not be surprised that a variety of theories on the nonanthropocentric side affirm that a variety of things are inherently valuable. Indeed, one measure of the "depth" of nonanthropocentric theories is how much they depart from the Kantian model, where such value is limited to individual human persons (at least amongst terrestrial beings). A version of inheritism that includes individual animals like the black bear is deeper than Kant's theory, but still like it in limiting such value to individuals. A deeper theory would be one that recognized the inherent value of *species as such*, for example, or one that attributed such value to *ecosystems*, and, in either case, denied that individuals have the sort of independent value that inherent value is. The theoretical limit, perhaps, is a theory that affirms the inherent value of the *biosphere itself* and sees the value of the individual as mythological, a product, perhaps, of a bankrupt individualistic paradigm in Western metaphysics. If we think of the best environmental ethical theory as the key with which we open the full range of our ethical questions as these relate to the natural order, the task before us is to decide what version of nonanthropocentric theory this is, how deep we go in parting company both with the Kantian and the sentientist tradition in ethics.

How shall we rationally decide this? How can we? One way is to follow Singer and refuse to go beyond sentientism. When, in the spirit of Dogen, Singer is asked to "think like a mountain," he finds, we know, "a perfect blank" and concludes that there is nothing to consider: Since there is nothing that matters experientially to the mountain, there is nothing of direct moral importance that can matter to us. Such is the provocative ambiguity of the invitation to 'think like a mountain,' however, that one might reach a very different conclusion. *Of course* one draws a "perfect blank" when one attempts to put oneself in a mountain's shoes. *Of course* there is nothing that matters experientially to the mountain, nothing that gives it pleasure or causes it pain, for example. To realize these truths is, one might say, the whole point of the exercise. Well, not quite the whole point since a truth half understood is misunderstood, and the other half of the truth, the half that Singer and other sentientists fail to understand, is that we carry prejudicial baggage with us if we assume that the moral status of the mountain depends on whether it can *experience* anything, pleasure and pain in particular. Isn't this assumption simply an unrecognized vestige of the anthropocentrism Singer and other sentientists triumphantly think they have put behind them? For consider: A mountain doesn't have to be one of us, be human, given the sentientist's views, to be of direct moral relevance; it just has to be *sufficiently like us*, be sentient, to count. Isn't that so close to anthropocentrism as to make us wonder how far we've gone beyond it? To reply that one draws 'a perfect blank' whenever one tries to 'think like a mountain' assumes that a clear and compelling answer has been given to this question. It does not give it. It is not difficult to imagine Dogen's tolerant smile over the sentientist's treatment of this question.

I think Dogen would be right to insist on the need for more from sentientists at this juncture, and right too (if Dogen took this step) to argue that the 'blank' state of mind we encounter when we 'think like a mountain' is not the answer some sentientists evidently think it is. Right on both points, however, Dogenites have their work cut out for them if, short of a preemptive appeal to an unarguable mysticism, they are to move us, rationally, to a deeper environmental ethic. The need for argument is not peculiar to sentientists, so that if, as seems to me, there is good reason to believe that standard sentientist arguments are weak,[15] it in no way follows that those who follow Dogen win by default. How, then, by way of positive argument, can an environmental ethic deeper than sentientism, deeper even than a version of inheritism that extends to the black bear and other individual animals — how can the case for a deeper theory proceed?

Among the possibilities that have been explored, three merit our attention. The first is cut from familiar theoretical cloth. Inherent value is postulated in the case of something (for example, species, ecosystems, the biosphere) to illuminate and unify our considered beliefs about right and wrong; theories that attempt to avoid postulating inherent value, we are to suppose, fail to offer the desirable illumination and unity. By way of example: Some have argued[16] that species *as such* must be viewed as having inherent value because (a) thoughtful people agree that it is wrong to render any species extinct and because (b) the only satisfactory way to account for this belief is by postulating independent, inherent value for species in and of themselves.

This approach cannot be any stronger than the success proponents have in convincing us that both (a) and (b) are true. Success is not easy to come by in either case. Although many people are enthusiastic about the immorality of destroying some species (for example, the great blue whale, the African elephant, and the Siberian tiger), moral vigor wanes in the case of obscure species of plants or species of lethal viruses. Comparatively few people are of the opinion that we would do something wrong if we killed the last four remaining specimens of *Phacelia argilaceae* (all of which are enclosed by a fence in an inhospitable region of Utah), and even fewer believe it would be wrong to destroy, *absolutely*, every trace of the smallpox virus *(Poxvirus variolae)*; most people, it seems, would happily consign that species to utter oblivion. So it is, at best, an unstable platform, this attempt to argue for the inherent value of species *as such* because otherwise we will be unable to unify and illuminate the moral beliefs thoughtful people have about the extinction of species. Whether right or wrong, most people, even thoughtful ones, seem to be selective when it comes to the species they think ought to be saved.

Or consider variations of the so-called "last man argument."[17] You are the last human being on earth. None will come after you, and you know it. You have the means to blow the earth to smithereens before you die; or you can leave it be, to work out its future destiny on its own, so to speak. What ought you to do? Some there are who think that thoughtful people will speak with one voice: Don't blow it up. There is room for robust skepticism on this point, however, and a skepticism that is dwarfed by the one that surrounds the suggestion that the *only* or *best* way to account for this presumed belief about the desirability of saving the earth is by attributing inherent value to it. Equally plausible, it seems, is the suggestion that destroying it when this is avoidable would be singularly ungrateful, like smashing the dinner plates after the host has dropped dead of a heart attack. Just as I owe the host, even when deceased, behaviour that displays my thanks for the opportunity to dine, so I owe the earth something like a debt of gratitude for my past life. Or so it may be argued. It is more in the nature of a leap of faith than a reasoned argument to conclude that we *must* attribute inherent value to the earth if we are to have any reason, as the last man, not to blow it to kingdom come.

A second possibility for deeper theories is to resurrect naturalism in ethics. Where we find certain *facts* (for example, facts of the form X-is-alive), there we also find *values* (of the form, say, X-is-inherently-good), and, once values take up independent lodging in the world, obligation cannot be far behind. From "X is inherently good" more than a few have derived "X ought not to be destroyed". But naturalism is a vision ill-suited to the dominant temper of the times, where the shadows of both Hume and Moore are still cast across the thought of most of their philosophical descendants. Even in the case of the most promising work among the new naturalists — Paul Taylor's ethic of respect for nature[18] — the centuries old doubts do not go away. With Taylor we can, I think, agree that living things are teleological centers of life, all 'striving' to realize their individual potential — their good, if you like, a good they have independently of their usefulness to us. But the good we find here seems an inadequate sort of good on which to erect human obligations. An oak tree that fully actualizes its natural propensities is, let us agree, a better oak tree than one that does not — is better *as an oak tree*, better *of its kind*. That something is good-of-its-kind, however, creates no obligation to preserve or protect it. Otherwise we would be obliged to rally round and save Henry Lee Lucas, who, as the confessed murderer of over 150 people, is the best of his kind, the most prolific murderer, we have yet encountered. If, in reply, we are told that it is exemplars of *natural* kinds that we are to preserve and protect, the case seems just as counterintuitive. A specimen of belladonna is good of its kind if it has the power to kill off the unwary hiker. Must we, therefore, act to save the most virulent strains, out of respect for their value? I do not think it unfair to give a negative answer to this question in particular and to resist in general the suggestion that living things that are good of their kind ought to be respected and preserved. This sort of goodness (good of its kind), which is, I think, naturalistic, is not equal to the theoretical task of grounding human obligations. Morally significant values, ones on which our duties are based, are not facts in the way naturalism assumes or requires. Or so it seems to me.

The third possibility worthy of consideration has mystical markings. Rooted in the awareness of the interconnectedness of all things (my body, for example, in all likelihood contains atoms from a long dead brontosaurus, from an even older dead star, from the body of Julius Caesar) — rooted in this awareness, a mystical environmental ethic transports us beyond the illusoriness of separateness, including the myth of the separateness of our own individual being, and replaces this pedestrian vision of the self and world with a more or less ineffable vision of the unity or sameness of all that is. Where, before, we took comfort in the ignorant sound of two hands clapping, we now listen to the wise timbre of the solitary hand.

It would be nice — or so many will suppose — if unbridled monism could be summarily dismissed. But it is both too old and too new for that, and the names and life-ways associated are too noble to allow a breezy rejection to count. "Merely to list the variations on [the] theme," writes Theodore Roszak,[19] himself an ardent supporter, "would fill a book. Lao Tzu teaching 'the great Tao flows everywhere' . . . the Vedic wisdom which can say of all things the eye may light upon '*tat tuam asi* — that's *you*! . . . the Avatamsaka Sutra that transfigures the universe into the Buddha's sacred body of light . . . the night Hermetic Uroborus inscribed 'One is All' . . . the *Wakan-Tanka* of the American Indians, whose presence made every object holy, as much the stone as man . . . Blake summoning us 'To see a world in a grain of sand' . . . Dylan Thomas discovering that 'The force that through the green fuse drives the flower drives my blood' . . .". A recent addition to this list, John Seed, the Australian environmentalist, expresses the unitary vision in these terms.[20]

> When humans investigate and see through their layers of anthropocentric self-cherishing, a most profound change in consciousness begins to take place. Alienation subsides. The human is no longer an outsider, apart. Your humaneness is then recognized as being merely the most recent stage of your existence, and as you stop identifying exclusively with this chapter, you start to get in touch with yourself as mammal, as vertebrate, as a species only recently emerged from the rain forest. As the fog of amnesia disperses, there is a transformation in your relationship to other species, and in your commitment to them . . . "I am protecting the rain forest" develops into "I am that part of the rain forest recently emerged into thinking." What a relief then: The thousands of

years of (imagined) separation are over and we begin to recall our true nature. That is, the change is a spiritual one, thinking like a mountain, sometimes referred to as deep ecology.

As your memory improves, as the implications of the sciences of evolution and ecology are internalised and replace the outmoded anthropocentric structures in your mind, there is identification with all life. There follows the realisation that the distinction between 'life' and 'lifeless' is a human construct. Every atom in this body existed before organic life emerged 4,000 million years ago. Remember your own childhood as minerals, as lava, as rocks? Rocks contain the potentiality to weave themselves into such stuff as this. We are the rocks dancing. Why do we look down on them with such a condescending air? It is they that are the immortal part of us.

It is hard to decide what to say of the stuff of which the unitary vision is made. It is tempting to dismiss it, not because the arguments are bad (more often than not, there are no arguments, good or bad), but because most of it is unintelligible to the outsider. On the other hand, it is tempting to be tempted, to give in to the pull of union-with-nature which, I assume, all of us feel at times in our life. (I do, in any event.) If the power and existence of the feeling were the marks of its truth, we would know where to stand. But feelings, alas, do not wear their veracity on their sleeve, so that we must, if we are to show respect for the ordinary canons of reason, think about, not merely experience, the unitary vision, test its mettle by critical reflection, not accept its validity on the grounds that it is psychologically compelling or because ancient sages and noble peoples have believed it. And here's the rub. For the noble vision does not fare well when subjected to tests which, administered in other quarters to other views, are fair.

For example: There are problems enough in making sense of my *identity* over time as a human person, if we accept a worldview that has human persons in it. How much more difficult must it be, therefore, to tie my identity to the rain forest or to 4 billion year old atoms. What can be the criterion of identity, given such a view? If I am the same as a rock because we both contain some of the same atoms of a more ancient bit of matter, what is it that makes this atom, now, the same as the atom it was then? I do not think we have any easy, or possibly any intelligible, answers ready to hand. It is not clear to me whether, in the end, it is the sound rather than the substance of the ideas that attracts us — their novelty, their psychological resonance, their romance. But not their truth.

Most proponents of the unitary vision are aware of the difficulties others find; nor are they short on replies. The limits of both time and my own knowledge make it impossible for me even to attempt to do justice to this debate here. The perennial philosophy does not lend itself to simple confirmation. Or disconfirmation. (Or, possibly, to neither!) I hope it is not unfair to note, however, that the gaze of the unitary vision seems not so much to avoid, as to raise to a different environment, the problems that plague more pedestrian accounts of the world and our place in it. If, for example, naturalism is not a credible theory of value given our ordinary, non-unitary vision, it is difficult to understand how the case is any different if, in place of natural facts, we have mystical ones. It is, that is, not clear to me how we can infer that something *is good*, in any morally significant sense of "good", simply from our knowledge of realization that something *is*. If, in reply, we are told that mystical knowledge of value is immediate, not inferential, so that in knowing the true nature of what is we also know, immediately, the truth about what is good and ought to be, then we ought, I think, to test this ice *very* carefully before skating on it. To advance a position that builds in its own immunity from criticism runs the risk of permitting nonsense to pass for truth. And the greater the possible truth, the greater the actual risk.

Some will view this reluctance to take such risks as a symptom of a deeper, more sinister uneducability. George Sessions, whose influential work I commend to your attention, may have this in mind when he voices his "fear that many Western philosophers and other intellectuals are so thoroughly entrenched in their Western academic training and methodologies and narrow specialities that they are going to be of very little help toward, and might actually constitute a reactionary hindrance to, the development of an ecological paradigm"[21] of the sort we find articulated, for example, by John Seed. Well, perhaps. But perhaps these "reactionaries," if not on the side of the angels, at least are on the side of what is true. The veracity of the unitary vision, the "new ecological paradigm," if accepted by enough of us, would move us to an environmental ethic deeper than the one I would personally endorse, the one that knows the feel and taste of honey dribbling down our fur. To go any deeper than this, to my mind at least, is to get in way over our heads when we can, and rationally should, avoid it.

NOTES

1. Arne Naess, "The Shallow and the Deep Long-Range Ecology Movements", *Inquiry*, Vol. 16 (1973), pp. 95–100.
2. As representative of the former view, see Gregory Kavka, "The Futurity Problem," in R.I. Skora and Brian Barry, eds. *Obligations to Future Generations* (Philadelphia: Temple University Press, 1978) pp. 186-203. The latter position finds expression in, for example, Annette Baier, "For the Sake of Future Generations," in Tom Regan, ed., *Earthbound: New Introductory Essays in Environmental Ethics* (New York: Random House, 1983). Additional references are found in Baier's "Suggestions for Further Reading."
3. As representative of the former view, see William Baxter, *People or Penguins: The Case for Optimal Pollution* (New York: Columbia University Press, 1974). The latter position finds expression in, for example, Mark Sagoff, "Ethics and Economics in Environmental Law," in Tom Regan, ed., *Earthbound, op. cit.* Additional references are found in Sagoff's "Suggestions for Further Reading."
4. As representative of the former view, see William Aiken, "Ethical Issues in Agriculture," in Tom Regan, ed., *Earthbound, op. cit.* The latter position finds expression in, for example, J. Baird Callicott, "Animal Liberation: A Triangular Affair," *Environmental Ethics* 2, no. 4 (Winter 1980), pp. 311–38. Additional references are found in Sagoff's "Suggestions for Further Reading."
5. As representative of the former view, see Alastaire Gunn, "Why Preserve Rare Species?" in Tom Regan, ed., *Earthbound, op. cit.* The latter position finds expression in, for example, Callicott's "Animal Liberation: A Triangular Affair," *op. cit.* Additional references are found in Gunn's "Suggestions for Further Reading."
6. These issues are pursued more fully in my *The Case For Animal Rights* (Berkeley: University of California Press, 1983), Chapter 4.
7. The point is made forcefully by both Bentham and Mill, for example. See their respective selections in Tom Regan and Peter Singer, eds., *Animal Rights and Human Obligations* (Englewood Cliffs: Prentice-Hall, 1976).
8. The point is pursued at length in my *The Case For Animal Rights, op. cit.*, Chapter 5.
9. See *The Case for Animal Rights*, Chapter 4, for a discussion of these issues.
10. Peter Singer, *Practical Ethics* (New York: Oxford University Press, 1982), p. 92. Singer refers to a weed, not a mountain, in the passage cited. The philosophical point remains the same.
11. See, for example, Immanuel Kant, *The Fundamental Principles of the Metaphysic of Morals*, many editions.
12. A fuller discussion is offered in Chapter 7 of *The Case for Animal Rights, op. cit.*
13. *Ibid.*

14. John Rodman, "The Liberation of Nature," *Inquiry*, 20 (1977), 83–131.
15. I argue this in, for example, "The Nature and Possibility of an Environmental Ethic," *Environmental Ethics*, 3 (1981), 19–34; reprinted in Tom Regan, *All That Dwell Therein: Essays on Animal Rights and Environmental Ethics* (Berkeley: University of California Press, 1982), pp. 184–205.
16. See, for example, the essay by Callicott cited above.
17. For a full discussion, see Robert Elliot, *An Environmental Ethic* (Ph.D. Dissertation, Queensland University).
18. Paul Taylor, "The Ethics of Respect for Nature," *Environmental Ethics*, 3, no. 3 (1981). Taylor's views are much deeper and more subtle than I am able to suggest here.
19. Theodore Roszak, *Where the Wasteland Ends* (New York: Doubleday Books, 1973), p. 398.
20. John Seed, "*Anthropocentrism Questioned*," in George Sessions and Bill Devall, eds., *Ecophilosophy V*, pp. 11–12.
21. George Sessions, *ibid*., p. 7. Session's address is Sierra College, Rocklin, California 95677.

QUESTIONS

1. Contrast anthropocentric environmental ethics with deep ecology.
2. Why does Regan reject a deep ecology approach to explaining and justifying animal rights? What justification does he put in its place?
3. What is the "mental states" theory of value and why do its proponents believe that it justifies the view that animals have rights? Kantians object to grounding morality on mental states or feelings. Why? Kantians have traditionally thought that only human beings have inherent moral value. Why? What are Regan's reasons for thinking that they are mistaken in this regard?
4. Why does Regan think that things lacking consciousness cannot possess inherent value?

AGAINST ANIMAL RIGHTS*

Jan Narveson

Professor Regan distinguishes three levels, as we might call them, of theoretical involvement with the environment:

1) the Anthropocentric, which views all such problems from the strictly human viewpoint;
2) the Sentientistic, which views them from the standpoint of all sentient creatures, not just humans; and
3) the Deep Ecologistic, which views them from the standpoint of the entire natural environment, including nonsentient entities.

In his paper, Regan rejects the first, accepts the second, and expresses rather more sympathy for the third than I think it deserves, although he does reject it as well. In the present comments, I shall be concerned with the way in which he argues for the position he holds, and supply some arguments for staying at the first level — not quite all of that either, in fact! I

From Environmental Ethics: Philosophical and Policy Perspectives, *edited by Philip P. Hanson. Burnaby: Institute for the Humanities/SPU Publications, 1986, pp. 119–123. Reprinted by permission of the Institute for the Humanities.*

shall also supplement his arguments against the third level, and make a specific criticism, one that will be seen to be crucial for purposes of environmental ethics, of *his* level-two position. (Not all level-two positions would be susceptible of this criticism, but those that did not would, I think, succumb to our combined criticisms of the third-level position.)

Let us begin by contemplating, for a moment, the subject of 'inherent value' as described by Regan. Following Kant, he suggests that this "type" of value is not reducible to "the value of that individual's mental states", nor with his usefulness to others or their attitudes to or beliefs about him, nor with any of his skills or "other virtues, including moral virtues"; and he suggests that "there is nothing in the notion of inherent value itself that necessarily limits its possession to what is capable of having mental states . . ." Is this right? Well, here we must make a distinction, at least. No doubt this may seem an academic point, but as a matter of fact *Kant's* notion of 'inherent value' was such that it certainly would *not* be possible for anything but minded entities to have it. In fact, Kant didn't think animals had it either, so far as that goes. The reason is that, on this concept of inherent value, to 'have' inherent value is to be a subject with values in a strong sense of the term "values" such that one must have a rational will to have them. People have 'inherent' dignity and moral worth by virtue of being moral beings, centres of moral decision-making. It is easy enough to see why the term "inherent value" is appropriate here: for beings of this kind are 'centres' of value — one is tempted to say 'originators' of value; and so nobody *else* needs to be on the scene in order for them to be subjects of value, since, so to speak, they already are. Nothing of this sort makes any sense regarding mountains, however.

But there is another sense of "inherent value" in which non-minded entities may be said to have it (sometimes). Consider, as perhaps the outstanding category of cases in question, the notion of aesthetic value. When we say that a certain musical performance is a fine one, or a certain painting a great one, we are making a judgement that does not call for completion along the lines of specifying the purpose to which the performance or painting in question contributes. It is not the point of a painting to be a means to some further, distinct state of affairs in the world. Mechanical devices, say, are good (or bad) 'for' something, but not works of art. Nevertheless, it would be absurd to say of a painting that its value is necessarily equal in all things that have any of it at all. Nor, in a sense, is its value "not dependent on . . . the attitudes and beliefs others have toward, or about" it. Of course it is a debatable issue whether beauty is 'in the eye of the beholder', but it would be absurd to claim that the eye of the beholder had absolutely nothing to do with it. We build museums and symphony halls in order that *we* may enjoy the experiences which great works of art afford us. We do *not* build them in order that the works of art *themselves* may get their just rewards for being great! I am sure that it is a matter of the most utter indifference to a painting where or how it happens to be lodged, or even whether it 'lives' or 'dies'! In the case of entities with Kantian-type 'inherent' value, on the other hand, it at least makes sense to suppose that they can be owed duties in their own right, and perhaps even that their existence constrains us independently of our own end, which is what Kant thought.

Having made this distinction, we can see that 'Deep Ecology' derives no benefit from the notion of inherent value. On the one hand, it makes no sense to attribute Kantian-type inherent value to the environment, so that road, together with Kantian conclusions about treating it as an end-in-itself, is out; and if our valuing of the environment is aesthetic, then it is at least not true that we ought to regard mountains and whatnot as having *rights*. Rather, our question would then be whether the beauty of various things in the environment outweighs the value of various alterations that would diminish that beauty. And that seems to me exactly the right sort of question to ask, as a matter of fact. But beauty is one of *our* interests, and that is how it enters the picture — i.e., *not* as 'inherent' in Regan's sense.

As an additional point, I would like to urge that the whole idea of Deep Ecology is hopeless for a different reason. The trouble with Nature is that everything is a part of it, including ourselves. *No matter what we do to it*, this will still be true. Should we blow up as much of our environment as we can with hydrogen bombs, the smithereens into which we blow it will be just as 'natural', just as much 'whole system', as it is now or ever was. It is, then, useless to try to do anything to 'preserve' Nature: anything you can conceivably do to it will leave it just as much Nature as ever. When we are concerned about our environment, then, what makes this concern coherent is precisely that it is *our* environment, and that so viewed, we are better off if it is in some conditions rather than others: it looks nicer, smells better, leaves us in a better state of health, affords us with more of the things we want. To imagine that Nature in its own right has interests conflicting with ours, and interests which take precedence over or are even equal to ours, is simply to go off a conceptual deep end. 'Deep' Ecology is too deep — indeed, a bottomless pit.

Next, we need to observe something about the character of Regan's concern with animals. On his view, animals are people, as it were: that is, we have duties to them as individuals, duties not to kill or harm them, to sustain them in good health, and so on. Even if we have any such duties at all, in general — which I doubt — I don't accept Regan's reasons for thinking that we have them. But rather than arguing about that here, I just wish to point out that this is not the kind of moral relation to animals that will capture one of the concerns many or most people do have regarding the animal part of our environment. That concern is for the preservation of *species*, not individuals. It is environmental and ecological, rather than personal. A given species exists and is preserved if it has members — *any* members. And it flourishes at some optimal size, which can be either fallen short of *or* exceeded. In the latter case, it might be environmentally sound to declare open season for awhile and thin down the population. In the former, it might be well to capture a few sound specimens and have them breed in safe captivity for awhile. But this is not the sort of treatment that John Q. Bear should get if he literally has *rights*. We can't shoot a few million Chinese or Indians just because there are too many of them. And on the other hand, we do not owe it to anybody that we, for instance, capture a few females and shack him and them up together in a motel for a few years until they restore the right population density to their particular biological variety of *Homo sapiens*.

For similar reasons, the whole idea of doing environmental ethics by positing rights on the part of the things we are concerned to protect is completely misguided. Forests, mountains, species — these simply aren't the sort of things that can sensibly be thought to have rights. And while particular animals can, perhaps, be alleged without actual self-contradiction to have rights, I am very far from persuaded that they do, and in any case it is quite clear that the preservation or protection of individual animals as such simply isn't where the action is when it comes to environmental ethics.

Let us return to the Reganian position, that animals have rights in their own right. His arguments for this, mainly, are two: first, that we are required to acknowledge such rights when we consider such cases as those of the senile, the feeble-minded, or infant humans. And second, that we can sympathize with sentient beings, because we are sentient ourselves, and if our own claims to good treatment are based on our own sentience, then we must extend those to all sentient creatures, in consistency. I reject both of these arguments. The fact that one can sympathize with another entity, come to realize that it has a point of view, does not rationally commit one to giving it rights, including those one wants in those same respects on one's own behalf. Something more is needed: to wit, the capacity to act in such a way as to make it in our interest to extend those rights. We do sympathize strongly with marginal humans, and more especially do those who are near and dear to them. This, I think, is sufficient basis to extend the rights it clearly is in our interest to extend to all normal humans to marginal cases as well; but that basis is clearly lacking for animals.[1] But I cannot here develop this more robust theory of rights.[2] I just don't think that rights are as easily come by as Regan thinks!

But rights certainly do come into these questions: not rights of animals or plants or mountains, but rights of plain old people such as ourselves. Where they come into it — and in a very big way — is in the possibility that certain humans have the right to do things to the environment that certain *other* humans don't like. In these possibilities lie, I think, all of the problems of environmental ethics currently exercising responsible people. That's quite enough, in my judgment, without going further and taking on the problems of animals for their own sakes, or of trees or canyons for theirs.

One can view certain questions about the treatment of animals in this light. Suppose you wish to mistreat an animal, in my view of how animals should be treated: e.g., to whip it, or to stick electrodes into it, or to eat it. If it is *my* animal, there is no conceptual problem: I then have the right to insist that you refrain from doing those things to it. But what if it is yours? Then, it would seem, I do not. I have only the right to request that you refrain, and to attempt to persuade you to my point of view. That is not enough to satisfy enthusiasts for animal rights, however. They want recognition of a right on the part of the animal itself. But there is another possibility to consider. What if they have the right to an environment in which animals do not suffer? Perhaps that would be like the right to clean air. Armed with such a right, if we have it, we can insist that others clean up their air-polluting acts on our accounts. I am inclined to think that we do have such a right, but in this commentary cannot develop the case for it.

But would a right to an environment free of suffering animals be enough like a right to clean air so that I could act similarly against a torturer of animals? This is problematic. We need to ask what the right to clean air would be based on, if we have one. Is it the right to health, so that others may not do what is injurious to my health, such as to insert smoke into my lungs? I don't think so. It doesn't negatively affect my health if you put your hand gently but firmly against my chest, thus preventing my further progress in that direction. But unless it is a direction I have no right to go in, you don't have the right to do that. I can insist that you get your hands off me just because the body you are putting them on is mine. However, with others' pains, things are different. It may well not be bad for my *health* at all if my environment is full of suffering animals (or people, for that matter). And if it isn't then the snag is that I do not obviously *own* the parts of my environment that are negatively affected, in my view, when the animals in it suffer. While I also do not own those parts of the environment that are immediately affected by pollution, I do own the body which is eventually visited with those bad effects. What sort of claim is available here? So long as tastes differ at all, we logically *cannot all* have the right to any sort of environment we like: what is an improvement to you is then a deterioration to me.

We do in fact agree to a very substantial extent on some aspects of these problems. Being sympathetic creatures, we don't like the pains of others, even when those others are animals. And most of us would classify grime-covered slums as eyesores, and the Place Des Arts as attractive. Yet we don't have the right to require a slum-dweller to clean up his act at the slum-dweller's expense; nor, I think, have we the right to prevent sealers from clubbing small seals for the sake of their valuable hides, even though nearly all of us, including probably the sealer, would rather that those animals not undergo such a fate. Even substantial identity of tastes doesn't solve all problems here; and in fact there is substantial diversity in the case of many of the issues of environmental ethics. Since we have a truly common interest in health, further information linking these issues to issues of human health is likely to be of enormous assistance in solving them, but I do not suppose that all of them will succumb to that treatment.

NOTES

* This commentary is not a transcript of my adlibbed remarks on the occasion of my response to Tom Regan at the environmental ethics workshop. I am dealing more fully with some aspects of his paper, and develop much less than I did on that occasion the alternative position on these matters that I am partial to.
1. See my "Animals Rights Revisited", in Harlan Miller and William Williams, eds., *Ethics and Animals* (Clifton, New Jersey: Humana Press, 1983).
2. The fundamentals of my current views are to be found in "Human Rights: Which, if Any, There Are", in *NOMOS XXIII: Human Rights* (New York University Press, 1981); edited by J. Roland Pennock & John W. Chapman.

QUESTIONS

1. Narveson gives an alternate reading of Kant from that of Regan. What are the main points of difference? Are these two readings as important to the issue of animal rights as Narveson makes out? Why or why not?
2. Narveson argues that things like mountains can have inherent value. Why does he think this view is consistent with rejecting Deep Ecology?
3. Narveson seems to suggest that a central concern of environmental ethics, namely the preservation of species, is not addressed by a focus on animal rights. Is he right about this?
4. Do all of the problems of environmental ethics currently exercising responsible people flow from the possibility that certain human beings have the right to do things to the environment that certain other human beings don't like, as Narveson claims?

ETHICS OF WASTES: THE CASE OF THE NUCLEAR FUEL CYCLE

Andrew Brook

In Canada and the United States, we consume a huge amount of energy and other goods relative to other parts of the world and are totally dependent on large industries. Among the problems created by this way of life, the vast quantity of often dangerous wastes we produce is among the more difficult. A particularly interesting case study for the ethics of wastes and their management is the nuclear power industry. It presents some major waste management problems, problems that will require enormous amounts of money and labour to solve.

Reprinted by permission of Andrew Brook.

What to do about nuclear wastes is a policy question; policy questions always have moral questions at their heart. Those posed by nuclear energy tax the full resources of modern moral philosophy. In a classic study of two decades ago, Arthur Porter put it this way:

> . . . an assessment of the value of nuclear power . . . ultimately requires an examination of the acceptability to society of the risk and benefits of the technology, relative to other options. This process is, by definition, extremely difficult since value judgments of a particularly complex kind, transcending nuclear power per se, are clearly involved. Indeed, whose values are to be judged worthy and how this assessment is to be accomplished with justice are pertinent questions.[1]

All this is just as true today as it was when Porter wrote it. Of the wide range of cost/risk/ benefit issues to which Porter alludes, we will concentrate on those resulting from the wastes created by nuclear power. The major wastes in the nuclear industry are the wastes from the mining and milling process used to create uranium fuel and the wastes left behind when this fuel is used to generate electricity in a reactor. We will focus on what are called high level wastes, the wastes created by burning fuel in a reactor. Our aim is to determine the values that should govern policy questions about these wastes and how to apply these values in a variety of contexts. The most central ethical question concerns our obligations to future generations.

Ethical decisions always underlie policy decisions. The former are often made in an analytic vacuum that we would not begin to accept for making design decisions or investment decisions. Similarly, cost/benefit assessments are often carried out with very narrow notions of what can properly be classed as costs or benefits. Here is how an ideal method for settling ethical issues in policy contexts might work. First we would collect the relevant facts: what are the problems, what are the possible solutions? We would next identify basic ethical principles such as fairness in the distribution of costs, risks and benefits over populations and times and liberty for the people concerned, and so on. Then we would lay out criteria for setting costs against costs, benefits against benefits, etc., both considered broadly enough to include full social costs and benefits, direct and indirect. Finally, we would apply the principles and criteria to the facts. We will carry this method out as fully as a short paper allows. We will sketch the relevant facts about the nuclear fuel cycle, identify relevant values, and lay out some of the relevant costs and benefits.

High-Level Reactor Wastes

The best known wastes in the nuclear industry are the high level wastes produced by nuclear reactors. In Canada, nuclear reactors are concentrated in Ontario, where they generate about 50% of the province's electricity. Quebec and New Brunswick also have reactors. Nuclear reactors generate electricity by setting up a controlled chain reaction in the radioactive component of uranium fuel, uranium 235. This fuel is manufactured into pellets held in tubes tied together into circular bundles and these bundles are inserted into long tubes inside the reactor. The chain reaction in this fuel generates an enormous amount of heat. This heat is used to superheat steam, which then powers turbines connected to electrical generators. In the course of the uranium being 'burned', the industry term for the chain reaction, a number of highly radioactive materials come into existence inside the fuel bundles — radioactive strontium, cesium, americium, and so on — and the metal holding the pellets also becomes radioactive.

One important new mineral is plutonium, which is dangerous radiologically and also chemically — the radiation from a minute amount on the inside of the lungs can cause lung cancer. Plutonium is more toxic chemically than almost any other material. Plutonium also poses a security risk; it can be refined into bomb grade material. Of the two atomic bombs dropped on Japan by the United States, one used refined plutonium, the other heavily enriched uranium 235.[2]

The radioactivity in spent fuel increases many orders of magnitude when burned.[3] Natural processes of radioactive decay restore the spent fuel to something like the radioactivity it once had but that takes 300 to 800 years (after about 500 years, the radioactivity of the fuel has decreased 200,000 times[4]). Different radioactive materials decay at rates that vary by orders of magnitude; plutonium, for example, has a halflife of about 24,000 years, which make wastes in which it occurs particularly long lived.[5]

Compared to the amounts of wastes produced by other industrial processes, the volume of high level wastes produced by a reactor is quite small, however. A pellet of fuel roughly the size of a large marble produces enough electricity to power an average house for a year. By comparison, it would take many *tons* of coal producing many *tons* of CO_2 and a large amount of fly ash to produce the same amount of electricity. By comparison, all the high level wastes ever produced in Canada weigh less than 25,000 tons. In fact, all the high level waste produced by Canadian reactors in a history that is now about forty five years long is still stored onsite, first in large pools of water for six years or so, then in thick concrete containers as the fuel becomes less active. This form of storage is adequate to ensure that there is almost no release of radioactivity to the atmosphere so long as nothing goes wrong. The proviso, 'so long as nothing goes wrong', is important, however; these methods need constant monitoring and maintenance. They are thus the very opposite of being a passive, permanent solution requiring no further human intervention.

Mine/Mill Wastes

To make the fuel burned in reactors, uranium ore is mined and milled to extract the uranium and then fabricated into fuel. This process produces large quantities of low level wastes. The amounts of these wastes are huge — well over 150 million tonnes of these wastes now exist in Canada alone — and they may lead to more exposure to radiation than any other part of the fuel cycle.[6] Because the volumes are so huge, and also because much of the waste is fluid, these 'low level' wastes may well be a more intractable problem than high level wastes. Currently, no good scheme for managing them has ever been devised. Thus they eminently deserve to be studied from the ethical point of view. In this paper, however, we will focus on high level wastes. One reason is that a promising scheme has been devised for dealing with these wastes and it is in need of careful ethical assessment.[7]

Long-Term Management of High-Level Wastes

High level wastes are contained in highly corrosion-resistance structures. Thus, they will not disperse for a long period of time, though still well before the radioactive materials in them decay to insignificant levels. Release via a massive uncontained explosion and fire on the model of the Chernobyl disaster is unlikely in Canada or the United States. What exploded in Chernobyl was active fuel in which a chain reaction was taking place within a reactor. All reactors outside the former Soviet countries have massive reinforced concrete containment shells. When the fuel is spent and removed from the reactor, there is no longer a chain reaction. The dangers become heat and extremely high levels of radioactivity. And the major risk is over the long term. Over time, the risk that the active monitoring of water tanks and concrete containers needed to ensure safety will decrease or even cease altogether obviously increases. If the monitoring and necessary repairs, etc., ceased, living beings could spend dangerous amounts of time around the concrete containers. Further, in the medium term any spent fuel not in containers, and in the long term these containers themselves, would deteriorate, allowing the spent fuel to dissipate.

A method for permanent disposal of spent fuel has been undergoing research and development for a couple of decades now. The method involves sinking mine shafts into stable, waterproof structures of plutonic rock in the Canadian Shield.[8] The spent fuel, which is itself highly resistant to corrosion, would be put into lead containers. These containers would be placed in cavities lined with clay at the bottom of the shaft (clay lined to prevent any possible moisture penetration.) The shafts would then be backfilled with clay or concrete, effectively isolating the wastes from the environment and making any contact between them and living beings highly unlikely. The aim is to achieve a level of isolation such that there would not be more than one chance in a million per year that a maximally exposed creature would develop a fatal cancer or serious genetic defect, and that this isolation be assured for at least 10,000 years without active intervention. We receive much more radiation than this every year from the radium found in all rock, concrete and soil, from X-rays, from air travel, and so on.

Everything to do with nuclear power is contentious, but nuclear wastes have one feature that distinguishes them from other nuclear issues: they are already with us. Thus there is no longer any question about whether to bring them into existence. This means that many of the ethical issues that are central to decisions about nuclear power, issues arising from such questions as whether to build more reactors or phase out the ones we already have, do not arise. The principal ethical issue that remains is this: are we obliged to assume the costs of disposing of these wastes, and as permanently as possible, or is it permissible for us to pass at least some of the costs of dealing with them on to future generations? This issues breaks into two questions:

1. What are our obligations? and,
2. To what beings: just human beings, or all creatures, ecosystems, and the biosphere as a whole?

Values for the Facts

Our task now is to identify values appropriate to the facts about wastes from the nuclear fuel cycle. Nuclear wastes have two useful features as a test case for ethical issues of waste management:

1. Nobody currently alive and nobody for a number of generations is going to benefit much from finding a more permanent solution to them; the current solution will protect us and a number of generations to come quite adequately. (Spent fuel does have one possible near benefit, but exploiting it is actually made more difficult by long term disposal, a point to which we will return.) Thus managing them does not give rise to difficult questions about distribution of benefits: who should get, or be allowed to use, how much of what, when and

how?, and similar questions of distributive justice. Wastes raise primarily cost questions: given that they have to be managed for many thousands of years, who is obliged to assume the costs of doing so? This simplifies the ethical situation.

2. Because nobody alive now or for some time is going to benefit much from finding a more permanent solution than the one already in place, finding a more permanent solution will not be motivated by self-interest. Thus, the arguments in its favour have to be moral ones alone.

What are our obligations with respect to nuclear wastes? A number of issues need to be distinguished:

1. *Principles.* What are the general principles that should guide our ethical thinking about the disposal of nuclear wastes?
2. *Scope.* Are our obligations restricted to humans or do they extend to other creatures? To the environment? To the biosphere as a whole? To future generations as well as to the current one? Only to people, animals and ecologies close to us or over the whole surface of the planet?
    1. and 2. cover the two issues identified at the end of the last subsection. Other partly moral, partly conceptual issues are also highly relevant:
3. *Discounting.* Are creatures of other kinds or far distant future generations of our own kind worth less morally than people existing now?
4. *Cost/risk/benefit.* Given that better solutions to a waste management problem tend to cost more money, what, all aspects of risk, cost and benefit considered, is the optimal expenditure on this problem versus other social problems and demands?
5. *Moral assessment and risk assessment.* How should risk assessments shape our moral assessment?
6. *Uncertainty.* Given that we can never be certain about any outcome in a complex industrial system and given that the further we project into the future, the more uncertain we become, how can we reach ethical conclusions in the face of such uncertainty?
7. *Reducing risk vs. retaining benefits.* What is the appropriate balance between reducing the risks contained in high level wastes and leaving open the possibility of exploiting the very considerable economic potential that the fuel rods still contain?
8. *Procedural issues.* What procedures would allow us to arrive at fair and democratic decisions, and who should have what roles in them?

1. Principles   What principles should govern our ethical thinking about deep disposal?[9] One is a principle of distributional equity: costs, risks and benefits must be distributed equitably, at a time and across time. A second is that liberty is a particularly central good (benefit), at least for members of the human species, and any reduction of liberty requires particularly powerful justification. We need to narrow both notions down.

The part of the principle of distributional equity of relevance here is this:

A. Fairness. Those who benefit should bear the costs.

It follows from this principle that, since the people now alive have reaped most of the benefits of the activities that have created the high level wastes we are considering, we have an obligation to bear the costs of disposing of them, and disposing of them permanently. I do not think that there is any way around this.

That may appear to settle the matter and so far as identifying our obligations on *this* issue, it does. But obligations can be overridden if there are conflicting obligations that are even stronger. We will take up this issue in 4. below. Furthermore, even if A. settles our intergenerational obligations, there is also a tricky interregional issue. Most of the beneficiaries of nuclear power live in or near large centres; people in the outlying regions have reaped few benefits. Yet any long term solution to the wastes will inevitably be constructed in some outlying region; that's where the appropriate rock structures are found and there is room to build a large mine complex.

To see our way to the most ethical solution here, I think the word 'inevitably' is important: if any long term disposal facility must be built in the hinterland, then there are only two choices: construction in the hinterland or forego a long term solution and continue the short term procedures now in place. If so, then disposal in the hinterland is the fair*est* long term solution possible, even if it is not entirely fair. If we adopted it, we would still be obliged, of course, to ensure that the costs to present and future beings in the area selected are kept as low as feasible, that benefits be maximized, and that any differential in costs is accompanied by fair compensation. The secure, well paid jobs that go with a waste disposal facility would be one compensatory benefit.

The aspect of the ethics of liberty of relevance to nuclear wastes is this:

> B. *Liberty.* Our actions must infringe on the lives of other beings to the smallest extent reasonably possible.

This principle applies particularly obviously to human beings but it may well apply to many other beings, too, as we will see below. Here are some of the ways in which the management, or perhaps more accurately *mis*management, of high level wastes could restrict liberty: causing pain; damaging bodies; harming abilities; imposing significant protection costs; spoiling ecosystems; reducing opportunities; and so on. Some of the examples I just gave concerned freedom *from* (freedom from unnecessary pain, unnecessary costs, etc.) and some concerned freedom *to* (not harming the field of opportunities available). With this distinction, we can spell out the demand of liberty this way:

> B'. We must choose the solution to the disposal of high level wastes that will reduce future beings' freedom from costs and harms and limit their freedom to pursue their life as they would live it to the minimum extent reasonably possible.

Note that even this longer version of the principle of liberty is weaker than some would argue it should be. It says nothing about *enhancing* freedom from or freedom to.

Of course, protecting the liberty of future beings requires that we restrict our own liberty in certain ways. In particular, the liberty to spend the resources needed to dispose of nuclear wastes permanently on things of immediate benefit to us must go. Thus, the demands of fairness and the liberty of future beings are in conflict with enhancing our own liberty. To resolve this conflict, we have to look deeper.

Here is a principle that can start to resolve the conflict:

C. *Equal worth*. Prior to considerations of morally relevant distinguishing qualities, each person has the same value as any other.

The argument for it is a general principle of rationality: unless we treat similar things as similar, it would be impossible to make general, comparative judgments about them at all. If so, it would be irrational to assign two relevantly similar people different moral value. This argument grounds the ethical principle of equal *prima facie* worth on a general consideration about what is required for rationality as a whole.

To be sure, discriminatory assignments of value can be justified — so long as there is a morally relevant difference. And we could be quite generous about what such differences might be.[10] Other kinds of partiality might also be allowable. For example, only a few people (including myself) are within my control; partiality toward these people will increase the chances of my doing what I can to procure and distribute things of value in this world. Similarly, special bonds of affection may justify special concern, if the loss of those bonds would seriously undermine my life having any point or purpose in my eyes, seriously undercut my self-confidence, and so on. All these would reduce my chances of doing something of value. (Williams has explored arguments for partiality to some people and also for partiality to humans over other beings, an issue directly related to Scope below.[11])

Some differences are not morally relevant, however. Self-interest, maximizing (or a desire to maximize) one's own benefits and minimizing one's costs simply because the benefits and costs would accrue to me, is not, for example. Here there is no relevant difference between me and anyone else; as the nineteenth century philosopher Henry Sidgwick put it, mere numerical difference makes no moral difference. Similarly, the collective self-interest of one's own generation is not by itself a morally relevant difference between one's own generation and future generations. In general, no one person (even if he is me) and no one generation (even if it is mine) have features that justify giving that person or generation preferential treatment in the distribution of costs and benefits.

Since we are the ones enjoying the benefits of nuclear energy, any passing on of the costs of the activities involved would constitute just such a discriminatory assignment of costs and benefits. From this we can conclude that we have a moral obligation to find a permanent, passive solution to the problem of nuclear wastes. If we were passing on additional benefits as large as the benefits we are enjoying and if we were also assuming half the costs of these benefits, the conclusion would not hold. But it seems unlikely that we are doing so. Of course, the principle of fairness is just an instantiation of the equal worth principle. But it is possible to argue for the latter in ways not open to the former, not directly.

It seems to me that the conclusion of the discussion above is clear: we have an ethical obligation to find a permanent, passive solution to the problem of radioactive waste management. A true ethical sceptic or someone with a strong interest in ignoring the problem of nuclear wastes might still try to wiggle out, but to refuse to accept such arguments as ethically binding would be pretty much to get out of the business of justifying courses of action, finding good and sufficient reasons for what we do, altogether. Moreover, we do care about these principles — they are deeply embedded in our view of how interpersonal relations ought to be governed, and therefore in our notions of self-respect and sense of decency.

Return now to the suggestion that liberty is a distinctively human good and therefore that the analysis above applies only to human beings. We take up the general issue of obligations to the nonhuman in the next section but on this specific issue, I think we can say the following: 1. Animals do care about their own liberty; think of how animals suffer when caged. 2. Disease, radioactive poisoning, etc., limit the liberty of animals just as much as of humans.

2. Scope   Questions of scope come in a number of dimensions. To how many kinds of creatures do our obligations extend, just to humans or also to other creatures, the various ecologies, and the biosphere as a whole? Over what space — to people, animals and ecologies close to us or across the whole planet? And over what span of time — just to us or to future generations, too? We are most apt to reach ethical judgments that can be defended if we take the widest possible scope: All beings, not just humans; everywhere on the planet, not just in our own communities; and at all times, not just now and in the immediate future. If something has the capacity to be harmed, it has interests, and if it has interests, the principle of equal worth can be applied, *mutatis mutandis*, to argue that it would be unfair to load a discriminatory mix of costs and benefits on it. Quantifying 'discriminatory' over members of various species, the species themselves, their ecosystems, etc., will be a difficult task but it will be an unavoidable one if we wish our waste management decisions to be ethical over the scope of the whole biosphere.[12]

3. Discounting   Even if we do consider everything everywhere and at all times, does it all have to be given *equal* consideration? This is the difficult issue of discounting. In economics, discounting is clearly justified. An economic benefit in the distant future is worth less to me now than one immediately available to me. Is there anything comparable in ethics? Is it ever ethical to value far distant beings, beings far in the future, beings very different from us (earth worms, say, or bacteria) less than we value ourselves and the human beings immediately around us?

This issue tends to break down into two subissues. One concerns *human* beings far distant from us in space or time, the other concerns *all other* beings. In connection with the first, I cannot see any ethical justification for valuing one human being less than another, no matter where or when that human being may live. By contrast, we might be able to make a case for valuing some forms of life less than others: even if we want to keep plentiful *examples* of each kind of life, even down to bacteria, etc., it is far less clear that each *individual* in many lifeforms deserves the same concern as we extend to human individuals.

All this raises a number of difficulties for the principles enunciated earlier. For beings where preservation of genetic material may be more important than protection of the well-being or even the existence of individuals, liberty is at most a far smaller concern. Likewise, with such beings we switch from the worth of individuals to the worth of types, something anathema to the ethics of human beings. And so on. When one combines these complications with the uncertainties that still infect the notion of discounting for the future in general, I think we rapidly find ourselves completely at sea. For these reasons, I will restrict my discussion of discounting to human beings.

For distant human beings, especially human beings distant in time, we might try to use the economist's notion of discounting to justify extending less concern to them than we extend to human beings living now. It would argue that future generations, like other things in the future, are worth less than the equivalent things right now. This is the principle that a bird in the hand is worth two in the bush. In financial contexts it can be argued for on a number of bases: uncertainties or probabilities, rates of return on present wealth, and so on. The economist's notion probably has no relevance to moral questions. One discounts the economic value of the future on the basis of its value for us (now); one considers the moral worth of future generations on the basis of their value, period — their value for anyone, including themselves.

There are, however, other discounting principles. Some people might argue that far distant people, just by being so far distant, are worth less per head than people currently alive. While this does not seem a morally relevant difference, being mere location in time, two other discounting principles are perhaps more plausible.

1. *Nature of future persons.* The farther we move into the future, the greater the probability that persons alive then will be different from us in one or another of a number of relevant ways: they may be immune to radiological damage and chemical poisoning; though still at risk, such risks may no longer affect their interests; their forms of social life may be so different from ours that their moral worth is reduced; they may be such moral monsters that they would not merit our moral concern. These all seem to be very remote possibilities.
2. *Existence of future persons.* The farther we move into the future, the greater the probability that no persons will exist at all. This claim is sound but ignores the fact (as does the first) that significant damage from nuclear wastes could occur within a few hundred years if nothing more is done, a period short enough to reduce the probability considerably.

To see the real moral force of these discounting principles, it is essential to distinguish between *epistemic possibility* ('It may, I just don't know') and *real probability* ('It may; reliable calculation reveals a chance of . . ., which is more than insignificant'). If we just don't know, we can ensure that we have met our obligations (though we don't, of course, know that we have them either) only by acting as though there will, in the future, be people, and people relevantly like us. And even if we do know that there is some real probability that there won't be, this probability must, I think, be fairly high before our obligation to act as though there will be is significantly reduced — though this point is controversial. So long as there is any significant probability that there will be relevantly similar people, there is a probability that we have obligations. Thus any discounting principle of which I am aware seems to have only a negligible effect on our obligations to future generations.

In addition to the question of temporal scope and discounting, there is an important ethical issue that arises with spatial scope and consideration of beings elsewhere on the planet. Canada is not the only country with nuclear waste disposal problems. Indeed, compared to the problems faced by the United States, Russia or any other bomb producing country, our problems are pretty small. Both the United States and Russia have literally hundreds of times as much high level waste in storage as we do. If we can find a passive, permanent solution to our own high level wastes, do we have an obligation to use it to help other countries deal with theirs?

The issues here are practical and political as well as ethical. On the practical side, there is the issue of transportation and the dangers inherent in moving highly toxic wastes such long distances. On the political side, there is the fact that both the United States and Russia have been massively less responsible in their management of high level wastes than Canadians have been, Russia in particular. Nevertheless, a question does arise about whether we have obligations to peoples in other parts of the world as they face their nuclear waste problems.

4. Cost/Risk/Benefit   Earlier we looked at the implications of principles of fairness and protection of liberty for the management of nuclear wastes. Another principle is also important, indeed can overrule the demands of fairness and liberty in some contexts. It is the broadly utilitarian principle that we should strive to get the maximum benefit, that is to say, to do the greatest good, for each expenditure of resources and incurring of risk. The argument for this principle is very simple: anything else wastes resources. The mechanism for applying it is cost/risk/benefit analysis.

Cost/risk/benefit analysis is the activity of assessing the benefits of a proposal, the costs of achieving those benefits, and the risks involved. More precisely, it consists of analyzing financial risks — financial costs times probability of incurring them; nonfinancial risks — harms times probability of incurring them and costs of rectifying them; and both the probability and the size of the benefits that would accrue.

Sometimes benefits are so great or costs relative to a benefit so high that neither an analysis nor additional moral judgment is needed to decide what should be done. For example, no competent cost/risk/benefit analysis of hospitals is going to question whether we should keep them — though there can certainly be disagreement about how many we need, what kind, and where, as we are seeing! We view health as a benefit that can be traded off against other things only down to a certain level (though that level may be falling right now). At the other extreme, no competent public authority would allocate $1m to fix a few potholes. But benefits and/or costs are often not so clear.

In particular, better management of wastes is a benefit that we have historically viewed as readily tradeable for other benefits, lower debt loads for example. For this reason, we tend to make decisions about waste management on a comparative basis: for a given expenditure, what is the greatest benefit we can attain, and at what overall cost of resources and harms? I think that this is the right approach and that we should do it on the widest possible basis. In considering radiological wastes, we should take into account, for example, the fact that non-radiological toxins have no halflife. In considering an expenditure of resources to dispose of radioactive wastes, we should consider what else we could accomplish for the same money. And not just for us; also for people elsewhere and well into the future, and for beings of other kinds. (We are part of the 5% of the population of the world that uses 40% of the world's resources; we can afford to be generous.)

Here is one central issue: for a given cost, at a given probability or risk level, what is the greatest obtainable benefit? To meet our obligations to future generations with respect to the hazards in radioactive wastes would cost a lot. Would the benefit conferred on living things as a whole from expending resources on these wastes be as great as the benefits we could confer by expending the resources in some other way?

Some answers to this question might well cancel obligations arising from application of the principles of fairness and liberty. Suppose that the answer to the above question is no, that achieving a permanent solution to nuclear wastes would not be a benefit as great as we could achieve by expending the same resources in other ways. Suppose further that the greater benefit can be secured with as much fairness and protection of liberty across species, space, and time as would be true of a permanent disposition of nuclear wastes. In this situation, our obligations with respect to nuclear wastes would either be cancelled or greatly reduced. Resources can be expended only once, and we can obtain a greater benefit with as much fairness, etc., by expending them another way. Therefore, we are obliged to expend them the other way. If we have spent them some other way, we cannot expend them on nuclear wastes. But ought implies can. Therefore, our obligation to expend the resources on nuclear wastes is either cancelled or at least greatly reduced.

Whether the answer is no is a complicated, partly philosophical, partly factual question: philosophical to the extent that we would need criteria for comparing costs and ranking benefits; factual for reasons that are perfectly obvious. A couple of examples of possible alternative expenditures of the relevant resources may serve to highlight not only the complexity but also the practical reality of both the philosophical and the factual issues. There is increasing evidence that one unhappy byproduct of modern medicine is what one might call pollution of the human gene pool. The exponential increase and spread of diabetes is one example. Certainly passing on a sound gene pool would be a great benefit to future generations. An even simpler example is CO_2 and other 'greenhouse gas' emissions; all fossil fuel power generation releases vast quantities of CO_2 and also SO_2, as well as fly ash, particulate carbon and even radiation. (Some authorities suggest that the radon and other radioactive materials released when some coal is burned in a normal operation exceed the amount of radioactivity likely to be released from a nuclear power plant during the most seriously likely breakdown or accident.) Or what about the benefits of winding 'big energy' options such as nuclear, fossil and hydro generation down and substituting 'small' options such as conservation and solar and wind generation?

Would the benefit of improvements in the gene pool or in levels of greenhouse gas and other emissions or in conversion to small energy options be as great as the benefit of freedom from the dangers of radioactive poisoning from reactor wastes or uranium tailings? And could they be secured for a similar expenditure of resources? I doubt that anyone knows the answer to these questions. But the questions must be asked. As Bodde has put it, "our duty is to create solutions to the disposal of radioactive wastes in the context of other threats to human existence, rather than in isolation" — and not just to human existence![13] Rational public policy requires answers to thousands of similar questions. Ask yourself: What *would* the balance be if the comparison were with renewable energy? And what would it be if the comparison were with heavy metal contamination? (Heavy metals have no halflife and retain their toxicity forever.)

These hypothetical cost/benefit questions are still artificially simplistic. The real cost/benefit questions (and hence the real moral questions) also include:

1. When we allocate resources to create a new benefit, how should the new benefits in turn be used? For example, should we use it to expand wealth or to enhance health, safety or make other gains in liberty?
2. Then distributional questions arise: additional wealth or liberty for what beings, over what space and what time? We are clearly permitted to consume some benefits, but it is equally clear that if we are to honour the principles of the equal worth of every person and the worth of all that lives, we cannot consume as much as we like unless we can leave others with the same largesse. Within these parameters, however, lies an enormous range of options, both with respect to us and others alive now, us and future generations, and us and other kinds of being.
3. Technical questions, such as whether the principle of equal worth can be realized in equal cost/benefit *ratios*, or whether equal cost/benefit *distributions* (so that everyone gets the same amount of each, and not just the same ratio) are required. This question too needs to be asked for nonhuman as well as human beings.[14]

And so on, almost without limit. Public policy that is rational from the cost/benefit point of view (and therefore public policy that meets even the necessary conditions of moral soundness) is extraordinarily complicated — something that will come as no surprise to those familiar with the deep and sometimes unavoidable vacuum in which many policy decisions are taken.[15]

It is perhaps worth noting, before we leave this topic, that cost/benefit issues may also be relevant to our previous discussion of probability and obligations. There I argued that the probability of there not being relevantly similar people, or people at all, must be determinate and fairly high before our obligations are significantly reduced. This argument may have to be modified in the following way. If the costs of meeting these obligations are high enough that great benefits could otherwise be achieved, our obligations may fall faster than would otherwise be the case. The same might be argued, *mutatis mutandis*, for other creatures, ecological systems, etc.

5. Moral Assessment and Risk Assessment   Costs and benefits and other aspects of resource utilization always have risks attached: there is a risk that expending resources will not achieve the targeted benefit, that something in the process will have unintended side effects, and so on. How should assessment of risks guide our ethical assessments? In my view, no matter how well technological risk assessment based in probability calculations is done, it never settles the ethical questions. Of course, this does not imply that risk assessments have no role to play. Even if we should always do a separate ethical assessment, we must also ground it in the best knowledge of the facts available. This is what the regime of risk assessment can provide. Nevertheless, after all the facts are in, we still have to apply our ethical principles and make an independent determination of what we ought to do.

Here is an easy example to demonstrate that level of risk and level of ethical seriousness are not the same thing. Consider the spate of children run over by school buses every year. With these accidents, increased moral acceptability is not linear with decreasing risk. Reducing the frequency of such accidents would not be enough to make the ones that remain morally acceptable. No such accidents are acceptable. That implies that the only acceptable level of risk in this case is the lowest level we can attain. In short, risk and moral acceptability are not in a linear relationship.

Here is another way in which risk assessment does not settle the ethical questions. In Canada, we generate electricity primarily in three ways: nuclear fission, burning fossil fuels (coal, oil or natural gas), and hydro power. Compare nuclear to fossil fuel generation. These technologies clearly have very different harm/probability profiles. The harms that nuclear power can inflict are catastrophically severe, as Chernobyl demonstrated, but the probability of incurring them is generally thought to be quite low, at least in Canada. By contrast, with fossil fuel, we are virtually certain to incur the harms they can produce, harms such as the CO_2 and SO_2 emissions and release of radium and other radioactive and/or toxic elements already mentioned and also depletion of a nonrenewable resource. But these harms are generally considered less significant than those that a nuclear disaster can inflict. Whether we are right to consider the harms inflicted by burning fossil fuels relatively less significant might be debated, but the point I want to make here is this. Only by a separate ethical assessment in the light of our various visions of the good life for ourselves and other kinds of being can one assess the high harm/low probability risks of nuclear power against low harm/high probability risks such as we find with fossil fuels.

Other philosophically difficult questions arise about risks, too. For example, how does diminishing level of risk work, or rather, how should it work, as a discounter of costs? It is quite clear that it does do so: in connection with the nuclear industry we have been able to accept some potential costs that would be quite horrendous because we have been able to convince ourselves that the risk of having to pay them is quite low. Since we cannot avoid running some low risks of high costs in whatever we do, it seems clear that some discount factor must be morally acceptable. But how much a cost can be discounted as the probability of risk moves to very small figures is totally unclear. It is an important question in connection with the nuclear industry generally and in connection with our relation to future generations in particular. The principle of equal worth is unlikely to be able to help us with it.

Second, is there such a thing as an absolutely unacceptable cost, however low the risk and whatever the benefit? Given the Doomsday aura that surrounds certain aspects of the nuclear industry, this is a question that some people have asked. Even the principles, let alone the criteria and facts, for an adequate answer probably do not exist.

A third starts from the idea that the depletion of nonrenewable resources is itself a cost being imposed on future generations. Classical economic cost/benefit analysis does not seem well suited to thinking about this kind of cost, there being no possible benefit that could compensate for it. Criteria for assigning cost values to questions of depletion are needed, and might be difficult to find.

6. Uncertainty   We can never be certain about any outcome in a complex industrial system and the further we move into the future, the more uncertain we become. How can we reach ethical conclusions in the face of such uncertainty?

One of the most ethically vexing aspects of the nuclear industry or any other big, technologically complex system flows from the limits of knowledge. Though I have spoken about many factual issues above as though the relevant facts are known with a high degree of certainty, in fact that is not always the case. It would have taken many detailed qualifications to identify even the most important limits to certainty but that does not mean that they do not exist. This compounds the problem of risk assessment: not only must we try to assess the level of risk in each relevant context, risk being a matter of the size of a danger times the probability of it occurring, we must also recognize that there are uncertainties built into these calculations so large that our conclusions could be seriously in error.

There is probably no good ethical way to take account of this limitation. The best we can do from the moral point of view is to err on the side of caution. Where we are dealing with the health and safety of large numbers of humans and other living things over large ecologies and geological periods of time, we can be sure that we have met our obligations in the face of uncertainty only if we build the worst outcomes that are at all likely into our analyses at all relevant points.

7. Reducing Risk Vs. Retaining Benefits   As well as posing very serious risks of radiological and chemical poisoning, spent nuclear fuel also houses a huge potential benefit. As was noted earlier, one of the results of fissioning uranium is an even heavier and more fissionable metal, plutonium. Plutonium does not exist in nature but substantial amounts of it are contained in spent reactor fuel. Since it is just as good a reactor fuel as uranium, it would generate enormous amounts of additional energy if it were to be 'burned' in its own controlled chain reaction. This gives rise to a tricky ethical question.

On the one hand, we want to protect future generations from the risks posed by spent fuel — unprotected contact and diversion for weapons. On the other hand, we do not want to cut them off from a potentially huge benefit. What is the optimal balance between reducing these hazards over a geological time frame and leaving this potential benefit available to future generations? In the light of the diversion risk, should we make it impossible for future generations to use this resource at all? It does have potential to be used to make bombs — it could be diverted and purified into weapons grade material.

8. Procedural Issues   My comments on procedural ethics will be very sketchy; the topic requires a paper of its own. In connection with the management of nuclear wastes, a number of important ethical issues arise that have to do with procedures. Who should make the decisions? What procedures will allow all stakeholders to have a fair say? What procedures will generate the best decisions? (These are not necessarily the same.) How can we prevent the majority from tyrannizing minorities; should communities have veto power, for example, over the location of a facility in their area? (This is a basic problem of all democratic decision making.) Can compensation justify overruling a community's or an individual's objections? And how should the wishes of people with views very different from ourselves be taken into account?

This last question is pressing with respect to the geological deep disposal proposal. The facility is likely to be built in northern Ontario. If it is, aboriginal people will be far more affected by the facility than by any other aspect of the nuclear fuel cycle. Yet, not only have they not received many benefits from the power thus generated, they tend to view the world and our place in it in a way that is quite antithetical to big power or any other system that imposes heavy environmental demands. How should these people enter the decision making process, in particular the process of choosing a site?

The Current Proposal

We have now discussed the eight considerations introduced earlier: principle; scope; discounting; cost/risk/benefit; moral assessment and risk assessment; uncertainty; reducing risk vs. retaining benefits; and procedures. Let us now ask how well the current proposal to bury spent fuel in plutons in the Canadian Shield does when assessed against these desiderata.

1. Deep geological disposal of high level wastes probably achieves fairness and protects future liberty better than any other proposal.
2. Deep disposal seems likely to provide protection of the widest scope compared to other concepts, in all three dimensions, that is, kind of being, time, and place.
3. Because of its long time frame, deep disposal discounts future generations of people and other living things less than any other concept.
4. Concerning costs and benefit, the deep disposal concept clearly forces those who benefit to assume the costs. On the issue of achieving the greatest benefit for a given cost, however, I wonder if the deep disposal concept may not be less than optimal. I suspect that greater social and ecological goods could be attained by building a less secure facility and expending some of the funds in other ways. I have in mind things such as other protections for ecosystems, population control, and of course the perennial demands of feeding the hungry, helping people find sustainable ways to provide for themselves, and achieving a fairer distribution of resources.

5. Because deep disposal reduces risk as far as is reasonably achievable, given current knowledge, it does as well at satisfying our moral demands for risk reduction as any concept is likely to do.

6. At least half a billion dollars worth of research has been done in connection with the deep disposal concept. Thus this proposal probably reduces the uncertainties in our knowledge farther than other concepts.

7. Recovering the plutonium contained in spent fuel buried in plutonic rock would be expensive but not impossible. So a balance is struck between minimization of harm and retrievability of possible benefits, though one favouring minimization of harm.

8. Since most of the important procedural issues will arise as the proposal is considered in the public arena and decisions are made about commencement, site, etc., it is too early to say how the proposal stacks up procedurally.

Application to Other Issues

The methodology we have used for determining our obligations in connection with nuclear wastes could be applied to many other issues, too. Within the nuclear industry, some nonenvironmental issues to which it could be applied include: uranium mining and an economy based on exploitation of natural resources; marketing nuclear technology; terrorism and the weapons risk; consumption vs. conservation in industrial economies; the creation of a technological 'priesthood' having esoteric knowledge not possessed by the rest of us and having a lot of power in society by virtue of their control of large industrial complexes; and other industrial and social structure issues.

The moral analysis offered above can be applied to other social and environmental issues. I have used it, for example, in connection with land use policy in British Columbia. The issues such as soil depletion, biomass depletion, and diversion of land from agriculture to housing, transportation and industry have essentially the same moral structure as the issue of nuclear wastes. They are all situations in which gaining a benefit for ourselves now will impose large costs on future generations of humans and other beings with little by way of compensating benefits unless we do something. Yet the costs of doing anything effective would be quite high and yield little if any direct benefit to us. The moral issue is also the same: Do we have an obligation to assume costs of our current activities such as these, saving future generations from having to do so?

More analyses are needed before definitive moral conclusions can be reached about nuclear energy and the environment, both factual and criterial analyses. Much has been done — a number of fairly well founded standards now exist, for example, and a promising proposal for a high level waste disposal facility is under consideration. But more remains to be done and we still do not have an integrated ethical framework within which to think about the industry and what surrounds it as a whole.

The biggest problem may not be the lack of a clear ethical framework, however. In many areas of social policy, what we are obliged to do is actually quite clear. The problem is to muster the personal and political will and the resources to do it. I think that we know what we should do about nuclear wastes: find the most permanent, passive solution to them that comes at a reasonable cost, given the costs of other potential benefits, and that will not make future exploitation of the fuel impossible. How do we marshall the will and the resources to do it?[16]

NOTES

1. Royal Commission on Electric Power Planning, *A Race Against Time* (known as the Porter Commission Report after the Chair of the Commission, Arthur Porter) Toronto: Queen's Printer, 1978, p. 153.
2. Here is what is meant by saying that uranium is enriched. In nature, more than 99% of uranium is of the isotope 238, less than 1% is 235, the fissionable material. In bombs, enough of the 238 is removed to raise the portion of 235 to roughly 70% of the total. The fuel in most reactors is enriched, too, but the ratio of 235 is increased only to about 7%, not to 70% or more as in bombs. Candu reactors use unenriched fuel, in which the fissionable 235 makes up only about .7% of the total. Among other things, this makes Candu fuel more difficult to use as raw material for bombs.
3. An order of magnitude is ten times larger or smaller than the initial amount. So if X is two orders of magnitude larger than Y, then X is 100 times (10x10) larger than Y.
4. "300 to 800 years": see the report of the Advisory Panel on Tailings of the Atomic Energy Control Board, "An Appraisal of Current Practices for the Management of Uranium Mill Tailings" (AECB 1156). '200,000 times less': *Environmental Impact Statement on the Concept for the Disposal of Canada's Nuclear Fuel Wastes* Atomic Energy of Canada Ltd 10721, COG-93–11, 1994. Unless otherwise noted, facts cited concerning high level wastes are taken from this document.
5. A half-life is the time it takes the radioactivity in a material to diminish by one half. Thus plutonium is half as radioactive after 24,000 years, one quarter as radioactive after 48,000 years, one eighth as radioactive after 72,000 years, and so on.
6. American Physical Society, "Report to the American Physical Society by the Study Group on Nuclear Fuel Cycles and Waste Management," *Review of Modern Physics* 50 (January 1978), pp. 1–186.
7. There is an article on the ethics of managing low level uranium mine/mill waste by the same author in earlier editions of *Contemporary Moral Issues*.
8. Unlike most rock, plutonic rock has few cracks or fissures and is highly impermeable. Over one thousand possibly suitable structures have been identified.
9. At this point, some ethicists would introduce the leading metaethical positions such as libertarianism, contractarianism, utilitarianism, and various egalitarian and deontological approaches. An interesting example is contained in Ch. 6 of the first reference document for *Environmental Impact Statement on the Concept for the Disposal of Canada's Nuclear Fuel Wastes*, Atomic Energy of Canada Ltd 10721, COG-93-11, 1994. The background document is entitled *The Disposal of Canada's Nuclear Fuel Waste: Public Involvement and Social Aspects*, M. Greber et al., AECL 10712, COG-93-2, 1994. Some of this moral background can also be found in R. Gaizauskas, "A Philosophical Examination of Our Responsibility to Future Generations." Project for the AECB (AECB: Ottawa, 1977). I have adopted a different strategy.*
10. We could even go so far as to weigh personal attributes differentially without violating the principle, though many would consider these morally *ir*relevant: for some people and in some contexts, having Beethoven's powers may make him more valuable than John Smith. Likewise for other kinds of genius, sensitivity, and maybe even personal beauty, grace or charm.
11. Williams, B. *Ethics and the Limits of Philosophy* Cambridge, MA: Harvard University Press 1985, see esp. Ch. 6.
12. Holmes Rolston mounts an argument along these lines connecting interests to moral worth in *Environmental Ethics*,

    An argument diametrically opposed to the thrust of his and my analysis has enjoyed some currency in libertarian and contractarian circles. It urges that we have no obligations to future generations, to other creatures, or even to many contemporary persons, as follows:
    1. We have obligations only where someone has rights; rights are conferred by explicit or implicit agreement of others.
    2. Only actual, not possible, persons can enter into agreements and thereby gain rights. Very few even of them have entered any such agreements with me or people with whom I share rights.

3. In particular, no future person could enter agreements or have rights; to contract, you have to be alive.
4. Hence no future person can have rights now.
5. Hence we have no obligation now to future persons.
6. Likewise, *mutatis mutandis*, for other species, most other people alive now, and so on.
    Even if we accept 1. to 3., however, 4. does not follow. First, a person's rights may extend further in time than the person does. Thus *any* actual person, no matter at what time he or she is actual, may well have rights now. Second, the argument as a whole assumes that we have no obligations to people and other beings that are not conferred by agreement. Against this view, a powerful argument can be mounted that people and other beings have *intrinsic* value, value that does not depend on whether others acknowledge it or bind themselves by agreement to respect it.
13. Bodde, D. L. Radioactive wastes: pragmatic strategies and ethical perspectives. In D. Maclean and P. G. Brown, eds. *Energy and the Future*. Totowa NJ: Rowman and Littlefield 1983, p. 121.
14. To some extent, this is merely an academic question. Some level of cost is unavoidable to any being who has to service a body, so any strict adherence even to the ratio interpretation will achieve at least some measure of distributional equity.
15. In some contexts, at least three further cost/benefit questions would have to be addressed. Fortunately, they do not affect our obligations with respect to nuclear wastes. (i) Are total benefits of an activity greater than minimum total costs? With respect to nuclear wastes, the answer is almost certainly yes. (ii) Are sufficient total resources available at all? The answer is again yes, though the real question here is whether sufficient resources can reasonably be made available; and were the answer not yes, we would have to go into that very difficult question in a serious way. (iii) Will future generations be able to secure the same benefits for themselves much more cheaply than we can? Although the answer is probably no, the whole question can be rejected, if my earlier argument is sound, because it is we who are reaping the benefits of nuclear power and so there is no sound moral reason in general that future generations should be made to assume any of the costs.
16. I would like to thank Christine Koggel and especially Wesley Cragg for very helpful comments and suggestions.

*   Editor's Note: The AECB studies may be obtained by writing to: Atomic Energy Control Board, 280 Slater St., P.O. Box 1046, Ottawa K1P 5S9. Atomic Energy of Canada Ltd. documents can be obtained from: AECL Research, Whiteshell Laboratories, Pinawa, Manitoba R0E 1L0. The material you wish to obtain should be identified by name and date or number as indicated above.

QUESTIONS

1. Andrew Brook sets out three principles that he suggests should guide our thinking about the disposal of nuclear wastes. What are those principles? Are they similar to or different from the principles that the authors/editors of this book have articulated in the introductions to the chapters of this book?
2. Do we have obligations to future generations? What are Brook's views on this subject? Does he present convincing arguments to support his view?
3. Brook identifies eight issues that ought to guide our thinking about the disposal of nuclear wastes. Do you agree with this list? Can the issues be given an order of priority?
4. Is Brook right in thinking that Canadians have a moral obligation to endorse and finance the deep disposal proposal for nuclear wastes that he describes in his paper?

SUGGESTIONS FOR FURTHER READING

- Susan J. Armstrong and Richard Botzler, eds., *Environmental Ethics: Divergence and Convergence* (New York: McGraw-Hill, 1993). This is an excellent anthology covering a wide range of issues. Intended as a text, the book is also an excellent though challenging introduction to the topic of environmental ethics.
- Raymond Bradley and Stephen Duguid, eds., *Environmental Ethics: Philosophical and Policy Perspectives* (Vancouver: University of British Columbia Press, 1988). See previous note.
- G.H. Brundtland, *Our Common Future* (Oxford: Oxford University Press, 1987). This is the report of the World Commission on Environment and Development referred to often as the Brundtland Report. Its impact was felt around the world when it was published and it continues to shape the debate over environmental concerns.
- Conrad G. Brunk, Lawrence Haworth, and Brenda Lee, *Value Assumptions in Risk Assessment: A Case Study of the Alachlor Controversy* (Waterloo: Wilfrid Laurier University Press, 1991). This is an excellent study of the role of values in risk assessment built on a detailed analysis of a risk analysis of agricultural chemical alachlor.
- Wesley Cragg and Mark Schwartz, "Sustainability and Historical Injustice: Lessons from the Moose River Basin," *Journal of Canadian Studies* vol. 31, no. 1 Spring 1996.
- Alex Davidson and Michael Dence, eds., *The Brundtland Challenge and the Cost of Inaction* (The Institute for Research on Public Policy, P.O. Box 3670 South Halifax, Nova Scotia, 1988). This is a report on two workshops on environmental issues held in 1988 in Hull, Quebec, and at the University of Waterloo. The workshops were sponsored by the Institute and the Royal Society of Canada. The report identifies the issues that participants at the workshop regarded as pressing and the recommendations that resulted.
- Robert Elliot and Arran Gare, eds., *Environmental Philosophy* (Queensland: University of Queensland Press, 1983). This is another valuable collection on the general topic of environmental ethics. Contributors are drawn from Canada, the United States, Great Britain, and Australia.
- Al Gore, *Earth in the Balance* (Boston, New York, and London: Houghton Mifflin Company, 1992). Written prior to Gore's election as vice-president of the United States, this book is an appeal to government, business, and the public at large to take notice of approaching environmental crises caused by abusive development and ecological insensitivity.
- Philip Hanson, ed., *Environmental Ethics: Philosophical and Policy Perspectives* (Vancouver, Simon Fraser Publications, 1986). This book and the next one are anthologies resulting from seminars held in the 1980s in British Columbia. They introduce the concerns of a variety of authors who are prominent in the field.
- Arne Naess, *Ecology, Community and Lifestyle* (Cambridge: Cambridge University Press, 1989). In this book the father of deep ecology traces the deep ecology movement and outlines his environmental philosophy, which is described as ecosophy.
- Ernest Partridge, ed., *Responsibilities to Future Generations: Environmental Ethics* (Buffalo: Prometheus Books, 1981). This collection includes many contributions on the subject of our obligations to posterity. It is helpful because of both the variety of discussions of the issues and the way it traces the development of a variety of themes in the last decade.

- John Passmore, *Man's Responsibility for Nature* (London: Duckworth, 1974). This book, now regarded as something of a classic in the field, evaluates a variety of views of nature found in Western literature and concludes by formulating a conservation ethic.
- Peter Singer, *Animal Liberation* (New York: Random House, 1990). This is the second edition of a book that has had a great influence in shifting attitudes on the part of many people toward animals. In it the author argues that animals do have rights that should be respected and seeks to understand the implications for our relationship to them of that finding.
- Alex Wellington, Alan Greenbaum, and Wesley Cragg, eds., *Canadian Issues in Applied Environmental Ethics* (Peterborough: Broadview Press, 1997). This book is an anthology of articles published for the first time in this collection. Topics include the environment and the economy, ethical issues relating to non-human animals, mining, fishing, and Native hunting.

Chapter 9

Business Ethics

Introduction

The idea that business should be conducted ethically is as old as ethics itself. The economy, after all, is just another arena in which human beings interact with a view to accomplishing their goals and objectives. Why then, it might be asked, is the expression "business ethics" so often thought to be an oxymoron? Finding the answer to this question lies at the heart of the study of business ethics. It will also lead us to consider the point and purpose of ethical values.

Profit maximization, many assume, is the goal of business. On this view, the purpose of business is to generate profits for owners and shareholders. To paraphrase some well-known commentators, the proper focus of business is profits. People with altruistic impulses should express them elsewhere.

For many, this view, when couched in relatively moderate language, is persuasive. Business is a hard-nosed, competitive affair. To be successful business people must put profits before people. Indeed, or so some would argue, when business does not put profits before people, people ultimately suffer.

The tension this view of business generates for ethics is obvious. The focus of ethics is people, their obligations, rights, and welfare. If the guiding principle of ethics is the golden rule — do unto others as you would have them do unto you — then on the profit maximization view, for business, an appropriate guiding principle would be "caveat emptor," let the buyer beware. This view has led many to say that it is not the job of business people to address issues of poverty, or discrimination, labour, or human rights issues. These issues are best left to governments to sort out. If business has any ethical obligations, they are simply to obey the law and generate profits. Is there then anything more than just a narrow place for ethics in business?

The importance of ethics in our lives is testimony to a number of fundamental truths about the human condition. Human beings are social animals who need each other to meet even their most basic needs. Taken as isolated individuals we are virtually defenceless in the face of serious attack. In absence of substantial social supports, none of us would survive infancy or childhood. Even as adults, our survival, to say nothing of the quality of our lives, is directly dependent on the assistance and cooperation of others.

What this suggests is that ethics is indeed about people. More particularly, however, it is about creating the conditions for cooperation between and among people. Ethics sets the parameters of cooperation. Respect for those parameters creates the conditions in the absence of which cooperation is difficult or perhaps impossible.

Business is an example of an area of human activity that rests on cooperation. This is obviously true of large business organizations. It is equally true of small ones. Any business needs suppliers, methods of communication, places to do business, clients, and so on, all of which assume cooperative interaction.

This observation, however, is sure to be countered by a second one. Business needs a modicum of cooperation. But in our society at least, private enterprise is grounded on competition. Cooperation, it might be argued, is peripheral to a free-enterprise economy.

This objection, which articulates widely shared assumptions about the nature of competition, misses a vital point. Competitive activity is intensely cooperative. Business people cannot compete without the cooperation of employees, suppliers, the government, customers, and the public generally. In each case, the less certain the ethical environment, the higher the cost of doing business.

Let us take this thesis one step further. If business is a fundamentally cooperative activity, we should expect that success in business is a function of the capacity of a business to facilitate and encourage cooperation. Further, if ethics provides the parameters of cooperation, we should expect those businesses that take ethics seriously to be more likely to succeed than those that do not.

It is hard to see that there could be obstacles to ethical business practice when ethical business practice enhances the pursuit of profit or when it carries with it no obvious or serious costs. Unfortunately, this is not always the case. And, when it is not, is it reasonable to assume that members of the business community, or anyone else, for that matter, should put business interests aside and pursue an alternative good? Both past and recent business history suggests that when making money is involved, it cannot be assumed that ethics will be given a high priority.

Background Considerations

The history of business in the industrialized world is in essence the history of the corporation. It is true that codified laws allowing for the creation of organizations whose purpose is to carry on commercial transactions have a history going back to the Code of Hammurabi in 2083 B.C. The history of the modern investor-owned corporation, however, can be traced to the early modern period of European history with the actual incorporation of business enterprises. Monarchs normally granted authority to form (business) organizations in the form of letters patent. The grant usually permitted the creation of a monopoly for the purpose of achieving some specific public goal such as the building of a road or canal. As time went on the public purposes for which charters were granted constantly expanded and, eventually, chartering private corporations became the common way to deal with public needs. The charter granted to the Governor and Company of Adventurers Trading into Hudson Bay is a case in point. This charter assigned the company "the exclusive right to trade and commerce," "possession of the lands, mines, minerals, timber, fisheries etc." as well as the "full power of making laws, ordinances and regulations at pleasure and of revoking them at pleasure." The "full power of making laws" carried with it both rights and obligations.

The legal framework within which corporations operate underwent significant modification beginning early in the 19th century in response in part to charges of favouritism, corruption, and unfair monopolies. As a result, the mercantile idea that corporations should be chartered only when their activities would advance public goods was gradually replaced with a legislated framework requiring only that those wishing to incorporate register their companies following a set of largely formal and non-demanding bureaucratic procedures. Incorporation thus became a legal right that could be activated with minimal effort. It has been suggested that these changes laid the foundations for the emergence of big business or the large modern corporation. They also had the effect of disentangling incorporation from the notion that corporations, in return for the privilege of incorporation, should serve public interests as identified in their charter of incorporation.

What emerged in law to take its place was the view that the primary obligation of corporations was to serve the interests of their shareholders. This view emerged to dominate discussions of the ethical responsibilities of business in general and private sector corporations in particular throughout much of the twentieth century.

The Current Situation

Throughout most of the second half of the twentieth century, the industrialized democracies resolved the tension between ethics and profit-seeking by allocating the task of setting standards to government, while allocating responsibility for generating economic wealth to business. (The case for this allocation of responsibilities is set out in the third reading in this chapter, "Human Rights and Business Ethics: Fashioning a New Social Contract.") The end of the Cold War in the 1990s as well as the increasing economic importance and impact of globalization, however, have thrown that allocation of responsibilities into doubt. In today's world, multinational corporations drive economic development in both the developed and the developing world. Globalization has given business the capacity to determine where and to a large extent under what conditions they will do business. In the last two decades, governments in all parts of the world have found themselves often competing for investment dollars by creating attractive regulatory environments in what some people have described as a "race to the bottom." The result has been increasing concern about the ethical responsibilities of corporations to their stakeholders, that is to say the people and the communities impacted by their activity.

Paralleling the emergence of corporate power and influence and the decline in the willingness and also the capacity of governments to set adequate labour, environmental, and human rights standards of business conduct has been the emergence of voluntary sector organizations concerned with tracking and influencing standards of business conduct. The conditions that have facilitated the growth of the multinational corporation capable of doing business anywhere in the world have also facilitated the emergence of global voluntary sector organizations such as Amnesty International, Transparency International, The World Wildlife Fund, Human Rights Watch, and Greenpeace, to name just a few. These organizations have learned how to mobilize public opinion with a view to bringing pressure to bear on the operations of multinational corporations. Increasingly, corporations are finding themselves exposed to damaging criticism of the conditions under which the products they sell are produced, as the recent experiences of firms such as Nike, Shell, and Talisman illustrate. Increasingly, therefore, business is being challenged to look carefully at the ethical principles underlying their commercial activities.

The Moral Dimension

The work of business ethics revolves essentially around two questions: Why be ethical? And what does ethics require of people engaged in the business of business? The fact that business ethics revolves around these two questions, however, has a perplexing character. The perplexity derives from the fact that the challenge these questions pose is not confined to the realm of business, but rather is endemic to the human condition. In practical terms, individuals and groups encounter the challenge posed by the questions "Why be ethical?" whenever they are faced with situations in which the "efficient" way of accomplishing their goals and objectives clashes with moral values. And, practically speaking, the second question is a common companion for those working in areas such as medicine or new technologies or politics in which the facts are not clear, or impacts are hard to predict, or moral dilemmas involving the apparent conflict of moral principles are encountered, or borderline cases are at issue.

Seen from this perspective, business people and organizations are not a special case. Like everyone else, they face the challenge of deciding whether their activities will be guided by ethical principles when ethics and self-interest appear to diverge in significant ways. And like everyone else, they face the challenge of applying moral values in complex environments in which their application is neither clear nor straightforward.

All of this is quite true, of course. However, it is incomplete, particularly with respect to investor-owned corporations in market economies. Practically speaking, the measure of success for managers and corporations is profits. And the most obvious and unavoidable obligations of managers and the investor-owned companies they manage flow to shareholders who are the putative owners.

The effect of this profit-oriented mindset is to put business managers within a tightly constrained moral environment quite unlike the type of moral environments in which moral agents otherwise are likely to find themselves. Seen from a moral perspective, the view that the primary obligation of business managers is to maximize profits places severe limits on the capacity and the obligation of people engaged in business activity to consider the wider social, environmental, and economic impact of their activities on people and the communities in which they do business.

These considerations give rise to a number of questions: Is it the case that the primary obligation of business is to maximize profits? Is good ethics good business? Do business managers have an obligation to go beyond concern for profits to consider the impact of their activities on all those likely to be impacted by what they do? If business has wider ethical obligations, how should those obligations be determined? What are the obligations of the people, professionals for example, who are employed by business firms?

These questions have been given new urgency in the new millennium by the moral failures that have resulted in the destruction of what were only a short time prior some of the world's most admired and respected corporations. Enron is a case in point. In the pursuit of profits, the management, auditors, and the board of Enron engaged in unethical business practices that led to the collapse of the company, and with it the jobs and pensions of their employees and the financial security and well-being of their investors and many other stakeholders. The subsequent collapse of companies such as MCI-WorldCom, Global Crossing, and Arthur Andersen, the firm responsible for auditing Enron, indicated that similar practices had become common in the American business community. As a result, governments, corporations, civil society, and the public generally have launched into a reexamination of widespread assumptions about the ethical responsibilities of multinational corporations and the business community generally.

The Readings

The first reading by Wesley Cragg argues that globalization has undermined the effectiveness of a post-War understanding that resulted in the allocation of responsibility for the generation of economic wealth to the private sector and responsibility for ensuring that that wealth was equitably distributed to the public sector of industrialized societies. What is now needed, the article proposes, is a new social contract that allocates a much wider range of ethical responsibilities to business, including the obligation to respect and to encourage respect for fundamental human rights as set out in the United Nations Declaration of Human Rights. The second, third, and fourth readings provide evidence that a new social contract may be emerging. The first of this trilogy is the International Code of Ethics for Canadian Business. This Code resulted from the initiative of a group of Calgary-based oil companies and was carried forward by the Canadian Exporters and Manufacturers Association and subsequently endorsed by Lloyd Axworthy, who was at the time the Minister of Foreign Affairs in the Canadian Government. The second reading in the trilogy sets out "The Global Compact," an initiative of Kofi Annan, the Secretary-General of the United Nations. It takes the form of a voluntary social contract binding those that sign it to respect relevant UN conventions, for example the UN Declaration of Human Rights. The third reading in the trilogy is written by Craig Mackenzie, the head of Investor Responsibility, a new and significant unit of a very large British investment company called Insight Investment. It is a statement directed to actual and potential investors by Insight Investment, setting out a new direction in their investment policy. It therefore is intended for commercial markets, not academic audiences. Nonetheless, it is an excellent account of what the first reading describes as a "new social contract." The reading details both the actual and potential social benefits of what it describes as "free-market globalization," as well as the problems that must be addressed if economic development is going to contribute to global and fairly shared economic development directed toward the eradication of poverty, protection of the environment, respect for human rights, and the development of democratic institutions.

The fifth reading by Doreen McBarnet asks "What is corporate responsibility and to whom is business accountable?" She offers a systematic overview of the movement toward greater corporate accountability and then asks what is required if it is to prove effective.

Finally, Conrad Brunk examines the role of professionals in a technological society. Although this article was written well before the recent spate of corporate moral disasters, it forseees in a remarkably clear way the need for a clear understanding of the role of ethics in professional training and work as well as the consequences of a failure to acknowledge that role and then to put it effectively into practice for ethical business practice.

HUMAN RIGHTS AND BUSINESS ETHICS: FASHIONING A NEW SOCIAL CONTRACT[1]

Wesley Cragg

In 1948, the United Nations Declaration of Human Rights was adopted by the United Nations. In the intervening fifty years, it has been formally endorsed by most of the countries of the world. The Declaration itself was a response to human rights abuses that preceded and accompanied the Second World War, a global war that created a global moral crisis to which the United Nations Declaration was a collective and global response.
The Universal Declaration began:

> *Whereas recognition of the inherent dignity and of the equal and inalienable rights of all members of the human family is the foundation of freedom, justice and peace in the world, and*
> *Whereas disregard and contempt for human rights have resulted in barbarous acts which have outraged the conscience of mankind, and, the advent of a world in which human beings shall enjoy freedom of speech and belief, **and freedom from fear and want** has been proclaimed as the highest aspiration of the common people ...*

The General Assembly:

> *Proclaims this Universal Declaration of Human Rights as a common standard of achievement of all peoples and all nations, to the end that every individual and **every organ of society** ... shall strive to ... secure their universal and effective recognition and observance ... .*

In the years following the proclamation, it came to be widely assumed that the Declaration of Human Rights was addressed principally to governments. In the liberal democracies of the developed world, governments, urged on by their citizens, did proceed to take up the challenge. Human rights were enshrined in constitutions; the Canadian constitution is an example. Laws designed to protect minorities from discrimination were passed. Provision was made for refugees, though it was not always as generous as it might be. A social safety net was put in place to protect the poor including health insurance, unemployment insurance, old age security and so on. Constitutional guarantees were put in place to restrain governments in the exercise of their powers thus protecting freedom of expression and of the press, freedom of assembly, the right to a fair trial and so on.

One consequence of the assumption that protecting and enhancing human rights was a government responsibility, however, was a *de facto* division of responsibilities between governments and the private sector. The private sector assumed primary responsibility for generating wealth while the public sector accepted responsibility for ensuring respect for human rights including freedom from "fear and want."

Let me describe this arrangement as a tacit social contract. It is this "contract" that I want to examine and evaluate in what follows.

Published in The Journal of Business Ethics, *Vol. 27, Nos. 1–2, pp. 205–214.*

Reprinted in: Business Challenging Business Ethics: New Instruments for Coping with Diversity in International Business, *Eds. Jacek Sójka and Johan Wempe, Dordrecht/Boston/London: Kluwer Academic Publishers, 2000, pp. 205–214.*

Establishing the existence of a "contract" or a general understanding of respective responsibilities in complex societies or tracing causally its impact is not an exact science. However, I do want to suggest that understanding the division of responsibilities between business and government in the post-War industrialized world as forming a tacit social contract is illuminating however difficult it might be to prove its existence. It is illuminating, I want to suggest, because it highlights the striking character of that division of responsibilities and its implications for the way in which much of the private sector perceives its role and responsibilities. Specifically, as generators of wealth, many private sector corporations and business people have been persuaded to the view that their sole social responsibility is simply to maximize profits in lawful ways. As a result, many in the corporate world tend to pay little attention to human rights issues as a corporate responsibility.

The evidence supporting the existence of a tacit understanding of the social responsibilities of the private sector is extensive and multi dimensional. There are for example the theories of management that emerged in powerfully articulate forms in the sixties and seventies that argued that a corporation's sole obligation is wealth maximization for the benefit of its owners or shareholders whose property it is. As Milton Friedman put it both simply and elegantly, the social responsibility of the modern corporation is simply to maximize profits. To go beyond this objective is a misuse of power that is doomed to fail and in the process impede the exercise on the part of civil authorities of their own proper responsibilities.[2]

One would expect that companies that see profit maximization as their primary obligation to define their social and ethical responsibilities narrowly. They would regard themselves as having a limited number of informal obligations defined by local conventions and culture. These would include obligations owed by the company to employees and the reciprocal obligations of employees to their employer. Other obligations would be those set out in contracts with employees, suppliers, customers, clients and so on. Taken together, these informal and contractual obligations could be anticipated to include: honesty in financial transactions, respect for company property, avoidance of conflict of interest, meeting contractual obligations, respect for the law and respect for basic rules of civility.

One would also expect that when companies with this management orientation went beyond their ethical duties narrowly defined and their legal obligations, it would be for clearly defined public relations purposes governed by enlightened self-interest.

In short, as Milton Friedman suggested, where the primary obligation is wealth maximization, obligations to stakeholders can be expected to be defined by the law, prevailing ethical customs and good public relations.

There is a good deal of evidence to suggest that this view has become the dominant view since the Second World War. The codes of conduct that have become common features of corporate policy and public relations in the last three or four decades are one rich source of supporting documentation.[3] What they reveal is a focus on "measures designed to protect the firm from wrongful acts by its employees."[4] That is to say, the primary purpose of codes of conduct historically has been the protection of the corporations. Public relations also emerges as a key factor in this regard. Thus, a 1978 UK study of advertising codes of ethics around the world found that for example, "industry will dedicate resources to code administration only if it expects benefits such as consumer goodwill or the removal of government legislation", a view that studies of Canadian and American codes have echoed.[5]

Further evidence comes directly from the private sector itself. A good example is a statement by François Vincke Secretary General of PetroFina, who says in a recent discussion of the International Chamber of Commerce's campaign against bribery that "until recently, ...

corporate responsibility was dictated by the law, or to put it in even simpler terms: the ethical code of a company was the criminal code."[6] Perhaps even more persuasive is a report to the OECD by a business sector advisory group which states categorically that: "Most industrialized societies recognize that generating long-term economic profit is the corporations primary objective."[7] The authors of the report acknowledge that ethics and ethics codes have a clear place in corporate governance whose goal is profit maximization. However, those ethical values must connect directly or indirectly to enhancing the bottom line. Furthermore, corporations that go beyond these ethical parameters should disclose their social agenda. The implication is clear. Commitment to respect human rights in international commerce even where it is not mandated by law implies a willingness to diverge from the goal of maximizing long term economic profitability.[8] There is no parallel suggestion that companies that propose not to respect international human rights and other ethical standards in their operations disclose this fact as well. Thus implicit among the assumptions of the report is the tacit understanding that the primary ethical obligation of a modern corporation is to maximize profitability within the constraints of law. This implication is reinforced by the report's suggestion that where important social objectives are at stake, governments will have to assume the leadership position.[9]

This view has come to dominate the thinking not only of business but also of governments and international economic institutions established to deal with the growth of international trade. Its effect has been to separate economics, which in the minds of many means "the science of profit maximization," from any ethical values beyond those required to ensure the achievement of the corporations primary objective, namely profit maximization.

The Post-War Social Contract Evaluated

The post-War period has seen remarkable growth in respect for human rights and economic wealth for industrialized countries. While not everyone has shared equally in the wealth generated, it is unarguable that the economic wealth available to the citizens of the industrialized world today is many times greater than the wealth available to citizens of the same countries either before or after the war. Respect for human rights has also become an entrenched feature of the industrialized world's political and social systems. Once again, not everyone has benefitted equally. But it is surely evident that human rights and related moral principles are more widely respected and constitutionally entrenched than was the case fifty years ago. The benefits have been enormous.

We might therefore describe the outcome of the tacit social contract that has guided post-War economic development in the developed world as follows: profit maximization + a free market + the law = economic wealth (development).

This formula, though apparently widely endorsed, has nonetheless come under considerable scrutiny in recent years. Two factors have been particularly influential. First is a series of "moral crises" involving illegal or unethical conduct on the part of employees and senior management acting in what they thought was the best interests of their employers that resulted in significant damage to a number of large and apparently successful corporations. What these crises have revealed is that the mantra of profit maximization can work both for and against corporations and their shareholders by rationalizing unethical and illegal actions. Cutting ethical corners, which many have come to believe is at least sometimes the price that tough minded business people have to pay to compete successfully, can backfire resulting in serious public relations costs and financial penalties.

The Lockheed bribery scandal in the late 1970s was for many the first clear warning sign. Both the actions of Lockheed senior management and subsequent investigations on the part of the U.S. Senate made it painfully clear that respected business leaders were prepared to condone bribery in foreign business transactions if that is what it took to beat the competition. Particularly important for our purposes, however, was the fact that those condoning corruption saw it as justifiable in the international market if it did not involve breaking the laws of the corporation's own country or what were seen as the moral conventions of the country in which it took place. Even more insidious was what appeared to be an implied suggestion that similar conduct might also be justified in the home market if competing successfully demanded it. This conclusion was relatively easily rationalized if law was equated with law enforcement and risks associated with skirting the law were carefully and rationally calculated.

The Bhopal disaster further illustrated ambiguities about how the social contract was to be interpreted in international commerce. Against what laws and environmental regulations should management be judged, India's or those of the country in which a company was headquartered, in this case the United States? What moral conventions, for example with regard to health and safety standards, should prevail, those of the host country or those of the parent?

Increasingly, companies also have also begun to realize that the mantra of profit maximization can be turned against a corporation when it becomes the frame of reference for individual employees. This knowledge in turn has made it more and more difficult for senior management to accept the idea that "business is business and ethics is ethics" particularly when confronted with employee fraud and other forms of unethical activity,[10] a lesson driven home for many by the collapse of Barrings Bank.

For many, what these developments have stimulated over the past two decades is the growing realization that ethics and business are much more closely connected than the tacit social contract, forged in the post-War period, would suggest. The remedy offered has been to develop better articulated and more robust understandings of the role of ethics in leadership and corporate culture. The result has been the growth of interest in corporate codes of conduct that set out acceptable standards of conduct for both corporations and their employees.

What is more, decisions to create codes and build more ethical corporate cultures have had some surprising results. Many corporations have discovered that substantial positive benefits can flow from building a reputation as an ethical company. Employees prefer to work for ethical companies. A reputation for ethical business practices attracts better qualified, better motivated job applicants. Employee morale and public relations benefit. Long term profitability can be enhanced and so on. These discoveries have added additional weight to the view that ethics and business are related and that indeed there is a place for ethics in free market economies.

The difficulty is that the resulting codes are largely self serving. Their primary function, as Craig Forcese points out in his two volume study for the International Centre for Human Rights and Democratic Development (Montreal, Canada), has been to ensure that the corporation and its employees meet their reciprocal obligations to each other and to the law and act in ways that enhance the corporation's public image. Hence corporate codes have not been extended, for the most part, to cover issues like respect for human rights.

Of course, human rights are covered in the country in which corporations are headquartered since they are embedded in the legal structures of the industrialized world. Hence, in those contexts explicit reference to human rights values is redundant. However, the laws of industrialized states do not as a rule extend beyond their borders. Hence they do not govern corporate operations abroad, specifically in the developing world. As a result, current interest in ethics codes has not altered in any fundamental way the post-War social contract.

The second factor relevant to an evaluation of the post-War conception of the social responsibilities of corporations is globalization. Globalization is a complex phenomenon and not easily characterized accurately. What can be said, however, is that it has had dramatic impacts on the legal environment in which corporations, particularly multinational corporations, conduct business. These changes in turn have significant implications for corporations and the post-War social contract.

First is the fact of corporate power. The largest transnational corporations have budgets that dwarf those of most of the world's nations. This power has been enhanced by corporate mobility. In today's world, corporations have a great deal of freedom in deciding where to do business. They can choose the countries in which they invest. They can choose their suppliers. And their suppliers can choose with remarkable freedom where in turn they will produce the goods and services they offer. An equally important parallel development has been advances in communications technology that allow the movement of capital virtually instantaneously from one country to another.

The effect of these developments has been to give multinational corporations remarkable freedom to choose the legal systems that will govern their operations. Corporations are now free to seek out those environments in which the laws in place provide the most favourable conditions for maximizing profits. This fact in turn has given corporations a powerful tool for persuading the countries in which they do business to create a favourable legal environment, namely one that puts the fewest possible regulatory constraints on the conduct of business. Thus, various states have made themselves into havens for firms seeking to avoid tax and banking restrictions, corporate disclosure and other regulatory regimes in their home country.

Globalization has also provided nation states with an incentive to engage in "regulatory competition." The temptation to attract investment by promising a legal environment that minimizes labour or environmental standards, for example, is obvious. The result has been what some have described as a "race to the bottom."[11]

In contrast, while globalization has strengthened the capacity of multinational corporations to choose and shape the regulatory environment in which they operate, it has weakened the capacity of nation states to regulate business activity. Law as we know it is the creation of nation states. The jurisdiction of national legal systems is bounded by the principle of extraterritoriality limiting the capacity of states to project their domestic law abroad. The ability of states to control the legal environment regulating international commerce has been further weakened by free trade agreements such as NAFTA and the WTO.[12] The effect of these factors both apart and in combination has been to put much of the activity of multinationals beyond the effective reach of any one country's legal system.

Parallelling these developments has been the emergence and increasing importance of transnational agencies and institutions, for example the OECD. However, to date, few if any of these agencies and institutions — the European Union is the single obvious, but still limited, exception — have been willing or able to stand proxy for the state, to make regulatory standards effective across national boundaries. Even when they are able to "legislate" (e.g. the ILO) many countries refuse to treat such regulatory standards as legally binding until and unless they are expressly incorporated into domestic law. When they are able to "adjudicate" (e.g. the United Nations or the World Court) they seldom have at their disposal effective regimes of enforcement, and sanctions must still be applied by states.

Nor is globalization the only obstacle to state regulation. The popularity of neo-conservative policies has led many governments in the developed world to reduce state regulation of the economy, taxation and state expenditure thus liberating market forces and, hopefully, stimulating investment, jobs and general prosperity. While the state has by no means disappeared and has even deployed its coercive powers more vigorously in certain fields of social control, for example the bribery of foreign public officials, in many areas, business is being freed from many of the constraints which had been imposed over half a century of interventionist state policies.[13]

The result of these domestic and global shifts is the apparent emergence of what might be called a regulatory vacuum with regard to many aspects of international commerce. It is a vacuum furthermore which many corporations have shown considerable willingness to exploit. Thus, it is now painfully obvious that many business leaders are prepared to ignore some of the most basic norms of human behaviour in the name of profit maximization. It is equally obvious that many of their competitors feel compelled to follow their lead or lose an important competitive advantage.

What are the implications of these developments for an evaluation of what I have described as the economic assumptions underlying the post-War social contract, namely that "free markets + profit maximization + the law = economic wealth (development)"? It would appear to be this. Where corporations are able to control the legal environment that governs their activities then "law" drops from the equation. When law is removed from the equation, the formula equates unconstrained profit maximization with the generation of economic wealth and development.

The most appropriate moral characterization of unconstrained profit maximization is greed. It is perhaps unsurprising, therefore, given the account just offered, that we have seen serious efforts over the past two decades, particularly on the part of a few private sector commentators and "cutting edge" business tycoons, to rehabilitate greed. The 1980s, for example, are now widely known in North America as the greed decade. It was a decade in which a few enormously "successful" entrepreneurs toured business schools extolling the virtues of greed. It was also a decade in which an undisciplined pursuit of profits caused a spectrum of disasters from the wide spread collapse of financial institutions (in the United States, for example) to the destruction of fishing stocks that had been the source of livelihood and subsistence for communities for centuries (in Canada's Maritime provinces, for example). And it was a decade that ended in a damaging recession from which many communities in the industrial world began to recover only after almost another decade steady economic growth.

In 1990s, the collapse of the "tiger" economies and the spread of "the Asian flu" is widely agreed to have involved two factors. The first was the lack of accountability and the apparently irresponsible use of power on the part of Asian financial institutions and conglomerates. But equally important has been the pursuit of profits at any cost on the part of investment managers and financial institutions in the industrialized democracies.[14]

Hedge funds provide an excellent example of management for profit maximization in a global economy in which legal constraints are minimal. These funds are managed with a view to making as much money as possible in as short a period of time as possible for wealthy investors. Global financial markets are largely unregulated. Hedge funds exploit that fact for the benefit of their managers and shareholders. In the process, they have been known to seriously destabilize financial systems around the world.

The story of Long-Term Capital Management illustrates the phenomenon. This hedge fund was managed by some of the world's most gifted and knowledgeable money managers who used the financial resources of some of the world's largest and most powerful financial institutions and their own talents to gamble on the movement of money markets. The result was the near collapse of the financial systems of the industrialized world, an outcome that was avoided only by the intervention of the American Federal Reserve Board.[15] In reviewing these events, surely the name, Long-Term Capital Management, is not without significance. Neither is the fact that two of the managers of the fund at the time of its collapse were Nobel laureates. But perhaps most important is the obvious implication that greed under the guise of profit maximization can have very destructive impacts on a global market economy.

In this environment, ethics that goes beyond the bounds of corporate self interest is seen as not simply irrelevant to economic development but also an impediment forcing corporations to choose between ethics, including respect for human rights, and profits. Equally important, there is no evidence that an economy built simply on unconstrained profit maximization will result in economic development let alone minimally equitable development of the sort that has characterized the post-War economies of the industrialized world.

How then are these post-War developments to be characterized, ethically speaking? As already noted, the unrestrained pursuit of profit maximization is simply another word for greed. And greed has been condemned as personally and socially destructive by all of the world's great religions and by moral leaders at virtually every stage of the development of human civilization. Furthermore, there is today no shortage of evidence confirming that view. What that evidence suggests is that unrestrained profit maximization or greed is the enemy not the driving force of a free market economy.

Building a New Social Contract

What then are the lessons to be learned from the post war experience? The first, surely, is the need to reexamine the ethical foundations of market economies and the relative responsibilities of the private and public sectors in ensuring that business activity leads to equitable economic development. A second and equally important lesson is that events provoking global crises and changes can provoke the kind of serious rethinking of responsibilities that seems now to be required. The 1948 Declaration of Human Rights stands as a powerful example, coming as it did as a response to the moral crisis provoked by the horrors of the Second World War. A second example is the rethinking that many corporations have undergone in the past three decades faced with moral crises caused by ethically questionable state and corporate conduct.[16] Most recently, events in Seattle in response to World Trade Organization meetings designed to facilitate further economic globalization have provoked calls for serious reevaluation of the values driving the new economy. A third lesson, however, must be added to the previous two. As was the case in 1948, events over the past half century have given rise to resources, insights and experience that are now available to guide the process of reexamination and development of new standards if we choose to use them.

Let me conclude by highlighting some of those resources, insights and experience. Note first that in response to the damaging effects of corruption on economic development, some of the world's most influential international economic institutions (e.g., the World Bank, the International Monetary Fund, the Asian Development Bank) are now beginning slowly to accept that ethics and economics are integrally related. One consequence of this reexamination is the recently concluded Organization for Economic Cooperation and Development convention calling on member countries to criminalize the bribery of foreign public officials. This convention has emerged from the realization on the part of a number of powerful multinational corporations that corruption is inconsistent with the operation of a market economy and a serious impediment to economic development. Equally important has been the realization that the problem of corruption cannot be solved by individual corporations or the public or private sectors acting alone. Finally, events leading up to the creation of the convention have illustrated the impact that NGOs, Transparency International in this case, can have in bringing about coordinated actions by national governments and international institutions in dealing with this kind of global problem.

The OECD and its nation state members have also developed Corporate Governance Guidelines and Guidelines for Multinational Enterprises. In both cases, there is evidence that the industrialized nations and their international institutions are moving beyond understandings of corporate social responsibilities that have dominated corporate and government thinking since the Second World War.

Second, faced with the need to provide principles and codes to guide corporations in the global market place, coalitions of business leaders, religious leaders and members of civil society are forming with a view to articulating model international codes of conduct. Two examples are the *CAUX Round Table Principles for Business* and *An Interfaith Declaration by Christians, Muslims and Jews*. The Interfaith Declaration builds on the values of justice, mutual respect, stewardship and honesty. The Caux Principles are grounded on two moral concepts, the Japanese concept of "kyosei" which means living and working together for the common good, and the concept of human dignity. Both these statements give a central place to respect for human rights in business activity.

Third, a number of governments have begun to develop codes for the conduct of international business. A good example is the "Standard of Principles for Canadian Business." This code highlights respect for human rights and social justice. The American government has also published a statement on Model Business Principles and has become heavily involved in negotiations with American multinational companies in the apparel industry. And while these efforts cannot be said to have been particularly influential to date, they do indicate a growing awareness that ethics has a serious role to play in the private sector.

Fourth, increasingly, multinational corporations too are recognizing that the old social contract is no longer valid. The best indication of this is the development of corporate codes that explicitly recognize that one of the central ethical obligations of business is to ensure respect for human rights in their own operations. An example is the Code of Conduct for Alcan Aluminum Ltd., a Canadian multinational company in the aluminum business. This code states that "Alcan is guided by principles of non-discrimination and respect for human rights and freedoms." Placer Dome, a Canadian mining company, is a second example of a multinational corporation that has recently made a public commitment to operating world wide in accordance with principles of sustainable development which include respect for the human rights.

What these developments indicate is that segments of the business community are increasingly aware that ethics and economics are closely related. Thus, the Pacific Basin Economic Council Charter on Standards for Transactions Between Business and Government links good governance and economic growth and calls for honesty, integrity, transparency and accountability in business transactions as a key to building public confidence in business and government.

Fifth, civil society is beginning to play a central role in the growing awareness that respect for human rights is a private sector as well as a public sector responsibility. International coalitions are beginning to create new benchmarks and tools for assessing corporate social performance. AA1000, developed by the Institute for Social and Ethical Accountability,[17] is a first attempt to generate an internationally recognized auditing standard. SA 8000 is a performance oriented labour rights standard linking directly to the work of the International Labour Organization. SA8000 is intended to play a role in social accountability similar to the ISO environmental management standards that are now widely used to encourage environmentally responsible business practices. These initiatives are slowly becoming influential factors reshaping public and corporate understandings of the responsibilities of transnational corporations.

Finally, perhaps of most significance is the leadership being offered by a small number of transnational corporations that have committed themselves to competitive business practices consistent with respect for human rights in all aspects of their operations. What is unique about these corporate leaders is their commitment to allowing and encouraging independent evaluation and monitoring of the impact of their codes on the way they do business. An excellent recent example is a decision on the part of Levi Strauss, a large multinational corporation in the apparel industry whose code sets out "Terms of Engagement" for its suppliers that require respect for employee human and labour rights, to obtain an independent evaluation of the effectiveness of its "Terms of Engagement" in its business operations in the Dominican Republic. In pursuit of this objective, Levi Strauss engaged a group of four NGOs including Oxfam (England) to undertake an independent study. That study has now been concluded and its results are publicly available. This private sector/civil society "partnership" model as a way of building ethics back into the global market is now being explored by corporations in manufacturing, resource extraction and retailing around the world.

What then is to be learned from these developments?

1. We need a new social contract to frame business activities in the emerging global market place. The widespread view in the private sector that the protection of human rights is a government, not a corporate responsibility is not tenable in a global economy. As the Pacific Basin Economic Council points out in its Charter, the purpose of trade liberalization is to promote development that increases living standards. Both traditional wisdom and recent experience demonstrate that free domestic or global markets that ignore internationally recognized ethical norms do not promote economic development and improve living standards. What they do promote is the reallocation of existing wealth from those who are already poor to those who are already rich.
2. The new social contract must include recognition on the part of the business community that they have an obligation to operate in all aspects of their operations within the framework of policies and codes that encompass respect for human rights and other values of fundamental human importance, for example environmental protection.
3. The new social contract must acknowledge that building respect for fundamental human values in the private sector requires business and government partnerships. It is clear that national government and international regulation is essential to creating a level economic playing field for the conduct of international commerce. It should be equally clear that government and international regulation is required to protect the market and those it is designed to benefit from the worst vices of an outdated business culture which is

prepared to tolerate and even encourage crony, casino and rogue capitalism and where greed is extolled as the driving force of business activity.

4. The new social contract needs to ensure a significant role for civil society in monitoring the adherence of corporations to the codes they adopt. This cooperation should be based on private sector/civil society partnerships whose goal is to work together for benefit of all stakeholders.

5. Finally and perhaps most important, we need to remind ourselves, as Gandhi and others have pointed out, that commerce without conscience is a formula for human exploitation, not human development.

NOTES

1. This research was funded in part by a SSHRC Strategic Funding Grant in support of a York University project entitled "Voluntary Codes: The Regulatory Norms of a Globalized Society?" The paper was first read to a conference in Bangkok, Thailand on Human Rights and Business Ethics marking the 50th anniversary of the UN Declaration of Human Rights. The Bangkok conference was funded in part by the Canadian International Development Agency. I would like to thank the Social Sciences and Humanities Council and the CIDA for their support. For further information about the voluntary codes study, please contact Wesley Cragg.

2. See for example: "The Social Responsibility of Business is to Increase Profits" in The New York Times Magazine (Sept. 13, 1970).

3. American surveys indicate that "by the late 1980s as many as 77% of large US corporations had some sort of corporate code of conduct." "A 1981 survey of 125 of the largest Canadian businesses ranked by revenue found that 49% of the 51 responding corporations had 'corporate statements of objectives'" (Forcese, 1997, p. 14).

4. Ibid., p. 14.

5. Ibid., p. 12.

6. Vincke et al. 1999, p. 15.

7. Ira M. Millstein (Chairman), April 1998.

8. Ibid. p. 25.

9. Ibid. p. 70

10. Recent studies indicate the dimensions of the problem. A study by a Canadian accounting and consulting firm recently revealed that large Canadian corporations each lost on average $1.3 million (Can.) from fraud in 1997. Similar studies in the United States have revealed that white collar crime may cost the private sector as much as $100 billion (US) each year. In 1994, a study of over 4000 U.S. employees found that 31% of employees surveyed had observed conduct at work over the course of a year that violated either the law or the policies of the company for which they worked. Further, fewer than half of the 31% reported the misconduct they had observed to their employer.

11. See, for example, Roy Culpeper and Gail Whiteman's analysis in "The Corporate Stake in Social Responsibility" (Culpeper *et al.*1998).

12. The ongoing dispute over European Union regulations governing the import of bananas and the conflict between Europe and Canada over the export of beef that have been exposed to genetic engineering are obvious cases in point. In both cases, attempts to regulate goods has been struck down by the WTO.

13. See for example, Arthurs, 1997.

14. For an interesting discussion of these and other aspects of the Asian economic crisis see Jomo, 1998.

15. See for example comments attributed to Paul Volcker, former chairman of the U.S. Federal Reserve Board, by Mathew Ingram in *The Globe and Mail*, Monday, Sept. 13, 1999. In an article entitled "The world according to Paul Volcker," Volcker is said to have described the activities of Long Term Capital as completely unregulated and speculative. He is described as saying further that their activities threatened to destabilize a substantial portion of the U.S. financial industry.

16. I have in mind here examples like South African apartheid, corporate moral crises like the Lockheed, Bophal, Exon Valdez scandals, and the collapse of the "tiger" economies in the 1990s. Most recently, a Canadian Oil Company, Talisman, has been faced with scrutiny on the part of the Canadian and American governments, INGO's in Canada and abroad and a number of Canadian and American pension funds. At issue is its participation in an oil extraction and export project in an oil field in an area of the country wracked by civil war. The controversy has depressed the value of its shares. In response to the criticism, the company has had to examine its operating policies. It continues to defend its investment and involvement in the Sudan but is also beginning to take steps to define its ethical obligations. It has also signed a code of conduct for Canadian companies doing business internationally that recognizes that corporations have obligations to protect and respect human rights in their international operations.
17. Located in London England.

REFERENCES

Arthurs, H.W.: 1997, "'Mechanical Arts and Merchandise': Canadian Public Administration in the New Economy", *McGill Law Journal* 42:1, 29-61.

Culpeper, Roy and Gail Whitmen: 1998, "The Corporate Stake in Social Responsibility", *Canadian Corporations and Social Responsibility*, Canadian Development Report 1998, (Reneuf Publishing, Ottawa, Canada), pp. 13-35.

Forcese, Craig: 1997, (No. 1) *Commerce with Conscience: Human Rights and Corporate Codes of Ethics* (International Centre for Human Rights and Democratic Development, Montreal, Canada).

Forcese, Craig: 1997 (No. 2), *Putting Conscience into Commerce: Strategies for Making Human Rights Business as Usual* (International Centre for Human Rights and Democratic Development, Montreal, Canada).

Jomo, K.S.: 1998, *Tigers in Trouble* (Zed Books, London and New York).

Millstein, Ira M. (Chairman): 1998, *Corporate Governance: Improving Competitiveness and Access to Capital in Global Markets*, A Report to the OECD by the Business Advisory Group on Corporate Governance, Organization for Economic Co-operation and Development, (OECD, Paris, France).

Vincke, François, Fritz Heiman, and Ron Katz: 1999, *Fighting Bribery: A corporate manual*, (International Chamber of Commerce, Paris, France).

QUESTIONS

1. What is a social contract? Why does Wesley Cragg describe the post-War understanding of the economic and social responsibilities of corporations as a social contract?
2. What evidence does Cragg offer for the view that the post-War social contract needs to be significantly revised?
3. What is the role and impact of globalization on these developments?
4. What does Cragg point to in claiming that there is evidence of a new social contract emerging?

INTERNATIONAL CODE OF ETHICS FOR CANADIAN BUSINESS

Vision

Canadian business has a global presence that is recognized by all stakeholders as economically rewarding to all parties, acknowledged as being ethically, socially and environmentally responsible, welcomed by the communities in which we operate, and that facilitates economic, human resource and community development within a stable operating environment.

Beliefs

We believe that:
- we can make a difference within our sphere of influence (our stakeholders)
- business should take a leadership role through establishment of ethical business principles
- national governments have the prerogative to conduct their own government and legal affairs in accordance with their sovereign rights
- all governments should comply with international treaties and other agreements that they have committed to, including the areas of human rights and social justice
- while reflecting cultural diversity and differences, we should do business throughout the world consistent with the way we do business in Canada
- the business sector should show ethical leadership
- we can facilitate the achievement of wealth generation and a fair sharing of economic benefits
- our principles will assist in improving relations between the Canadian and host governments
- open, honest and transparent relationships are critical to our success
- local communities need to be involved in decision-making for issues that affect them
- multi-stakeholder processes need to be initiated to seek effective solutions
- confrontation should be tempered by diplomacy
- wealth maximization for all stakeholders will be enhanced by resolution of outstanding human rights and social justice issues
- doing business with other countries is good for Canada and vice versa

Values

We value:
- Human rights and social justice
- Wealth maximization for all stakeholders
- Operation of a free market economy
- A business environment which mitigates against bribery and corruption
- Public accountability by governments
- Equality of opportunity
- A defined code of ethics and business practice
- Protection of environmental quality and sound environmental stewardship
- Community benefits
- Good relationships with all stakeholders
- Stability and continuous improvement within our operating environment

Principles

    A. Concerning Community Participation and Environmental Protection, we will:

- strive within our sphere of influence to ensure a fair share of benefits to stakeholders impacted by our activities
- ensure meaningful and transparent consultation with all stakeholders and attempt to integrate our corporate activities with local communities as good corporate citizens
- ensure our activities are consistent with sound environmental management and conservation practices
- provide meaningful opportunities for technology cooperation, training and capacity building within the host nation

    B. Concerning Human Rights, we will:

- support and promote the protection of international human rights within our sphere of influence
- not be complicit in human rights abuses

    C. Concerning Business Conduct, we will:

- not make illegal and improper payments and bribes and will refrain from participating in any corrupt business practices
- comply with all applicable laws and conduct business activities in a transparent fashion
- ensure contractor's, supplier's and agent's activities are consistent with these principles

    D. Concerning Employees Rights and Health & Safety, we will:

- ensure health and safety of workers is protected
- strive for social justice and promote freedom of association and expression in the workplace
- ensure consistency with universally accepted labour standards, including those related to exploitation of child labour

Application

The signators of this document are committed to implementation with their individual firms through the development of operational codes and practices that are consistent with the vision, beliefs, values and principles contained herein.

THE GLOBAL COMPACT: CORPORATE CITIZENSHIP IN THE WORLD ECONOMY

Kofi Annan, Secretary-General, United Nations

Let us choose to unite the power of markets with the authority of universal ideals. Let us choose to reconcile the creative forces of private entrepreneurship with the needs of the disadvantaged and the requirements of future generations.

Overview

United Nations Secretary-General Kofi Annan first proposed the Global Compact in an address to The World Economic Forum on 31 January 1999. The Global Compact's operational phase was launched at UN Headquarters in New York on 26 July 2000. The

Secretary-General challenged business leaders to join an international initiative — the Global Compact — that would bring companies together with UN agencies, labour and civil society to support nine universal principles in the areas of human rights, labour and the environment.

Through the power of collective action, the Global Compact seeks to advance responsible corporate citizenship so that business can be part of the solution to the challenges of globalisation. In this way, the private sector — in partnership with other social actors — can help realize the Secretary-General's vision: a more sustainable and inclusive global economy.

Today, hundreds of companies from all regions of the world, international labour and civil society organizations are engaged in the Global Compact. The Global Compact is a direct initiative of the Secretary-General; its staff and operations are lean and flexible.

The Global Compact is a voluntary corporate citizenship initiative with two complementary objectives:

* Making the Global Compact and its principles part of business strategy and operations
* Facilitating cooperation among key stakeholders and promoting partnerships in support of UN goals

To achieve these objectives, the Global Compact offers facilitation and engagement through several mechanisms: Policy Dialogues, Learning, Local Networks and Partnership Projects.

The Global Compact is not a regulatory instrument — it does not "police", enforce or measure the behavior or actions of companies. Rather, the Global Compact relies on public accountability, transparency and the enlightened self-interest of companies, labour and civil society to initiate and share substantive action in pursuing the principles upon which the Global Compact is based.

The Global Compact is a network. At its core are the Global Compact Office and four UN agencies: Office of the High Commissioner for Human Rights; United Nations Environment Programme; International Labour Organization; United Nations Development Programme. The Global Compact involves all the relevant social actors: governments, who defined the principles on which the initiative is based; companies, whose actions it seeks to influence; labour, in whose hands the concrete process of global production takes place; civil society organizations, representing the wider community of stakeholders; and The United Nations, the world's only truly global political forum, as an authoritative convener and facilitator.

The Nine Principles

The Global Compact's principles in the areas of human rights, labour and the environment enjoy universal consensus being derived from:

* The Universal Declaration of Human Rights
* The International Labour Organization's Declaration on Fundamental Principles and Rights at Work
* The Rio Declaration on Environment and Development

The nine principles are:

Human Rights

Principle 1: Businesses should support and respect the protection of international human rights within their sphere of influence; and

Principle 2: make sure their own corporations are not complicit in human rights abuses.

Labour Standards

Principle 3: Businesses are asked to uphold the freedom of association and the effective recognition of the right to collective bargaining;

Principle 4: the elimination of all forms of forced and compulsory labour;

Principle 5: the effective abolition of child labour; and

Principle 6: the elimination of discrimination in respect of employment and occupation.

Environment

Principle 7: Businesses are asked to support a precautionary approach to environmental challenges;

Principle 8: undertake initiatives to promote greater environmental responsibility; and

Principle 9: encourage the development and diffusion of environmentally friendly technologies.

Why Participate

There are numerous benefits to participating in the Global Compact. These include:

- Producing practical solutions to contemporary problems related to globalisation, corporate responsibility and sustainable development in a multi-stakeholder context.
- Rallying around universal principles and responsible corporate citizenship to make the global economy more sustainable and inclusive.
- Leveraging the UN's global reach and convening power with governments, business, labours, civil society and other stakeholders.
- Sharing good practices and learnings.
- Accessing the UN's broad knowledge in development issues and its practical reach worldwide.

INVESTORS, CODES AND CORPORATE RESPONSIBILITY

Craig Mackenzie

Introduction

Insight Investment is a large institutional shareholder. We are committed to encouraging the companies in which we invest to achieve high standards of corporate responsibility. We believe that investors have a moral obligation and a long-term interest in doing so. But what standards should Insight encourage? What principles should guide our work? Where should we focus our efforts in order to do the most good? This paper records the results of our opening analysis of these questions. It also introduces Insight's Global Business Principles Project, which aims to contribute to providing a basis for more effective and coherent investor activity in this area in the future.

Companies create immense benefits for society, through the provision of products and services, and through the creation of jobs and wealth. The expansion of private enterprise in developing countries in recent decades is one factor which has helped to raise the living standards of hundreds of millions of people — in the last 20 years the number of people living on less than $1 a day has fallen by 200m despite large growth in overall population (Source: World Bank). The continued expansion of free trade and private investment is an important part of any plausible attempt to raise the standard of living of the 1.2 billion people who remain in the most extreme poverty.

However, it goes without saying that free-market globalisation is not without serious problems. A particularly controversial aspect of globalisation relates to the role of multinational companies in development. Amongst other things, global companies are charged with complicity in human rights abuses, exploitation of sweatshop labour conditions, irresponsible product marketing, involvement in bribery and corruption, the improper use of political influence, and contribution to all manner of environmental destruction.

The charge of corporate irresponsibility is not new. Ever since the rise of corporations, there have been allegations of corporate irresponsibility (both the British East India Company and Cecil Rhodes' British South Africa Company, for example, were heavily criticised in their time). However, in recent years, as a result of the rapid globalisation of business, these challenges have become significantly more widespread in terms of the sheer volume of companies involved; they have also become more widely reported as a result of the globalisation of the media, and the emergence of new media technologies such as the internet. This trend is likely to continue. Section 2 of this paper outlines why the problem of corporate irresponsibility is particularly acute in developing countries.

In the face of these challenges, there are strong ethical and commercial reasons for companies to demonstrate corporate social responsibility. This principle is now widely accepted by companies, governments and wider civil society. Much of the time, on many issues, companies fulfil this responsibility simply by obeying the law. But this is not always the case. In some circumstances, if companies are to demonstrate corporate responsibility, they must go beyond legal compliance, respecting wider ethical principles.

Such principles now exist in the form of various international codes and standards, but, for various reasons, they are not widely or fully respected by companies. The third section argues that the starting point for developing more responsible global corporate practice is to encourage greater understanding and respect for global principles by the business community.

In the last decade, investors have become a powerful force for corporate accountability with regard to questions of corporate governance, but they have for the most part, been silent on the question of corporate responsibility. There is a growing acceptance of the need to address this wider agenda both on grounds of moral responsibility and on the grounds of self-interest. Investors have a responsibility, an interest and a substantial opportunity to play a powerful role in encouraging more responsible business practice. The fourth section describes the role that we believe investors should play in providing support, encouragement and accountability for companies in their efforts to respect global business principles. The final section outlines Insight Investment's Global Business Principles Project: a practical initiative by one large institutional investor to encourage greater understanding and respect for global business principles.

This document is a preliminary analysis of what is a very large and complex set of questions. The questions we consider here take us well beyond the conventional sphere of expertise of investment institutions. Nevertheless, we believe that it is incumbent upon us to be clear in advance about the analytical basis of the programme of activity on which we will be embarking in the coming years. This work is a contribution to an emerging debate, and by no means Insight Investment's last word on the subject. We greatly welcome comments and criticisms from those with interest and expertise on the issues raised below.

In the Firing Line

In recent years, western companies from a range of industrial sectors have been hit by controversies over their operations in developing countries. The companies concerned in each case have often strenuously denied the allegations against them. But the sheer frequency of such controversies, together with the fact that these are often supported by influential and international coalitions of campaigners and critics, illustrates the risks for firms which neglect, or are perceived to neglect, basic principles of ethical behaviour.

- Various manufacturers and retailers of clothing and sportswear have been attacked in high-profile campaigns over alleged "sweatshop" conditions in contract factories in Asia, Africa and Latin America. Among the allegations against them: payment of low wages, forced overtime, intimidation and physical punishment of workers, the employment of under-age children, and failures to control the use of toxic chemicals in factories.
- Many of the world's largest oil and mining companies have at various times in recent years been accused of: involvement in human rights abuses, destroying local environments, ignoring the land rights of indigenous people, and fuelling conflict through their payment of royalties to warmongering governments.
- Some companies have seen their product markets seriously threatened by public concerns (the "conflict diamonds" campaign, for example, at one point posed a significant threat to diamond sales); others have encountered major security risks to personnel and to their upstream assets as a result of local community unrest (this has been true, for example, in Nigeria, Indonesia and Papua New Guinea).
- Construction companies and others involved in building or financing hydroelectric dams have been variously accused of complicity in environmental destruction and of neglecting the rights of indigenous people. Dam projects in Turkey, Malaysia and China have attracted particular attention in recent years.
- Electricity and water utilities have also become embroiled in controversies in a number of their recent forays into developing countries. Typically driving protests against these sort of companies — whether the project in question is to build a new power plant in Asia or to run a water and sewage system in Latin America — is local opposition over the level of tariffs charged to consumers.
- A number of tobacco firms and also food companies have been criticised over their allegedly irresponsible marketing tactics in developing countries. Chocolate manufacturers, meanwhile, have recently been hit by allegations that child slave labour is involved in producing the cocoa which they source from West Africa.
- Arms manufacturers have long attracted public ire for selling weapons to countries with poor human rights records. Campaigns have often focused on the promotion of arms sales by home governments, as well as on the companies themselves.
- In a major recent controversy that raised concerns across the corporate world about the protection of intellectual-property rights, pharmaceuticals companies have been attacked

over the high price of their HIV drugs in developing countries — as well as over the cost of their treatments for other diseases prevalent in the third world. To head off such criticisms, some firms have lowered their prices for certain drugs and also funded various community health projects.

- Finally, there are signs that major media and information technology firms are now also starting to come into the firing line. A number of them, for example, have come under pressure from western human rights campaigners to uphold human rights and principles of free speech in undemocratic developing countries, such as China. Thus the companies are being encouraged to refuse demands by local officials that they censor the content of their offerings or that they hand over information on any of their customers who happen to be political dissidents.

2. Globalisation and Corporate Responsibility

We believe that the greatest challenge of corporate responsibility lies with company activities in the developing world, for three reasons: the dramatic increase in the scale of Western business activity there in recent decades; the particularly acute ethical challenges for business in many developing countries; and the lack of state capacity to regulate business.

2.1 The Rise of Global Investment

Over the last few decades, there has been a rapid expansion of investment in the developing world by Western companies: in 2001, for example, foreign direct investment (FDI) inflows to developing nations totalled $205 billion, compared with only $8 billion in 1980 (Source: UNCTAD). British and continental European multinationals that form the bulk of Insight Investment's shareholdings thus now have significant exposure to economies in Asia and Latin America and, although often to a lesser extent, in Africa.

At present, the majority of FDI still takes place between industrialised nations; also the current economic downturn has led to a retrenchment, though far from abandonment, of companies' foreign investment plans. Looking beyond the immediate future, however, developing countries are widely expected to provide an important source of future profitability for many of the world's multinationals. Whereas in the West, few economic sectors provide opportunities for rapid market growth, economies such as China and India, as well as a number of others in Asia, and several in Latin America and Africa, offer companies the potential of large populations eager for consumer goods and major cost advantages as locations for industrial production. The vast natural resources of many developing countries will also provide very attractive opportunities for continuing investment by multinational oil, mineral and other natural resource companies. (1)

2.2 Ethically Challenging Business Environment

A second reason why the challenge of corporate responsibility is particularly demanding in developing countries arises from the political, economic and other disadvantages frequently faced by these countries. Problems in the developing world — including, for example, corruption, human rights abuses, conflict, poverty and disease — are often more widespread or more intractable than in the West. Most of the world's most severe local air and water pollution problems, for example, can be found in developing countries — as can many of the world's most bio-diverse and threatened ecosystems. Companies operating in such regions cannot avoid becoming embroiled in these issues. Similarly, the scale of poverty and of epidemic diseases, such as HIV, in parts of the third world, combined with the difficulties faced by indigenous or international institutions in dealing with such problems, creates unavoidable demands on companies to step into the breach. In some situations, people are so poor and vulnerable that any negative corporate impact is devastating. Conversely, companies are sometimes so economically and political powerful that their presence can impose substantial disruptions on local society.

2.3 Lack of Regulatory Capacity

A third, related problem associated with corporate activity in the developing world arises from the fact that systems of state regulation, and state capacity more generally, are often relatively incomplete or under-resourced compared to those in Western countries. Over many decades, and sometimes over centuries, rich countries have built elaborate systems of law relating to every aspect of corporate activity, establishing principles of acceptable conduct and strict limits to behaviour. The systems provide a very clear guide to corporate activity in rich countries. And should companies overstep the mark, there are small armies of inspectors, investigators, auditors and other officials to check and punish infringements.

These frameworks are often significantly less complete in developing countries, and the regulatory authorities have dramatically less capacity to respond to infringements. In fact, in certain poor countries, the institutions of the state fail to operate as they should on a very fundamental level: they may be riddled with corruption, for example, they may be incapacitated by ethnic divisions, or they may be used by elites as instruments of repression against minorities or against the population as a whole. Furthermore in rich countries, other institutions of civil society — the press, the trade unions, consumer groups, universities, single-issue campaigners and others — are relatively strong and well resourced, providing additional sources of corporate scrutiny. In poor countries, these institutions — while often increasingly active — are rarely as strong.

Sometimes the problem is not simply a regrettable lack of government capacity to regulate companies. In some situations governments deliberately choose not to impose regulations on companies. In a competitive effort to create lower-cost business environments to attract foreign investment, governments have sometimes deliberately reduced regulatory requirements for business, often in special economic zones. In some cases, companies have actively encouraged governments to do this. This raises difficult questions about the legitimacy of trade-offs between economic growth and basic rights and welfare of those impacted, particularly in the light of the uneven distribution of the resulting economic benefits.

2.4 Corporate Responsibility is Not Only a Developing Country Problem

It perhaps goes without saying that the suggestion that the greatest challenge of corporate responsibility lies in poor countries does not imply an absence of corporate responsibility problems in industrialised countries. As the collapse of Enron and other recent scandals have illustrated, regulations on corporate governance in the West have sometimes proved insufficient to prevent behaviour by companies that is unethical and financially disastrous. Similarly, complying with minimum environmental, human rights and labour regulations may not be sufficient for companies who want to persuade public and political opinion in the West that they are responsible corporate citizens.

Nonetheless, the more comprehensive nature of regulatory systems in rich countries, combined with their generally higher levels of state provision and governance means that companies — by and large — can ensure that they fulfil their basic social responsibilities (and thereby also contain the risk of public uproar and political resistance), simply by complying fully with the law.

It should therefore be no surprise that some companies find it relatively easy to conduct themselves in a responsible way in rich countries, and so much more difficult to do so in developing countries.

2.5 Controversies

A closer look at just a few of the high-profile controversies that have recently engulfed Western multinationals in developing countries will illustrate the nature of the problem. (For further examples, see, In the Firing Line, p. 485.)

2.5.1 Child Labour. In the case of the child-labour allegations which have damaged the brands of a series of Western retailers such as Nike, companies have found themselves inextricably entangled in a complex social problem for which government solutions are lacking. Many of the alleged underage workers in question have been discovered in locally-owned factories in Asia from which the retailers source their products, or in their subcontractors even further down the supply chain. The depth of poverty in many Asian countries means that child labour is frequently widespread throughout the economy. The most severe problem is not that children are working in factories, but that they are often employed in abysmal and exploitative conditions, with few rights; together with the fact that they are simultaneously being denied access to the education which may provide their route out of poverty. The situation is exacerbated by the incapacity of local governments to enforce domestic laws against abusive child labour, or to provide economic and educational alternatives for poor families and their children. In order to fulfil their social responsibilities, therefore, many Western retailers have attempted to adopt (though not always successfully) a regulatory role themselves: that is, they have tried to establish monitoring systems to ensure that their local contractors are abiding by legal requirements — and also, in some cases, to provide education for local children.

2.5.2 Human Rights Controversies. Similarly, Western companies such as Enron, Premier Oil, Rio Tinto, Shell, TotalFinaElf, Unocal, and many others, have become embroiled in human rights controversies. As a result, some companies have begun to accept that their human rights responsibilities need to extend beyond mere acceptance of the local situation as it stands and of the role played by host governments. For it has often been multinationals' alleged complicity in rights abuses committed by government security forces or other arms of the state that has been the source of international uproar. In Indonesia, China, Nigeria, and Burma, among other countries, foreign firms have been accused of turning a blind eye to state abuses in this way. The precise ethical principles that corporations should follow in such situations remain a subject of heated international debate.

2.5.3 AIDS in Africa. The AIDS crisis in Africa, meanwhile, has also created new, and uncertain, responsibilities for foreign companies that go beyond legal requirements. Some companies such as the mining giant, Anglo American, for example, have recently begun to subsidise, or provide for free, HIV treatment for their workers — a pressing social need given the failure of state healthcare provision in many African countries. Similarly many pharmaceuticals companies, such as Britain's GlaxoSmithKline, have responded to intense international pressure to reduce the price of their HIV drugs throughout the developing world.(2)

2.5.4 Environmental Damage. A final, and perhaps most obvious, example are the controversies relating to corporate environmental behaviour. Driving the criticism in many of these cases has been a widespread public suspicion (whether fair or not) that companies are taking advantage of the weaker systems of environmental regulation — and in particular weaker enforcement of local laws — which are often found in developing countries. Again, intense debate continues over the correct standards that companies should uphold globally on a number of environmental issues.

2.6 Reversing Globalisation is Not a Solution

Some anti-globalisation critics seem to believe that the answer to the problems described above is for multinational companies to withdraw their investment from the developing world. Hostility to foreign investment in developing countries is misplaced. In fact, we would argue it ought to be encouraged rather than curtailed. The key question is not the level of FDI, but the manner in which it is employed. Provided host governments ensure that they maximise, and manage well, the economic benefits which this investment can bring (such as employment, tax revenues, skills and technology transfer), foreign investment can be a powerful driver for sustainable development and poverty-reduction — as several Asian countries have demonstrated during the last 30 years. In itself, foreign capital may not guarantee a country's economic success; but rarely have nations lifted themselves out of poverty simply by shutting themselves off from global markets.

2.7 Interests

While there are strong reasons to hope that investment in developing countries will continue to grow, anti-globalisation protestors have good reason to be concerned about the problems to which Western multinationals contribute. The controversies listed above are serious and, in many cases, companies cannot legitimately escape blame for their contribution to the problems. One reason for the existence of these problems is that some businesses profit in the short-term precisely from the absence of explicit systems of rules, regulations, and social expectations. This fact fuels much of the protesters' sense of injustice. However, we would argue that, in general, it is not in the long-term financial interests of companies and their shareholders for these problems to persist. For what is at stake when they become embroiled in controversies is not just the immediate corporate reputation. Also under threat is their "licence to operate," the broad public and political acceptance which underpins the actual security and stability of their investments and markets over the long term. Section 4 explains this point more fully.

2.8 The Need for a Long-term Solution

The growing exposure of Western companies to difficult and relatively unregulated developing world business environments has created a major challenge for global multinationals. It is not a new challenge — companies have been plying their trade around the world for at least 200 years — but it is a challenge that has been growing in scale and significance. The existence of a substantial international backlash to globalisation means that the challenge of corporate responsibility must be met if we are to safeguard the historic economic opportunities which globalisation offers. How then should the challenge of corporate responsibility be addressed?

3. Global Ethical Principles

In the long-term, the solution to the problem of corporate responsibility in developing countries is for these countries to establish comprehensive and fully effective systems of democratically accountable state regulation of business. Companies have a role in fostering this long-term solution and a responsibility not to obstruct it. However, the reality is that in many countries this solution is many years away. Considerable gaps in government regulation will remain for some time to come. We believe that the only practicable short-term answer is for stronger self-regulation by companies. But regulation according to what principles?

3.1 Fundamental Values

We believe that the solution is for companies to regulate their behaviour according to legitimate ethical principles, especially those that have been codified in internationally authoritative conventions and guidelines. This solution is now widely supported both by governments and by many leading companies who have made public commitments to respect global business principles.

The appropriateness of ethical standards is inevitably a matter of considerable debate, but there are a number of core ethical principles that are the subject of widespread consensus: principles relating to honesty, the keeping of promises, the avoidance of harm, the provision of aid to those in need, respect for human rights and dignity, and ideas about fairness and equity. While there is scope for disagreement about the application of these principles in practice, there is little serious practical disagreement about their basic legitimacy.

These principles are so much part of the background expectations of people in the modern world — including business people — that they form an essential basis for practical corporate responsibility. Most people in business are honest without having to be told to be so, simply because they believe it is right that they should be so.

However, a growing number of companies are choosing not to depend solely on the moral virtues of their staff, and are making explicit statements of the principles that they believe should govern their business (Shell, BP, Philips, and Novo Nordisk are among a rapidly expanding constellation of companies with such commitments). While such policy commitments help to provide guidance to those whose moral integrity is lacking, more importantly they can make it easier for employees to make the right decision when faced with conflicts.

Well-crafted company codes are a very valuable basis for corporate self-regulation. However, there are fundamental questions of legitimacy about company-authored codes. Is it right that companies should set their own standards of behaviour?

3.2 International Norms

We believe that the most credible basis for global business principles is provided by the extensive body of international norms, established by the United Nations and ratified by governments (See accompanying text). Most important of all is the Universal Declaration of Human Rights (UDHR) and its associated conventions and instruments. Also important are the UN conventions relating to sustainable development.

The UDHR is addressed primarily to governments, however it also requires that 'every organ of society …shall strive by teaching and education to promote respect for these rights and freedoms and by progressive measures, national and international, to secure their universal and effective recognition and observance …'(3) Companies are among the most powerful organs of modern society. The central basis for global business principles, we believe, is the imperative for companies to play their part in respecting, promoting and securing these rights and freedoms. The question of what can legitimately be expected by companies in this regard is a large one. The demands the UDHR and other international conventions place on business are by no means self-explanatory. Their application in the myriad circumstances of business practice requires considerable interpretation and discussion. Fortunately, considerable progress has already been made in this area. With regard to the UDHR itself, there is now specific guidance (see the UN Human Rights Principles and Responsibilities for Transnational Corporations (4)). More broadly there are two particularly important Codes:

- OECD Guidelines for Multinational Enterprises (5)
- ILO Tripartite Declaration of Principles Concerning Multinational Enterprises and Social Policy (6)

Both these codes have been adopted by governments in consultation with business and trades unions. Both refer to wider international norms. In addition to these government-sponsored principles and guidelines, there are a bewildering array of codes, management standards, and reporting standards relating to corporate responsibility. Among the most important are:

- UN Global Compact (7)
- Global Sullivan Principles (8)
- ISO14001 (9)
- SA8000 (10)
- The Global Reporting Initiative (11)
- AA1000 (12)

International Principles

There is a growing body of internationally agreed principles, some with general application and some relating specifically to business. Here are what we suggest are the most important:

1. United Nations Universal Declaration of Human Rights (1948). UDHR is the most widely recognized human rights standard. It is the basis for most other human rights principles embodied in international agreements, national laws and voluntary standards. While the UDHR itself is not binding on governments, the International Covenant on Civil and Political Rights (ICCPR) and the International Covenant on Economic, Social and Cultural Rights (ICESCR), agreed in 1966 are legally binding on signatories. While the UDHR is addressed primarily to governments, it does enjoin companies and all other organs of society to respect, protect and secure human rights. A UN committee is currently drafting specific guidance for business on this topic.
2. OECD Guidelines for Multinational Enterprises (1976, amended 2000). The OECD Guidelines are non-binding recommendations to companies made by its thirty member nations. They offer, among other things, basic advice on disclosure, industrial relations, environmental management and combating corruption. They also recommend that companies attempt to apply such principles throughout their supply chain and with business partners. The guidelines explicitly encourage sustainable development but stop short of providing a decision-making framework for companies seeking to operationalise this broad recommendation. Though voluntary, the OECD Guidelines do have a mechanism for enforcement using a system of National Contact Points.

3. International Labour Organisation Tripartite Declaration of Principles Concerning Multinational Enterprises and Social Policy (1997). The ILO Declaration principally reflects the perspectives of labour relations with business and government. Prescriptive in character, it promotes freedom of association, collective bargaining, the effective end of child labour and forced labour, employment creation, highest standards of health and safety, elimination of discrimination, and training of local people. In general, although non-binding, it does offer robust recommendations for industrial dispute avoidance and reconciliation.

4. United Nations Conference on Environment and Development Declaration of Principles, Rio de Janeiro (1992).The Rio Declaration demonstrates the commitment of 172 nations to the principles of sustainable development. It is broad in focus and aspirational in tone and, therefore, not binding in law. It includes what is widely regarded as the pre-eminent definition of sustainable development but does not provide a decision-making framework for balancing the many dimensions of sustainability that can come into conflict. The Declaration did, however, succeed in reinforcing the concepts of 'polluter pays' and the 'precautionary principle'.[13]

5. UN Framework Convention on Climate Change (1992) is a framework for science-based initiatives on climate change. The subsequent Kyoto Protocol (1997) establishes binding greenhouse gas reduction targets for governments. Some leading companies have adopted the Kyoto targets and mechanisms.

6. UN Convention on Biological Diversity (1992). The CBD has three main goals: the conservation of biodiversity; its sustainable use; and sharing the benefits arising from commercial use of genetic resources in a fair and equitable way. Binding to over 170 ratifying countries, the provisions of the CBD only offer vague guidance for specific corporate behaviour. However, the CBD clauses on intellectual property and benefit sharing of genetic resources do warrant careful attention from relevant sectors (for example, biotechnology, forestry and tourism) as over 100 countries are now introducing laws based on the convention.

3.3 Corporate Compliance

In the last ten years, the number of companies recognising the need to make formal commitments to respecting global business principles has grown dramatically. One defining feature of corporate responsibility leaders is their willingness to make themselves accountable for voluntary compliance with such principles. These companies have, in many cases, embarked on a long-term programme to develop a clearer understanding of how these principles may be reflected in practice, and some have developed a body of management systems to regulate company activities to ensure compliance with the principles endorsed.

However, these leading companies are very much in the minority. Many companies still have not formally endorsed relevant codes. Of those who have endorsed the codes, anecdotal evidence indicates that few have adopted a comprehensive approach to their adoption throughout the business. Why do companies fail to respect international principles?

3.3.1 Denial of Corporate Social Responsibility. One reason is that many companies hold the view, whether explicitly or implicitly, that their only responsibility is to create shareholder value within the law. If taken seriously, this would imply that they have no obligation to respect ethical principles that are not directly backed by legal requirements. We believe that this position is morally untenable. The demands morality places on people, whether individually or collectively in companies, derives from our common humanity, and not from the contingencies of legislation. Companies have a moral obligation to behave responsibly whether or not they are legally compelled to do so.

Whether for ethical or commercial reasons, many companies now publicly accept the need to go beyond legal compliance in their desire to behave responsibly, but this acceptance is by no means universal. There are a variety of more practical reasons why companies fail to comply with authoritative ethical principles.

3.3.2 Ignorance of Problems. In the last decade, a large number of companies have exposed themselves to business in developing countries for the first time. In a significant number of cases, companies have been unprepared for the cultural, social, economic, religious, regulatory and political differences between the business environment in an emerging economy and the one back home. Too many executives seem to be unaware of the large problems that they are likely to face, until they are confronted with them.

3.3.3 Lack of Understanding of Principles. Even where companies are aware of the existence of problems, they may not turn to international principles as a solution. While few people in business are likely to be ignorant of the UDHR, rather more are unaware of the obligations it places on companies, and how those obligations may be interpreted in particular settings. Much the same is true of the OECD and ILO Guidelines.

3.3.4 Conflicts Between Principles. There is nothing inherent about moral principles that suggests that they will never be in conflict with one another. In practice principles are frequently in conflict. There are conflicts between different rights, between different welfare goals, and between rights and welfare goals. The economic necessity in the poorest families for children to work conflicts with children's right to be free from work and to receive an education. Addressing such conflicts with care and wisdom is one of the biggest challenges for global business principles.

3.3.5 Conflicts with Local Laws. Another set of challenges relates to the relationship between global business principles and local laws. How do global principles relate to local laws? What happens when principles and laws conflict? When should companies respect the law rather than principle and vice-versa?

3.3.6 Gaps. On some issues, consensus on appropriate principles has not yet emerged. How much can reasonably be expected of companies in response to the global AIDS crisis? What principles should govern the use of genetically modified organisms? What role should companies play with regard to climate change?

3.3.7 Limits. There are important questions about where the responsibilities of companies end and where the responsibility of customers, suppliers, governments and the international community begins. In deciding how responsibilities should be shared between different agents, the resulting distribution of burdens and benefits should be considered. Not least, because principles that impose too great a burden on companies' operations in developing countries will drive these companies away, thereby removing the benefits of investment. A balance is needed that accommodates the reasonable desire of companies to profit from developing-country business relationships, while establishing clear corporate obligations to protect the interests and rights of those affected by their activities.

3.4 Encouraging Compliance with Global Business Principles

We believe that a central part of meeting the challenge of corporate responsibility is for companies to comply with global business principles. In order to achieve greater compliance, there is a need to encourage greater understanding and to address the issues indicated above. There is also a need for more companies to commit themselves fully to adhering to the standards established by global business principles. Shareholders, particularly large institutional shareholders and their fund managers, have an important role to play in promoting this change.

5. The Global Business Principles Project

At Insight, we accept that investors have a responsibility and an interest in supporting and encouraging high standards of ethical conduct by the companies in which we invest. We believe that it is right that we focus our efforts in this regard where they are most needed. As we have argued, we believe investor involvement is most needed with regard to companies' business activities in developing countries. We also believe that the best thing we can do to address the challenge of developing-country corporate responsibility is to provide support and encouragement to companies in their efforts to comply with legitimate global business principles, and to play a part in holding them accountable for compliance.

In order to make progress with these tasks, it is important that we are clear about the ethical principles with which we can reasonably expect companies to comply. Insight has therefore established its Global Business Principles Project to help gain greater clarity about these principles, and to provide a basis for our engagement with companies. This paper is the first step in the project. It has tried to establish the case for a focus on the challenge of corporate responsibility in developing countries and the outlines of a solution based on compliance with global business principles. Our conclusions are provisional, and we invite comment from interested parties. This document is only the first small step. Our core activities in taking the project forward include:

5.1 Research and Debate

As we have made clear, one of the major obstacles that blocks greater attention to global business principles by companies and their shareholders is a lack of agreement about the role that principles should play in practice. Insight will be commissioning research and hosting debates on a number of topics in order to gain greater understanding and agreement about principles. We seek to work in partnership in this endeavour with companies, investors and other stakeholder groups. We welcome expressions of interest in collaboration from such organisations.

5.1.1 Comparative Analysis. An important first step is to understand the scope and limitations of existing authoritative business principles. How do existing codes compare in their coverage of different problems of corporate responsibility? Are there any important omissions? How do codes relate to more fundamental ethical ideas? How do they vary in the stringency and specificity of their requirements? How do they contrast in their legal status and their monitoring systems? These are some of the important questions we will be considering in our comparative analysis of existing codes.

5.1.2 Issue-Specific Principles. We will be looking at a selection of specific issues that are important to the companies and business sectors in which we have substantial holdings in order to identify and test appropriate principles. For example, we have holdings in a number of companies that have extensive supply chains in developing countries where poor labour conditions are a serious problem. In spite of several years of active exploration of this topic, there is still considerable confusion among many companies about what they should be doing to address this difficult issue. Other topics we are evaluating as candidates for investigation include: bribery and corruption, access to medicines, the relevance of civil and political human rights to business, the marketing of dangerous products, the use of toxic chemicals, and climate change.

5.1.3 Cross-Cutting Principles. There are a number of problems regarding corporate practice in developing countries that cut across numerous specific corporate responsibility issues. For example, there are fundamental issues of principle regarding the appropriate relationship between companies and governments, particularly governments that lack democratic legitimacy. There are also important cross-cutting questions of principle about the appropriate division of responsibility for problems between companies and their suppliers. While companies have responsibility for their own actions, under what circumstances do they have responsibilities for those of their suppliers? What aspects of the company-supplier relationship strengthen a company's moral involvement, and what aspects weaken this involvement?

Another cross-cutting topic relates to the distinction between binding moral duties and corporate action 'beyond the call of duty'. On some issues companies seem to have a clear moral obligation to take action. But on others, though their contribution may be valuable, there is no moral requirement on them to act. For example, to what extent should companies be expected to contribute to the development of basic infrastructure — such as water supply and sanitation — in the communities in which they operate in poor countries? There is a great need for such development, and, to some extent, companies have the ability to contribute to it, but should they be expected to shoulder this burden?

A third important cross-cutting issue relates to the tensions between the short-term creation of shareholder value and moral obligations. Shareholders have the legal and moral right to demand that company directors act in good faith and with due care to produce returns on their investments. They have placed their capital at risk and may reasonably expect a sincere effort from the company to produce an acceptable return. However, morality — as expressed in global business principles — imposes limits on the means by which companies can pursue value for shareholders. There are, therefore, very real practical tensions between business imperatives and the demands of principled corporate conduct.

The payment of bribes to public officials is prohibited by law and by global business principles, but refusal to pay bribes can lead to the loss of lucrative contracts. In such cases the demands of morality can conflict with the short-term financial interests of shareholders. Of course, in the long term, we would argue that it is in all of our interests that corruption is ended. But this does not help companies who are penalised in the short term. Companies, investors and governments need to understand the dynamics of these conflicts of interest, and to seek methods — including government intervention where appropriate — to remedy them.

5.2 Engagement and Accountability

The second element of the Global Business Principles Project is to seek to use our legitimate influence as shareholders to encourage high standards of compliance with global business principles.

5.2.1 Insight's Use of the Principles. We believe that we need to promote understanding of global business principles, in order to establish the basis on which we can fulfil our responsibility as investors to encourage principled corporate conduct. However, we do not believe that, as investors, we have any special capability to fulfil this role. We do, however, have a unique and crucial role with regard to providing support and encouragement to companies in their efforts to comply with global business principles, and most important of all, playing a part in holding companies accountable for compliance with these principles. If companies are to make a substantial and sustained effort to comply with global business principles, it is crucial that they have the active support of shareholders. Too often, in the past, shareholders have ignored — or even dismissed — company activities in this area. Company law, on both sides of the Atlantic, gives shareholders particular authority to hold company directors accountable for their running of the company. Where companies fail to respect legitimate global business principles, shareholders have a role that is uniquely theirs: requesting and, if necessary, demanding accountability from the board.

5.2.2 What will Insight Expect to See from Companies? In order to rise to the challenge of corporate responsibility, we believe that companies must:

- Make public their commitment to adhere to relevant ethical principles
- Establish objectives and expectations with regard to application of specific principles to specific problems
- Set up systems of training, guidance and support for staff
- Establish specific new management systems, where appropriate
- Monitor the company's level of achievement of compliance with principles
- Publish a record of the company's performance in adhering to relevant principles

As the Global Business Principles Project progresses, Insight will make clear through its own policy documents, its understanding of good practice with regard to particular corporate responsibility problems and principles.

5.2.3 Policy. Through our programmes of research and debate, Insight hopes to gain greater clarity and agreement about the appropriate application of global principles to corporate practice. As we do so, we will formulate and publish statements of policy in which we will set out our understanding of the appropriate standards of principled business conduct with regard to various corporate responsibility issues. These policy statements will guide our subsequent activity. It is against these policies that our clients, companies and the wider public may hold us accountable for our activities.

5.2.4 Company Analysis. On the basis of our policy, Insight will then, through its own research and that supplied by research agencies, evaluate the extent of company commitments to, and compliance with, global business principles.

5.2.5 Engagement. Where we find apparently inadequate levels of corporate responsibility, we will contact companies to express our support for global business principles, and to encourage improvement. We will also request an account from companies of their reasons for non-compliance with global business principles.

Our experience leads us to believe that many companies will welcome the support and encouragement of shareholders on this topic. Where companies are less receptive, we will use the more formal methods available to shareholders for achieving corporate accountability. In all of our activity, Insight will be guided by the principles set out in our Policy on Corporate Governance and Corporate Responsibility. Among other things, this policy makes clear that Insight believes that investors must themselves be accountable for their actions, to their clients, to the companies they are shareholders in, and to wider society. We will therefore be publishing regular accounts of our activities.

Insight looks forward to working with companies, investors and other stakeholders in pursuing the goals of the Global Business Principles Project in the coming months. To follow our progress, submit comments, and to register for future updates, please visit our Web site: www.insightinvestment.com/responsibility

NOTES

1. For further information on FDI trends and prospects, see the World Bank's "Global Development Finance 2002"
2. See, for example, GlaxoSmithKline's website: http://www.gsk.com/community/downloads/facing_the_challenge.pdf; also see Oxfam's website: http://www.oxfam.org.uk/cutthecost/index.html
3. Universal Declaration of Human Rights: http://www.un.org/Overview/rights.html
4. http://www1.umn.edu/humanrts/PrinciplesWithCommentary5final.html
5. http://www.oecd.org/EN/home/0,,EN-home-93-3-no-no-no-93,00.html
6. http://www.ilo.org/public/english/employment/multi/index.htm
7. http://65.214.34.30/un/gc/unweb.nsf/content/thenine.htm
8. http://www.globalsullivanprinciples.org/principles.htm
9. http://www.iso.ch/iso/en/prods-services/otherpubs/iso14000/index.html
10. http://www.cepaa.org/sa8000_review.htm
11. http://www.globalreporting.org/GRIGuidelines/index.htm
12. http://www.accountability.org/aa1000/default.asp
13. http://www.globalreporting.org/GRIGuidelines/index.htm;
    http://www.accountability.org.uk/aa1000/default.asp.

These standards often incorporate specific reference to the UDHR and other international norms, but in many cases they go further, incorporating a variety of other principles of good practice.

QUESTIONS

1. What reasons does Craig Mackenzie offer for the view that investors have a moral obligation and a long-term interest in encouraging companies in which they invest to achieve high standards of corporate responsibility?
2. What evidence does Mackenzie provide to support his view that the problems of corporate irresponsibility are particularly acute in developing countries?
3. What are the global principles that Mackenzie suggests should provide the starting point for developing more responsible global corporate practice?
4. Is Mackenzie's analysis of the responsibilities of investors sound? Is it realistic?

THE NEW CORPORATE ACCOUNTABILITY

Doreen McBarnet

What is corporate responsibility and to whom is business accountable? These questions used to have easy answers, at least in the Milton Friedman school of thought. 'Responsibility' and 'accountability' were defined by law. 'Accountability' was to shareholders, and management's responsibility was to maximise 'the bottom line.' There is a growing discourse, however, of a much wider concept of corporate responsibility and accountability, not just among philosophers or social critics but in the business community itself. The new image focuses not on the bottom line but on the 'triple bottom line' of economic, social and environmental responsibility. Accountability is not just to shareholders but to 'stakeholders,' often very widely defined. And both responsibility and accountability are defined not by legal obligations but by a much wider remit.

The first section of the paper offers a simple illustration of developments in the concept of corporate responsibility. The second reviews a range of social and economic forces which have been identified as driving the new approach to corporate responsibility. These could be seen as constituting a 'new accountability.' Indeed a whole discourse is developing, with new buzzwords, new gurus, and new clichés. The third section of the paper begins to look behind the discourse, to ask: who is driving? Is the new responsibility more than just discourse? Is the discourse more important than the empirical reality? Is the new accountability, reality or image, desirable?

Corporate Responsibility: From Bottom Line to Triple Bottom Line

The classic referent for the narrow concept of corporate responsibility is Milton Friedman, who famously declared

> The social responsibility of business is to increase its profits.[1]

To Friedman, and to others who take this stance,[2] accountability is to shareholders; the criterion of stewardship and responsibility is financial, maximising the 'bottom line'; and the only legitimate constraint on the pursuit of profit is the obligation to comply with the law.

The Friedman stance is however, just one end of the spectrum in the current discourse of corporate responsibility. Compare that position, with, for example, the public stance taken by Royal Dutch/Shell, which is commonly cited as epitomising a very different approach.[3] In its first annual *social* report Shell set out its vision of corporate responsibility in the following terms. First,

> The Royal Dutch/Shell Group is commercial in nature and its primary responsibility has to be economic — wealth generation, meeting customer needs, providing an acceptable return to investors, and contributing to overall economic development.[4]

So far this is pure Friedman. But the report goes on:

> But there is also an inseparable responsibility to ensure that our businesses are run in a way that is ethically acceptable to the rest of the world and in line with our own values.[5]

Indeed the report is summarised as describing

> how we, the people, companies and businesses that make up the Royal Dutch/Shell
> Group, are striving to live up to our responsibilities — financial, social and environmental.[6]

Note the differences from the Friedman school of thought. First, responsibility is defined not in terms of the bottom line but in terms of a *triple* bottom line — financial, social and environmental.[7] Second, accountability is defined as owed not just to shareholders, or even to the wider remit of stakeholders[8] as in, for example, continental European concepts of corporate governance — shareholders *plus* employees, consumers, suppliers. Rather Shell announces itself responsible to all of those categories[9] *and* to 'society at large,'[10] indeed to 'the *rest of the world*.'[11] Thirdly, Shell holds itself up as accountable not just on *legal* obligations, but according to what is *'ethically acceptable'*[12] to the rest of the world and 'ourselves.' 'This report', states the opening line, 'is about values.'[13] The company has set out a statement of principles[14] and in its social reports it accounts for its performance according to those principles, with 'external verification.'[15]

The Shell Report provides a particularly clear illustration of the other end of the spectrum in the current discourse on corporate responsibility, and it demonstrates the overt introduction of the language of ethics into business's public depiction of its role. But Shell is not so much a special case as part of a trend. All of the US's Fortune 500 corporations have codes of conduct,[16] and as at March 1999, 70% of the UK's FTSE350 were making some disclosure about environmental and social issues.[17] The language of ethics turns up repeatedly in business discourse. In the UK, the FTSE (The Financial Times Stock Exchange Index) has introduced in 2001 the FTSE4Good index for ethically high scorers. And this is just the latest in the line of a burgeoning field of 'ethical investment,' reckoned to have grown tenfold over the last 10 years.[18] There are banks expressly describing themselves as 'ethical banks,' there are ethical audits and ethics consultancies.

Discussion of the moral responsibilities of business has come out of the classroom and into both the financial press and the boardroom. Why?

Drivers

In academic analysis, in media analysis, and in discussion within business itself, a number of 'drivers'[19] of this new discourse of business ethics and corporate responsibility have been and can be identified. Some drivers are 'old', the need to respond to crises, for example, though the nature of that response could be seen as innovative. Some are new, indexing a changing global context.

'Old' Drivers: Crisis Management

What Shell itself has described as its 'transformation'[20] did not take place in a vacuum. It was a response to major PR crises resulting from both environmental, and, especially, human rights issues. 'Shell in Nigeria' has become a classic case study for business schools.[21] The company's operation in a state run by a military dictatorship accused of major human rights abuses, the impact of oil extraction on the Ogoni people and the Delta environment, the execution of Ken Saro-Wiwa, the campaigns of human rights organisations pointing the finger not just at the Nigerian dictatorship but at Shell, amounted to a PR disaster, which was only exacerbated when Shell's plan to dump its Brent Spar oil rig at sea was met by much publicised resistance by Greenpeace.[22]

In that context the new philosophy of corporate responsibility adopted by the company can be seen as a response to a very old driver of crisis management. Indeed a study by Arthur Andersen and the London Business School found that the motivation for introducing codes of conduct in 22% of companies surveyed was 'negative publicity.'[23] Other examples come readily to mind, with British Airways introducing a code of conduct after Virgin accused it of 'dirty tactics,' or NatWest Bank doing so after the Blue Arrow affair.[24]

If the stimulus is not novel, however, the nature of the response is. Shell in particular, instead of sticking to its original response to criticism over its role in Nigeria (a Friedmanesque denial of responsibility — 'Nigeria makes its rules and it is not for private companies such as us to comment on such processes in the country'[25]) switched tack to acknowledge that 'not to take action could itself be a political act,'[26] and to commit itself in the future to a wider concept of responsibility. Its new Statement of Principles made an express commitment to 'express support for fundamental human rights,'[27] while subsequent reports have documented its attention to human rights issues, including dilemmas faced[28] and it has produced a 'management primer' on human rights.[29]

'New' Drivers

More generally the growth in business discourse of a wider concept of corporate responsibility has also been attributed[30] to a range of new socio-political, economic and strategic developments.

Globalisation and Civil Society

One recurrent theme in analyses of drivers of the new corporate responsibility is the ubiquitous if hazy 'globalisation', including the global economy, the role of civil society and the new technology.

Globalisation refers in part to the development of worldwide consumer markets and production. There is nothing new in the use by first world companies of third world labour pools for cheap labour far from the constraints of first world health and safety, minimum wage, environmental or other laws. Nor indeed is organised protest by civil society new. Witness, historically, the critics of slavery. Global non-governmental (NGO) activity has however become a key part of the discussion of globalisation, and identified as one of the drivers of the new corporate responsibility.

NGOs monitor, investigate and campaign against corporate activity. Greenpeace, with its environmental concerns, and Amnesty International and Pax Christi, with their focus on human rights, played major parts in the public attacks on Shell. NGOs such as Earthrights International and the Centre for Constitutional Rights have been involved in legal action against corporations, as in the pursuit, through the US courts, of Unocal and Shell in relation to human rights issues in Myanmar (Burma) and Nigeria.

Another tactic is to buy shares in order to protest as shareholders at annual general meetings (AGMs). BP, for example, at its 2001 AGM, faced boisterous criticism of the human rights and environmental implications of its exploration strategies.[31] Even where the protestors are very much in the minority, and the vote lost, this strategy ensures the generation of significant publicity.

The broader anti-globalisation and anti-capitalism movements, and what we might think of as 'NGNs' — non-governmental *networks* — are also identified[32] as highly significant drivers.

Businesses can also face a situation where activists' techniques, for example in the case of animal rights movements, move beyond protest to violence and threats of violence against corporate executives, sometimes to significant effect, as in the Royal Bank of Scotland's decision to withdraw from funding of Huntingdon Life Sciences, a core target of UK animal rights activists.

Globalisation: The New Technology

All of this can be seen as aided by the new technology, expanding easy global communication, and making for instant worldwide publicity. There is now, it is frequently said, 'no hiding place' for corporate activity. The internet not only allows for the organisation of networks of protest on the streets, but provides a ready forum for instant criticism and publicity, with Web sites on all kinds of issues, pointing the finger at specific companies. The Greenpeace Web site offers a shoppers' guide on such issues as GM foods, with, for example, Kellogg's self-presentation in the UK as a GM free company, undermined by the Web site observation that it was still using GM crops in the US. Amnesty International has produced world maps highlighting countries where there is 'corporate risk' with regard to human rights, and naming companies operating there.

All this can be seen as resulting in a new *de facto* accountability, that goes beyond that required by law. Take another classic case, that of Nike. Nike, like many other multinational companies, has its shoes and clothing produced in cheap labour countries by independent suppliers. Some of its Vietnamese, Indonesian and Chinese suppliers have been exposed as using child labour, requiring employees to work long hours (beyond even the high legal maximum of the countries in question), at less than even the low statutory minimum wage, and in some places in conditions where carcinogens in the air were above the permitted level.[33] In short, both Nike's own code of conduct, and in some cases, local law, were being broken, but not by Nike. Under traditional criteria Nike was neither accountable nor responsible.

But Nike was *held* responsible and held to account by civil society campaigners. Again the Nike experience has become an icon of what can go wrong if companies stick to too narrow a notion of corporate responsibility — demonstrations, protests, 'shoe-ins' where Nike trainers were publicly thrown away, very public rejection of sponsorship, weeks of Garry Trudeau anti-Nike cartoons, and a fall in profits.[34]

Trends in Business Practice: Outsourcing and Branding

The Nike case demonstrates another contextual factor — trends in business practice such as outsourcing and branding. Nike was particularly vulnerable to such adverse publicity, because of the importance to its business of the Nike brand. Indeed Nike is in a sense only a brand. Production is all subcontracted. The functions of the Nike corporation itself consist of design, marketing, and finance; Nike's role is the creation and management of a brand. In its emphasis on branding, however, it can be seen to have created its own nemesis.[35] The very fact that the name is so well known makes it an easy target for critique.[36] At the same time the trend to outsourcing and subcontracting means companies have less direct control over the conditions under which their products are made. Though this can be seen cynically as an advantage when no responsibility or accountability is attached, it becomes a source of risk when the 'new accountability' is brought into play.

Employees and The New Economy

The trend to outsourcing, incidentally, points to another aspect of what is sometimes presented as 'the new economy,' characterised by much less long term job security on the one hand, and employee loyalty, on the other. Business discussion of the drivers of a wider notion of corporate responsibility routinely refers to the importance of corporate values and corporate citizenship in attracting and keeping 'the best and the brightest minds'[37], and countering the 'garage millionaire syndrome.'[38]

Market Factors: Consumers and Investors

Market factors can also be seen as key contextual drivers. Traditional legal definitions of responsibility can (theoretically at least[39]) be enforced through legal sanctions, but civil society campaigns to enforce a notion of corporate responsibility that goes *beyond* legal requirements depend for their effectiveness on market reactions.[40] In other words, attacking brands on ethical and social grounds would be ineffective if consumers and investors did not care. Further drivers are therefore identified in what is seen as a growing trend to what we might think of as 'concerned consumption' (the so-called 'purse power'),[41] 'ethical banking'[42] and ethical investment, including funds which screen companies by triple bottom line criteria rather than simply on the basis of financial performance or value.

Market forces can also impact on companies via corporate governance channels. The role of NGOs as minority shareholders at AGMs has already been noted, and larger shareholders such as pension funds can play a similar role, via, for example shareholder resolutions. Shell's activities in relation to human rights and environmental issues are now externally audited as a result of pension fund action of just this sort, with investment adviser PIRC challenging at a Shell Transport and Trading AGM in 1997[43] and management taking the point on board. CALPERS (the Californian Public Employees Retirement Scheme Fund with international investment capacity in excess of $74,000 million[44]) announced in February 2002 that it was pulling out of investment in businesses in Thailand, Indonesia, Malaysia, and the Philippines because they did not meet CALPERS' ethical criteria. A key issue, with echoes of the Nike experience, was labour conditions.[45]

Legal and Regulatory Developments

The market also operates in a legal and regulatory context, and though the role of law and regulation has been less marked in discussion of drivers of the new corporate responsibility (perhaps because it is rather more prosaic than globalisation or corporate martyrdom), it should be added to the catalogue. For example, a particular fillip has been given to 'ethical investment' by a recent development in UK law. Pension funds have been required by law since July 2000 to disclose whether and how social, environmental and ethical issues influence their investment policy. Though this of itself does not require pension funds to invest 'ethically,' increasing transparency can itself result in a shift of policy to avoid potential criticism.

Likewise the proliferation of codes of conduct in the US may be set in the context of the tougher penalties introduced by the Foreign Corrupt Practices Act, *and* the Sentencing Commission's guidelines that those penalties should be modified if the corporation in question had a code of conduct and an active programme for its propagation and enforcement.[46]

The importance of reputation has been implicit in factors already discussed such as PR crisis management and branding. In the Arthur Andersen / LBS survey of UK companies with codes of conduct, 72% gave 'reputation' as the prime motivation, and the authors note that 'heavily branded companies are more likely to manage business ethics.'[47] Indeed 'reputation,' 'reputation risk' and 'reputation management' are key notions that crop up again and again in contemporary UK business discourse.[48] They also crop up in contemporary UK business regulation. The London Stock Exchange's Combined Code on Corporate Governance, based on the Turnbull Report of 1999, includes reputation as an asset to be protected by companies, and requires internal reviews and reputational risk management, with, it has been suggested, directors potentially open to attack for breach of fiduciary duties if they do not pay this issue sufficient attention.[49]

These developments can be seen as both a product of the new accountability and a new factor within it.

International initiatives are also relevant. There are a number of ongoing attempts to extend the ambit of the UN's Declaration of Human Rights into business via codes of practice with the backing of the UN, OECD and NGOs like Amnesty International. There are also national legislative initiatives (for example, in Australia) aimed at requiring multinational corporations to meet internationally agreed human rights, environmental codes, and employee and consumer rights.

The Ethics Industry

There is another factor which should be added to the usual list of 'drivers', one which, again, can be seen as both a product and a constituent part of the 'new accountability.' This is the emergence of a whole new ethics industry. As well as ethical investment funds and banks, there are ethics consultancies, ethics standard setting organisations, ethics certification firms — all with a vested interest in selling 'ethics' to business.

The big accountancy firms now include ethics and reputation risk management services, as well as green and social responsibility audits. The 1999 Arthur Andersen / LBS survey of companies with codes of conduct also, of course, marketed the services of Arthur Andersen's own 'Ethics and Responsible Business Practices consulting group,' arguing, (ironically, in the wake of Andersen's own recent experiences *vis à vis* Enron), that with reputation an 'increasingly valuable corporate asset,' companies need 'robust programmes for guiding employee behaviour' and expressing concern that 'adoption of programmes to manage business ethics risk is by no means evident in all large companies.' Significantly, the authors add to their argument on the need for companies to adopt these programmes: 'the prize for those which can do so successfully is competitive advantage.'[50]

Ideology: Good Business

The emphasis on competitive advantage takes us to another facet of the context for the new corporate responsibility, the recurrent presentation of the idea that being 'good,' or being seen to be 'good' is good business. In other words in the last analysis the triple bottom line is elided with the bottom line. The clear message is that the new corporate responsibility is not in conflict with the old. Businesses benefit financially by adopting a broader ethical approach. Business ethics become good business strategy.[51] Shell poses the question: 'Profits and principles: does there have to be a choice?'[52] Amnesty International in its guide for business, *Human Rights: is it any of your business?* reminds companies of 'the business case for human rights':

> companies have a direct self-interest in using their legitimate influence to protect and promote the human rights of their employees and of the communities within which they are investing and/or operating... Corporate reputation, licence to operate, brand image, employee recruitment and retention, share value — all these key commercial concerns are affected by society's perception of a company's behaviour with regard to human rights.[53]

The ideology of good business can be seen as a justification for a change of approach driven by other factors, or as a driver itself, a means of persuading business into a change of approach. It may also be seen as an indication that any assumption of real change needs very careful scrutiny indeed. In the next section we move from uncritical review of the 'new accountability' to make a start, at least, at unpacking it by asking: who is driving? Is the new corporate responsibility (and accountability) more than just discourse? Is the discourse more important than the empirical reality? Is the new accountability, reality or image, desirable?

Who is Driving?

Though in the previous section the notion of 'drivers' was used uncritically, as the literature uses it, it does in fact need scrutiny. Identifying the 'drivers' of the new ethics has also become part of the discourse of the new ethics, and there is a good deal of assumption mixed in with the facts. There is also a confluence of analysis *of* businesses, and the context in which they are operating, with explanation *by* businesses adopting a new approach — indeed explanation, in part, to shareholders operating under the *old* accountability.

The notion of 'drivers' suggests an image of business as reactive to a changing context, but business can be seen as being both reactive and proactive. Business may lead and create the ethical market, without the prompting of a crisis or other drivers. It may also react to a new context, partly of its own making, but then go on to proactively use and develop the discourse of change. Shell's new image was a response to a tough situation (and arguably also an expression of genuine concern on the part of executives). Nonetheless it now chooses to make its social conscience a key part of its PR and advertising campaigns. Shell no longer advertises its oil or petrochemicals products; it advertises its corporate citizenship.

Consider this newspaper advertisement for Shell — in this case focussed on environmental rather than human rights issues — illustrated with a photograph of piles of barrels of obsolete insecticide.

> Cover up or clean up?
> It wasn't our pollution. The insecticide was owned by the government and had been provided by aid organisations to combat locusts. However we had produced it some thirty years before, so we willingly agreed to assist in its safe collection and incineration. It's part of our commitment to sustainable development, balancing economic progress with environmental care and social responsibility. Because do we really profit if the world doesn't?[54]

The answer to that is of course 'yes,' as companies have been profiting for generations. But what we see here is a bid to profit from a good deed, or to do a good deed for profit.

'Good business' is not done quietly. Shell's declared commitment to the triple bottom line is not simply a code of conduct; it is a market brand. This is not new. The whole basis of the Bodyshop brand was its ethical stance — an entirely proactive strategy.

The new accountability is also the new market opportunity and the concerned consumer can be seen as a creation of market supply as well as of civil society demand. The new accountability may make companies vulnerable, but that market vulnerability can also be converted to market opportunity. Union Carbide, infamous for the Bhopal tragedy, went on to become a leader in advising companies on using hazardous technologies safely in developing countries.[55]

The language of *strategic* citizenship,[56] of principles *and* profits,[57] of good business as a source of competitive advantage, the idea that altruism pays, may be a discursive way of bridging the old accountability and the new, denying a conflict of interest between profit maximisation (at least in the long run) and doing the right thing. Companies are after all still *legally* accountable to shareholders. It could, on the other hand, suggest a co-opting of critique — new wine in old bottles. And if the message is that altruism pays is it then altruism? If this is the motivation, are we talking about ethics at all? One might argue that pragmatically the philosophical point is irrelevant if the practical outcome is beneficial. But is it? And if so, how far?

Just Discourse?

Much is made of the proliferation of corporate codes of conduct, but, as is increasingly acknowledged, codes also need to be effectively implemented and monitored. Webley's survey of UK companies in 1995 found that a third of employees in respondent companies were not issued with the company's code, a third provided no mechanism for raising issues, and less than 40% required managers to certify the code was being applied.[58] Companies need to look to their structure of both sanctions and rewards. What happens to whistleblowers? What happens to the employee who loses a contract by refusing to bribe or to work in a context of human rights abuse? There are issues of interpretation. Embedding ethics in the corporate culture is declared as the aim but how is it best accomplished?[59] Where production is via subcontractors or goods bought in from external suppliers how is their practice monitored? Are codes effectively percolated to all parts of an organisation and other relevant sectors? According to Klein, until 1998 Nike and Gap (which has also attracted criticism over child labour in its suppliers' factories) only published their codes of conduct in English and did not distribute them to the (Asian) factory workers producing their brand.[60]

And what *is* the ethical stance? Codes may denigrate child labour, but is simply prohibiting child labour appropriate where children, for example AIDS orphans in Zimbabwe, are the family earners? How far should implementation be tempered by ethical judgement? Companies may deal with unethical practices by their suppliers by imposing ethical codes upon them. But is it ethical to impose ethical codes — and the costs of meeting them — on third world suppliers, without improving the terms of trade?[61]

Ethical investment needs a closer look too. How ethical is it? What do ethical funds mean by ethics? By what criteria do they measure ethical practice? How and how effectively do they make their assessments? What is the impact of the development of 'light green' as well as 'dark green' environmental measures, with less rigorous standards? What is the impact of the ethical fund policy of 'engagement' — including in the 'investable' categories companies which have poor ethical records but are trying to improve? Or companies that are 'best in class', in a sector which fails on rigorous ethical criteria — arms trading perhaps — but is seen as 'less unethical' than its competitors. Lewis and Mackenzie[62] see engagement as the more active form of ethical investment, since it seeks to alter companies in the direction of a wider concept of corporate responsibility, rather than simply rewarding those taking it on on their own. But these approaches could also be seen as expanding ethical investment only by diluting it. There is also the issue of transparency: are all investors in 'ethical funds' fully aware of these policies?

For its part, ethical and triple bottom line reporting needs to be subjected to the same scrutiny as conventional financial reporting (which has not stood up well in the light of either empirical research or the lessons of practical experience[63]). Likewise ethical audit. How independent are the auditors? What standards do they apply? How adequate are they? How, and how creatively, are those standards interpreted and applied?

These are empirical questions.[64] Only with a solid empirical base can the reality of the new corporate responsibility in practice, or even as potential, be properly assessed. Till then there remains plenty of discourse, on both the practical fulfilment of a new business ethics, and on its inevitability, given the driving forces, the pressures for change, outlined above. But how real are those forces?

Drivers or Discourse

The discourse is real enough, and pervasive, not only in corporate reports but in public debate on business by business, in the invocations of NGOs, in the sales pitch of the ethics industry, in management texts and in the books of business gurus. For example:

- At a recent business forum, Jane Nelson, director of the Prince of Wales Business Leaders Forum, listed as drivers the now familiar inventory of: consumers, governments, inter-governmental organisations, civil society, brands, reputations, new markets, and stake-holders; as the social issues being raised: human rights, labour rights, anti-corruption, poverty and climate change. She concluded: 'There seems to be only one certainty. These issues are not likely to disappear and they call for some fundamental changes in the way companies are managed and led.'[65]
- In a pull-out poster Amnesty International declares: 'The pressures on transnational companies to avoid doing harm and to exercise their legitimate influence for good are growing.'[66] In its management primer on human rights its list of drivers includes: shareholders, ethical investment, consumers, the internet, social auditing, regulatory and normative pressures.[67]
- In their influential textbook *Corporate Citizenship*, McIntosh *et al.* outline a rapidly changing environment, including, again: a global economy, technological revolution, pro-liferation of information (which campaigners can use to advantage), wider consumer choice, changing working patterns, and they conclude: in this environment: 'corporate cit-izenship…is no longer discretionary.'[68]

Over and over again we find similar lists of pressures, drivers, forces, the same conclusion of inevitable change in the direction of a new corporate responsibility. But these are logical hypotheses. They too need empirical testing. Indeed, even at the level of logical hypothesis there are questions to be asked.

Take the issue of branding, the exposure to investigation and adverse publicity that this can produce, and the role of NGOs in doing this. The case studies are graphic enough, but are Nike and Gap the only companies using sweated labour? Branding may make some companies particularly vulnerable to public critique, but what of the many anonymous producers involved in the same practices? Where are the NGO or NGN investigations of and protests against them? One company may suffer but does business in general? People burning their Nike trainers need to replace them. Are the new sources any more ethical than the old? Klein, for all her emphasis on the role of civil society, recognises the limits of the brand boomerang and is thrown back in her conclusion on calls for international regulation of the old-fashioned variety as a means of controlling corporate practice.[69] There are limits to the range and rigour of the new accountability. NGO legal action too places huge demands on resources and is necessarily targeted.

That is not of course to deny in any way the role of NGOs in drawing attention to problems, their traditional role indeed of 'constructing a social problem' that then demands attention by other agencies. And they go far beyond that. Even single cases can have huge precedential effect. It nonetheless raises the question of how extensively business as a whole is likely to be 'driven' by these forces into a new corporate responsibility.

There is also a huge resource imbalance between the activists of civil society and the corporations they are confronting, which may well have an effect on legal battles, PR battles, and battles to lobby for governmental and intergovernmental action.

How strong as yet are the new market forces? The question of just how ethical 'ethical investment' is has already been raised, and this has implications for its role as a force for change. Likewise the concerned consumer is as yet only a niche market. All of this may change, take on its own momentum, but we are as yet very far from being in the world of irresistible market forces pressing for respect for human rights.

And how real is the pressure of the new economy? The management fear of losing bright employees to the garage millionaire syndrome is of little relevance to most employees, who can as readily be seen as disempowered rather than empowered by the new economy.

The reality is that the discourse of drivers tends to take the exception and treat it as the rule.

Not all the drivers listed are 'just discourse.' The ethics industry is very real, but any assumption that it will stimulate ethical corporate practice will depend on how it functions in practice. We cannot simply assume the logical consequence of a new ethical world. Law and regulation can be weak or strong. But again one cannot assume logical causal chains. Personal liability for directors, for example, may well focus the management mind, but it can also, counter-intuitively, reduce the likelihood of punitive action because it is seen as draconian.[70]

And then there is the discourse of 'good business' — 'profits and principles: does there have to be a choice?' — with the clear implication that the answer is: no. But the answer is yes; sometimes there does have to be a choice. Though there is sense in the argument that long term sustainability of business requires attention to more than short term profit, how long term are how many shareholders willing to be? The 'good business' approach is in fact a sleight of hand that hides the real conflicts involved in pursuing profits *and* principles. The real test is what happens when there has to be a choice.

For a *sustainable business ethics* to develop there will need to be a move away from a discursive conjoining of profit and principle, which essentially ducks the issue, to an acknowledgement that ethics involves conflict and choice, and that, for the ethical business in a situation of conflict, the exercise of that choice must be in favour of principle at the expense of profit. What we need to know is how much of business is taking, or is willing to take, *that* approach to corporate responsibility, and whether those with an interest in the *old* accountability will let it.

A Desirable Development?

It is worth mentioning briefly that there is also the question of whether a new accountability of the kind outlined above, even if it is realisable, is desirable. For example, some of the forms of protest engaged in the new accountability, effective as they may be, raise significant questions for democracy and the rule of law. The idea of a code of conduct for NGOs has already been raised.[71] Vigilante tactics such as those employed by animal rights activists can also produce a backlash of repressive law with wider consequences.

Indeed even the discourse of the new accountability has its dangers. Debora Spar, professor at Harvard Business School, has argued that brand based regulation is so successful that we no longer need regulation. We have, she says, the 'spotlight phenomenon' now:

> Firms will cut off abusive suppliers or make them clean up because it is now in their financial interest to do so.[72]

This is both a huge assumption and a dangerous proposal. Regulation is already of limited effect, and while such developments as the 'spotlight phenomenon' may indeed be valuable supplements, we are a long way from the situation where regulation can be entirely replaced by market forces.

Discourse as Driver

This critique is not intended as yet another work of Jonah sociology, spreading messages of gloom and acting as a damper on all hope of social change. Its goal is merely to urge careful interpretation of the current discourse of both the new corporate responsibility and the new context of accountability, and to press the need for research that probes beneath the surface of that discourse. And a sociological perspective *can* offer positive messages too.

In this essay we have already analysed the notion of drivers as discourse, but by way of conclusion we can close the loop by considering the role of discourse as driver, because discourse, even if it is 'just discourse' can have significant repercussions on social practice.[73]

A number of leading companies are adopting 'good corporate citizenship' as, in effect, their brand image. We might think of this as 'halo-branding.' If Nike's branding focussed on the cool customer, Shell's focuses on the ethical company, and of course by extension, the ethical customer and investor. Moral is the new cool. But this is a different kind of image, and one that is hard to live up to. Indeed it can be seen as feeding into the 'new accountability.' NGOs are well aware of this potential for shortfall, and the leverage it can provide. Witness Peter Frankental of Amnesty International:

> From an NGO perspective, a company that ties its flag to the mast of human rights is offering a hostage to fortune. If it fails to deliver on its stated commitments, its credibility will be at stake.[74]

While this of itself does nothing to resolve the issue of the limits of NGO action raised earlier, it does suggest that it will be difficult for at least high profile companies to ignore their own declared principles, without an overt change of management style (or management), a reversion to the old accountability with profit as the trump card, or the construction of some new creative response.

All of these scenarios are of course possible. Indeed it is just how the multiplicity of possible scenarios will in fact play out that is the fascination of this area. If philosophers are concerned with how the new business ethics *should* develop, sociologists are concerned with how it *is* developing and how it will. Probing the dynamics of that development will be one of the more interesting research challenges of the immediate future, and one with significant practical implications.

NOTES

1. M Friedman 'The social responsibility of business is to increase its profits' *New York Times Magazine*, 13 September 1970; and see M Friedman *Capitalism and freedom* (Chicago University Press, 1962). This position is also justified in terms of the success of capitalism in increasing wealth which benefits society as a whole, though of course this does not deal with distributive issues.
2. See E Sternberg *Corporate Governance* (Institute of Economic Affairs,1998)
3. The following analysis is based on Shell documents, case studies on Shell, and discussions with senior Shell executives.
4. The Shell Report *Profits and principles — does there have to be a choice?* (1998): 3.
5. The Shell Report *Profits and principles — does there have to be a choice?*, p 3
6. The Shell Report *Profits and principles — does there have to be a choice?*, p 2
7. Elkington J *Cannibals with forks: the triple bottom line of 21ˢᵗ century business* (Capstone 1997)
8. See for example R E Freeman *Strategic management: a stakeholder approach* (Boston: Pitman, 1984)
9. Royal Dutch/Shell Group *Statement of General Business Principles* 1997, principle 2
10. The Shell Report *Profits and principles — does there have to be a choice?*, p 3
11. The Shell Report *Profits and principles — does there have to be a choice?*, p 3
12. The Shell Report *Profits and principles — does there have to be a choice?*, p 3
13. The Shell Report *Profits and principles — does there have to be a choice?*, p 3
14. Royal Dutch/Shell Group *Statement of General Business Principles* 1997
15. External verification by KPMG Price Waterhouse of Shell's assertions on its policies and strategies for implementing them. (The Shell Report *Profits and principles — does there have to be a choice?*, p 52) In this report however Shell recognised the distinction between external verification of the 'accuracy of the data' and 'the assurance process by which the quality of performance against stated objectives can be judged.' (Shell Report *Profits and principles — does there have to be a choice?*, p 51) In the 1999 report they recognise that new criteria are needed for measuring social performance and commit themselves to working with others to find the best means. (The Shell Report 1999 *People, planet and profits* p37)
16. *Financial Times* 5 August 1999
17. P Williams *The Financial Director* March 1999
18. *Guardian* 3 November 2001
19. I use the term uncritically for the moment in order to explore contextual issues, but the notion of 'drivers' needs scrutiny too. See ahead.
20. The Shell Report *Profits and principles — does there have to be a choice?*, p 2 and see P Mirvis 'Transformation at Shell', *Business and Society Review* 105, no. 1 (2000), 63-84
21. Including my own MBA course on Business Ethics at Oxford's Said Business School, and see Harvard Business School case studies *Royal Dutch/Shell in Nigeria* (Boston: Harvard Business School Publishing 9-399-126, Rev. April 20 2000), and *Royal Dutch/Shell in transition* (Boston: Harvard Business School Publishing 9-300-039, October 4, 1999) and management texts, for example McIntosh M, D Leipziger, K Jones, G Coleman *Corporate Citizenship* (FT/Pitman, 1998). See too P. Mirvis 'Transformation at Shell', *Business and Society Review* 105, no. 1 (2000), 63-84, and G. Chandler 'Oil companies and human rights', *Business ethics: a European Review* 7, no.2 (1998): 69-72
22. Even though Greenpeace's claims were in fact based on erroneous assumptions, as was later acknowledged.

23. Arthur Andersen / London Business School. *Ethical Concerns and reputation risk management,* Arthur Andersen, 1999

24. Simon Webley 'The nature and value of internal codes of ethics', paper presented at the conference on *The importance of human rights in international business,* University of Exeter, 15-17 September 1998

25. Eckbert Imomoh, General Manager Eastern Division, Shell Petroleum, on 18 April 1996 on *Africa Express,* Channel 4 TV, UK, cited in McIntosh M, D Leipziger, K Jones, G Coleman *Corporate Citizenship,* p 123, fn 73.

26. Mark Moody Stuart, Chairman of the Committee of Managing Directors, Shell Group, quoted in Harvard Business School case *Royal Dutch/Shell in transition* (Boston: Harvard Business School Publishing 9-300-039, October 4, 1999) p 7.

27. Royal Dutch/Shell Group *Statement of General Business Principles,* 1997, principle 2. e.

28. See for example The Shell Report 1999 *People, planet and profits* p 28 on its approach to child labour in Brazil (not in its own company) and its report on its actions in Nigeria.

29. Shell International Petroleum Company *Business and Human Rights: a management primer* 1998

30. See for example, McIntosh M, D Leipziger, K Jones, G Coleman *Corporate Citizenship*; S Zadek 'Balancing performance, ethics, and accountability', *Journal of Business Ethics* 17 no. 13 (1998): 1421-1441; Naomi Klein, *No logo* (Flamingo, 2000)

31. London, 19 April 2001.

32. For example, Klein, *No Logo*

33. In November 1997 an employee leaked a report by the company's auditors exposing conditions in Vietnamese factories supplying it (*Guardian* 13 June 1998), and the story has featured repeatedly in all forms of media since.

34. Which Nike itself attributed to its association with child labour.

35. Klein *No logo* is particularly associated with this argument.

36. What Klein labels the 'brand boomerang', *No Logo*: 345

37. BP Chief Executive Officer Sir John Browne 'Large companies cannot afford to disappoint' in M MacIntosh (ed) *Visions of ethical business, (*www. business-minds.com, 2000) at p 24

38. BT spokesman, quoted in *Financial Times* 31 March 1999

39. Socio-legal research demonstrates that in practice this is often harder than might be expected.

40. Though there are also strategies of challenging narrow definitions in the courts and through lobbying for wider legislative remits.

41. Evidenced for example in consumer support for the Fair Trade movement. See K Jones 'Global sourcing', in C Moon, C Bonny et al (eds) *A Guide to Business Ethics* (Profile Books, 2001); K Bird and D R Hughes 'Ethical consumerism: the case of "fairly- traded" coffee', *Business Ethics: a European Review* 6 no. 3 (1997): 159-67.

42. Examples in the UK are Triodos and the Co-operative Bank.

43. The motion was defeated but 10% of shareholders supported the resolution, and management introduced independent verification. And see McIntosh et al *Corporate Citizenship,* p 124.

44. The value quoted in McIntosh M D Leipziger, K Jones, G Coleman *Corporate Citizenship,* p 90, which was published in 1998.

45. Business Week Online, 25 February 2002.

46. Simon Webley 'The nature and value of internal codes of ethics', paper presented at the conference on *The importance of human rights in international business,* University of Exeter, 15-17 September 1998

47. Arthur Andersen / London Business School. *Ethical Concerns and reputation risk management*, p 12

48. See for example Kay J *Foundations of corporate success,* Oxford: Oxford University Press, 1998, and see Charles Forbrun's work on 'reputational capital': Charles Forbrun *Reputation: realizing value from the corporate image* (Boston: Harvard Business School Press, 1996)

49. Interview with in-house Head of Legal Department of international corporation; and see Philip Goldenberg, partner Berwin Leyton, quoted in the *Financial Times* 9 March 2002.

50. Arthur Andersen / London Business School. *Ethical Concerns and reputation risk management*, p 7

51. For example McIntosh et al *Corporate Citizenship*

52. Royal Dutch/Shell Group Report *Profits and principles — does there have to be a choice?* 1997
53. Amnesty International/Prince of Wales Forum, 2000, p 24.
54. Repeated newspaper advertisement. See, for example, *Financial Times* 12 September 1999. And BP's logo on its petrol pumps is now a stylised flower.
55. T Donaldson 'Values in tension.' *Harvard Business Review* (1996) September: 48-62, at 53.
56. McIntosh et al *Corporate Citizenship*
57. The Shell Report *Profits and principles — does there have to be a choice?* 1997
58. A Doig and J Wilson 'The effectiveness of codes of conduct', *Business Ethics: a European Review* 7 no. 3 (1998): 140-49, at p 142, citing Simon Webley's Institute of Business Ethics Survey 1995
59. See R Warren 'Codes of ethics: bricks without straw', *Business Ethics: a European Review* 2 no. 4 (1993) for why codes may not be enough for active business ethics. And see A Doig and J Wilson 'The effectiveness of codes of conduct', *Business Ethics: a European Review* 7 no. 3 (1998): 140-49
60. Klein *No Logo*, p 431
61. Fiona King 'Reality check on corporate social responsibility and corporate citizenship', in M McIntosh et al *Visions of ethical business* (www. business-minds.com, 2000)
62. A Lewis and C Mackenzie 'Support for investor activism among UK ethical investors', *Journal of Business Ethics* 24 no. 3 (2000): 215-217
63. See, for example, McBarnet and Whelan *Creative accounting and the cross-eyed javelin thrower* (John Wiley, 1999) on off-balance sheet financing, and the collapse of Enron which has brought home its implications.
64. Though a body of academic research is developing, the discourse, or certainly the business discourse, does not tend to be evidence based except in the sense of referring to famous case studies, and that may be misleading as the basis of the kind of general conclusions that are drawn. A lot more research, and particularly qualitative research, is also required. The bulk of research to date is quantitative or at macro level.
65. J Nelson 'Innovations in executive development: building socially-aware business leaders' in M MacIntosh (ed) *Visions of ethical business*
66. Amnesty International newsletter November 2000
67. Amnesty International *Human Rights: is it any of your business?* Amnesty International / Prince of Wales Business Leaders Forum, 2000
68. McIntosh et al *Corporate Citizenship*, pp xxii-xxiii
69. Klein *No Logo*, pp 422, 424, 437
70. See McBarnet and Whelan *Creative accounting and the cross-eyed javelin thrower* on the issue of personal liability in relation to creative accounting.
71. *Financial Times* 11 July 2000
72. D Spar 'The spotlight on the bottom line' *Foreign Affairs,* 13 March 1998, cited in Klein *No Logo* p 434
73. E P Thompson *Whigs and Hunters* (Allen Lane, 1975) is the classic citation for the practical impact of the discourse of the rule of law
74. P Frankental 'Can branding reinforce human rights?' in M McIntosh et al *Visions of ethical business* (www. business-minds.com, 2000)

BIBLIOGRAPHY

Amnesty International. *Human Rights: is it any of your business?* Amnesty International / Prince of Wales Business Leaders Forum, 2000.

Arthur Andersen / London Business School. *Ethical Concerns and reputation risk management,* Arthur Andersen, 1999.

Bird K. and D. R. Hughes 'Ethical consumerism: the case of "fairly-traded" coffee,' *Business Ethics: a European Review* 6 no. 3 (1997): 159-67.

Browne J. 'Large companies cannot afford to disappoint' in M MacIntosh (ed.) *Visions of ethical business,* www. business-minds.com, 2000.

Chandler G. 'Oil companies and human rights,' *Business ethics: a European Review* 7, no. 2 (1998): 69–72.

Doig A. and J. Wilson 'The effectiveness of codes of conduct,' *Business Ethics: a European Review* 7 no. 3 (1998): 140–49.

Donaldson T. "Values in tension." *Harvard Business Review* (1996) September: 48–62.

Elkington J. *Cannibals with forks: the triple bottom line of 21st century business,* Capstone, 1997.

Forbrun C. *Reputation: realizing value from the corporate image.* Boston: Harvard Business School Press, 1996.

Frankental P. 'Can branding reinforce human rights?' in M. McIntosh *et al.* *Visions of ethical business,* www.business-minds.com, 2000.

Freeman R. E. *Strategic management: a stakeholder approach,* Boston: Pitman, 1984.

Friedman M. *Capitalism and freedom*, Chicago University Press, 1962.

Friedman M. 'The social responsibility of business is to increase its profits' *New York Times Magazine*, 13 September 1970.

Harvard Business School case study *Royal Dutch/Shell in Nigeria.* Boston: Harvard Business School Publishing 9-399-126, Rev. April 20, 2000.

Harvard Business School case study *Royal Dutch/Shell in transition.* Boston: Harvard Business School Publishing 9-300-039, October 4, 1999.

Jones K. 'Global sourcing,' in C. Moon, C. Bonny *et al.* (eds.) *A Guide to Business Ethics* Profile Books, 2001.

Kay J. *Foundations of corporate success,* Oxford: Oxford University Press, 1998.

King F. 'Reality check on corporate social responsibility and corporate citizenship,' in M. McIntosh *et al.* *Visions of ethical business,* www.business-minds.com, 2000.

Klein N. *No logo*, London: Flamingo, 2000.

Lewis A. and C. Mackenzie 'Support for investor activism among UK ethical investors', *Journal of Business Ethics* 24 no. 3 (2000): 215–217.

McBarnet D. and C. Whelan *Creative accounting and the cross-eyed javelin thrower,* Chichester: John Wiley, 1999.

McIntosh M., D. Leipziger, K. Jones, G. Coleman *Corporate Citizenship.* London: FT/Pitman, 1998.

Mirvis P. 'Transformation at Shell', *Business and Society Review*, 105:1(2000) 63–84.

Nelson J. 'Innovations in executive development: building socially- aware business leaders' in M. McIntosh *et al.* *Visions of ethical business,* www.business-minds.com, 2000.

Spar D. 'The spotlight on the bottom line' *Foreign Affairs*, 13 March 1998.

Sternberg E. *Corporate Governance*, London, Institute of Economic Affairs, 1998.

Thompson E. P. (1975) *Whigs and Hunters*, London, Allen Lane.

Warren R. 'Codes of ethics: bricks without straw,' *Business Ethics: a European Review* 2 no. 4 (1993).

Webley S. 'The nature and value of internal codes of ethics,' paper presented at the conference on *The importance of human rights in international business*, University of Exeter, 15–17 September 1998.

Zadek S. 'Balancing performance, ethics, and accountability,' *Journal of Business Ethics* 17 no. 13 (1998): 1421–1441.

QUESTIONS

1. What is the business case for business ethics? Why is so much emphasis placed on it?
2. What is "the new accountability"? What is "driving" the new accountability? Why does Doreen McBarnet think that the new emphasis on corporate responsibility and corporate accountability need careful scrutiny?
3. McBarnet suggests that "even the discourse of the new accountability has dangers." Why is this?
4. Is there tension between the business case and the ethics case for ethical corporate conduct? If so, which approach should prevail?

PROFESSIONALISM AND RESPONSIBILITY IN THE TECHNOLOGICAL SOCIETY

Conrad G. Brunk

In late 1984 Canada's first astronaut rocketed into space aboard the American space shuttle Challenger to help demonstrate to the world, or at least to his own countrymen, the technological wonders of the Canadian-built "Canadarm" — the robotic arm with which the astronauts launch and retrieve satellites of various kinds. As the shuttle circled the earth, performing with an uneven degree of success its televised tasks, rumours began to circulate in the media that this mission included darker and more ominous purposes than the official space administration statements cared to mention.

Of course, these rumours were not news to anyone who had taken the time to read between the superficial headlines about the space shuttle project. It is was well known that the shuttle was a central element of the American drive to place in space military weapons of various kinds, ranging from military intelligence and missile guiding satellites to anti-satellite weapons and eventually President Reagan's "Star Wars" anti-ballistic-missile defense system.

Soon after Marc Garneau's triumphant return, he was asked by an unusually probing CBC interviewer how he felt about the military aspects of the space mission in which he had just participated. Garneau responded that he was opposed to the militarization of space, but that he did not see his participation in the shuttle mission as inconsistent with this view. He had not himself worked directly with any weapon, he explained, but only with "space technology, space science, and life science experiments."[1] These he considered purely "civilian" tasks. He expressed no ethical qualms at all about the fact that the space shuttle was by nearly all accounts the primary vehicle for the American militarization of space. He seemed able to view his own participation in the project in isolation from the larger system of which his role was an integral part. He was a professional merely doing his job and doing it well; and the job he defined, not as assisting in the militarization of space, but as contributing to human scientific and technological understanding. All potential cognitive dissonance in this man appeared on the surface to be neatly resolved.

Garneau, like most of his colleagues in the various professions, appears to be a man of high moral conscience, who seeks to live according to the system of values he espouses. We

Adapted from "Professionalism and Responsibility in the Technological Society," Conrad G. Brunk, Benjamin Eby Lecture, February 3, 1985, Conrad Grebel College, Waterloo, Ontario. Originally published in Conrad Grebel Review. *Copyright © 1985, Conrad Grebel College. Reprinted by permission.*

have no reason to charge him with "hypocrisy" in the sense that he is publicly espousing a commitment to moral values belied by his own behavior. His situation is not so simple as that. Garneau, if pushed on the matter, would probably be able to give a consistent justification for what might appear to be inconsistent behavior, and his justification would be found to be perfectly acceptable by most of his professional colleagues. His justification could appeal to principles of professional morality widely accepted in our society. It is these principles of the prevailing professional morality in our society that are my concern.

Garneau's situation is a paradigm of one of the most intractable problems of moral responsibility of our age. On the one hand, he expresses strong moral opposition to a policy pursued by the society of which he is a member — in this case the use of space for the proliferation of military weapons. On the other hand, he lends his personal participation to a project which is an integral part of the implementation of the very policy he opposes. He is just like the research biologist who, having devoted herself to the development, through recombinant DNA, of an artificial organism for the production of insulin for diabetes, finds that she can fund her research only by participation in a project that is using her findings to produce a new, and of course illegal, biological weapon.

These examples could be multiplied by the thousands. They are part of the everyday experience of people, not only professionals, whose work involves them in one way or another in economic, social, and technological institutions and systems not of their own making. These institutions and systems, of course, are never perfect from the point of view of any one individual's moral outlook. They are always a mixture of good and evil, of justice and injustice, and thus participation in them is always fraught with moral ambiguity. There is really nothing new about this. For whenever people decide to act in cooperation with others to achieve some otherwise unattainable purpose they face the necessity of accommodating their own moral goals to those of the others with whom they cooperate.

But it is not just this kind of ambiguity which is involved in the situation of Marc Garneau. There is a more significant aspect than the simple model of choosing the lesser evil or the greater good captures. It has to do with the way the individuals in these situations find ways to escape moral choice and moral responsibility altogether. In these cases the actors may not even see a tragic choice of the lesser evil or greater good. Rather, they fail to see any choice whatever. If pushed to make a judgment about the militarization of space, for example, Garneau might well agree that the escalating arms race, particularly its expansion into space, poses dangers to humanity that far outweigh the limited goods achieved by space technology generally. Even if he would not go this far, still, he apparently believes that the development of space technology for peaceful purposes *could* and *ought* to go forward without the military component. Yet he does not see this as *his own* moral responsibility in any sense. Hence, he does not feel morally or professionally compromised.

The political scientist and philosopher Hannah Arendt addressed this question in her profound book, *Eichmann in Jerusalem*, in which she attempts to understand the mind and moral rationalization of Adolf Eichmann, the self-proclaimed "construction engineer" who engineered the massive program of arrest and transportation of millions of German Jews to the Nazi death camps during the Second World War. What intrigued Arendt as she sat through the long Jerusalem trial in which Eichmann was convicted by an Israeli court of crimes against humanity, was how a man who evidenced virtually no hatred or even prejudice against the Jewish people provided his full and energetic leadership to this "Final Solution to the Jewish Problem." This was a problem for the court, for it is an established principle in all law, that people ought not to be found guilty of a crime unless it can be shown that they acted intentionally. Eichmann knew full well that the Final Solution was, as he himself put it, "One of the greatest crimes ever committed in the history of humanity," nevertheless he did not consider his own participation in it to be wrong. It was not wrong because, he claimed, he had himself never killed, nor even borne ill-will toward, any Jew. He had only done what any good professional who was given an assignment would have done, and he had done it to the very best of his ability. As Arendt put it, "Except for an extraordinary diligence in looking out for his personal advancement, he had no motives at all. And this diligence in itself was in no way criminal; he certainly would never have murdered his superior in order to inherit his post. He *merely*, to put the matter colloquially, *never realized what he was doing*" (emphasis in original).[2]

This is the moral reality which Arendt attempts to capture in the subtitle of the book, "A Report on the Banality of Evil." It is the "banality" of even the horrendous evil of the Nazi holocaust that troubles her, for it is this banality that allows even well-intentioned and conscientious people in the society to participate in seemingly limitless evil. The banality of evil consists in the fact that there are evil consequences without evil actors, and often evil without evil actions. And, where there are no evil actors or actions to be found, no one takes responsibility for the evil that is done.

What is it about our society that makes this escape from responsibility so easy and so pervasive? Arendt, along with many others, suggests that it is in the nature of any kind of bureaucratic structure to define responsibilities within each role or office of the bureaucracy so narrowly that few, if any, in the bureaucracy have any real control over the policies adopted and pursued by it. In other words, it is a function of *role specialization*. When any social task is divided up into smaller, specialized tasks, the sense of participation in the larger task is dissipated. Persons see themselves as responsible only for their immediate task and less responsible for the larger one. The greater the specialization of the overall task, the less the sense of responsibility felt by those performing the specialized tasks.

It is commonly noted by social observers that among the most significant aspects of the industrial-technological society are specialization and its closely related partner, professionalism. It is important to look at these two phenomena together if we are to gain a deeper understanding of the way in which we exercise, or fail to exercise, responsible moral control over the institutions we create. As society becomes scientifically and technologically more advanced, it also requires at the same time greater degrees of specialization. No one can be an expert on many things in a time when the body of scientific and technical knowledge is so large and expanding so fast that it far outruns the ability of any one person to keep up with more than a small portion of it. At the same time that greater specialization is required, so, it seems, more professionalism emerges.

There is not complete agreement about how to define a "professional." The claim to professionalism is made by increasing numbers of people in increasing kinds of activities, so that everyone from the plumber to the chimney sweep calls themselves "professionals." The claim to be a professional certainly arises in part out of the fact that more types of jobs in our society demand the kind of highly specialized training in an esoteric body of knowledge that was previously required only in the traditional professions of medicine, law, nursing, teaching, engineering, and the like. In addition, professionals have usually been thought of as people who, because they perform an essential service to others who must rely upon their knowledge completely, and hence are in a position to take advantage of their clients, must be persons of extraordinary integrity and altruism. Since professionals are accorded a special place in society, it is expected that in return they exercise special virtue in looking after the public good. The Hippocratic oath, which for centuries has been taken by initiates into the medical profession, is a classic expression of this "professional ethic of special virtue."

It is a common observation that the infamous scandals of the Watergate affair, involving professionals of every sort, from Agnew the engineer to the lawyers, Nixon, Mitchell, and Dean, began a major "crisis of confidence" in the professions in Western society. A major fallout from this era has been strong renewal of interest in "professional ethics" among nearly all the traditional professions. The professions came quickly to the realization that if they did not maintain at least the appearance of ethical integrity in the exercise of their skill for the public good, society, through government regulation, would maintain it for them.

Out of this has arisen an important debate about whether professionalism is or is not a good thing. Does professionalism in fact instill a greater sense of responsibility for the social good in the professional, or does it merely provide a cloak for self-serving, monopolistic practices? I want to look at this question from the point of view of how professionalism functions in a technological society such as our own, with all the dynamics for degeneration into the banality of evil which Arendt observes. The question I want to address is whether "professional ethics" and the notion of "professional responsibility" involved in such ethics act in our society as a significant check upon the descent into the banality of evil, or whether they in fact accelerate and rationalize such a descent.

This question is important, if for no other reason than that the greatest dangers faced by humanity today are dangers posed by the development and use of technology. Nuclear technology, in both its military and civilian uses, carries with it, we now know with certainty, the possibility of human extinction on this planet. So does the new recombinant DNA technology, which many some experts believe poses as great a risk to the human species as nuclear technology, if not greater. In a very obvious and incontrovertible sense we are all dependent upon the professional technologists who develop, and to a greater or lesser extent preside over, these technologies. We all trust that the recombinant DNA researchers will take the precautions necessary to insure that a newly synthesized deadly organism will not be released uncontrolled into our environment. To what extent is our faith well-founded and to what extent is it a blind faith? Can we really rely upon "professional ethics" to save us? If not, upon what can we rely?

If moral responsibility is not exercised by the professional technologists themselves, it is not likely to be exercised effectively by anyone else. If technology is to be brought under human control so that it serves legitimate human ends, it will be because those professional technicians — the scientists, the researchers, the engineers, and the advisors to the politicians — exercise responsible moral judgment at the very source of technological development itself. If moral responsibility is abdicated here, technology will certainly chart its own course independent of human purposes, and it will become the responsibility of the great, anonymous "No One." And the great "No One," we know well from recent history, seems prone to misdeeds of limitless horror.

Whether or not even the exercise of professional responsibility can save us depends upon how professional responsibility is conceived. There is always a "professional ethic" at work among professionals. It is clear from the statements of Adolf Eichmann at his trial that he considered himself to have adhered scrupulously to the ethic of his profession. This is in the very nature of the self-concept of a professional. So, clearly, it is not professional ethics *per se* that are needed, but professional ethics of a certain kind — of a kind that actually takes responsibility in some way for the policies and practices of the system in which one plays a professional role.

It is my view that the prevailing conception of professional ethics and professional responsibility in our society in fact serves to rationalize the kind of escape from responsibility that we see evidenced by Eichmann, Garneau, and all those professionals who define their sphere of moral responsibility so narrowly as to exclude everything beyond their actions in their immediate role. In doing so it gives over to the Anonymous Other — the "No One" — all responsibility for the ultimate corporate outcome. How does the prevailing professional ethic move in this direction?

One way it does so is by focusing moral attention upon the actions of *individuals* rather than upon the *corporate* actions of a whole profession or institution in which the professional functions. This focus is clearly evident in the traditional Codes of Ethics for various professionals, whether physicians, nurses, or engineers. A primary principle in these Codes is the principle of "loyal agency," or the duty always to serve the interest of the client or employer in a loyal and faithful manner. A clear implication of this principle is that when one acts as the agent of others, their values are the ones that ought to control the situation. If those values conflict with your own, you must, in the interest of professionalism, place your own values in suspension. Since you are acting on behalf of others, the action is in a sense *theirs*, not your own, hence the responsibility is *theirs*, not your own.

So, for example, the lawyer hired by a chemical company to defend the latter in a suit brought against it by the government for illegal dumping of toxic chemicals, if she is truly "professional," will not concern herself with whether the company really is guilty of the offense. Indeed it would be considered by many of her colleagues extremely "unprofessional" if she conducted her defense of the company according to her own view of how laws should be applied to companies whose activities threaten the environment, especially if that view is not completely consonant with the interests of the company. Her proper professional role, it is said, is to represent *only* the interests of the company for whom she acts as an agent, not to represent all the interests relevant to a just settlement of the case. In this way the lawyer abdicates completely her responsibility for a just outcome of the case. She sees the responsibility lying somewhere else.

Of course everyone else, following their professional ethic, will reason the same way. They will see their moral responsibility being fulfilled if only they are loyal to the demands of their specific role as interpreted by their superior. Even the managers of the chemical company will not see it as *their* responsibility to clean up the toxic chemicals unless legally required to do so. Their professional managerial responsibility is to be loyal stewards of the stockholders who hired them to produce a maximum return on their investment in the company by producing chemical products in the most profit-maximizing way.

How is this ethical isolationism justified in terms of conventional morality? What are the ways in which professionals, and others, reach the conclusion that the evil done by the institutions in which they play a role is "not their business"? It is important to look at some of the typical rationalizations or excuses called upon by the traditional professional ethic, and to see how they stand up to critical scrutiny.

One common rationalization is the "Appeal to Expert Authority," or what might be called the "Appeal to Technical Ignorance." This excuse seems to be endemic to technological society with its high degree of specialization and division of labour. It reasons thus: "It isn't professional for me to make a firm moral judgment about what my profession or the institution of which it is a part is doing, even though privately I do have serious doubts about what it is doing. But I am not an expert in that kind of problem, so it is best to keep my mouth shut and leave it to the experts. I have no option but to trust their judgment since they know more than I do."

One of the most important features of modern technological society is that as more aspects of life become technically and politically sophisticated, the more we depend upon the technical experts to deal with more and more of our problems. Five years ago I would have written this article with a pencil. If it had broken down I would have been able to deal with the situation myself. But today I have written it on a computer. If it suddenly begins to scramble my text and print out nonsense, chances are that I will be at a loss to repair the problem. I am dependent upon the computer expert. I have to defer to his judgment.

But suppose he tells me that he knows a quick fix for my problem. He knows how to break the protection code on a software package that will repair my program in a jiffy. Normally it sells for 200 dollars, but if he cracks the code he can copy it for me free. Now, who is the "expert"? He may know far more than I do about computer software, but does that mean he is a better judge than I am about the ethics of computer theft? The path of least resistance here, of course, is not to ask any questions, but to fall back upon the "Appeal to Technical Ignorance" which absolves me from all responsibility for the way this technical expert solves my problem.

The "Appeal to Expert Authority" is widespread in our society. But "experts" are not necessarily in any better position to make a responsible moral choice than non-experts — in fact, in many cases they may be in a worse position, for their role may make them even less objective, more biased, and under greater pressure to tailor their opinion to the requirements of their role. Being a technical expert is not the same as being a moral expert. Neither is it necessarily true that because the technical expert knows more about the facts he or she is in a better position to make a reasoned moral judgment. Technical experts can be moral morons just as ethics experts can be technical morons — and, of course, the latter can make mistakes as disastrous as the former.

Further, technical experts themselves do not agree about the moral implications of the technologies they design and control. Their assessment of the risks and probable consequences of certain technological decisions can be as influenced by their own normative biases as the assessments of non-experts. It is a grave mistake to believe that the experts are in a preferred position to make the most reliable moral judgment, and a society that leaves moral judgments up to the experts in their field is a society that is asking most of its members to abdicate moral responsibility.

One version of the "Appeal to Expert Authority" is especially characteristic of the modern bureaucratic society. It appeals to the fact that since society has created other professional roles specifically to look after the larger social interests, it is not proper to concern oneself with this interest in one's own profession. It escapes moral responsibility by claiming, "It's not my role to look after the problem of long-term public welfare because it will be looked after by those trained for exactly that job." In our bureaucratic society this argument takes advantage of the fact that government establishes all kinds of regulatory agencies with their arsenals of regulations as a way of protecting society from the threat of unrestrained technological adventure.

It is commonly charged that extensive government regulatory intervention in society stifles creativity and initiative, and to some extent this is true. It may also be true that it stifles the sense of moral responsibility as well, by creating the expectation that "Big Brother" will look after the implications of our professional and technological activities. Even though I believe that the price we pay for government regulation is often worth it, yet, on this issue government control may not be the solution because government regulation can never fully substitute for a sensitive and morally responsible professional conscience. This is not so only because government experts, too, are not always necessarily trustworthy in their moral judgment, but also because it simply is not always possible to counter the full weight of the technological establishment whose interests simply overwhelm the political power of the government regulatory bodies.

There is a second important rationalization for the ethical isolationism which refuses to take moral responsibility beyond the immediate professional role. It relies upon a very narrow definition of professionalism as the performance of purely technical skills. Thus, it claims that it is simply "unprofessional" to use one's professional status to make judgments about any issue that goes beyond one's own area of technical competence. It identifies professional responsibility with technical competence. This view is bolstered by the positivistic assumption, still embraced by many in the scientific and technological community, that normative judgments of any kinds are subjective matters of opinion, and it is an abuse of one's role to put them forward as "professional" opinions. Only those problems which can be reduced to their technical dimensions are amenable to professional judgment.

This rationalization can take several different courses. One is to turn every question of social or moral value into a purely technical question, thereby disguising a moral choice as a technical one. For example, physicians who sat on the therapeutic abortion committees of Canadian hospitals had to decide whether to permit any abortion to be performed in their hospital according to what appeared to be a purely technical, that is to say *medical*, standard. They were supposed to decide whether or not the pregnancy in each case before them constitute a threat to the life or health of the mother. Even though the choice the physicians were forced to make was clearly a value choice — between the severity of risk to the mother and the life of the unborn child — both the Therapeutic Abortion Act and the professional ethic of these physicians conspired as best they could to make this appear as a purely "medical" decision. Everyone involved, including the patient and the public, feels more comfortable if the doctors can emerge from their deliberations to announce that an abortion is or is not "medically indicated" in this case. The comfort stems from the illusion that they avoided making a moral choice about abortion for which they have to take moral responsibility. Most significantly, the doctors here have avoided the appearance of "unprofessional action," which they would risk if they were to emerge with the announcement that in their opinion it would be *wrong* to perform this abortion even though, medically speaking, there is some risk to the mother's health (or that it would be *right* even though there is no significant risk).

A second way the "It's Not Professional" rationale is used in the prevailing individualist professional ethic is to admit the importance of both moral and technical questions, but to make a strong distinction between personal, professional morality and politics or political morality. Professional morality is then limited, as we have seen, to matters of personal conduct such as honesty, loyalty, collegiality, and reliability. Any evaluation of the professional role itself or the institution of which it is a part is considered "political," not moral, and therefore is beyond the bounds of professional morality. When one is making these "political" judgments, one is speaking not as a professional, but as a private citizen, a member of a public interest group, or in some other non-professional role. Hence, to speak out or take a stand on these matters "as a professional" is to abuse one's role — to pose as an expert in an area where one is not.

This rationalization divides the moral agent up into different insular roles. It allows the nuclear physicist to be concerned about the an escalating arms race and the policies of his government with respect to it *in his role as a private citizen*, but when he goes to the university lab to pursue his enhanced radiation research funded by the defense department, research which he knows is part of a larger project to develop a neutron bomb, he must not bring his moral convictions into that area of his professional life. That would be an abuse of his professional position. He might well vote for the peace candidate in the next election, and even write a letter on the issue to the newspaper as long as he could make it clear that he was not speaking "as a nuclear physicist."

None of these rationalizations of the denial of professional moral responsibility for one's role and its place in the larger scheme of things has the pervasive influence and appeal to deep-seated moral assumptions in our culture as the third and final one I would like to consider. This is the appeal to one form or another of what the classical economist Adam Smith called the "Invisible Hand." The Invisible Hand, for Smith, was that benevolent principle he believed to be at work in the capitalist free market whereby the unrestrained self-interest and greed of capitalists interested in nothing but the maximization of their own profits would mysteriously result in the maximum welfare of everyone in society. The Invisible Hand, in other words, turns selfish motivations into altruistic results. It was due to the working of this great Invisible Hand that Smith believed an unrestrained laissez faire economy, in which each entrepreneur sought only his or her own profit and ignored completely the good of others or of society as a whole, would ironically make everyone better off. A deep faith in the Invisible Hand has been the fundamental premise of laissez faire economists from Adam Smith to the contemporary "neo-classical" economists.

The dogma of the Invisible Hand has been invoked as a justification for radical individualism far beyond the province of economic behavior. Nowhere has its influence been felt more profoundly than in the area of professional ethics where it is believed to turn narrow professional self-interest on the part of each professional into the general good. Just as Adam Smith's Invisible Hand theory prompted businesspeople not to worry about the social consequences of the products they market, the production procedures they used, or the conditions of work in their establishment, because the marketplace will make it all turn out right, so it tells modern professionals not to make it their business to worry about the social consequences of their professional roles or the institutions of which those roles are a part, because in the whole scheme of things these problems are sure to take care of themselves.

The modern Invisible Hand is invoked in a variety of forms. One form is just an updated version of Adam Smith's benevolent free market. In this view the Invisible Hand of the free market will turn professional as well as economic egoism and greed into social well-being. If only we insure that the market is really free and that all externalities are actually paid for, it will in the long run naturally weed out all the socially detrimental practices. If the chemical engineer develops insect control chemicals that are also carcinogenic, the consuming public will discover this soon enough, and their market behaviour will spur the development by another engineer of a less carcinogenic chemical. In the meantime, neither of them needs to worry about the problem of increasing cancer rates — it will look after itself.

A second form of the Invisible Hand operates, not through the laissez faire economic marketplace, but through the so-called "free marketplace of ideas." Here the assumption is that it does not matter so much if the viewpoint expressed by each lawyer in the courtroom or the story published by the journalist is "the whole truth and nothing but the truth" as far as he or she knows it, because as long as everyone else's viewpoint is freely fed into the system, the greatest approximation to the truth will emerge.

There is a third version of the Invisible Hand idea which is probably the most widely accepted or assumed by professionals in our day, especially by professional technologists. While it may not generally be thought of as an Invisible Hand, I think it functions in the logic of justification for ethical isolationism in much the same way as the previously considered Invisible Hand arguments. It, too, is an article of faith in a benevolent force presiding over human actions and institutions which protects them from their own worst mistakes. It is faith in what Amatai Etzioni has called the "Technological Fix" — the belief that for every human problem, including especially the harmful and dehumanizing consequences of certain technologies, there is a technological solution. It is an Invisible Hand argument because it assumes not only that there is for every technological problem a technological fix *theoretically* available, but also that this fix will *actually* be implemented in time to prevent irremediable harm to the human community.

Upon this article of faith the nuclear physicists employed by the nuclear power industry almost unanimously supported the increased reliance upon the nuclear production of electricity, despite the fact that there was not at the time any known way to store safely the highly toxic radioactive waste. So the nuclear generating plants of the world are piling up this waste in temporary holding tanks in anticipation of the "inevitable" technological solution.

This faith in technological fix spurs technological development in all directions, seemingly without regard to the potential hazards, and the faith is so deeply and firmly entrenched that any professional scientists or engineer who suggests seriously that research or development of certain technologies are so inherently risky that they ought not to be pursued at all, is viewed by his or her colleagues as an irresponsible alarmist if not a traitor to the profession. Belief in the Invisible Technological Hand not only leads to abdication from responsibility for the risks imposed by one's own professional involvement in technology, but it can also spur the professional technologists and their political allies on to the serious advancement of technological solutions which are themselves fraught with even more serious risks — all in the belief that it may be the final technological fix.

Do we have good reasons to share with the true believers their abiding faith in the benevolence and trustworthiness of the Invisible Hand in any of its guises? The history of massive poverty and exploitation, to say nothing of unrestrained environmental degradation, produced by the free marketplace wherever it has been most closely associated is too clear to be denied by anyone who is not fervently committed to the dogma.

But what about the great Invisible Technological Hand? Is there evidence to support faith in its benevolent touch upon the sweaty brow of the technological society? Or is there evidence to the contrary? In the remainder of this paper I want to advance at least one important ground for reasonable doubt. That there is an Invisible Hand at work in the technological institutions of our society I do not doubt. Indeed, I suspect that there likely is more than just one such Hand, and if only one of them is anything less than benign there is good reason to doubt that the technological institutions can take care of themselves apart from conscientious moral responsibility exercised by the technological professionals themselves.

There is, in my view, an important Invisible Hand at work in our technological society, which is not necessarily benign. It is that force at work within technology itself which various writers from Jacques Ellul to Anatol Rapoport have referred to as the "Technological Imperative." It is a dynamic inherent within technology, (and essential to its growth and survival), which means that it is not morally neutral and is often morally detrimental. In a recent paper, Anatol Rapoport has illustrated the inherent dynamic of the technological imperative especially as it works in the case of military technology.[3] To understand what Rapoport means by the "technological imperative" one must also understand his "systems theory" approach to the problem, where technology is viewed as a social system evolving in certain directions depending upon the demands made upon it by its environment. The "environment" of the technological systems, and of technology itself, is the human community, especially as it is represented by the professional technologists. Viewed in this way, technological evolution is a response to the needs of its environment, which in this case are the needs of the human community. This is the aspect of technology that the technological optimists see best — technology as the servant of humanity.

However, from the perspective of systems theory, it is possible to view the matter the other way around. A biological species evolves in response to the "needs" of the other biological systems in its environment, but it also becomes part of the environment in which the other biological systems evolve in response to *its* needs. The same thing is true of institutional — what Rapoport calls "symbolic" — systems. They too become an environment for the human beings who created them, and the human community then also evolves in directions which serve their needs. This is clearly true of the institution of technology and its various technological sub-systems such as the system of military technology. Viewed in this way, it can be seen that human beings, especially the technological professionals, adapt their behaviour to the "needs" of the technological system. In this sense human beings become the servants of technology.

Rapoport sees the technological imperative as the internal needs of technological systems which determine the responses of the successful, innovative technologist. So, for example, one can speak of the "need" within missile technology for accurate guidance systems, radar evasion or "stealth" techniques, increased speed, range and so on. These "needs" are all internal to the missile technology itself. The persons who then are "selected for" in the professional community are those persons who are most closely attuned to these technological "needs". And, importantly, the needs of technology are not necessarily the real needs of the human community it supposedly serves, for technology has its own system of "needs."

What are some of the typical "needs" of values intrinsic to technology itself which can be identified as part of the technological imperative? 1. *Efficiency*. Technologically speaking, performing a task in less time and with less human energy is intrinsically better. 2. *Complexity*. Higher technology is intrinsically better than lower technology (because it reflects an intellectual advance or "breakthrough"). 3. *Technical "Elegance."* This is an aesthetic quality similar to that which obtains in science or mathematics, so that the more elegant the system, the better. 4. *Self-perpetuation*. This is a value intrinsic to all organic and social systems. It is the inherent drive to survive, to grow, to gain power, and to reproduce oneself. In the case of technology it manifests itself in the following maxims: More technology is better than less; technology dependent upon yet more technology is better; the technically possible is good and should therefore become actual, etc.

These values intrinsic to technology, which give the "imperative" to develop along certain paths, help to constitute what Robert Oppenheimer once called "the lure of the technically sweet." This lure is what most attracted the brilliant team of professional scientists, mathematicians and engineers headed by Oppenheimer in the Manhattan Project to devote their energies to the development of the first atomic bomb. Said Oppenheimer later, in reflection upon what he came to see as a regrettable part of his professional past:

> It is my judgment in these things that when you see something that is technically sweet you go ahead and do it and you argue about what to do about it only after you have had your technical success. That is the way it was with the atomic bomb.[4]

It was this realization that led Oppenheimer to speak out against the further development of the far more powerful hydrogen bomb. Its development, too, was driven on by the technological imperative and the lure to the professional defence community of its "technical sweetness." On this issue Oppenheimer threw aside the canons of the isolationist professional ethic and publicly opposed the devotion of scientific energy to the development of the hydrogen bomb. But his voice and the voices of other technological professionals who followed him were silenced. They were silenced because their appeal to moral and political ends (i.e., that the hydrogen bomb would stimulate an open-ended arms race to mass suicide) did not, as Rapoport notes, fit the mentality of the professional elite who had become the servants of the technology.

What is the import of this "technological imperative" for professional responsibility? First, if such an imperative operates within technology it means that the technological professionals are the primary instruments through which the technological systems will have their needs met. Or, put more bluntly, the professionals are the primary servants of technology, and their professional success is a measure of the degree to which they have learned to serve their "master." However, they will not see it that way. Their view will be the one of human purposes being served by the technological servant, and they will always be able to cite the human, social and political purposes which, if realized, would justify the course already charted by the imperatives of the technology itself. So, the defense professionals are always able to cite the strategic considerations that demand a further buildup of their nuclear arsenal — it is essential to counter the technological developments on the other side.

Secondly, if the professionals are the primary instruments through which the technological imperative actualizes itself, we ought not to be surprised to find that the professional ethic which has evolved in the professional community tends to serve the demands of the technological imperative rather than to place effective limits upon it. This is precisely how, in my view, the canons of professional morality I have cited function. The various rationalizations for the restriction of one's professional moral choice to the narrow confines of loyalty, honesty, and technical competence in one's role are all ways in which the professional retreats from the opportunity to challenge or redirect the course of the technological imperative. The Invisible Technological Hand is not necessarily benign. In the case of some of the new technologies there is good reason to fear that it is downright malevolent. If this is true, any professional ethic which relies upon the good graces of the Invisible Hand constitutes a form of moral irresponsibility founded upon false hope.

Third, if it is true that the prevailing professional ethic is the rationalization of the technological imperative, it means that the influence of this internal dynamic of technology is greatly strengthened through the community of technological professionals. The professional establishment itself becomes a powerful political force on the side of the technological imperative. This is one reason why some of the rationalizations I reviewed earlier, which escape personal responsibility by assigning it to other roles such as government regulators, other more knowledgeable experts, or to other nonprofessional roles like the roles of responsible citizens, are not very reliable solutions either. For if our society becomes increasingly professionalized, and if this professionalism is guided by the traditional professional ethic, then as the power of the technological imperative expands, there will be fewer non-professional "others" left who are free to make moral judgments, and it will become more difficult for them to counter its influence. This certainly is one reason, among others, why government regulatory agencies have been notoriously limited in their ability to curb many of the well-known and foreseen detrimental impacts of technology upon the social and biological environments.

Is there any solution to this problem? Can the combined forces of the technological imperative and the professional establishment which serves its needs be countered effectively so that technology truly does serve the moral ends of humanity? The prospects, I think, are not good. But I have one suggestion which I think would constitute an important step in the direction of technological responsibility. That step is the adoption of a new professional ethic which rejects the rationalizations for ethical isolationism and escape from responsibility characteristic of the prevailing professional ethic, and infuses the technological establishment itself with a moral conscientiousness that places limits upon the Invisible Technological Hand *from the inside*. Moral convictions.

A responsible professional ethic, then, must be an Ethic of Conscientious Professionalism, which always takes a broader, structural view of the system of the institution in which the professional role functions, and takes as *at least one* important consideration in decision-making, the moral significance of the larger work.

An Ethic of Conscientious Professionalism must always be prepared to address and answer the question, "How far am I prepared to go in participation with this system? Where do I draw the line in my participation with a system I can no longer justify?" It must be prepared to take the difficult step of conscientious refusal to participate in the system or in aspects of the system. This is not an easy thing to do, because it almost always implies great personal sacrifice, including the loss of professional standing in the eyes of one's colleagues, and even banishment from the profession. This is the price one pays as well for even the lesser "offense" of blowing the whistle on actions of one's professional colleagues or employers that pose grave threats to the public welfare.

A responsible Ethic of Conscientious Professionalism embraces the principle that with increased knowledge and power comes increased responsibility. So, it is precisely because the professional has greater understanding of the implications for good or ill of the technology or skill she practices that she also has a greater responsibility to protect the social good. Thus, not only is it not *inappropriate* for the professional to take public moral stands on matters concerning the moral impact of her profession on society (as we have seen the traditional professional ethic says), but it is a positive professional *responsibility*. It is as appropriate for the nuclear physicist to warn of the dangers of nuclear power plants and weapons as anyone else, indeed, she usually has a greater obligation than anyone else to do so.

One of the positive developments in the direction of a more responsible professional ethic in our society has been the recent phenomenon of professionals organizing themselves *as professionals* to exercise an influence upon the political decisions being made affecting the use of their profession for the public good. The organization of academics into Science for Peace, medical doctors into Physicians for Social Responsibility, and even retired NATO military generals into Generals for Peace, are important examples of professionals taking their social responsibilities as professionals seriously.

The sense that the narrow blinkers of traditional professional ethics must be removed and the horizon of moral responsibility expanded is finding its way even into the center of the traditional professional establishment. It is reflected in the fact that the Codes of Ethics of various professions have begun to shift their emphasis from the narrow concerns about loyalty to client or employer, honesty in dealing with one's colleagues, bringing honor upon the profession, and so on, to a recognition of the duty to use the profession in the service of the public good. The Codes of Ethics of the various professional engineering associations have made dramatic changes in this regard in recent years. Nearly all of them expound the principle that the engineer shall "regard his duty to public welfare as paramount."[5] Whether, or to what extent, this sentiment will actually translate itself into practice remains to be seen. It is nevertheless significant that the profession has at least come to acknowledge the principle.

I have argued that the traditional professional ethic and its typical rationalizations for not taking seriously a profession's broad impact upon the social welfare of the practice of that profession constitutes a serious avoidance of moral responsibility. It is an escape that permits other forces, whose influences are not always for the social good, to take over and determine the course of our social development, independent of the very values we espouse. The traditional ethic may even be the rationale by which professionals become the blind servants of such alien forces as the Technological Imperative. What is needed is a new Professional Ethic which sensitizes us to the way in which we are drawn into the service of these forces, and instills in us a vigilant responsibility for the future of humanity and its habitat.

NOTES

1. *Engineering Dimensions* 6 (January/February, 1985) p. 22
2. Hannah Arendt, *Eichmann in Jerusalem: A Report on the Banality of Evil* (New York: Viking Press, 1963) p. 287
3. Anatol Rapoport, "The Technological Imperative." Unpublished paper presented at the University of Waterloo Conference on Philosophy and Nuclear Arms, September 28-30, 1984
4. Robert Jungk, *Brighter Than a Thousand Suns* (Harmondsworth: Penguin Books, 1964) p. 266
5. See, for example, the *Code of Ethics*, Association of Professional Engineers in Ontario, Sec. 2a

QUESTIONS

1. What are the conventional principles of professional morality that in Conrad Brunk's view are widely accepted in our society? Do you agree with his account in this regard?
2. Why does Brunk claim that our involvement as individuals with various institutions in our society is always "fraught with moral ambiguity"? Is he right about this? Is his example of Adolf Eichmann's role in the mass execution of Jews in Germany in the 1930s and 1940s a good illustration of the problem? Can you think of others that are more recent and more closely connected to our contemporary situation?
3. Do you agree that ethics is central to the role of professionals? Why does Brunk think that the moral ambiguity that individuals face through their participation in the activities of social institutions is particularly acute for professionals? Is he right about this?
4. What is "the Invisible Hand" of Adam Smith? What role does it play in the rationalization of the denial of moral responsibility of professionals for critical scrutiny of their role in practices that have serious implications for the welfare of the wider community in which they live and work?
5. What is the technological imperative? What are the values which are central to its impact?
6. When all is said and done, what are the moral obligations of professionals in our society in Brunk's view? Is his account of the matter sound? Does it help to understand the moral disasters that have led to the failure of companies and firms such as Enron, WorldCom, Global Crossing, Bre-X, or Arthur Andersen?

SUGGESTIONS FOR FURTHER READING

There are very few topics in applied ethics that have produced a flood of commentary equal to that in the field of business ethics. What follows are some suggestions of readings organized under some general headings.

Business Ethics Journals

- *Journal of Business Ethics* and *Business Ethics Quarterly*

Ethics and Globalization

- Thomas Friedman, *The Lexus and the Olive Tree* (Anchor Books: New York, 2000). This book is written by an American author and has the subtitle: "Understanding Globalization."
- Noreena Hertz, *The Silent Takeover: Global Capitalism and the Death of Democracy* (Arrow Books: London, 2001). This book by a British author looks at the impact of globalization on democratic institutions and practices.
- Naomi Klein, *No Logo* (Flamingo, Harper Collins Publishers: London, 2000). This is a very influential book by a Canadian author that articulates the case against globalization.

Corporate Citizenship

- Malcolm McIntosh et al., *Living Corporate Citizenship: Strategic routes to socially responsible business* (Prentice Hall: London, 2003). This book explores the implications of the UN Global Compact for corporate citizenship.
- Simon Zadek, *The Civil Corporation: the new economy of corporate citizenship*, (Earthscan: London, 2001). Simon Zadek is the head of a British consultancy firm called AcountAbility located in London, England. He is closely associated with the development of social auditing standards for verifying the social performance of corporations.

Academic Texts

- John Boatright, *Ethics and Finance* (Blackwell: Oxford, 1999). The focus in this book is financial services. However, it is a good analysis of the role of ethics within the context of the conventional view that the role of business is to maximize profits.
- Thomas Donaldson and Thomas Dunfee, *Ties that Bind: A Social Contracts Approach to Business Ethics* (Harvard Business School Press: Boston, 1999). This book applies social contract theory to understanding the moral obligations of business in global markets.

Canadian Books

- Fredrick Bird, *The Muted Conscience: Moral Silence and the Practice of Ethics in Business* (Quorum Books: Westport, Connecticut, 2002). This book examines moral silence in the business community and the reasons for it and concludes by examining ways in which moral silence can and has been overcome.
- Deborah Poff and Wilfred Waluchow, *Business Ethics in Canada* (Prentice Hall: Scarborough, 1999). This is an anthology of writing covering a wide range of topics and intended for undergraduate classroom use.

Chapter 10

War, Terrorism, and the War against Terrorism

Introduction

We have already observed in previous chapters that human beings need the help and cooperation of others if they are to meet even their most basic needs. To survive, we need food, shelter, and clothing. Given the conditions of modern life, none of us could provide these things for ourselves isolated from the assistance of others. When we add to this list the way in which our personal welfare is shaped by the social and economic environment in which we live, an important additional dimension is added to this fact of mutual dependence.

Our vulnerability to violence, against which our defences are in many circumstances strikingly limited illustrates this mutual interdependence.

In light of the need that individuals have to join in communities, it is perhaps ironic that one type of violence to which people are particularly vulnerable is violence inflicted on them by communities or groups. This is true both of the communities in which they have membership, their own country, for example, and also communities with which they have no formal association, for instance other countries.

Given their vulnerability to violence, what actions are individuals or the groups of which they are a part justified in taking to protect things they value, their lives, their possessions, and their autonomy or independence from others?

This question might seem to have a simple answer: A group is entitled to take whatever steps are necessary to protect what legitimately belongs to their members from any illegitimate threat. However, this response hides a number of complex issues behind a deceptively simple façade. To begin with, if a community uses force to protect itself against what it regards as unjustifiable threats, it will almost inevitably threaten the lives and properties of others, many of whom may not be parties to or responsible for the dispute to which the community is responding. Furthermore, the methods of defence chosen may require a community to override the objections of some of its own members and coerce their cooperation under conditions that may mean substantial loss of life and destruction of property on the part of those whose cooperation is required.

Secondly, when a group uses force to protect what it regards as its legitimate interests, it is imposing its own view of what its legitimate interests are as well as what counts as an illegitimate threat. To those faced with an unprovoked attack, these problems may not seem particularly significant. However, in our modern world, the disputes that frequently give rise to international conflict are complex and not easily resolved, particularly given prevailing notions of sovereignty and the absence of greed upon procedures for adjudicating differences.

Finally, the answer posed raises serious problems about what constitutes an illegitimate threat and what countermeasures are justified in particular circumstances. Is the decision of a country to purchase new sophisticated weapons or increase the size of its armed forces properly regarded as an illegitimate threat? Note that each has been so regarded already in this century and each has been thought to justify armed attack by those who saw themselves threatened. Are nations justified in using any weapon at their disposal, whatever their destructive potential, to deal with any threat regardless of its character? Are there types of weapons that should not be used or even developed by countries even when the alternative may be defeat or destruction at the hands of an enemy?

These are the questions that face those concerned with the morality of modern warfare.

Background Considerations

The past century was a remarkable one viewed from the perspective of international conflict. The planet endured two world wars and innumerable regional conflicts. The fact of conflict is not a twentieth or twenty-first century phenomenon, of course. But the destructive quality of modern international conflicts is a new development in human history. This is in large part a product of modern technology that has opened the door to the relatively inexpensive production of biological, chemical, and nuclear weapons of mass destruction.

For many people, developing rules proscribing the use of weapons of mass destruction has been regarded as in many ways the most pressing moral imperative of our age. It is clear that real progress in fact has resulted from international efforts in this regard. There now are widely accepted international conventions prohibiting the use of chemical and biological weapons. And the collapse of the Cold War had until recently lead many to believe that the once-real danger of nuclear war with its very serious implications for the future of life on this planet had receded to such a degree that it was no longer a serious threat.

However, weapons of mass destruction are not the only concern. Though what are called conventional weapons are not weapons of mass destruction, they are nevertheless vastly more destructive than the weapons available as recently as even the Second World War. Further, the capacity of belligerents to deliver those weapons to their targets in large numbers has increased exponentially, as the readings in this chapter make clear.

The nature of modern warfare has also made it increasingly difficult to differentiate between military units carrying on a conflict and civilian populations. As a result, it is virtually certain that military conflict, when it occurs, will result in substantial direct or indirect civilian casualties. Under what conditions, therefore, is the use of force in resolving international conflict morally justifiable?

The Current Situation

The Cold War ended with the collapse of the Soviet Union more than a decade ago. Many believed at that time that international tensions would ease. Many more hoped that international conflict would become a relic of the past. Neither has proven to be the case. While the threat of global nuclear war has virtually disappeared, and with it the fear of nuclear annihilation, regional and national or civil conflicts that were held in check by superpower rivalry have emerged in many parts of the globe. So too has the threat of terrorism. As a consequence, the last decade of the last century saw violent regional and civil conflict in virtually every region of the world with the exception of North America. The attacks of September 11,

2001, were a severe shock to the American people. A country that had for much of its history been buffered from the direct impact of war suddenly realized that it too was vulnerable to terrorist attack.

The response was dramatic: the declaration of war on terrorism; dramatic changes in American foreign policy; the invasion of Afghanistan with a view to destroying the terrorist training bases of al Qaeda and the Taliban government that supported them; and finally an attack on Iraq. The attack on Afghanistan was supported by a wide coalition of countries. However, when the United States turned its attention to Iraq, support for military intervention became more restrained and worldwide criticism began to form. The focus of much of what follows is on those developments.

What is it about war that makes it an issue? The answer is relatively straightforward. On the one hand, when nations decide to go to war, they do so in the name of values that normally attract moral commendation: courage, loyalty, altruism, the defence of freedom, and so on. On the other hand, war involves deliberately inflicted death, destruction, and human suffering. Put another way, war virtually requires that combatants set aside and ignore principles and values in dealing with the enemy that they would otherwise regard as sacrosanct.

Some have argued that moral considerations have no bearing on the use of military force to accomplish national objectives either because they reject morality itself or because they are "political realists." Political realists typically argue that morality has to do with relations between and among individuals but has no relevance to the conduct of groups, particularly nation states. A second view argues that war is justified, but only when it can be shown to be "just."

"Just" war theory has a long history. Its relevance to modern discussions of the ethics of war was demonstrated by the role it played in discussions that preceded and followed the Persian Gulf war, and the wars in Afghanistan. On the other hand, it seems to have played a less prominant role in justifying and subsequently evaluating the war on Iraq.

The Readings

The readings in this chapter have an unusual character. All the chapters in this book have begun with readings drawn from court cases or popular debate, government reports or the media. In this chapter, the space devoted to putting the philosophical discussion in the context of ongoing public discussion is more extensive. The goal is to capture in a way as balanced as possible the different views that were expressed before, during, and after the invasion of Iraq. The first of these readings is an article written by Jimmy Carter for the New York Times prior to the actual invasion. In the article, Carter, a former President of the United States, evaluates the justifiability of an invasion of Iraq against "just" war criteria. He concludes that an invasion of Iraq by the United States would not be morally acceptable.

One of the staunchest allies of the United States as preparations for an invasion of Iraq proceeded was Tony Blair, Prime Minister of the United Kingdom. Although the early justifications of war focused on terrorism and the fear that Saddam Hussein, the President of Iraq, was developing weapons of mass destruction. Tony Blair in particular shifted the focus of his justification for military intervention prior to the actual invasion of Iraq to the brutality and human rights violations of the Iraqi regime. That justification is set out by Tony Blair in a speech made at a time when both the sentiment within his own party and public opinion in the United Kingdom were heavily weighted against an invasion of Iraq that was not sanctioned by the Security Council of the United Nations.

In contrast to Tony Blair's justification of the coming war, Mohamad Byden, a Muslim, Iraqi American, evaluates the various arguments for going to war with Iraq from Muslim and Arab historical perspectives. Emphasizing the dangers of unilateral American action, he rejects the moral justifications for war of the kind examined by Al Gore and endorsed by Tony Blair.

Michael Ignatieff, writing for the Observer, a well-known British newspaper, while the invasion of Iraq was underway, took up the issue of the terrorism and security. He argues that, in light of terrorism and the events of September 11, 2001, faced with the threat that a rogue state might "transfer chemical, biological and nuclear weapons to suicide bombers," the United States and Great Britain have no choice but to invade Iraq to remove Saddam Hussein and his rogue regime from power.

Taken together, these first readings provide a relatively comprehensive picture of the kinds of moral arguments and justifications that were used and continue to be used both to criticize and to justify the decision by the Government of the United States and its allies to go to war to depose the Government of Iraq led by Suddam Hussein.

The next set of readings stands back from direct involvement in the debate with a view to examining the validity of the kinds of arguments set out in the first set of readings. Trudy Govier begins by setting out a number of fallacies that are frequently relied on to justify military action. She follows this analysis with a discussion of the three dominant theories used to support and evaluate justifications for war: realism, "just" war theory, and pacifism. Govier then rejects realism as logically arbitrary and incompatible with a widely endorsed emphasis on such things as human rights. Setting aside the case for pacifism, she tests the justifications of the invasion of Iraq against "just" war theory which sets out moral criteria that, if satisfied, justify going to war, and concludes that judged by those criteria, the war against Iraq was not and is not morally justifiable.

The final two readings take up the third of the three options set out by Trudy Govier, namely, the merits of pacifism. Jan Narveson looks at the various doctrines that have been called pacifism, examining each in turn. He concludes that none of the doctrines that has been used to justify a pacifist response to violence and aggression is plausible or coherent. Conrad Brunk responds to Narveson's analysis with an alternative account of pacifism and its various formulations, arguing that pacifism is logically and morally coherent and is a defensible response to international conflict.

JUST WAR OR A JUST WAR?

President Jimmy Carter

Profound changes have been taking place in American foreign policy, reversing consistent bipartisan commitments that for more than two centuries have earned our nation greatness. These commitments have been predicated on basic religious principles, respect for international law, and alliances that resulted in wise decisions and mutual restraint. Our apparent determination to launch a war against Iraq, without international support, is a violation of these premises.

Jimmy Carter, the 39th president of the United States, is chairman of the Carter Center in Atlanta and winner of the 2002 Nobel Peace Prize.

As a Christian and as a president who was severely provoked by international crises, I became thoroughly familiar with the principles of a just war, and it is clear that a substantially unilateral attack on Iraq does not meet these standards. This is an almost universal conviction of religious leaders, with the most notable exception of a few spokesmen of the Southern Baptist Convention who are greatly influenced by their commitment to Israel based on eschatological, or final days, theology.

For a war to be just, it must meet several clearly defined criteria.

The war can be waged only as a last resort, with all nonviolent options exhausted. In the case of Iraq, it is obvious that clear alternatives to war exist. These options previously proposed by our own leaders and approved by the United Nations were outlined again by the Security Council on Friday. But now, with our own national security not directly threatened and despite the overwhelming opposition of most people and governments in the world, the United States seems determined to carry out military and diplomatic action that is almost unprecedented in the history of civilized nations. The first stage of our widely publicized war plan is to launch 3,000 bombs and missiles on a relatively defenseless Iraqi population within the first few hours of an invasion, with the purpose of so damaging and demoralizing the people that they will change their obnoxious leader, who will most likely be hidden and safe during the bombardment.

The war's weapons must discriminate between combatants and noncombatants. Extensive aerial bombardment, even with precise accuracy, inevitably results in "collateral damage." Gen. Tommy R. Franks, commander of American forces in the Persian Gulf, has expressed concern about many of the military targets being near hospitals, schools, mosques and private homes.

Its violence must be proportional to the injury we have suffered. Despite Saddam Hussein's other serious crimes, American efforts to tie Iraq to the 9/11 terrorist attacks have been unconvincing.

The attackers must have legitimate authority sanctioned by the society they profess to represent. The unanimous vote of approval in the Security Council to eliminate Iraq's weapons of mass destruction can still be honored, but our announced goals are now to achieve regime change and to establish a Pax Americana in the region, perhaps occupying the ethnically divided country for as long as a decade. For these objectives, we do not have international authority. Other members of the Security Council have so far resisted the enormous economic and political influence that is being exerted from Washington, and we are faced with the possibility of either a failure to get the necessary votes or else a veto from Russia, France and China. Although Turkey may still be enticed into helping us by enormous financial rewards and partial future control of the Kurds and oil in northern Iraq, its democratic Parliament has at least added its voice to the worldwide expressions of concern!

The peace it establishes must be a clear improvement over what exists. Although there are visions of peace and democracy in Iraq, it is quite possible that the aftermath of a military invasion will destabilize the region and prompt terrorists to further jeopardize our security at home. Also, by defying overwhelming world opposition, the United States will undermine the United Nations as a viable institution for world peace.

What about America's world standing if we don't go to war after such a great deployment of military forces in the region? The heartfelt sympathy and friendship offered to America after the 9/11 attacks, even from formerly antagonistic regimes, has been largely dissipated; increasingly unilateral and domineering policies have brought international trust in our country to its lowest level in memory. American stature will surely decline further if we launch a war in clear defiance of the United Nations. But to use the presence and threat of our military power to force Iraq's compliance with all United Nations resolutions with war as a final option will enhance our status as a champion of peace and justice.

I WANT TO SOLVE THE IRAQ ISSUE VIA THE UNITED NATIONS

Prime Minister Tony Blair

We've been in power for six years now. Through the election wins, the popular changes and yes, the tougher decisions.

. . .

The progress we have made, we have made together. I know it is tough right now. I know it is an uncertain time for our country. But we will come through this and we will come through it together.

We will come through it by holding firm to what we believe in. One such belief is in the United Nations. I continue to want to solve the issue of Iraq and weapons of mass destruction through the UN. That is why last November we insisted on putting UN inspectors back into Iraq to disarm it.

Dr Blix reported to the UN yesterday and there will be more time given to inspections. He will report again on 28 February. But let no one forget two things. To anyone familiar with Saddam's tactics of deception and evasion, there is a weary sense of déjà vu. As ever, at the last minute, concessions are made. And as ever, it is the long finger that is directing them. The concessions are suspect. Unfortunately the weapons are real.

Last year, 12 long years after the UN first gave him 15 days to produce a full audit of his chemical, biological and nuclear weapons programmes and he denied he had any, we passed UN Resolution 1441. It gave him a "final opportunity" to disarm. It instructed him to co-operate fully with the UN inspectors. Why was the inspection regime so tough? Because for 12 years, he had played a game with the inspectors.

In 1991 Iraq denied it had a biological weapons offensive programme. For four years the inspectors toiled. It was not until 1995 that Saddam's son-in-law defected to Jordan, explained the true biological weapons programme and it was partially dealt with. He was, of course lured back to Iraq and then murdered.

The time needed is not the time it takes the inspectors to discover the weapons. They are not a detective agency. We played that game for years in the 1990s. The time is the time necessary to make a judgment: is Saddam prepared to co-operate fully or not. If he is, the inspectors can take as much time as they want. If he is not, if this is a repeat of the 1990s — and I believe it is — then let us be under no doubt what is at stake.

By going down the UN route we gave the UN an extraordinary opportunity and a heavy responsibility. The opportunity is to show that we can meet the menace to our world today together, collectively and as a united international community. What a mighty achievement that would be. The responsibility, however, is indeed to deal with it.

Speech by Prime Minister Tony Blair at Labour's local government, women's and youth conferences, SECC, Glasgow. Saturday 15 February 2003. Reprinted by permission.

The League of Nations also had that opportunity and responsibility back in the 1930s. In the early days of the fascist menace, it had the duty to protect Abyssinia from invasion. But when it came to a decision to enforce that guarantee, the horror of war deterred it. We know the rest. The menace grew; the League of Nations collapsed; war came.

Remember: the UN inspectors would not be within a thousand miles of Baghdad without the threat of force. Saddam would not be making a single concession without the knowledge that forces were gathering against him. I hope, even now, Iraq can be disarmed peacefully, with or without Saddam. But if we show weakness now, if we allow the plea for more time to become just an excuse for prevarication until the moment for action passes, then it will not only be Saddam who is repeating history. The menace, and not just from Saddam, will grow; the authority of the UN will be lost; and the conflict when it comes will be more bloody. Yes, let the United Nations be the way to deal with Saddam. But let the United Nations mean what it says; and do what it means.

What is the menace we speak of? It is not just Saddam. We are living through insecure times. Wars; terrorist threats; suddenly things that seem alien to us are on our doorstep, threatening our way of life.

Let me try to make sense of it. For hundreds of years, Europe was at war, the boundaries of many nations shifting with each passing army, small countries occupied and re-occupied, their people never at peace. Large countries fought each other literally for decades at a time with only the briefest respite to draw breath before the resumption of hostilities. For my father's generation that was the Europe they were brought up in. Today in Europe former enemies are friends, at one, if not always diplomatically. The EU is a massive achievement of peace and prosperity now set to welcome in the nations who suffered from the other great tyranny of my father's life time and my own: the Soviet Union. For the first 40 years of my life, the reality was the Communist bloc versus the West. Today the Cold War is over. The EU is set to grow to 25, then 30 then more nations. Russia is our partner and we, hers, in her search for a new and democratic beginning. China is developing as a Socialist market economy and is the ally of Europe, and the US.

We don't wake up and fear Russia or China as we did. America is not focussed on the struggle for ideological hegemony between Communism and liberal democracy. The issue is not a clash for conquest between the big powers.

But the old threat has been replaced by a new one. The threat of chaos; disorder; instability. A threat which arises from a perversion of the true faith of Islam, in extremist terrorist groups like Al Qaida. It arises from countries which are unstable, usually repressive dictatorships which use what wealth they have to protect or enhance their power through chemical, biological or nuclear weapons capability which can cause destruction on a massive scale.

What do they have in common these twins of chaos — terrorism and rogue states with Weapons of Mass Destruction? They are answerable to no democratic mandate, so are unrestrained by the will of ordinary people. They are extreme and inhumane. They detest and fear liberal, democratic and tolerant values. And their aim is to de-stabilise us.

September 11th didn't just kill thousands of innocent people. It was meant to bring down the Western economy. It did not do so. But we live with the effects of it even today in economic confidence. It was meant to divide Muslim and Christian, Arab and Western nations, and to provoke us to hate each other. It didn't succeed but that is what it was trying to do.

These states developing Weapons of Mass Destruction, proliferating them, importing or exporting the scientific expertise, the ballistic missile technology; the companies and individuals helping them: they don't operate within any international treaties. They don't conform to any rules. North Korea is a country whose people are starving and yet can spend billions of dollars trying to perfect a nuclear bomb. Iraq, under Saddam became the first country to use chemical weapons against its own people. Are we sure that if we let him keep and develop such weapons, he would not use them again against his neighbours, against Israel perhaps? Saddam the man who killed a million people in an eight year war with Iran, and then, having lost it, invaded Kuwait? Or the other nations scrabbling to get a foot on the nuclear ladder, are we happy that they do so?

And the terrorist groups already using chemical and biological agents with money to spend, do we really believe that if Al Qaida could get a dirty bomb they wouldn't use it? And then think of the consequences. Already there is fear and anxiety, undermining confidence. Think of the consequences then. Think of a nation using a nuclear device, no matter how small, no matter how distant the land. Think of the chaos it would cause.

That is why Saddam and Weapons of Mass Destruction are important.

Every time I have asked us to go to war, I have hated it. I spent months trying to get Milosevic to stop ethnic cleansing in Kosovo, delaying action while we negotiated endlessly. I agreed with President Bush not to strike Afghanistan after September 11th but instead to offer the Taliban, loathsome though they were, an ultimatum: yield up Al Qaida and we will let you stay. We used force in the end, but in Kosovo only as a last resort, and though I rejoiced with his people at the fall of Milosevic, as I rejoiced with the Afghan people at the fall of the Taliban, I know that amid the necessary military victory there was pain and suffering that brought no joy at all.

At every stage, we should seek to avoid war. But if the threat cannot be removed peacefully, please let us not fall for the delusion that it can be safely ignored. If we do not confront these twin menaces of rogue states with Weapons of Mass Destruction and terrorism, they will not disappear. They will just feed and grow on our weakness.

When people say if you act, you will provoke these people; when they say now: take a lower profile and these people will leave us alone, remember: Al Qaida attacked the US, not the other way round. Were the people of Bali in the forefront of the anti-terror campaign? Did Indonesia 'make itself a target'? The terrorists won't be nice to us if we're nice to them. When Saddam drew us into the Gulf War, he wasn't provoked. He invaded Kuwait.

So: where has it come to? Everyone agrees Saddam must be disarmed. Everyone agrees without disarmament, he is a danger.

No-one seriously believes he is yet co-operating fully. In all honesty, most people don't really believe he ever will. So what holds people back? What brings thousands of people out in protests across the world? And let's not pretend, not really that in March or April or May or June, people will feel different. It's not really an issue of timing or 200 inspectors versus 100. It is a right and entirely understandable hatred of war. It is moral purpose, and I respect that.

It is as one woman put it to me: I abhor the consequences of war.

And I know many in our own Party, many here today will agree with her; and don't understand why I press the case so insistently. And I have given you the geo-political reason — the threat of Weapons of Mass Destruction and its link with terrorism. And I believe it.

If I am honest about it, there is another reason why I feel so strongly about this issue. It is a reason less to do with my being Prime Minister than being a member of the Labour Party, to do with the progressive politics in which we believe. The moral case against war has a moral answer: it is the moral case for removing Saddam. It is not the reason we act. That must be according to the United Nations mandate on Weapons of Mass Destruction. But it is the reason, frankly, why if we do have to act, we should do so with a clear conscience.

Yes, there are consequences of war. If we remove Saddam by force, people will die and some will be innocent. And we must live with the consequences of our actions, even the unintended ones.

But there are also consequences of "stop the war."

If I took that advice, and did not insist on disarmament, yes, there would be no war. But there would still be Saddam. Many of the people marching will say they hate Saddam. But the consequences of taking their advice is that he stays in charge of Iraq, ruling the Iraqi people. A country that in 1978, the year before he seized power, was richer than Malaysia or Portugal. A country where today, 135 out of every 1000 Iraqi children die before the age of five — 70% of these deaths are from diarrhoea and respiratory infections that are easily preventable. Where almost a third of children born in the centre and south of Iraq have chronic malnutrition.

Where 60% of the people depend on Food Aid.

Where half the population of rural areas have no safe water.

Where every year and now, as we speak, tens of thousands of political prisoners languish in appalling conditions in Saddam's jails and are routinely executed.

Where in the past 15 years over 150,000 Shia Moslems in Southern Iraq and Moslem Kurds in Northern Iraq have been butchered; with up to four million Iraqis in exile round the world, including 350,000 now in Britain.

This isn't a regime with Weapons of Mass Destruction that is otherwise benign. This is a regime that contravenes every single principle or value anyone of our politics believes in.

There will be no march for the victims of Saddam, no protests about the thousands of children that die needlessly every year under his rule, no righteous anger over the torture chambers which if he is left in power, will be left in being.

I rejoice that we live in a country where peaceful protest is a natural part of our democratic process.

But I ask the marchers to understand this.

I do not seek unpopularity as a badge of honour. But sometimes it is the price of leadership. And the cost of conviction.

But as you watch your TV pictures of the march, ponder this:

If there are 500,000 on that march, that is still less than the number of people whose deaths Saddam has been responsible for.

If there are one million, that is still less than the number of people who died in the wars he started.

Let me read from an e-mail that was sent by a member of the family of one of those four million Iraqi exiles. It is interesting because she is fiercely and I think wrongly critical of America. But in a sense for that reason, it is worth reading.

She addresses it to the anti-war movement.

In one part, she says:

You may feel that America is trying to blind you from seeing the truth about their real reasons for an invasion. I must argue that in fact, you are still blind to the bigger truths in Iraq.

Saddam has murdered more than a million Iraqis over the past 30 years, are you willing to allow him to kill another million Iraqis?

Saddam rules Iraq using fear — he regularly imprisons, executes and tortures the mass population for no reason whatsoever — this may be hard to believe and you may not even appreciate the extent of such barbaric acts, but believe me you will be hard pressed to find a family in Iraq who have not had a son, father, brother killed, imprisoned, tortured and/or "disappeared" due to Saddam's regime.

Why it is now that you deem it appropriate to voice your disillusions with America's policy in Iraq, when it is right now that the Iraqi people are being given real hope, however slight and however precarious, that they can live in an Iraq that is free of its horrors?

We will give the e-mail to delegates. Read it all. It is the reason why I do not shrink from action against Saddam if it proves necessary. Read the letter sent to me by Dr Safa Hashim, who lives here in Glasgow, and who says he is writing despite his fears of Iraqi retribution.

He says the principle of opposing war by the public is received warmly by Iraqis for it reveals the desire of people to avoid suffering. But he says it misses the point — because the Iraqi people need Saddam removed as a way of ending their suffering.

Dr Hashim says:

The level of their suffering is beyond anything that British people can possible envisage, let alone understand his obsession to develop and possess weapons of mass destruction. Do the British public know that it is normal practice for Saddam's regime to demand the cost of the bullet used in the execution of their beloved family members and not even to allow a proper funeral?

If the international community does not take note of the Iraqi people's plight but continues to address it casually this will breed terrorism and extremism within the Iraqi people. This cannot be allowed to happen.

Remember Kosovo where we were told war would de-stabilise the whole of the Balkans and that region now has the best chance of peace in over 100 years?

Remember Afghanistan, where now, despite all the huge problems, there are three million children in school, including for the first time in over two decades one and a half million girls and where two million Afghan exiles from the Taliban have now returned.

So if the result of peace is Saddam staying in power, not disarmed, then I tell you there are consequences paid in blood for that decision too. But these victims will never be seen. They will never feature on our TV screens or inspire millions to take to the streets. But they will exist nonetheless.

Ridding the world of Saddam would be an act of humanity. It is leaving him there that is in truth inhumane.

And if it does come to this, let us be clear: we should be as committed to the humanitarian task of rebuilding Iraq for the Iraqi people as we have been to removing Saddam.

And there will be no stability in the Middle East until there is lasting peace between Israelis and Palestinians based on a secure Israel and a viable Palestinian state. I promise we will not rest until we have used every drop of our influence to achieve it.

OF DRUNKEN COWBOYS AND ARABIAN KNIGHTS: WEIGHING THE MORALITY OF A WAR AGAINST IRAQ

Mohamad Bydon

> *On the last day,*
> *I kissed my sheik's tomb*
> *And said so-long,*
> *And went.*
> *Baghdad is no longer*
> *But a graveyard for the beloved and a love poem that I lost.*
> —Abdel Wahab al-Bayati, Iraqi poet in exile

On Detroit's Warren Avenue, a mosque welcomed passersby and worshippers with a large banner: "No to Saddam Hussein; No to UN Sanctions; Yes to Iraq." Founded by Iraqi Shi'ites seeking refuge in the United States after the Gulf War, the mosque is home to some of the most fervent anti-Saddam sentiments anywhere outside of Donald Rumsfeld's Pentagon. The worshippers tell horrifying tales of persecution and torture at the hands of Saddam's secular, and formerly pro-Western, regime. Although they make up 55–60 percent of Iraq's population, the Shi'ites have no representation in the central government that rules Iraq. They are forbidden from participating in their religious rituals, for which the punishment can include amputation, branding, or even execution. (In the past, physicians who refused to administer such punishments or who performed reconstructive surgery on the victims were themselves executed.) The Shi'ites have also seen their holy mosques and shrines — most notably the tombs of Imam Ali and Imam Husayn — desecrated at the hands of Iraqi security forces. Those who organized to fight Saddam's rule were quashed through a major military offensive in which Iraqi troops massacred innocent villagers, bulldozed civilian homes, and even drained the Amara and Hammar marshes used by the guerrilla fighters for cover. Shi'ite clergymen (including some of my own family members) were imprisoned or "disappeared."

Like Saddam's oppression of the Kurds and his use of biological weapons against the Islamic government in Iran, his brutalization of the Shi'ites was conducted with American knowledge at a time when his regime was receiving generous supplies of weapons and aid from Washington. The end of the Iran-Iraq war coincided with a major rift in American-Iraqi relations that culminated in the Persian Gulf War. Largely due to conversations with U.S. Ambassador April Glaspie just days before his invasion of Kuwait, Saddam Hussein mistakenly believed that the United States would not interfere in the conflict. When President George Bush began forming an international coalition to fight for the "liberation"—though not the democratization — of Kuwait, the nations of the world jumped aboard. The war to restore Kuwait's conservative but oil-friendly monarchy devastated the Iraqi army. While American losses numbered in the low hundreds, estimates of Iraqi deaths range from twenty thousand to one hundred thousand. The numbers include a vicious American massacre of thousands of retreating Iraqi troops on the now infamous "Highway to Hell," as well as the U.S. Air Force's obliteration of the Amiriya bomb shelter in Baghdad, killing six hundred to one thousand civilians.

From "Of Drunken Cowboys and Arabian Knights: Weighing the Morality of a War Against Iraq," Tikkun, Vol. 17, No. 6, pp. 17–20. Reprinted from TIKKUN: A Bimonthly Jewish Critique of Politics, Culture & Society, www.tikkun.org

As the war proceeded, the Shi'ites of Iraq saw an opportunity to overthrow Saddam. Most of the men in the Detroit-area mosque joined the Shi'ite resistance at the time of the Gulf War. Their stories of repression at the hands of Saddam are quickly followed by shocking episodes of the American role in the annihilation of their movement for the liberation of Iraq. This was not merely a matter of American indifference to their fate, evidenced by scenes of U.S. troops watching as Iraqi soldiers crushed entire Shi'ite communities. Rather, the American army played an active role in suppressing Shi'ite resistance to Saddam— first by moving U.S. army divisions to block Shi'ite fighters from accessing deserted Iraqi armories, and then by allowing Saddam's forces to fly armed helicopters into revolting Shi'ite villages. Although these American policies were driven by a fear of the unknown and an overarching desire to retain the territorial integrity of Iraq, there can be little doubt that America's refusal to aid the Shi'ites and Kurds after encouraging them to rebel has hurt our image among the people of the Middle East.

The Iraqi Shi'ites in Detroit differ on this current administration's hawkish plans towards Iraq. As first-hand victims of Saddam's repression, they speak with a moral authority lacking in the empty rhetoric of the Pentagon's militaristic neo-conservatives. Yet they do not see this as a clear-cut issue. Whereas some of them support any military campaign that would oust Saddam, others are more cautious, fearing for their own family members in Iraq and wanting to avoid a bloody civil strife similar to the one that broke out between Kurdish factions in northern Iraq between 1994 and 1997. As Iraqi expatriate Ala Fa'ik told the *Detroit News*, "Saddam Hussein is a thug who has abused people for more than twenty years while the whole world was watching…. His regime has hurt all Iraqis—the Chaldeans, the Muslims; he even imprisoned his own brother. But an American invasion would be very hurtful. My preference is to have change happen by the Iraqi people themselves." Recently, the Iraqi-American Conference for a Free and Democratic Iraq met in the Detroit-area where nearly 170,000 Iraqi Chaldeans, Shi'ites, and Kurds reside. The delegates voted against an invasion of Iraq, insisting that change must come from within rather than by decree of a superpower that has always placed its own interests ahead of those of the Iraqi people.

Similar sentiments can be found among Kurds in the Middle East. In Beirut, Lebanon, a Kurdish rights activist who helped defend PKK leader Abdullah Ocalan and who has been to Iraq at least five times in the past few years, tells me that the Kurdish people are not in agreement about the attack on Iraq. Many fear that a post-Saddam central government will strip them of their current autonomy, placing them once again under Baghdad's thumb. Kurdistan is today relishing in what many have called a "Golden Age"; the prospect of exchanging its new-found freedoms for Richard Perle's vision of a new Middle East is rather unappealing. Additionally, the Kurds remember the last time they challenged Saddam. On March 15, 1988, Iranian forces occupied the town of Halabja in northern Iraq. Kurdish leader Jalal Talabani, who is being courted by the current Bush administration, allied his faction with the fiercely anti-American Islamic Republic of Iran and provided armed Kurds to fight alongside the Iranian army. Saddam's government used the Iranian-Kurdish alliance to label the Kurds a fifth column fighting alongside Iraq's enemy during a time of war. The next morning, Iraqi Migs and Mirages dropped chemical weapons on Halabja, killing five thousand innocent Kurds. The bombing marked the beginning of the Anfal campaign, during which one hundred thousand Kurds were "disappeared" as four thousand Kurdish villages were razed to the ground.

Members of the current American administration cite the Halabja bombing as evidence that Saddam Hussein's Iraq belongs on the exclusive list of "evil" nations. Yet they conveniently ignore the American position at the time of the bombing. Saddam in 1988 was considered a pro-Western ruler who had brought modernity to his country while fighting the backward Islamic regime in Tehran. The progress of Saddam's chemical and biological programs was well known to his American supporters, as was his use of such weapons against Iran. After Saddam's air force used chemical weapons against the Kurds of Halabja, the United States worked hard to prevent the United Nations Sub-Committee on Human Rights from condemning Iraq (in a vote of eleven to eight, the sub-committee decided not to issue any condemnation). The U.S. administration at the time went on to veto a Congressional resolution urging sanctions against Iraq and even approved $1 billion worth of U.S. foreign aid to Iraq a mere six months after Halabja. On the long list of Middle Eastern dictators and human-rights violators, Saddam was "our S.O.B." It was only when he challenged American oil interests that he fell from grace and earned himself a spot within the so-called Axis of Evil.

Since last November, the Bush administration has been leveling charges against Iraq, preparing the American people for war against a third-world nation handcuffed by sanctions and regularly bombed by U.S. and British warplanes patrolling the no-fly-zones. The national discourse in this country over policy towards Iraq has been led by the right wing of American politics. Republican pundits from administrations past and present have debated the merits of an invasion to the backdrop of the Democratic Party's deafening silence. While the hawks dream of an oil-rich Jeffersonian democracy in Baghdad (and on the board of OPEC), the peaceniks have clamored to find their voice. Thus far, the anti-war position is revolving around questions of possible American casualties, an unwanted occupation of Baghdad, and the lack of allied support. While these are legitimate considerations, few among the cautious have attempted to make the case that we do not have a moral justification for launching an attack upon Iraq. Interestingly, the moral case was made most succinctly by House majority leader Dick Armey in an interview with journalist Jake Tapper: "I was trying to talk about who we are as a nation. I think we're somebody special. And we're not an aggressor. When somebody is compromising the freedom of somebody else on the globe—as was the case when Saddam Hussein had Iraq invade Kuwait—we ought to be there. But to attack just when we've got a fruitcake running around some country using it as a venue, I don't see a need."

Our European allies have been crying foul as the Bush administration has changed—unilaterally, of course—the definition of our "enemies" from those who kill Americans to those who use terrorism as a tactic to those who harbor terrorists and most recently to those who pursue weapons of mass destruction. With Osama bin Laden (remember him?) reportedly still alive and at the helm of Al Qaeda, President Bush is pursuing Iraq with an obsession so fervent that it must be called to question.

Republicans from past administrations have challenged George Bush on his unlikely claim that Iraq is an imminent threat that must be pre-empted. Few in number are the experts who believe that Iraq will launch a war against America in the near or distant future. Arguments that Iraq is a threat to regional stability have been lost on Middle Eastern leaders, the likely victims of any Iraqi chemical or biological aggression. From Jordan to Egypt to Saudi Arabia, our friends and allies in the Arab world see our own sprawling and indefinite war as a greater threat to their nations than the tattered Iraqi army. Even the Israeli army's Chief of Staff, General Moshe Yaalon dismissed the possibility of an Iraqi attack on Israel when, responding to a question about Iraq's chemical, biological, or nuclear capabilities, he said, "The Iraqi threat does not keep me awake at night. We are fully capable of defending ourselves ... [Iraq] does not constitute an existential threat to Israel."

Meanwhile, George Bush insists—in between golf strokes—that Saddam is "thumbing his nose" at the world, though nobody else in the world seems to see it that way. The international community is nervously watching as the major hegemonic power of the world cocks its fist and waits for the right moment to launch an unprovoked war against an impoverished third-world country. As our ally Israel continues its decades-old defiance of UN Resolution 487 calling for UN inspections of Israeli nuclear facilities, Republicans speak with authority about Iraq's outrageous refusal to abide by UN resolutions. Never mind that the resolution ending the Gulf War calls for regional, and not simply Iraqi, disarmament. Never mind that no nation would allow inspectors into its military facilities when it is on the verge of war with a Goliath state, especially when these inspectors have been used as spies in the past. In 1998, UN inspectors defied their mandate and handed over information on Iraq's conventional weapons facilities and presidential palaces to American officials, who proceeded to launch a military offensive against the Iraqi government using the information. As Operation Desert Fox began, the UN inspectors were evacuated voluntarily from the country in order to guarantee their safety during the bombing campaign. The Iraqi people, predictably, were not so fortunate. The American and British assault of 1998 killed hundreds of Iraqi civilians, although an early Pentagon estimate set the figure at ten thousand. In the aftermath of the devastating bombings, Iraqi protests that the UN inspectors had acted as spies fell on deaf ears, despite corroborating statements from several inspectors. Iraq retaliated by refusing to readmit the UN inspectors.

For his part, President Bush openly talks about the inherent evil of any nation possessing weapons of mass destruction, despite the fact that we and many of our allies possess large stockpiles of such weapons. Hawkish experts counter that if Saddam had biological or chemical weapons, he would definitely use them against our friends or allies. But in making such statements, they conveniently ignore history. It is important to remember that Saddam has never used weapons of mass destruction without tacit American approval, nor has the United States ever been the target of his aggression. While military experts disagree on his current capabilities, we know that at the start of the Gulf War he did in fact have extensive biological and chemical weapons programs. As the war proceeded, Saddam bombed Tel Aviv and Riyadh, occupied Kuwait City, torched miles of oil fields, and fought off allied forces, all with conventional weapons. He refrained from using his considerable stockpiles of chemical and biological weapons for one simple reason: American leaders made it clear to him that if he did use them, his entire regime would be removed from power. Saddam has never been deeply ideological. Like all dictators, he understands above all else how to stay in power. If it means the continuation of his regime, Saddam Hussein will avoid picking fights with trigger-happy cowboys. After all, does anyone truly believe that Iraq will attack us if we do not first attack Iraq? Even Madeleine Albright, hardly a pacifist, recently noted that the decade-long containment of Iraq and Saddam Hussein's ambitions has been successful. "Today, American and British planes enforce no-flight zones over 40 percent of [Saddam Hussein's] country and a maritime force prevents weapons from reaching Iraq by sea. Saddam Hussein's military is far weaker than it was a decade ago. And he must surely be aware that if he ever again tries to attack another country he will be obliterated." Indeed, the Iraqi army today is a shell of what it once was, unable to enter large parts of Iraq proper much less launch a world war. But even during the Gulf War, when Saddam's army was as strong as it had ever been, Iraqi soldiers regularly surrendered to European journalists and tv crews, mistaking them for the American army.

Nevertheless, bomb-dropping hawks continue to insist that Iraq is an imminent threat to America as flag-waving patriots have used Saddam's past brutality to claim our own moral superiority in this upcoming battle. Yet the post-war sanctions sustained with American pressure have resulted in death tolls so vast that they far outnumber any massacres committed by Saddam's forces. According to the United Nations, the sanctions have been responsible for the death of 1.5 million Iraqis. Conservative pundits argue that the deaths have been caused by the Iraqi government which has hoarded oil revenues. But it should be noted that the majority of these deaths came before the oil-for-food program allowed Iraq to sell oil on the worldwide market. Additionally, before the sanctions came into effect, the Iraqi people had one of the highest living standards in the third world and a medical infrastructure that was the envy of many developing nations. The post-war thwarting of Iraq has impacted children most severely: UNICEF estimates that 500,000 Iraqi children below the age of five have died as a result of restrictions placed by the sanctions.

In a 1996 interview with Madeleine Albright, *60 Minutes* reporter Lesley Stahl questioned the Secretary of State on sanctions against Iraq: "We have heard that a half million children have died. I mean, that's more children than died in Hiroshima. Is the price worth it?" Albright's response, in which she did not deny that these deaths were indeed caused by the sanctions, is still quoted in the Arab world as evidence of the true face of America: "I think this is a very hard choice, but the price — we think the price is worth it."

Today, American officials openly talk about a "war of liberation" for Iraq while defending Vladimir Putin's genocidal campaign in Chechnya and Ariel Sharon's brutal offensive in the West Bank. Although the fear of creating a double standard or the weight of our own history is not reason enough to oppose a war on Iraq, the precedent of unprovoked war is. While the Bush administration has pressured the United Nations and various allies into submission on the question of a stiffer policy towards Iraq, the Pentagon's war designs remain troubling. The *Christian Science Monitor* recently remarked that in "pressing his case against Iraqi leader Saddam Hussein, [George Bush] is asking the world to alter the founding principles of the post-World War II international order…. Mr. Bush is challenging United Nations rules on sovereignty and the acceptable use of force that have underpinned global relations for three generations." Echoing these concerns, a University of Virginia professor wrote for the *Washington Post*: "One common philosophical argument for democracy is that democratic regimes are particularly unlikely to start wars. Our nation now finds itself on the verge of initiating war against another sovereign nation. We have not been attacked by Iraq, and we have thus far failed to produce convincing evidence that Iraq has aided, or plans to aid, those who have attacked us. If we go to war, we will be the initiators of aggression." Dr. Talbot Brewer went on to warn that on the question of waging war, America may no longer function as a genuine democracy.

There is much more at stake in a U.S.-launched war against Iraq than the administration hawks would lead us to believe. Our moral compass as a nation must guide us through these difficult times to ensure that we remain true to our ideals, which have never been represented by the world-view of neo-conservatism. If we allow this President to challenge sovereign nations and foreign governments at will, we will have made him the moral arbiter of the world. Given such a mandate, George Bush — with sword, pistol, and Franklin Graham at his side — would launch America into a war the consequences of which may not be felt for decades.

FRIENDS DISUNITED

Michael Ignatieff

As I write this, in safety half a world away, oil fields blaze in southern Iraq, tanks race through the desert towards Baghdad and the first bodies are returning home for burial. It is a moment that confirms the worst fears of those who opposed the war, and encourages those who support the war to pray for a swift victory.

In ordering troops to cross the Iraqi border, President Bush and Tony Blair have themselves crossed into the dark and unfamiliar terrain of the new world order created by 9/11, while their former allies and friends remain on the other side, wishing they could still live in the safety and collective security of the world that existed before 9/11. In that now vanished world of the 1990s, Saddam Hussein pretended to disarm, and countries such as France, Russia and China were happy to pretend to inspect.

In the world after 9/11, suddenly this pretence is no longer good enough. As long as there was as much as a 1% chance that rogue states would transfer chemical, biological and nuclear weapons to suicide bombers, Britain and the United States knew where their national interests lay, and they did not lie in deferring to the reluctance of their allies at the United Nations.

Now that combat has commenced, those, like me, who support the war need to be honest enough to address some painful questions.

Who wants to live in a world where there are no stable rules for the use of force by states? Not me. Who wants to live in a world ruled by the military power of the strong? Not me. How will we oblige American military hegemony to pay "decent respect to the opinions of mankind"? I don't know. When the smoke of battle lifts, those who support the war will survey a battle zone that will include the ruins of the multilateral political order created in 1945.

To support the war entails a commitment to rebuild that order on new foundations. To support the war entails other discomforts as well. It means remaining distinct from the company you keep, supporting a swift and decisive victory, while maintaining your distance from the hawks, the triumphalists, the bellowing commentators who mistake machismo for maturity.

Back in the 60s, when I marched against the war in Vietnam, I learned that it is a mistake to judge a cause by the company it makes you keep. I slogged through the streets with Trotskyites who thought America was an evil empire, and I stood arm in arm with pacifists who made me wonder whether they would have fought Hitler. Since I was anti-communist, I actually had more in common with the liberal hawks who thought they were defending south Vietnam against advancing communist tyranny. But I believed that nothing could save the weak and corrupt south Vietnamese government.

This time over Iraq, I don't like the company I am keeping, but I think they are right on the issue. I much prefer the company on the other side, but I believe they are mistaken.

I don't like President Bush's domestic policies. He should be helping state and local government maintain jobs and services, especially for the poor. His attack on affirmative action turns back decades of racial progress. The tax breaks for the rich are unjust. His deficits are mortgaging the future.

It is wrong to deny all rights of due process to the so-called illegal combatants on Guantanamo and the military brigs. The president's attorney-general is dangerously cavalier about the civil liberties he is supposed to protect. The bullying tone the president adopted in his diplomacy at the UN made it difficult to secure UN support. But I still think that Bush is right when he says Iraq would be better off if Saddam were disarmed and, if necessary, replaced by force.

It is worth remembering that Blair has similar difficulties with the company he is keeping. He disagrees with the president on the global environment, and his third-way politics are about as far from Texas conservatism as the distance, right now, between Washington and Paris. But he understands that the choice is not about the company you keep, but between alienating old, but essentially pacifist, friends and appeasing a tyrant.

A lot of my friends think that supporting Bush on this issue is naive. The company you keep, they argue, matters in politics. If you can't trust him on other issues, you have no reason to trust him on this one. If he is so cavalier about freedom at home, what makes you believe that he will say what he means about staying the course to create freedom in Iraq?

My friends also imply that the company I am keeping in this war is a definition of what kind of person I am. So where we all stand has become a litmus test of our moral identities. But this shouldn't be the case. Opposing the war doesn't make you an anti-globalist, an anti-semite or an anti-American, any more than supporting the war makes you an apologist for American imperialism. In fact in moral terms the war is not a clash of competing moral identities, but rather a battle within each of us to balance competing ethical claims. Sometimes it's easier to see this in the positions of the other side than in your own.

Recently, 14,000 "writers, academics and other intellectuals" — many of them friends of mine — published a petition against the war, while condemning the Iraqi regime for its human rights violations and supporting "efforts by the Iraqi opposition to create a democratic, multi-ethnic and multi-religious Iraq." But since they say that "the decision to go to war at this time is morally unacceptable," I wonder what their support amounts to. Their balancing act amounts to a pat on the head to Kanan Makiya and all the Iraqis risking their lives to create a decent society. They don't want a pat on the head. What they want is a rapid and decisive American victory.

The problem is not that overthrowing Saddam by force is "morally unjustified." Who seriously believes that 25 million Iraqis would not be better off if Saddam were overthrown?

The issue is whether it is prudent to do so, whether the risks are worth running.

Evaluating risks is not the same as making moral choices. It is impossible to be certain that improving the human rights of 25 million people is worth the cost, because no one knows what the cost will be. Besides, even if they could be known — what the philosophers call "consequential" justifications — that 25 million people will live better runs smack against "deontological" objections, namely that good consequences cannot justify killing people. I think the consequential justifications can override the deontological ones, but only if the gains in human freedom are large and the human costs are low. But let us admit it, the risks are large: the war may be bloody, the peace may be chaotic, and what might be good, in the long term, for Iraqis might not be so good for UK and US security. Success in Iraq might win America friends, or it might increase the anger of the Muslim world.

It would be great if moral certainty made risk assessment easier, but it doesn't actually do so. What may be desirable from a moral point of view may be so risky that we would be foolish to try. So what do we do? Isaiah Berlin used to say that we just have to "plump" for one option or the other in the absence of moral certainty or perfect knowledge of the future. I have plumped and many of my friends have plumped otherwise, but I do know this: we should also try to decide for ourselves, regardless of the company we keep.

During Vietnam, I marched with people who thought America was the incarnation of imperial wickedness, and I marched against people who thought America was the last best hope of mankind. Both positions seemed hopelessly ideological, and at the same time, narcissistic. The issue was not fundamentally about our souls; it was about what was right for the people of Vietnam. Just as in Vietnam, the debate over Iraq has become a referendum on American power, and what you think about Saddam seems to matter much less than what you think about America.

But the fact is that America is neither the redeemer nation, nor the evil empire. It isn't always right, but it isn't always wrong. Ideology cannot help us here. In the weeks and years ahead, the choices are not about who we are or what company we should keep nor even about what we think America is or should be. They are about what risks are worth running, when our safety depends on the answer, and when the freedom of 25 million people hangs in the balance.

THE LOGIC OF WAR

Trudy Govier

In this paper, I first consider some lines of argument that are demonstrably fallacious or incorrect and are used to support war; I next consider the 2003 invasion of Iraq by the United States and the United Kingdom within the framework of Just War Theory.

A. Arguments for War: a Logical Analysis

It may seem surprising, but it's true: bad logic is a cause of violence. What I mean by this is that some standard arguments people appeal to when they attempt to justify war are based on bad logic. Not only do leaders and pundits use and repeat bad arguments when seeking to justify war and other forms of political violence to the public, members of the public often accept such discourse uncritically, reproducing the fallacies with fatal effect. The idea that logic contributes to war may seem implausible when we consider some of the other factors such as competition for power, greed, domination, racism, social inequality, fear, humiliation, resentment, and the desire for revenge. Religious and ideological difference matter a lot. But so do arguments and patterns of thinking.

Bad arguments and careless logic can be found in many places, concerning many subjects — including, it must be admitted, the rhetoric of opponents of war. The point here is not that fallacies and careless arguments are unique to the topic of violence. Rather it is that because of the extraordinary damage and suffering war implies, our arguments on that topic merit an especially careful and rigorous scrutiny.

False Analogies

To list all the errors of reasoning connected with our thinking about violence is not possible, but one type of reasoning that merits special attention is arguments from analogy. Arguments from historical analogy are often shockingly weak. The all-time rhetorical favorite strategy is to enlist the assistance of Hitler, who is brought in and compared to some contemporary demonized leader. 'Appeasement' as practiced by British Prime Minister Chamberlain when he visited Hitler in 1938 was later judged to be a serious and immoral mistake. On this basis, 'appeasement' has come to have a very bad name indeed, and people often evoke Chamberlain's approach to argue against diplomacy and in favour of war. Because war was needed to defeat Hitler, they claim that we also need war in some present case. Saddam Hussein was compared to Hitler in 1991 and again in 2003, and Slobodan Milosevic was compared to Hitler in 1999. During the Cold War, Hitler was often cited in arguments against arms control agreements between NATO and the Warsaw Pact. Pretty well everybody agrees about Hitler and the need for a war against him, so critics of contemporary militarism can be made to look naïve and or even wicked if they can be portrayed as equivalent to defenders of the 'appeasement' of 1939. A moment's thought should suffice to show that such references amount to propaganda as distinct from serious analysis. Hitler's military forces and territorial strength vastly exceeded those of Saddam Hussein and Slobodan Milosevic, and the Soviet Union never had the genocidal goals of Nazi Germany.

All too often, a complex situation of the past is summed up in a kind of 'nutshell' description, telling us what lesson 'history' supposedly *taught* in that case.[1] Then, on the cavalier assumption that the present situation resembles the selected case from the past, the supposed lesson is applied to the present problem. It was often argued, based on the bombings of Serbia/Kosovo by NATO forces in the spring of 1999 and Afghanistan by the United States and Britain in the fall of 2001, that bombing Iraq would suffice to defeat the Saddam Hussein regime and bring positive change. These nutshell analogies presuppose that the Kosovo and Afghanistan campaigns were successful and cite them as precedents to support aerial attacks on Iraq.

Tony Blair cited Kosovo and Afghanistan when he argued that Britain should assist in 'regime change' in Iraq.

> Remember Kosovo where we were told war would de-stabilize the whole of the Balkans and that region now has the best chance of peace in over 100 years?
> Remember Afghanistan, where now, despite all the huge problems, there are three million children in school, including for the first time in two decades one and a half million girls and where two million Afghan exiles from the Taliban have now returned.[2]

Both in the case of Serbia/Kosovo and in the case of Afghanistan, the nutshell summary of 'success' is incorrect. The situation for human rights in Kosovo after the 1999 war has been deplorable: over 50,000 international personnel are involved in running the territory; there are numerous acrimonious disagreements between Kosovo Albanians and peacekeeping personnel and there have been thousands of revenge attacks. Several years after the (supposed) success of this campaign, the Canadian Department of Foreign Affairs and International Trade was still warning Canadian citizens not to travel in the area because it was too dangerous.[3]

As for Afghanistan, at the time of writing (May, 2003), some sixteen months after the defeat of the Taliban regime and the much-advertised establishment of law and democracy in that country, warlordism, corruption, and chaos prevail outside the capital city of Kabul. In some village areas, families who send their daughters to school are threatened with punishment by death. Many of the promised funds for reconstruction have not been provided by the international community. Taliban and al-Qaeda forces are continuing to stage destructive guerrilla attacks, the Karzi government survives only with considerable protection from international forces, and, due to opposition by the United States, there are no peacekeeping personnel outside the Kabul area. As with Kosovo, it is a gross misstatement to say that bombing *succeeded* in this case. The nutshell premises on which analogy arguments from Kosovo and Afghanistan are erected to support further campaigns are simply false. Moreover, the similarities between Iraq and these other places is superficial at best. Even if it were true that bombing had 'worked' against Serbia and Taliban Afghanistan, that wouldn't support a prediction that it would 'work' against the solidly entrenched and resource-rich regime of Saddam Hussein. These analogies fall apart the minute they are subjected to serious scrutiny.

False Dichotomies

False Dichotomies are characteristic of much thinking about violence and war. A dichotomy is a binary opposition of the form A or B — the assumption being that A and B are the only possibilities. Such a dichotomy is a false one when A and B are not the only possibilities. The error will be familiar to many. We so easily make opposition into exclusive alternatives. We think in false dichotomies whenever we assume that what is not good is bad; he who does not succeed is a failure, and so on. Obviously, many people and many things are neither successful nor failures, but something in between. The same can be said of 'fat' and 'thin' and 'friend' and 'enemy.' Your friend is not your enemy and your enemy is not your friend — but there is a whole middle range of people who are neither your friend nor your enemy. To believe otherwise is to engage in paranoiac thinking. This is a route to insanity.[4] When we think in false dichotomies of *either/ors*, we over-simplify and fail to remember the *neither/nors* — instances of ambiguity, complexity, indeterminacy that for various reasons fall in the middle of the spectrum we have severed into two poles.

President George W. Bush's statement, shortly after the attacks of September 11, 2001, that "you are either with us or with the terrorists" provides a classic example of a false dichotomy. It was a rhetorical attempt to structure the world into Good and Evil, leaving honest intellectuals and sceptics no place to stand. The idea that the Bad Guys are worse than Bad, being, in fact, Evil, and even, according to the rhetoric, members of an Axis of Evil, supports an especially insidious polarization between the Good Side and the Evil Others. The term 'evil' is so strong that we are highly unlikely to accept that it has any application to ourselves and our own side. ('I might have a fault or two, I might have done some bad things on occasion, I might have a few flaws of character, sure; but I would never actually be *evil* — and the same is true for my group and my nation.') The rhetoric of the Bush administration structures for its audience a dangerously distorted picture of a world polarized between good and evil. Stark and exaggerated dichotomies of good and evil, friend and enemy, polarize reality and paralyze thought.[5] Defense analyst Gwynne Dyer explained North Korea's nuclear threats in 2002-2003 in just this way, alleging that they were the result of that country's shocked anger at suddenly being described as a member of an "axis of evil."[6]

In contexts of action and policy, false dichotomies take the form of failing to consider alternatives. They pose to us false dilemmas, supporting war and violence because we assume that we face a stark choice between a *violent* response and doing *nothing* at all. 'Well what *are* you going to do? Just sit there?,' people often ask. They treat the question as purely rhetorical on the assumption that the critics of violence can provide no answer. The underlying assumption is that if we refuse to resort to violence, we can do nothing at all. This assumption represents a false dichotomy because alternatives do exist. In the particular context of the 2003 war against Iraq, the dichotomy of '*war or nothing*' or '*war or prop up a dictator who will endanger the world*' neglected such alternatives as the prolonged and intrusive presence of international inspectors in Iraq, the exiling of Saddam Hussein from his country, or the strengthening of the Iraqi people to the point where a nonviolent social revolution would have become possible.

Our Side Bias

Making an exception of your own case — describing yourself in more flattering terms than you would apply to relevantly similar others, or judging yourself by standards less strict than those you would apply to others — amounts to mistaken logic as well as mistaken ethics. Such self-favouring constitutes a *bias* towards your own side. Feminists used to satirize bias against women by pointing out the differential emotional implications of certain words used, characteristically, to describe men and women. While men who spoke up in meetings were *assertive* (a pro word), women who did the same were *aggressive* (for women, a con word).[7] In the politics and rhetoric of violence, our side resorts to just war in a good cause, while the other side are violent aggressors or terrorists.

So far as war and violence are concerned, the devastation wrought by violence seems painfully clear when we feel it on *Our* Side, but is, for many people, far less obvious when we impose it on *Them*. The 3000 deaths from the terrorist attacks on the United States on September 11, 2001 were deplorable and understood and publicized as such, while casualties in foreign wars receive far less attention in most western media.

In the use of such terms as 'just cause,' 'war,' 'troops,' 'terrorists,' 'revolutionaries,' and 'freedom fighters' double standards abound. In much of the Arab world, those we call 'suicide bombers' do not commit suicide. Suicide is deemed to be wrong in Islam, and these people do no wrong, because they are heroes. Those we castigate as suicide bombers are, for many in the Arab world, martyrs. To many in the West, a double standard would be apparent here, in the way the pejorative and honorific terms are applied. However, we tend to find it much harder to identify our own double standards, for example the view that bombing by a *state*, even with resultant deaths of innocent civilians, may count as a rightful, even heroic, action in a just war, whereas, by contrast, explosive attacks by *non-state agents* who kill innocent civilians are deemed deplorable and merit the harsh epithet, 'terrorism.'

The case of weapons of mass destruction in Iraq provides an even more powerful example. Between the fall of 2002 and the American invasion of Iraq in March, 2003, there was an enormous amount of publicity and public debate about weapons of mass destruction in Iraq. Yet virtually *nothing* was said about the possession of such weapons by Iraq's accusers: the United States and Britain. Clearly, it would be dangerous and seriously wrong for a nation to use weapons of mass destruction. Any nation could at some point have leaders who could make risky and unwise decisions in times of conflict. Thus it is dangerous for *any* nation to possess weapons of mass destruction. Concern about weapons of mass destruction supports arguments for generalized disarmament. To suppose that Iraqi or Arab weapons of mass destruction are dangerous and must be destroyed, while weapons of mass destruction in the hands of such countries as the United States are safe and serve to deter aggression amounts to an appalling instance of Our Side Bias.[8] The gross selectivity implicit in such thinking is plainly inadequate — logically, ethically, politically, and legally.

The problem of ridding the world of weapons of mass destruction is a general problem and it is enormous and profound. This problem does not concern only the weapons of countries identified by the George W. Bush administration as being located on some axis of evil. Nor is it a problem that can be solved by pitting the Good Guys against the Bad Guys in a battle to the death. It is a hugely complex *political* problem requiring a negotiated and closely administered solution.

The John Wayne Fallacy[9]

A major problem with our thinking about violence is the highly unrealistic nature of our expectations about what it can accomplish. Among the many sources of unreflective thinking in this area is the fact that our expectations arise from fictional narrative more than from real experience. We have unrealistic expectations that the 'story' will simply end because stories do end. Because of these expectations, we expect an ending in real life, and we expect violence to be a means that will provide it. In western movies, for instance, plots are structured around competition between the Good Guys and the Bad Guys. The Bad Guys have caused a problem and the Good Guys solve it by winning a physical victory over them in a violent struggle. This victory will be certain when they eliminate the Bad Guys, which they will do by killing them off. The clear victory of the Good Guys provides a satisfying ending. In a typical final scene, the Good Guy, in the person of John Wayne or some other stereotypically heroic type, stands victorious, holding his rifle at his side. Or he strides triumphantly off into a pink and orange sunset, the implication being that he has solved the problem by killing off the Evil Ones and leaves a better world behind him. The narrative ends at the point of victory, when the conquering hero has supposedly made his world happy and safe.

In real life — as distinct from the movies — there are serious after-effects when physical violence is used. War, terrorism, and violent revolution are notoriously painful in appalling ways. People are killed and injured, usually in strikingly large numbers, and many suffer terribly. The resentment and hatred in survivors propels quests for retaliation and revenge; thus violence has a decided tendency to provoke more of itself. Power struggles emerge. Charismatic ideologues may come to the fore. Needed facilities for water, sewage, and power generation are disrupted, with the result that thousands of people lack necessities of modern life. Physical and cultural environments are seriously damaged. Economies are shattered. The people who live through all this are real human beings, not characters on a screen.

John Wayne and the other heroes of violent drama never have to clean up after the struggle. Movies never show these people removing debris, treating the sick and injured, rebuilding hospitals, schools, highways, and bridges, restoring power lines and factories, struggling to contain looting and smashing, trying to get prosthetic limbs for small children who have lost arms and legs in bombing campaigns, negotiating desperately with discredited police from the other side, or trying to reconcile hostile people so that coexistence becomes possible. In fiction, violence marks the end and the solution, but in the real world, it is not like that. Forgetting about the aftermath might be all right for a movie script, but it's painfully inadequate as the resolution to a serious political conflict. Just a little common sense should tell us that killing and generalized, authorized mayhem will produce an awful mess in physical and human terms.

George W. Bush made token reference to the situation of the people of Iraq, but comments before the war indicate that he did not fully appreciate the anarchy and devastation that would follow in the wake of war.

Some worry that a change of leadership in Iraq could create instability and make the situation worse. The situation could hardly get worse, for world security and for the people of Iraq. The lives of Iraqi citizens would improve dramatically if Saddam Hussein were no longer in power. . . Freed from the weight of oppression, Iraq's people will be able to share in the progress and prosperity of our time. If military action is necessary, the United States and our allies will help the Iraqi people rebuild their economy, and create the institutions of liberty in a unified Iraq at peace with its neighbors.[10]

Here, the U.S. President did at least allude to the situation of post-war Iraq, but he skirts over enormous difficulties, appearing to believe that once oppression is lifted (by a military victory), progress would follow easily. Al Gore was among many who expressed doubts about any rebuilding of Iraq under American leadership, noting that it was official Bush doctrine that the U.S. should not be involved in nation-building. Gore urged that military intervention would impose responsibilities for involvement in reconstruction of the country.

If we go in there and dismantle them — and they deserve to be dismantled — but then we wash our hands of it and walk away and leave it in a situation of chaos, and say, "That's for y-all to decide how to put things back together now," that hurts us.[11]

Justifications for Violence

In their most general form, arguments to justify violence have a fairly simple structure. First, there is a just or morally defensible goal that we must reach by some means or other. Second, by using physical violence as a means, we can arrive at that goal. Third, no other means will get us there. From these premises, we arrive at the conclusion that physical violence is justified 'as a last resort.'

We can set out such a line of argument as follows.

P1 — Our goal, G, is just.
P2 — We can achieve G by using a violent means, V.
P3 — We cannot achieve G by any means other than V.

Therefore,

C — We are justified in using V to achieve G.

Now there is nothing *fallacious* in principle about arguments of this general type. They need not involve any erroneous *reasoning* in moving from the premises to the conclusion. Rather, the problem is that careless and self-indulgent thinking is far too often involved in our acceptance of the three premises.

Often, motives are mixed and goals are confused and we accept such a premise as P1 with far too little self-criticism and even, sometimes, with a failure to clearly articulate what our goal, G, is.[12] (P1, in effect, states what is called the '*Just Cause*' condition in Just War Theory.) "Our Side Bias" tends to make us indulgent in judging our own goals. The second problem comes with P2. This is where the John Wayne fallacy enters the picture and discourages us from thinking realistically about what the effects of the resort to violence are likely to be. By applying bombs to a bad situation, there is a very significant likelihood of making it worse. (These considerations, applied to P2, incorporate at least two other conditions in Just War

Theory: those of *Proportionate Harm* and *Likelihood of Emergent Peace*.) Now, we arrive at P3. (This premise is captured in Just War Theory in the condition, *Exhaustion of Alternatives*.) Premises of this sort get much of their plausibility from the falsely dichotomous assumption that there is no alternative to violence as a means of reaching our goal.

There is no need to go the route of absolute pacifism to criticize most arguments purporting to justify wars. Judicious *skepticism* will take us a long way in the same direction.

B. Just War Theory and the Attack on Iraq in 2003

Just War Theory and Its Two Main Rivals

The ethical perspective of Just War Theory can best be understood by contrasting it with two other influential perspectives on war and peace: those of Pacifism, and *realpolitik*. (The latter is known as Realism in international relations theory). Pacifists oppose all war. Just War theorists distinguish between morally permissible (just) wars and morally impermissible (unjust) wars. Realists disallow evaluations of war by moral standards and urge that war can be supported when, and only when, it is in the national interest of the state that has recourse to it.

Pacifism is the view that war, institutionalized large-scale violence as a response to conflicts about the locus of political power, is never morally justified. Just War Theory originally developed as a departure from early Christian pacifism, expressed in the teachings of Jesus as portrayed in the New Testament. It was a concession Christianity made to state power when the religion became established as a state religion as distinct from a religion held by a minority sect.

Pacifists contend that Just War Theory fails to address the fundamental moral problem of war which is that, because of what war is, it necessarily involves the deliberate wounding and destruction of human bodies in the pursuit of political goals. Just War Theory seeks to provide criteria for judging which wars are morally legitimate and which are not. Pacifists regard Just War Theory as ill-founded because they deny that any war could be just. For a pacifist, the idea of a just war fails to acknowledge the depth of the fundamental moral problem of war, which is that it requires the deliberate killing of large numbers of people in the pursuit of political goals. [13]

Realists, on the other hand regard pacifism as ill-founded because they think that moral standards do not apply to such topics as war in which power politics dominate all other considerations.

Realism is the view of a significant school in the field of international relations. Realist scholars observe the real relations of states and conclude that morality has little bearing on them. Some analysts believe that idealistic goals (as pursued, for instance, by Woodrow Wilson after the first world war) are unrealistic and dangerous for relationships between states. Moral pretensions can lead to crusades and naivete; they can also betray national interests, which are the true guide to the conduct of relationships between states. For this and other reasons, Realists argue that morality should be kept out of international relations. According to Realists, moral judgments are the stuff of philosophers and theologians. They belong in the classroom and the pulpit, not Cabinet chambers or on the battlefield.

Few philosophers are sympathetic to Realism. The exemption of a substantial area of human life from ethical scrutiny and evaluation seems not only logically arbitrary, but untrue to the social realities of colloquial and academic talk about international relations, in which such ethically substantial terms as 'human rights,' 'dictator,' 'refugee,' and 'transgression' are used with great frequency. [14]

A Short Version of Just War Theory

To qualify as a just war, a war must satisfy ALL of the following conditions: [15]

1. *Just Cause*. The war must be fought for a just cause. The most obvious just cause is self-defence, but there are others; going to the defence of an ally who had been attacked would commonly be regarded as a just cause.
2. *Legitimate Authority*. The war must be declared by a competent legitimate political authority. That is to say, the authorized legal government of the state, collectively or through its authorized representative, must make the decision to go to war. (The word 'competent' in this context should not be taken to mean knowledgeable or wise but rather to refer to the legitimacy of the government as authorized by its people and recognized within the international community and to its capacity to exercise control and maintain order within its assigned and recognized territory.)
3. *Exhaustion of Alternatives*. The war must be undertaken as a last resort in the sense that all the nonviolent alternatives to resolve the conflict in question and pursue the Just Cause must have been exhausted so that war is truly the last resort.
4. *Rightful Intentions*. The nation must enter the war with "rightful intentions" in the sense that its intentions must be properly related to its just cause and must remain within those bounds. If a cause is deemed just, but the state in question is pursuing several other, questionable, goals at the same time, the war loses its claim to be just.
5. *Likelihood of Emergent Peace*. There must be a reasonable likelihood that the outcome of the war will be successful. This condition is sometimes narrowly interpreted as victory for the side with the just cause. However, one may argue for broader interpretations, according to which success in a war requires not only military victory for the 'right' side but, in addition, the establishment of a viable peace in the aftermath of the war. The broader interpretation seems reasonable: after all, if a war leaves in its wake all the makings for further wars, winning it does not constitute any kind of sustainable success.[16]
6. *Proportionate Harm*. The total harm that is likely to result from the war must be less than the benefit that is likely to result if the war is successfully conducted and brought to a conclusion. When entering into the war, it must be reasonable to predict that one can achieve a result that is better overall than the result of not going to war.
7. *Discrimination*.[17] A distinction between combatants and civilians must be maintained in the conduct of the war. A fundamental presumption of Just War Theory is that enemy combatants are non-innocent because they are threats to those fighting for a just cause, whereas enemy civilians are innocent (they do not constitute such a threat). In conducting a just war one is entitled to intentionally kill enemy combatants but one is not (with some exceptions) entitled to intentionally kill civilian persons. The exception is that sometimes civilians will unavoidably, even foreseeably, be killed as a corollary of attacks on military targets. Such deaths should be minimized. They are often referred to, on the presupposition of this sort of framework, as *collateral damage*.
8. *Proportionate Means*. Within the war, a principle of proportional harm (or evil) to benefit (or good) must be observed for every specific tactic and campaign.

The first six of these conditions have to do with resorting to war; these are called conditions of *jus ad bellum*. The next two conditions have to do with the way the war is conducted; these are called conditions of *jus in bello*. In principle, the justice of going to war in the first place is separable from the justice of how the war is conducted. For example, a war could be waged for a just cause and yet fail to sufficiently observe the distinction between combatant and civilian personnel.

Just War Theory and the Attack on Iraq in 2003

So far as Just War Theory is concerned, there is an interesting rhetorical contrast between the March 2003 attack and the Gulf War of 1991. In 1991, the notion of a *just war* was frequently appealed to by George Bush; Iraq had aggressively attacked Kuwait with the intent of annexing it and was an unjust aggressor; thus the liberation of Kuwait seemed to clearly satisfy the *Just Cause* condition. In 2003, however, the rhetoric of *just war* was not common. The appeal was made, rather to weapons of mass destruction in Iraq and alleged links between Iraq and terrorism. Nevertheless, it is relevant to assess the 2003 war from the perspective of Just War Theory, because, in Western thinking, that theory represents a prominent consensus about the legitimacy of war. [18]

At time of writing, there is not sufficient knowledge to apply all of the conditions of Just War Theory in this context. With regard to several of them — including the extremely important condition of *Discrimination* — one can only reserve judgment. Nevertheless, there are some truly alarming reports.

Writing for the British paper, *The Independent*, John Pilger quoted Red Cross doctors describing "incredible" levels of civilian casualties. Pilger believed that Western observers were callous about the suffering of the Iraqi people. He said:

> Imagine: what did Commander Andrew McKendrick's 30 missiles hit? How many did they kill or maim in a population nearly half of which are children? . . . perhaps each of your missiles had a sensory device that could distinguish George Bush's evil-doers from toddlers. What is certain is that your targets did not include the Ministry of Oil. [19]

Pilger claimed that what Bush and Blair described as liberation was no such thing: it was "bloody conquest".

Writing for the *Boston Globe* early in April, 2003, Elizabeth Neuffer reported that up to 100 casualties per hour were arriving in Baghdad hospitals during the bombing campaign and that far more Iraqi deaths were expected as ground fighting came to that city. She quoted defence analyst William M. Arkin as warning that the civilian casualties would "reverberate loudly" once the war was over. [20] A Reuters story by Samia Nakhoul described the "daily horror" of civilian casualties during the war:

> At the Kindi hospital, staff were overwhelmed by the sharp rise in casualties since U.S. ground troops moved north to Baghdad on Thursday and intensified their aerial assault. Ambulance after ambulance raced in with casualties from around the capital. Victim after victim was rushed in, many carried in bed sheets after the stretchers ran out. Doctors struggled to find them beds. Staff had no time even to clean the blood from trolleys. Patients' screams and parents' cries echoed across the ward... . "During the bombardment, hospitals received up to 100 casualties per hour," ICRC spokesman Roland Huguenin-Benjamin told Reuters on Sunday. [21]

When this essay was written in May, 2003, there were no reliable estimates of total casualties. [22] Nor was it possible to know the medium or long-term consequences of the unseating of Saddam Hussein's regime. Thus it was not possible to make a reasonable judgment about whether the conditions of *Proportionate Harm* and *Proportionate Means* were satisfied.

Nevertheless, we need not remain agnostic about the issue of what Just War Theory would say about this particular war. To qualify as just, a war must satisfy *all* the conditions of the theory. The *Just Cause* condition has claim to be more fundamental than others, both from a commonsense point of view and because, in the logic of Just War Theory, it is presupposed by several others. If there is no just cause, there is no room for considering whether alternative ways of getting to one's just goal have been exhausted. Nor is there any point in applying the *Rightful Intentions* condition. The condition of *Proportionate Harm* will be similarly inapplicable.

Thus a fundamental question is whether the United States, the United Kingdom, and their coalition partners had a *just cause*. Even posing the question reveals an immediate problem, because it is so unclear what their motivation was. For several months prior to the war, the most prominent public goal was ridding the world of the *weapons of mass destruction* possessed by Iraq under the regime of Saddam Hussein. This professed goal received a vast amount of attention until just before the war. But the problem with Iraq's weapons of mass destruction as a just cause for the war is that U.N. inspectors under the auspices of the Security Council of the United Nations had found no such weapons in Iraq. Many were not impressed by the insistence of President George W. Bush and Prime Minister Tony Blair that these *weapons must exist, though they had not been discovered* and that the Iraqis had failed to reveal weapons '*known*' to exist in a context in which accredited inspectors implementing intrusive monitoring techniques over a prolonged period simply could not find them. These doubts were borne out when U.S. and U.K. troops failed to find the alleged weapons during or after the war.

A second 'justifying' cause may be found in the notion of pre-emptive security. This concept was officially endorsed by the United States in a government policy statement of September, 2002. The statement was an attempt to legitimize self-defence even for cases in which an attack was neither in progress or imminent. For both Just War Theory and international law, a nation is deemed to have a right to defend itself if it is *actually attacked*. It is also deemed to have such a right in the context of an *imminent* attack. The desire to extend the right so as to allow pre-emptive self-defence against *possible* attacks was inspired by the traumatic surprise attacks of September 11, 2001. The idea is that a prospective enemy in the form of a 'rogue state' or 'evil state' could be in a position to do terrible damage to the United States and such a risk had to be eliminated before it materialized in the form of an actual or imminent attack.

If Fred punches Joe, he is attacking him and Joe is entitled to defend himself. If Fred stands near Joe and waves a baseball bat close to Joe's head, while verbally threatening him, Joe may reasonably judge that an attack from Fred is imminent. Assuming its imminence, he is entitled to defend himself before Joe's attack is fully underway. But suppose that Fred is several miles away from Joe and Joe has heard rumours to the effect that Fred doesn't like him and is buying a gun. Feeling threatened, Joe decides that he needs to attack Fred first in order to protect himself. This is pre-emptive security.

The Iraq of Saddam Hussein was regarded as an enemy of the United States and it was believed that Iraq had, or could have, weapons of mass destruction, which it might someday use to attack the United States. Thus, based on its doctrine of pre-emptive self-defence, the

United States asserted the right to attack Iraq in its own security interests, as broadly defined by the doctrine of pre-emption. Former U.S. Vice President Al Gore noted some of the deep problems with this doctrine.

> Now we have seen the assertion of a brand new doctrine called "preemption," based on the idea that . . . the United States cannot wait for proof of a fully established mortal threat, but should rather act at any point to cut that short. The problem with preemption is that in the first instance it is not needed . . . But that is a relatively minor issue compared to the longer-term consequences that I think can be foreseen for this doctrine. To begin with, the doctrine is presented in open-ended terms, which means that if Iraq is the first point of application, it is not necessarily the last. In fact, the very logic of the concept suggests a string of military engagements against a succession of sovereign states: Syria, Libya, North Korea, Iran . . . (T)he implication is that wherever the combination exists of an interest in weapons of mass destruction together with an ongoing role as host to or participant in terrorist operations, the doctrine will apply ... (I)f the Congress approves the Iraq resolution just proposed by the administration, it would be simultaneously creating the precedent for preemptive action anywhere, anytime this or any future president as a single individual, albeit head of state, decides that it is time.[23]

A highly significant problem with pre-emptive self-defence as an authorization to resort to military force is that it is clearly *not* universalizable. Gore noted this point.

> If other nations assert that same right, then the rule of law will quickly be replaced by the reign of fear. Any nation that perceives circumstances that could eventually lead to an imminent threat would be justified under this approach in taking military action against another nation.[24]

The pre-emptive security approach will only be tenable if it is not generalized. Thus its plausibility depends absolutely on Our Side Bias. The name for this kind of approach is *unilateralism*. Given the interdependence of the people and nations, unilateralism is not a tenable doctrine. If all states claimed the right to use military force in the quest for pre-emptively defined security, the result would be anarchy and mayhem. For one state in particular to claim that right only for itself is clearly not acceptable. Logically and ethically, it cannot be justified. Politically, it is unlikely to win allies and friends. And legally it is too partial to be compatible with the rule of law.

John Currie, who teaches international law at the University of Ottawa, said:

> Right now, the U.N. Charter bans war unless it's authorized by the Security Council. Or, it says, "if an armed attack occurs," a state can act in self-defence. Over time, these words have been interpreted to allow action against "an imminent attack". Now, if Bush gets his way, that would expand to allow for "a pre-emptive attack." . . . The U.S. and its allies have acted by claiming all sorts of unprecedented justifications in international law.[25]

No just cause is to be found in the notion of pre-emptive self-defence.

Linked to this second 'justifying' cause was the claim that Saddam Hussein's government was in some way connected to Osama bin Laden and al-Qaeda. Though alleged by both Bush and Blair, that link was never supported by good evidence and was deemed to be highly tenuous, even by some observers close to the U.S. administration.

The notion of 'regime change' was also prominent in public discussions before the war. The regime of Saddam Hussein was brutal. It was characterized by appalling suppression, torture, gruesome underground prisons, a prison especially for children, abduction, and disappearances for even extremely minor 'offences.' It was argued that such a regime clearly needed to be changed, and the attack was justified in order to do so. There were many variants of the argument. Some emphasized the danger of Saddam Hussein to the world at large or to the United States in particular. Others argued that the regime needed to be changed because his neighbours were at risk. Others stressed the damage to the people of Iraq. Given the weakness of Iraq by 2003, the most plausible argument for regime change would be this last one. Realistically, at that time there was little danger of an impoverished, weakened, and largely disarmed Iraq attacking the United States or any other country.

The most plausible argument for a just cause in the case of this war would begin with the claim that regime change was necessary in order to liberate the Iraqi people from their own dictator. Eventually this notion was emphasized by Tony Blair, who faced considerable vocal opposition to the war, and several key resignations from his Cabinet. One key resignation was that of Robin Cook. Cook was the leader of the House of Commons and had been Foreign Secretary in Blair's Labour Government. Just before the war, he resigned, saying:

> If we believe in an international community based on binding rules and institutions, we cannot simply set them aside when they produce results that are inconvenient to us. I cannot defend a war with neither international agreement nor international support. . . . Britain is not a superpower. Our interests are best protected, not by unilateral action, but by multilateral agreement and a world order governed by rules. .. Iraq's military strength is now less than half its size at the time of the last (1991) Gulf War. Ironically, it is only because Iraq's military forces are so weak that we can even contemplate invasion.
>
> I believe that the prevailing mood of the British public is sound. They do not doubt that Saddam Hussein is a brutal dictator. But they are not persuaded he is a clear and present danger to Britain.[26]

Blair argued that an attack against Iraq would remove the evil regime, terminate gross violations of human rights, and make it possible to democratize Iraq.

The Bush administration referred to the liberation, bringing freedom to the Iraqi people, establishing a democratic government there, and even, possibly, using this success as a stepping stone to the democratization of the whole Middle East region. An essay in the *New York Times* described the theory:

> As the war in Iraq began last week, some prominent members of the Bush administration were repeating their hope that the removal of Saddam Hussein will be the catalyst for a wave of democratic reform throughout the Middle East. In making their case these planners have revived a staple of cold-war thinking, the domino theory: the idea that sudden change in the leadership of one nation can set off a chain reaction in its neighbor, transforming an entire region. ... In today's unipolar world, a so-called positive or reverse domino theory has emerged. It envisions democracy as the great insurgent movement in our time, with the United States leading the revolution.[27]

The writer went on to point out that the theory of positive dominoes was not plausible and had been deemed too optimistic by George J. Tenet, the U.S. director of central intelligence.

There are logical problems both about analogy and about causation in connection to the original negative domino theory. According to that theory, if one country fell to communism, its neighbours would do so as well, like a line of tumbling dominoes. The counterpart positive domino theory has logically similar problems with regard to analogy and causation. The countries to be affected differ from each other in many relevant respects. Even if Iraq were (somehow) to be democratized as a result of the war, any claim that the trend would spread to such neighbours as Syria and Saudi Arabia seems quite implausible because these are countries with quite different circumstances and histories.

There are four fundamental obstacles to counting the democratization of Iraq as a just cause for the war. The first problem is that war is not plausible as a method of democratization. The second problem is that are so many other brutally repressive regimes in the world that were not selected by the U.S. administration as targets of attack. The third problem is that international law does not permit one state to judge that some other state has an 'evil' regime that needs 'regime change' and launch a military invasion in order to implement its judgment. To authorize invasion in all such contexts would be an international legal innovation risking chaos. The fourth problem is that there was simply too much evidence of other motivating factors to make it at all plausible to believe that the goal was the liberation of the Iraqi people.

Guarantee of access to Iraq's enormous oil resources appeared to many to be a powerful factor behind this war. Peace demonstrators made the accusation when they shouted "No blood for oil," and many Iraqis screamed their suspicions in large demonstrations. They claimed that foreign troops had come, not to liberate them, but to take their oil. Evidence for such claims lay in the fact that in the turbulent days when the Saddam Hussein regime had fallen and there was not effective government, U.S. troops protected oil fields and refineries, while hospitals, schools, and other public institutions were smashed and looted. At the same time, the United States was consolidating four military bases in Iraq. These were to be permanent staging points for American military power in the region, and they were to make possible the withdrawal of U.S. troops from Saudi Arabia.

Comments from some American soldiers indicated sentiments of revenge for the September 11 attacks on the United States, although such sentiments were sadly ill-founded given that there was no evidence of Iraqi involvement in those attacks. Several commentators believed that George W. Bush sought a continuing role as 'leader of a nation at war' to ensure his re-election in 2004.[28] The desire, on the part of the United States, to demonstrate its military might and will to dominate to any potentially rebellious nation was another factor.

With so many motives and so much at stake, the idea that the United States and the United Kingdom attacked Iraq to liberate its people was not credible to the careful observer.

And indeed, many spoke eloquently on the point. Edward Said, for instance, said:

This is the most reckless war in modern times. It is all about imperial arrogance unschooled in worldliness, unfettered either by competence or experience, undeterred by history or human complexity, unrepentant in its violence and the cruelty of its technology. What winning, or for that matter losing, such a war will ultimately entail is unthinkable. But pity the Iraqi civilians who must still suffer a great deal more before they are finally 'liberated.'[29]

Robert Fisk, a renowned reporter for the British paper, *The Independent*, remained in Baghdad and wrote about heart-breaking scenes on streets and in hospitals, and a general atmosphere of fear and insecurity.

It could be argued that liberating the Iraqi people from a brutal dictatorship would be a morally worthy thing to do and would constitute a just cause from a moral perspective — though it would not qualify as such under international law as that law presently stands. The point can be argued in the abstract. However, we need not pause to address it here. There are simply too many mixed motives, some clearly imperialistic and unilateralist, to make *democratization* plausible as a *just cause* in this case. In this instance, there is no just cause to be found. And for that reason, the war does not count as just according to the criteria of Just War Theory.

Even within a few weeks following the war, there was abundant evidence of widespread destruction and anti-Americanism. The chances of establishing a viable democratic regime in Iraq seemed small. My personal prediction would not be for success in the tasks of democratization and reconstruction. For the sake of the injured and overburdened people of Iraq, I can only hope to be wrong.

NOTES

1. The 'history' that 'teaches' such a 'lesson' is clearly not that of the careful historian.
2. Tony Blair, "I want to solve the Iraq issue via the United Nations," speech February 15, 2003; reprinted here.
3. For a brief discussion of what caused the fall of Milosevic, see Gene Sharp, "Serbia's Struggle for Freedom," *Peace Magazine*, October-December 2001, 81 — 20. I discuss this story in my essay "Power" in *A Delicate Balance: What Philosophy Can Tell us about Terrorism* (Boulder, CO: Westview Press 2002).
4. The cases said here to be in the middle of the spectrum differ in ways that are logically interesting but the logical intricacies cannot be discussed here.
5. Antje Krog, quoting Wilhelm Verwoerd in *Country of My Skull* (Cape Town: CTP Printers 1998) says that ambiguity is an early casualty of war; we might say Truth is the first casualty and Ambiguity a close second. 2003.
6. Public lecture presented at the University of Calgary, March 5, 2003. Relying on reports from David Frum, the Canadian speech-writer who was the original author of the "axis of evil" phrase, Dyer claimed that North Korea was included almost arbitrarily, because an "axis" should have more than two members, and it would be impolitic to have only Muslim countries on it. On Dyer's account, North Korea reacted with shock and horror to that inclusion, and the political struggles between it and the U.S. began to be severely aggravated at that point.
7. This kind of Double Standard would seem to be far less prevalent now than it was twenty or thirty years ago.
8. But what about the following objection? 'Powers such as the United States, Britain, France, Russia, and China have possessed nuclear weapons for over fifty years without using them, whereas North Korea, and Iraq, if they should get them, are 'new players' in this 'game' and players not known to be reliable. Furthermore, in the case of Iraq, Saddam Hussein has an especially bad record, since he has started two major wars in the period 1980 — 1983. And his regime is nondemocratic, grossly abusive, and lacking in all scruples.' By such considerations, one could construct an argument to the effect that Iraq is relevantly different from the United States and other established nuclear powers so far as its possession of weapons of mass destruction is concerned. Such arguments can indeed be made. I grant that they merit attention, although in my opinion, they do not suffice to outweigh the basic argument that any country, democratic or not, can have an unwise and rash leadership. (Indeed George W. Bush seems amply to confirm this point in his own person.)
9. My own label. This is not a standard textbook fallacy.

10. Cincinnati Museum Centre — Cincinnati Union Terminal, October 2002 (accessed at http://www.whitehouse.gov/news/releases/2002/10/20021007-8.html)

11. Al Gore, "Iraq and the War on Terrorism," Speech to the Commonwealth Club, September 23, 2002 (accessed at (http://www.commonwealthclub.org/archive/o2/02-09gore-speech.html). It is noteworthy that Gore is similar to Bush in some crucial respects, despite disagreeing with this unilateralist approach. He accepts the commitment to an expanding war against terrorism and he does not question the assumption that there were threatening weapons of mass destruction in large numbers in Iraq. He also objects to the failure to take rebuilding seriously on the grounds that it will damage the reputation of the United States, and not on the grounds of the wellbeing or illbeing of the Iraqi people.

12. Gwynne Dyer claimed that the main goal of George W. Bush was to establish himself as a leader based on military success, that Iraq had replaced al-Qaeda as enemy after the defeat of the Taliban in Afghanistan.

13. My own position is not one of general pacifism, but rather one of *skepticism about the merits of arguments purporting to justify the use of violence to solve problems and resolve conflicts*. Since war is such a serious matter, I believe that the arguments for it should be extremely compelling. And I find that in many cases, they are not. I argued this in the case of the 1991 Gulf War in "Was the Gulf War a Just War?" which appeared in the third edition of this anthology (*Contemporary Moral Issues*), pages 476 — 488.

14. A thorough critical discussion of Realism may be found in Robert Holmes, *On War and Morality* (Princeton, NJ: Princeton University Press 1989).

15. This section is adopted, with some amendments, from my earlier essay, "Was the Gulf War a Just War?"

16. This point is ably argued by Duane Cady in *From Warism to Pacifism* (Philadelphia: Temple University Press 1989).

17. Note that in this context, unlike many others in moral thinking, the notion of *Discrimination* is a positive one. We are supposed to discriminate between combatants and noncombatants; killing the former is permissible in wars, whereas killing the latter is generally not.

18. I say this without personally supporting Just War Theory. I have in fact a number of fundamental doubts about that theory, many of which concern the applicability of the *Discrimination* condition to war as currently practiced. But I do not have the space to explain these concerns here.

19. John Pilger, "The unthinkable is becoming normal." *The Independent*, April 21, 2003.

20. Elizabeth Neuffer, "Casualties: City battles will boost growing civilian toll," *Boston Globe*, April 7, 2003.

21. "Iraqi Hospitals Offer Snapshot of War Horror," Reuters report April 6, 2003; accessed at http://www.reuters.com/newsArticle.jhtml?type=focusIraqNews&st.

22. By late May, 2003, Paul Rogers, of the Peace Studies Program at Bradford University, U.K., was estimating a total of some 20,000 Iraqi deaths; that figure included both military and civilian deaths.

23. Al Gore, "Iraq and the War on Terrorism," Speech September 23, 2002 (see note 11 above).

24. *Ibid*.

25. John Currie, CBC *Commentary*, March 26, 2003.

26. Robin Cook, "Why I had to leave Blair's Cabinet: This will be a war without support at home or agreement abroad," *Counterpunch*, March 18, 2003.

27. Sam Tanenhaus, "From Vietnam to Iraq: The Rise and Fall and Rise of the Domino Theory", *New York Times* March 25, 2003.

28. See note 5.

29. Edward Said, "The Academy of Lagado," *London Review of Books*, April 17, 2003.

QUESTIONS

1. Given Trudy Govier's account of Realism and Just War Theory, into which of these categories would you put the authors of the readings that precede this one? Does trying to discern the theoretical basis of their justification or their criticism of the "war on terrorism" and its specific manifestation in Afganistan and Iraq help to evaluate the positions they take?

2. What are Govier's reasons for rejecting Realism as the basis for resolving international conflict? Are they convincing?
3. Does Just War Theory provide a sound basis for evaluating the invasion of Afghanistan and Iraq?

PACIFISM: A PHILOSOPHICAL ANALYSIS

Jan Narveson

Several different doctrines have been called "pacifism," and it is impossible to say anything cogent about it without saying which of them one has in mind. I must begin by making it clear, then, that I am limiting the discussion of pacifism to a rather narrow band of doctrines, further distinctions among which will be brought out below. By "pacifism," I do *not* mean the theory that violence is evil. With appropriate restrictions, this is a view that every person with any pretensions to morality doubtless holds: Nobody thinks that we have a right to inflict pain wantonly on other people. The pacifist goes a very long step further. *His* belief is not only that violence is evil but also that it is morally wrong to use force to resist, punish, or prevent violence. This further step makes pacifism a radical moral doctrine. What I shall try to establish below is that it is in fact, more than merely radical — it is actually incoherent because self-contradictory in its fundamental intent. I shall also suggest that several moral attitudes and psychological views which have tended to be associated with pacifism as I have defined it do not have any necessary connection with that doctrine. Most proponents of pacifism, I shall argue, have tended to confuse these different doctrines, and that confusion is probably what accounts for such popularity as pacifism has had.

It is next in order to point out that the pacifistic attitude is a matter of degree, and this in two respects. In the first place, there is the question: How much violence should be resisted, and what degree of force is one not entitled to use in resisting, punishing, or preventing it? Answers to this question will make a lot of difference. For example, everyone would agree that there are limits to the kind and degree of force with which a particular degree of violence is to be met: we do not have a right to kill someone for rapping us on the ribs, for example, and yet there is no tendency toward pacifism in this. We might go further and maintain, for example, that capital punishment, even for the crime of murder, is unjustified without doing so on pacifist grounds. Again, the pacifist should say just what sort of a reaction constitutes a forcible or violent one. If somebody attacks me with his fists and I pin his arms to his body with wrestling holds which restrict him but cause him no pain, is that all right in the pacifist's book? And again, many non-pacifists could consistently maintain that we should avoid, to the extent that it is possible, inflicting a like pain on those who attempt to inflict pain on us. It is unnecessary to be a pacifist merely in order to deny the moral soundness of the principle, "an eye for an eye and a tooth for a tooth." We need a clarification, then, from the pacifist as to just how far he is and is not willing to go. But this need should already make us pause, for surely the pacifist cannot draw these lines in a merely arbitrary manner. It is his reasons for drawing the ones he does that count, and these are what I propose to discuss below.

"Pacifism: A Philosophical Analysis" appeared in Ethics, *Vol 75, pp. 259–271, copyright 1965 by The University of Chicago Press (Chicago: The University of Chicago Press). It is reprinted here with the permission of the author and The University of Chicago Press.*

The second matter of degree in respect of which the pacifist must specify his doctrine concerns the question: Who ought not to resist violence with force? For example, there are pacifists who would only claim that they themselves ought not to. Others would say that only pacifists ought not to, or that all persons of a certain type, where the type is not specified in terms of belief or non-belief in pacifism, ought not to resist violence with force. And, finally, there are those who hold that everyone ought not to do so. We shall see that considerations about this second variable doom some forms pacifism to contradiction.

My general program will be to show that (1) only the doctrine that everyone ought not to resist violence with force is of philosophical interest among those doctrines known as "pacifism"; (2) that doctrine, if advanced as a moral doctrine, is logically untenable; and (3) the reasons for the popularity of pacifism rest on failure to see exactly what the doctrine is. The things which pacifism wishes to accomplish, insofar as they are worth accomplishing, can be managed on the basis of quite ordinary and conservative moral principles.

Let us begin by being precise about the kind of moral force the principle of pacifism is intended to have. One good way to do this is to consider what it is intended to deny. What would non-pacifists, which I suppose includes most people, say of a man who followed Christ's suggestion and, when unaccountably slapped, simply turned the other cheek? They might say that such a man is either a fool or a saint. Or they might say, "It's all very well for him to do that, but it's not for me"; or they might simply shrug their shoulders and say, "Well, it takes all kinds, doesn't it?" But they would *not* say that a man who did that ought to be punished in some way; they would not even say that he had done anything wrong. In fact, as I have mentioned, they would more likely than not find something admirable about it. The point, then, is this: The non-pacifist does *not* say that it is your *duty* to resist violence with force. The non-pacifist is merely saying that there's nothing wrong with doing so, that one has every right to do so if he is so inclined. Whether we wish to add that a person would be foolish or silly to do so is quite another question, one on which the non-pacifist does not *need* to take any particular position.

Consequently, a genuine pacifist cannot merely say that we may, if we wish, prefer not to resist violence with force. Nor can he merely say that there is something admirable or saintly about not doing so, for, as pointed out above, the non-pacifist could perfectly well agree with that. He must say, instead, that, for whatever class of people he thinks it applies to, there is something positively wrong about meeting violence with force. He must say that, insofar as the people to whom his principle applies resort to force, they are committing a breach of moral duty — a very serious thing to say. Just how serious, we shall ere long see.

Next, we must understand what the implications of holding pacifism as a moral principle are, and the first such implication requiring our attention concerns the matter of the size of the class of people to which it is supposed to apply. It will be of interest to discuss two of the four possibilities previously listed, I think. The first is that in which the pacifist says that only pacifists have the duty of pacifism. Let us see what this amounts to.

If we say that the principle of pacifism is the principle that all and only pacifists have a duty of not opposing violence with force, we get into a very odd situation. For suppose we ask ourselves, "Very well, which people are the pacifists then?" The answer will have to be "All those people who believe that pacifists have the duty not to meet violence with force." But surely one could believe that a certain class of people, whom we shall call "pacifists," have the duty not to meet violence with force without believing that one ought not, oneself, to meet violence with force. That is to say, the "principle" that pacifists ought to avoid meeting violence with force, is circular: It presupposes that one already knows who the pacifists are. Yet this is precisely what that statement of the principle is supposed to answer! We are supposed to be able to say that anybody who believes that principle is a pacifist; yet, as we have seen, a person could very well believe that a certain class of people called "pacifists" ought not to meet violence with force without believing that he himself ought not to meet violence with force. Thus everyone could be a "pacifist" in the sense of believing that statement and yet no one believe that he *himself* (or anyone in particular) ought to avoid meeting violence with force. Consequently, pacifism cannot be specified in that way. A pacifist must be a person who believes either that he himself (at least) ought not to meet force with force or that some larger class of persons, perhaps everyone, ought not to meet force with force. He would then be believing something definite, and we are then in a position to ask why.

Incidentally, it is worth mentioning that when people say things such as "Only pacifists have the duty of pacifism," "Only Catholics have the duties of Catholicism," and, in general, "Only X-ist have the duties of X-ism" they probably are falling into a trap which catches a good many people. It is, namely, the mistake of supposing that what it *is* to have a certain duty is to *believe* that you have a certain duty. The untenability of this is parallel to the untenability of the previously mentioned attempt to say what pacifism is. For, if having a duty is believing that you have a certain duty, the question arises, "*What* does such a person believe?" The answer that must be given if we follow this analysis would then be, "He believes that he believes that he has certain duty"; and so on, ad infinitum.

On the other hand, one might believe that having a duty does not consist in believing that one has and yet believe that only those people really have the duty who believe that they have it. But in that case, we would, being conscientious, perhaps want to ask the question, "Well, *ought* I to believe that I have that duty, or oughtn't I?" If you say that the answer is "Yes," the reason cannot be that you already do believe it, for you are asking whether you *should*. On the other hand, the answer "No" or "It doesn't make any difference — it's up to you," implies that there is really no reason for doing the thing in question at all. In short, asking whether I ought to believe that I have a duty to do *x* is equivalent to asking whether I should *do x*. A person might very well believe that he ought to do *x* but be wrong. It might be the case that he really ought *not* to do *x*; in that case the fact that he believes he ought to do *x*, far from being a reason why he ought to do it, is a reason for us to point out his error. It also, of course, presupposes that he has some reason other than his belief for thinking it is his duty to do *x*.

Having cleared this red herring out of the way, we must consider the view of those who believe that they themselves have a duty of pacifism and ask ourselves the question: What general kind of reason must a person have for supposing a certain type of act to be *his* duty, in a moral sense? Now, one answer he might give is that pacifism as such is a duty, that is, that meeting violence with force is, as such, wrong. In that case, however, what he thinks is not merely that *he* has this duty, but that *everyone* has this duty.

Now he might object, "Well, but no; I don't mean that everyone has it. For instance, if a man is defending, not himself, but *other* people, such as his wife and children, then he has a right to meet violence with force." Now this, of course, would be a very important qualification to his principle and one of a kind which we will be discussing in a moment. Meanwhile, however, we may point out that he evidently still thinks that, if it weren't for certain more important duties, everyone would have a duty to avoid meeting violence with force. In other words, he then believes that, other things being equal, one ought not to meet violence with force. He believes, to put it yet another way, that if one does meet violence with force one must have a special excuse or justification of a moral kind; then he may want to give some account of just which excuses and justifications would do. Nevertheless, he is now holding a general principle.

Suppose, however, he holds that no one *else* has this duty of pacifism, that only he himself ought not to meet force with force, although it is quite all right for others to do so. Now if this is what our man feels, we may continue to call him a "pacifist," in a somewhat attenuated sense, but he is then no longer holding pacifism as a *moral* principle or, indeed, as a principle at all.[1] For now his disinclination for violence is essentially just a matter of taste. I like pistachio ice cream, but I wouldn't dream of saying that other people have a duty to eat it; similarly, this man just doesn't *like* to meet force with force, although he wouldn't dream of insisting that others act as he does. And this is a secondary sense of "pacifism," first, because pacifism has always been advocated on moral grounds and, second, because non-pacifists can easily have this same feeling. A person might very well feel squeamish, for example, about using force, even in self-defense, or he might not be able to bring himself to use it even if he wants to. But none of these has anything to do with asserting pacifism to be a duty. Moreover, a mere attitude could hardly license a man to refuse military service if it were required of him, or to join ban-the-bomb crusades, and so forth. (I fear, however, that such attitudes have sometimes caused people to do those things.)

And, in turn, it is similarly impossible to claim that your support of pacifism is a moral one if your position is that a certain selection of people, but no one else, ought not to meet force with force, even though you are unprepared to offer any reason whatever for this selection. Suppose, for example, that you hold that only Arapahoes, or only the Chinese, or only people more than six feet high have this "duty." If such were the case, and no reasons offered at all, we could only conclude that you had a very peculiar attitude toward the Arapahoes, or whatever, but we would hardly want to say that you had a moral principle. Your "principle" amounts to saying that these particular individuals happen to have the duty of pacifism just because they are the individuals they are, and this, as Bentham would say, is the "negation of all principles." Of course, if you meant that somehow the property of being over six feet tall *makes* it your duty not to use violence, then you have a principle, all right, but a very queer one indeed unless you can give some further reasons. Again, it would not be possible to distinguish this from a sheer attitude.

Pacifism, then, must be the principle that the use of force to meet force is wrong *as such*, that is, that nobody may do so unless he has a special justification.

There is another way in which one might advocate a sort of "pacifism," however, which we must also dispose of before getting to the main point. One might argue that pacifism is desirable as a tactic: that, as a matter of fact, some good end, such as the reduction of violence itself, is to be achieved by "turning the other cheek." For example, if it were the case that turning the other cheek caused the offender to break down and repent, then that would be a very good reason for behaving "pacifistically". If unilateral disarmament causes the other side to disarm, then certainly unilateral disarmament would be a desirable policy. But note that its desirability, if this is the argument, is due to the fact that peace is desirable, a moral position which anybody can take, pacifist or no, plus the purely contingent fact that this policy causes the other side to disarm, that is, it brings about peace.

And, of course, that's the catch. If one attempts to support pacifism because of its probable effects, then one's position depends on what the effects are. Determining what they are is a purely empirical matter, and, consequently, one could not possibly be a pacifist as a matter of pure principle if his reasons for supporting pacifism are merely tactical. One must, in this case, submit one's opinions to the governance of fact.

It is not part of my intention to discuss matters of fact, as such, but it is worthwhile to point out that the general history of the human race certainly offers no support for the supposition that turning the other cheek always produced good effects on the aggressor. Some aggressors, such as the Nazis, were apparently just "egged on" by the "pacifist" attitude of their victims. Some of the S.S. men apparently became curious too see just how much torture the victim would put up with before he began to resist. Furthermore, there is the possibility that, while pacifism might work against some people (one might cite the British, against whom pacifism in India was apparently rather successful — but the British are comparatively nice people), it might fail against others (e.g., the Nazis).

A further point about holding pacifism to be desirable as a tactic is that this could not easily support the position that pacifism is a *duty*. The question whether we have no *right* to fight back can hardly be settled by noting that not to fight back might cause the aggressor to stop fighting. To prove that a policy is a desirable one because it works is not to prove that it is *obligatory* to follow it. We surely need considerations a good deal less tenuous than this to prove such a momentous contention as that we have no *right* to resist.

It appears, then, that to hold the pacifist position as a genuine, full-blooded moral principle is to hold that nobody has a right to fight back when attacked, that fighting back is inherently evil, as such. It means that we are all mistaken in supposing that we have a right of self-protection. And, of course, this is an extreme and extraordinary position in any case. It appears to mean, for instance, that we have no right to punish criminals, that all of our machinery of criminal justice is, in fact, unjust. Robbers, murderers, rapists, and miscellaneous delinquents ought, on this theory, to be let loose.

Now, the pacifist's first move, upon hearing this, will be to claim that he has been misrepresented. He might say that it is only one's *self* that one has no right to defend, and that one may legitimately fight in order to defend other people. This qualification cannot be made by those pacifists who qualify as conscientious objectors, however, for the latter are refusing to defend their fellow citizens and not merely themselves. But this is comparatively trivial when we contemplate the next objection to this amended version of the theory. Let us now ask ourselves what it is about attacks on *other* people which could possibly justify *us* in defending them, while we are not justified in defending ourselves? It cannot be the mere fact that they are other people than ourselves, for, of course, everyone is a different person from everyone else, and if such a consideration could ever of itself justify anything at all it could also justify anything whatever. That mere difference of person, as such, is of no moral importance, is a presupposition of anything that can possibly pretend to be a moral theory.

Instead of such idle nonsense, then, the pacifist would have to mention some specific characteristic which every *other* person has which we lack and which justifies us in defending them. But this, alas, is impossible, for, while there may be some interesting difference between *me*, on the one hand, and everyone else, on the other, the pacifist is not merely addressing himself to me. On the contrary, as we have seen, he has to address himself to everyone. He is claiming that each person has no right to defend himself, although he does have a right to defend other people. And, therefore, what is needed is a characteristic which distinguishes *each* person from everyone else, and not just *me* from everyone else — which is plainly self-contradictory. If the reader does not yet see why the "characteristic" of being identical with oneself cannot be used to support a moral theory, let him reflect that the proposition "Everyone is identical with himself" is a trivial truth — as clear an example of an analytic proposition as there could possibly be. But a statement of moral principle is not a trivial truth; it is a substantive moral assertion. But non-tautologous statements, as everyone knows, cannot logically be derived from tautologies, and, consequently, the fact that everyone is identical with himself cannot possibly be used to prove a moral position.

Again, then, the pacifist must retreat in order to avoid talking idle nonsense. His next move, now, might be to say that we have right to defend all those who are not able to defend themselves. Big, grown-up men who are able to defend themselves ought not to do so, but they ought to defend mere helpless children who are unable to defend themselves.

This last, very queer theory could give rise to some amusing logical gymnastics. For instance, what about groups of people? If a group of people who cannot defend themselves singly can defend themselves together, then when it has grown to that size ought it to stop defending itself? If so, then every time a person *can* defend someone else, he would form with the person being defended a "defensive unit" which was able to defend itself, and thus would by his very presence debar himself from making the defense. At this rate, no one will ever get defended, it seems: The defenseless people by definition cannot defend themselves, while those who can defend them would enable the group consisting of the defenders and the defended to defend themselves, and hence they would be obliged not to do so.

Such reflections, however, are merely curious shadows of a much more fundamental and serious logical problem. This arises when we begin to ask: But why should even defenseless people be defended? If resisting violence is inherently evil, then how can it suddenly become permissible when we use it on behalf of other people? The fact that they are defenseless cannot possibly account for this, for it follows from the theory in question that everyone ought to put himself in the position of people who are defenseless by refusing to defend himself. This type of pacifist, in short, is using the very characteristic (namely, being in a state of not defending oneself) which he wishes to encourage in others as a reason for denying it in the case of those who already have it (namely, the defenseless). This is indeed self-contradictory.

To attempt to be consistent, at least, the pacifist is forced to accept the characterization of him at which we tentatively arrived. He must indeed say that no one ought ever to be defended against attack. The right of self-defense can be denied coherently only if the right of defense, in general, is denied. This in itself is an important conclusion.

It must be borne in mind, by the way, that I have not said anything to take exception to the man who simply does not wish to defend himself. So long as he does not attempt to make his pacifism into a principle, one cannot accuse him of any inconsistency, however much one might wish to say that he is foolish or eccentric. It is solely with moral principles that I am concerned here.

We now come to the last and most fundamental problem of all. If we ask ourselves what the point of pacifism is, what gets it going, so to speak, the answer is, of course, obvious enough: opposition to violence. The pacifist is generally thought of as the man who is so much opposed to violence that he will not even use it to defend himself or anyone else. And it is precisely this characterization which I wish to show is far from being plausible, morally inconsistent.

To begin with, we may note something which at first glance may seem merely to be a matter of fact, albeit one which should worry the pacifist, in our latest characterization of him. I refer to the commonplace observation that, generally speaking, we measure a man's degree of opposition to something by the amount of effort he is willing to put forth against it. A man could hardly be said to be dead set against something if he is not willing to lift a finger to keep it from going on. A person who claims to be completely opposed to something yet does nothing to prevent it would ordinarily be said to be a hypocrite.

As facts, however, we cannot make too much of these. The pacifist could claim to be willing to go to any length, short of violence, to prevent violence. He might, for instance, stand out in the cold all day long handing out leaflets (as I have known some to do), and this would surely argue for the sincerity of his beliefs.

But would it really?

Let us ask ourselves, one final time, what we are claiming when we claim that violence is morally wrong and unjust. We are, in the first place, claiming that a person *has no right* to indulge in it, as such (meaning that he has no right to indulge in it, *unless* he has an overriding justification). But what do we mean when we say that he has no right to indulge in it? Violence, of the type we are considering, is a two-termed affair: one does violence *to* somebody, one cannot simply "do violence." It might be oneself, of course, but we are not primarily interested in those cases, for what makes it wrong to commit violence is that it harms the people to whom it is done. To say that it is wrong is to say that those to whom it is done have a right *not* to have it done to them. (This must again be qualified by pointing out that this is so only if they have done nothing to merit having the right abridged.)

Yet what could that right to their own security, which people have, possibly consist in, if not a right at least to defend themselves from whatever violence might be offered them? But lest the reader think that this is a gratuitous assumption, note carefully the reason why having a right involves having a right to be defended from breaches of that right. It is because the prevention of infractions of that right is precisely what one has a right to when one has a right at all. A right just *is* a status justifying preventive action. To say that you have a right to *X* but that no one has any justification whatever for preventing people from depriving you of it, is self-contradictory. If you claim a right to *X*, then to describe some action as an act of depriving you of *X*, is logically to imply that its absence is one of the things that you have right to.

Thus far it does not follow logically that we have a right to use force in our own or anyone's defense. What does follow logically is that one has a right to whatever may be necessary to prevent infringements of his right. One might at first suppose that the universe *could* be so constructed that it is never necessary to use force to prevent people who are bent on getting something from getting it.

Yet even this is not so, for when we speak of "force" in the sense in which pacifism is concerned with it, we do not mean merely physical "force." To call an action a use of force is not merely to make a reference to the laws of mechanics. On the contrary, it is to describe whatever is being done as being a means to the infliction on somebody of something (ordinarily physical) which he does not want done to him; and the same done to him; and the same is true for "force" in the sense in which it applies to war, assault and battery, and the like.

The proper contrary of "force" in this connection is "rational persuasion." Naturally, one way there *might* be of getting somebody not to do something he has no right to do is to convince him he ought not to do it or that it is not in his interest to do it. But it is inconsistent, I suggest, to argue that rational persuasion is the only morally permissible method of preventing violence. A pragmatic reason for this is easy enough to point to: Violent people are too busy being violent to be reasonable. We cannot engage in rational persuasion unless the enemy is willing to sit down and talk; but what if he isn't? One cannot contend that every human being can be persuaded to sit down and talk before he strikes, for this is not something we can determine just by reasoning: it is a question of observation, certainly. But these points are not strictly relevant anyway, for our question is not the empirical question of whether there is some handy way which can always be used to get a person to sit down and discuss moral philosophy when he is about to murder you. Our question is: *If* force is the only way to prevent violence in a given case, is its use justified *in that case*? This is a purely moral question which we can discuss without any special reference to matters of fact. And, moreover, it is precisely this question which we should have to discuss with the would-be violator. The point is that if a person can be rationally persuaded that he ought not to engage in violence, then precisely what he would be rationally persuaded of if we were to succeed would be the proposition that the use of force is justifiable to prevent him from doing so. For note that if we were to argue that only rational persuasion is permissible as a means of preventing him, we would have to face the question: Do we mean *attempted* rational persuasion, or *successful* rational persuasion, that is, rational persuasion which really does succeed in preventing him from acting? Attempted rational persuasion might fail (if only because the opponent is unreasonable), and then what? To argue that we have a right to use rational persuasion which also succeeds (i.e., we have a right to its success as well as to its use) is to imply that we have a right to prevent him from performing the act. But this, in turn, means that, if attempts at rational persuasion fail, we have a right to the use of force. Thus what we have a right to, if we ever have a *right* to anything, is not merely the use of rational persuasion to keep people from depriving you of the thing to which you have the right. We do indeed have a right to that, but we also have a right to anything else that might be necessary (other things being equal) to prevent the deprivation from occurring. And it is a logical truth, not merely a contingent one, that what *might* be necessary is *force*. (If merely saying something could miraculously deprive someone of the ability to carry through a course of action, then those speech-acts would be called a type of force, if a very mysterious one. And we could properly begin to oppose their use for precisely the same reasons as we now oppose violence.)

What this all adds up to, then, is that *if* we have any rights at all, we have a right to use force to prevent the deprivation of the thing to which we are said to have a right. But the pacifist, of *all* people, is the one most concerned to insist that we do have some rights, namely, the right not to have violence done to us. This is logically implied in asserting it to be a duty on everyone's part to avoid violence. And this is why the pacifist's position is self-contradictory. In saying that violence is wrong, one is at the same time saying that people have a right to its prevention, by force if necessary. Whether and to what extent it may be necessary is a question of fact, but, since it is a question of fact only, the *moral* right to use force on some possible occasions is established.

We now have an answer to the question. How much force does a given threat of violence justify for preventive purpose? The answer, in a word, is "Enough." That the answer is this simple may at first sight seem implausible. One might suppose that some elaborate equation between the aggressive and the preventive force is needed: the punishment be proportionate to the crime. But this is a misunderstanding. In the first place, prevention and punishment are not the same, even if punishment is thought to be directed mainly toward prevention. The punishment of particular crime logically cannot prevent *that* instance of the crime, since it presupposes that it has already been performed: and punishment need not involve the use of any violence at all, although law-enforcement officers in some places have a nasty tendency to assume the contrary. But preventive force is another matter. If a man threatens to kill me, it is desirable, of course, for me to try to prevent this by the use of the least amount of force sufficient to do the job. But I am justified even in killing him *if* necessary. This much, I suppose, is obvious to most people. But suppose his threat is much smaller: suppose that he is merely pestering me, which is a very mild form of aggression indeed. Would I be justified in killing him to prevent this, under any circumstances whatever?

Suppose that I call the police and they take out a warrant against him, and suppose that when the police come, he puts up a struggle. He pulls a knife or a gun, let us say, and the police shoot him in the ensuing battle. Has my right to the prevention of his annoying me extended to killing him? Well, not exactly, since the immediate threat in response to which he is killed is a threat to the lives of the policemen. Yet my annoyer may never have contemplated real violence. It is an unfortunate case of unpremeditated escalation. But this is precisely what makes the contention that one is justified in using enough force to do the job, whatever amount that may be, to prevent action which violates a right less alarming than at first sight it seems. For it is difficult to envisage a reason why extreme force is needed to prevent mild threats from realization except by way of escalation, and escalation automatically justifies increased use of preventive force.

The existence of laws, police, courts, and more or less civilized modes of behavior on the part of most of the populace naturally affects the answer to the question of how much force is necessary. One of the purposes of a legal system of justice is surely to make the use of force by individuals very much less necessary than it would otherwise be. If we try to think back to a "state of nature" situation, we shall have much less difficulty envisaging the need for large amounts of force to prevent small threats of violence. Here Hobbes's contention that in such a state every man has a right to the life of every other becomes understandable. He was, I suggest, relying on the same principle as I have argued for here: that one has a right to use as much force as necessary to defend one's rights, which includes the right of safety of person.

I have said that the duty to avoid violence is only a duty, other things being equal. We might arrive at the same conclusion as we have above by asking the question: Which "other things" might count as being *un*equal? The answer to this is that whatever else they may be, the purpose of preventing violence from being done is necessarily one of these justifying conditions. That the use of force is never justified to prevent initial violence being done to one logically implies that there is nothing wrong with initial violence. We cannot characterize it as being wrong if preventive violence is not simultaneously being characterized as justifiable.

We often think of pacifists as being gentle and idealistic souls, which in its way is true enough. What I have been concerned to show is that they are also confused. If they attempt to formulate their position using our standard concepts of rights, their position involves a contradiction: Violence is wrong, *and* it is wrong to resist it. But the right to resist is precisely what having a right of safety of person is, if it is anything at all.

Could the position be reformulated with a less "committal" concept of rights? I do not think so. It has been suggested[2] that the pacifist need not talk in terms of this "kind" of rights. He can affirm, according to this suggestion, simply that neither the aggressors nor the defenders "have" rights to what they do, that to affirm their not having them is simply to be against the use of force, without this entailing the readiness to use force if necessary to protect the said rights. But this will not do, I believe. For I have not maintained that having a right, or believing that one has a right, entails a *readiness* to defend that right. One has a perfect right not to resist violence to oneself if one is so inclined. But our question has been whether self-defense is justifiable, and not whether one's belief that violence is wrong entails a willingness or readiness to use it. My contention has been that such a belief does entail the justifiability of using it. If one came upon a community in which no sort of violence was ever resisted and it was claimed in that community that the non-resistance was a matter of conscience, we should have to conclude, I think, not that this was a community of saints, but rather that this community lacked the concept of justice — or perhaps that their nervous systems were oddly different from ours.

The true test of the pacifist comes, of course, when he is called upon to assist in the protection of the safety of other persons and not just of himself. For while he is, as I have said, surely entitled to be pacific about his own person if he is so inclined, he is not entitled to be so about the safety of others. It is here that the test of principles comes out. People have a tendency to brand conscientious objectors as cowards or traitors, but this is not quite fair. They are acting as if they were cowards or traitors, but claiming to do so on principle. It is not surprising if a community should fail to understand such "principles," for the test of adherence to a principle is willingness to act on it, and the appropriate action, if one believes a certain thing to be grossly wrong, is to take steps to prevent or resist it. Thus people who assess conscientious objection as cowardice or worse are taking an understandable step: from an intuitive feeling that the pacifist does not really believe what he is saying they infer that his actions (or inaction) must be due to cowardice. What I am suggesting is that this is not correct: The actions are due, not to cowardice, but to confusion.

I have not addressed myself specifically to the question whether, for instance, conscription is morally justifiable, given that the war effort on behalf of which it is invoked is genuinely justifiable. Now, war efforts very often aren't justifiable (indeed, since at least one of the parties to each war must be an aggressor, a minimum of 50 percent of war efforts must be unjustifiable); but if they ever are, is it then justifiable to conscript soldiers? In closing, I would suggest an answer which may seem surprising in view of my arguments a few pages back. My answer is that it is, but in the case of conscientious objectors, the only justifiable means of getting them to comply is rational persuasion.

The reason is that, in showing that self-defense is morally justifiable, one has not simultaneously shown that the defense of other people is morally *obligatory*. The kinds of arguments needed to show that an act is obligatory are quite different from those which merely show that it is justified. And, since what has been shown is that self-defense is justifiable and not obligatory, the only conclusion that can be immediately inferred from this is that defense of others is also justifiable and not obligatory. Would it be possible to show that the defense of others (at least in some circumstances) is obligatory and not merely justifiable, without at the same time showing that self-defense is obligatory and not merely justifiable?

The only thing I can suggest here is that the answer requires us to speculate about the obligations of living in a community. If a community expects its members to assist in the common defense when necessary, it can make this clear to people and give them their choice either to be prepared to meet this obligation or to live somewhere else. But a community of pacifists would also be quite conceivable, a community in which no citizen could expect the others to defend him as part of their community responsibilities. One might not care to live in such a community, but then, a pacifist might not care to live in our sort. When the community is a whole nation of present-day size, it is much more difficult to put the issue clearly to each citizen in advance. But the upshot of it is that (1) the issue depends upon what sort of community we conceive ourselves to have; (2) we do not have clearly formed views on this point; (3) there is no basic moral duty to defend others; (4) we therefore have no direct right to force people to become soldiers in time of justified wars; (5) but we do have a right to deny many basic community services to people who will not assist us in time of need by contributing the force of their arms; and so (6) the only thing to do is to try to argue conscientious objectors into assistance, pointing to all of the above factors and leaving them their choice.

Too much can easily be made of the issue of conscription *versus* voluntary service in time of war. (In time of peace, we have another issue altogether; my arguments here apply only when there is clear justification for defensive measures.) It must be remembered that there is a limit to what law can do in "requiring" compliance, and the pacifist is precisely the person who cannot be reached by the ordinary methods of the law, since he has made up his mind not to be moved by force. The philosophical difference lies, not in the question of whether compliance is ultimately voluntary, since with all laws it to some extent must be, but in the moral status which military service is presumed to have. The draft is morally justifiable if the defense of persons is considered a basic obligation of the citizen. In contemporary communities, it seems to me that there is good reason for giving it that status.

Many questions remain to be discussed, but I hope to have exposed the most fundamental issues surrounding this question and to have shown that the pacifist's central position in untenable.

NOTES

1. Compare, for example, K. Baier, *The Moral Point of View* (Cornell, 1958), p. 191.
2. I owe this suggestion to my colleague, Leslie Armour.

QUESTIONS

1. Why does Jan Narveson think that the thesis that people ought not to resist violence with force is of philosophical interest?
2. Given Trudy Govier's description of Realism and Just War Theory, is Narveson a Realist or a Just War theorist?
3. Are Narveson's definitions of pacifism plausible seen from the perspective of pacifists? Can you formulate an account that is plausible but not vulnerable to Narveon's *logical* (as opposed to moral) criticisms?
4. Would it be fair to say that Jan Narveson believes that people are entitled to resist violence with violence? If so, what reasons does he give for his view? Are his reasons persuasive?

IS PACIFISM MORALLY COHERENT? A REPLY TO NARVESON

Conrad Brunk

Although pacifist dissent from the mainstream morality of "justified violence" has persisted throughout the recorded history of humanity, it has never been widely embraced as a principle of personal conduct, to say nothing of an operative principle of social order. This is true despite the fact that versions of pacifism have been espoused by the founders and influential figures in several of the major world religions, including Christianity. The pacifism of both Jesus and the Buddha, for example found little acceptance in the mainstreams of the religious traditions they fostered, except among the first few generations of believers. These were typically persecuted or reviled minorities who challenged the mores and practices of their society and, thus, found themselves at the edges of the social mainstream.

By permission of Conrad Brunk, Conrad Grebel College, affiliated with the University of Waterloo.

The religious exponents of pacifism rarely have put forward their teaching in the systematic manner of a world view or social philosophy. The pacifism of Jesus, for example, is expressed only in cryptic, aphoristic utterances whose implications for the whole of life or social order are left largely unspecified. When the third and fourth generation systematizers of a new religion take up the task of incorporating the teachings of its founder into a comprehensive, systematic theology or philosophy, the pacifism of the latter usually becomes relativized, contextualized, idealized, or otherwise relegated to the edges of the new dogma. The ways in which Christian theologians from Augustine and Aquinas to Luther and Niebuhr have circumvented the radical pacifist utterances of Jesus in their justifications of Christian participation in "just wars" are widely recognized cases in point.

Few of the well-known modern expositors of pacifism, such as Tolstoi, Gandhi, or even the philosopher Bertrand Russell, provide the kind of systematic defence of the doctrine that social and moral philosophers generally require. Pacifist writers tend to argue their case either on grounds that the position follows logically form some teaching of a moral authority (e.g., Jesus, the New Testament) or from the obvious opprobrium of particular wars or types of wars. Tolstoi is an example of both the first and second approach, Russell of the second. To be sure, Gandhi's doctrine of Satyagraha or nonviolent pursuit or truth and justice was an integral part of a larger philosophy, but, like Jesus' principle of "love of neighbour," it, too, had to be given its systematic expression by later expositors.[1]

It is not surprising that pacifism has not attracted a great deal of serious attention from moral philosophers and that, when it has, it has often been caricatured as "bizarre and vaguely ludicrous."[2] This is so because, from a philosophical point of view, it is not at all evident what the doctrine is. Its fundamental moral premises, the logic of its arguments, and precisely what actions or policies it prohibits or requires in particular circumstances are not always clearly specified. This problem is exacerbated by the fact that there are nearly as many versions of pacifism as there are pacifists, making it easy for critics of the doctrine to choose the most bizarre and ludicrous expressions of it as easy targets for devastating philosophical assault.

My aim is to clarify what I take to be the fundamental logic and central claims of at least some varieties of pacifism and to defend them from several of the more commonly advanced philosophical criticisms against the doctrine in general. One of the interesting features of the philosophical debate about pacifism is the fact that it has concentrated on the internal logic and consistency of the doctrine, rather than upon its substantive claims about what kind of behaviour is permissible or impermissible from a moral point of view. In this debate those who have defended pacifism from the charge of internal inconsistency often note that, nonetheless, they consider it to be profoundly wrong. But this substantive claim is itself more often asserted as self-evident than argued for.[3]

Although I believe that a much stronger philosophical case for the substantive claims of pacifism can be made than is generally held, I wish to limit my defence of it here primarily to the *a priori* case made against it. The most widely published and discussed example of this case aginst pacifism has been made by Jan Narveson.[4] Although there have been a variety of published replies made to Narveson's various arguments,[5] in my view they have not successfully clarified how these *a priori* arguments misconstrue the claims actually made by pacifists themselves, nor how these claims rely upon more generally shared ethical assumptions. After clarifying the nature of various pacifist claims, I will summarize four types of arguments made by Narveson against pacifism and show how each of them fails against at least certain versions of the doctrine.

What Pacifism Is

It is not an easy task to clarify what kinds of claims pacifists in fact make, because pacifism takes a variety of forms.[6] Different pacifist views can be categorized according to what kinds of normative claims they make (i.e., what kind of behaviour is approved or disapproved) and the kinds of reasons or justifications given for the normative claims. Narveson takes pacifism to be the view that all "violence is evil," and that "it is morally wrong to use force to resist, punish or prevent violence."[7] Further, he holds that pacifism "must be the principle that the use of force to meet force is wrong as *such*," that is, it must be a matter of "pure principle."[8] Ignoring for the moment Narveson's conflation of the two very distinct concepts of force and violence in these statements, it should be noted that this pacifism against which he argues is only one of many possible versions. This definition does not count as "pacifist" any view that accepts the use of forceful or even violent resistance of certain kinds, as well as any view based upon consequentialist considerations. Narveson dismisses the consequentialist version as a "merely tactical" position that is clearly empirically false.[9]

It may be true that the most historically enduring varieties of pacifism have taken the "principled," nonresistant form Narveson criticizes. Since most of these pacifisms were founded upon religious morality, they took the proscription against violence or war as a matter of principle, usually as a divine injunction or calling. This would be true of some of the historic "peace churches," such as the Mennonites and the Amish as well as the Christian pacifism of Tolstoi. But it would not be true of the Satyagraha of Gandhi or of the pacifism of many modern Quakers, which fits much more closely the mould of what Narveson calls "tactical" pacifism. Gandhi, for example, was perfectly willing to admit that *if* violence were the only means of successfully resisting certain evils, then it would be not only justifiable to use violence, but *morally preferable* to do so.[10] He believed, however, that as a matter of fact it was rarely, if ever, the only available means. Even those pacifists who base their opposition to violence or war on what Narveson calls "pure principle" would rarely hold this as an *absolute* prohibition. Many religious pacifists are willing to admit the *theoretical* possibility of legitimate violence, or even war, but would not permit it in the circumstances where the nonpacifist generally considers these to be legitimate.[11]

Narveson objects that Ganhdi, and others who argue the case for nonviolence or pacifism on grounds other then pure principle, are not really pacifists. Their position, he says, is morally indistinguishable from that of the nonpacifist, because the two would agree if it were not for their different assessment of the "contingent fact" about the efficacy of the pacifist approach to conflict.[12] But it is, indeed, a puzzling claim that there is no significant *moral* difference between those who embrace a certain moral rule (e.g., nonviolence) because they have one view of the facts and those who do not embrace the rule because they have a substantially different view of the facts. Would Narveson hold, for example, that two so-called "rule utilitarians" who adopted opposite viewpoints on a question like the morality of capital punishment, because they made different assessments of the social consequences of the practice, had no significant *moral* disagreement?

What is distinctive about pacifism as a moral doctrine are the substantive moral *rules* about violence, war, and so forth, that it embraces, not the justificatory *grounds* for these moral rules. A pacifism adopted on rule-utilitarian grounds,[13] for example, is no less a *pacifism* than one adopted on *a priori* grounds. Narveson is free, of course, to limit the reference of the term in this way for the purpose of his argument, but in doing so his reader must bear in mind that he does not make a case against many, perhaps a majority, of those who are commonly regarded as "pacifists" and who would regard themselves as such. Certainly, in popular parlance the term "pacifist" refers generally to those persons who, at a minimum, view their participation in warfare as morally illegitimate, whatever else they may believe about the use of violence, force, or even homicide, and whatever grounds they may have for holding this view.

Since a pure *a priori* pacifism, however, does not build its case upon the "contingent facts," one cannot effectively undermine it by pointing to the facts, such as the fact that non-resistance or nonviolence is often not an effective means of countering evil and injustice. The most effective argument against it will be *a priori* as well, as Narveson recognizes on choosing this line of attack. He must show that there is some flaw in the internal logic of the *a priori* pacifist view. To do this, attention has to be focused upon the content of the principle or rule itself, which this kind of pacifist affirms. So it will make a difference just what the content of the principle rule is.

It is here that Narveson's argument suffers from too narrow a view of the various substantive principles a pacifist might adopt. Pacifists commonly adopt one of the following moral rules, which they take as definitive of their pacifism. They are listed in order of the decreasing generality of the class of behaviours they counsel against.

1. It is morally impermissible to use force, coercion, or violence against another person. (The *Nonresistance Principle*)
2. It is morally impermissible to use violence, defined as the intentional infliction of serious physical or psychological injury upon another person. (The *Nonviolence Principle*)
3. It is morally impermissible to use *lethal* violence against another person. (The *No-Homicide Principle*)
4. It is morally impermissible to engage in the organized mass violence and killing of warfare. (The *No-War* or *Conscientious Objector Principle*)

Only Principle 1, the Nonresistance Principle, expresses the view Narveson ascribes to pacifism generally, namely that all acts of resistance to evil are morally prohibited. The latter three principles accept the legitimacy of some type of resistance to aggression, differing only in the *limits* they would place upon this resistance. The Nonviolence Principle accepts the legitimacy of coercive or even forceful resistance. It is the operative principle in the pacifism of such persons as Gandhi, Martin Luther King, and A.J. Muste, all of whom found non-resistant pacifism to be morally as objectionable as nonpacifist violence.[14] Albert Camus' "Neither Victims Nor Executioners"[15] is an example of a call for a pacifism based primarily on the no-homicide principle, and the pacifism often expressed by members of popular anti-war and disarmament movements is often expressed primarily in terms of the No-War or Conscientious Objector Principle.

Pacifism is often confused with passivism, or the view that one ought to respond to aggression and injustice with passivity, or at least with no more response than moral persuasion. It should be clear that only a pacifism of complete nonresistance could reasonably be characterized as passivistic. When the concepts of force and coercion themselves are carefully defined, it is questionable whether even the most disciplined nonresistant passivists are able actually to conduct their everyday tasks of child-rearing and other personal relationships in accordance with their espoused principle. But it should also be clear that the oft-cited charge against pacifism, that it denies one's own status as a person by passively accepting degradation by the aggressor,[16] applies, if at all, only to a pure, nonresistant pacifism. All other versions of the doctrine permit, and often demand, uncompromising resistance to evil. Their only disagreement with nonpacifists on this point concerns the limits they would place upon the means of resistance. Most nonpacifists agree that some limit must be placed on the means of resisting aggression. Once this point is clarified, the fundamental debate between the two appears in a completely different light from that which Narveson casts on it.

The "Rights" Argument Against Pacifism

One of the *a priori* arguments levelled against pacifism is that the doctrine contradicts itself by undermining the very premises upon which it is based. Narveson formulates two versions of this argument in his attack upon pacifism. The first claims that the pacifist belief about violence is founded upon, or presupposes, the conviction that all persons have a right not to have violence used against them. This is so, he says, because, "what makes [violence] wrong is that it harms the people to whom it is done. To say that it is wrong is to say that those to whom it is done have a right not to have it done to them." Further, according to Narveson, when one has a right to something (e.g., the forbearance of others), this implies that "one has a right to whatever may be necessary to prevent infringements of his right."[17] Since violence sometimes would appear to be the only means by which one can protect oneself or others against violence, it follows that one has a right to use that violence. Therefore, in denying that the use of violence is ever justified, the pacifist is denying the very right upon which the proscription of violence is founded.

There are several responses the pacifist might make to this critique. The first is to deny that there is any such right against violence entailed by the duty not to use violence. Narveson simply asserts without argument that "to say that [violence] is wrong is to say that those to whom it is done have a right *not* to have it done to them." The assumption here that every moral duty entails a correlative *right* on the part of another to the performance of the duty, especially a right in Narveson's strong sense of the term, is far from self-evident, and is, in fact, not accepted by many moral theorists.[18] It is certainly not accepted by most pacifists. There is no *logical* difficulty in asserting a case of a duty to do (or not do) X without asserting a correlative right on the part of some person P to guarantee performance of that duty. Indeed, the commonly asserted duties to the natural environment, to future generations, or to oneself would seem to be just such cases. In any case, the burden of proof seems to be upon Narveson to show that duties without correlative rights are logical impossibilities. At least he must show that the duty not to use violence is necessarily of this character.

Many pacifists would, thus, deny that there is any "right" in Narveson's sense not to be victimized by violence. Most religious and ethical defences of pacifism make no appeal to such a right. In the case of religious pacifism, at least, the doctrine is usually part of a decidedly nonrights-oriented moral perspective — that is to say, it is commonly founded in a "duty-based" or "virtue-based" morality.[19] For example, the historical "peace church" groups (e.g., Quakers, Mennonites, Amish) shy away from appeals to rights precisely because they involve egoistic and individualistic values as well as coercive means of enforcement, which are contrary to the communal values of mutuality, altruism, and nonresistance central to their religious outlook.[20] This kind of pacifism derives its moral rejection of force, coercion, violence, not from any "right" not to be victimized by these things, but from the value or virtue of responding to aggression in other ways. I know of no defence of pacifism that makes its case on the grounds that there is a "right" not to be victimized by violence.

Yet, even were a pacifist to make the case against violence on the basis of a right not to be victimized by it, Narveson's argument that the pacifist's absolute proscription of violence contradicts this right does not follow. As we have seen, Narveson argues that having a right *logically* entails the right to do "whatever may be necessary to prevent infringements of [the] right." He has to hold this strong view of the right against violence in order for the argument to work, for his complaint against pacifists is that when they place limits upon the means they may justifiably use in defence against a violent aggressor they in effect deny that one has the right to defend oneself.

But surely this concept of a right is problematic in the extreme. If taken simply as Narveson asserts it, it would imply that if I have a right to keep the penny I have earned, I have a right to kill anyone who tries to steal it from me if that is the only means by which I can do so. Otherwise, I would not have a genuine "right" to the penny. Our legal system clearly does not interpret my property rights in this strong sense. In fact, it would quite appropriately hold me guilty of criminal homicide were I to defend my right in this way. This is so not just because it is the law that gives me the right to my penny and the law alone that may appropriately enforce my right. In relatively just societies, the law does not have the right to kill persons who would steal my penny, should that turn out to be the only means of deterring them. Surely Narveson would not want to argue that the law is thus denying the very right to property it also asserts by placing this limit on the defence of the right.

Perhaps he does not really mean to take the concept of "necessary means" this far. Narveson might argue that one has the right to use only means that are *proportionate* in some sense to the value being defended. That is, in defending a right, one may not violate the more important right of another (e.g., one may not take life in defence of property). One, however, has a right to take life to defend life, use violence to prevent violence, and so forth, and this is what the pacifist, of course, denies.[21] But even this will not save the argument, for several reasons. First, there are commonly recognized cases in law and morality where life may not legitimately be taken in defence of the right to life. If, for example, the life that must be taken is that of an "innocent" third party, the law will not view such homicide as justified. If someone threatens to kill me unless I in turn kill some third person who poses no threat to me or to anyone else, the law in most jurisdictions in the western world will hold me guilty of criminal homicide, not even excusing my action on grounds of duress. Do these legal jurisdictions thereby contradict their own assertion of a legal right to life?[22]

Narveson might respond by pointing out that the difference in this latter example is that the innocent third party has in no way "forfeited" his or her right to life, as has the aggressor who threatens my life or bodily integrity. So the former's right to life still stands on par with my own right. Still, why should the law and common morality require me to place greater weight on the other's right to life than my own? Here law and common moral intuitions make exactly the same moral judgment as does the pacifist in not permitting me to prefer my own right to the equal rights of others.

Here we can see the crux of the argument between the pacifist and the nonpacifist. The latter at this point appeals to a theory of "forfeiture" of rights that makes the taking of an aggressor's life a legitimate means of defending one's own right.[23] But, it is just this idea of "forfeiture" of the right not to be killed, victimized by violence, forced, coerced that the pacifist denies. There is no necessary disagreement with the nonpacifist on the logic of rights, even on the matter of the right to defend one's rights. Nor is there disagreement on whether there are limits on the means of defending one's rights. The disagreement turns on the substantive moral question of the conditions, if any, under which a person forfeits these rights, and the pacifist rejects the nonpacifist accounts of this alleged forfeiture. In particular, pacifists typically deny that the aggression of others necessarily constitutes a forfeiture of their rights against violence, killing, and the like, and thus are committed to the view that such means of defending one's rights are not morally appropriate.[24]

So, even if pacifists accepted Narveson's account of the right against violence or killing, there would be no contradiction at all in their also holding that the defence of that right should be limited to nonviolent or nonlethal means. Only a pacifism based upon the pure Nonresistance Principle as defined earlier would have any difficulty accepting this concept of a right against violence. And even this radical form of pacifism could accept a weaker form of the right against violence. A nonresistant pacifist could hold that such a right entails the right to "claim" performance of the correlative duty on the part of a potential aggressor, but not the right to enforce it by forceful or coercive means. This may not be the concept of a "right" normally invoked in the legal sense, or even in many theories of moral rights, but it may be the sense, and the only sense, in which a nonresistant pacifist might admit the existence of rights. There is no contradiction, nor even any manifest implausibility, in such a conception of moral rights. Most nonresistant pacifists would likely hold that because force and coercion are morally problematic, this is good reason for rejecting altogether rights in the sense Narveson conceives of them.

The Argument From the Absolute Evil of Violence

Narveson has also put forward a second, consequentialist version of the argument that pacifism undermines its own basic premises. He argues that pacifists presumably adopt the absolute rule against the use of violence because they believe that the evil inflicted upon a person in an act of violence is absolute or irredeemable.[25] If they do hold such a belief, then just the opposite conclusion from the one the pacifist draws from it would follow. The reason is that often there are situations where the choice one faces is between one course of action involving a certain amount of violence (e.g., the violence of one's defence), and another course of action involving a greater amount violence (e.g., the violence that would be perpetrated by the aggressor if one did not resist). Says Narveson, "If violence is absolutely evil, then the reasonable thing to do would seem to be to minimize it — to do what produces least of this irredeemable evil."[26] And, if my own violent defence in fact minimizes this evil, then the absolute and irredeemable character of violence commits me to this action. But this is just what the pacifists thinks he or she ought not to do.

The first thing to note about this argument is its consequentialist character. It holds that pacifism must be committed to the view that violence is the supreme harm that can be done to another, and it is this and only this evil consequence that makes the action morally wrong. On the consequentialist paradigm of ethics, it is only the *amount* of good and evil in the consequences resulting from an action that can determine the latter's moral character, and the primary objective of moral action is to maximize the good and minimize the evil. Thus, it comes as a surprise to few moral theorists, and least of all to pacifists, to hear the argument that *if* it is theoretically possible that the use of violence may on occasion be necessary to prevent the occurrence of greater violence, and *if* all action ought to aim at the goal of maximizing good and minimizing evil, then the pacifist's absolute prohibition on the use of violence is quite wrong.

One response that some defenders of pacifism have made to this line of argument is that it fails to take seriously the implication of saying that the harm of violence or killing is "absolute," namely that the sum of the evil of two (or a million) absolutes is no greater than that of one, any more than the sum of two or more infinities is greater than one infinity. This being the case, the pacifist could defeat the consequentialist argument on its own grounds by denying the theoretical possibility of one act of violence being a lesser evil than another or even many others. This line of defence, however, is problematic because it succeeds in avoiding the charge of inconsistency at the cost of putting forward a highly implausible view of moral accounting. For, whatever the gravity of the evil of violence or homicide, surely it must be true that, all other things being equal, the violent death of a thousand persons is worse than the death of one. Pacifism, however, can be defended on other grounds consistent with this recognition.

The other response to the consequentialist objection, and the one that would surely be made by the *a priori* pacifist against whom Narveson directs his argument, is simply to deny the validity of the consequentialist paradigm of ethics itself. That is to say, the *a priori* pacifist simply does not admit the thesis that the sole criterion of right action is the balance of good over evil resulting from the action, nor, consequently, that the quantity of violence resulting from a choice among various actions is the *sole* determinant of the morality of the choice. This is precisely the respect in which the pacifism in question is *a priori*. The rule against violence, etc., is not derived solely from a determination of the quantity of good or evil resulting in every case, but from some intrinsic character of the act of violence (or force or killing) itself. In the case of the divine command pacifist, the rule is directly derived from the perceived will of God; in the case of a rationalist pacifism, from a principle such as the Kantian principle of respect for persons as ends, and so on.

Here again it is evident that the pacifist doctrine need not appeal to some unique, esoteric structure of ethics. It does, however, generally side with one of the important traditions in ethical theory against the consequentialist, or at least a simple act utilitarian, tradition. The pacifist's absolute rejection of violence is no different in its *logic* from any deontological moral claim that demands adherence to a rule, such as a rule of justice, for example, even in circumstances where the good is not maximized thereby. Its logic is solidly in the ethical traditions that hold, for example, that good may not be maximized by means that deny the fundamental rights of others, that a just war may not be fought by unjust means even if its aims are put in jeopardy, and so on. Narveson's argument against pacifism at this point is painted with such broad strokes that it challenges far more than only pacifism: it challenges all non-consequentialist theories of ethics. One might note that it even challenges the theory of rights that forms the basis of Narveson's first argument against pacifism above. For, it is commonly held that one of the significant things about having rights is that they cannot justifiably be violated simply on a showing that the greater good is served thereby.[27]

The Argument From the Concern for "Clean Hands"

A common argument against the pacifist is that there is surely something wrong with an ethic that permits a greater amount of violence to occur, as long as that violence is done at the hands of someone else. Even on most nonconsequentialist ethical theories if violence is an evil, to say nothing of a supreme evil, then surely there must be a duty to *prevent* aggressors from inflicting this evil upon others, if not oneself. And if there is such a duty, if the violence being threatened by others is greater than the violence required to prevent it, then surely the latter violence must be justified. But since this is precisely what pacifists deny, it is clear that for them it is more important that they not *do* violence than that violence be prevented. Such a preoccupation with one's own moral action, Navreson charges, cannot be justified. It reflects a kind of self-centred concern with the purity of one's own soul and myopic neglect of the interests of others incompatible with the very idea of morality itself. "What it comes down to," he says, "is that pacifists want, so to speak, to keep their own hands clean. Never mind how many others will be murdered, raped, tortured by their refusal to use violence if it is necessary to prevent that. The interests of their own souls come first!"[28]

This criticism, unlike the previous ones we have considered, is not that pacifism is internally inconsistent or incoherent in some way, but that it is simply morally irresponsible. Pacifists apparently take the view that they bear responsibility only for their own actions and not for the consequences of actions by others. If a madman threatens to murder several people unless the pacifist bystander stops him with the necessary violence of which he or she is capable, is the latter not responsible for the deaths of those murdered if he or she does not intervene? Many critics of pacifism assert that the pacifist is responsible for the deaths. Narveson does not go quite this far, however. He recognizes that there is something quite wrong in saying *simpliciter* that the pacifist is responsible for the deaths, since surely the responsibility is primarily the murderer's. Yet, he says, "It certainly was a *result* of [the pacifist's] nonaction that those people died, in the circumstances. And can't [he or she] be blamed for that?"[29]

Of course, whether or not pacifists are to be "blamed" or held "responsible" for the inaction that allowed these deaths depends upon whether they have failed in the performance of their moral obligations. It is simply question-begging to say that they are to blame, because what is at issue is whether or not the refusal to prevent the deaths by violent means *was* such a failure. That it was a moral failure is precisely what pacifists deny, and it is this denial that must be shown to be mistaken. Why do pacifists believe that the refusal to defend with violence the murderer's innocent victims is not an abdication of moral responsibility? Is it because they hold the view that "one can be blamed only for action rather than inaction," as Narveson suggests?[30] I see nothing that would commit pacifists to this admittedly indefensible view. They need hold only that the action required in this case to prevent the evil is a *morally unacceptable means* of preventing the evil. Pacifists might well hold that there is in general a duty to prevent harm to others and to do good for others. In fact, most pacifist groups espouse stronger duties of benef- icence (e.g., "serving one's neighbour," "defending the oppressed") than are generally held in popular, nonpacifist morality. But, in addition, they hold that there are moral limits on the means by which such beneficence is to be accomplished.

Again, the pacifist logic at this point is no different from any standard deontological or nonconsequentialist view of morality. Following nearly all ethical theories of this type, paci- fists would appear to presuppose a significant moral distinction in certain circumstances between "doing" evil and "permitting" evil to occur. This seems to be in the very nature of nonconsequentialist theories; for since the theories hold certain features of actions them- selves to be "wrong-making" or "right-making," it is essential for them to rely upon some theory of action that provides criteria for distinguishing between "action" and "non-action" or "doing" and "permitting." I am not sure that pacifist doctrine has been any more success- ful at providing a satisfactory account of this distinction than have other ethical theorists who espouse it,[31] or have the modern legal systems in which it is firmly entrenched. But here again, the distinction itself is not unique to pacifism. The debate on the morality of euthana- sia has focused on just this issue, with one side arguing that there is an important distinction between "killing" a person and only "permitting" the person to die, which sometimes makes a difference in the moral character of the two actions, and the other side arguing that there is no difference at all.[32]

What, then, is to be made of Narveson's charge that pacifists' concern with not doing violence is primarily a self-centred concern with keeping their own souls pure and hands clean? Having carefully laid out the logic of the pacifist argument, it is evident how the charge quite widely misses its mark. Pacifists do not argue that the *reason* for not using violence (or whatever) in self-defence is that it would soil their hands. Indeed, the claim that one has soiled one's hands makes no sense unless it is already assumed that the action was morally wrong.

One cannot sacrifice one's moral integrity ("soil one's hands") unless one has done what is (for other reasons) at least *prima facie* wrong. And, of course, pacifists claim to have *independent* reasons for believing violent (or whatever) actions to be wrong — reasons of the kind we have cited above. The fact that Narveson and other nonpacifists do not accept the pacifist's reasons as legitimate does not imply in any way that pacifists' concern is primarily with the purity of their own souls.[33] If pacifism's claims are to be defeated, it still must be shown that the reasons it gives for the moral unacceptability of violence (or whatever) do not work. As we have seen, Narveson's argument against these reasons succeeds only insofar as it succeeds against the whole deontological or "absolutist" enterprise in ethics.

The Universalizability Argument Against Pacifism

In his early article against pacifism,[34] Narveson also argued that certain claims made by some pacifists fail to pass the test of morality at all. He is concerned in particular with pacifists who appear to hold that the pacifist constraints on behaviour are to be embraced only by certain people, e.g., those who choose to be pacifists. In other words, these pacifists believe that not *everyone* has the duty to refrain from violence. For some people it is permissible to use violence, perhaps even obligatory. Such a viewpoint, Narveson argues, can hardly be putting forward a *moral* claim about the use or nonuse of violence. At best it is merely a statement of this person's personal distaste of violence, and this is a position entirely consistent with the nonpacifist's claim that violence is morally permissible under certain conditions. If the pacifist's refusal of violence is a claim of moral principle, then certainly it must be the view that violence is wrong not only for him or her, but for anyone, and that the nonpacifist's view that it is permissible is incorrect. In addition, Narveson holds that pacifism cannot merely be the view that "there is something admirable or saintly about not [using violence], for . . . the non-pacifist could perfectly well agree with that. He must say, instead, that, for whatever class of people he thinks it applies to, there must be something *positively wrong* about meeting violence with force."[35]

Although Narveson does not put it in so many words, I take the thrust of his argument here to be that for claims to be *moral*, they must be universalizable in the sense theorists such as Hare and Baier have urged they must be.[36] This means that one cannot claim moral duties or permissions for oneself that would not apply with equal force to all others in similar situations. But this is just what certain pacifists appear to claim. Much that Narveson has to say about this kind of pacifism I think is correct. He is quite right to point out that the fact that one believes pacifism to be true while others do not is no reason at all for concluding that one has the duty to act pacifistically while the others have no such duty. Further, if pacifism cannot be recommended on moral grounds as a principle that ought to be followed by everyone, then it is not an ethic in the full sense of the word. It is in danger of becoming simply a personal preference or vocational choice that does not challenge nonpacifist morality in any way.

Many pacifist claims appear to fall into the trap Narveson has identified. Some of the traditional religious pacifist groups have sometimes expressed their nonresistant pacifism in dualistic terms, holding that nonresistance is a duty only for Christians (or even only for Christians of their own particular persuasion), and that violence is not only permissible for others but, in the case of those who govern society, a positive duty.[37] Other pacifist writers have espoused the view as a personal ideal or "vocation" to which it is appropriate, though not obligatory, for certain people to commit themselves.[38] These types of "pacifism" are attractive to many people because they are more "realistic" about the necessity of violence in the maintenance of social order, while at the same time affirming that pacifist commitments play an important social role as a witness to an important moral ideal. But it is just this willingness to condone, even recommend, violence in those contexts where the nonpacifist views it as appropriate that renders it innocuous as a *social* ethic.

The validity of Narveson's complaint against these versions of pacifism lies in just this idea of a "social ethic." What Narveson means by an ethic of "moral principle" is a body of rules and principles by which the members of a society can order their lives in some kind of cooperative enterprise. Clearly, pacifists who do not see their pacifism as relevant to just this situation, but relegate it to restricted social roles or spheres of behaviour, are not espousing a "social ethic." As one writer has put it, this kind of pacifism offers no more a critique of the social institutions of violence and war than the practice of celibacy offers a critique of the institution of marriage![39]

But if these nonuniveralizable versions of pacifism do not count as a social ethic, does this mean that they are not moral views at all? This, I think, is too strong a claim. I see no reason to limit the concept of morality to the level of duties, rights, and principles, nor to the sphere of social rules. The moral life also includes the sphere of ideals, of supererogatory goods, of virtues, and the like. These do not always give rise to universalizable rules and principles nor to strict obligations. Not everything that is good or virtuous is also morally required. As J. O. Urmson, among others, has pointed out, the saint and the hero are persons who are generally considered to have adopted a better way of life than the rest of us who merely do our duty, but their example is not universalizable.[40]

There is no inconsistency in a pacifism that simply holds the life of nonviolence to be better than one reliant upon violence, nor is there any reason to insist that commitment to such an ideal is not a moral commitment. It may even be that the personal commitment one makes to this ideal could give rise to a nonuniversalizable duty to live in accordance with it, as Craig Ihara has argued.[41] Such a view, however, runs into trouble if it also asserts a positive duty on the part of others to use violence in defence of certain values. For, certainly, commitment to an ideal is not morally justifiable if it conflicts with the universalizable obligations of general morality.

There is another way in which a kind of "dualistic" pacifism could circumvent Narveson's universalizability objection. Many religious pacifists, as we have seen, hold the view that their pacifist principles ought not to be imposed upon the society at large as a rule of social policy. Thus, it appears that they do not hold the rule of nonviolence (or whatever) to be a universal obligation, and hence their pacifism fails to achieve the status of a social ethic that in any way challenges nonpacifism. But this need not necessarily be true. Such a pacifism could take the position that the pacifist rules of behaviour do prescribe a morally *preferable* way of life, which ideally ought to be adopted by everyone. Yet, it might also hold that this moral obligation ought not to be imposed (e.g., by the coercive institutions of politics and law) upon a society that is unwilling to accept the severe discipline of pacifism or its sometimes sacrificial consequences. This pacifism holds that what is morally right is not necessarily always the best as an enforced social *policy*. There is nothing unique, or even widely controversial, about the claim that there are sometimes good moral reasons for not trying to enforce the highest moral standards as social policy. This is reflected in the widely held view that morality ought not always be enforced by law. So, Christian pacifists might hold the view that, while in some ultimate sense everyone ought to follow the nonviolent moral example of Jesus, nevertheless, in a society where most people in fact do not accept this discipline (even thought they ought), it would be wrong to advocate a pacifist social policy for that society, because such a course would involve the imposition of certain sacrifices (brought on by the pacifist stance) that are not voluntarily accepted by those uncommitted to the ethic. Such pacifists might even hold that, given society's unwillingness to embrace the pacifist discipline, the next best alternative social policy is a system of morally sanctioned and constrained violence, as advocated in the traditional theory of the "just war," for example. They, of course, could still refuse violence for themselves as a violation of moral duty and, thus, as a matter of conscience. Indeed, it would be inconsistent for them not to do so.

This form of apparently "dualistic" pacifism would meet the universalizabilty test so long as it viewed pacifism as a possible, and preferable, moral alternative for society, even given the kind of violent aggression that is bound to occur in the world as it is. Most nonpacifists, of course, hold that society could not be organized in a morally acceptable way on pacifist principles. But it is on this substantive, normative issue that the debate between pacifists and nonpacifists is properly focused.

Perhaps it is not purely coincidental that many of the religious pacifist groups have tended to view themselves as sectarian remnants of the true (pacifist) faith, destined to perennial exclusion from the irredeemable social mainstream. Their "dualistic" morality, which condones violence within the social order while rejecting it for themselves, is not so much a denial of the ultimate universality of the pacifist norm as it is a stoic acceptance of the fact that the social order will never embrace true faith and righteousness. For them, the question of whether pacifism is a social ethic for the world does arise — not because the ethic is not universalizable, but because the question is purely hypothetical.

Conclusion: Pacifism and Faith

I have tried to show that certain attempts to undermine the pacifist ethic on *a priori* grounds are unsuccessful. They fail because they do not take seriously enough the varied ways in which the case for the doctrine can be, and often is made. Hence, they miss the way the structures of the pacifist arguments follow rather conventional patterns of moral argument, relying upon concepts well-established in various ethical theories. The case, then, is not so much against pacifism as it is against these larger ethical traditions.

If the case against pacifism is to be made, then, it must be made on the grounds that its substantive normative claims about the illegitimacy of force, coercion, violence, killing, or war are unacceptable on moral grounds. This, of course, is what most people believe. Even those who have argued, as I have, that the *a priori* case against pacifism fails, usually are quick to add, as does Tom Regan, that "pacifism is false, and profoundly so. . . ."[42] This verdict seems obvious to most people because of the apparently overwhelming evidence of the unpalatable consequences resulting from the refusal to use violent means of defence against aggression. While the effectiveness of violence in resisting aggression and injustice is vastly overrated in prevailing popular and philosophical morality,[43] and the effectiveness of nonviolent forms of resistance woefully underrated and unexplored by a society preoccupied with violent "technological fixes" to human conflict,[44] nevertheless it must be admitted that there certainly are times and circumstances in which adherence to nonviolence results in the tragic sacrifice of innocent lives and fundamental human values.[45] For this reason it is no mere coincidence that pacifisms of absolute principle tend to be most strongly embraced within religious communities, where it is combined with an eschatological faith in a sovereign deity who will, in the long run, insure that these sacrifices are turned to some higher good, and that justice will prevail. For those without such faith the wait for the long run will seem morally irresponsible.

The philosopher Elisabeth Anscombe has shown that this kind of faith is often needed to undergird even a nonpacifist adherence to absolute limits on one's means of defence. In her article, "War and Murder," in which she defends the Catholic "Just War" prohibition on the killing of innocent civilians in the conduct of war and argues strongly against the pacifist prohibition on all killing in war, she says:

> It is not a vague faith in the triumph of "the spirit" over force (there is little enough warrant for that), but a definite faith in the divine promises, that makes us believe that the Church cannot fail. Those, therefore, who think they must be prepared to wage a war with Russia involving the deliberate massacre of cities, must be prepared to say to God: "We had to break your law, lest your Church fail. We could not obey your commandments, for we did not believe your promises."[46]

Anscombe could not have expressed more poignantly the faith of the religious pacifist. Ultimately, it may be the faith of all absolute pacifism.

NOTES

1. In the case of Gandhi, this expositor is Joan Bondurant in *Conquest of Violence* (Berkeley: U. of Calif. Press, 1967).
2. This characterization of pacifism is cited by Jan Narveson in his article, "Is Pacifism Consistent?" *Ethics*, vol. 78 (1968): 148. It is repeated by Tom Regan in "A Defense of Pacifism," *Canadian Journal of Philosophy*, vol. 2, no. 1 (1972): 73—86.
3. See, for example, Tom Regan, *op. cit.*
4. The first, and most widely reprinted of Narveson's articles against pacifism was his "Pacifism: A Philosophical Analysis," in *Ethics*, vol. 75 (1965): 259—71. Reprinted in Richard Wasserstrom, ed., *War and Morality* (Belmont: Wadsworth Publishing Co., 1970), 63—77. All page references to this article are to this reprinted version. The second was a reply to several critics in "Is Pacifism Consistent?," *op. cit.*, and the latest was a section on pacifism in his chapter, "Violence and War," in Tom Regan, *Matters of Life and Death: New Introductory Essays in Moral Philosophy* (New York: Random House, 1989), 109—147.

   In fairness to Professor Narveson, it should be said that the articles to which this paper responds do not represent accurately his most recent thinking or writing on the matter. He kindly consented to read and respond to a draft of this paper, and his comments were very helpful in clarifying some of the points in the paper. While his general position has not changed, and he would not accept most of the arguments I advance here, it is clear that he would state his position in a somewhat different manner.
5. Among these replies are the following: M.J. Whitman, "Is Pacifism Self-Contradictory?," *Ethics*, vol. 76 (1966): 307–8. Ronald B. Miller, "Violence, Force and Coercion," in *Violence: Award Winning Essays in the Council for Philosophical Studies Competition.* Edited by Jerome Shaffer (New York, David McKay, 1971), 11–44. Tom Regan, "A Defense of Pacifism," *op. cit.* Craig K. Ihara, "In Defense of a Version of Pacifism," *Ethics*, vol. 88 (July 1978): 369—74. A recent, excellent reply is by Cheyney C. Ryan, "Self-Defense, Pacifism, and the Possibility of Killing," *Ethics*, vol. 93 (April 1983): 508—24.
6. John H. Yoder analyses 18 different versions of religious pacifism in his book *Nevertheless: The Varieties of Christian Pacifism* (Scottdale: Herald Press, 1971).

7. Narveson, "Pacifism: A Philosophical Analysis," *op. cit.*, 63.
8. Ibid, 68.
9. Ibid.
10. For example, Gandhi wrote, "I do believe that where there is only a choice between cowardice and violence, I would advice violence." *Young India* (August 11, 1920), as quoted in Bondurant, *op. cit.*, 28.
11. A good example of this is the pacifism of the Jehovah's Witnesses, which abjures all participation in warfare except for the coming War of Armageddon into which they believe they will be led by God Himself. An interesting case arose in the U.S. Supreme Court concerning whether JW's qualified for the conscientious objector exemption under the Selective Service Act. The Act required that to qualify for this exemption one must be opposed to participation in "war in any form." The Selective Service officials had refused CO status to a JW because of his admission that he would fight in the War of Armageddon, but the Supreme Court reversed this decision on the grounds that, whatever the War of Armageddon was, it was not a "real shooting war" of the kind Congress had in mind when drafting the Act. *Sicurella v. United States*, 348 U.S. 385 (1955), 391.
12. Narveson, "Pacifism: A Philosophical Analysis," *op. cit.*, 68.
13. An example of such a Rule Utilitarian argument is to be found in Martin Benjamin, "Pacifism for Pragmatists," *Ethics*, vol. 83 (April 1973): 196–213.
14. The distinctions between force, coercion, and violence, which are well-defined in political science and philosophy, seem to be lost upon many of the participants in the debate over pacifism, where "force" is used as a global reference to what the pacifist rejects. In this paper I follow the standard definitions of these terms. "Force" in human relations refers to the exertion of physical or psychological power against another person in a manner that completely overrides the latter's choice. One who is the object of force does not in any sense "act" but is acted upon. Force can be used in nonviolent (nonharmful) as well as violent ways, as when an unwilling child is forcefully (but nonharmfully) pulled from the path of an oncoming truck. "Force" is in stark contrast with "coercion," a rather complex concept that, roughly speaking, involves inducing another to choose to act in a way that he or she would prefer not to act had the coercer not worsened the conditions of his or her choice with threats, etc. Coercion, like force, can be accomplished either nonviolently, as when mother says, "Eat your spinach or you will not be allowed to go out to play," or violently, if the threatened sanction is an act of violence. The concept of violence is also very complex. But unlike force and coercion, it necessarily involves the infliction of serious injury or harm upon another person.
15. First published in English in *Politics*, July–August 1947. Reprinted in Peter Mayer, *The Pacifist Conscience* (Chicago: Henry Regnery Co., 1967), 423–39.
16. An example of this argument appears in the article by Cheyney C. Ryan, *op. cit.*, 522ff. Says Ryan, "That the refusal to allow others to treat one as an object is an important step to defining one's own integrity is a point well understood by revolutionary theorists such as Fannon [sic]. It is a point apparently lost to pacifists like Gandhi, who suggested that the Jews in the Warsaw Ghetto would have made the superior moral statement by committing collective suicide, since their resistance proved futile anyway. . . . Our real concern is what the refusal to intervene would express about our relationships and ourselves, for one of the ways we acknowledge the importance of a relationship is through our willingness to take such actions, and that is why the problem in such cases is how we can bring ourselves *not* to intervene (how is passivity possible)." Such a statement, typical of pacifism's critics, completely misses the central core of the Gandhian philosophy of nonviolent resistance.
17. "Pacifism: A Philosophical Analysis," *op. cit.*, 72.
18. See, for example, the discussion of the correlation of duties and rights by Joel Feinberg in *Social Philosophy* (Englewood Cliffs: Prentice-Hall, 1973), Chap. 4. It should be noted that a rejection of the view that all duties imply correlative rights need not entail a rejection of the other side of the correlativity thesis — that all rights imply duties. Certainly the pacifist need not reject this, the move widely accepted, version of the correlativity of rights and duties. Narveson's argument at this point rests upon the *two-way* correlativity thesis, since his point is that if pacifists think that violence (or whatever) is wrong, they are committed to thinking that they have a right not to have violence used against them.

19. For an example of the latter kind of argument for pacifism, see Stanley Hauerwas, *A Community of Character* (Notre Dame: Notre Dame U. Press, 1981) and *The Peaceable Kingdom* (Notre Dame: Notre Dame U. Press, 1983).

20. This is because, whatever else "rights" are, they do more than merely express the correlative duty of action or forbearance. Moral and legal philosophers have pointed out that to assert a right is to in some sense make a *claim* upon someone (the one who has the duty, and "against" whom one has the right) to the performance of the duty. This claim may take the form of pressures that range all the way from coercive threats of violence or of legal sanctions to mere moral "demands" or even "reminders." It is the more coercive of these claims that are antithetical to certain forms of pacifism.

21. Narveson himself suggests this when he says that we have a right "to anything else that might be necessary (*other things being equal*). . . ." (Emphasis mine.) "Pacifism: A Philosophical Analysis," *op. cit.*, 73.

22. This counter-example to Narveson of the "innocent third party" is made with great clarity by Cheyney Ryan, *op. cit.*, 517ff.

23. The importance of the "forfeiture" argument to a theory of just killing is recognized by Michael Walzer in his classic book, *Just and Unjust Wars* (New York: Basic Books, 1977). Walzer devotes six chapters (Part III) to the development of such a theory.

24. Cheyney Ryan has done an excellent job of analysing the various theories of "forfeiture" put forward by nonpacifists, and showing the difficulties involved in them. In the absence of a plausible accounting of "forfeiture," the pacifist rejection of the thesis, Ryan suggests, remains a plausible alternative. Ryan also makes the point I have made here that the disagreement between the pacifist and nonpacifist is not on the question of whether there are limits on the defence of one's rights, but on *what* the limits are. Ryan, *op. cit.*

25. This agreement appears in Narveson's "Violence and War," *op. cit.*, 118ff.

26. Ibid., 119.

27. That is, as Ronald Dworkin puts it, rights "trump" utilities. *Taking Rights Seriously* (Cambridge: Harvard U. Press), Chap. 8.

28. Narveson, "Violence and War," *op. cit.*, 120.

29. Ibid.

30. Ibid.

31. See the defence of this distinction by Philippa Foot, "The Problem of Abortion and the Doctrine of Double-Effect," in James Rachels, ed., *Moral Problems* (New York: Harper and Row, 1971), 29–41.

32. In this debate James Rachels puts forward the "no difference" position in his article, "Active and Passive Euthanasia," *The New England Journal of Medicine*, vol 292, no. 2 (January 9, 1975): 78–80. The argument against the distinction is similar to Narveson's against the pacifist. Both hold that where the foreseen consequences of action and inaction are the same, the moral character of the latter is the same. This, of course, is to defeat the deontological distinction by asserting a teleological or consequentialist criterion. For an argument against Rachels, see Tom Beauchamp and James Childress, *Principles of Biomedical Ethics*, 2nd ed. (Oxford: Oxford U. Press, 1983), 117ff.

33. This point was made clear to me by Thomas Nagel in his "War and Massacre," in Cohen, Nagel, and Scanlon, *War and Moral Responsibility*. (Princeton: Princeton U. Press, 1974), 12. Nagel shows how the "pure hands" argument fails against all forms of "absolutist" ethics, such as the just war theory rejection of the thesis that killing noncombatants is sometimes necessary in war. My argument is that this absolute prohibition in just war theory is identical in its logic to the pacifist rejection of all killing or violence.

34. "Pacifism: A Philosophical Analysis," *op. cit.*, 67ff.

35. Ibid., 65.

36. R. M. Hare, *The Language of Morals* (Oxford: Oxford U. Press, 1952) and Kurt Baier, *The Moral Point of View* (Cornell: Cornell U. Press, 1958).

37. For a statement of this position by a Mennonite, see Guy F. Hershberger, *War, Peace and Nonresistance* (Scottdale, PA: Herald Press, 1944). Not all Mennonite writers would express the doctrine of pacifism in this way, however. For a modified view, see John H. Yoder, *The Christian Witness to the State* (Newton, KA: Faith and Life Press, 1964).

38. This version of pacifism is defended by Craig K. Ihara, *op. cit.*, and by John Miller, "Schleitheim Pacifism and Modernity," *Conrad Grebel Review*, vol. 3, 2 (Spring 1985), 155–64.

39. I have been unable to recall where I came across this analogy, but it is not my own. It is important to recognize the implications of this analogy in both directions. For even if celibacy does not constitute a moral critique of marriage or human sexuality, this is not generally considered a reason for believing that the commitment to celibacy is in no sense *moral*. Further, it is not implausible to call into question the appropriateness of the entire analogy, for in a certain sense celibacy *is* a critique of human sexuality (at least in the minds of those who choose it as a moral virtue). The critique is something like the following: There is something about sex and/or marriage that detracts people from the "higher" goods in life (e.g., contemplation, spirituality, freedom to serve humanity, etc.), which is not to say that it has no other redeeming virtues, or, at least, that it is not a "necessary evil" (for the procreation of the species). Something like this seems to be implied in the view of the commitment to celibacy as *moral*. This can be seen in other types of moral heroism or sainthood, such as, for example, the "Mother Theresa" commitment to extreme altruism. The fact that this is seen as a *moral* commitment has nothing to do with the fact that the rest of humanity who do not exhibit this kind of concern for human welfare are somehow not living rightly, but rather it points out the evil inherent in the propensity of the rest of us to prefer our own interests over those of others, often to their detriment. This is part of what makes Mother Theresa and others like her, not just persons who have chosen a particular vocation rather than another (which choice has no inherent moral quality at all), but rather *moral* saints or heroines.

    In the same way the choice of pacifism as a personal moral commitment *is* a kind of critique of violence and war, and can be viewed in the same way as other kinds of moral heroism and sainthood.

40. J. O. Urmson, "Saints and Heroes," in *Essays in Moral Philosophy*, ed. A.I. Meldon (Seattle: University of Washington Press, 1958).

41. Ihara, *op. cit.*

42. Regan, "A Defense of Pacifism," *op. cit.*, 452.

43. It is rarely recognized in the popular debates about the relative effectiveness of violence and non-violence that in violent conflict the theoretically highest success rate can be only 50 percent. This is because the successful violence of the winner entails the unsuccessful violence of the loser. In reality, of course, the success rate is much lower than 50 percent because often *both sides* are losers. Whatever else may be said about the efficacy of nonviolence, it does not have this theoretical limit on its success, since it permits both sides of a conflict to "win."

44. For an excellent study of the potential for nonviolent forms of resistance, and exploration of the hidden historical examples of its successful use, see Gene Sharp, *The Politics of Nonviolent Action* (Boston: Porter Sargent, 1973).

45. Of course, we must remind ourselves that, as the tragic history of humanity clearly demonstrates, these same outcomes are the regular consequences of *violent* resistance as well. These outcomes are generally not seen as reasons to doubt the efficacy of violence, probably because of an *a priori* conception of violence as "the utmost one can *do*." The corollary of this view is that nonviolent response is not "doing the utmost," and, hence, is morally irresponsible. Perhaps this is why all the empirical evidence in history of the *failure* of violence to achieve justice or prevent evil does not seem to be counted as counter-evidence in the ethical debate. Cases of the failure of nonviolence, on the other hand, are conclusive evidence of its inefficacy.

46. Elizabeth Anscombe, "War and Murder," reprinted in Wasserstrom, *op. cit.*, 53.

QUESTIONS

1. What is the *a priori* case against pacifism?
2. Is there an important distinction between resisting violence with violence and resisting violence with force? Why or why not?
3. Is Brunk successful in arguing that the right not to be victimized by violence does not, taken by itself, imply the right to use force to resist violence?

4. Is Narveson right to think that if violence is evil the right thing to do is to minimize it even if doing so requires recourse to violent means?

5. How does Brunk defend the view that it is not always good social policy to require that people do what is morally right.

SUGGESTIONS FOR FURTHER READING

For a number of recent discussions of war and its justifications, look carefully at Trudy Govier's footnotes. In addition, the following are worth consulting:

The various speeches of George W. Bush can be found at the American White House Web site. We had proposed to use one of his speeches as a reading but learned in seeking copyright permission that the White House prohibits the reprinting of Presidential speeches in any form.

Virtually all of the major Canadian papers and magazines together with all major international newspapers and magazines covering public affairs carried extensive commentary on the pros and cons of the invasion of Iraq as it was debated in the United Nations and then initiated by the United States, Great Britain, and the other countries that participated in the invasion. Back issues of newspapers and quality magazines, Macleans for example, can be found in libraries and through newspaper Web sites. One interesting example of that commentary is "A Letter to America" by Margaret Atwood in the Friday, March 28, 2003 edition of the *Globe and Mail* in the Comment section at A17.

Throughout the period before, during, and after the war on Iraq, the journal *Tikkun* carried a series of articles examining the war from a number of difference perspectives. The commentaries are relatively short and accessible and well worth consulting.

Other Suggestions

- Elliot Abrams, "Close calls: intervention, terrorism, missile defense, and 'just war' today," Washington D.C., Ethics and Public Policy Centre, 1998.
- Karl von Clausewitz, *On War* (Princeton, N.J.: Princeton University Press, 1976). Clausewitz is one of the most famous theoreticians of the realist school. He argues that the very idea of international relations requires that nations act from self-interest. He argues that moderation in war is an absurdity, and defends the doctrine of military necessity, namely that a state is justified in doing whatever is necessary to attain a war's objectives.
- Alan M. Dershowitz, *Why (understanding the threat) Terrorism (responding to the challenge) Works*, New Haven and London: Yale University Press, 2002. The subject of this book is state-sponsored terrorism. The book begins with a discussion of how to stop harmful conduct and then applies those general approaches to deterring terrorism. The author argues that the actions and policies of the UN and Europe since 1968 have violated basic rules of deterrence and provided incentives for terrorist activity.
- Andrew Fiala, "Pacifism and the War on Terror," *The Humanist,* November/December, 2002. The author, an American professor of philosophy, offers a defence of what he calls "practical pacifism."

- J.L. Holgzrefe and Robert O. Keohane, Eds., *Humanitarian Intervention: Ethical, Legal and Political Dilemmas*, Cambridge University Press, 2003. Many of the arguments for the war in Iraq have focused on the obligation and the right of the international community, with or without a UN mandate, to intervene militarily to stop serious abuse of human rights by governments like that of Saddam Hussein. The contributors to this book seek to identify strategies designed to resolve or at least reduce the tension between protecting human rights through international military action and respect for national sovereignty.
- Robert L. Holmes, *On War* (Princeton N.J.: Princeton University Press, 1989). This book, which is referred to by Trudy Govier, is an excellent recent discussion of the morality of both conventional and nuclear war. The author defends the view that modern warfare cannot be justified, morally speaking. The book contains a careful evaluation of the three approaches to an evaluation of the moral dimension of war mentioned in the introduction — political realism, Just War Theory, and pacifism.
- Ted Honderich, *After the Terror*, New York: Columbia University Press, 2002. This book takes up the question of the "root causes" of terrorism and argues that the wealthy industrialized world is partially responsible for terrorism because it has not intervened to create the conditions for longer and better lives on the part of the millions of people in the world today who live under conditions of severe poverty and depravation.
- National Conference of Catholic Bishops, "The Challenge to Peace: God's Promise and Our Response" (a pastoral letter), *The Chicago Catholic*, June 24 to July 1, 1983. Probably the most important recent contribution to the Just War debate. It surveys the traditional views of the use of military force by the Roman Catholic Church and applies those views to an assessment and a moral critique of American nuclear defence policies and armaments.
- Brian Orend, "Evaluating Pacifism," *Dialogue* XL (2001). The author develops what he describes as a rigorous, sympathetic account of pacifism and then critically evaluates its merits from the perspective of Just War Theory. He concludes that pacifism is not a viable approach to violence and war.

Chapter 11

Tools and Theories

Introduction

The goal of contributors to a book like this one is to provide answers to questions about how we determine as individuals and as a society the morally appropriate solutions to difficult practical issues. The fact that the issues are contemporary and the readings for the most part current may mislead us into thinking that reflections on morality are a recent phenomenon. While it is true that critical reflections on practical moral issues of the sort we have examined in this book are fairly recent, for thousands of years philosophers have been concerned with providing theories that explain the role of morality in daily life. Many of these theories have been at the level of generalized accounts of what morality is and of how we come to know what we ought to do. In this chapter, we provide a selection of some of these moral theories and consider some of the connections between these theories and the resolution of moral issues.

As noted in the Preface, in this book we have adopted the approach that theory and practice are connected and that one need not learn the theory first in order to apply it to practical issues or to understand the issues themselves. Moral philosophers have always been concerned to connect theory and practice. Philosophers such as Plato, Aristotle, Kant, Hume, and Mill provided general theories about how we ought to live at the same time as they examined practical issues such as capital punishment, poverty, sexuality, and the treatment of animals, for example. In the twentieth century, however, positivism and analytical philosophy directed attention away from the resolution of issues, considered now not to be the proper domain of philosophy, to an examination of the use and function of the language of morality. Many moral philosophers became convinced that their proper job was linguistic and conceptual analysis.

Since the latter half of the twentieth century, however, this trend has been reversed. Two publications in particular illustrate that change. John Rawls's *A Theory of Justice* and the journal, *Philosophy & Public Affairs*, came out in 1971 and succeeded in once again legitimizing the examination of practical issues. By providing a theory of justice and generating principles that were to form the background structure of a just society, Rawls's highly influential work turned attention back to applying theory to practice. Rawls's theory is examined by several authors in this book, including Christine Koggel in the poverty chapter and Annette Baier in this chapter. Judith Jarvis Thomson's article on abortion in the first issue of *Philosophy & Public Affairs* is also regarded by many as signalling a decisive shift back toward the explicit examination of practical issues.

Technology has also played a role in directing attention back to practical problems. With technological advances have come new moral dilemmas with respect to issues such as abortion and assisted reproduction, euthanasia, pornography, the environment, business, and war. These developments not only demand our immediate attention, but highlight the need for critical tools that allow us to evaluate the complex and multiple dimensions of these practical issues. These technological advances have also breathed new life into the project of using insights from the kind of theories presented in this chapter as critical tools for evaluating moral issues. This development is reflected in a number of contributors to this book whose conclusions on the moral issues they are examining are derived from the application of specific moral theories.

The resurgence of practical ethics has also brought with it, however, close critical examination of traditional moral theories themselves. This has been stimulated at least in part by growing awareness of the entrenched character of discrimination in both modern and traditional societies, widespread resistance to its eradication, and the apparent insensitivity of traditional moral theorists to its pervasiveness and importance. Issues in chapters such as equality and discrimination, aboriginal rights, and poverty focus attention on these concerns, although there continues to be deep disagreement about where and how principles of equality are appropriately applied.

How might we distinguish what we do when we critically examine practical moral issues and what we do when we provide theories of morally right action? As a first attempt, we can say that any human activity can be approached at two levels. We might call the first the level of participation and the second the level of reflection. Thus, for example, we can participate in a game such as hockey or chess. Or we can stand back and reflect on the nature of the game and how it is played.

Resolving moral issues can be thought of as an activity. And, as with any human activity, we can, if we wish, participate by becoming involved in discussions aimed at resolving particular issues. Or we can stand back and reflect on the nature of morality and how moral problems are solved. As with most activities, of course, serious reflection presupposes some direct experience with the activity itself. That is one of the reasons the approach to moral issues that has dominated this book has been that of participant in the activity of resolving concrete moral issues. However, participation in the resolution of concrete moral issues presupposes certain commitments to particular principles and theoretical foundations. It also raises questions that are genuinely interesting in their own right, questions that can be approached only by reflecting on our own attempts, as well as the attempts of others, to resolve particular moral problems.

What kinds of questions are suggested by discussion and argument in previous chapters? We shall highlight just two. First, one of the striking features of the readings collected in this anthology is the extent to which those who have made serious efforts to develop and support positions on particular issues disagree. What are we to conclude from this fact? One possible response is simply to throw up our hands in frustration and go on to some more "productive" activity. But this response has serious implications. The issues we have been examining are important and virtually unavoidable. If we cannot resolve them through rational discussion, how are they going to be resolved? Some would argue (as for example in the euthanasia, capital punishment, or pornography debates) that the position of the majority should prevail. But this, too, has worrisome implications that require careful exploration. It would seem, on reflection, that there is no "easy" way to escape the fact that well-intentioned people do disagree on moral questions. Why is this so? Does it tell us something of importance about the nature of morality?

Asking whether moral issues can be resolved would seem to lead to further questions: Is the resolution of moral issues a general responsibility? Or is it a task that can be or ought to be assigned to experts? There is one sense in which responsibility for resolving moral problems clearly cannot be assigned to others. If I am faced with a request by an ill person that she be helped in terminating her life, then I must respond to the request. No one else can do it for me. In this sense we cannot assign responsibility for our own behaviour to others. But it is always possible to seek advice in deciding what to do. We might then rephrase our question by asking whether moral philosophers are a good source of advice for those who are faced with difficult moral problems.

Consideration of all these questions has given rise to a number of positions, many of which are reflected in the readings in previous chapters. Faced with disagreement on moral questions, some philosophers have opted for a position of moral relativism (discussed in this chapter by David Wong). Others reject this view. An alternative position might be that not all moral disputes are alike. In some cases agreement can be achieved and in some cases it cannot. Finally, some have argued that there are basic principles that no agent could rationally reject. If moral argument is built on those principles, agreement should be possible. This view would seem to be implied by Andrew Brook in his discussion of our obligation to future generations (Chapter 8) and by J.T. Stevenson in his discussion of aboriginal rights (Chapter 6).

Further reflection on the features of moral argument and the nature of morality reveals another dimension to the activity of examining moral issues, one that is less visible because it operates at the level of assumptions about the nature of human beings and social relations. The readings in this chapter explore this dimension of morality and provide us with various views about the nature of human beings, morality, and social relations. The idea that our embeddedness in social relations is relevant to the identification, examination, and analysis of moral issues has been a recurring theme in this book and is particularly evident in the chapters on discrimination, aboriginal rights, poverty, the environment, and business ethics.

The Readings

Immanuel Kant takes the human capacity to reason to be the basis for describing human beings as "ends in themselves" and as having "absolute worth." This capacity, he argues, distinguishes us from non-human animals in that it enables people to deliberate and make decisions about what they ought to do, decisions that are an obvious vital part of morality. Based on this understanding of human nature, Kant formulates what he calls the categorical imperative, "act only on that maxim whereby thou canst at the same time will that it should become a universal law," as the basis for determining morally right action.

The reading by John Stuart Mill assumes a conception of the nature of morality different from that defended by Kant. While Mill agrees that rationality is a unique and valuable human capacity, he looks to the consequences of human action to determine morally right action. He argues that "pleasure, and freedom from pain, are the only things desirable as ends" and that a calculation of happiness specified in terms of both the quantity and quality of pleasure should form the basis for morality. In calculating the happiness that will result, Mill distinguishes himself from consequentialist accounts by egoists, who argue that our own interests should count for more. Mill argues that everyone's interests count equally; there is no justification for giving more value to one's own interests than to the interests of anyone else affected by one's actions. The greatest happiness principle dictates that morally right action is that which produces the greatest happiness for the greatest number of people.

The third reading by David Wong presents an approach that is sceptical of the project in which each of the authors thus far has been engaged, the project of determining morally right action on the basis of a formula that holds for all people in all places and at all times. By providing examples of deep disagreements about moral practices in various cultures, Wong sounds a warning against complacency in a belief that we can formulate universal principles that dictate duties that are absolutely without exception. This belief, he argues, has and can result in a disrespect for people from different cultures. Wong defends a form of relativism that he sees as occupying the middle ground between universalism and the extreme version of relativism that holds that all moralities are equally true.

In the fourth and final reading, Annette Baier also reflects on the tendency in traditional moral theory to formulate universal principles. However, Baier focuses attention on both the contexts within which the theories were formulated and the assumptions about people and social relations underlying these theories. She distinguishes two sorts of approaches to thinking about morality, one that sees justice as a primary virtue and values individual rights, and one that emphasizes our interdependency and values relationships and responsibilities to others. Like other theorists defending the second approach of an ethic of care, Baier connects this way of thinking about morality to people who have been and continue to be disadvantaged, and argues that this approach offers important insights that can and should be incorporated by the justice approach, which has dominated moral and political theory. A care approach moves the focus from the task of determining individual rights and settling conflicting rights to the social and political contexts within which relationships are formed and responsibilities are created. The reading by Baier represents but one approach critical of traditional moral theory in the important and growing area of feminist ethics. It turns out that this approach is central to many of the readings that take the analysis of equality and discrimination to be relevant to an assessment of moral issues.

THE CATEGORICAL IMPERATIVE

Immanuel Kant

Nothing can possibly be conceived in the world, or even out of it, which can be called good without qualification, except a *good will*. Intelligence, wit, judgment, and the other *talents* of the mind, however they may be named, or courage, resolution, perseverance, as qualities of temperament, are undoubtedly good and desirable in many respects; but these gifts of nature may also become extremely bad and mischievous if the will which is to make use of them, and which, therefore, constitutes what is called *character*, is not good. It is the same with the *gifts of fortune*. Power, riches, honor, even health, and the general well-being and contentment with one's condition, which is called *happiness*, inspire pride, and often presumption, if there is not a good will to correct the influence of these on the mind, and with this also to rectify the whole principle of acting, and adapt it to its end. The sight of a being who is not adorned with a single feature of a pure and good will, enjoying unbroken prosperity, can never give pleasure to an impartial rational spectator. Thus a good will appears to constitute the indispensable condition even of being worthy of happiness.

* * * * * * *

From Fundamental Principles of the Metaphysics of Morals *(1785), translated by T.K. Abbott.*

An action done from duty derives its moral worth, *not from the purpose* which is to be attained by it, but from the maxim by which it is determined, and therefore does not depend on the realization of the object of the action, but merely on the *principle of volition* by which the action has taken place, without regard to any object of desire. It is clear from what precedes that the purposes which we may have in view in our actions, or their effects regarded as ends and springs of the will, cannot give to actions any unconditional or moral worth. In what, then, can their worth lie if it is not to consist in the will and in reference to its expected effect? It cannot lie anywhere but in the *principle of the will* without regard to the ends which can be attained by the action. For the will stands between its *a priori** principle, which is formal, and its *a posteriori*† spring, which is material, as between two roads, and as it must be determined by something, it follows that it must be determined by the formal principle of volition when an action is done from duty, in which case every material principle has been withdrawn from it.

The third proposition, which is a consequence of the two preceding, I would express thus: *Duty is the necessity of acting from respect for the law*. I may have *inclination* for an object as the effect of my proposed action, but I cannot have *respect* for it just for this reason that it is an effect and not an energy of will. Similarly, I cannot have respect for inclination, whether my own or another's; I can at most, if my own, approve it; if another's, sometimes even love it, that is, look on it as favorable to my own interest. It is only what is connected with my will as a principle, by no means as an effect — what does not subserve my inclination, but overpowers it, or at least in case of choice excludes it from its calculation — in other words, simply the law of itself, which can be an object of respect, and hence a command. Now an action done from duty must wholly exclude the influence of inclination, and with it every object of the will, so that nothing remains which can determine the will except objectively the *law*, and subjectively *pure respect* for this practical law, and consequently the maxim that I should follow this law even to the thwarting of all of my inclinations.

Thus the moral worth of an action does not lie in the effect expected from it, nor in any principle of action which requires to borrow its motive from this expected effect. For all these effects — agreeableness of one's condition, and even the promotion of the happiness of others — could have been also brought about by other causes, so that for this there would have been no need of the will of a rational being; whereas it is in this alone that the supreme and unconditional good can be found. The pre-eminent good which we call moral can therefore consist in nothing else than *the conception of law* in itself, *which certainly is only possible in a rational being*, in so far as this conception, and not the expected effect, determines the will. This is a good which is already present in the person who acts accordingly, and we have not to wait for it to appear first in the result.

* * * * * * *

The conception of an objective principle, in so far as it is obligatory for a will, is called a command (of reason), and the formula of the command is called an Imperative.

All imperatives are expressed by the word *ought* [or *shall*], and thereby indicate the relation of an objective law of reason to a will which from its subjective constitution is not necessarily determined by it (an obligation). They say that something would be good to do or to forbear, but they say it to a will which does not always do a thing because it is conceived to

---

* *a priori*: known prior to sense experience
† *a posteriori*: known as the result of sense experience

be good to do it. That is practically *good*, however, which determines the will by means of the conceptions of reason, and consequently not from subjective causes, but objectively, that is, on principles which are valid for every rational being as such. It is distinguished from the *pleasant* as that which influences the will only by means of sensation from merely subjective causes, valid only for the sense of this or that one, and not as a principle of reason which holds for every one.

A perfectly good will would therefore be equally subject to objective laws (viz., laws of good), but could not be conceived as *obliged* thereby to act lawfully, because of itself from its subjective constitution it can only be determined by the conception of good. Therefore no imperatives hold for the Divine will, or in general for a *holy* will; *ought* is here out of place because the volition is already of itself necessarily in unison with the law. Therefore imperatives are only formulae to express the relation of objective laws of all volition to the subjective imperfection of the will of this or that rational being, for example, the human will.

* * * * * * *

Finally, there is an imperative which commands a certain conduct immediately, without having as its condition any other purpose to be attained by it. This imperative is *categorical*. It concerns not the matter of the action, or its intended result, but its form and the principle of which it is itself a result; and what is essentially good in it consists in the mental disposition, let the consequence be what it may. This imperative may be called that of *morality*.

* * * * * * *

There is therefore but one categorical imperative, namely, this: *Act only on that maxim whereby thou canst at the same time will that it should become a universal law.*

Now if all imperatives of duty can be deduced from this one imperative as from their principle, then, although it should remain undecided whether what is called duty is not merely a vain notion, yet at least we shall be able to show what we understand by it and what this notion means.

Since the universality of the law according to which effects are produced constitutes what is properly called *nature* in the most general sense (as to form) — that is, the existence of things so far as it is determined by general laws — the imperative of duty may be expressed thus: *Act as if the maxim of thy action were to become by thy will a universal law of nature.*

We will now enumerate a few duties, adopting the usual division of them into duties to ourselves and to others, and into perfect and imperfect duties.

1. A man reduced to despair by a series of misfortunes feels wearied of life, but is still so far in possession of his reason that he can ask himself whether it would not be contrary to his duty to himself to take his own life. Now he inquires whether the maxim of his action could become a universal law of nature. His maxim is: From self-love I adopt it as a principle to shorten my life when its longer duration is likely to bring more evil than satisfaction. It is asked then simply whether this principle founded on self-love can become a universal law of nature. Now we see at once that a system of nature of which it should be a law to destroy life by means of the very feeling whose special nature it is to impel to the improvement of life would contradict itself, and therefore could not exist as a system of nature; hence that maxim cannot possibly exist as a universal law of nature, and consequently would be wholly inconsistent with the supreme principle of all duty.

2. Another finds himself forced by necessity to borrow money. He knows that he will not be able to repay it, but sees also that nothing will be lent to him unless he promises stoutly to repay it in a definite time. He desires to make this promise, but he has still so much conscience as to ask himself: Is it not unlawful and inconsistent with duty to get out of a difficulty in this way? Suppose, however, that he resolves to do so, then the maxim of his action would be expressed thus: When I think myself in want of money, I will borrow money and promise to repay it, although I know that I never can do so. Now this principle of self-love or of one's own advantage may perhaps be consistent with my whole future welfare; but the question now is, Is it right? I change then the suggestion of self-love into a universal law, and state the question thus: How would it be if my maxim were a universal law? Then I see at once that it could never hold as a universal law of nature, but would necessarily contradict itself. For supposing it to be a universal law that everyone when he thinks himself in a difficulty should be able to promise whatever he pleases, with the purpose of not keeping his promise, the promise itself would become impossible, as well as the end that one might have in view in it, since no one would consider that anything was promised to him, but would ridicule all such statements as vain pretenses.

3. A third finds in himself a talent which with the help of some culture might make him a useful man in many respects. But he finds himself in comfortable circumstances and prefers to indulge in pleasure rather than to take pains in enlarging and improving his happy, natural capacities. He asks, however, whether his maxim of neglect of his natural gifts, besides agreeing with his inclination to indulgence, agrees also with what is called duty. He sees then that a system of nature could indeed subsist with such a universal law, although men (like the South Sea islanders) should let their talents rest and resolve to devote their lives merely to idleness, amusement, and propagation of their species — in a word, to enjoyment; but he cannot possibly *will* that this should be a universal law of nature, or be implanted in us as such by a natural instinct. For, as a rational being, he necessarily wills that his faculties be developed, since they serve him, and have been given him, for all sorts of possible purposes.

4. A fourth, who is in prosperity, while he sees that others have to contend with great wretchedness and that he could help them, thinks: What concern is it of mine? Let everyone be as happy as Heaven pleases, or as he can make himself; I will take nothing from him nor even envy him, only I do not wish to contribute anything to his welfare or to his assistance in distress! Now no doubt, if such a mode of thinking were a universal law, the human race might very well subsist, and doubtless even better than in a state in which everyone talks of sympathy and good-will, or even takes care occasionally to put it into practice, but, on the other side, also cheats when he can, betrays the rights of men, or otherwise violates them. But although it is possible that a universal law of nature might exist in accordance with that maxim, it is impossible to *will* that such a principle should have the universal validity of a law of nature. For a will which resolved this would contradict itself, inasmuch as many cases might occur in which one would have need of the love and sympathy of others, and in which, by such a law of nature, sprung from his own will, he would deprive himself of all hope of the aid he desires.

These are a few of the many actual duties, or at least what we regard as such, which obviously fall into two classes on the one principle that we have laid down. We must be *able to will* that a maxim of our action should be a universal law. This is the canon of the moral appreciation of the action generally. Some actions are of such a character that their maxim cannot without contradiction be even *conceived* as a universal law of nature, far from it being possible that we should *will* that it *should* be so. In others, this intrinsic impossibility is not found, but still it is impossible to *will* that their maxim should be raised to the universality of a law of nature, since such a will would contradict itself. It is easily seen that the former violate strict or rigorous (inflexible) duty; the latter only laxer (meritorious) duty. Thus it has been completely shown by these examples how all duties depend as regards the nature of the obligation (not the object of the action) on the same principle.

If now we attend to ourselves on occasion of any transgression of duty, we shall find that we in fact do not will that our maxim should be a universal law, for that is impossible for us; on the contrary, we will that the opposite should remain a universal law, only we assume the liberty of making an *exception* in our own favor or (just for this time only) in favor of our inclination. Consequently, if we considered all cases from one and the same point of view, namely, that of reason, we should find a contradiction in our own will, namely, that a certain principle should be objectively necessary as a universal law, and yet subjectively should not be universal, but admit of exceptions. As, however, we at one moment regard our action from the point of view of a will wholly conformed to reason, and then again look at the same action from the point of view of a will affected by inclination, there is not really any contradiction, but an antagonism of inclination to the precept of reason, whereby the universality of the principle is changed into a mere generality, so that the practical principle of reason shall meet the maxim half way. Now, although this cannot be justified in our own impartial judgment, yet it proves that we do really recognize the validity of the categorical imperative and (with all respect for it) only allow ourselves a few exceptions which we think unimportant and forced from us.

* * * * * * *

Supposing, however, that there were something *whose existence* has *in itself* an absolute worth, something which, being *an end in itself*, could be a source of definite laws, then in this and this alone would lie the source of a possible categorical imperative, that is, a practical law.

Now I say: Man and generally any rational being *exists* as an end in himself, *not merely as a means* to be arbitrarily used by this or that will, but in all his actions, whether they concern himself or other rational beings, must be always regarded at the same time as an end. All objects of the inclinations have only a conditional worth; for if the inclinations and the wants founded on them did not exist, then their object would be without value. But the inclinations themselves, being sources of want, are so far from having an absolute worth for which they should be desired that, on the contrary, it must be the universal wish of every rational being to be wholly free from them. Thus the worth of any object which is *to be acquired* by our action is always conditional. Beings whose existence depends not on our will but on nature's, have nevertheless, if they are rational beings, only a relative value as means, and are therefore called *things*; rational beings, on the contrary, are called *persons*, because their very nature points them out as ends in themselves, that is, as something which must not be used merely as means, and so far therefore restricts freedom of action (and is an object of respect). These, therefore, are not merely subjective ends whose existence has a worth *for us* as an effect of our action, but *objective ends*, that is, things whose existence is an end in itself — an end, moreover, for which no other can be substituted, which they should subserve *merely* as means, for otherwise nothing whatever would possess *absolute worth*; but if all worth were conditioned and therefore contingent, then there would be no supreme practical principle of reason whatever.

If then there is a supreme practical principle or, in respect of the human will, a categorical imperative, it must be one which, being drawn from the conception of that which is necessarily an end for everyone because it is *an end in itself*, constitutes an *objective* principle of will, and can therefore serve as a universal practical law. The foundation of this principle is: *rational nature exists as an end in itself*. Man necessarily conceives his own existence as being so; so far then this is a *subjective* principle of human actions. But every other rational being regards its existence similarly, just on the same rational principle that holds for me, so that it is at the same time an objective principle from which as a supreme practical law all laws of the will must be capable of being deduced. Accordingly the practical imperative will be as follows: *So act as to treat humanity, whether in thine own person or in that of any other, in every case as an end withal, never as means only*. We will now inquire whether this can be practically carried out.

To abide by the previous examples:

First, under the head of necessary duty to oneself: He who contemplates suicide should ask himself whether his action can be consistent with the idea of humanity *as an end in itself*. If he destroys himself in order to escape from painful circumstances, he uses a person merely as a *means* to maintain a tolerable condition up to the end of life. But a man is not a thing, that is to say, something which can be used merely as means, but must in all his actions be always considered as an end in himself. I cannot, therefore, dispose in any way of a man in my own person so as to mutilate him, to damage or kill him. (It belongs to ethics proper to define this principle more precisely, so as to avoid all misunderstanding, for example, as to the amputation of the limbs in order to preserve myself, as to exposing my life to danger with a view to preserve it, etc. This question is therefore omitted here.)

Secondly, as regards necessary duties, or those of strict obligation, towards others: He who is thinking of making a lying promise to others will see at once that he would be using another man *merely as a means*, without the latter containing at the same time the end in himself. For he whom I propose by such a promise to use for my own purposes cannot possibly assent to my mode of acting towards him, and therefore cannot himself contain the end of this action. This violation of the principle of humanity in other men is more obvious if we take in examples of attacks on the freedom and property of others. For then it is clear that he who transgresses the rights of men intends to use the person of others merely as means, without considering that as rational beings they ought always to be esteemed also as ends, that is, as beings who must be capable of containing in themselves the end of the very same action.

Thirdly, as regards contingent (meritorious) duties to oneself: It is not enough that the action does not violate humanity in our own person as an end in itself, it must also *harmonize with* it. Now there are in humanity capacities of greater perfection which belong to the end that nature has in view in regard to humanity in ourselves as the subject; to neglect these might perhaps be consistent with the *maintenance* of humanity as an end in itself, but not with the *advancement* of this end.

Fourthly, as regards meritorious duties towards others: The natural end which all men have is their own happiness. Now humanity might indeed subsist although no one should contribute anything to the happiness of others, provided he did not intentionally withdraw anything from it; but after all, this would only harmonize negatively, not positively, with *humanity as an end in itself*, if everyone does not also endeavor, as far as in him lies, to forward the ends of others. For the ends of any subject which is an end in himself ought as far as possible to be *my* ends also, if that conception is to have its *full* effect with me.

This principle that humanity and generally every rational nature is *an end in itself* (which is the supreme limiting condition of every man's freedom of action), is not borrowed from experience *first*, because it is universal, applying as it does to all rational beings whatever, and experience is not capable of determining anything about them; *secondly* because it does not present humanity as an end to men (subjectively), that is, as an object which men do of themselves actually adopt as an end; but as an objective end which must as a law constitute the supreme limiting condition of all our subjective ends, let them be what we will; it must therefore spring from pure reason. In fact the objective principle of all practical legislation lies (according to the first principle) in *the rule* and its form of universality which makes it capable of being a law (say, for example, a law of nature); but the *subjective* principle is in the *end*; now by the second principle, the subject of all ends is each rational being inasmuch as it is an end in itself. Hence follows the third practical principle of the will, which is the ultimate condition of its harmony with the universal practical reason, viz., the idea of *the will of every rational being as a universally legislative will*.

On this principle all maxims are rejected which are inconsistent with the will being itself universal legislator. Thus the will is not subject to the law, but so subject that it must be regarded *as itself giving the law*, and on this ground only subject to the law (of which it can regard itself as the author).

QUESTIONS

1. According to Immanuel Kant, how do I determine what actions are morally right?
2. Kant tells us to treat people "as ends and never as means only." What does he mean by this? What is the relevance of this precept for the categorical imperative?
3. Why, according to Kant, do I have a duty not to take my own life?
4. Using the example of lying, illustrate how Kant would have us decide if lying can be morally permissable. Is Kant's answer satisfactory? If not, is this a good reason to reject Kant's formulation of the Categorical Imperative?

UTILITARIANISM

John Stuart Mill

Chapter II. What Utilitarianism Is

. . . The creed which accepts as the foundation of morals, Utility, or the Greatest Happiness Principle, holds that actions are right in proportion as they tend to promote happiness, wrong as they tend to produce the reverse of happiness. By happiness is intended pleasure, and the absence of pain; by unhappiness, pain, and the privation of pleasure. To give a clear view of the moral standard set up by the theory, much more requires to be said; in particular, what things it includes in the ideas of pain and pleasure; and to what extent this is left an open question. But these supplementary explanations do not affect the theory of life on which this theory of morality is grounded — namely, that pleasure, and freedom from pain, are the only things desirable as ends; and that all desirable things (which are as numerous in the utilitar-

From Utilitarianism *(1861).*

ian as in any other scheme) are desirable either for the pleasure inherent in themselves, or as means to the promotion of pleasure and the prevention of pain.

Now, such a theory of life excites in many minds, and among them in some of the most estimable in feeling and purpose, inveterate dislike. To suppose that life has (as they express it) no higher end than pleasure — no better and nobler object of desire and pursuit — they designate as utterly mean and grovelling; as a doctrine worthy only of swine, to whom the followers of Epicurus were, at a very early period, contemptuously likened; and modern holders of the doctrine are occasionally made the subject of equally polite comparisons by its German, French, and English assailants.

When thus attacked, the Epicureans have always answered, that it is not they, but their accusers, who represent human nature in a degrading light; since the accusation supposes human beings to be capable of no pleasures except those of which swine are capable. If this supposition were true, the charge could not be gainsaid, but would then be no longer an imputation; for if the sources of pleasure were precisely the same to human beings and to swine, the rule of life which is good enough for the one would be good enough for the other. The comparison of the Epicurean life to that of beasts is felt as degrading, precisely because a beast's pleasures do not satisfy a human being's conceptions of happiness. Human beings have faculties more elevated than the animal appetites, and when once made conscious of them, do not regard anything as happiness which does not include their gratification. I do not, indeed, consider the Epicureans to have been by any means faultless in drawing out their scheme of consequences from the utilitarian principle. To do this in any sufficient manner, many Stoic, as well as Christian elements require to be included. But there is no known Epicurean theory of life which does not assign to the pleasures of the intellect, of the feelings and imagination, and of the moral sentiments, a much higher value as pleasures than to those of mere sensation. It must be admitted, however, that utilitarian writers in general have placed the superiority of mental over bodily pleasures chiefly in the greater permanency, safety, uncostliness, & c., of the former — that is, in their circumstantial advantages rather than in their intrinsic nature. And on all these points utilitarians have fully proved their case; but they might have taken the other, and, as it may be called, higher ground, with entire consistency. It is quite compatible with the principle of utility to recognise the fact, that some *kinds* of pleasure are more desirable and more valuable than others. It would be absurd that while, in estimating all other things, quality is considered as well as quantity, the estimation of pleasures should be supposed to depend on quantity alone.

If I am asked, what I mean by difference of quality in pleasures, or what makes one pleasure more valuable than another, merely as a pleasure, except its being greater in amount, there is but one possible answer. Of two pleasures, if there be one to which all or almost all who have experience of both give a decided preference, irrespective of any feeling of moral obligation to prefer it, that is the more desirable pleasure. If one of the two is, by those who are completely acquainted with both, placed so far above the other that they prefer it, even though knowing it to be attended with a greater amount of discontent, and would not resign it for any quantity of the other pleasure which their nature is capable of, we are justified in ascribing to the preferred enjoyment a superiority in quality, so far outweighing quantity as to render it, in comparison, of small account.

Now it is an unquestionable fact that those who are equally acquainted with, and equally capable of appreciating and enjoying, both, do give a most marked preference to the manner of existence which employs their higher faculties. Few human creatures would consent to be changed into any of the lower animals, for a promise of the fullest allowance of a beast's pleasures; no intelligent human being would consent to be a fool, no instructed person would be an ignoramus, no person of feeling and conscience would be selfish and base, even though they should be persuaded that the fool, the dunce, or the rascal is better satisfied with his lot than they are with theirs. They would not resign what they possess more than he, for the most complete satisfaction of all the desires which they have in common with him. If they ever fancy they would, it is only in cases of unhappiness so extreme, that to escape from it they would exchange their lot for almost any other, however undesirable in their own eyes. A being of higher faculties requires more to make him happy, is capable probably of more acute suffering, and is certainly accessible to it at more points, than one of an inferior type; but in spite of these liabilities, he can never really wish to sink into what he feels to be a lower grade of existence. We may give what explanation we please of this unwillingness; we may attribute it to pride, a name which is given indiscriminately to some of the most and to some of the least estimable feelings of which mankind are capable; we may refer it to the love of liberty and personal independence, an appeal to which was with the Stoics one of the most effective means for the inculcation of it; to the love of power, or to the love of excitement, both of which do really enter into and contribute to it: but its most appropriate appellation is a sense of dignity, which all human beings possess in one form or other, and in some, though by no means in exact, proportion to their higher faculties, and which is so essential a part of the happiness of those in whom it is strong, that nothing which conflicts with it could be, otherwise than momentarily, an object of desire to them. Whoever supposes that this preference takes place at a sacrifice of happiness — that the superior being, in anything like the equal circumstances, is not happier than the inferior — confounds the two very different ideas, of happiness, and content. It is indisputable that the being whose capacities of enjoyment are low, has the greatest chance of having them fully satisfied; and a highly-endowed being will always feel that any happiness which he can look for, as the world is constituted, is imperfect. But he can learn to bear its imperfections, if they are at all bearable; and they will not make him envy the being who is indeed unconscious of the imperfections, but only because he feels not at all the good which those imperfections qualify. It is better to be a human being dissatisfied than a pig satisfied; better to be Socrates dissatisfied than a fool satisfied. And if the fool, or the pig, is of a different opinion, it is because they only know their own side of the question. The other party to the comparison knows both sides.

It may be objected, that many who are capable of the higher pleasures, occasionally, under the influence of temptation, postpone them to the lower. But this is quite compatible with a full appreciation of the intrinsic superiority of the higher. Men often, from infirmity of character, make their election for the nearer good, though they know it to be the less valuable; and this no less when the choice is between two bodily pleasures, than when it is between bodily and mental. They pursue sensual indulgences to the injury of health, though perfectly aware that health is the greater good. It may be further objected, that many who begin with youthful enthusiasm for everything noble, as they advance in years sink into indolence and selfishness. But I do not believe that those who undergo this very common change, voluntarily choose the lower description of pleasures in preference to the higher. I believe that before they devote themselves exclusively to the one, they have already become incapable of the other. Capacity for the nobler feelings is in most natures a very tender plant, easily killed, not only by hostile influences, but by mere want of sustenance; and in the majority of young persons it speedily dies away if the occupations to which their position in life has devoted them, and the society into which it has thrown them, are not favourable to keeping that higher capacity in exercise. Men lose their high aspirations as they lose their intellectual tastes, because they have not time or opportunity for indulging them; and they addict themselves to inferior pleasures, not because they deliberately prefer them, but because they are either the only ones to which they have access, or the only ones which they are any longer capable of enjoying. It may be questioned whether any one who has remained equally susceptible to both classes of pleasures, ever knowingly and calmly preferred the lower, though many, in all ages, have broken down in an ineffectual attempt to combine both.

From this verdict of the only competent judges, I apprehend there can be no appeal. On a question which is the best worth having of two pleasures, or which of two modes of existence is the most grateful to the feelings, apart from its moral attributes and from it consequences, the judgment of those who are qualified by knowledge of both, or, if they differ, that of the majority among them, must be admitted as final. And there needs be the less hesitation to accept this judgment respecting the quality of pleasures, since there is no other tribunal to be referred to even on the question of quantity. What means are there of determining which is the acutest of two pains, or the intensest of two pleasurable sensations, except the general suffrage of those who are familiar with both? Neither pains nor pleasures are homogeneous, and pain is always heterogeneous with pleasure. What is there to decide whether a particular pleasure is worth purchasing at the cost of a particular pain, except the feelings and judgment of the experienced? When, therefore, those feelings and judgment declare the pleasures derived from the higher faculties to be preferable *in kind*, apart from the question of intensity, to those of which the animal nature, disjoined from the higher faculties, is susceptible, they are entitled on this subject to the same regard.

I have dwelt on this point, as being a necessary part of a perfectly just conception of Utility or Happiness, considered as the directive rule of human conduct. But it is by no means an indispensable condition to the acceptance of the utilitarian standard; for that standard is not the agent's own greatest happiness, but the greatest amount of happiness altogether; and if it may possibly be doubted whether a noble character is always the happier for its nobleness, there can be no doubt that it makes other people happier, and that the world in general is immensely a gainer by it. Utilitarianism, therefore, could only attain its end by the general cultivation of nobleness of character, even if each individual were only benefitted by the nobleness of others, and his own, so far as happiness is concerned, were a sheer deduction from the benefit. But the bare enunciation of such an absurdity as this last, renders refutation superfluous.

According to the Greatest Happiness Principle, as above explained, the ultimate end, with reference to and for the sake of which all other things are desirable (whether we are considering our own good or that of other people), is an existence exempt as far as possible from pain, and as rich as possible in enjoyments, both in point of quantity and quality; the test of quality, and the rule for measuring it against quantity, being the preference felt by those who, in their opportunities of experience, to which must be added their habits of self-consciousness and self-observation, are best furnished with the means of comparison. This, being, according to the utilitarian opinion, the end of human action, is necessarily also the standard of morality; which may accordingly be defined, the rules and precepts for human conduct, by the observance of which an existence such as has been described might be, to the greatest extent possible, secured to all mankind; and not to them only, but, so far as the nature of things admits, to the whole sentient creation. . . .

I must again repeat, what the assailants of utilitarianism seldom have the justice to acknowledge, that the happiness which forms the Utilitarian standard of what is right in conduct, is not the agent's own happiness, but that of all concerned. As between his own happiness and that of others, utilitarianism requires him to be as strictly impartial as a disinterested and benevolent spectator. In the golden rule of Jesus of Nazareth, we read the complete spirit of the ethics of utility. To do as one would be done by, and to love one's neighbour as oneself, constitute the ideal perfection of utilitarian morality. As the means of making the nearest approach to this ideal, utility would enjoin, first, that laws and social arrangements should place the happiness, or (as speaking practically it may be called) the interest, of every individual, as nearly as possible in harmony with the interest of the whole; and secondly, that education and opinion, which have so vast a power over human character, should so use that power as to establish in the mind of every individual an indissoluble association between his own happiness and the good of the whole; especially between his own happiness and the practice of such modes of conduct, negative and positive, as regard for the universal happiness prescribes: so that not only he may be unable to conceive the possibility of happiness to himself, consistently with conduct opposed to the general good, but also that a direct impulse to promote the general good may be in every individual one of the habitual motives of action, and the sentiments connected therewith may fill a large and prominent place in every human being's sentient existence. If the impugners of the utilitarian morality represented it to their own minds in this its true character, I know not what recommendation possessed by any other morality they could possibly affirm to be wanting to it: what more beautiful or more exalted developments of human nature any other ethical system can be supposed to foster, or what springs of action, not accessible to the utilitarian, such systems rely on for giving effect to their mandates.

· · · · · · ·

Chapter IV. Of What Sort of Proof the Principle of Utility Is Susceptible

It has already been remarked, that questions of ultimate ends do not admit of proof, in the ordinary acceptation of the term. To be incapable of proof by reasoning is common to all first principles; to the first premises of our knowledge, as well as to those of our conduct. But the former, being matters of fact, may be the subject of a direct appeal to the faculties which judge of fact — namely, our senses, and our internal consciousness. Can an appeal be made to the same faculties on questions of practical ends? Or by what other faculty is cognizance taken of them?

Questions about ends are, in other words, questions about what things are desirable. The utilitarian doctrine is, that happiness is desirable, and the only thing desirable, as an end; all other things being only desirable as means to that end. What ought to be required of this doctrine — what conditions is it requisite that the doctrine should fulfil — to make good its claim to be believed?

The only proof capable of being given that an object is visible, is that people actually see it. The only proof that a sound is audible, is that people hear it: and so of the other sources of our experience. In like manner, I apprehend, the sole evidence it is possible to produce that anything is desirable, is that people do actually desire it. If the end which the utilitarian doctrine proposes to itself were not, in theory and in practice, acknowledged to be an end, nothing could ever convince any person that it was so. No reason can be given why the general happiness is desirable, except that each person, so far as he believes it to be attainable, desires his own happiness. This, however, being a fact, we have not only all the proof which the case admits of, but all which it is possible to require, that happiness is a good: that each person's happiness is a good to that person, and the general happiness, therefore, a good to the aggregate of all persons. Happiness has made out its title as *one* of the ends of conduct, and consequently one of the criteria of morality.

But it has not, by this alone, proved itself to be the sole criterion. To do that, it would seem, by the same rule, necessary to show, not only that people desire happiness, but that they never desire anything else. Now it is palpable that they do desire things which, in common language, are decidedly distinguished from happiness. They desire, for example, virtue, and the absence of vice, no less really than pleasure and the absence of pain. The desire of virtue is not as universal, but it is as authentic a fact, as the desire of happiness. And hence the opponents of the utilitarian standard deem that they have a right to infer that there are other ends of human action besides happiness, and that happiness is not the standard of approbation and disapprobation.

But does the utilitarian doctrine deny that people desire virtue, or maintain that virtue is not a thing to be desired? The very reverse. It maintains not only that virtue is to be desired, but that it is to be desired disinterestedly, for itself. Whatever may be the opinion of utilitarian moralists as to the original conditions by which virtue is made virtue; however they may believe (as they do) that actions and dispositions are only virtuous because they promote another end than virtue; yet this being granted, and it having been decided, from considerations of this description, what *is* virtuous, they not only place virtue at the very head of the things which are good as means to the ultimate end, but they also recognise as a psychological fact the possibility of its being, to the individual, a good in itself, without looking to any end beyond it; and hold, that the mind is not in a right state, not in a state comfortable to Utility, not in the state most conducive to the general happiness, unless it does love virtue in this manner — as a thing desirable in itself, even although, in the individual instance, it should not produce those other desirable consequences which it tends to produce, and on account of which it is held to be virtue. This opinion is not, in the smallest degree, a departure from the Happiness principle. The ingredients of happiness are very various, and each of them is desirable in itself, and not merely when considered as swelling an aggregate. The principle of utility does not mean that any given pleasure, as music, for instance, or any given exemption from pain, as for example health, are to be looked upon as a means to a collective something termed happiness, and to be desired on that account. They are desired and desirable in and for themselves; besides being means, they are a part of the end. Virtue, according to the utilitarian doctrine, is not naturally and originally part of the end, but it is capable of becoming so; and in those who love it disinterestedly it has become so, and is desired and cherished, not as a means to happiness, but as a part of their happiness.

To illustrate this farther, we may remember that virtue is not the only thing, originally a means, and which if it were not a means to anything else, would be and remain indifferent, but which by association with what it is a means to, comes to be desired for itself, and that too with the utmost intensity. What, for example, shall we say of the love of money? There is nothing originally more desirable about money than about any heap of glittering pebbles. Its worth is solely that of the things which it will buy; the desires for other things than itself, which it is a means of gratifying. Yet the love of money is not only one of the strongest moving forces of human life, but money is, in many cases, desired in and for itself; the desire to possess it is often stronger than the desire to use it, and goes on increasing when all the desires which point to ends beyond it, to be encompassed by it, are falling off. It may be then said truly, that money is desired not for the sake of an end, but as part of the end. From being a means to happiness, it has come to be itself a principal ingredient of the individual's conception of happiness. The same may be said of the majority of the great objects of human life — power, for example, or fame; except that to each of these there is a certain amount of immediate pleasure annexed, which has at least the semblance of being naturally inherent in them; a thing which cannot be said of money. Still, however, the strongest natural attraction, both of power and of fame, is the immense aid they give to the attainment of our other wishes; and it is the strong association thus generated between them and all our objects of desire, which gives to the direct desire of them the intensity it often assumes, so as in some characters to surpass in strength all other desires. In these cases the means have become a part of the end, and a more important part of it than any of the things which they are means to. What was once desired as an instrument for the attainment of happiness, has come to be desired for its own sake. In being desired for its own sake it is, however, desired as *part* of happiness. The person is made, or thinks he would be made, happy by its mere possession; and is made unhappy by failure to obtain it. The desire of it is not a different thing from the desire of happiness, any more than the love of music, or the desire of health. They are included in happiness. They are some of the elements of which the desire of happiness is made up. Happiness is not an abstract idea, but a concrete whole; and these are some of its parts. And the utilitarian standard sanctions and approves their being so. Life would be a poor thing, very ill provided with sources of happiness, if there were not this provision of nature, by which things originally indifferent, but conducive to, or otherwise associated with, the satisfaction of our primitive desires, become in themselves sources of pleasure more valuable than the primitive pleasures, both in permanency, in the space of human existence that they are capable of covering, and even in intensity.

Virtue, according to the utilitarian conception, is a good of this description. There was no original desire of it, or motive to it, save its conduciveness to pleasure, and especially to protection from pain. But through the association thus formed, it may be felt a good in itself, and desired as such with as great intensity as any other good; and with this difference between it and the love of money, of power, or of fame, that all of these may, and often do, render the individual noxious to the other members of the society to which he belongs, whereas there is nothing which makes him so much a blessing to them as the cultivation of the disinterested love of virtue. And consequently, the utilitarian standard, while it tolerates and approves those other acquired desires, up to the point beyond which they would be more injurious to the general happiness than promotive of it, enjoins and requires the cultivation of the love of virtue up to the greatest strength possible, as being above all things important to the general happiness.

It results from the preceding considerations, that there is in reality nothing desired except happiness. Whatever is desired otherwise than as a means to some end beyond itself, and ultimately to happiness, is desired as itself part of happiness, and is not desired for itself until it has become so.

QUESTIONS

1. How does John Stuart Mill justify his claim that "pleasure, and freedom from pain, are the only things desirable as ends"?
2. What is the Utilitarian formula for determining morally right action?

3. What does Mill mean when he says that "it is better to be a human being dissatisfied than a pig satisfied; better to be Socrates dissatisfied than a fool satisfied"?
4. What is the Greatest Happiness Principle? Do you think that a theory of morality should be based on a calculation of happiness?

RELATIVISM

David Wong

i Introduction

Moral relativism is a common response to the deepest conflicts we face in our ethical lives. Some of these conflicts are quite public and political, such as the apparently intractable disagreement in the United States over the moral and legal permissibility of abortion. Other conflicts inviting the relativistic response are of a less dramatic but more recurrent nature. This author's experience as a first-generation Chinese American exemplifies a kind of conflict that others have faced: that between inherited values and the values of the adopted country. As a child I had to grapple with the differences between what was expected of me as a good Chinese son and what was expected of my non-Chinese friends. Not only did they seem bound by duties that were much less rigorous in the matter of honouring parents and upholding the family name, but I was supposed to feel superior to them because of that. It added to my confusion that I sometimes felt envy at their freedom.

Moral relativism, as a common response to such conflicts, often takes the form of a denial that any single moral code has universal validity, and an assertion that moral truth and justifiability, if there are any such things, are in some way relative to factors that are culturally and historically contingent. This doctrine is *meta-ethical* relativism, because it is about the relativity of moral truth and justifiability. Another kind of moral relativism, also a common response to deep moral conflict, is a doctrine about how one ought to act toward those who accept values very different from one's own. This *normative* moral relativism holds that it is wrong to pass judgement on others who have substantially different values, or to try to make them conform to one's values, for the reason that their values are as valid as one's own. Another common response to deep moral conflict, however, contradicts moral relativism in its two major forms. It is the universalist or absolutist position that both sides of a moral conflict cannot be equally right, that there can be only one truth about the matter at issue. This position is so common, in fact, that William James was led to call us 'absolutists by instinct' (James, 1948). The term 'universalism' will be used hereafter, because 'absolutism' is used not only to refer to the denial of moral relativism, but also to the view that some moral rules or duties are absolutely without exception.

ii Meta-Ethical Relativism

The debate between moral relativism and universalism accounts for a significant proportion of philosophical reflection in ethics. In ancient Greece at least some of the 'Sophists' defended

From A Companion to Ethics, *edited by Peter Singer. From the* Blackwell Companions to Philosophy. *Oxford: Basil Blackwell Publishers, 1993. Reprinted by permission of Basil Blackwell Publishers.*

a version of moral relativism, which Plato attempted to refute. Plato attributes to the first great Sophist, Protagoras, the argument that human custom determines what is fine and ugly, just and unjust. Whatever is communally judged to be the case, the argument goes, actually comes to be the case (*Theaetetus*, 172ab; it is unclear, however, whether the real Protagoras actually argued in this manner). Now the Greeks, through trade, travel, and war, were fully aware of wide variation in customs, and so the argument concludes with the relativity of morality. The question with this argument, however, is whether we can accept that custom determines in a strong sense what is fine and ugly, just and unjust. It may influence what people *think* is fine and just. But it is quite another thing for custom to determine what is fine and just. Customs sometimes change under the pressure of moral criticism, and the argument seems to rely on a premise that contradicts this phenomenon.

Another kind of argument given for relativism is premised on the view that the customary ethical beliefs in any given society are functionally necessary for that society. Therefore, the argument concludes, the beliefs are true for that society, but not necessarily in another. The sixteenth-century essayist, Michel de Montaigne, sometimes makes this argument ('Of custom, and not easily changing an accepted law', in Montaigne, 1595), but it has had its greatest acceptance among anthropologists of the twentieth century who emphasize the importance of studying societies as organic wholes of which the parts are functionally interdependent. The problem with the functional argument, however, is that moral beliefs are not justified merely on the grounds that they are necessary for a society's existence in anything like its present form. Even if a society's institutions and practices crucially depend on the acceptance of certain beliefs, the justifiability of those beliefs depends on the moral acceptability of the institutions and practices. To show that certain beliefs are necessary for maintaining a fascist society, for instance, is not to justify those beliefs.

Despite the weaknesses of these arguments for moral relativism, the doctrine has always had its adherents. Its continuing strength has always been rooted in the impressiveness of the variation in ethical belief to be found across human history and culture. In an ancient text (*Dissoi Logoi* or the *Contrasting Arguments*; Robinson, 1979) associated with the Sophists, it is pointed out that for the Lacedaemonians, it was fine for girls to exercise without tunics, and for children not to learn music and letters, while for the Ionians, these things were foul. Montaigne assembled a catalogue of exotic customs, such as male prostitution, cannibalism, women warriors, killing one's father at a certain age as an act of piety, and recites from the Greek historian Herodotus the experiment of Darius. Darius asked Greeks how much they would have to be paid before they would eat the bodies of their deceased fathers. They replied that no sum of money could get them to do such a thing. He then asked certain Indians who customarily ate the bodies of their deceased fathers what they would have to be paid to burn the bodies of their fathers. Amidst loud exclamations, they bade him not to speak of such a thing (Montaigne's 'Of custom' (1595), and Herodotus, *Persian Wars*, Book III, 38).

But while many have been moved by such examples to adopt moral relativism, the argument from diversity does not support relativism in any simple or direct way. As the Socrates of Plato's dialogues observed, we have reason to listen only to the wise among us (*Crito*, 44cd). The simple fact of diversity in belief is no disproof of the possibility that there are some beliefs better to have than the others because they are truer or more justified than the rest. If half the world still believed that the sun, the moon, and the planets revolved around the earth, that would be no disproof of the possibility of a unique truth about the structure of the universe. Diversity in belief, after all, may result from varying degrees of wisdom. Or it may be that different people have their own limited perspectives of the truth, each perspective being distorted in its own way.

It is sometimes thought that the extent and depth of disagreement in ethics indicates that moral judgements are simply not judgements about facts, that they assert nothing true or false about the world but straightforwardly express our own subjective reactions to certain facts and happenings, whether these be collective or individual reactions (e.g. see C. L. Stevenson, *Ethics and Language,* 1944). A more complicated view is that moral judgements purport to report objective matters of fact, but that there are no such matters of fact (see J. L. Mackie, *Ethics: Inventing Right and Wrong*, 1977). The success of modern science in producing a remarkable degree of convergence of belief about the basic structure of the physical world probably reinforces these varieties of scepticism about the objectivity of moral judgements. It is hard to deny that there is a significant difference in the degree of convergence of belief in ethics and in science. Yet there are possible explanations for that difference that are compatible with claiming that moral judgements are ultimately about facts in the world. These explanations might stress, for instance, the special difficulties of acquiring knowledge of subjects that pertain to moral knowledge.

An understanding of human nature and human affairs is necessary for formulating an adequate moral code. The enormously difficult and complex task of reaching such an understanding could be a major reason for differences in moral belief. Furthermore, the subject matter of ethics is such that people have the most intense practical interest in what is established as truth about it, and surely this interest engenders the passions that becloud judgement (for a reply in this spirit see Nagel, 1986, pp. 185–88). Universalists could point out that many apparently exotic moral beliefs presuppose certain religious and metaphysical beliefs, and that these beliefs, rather than any difference in fundamental values, explain the apparent strangeness. Consider, for example, the way our view of Darius' Indians would change if we were to attribute to them the belief that eating the body of one's deceased father is a way of preserving his spiritual substance. Finally, some of the striking differences in moral belief across societies may not be rooted in differences in fundamental values but in the fact that these values may have to be implemented in different ways given the varying conditions that obtain across societies. If one society contains many more women than men (say, because men are killing each other off in warfare), it would not be surprising if polygamy were acceptable there, while in another society, where the proportion of women to men is equal, monogamy is required. The difference in accepted marriage practice may come down to that difference in the proportion of women to men, and not to any difference in basic moral ideals of marriage or of the proper relationships between women and men.

The mere existence of deep and wide disagreements in ethics, therefore, does not disprove the possibility that moral judgements can be objectively correct or incorrect judgements about certain facts. Moral relativists must chart some other more complicated path from the existence of diversity to the conclusion that there is no single true or most justified morality. I believe (and have argued, in *Moral Relativity*, 1984) that the relativist argument is best conducted by pointing to particular kinds of differences in moral belief, and then by claiming that these particular differences are best explained under a theory that denies the existence of a single true morality. This would involve denying that the various ways that universalists have for explaining ethical disagreement are sufficient for explaining the particular differences in question. (For another strategy of argument that relies more on an analysis of the meaning of moral judgements, see Harman, 1975.)

One apparent and striking ethical difference that would be a good candidate for this sort of argument concerns the emphasis on individual rights that is embodied in the ethical culture of the modern West and that seems absent in traditional cultures found in Africa, China, Japan and India. The content of duties in such traditional cultures instead seems organized around the central value of a common good that consists in a certain sort of ideal community life, a network of relationships, partially defined by social roles, again, ideal, but imperfectly embodied in ongoing existing practice. The ideal for members is composed of various virtues that enable them, given their place in the network of relationships, to promote and sustain the common good.

Confucianism, for instance, makes the family and kinship groups the models for the common good, with larger social and political units taking on certain of their features, such as benevolent leaders who rule with the aim of cultivating virtue and harmony among their subjects. Moralities centred on such values would seem to differ significantly from ones centred on individual rights to liberty and to other goods, if the basis for attributing such rights to persons does not seem to lie in their conduciveness to the common good of a shared life, but in a moral worth independently attributed to each individual. By contrast a theme frequently found in ethics of the common good is that individuals find their realization as human beings in promoting and sustaining the common good. Given this assumption of the fundamental harmony between the highest good of individuals and the common good, one might expect the constraints on freedom to have greater scope and to be more pervasive when compared to a tradition in which no such fundamental harmony between individual and common goods is assumed.

If the contrast between the two types of morality is real, it raises the question of whether one or the other type is truer or more justified than the other. The argument for a relativistic answer may start with the claim that each type focuses on a good that may reasonably occupy the centre of an ethical ideal for human life. On the one hand, there is the good of belonging to and contributing to a community; on the other, there is the good of respect for the individual apart from any potential contribution to community. It would be surprising, the argument goes, if there were just one justifiable way of setting a priority with respect to the two goods. It should not be surprising, after all, if the range of human goods is simply too rich and diverse to be reconciled in just a single moral ideal.

Such an argument could be supplemented by an explanation of why human beings have such a thing as a morality. Morality serves two universal human needs. It regulates conflicts of interest between people, and it regulates conflicts of interest within the individual born of different desires and drives that cannot all be satisfied at the same time. Ways of dealing with those two kinds of conflict develop in anything recognizable as human society. To the extent that these ways crystallize in the form of rules for conduct and ideals for persons, we have the core of a morality. Now in order to perform its practical functions adequately, it may be that a morality will have to possess certain general features. A relatively enduring and stable system for the resolution of conflict between people, for instance, will not permit the torture of persons at whim.

But given this picture of the origin and functions of morality, it would not be surprising if significantly different moralities were to perform the practical functions equally well, at least according to standards of performance that were common to these moralities. Moralities, on this picture, are social creations that evolve to meet certain needs. The needs place conditions on what could be an adequate morality, and if human nature has a definite structure, one would expect further constraining conditions on an adequate morality to derive from our nature. But the complexity of our nature makes it possible for us to prize a variety of goods and to order them in different ways, and this opens the way for a substantial relativism to be true.

The picture sketched above has the advantage of leaving it open as to how strong a version of relativism is true. That is, it holds that there is no single true morality, yet does not deny that some moralities might be false and inadequate for the functions they all must perform. Almost all polemics against moral relativism are directed at its most extreme versions: those holding that all moralities are equally true (or equally false, or equally lacking in cognitive content). Yet a substantial relativism need not be so radically egalitarian. Besides ruling out moralities that would aggravate interpersonal conflict, such as the one described above, relativists could also recognize that adequate moralities must promote the production of persons capable of considering the interests of others. Such persons would need to have received a certain kind of nurturing and care from others. An adequate morality, then, whatever else its content, would have to prescribe and promote the sorts of upbringing and continuing interpersonal relationships that produce such persons.

A moral relativism that would allow for this kind of constraint on what could be a true or most justified morality might not fit the stereotype of relativism, but would be a reasonable position to hold. One reason, in fact, that not much progress has been made in the debate between relativists and universalists is that each side has tended to define the opponent as holding the most extreme position possible. While this makes the debating easier, it does nothing to shed light on the vast middle ground where the truth indeed may lie. Many of the same conclusions could be drawn about the debate over normative moral relativism: much heat, and frequent identification of the opponent with the most extreme position possible.

iii Normative Relativism

The most extreme possible position for the normative relativist is that no-one should ever pass judgement on others with substantially different values, or try to make them conform to one's own values. Such a definition of normative relativism is usually given by its opponents, because it is an indefensible position. It requires self-condemnation by those who act according to it. If I pass judgement on those who pass judgement, I must condemn myself. I am trying to impose a value of tolerance on everyone, when not everyone has that value, but this is not what I am supposed to be doing under the most extreme version of normative relativism. Philosophers are usually content with such easy dismissals of the most extreme version of normative relativism, but there is reason to consider whether more moderate versions might be more tenable. The reason is that normative relativism is not just a philosophical doctrine but a stance adopted toward morally troubling situations.

Anthropologists are sometimes identified with this stance, and it is instructive to understand how this identification emerged from a historical and sociological context. The birth of cultural anthropology in the late nineteenth century was in part subsidized by colonizing governments needing to know more about the nature and status of 'primitive' peoples. Influenced by Darwinian theory, early anthropological theory tended to arrange the peoples and social institutions of the world in an evolutionary series, from primordial man to the civilized human being of nineteenth-century Europe. Many anthropologists eventually reacted against the imperialism of their governments and to its rationalization supplied by their predecessors. More importantly, they came to see the peoples they studied as intelligent men and women whose lives had meaning and integrity. And this led to questioning the basis for implicit judgements of the inferiority of their ways of life, especially after the spectacle of the civilized nations in brutal struggle with one another in the First World War (see, for example, Ruth Benedict, *Patterns of Culture*, 1934, and more recently, Melville Herskovits, *Cultural Relativism: Perspectives in Cultural Pluralism*, 1972).

The normative relativism of some of the anthropologists of that period, then, was a response to real moral problems concerning the justifiability of colonization and more generally concerning intervention in another society so as to cause major changes in previously accepted values or in people's ability to act on those values. No simple version of normative relativism is the answer to these problems, as was illustrated by the fact that an ethic of non-judgemental tolerance would self-destruct when used to condemn the intolerant. The inadequacy of the simple versions also is illustrated by the swing in anthropology on the question of normative relativism after the Second World War. That war, many realized, was a battle against enormous evil. Such a realization brought vividly to the forefront the necessity of passing judgement at least sometimes and of acting on one's judgement. And accordingly there was a new trend within cultural anthropology toward finding a basis for making judgements that would depend on criteria to be applied to all moral codes.

A more reasonable version of normative relativism would have to permit us to pass judgement on others with substantially different values. Even if these different values are as justified as our own from some neutral perspective, we still are entitled to call bad or evil or monstrous what contradicts our most important values. What we are entitled to do in the light of such judgements, however, is another matter. Many of us who are likely to read this book would be reluctant to intervene in the affairs of others who have values substantially different from ours, when the reason for intervention is the enforcement of our own values, and, when we think that we have no more of an objective case for our moral outlook than the others have for theirs. The source of this reluctance is a feature of our morality. A liberal, contractualist outlook is very much part of our ethical life in the postmodern West, whether we acknowledge it or not. We want to act toward others in such a way that our actions could be seen as justified by them if they were fully reasonable and informed of all relevant facts. If we hold a meta-ethical moral relativism, however, then we must recognize that there will be occasions when some otherwise desirable course of action toward others with different values will violate this feature of our morality.

At that point, there is no general rule that will tell us what to do. It would seem to depend on what other values of ours are at stake. If a practice performed by others were to involve human sacrifice, for example, then the value of tolerance might indeed be outweighed, and we may decide to intervene to prevent it. The disagreement over the legal permissibility of abortion demonstrates how difficult the weighing can be, however. Consider the position of those who believe that abortion is morally wrong because it is the taking of life that has moral status. Within this group some seem undisturbed by the fact that there is deep disagreement over the moral status of the fetus. They wish to prohibit abortion. But others in this group, while holding that abortion is wrong, admit that reasonable persons could disagree with them and that human reason seems unable to resolve the question. For this reason they oppose legal prohibitions of abortion. The former believe that the latter do not take the value of human life seriously, while the latter believe that the former fail to recognize the depth and seriousness of the disagreement between reasonable persons.

Each position has some force, and clearly normative relativism offers no simple solution to the dilemma. What the doctrine provides, however, is a set of reasons for tolerance and non-intervention that must be weighed against other reasons. The doctrine applies not only to proposed interventions by one society in another, but also, as in the case of abortion, to deep moral disagreements within pluralistic societies containing diverse moral traditions. If meta-ethical relativism is true, even if only with respect to a limited set of moral conflicts such as abortion, then our moral condition is immeasurably complicated. We must strive to find what will be for us the right or the best thing to do, and also deal with the feelings of unease caused by the recognition that there is no single right or best thing to do. This task, no matter how difficult, is not the end of moral reflection. It instead may be the beginning of a different sort of reflection that involves on the one hand an effort to reach an understanding with those who have substantially different values, and on the other the effort to stay true to one's own values. Some of those who believe that abortion is the taking of a life with moral status, for instance, have chosen to oppose it by placing their efforts into organizations that aim to lessen the perceived need for abortion, organizations that aid unwed mothers, for example.

One final issue regarding relativism needs addressing. Relativism has a bad name in some quarters because it is associated with a lack of moral conviction, with a tendency toward nihilism. Part of the reason for the bad name may be the identification of relativism with its most extreme forms. If these forms are true, then everything is permitted, on someone's morality. But another reason for the bad name is the assumption that one's moral confidence, one's commitment to act on one's values, is somehow dependent on maintaining the belief that one's morality is the only true or the most justified one. But surely some reflection will reveal that such a belief alone would not guarantee a commitment to act. The commitment to act involves a conception of what one's morality means to the self, whether it be the only true one or not. It involves making a connection between what one desires, what one aspires to, and the substantive content of one's moral values. It is being able to see morality as important to us in these ways that allows us to avoid nihilism. The belief that our morality is the only true or most justified one does not automatically create this kind of importance, nor is it a necessary condition for this kind of importance, because the values I may see as important and part of what makes life most meaningful to me may not have to be values that all reasonable persons would accept or recognize to be true.

Here, as in other matters concerning relativism, the emotion provoked by the mere name tends to muddle the issues and to polarize unnecessarily. When we get through defending and attacking what most people conceive as relativism or what they associate with it, then most of the real work remains to be done. What is left is a moral reality that is quite messy and immune to neat solutions. But why should we have expected anything else?

REFERENCES

Benedict, R.: *Patterns of Culture* (New York: Penguin, 1934).

Harman, G.: 'Moral relativism defended', *Philosophical Review* 84 (1975), 3–22.

Herodotus: *The Persian Wars*, trans. George Rawlinson (New York: Modern Library, 1942).

Herskovits. M.: *Cultural Relativism: Perspectives in Cultural Pluralism* (New York: Vintage, 1972).

James, W.: 'The will to believe', *Essays in Pragmatism*, ed. Aubrey Castell (New York: Hafner, 1948).

Mackie, J.L.: *Ethics: Inventing Right and Wrong* (Harmondsworth: Penguin, 1977).

Montaigne, M. de: *Complete Essays* (1595); trans. Donald M. Frame (Stanford: Stanford University Press, 1973).

Nagel, T.: *The View from Nowhere* (New York: Oxford University Press, 1986).

Plato: *Crito* and *Theaetetus*; trans. E. Hamilton and H. Cairns, *Collected Dialogues of Plato* (Princeton: Princeton University Press, 1961).

Robinson, T. M., trans.: *Contrasting Arguments: an edition of the Dissoi Logoi* (New York: Arno Press, 1979).

Stevenson, C. L.: *Ethics and Language* (New Haven: Yale University Press, 1944).

Wong, D. B.: *Moral Relativity* (Berkeley: University of California Press, 1984).

QUESTIONS

1. What does David Wong mean by the term *meta-ethical* relativism?
2. Do you think that an appropriate response to conflicts and disagreements about morality is to conclude that moral truth and justifiability are "relative to factors that are culturally and historically contingent"?
3. What is the distinction drawn by Wong between *normative* moral relativism and universalism?
4. According to Wong, what prompted the development of normative relativism? What reasons does Wong provide for rejecting the most extreme version of normative relativism?
5. Do you think that Wong's account of a "more reasonable version of normative relativism" addresses the concerns he himself raises about relativism as a theory about morality?

THE NEED FOR MORE THAN JUSTICE

Annette C. Baier

In recent decades in North American social and moral philosophy, alongside the development and discussion of widely influential theories of justice, taken as Rawls takes it as the 'first virtue of social institutions,'[1] there has been a counter-movement gathering strength, one coming from some interesting sources. For some of the most outspoken of the diverse group who have in a variety of ways been challenging the assumed supremacy of justice among the moral and social virtues are members of those sections of society whom one might have expected to be especially aware of the supreme importance of justice, namely blacks and women. Those who have only recently won recognition of their equal rights, who have only recently seen the correction or partial correction of longstanding racist and sexist injustices to their race and sex, are among the philosophers now suggesting that justice is only one virtue among many, and one that may need the presence of the others in order to deliver its own undenied value. Among these philosophers of the philosophical counter-culture, as it were — but an increasingly large counterculture — I include Alasdair MacIntyre,[2] Michael Stocker,[3] Lawrence Blum,[4] Michael Slote,[5] Laurence Thomas,[6] Claudia Card,[7] Alison Jaggar,[8] Susan Wolf[9] and a whole group of men and women, myself included, who have been influenced by the writings of Harvard educational psychologist Carol

From the Canadian Journal of Philosophy, *Supplementary Vol. 13, 1987, pp. 41–56. Published by the University of Calgary Press. Reprinted by permission of* Canadian Journal of Philosophy *and Annette C. Baier.*

Gilligan, whose book *In a Different Voice* (Harvard 1982; hereafter D.V.) caused a considerable stir both in the popular press and, more slowly, in the philosophical journals.[10]

Let me say quite clearly at this early point that there is little disagreement that justice is a social value of very great importance, and injustice an evil. Nor would those who have worked on theories of justice want to deny that other things matter besides justice. Rawls, for example, incorporates the value of freedom into his account of justice, so that denial of basic freedoms counts as injustice. Rawls also leaves room for a wider theory of the right, of which the theory of justice is just a part. Still, he does claim that justice is the 'first' virtue of social institutions, and it is only that claim about priority that I think has been challenged. It is easy to exaggerate the differences of view that exist, and I want to avoid that. The differences are as much in emphasis as in substance, or we can say that they are differences in tone of voice. But these differences do tend to make a difference in approaches to a wide range of topics not just in moral theory but in areas like medical ethics, where the discussion used to be conducted in terms of patients' rights, of informed consent, and so on, but now tends to get conducted in an enlarged moral vocabulary, which draws on what Gilligan calls the ethics of *care* as well as that of *justice*.

For 'care' is the new buzz-word. It is not, as Shakespeare's Portia demanded, mercy that is to season justice, but a less authoritarian humanitarian supplement, a felt concern for the good of others and for community with them. The 'cold jealous virtue of justice' (Hume) is found to be too cold, and it is 'warmer' more communitarian virtues and social ideals that are being called in to supplement it. One might say that liberty and equality are being found inadequate without fraternity, except that 'fraternity' will be quite the wrong word, if as Gilligan initially suggested, it is *women* who perceive this value most easily. ('Sorority' will do no better, since it is too exclusive, and English has no gender-neutral word for the mutual concern of siblings.) She has since modified this claim, allowing that there are two perspectives on moral and social issues that we all tend to alternate between, and which are not always easy to combine, one of them what she called the justice perspective, the other the care perspective. It is increasingly obvious that there are many male philosophical spokespersons for the care perspective (Laurence Thomas, Lawrence Blum, Michael Stocker) so that it cannot be the prerogative of women. Nevertheless Gilligan still wants to claim that women are most unlikely to take *only* the justice perspective, as some men are claimed to, at least until some mid-life crisis jolts them into 'bifocal' moral vision (see D.V., ch. 6).

Gilligan in her book did not offer any explanatory theory of why there should be any difference between female and male moral outlook, but she did tend to link the naturalness to women of the care perspective with their role as primary care-takers of young children, that is with their parental and specifically maternal role. She avoided the question of whether it is their biological or their social parental role that is relevant, and some of those who dislike her book are worried precisely by this uncertainty. Some find it retrograde to hail as a special sort of moral wisdom an outlook that may be the product of the socially enforced restriction of women to domestic roles (and the reservation of such roles for them alone). For that might seem to play into the hands of those who still favor such restriction. (Marxists, presumably, will not find it so surprising that moral truths might depend for their initial clear voicing on the social oppression, and memory of it, of those who voice the truths.) Gilligan did in the first chapter of D.V. cite the theory of Nancy Chodorow (as presented in *The Reproduction of Mothering* [Berkeley 1978]) which traces what appears as gender differences in personality to early social development, in particular to the effects of the child's primary caretaker being or not being of the same gender as the child. Later, both in 'The

Conquistador and the Dark Continent: Reflections on the Nature of Love' (*Daedalus* [Summer 1984]), and 'The Origins of Morality in Early Childhood', she develops this explanation. She postulates two evils that any infant may become aware of, the evil of detachment or isolation from others whose love one needs, and the evil of relative powerlessness and weakness. Two dimensions of moral development are thereby set — one aimed at achieving satisfying community with others, the other aiming at autonomy or equality of power. The relative predominance of one over the other development will depend both upon the relative salience of the two evils in early childhood, and on early and later reinforcement or discouragement in attempts made to guard against these two evils. This provides the germs of a theory about *why*, given current customs of childrearing, it should be mainly women who are not content with only the moral outlook that she calls the justice perspective, necessary though that was and is seen by them to have been to their hard won liberation from sexist oppression. They, like the blacks, used the language of rights and justice to change their own social position, but nevertheless see limitations in that language, according to Gilligan's findings as a moral psychologist. She reports their discontent with the individualist more or less Kantian moral framework that dominates Western moral theory and which influenced moral psychologists such as Lawrence Kohlberg,[11] to whose conception of moral maturity she seeks an alternative. Since the target of Gilligan's criticism is the dominant Kantian tradition, and since that has been the target also of moral philosophers as diverse in their own views as Bernard Williams,[12] Alasdair MacIntyre, Philippa Foot,[13] Susan Wolf, and Claudia Card, her book is of interest as much for its attempt to articulate an alternative to the Kantian justice perspective as for its implicit raising of the question of male bias in Western moral theory, especially liberal-democratic theory. For whether the supposed blind spots of that outlook are due to male bias, or to non-parental bias, or to early traumas of powerlessness or to early resignation to 'detachment' from others, we need first to be persuaded that they *are* blind spots before we will have any interest in their cause and cure. Is justice blind to important social values, or at least only one-eyed? What is it that comes into view from the 'care perspective' that is not seen from the 'justice perspective'?

Gilligan's position here is most easily described by contrasting it with that of Kohlberg, against which she developed it. Kohlberg, influenced by Piaget and the Kantian philosophical tradition as developed by John Rawls, developed a theory about typical moral development which saw it to progress from a pre-conventional level, where what is seen to matter is pleasing or not offending parental authority-figures, through a conventional level in which the child tries to fit in with a group, such as a school community, and conform to its standards and rules, to a post-conventional critical level, in which such conventional rules are subjected to tests, and where those tests are of a Utilitarian, or, eventually, a Kantian sort — namely ones that require respect for each person's individual rational will, or autonomy, and conformity to any implicit social contract such wills are deemed to have made, or to any hypothetical ones they would make if thinking clearly. What was found when Kohlberg's questionnaires (mostly by verbal response to verbally sketched moral dilemmas) were applied to female as well as male subjects, Gilligan reports, is that the girls and women not only scored generally lower than the boys and men, but tended to *revert* to the lower stage of the conventional level even after briefly (usually in adolescence) attaining the post-conventional level. Piaget's finding that girls were deficient in 'the legal sense' was confirmed.

These results led Gilligan to wonder if there might not be a quite different pattern of development to be discerned, at least in female subjects. She therefore conducted interviews designed to elicit not just how far advanced the subjects were towards an appreciation of the nature and importance of Kantian autonomy, but also to find out what the subjects themselves saw as progress or lack of it, what conceptions of moral maturity they came to possess by the time they were adults. She found that although the Kohlberg version of moral maturity as respect for fellow persons, and for their rights as equals (rights including that of free association), did seem shared by many young men, the women tended to speak in a different voice about morality itself and about moral maturity. To quote Gilligan, 'Since the reality of interconnexion is experienced by women as given rather than freely contracted, they arrive at an understanding of life that reflects the limits of autonomy and control. As a result, women's development delineates the path not only to a less violent life but also to a maturity realized by interdependence and taking care' (D.V., 172). She writes that there is evidence that 'women perceive and construe social reality differently from men, and that these differences center around experiences of attachment and separation . . . because women's sense of integrity appears to be intertwined with an ethics of care, so that to see themselves as women is to see themselves in a relationship of connexion, the major changes in women's lives would seem to involve changes in the understanding and activities of care' (D.V., 171). She contrasts this progressive understanding of care, from merely pleasing others to helping and nurturing, with the sort of progression that is involved in Kohlberg's stages, a progression in the understanding, not of mutual care, but of mutual *respect*, where this has its Kantian overtones of distance, even of some fear for the respected, and where personal autonomy and *in*dependence, rather than more satisfactory interdependence, are the paramount values.

This contrast, one cannot but feel, is one which Gilligan might have used the Marxist language of alienation to make. For the main complaint about the Kantian version of a society with its first virtue justice, construed as respect for equal rights to formal goods such as having contracts kept, due process, equal opportunity including opportunity to participate in political activities leading to policy and law-making, to basic liberties of speech, free association and assembly, and religious worship, is that none of these goods do much to ensure that the people who have and mutually respect such rights will have any other relationships to one another than the minimal relationship needed to keep such a 'civil society' going. They may well be lonely, driven to suicide, apathetic about their work and about participation in political processes, find their lives meaningless and have no wish to leave offspring to face the same meaningless existence. Their rights, and respect for rights, are quite compatible with very great misery, and misery whose causes are not just individual misfortunes and psychic sickness, but social and moral impoverishment.

What Gilligan's older male subjects complain of is precisely this sort of alienation from some dimly glimpsed better possibility for human beings, some richer sort of network of relationships. As one of Gilligan's male subjects put it, 'People have real emotional needs to be attached to something, and equality does not give you attachment. Equality fractures society and places on every person the burden of standing on his own two feet' (D.V., 167). It is not just the difficulty of self reliance which is complained of, but its socially 'fracturing' effect. Whereas the younger men, in their college years, had seen morality as a matter of reciprocal noninterference, this older man begins to see it as reciprocal attachment. 'Morality is . . . essential . . . for creating the kind of environment, interaction between people, that is a prerequisite to the fulfillment of individual goals. If you want other people not to interfere with your pursuit of whatever you are into, you have to play the game,' says the spokesman for traditional liberalism (D.V. 98). But if what one is 'into' is interconnexion, interdependence rather than an individual autonomy that may involve 'detachment,' such a version of morality will come to seem inadequate. And Gilligan stresses that the interconnexion that her mature women subjects, and some men, wanted to sustain was not merely freely chosen interconnexion, nor interconnexion between equals, but also the sort of interconnexion that can obtain between a child and her unchosen mother and father, or between a child and her unchosen older and younger siblings, or indeed between most workers and their unchosen fellow workers, or most citizens and their unchosen fellow citizens.

A model of a decent community different from the liberal one is involved in the version of moral maturity that Gilligan voices. It has in many ways more in common with the older religion-linked versions of morality and a good society than with the modern Western liberal ideal. That perhaps is why some find it so dangerous and retrograde. Yet it seems clear that it also has much in common with what we can call Hegelian versions of moral maturity and of social health and malaise, both with Marxist versions and with so-called right-Hegelian views.

Let me try to summarize the main differences, as I see them, between on the one hand Gilligan's version of moral maturity and the sort of social structures that would encourage, express and protect it, and on the other the orthodoxy she sees herself to be challenging. I shall from now on be giving my own interpretation of the significance of her challenges, not merely reporting them.[14] The most obvious point is the challenge to the individualism of the Western tradition, to the fairly entrenched belief in the possibility and desirability of each person pursuing his own good in his own way, constrained only by a minimal formal common good, namely a working legal apparatus that enforces contracts and protects individuals from undue interference by others. Gilligan reminds us that noninterference can, especially for the relatively powerless, such as the very young, amount to neglect, and even between equals can be isolating and alienating. On her less individualist version of individuality, it becomes defined by responses to dependency and to patterns of interconnexion, both chosen and unchosen. It is not something a person *has*, and which she then chooses relationships to suit, but something that develops out of a series of dependencies and interdependencies, and responses to them. This conception of individuality is not flatly at odds with, say, Rawls's Kantian one, but there is at least a difference of tone of voice between speaking as Rawls does of each of us having our own rational life plan, which a just society's moral traffic rules will allow us to follow, and which may or may not include close association with other persons, and speaking as Gilligan does of a satisfactory life as involving 'progress of affiliative relationship' (D.V., 170) where 'the concept of identity expands to include the experience of interconnexion' (D.V., 173). Rawls can allow that progress to Gilligan-style moral maturity may be *a* rational life plan, but not a moral constraint on every life-pattern. The trouble is that it will not do just to say 'let this version of morality be an optional extra. Let us agree on the essential minimum, that is on justice and rights, and let whoever wants to go further and cultivate this more demanding ideal of responsibility and care.' For, first, it cannot be satisfactorily cultivated without closer cooperation from others than respect for rights and justice will ensure, and, second, the encouragement of some to cultivate it while others do not could easily lead to exploitation of those who do. It obviously *has* suited some in most societies well enough that others take on the responsibilities of care (for the sick, the helpless, the young) leaving them free to pursue their own less altruistic goods. Volunteer forces of those who accept an ethic of care, operating within a society where the power is exercised and the institutions designed, redesigned, or maintained by those who accept a less communal ethic of minimally constrained self-advancement, will not be the solution. The liberal individualists may be able to 'tolerate' the more communally minded, if they keep the liberals' rules, but it is not so clear that the more communally minded can be content with just those rules, nor be content to be tolerated and possibly exploited.

For the moral tradition which developed the concept of rights, autonomy and justice is the same tradition that provided 'justifications' of the oppression of those whom the primary right-holders depended on to do the sort of work they themselves preferred not to do. The domestic work was left to women and slaves, and the liberal morality for right-holders was surreptitiously supplemented by a different set of demands made on domestic workers. As long as women could be got to assume responsibility for the care of home and children, and to train their children to continue the sexist system, the liberal morality could continue to be the official morality, by turning its eyes away from the contribution made by those it excluded. The long unnoticed moral proletariat were the domestic workers, mostly female. Rights have usually been for the privileged. Talking about laws, and the rights those laws recognize and protect, does not in itself ensure that the group of legislators and rights-holders will not be restricted to some elite. Bills of rights have usually been proclamations of the rights of some in-group, barons, landowners, males, whites, non-foreigners. The 'justice perspective,' and the legal sense that goes with it, are shadowed by their patriarchal past. What did Kant, the great prophet of autonomy, say in his moral theory about women? He said they were incapable of legislation, not fit to vote, that they needed the guidance of more 'rational' males.[15] Autonomy was not for them, only for first class, really rational, persons. It is ironic that Gilligan's original findings in a way confirm Kant's views — it seems that autonomy really may not be for women. Many of them reject that ideal (D.V., 48), and have been found not as good at making rules as are men. But where Kant concludes — 'so much the worse for women,' we can conclude — 'so much the worse for the male fixation on the special skill of drafting legislation, for the bureaucratic mentality of rule worship, and for the male exaggeration of the importance of independence over mutual interdependence.'

It is however also true that the moral theories that made the concept of a person's rights central were not just the instruments for excluding some persons, but also the instruments used by those who demanded that more and more persons be included in the favored group. Abolitionists, reformers, women, used the language of rights to assert their claims to inclusion in the group of full members of a community. The tradition of liberal moral theory has in fact developed so as to include the women it had for so long excluded, to include the poor as well as rich, blacks and whites, and so on. Women like Mary Wollstonecraft used the male moral theories to good purpose. So we should not be wholly ungrateful for those male moral theories, for all their objectionable earlier content. They were undoubtedly patriarchal, but they also contained the seeds of the challenge, or antidote, to this patriarchal poison.

But when we transcend the values of the Kantians, we should not forget the facts of history — that those values were the values of the oppressors of women. The Christian church, whose version of the moral law Aquinas codified, in his very legalistic moral theory, still insists on the maleness of the God it worships, and jealously reserves for males all the most powerful positions in its hierarchy. Its patriarchal prejudice is open and avowed. In the secular moral theories of men, the sexist patriarchal prejudice is today often less open, not as blatant as it is in Aquinas, in the later natural law tradition, and in Kant and Hegel, but is often still there. No moral theorist today would say that women are unfit to vote, to make laws, or to rule a nation without powerful male advisors (as most queens had), but the old doctrines die hard. In one of the best male theories we have, John Rawls's theory, a key role is played by the idea of the 'head of a household.' It is heads of households who are to deliberate behind a 'veil of ignorance' of historical details, and of details of their own special situation, to arrive at the 'just' constitution for a society. Now of course Rawls does not think or say that these 'heads' are fathers rather than mothers. But if we have really given up the age-old myth of women needing, as Grotius put it, to be under the 'eye' of a more 'rational' male protector and master, then how do families come to have any one 'head,' except by the death or desertion of one parent? They will either be two-headed, or headless. Traces of the old patriarchal poison still remain in even the best contemporary moral theorizing. Few may actually say that women's place is in the home, but there is much muttering, when unemployment figures rise, about how the relatively recent flood of women into the work force complicates the problem, as if it would be a good thing if women just went back home whenever unemployment rises, to leave the available jobs for the men. We still do not really have a wide acceptance of the equal right of women to employment outside the home. Nor do we have wide acceptance of the equal duty of men to perform those domestic tasks which in no way depend on special female anatomy, namely cooking, cleaning, and the care of weaned children. All sorts of stories (maybe true stories), about children's need for one 'primary' parent, who must be the mother if the mother breastfeeds the child, shore up the unequal division of domestic responsibility between mothers and fathers, wives and husbands. If we are really to transvalue the values of our patriarchal past, we need to rethink all of those assumptions, really test those psychological theories. And how will men ever develop an understanding of the 'ethics of care' if they continue to be shielded or kept from that experience of caring for a dependent child, which complements the experience we all have had of being cared for as dependent children? These experiences form the natural background for the development of moral maturity as Gilligan's women saw it.

Exploitation aside, why would women, once liberated, not be content to have their version of morality merely tolerated? Why should they not see themselves as voluntarily, for their own reasons, taking on *more* than the liberal rules demand, while having no quarrel with the content of those rules themselves, nor with their remaining the only ones that are expected to be generally obeyed? To see why, we need to move on to three more differences between the Kantian liberals (usually contractarians) and their critics. These concern the relative weight put on relationships between equals, and the relative weight put on freedom of choice, and on the authority of intellect over emotions. It is a typical feature of the dominant moral theories and traditions, since Kant, or perhaps since Hobbes, that relationships between equals or those who are deemed equal in some important sense, have been the relations that morality is concerned primarily to regulate. Relationships between those who are clearly unequal in power, such as parents and children, earlier and later generations in relation to one another, states and citizens, doctors and patients, the well and the ill, large states and small states, have had to be shunted to the bottom of the agenda, and then dealt with by some sort of 'promotion' of the weaker so that an appearance of virtual equality is achieved. Citizens collectively become equal to states, children are treated as adults-to-be, the ill and dying are treated as continuers of their earlier more potent selves, so that their 'rights' could be seen as the rights of equals. This pretence of an equality that is in fact absent may often lead to desirable protection of the weaker, or more dependent. But it somewhat masks the question of what our moral relationships *are* to those who are our superiors or our inferiors in power. A more realistic acceptance of the fact that we begin as helpless children, that at almost every point of our lives we deal with both the more and the less helpless, that equality of power and interdependency, between two persons or groups, is rare and hard to recognize when it does occur, might lead us to a more direct approach to questions concerning the design of institutions structuring these relationships between unequals (families, schools, hospitals, armies) and of the morality of our dealings with the more and the less powerful. One reason why those who agree with the Gilligan version of what morality is about will not want to agree that the liberals' rules are a good minimal set, the only ones we need pressure *everyone* to obey, is that these rules do little to protect the young or the dying or the starving or any of the relatively powerless against neglect, or to ensure an education that will form persons to be *capable* of conforming to an ethics of care and responsibility. Put baldly, and in a way Gilligan certainly has not put it, the liberal morality, if unsupplemented, may *unfit* people to be anything other than what its justifying theories suppose them to be, ones who have no interest in each others' interests. Yet some must take an interest in the next generation's interests. Women's traditional work, of caring for the less powerful, especially for the young, is obviously socially vital. One cannot regard any version of morality that does not ensure that it gets well done as an adequate 'minimal morality,' any more than we could so regard one that left any concern for more distant future generations an optional extra. A moral theory, it can plausibly be claimed, cannot regard concern for new and future persons as an optional charity left for those with a taste for it. If the morality the theory endorses is to sustain itself, it must provide for its own continuers, not just take out a loan on a carefully encouraged maternal instinct or on the enthusiasm of a self-selected group of environmentalists, who make it their business or hobby to be concerned with what we are doing to mother earth.

The recognition of the importance for all parties of relations between those who are and cannot but be unequal, both of these relations in themselves and for their effect on personality formation and so on other relationships, goes along with a recognition of the plain fact that not all morally important relationships can or should be freely chosen. So far I have discussed three reasons women have not to be content to pursue their own values within the framework of the liberal morality. The first was its dubious record. The second was its inattention to relations of inequality or its pretence of equality. The third reason is its exaggeration of the scope of choice, or its inattention to unchosen relations. Showing up the partial myth of equality among actual members of a community, and of the undesirability of trying to pretend that we are treating all of them as equals, tends to go along with an exposure of the companion myth that moral obligations arise from freely *chosen* associations between such equals. Vulnerable future generations do not choose their dependence on earlier generations. The unequal infant does not choose its place in a family or nation, nor is it treated as free to do as it likes until some association is freely entered into. Nor do its parents always choose their parental role, or freely assume their parental responsibilities any more than we choose our power to affect the conditions in which later generations will live. Gilligan's attention to the version of morality and moral maturity found in women, many of whom had faced a choice of whether or not to have an abortion, and who had at some point become mothers, is attention to the perceived inadequacy of the language of rights to help in such choices or to guide them in their parental role. It would not be much of an exaggeration to call the Gilligan 'different voice' the voice of the potential parents. The emphasis on care goes with a recognition of the often unchosen nature of the responsibilities of those who give care, both of children who care for their aged or infirm parents, and of parents who care for the children they in fact have. Contract soon ceases to seem the paradigm source of moral obligation once we attend to parental responsibility, and justice as a virtue of social institutions will come to seem at best only first equal with the virtue, whatever its name, that ensures that each new generation is made appropriately welcome and prepared for their adult lives.

This all constitutes a belated reminder to Western moral theorists of a fact they have always known, that as Adam Ferguson, and David Hume before him emphasized, we are born into families, and the first society we belong to, one that fits or misfits us for later ones, is the small society of parents (or some sort of child-attendants) and children, exhibiting as it may both relationships of near equality and of inequality in power. This simple reminder, with the fairly considerable implications it can have for the plausibility of contractarian moral theory, is at the same time a reminder of the role of human emotions as much as human reason and will in moral development as it actually comes about. The fourth feature of the Gilligan challenge to liberal orthodoxy is a challenge to its typical *rationalism*, or intellectualism, to its assumption that we need not worry what passions persons have, as long as their rational wills can control them. This Kantian picture of a controlling reason dictating to possibly unruly passions also tends to seem less useful when we are led to consider what sort of person we need to fill the role of parent, or indeed want in any close relationship. It might be important for father figures to have rational control over their violent urges to beat to death the children whose screams enrage them, but more than control of such nasty passions seems needed in the mother or primary parent, or parent-substitute, by most psychological theories. They need to love their children, not just to control their irritation. So the emphasis in Kantian theories on rational control of emotions, rather than on cultivating desirable forms of emotion, is challenged by Gilligan, along with the challenge to the assumption of the centrality of autonomy, or relations between equals, and of freely chosen relations.

The same set of challenges to 'orthodox' liberal moral theory has come not just from Gilligan and other women, who are reminding other moral theorists of the role of the family as a social institution and as an influence on the other relationships people want to or are capable of sustaining, but also, as I noted at the start, from an otherwise fairly diverse group of men, ranging from those influenced by both Hegelian and Christian traditions (MacIntyre) to all varieties of other backgrounds. From this group I want to draw attention to the work of one philosopher in particular, namely Laurence Thomas, the author of a fairly remarkable article[16] in which he finds sexism to be a more intractable social evil than racism. In a series of articles, and a forthcoming book,[17] Thomas makes a strong case for the importance of supplementing a concern for justice and respect for rights with an emphasis on equally needed virtues, and on virtues seen as appropriate *emotional* as well as rational capacities. Like Gilligan (and unlike MacIntyre) Thomas gives a lot of attention to the childhood beginnings of moral and social capacities, to the role of parental love in making that possible, and to the emotional as well as the cognitive development we have reason to think both possible and desirable in human persons.

It is clear, I think, that the best moral theory has to be a cooperative product of women and men, has to harmonize justice and care. The morality it theorizes about is after all for all persons, for men and for women, and will need their combined insights. As Gilligan said (D.V., 174), what we need now is a 'marriage' of the old male and the newly articulated female insights. If she is right about the special moral aptitudes of women, it will most likely be the women who propose the marriage, since they are the ones with more natural empathy, with the better diplomatic skills, the ones more likely to shoulder responsibility and take moral initiative, and the ones who find it easiest to empathize and care about how the other party feels. Then, once there is this union of male and female moral wisdom, we maybe can teach each other the moral skills each gender currently lacks, so that the gender difference in moral outlook that Gilligan found will slowly become less marked.

NOTES

1. John Rawls, *A Theory of Justice* (Harvard University Press)
2. Alasdair MacIntyre, *After Virtue* (Notre Dame: Notre Dame University Press)
3. Michael Stocker, 'The Schizophrenia of Modern Ethical Theories,' *Journal of Philosophy* 73, 14, 453–66, and 'Agent and Other: Against Ethical Universalism,' *Australasian Journal of Philosophy* 54, 206–20
4. Lawrence Blum, *Friendship, Altruism and Morality* (London: Routledge & Kegan Paul 1980)
5. Michael Slote, *Goods and Virtues* (Oxford: Oxford University Press 1983)
6. Laurence Thomas, 'Love and Morality,' in *Epistemology and Sociobiology*, James Fetzer, ed. (1985); and 'Justice, Happiness and Self Knowledge,' *Canadian Journal of Philosophy* (March, 1986). Also 'Beliefs and the Motivation to be Just,' *American Philosophical Quarterly* 22 (4), 347–52
7. Claudia Card, 'Mercy,' *Philosophical Review* 81, 1, and 'Gender and Moral Luck,' forthcoming.
8. Alison Jaggar, *Feminist Politics and Human Nature* (London: Rowman and Allanheld 1983)
9. Susan Wolf, 'Moral Saints,' *Journal of Philosophy* 79 (August, 1982), 419–39
10. For a helpful survey article see Owen Flanagan and Kathryn Jackson, 'Justice, Care & Gender: The Kohlberg-Gilligan Debate Revisited,' *Ethics*
11. Lawrence Kohlberg, *Essays in Moral Development*, vols. I & II (New York: Harper and Row 1981, 1984)
12. Bernard Williams, *Ethics and the Limits of Philosophy* (Cambridge: Cambridge University Press 1985)
13. Philippa Foot, *Virtues and Vices* (Berkeley: University of California Press 1978)
14. I have previously written about the significance of her findings for moral philosophy in 'What Do Women Want in a Moral Theory?' *Nous* 19 (March 1985), 'Trust and Antitrust,' *Ethics* 96 (1986), and in 'Hume the Women's Moral Theorist?' in *Women and Moral Theory*, Kittay and Meyers, ed., forthcoming.
15. Immanuel Kant, *Metaphysics of Morals*, sec. 46
16. Laurence Thomas, 'Sexism and Racism: Some Conceptual Differences,' *Ethics* 90 (1980), 239–50; republished in *Philosophy, Sex and Language*, Vetterling-Braggin, ed. (Totowa, NJ: Littlefield Adams 1980)
17. See articles listed in note 6, above. The book has the title *A Psychology of Moral Character*.

QUESTIONS

1. What are some of the differences in the two approaches to morality that Annette Baier outlines in her summary of Carol Gilligan's account of an ethic of care and John Rawls's defence of justice?
2. According to Baier, how does reasoning about moral problems in terms of relationships and an interconnection with others challenge what she refers to as "the individualism of the Western tradition"?
3. Does the perspective of the ethic of care adopted by those on the margins of society force us to reject the kind of moral theory offered by Kant?
4. Do you think that the approach to morality defended by Baier can be harmonized with a justice approach, as she suggests?

SUGGESTIONS FOR FURTHER READING

There are three ways to proceed in an exploration of the ideas introduced in this chapter. The first is to look for general guides that are designed for those who teach ethics and that provide bibliographies, resources, and links to various associations and institutions. The first list is a Web site that provides just these things. The second is to go directly to the main sources: either to the larger works by the authors in the chapter or to the works referred to in the notes appended to some of the contributions. The second list provides a sample of this kind of reading. The third approach is to examine books that provide an overview of the field of moral philosophy as well as suggestions for approaching primary sources. This approach is suggested in the third group of readings.

Web site

Ethics Updates. A Web site founded in 1994, edited by Lawrence M. Hinman, and designed primarily to be used by ethics instructors and their students. It provides updates on current literature that relates to ethics. URL: http://ethics.acusd.edu/index.html

A Selection of Theoretical Works

- Will Kymlicka, *Contemporary Political Philosophy* (Oxford: Clarendon Press, 1990). This book provides a useful survey of dominant and influential political theorists; in particular, of liberal theorists such as Ronald Dworkin and John Rawls.
- Ronald Dworkin, *Taking Rights Seriously* (London: Duckworth, 1978). Dworkin distinguishes between the formal and substantive approaches to equality, calling the first, "the right to equal treatment" and the second, "the right to treatment as an equal." He applies these approaches to such issues as affirmative action and pornography.
- John Rawls, *A Theory of Justice* (Cambridge, MA: Harvard University Press, 1971). This book has had a big impact on moral and political theory, as is evident in Annette Baier's critique of Rawls's account of justice in her reading in this chapter. Rawls sets forth principles of justice that "free and rational persons would accept in an initial position of equality."
- David Gauthier, *Morals by Agreement* (Oxford: Clarendon Press, 1986). In this book, Gauthier develops a contractarian rationale for moral behaviour. The result is a theory of morality that identifies the moral principles that would emerge from agreement among rational persons, who acknowledge a distinction between what they may and may not do by recognizing a place for mutual constraint.
- Thomas Hurka, *Perfectionism* (New York: Oxford University Press, 1993). Hurka revives virtue theory by providing an account of the human good by reference to human nature and what it means to use our rational capacities to form and pursue interests, projects, and goals.
- Carol Gilligan, *In a Different Voice: Psychological Theory and Women's Development* (Cambridge, Mass.: Harvard University Press, 1982). This is another book that has had a large impact on moral theory in particular. A number of authors in this collection, including Susan Sherwin, Christine Koggel, and Annette Baier, have summarized or made references to Gilligan's work on an ethic of care and its connections to women.

- Alasdair MacIntyre, *After Virtue: A Study in Moral Theory* (London: Duckworth, 1981). Recognized as a controversial re-evaluation of contemporary moral philosophy, this book offers an analysis of various moral theories in the context of an examination of history and tradition.

Books

- D.D. Raphael, *Moral Philosophy*, 2nd ed. (Oxford: Oxford University Press, 1994). This book is intended as an introduction to the subject and requires no previous knowledge of philosophy. Written expressly for beginners, it makes a point of showing the connections between abstract ethics and practical problems in law and government and in the social sciences generally.
- James Rachels, *The Elements of Moral Philosophy* (New York: Random House, 1986). In the course of providing a survey of traditional moral theory, Rachels also gives reasons for endorsing or rejecting the "contending ideas, theories, and arguments" in the area of moral philosophy.
- Paul W. Taylor, *Principles of Ethics: An Introduction* (Belmont, California: Wadsworth Publishing Company, 1975). The chief merit of this book as an introduction to moral philosophy is that it discusses some of the most important perennial topics encountered in moral philosophy, topics such as relativism, egoism, and freedom of the will. The book also includes lists of suggested readings that might prove helpful.
- Mary Warnock, *Ethics Since 1900* (Oxford: Oxford University Press, 1978). This, too, is an introductory text. However, its approach is quite different from that used by Taylor. Warnock surveys the development of modern moral philosophy by introducing some of the major moral philosophers and philosophical schools of the twentieth century.
- David Rosenthal and Fadlou Shahadi (eds.), *Applied Ethics and Ethical Theory* (Salt Lake City: University of Utah Press, 1988). A collection of articles by philosophers such as Ruth Macklin, Dale Jamieson, Onora O'Neill, and Frances Kamm, who examine the connections between moral theory and practical issues, and address the specific issue of whether we can apply theory to practice.
- Hugh LaFollette (ed.), *The Blackwell Guide to Ethical Theory* (Malden, MA: Blackwell Publishers, 2000). This is a comprehensive collection by leading theorists who discuss the themes and problems and evaluate the arguments of the main normative and meta-ethical theories.
- Samantha Brennan (ed.), *Feminist Moral Philosophy*, in *Canadian Journal of Philosophy*. Supplementary Volume, no. 28, 2003. The contributors to this volume explore recent feminist developments in moral philosophy and their connection to mainstream moral theory by reworking traditional concepts of moral philosophy or applying traditional moral theory to feminist problems.

Notes on the Contributors

Kofi Annan is Secretary-General of the United Nations. He earned his master's degree in management from the Massachusetts Institute of Technology (MIT).

Annette C. Baier is retired from the Department of Philosophy at the University of Pittsburgh. She has numerous publications on moral theory, including *Moral Prejudices: Essays on Ethics* (1994), and *Postures of the Mind: Essays on Mind and Morals* (1985).

Jerome E. Bickenbach is Queen's Research Chair in the Philosophy Department at Queen's University. He is the editor of *Canadian Cases in the Philosophy of Law* (1991) and the author of *Physical Disability and Social Policy* (1993).

Tony Blair, an Oxford-educated barrister, has been Prime Minister of the United Kingdom since 1997.

Andrew Brook is Professor of Philosophy, Director of the Institute of Interdisciplinary Studies, and Chair of the Cognitive Science Management Committeee at Carleton University.

Alan Brudner is a Hegel scholar and teaches at the University of Toronto in the Departments of Law and Political Science.

Conrad G. Brunk is the Director of the Centre for Studies in Religion and Society at the University of Victoria, previously posted as Professor of Philosophy and Academic Dean at Conrad Grebel University College, University of Waterloo.

Mohamad Bydon is a graduate student at Johns Hopkins University in Baltimore, Maryland. He was a Senior Fellow in Near Eastern Studies at Dartmouth College in Hanover, New Hampshire.

Jimmy Carter was the 39th President of the United States. After leaving office, he founded the Carter Center, a non-profit organization promoting peace, human rights, democracy, and economic development worldwide.

Lorenne Clark is a former Professor of Philosophy at the University of Toronto, and practised law for several years in Nova Scotia.

Wesley Cragg is the George R. Gardiner Professor of Business Ethics in the Philosophy Department and Schulich School of Business at York University. He is widely published, with recent texts including *Canadian Issues in Applied Environmental Ethics* (1999) and *The Practice of Punishment: Toward a Theory of Restorative Justice* (1992).

Sue Dwyer taught in the Philosophy Department at McGill University and is currently an Associate Professor of Philosophy at the University of Maryland, Baltimore County.

Jason T. Eberl is Assistant Professor and Graduate Co-director in the Department of Philosophy at Indiana University-Purdue University Indianapolis.

Jane English, now deceased, taught philosophy at the University of North Carolina, Chapel Hill, at the time the article included was first published.

George Erasmus served as President of the Dene Nation from 1976 to 1983 and was National Chief of the Assembly of First Nations from 1985 to 1991. He was Co-chair of the Royal Commission on Aboriginal Peoples, and is currently President and Chair of the Aboriginal Healing Foundation.

Marilyn Frye is the author of *The Politics of Reality: Essays in Feminist Theory* (1983) and *Willful Virgin: Essays in Feminism* (1992). She teaches in Women's Studies and the Department of Philosophy at Michigan State University.

Northrop Frye, now deceased, is one of Canada's eminent literary scholars. His essays on Canadian culture are collected in a small volume entitled *Divisions on a Ground* (1982).

David Gauthier is a former Chair of Philosophy at the University of Toronto. He currently teaches at the University of Pittsburgh and is the author of *Morals by Agreement* (1986).

Trudy Govier formerly Associate Professor of Philosophy at Trent University, is a professional speaker and author, having recently published *A Delicate Balance: What Philosophy Can Tell Us About Terrorism* (2002).

Leo Groarke teaches philosophy at, and is the Dean of the Brantford Campus of, Wilfred Laurier University.

Michael Ignatieff, Professor of the Practice of Human Rights Policy, is Director of the Carr Center of Human Rights Policy at Harvard University. He is an acclaimed author and regular contributor to BBC programming.

Immanuel Kant was a prominent 18th-century German philosopher who made significant contributions in all areas of philosophy. Some of his important works are *Critique of Pure Reason*, *Prolegomena to All Future Metaphysics*, and *The Principles of the Metaphysics of Morals*.

Steve Kerstetter is a freelance social policy consultant and research associate with the Canadian Centre for Policy Alternatives. He retired in 2000 as Director of the National Council of Welfare.

Christine M. Koggel is Associate Professor and Chair of the Philosophy Department at Bryn Mawr College, Pennsylvania. She has served two terms as a member of the Canadian Philosophical Association's Standing Committee on Equity Issues and is the author of *Perspectives on Equality* (1998) as well as numerous journal articles.

Antonio Lamer is a retired Chief Justice of the Supreme Court of Canada.

Craig Mackenzie is, in addition to being a member of several business ethics and advisory boards, Head of Socially Responsible Investment at the asset management arm of HBOS plc, one of Europe's largest banks.

Doreen McBarnet is a Reader in Sociology at the Centre for Socio-Legal Studies, Wolfson College, University of Oxford.

Michael McDonald is the Chair of the W. Maurice Young Centre for Applied Ethics at the University of British Columbia. He is the former editor of *Dialogue*, the official journal of the Canadian Philosophical Association.

Wendy McElroy is a Fellow of the Center for Libertarian Studies and a member of the Association of Libertarian Feminists. Her recent works include the anthologies *Freedom, Feminism, and the State* (1986; 1991), and *Liberty for Women* (2002).

Peggy McIntosh is Associate Director of the Wellesley College Center for Research on Women (in Wellesley, Massachusetts), and founder and Co-director of National S.E.E.D. Project on Inclusive Curriculum. She has held teaching posts at Harvard, Trinity, and elsewhere.

William R. McIntyre is a former justice of the Supreme Court of Canada.

Beverley McLachlin is Chief Justice of the Supreme Court of Canada.

Mary Midgley, formerly a member of the University of Newcastle, England, is now retired. She is well known for her writing in applied ethics.

John Stuart Mill is best known for his development of utilitarianism from foundations set out by Jeremy Bentham in the early nineteenth century.

Jan Narveson, the author of *Moral Matters* (1993) and *Respecting Persons in Theory and Practice* (2002), teaches at the University of Waterloo.

Jeffrey Nisker is Chair of Reproductive Endocrinology at the University of Western Ontario, a member of the Canadian Bioethics Society Board of Directors, and Co-chair of the Health Canada Advisory Board on Reproductive Technologies and Genetics.

Patrick Nowell-Smith is a former member of the Department of Philosophy at York University. He is now retired and living in Wales.

Bruce Porter was Director of the Centre for Equality Rights in Accommodation in Toronto from 1986-2002. Currently, he is Coordinator of the Charter Committee on Poverty Issues, Director of Social Rights Advocacy Centre, and acts as a human rights consultant.

James Rachels, now deceased, taught philosophy at the University of Alabama at Birmingham. He is the author of *The Elements of Philosophy* (1986) and *Can Ethics Provide Answers? And Other Essays in Moral Philosophy* (1997).

Tom Regan is a member of the Department of Philosophy and Religion at North Carolina State University. He has written numerous articles and books, including *The Case for Animal Rights* (1984).

Melanie Rock holds a Ph.D. in Anthropology and is Assistant Professor in the Department of Community Health Sciences at the University of Calgary.

Joe Sanders, a lawyer and political consultant, was an advisor to the National Indian Brotherhood from 1981 to 1991.

Amartya Sen is the 1998 Nobel Laureate in Economics. He is Master of Trinity College at the University of Cambridge, and has held teaching positions at Harvard University, Oxford University, and the London School of Economics, among others.

Laura Shanner is Associate Professor at the John Dossetor Health Ethics Centre at the University of Alberta with special interest in reproduction and genetics.

Susan Sherwin has written extensively on ethical issues from a feminist perspective, work which includes the book *No Longer Patient: Feminist Ethics & Health Care* (1992). She teaches philosophy at Dalhousie University in Halifax.

Rosalind S. Simson teaches in the Departments of Philosophy and Women's Studies at Hobart and William Smith Colleges in Geneva, NY.

Brian Slattery is a Fellow of the Royal Society of Canada and Professor in the Osgoode Hall Law School at York University. He recently acted as senior researcher and advisor to the Royal Commission on Aboriginal Peoples.

Margaret A. Somerville is Chair of the Faculty of Law at McGill University, a member of the Faculty of Medicine, and was founding Director of the McGill Centre for Medicine, Ethics and Law.

John Sopinka is a justice with the Supreme Court of Canada.

J.T. Stevenson has written extensively in the field of applied ethics and the history of Canadian political and social thought. He is Professor Emeritus at the University of Toronto.

Pierre Elliott Trudeau, Canada's Prime Minister from 1968-1979 and 1980-1984, died September 28, 2000.

Adrian Alex Wellington has graduate degrees in philosophy, law, and environmental studies. She teaches courses in professional and applied ethics, and philosophy of law at Ryerson University.

Bertha Wilson is a former justice of the Supreme Court of Canada.

David B. Wong is the author of *Moral Relativity* (1984). He is a Professor of Philosophy at Duke University in Durham, North Carolina.